STANLEY GIBBONS

OVERSEAS 1

FOREIGN STAMP CATALOGUE

A-C

D1513825

STANLEY GIBBONS PUBLICATIONS LTD

391 Strand London WC2R 0LX

Telephone 01-836 9707

By appointment to H.M. the Queen, Stanley Gibbons Ltd, Philatelists

Retail Price in UK £3·25

Made and Printed in Great Britain by Balding + Mansell Ltd, London & Wisbech

Contents of this Volume

For complete Index see end of catalogue

The Stanley Gibbons Group
Philatelists & Publishers/Established 1856

Our Addresses . . .

London

Stanley Gibbons Limited
391 Strand, London, WC2R 0LX
Telephone: 01–836 9707
Telegrams: Philatelic, London, W.C.2
Cables: Stangib, London, WC2B 5HD
Telex: 28883

Shop Department
391 Strand, London, W.C.2
*Open Monday–Friday 9 a.m. to 5.30 p.m. and
Saturday 9.30 a.m. to 12.30 p.m.*

Specialist and Rare Stamp Department
Romano House, 399 Strand, London, W.C.2
Telephone: 01–836 9707
*Open Monday–Friday 9 a.m. to 5 p.m. and
Saturday 9.30 a.m. to 12 noon (excluding
Summer Saturdays)*

Stanley Gibbons Auctions Ltd
Drury House, Russell Street, Drury Lane,
London, WC2B 5HD
Telephone: 01–836 7941
Cables: Philators, London, W.C.2

Stanley Gibbons Publications Ltd
Drury House, Russell Street, Drury Lane,
London, WC2B 5HD
Telephone: 01–836 2005 and 4136

Birmingham

Trade Publications Division
StanGib House, Sarehole Road
Birmingham, B28 8EE
Telephone: 021–777 7255

New York

StanGib Limited
StanGib Building, 595 Fifth Avenue,
New York, N.Y. 10017, U.S.A.
Telephone: 212–PL8–2210
Cables: Stangib, New York
*This has no connection with Stanley Gibbons
Incorporated, of New York.*

OVERSEAS Volume 1

Following the publication last year of the three-volume Europe Catalogue we now have pleasure in presenting the first volume of the new Foreign Overseas Catalogue.

FEATURES OF THIS NEW CATALOGUE

- Prices completely reviewed and updated to follow market trends

- Set prices included

- Fully revised catalogue listings

- Latest new issues

- Comprehensive indexes to Foreign Overseas countries and places, with helpful cross references throughout the text

- Indispensable information section and International Philatelic Glossary

- Interesting historical background notes

- Currency conversion tables

V.A.T.: Stanley Gibbons have absorbed Value Added Tax, therefore all prices reflect the international market and are tax inclusive.

Introducing this volume . . .

The New Shape of the Gibbons Catalogue

This is the first British stamp catalogue ever to be computer type-set and it was prepared in Uppsala, Sweden. It is one of the first British contracts to be given to Bemrose/Almqvist & Wiksell, a new Anglo-Swedish company based in London. The printing was done by Balding + Mansell in Wisbech, Cambridgeshire. Publication of this volume was delayed by the long and complicated job of programming but it is expected that this new computer setting will pave the way for more rapid and efficient production in the future.

The incredible increase in the number of new issues emanating from nearly every stamp-issuing country coupled with the consequent limitation in the number of countries the individual can collect has forced major changes in catalogue publishing.

Whilst the old "Part I" volume still continues as the *British Commonwealth Catalogue*, the last editions of "Part II" *Europe and Colonies* and "Part III" *America, Asia and Africa* were those of 1970. During 1970–71 we published twelve foreign Sectional Catalogues, each containing a small group of countries, but on the whole the demand was not sufficient to encourage us to complete the work in this form, which would have entailed up to forty Sections.

In 1972 we published a fully revised and completely reset catalogue of Europe in three volumes and these have been very well received, proving an immediate success. A great deal of thought and experiment was put into how to present the rest of the foreign countries in convenient-sized uniform books. We considered arranging them by continent, but this would have meant either having volumes of very unequal size or devoting two to some continents which would have been unsatisfactory. Finally we opted for four foreign overseas volumes of about equal length with the countries arranged in basically alphabetical order on the lines of the European volumes. The other Overseas volumes will cover D to J, K to P and Q to Z.

New Arrangement of Countries

Those countries that have been independent since they started issuing stamps presented no problem in putting into alphabetical order. We were then left with a large number of colonial territories which sometimes joined larger units, such as French Equatorial Africa or French West Africa, only to split up again later and become fully independent and usually changing their names. The logical thing was to list them in alphabetical order under their present titles preceded by the issues of the colonial territories that now form part of them. This geographical concept is extended to show occupation issues after the country occupied rather than after the occupying power, and this also applies to Post Offices Abroad. Islands forming part of an archipelago are also listed together, e.g. Anjouan, Great Comoro, Mayotte and Mohéli are listed under Comoro Islands followed by the general issues.

Cross References

Cross references for all foreign overseas stamp-issuing places that are not in strict alphabetical order indicate where the stamps will be found, either elsewhere in this volume or in the volumes that will follow. In addition to the index to this book there is a separate index giving the remaining foreign overseas countries.

References to catalogue or type numbers in foreign overseas countries not in this volume relate to the numbers at present appearing in the 1970 Catalogues or the Sectionals.

Classes of Use

As in the Europe volumes the Postage Due, Express, Newspaper, Official stamps, etc., are listed with the ordinary stamps in chronological order with prefix letters indicating their class and they are numbered in sequence for easy reference. We no longer use the "A" and "C" prefix letters to indicate Air or Charity stamps as we do not regard these as being separate classes of use, but there are a very few exceptions where to have done this would have entailed renumbering a very large number of stamps. Such an exception will be found in the air stamps of the United States.

Prices and Value Added Tax

As it is now some years since the prices of many of the countries in this volume were revised, every price quotation has been looked at and most of them have been altered to bring them into line with current market conditions. Set prices have been introduced wherever possible making it easier to value collections and they show particularly marked reductions in sets containing a number of stamps quoted at the minimum price of 5p.

All the prices are on a tax inclusive basis as Stanley Gibbons Ltd are able to absorb V.A.T. on stamps due to their vast exports and the fact that much of their business is in stamps over 100 years old, these two categories not being taxable. However, as in the past, price changes will reflect the international market.

Revision in the Catalogue Lists

Historical Notes

Mr. B. St. G. Drennan, F.R.P.S., L., who was responsible for the historical notes which were introduced in the Europe volumes, has continued with his painstaking researches to produce illuminating notes for this foreign overseas volume. Here they are all the more necessary by reason of the coming together of issues for the same area which were formerly listed under various headings. We particularly commend the comprehensive notes dealing with the chequered history of China in the new list.

General

As the whole work has been reset we have taken the opportunity to make improvements in every country, both by modernising the style in the interests of clarity, and by adding stamps and errors that have come to light since the countries were last rewritten. There is only space to refer to the most major changes :—

Afghanistan. Just as we were going to press Herr Horst G. Dietrich revealed the results of many years of research into the issues of 1293/5 (Mohammedan dates). He has demonstrated that the Afghan post offices in Kandahar and Herat had not been established at the time when the stamps attributed to them were put on the market and that they must be regarded as fakes or bogus. They have therefore been deleted and colour descriptions of the remaining issues have been amended. It also appears that the conversion of the Mohammedan dates to those of the Gregorian calendar for the years 1870 to 1878 are not quite accurate and that they should read one year later. This information reached us too late for the dates to be changed in this edition. We are grateful to Herr Dietrich for his help.

Other changes: 1880 issue listed in tabulated form under the four types of paper used but the status of some of these remains in doubt. Newspaper stamps listed as such instead of with the definitives. The former long definitive sets ranging through 1932–46, 1939–65 and 1951–62 broken down into six separate sets with more illustrations to help identification. 1961–64 Agency issues formerly excluded owing to their limited use now recorded in the Appendix.

Arabian Gulf States. We are indebted to Mr. A. N. Donaldson for vetting our lists of Abu Dhabi, Ajman and Bahrain.

Argentine Republic. All issues to 1924 rewritten. Relisting of complicated definitives from 1954 in more convenient sets with extra illustrations, followed by the relevant Officals. In this we have been greatly helped by the Rev. J. N. T. Howat. Departmental Officials remain tabulated at the end but the general Officials integrated.

Bolivia. Clearer listing of first issue. Eudes & Chassepot printing of 1895 on thick paper restored as the stamps did postal duty ; but they are priced only for postally used. In this we relied on the careful re-statement of the views of experts in an article by Commander D. L. Gordon in *The Mainsheet.*

Burundi. Amplified listing of first issue based on researches by Monsieur C. Celis. As the volume of new issues has diminished and is on a par with Rwanda, stamps formerly recorded in the Appendix now listed in full.

Canal Zone. Recently discovered errors in the early issues added as well as booklet panes since we list them in the corresponding issues of the United States.

Chile. Major revision in the periods 1879–1932 and 1955–58.

China. This is completely rewritten from beginning to end with a great deal of help from a team of leading members of the China Philatelic Society of London. In fact several thousand stamps have been added, the whole job co-ordinated by Mr. B. St. G. Drennan, F.R.P.S., L., who worked for many months on this. It has been a labour of love.

Placed first comes the list of *Shanghai,* revised in the light of the published work of the late L. F. Livingston with further help from Mr. Peter Holcombe. In the *Imperial issues* of China many errors added and new enlarged illustrations distinguishing the London and first and second Peking

printings of the 1913–33 issues. *Provincial surcharges* of 1940–43 listed in full with illustrations for which we are indebted to Mr. James Negus, F.R.P.S., L. For many additions in the provincial Silver Yuan and "unit" issues of 1949 we must thank Wing Cdr. P. I. Padget F.R.P.S., L.

The biggest single contribution is the first listing in any general catalogue of the early *Communist local, border area and regional issues* starting in 1929, the combined work of Mr. R. F. Lankester, who built up most of his very fine collection when he was resident in China, and of Mr. Drennan who also has a fine collection. The most difficult problem was the illustrations as many of these stamps are very primitive and also rare. In many cases we had no access to stamps so that some of the illustrations may be unclear, but they will serve to identify the stamps until opportunities occur to make new illustrations from the stamps.

In the *Chinese Provinces* there is a new list of *Manchukuo* compiled by Mr. Negus based on the handbook by Mrs. Helen Zirkle published by the Collectors Club of New York. Communist issues for *North East China* amplified. Stamps of the *Ili Republic* added after Sinkiang. *Tibet* follows here.

Taiwan starts with the first comprehensive listing in any general catalogue of the very complicated issues, first as a Chinese Province in 1888–95 and then the temporary Black Flag Republic of 1895 before the island was ceded to Japan. For painstaking work on these issues we must thank Mr. E. N. Lane, Wing Cdr. Padget and Mr. Peter Holcombe.

After the Foreign Post Offices in China and the German leased territory of Kiaochow the list ends with the *Japanese Occupation issues.* In *Mengkiang* and in the five "Districts" of *North China* we now list both the large and the small overprints; for these we are again indebted to Mr. Negus.

Cilicia. Completely rewritten, simpler to follow with considerable additions.

Colombia and States. Also completely rewritten with many changes in the early issues where names of printers have been inserted based on a recent article by Mr. John Swales in *The Mainsheet.* Careful distinction between local issues made during the Civil War of 1899–1902 in areas cut off from the capital and the true contemporary issues for those states that still had the right to issue their own stamps. The 1920 Compania Colombiana de Navegacion Aeréa stamps added under the Private Air Companies.

Costa Rica. Early issues rewritten. In these we have derived much help from *The Oxcart*, organ of The Society of Costa Rica Collectors.

Cuba. Issues of the Spanish Colony, U.S. Administration and Republic now listed all in one place. The 1937 Association of American Writers and Artists set now listed as generally recognised in the U.S.A.

Former French Colonies. These now have contemporary spellings and the colonial and independent issues are united. Many errors, etc., added in *Algeria, Cameroun, Central African Republic, Chad,* the *Comoro* group and *Congo.*

STANLEY GIBBONS PUBLICATIONS LTD.

May we help?

We would like to help you build your collection and therefore remind you that the prices quoted in this catalogue are our selling prices at the time this book went to press.

Ideally, we hope you'll visit our 391 Strand Shop or our Specialist and Rare Stamp showrooms at Romano House, 399 Strand, for here you can see everything, but equally our Approval Service can send you, no matter where you live, attractive selections of most countries. For stamps priced at £1 or over in this catalogue we welcome collectors Want Lists. Our Specialist File can register your special requirements if we cannot offer immediately.

In every way we can help you enjoy a lifetime's hobby—that is just what we are doing for many thousands of collectors throughout the world—so the important thing is to contact us.

Stanley G bbons

For your Information . . .

Prices

Condition

Our prices are for stamps in fine average condition, and in issues where condition varies, generally in the older "classic" issues, we may ask more for the superb and less for the substandard. Prices for used stamps are for postally used (or cancelled-to-order in some modern issues).

Gum

In the case of unused stamps our prices are for fine average condition, which ranges between lightly hinged and part original gum and this varies from issue to issue. New issues are supplied unmounted for six months from date of issue, after which they may be supplied mounted.

Price Alterations

All prices are subject to change without notice and we give no guarantee to supply all stamps priced. Prices quoted for albums, publications, etc, advertised in this catalogue are also subject to change without notice.

Guarantee

All stamps are guaranteed genuine originals in the following terms:—

If not as described, and returned by the purchaser within six years, we undertake to refund the price paid to us and our liability will thereby be dis-

charged. If any stamp is certified as genuine by the Expert Committee of the Royal Philatelic Society, London, or of the British Philatelic Association Limited, the purchaser shall not be entitled to make any claim against us for any error, omission or mistake in such certificate.

Finally please note . . .

Our terms are cash with order unless you have established a credit account.

Stanley Gibbons catalogue numbers are recognised universally and any individual stamp can be identified by quoting the catalogue number (the one at the left of the column) prefixed by the country name and the letters 'S.G.' Do not confuse the catalogue number with the bold face Type numbers which refer to illustrations.

Whilst we welcome information and suggestions we must ask correspondents to include the cost of postage for the return of any stamps submitted plus registration (20p) where appropriate.

Where information is solicited purely for the benefit of the enquirer we regret we cannot undertake to reply unless stamps or reply coupons are sent to cover the postage.

Watermarks are normally shown as seen from the FRONT of the stamp. Where no watermark is noted, the stamps are without distinctive watermark.

We do not list inverted or reversed watermarks as separate varieties in this Catalogue.

Stamps not listed in this catalogue (unless they are new issues) are almost certainly not adhesive postage stamps but Revenue, Local or other issues outside its scope.

We regret we do not give opinions as to the genuineness of stamps, nor do we identify stamps or number them by our Catalogue.

The recognised Expert Committees in this country are those of the Royal Philatelic Society, 41 Devonshire Place, London, W1N 1FE, and of the British Philatelic Association Ltd., 446 Strand, London, WC2R 0RA. These Expert Committees do not undertake valuations under any circumstances and fees are payable for their services.

Information for the collector

The anatomy of a postage stamp is made up of the following parts: paper, watermark, printing process, separation and gum which are briefly dealt with in the following notes. More detailed information is contained in *Stamp Collecting*, by Stanley Phillips published by us at £1.25.

Paper

Many of the early issues were printed on hand-made paper, which was produced sheet by sheet, but most stamps are printed on machine-made paper which is turned out in continuous rolls. The greatest variation in paper is, therefore, to be found on the early issues. The following is a description of the main types of paper used in stamp production:—

Wove paper, on which the great majority of stamps are printed, has a plain, even texture which is created when the wet pulp is brought into contact with finely-netted wire gauze mesh (i.e., the "dandy roll") of the paper-making machine. Unless otherwise stated in the catalogue, it can be assumed that all stamps are on wove paper.

Laid paper is similarly impressed in the wet state, but with closely-set parallel lines, either vertically or horizontally laid.

Quadrillé (or squared) paper is a form of laid paper where crossed lines produce squares or rectangles.

Bâtonné paper is a thin, "bank" letter paper watermarked with well-spaced parallel lines (intended as a guide to neat writing). This can be either wove or laid and in the latter case the laid lines come between the "batons" (French for a staff).

Granite paper, used for many of the stamps of Switzerland, can be easily distinguished by the coloured lines in its texture.

Granite   Quadrillé

Moiré   Burelé band

Kinds of Paper

Paper is sometimes coated or *chalk-surfaced* and this was often used to make it difficult to clean off postmarks and use the stamps again. In the Catalogue all stamps are deemed to be on "ordinary paper" unless described as "chalky" or "chalk-surfaced". There are degrees of coating and our definition of chalk-surfaced paper applies to paper which shows a black line when touched with silver. *Enamel* and *glazed* papers are other forms of coating which are often found in the stamps of Portugal and Colonies.

Coloured paper. Unless otherwise stated, stamps are printed on white paper, but where a coloured paper is used (and by this we mean coloured right through), the colour of the paper is given in italics, thus:—

Black/*yellow* (=black on yellow)

Toned paper can be expressed as paper which is off-white but which could not be described as being of any definite colour. There is a tendency nowadays, to introduce specially white paper (either ordinary or chalky), as in Great Britain, Australia, New Zealand, etc.

Native papers, made from rice or silk fibre, are very distinctive and are found in early issues of China, Japan and Indian Native States.

Manilla paper, made from manilla hemp or wood fibre, is normally used for cheap envelopes and newspaper wrappers. It is coarse, usually brown in colour, and may be wove or laid.

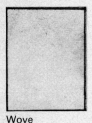
Wove   Laid

Moiré consists of a very fine pattern and examples of this are found on the backs of early Mexican stamps.

Burelage is a fine pattern or network *printed* on the face of the stamp beneath the design or on the back, another device to discourage forgery or tampering with the postmark. There are examples in the early issues of Denmark, in Queensland and the 1932 issue of Venezuela.

Ribbed paper is distinguished by very fine parallel lines on the front and back, and there are examples of this on the first issue of Austria, and in many stamps of Switzerland.

Silk threads. Coloured silk threads embodied in the paper. This was used as an experiment by John Dickinson but the best known examples are in the early issues of Switzerland.

Papers come in a wide range of thicknesses from *pelure*, a very thin, hard, tough paper which is translucent, to thick *"carton"* paper.

The recognition of paper assumes importance when classifying stamps which were successively printed on different kinds of paper.

Watermarks

A watermark is a device or pattern produced by pressure on the wet paper pulp during manufacture thereby thinning the paper. It can usually be seen when a stamp is held up to the light or laid face down on a black watermark detector or tray. If still obscure, a few drops of benzine (petroleum ether 40/60) on the stamp should reveal the watermark, but note that this can affect the colours of a photogravure stamp. Remember also that benzine is highly inflammable.

A device which occurs once on every stamp is called a *single* watermark; a *multiple* watermark is a device repeated closely throughout the sheet so that each stamp shows parts of several devices. A *sheet* watermark is a pattern extending over a part of a sheet, sometimes repeated several times in the sheet. In sheet watermarks there are usually a number of stamps in the sheet without watermark. A *papermakers'* watermark usually consists of a name or a device without postal significance (in contradistinction to a sheet watermark supplied to the order of the postal authority) and only occupies a very small part of the sheet. These are normally ignored as most of the stamps would be without watermark, although copies bearing a portion of the watermark may be worth a premium. Some

British Colonial issues have watermarks in the sheet margins in addition to those on the stamps, such as the words "CROWN AGENTS" or the name of the Colony. These are ignored in the Catalogue as they do not normally affect the stamps unless the watermark is misplaced and individual letters happen to fall on the row of stamps adjoining the margin.

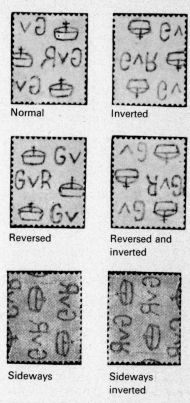

Normal   Inverted

Reversed   Reversed and inverted

Sideways   Sideways inverted

The above illustrations showing positions of watermarks are as seen when looking at the backs of the stamps.

Watermarks normally read correctly through the front of the stamp, showing in reverse on the back. Hence in the Catalogue they are always described as seen from the *front* of the stamp. Sometimes watermarks occur sideways, inverted or reversed, etc. We normally list sideways watermarks, but *inverted and reversed watermarks are outside the scope of this catalogue.* They are caused through feeding the paper incorrectly and in the older issues sheets were often fed quite indiscriminately so that inverted and reversed watermarks in these issues are often relatively common.

Printing Processes

There are four main processes used for printing postage stamps: Recess-printing, Photogravure, Typography and Lithography.

Recess-printing. In this process, also known as Line-engraving, Intaglio, or *Taille douce,* the design is cut into the plate which is then inked and wiped so that the ink remains only in the recesses. The paper is then placed against the plate under great pressure, whereby the ink is picked up from the grooves and, in the form of the stamp design, stands out in relief on the paper. The raised image can usually be felt with the finger.

The *Die* is the engraved original from which printing plates (or cylinders) are produced in recess-printing, photogravure or typography. New plates made from the original die sometimes show slight differences from the original plates and dies are sometimes re-engraved, often producing marked differences.

Photogravure, also called Rotogravure, Heliogravure, etc., is basically another form of recess-printing. The photograph design is chemically treated and transferred to a copper plate and etched. The surface of the plate holds the ink in a number of tiny cells (or dots) caused by the superimposition of a fine grid or screen; the intensity of colour varies according to the depth of the cells. In modern photogravure the "plate" is usually a cylinder in high-speed, multicolour rotary presses. Some of these print individually cut sheets but in really fast printing the paper is fed "in the web" from large rolls and is cut into sheets afterwards.

Typography, also called Surface-printing or Letterpress-printing, is the opposite to recess-printing in that the image is in "relief" on the plate. When the ink is applied by a roller only the raised portions, i.e. the design, receive the ink. The effect of pressure in printing usually causes the design to stand out in relief on the back of the stamp.

Lithography. Here the design is transferred to the plate or "stone" in a special greasy ink. The flat surface is then moistened so that when the printing ink is applied it adheres only to the greased portion which may then be impressed on the paper. In *offset-lithography,* the image is taken up by a rubber "blanket" which "offsets" it onto the paper, while in modern *photo-lithography* the stamp design is photographically processed onto an etched zinc plate which is attached to the cylinder of a rotary press.

Delacryl is an advanced and refined form of lithography using improved screens which was developed by De La Rue and Co. in 1966.

Embossing was used in some early issues, notably in the 1847–54 issue of Great Britain, Gambia, Heligoland, Sardinia, etc. The relief effect is achieved by the use of two dies, one engraved in relief and the other in recess, between which the paper is pressed. This can be done with or without colour.

This is the process often used for printing postal stationery. Embossed stamps cut from envelopes etc. should not be confused with embossed postage stamps, which must be adhesive to qualify for listing in the Catalogue.

Gold Blocking and Embossing. Gold blocking is the transfer and adhesion of foil to paper under heat and pressure. Embossing on stamps raises the design above the surrounding areas of paper. This may be achieved either on foil blocking and embossing machines or by printing and embossing on the photogravure machine. Examples are found in modern commemorative issues of Great Britain.

Type-set is the term given to stamps printed from movable type so that each stamp in the sheet is set up separately, generally producing a number of varieties. This process is sometimes resorted to when the ordinary facilities for stamp production are lacking and examples are found in the Postmasters' stamps of United States and Confederate States. A few stamps have been produced on *typewriters,* notably Long Island and Uganda.

In recent times it is not unusual to find stamps produced by a combination of two or more processes.

Appearance of the Printing Unit:

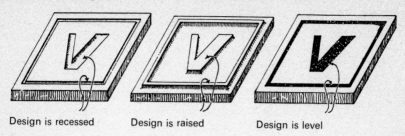

Design is recessed   Design is raised   Design is level

Sectional View through Middle showing Shape of Printing Surface:

Sectional View of stamp showing effect of Pressure on the Paper:

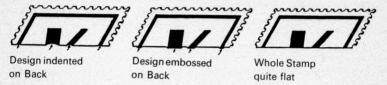

Design indented   Design embossed   Whole Stamp
on Back   on Back   quite flat

Separation

The very first postage stamps were *imperforate* as there were no means available for perforating stamps. They had to be separated by scissors, hence the importance of wide margins when collecting imperf. stamps, particularly where the stamps later appeared with perforations which could be trimmed off so as to create imperf. stamps. Imperf. errors of stamps which normally exist only perforated are usually listed in pairs where pairs are known to exist.

Rouletting was the next form of separation to be introduced. It is a form of perforation in which the paper is partly cut through but no paper is removed. This may be done with a wheel or a series of wheels with small points on their circumference. The various types of roulette are usually expressed in French terms descriptive of the type of cut or the appearance of the edges of the stamps when separated. Thus *Percé* ("pierced") *en arc* is a roulette in which the cuts are curved; *Percé en lignes* implied straight cut; *Percé en croix* means cuts in the shape of little crosses, forming lozenges with the outer corners open; and *Percé en scie* is applied to the distinctive saw-toothed roulette, where the edges of the stamps are like the edge of a saw. *Percé en points* means pin roulette, often called pin

perforation in error. In addition there are oblique roulette, serpentine roulette and zig-zag roulette. Roulettes are sometimes indicated by the measurements of a perforation gauge.

Perforation was invented by Henry Archer and first used in Great Britain stamps in 1850. It differs from rouletting in that a part of the paper is punched out by a series of holes between the stamps.

Forms of Separation

Roulette   Imperforate

Percé en arc

Serpentine roulette

Zig-zag roulette

Perforation

Comb Perforation

A *line perforation* is produced by a machine with one line of pins which punches a single row of holes at a time. A *comb perforation* is the result of a machine punching three sides of each stamp in a row at the same time. When a whole sheet of stamps is perforated in one operation by punches arranged in transverse rows, the result is called a *harrow* perforation.

As a general rule a line perforation produces irregular corners on a stamp and a comb perforation regular ones, but sometimes a line-perforated stamp has perfect corners, because of a chance matching intersection of the rows of holes. Also, a comb-perforated stamp may have irregular corners due to an imperfection in the comb. Difficulties in distinguishing line or comb perforated stamps can usually be resolved by the study of a corner marginal block of four.

The "gauge" of a perforation is measured by the number of holes in a space of two centimetres, indicated by a perforation gauge. In the Catalogue they are normally given to the nearest half and the *Instanta Gauge* is our standard. Where perforations are exactly on the Quarter or Three-quarter measurement, the Catalogue quotes the higher figures, i.e. $11\frac{3}{4}\times12\frac{1}{4}=12\times12\frac{1}{2}$.

The various perforations are expressed as follows:—

Perf. 14: Perforated alike on all sides.

Perf. 14×15: Compound perforation. The first figure refers to top and bottom, the second to left and right sides.

Perf. 14, $14\frac{1}{2}$: Perforated approximately $14\frac{1}{4}$.

Perf. 14–15: Perforations are irregular in the sheet, and stamps may measure anything between 14 and 15.

Perf. compound of 14 *and* 15: This is a general description indicating that two gauges of perforation have been used, but not *necessarily* on opposite sides of the stamp. It could be one side in one gauge and three in the other; or two adjacent sides with the same gauge. Where more precise detail is required we give the perforations starting with that at the top and proceeding clockwise: i.e. 14×14×15×14 indicates perf. 15 at bottom and perf. 14 on the other three sides.

Perf. 11 *and* 14 *mixed*: This indicates stamps that were perforated in one gauge, and re-perforated in another.

Imperf. × *perf.* 14 means imperf. at top and bottom and perf. 14 at sides, whilst *Perf.* 14 × *imperf.* means the reverse.

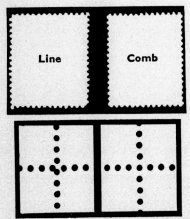

Examples of Line and Comb Perforation

Imperf. × perf.

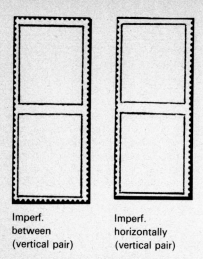

| Imperf. between (vertical pair) | Imperf. horizontally (vertical pair) |

Imperf. between is a common type of variety in which one row of perforations has been missed. Thus *Imperf. between* (*vert. pair*) means a vertical pair which is imperf. horizontally between the stamps.

Imperf. horiz. (*vert. pair*) means a vertical pair which is imperf. horizontally not only between the two stamps but also on the top and bottom, showing that it comes from a sheet on which several of the rows were not perforated horizontally. Naturally the missing perforations can just as easily occur in the vertical rows and these are collected in horizontal pairs.

In this Catalogue we do not list stamps which are merely imperf. between stamp and margin.

Gum

The gum normally used on stamps has been Gum Arabic until the late sixties when synthetic adhesives were introduced. Harrison and Sons Ltd, for instance use *Polyvinyl Alcohol*, known as PVA. This is almost invisible except for a slight yellowish tinge which was incorporated to make it possible to see that the stamps have been gummed. Because of its advantages in hot countries, as stamps do not curl and sheets are less likely to stick together, it is probable that it will be used by other printers. Gum arabic and PVA are not distinguished in the lists. Stamps described as being *Self-adhesive* are issued on backing paper from which they are peeled off and reaffixed to mail. There are examples of this in Sierra Leone.

All stamps are assumed to have gum of some kind and where they are without gum this is stated.

Used Stamps

Our used prices are normally for stamps postally used but may be for stamps "cancelled-to-order" where this practice exists.

Pen-cancellation usually denotes fiscal use and such stamps are outside the scope of this catalogue but occasionally postally used copies were pen-cancelled, as in the first issue of Finland.

Luminescence

This term refers to stamps issued overprinted with *fluorescent* or *phosphorescent* bands or printed on paper or with ink containing fluorescence or phosphorescence. These stamps are for use in connection with electronic mail-sorting machines and are now issued by a number of countries which have a very heavy flow of mail. Where this is applied in the form of bands, as in Japan, Great Britain and Canada, they are visible to the naked eye and so are listed. The general practice is now to treat the whole stamp and these can be distinguished by the use of ultra-violet lamps of the correct range. Such stamps are listed only when there are also some other means of distinguishing them. Where this is not so, they are recorded in footnotes or headings.

Colours

Where two or more colours are used, the central portion of the stamp is in the first colour given and other colours are in the order of appearance moving from the centre of the stamp unless otherwise stated. Where four or more colours are used the term multicoloured is usually employed. Where more than one colour is used the stamps are usually printed in more than one operation. This frequently produces some variation in registration resulting sometimes in unusual varieties, but these are outside the scope of this catalogue. However, major errors such as inverted centres are listed. Aniline colours are derived from coal-tar and have a particular brilliance which generally shows through the back of the stamp.

The following and similar abbreviations are in general use throughout the catalogue to avoid unnecessary overrunning of lines:—Bl. (blue); blk. (black); bwn., brn. (brown); car., carm. (carmine); choc. (chocolate); clar. (claret); emer. (emerald); grn. (green); ind. (indigo); mag. (magenta); mar. (maroon); mve. (mauve); ol. (olive); orge. (orange); pk. (pink); pur. (purple); scar. (scarlet); sep. (sepia); turq. (turquoise); ultram. (ultramarine); verm. (vermilion); vio. (violet); yell. (yellow).

Colours of overprints and surcharges are in black unless otherwise stated. Other colours are given either in the heading or by the following abbreviations in brackets after the description of the stamp, thus (B.)=blue, (Br.)=brown, (C.)= carmine, (G.)=green, (Mag.)=magenta, (Mve.) =mauve, (Ol.)=olive, (O.)=orange, (P.)=purple, (Pk.)=pink, (R.)=red, (Sil.)=silver, (V.)=violet, (Vm.) or (Verm.)=vermilion, (W.)=white, (Y.)= yellow.

Booklets

Booklet stamps are only listed where they can be distinguished by their perforations.

Coils

Coil stamps are issued in rolls for use in automatic vending machines. They are only listed where there are perforation or other differences to distinguish them.

Fiscals

This catalogue is restricted to stamps which are valid for postal use. Many stamps have validity for both postal and fiscal use, i.e. on documents, as revenue or receipt stamps, etc. Others are issued for fiscal use only and these are only listed where they have been expressly authorised for use as postage stamps, usually owing to a temporary shortage. Where fiscal stamps are overprinted for postal use they are included in the ordinary listing but where this is not the case they are known as *Postal Fiscal* stamps and listed under this heading.

Double Prints

This results from a sheet of stamps going through the press twice and such authenticated errors are listed. However, a similar effect can be obtained in offset-litho where the second impression is obtained by contact with the "blanket" and the impression is usually fainter. "Blanket" offsets are outside the scope of this Catalogue.

Bisects

Occasionally during a temporary shortage of stamps of a particular value stamps of a higher denomination are bisected (or trisected etc.) and used on the mail. These are only listed where the practice has been expressly authorised and the prices quoted are for stamps used on large piece or cover and dated during the period of authorisation.

Re-entry

A kind of variety found on recess-printed stamps in which the whole or part of the design is duplicated or deepened. If the roller-die is incorrectly rocked on the plate the impression can be scraped off and the roller-die is "re-entered" in the correct position and may thus produce a double impression of part of the design.

Se-tenant

(=joined together). Stamps of different denominations joined together or a variety in pair with normal, etc.

Tête-bêche

Stamps or overprints printed upside down in relation to one another. These are sometimes errors in the positioning of clichés within the plate, or come about through special arrangements of sheets used for making up into booklets.

Illustrations

Illustrations of stamps in this catalogue are $\frac{3}{4}$ linear size; overprints, surcharges and watermarks are normally actual size.

Stamps in sets that are not illustrated are the same size and format as the value shown unless otherwise indicated.

Prices

The prices in the left-hand column are for unused stamps and those in the right-hand column for used. Prices are given in new pence and pounds. 100 pence (p)=1 pound (£1).

The minimum price quoted is 5p. This represents a handling charge rather than a basis for valuing common stamps. Where the actual value of a stamp is less than 5p this may be apparent when set prices are shown, particularly for sets including a number of 5p stamps. It therefore follows that in valuing common stamps the 5p catalogue price should not be reckoned automatically since it covers a variation in real scarcity and can mean anything between the handling charge and the old 1s. 3d. price.

Set prices are generally for one of each value in the set excluding shades, dies, etc., but including major colour changes. Where there are alternative shades, etc., generally the cheapest is included and the number of stamps in the set is always stated.

Printers

The names of the following printers are often given in abbreviated form:—

A.B.N. Co.	American Bank Note Co., New York.
A. & M.	Alden & Mowbray Ltd., Oxford.
Aspioti-Elka (Aspiotis)	Aspioti-Elka, Corfu, Greece.
B.W.	Bradbury Wilkinson & Co., Ltd.
Continental B.N. Co.	Continental Bank Note Co.
Courvoisier	Imprimerie Courvoisier S.A., Le-Chaux-de-Fonds, Switzerland.
D.L.R.	De La Rue & Co., Ltd., London.
Enschedé	Joh. Enschedé en Zonen, Haarlem, Netherlands.
Format	Format International Security Printers, Ltd., London.
Harrison	Harrison & Sons, Ltd., London.
J.W.	John Waddington of Kirkstall, Ltd.
P.B.	Perkins Bacon Ltd., London.
Questa	Questa Colour Security Printers, Ltd.
Waterlow	Waterlow & Sons, Ltd., London.

Abbreviations Used

Anniv.	Anniversary.
B.A.	Buenos Aires.
C, c	Chalky paper.
Des.	Designer; designed.
Diag.	Diagonal; diagonally
Eng.	Engraver; engraved.
F.C.	Fiscal Cancellation.
Horiz.	Horizontal; horizontally.
Imp., Imperf.	Imperforate (not Perforated).
Inscr.	Inscribed.
L.	Left.
Litho.	Lithographed.
mm.	Millimetres.
MS	Miniature sheet.
N.Y.	New York.

O, o	Ordinary paper.
Opt(d).	Overprint(ed).
P or P-c.	Pen-cancelled.
P., Pf. or Perf.	Perforated.
Pr.	Pair.
Percé en arc.	Perforated in curves.
Percé en scie.	Perforated with a saw-edge.
Photo.	Photogravure.
Pin Perf.	Perforated without removing any paper.
Ptd.	Printed.
R.	Right.
Recess,	Recess-printed.
Roto.	Rotogravure.
Roul.	Rouletted—a broken line of cuts.
S.	SPECIMEN (overprint).
Surch.	Surcharge(d).
T.C.	Telegraph Cancellation.
T.	Type.
Typo.	Typographed.
Un.	Unused.
Us.	Used.
Vert.	Vertical; Vertically.
W. or wmk.	Watermark.
Wmk. s.	Watermark sideways.

(†) = Does not exist.

(—) (or a blank price column) = Exists, or may exist, but price cannot be quoted.

/ between colours means "on" and the colour following is that of the paper on which the stamp is printed.

Arabic Numerals

As in the case of European figures, the details of the Arabic numerals vary in different stamp designs, but they should be readily recognised with the aid of this illustration.

•	١	٢	٣	٤	٥	٦	٧	٨	٩
0	1	2	3	4	5	6	7	8	9

INTERNATIONAL PHILATELIC GLOSSARY

English	French	German	Spanish	Italian
Agate	Agate	Achat	Agata	Agata
Air stamp	Timbre de la poste aérienne	Flugpostmarke	Sello de correo aéreo	Francobollo per posta aerea
Apple-green	Vert-pomme	Apfelgrün	Verde manzana	Verde mela
Barred	Annulé par barres	Balkenentwertung	Anulado con barras	Sbarrato
Bisected	Timbre coupé	Halbiert	Partido en dos	Frazionato
Bistre	Bistre	Bister	Bistre	Bistro
Bistre-brown	Brun-bistre	Bisterbraun	Castaño bistre	Bruno-bistro
Black	Noir	Schwarz	Negro	Nero
Blackish Brown	Brun-noir	Schwärzlichbraun	Castaño negruzco	Bruno nerastro
Blackish Green	Vert foncé	Schwärzlichgrün	Verde negruzco	Verde nerastro
Blackish Olive	Olive foncé	Schwärzlicholiv	Oliva negruzco	Oliva nerastro
Block of four	Bloc de quatre	Viererblock	Bloque de cuatro	Bloco di quattro
Blue	Bleu	Blau	Azul	Azzurro
Blue-green	Vert-bleu	Blaugrün	Verde azul	Verde azzurro
Bluish Violet	Violet bleuâtre	Bläulichviolett	Violeta azulado	Violetto azzurrastro
Booklet	Carnet	Heft	Cuadernillo	Libretto
Bright Blue	Bleu vif	Lebhaftblau	Azul vivo	Azzurro vivo
Bright Green	Vert vif	Lebhaftgrün	Verde vivo	Verde vivo
Bright Purple	Mauve vif	Lebhaftpurpur	Púrpura vivo	Porpora vivo
Bronze-green	Vert-bronze	Bronzegrün	Verde bronce	Verde bronzo
Brown	Brun	Braun	Castaño	Bruno
Brown-lake	Carmin-brun	Braunlack	Laca castaño	Lacca bruno
Brown-purple	Pourpre-brun	Braunpurpur	Púrpura castaño	Porpora bruno
Brown-red	Rouge-brun	Braunrot	Rojo castaño	Rosso bruno
Buff	Chamois	Sämisch	Anteado	Camoscio
Cancellation	Oblitération	Entwertung	Cancelación	Annullamento
Cancelled	Annulé	Gestempelt	Cancelado	Annullato
Carmine	Carmin	Karmin	Carmín	Carminio
Carmine-red	Rouge-carmin	Karminrot	Rojo carmín	Rosso carminio
Centred	Centré	Zentriert	Centrado	Centrato
Cerise	Rouge-cerise	Kirschrot	Color de ceresa	Color Ciliegia
Chalk-surfaced paper	Papier couché	Kreidepapier	Papel estucado	Carta gessata
Chalky Blue	Bleu terne	Kreideblau	Azul turbio	Azzurro smorto
Charity stamp	Timbre de bienfaisance	Wohltätigkeits- marke	Sello de beneficenza	Francobollo di beneficenza
Chestnut	Marron	Kastanienbraun	Castaño rojo	Marrone
Chocolate	Chocolat	Schokolade	Chocolate	Cioccolato
Cinnamon	Cannelle	Zimtbraun	Canela	Cannella
Claret	Grenat	Weinrot	Rojo vinoso	Vinaccia
Cobalt	Cobalt	Kobalt	Cobalto	Cobalto
Colour	Couleur	Farbe	Color	Colore
Comb-perforation	Dentelure en peigne	Kammzähnung, Reihenzähnung	Dentado de peine	Dentellatura e pettine
Commemorative stamp	Timbre commémoratif	Gedenkmarke	Sello conmemorativo	Francobollo commemorativo
Crimson	Cramoisi	Karmesin	Carmesí	Cremisi
Deep Blue	Bleu foncé	Dunkelblau	Azul oscuro	Azzurro scuro
Deep Bluish Green	Vert-bleu foncé	Dunkelbläulichgrün	Verde azulado oscuro	Verde azzurro scuro
Design	Dessin	Markenbild	Diseño	Disegno
Die	Matrice	Urstempel, Type, Platte	Cuño	Conio, Matrice
Double	Double	Doppelt	Doble	Doppio
Drab	Olive terne	Trüboliv	Oliva turbio	Oliva smorto
Dull Green	Vert terne	Trübgrün	Verde turbio	Verde smorto
Dull Purple	Mauve terne	Trübpurpur	Púrpura turbio	Porpora smorto

English	French	German	Spanish	Italian
Embossing	Impression en relief	Prägedruck	Impresión en relieve	Impressione a relievo
Emerald	Vert-eméraude	Smaragdgrün	Esmeralda	Smeraldo
Engraved	Gravé	Graviert	Grabado	Inciso
Error	Erreur	Fehler, Fehldruck	Error	Errore
Essay	Essai	Probedruck	Ensayo	Saggio
Express letter stamp	Timbre pour lettres par exprès	Eilmarke	Sello de urgencia	Francobollo per espresso
Fiscal stamp	Timbre fiscal	Stempelmarke	Sello fiscal	Francobollo fiscale
Flesh	Chair	Fleischfarben	Carne	Carnicino
Forgery	Faux, Falsification	Fälschung	Falsificación	Falso, Falsificazione
Frame	Cadre	Rahmen	Marco	Cornice
Granite paper	Papier avec fragments de fils de soie	Faserpapier	Papel con filamentos	Carto con fili di seta
Green	Vert	Grün	Verde	Verde
Greenish Blue	Bleu verdâtre	Grünlichblau	Azul verdoso	Azzurro verdastro
Greenish Yellow	Jaune-vert	Grünlichgelb	Amarillo verdoso	Giallo verdastro
Grey	Gris	Grau	Gris	Grigio
Grey-blue	Bleu-gris	Graublau	Azul gris	Azzurro grigio
Grey-green	Vert gris	Graugrün	Verde gris	Verde grigio
Gum	Gomme	Gummi	Goma	Gomma
Gutter	Interpanneau	Zwischensteg	Espacio blanco entre dos grupos	Ponte
Imperforate	Non-dentelé	Geschnitten	Sin dentar	Non dentellato
Indigo	Indigo	Indigo	Azul indigo	Indaco
Inscription	Inscription	Inschrift	Inscripción	Dicitura
Inverted	Renversé	Kopfstehend	Invertido	Capovolto
Issue	Émission	Ausgabe	Emisión	Emissione
Laid	Vergé	Gestreift	Listado	Vergata
Lake	Lie de vin	Lackfarbe	Laca	Lacca
Lake-brown	Brun-carmin	Lackbraun	Castaño laca	Bruno lacca
Lavender	Bleu-lavande	Lavendel	Color de alhucema	Lavanda
Lemon	Jaune-citron	Zitrongelb	Limón	Limone
Light Blue	Bleu clair	Hellblau	Azul claro	Azzurro chiaro
Lilac	Lilas	Lila	Lila	Lilla
Line perforation	Dentelure en lignes	Linienzähnung	Dentado en linea	Dentellatura lineare
Lithography	Lithographie	Steindruck	Litografía	Litografia
Local	Timbre de poste locale	Lokalpostmarke	Emisión local	Emissione locale
Lozenge roulette	Percé en losanges	Rautenförmiger Durchstich	Picadura en rombos	Perforazione a losanghe
Magenta	Magenta	Magentarot	Magenta	Magenta
Margin	Marge	Rand	Borde	Margine
Maroon	Marron pourpré	Dunkelrotpurpur	Púrpura rojo oscuro	Marrone rossastro
Mauve	Mauve	Malvenfarbe	Malva	Malva
Multicoloured	Polychrome	Mehrfarbig	Multicolores	Policromo
Myrtle-green	Vert myrte	Myrtengrün	Verde mirto	Verde mirto
New Blue	Bleu ciel vif	Neublau	Azul nuevo	Azzurro nuovo
Newspaper stamp	Timbre pour journaux	Zeitungsmarke	Sello para periódicos	Francobollo per giornali
Obliteration	Oblitération	Abstempelung	Matasello	Annullamento
Obsolete	Hors (de) cours	Ausser Kurs	Fuera de curso	Fuori corso
Ochre	Ocre	Ocker	Ocre	Ocra
Official stamp	Timbre de service	Dienstmarke	Sello de servicio	Francobollo di servizio
Olive-brown	Brun-olive	Olivbraun	Castaño oliva	Bruno oliva
Olive-green	Vert-olive	Olivgrün	Verde oliva	Verde oliva
Olive-grey	Gris-olive	Olivgrau	Gris oliva	Grigio oliva

English	French	German	Spanish	Italian
Olive-yellow	Jaune-olive	Olivgelb	Amarillo oliva	Giallo oliva
Orange	Orange	Orange	Naranja	Arancio
Orange-brown	Brun-orange	Orangebraun	Castaño naranja	Bruno arancio
Orange-red	Rouge-orange	Orangerot	Rojo naranja	Rosso arancio
Orange-yellow	Jaune-orange	Orangegelb	Amarillo naranja	Giallo arancio
Overprint	Surcharge	Aufdruck	Sobrecarga	Soprastampa
Pair	Paire	Paar	Pareja	Coppia
Pale	Pâle	Blass	Pálido	Pallido
Pane	Panneau	Gruppe	Grupo	Gruppo
Paper	Papier	Papier	Papel	Carta
Parcel post stamp	Timbre pour colis postaux	Paketmarke	Sello para paquete postal	Francobollo per pacchi postali
Pen-cancelled	Oblitéré à plume	Federzugentwertung	Cancelado a pluma	Annullato a penna
Percé en arc	Percé en arc	Bogenförmiger Durchstich	Picadura en forma de arco	Perforazione ad arco
Percé en scie	Percé en scie	Bogenförmiger Durchstich	Picado en sierra	Foratura a sega
Perforated	Dentelé	Gezähnt	Dentado	Dentellato
Perforation	Dentelure	Zähnung	Dentar	Dentellatura
Photogravure	Photogravure, Heliogravure	Rastertiefdruck	Fotograbado	Rotocalco
Pin perforation	Percé en points	In Punkten durchstochen	Horadado con alfileres	Perforato a punti
Plate	Planche	Platte	Plancha	Lastra, Tavola
Plum	Prune	Pflaumenfarbe	Color de ciruela	Prugna
Postage Due stamp	Timbre-taxe	Portomarke	Sello de tasa	Segnatasse
Postage stamp	Timbre-poste	Briefmarke, Frei-marke, Postmarke	Sello de correos	Francobollo postale
Postal fiscal stamp	Timbre fiscal-postal	Stempelmarke als Postmarke ver-wendet	Sello fiscal-postal	Fiscale postale
Postmark	Oblitération postale	Poststempel	Matasello	Bollo
Printing	Impression, Tirage	Druck	Impresión	Stampa, Tiratura
Proof	Épreuve	Druckprobe	Prueba de impresión	Prova
Provisionals	Timbres provisoires	Provisorische Mark-en, Provisorien	Provisionales	Provvisori
Prussian Blue	Bleu de Prusse	Preussischblau	Azul de Prusia	Azzurro di Prussia
Purple	Pourpre	Purpur	Púrpura	Porpora
Purple-brown	Brun-pourpre	Purpurbraun	Castaño púrpura	Bruno porpora
Recess-printing	Impression en taille douce	Tiefdruck	Grabado	Incisione
Red	Rouge	Rot	Rojo	Rosso
Red-brown	Brun-rouge	Rotbraun	Castaño rojizo	Bruno rosso
Reddish Lilac	Lilas rougeâtre	Rötlichlila	Lila rojizo	Lilla rossastro
Reddish Purple	Pourpre-rouge	Rötlichpurpur	Púrpura rojizo	Porpora rossastro
Reddish Violet	Violet rougeâtre	Rötlichviolett	Violeta rojizo	Violetto rossastro
Red-orange	Orange rougeâtre	Rotorange	Naranja rojizo	Arancio rosso
Registration stamp	Timbre pour lettre chargée (recom-mandée)	Einschreibemarke	Sello de certificado	Francobollo per lettere raccoman-date
Reprint	Réimpression	Neudruck	Reimpresión	Ristampa
Reversed	Retourné	Umgekehrt	Invertido	Rovesciato
Rose	Rose	Rosa	Rosa	Rosa
Rose-red	Rouge rosé	Rosarot	Rojo rosado	Rosso rosa
Rosine	Rose vif	Lebhaftrosa	Rosa vivo	Rosa vivo
Roulette	Perçage	Durchstich	Picadura	Foratura
Rouletted	Percé	Durchstochen	Picado	Forato
Royal Blue	Bleu-roi	Königblau	Azul real	Azzurro reale

English	French	German	Spanish	Italian
Sage-green	Vert-sauge	Salbeigrün	Verde salvia	Verde salvia
Salmon	Saumon	Lachs	Salmón	Salmone
Scarlet	Écarlate	Scharlach	Escarlata	Scarlatto
Sepia	Sépia	Sepia	Sepia	Seppia
Serpentine roulette	Percé en serpentin	Schlangenliniger Durchstich	Picado a serpentina	Perforazione a serpentina
Shade	Nuance	Tönung	Tono	Gradazione de colore
Sheet	Feuille	Bogen	Hoja	Foglio
Slate	Ardoise	Schiefer	Pizarra	Ardesia
Slate-blue	Bleu-ardoise	Schieferblau	Azul pizarra	Azzurro ardesia
Slate-green	Vert-ardoise	Schiefergrün	Verde pizarra	Verde ardesia
Slate-lilac	Lilas-gris	Schieferlila	Lila pizarra	Lilla ardesia
Slate-purple	Mauve-gris	Schieferpurpur	Púrpura pizarra	Porpora ardesia
Slate-violet	Violet-gris	Schieferviolett	Violeta pizarra	Violetto ardesia
Special delivery stamp	Timbre pour exprès	Eilmarke	Sello de urgencia	Francobollo per espressi
Specimen	Spécimen	Muster	Muestra	Saggio
Steel Blue	Bleu acier	Stahlblau	Azul acero	Azzurro acciaio
Strip	Bande	Streifen	Tira	Striscia
Surcharge	Surcharge	Aufdruck	Sobrecarga	Soprastampa
Tête-bêche	Tête-bêche	Kehrdruck	Tête-bêche	Tête-bêche
Tinted paper	Papier teinté	Getöntes Papier	Papel Coloreado	Carta tinta
Too-late stamp	Timbre pour lettres en retard	Verspätungsmarke	Sello para cartas retardadas	Francobollo per le lettere in ritardo
Turquoise-blue	Bleu-turquoise	Türkisblau	Azul turquesa	Azzurro turchese
Turquoise-green	Vert-turquoise	Türkisgrün	Verde turquesa	Verde turchese
Typography	Typographie	Buchdruck	Tipografia	Tipografia
Ultramarine	Outremer	Ultramarin	Ultramar	Oltremare
Unused	Neuf	Ungebraucht	Nuevo	Nuovo
Used	Oblitéré, Usé	Gebraucht	Usado	Usato
Venetian Red	Rouge-brun terne	Venezianischrot	Rojo veneciano	Rosso veneziano
Vermilion	Vermillon	Zinnober	Cinabrio	Vermiglione
Violet	Violet	Violett	Violeta	Violetto
Violet-blue	Bleu-violet	Violettblau	Azul violeta	Azzurro violetto
Watermark	Filigrane	Wasserzeichen	Filigrana	Filigrana
Watermark sideways	Filigrane couché	Wasserzeichen liegend	Filigrana acostado	Filigrana coricata
Wove paper	Papier ordinaire, Papier uni	Einfaches Papier	Papel avitelado	Carta unita
Yellow	Jaune	Gelb	Amarillo	Giallo
Yellow-brown	Brun-jaune	Gelbbraun	Castaño amarillo	Bruno giallo
Yellow-green	Vert-jaune	Gelbgrün	Verde amarillo	Verde giallo
Yellow-olive	Olive jaunâtre	Gelboliv	Oliva amarillo	Oliva giallastro
Yellow-orange	Orange jaunâtre	Gelborange	Naranja amarillo	Arancio giallastro
Zig-zag roulette	Percé en zigzag	Sägezahnartiger Durchstich	Picado en zigzig	Perforazione a zigzag

Abu Dhabi

1000 Fils = 1 Dinar

The largest of the Trucial States on the Persian Gulf which comprise Abu Dhabi, Ajman, Dubai, Fujeira, Ras al Khaima, Sharjah and Umm al Qiwain; these are so called after the Perpetual Maritime Truce agreement with the United Kingdom of May 1853 under which their Shaikhs undertook to give up piracy and the slave trade.

Abu Dhabi had a British postal administration till 1 January 1967, when the shaikhdom took over the postal service. Earlier issues are listed in the British Commonwealth Catalogue.

9   **10**

Shaikh Zaid bin Sultan al Nahayyan

(Recess (Nos. 26/33) or litho (Nos. 34/7) De La Rue)

1967–69. (a) T **9** and various other designs. P 13×13½ (1 April 1967).

26	–	5 f. red and deep green	..	5	5
27	–	15 f. red and deep brown	..	5	5
		a. Surch "25" in Arabic numerals (13.12.69) (on cover)*			
28	–	20 f. red and deep blue	..	5	5
29	–	35 f. red and deep reddish violet	..	5	8
30	9	40 f. bluish green	..	8	10
31		50 f. brown	..	10	10
32		60 f. new blue ..	..	10	12
33		100 f. carmine	..	20	20
34	–	125 f. olive-brown and apple-green	..	20	25
35	–	200 f. brown and greenish blue	..	30	35
36	–	500 f. bright violet and orange ..	..	85	90
37	–	1 d. ultramarine and yellow-green	..	1·75	1·90
26/37		Set of 12	..	3·75	4·00

Designs: Vert (as T **9**)—5 f. to 35 f. National flag. Horiz (47×27 mm)—125 f. Antelope; 200 f. Falcon; 500 f., 1 d. Palace. Each with portrait of ruler.

*Due to heavy demand for the 5 f. and 20 f. values during December 1969 the Director of Posts surcharged a limited quantity of the 15 f. stamp with "25" (f.) in Arabic figures by means of a numbering machine.

Nearly all of these provisionals were sold over the Post Office counters between 13 Dec and 24 Dec and must be used on cover during this period.

(Photo Harrison)

     (b) T **10**. P 14½×14 (6 Aug 1967)

38	10	40 f. deep bluish green	..	8	8
39		50 f. brown	..	8	10
40		60 f. new blue..	..	10	10
41		100 f. carmine ..	..	15	20
38/41		Set of 4	..	40	45

11 Human Rights Emblem and Shaikh Zaid

(Photo Harrison)

1968 (1 Apr). Human Rights Year. P 14½×14.

42	11	35 f. multicoloured	..	5	8
43		60 f. multicoloured	..	10	10
44		150 f. multicoloured	..	25	30

12 Arms and Shaikh Zaid

(Des and photo Harrison)

1968 (6 Aug). Shaikh's Accession Anniversary. P 14×14½.

45	12	5 f. black, silver, red and green	..	5	5
46		10 f. black, silver, red and orange	..	5	5
47		100 f. black, gold, red and mauve	..	20	20
48		125 f. black, gold, red and light blue	..	25	30
45/8		Set of 4 ..	..	50	55

13 New Construction

(Des V. Whiteley. Litho De La Rue)

1968–69. 2nd Anniv of Shaikh's Accession. "Progress in Abu Dhabi". T **13** and similar horiz designs. Multicoloured. P 12½×13 (10 f.) or 12 (others).

49	5 f. Type **13** (17.12.68) ..	..	5	5
50	10 f. Airport buildings (46½×34 mm) (1.1.69) ..	..	5	5
51	35 f. Shaikh Zaid, bridge and falcon (59×34 mm) (1.1.69) ..	..	5	8

14 Petroleum Installations

(Des A. Larkins. Litho De La Rue)

1969 (6 Aug). Third Anniversary of Shaikh's Accession. Petroleum Industry. T **14** and similar horiz designs. Multicoloured. P 14.

52	35 f. Type **14** ..	..	5	5
53	60 f. Marine drilling platform	..	10	10
54	125 f. Separator platform, Zakum field	..	20	20
55	200 f. Tank farm ..	..	35	35
52/55	Set of 4 ..	..	65	70

15 Shaikh Zaid   **16** Arab Stallion

(Litho De La Rue)

1970 (1 Jan)–**1971**. *T* **15/16** *and similar designs.* *P* 14.

56	**15**	5 f. multicoloured (1.4.70)	..	5	5
57	–	10 f. multicoloured	..	5	5
58	**15**	25 f. multicoloured (1.4.70)	..	5	5
59	–	35 f. multicoloured (1.7.70)	..	5	5
60	–	50 f. multicoloured	..	8	8
61	**15**	60 f. multicoloured (1.4.70)	..	10	10
62	–	70 f. multicoloured	..	10	10
63	**15**	90 f. multicoloured (1.4.70)	..	15	20
64	**16**	125 f. multicoloured (18.1.71)	..	20	25
65	–	150 f. multicoloured (18.1.71)	..	25	30
66	–	500 f. multicoloured (18.1.71)	..	85	90
67	–	1 d. multicoloured (18.1.71)	..	1·75	1·90
56/67		*Set of* 12	..	3·50	4·00

Designs: *Vert* (as *T* **15**)—10, 35, 50, 70 f. Similar portrait, but without scroll at foot and country name larger. *Horiz* (as *T* **16**)—150 f. Gazelle; 500 f. Fort Jahili; 1 d. Great Mosque. Face value is in Arabic only on No. 67.

17 Shaikh Zaid and "Mount Fuji" (T. Hayashi)

(Litho Kyodo Printing Co Ltd, Japan)

1970 (10 July). *"Expo 70" World Fair, Osaka, Japan.* *P* 13.

68	**17**	25 f. multicoloured	..	5	5
69	–	35 f. multicoloured	..	5	5
70	–	60 f. multicoloured	..	10	10

18 Abu Dhabi Airport   **19** Pres. Nasser

(Litho De La Rue)

1970 (22 Sept). *4th Anniversary of Shaikh's Accession. Completion of Abu Dhabi Airport.* *T* **18** *and similar multicoloured designs.* *P* 13½ × 14 (150 f.) or 14 × 13½ (*others*).

71	25 f. Type **18**	..	5	5
72	60 f. Airport entrance	..	10	10
73	150 f. Aerial view of Abu Dhabi (*vert*)	..	25	30

(Litho De La Rue)

1971 (3 May). *Gamal Nasser (President of Egypt) Commemoration.* *P* 14.

74	**19**	25 f. black and pink	..	5	5
75		35 f. black and lilac	..	5	5

20 Motorised Patrol

(Litho De La Rue)

1971 (6 Aug). *5th Anniversary of Shaikh's Accession. Defence Force.* *T* **20** *and similar horiz designs.* *Multicoloured.* *P* 13½.

76	35 f. Type **20**	..	5	5
77	60 f. Patrol-boat	..	10	10
78	125 f. Armoured car	..	20	20
79	150 f. "Hunter" jet-fighters	..	25	25
76/79	*Set of* 4	..	55	55

UNITED ARAB EMIRATES

Following the withdrawal of British forces from the Gulf and the ending of the Anglo-Trucial States treaties six of the states, Abu Dhabi, Ajman, Dubai, Fujeira, Sharjah and Umm al Qiwain, formed an independent Union on 2 December 1971. The seventh state, Ras al Khaima, joined during February, 1972. Each emirate continued to use its own stamps, pending the introduction of a unified currency. A Union Postal administration came into being on 1 Aug 1972.

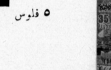

5 Fils

(21)   **22** Dome of the Rock

(Surch by NITCO Printing Press, Abu Dhabi)

1971 (8 Dec). *No.* 60 *surch with T* **21** *in green.*

80	5 f. on 50 f. multicoloured	..	75	75
	a. Surch albino	..		

No. 80 was surcharged to meet the seasonal demand for the local greetings card rate and was only on sale from the 8th to the 18th December, when further supplies of No. 56 arrived.

(Litho De La Rue)

1972 (3 June). *Dome of the Rock, Jerusalem.* *T* **22** *and similar vert views.* *Multicoloured.* *P* 13½.

81	35 f. Type **22**	..	5	5
82	60 f. Mosque entrance	..	10	10
83	125 f. Mosque dome	..	20	20

UAE

(23)

(Optd by National Printing Press, Abu Dhabi)

1972 (Aug). *Provisional Issue. Nos. 56/67 optd with T 23 and similar types.*

84	**15**	5	f. multicoloured (1.8)	..	..	5	5
			a. Opt inverted	..	..		
85	–	10	f. multicoloured (1.8)	..	..	5	5
86	**15**	25	f. multicoloured	..	..	5	5
87	–	35	f. multicoloured	..	..	5	5
88	–	50	f. multicoloured	..	..	8	8
89	**15**	60	f. multicoloured (1.8)	..	..	10	10
90	–	70	f. multicoloured	..	..	10	10
91	**15**	90	f. multicoloured	..	..	15	20
92	**16**	125	f. multicoloured	..	..	20	25
93	–	150	f. multicoloured	..	..	25	30
94	–	500	f. multicoloured	..	..	85	90
95	–	1	d. multicoloured	..	..	1·75	1·90
84/95			*Set of* 12	..	..	3·50	4·00

Although overprinted "UAE" these stamps were initially only on sale in Abu Dhabi. Later, supplies of the 10 and 25 f. values were sent to Dubai and to Sharjah to meet shortages of stamps there.

The stamps of Abu Dhabi were superseded by those of United Arab Emirates on 1 January 1973.

ABYSSINIA. See Ethiopia.

Afghanistan

1870. 12 Shahi=6 Sanar=3 Abasi=1 Rupee
1920. 60 Paisa=2 Kran=1 Rupee
1926. 100 Poul (Pul)=1 Afghani (Rupee)

The Kabuli ordinary rupee of raw silver was worth 60 paisa but there was also a Kabuli sterling rupee of refined silver which was worth 66 paisa

Afghanistan first became a kingdom under Afghan rule in 1747. The title of the ruler in 1868, when Sher Ali established his authority, was that of Amir.

Amir Sher Ali

9 June 1863–1866; 1868–21 February 1879

DATES OF ISSUE. All the circular and some of the rectangular stamps bear the Mahommedan date of issue in the following numerals:

١	٢	٣	٤	٥
1	2	3	4	5

٦	٧	٨	٩	٠
6	7	8	9	0

These must be understood for correct identification and the approximate positions of the dates are shown by the arrows in the illustrations.

CANCELLATIONS. The usual form of cancellation up to 1891 consisted of cutting or tearing off a portion of the stamp, and used specimens are therefore found in apparently damaged condition.

PRICES. The prices quoted for the circular stamps are for cut-square specimens and where these are used, with "cancelling tear". Stamps cut round, both unused and used, are worth only a fraction of these prices.

VALIDITY. Until 1928 when Afghanistan joined the U.P.U. the stamps were only valid for internal use, foreign mail having to be franked in addition with Indian stamps.

1870–1900 ISSUES. These were all lithographed locally and issued imperforate and without gum. The stamps were drawn separately on the plates and differ in detail.

2 Shahi

1870–71. Dated 1288. Medium laid paper, white to yellowish.

1	1	Shahi, black (Pl. A)	..	..	.. 50·00 12·00
2		Shahi, black (Pl. B)	..	..	.. 12·00 7·00
3		Shahi, black (Pl. C)	..	..	.. 18·00 5·00
4	2	Shahi, black (Pl. D)	..	..	.. 30·00 7·00
5	1	Sanar, black (Pl. B)	..	..	.. 25·00 12·00
6		Sanar, black (Pl. C)	..	..	.. 10·00 5·00
7	2	Sanar, black (Pl. D)	..	..	.. 25·00 10·00
8	1	Abasi, black (Pl. C)	..	..	.. 10·00 5·00
9	2	Abasi, black (Pl. D)	..	..	.. 12·00 5·00

The four plates were each of 15 stamps. Plates B, C and D were of mixed values. The make up and characteristics of the plates are as follows:—

Pl. A. Both circles dotted. Outer circle 30 mm diam. Plate entirely of "Shahi" types.

Pl. B. Both circles dotted. Outer circle 28 mm diam. Ten "Shahi" and five "Sanar" types.

Pl. C. Both circles dotted. Outer circle 28 mm diam. Outer circle narrower. Five "Shahi", five "Sanar" and five "Abasi" types.

Pl. D. Outer circle dotted. Inner circle round lion's head plain. Five "Shahi, five "Sanar" and five "Abasi" types.

1 Shahi

Sanar

Abasi

3 6 Shahi   1 Rupee

5

1871–72. *Dated 1289. Thin yellowish wove paper.*

10	**3**	6 Shahi, reddish purple ..	..	..	£120	75·00
11		1 rupee, reddish purple ..	..	..	£150	£100

Plate of four stamps, two types of each value. Position of date varies in each type.

1872–73. *Dated 1290. Medium laid paper, white to yellowish.*

13	**5**	Shahi black	..	..	..	..	75	75
14		Shahi, purple	..	..	..	..	£100	75·00

Plate of sixty types. Forgeries exist of No. 14.

4

Abasi   ½ Rupee   1 Rupee

1873–74. *As T 5 but dated 1291. Medium white laid paper.*

15	**5**	Abasi, black	..	..	..	..	12·00	8·00
16		½ rupee, black	..	..	..	..	6·00	5·00
17		1 rupee, black	..	..	..	..	7·00	6·00

Plate of fifteen stamps, five types of each value.

(a)   *(b)*

Abasi

1872–73. *Dated 1290. Medium white laid paper.*

12	**4**	Shahi, black	..	..	..	5·00	2·50
		a. Right-hand ornament missing *(a)*	..	80·00	65·00
		b. Right-hand ornament roughly restored on stone *(b)*	..	..	12·00	6·00

Plate of fifteen types. In its original state. The third (last) stamp in the second row had no external ornament at right *(a)*. The ornament was roughly added on the stone during printing and appears as *(b)*.

6 Sanar   *(a)*

1874–75. *Dated 1292. Thick white laid paper. Stamps printed in black or purple.*

			A. Black	B. Purple
			35·00 25·00	5·00 5·00
18	**6**	Sanar	35·00 25·00	5·00 5·00
		a. Wide outer circle (a) ..	80·00 60·00	40·00 25·00
19		Abasi	50·00 35·00	7·00 8·00

Plate of fifteen stamps: ten "Sanar" types and five "Abasi" types. No. 18a is the last stamp in the sheet.

7½ Rupee

(a) Shahi   (b) Shahi   Sanar

     (img)   (img)   (img)

(c) Abasi   (d) Abasi   (e) Rupee   (f) Rupee

1875–76. *Dated 1293. So-called "tablet" issue. The value is in a white tablet below the lion's head.*

A. White laid paper. B. White laid card paper

				A	B
20	**7**	Shahi, black (a)	..	50·00 25·00	— 50·00
21		Shahi, black (b)	..	50·00 25·00	— 50·00
22		Sanar, black ..	..	70·00 30·00	— 60·00
23		Abasi, black (c)..	..	80·00 30·00	— 50·00
24		Abasi, black (d)	..	£100 40·00	— 75·00
25		½ rupee, black ..	..	50·00 30·00	— 70·00
26		Rupee, black (e)	..	90·00 40·00	— 75·00
27		Rupee, black (f)	..	£175 55·00	— 90·00

White laid paper

28	**7**	Shahi, purple (a)	..	75·00 35·00
29		Shahi, purple (b)	..	75·00 35·00
30		Sanar, purple ..	..	75·00 40·00
31		Abasi, purple (c)	..	80·00 40·00
32		Abasi, purple (d)	..	£170 60·00
33		½ rupee, purple ..	..	15·00
34		Rupee, purple (e)	..	15·00
35		Rupee, purple (f)	..	35·00

The value on Types (c) and (e) reads "abasi" or "rupee" but on Types (d) and (f) the value is expressed as "one abasi" or "one rupee".

Plate of twenty-four stamps: twelve "Shahi" types and three types each of the other values, as follows:—
Shahi: 6 of (a), 6 of (b).   ½ rupee: 3
Sanar: 3.   Rupee: 2 of (e), 1 of (f).
Abasi: 2 of (c), 1 of (d).

8 Sanar

(a) Shahi   (b) Shahi   Abasi   ½ Rupee   1 Rupee

1875–76. *Dated 1293. Inscriptions on white ground. Medium white laid paper.*

Four series in different colours, one for each Post Office

A. Peshawar. *Grey.*   C. Kabul. *Greenish grey, brownish green, yellow-brown.*
B. Jalalabad, *Purple to violet.*   D. Tashkurghan (Khulm). *Grey-black, brownish black.*

							A		B		C		D	
36	**8**	Shahi (a)	..	..	..	..	1·50	1·00	4·00	1·00	6·00	1·75	30·00	20·00
37		Shahi (b)	..	..	..	..	2·50	1·50	9·00	2·00	—	3·75	—	—
38		Sanar ..	..	..	..	..	5·00	2·50	5·00	2·00	10·00	4·25	45·00	25·00
39		Abasi ..	..	..	..	..	6·00	2·50	9·00	3·50	16·00	8·00	100·00	50·00
40		½ rupee ..	..	..	..	..	7·00	3·00	16·00	6·00	16·00	12·00	70·00	70·00
41		1 rupee ..	..	..	..	..	7·00	3·00	17·00	7·00	24·00	24·00	80·00	80·00

The above Post Offices were opened in 1871. We no longer list stamps for Kandahar and Herat. In Kandahar there was a British Field Post Office but a local office was not opened there until 1883 or 1884 and mail was routed to India via Chaman as the route to Kabul was not established until 1906. The Herat office did not open until 1908. Stamps in jet-black and in bright green shades are fakes. Stamps in very pale brown on whiter paper are reprints made in Peshawar.

Two plates of twenty-four stamps each: Plate A, twenty-four "Shahi" types (20 of (a) and 4 of (b)). Plate B, twelve "Sanar" types, six "Abasi" types and three types each of ½ rupee and 1 rupee.

9 Shahi

Sanar

Abasi

½ Rupee

1 Rupee

(a) Full date 1294

(b)
Abbreviated
date 94

1876–77. *Dated* 1294. *Medium white laid paper. Variations in colours for Kabul and Tashkurghan.*
A. Peshawar. *Grey.*
B. Jalalabad. *Purple to violet.*
C. Kabul. *Greenish grey, olive-grey.*
D. Tashkurghan (Khulm). *Yellow-brown, brown.*

				A		B		C		D	
42	9	Shahi (*a*)		2·40	2·00	3·00	2·00	—	3·00	2·40	1·00
43		Shahi (*b*)		60	50	65	45	2·40	1·50	65	40
44		Sanar (*b*)		1·50	50	1·75	35	4·75	1·50	2·10	65
45		Abasi (*a*)		3·50	2·00	4·75	3·00	12·00	10·00	8·50	4·00
46		Abasi (*b*)		2·40	75	3·50	1·25	9·50	8·00	4·75	2·50
47		½ rupee (*a*)		4·25	3·50	5·50	3·00	14·00	12·00	8·50	5·00
48		1 rupee (*a*)		4·25	3·50	5·50	3·00	14·00	12·00	8·50	5·00

As with the previous issue stamps in black, bright green and also sage-green on wove paper are fakes.
Plate of forty stamps: twenty-five "Shahi" types (4 of (*a*) and 21 of (*b*)), eight "Sanar" types, three "Abasi" types (1 of (*a*) and 2 of (*b*)) and two types each of ½ rupee and 1 rupee.

10 Shahi

Sanar

Abasi

½ Rupee

1 Rupee

11 Shahi

1877–78. *Dated* 95. *Medium white laid paper. Colours as last.*

				A		B		C		D	
49	10	Shahi		35	35	40	35	†		5·50	1·75
50		Sanar		40	30	35	30	60	50	75	65
51		Abasi		1·10	1·10	1·60	1·40	1·75	1·50	2·10	1·75
52		½ rupee		2·40	2·00	4·75	3·00	5·50	4·00	7·00	4·50
53		1 rupee		2·40	2·00	5·50	3·00	5·50	4·50	7·00	4·50

Two plates of forty stamps each. Plate A, forty "Shahi" types. Plate B, thirty "Sanar" types, six "Abasi" types, and two types each of ½ and 1 rupee.

1878. As last, but new (so-called "Skeleton") type.

54	11	Sh		65	30	60	50	25	20	25	20

Plate of forty "Shahi" types. No. 54 in yellow-brown is known on thick white laid card-paper.

PAPERMAKER'S WATERMARK. All the foregoing may be found with papermaker's watermark "LESCHALLAS" and "PRO BONO PUBLICO" with ornamental designs.

Amir Yakub Khan, February–19 October 1879

Amir Abdurrahman Khan, 22 July 1880–1 October 1901

12 1 Abasi

2 Abasi

1 Rupee

1880. *Dated* 1298. *Handstamped in the following colours:—*

Purple:	*Pale, dull and deep purple; mauve, violet-purple; brown-purple; black-purple.*
Lake:	*Carmine, pale and deep carmine; lake, carmine-lake, deep lake; magenta; brown-lake; dull red.*
Brown:	*Pale and deep red-brown; yellow-brown; brown, deep brown; orange-brown, orange-red-brown.*
Black:	*Grey-black; brownish black; purple-black; deep black.*
Orange:	*Pure orange.*
Green:	*Bright green.*
Blue:	*Deep blue.*

A. *Thin laid bâtonné (including surface ribbed bâtonné)*
B. *Laid.*   C. *Wove.*   D. *Thin wove bâtonné*

I. *On white papers*

			A		B		C		D	
55	**12**	1 a. purple	55	45	—	—	4·75	2·50	†	
56		1 a. lake	90	50	—	—	3·00	1·50	2·00	
57		1 a. brown	90	50	—	—	—	2·00	1·75	1·50
58		1 a. black	5·50	2·50	†		—	—	†	
59		2 a. purple	90	50	—	—	—	—	†	
60		2 a. lake	1·25	1·25	—	—	†		2·75	
61		2 a. brown	1·25	1·00	†		4·75	—	—	—
62		2 a. black	5·50	3·25	—	—	—	—	1·50	1·25
63		1 r. purple	90	60	†		4·75	—	—	
64		1 r. lake	1·50	1·25	†		—	2·25	2·75	—
65		1 r. brown	3·50	3·00	†		—	—	1·60	—
66		1 r. black								†	

II. *On various coloured papers*

			A		B		C		D	
67	**12**	1 a. purple/yellow		1·50	†		13·00	—		
68		1 a. lake/yellow	3·25	1·50	†		85	—	†	
69		1 a. brown/yellow	6·50	—			—	—		
70		1 a. black/yellow	11·00	—	†		6·50	—	†	
71		1 a. green/yellow	†		†		11·00	—		
72		1 a. lake/orange	2·25	3·00	†		1·40	—	†	
73		1 a. purple/pink	2·75	3·00	†		3·50	—	†	
74		1 a. lake/pink	1·40	3·00	†		2·25	—	†	
75		1 a. brown/pink			†		8·50	20·00	†	
76		1 a. black/pink	11·00	—			—	—	†	
77		1 a. green/pink	†		†		5·50	3·00	†	
79		1 a. lake/lavender	1·60	2·00	†		†		†	
80		1 a. brown/lavender			†		8·50	6·00	—	—
81		1 a. black/lavender	8·50	10·00	†		—	—	—	—
82		1 a. orange/lavender	†		†		†		5·50	8·00
83		1 a. purple/green	5·50	8·00	†		5·00	3·00	†	
84		1 a. lake/green	1·10	8·00	†		—	—	†	
85		1 a. brown/green	1·60	6·00	†		—	6·00	3·50	—
86		1 a. black/green	16·00	20·00	†		—	—	—	
87		1 a. blue/green	†		11·00	—	†		†	
88		1 a. purple/blue	—	—	†		6·50	4·00	†	
89		1 a. lake/blue	—	—	†		†		—	5·00
90		1 a. brown/blue	†		†		11·00	—	—	—
91		1 a. black/blue	†		†		—	—	—	—
92		1 a. orange/blue	†		†		†		5·50	—
93		2 a. lake/yellow	1·40	1·25	†		3·00	—	†	
94		2 a. brown/yellow	—	10·00	—	—	—	—	†	
95		2 a. black/yellow	5·50	10·00	†		—	—	†	
96		2 a. lake/orange	†		†		2·25	—	†	
97		2 a. lake/pink	2·25	—	†		3·75	—	†	
98		2 a. brown/pink	—	5·00	†		—	—	†	
99		2 a. black/pink	—	5·00	†		16·00	—	†	
100		2 a. purple/lavender	†		—	—	—	6·00	—	4·50
101		2 a. lake/lavender	2·10	—	†		†		†	
102		2 a. brown/lavender	—	—	†		11·00	—	†	
103		2 a. black/lavender	16·00	—	†		22·00	—	†	
104		2 a. lake/green	1·75	—	†		—	—	†	
105		2 a. brown/green	—	—	†		6·50	—	†	
106		2 a. black/green	†		†		—	5·00	†	
107		2 a. blue/green	†		—	—	†		†	
108		2 a. purple/blue	†		†		—	6·00	†	
109		2 a. brown/blue	†		†		—	5·00	†	
110		2 a. black/blue	†		†		—	—	—	5·50

111	12	1 r. purple/yellow	6·50	—	†		†		†
112		1 r. lake/yellow	3·50	3·25	†	3·00	3·25		†
113		1 r. brown/yellow	6·50	—	—	—	—		†
114		1 r. blue/yellow	6·50	—	†		†		†
115		1 r. black/yellow	6·50	—	†		†		†
116		1 r. lake/orange		†	†	2·75	3·00		†
117		1 r. lake/pink	2·25	3·00	†	3·50	8·00		†
118		1 r. brown/pink	9·50	—	†	8·50	—		†
119		1 r. black/pink	—	—	—	—	5·50	—	†
120		1 r. blue/pink	—	—	†		†		†
121		1 r. lake/lavender	2·10	—	†		†		†
122		1 r. brown/lavender	—	—	†	13·00	8·00		†
123		1 r. black/lavender	27·00	—	†		†		†
124		1 r. purple/green	—	—	†		†	6·00	
125		1 r. lake/green	2·10	5·00	†		†		†
126		1 r. brown/green		†	†	8·50	8·00		†
127		1 r. black/green		†	†		†		†
128		1 r. blue/green	11·00	—	—	—	†		†
129		1 r. purple/blue		†	†	27·00	—		†
130		1 r. brown/blue		†	†	—	—		†
131		1 r. black/blue		†	†	22·00	—	22·00	—

The laid and wove papers may be found thick and thin.
It is doubtful whether all the stamps on coloured papers were actually issued.

13 Type **12** re-drawn, wide outer circle

1889–90. *Dated* 1298. *Handstamped in the following colours:—*

Purple: *Pale, dull, and deep purple; mauve; violet-purple; brown-purple.*
Lake: *Deep carmine; lake; carmine-lake; deep lake; magenta.*
Red: *Dull red.*
Brown: *Red-brown.*
Green: *Bright green.*

(a) *Thin laid bâtonné paper (including surface-ribbed bâtonné)*

132	13	1 a. purple	1·25	1·25
133		1 a. purple/yellow	6·00	6·00
134		1 a. lake	1·25	1·25
135		1 a. red	1·50	1·50
136		1 a. brown	3·50	3·00

(b) *Wove paper*

137	13	1 a. brown-red		
138		1 a. green	7·00	

14

15

16

R 1

1892. *Dated* 1309. *Pelure paper.*

139	14	1 a. grey-blue			45	45
		a. Tête-bêche (pair)			2·75	2·75
140	15	2 a. grey-blue			2·40	2·40
141	16	1 r. grey-blue			5·00	5·00

Each sheet of 178 stamps was made up of 1 a., 130 (3rd stamp in 2nd row, inverted); 2 a., 36; and 1 r., 12.

1892. REGISTRATION. *Dated* 1309. *Pelure paper.*

R142	R 1	1 r. slate-blue		25	40
		a. Tête-bêche (pair)		4·50	

Printed in sheets of 110 (11×10), the 35th stamp being inverted.
Beware of forged cancellations on this and later registration stamps.

17   **R 2**
National Coat-of-Arms. (Repeated with variations on T **18/26**)

1893. *Dated* 1310 (*see arrow*). *Black on thin coloured wove paper.*

142	17	1 a. yellow-green	55	55
		a. Emerald-green	65	65
		b. Blue-green (to deep)	80	70
143		1 a. rose (to deep)	70	65
		a. Carmine	80	70
		b. Salmon-pink	70	60
		c. Crimson	70	60
		d. Brown-rose	1·00	1·00
144		1 a. lilac	1·00	70
		a. Lilac-rose	65	60
		b. Magenta	80	80
		c. Violet (to deep)	70	70
145		1 a. yellow (to bright)	55	55
		a. Greenish yellow	70	50
		b. Orange-yellow	1·25	1·25
146		1 a. salmon	70	60
		a. Bright orange	80	80
147		1 a. blue (to deep)	1·40	1·40
		a. Indigo	1·40	1·40

1894. REGISTRATION. *Dated* 1311. *Thin wove paper.*

R148	R 2	1 r. black/green		35	45

18 2 Abasi   1 r. (value)

R 3

1894–95. *Undated. Thin wove paper.* (*a*) *POSTAGE.*
148   **18** 2 a. black/*green* .. .. 2·00 1·50
149   1 r. black/*green* .. .. 2·25 1·50
          (*b*) *REGISTRATION*
R150 R 3 2 a. black/*green* .. .. 1·75 2·00
   Each sheet of 48 stamps was made up of 2 a., 24; 1 r., 12; and 2 a. Registration, 12.

R 4   19

1898. *REGISTRATION. Undated. Black on thin coloured wove paper.*
R151 R 4 2 a. green (shades) .. .. 80 1·00
R152   2 a. magenta (shades) .. 1·10 1·25
R153   2 a. deep rose .. .. 1·40 1·40
R154   2 a. yellow .. .. 95 1·10
        a. Orange .. .. .. 1·25 1·40
        b. Salmon .. .. .. 1·00 1·10

1899–1900. *Dated 1316. Black on thin coloured wove paper.*
150 **19** 2 a. blue-green 55 55
151   2 a. lilac-rose .. .. 1·40 1·40
152   2 a. rose-red .. .. 1·40 1·40
153   2 a. deep violet 55 55
154   2 a. pale yellow .. .. 1·10 1·10
        a. Orange-yellow 80 80
155   2 a. bright blue .. ..

Amir Habibullah Khan
1 October 1901–19 February 1919

20 1 Abasi   **21** 2 Abasi   **22** 1 Rupee

(Eng Mahmud Masi. Recess)
1907–08.
          (*a*) *Imperf* (Mar 1907–08)
156 **20** 1 a. blue .. .. .. 1·50 40
        a. Blue-green 75 65
        b. Emerald-green (1908) .. 2·00 1·00
157 **21** 2 a. blue 35 25
158 **22** 1 r. green 55 50
         (*b*) *Zigzag roulette* (1907)
159 **20** 1 a. green .. .. .. 6·00 5·00
160 **21** 2 a. blue .. .. .. 8·00 5·00
161 **22** 1 r. blue-green .. .. 10·00 8·00
    (*c*) *Perf* 12 (on 2, 3 or 4 sides) (1908)
162 **20** 1 a. green .. .. .. 1·50 1·00
163 **21** 2 a. blue 35 30
164 **22** 1 r. blue-green 75 75
        a. Imperf between (pair) .. 4·75 4·75
   The above exist with portions of watermark "HOWARD & JONES LONDON" in double-lined capitals.
   Printed in small panes giving *tête-bêche* pairs separated by gutter margins.

23 2 Paisa   **24** 1 Abasi

25 2 Abasi   **26** 1 Rupee

1909 (23 Jan)–**19.** *P* 12. *Typo.*
165 **23** 2 p. olive-brown (1913) .. 25 30
        a. Imperf between (vert pr) ..
        b. Laid paper .. ..
166 **24** 1 a. blue 10 8
        a. Imperf (1910) 45 45
        b. Imperf between (pair) .. 2·00 2·00
167   1 a. red (10.16) 8 8
168   1 a. carmine-rose (1918) .. 8 8
        a. Imperf .. ..
169 **25** 2 a. green 15 15
        a. Imperf (1910) 90
        b. Imperf between (horiz pr)
170   2 a. yellow (10.16) 25 25
        a. Bistre (1919) 25 25
        b. Imperf between (horiz pr)
171 **26** 1 r. red-brown 30 30
172   1 r. bright bistre (10.16) .. 30 30
        a. Yellow-olive (1919) .. 30 45
   No. 165 was used on postcards.
   Nos. 165, 166, 169 and 171 are found on paper watermarked "HOWARD & JONES LONDON".

P 1 3 Shahi   O 1

1 Kran

1 Rupee

2 Rupees

1909–18. *PARCEL POST. Typo. P* 12.

P173	P 1	3 s. olive-brown		12	20
		a. Imperf between (horiz pair)			
		b. Buff (1911–12?)			
P174		3 s. green (10.16)		15	15
P175		1 k. grey-olive		15	30
		a. Yellow-olive			
		b. Grey (1911–12?)			
P176		1 k. rose-red (10.16)		30	50
P177		1 r. orange		50	50
P178		1 r. olive-grey			
P179		1 r. orange-brown (10.16)		35	35
		a. Deep brown (1918)			
P180		2 r. scarlet		65	75
P181		2 r. blue (10.16)		85	85
		a. Imperf between (pair)		3·25	3·25

The above Parcel Post stamps may sometimes be found showing portions of the paper-maker's watermark "HOWARD & JONES LONDON" in double-lined capitals.

1909–22. *OFFICIAL. Typo. P* 12.

O173	O 1	(No value) red		25	30
		a. Thick cream paper			
		b. Laid paper (1920?)			
O174		(No value) carmine (1922)		25	30

King Amanullah
28 February 1919–14 January 1929

In 1919 Afghanistan proclaimed her complete independence both in internal and external affairs. This was recognised by the Government of India on 8 August 1929.

27 Royal Star of Order of Independence

P 2 Old Habibia College, Kabul

(Des Ghulam Mohamed Khan. Typo)

1920 (Sept). *New Currency. First Anniv of End of War of Independence. Large size* 39×47 *mm. P* 12.

173	**27**	10 p. carmine			5·00	2·50
		a. Rose-red			5·00	2·50
174		20 p. maroon			10·00	5·00
175		30 p. blue-green			15·00	7·00

Printed in sheets of two stamps.

1921 (Mar?). *PARCEL POST. Typo. P* 12.

P182	**P 2**	10 p. chocolate			20	20
		a. Tête-bêche (pair)			1·00	1·00
		b. Laid paper				
P183		15 p. red-brown			25	25
		a. Tête-bêche (pair)			1·00	1·00
P184		30 p. bright magenta			60	60
		a. Tête-bêche (pair)			2·25	2·25
		b. Thick laid paper			2·25	2·25
P185		1 r. turquoise-blue			1·00	1·00
		a. Tête-bêche (pair)			4·00	4·00

There were several printings in different shades in sheets of two stamps and in sheets of four arranged in a block or strip. The perforations are usually on only one or two sides.
No. P184b has a papermaker's watermark.
All values are found in at least two different types, the differences being mainly in the clouds.

I	II	III	IV

1922 (April)–**27**. *Second Anniv of End of War of Independence. Small size* 22½×28½ *or* 23×29 *mm.*

(a) P 12

176	**27**	10 p. red (*shades*) (I)			25	25
		a. Error. Maroon			6·00	7·00
177		10 p. red (*shades*) (II) (6.22)			8	8
		a. Error. Lilac-brown				
178		20 p. maroon (*shades*) (III)			10	10
179		20 p. lilac-brown (*shades*) (IV) (1925)			20	20
180		30 p. blue-green			20	20
		a. Tête-bêche (pair)			1·00	1·00
		b. Green			15	15
		ba. Tête-bêche (pair)			1·00	1·00
		c. Apple-green (1924?)			12	12
		ca. Tête-bêche (pair)			90	90

(b) P 11

180d	**27**	10 p. rose (II) (9.27?)			

Settings:—10 p. Type I ("10" in centre of label), sheet of 16 (4×4). 10 p. Type II ("10" to right of label), sheets of 20 (4×5) or 25 (5×5). 20 p. Sheets of 16 (4×4), all Type III; sheets of 25 (5×5), 8 Type III, 17 Type IV. 30 p. Sheets of 16 (4×4), first stamp in last row inverted.

28 "5th Year of Independence of Afghanistan"

1923 (26 Feb). *5th Independence Day. Handstamped with* T **28**, *in black.*

(a) POSTAGE

181	**27**	10 p. rose (I)			2·50	2·50
		aa. Type II				
181a		20 p. lilac-brown (III)				
		b. Type IV				
182		30 p. blue-green			2·50	2·50
		a. Tête-bêche (pair)				

All values exist with the handstamp in blue.

(b) PARCEL POST

P183	**P 2**	10 p. chocolate			6·00
P184		15 p. red-brown			6·00
P185		30 p. bright magenta			

29 Crest of King   29a
Amanullah

(Des Ghulam Mohamed Khan. Typo)

1924 (24 Feb). *6th Independence Day. Small size* 24×32 *mm. P* 12.
183 **29** 10 p. chocolate   ..   ..   ..   3·00   2·50
    a. Tête-bêche (pair)   ..   ..   5·00   4·75
Printed in blocks of 4, *tête-bêche* vertically.

1924–26. *Typo. P* 12.
183b **29a** 5 k. blue (1926?)   ..   ..   2·50
183c   5 r. magenta   ..   ..   1·75
        d. Bright violet (1925?)   ..   1·75
Printed in sheets of 4.

F 1

POSTAGE DUE CANCELLATIONS. The above cancellation was applied to incoming foreign mail arriving without Afghan postage stamps to denote that the internal postage had to be collected. It was occasionally used between 1921 and 1925 but was seldom needed as current Afghan stamps could be purchased at the extra-territorial Afghan post offices at Peshawar and Quetta. However, this privilege was withdrawn on 1 January 1925 after which inadequately franked incoming mail greatly increased. Most of this mail passed through Kabul where the stamps and cancellations were applied. The use of postage due cancellations ceased on 1 April 1928 when Afghanistan joined the Universal Postal Union.
    These were formerly listed as postage due stamps but they are really cancellation marks and not overprints.

1925 (Feb). *7th Independence Day. Larger size* 29×37 *mm. P* 12.
184 **29** 10 p. red-brown   ..   ..   ..   2·50   1·75
Printed in sheets of 8, in two panes of 4 arranged vertically and separated by a gutter margin. Sometimes the panes are *tête-bêche.* Perforations are between the stamps and usually in the top and bottom margins.

1925 (Aug). *POSTAL FISCAL. Typo. P* 12.
F185 **F 1** 1 sh. bistre-brown   ..   ..   —   1·00
F186   1 sh. red-orange   ..   ..   —   5·00
    Owing to a shortage of postage stamps between August 1925 and January 1926 in Mazar-i-Sherif and district the postmaster authorised the use of the above receipt tax stamps of 1909 and 1917 respectively for use as postage stamps.

1926 (27 Feb). *7th Anniv of Independence. Size* 26×33 *mm. P* 12.
185 **29** 10 p. violet-blue   45   45
    a. Imperf (pair)   ..   ..   1·25   1·25
    b. Imperf between (vert pair)   2·50   2·75
    c. Imperf between (horiz pair)   3·25   3·75
Printed in sheets of 8, in two panes of 4, side by side, arranged *tête-bêche; also in sheets of 4.

30 Crest of King Amanullah

Independence Issues. The declaration of independence took place on 28 February 1919, the date of the installation of King Amanullah. The local custom was to celebrate an event by the day rather than the anniversary, thus in 1926 the stamp commemorated the 7th Independence Day although it was the sixth anniversary by western reckoning. In the years 1926–28 the 7th to 9th *anniversaries* were commemorated. From 1931 the local custom was resumed when the 13th independence day was commemorated, although some confusion arose later when some stamps were wrongly inscribed "Anniversary". It was also in 1931 that the date was changed to that of the armistice, 24th August 1919, that ended the war, mainly because the weather was more suitable for the celebrations. Exceptionally in 1937/9 the celebrations took place in May because August was too hot.
    The stamps were normally put on sale at the beginning of the celebrations for a period of two weeks after which the remainders were sent to the Philatelic Bureau in Kabul for sale there at double face value.

1927 (26 Feb). *8th Anniv of Independence. P* 12.
    (a) *Typo in line (white background)*
186 **30** 10 p. magenta   55   55
    a. Imperf between (pair)   ..   3·25
    b. Imperf (pair)
    (b) *Typo in half-tone (dotted background)*
187 **30** 10 p. magenta   65   65
    a. Imperf between (pair)   ..   3·25
    b. Imperf (pair) with gutter margin
Printed in sheets of 8, in two panes of 4, side by side, arranged *tête-bêche* with outer margins imperf.

31   32

33   34 Crest of King Amanullah

T **31/3, 35/9** and **41,** National Seal

1927. *New Currency. Typo.*
    A. *Imperf* (29 Oct).   B. *P* 11 (2, 3 *or* 4 *sides*) (Nov)

		A		B	
188 **31** 15 p. rosine	..	8	8	8	8
a. Imperf between (horiz pair)		†		—	
b. Perf 12	..	†		—	
189 **32** 30 p. blue-green	..	10	8	10	8
a. Imperf between (pair)	..	†		—	
190 **33** 60 p. light blue	..	30	30	25	25
a. Tête-bêche (pair)	..	—	—	75	75
b. Imperf between (vert pair)		†		—	

Sheets—Imperf: 15 p. 9 (3×3); 30 p. 6 (3×2); 60 p. 8 (2×4), the lower pane *tête-bêche.* Perf: At first as the

imperf sheets but later in larger sheets: 15 p. 18 (6×3), 30 p. 16 (4×4); 60 p. 12 (3×4).
See also Nos. 208 and 213 for new colours.

1928 (Feb). *9th Anniv of Independence. Typo. P 11×imperf at outer edges.*
191 **34** 15 p. rosine 25 20
   a. Tête-bêche (pair) 85 85
   b. Imperf between (pair) 85 85
   c. Imperf (pair) .. ..
   d. Do. Tête-bêche (pair) .. ..
In sheets of 8 (2×4), middle rows *tête-bêche* vertically.
A 15 p. stamp similar to Type **34** was not issued and is believed to have been prepared for the 10th Anniversary of Independence.

P 3   P 4

1928. *PARCEL POST. Typo. P 11 or 11×imperf.*
P192 **P 3** 2 a. orange 40 45
   a. Imperf (pair) .. ..
P193 **P 4** 3 a. green 75 75
   2 a. in sheets of 8 (2×4) normally perforated all round; 3 a. in sheets of 4 with imperf outer margins.
See also Nos. P214/5 for new colours.

35   36

37   38   39

1928. *NEWSPAPER. Typo. Size 39×22¾ mm. P 11.*
N192 **35** 2 p. blue *to* indigo (*thick cream paper*) 75 50
   a. Thin white paper 80 80
   b. Imperf between (pair) .. ..
In sheets of 16 (4×4).
Stamps for the newspaper rate are no longer listed amongst the definitive issues as they were only valid for use on newspapers.
See also No. N205.

1928. *Typo. P 11.*
193 **36** 10 p. dull green 5 5
   a. Tête-bêche (pair) .. .. 2·50 2·50
   b. Imperf between (pair) 50 60
   c. Perf 11×12 .. .. ..
   d. Perf 12 .. .. ..
194 **37** 25 p. carmine 8 8

195 **38** 40 p. ultramarine 10 10
   a. Tête-bêche (pair) .. .. 1·60 1·50
   b. Imperf (pair) .. ..
   c. Imperf tête-bêche (pair)
   d. Imperf between (horiz pair) .. 85
   e. Do. Tête-bêche (pair) .. .. 2·75
   f. Imperf between (vert pair)
196 **39** 50 p. scarlet 15 15
   Sheets: 10 p. first in sheets of 12 (3×4) No. 6 being *tête-bêche* and then sheets of 20 (4×5). Other values sheets of 20 (5×4), No. 17 of the 40 p. being *tête-bêche*.
See also Nos. 206 etc. for new colours.

Amir Inayatullah Khan
14–17 January 1929
Amir Habibullah
17 January–16 October 1929

40 "Amir Habibullah, 1347. Defender of the Faith of Mohamed; Prophet of God"

1929 (Jan?). *Handstamped as T* **40**. A. *Imperf.* B. *P* 11 (2, 3 or 4 *sides*).

                            A   B

(a) NEWSPAPER
197 **35** 2 p. dull bl *to* ind .. .. .. † 1·25

(b) POSTAGE
198 **36** 10 p. dull green .. .. .. † 1·25
199 **31** 15 p. rosine .. .. .. 1·00 1·25
200 **37** 25 p. carmine .. .. .. † 1·75
201 **32** 30 p. blue-green .. .. 1·40 2·00
202 **38** 40 p. ultramarine .. .. † 2·00
   a. Tête-bêche (pair) .. .. † 25·00
203 **39** 50 p. scarlet .. .. .. † 3·75
204 **33** 60 p. light blue .. .. 3·00 4·00

(c) OFFICIAL
O205 **O 1** (No value) red .. .. .. † 5·00
O206 (No value) carmine .. .. † 5·00
This handstamp was also applied to the Parcel Post stamps but owing to the very restricted postal service during the revolt it is most unlikely that any were used.
Forgeries of this handstamp are common.
Prices are for unused stamps. Used stamps with genuine cancellations are very rare.

King Mohamed Nadir Shah
16 October 1929–8 November 1933

1929–31. *NEWSPAPER. Colour changed. Size 42½×25 mm. Thick or thin paper.* A. *P* 11 (Dec? 1929). B. *P* 12 (July? 1931).
                            A   B
N205 **35** 2 p. rose-carmine .. 10 10 — —
   a. Imperf between (pair) .. .. 1·40 — †
In sheets of 6 (2×3).

41

1929–31. *New type and colours changed. Thick or thin paper.* A. *P* 11 (Nov 1929). B. *P* 12 (July? 1931).

			A	B
206	36	10 p. dull purple	45	45	†
207		10 p. brown	12	12	— —
		a. Imperf (pair)			†
		b. Imperf between (horiz pair)	65	—	— —
208	31	15 p. ultramarine	15	15	— —
209	37	25 p. blue-green	25	25	— —
210	41	30 p. green	20	20	— —
		a. Arabic "30" missing	†		— —
211	38	40 p. carmine	25	25	— —
		a. Tête-bêche (pair)	2·75	2·75	— —
		b. Imperf between (vert pair)	1·60	1·60	†
212	39	50 p. deep blue	45	45	— —
213	33	60 p. black	45	45	— —

Sheets: 10 p. 20 (4×5), 15 p. 18 (6×3), 30 p. 10 (5×2), others 20 (5×4), No. 17 of the 40 p. being *tête-bêche*.

1929 (Dec?). *PARCEL POST. Colours changed. P* 11 *on 2, 3 or 4 sides.*

P214	**P 3**	2 a. green	50	50
		a. Imperf between (vert pair)		
P215	**P 4**	3 a. brown	90	1·00

Parcel Post stamps were discontinued in 1932.

DESIGNER. Abdul Gafour Khan Brishna designed all the Independence Day issues from 1931 to 1947.

42 Independence Memorial

43

1931 (24 Aug). *13th Independence Day. Litho. Laid paper. P* 12.

214	**42**	20 p. red	20	20

(Des Abdul Hamid Khan. Typo)
Two Types.
I. Numerals shaded in places. Size 21×29 mm.
II. Numerals unshaded. Size 21¾×30 mm.

1932–38. *NEWSPAPER. Medium white wove paper. P* 11¾ (line).

N215	**43**	2 p. brown-red *to* claret (I)	5	5
N216		2 p. olive-black (I) (1934)	5	5
N217		2 p. bronze-green *to* grey-green (I) (1934)	5	5
N218		2 p. deep black *to* slate (II) (1936)	5	5
		a. Imperf (pair) (1937)		
N219		2 p. vermilion (II) (1938)	5	5
		a. Imperf (pair)		
		b. Perf 11¾×11		
N220		2 p. carmine *to* rose (II) (1938)	5	5
		a. Imperf (pair)		

Forgeries exist which differ in size, paper or perforation.

COLOURS. Many stamps of the above and following issues, and particularly those in use over a long period, show wide variations of shade, too numerous to list.

44

45
National Council Chamber

46 National Assembly Building   **47** Council Chamber

48 Council Chamber   **49** National Assembly Building

(Des Abdul Gafour Khan Brishna. Typo)

1932. *Inauguration of National Council. P* 12.

215	**44**	40 p. olive-brown		12	8
216	**45**	60 p. violet		20	15
217	**46**	80 p. deep scarlet		25	25
218	**47**	1 a. black		80	70
219	**48**	2 a. ultramarine		90	60
220	**49**	3 a. grey-green		1·25	90
215/220		*Set of 6*		3·25	2·40

In sheets of 12, 40 p., 60 p. and 3 a. arranged 4×3, others 3×4.

For new colours see also Nos. 250/1.

50 Mosque at Balkh   **51** Kabul Fortress

52   **53**
Parliament House, Darul Funun, Kabul

54 Arch at Qualai Bust, Kandahar   **55** Memorial Pillar of Knowledge and Ignorance, Kabul

56 Independence
Memorial, Kabul

57 Minaret at Herat

58 Arch of Paghman

59 Ruins at Balkh

60 Minarets at Herat

61 Great Buddha at
Bamian

(Des Abdul Gafour Khan Brishna. Typo)

1932. *P* 12.

221	**50**	10 p. brown			5	5
222	**51**	15 p. brown			5	5
223	**52**	20 p. red			10	10
224	**53**	25 p. grey-green			8	5
225	**54**	30 p. red			10	8
226	**55**	40 p. yellow-orange			8	5
227	**56**	50 p. light blue			20	12
		a. Tête-bêche (pair)			75	75
228	**57**	60 p. deep blue			20	15
229	**58**	80 p. reddish violet			35	35
230	**59**	1 a. deep blue			35	25
231	**60**	2 a. purple			60	50
232	**61**	3 a. claret			1·00	90
221/232		Set of 12			2·75	2·40

See also Nos. 237/51.

62 Independence
Memorial

63 National Liberation
Monument, Kabul

1932 (Aug). *14th Independence Day. Litho. P* 12.

233	**62**	1 a. carmine			50	35

(Des Abdul Hamid Khan. Typo)

1932 (Nov). *Commemorative issue. P* 12.

234	**63**	80 p. brown-lake			25	25

64 Arch of Paghman

1933 (Aug). *15th Independence Day. Typo. P* 12.

235	**64**	50 p. pale bright blue			25	25

King Mohamed Zahir Shah, 8 November 1933

65 Independence Memorial

1934 (Aug). *16th Independence Day. Litho. No gum. P* 12.

236	**65**	50 p. yellow-green			25	25
		a. Tête-bêche (pair)			60	60

66 Royal Palace, Kabul

67 Hunters Canyon
Pass, Hindu Kush

(Des Abdul Gafour Khan Brishna. Typo)

1934–38. *As* 1932 *issues but colours changed and new values. P* 12.

237	**50**	10 p. deep violet			5	5
		a. Imperf (pair)				
238	**51**	15 p. emerald-green			5	5
239	**52**	20 p. bright magenta			5	5
240	**53**	25 p. rose-carmine			5	5
241	**54**	30 p. yellow-orange			10	5
242	**55**	40 p. black			12	12
243	**66**	45 p. deep blue			20	20
244		45 p. rose-carmine (1.1.38)			8	8
245	**56**	50 p. red-orange			10	5
246	**57**	60 p. deep violet			15	10
247	**67**	75 p. scarlet			35	35
248		75 p. deep blue (1.1.38)			20	12
		a. Perf 11×12				
249	**59**	1 a. bright magenta			30	25
250	**48**	2 a. slate			65	50
		a. Imperf (pair)				
251	**49**	3 a. deep ultramarine			1·00	90
237/251		Set of 15			3·00	2·50

Forgeries exist which differ in perforation, none matching the 11¾ of the above issue.

68 Independence Memorial

69 Firework Display

1935 (15 Aug). *17th Independence Day. Litho. P* 12.
252 **68** 50 p. blue 30 30

1936 (15 Aug). *18th Independence Day. Litho. P* 12.
253 **69** 50 p. bright magenta 30 30
　　　a. Imperf between (horiz pair) ..

70 Independence Memorial and Mohamed Nadir Shah

71 Mohamed Nadir Shah

1937 (27 May). *19th Independence Day. Litho.*
　　　　A. *P* 12.　B. *Imperf*
254 **70** 50 p. brown and violet　25　25　25　25

1938 (May). *20th Independence Day. Litho.*
　　　　A. *P* 11×12.　B. *Imperf*
255 **71** 50 p. choc & lt bl .. 25　25　45　45

72 Aliabad Hospital

74 Mohamed Nadir Shah

73 Pierre and Marie Curie

(Des Abdul Gafour Khan Brishna. Typo)

1938 (22 Dec). *OBLIGATORY TAX. International Anti-Cancer Fund. P* 12.
256 **72** 10 p. turquoise-green.. .. .. 1·50 1·50
257 **73** 15 p. blue .. .. 1·50 1·50

1939 (May). *21st Independence Day. Typo. P* 11.
258 **74** 50 p. carmine-red 20 20

75 Coat-of-Arms

(Des Abdul Hamid Khan. Litho)

1939 (Oct)–**61**. *NEWSPAPER. Various papers. P* 11, 12 *or compound.*
N259 **75** 2 p. blackish olive 5 5
　　　　　a. *Black* 5 5
N260　　2 p. reddish mauve (*No gum*) (1961) .. 5 5
For T **75** redrawn larger see Nos. N652/3.

76 Darul Funun, Parliament House, Kabul

77 Royal Palace, Kabul

78 Minarets at Herat

79 Independence Memorial

80 Ruins at Kandahar Fort

81 Independence Memorial and Mohamed Nadir Shah

82 Mohamed Zahir Shah

83 Sugar Mill, Baghlan

84 Mohamed Zahir Shah

(Des Abdul Gafour Khan Brishna. Typo)

1939 (Oct)–**47**. *Sizes in millimetres. Various papers. P* 11, 12 *or compound.*
259 **76** 10 p. purple *to* violet (36½×24) .. 5 5
260　　15 p. emerald-green (32×21) .. 5 5
261　　20 p. reddish purple (34×22½) .. 5 5
262 **77** 25 p. red (31×19) 8 5
263　　25 p. green (31×19) (21.3.42) .. 5 5
264　　30 p. orange (31×19) 8 5
265 **78** 35 p. orange (1.5.44) 15 15
266 **77** 40 p. grey (29×18) 10 5
267 **79** 45 p. red (21×28) 10 5
268　　50 p. orange (20×27).. .. 10 5
269　　60 p. violet (21×29) 10 8
270 **80** 70 p. violet (1.5.44) 20 15
271　　70 p. purple (1945?) 25 20
272 **81** 75 p. ultramarine (35½×21½) .. 50 20
273　　75 p. claret (35½×21½) (21.3.42) .. 15 8
274　　75 p. scarlet (35½×21½) (1944) .. 15 12
　　　　a. *Red-brown* (11.47) 20 15
275　　80 p. brown (34½×21) 20 10
276 **82** 1 a. bright purple (36½×20½) .. 25 10
　　　　a. Imperf (pair) .. ..

277 **84** 1 a. bright purple (35½×20) (8.42) .. 25 15
278 **83** 1 a. 25, ultramarine (21.3.42) .. 50 15
279 **84** 2 a. rose-carmine (35½×20) 50 30
     a. Copper-red (1946) 40 30
280 – 3 a. blue *to* indigo (35½×20) 60 30
259/280 *Set of 22* .. .. 4·00 2·25
Design:—3 a. As T **82** but head turned more to left.
Many additional shades exist.
A 1 a. 50 brown in Type **83** was prepared but had no postal validity.

85 Aeroplane over Kabul

O 2

(Des Abdul Gafour Khan Brishna. Typo)

1939 (Oct)–*47*. *AIR*. *Sizes in millimetres. Various papers.*
P 11, 12 *or compound*.
280*a* **85** 5 a. orange (35×22) 55 55
    aa. Imperf between (horiz pair) ..
    ab. Imperf (pair) (2.1.47) ..
280*b* 10 a. blue (35×22) 80 65
    ba. Imperf between (horiz pair) ..
    bb. Imperf (pair) (2.1.47) ..
280*c* 20 a. green (33×21) .. .. 1·50 1·25
    ca. Imperf between (horiz pair) ..
    cb. Imperf (pair) (2.1.47) ..
Various shades exist. For new colours, see Nos. 304/6.
Dangerous forgeries exist but differ slightly in sizes.

(Des Abdul Hamid Khan)

1939 (Oct)–*65*. OFFICIAL.

    (*a*) *Size* 22¼×28 *mm. Typo* (1939–40)
O281 **O 2** 15 p. emerald (*p* 11 *or* 12) 5 5
O282 30 p. yellow-brown (*p* 12) (1940) .. 8 8
O283 45 p. lake (*p* 11 *or* 12) 10 10
O284 1 a. magenta (*p* 11) 15 15

    (*b*) *Size* 24½×31 *mm. Typo. P* 11 (1954)
O285 **O 2** 50 p. carmine 8 8

    (*c*) *Size* 24×30½. *Litho. P* 11 (1965?)
O286 **O 2** 50 p. cerise.. .. .. 5 5
O281/286 *Set of 6* 45 45

86 Mohamed Nadir   **87** Arch of Paghman
Shah

1940 (23 Aug). *22nd Independence Day. Typo. P* 11.
281 **86** 50 p. grey-green 30 30

1941 (23 Aug). *23rd Independence Day. T* **87** *and another design. Typo. P* 12.
282 15 p. grey-green.. .. .. 1·25 50
283 50 p. red-brown 20 20
Design: (19×29½ *mm*)—15 p. Independence Memorial.

86 Independence   **87** Mohamed Nadir Shah and
Memorial   Arch of Paghman

1942 (23 Aug). *24th Independence Day. Typo. P* 12.
284 **86** 35 p. emerald-green.. .. .. 80 60
285 **87** 125 p. ultramarine 50 50

88 Independence   **89** Arch of Paghman
Memorial and
Mohamed Nadir
Shah

90 Independence Memorial and Mohamed Nadir Shah

1943 (Aug). *25th Independence Day. T* **88** *and similar design. Typo. P* 11×12 (35 *p*.) *or* 12×11 (1 a. 25).
286 35 p. carmine .. .. .. 1·25 1·00
287 1 a. 25, blue 45 45
Design: *Horiz*—35 p. Independence Memorial seen through archway and Mohamed Nadir Shah in oval frame.

1944 (Aug). *26th Independence Day. Typo. P* 12.
288 **89** 35 p. crimson.. .. .. 25 25
289 **90** 1 a. 25. violet-blue 50 50

91 Mohamed   **92** Mohamed Nadir Shah and
Nadir Shah and   Arch of Paghman
Independence
Memorial

1945 (Aug). *27th Independence Day. Typo. P* 12.
290 **91** 35 p. claret 25 25
291 **92** 1 a. 25, light blue 60 60

A regular new issue supplement to this
catalogue appears each month in

STAMP MONTHLY
—from your newsagent or by postal subscription
—details on request.

93 Independence
Memorial

94 Mohamed Nadir
Shah and
Independence
Memorial

1946 (Aug). *28th Independence Day. T 93 and similar designs inscr "1946". Typo. P 12.*
292   15 p. emerald   10   10
293   20 p. magenta   15   15
294   125 p. blue   60   60
Designs: *Horiz*—15 p. Mohamed Zahir Shah. *Vert*—125 p. Mohamed Nadir Shah.

1947 (Aug). *29th Independence Day. T 94 and similar designs inscr "1947". Typo. P 11½.*
295   15 p. yellow-green   10   10
296   35 p. magenta   12   12
297   125 p. blue   50   50
Designs: *Horiz*—15 p. Mohamed Zahir Shah and ruins of Kandahar Fort; 35 p. Mohamed Zahir Shah and Arch of Paghman.

95 Hungry Boy

96 Independence
Memorial

(Des Abdul Gafour Khan Brishna. Typo)

1948 (29 May). *Child Welfare Fund. T 95 and similar design. P 12.*
298 **95**   35 p. yellow-green   25   15
299   –   125 p. grey-blue   50   40
Designs: 125 p. Hungry boy in vert frame (26 × 33½ mm).
Unlike the later charity stamps the above issue was not for obligatory use. It was valid for one day only and then sold at the Philatelic Bureau at double face. There may have been a second printing as shades exist.

(Des Jalal Ludin Khan. Typo)

1948 (Aug). *30th Independence Day. T 96 and similar designs inscr "1948". P 12.*
300   15 p. green   10   10
301   20 p. magenta   12   12
302   35 p. blue   35   30
Designs: *Vert*—15 p. Arch of Paghman. *Horiz*—125 p. Mohamed Nadir Shah.

97 U.N. Symbol

98 Hungry Boy

(Des Abdul Gafour Khan Brishna. Typo)

1948 (24 Oct). *Third Anniv of U.N.O. P 12.*
303 **97** 1 a. 25, ultramarine   ..   ..   ..   2·50   2·25

UNITED NATIONS ISSUES. The above issue was only valid for one day. Later issues up to 1955 were obligatory tax stamps.

1948 (14 June). *AIR. As T 85 but colours changed.*
304 **85**   5 a. emerald-green   ..   ..   ..   3·75   3·75
305   10 a. orange   ..   ..   ..   3·75   3·75
306   20 a. greenish blue   ..   ..   3·75   3·75
The above exist imperforate.

(Des Jalal Ludin Khan. Typo)

1949 (28 May). *OBLIGATORY TAX. Child Welfare Fund. P 12.*
307   –   35 p. red-orange   30   30
308 **98** 125 p. ultramarine   60   60
Design: *Horiz*—35 p. As T 95 but 29 × 22½ mm.

OBLIGATORY TAX STAMPS. Between 1949 and 1959 these issues were for obligatory use for a few days (usually one day in the case of United Nations stamps) and could then be purchased usually at 50% over face value. From 1959 their use was voluntary, the charity premium being expressed on the stamps.

99 Victory Monument

100 Arch of Paghman

(Des Jalal Ludin Khan. Typo)

1949 (24 Aug). *31st Independence Day. T 99 and similar designs inscr "1949". P 12.*
309   25 p. green   12   12
310   35 p. magenta   15   15
311   1 a. 25, blue   30   30
Designs: *Horiz*—35 p. Mohamed Zahir Shah and ruins of Kandahar Fort; 1 a. 25, Independence Memorial and Mohamed Nadir Shah.

1949 (Oct). *OBLIGATORY TAX. Fourth Anniv of U.N.O. Typo. P 12.*
312 **100** 125 p. deep blue-green   ..   ..   4·00   4·00

101 Mohamed Zahir Shah and
Map of Afghanistan

102 Hungry Boy

1950 (1 Apr). *OBLIGATORY TAX. Return of Mohamed Zahir Shah from Visit to Europe. Typo. P 12.*
313 **101** 125 p. blue-green   45   45

1950 (28 May). *OBLIGATORY TAX. Child Welfare Fund. P 12.*
314 **102** 125 p. blue-green   45   45

103 Mohamed Nadir Shah

104

115 Flag

116 Mohamed Zahir Shah

117 Mohamed Zahir Shah

(Des Jalal Ludin Khan. Typo)

1950 (Aug). *32nd Independence Day.* P 12.
315	**103**	35 p. brown		12	12
316		125 p. blue ..	.. .. ..	30	30

1950 (Nov). *OBLIGATORY TAX. Fifth Anniv of U.N.O.* Typo. P 12.
317	**104**	1 a. 25, ultramarine ..	..	1·90	1·50

118 Mohamed Zahir Shah

119 Aeroplane over Kabul

105

106

1950 (22 Dec). *19th Anniv of Faculty of Medicine, Kabul.* Typo. P 12.

(a) POSTAGE
318	**105**	35 p. green ..	.. .. ..	20	20
319	**106**	1 a. 25, blue	.. .. ..	60	60

(b) OBLIGATORY TAX
320	**105**	35 p. carmine	.. .. ..	12	12
321	**106**	1 a. 25, black	.. .. ..	30	25

The 35 p. values measure 38½ × 25½ mm and the 1 a. 25 values 40 × 30 mm.

(T **109**, **116/7** recess; T **115** recess, flag litho; others photo Waterlow)

1951 (21 Mar). *With imprint "WATERLOW & SONS LIMITED LONDON" at foot.* P 12 (20, 30, 40, 70 p.), 12½ (10, 15, 25 p.), 12½ × 13 (60 p.), 13 (125 p., 2 a., 3a.), 13 × 12½ (50, 75, 80 p., 1 a.).
322	**107**	10 p. red-brown and yellow	..	5	5
323		15 p. red-brown and light blue	..	5	5
324	**108**	20 p. black ..	.. .. ..	75	20
325	**109**	25 p. green ..	.. .. ..	5	5
326	**110**	30 p. carmine	.. .. ..	8	5
327	**109**	35 p. violet ..	.. .. ..	5	5
328	**111**	40 p. red-brown	.. .. ..	12	5
329	**112**	45 p. blue	.. .. ..	8	5
330	**113**	50 p. greenish black	..	15	5
331	**114**	60 p. slate-black	..	15	5
332	**115**	70 p. black, red and green ..		10	5
333	**116**	75 p. carmine	.. ..	25	8
334	**117**	80 p. black and carmine	..	25	12
335		1 a. violet and green	..	20	12
336	**118**	125 p. black and purple	..	20	12
337		2 a. ultramarine	.. ..	30	12
338		3 a. ultramarine and black	..	65	20
322/338		*Set of 17*	.. .. ..	3·25	1·25

See also Nos. 425/425*l*.

(Recess Waterlow)

1951 (21 Mar)–**54**. *AIR. With imprint "WATERLOW & SONS LONDON" at foot.* P 13½.
339	**119**	5 a. red	.. .. ..	50	30
339*a*		5 a. deep green (24.3.54) ..		50	30
340		10 a. slate	.. .. ..	1·75	65
341		20 a. deep ultramarine	..	1·50	90

See also Nos. 415*a*/*c*.

107 Minaret at Herat

108 Buddha of Bamian

109 Mohamed Zahir Shah

110 Mosque at Balkh

111 Ruins at Kandahar Fort

120 Shepherdess

121 Arch of Paghman

112 Maiwand Victory Monument

113 View of Kandahar

114 Victory Towers, Ghazni

سال ٣٣ استقلال

(122)

سال ٣٤ استقلال

(123)

1951 (28 May). *OBLIGATORY TAX. Child Welfare Fund.*
T 120 and similar design. Typo. P 12.

342	35 p. green	..	..	20	20
343	125 p. ultramarine	..	..	35	35

Design: (34½ × 44 mm)—125 p. Young shepherd.

(Recess Waterlow)

1951 (25 Aug). *33rd Independence Day. T 121 and similar design optd with T 122, in violet. P 13½ × 13 (35 p.) or 13 (125 p.).*

344	35 p. black and green	..	20	20
345	125 p. blue	..	50	50

Design: (34 × 18½ mm)—125 p. Mohamed Nadir Shah and Independence Memorial.
See also Nos. 360/1 and 418/9.

IMPERFORATE STAMPS. From 1951 to 1964 many issues were made available imperforate from limited printings.

124 Flag of Pashtunistan

1951 (2 Sept). *OBLIGATORY TAX. Pashtunistan Day. T 124 and similar design. Typo. P 12.*

346	35 p. brown	..	..	40	40
347	125 p. blue	..	..	1·00	1 00

Design (42½ × 21½ mm)—125 p. Soldier.
Pashtunistan is an unrecognised country comprising the old British Indian "Northwest Frontier Province" and part of Baluchistan. The above and later issues were made to mark the proclamation of a Free Pashtunistan Government on 2 September 1948.

125 Dove and Globe

126 Avicenna (physician)

1951 (24 Oct). *OBLIGATORY TAX. United Nations Day. T 125 and vert design inscr "1944 1951". Typo. P 12.*

348	35 p. magenta	..	..	30	30
349	125 p. light blue (Dove and Globe)	..	1·40	1·40

1951 (4 Nov). *OBLIGATORY TAX. Twentieth Anniv of Faculty of Medicine. Typo. P 12.*

350	**126**	35 p. magenta	..	..	15	15
351		125 p. blue	..	..	50	50

127 Amir Sher Ali and First Stamp

128 Children and Postman

1951 (23 Dec). *OBLIGATORY TAX. 76th Anniv of U.P.U. T 127 and similar horiz design inscr "1951". Typo. P 12.*

352	**127**	35 p. brown	..	..	15	15
		a. Error. Bright blue	..	..	35·00	
353	–	35 p. magenta	..	..	15	15
354	**127**	125 p. bright blue	..		30	30
355	–	125 p. light blue	..		30	30
352/355		Set of 4	..	..	80	80

Design:—Nos. 353 and 355, Mohamed Zahir Shah and first stamp.
No. 352a results from a cliché of the 35 p. in the plate of the 125 p. bright blue and is found in pair. However, most were used before the error was discovered.

1952 (29 May). *OBLIGATORY TAX. Child Welfare Fund. T 128 and smaller horiz design inscr "PROTECTION DE L'ENFANCE 1952". Typo. P 12.*

356	35 p. brown	..	..	15	15
357	125 p. violet	..	..	35	35

Design: (33 × 23 mm)—125 p. Girl dancing.

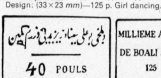

(129)   (130)

1952 (12 July). *OBLIGATORY TAX. Millenary of Birth of Avicenna (physician and philosopher). No. 326 surch with T 128 or 129, in violet.*

358	**110**	40 p. on 30 p. carmine	..	45	45
359		125 p. on 30 p. carmine	..	75	75

1952 (24 Aug). *34th Independence Day. As Nos. 344/5.*

(a) Optd in violet with T 123

360	**121**	35 p. black and green	..	15	15
361	–	125 p. blue	..	45	45

(b) Without opt

361a	**121**	35 p. black and green	..	1·00	1·00
361b	–	125 p. blue	..	..	1·00	1·00

131 Soldier and Flag of Pashtunistan

132 Orderly and Wounded Soldier

1952 (1 Sept). *OBLIGATORY TAX. Pashtunistan Day. Typo. P 11.*

362	**131**	35 p. red	..	..	10	10
363		125 p. deep blue	..	..	25	25

1952 (19 Oct). *OBLIGATORY TAX. Red Crescent Day. Litho. P 12.*

364	**132**	10 p. pale green	..	..	15	15

133

134 Staff of Aesculapius

1952 (25 Oct). *OBLIGATORY TAX. United Nations Day. Litho.* P 12.
365 **133** 35 p. rose-magenta 25 25
366 125 p. turquoise 65 65

1952 (2 Nov). *OBLIGATORY TAX. 21st Anniv of Faculty of Medicine. Litho.* P 12.
367 **134** 35 p. purple-brown.. .. 25 25
368 125 p. ultramarine 50 50

135 Stretcher Bearers and Wounded   **136** Prince Mohamed Nadir

1953 (10 May). *OBLIGATORY TAX. Red Crescent Day.* T **135** *and similar horiz design. Litho.* P 11.
369 **135** 10 p. pale emerald and orange-brn .. 15 15
370 — 10 p. chocolate and orange-brown .. 15 15
Design:—No. 370, Wounded soldier, orderly and eagle.

1953 (2 July). *OBLIGATORY TAX. Children's Day. Litho.* P 11.
371 **136** 35 p. orange 10 10
372 125 p. blue 25 25

137 Mohamed Nadir Shah and Flag-bearer   **138** Flags of Afghanistan and Pashtunistan

1953 (24 Aug). *OBLIGATORY TAX. 35th Independence Day.* T **137** *and vert design inscr "1953". Litho.* P 11.
373 35 p. emerald 10 10
374 125 p. violet 30 25
Design:—125 p. Independence Memorial and Mohamed Nadir Shah.

1953 (1 Sept). *OBLIGATORY TAX. Pashtunistan Day.* T **138** *and horiz design inscr "1953". Litho.* P 11.
375 35 p. red 10 10
376 125 p. blue 25 25
Design: (26 × 20 *mm*)—125 p. Badge of Pashtunistan.

139 U.N. Emblem   **140** Mohamed Nadir Shah   **141** Children's Band and Map of Afghanistan

1953 (24 Oct). *OBLIGATORY TAX. United Nations Day. Litho.* P 11.
377 **139** 35 p. mauve 35 35
378 125 p. ultramarine 75 75

1953 (2 Nov). *OBLIGATORY TAX. 22nd Anniv of Faculty of Medicine* (*wrongly inscr 23rd*). *Litho.* P 11.
379 **140** 35 p. orange 35 35
     a. Arabic figures corrected to "22nd" .. .. .. 2·00 2·00
380 125 p. blue 65 65
     a. "XXIII" changed to "XXII" and spelling corrected .. .. 2·25 2·25
In the 35 p. value the Arabic numeral which was corrected is the extreme right-hand figure in the second row of the inscription. No. 380 has the words "ANNIVERSAIRE" and "MÉDECINE" wrongly spelt "ANNIVERAIRE" and "MADE-CINE" and these were corrected in No. 380a.

1954 (5 July). *OBLIGATORY TAX. Child Welfare Fund. Typo.* P 11.
381 **141** 35 p. violet 10 10
382 125 p. bright blue 30 30

142 Mohamed Nadir Shah and Cannon   **143** Hoisting the Flag

1954 (Aug). *36th Independence Day. Typo.* P 11.
383 **142** 35 p. carmine 10 10
384 125 p. ultramarine 35 35

1954 (Sept). *OBLIGATORY TAX. Pashtunistan Day. Typo.* P 12.
385 **143** 35 p. chocolate 12 12
386 125 p. blue 30 30

144   **145** U.N. Flag and Map

1954 (17 Oct). *OBLIGATORY TAX. Red Crescent Day. Litho.* P 11.
387 **144** 20 p. red and blue 15 15

1954 (24 Oct). *OBLIGATORY TAX. United Nations Day and Ninth Anniv of United Nations. Typo.* P 12.
388 **145** 35 p. carmine 45 45
389 125 p. ultramarine .. .. 1·00 1·00

146 Globe and Clasped Hands   **147** Amir Sher Ali and Mohamed Zahir Shah

1955 (26 June). *Tenth Anniv of United Nations* (1st issue). T **148** *and similar vert design inscr "10 EME ANV. DES N.U.". Litho.* P 11.
390 35 p. green 35 35
391 125 p. turquoise-blue 75 75
Design: (28½ × 36 *mm*)—125 p. U.N. emblem and flags.

1955 (2 July). *85th Anniv of Postal Service. Litho.* P 11.
392 **147** 35 p. + 15 p. carmine-red .. 15 15
393 125 p. + 25 p. lavender-grey .. 35 35

148 Children on Swing

149 Mohamed Nadir Shah (centre) and Brothers

156

157 Mohamed Zahir Shah and Crescent

1955 (3 July). *Child Welfare Fund. Typo. P 11.*
394	148	35 p. + 15 p. green	..			20	20
395		125 p. + 25 p. violet	..	..	..	35	35

1955 (30 Aug). *37th Independence Day. T 149 and similar horiz design inscr "1955". Litho. P 11.*
396	149	35 p. pale ultramarine				10	10
397		35 p. bright mauve	..			10	10
398	–	125 p. pale violet	..			35	25
399	–	125 p. reddish purple	..	..		35	25

Design: 125 p. (2), Mohamed Zahir Shah and battle scene.

1956 (Sept). *Pashtunistan Day. Litho. P 11.*
411	156	35 p. + 15 p. reddish violet	..			12	12
412		140 p. + 15 p. sepia		..		35	35

1956 (18 Oct). *OBLIGATORY TAX. Red Crescent Day. Litho. P 11.*
413	157	20 p. light green and carmine			10	10

150

151 Red Crescent

152 U.N. Flag

1955 (5 Sept). *OBLIGATORY TAX. Pashtunistan Day. Litho. P 11.*
400	150	35 p. reddish brown				10	10
401		125 p. green	..			25	25

1955 (18 Oct). *OBLIGATORY TAX. Red Crescent Day. Litho. P 11.*
402	151	20 p. carmine-red and grey-green	..		12	12

1955 (24 Oct). *OBLIGATORY TAX. Tenth Anniv of United Nations (2nd issue). Litho. P 11.*
403	152	35 p. red-brown	..			35	35
404		125 p. ultramarine	..			75	75

158 Globe and Sun

159 Children on See-Saw

1956 (24 Oct). *United Nations Day and Tenth Anniv of Admission of Afghanistan. Litho. P 11.*
414	158	35 p. + 15 p. ultramarine	..		55	55
415		140 p. + 15 p. orange-brown		..	90	90

1957 (3 Feb)–62. *AIR. Colours changed. P 13½.*

(a) With imprint "WATERLOW & SONS LIMITED LONDON" at foot
415a	119	5 a. blue	..		35	20
415b		10 a. violet	..		70	50

(b) With imprint "THOMAS DE LA RUE & CO. LTD." at foot (1962)
415c	119	5 a. blue	..		75	40

1957 (20 June). *Child Welfare Fund. Litho. P 11.*
416	159	35 p. + 15 p. carmine	..		15	15
417		140 p. + 15 p. ultramarine	..		35	35

(160)

39 ^{em} Anv

(161)

1957 (24 Aug). *39th Independence Day. As Nos. 344/5 but optd with T 160 (35 p.) or 161 (125 p.).*
418		35 p. black and green (V.)			8	8
419		125 p. blue (V.)	..		20	20

153 Child on Slide

162 Pashtunistan Flag

163 Red Crescent Headquarters, Kabul

154 Independence Memorial and Mohamed Nadir Shah

1957 (1 Sept). *Pashtunistan Day. Litho. P 11.*
420	162	50 p. reddish purple	..		15	15
421		155 p. bright violet	..		30	30

1957 (17 Oct). *OBLIGATORY TAX. Red Crescent Day. Litho. P 11.*
422	163	20 p. blue and red	..		10	10

155 Exhibition Building

1956 (20 June). *Children's Day. Typo. P 11.*
405	153	35 p. + 15 p. violet-blue	..		15	15
406		140 p. + 15 p. brown	..		30	30

1956. *38th Independence Day. Litho. P 11.*
407	154	35 p. green (25 Aug)			10	10
408		140 p. ultramarine (8 Sept)	..		35	35

1956 (30 Aug). *International Exhibition, Kabul. Litho. P 11.*
409	155	50 p. chocolate	..		12	12
410		50 p. ultramarine	..		12	12

Postal validity was 35 p., 15 p. representing a premium.

164 U.N. Headquarters, New York

165 Royal Buzkashi (National Game)

1957 (24 Oct). *United Nations Day. Litho. P* 11.
423　164　35 p. + 15 p. chocolate　　..　　..　　15　15
424　　　140 p. + 15 p. blue　　..　　..　　35　35

(T **165** Photo Harrison)

1957 (23 Nov)–62. *T* **165** (*new value*) *and stamps of* 1951 *in new colours.*

(a) *With imprint* "WATERLOW & SONS LIMITED LONDON" *at foot* (*except* 140 p.)
425　110　30 p. bistre-brown (*p* 12)　..　　..　　5　5
425a　111　40 p. rose-red (*p* 12)　　　　..　　5　5
425b　113　50 p. yellow (*p* 13 × 12½)　..　　5　5
425c　114　60 p. bright blue (*p* 12½ × 13)　..　　5　5
425d　116　75 p. violet (*p* 12½)　　　　..　　8　5
425e　117　80 p. sepia and violet (*p* 13 × 12½)　8　5
425f　　　1 a. bright blue and bright
　　　　　carmine-red (*p* 13 × 12½)　..　　12　5
425g　165　140 p. brown-purple and deep
　　　　　olive-green (*p* 13½ × 14)　..　　25　12
425h　118　3 a. black and orange (*p* 13)　..　　35　15
425/425h　*Set of 9*　..　　..　　..　　90　50

(b) *With imprint* "THOMAS DE LA RUE & CO. LTD." *at foot*
(1962)
425i　116　75 p. bright violet (*p* 13 × 12)　..　　12　5
425j　117　1 a. bright blue and carmine
　　　　　(*p* 13 × 12)　　　..　　..　　15　5
425k　118　2 a. blue (*p* 13)　　..　　..　　30　12
425l　　　3 a. black and red-orange (*p* 13)　35　12
425i/l　*Set of 4*　..　　..　　..　　80　25

166 Children Bathing

167 Mohamed Nadir Shah and Old Soldier

1958 (22 June). *Child Welfare Fund. Litho. P* 11.
426　166　35 p. + 15 p. red　　..　　..　　10　10
427　　　140 p. + 15 p. chocolate　..　　..　　20　20

(Photo State Ptg Wks, Vienna)

1958. *40th Independence Day. P* 13½ × 14.
428　167　35 p. deep green (23 Aug)　..　　5　5
429　　　140 p. brown (6 Sept)　　..　　..　　15　15

168 Exhibition Buildings

169

1958 (23 Aug). *International Exhibition, Kabul. Litho. P* 11.
430　168　35 p. blue-green　　..　　..　　5　5
431　　　140 p. rose-red　　..　　..　　15　15

1958 (31 Aug). *Pashtunistan Day. Litho. P* 11.
432　169　35 p. + 15 p. light blue　　..　　10　10
433　　　140 p. + 15 p. red-brown　..　　15　15

170

171 Red Crescent on Map of Afghanistan

1958 (Sept). *Visit of President of Turkey. Litho. P* 11.
434　170　50 p. blue (13 Sept)　　..　　..　　10　10
435　　　100 p. chocolate (22 Sept)　..　　15　15

1958 (Oct). *OBLIGATORY TAX. Red Crescent Day. Litho. P* 11.
436　171　25 p. red and light emerald ..　　..　　5　5

172

173 Flags of U.N. and Afghanistan

(Photo State Ptg Wks, Vienna)

1958 (20 Oct). *"Atoms for Peace". P* 13½ × 14.
437　172　50 p. blue　　..　　..　　..　　20　20
438　　　100 p. purple　　..　　..　　..　　30　30

(Photo State Ptg Wks, Vienna)

1958 (23 Oct). *United Nations Day. P* 14 × 13½.
439　173　50 p. blue, red, green and black　..　　30　30
440　　　100 p. blue, red, black and green　..　　50　50

174 U.N.E.S.C.O. Headquarters, Paris

175 Globe and Torch

(Photo State Ptg Wks, Vienna)

1958 (13 Nov). *Inauguration of U.N.E.S.C.O. Headquarters Building, Paris. P* 13½ × 14.
441　174　50 p. green　　..　　..　　..　　25　25
442　　　100 p. olive-brown　..　　..　　35　35

(Photo State Ptg Wks, Vienna)

1958 (10 Dec). *Tenth Anniv of Declaration of Human Rights. P* 13½ × 14.
443　175　50 p. magenta　　..　　..　　25　25
444　　　100 p. brown-purple..　　..　　35　35

176 Tug-of-War

177 Mohamed Nadir Shah and Flags

1959 (23 June). *Child Welfare Fund. Litho. P* 11.
445　176　35 p. + 15 p. dull purple　..　　..　　10　10
446　　　165 p. + 15 p. bright mauve　..　　25　25

1959 (24 Aug). *41st Independence Day. Litho. P* 11.
447　177　35 p. red　　..　　..　　..　　8　8
448　　　165 p. violet ..　　..　　..　　20　20

178 Tribal Dance

179 Flag-sellers

1959 (Aug). *Pashtunistan Day. Litho. P* 11.
449　178　35 p. + 15 p. grey-green　　..　　8　8
450　　　165 p. + 15 p. yellow-orange　..　　20　20

1959 (17 Oct). *OBLIGATORY TAX. Red Crescent Day. Litho.*
P 11.
451 **179** 25 p. carmine and violet 5 5

180 Horseman   **181** "Uprooted Tree"

1959 (24 Oct). *United Nations Day. Litho. P* 11.
452 **180** 35 p. + 15 p. yellow-orange .. 10 10
453   165 p. + 15 p. turquoise-green .. 25 25

1960 (7 Apr). *World Refugee Year. Litho. P* 11.
454 **181** 50 p. red-orange 5 5
455   165 p. bright blue 15 15
MS455a 108 × 80 mm. Nos. 454/5. Imperf .. 3·75 3·75

182   **183**
Royal Buzkashi (national game)

1960–69. *Litho. P* 11.
456 **182** 25 p. rose (*shades*) (4.5.60) .. 8 8
      a. Error. Blue-green .. 6·00 6·00
457   25 p. violet (*shades*) (9.9.61) .. 5 5
458   25 p. yellow-olive (1963) 5 5
459   50 p. blue-green (*shades*) (4.5.60) 20 20
460   50 p. bright blue (*shades*) (9.9.61) 5 5
460a   50 p. yellow-orange (26.5.69) .. 20 20
461 **183** 100 p. yellow-olive (1961) .. 15 15
462   150 p. orange (28.6.64) .. 5 5
463   175 p. red-brown (9.11.60) .. 5 5
464   2 a. emerald (1961) 8 8
No. 456a occurred once in each sheet of the 50 p. blue-green. After a small number had been sold, the Post Office extracted the errors from the remaining unsold sheets.

184 Mother giving Ball to   **185** Aircraft over Mountains
     Children

1960 (22 June). *Child Welfare Fund. Litho. P* 11.
465 **184** 75 p. + 25 p. blue 8 8
466   175 p. + 25 p. green 15 15

1960 (24 July)–63. *AIR. Litho. P* 11 or 10½ (5 a.).
467 **185** 75 p. bluish violet 8 10
468   125 p. blue 12 10
469   5 a. yellow-olive (1963) 35 30

186 Independence Monument, Kabul

1960 (Aug). *42nd Independence Day. Litho. P* 11.
470 **186** 50 p. blue 5 5
471   175 p. bright mauve 15 15

187

1960 (1 Sept). *Pashtunistan Day. Litho. P* 11.
472 **187** 50 p. + 50 p. rose 10 10
473   175 p. + 50 p. deep ultramarine .. 25 25

188 Insecticide Sprayer   **189** Mohamed Zahir Shah

1960 (6 Sept). *Malaria Campaign Day. Litho. P* 11.
474 **188** 50 p. + 50 p. red-orange 30 30
475   175 p. + 50 p. red-brown 60 60

1960 (14 Oct). *Shah's 46th Birthday. Litho. P* 11.
476 **189** 50 p. red-brown 8 8
477   150 p. carmine 15 15

190 Ambulance

1960 (16 Oct). *Red Crescent Day. Litho. P* 11.
478 **190** 50 p. + 50 p. violet and red 10 10
479   175 p. + 50 p. blue and red 25 25

191 Teacher with Globe and   **192** Globe and Flags
     Children

1960 (23 Oct). *Literary Campaign. Litho. P* 11.
480 **191** 50 p. magenta 8 8
481   100 p. emerald-green 15 15

1960 (24 Oct–31 Dec). *United Nations Day. Litho. P* 11.
482 **192** 50 p. deep magenta 12 12
483   175 p. bright blue 25 25
MS483a 128 × 86 mm. Nos. 482/3. Imperf (31 Dec) .. .. 2·50 2·50

1960 للهـبـك ⊙⊙⊙ +2·5
(193) (194)

195 Mir Wais Nika
(patriot)

1960 (24 Dec). *Olympic Games, Rome. No. 463 optd with*
T 193.
484 **183** 175 p. red-brown (G.) .. 1·00 1·00
MS484a 86×62 mm. No. 484. Imperf 3·00 3·00

1960 (31 Dec). *World Refugee Year. Nos. 454/5 surch with*
T 194.
485 **181** 50 p. + 25 p. red-orange (B.) .. 1·50 1·50
486 165 p. + 25 p. bright blue (R.) .. 1·50 1·50
MS486a 108×80 mm. Nos. 485/6. Imperf .. 2·00 2·00

1960. *Litho. P 11.*
487 **194** 50 p. deep mauve 8 8
488 175 p. bright blue 20 20
MS488a 108×78 mm. Nos. 487/8. Imperf .. 60 60

1961–64 AGENCY ISSUES. Between 21 April 1961 and 15
March 1964 (both dates inclusive) very many issues were
made by an agency under the authority of a contract granted
by the Afghan Government. It soon became evident that only
token supplies were put on sale in Kabul for a few hours and
many of these sets contained denominations which were too
low for postal use. The lowest value that could be used was
25 p. except for the 2 p. newspaper rate for which special
stamps were issued. The lack of agency-produced stamps
throughout Afghanistan made it necessary for the post office
to issue its own locally produced stamps which we list. The
others are recorded in the Appendix to this volume.

196 Band Amir Lake   197 Independence
                          Memorial

(Photo State Ptg Wks, Vienna)

1961 (7 Aug). *P 13½ × 14.*
489 **196** 3 a. blue 20 15
490 10 a. reddish purple 60 50

1963 (23 Aug). *45th Independence Day. Litho. P 10½.*
491 **197** 25 p. light green 5 5
492 50 p. yellow-orange 8 8
493 150 p. dull magenta 15 10

198 "On Parade"   199 Assembly Building

1963 (31 Aug). *Pashtunistan Day. Litho. P 10½.*
494 **198** 25 p. light violet 5 5
495 50 p. light blue 8 5
496 150 p. red-brown 15 12

1963 (10 Sept). *National Assembly. Litho. P 10½.*
497 **199** 25 p. olive-brown 5 5
498 50 p. brown-red 5 5
499 75 p. chocolate 5 5
500 100 p. olive-green 8 5
501 125 p. reddish lilac 10 8
494/501 *Set of 5* .. 25 20

200 Balkh Gate   201 Kemal Atatürk

1963 (8 Oct). *Litho. P 11.*
502 **200** 3 a. deep brown (*shades*) 15 12

1963 (10 Oct). *25th Death Anniv of Kemal Atatürk. Litho.*
P 10½.
503 **201** 1 a. light blue 5 5
504 3 a. light reddish violet 15 15

202 Mohamed Zahir   203 Afghan Stamp of 1878
     Shah

1963 (15 Oct). *Shah's 49th Birthday. Litho. P 10½.*
505 **202** 25 p. green 5 5
506 50 p. grey-drab 5 5
507 75 p. carmine 5 5
508 100 p. chocolate 8 5
505/508 *Set of 4* .. 20 15

(Des G. C. Adams. Photo State Ptg Wks, Vienna)

1964 (28 Mar). *"Philately". Stamp Day. P 12.*
509 **203** 1 a. 25, black, emerald and gold .. 8 8
510 5 a. black, carmine and gold .. 20 20

204 Kabul International   205 Kandahar International
    Airport   Airport

(Photo State Ptg Wks, Vienna)

1964 (Apr). *AIR. Inauguration of Kabul International Airport.*
P 12×11.
511 **204** 10 a. green and bright purple .. 15 12
512 20 a. bright purple and deep green .. 30 25
513 50 a. turquoise-blue and deep blue .. 90 60

1964 (Apr). *AIR. Inauguration of Kandahar International Air-*
port. Litho. P 10½.
514 **205** 7 a. 75, chocolate .. 20 15
515 9 a. 25, light blue .. 25 20
516 10 a. 50, light green .. 25 20
517 13 a. 75, carmine .. 35 30

PRINTERS. The following issues to No. 649 were printed in
photogravure by the State Printing Works, Vienna, *unless*
otherwise stated.

206 Unisphere and Flags

207 "Flame of Freedom"

(Des G. C. Adams)

1964 (3 May). *New York World's Fair.* P 13½ × 14.
518 **206** 6 a. black, red and blue-green .. 15 15

1964 (12 May). *First U.N. "Human Rights" Seminar, Kabul.* P 14 × 13½.
519 **207** 3 a. 75, multicoloured 10 10

208 Snow Leopard

1964 (25 June). *Afghan Wild Life.* T **208** *and similar designs.* P 12.
520 25 p. blue and yellow 5 5
521 50 p. green and red 5 5
522 75 p. bright purple and turquoise-blue .. 10 10
523 5 a. deep brown and blue-green .. 20 20
520/523 *Set of 4* 30 30
Animals: *Vert*—50 p. Ibex. *Horiz*—75 p. Marco Polo sheep; 5 a. Yak.

209 Herat

210 Hurdling

1964 (12 July). *Tourist Publicity.* T **209** *and similar designs inscr* "1964". P 14 × 13½ (75 p.) *or* 13½ × 14 (*others*).
524 25 p. brown and violet-blue .. 5 5
525 75 p. blue and ochre 5 5
526 3 a. black, red and green .. 8 8
Designs: *Vert*—75 p. Tomb of Gowhar Shad. *Horiz*—3 a. Map and flag.

(Des G. C. Adams)

1964 (26 July). *Olympic Games, Tokyo.* T **210** *and similar designs.* P 12.
527 25 p. deep sepia, red and bistre.. .. 5 5
528 1 a. deep sepia, red and turquoise-blue 5 5
529 3 a. 75, deep sepia, red and yellow-grn 15 15
530 5 a. deep sepia, red and brown .. 20 20
527/530 *Set of 4* 40 40
MS530a 95 × 95 mm. Nos. 527/30. Imperf (sold at 15 a.) 50 50
Designs: *Vert*—1 a. Diving. *Horiz*—3 a. 75, Wrestling; 5 a. Football.

211 Afghan Flag

212 Pashtu Flag

(Des Khair Mohammad)

1964 (23 Aug). *46th Independence Day.* P 12.
531 **211** 25 p. multicoloured 5 5
532 75 p. multicoloured 5 5
On the above the Pushtu inscription "33rd Anniversary" is blocked out in gold.

(Des Khair Mohammad)

1964 (31 Aug). *Pashtunistan Day.* P 12.
533 **212** 100 p. multicoloured 5 5

213 Mohamed Zahir Shah

214 "Blood Transfusion"

1964 (14 Oct). *Shah's 50th Birthday.* P 14 × 13½.
534 **213** 1 a. 25, yellow-green and gold .. 5 5
535 3 a. 75, rose-red and gold 8 8
536 50 a. black and gold .. .. 1·10 1·10

(Des G. C. Adams. Litho Kabul)

1964 (18 Oct). *Red Crescent Day.* P 10½.
537 **214** 1 a. + 50 p. red and black 5 5

215 Badges of Afghanistan and U.N.

216 Doves with Necklace

(Des G. C. Adams)

1964 (24 Oct). *U.N. Day.* P 13½ × 14.
538 **215** 5 a. light blue, black and gold .. 12 12

(Des G. C. Adams)

1964 (9 Nov). *Women's Day.* P 13½ × 14.
539 **216** 25 p. blue, green and pink .. 5 5
540 75 p. blue, green and light blue .. 5 5
541 1 a. blue, green and silver .. 5 5

217 M. Jami

218 Lanceolated Jay

(Litho Kabul)

1964 (23 Nov). *550th Birth Anniv of Mowlana Jami (poet).* P 10½.
542 **217** 1 a. 50, cream, green and black .. 5 5

1965 (26 Apr). *Birds.* T 218 *and similar multicoloured designs.* P 13½×14 (1 *a.* 25) *or* 14×13½ (*others*).
543 1 a. 25, Type 218 .. .. .. 8 8
544 3 a. 75, White-capped "redstart" (*vert*) .. 12 12
545 5 a. Impeyan pheasant (*vert*) 20 20

219 I.T.U. Emblem and   **220** "The Red Town"
Symbols

1965 (17 May). *I.T.U. Centenary.* P 13½×14.
546 219 5 a. black, red and light blue .. 15 15

1965 (30 May). *Tourist Publicity.* T 220 *and similar vert designs inscr* "1965". *Multicoloured.* P 14×13½.
547 1 a. 25, Type 220 .. .. .. 5 5
548 3 a. 75, Bami Yan (valley and mountains) 10 10
549 5 a. Band-E-Amir (lake and mountains) 15 15

221 I.C.Y. Emblem   **222** Airliner and Emblem

1965 (26 June). *International Co-operation Year.* P 13½×14.
550 221 5 a. multicoloured 15 15

1965 (26 July). *10th Anniv of Afghan Airlines (ARIANA).* T 222 *and similar horiz designs.* P 13½×14.
551 1 a. 25, black, grey, new blue & pale bl 5 5
552 5 a. black, new blue and light purple .. 15 15
553 10 a. black, grey, new blue, grn & ochre 25 25
MS553a 90×90 mm. Nos. 551/3. Imperf .. 50 50
Designs:—5 a., 10 a. Airliner and emblem (different).

223 Mohamed Nadir   **224** Pashtu Flag
Shah

1965 (23 Aug). *47th Independence Day.* P 14×13½.
554 223 1 a. red-brown, black and grey-green 5 5

1965 (31 Aug). *Pashtunistan Day.* P 13½×14.
555 224 1 a. multicoloured 5 5

225 Promulgation of New Constitution   **226** Mohamed Zahir
Shah

1965 (11 Sept). *New Constitution.* P 13×13½.
556 225 1 a. 50, black and blue-green .. 8 8

1965 (14 Oct). *Shah's 51st Birthday.* P 14×13½.
557 226 1 a. 25, blackish brown, ultramarine and light salmon 5 5
558 6 a. indigo, bright purple & pale blue 20 15

227 First-Aid Post

1965 (16 Oct). *Red Crescent Day.* P 13½×14.
559 227 1 a. 50+50 p. red-brown, grn & red 5 5

228 U.N. and Afghan Flags   **229** Lizard (*Eublepharis macularius*)

1965 (3 Nov). *U.N. Day.* P 13½×14.
560 228 5 a. multicoloured 15 15

1966 (10 May). *Reptiles.* T 229 *and similar horiz designs. Multicoloured.* P 13½×14.
561 3 a. Type 229 .. .. .. 8 8
562 4 a. Lizard (*Agama caucasica*) .. 10 10
563 8 a. Tortoise 15 15

230 Cotton   **231** Footballer

1966 (29 June). *Agriculture Day.* T 230 *and similar horiz designs. Multicoloured. Litho.* P 13½×14.
564 1 a. Type 230 .. .. .. 5 5
565 5 a. Silkworm 15 15
566 7 a. Oxen 20 20

1966 (31 July). *World Cup Football Championships. Litho.* P 14×13½.
567 231 2 a. black and carmine-red .. 8 8
568 6 a. black and ultramarine .. 15 15
569 12 a. black and yellow-brown .. 35 35

232 Independence   **233** Pashtunistan Flag
Memorial

1966 (23 Aug). *Independence Day.* P 13½×14.
570 232 1 a. multicoloured 5 5
571 3 a. multicoloured 10 10

(Litho Kabul)

1966 (31 Aug). *Pashtunistan Day.* P 11.
572 233 1 a. light blue .. .: .. 5 5

234 Group of Afghans   **235** Map of Afghanistan

1966 (25 Sept). *Red Crescent Day. P* 13½ × 14.
573 **234** 2 a. + 1 a. bronze-green and scarlet ..   8   8
574   5 a. + 1 a. bistre-brown and magenta   15   15

1966 (3 Oct). *Tourist Publicity. T* **235** *and similar horiz designs inscr* "1966". *Multicoloured. P* 13½ × 14.
575   2 a. Type **235** ..   8   8
576   4 a. Hotel Kabul, former Palace of Abd-
    er-Rahman ..   10   10
577   8 a. Tomb of Abd-er-Rahman ..   20   20
MS578   111 × 80 mm. Nos. 575/7. Imperf   45   45

1966 (14 Oct). *Shah's 52nd Birthday. Portrait design similar to T* 226 *with position of inscriptions changed. Dated* "1966". *P* 14 × 13½.
579   1 a. slate-green ..   5   5
580   5 a. red-brown ..   12   12

236 Mohamed Zahir Shah   **237** Children Dancing
and U.N. Emblem

1966 (24 Oct). *U.N. Day. P* 12.
581 **236**   5 a. blackish green, light brown and
    bright green ..   15   15
582   10 a. crimson, light emer & lemon ..   30   30
The above are inscr "20TH ANNIVERSAIRE DES REFUGIES".

1966 (28 Nov). *Child Welfare Day. P* 13½ × 14.
583 **237**   1 a. crimson and yellow-green   8   8
584   3 a. + 2 a. brown and yellow   15   15
585   7 a. + 3 a. bronze-green and reddish
    purple ..   25   25

238 Construction of Power   **239** U.N.E.S.C.O.
Station   Emblem

1967 (7 Jan). *Afghan Industrial Development. T* **238** *and similar multicoloured designs. P* 14 × 13½ (5 a.) *or* 13½ × 14 *(others)*.
586   2 a. Type **238** ..   8   8
587   5 a. Handwoven carpet *(vert)* ..   15   12
588   8 a. Cement works *(horiz)* ..   20   15

1967 (6 Mar). *20th Anniv of U.N.E.S.C.O.* (in 1966). *Litho. P* 12½.
589 **239**   2 a. multicoloured ..   8   8
590   6 a. multicoloured ..   15   15
591   12 a. multicoloured ..   35   35

240 I.T.Y. Emblem   **241** Inoculation

1967 (11 May). *International Tourist Year. T* 240 *and similar horiz design. P* 12.
592   2 a. black, light blue and yellow   8   5
593   6 a. black, light blue and cinnamon   15   15
MS594   110 × 70 mm. Nos. 592/3. Imperf
(sold at 10 a.) ..   25   25
Design:—6 a. I.T.Y. emblem on map of Afghanistan.

1967 (6 June). *Anti-Tuberculosis Campaign. P* 12.
595 **241**   2 a. + 1 a. black and yellow ..   5   5
596   5 a. + 2 a. deep brown and pink ..   12   12

242 Hydro-Electric Power   **243** Macaco
Station

1967 (2 July). *Development of Electricity for Agriculture. T* 242 *and similar designs. P* 12.
597   1 a. lilac and blackish green   5   5
598   6 a. turquoise-blue and red-brown   15   10
599   8 a. blue and deep reddish purple   20   15
Designs: *Vert*—6 a. Dam. *Horiz*—8 a. Reservoir.

1967 (28 July). *Afghan Wildlife. T* 243 *and similar designs but horiz. P* 12.
600   2 a. indigo and buff ..   8   5
601   6 a. sepia and pale green (Hyena) ..   15   15
602   12 a. red-brown and pale blue (Gazelles)   30   20

244 "Saving the Guns at   **245** Pashtunistan Dancers
Maiwand" (after R. Caton
Woodville)

1967 (24 Aug). *Independence Day. P* 12.
603 **244**   1 a. chocolate-brown and orange-red   5   5
604   2 a. chocolate-brown and magenta ..   8   8

1967 (1 Sept). *Pashtunistan Day. P* 12.
605 **245**   2 a. violet and bright purple..   8   5

1967 (15 Oct). *Shah's 53rd Birthday. Portrait design similar to T* 226 *but with position of inscriptions changed. Dated* "1967". *P* 14 × 13½.
606   2 a. lake-brown ..   8   5
607   8 a. blue ..   15   12

246 Red Crescent   **247** U.N. Emblem and
Fireworks

1967 (18 Oct). *Red Crescent Day. P* 12.
608 **246**   3 a. + 1 a. red, black and yellow-olive   10   10
609   5 a. + 1 a. red, black and light blue ..   15   15

(Litho State Ptg Wks, Vienna)

1967 (24 Oct). *U.N. Day. P* 12.
610 **247**   10 a. multicoloured ..   25   20

248 Wrestling

249 Said Jamalluddin Afghan

1967 (20 Nov). *Olympic Games, Mexico City.* T **248** and similar horiz design. P 12.

611	4 a. reddish purple and olive-green	..	..	15	12
612	6 a. brown and deep cerise	..	..	20	15
MS613	100×65 mm. Nos. 611/2. Imperf	..		30	25

Design:—6 a. Wrestling—a "throw".

1967 (27 Nov). *Said Afghan Commemoration.* P 12.

614	**249** 1 a. reddish purple	..	..	5	5
615	5 a. bistre-brown	..	..	15	10

250 Bronze Vase

251 W.H.O. Emblem

1967 (23 Dec). *Archaeological Treasures (11th–12th century Ghasnavide era).* T **250** and similar vert design. P 12.

616	3 a. brown and light green	..	..	8	8
617	7 a. deep bluish green and light yellow (Bronze jar)	..	..	20	20
MS618	65×100 mm. Nos. 616/7. Imperf	..		30	25

1968 (7 Apr). *20th Anniv of World Health Organization.* P 12.

619	**251** 2 a. new blue and yellow-bistre	..	..	5	5
620	7 a. new blue and claret	..	..	15	15

252 Karakul Sheep

253 Map of Afghanistan

1968 (20 May). *Agriculture Day.* P 12.

621	**252** 1 a. black and yellow	..	..	5	5
622	6 a. blackish brown, black & lt blue		..	15	12
623	12 a. brown, blackish brown and cobalt	..	..	30	15

1968 (3 June). *Tourist Publicity.* T **253** and similar designs inscr "VISITEZ L'AFGHANISTAN 1968". P 13½×14 (2 a.) or 12 (others).

624	2 a. multicoloured	..	..	5	5
625	3 a. multicoloured	..	..	8	8
626	16 a. multicoloured	..	..	40	20

Designs: *Vert* (21×31 mm)—3 a. Tower; 16 a. Mosque.

254 Queen Humaira

255 Black Vulture

1968 (14 June). *Mothers' Day.* P 12.

627	**254** 2 a.+2 a. red-brown	..	..	10	10
628	7 a.+2 a. slate-green	..	..	20	20

1968 (3 July). *Wild Birds.* T **255** and similar vert designs. Multicoloured. P 12.

629	1 a. Type **255**	..	..	8	8
630	6 a. Eagle owl	..	..	20	15
631	7 a. Greater flamingoes	..	..	25	20

256 Horseman

257 Flowers on Gun-carriage

1968 (29 July). *Olympic Games, Mexico.* T **256** and similar designs. P 12 (2 a.) or 13½×14 (others).

632	2 a. multicoloured	..	..	8	8
633	8 a. multicoloured	..	..	20	15
634	12 a. multicoloured	..	..	35	20

Designs: *Vert* (21×31 mm)—2 a. Olympic flame and rings. *Horiz* (As T **256**)—12 a. Horse-riders galloping.

1968 (23 Aug). *Independence Day.* P 12.

635	**257** 6 a. multicoloured	..	..	15	15

258 Pashtunistan Flag

259 Red Crescent

1968 (31 Aug). *Pashtunistan Day.* P 12.

636	**258** 3 a. multicoloured	..	..	8	8

1968 (14 Oct). *Shah's 54th Birthday. Portrait design similar to* T **226** but differently arranged and in smaller size (21×31 mm). Dated "1968". P 12.

637	2 a. ultramarine	..		5	5
638	8 a. bistre-brown	..	..	20	20

1968 (16 Oct). *Red Crescent Day.* P 12.

639	**259** 4 a.+1 a. multicoloured	..		12	12

260 Human Rights Emblem

261 Maolala Djalalodine Balkhi

262 Temple Painting

1968 (24 Oct). *United Nations Day and Human Rights Year.* P 12.

640	**260** 1 a. brown, yellow-bistre and blackish green	..	..	5	5
641	2 a. black, yellow-bistre and bright bluish violet	..	..	5	5
642	6 a. bright bluish violet, yellow-bistre and deep slate-purple	..	..	15	15
MS643	101×65 mm. 260 10 a. red-orange, yellow-bistre and purple. Imperf			25	25

1968 (26 Nov). *Balkhi Commemoration.* P 12.

644	**261** 4 a. deep magenta & blackish green			10	10

1969 (2 Jan). *Archaeological Treasures (Bagram era).* T **262** and similar vert design inscr "1968". P 12.
645 1 a. lake, light yellow & dp bronze-green 5 5
646 3 a. dull purple and bright violet (Carved vessel) 10 8
MS647 101×66 mm. Nos. 645/6. Imperf (Sold for 10 a.) 25 25

263 I.L.O. Emblem

264 Red Cross Emblems

1969 (23 Mar). *50th Anniversary of International Labour Organization.* P 12.
648 **263** 5 a. black and olive-yellow 12 12
649 8 a. black and light turquoise-blue .. 20 15

(Litho State Ptg Wks, Vienna)

1969 (5 May). *50th Anniversary of League of Red Cross Societies.* P 14×13½.
650 **264** 3 a. +1 a. multicoloured 10 10
651 5 a. +1 a. multicoloured 15 15
Nos. 650/1 were only issued overprinted with two horiz gold bars, applied by litho in Kabul, obliterating "DE LA CROIX ROUGE INTERNATIONALE", and a similar inscr in Pushtu.

265 Coat-of-Arms (T **75** re-drawn)

1969 (26 May). *NEWSPAPER. Litho.* P 11.
N652 **265** 100 p. myrtle-green 5 5
N653 150 p. chocolate 8 8
T **265** is larger than T **75**, with different Pushtu inscr at top right.

266 Mother and Child

267 Map of Provinces

1969 (14 June). *Mothers' Day. Photo.* P 12.
654 **266** 1 a. +1 a. chocolate & orange-yell .. 5 5
655 4 a. +1 a. violet and mauve 12 12
MS656 121×81 mm. Nos. 654/5. Imperf (sold for 10 a.) 20 20

1969 (6 July). *Tourist Publicity. Badakshan and Pamir Region.* T **267** *and horiz views. Multicoloured. Photo.* P 13½×14.
657 2 a. Type **267** 5 5
658 4 a. Pamir landscape 10 10
659 7 a. Mountain mule transport 15 12
MS660 136×90 mm. Nos. 657/59. Imperf (sold for 15 a.) 35 35

268 Bust (Hadda era)

269 Mohamed Zahir Shah and Queen Humaira

1969 (3 Aug). *Archaeological Discoveries.* T **268** *and similar vert designs. Multicoloured. Photo.* P 14×13½.
661 1 a. Type **268** 5 5
662 5 a. Vase and jug (Bagram period) .. 12 12
663 10 a. Statuette (Bagram period).. .. 25 20

1969 (23 Aug). *Independence Day.* P 12.
664 **269** 5 a. Venetian red, deep blue & gold 12 12
665 10 a. blue-green, bright pur & gold .. 25 20

270 Map and Rising Sun **271** Mohamed Zahir Shah

1969 (31 Aug). *Pashtunistan Day. Typo.* P 10½.
666 **270** 2 a. red and light blue 5 5

1969 (14 Oct). *Shah's 55th Birthday. Photo.* P 12.
667 **271** 2 a. multicoloured 5 5
668 6 a. multicoloured 15 12

272 Red Crescent **273** U.N. Emblem, Afghan Arms and Flag

1969 (16 Oct). *Red Crescent Day. Photo.* P 12.
669 **272** 6 a. +1 a. multicoloured 15 12

1969 (24 Oct). *United Nations Day. Litho.* P 13½.
670 **273** 5 a. multicoloured 12 10

274 I.T.U. Emblem

275 Long-tailed Porcupine

Afghanistan 1970

1969 (12 Nov). *World Telecommunications Day. Litho.*
P 13½.
671 274 6 a. multicoloured 15 12
672 12 a. multicoloured 30 25

1969 (7 Dec). *Wild Animals. T 275 and similar vert designs.*
Multicoloured. Photo. P 12.
673 1 a. Type 275 .. .. 5 5
674 3 a. Wild boar 8 8
675 8 a. Bactrian red deer 20 15

276 Footprint on the Moon   **277** "Cancer the Crab"

1969 (28 Dec). *First Man on the Moon. Photo. P 13½.*
676 276 1 a. multicoloured 5 5
677 3 a. multicoloured 8 5
678 6 a. multicoloured 15 10
679 10 a. multicoloured 25 20
676/679 Set of 4 .. .. 45 35

1970 (7 Apr). *W.H.O. "Fight Cancer" Day. Photo. P 14.*
680 277 2 a. carmine, blackish grn & light grn 5 5
681 6 a. carmine, deep blue & light blue 15 12

278 Mirza Bedel   **279** I.E.Y. Emblem

1970 (6 May). *250th Death Anniv of Mirza Abdul Quader*
Bedel (poet). Photo. P 14 × 13½.
682 278 5 a. multicoloured 12 8

1970 (7 June). *International Education Year. Photo. P 12.*
683 279 1 a. black 5 5
684 6 a. carmine 15 10
685 12 a. myrtle-green 30 15

280 Mother and Child

1970 (15 June). *Mothers' Day. Photo. P 13½.*
686 280 6 a. multicoloured 15 8

281 U.N. Emblem, Scales   **282** Tourist Location Map
and Satellite

1970 (26 June). *25th Anniversary of United Nations. Photo.*
P 13½.
687 281 4 a. new blue, deep blue and yellow 10 8
688 6 a. new blue, deep blue and light
Venetian red 15 10

1970 (6 July). *Tourist Publicity. T 282 and horiz views dated*
"1970". Photo. P 12.
689 282 2 a. black, pale sage-grn & pale blue 5 5
690 – 3 a. multicoloured 8 8
691 – 7 a. multicoloured 15 12
Designs: (36 × 26 mm)—3 a. Lakeside palace; 7 a. Ruined
arch.

283 Quail   **284** Shah reviewing Troops

1970 (1 Aug). *Wild Birds. T 283 and similar horiz designs.*
Multicoloured. Photo. P 12.
692 2 a. Type 283 .. .. 5 5
693 4 a. Golden Eagle 10 10
694 6 a. Pheasant 15 12

1970 (23 Aug). *Independence Day. Photo. P 13½.*
695 284 8 a. multicoloured 20 15

285 Group of   **286** Mohamed Zahir
Pashtunistanis   Shah

1970 (31 Aug). *Pashtunistan Day. Typo. P 10½.*
696 285 2 a. ultramarine and red 5 5

1970 (14 Oct). *Shah's 56th Birthday. Photo. P 14 × 13½.*
697 286 3 a. reddish violet and deep green .. 8 8
698 7 a. light brown-purple & deep blue 15 10

287 Red Crescent   **288** U.N. Emblem and Plaque
Emblems

1970 (16 Oct). *Red Crescent Day. Typo. P 10½.*
699 287 2 a. black, red and gold 5 5

1970 (24 Oct). *United Nations Day. Photo. P 14.*
700 288 1 a. multicoloured 5 5
701 5 a. multicoloured 12 10

289 Afghan Stamps of   290 Global Emblem
1870

1970 (10 Nov). *Centenary of First Afghan Stamps. Photo. P 12.*
702 289 1 a. black, light turq-blue & salmon 5 5
703 4 a. black, light yellow and blue .. 10 10
704 12 a. black, cobalt and reddish lilac 30 20

1971 (17 May). *World Telecommunications Day. Photo. P 13½.*
705 290 12 a. multicoloured 30 20

291 *Callimorpha principalis*   292 Local Costume

1971 (30 May). *Butterflies. T 291 and similar horiz designs. Multicoloured. Photo. P 13½ × 14.*
706 1 a. Type 291 .. .. .. 5 5
707 3 a. *Epizygaenella species* 8 8
708 5 a. *Parnassius autocrator* 12 10

1971 (26 June). *U.N.E.S.C.O. Aid for Kuchani International Schools. Photo. P 13½.*
709 292 6 a. violet and yellow 15 12
710 10 a. maroon and light blue.. .. 25 20

293 Independence Memorial   294 Pashtunistan Flag
and Buildings

1971 (23 Aug). *Independence Day. Photo. P 13½.*
711 293 7 a. multicoloured 15 10
712 9 a. multicoloured 20 15

1971 (31 Aug). *Pashtunistan Day. Typo. P 10½.*
713 294 5 a. bright purple 12 10

295 Shah and Kabul Airport

1971. *AIR. T 295 and similar horiz design. Multicoloured. Photo. P 12½ × 13½.*
714 50 a. Type 295 .. .. .. 1·25 1·00
715 100 a. Shah, airline emblem and aircraft 2·50 2·00

296 Mohamed Zahir   297 Map, Nurse and
Shah   Patients

1971 (14 Oct). *Shah's 57th Birthday. Photo. P 12.*
716 296 9 a. multicoloured 20 15
717 17 a. multicoloured 40 35

1971 (16 Oct). *Red Crescent Day. Photo. P 14 × 13½.*
718 297 8 a. multicoloured 20 15

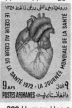

298 Racial Equality Year   299 Human Heart
Emblem

1971 (24 Oct). *United Nations Day. Photo. P 12.*
719 298 24 a. new blue 60 50

1972 (7 Apr). *World Health Day and World Heart Month. Photo. P 14 × 13½.*
720 299 9 a. multicoloured 20 15
721 12 a. multicoloured 30 20

300 *Tulipa lanata*   301 Buddha of Hadda

1972 (5 June). *Afghan Flora and Fauna. T 300 and similar multicoloured designs. Photo. P 14.*
722 7 a. Type 300 .. .. .. 15 10
723 10 a. Chukar (rock partridge) (*horiz*) .. 25 20
724 12 a. Lynx (*horiz*) 30 20
725 18 a. *Allium stipitatum* 40 35
722/725 Set of 4 .. .. .. 1·00 80

1972 (16 July). *Tourist Publicity. T* **301** *and similar horiz designs. Photo. P* 12.

726 3 a. blue and yellow-brown 8 8
727 7 a. turquoise-green and crimson .. 15 10
728 9 a. purple and myrtle-green 20 15
Designs:—7 a. Greco-Bactrian seal, 250 B.C.; 9 a. Greek temple, Ai-Khanum 3rd-2nd cent B.C.

302 Shah and Queen Humaira at Independence Parade

1972 (23 Aug). *Independence Day. Photo. P* 13½.
729 **302** 25 a. multicoloured 65 50

303 Wrestling

304 Pathan and Mountain View

1972 (26 Aug). *Olympic Games, Munich. T* **303** *and similar horiz designs, showing different wrestling holds. Photo. P* 13½.

730 4 a. multicoloured 10 10
731 8 a. multicoloured 20 15
732 10 a. multicoloured 25 20
733 19 a. multicoloured 45 35
734 21 a. multicoloured 50 45
730/734 *Set of 5* .. .. .. 1·40 1·10
MS735 160×110 mm. Nos. 730/4. Imperf
(sold for 60 a.) .. .. .. 1·50 1·50

1972 (31 Aug). *Pashtunistan Day. Photo. P* 12.
736 **304** 5 a. multicoloured 12 10

305 Mohamed Zahir Shah   306 Ruined Town and Refugees

1972 (14 Oct). *Shah's 58th Birthday. Photo. P* 14×13½.
737 **305** 7 a. greenish blue, black and gold .. 15 10
738 14 a. yellow-brown, black and gold 35 20

1972 (16 Oct). *Red Crescent Day. Photo. P* 14×13½.
739 **306** 7 a. black, red and light blue .. 15 10

307 E.C.A.F.E. Emblem   308 Ceramics

1972 (24 Oct). *United Nations Day. Photo. P* 13½.
740 **307** 12 a. black and cobalt 30 20

1973 (5 Feb). *Afghan Handicrafts. T* **308** *and similar multicoloured designs. Photo. P* 12.
741 7 a. Type **308** 15 10
742 9 a. Embroidered coat (*vert*) 20 15
743 12 a. Coffee set (*vert*) 30 20
744 16 a. Decorated boxes 40 30
741/744 *Set of 4* 95 70
MS745 110×110 mm. Nos. 741/4. Imperf
(sold for 45 a.) .. .. .. 1·00 1·00

AFRICA. See Portuguese Colonies (General Issues).

Ajman

1964. 100 Naye Paise = 1 Rupee
1967. 100 Dirhams = 1 Riyal (Saudi Arabian)

One of the Trucial States on the Persian Gulf. See notes under Abu Dhabi.

1 Shaikh Rashid bin Humaid al Naimi and Arab Stallion   **2** Kennedy in Football Kit

(Photo and litho Heraclio Fournier, Vitoria, Spain)

1964. *T* **1** *and similar horiz designs. Multicoloured. P* 14½.

(a) Size 34½ × 23 *mm* (20 June)

1	1 n.p. Type 1	..	..	5	5
2	2 n.p. Striped fish	..	..	5	5
3	3 n.p. Camel	..	..	5	5
4	4 n.p. Blue fish ..	..	..	5	5
5	5 n.p. Tortoise	..	..	5	5
6	10 n.p. Spotted fish	..	..	5	5
7	15 n.p. Stork	..	..	5	5
8	20 n.p. Gulls	..	..	5	5
9	30 n.p. Hawk	..	..	8	5

(b) Size 42½ × 27 *mm* (7 Sept)

10	40 n.p. Type 1	..	..	8	5
11	50 n.p. Striped fish	..	..	10	5
12	70 n.p. Camel	..	..	15	8
13	1 r. Blue Fish	..	..	20	10
14	1 r. 50, Tortoise ..	..	..	30	15
15	2 r. Spotted fish ..	..	..	35	15

(c) Size 53 × 34 *mm* (4 Nov)

16	3 r. Stork..	..	..	60	30
17	5 r. Gulls..	..	..	1·00	45
18	10 r. Hawk	..	..	1·90	90
1/18	*Set of* 18	..	..	4·50	2·40

IMPERFORATE STAMPS. Most of the following issues were also issued imperforate from limited printings.

(Photo State Ptg Wks, Vienna)

1964 (15 Dec). *President Kennedy Commemoration. T* **2** *and similar vert designs. P* 13½ × 14.

19	10 n.p. bright purple and green	..		5	5
20	15 n.p. reddish violet and turquoise-blue		5	5
21	50 n.p. blue and chestnut	..	..	10	5
22	1 r. deep bluish green and sepia	..	20	10
23	2 r. olive-brown and bright purple	..	40	20
24	3 r. red-brown and green	..		60	30
25	5 r. bistre-brown and bluish violet	..	95	45
26	10 r. red-brown and deep blue	..	1·90	90
19/26	*Set of* 8	..	..	3·75	1·90

MS26*a* 105 × 140 mm. Nos. 23/6 in new colours .. .. 3·75 3·75

Designs: Various pictures of Kennedy—15 n.p. Diving; 50 n.p. As naval officer; 1 r. Sailing with Mrs. Kennedy; 2 r. With Mrs. Eleanor Roosevelt; 3 r. With wife and child; 5 r. With colleagues; 10 r. Full-face portrait.

3 Start of Race

(Photo State Ptg Wks, Vienna)

1965 (12 Jan). *Olympic Games, Tokyo. T* **3** *and similar horiz designs. P* 13½ × 14.

27	5 n.p. slate-blue, red-brown and mauve		5	5
28	10 n.p. brown-red, bronze-green & lt blue	5	5
29	15 n.p. bistre-brown, violet & blue-green	5	5
30	25 n.p. black, blue and Venetian red	..	5	5
31	50 n.p. slate-violet, brown-purple & lt bl	10	5
32	1 r. ultram, black-green & reddish pur	..	20	10
33	1 r. 50, brn-pur, reddish vio & lt grn	..	30	15
34	2 r. blue, vermilion and ochre	..	..	40	20
35	3 r. reddish violet, chocolate & lt blue	..	60	30
36	5 r. reddish purple, deep green & yellow	95	45
27/36	*Set of* 10	..	..	..	2·50	1·25

MS36*a* 120 × 100 mm. Nos. 33/6 in new colours .. .. 2·25 1·50

Sports:—10 n.p., 1 r. 50, Boxing; 15 n.p. *T* **3**; 25 n.p., 2 r. Judo; 50 n.p., 5 r. Gymnastics; 1 r., 3 r. Sailing.

4 First Gibbons Catalogue and Alexandria (U.S.) 5 c. Postmaster's Stamp

1965 (6 May). *Stanley Gibbons Catalogue Centenary Exhibition, London. T* **4** *and similar horiz designs. Multicoloured. Photo. P* 13½.

37	5 n.p. Type **4**			5	5
38	10 n.p. Austria (6 k.) scarlet "Mercury" newspaper stamp	..	5	5
39	15 n.p. British Guiana "One Cent", 1856	5	5
40	25 n.p. Canada "Twelvepence Black", 1851		5	5
41	50 n.p. Hawaiian "Missionary" 2 c., 1851	10	5
42	1 r. Mauritius "Post Office" 2d. blue, 1847		20	10
43	3 r. Switzerland "Double Geneva" 5 c.+5 c., 1843	..	60	30
44	5 r. Tuscany 3 lire, 1860 ..	..		95	45
37/44	*Set of* 8	..	..	..	1·90	1·00

MS44*a* 2 sheets each 124 × 99 mm. Nos. 37, 40/1, 44 and 38/9, 42/3. *Two sheets* .. 3·75 3·75

The 5, 15, 50 n.p. and 3 r. also include the first Gibbons Catalogue and the others, the Gibbons "Elizabethan" Catalogue.

PAN ARAB GAMES
CAIRO 1965

(5)

الدَّوْرَة الرِّياضِتَّة العَرَبِتَّة
١٩٦٥ القَاهِرَة

(6)

1965 (27 Sept). *Pan Arab Games, Cairo. Nos. 29, 31 and 33/5 optd (a) With T* **5.**

45	15 n.p. bistre-brown, violet & blue-green	5	5
46	50 n.p. slate-violet, brown-pur & light bl	12	5
47	1 r. 50, brn-pur, reddish vio & light grn	35	15
48	2 r. blue, vermilion and ochre	50	20
49	3 r. reddish violet, chocolate & light bl ..	80	30

(b) With T **6**

50	15 n.p. bistre-brown, violet & blue-green	5	5
51	50 n.p. slate-violet, brn-pur & light blue ..	12	5
52	1 r. 50, brn-pur, reddish vio & light grn	35	15
53	2 r. blue, vermilion and ochre ..	50	20
54	3 r. reddish violet, chocolate & light bl ..	80	30
45/54	*Set of 10*	3·25	1·40

(Photo and litho Heraclio Fournier, Vitoria, Spain)

1965. *AIR. Designs similar to Nos. 1/9, but inscr "AIR MAIL". Multicoloured. P* 14½.

(a) Size 42½ × 25½ mm (15 Nov)

55	15 n.p. Type **1**	5	5
56	25 n.p. Striped fish	5	5
57	35 n.p. Camel	8	5
58	50 n.p. Blue fish	10	5
59	75 n.p. Tortoise	15	8
60	1 r. Spotted fish	20	10

(b) Size 53 × 34 mm (18 Dec)

61	2 r. Stork..	40	20
62	3 r. Gulls..	60	30
63	5 r. Hawk	95	45
55/63	*Set of 9*	2·25	1·10

(Photo and litho Heraclio Fournier, Vitoria, Spain)

1965 (Dec). *OFFICIAL. Designs similar to Nos. 1/9, additionally inscr "ON STATE'S SERVICE". Multicoloured. P* 14½.

(a) POSTAGE. Size 43 × 26 mm. (1 Dec)

O64	25 n.p. Type **1**	5	5
O65	40 n.p. Striped fish	10	5
O66	50 n.p. Camel	10	5
O67	75 n.p. Blue fish..	15	8
O68	1 r. Tortoise	20	10
O64/68	*Set of 5*	55	30

(b) AIR (18 Dec)
(i) Size 43 × 26 mm

O69	75 n.p. Spotted fish	15	8

(ii) Size 53 × 34 mm

O70	2 r. Stork	40	20
O71	3 r. Gulls	60	30
O72	5 r. Hawk	95	50
O69/72	*Set of 4*	1·90	1·00

(7)

(The pyramid device represents the watermark of the 1866 issue of Egypt)

1966 (2 Jan). *Stamp Centenary Exhibition, Cairo. (a) Nos. 38/9 and 41/3 optd with T* **7.**

73	10 n.p. multicoloured	5	5
74	15 n.p. multicoloured	5	5
75	50 n.p. multicoloured	10	5
76	1 r. multicoloured	20	10
77	3 r. multicoloured	60	30
73/77	*Set of 5*	90	50

(b) No. **MS**44*a optd with T* **7,** *(on each stamp)*

MS78	Two sheets each 124 × 99 mm as		
MS44*a*	.. ..	1·90	1·75

HAVE YOU READ THE NOTES AT THE BEGINNING OF THIS CATALOGUE?

These often provide answers to the enquiries we receive.

8 Sir Winston Churchill and Tower Bridge

1966 (22 Feb). *Churchill Commemoration. T* **8** *and similar horiz designs each including portrait of Churchill. Multicoloured. Litho. P* 13½.

79	25 n.p. Type **8**	5	5
80	50 n.p. Buckingham Palace	12	5
81	75 n.p. Blenheim Palace	15	8
82	1 r. British Museum	25	15
83	2 r. St. Paul's Cathedral in wartime ..	50	30
84	3 r. National Gallery and St. Martin's in the Fields Church	75	40
85	5 r. Westminster Abbey	1·25	60
86	7 r. 50, Houses of Parliament at night ..	1·90	90
79/86	*Set of 8*	4·50	2·25
MS87	101 × 120 mm. Nos. 85/6	3·00	2·00

9 Rocket

1966. *Space Achievements. T* **9** *and various multicoloured designs. Photo. P* 13½.

(a) POSTAGE. Size 32 × 32 mm (23 July)

88	1 n.p. Type **9**	5	5
89	3 n.p. Capsule	5	5
90	5 n.p. Astronaut entering capsule in space	5	5
91	10 n.p. Astronaut outside capsule in space	5	5
92	15 n.p. Astronauts and Globe	5	5
93	25 n.p. Astronaut in space	5	5
88/93	*Set of 6*	25	25
MS94	98 × 88 mm. 1 r. and 3 r. in designs of 15 n.p. and 10 n.p.	75	45

(b) AIR. Size 38 × 38 mm (22 Aug)

95	50 n.p. As Type **9**	10	5
96	1 r. Astronauts and Globe	20	10
97	3 r. Astronaut outside capsule in space	60	30
98	5 r. Capsule	95	45
95/98	*Set of 4*	1·60	80

≡ **Dh.** درهم =

(10)

1967 (19 Jan). *New Currency. Various issues with currency names changed by overprinting as T* **10.**

(a) POSTAGE. Nos. 1/18

99	1 d. on 1 n.p.	5	5
100	2 d. on 2 n.p.	5	5
101	3 d. on 3 n.p.	5	5
102	4 d. on 4 n.p.	5	5
103	5 d. on 5 n.p.	5	5
104	10 d. on 10 n.p.	5	5
105	15 d. on 15 n.p.	5	5
106	20 d. on 20 n.p.	5	5
107	30 d. on 30 n.p.	8	5
108	40 d. on 40 n.p.	8	5
109	50 d. on 50 n.p.	10	5
110	70 d. on 70 n.p.	15	8
111	1 r. on 1 r.	20	10
112	1 r. 50 on 1 r. 50	30	15
113	2 r. on 2 r.	40	20
114	3 r. on 3 r.	60	30

115	5 r. on 5 r.	..	..	..	95	45
116	10 r. on 10 r.	..	..	..	1·90	90
99/116	Set of 18	..	..	..	4·50	2·40

(b) AIR. Nos. 55/63

117	15 d. on 15 n.p.	..	..	5	5
118	25 d. on 25 n.p.	..	..	5	5
119	35 d. on 35 n.p.	..	..	8	5
120	50 d. on 50 n.p.	..	..	10	5
121	75 d. on 75 n.p.	..	..	15	8
122	1 r. on 1 r.	..	..	20	10
123	2 r. on 2 r.	..	..	40	20
124	3 r. on 3 r.	..	..	60	30
125	5 r. on 5 r.	..	..	95	45
117/125	Set of 9	..	..	2·25	1·25

(c) OFFICIAL. Nos. O64/72

O126	25 d. on 25 n.p.	..	..	5	5
O127	40 d. on 40 n.p.	..	..	8	8
O128	50 d. on 50 n.p.	..	..	8	10
O129	75 d. on 75 n.p. (No. O67)	..	..	12	15
O130	75 d. on 75 n.p. (No. O69)	..	..	12	15
O131	1 r. on 1 r.	..	..	15	20
O132	2 r. on 2 r.	..	..	35	35
O133	3 r. on 3 r.	..	..	55	60
O134	5 r. on 5 r.	..	..	90	95
O126/134	Set of 9	..	..	2·10	2·40

Nos. 19/44a and 79/98 were also surcharged in the new currency in limited quantities but they had little local usage.

11 Motor-car

1967 (20 Apr). *T* **11** *and similar horiz designs. Photo.*
P 12½ × 11½.

(a) POSTAGE

135	1 d. yellow-brown and black	..	..	5	5
136	2 d. new blue and brown	..	..	5	5
137	3 d. magenta and black	..	..	5	5
138	4 d. ultramarine and brown	..	..	5	5
139	5 d. emerald and black..	..	..	5	5
140	15 d. new blue and brown	..	..	5	5
141	30 d. brown and black	..	..	8	5
142	50 d. black and brown	..	..	8	5
143	70 d. bright reddish violet and black	..	12	5
135/143	Set of 9	..	..	50	35

(b) AIR

144	1 r. blue-green and brown	..	..	15	8
145	2 r. magenta and black	..	..	35	12
146	3 r. black and brown	..	..	55	25
147	5 r. yellow-brown and black	..	..	90	45
148	10 r. new blue and brown	..	..	1·75	85
144/148	Set of 5	..	..	3·25	1·50

Designs:—2 d., 2 r. Motor-coach; 3 d., 3 r. Motor-cyclist; 4 d., 5 r. Jetliner; 5 d., 10 r. Ocean liner; 15 d. Sailing ship; 30 d. Cameleer; 50 d. Arab horse; 70 d. Helicopter; 1 r. T **11**.

From June 1967 very many stamp issues were made by a succession of agencies which had been awarded contracts by the Ruler, sometimes two agencies operating at the same time. Several contradictory statements have been made as to the validity of some of these issues and for this reason they are recorded in the Appendix at the end of this volume.

On the withdrawal of British forces from the Gulf the defence treaties with the Trucial States were terminated on 2 December 1971 when Ajman joined with other states to form the United Arab Emirates. Accordingly all the stamp contracts had been terminated by 1 August 1972 and no further issues were authorised. The stamps of the United Arab Emirates were in use from 1 January 1973.

MANAMA

A dependency of Ajman

100 Dirhams=1 Riyal

1966 (5 July). *Nos. 10, 12, 14 and 18 of Ajman surch "Manama" in English and Arabic and new value.*

1	40 d. on 40 n.p. multicoloured	..	..	8	5
2	70 d. on 70 n.p. multicoloured	..	..	15	8
3	1 r. 50 on 1 r. 50, multicoloured	..	30	15
4	10 r. on 10 r. multicoloured	..	..	1·90	90
1/4	Set of 4	..	..	2·25	1·00

MANAMA المنامة
(1)

1967 (16 Aug). *Nos. 140/8 of Ajman optd with T* **1**.

(a) POSTAGE

5	15 d. new blue and brown (Br.)	..	..	5	5
6	30 d. brown and black (Bk.)	..	..	5	5
7	50 d. black and brown (Br.)	..	..	8	5
8	70 d. bright reddish violet and black (Bk.)	12	5
5/8	Set of 4	..	..	25	15

(b) AIR

9	1 r. blue-green and brown (Br.)..	..	15	8
10	2 r. black and brown (Br.)	..	..	55	25
11	3 r. black and brown (Br.)	..	..	55	25
12	5 r. yellow-brown and black (Bk.)	..	90	45
13	10 r. new blue and brown (Br.)	..	1·75	85
9/13	Set of 5	..	..	3·25	1·60

Later issues will be found in the Appendix at the end of this volume and the note after Ajman No. 148 also applies to Manama.

ALAOUITES. See under Latakia after Syria.

ALEXANDRETTA. See Hatay.

ALEXANDRIA. See Egypt (French Post Offices).

Algeria

1924. 100 Centimes = 1 Franc
1964. 100 Centimes = 1 Dinar

I. FRENCH DEPARTMENT

A French expedition to Algeria forced the Bey of Algiers to capitulate on 5 July 1830; but a long war against the Arabs of the interior did not end till the surrender of their leader, Abd-el-Kader, on 23 December 1847. From then on, in spite of further risings of the natives, many Europeans were settled in Algeria. Until 1924 French stamps were used without overprint.

PRINTERS. All the stamps of Algeria until 1958 were printed at the Government Printing Works, Paris, *unless otherwise stated.*

IMPERFORATE STAMPS. Many stamps exist imperforate in their issued colours but they were not valid for postage. Imperforate stamps in other colours are colour trials.

ALGÉRIE
(1)

ALGÉRIE
(2)

1924 (8 May)–**25**. *Stamps of France, 1900–25, optd as* T **1** *or* **2.**

1	11	½ c. on 1 c. slate (R.)		5	5
		a. Opt treble..		10·00	
2		1 c. grey (R.)		5	5
3		2 c. claret		5	5
4		3 c. orange-red (6.24)..		5	5
5		4 c. brown (B.) (7.24)		5	5
6	18	5 c. orange (B.)		5	5
7	11	5 c. blue-green (6.25) ..		5	5
8	30	10 c. green		5	5
9	18	10 c. green (1.25)		5	5
10	15	15 c. sage-green		5	5
11	30	15 c. green (6.25)		5	5
12	18	15 c. chocolate (B.) (11.25)		5	5
13		20 c. purple-brown (B.)		5	5
14		25 c. blue (R.)		5	5
15	30	30 c. scarlet (B.)		5	5
16	18	30 c. blue (R.) (9.25)		5	5
17		30 c. rosine (4.25)*		5	5
18		35 c. violet		5	5
19	13	40 c. red and pale blue..		5	5
20	18	40 c. olive (R.) (6.25)		5	5
21	13	45 c. green and pale blue (R.)		5	5
		a. Opt double		18·00	
22	30	45 c. red (B.) (2.25)		5	5
23		50 c. blue (R.)		5	5
24	15	60 c. mauve (7.24)		5	5
		a. Opt inverted		—	65·00
25		65 c. carmine (B.) (1.25)		5	5
26	30	75 c. blue (R.) (7.24)		5	5
		a. Opt double		10·00	
27	15	80 c. scarlet (12.25)		8	5
28		85 c. scarlet (B.) (7.24)		5	5
29	13	1 f. lake and yellow-green		15	5
30	18	1 f. 05, scarlet (11.25)..		12	5
31	13	2 f. red and blue-green		10	5
32		3 f. violet and blue (12.25)		25	12
33		5. f. blue and buff (R.)..		1·60	1·25
1/33		*Set of* 33		3·25	2·50

The overprint is T **2** on the 2 f. and similar but larger on the other oblong stamps, except on the 5 f., where it is similar to T **1**, but larger.

*No. 17 was only issued pre-cancelled and the price in the unused column is for stamps with full gum.

D **1**

D **2**

1926 (1 May)–**28**. *POSTAGE DUE. Typo.* $P 14 \times 13\frac{1}{2}$.

D34	D **1**	5 c. blue			5	5
D35		10 c. brown			5	5
D36		20 c. olive-green			5	5
D37		25 c. rosine			8	8
D38		30 c. carmine			5	5
D39		45 c. green			8	5
D40		50 c. dull claret			5	5
D41		60 c. green (2.28)			30	8
D42		1 f. claret/*straw*			5	5
D43		2 f. magenta (7.27)..			5	5
D44		3 f. deep blue (7.27)			5	5
D34/44		*Set of* 11			75	55

See also Nos. D249/52.

1926 (May)–**27**. *POSTAGE DUE. Typo.* $P 14 \times 13\frac{1}{2}$.

D45	D **2**	1 c. olive-green (6.26)			5	5
D46		10 c. violet			5	5
D47		30 c. bistre			5	5
D48		60 c. red			5	5
D49		1 f. bright violet (11.27)			1·50	40
D50		2 f. pale blue (7.27)			1·25	12
D45/50		*Set of* 6			2·75	60

Stamps of Type D **2** were employed to recover postage due from the sender in cases where the recipient refused delivery.

3 Street in the Casbah

4 Mosque of Sidi Abderahman

5 Grand Mosque

6 The Bay of Algiers

$\frac{1}{2}$
centime
(7)

(Des Watremetz (**3**), A. Montader (**4**), Anthony (**5**) and Brouty (**6**). Typo)

1926 (June)–**41**. $P 14 \times 13\frac{1}{2}$.

34	3	1 c. olive			5	5
35		2 c. claret			5	5
36		3 c. brown-orange			5	5
37		5 c. green			5	5
38		10 c. bright mauve			5	5
39	4	15 c. chestnut			5	5
40		20 c. green			5	5
41		20 c. carmine (11.26)			5	5
42		20 c. yellow-green (1941)*			5	5
43		25 c. green			5	5
44		25 c. light blue (11.27)			8	5
45		25 c. deep ultramarine (1939)			5	5
46		30 c. light blue			5	5
47		30 c. green (11.27)			15	8
48		35 c. violet			25	20
49		40 c. olive-green			5	5
50	5	45 c. plum			5	5
51		50 c. blue (7.26) ..			5	5
		a. *Indigo*			5	5
53		50 c. scarlet (7.30)			5	5
54		60 c. yellow-green (7.26)			5	5
55		65 c. sepia (8.27)			40	30
56	3	65 c. bright blue (1938)			5	5
57	5	75 c. carmine (7.26)			5	5
58		75 c. light blue (10.29)			45	5

59	5	80 c. red-orange (8.26)	..	8	8
60		90 c. red (8.27)	..	55	25
61	6	1 f. maroon and green..	..	10	5
62	5	1 f. 05, brown (8.26)	..	5	5
63		1 f. 10, bright magenta (8.27)	..	80	35
64	6	1 f. 25, ultramarine and blue (8.26)		15	15
65		1 f. 50, ultramarine and blue (8.27)		15	5
66		2 f. chocolate and blue-green (10.26)	..	30	5
67		3 f. vermilion and bright mauve (8.26)		55	12
68		5 f. mauve and scarlet (8.26)	..	1·00	12
69		10 f. carmine and brown (7.27)	..	8·00	5·00
70		20 f. yellow-green & bright vio (7.27)	..	35	35
34/70		Set of 36	..	13·00	7·50

*No. 42 pre-cancelled only. See note after No. 33.
For stamps as T **5**, but without "REPUBLIQUE FRAN-
ÇAISE", see Nos. 178/9, and for stamp as T **6**, but inscribed
"CENTENAIRE-ALGERIE", see France, No. 479.

1926. *Surch with T* **7.**

71	3	½ c. on 1 c. olive (R.)	..	5	5

(8) (9) (D 3)

1927 (Jan). *Wounded Soldiers of Moroccan War Charity
issue. Surch as T* **8.**

72	3	5 c. + 5 c. green	..	8	8
73		10 c. + 10 c. bright mauve		8	8
74	4	15 c. + 15 c. chestnut	..	8	8
75		20 c. + 20 c. carmine	..	8	8
76		25 c. + 25 c. green	..	8	8
77		30 c. + 30 c. light blue	..	8	8
78		35 c. + 35 c. violet	..	8	8
79		40 c. + 40 c. olive-green ..		8	8
80	5	50 c. + 50 c. deep blue (R.)	..	8	8
		a. Surch double (R. + Bk.)	..		
81		80 c. + 80 c. red-orange	..	8	8
82	6	1 f. + 1 f. maroon and green	..	8	8
83		2 f. + 2 f. chocolate and blue-green	..	2·75	2·75
84		5 f. + 5 f. mauve and scarlet	..	2·75	2·75
72/84		Set of 13	..	5·50	5·50

1927 (May). *Surch* (a) *with or* (b) *without bars as T* **9.**

85	4	10 on 35 c. violet (a)		5	5
86		25 on 30 c. light blue (a)		5	5
87		30 on 25 c. green (b)	..	5	5
88	5	65 on 60 c. yellow-green (b)	..	25	15
89		90 on 80 c. red-orange (b)	..	8	5
90		1 f. 10 on 1 f. 05, brown (a)	..	5	5
91	6	1 f. 50 on 1 f. 25, ultramarine & blue (a)		40	15
85/91		Set of 7	..	85	40

1927 (June). *POSTAGE DUE. Surch as Type D* **3,** *without
bars.*

D92	D 1	60 on 20 c. olive-green		15	5
D93		2 f. on 45 c. green	..	20	15
D94		3 f. on 25 c. rosine ..		5	5

(D 4) (D 5) (10)

1927 (June)–32. *POSTAGE DUE. Surch as Types D* **4** *or D* **5,**
with bars.

D95	D 2	10 c. on 30 c. bistre (10.32)	..	40	40
D96		1 f. on 1 c. olive-green		12	12
D97		1 f. on 60 c. red (10.32)	..	2·50	5
D98		2 f. on 10 c. violet ..		1·50	1·50
D95/98		Set of 4	..	4·00	1·75

1927 (Nov). *No. 5, surch with T* **10.**

92	11	5 c. on 4 c. brown	..	5	5

Minor variations in the shape of the "5" have been noted.

11 Railway Terminus, Oran   **12** Bay of Algiers, after
painting by Verecque

(Recess Institut de Gravure, Paris)

1930 (Mar). *Centenary of French Occupation. As T* **11** (*inscr*
"CENTENAIRE DE L'ALGERIE"). *P* 12½.

93		5 c. + 5 c. orange	..	1·25	1·25
94		10 c. + 10 c. olive-green ..		1·25	1·25
95		15 c. + 15 c. sepia	..	1·25	1·25
96		25 c. + 25 c. slate	..	1·25	1·25
97		30 c. + 30 c. scarlet	..	1·25	1·25
98		40 c. + 40 c. yellow-green		1·25	1·25
99		50 c. + 50 c. ultramarine..		1·25	1·25
100		75 c. + 75 c. bright purple	..	1·25	1·25
101		1 f. + 1 f. vermilion	..	1·25	1·25
102		1 f. + 1 f. 50, deep ultramarine..		1·25	1·25
103		2 f. + 2 f. carmine	..	1·25	1·25
104		3 f. + 3 f. deep green	..	1·25	1·25
105		5 f. + 5 f. carmine and deep green	..	2·00	2·25
		a. Centre inverted	..	65·00	
93/105		Set of 13	..	15·00	15·00

Designs: *Horiz*—10 c. Constantine; 15 c. The Admiralty,
Algiers; 25 c. Algiers; 30 c. Ruins of Timgad; 40 c. Ruins of
Djemila. *Vert*—50 c. Ruins of Djemila; 75 c. Tlemçen; 1 f.
Ghardaia; 1 f. 50 Tolga; 2 f. Touaregs; 3 f. Native Quarter,
Algiers; 5 f. The Mosque, Algiers.

(Recess Institut de Gravure)

1930 (4 May). *North African International Philatelic Exhibition. P* 12½.

106	12	10 f. + 10 f. purple-brown	..	2·50	2·50
		a. Perf 11	..	2·50	2·50

The premium included the cost of entry into the Exhibition.

13 Colomb Bechar-   **14** Arc de Triomphe, Lam-
Oued   bèse

15 Admiralty and Peñon Ligh-   **16** Moslem
thouse, Algiers   Cemetery, Tlemçen

(Eng H. Cheffer (A and **14**), Das (**13**), J. Piel (B), G. Hourriez
(**15**), Feltesse (C and **16**) and A. Delzers (D). Recess)

1936–40. *T* **13**/**16** *and similar designs. P* 13.

107	A	1 c. ultramarine	..	5	5
108	13	2 c. purple	..	5	5
109	14	3 c. green	..	5	5
110	B	5 c. bright magenta ..		5	5
111	15	10 c. emerald-green	..	5	5
112	C	15 c. scarlet	..	5	5
113	16	20 c. green	..	5	5
114	D	25 c. purple	..	10	5
115	B	30 c. emerald-green ..		8	5

116	C	40 c. maroon	..	..	5	5
117	**16**	45 c. blue	..	..	12	10
118	**15**	50 c. scarlet	..	..	15	5
119	A	65 c. red-brown	..	..	45	40
120		65 c. rose-carmine (1937)	..		8	5
121		70 c. red-brown (1939)	..		5	5
122	**13**	75 c. slate	..	..	5	5
123	**14**	90 c. scarlet	..	..	15	15
124		90 c. scarlet* (1939)	..		5	5
125	D	1 f. brown	..	..	5	5
126	**15**	1 f. 25, bright violet	..	..	12	5
127		1 f. 25, rose-carmine (1939)	..		5	5
128	**13**	1 f. 50, turquoise-blue	..	..	20	5
129		1 f. 50, rose-carmine (1940)	..		8	5
130	B	1 f. 75, orange-red	..	..	5	5
131	**14**	2 f. maroon	..	..	5	5
132	A	2 f. 25, emerald-green	..		1·50	1·25
133	D	2 f. 25, turquoise-blue* (1939)	..		5	5
134	B	2 f. 50, ultramarine (1940)	..		5	5
135	**16**	3 f. rose-magenta	..	..	5	5
136	D	3 f. 50, turquoise-blue	..	..	25	25
137	**15**	5 f. slate	..	..	5	· 5
138	**13**	10 f. orange-red	..	..	5	5
139	C	20 f. turquoise-blue	..	..	15	15
107/139		*Set of 33*	..	..	4·00	2·40

Designs: *Horiz*—A, A halt in the Sahara; B, Ghardaia, Mzab; C, Marabouts, Touggourt; D, El Kebir Mosque, Algiers.
*Nos. 124 and 133 have figures of value in colour on white background.
For 1 f. 50, rose-carmine, as No. 129, but without "RF" in side panels, see No. 180.

17 Exhibition Pavilion   **18** Constantine in 1837

(T **17**/8 Des M. Racim. Eng J. Piel. Recess)

1937. *Paris International Exhibition.* P 13.

140	**17**	40 c. green	..	..	15	10
141		50 c. rose-carmine	..	..	5	5
142		1 f. 50, blue	..	..	20	10
143		1 f. 75, brownish black	..	..	25	20
140/143		*Set of 4*	..	..	60	40

1937. *Centenary of Capture of Constantine.* P 13.

144	**18**	65 c. carmine	..	..	12	5
145		1 f. brown	..	..	80	12
146		1 f. 75, greenish blue	..	..	5	5
147		2 f. 15, bright purple	..	..	5	5
144/147		*Set of 4*	..	..	90	25

19 Ruins of Roman Villa

(Eng J. Piel. Recess)

1938 (Oct). *Centenary of Philippeville.* P 13.

148	**19**	30 c. green	..	..	15	12
149		65 c. ultramarine	..	..	5	5
150		75 c. purple	..	..	15	12
151		3 f. carmine	..	..	60	60
152		5 f. brown	..	..	1·00	50
148/152		*Set of 5*	..	..	1·75	1·25

1918 - 11 Nov. - 1938
0.65 + 0.35

(20)

1938 (11 Nov). *20th Anniv of Armistice Day.* No. 132 surch with T **20**.

153		65 c. + 35 c. on 2 f. 25, emerald-grn (R.)		10	10
	a. Surch inverted ·	..	..	..	28·00	

0,25

(21)

1938. *No. 118 surch with T* **21**.

154	**15**	25 c. on 50 c. scarlet	..	..	5	5
		a. Surch inverted	..	..	7·00	5·00
		b. Surch double	..	..	7·00	5·00
		c. Pair, one without surch	..		15·00	

22 Caillié, Lavigerie and Duveyrier

(Des and eng J. Piel and M. Racim. Recess)

1939. *Sahara Pioneers' Monument Fund.* P 13.

155	**22**	30 c. + 20 c. emerald-green	..	..	15	15
156		90 c. + 60 c. carmine	..	..	15	15
157		2 f. 25 + 75 c. ultramarine	..	..	1·75	1·75
158		5 f. + 5 f. black	..	..	3·00	3·00
155/158		*Set of 4*	..	..	4·50	4·50

23 Vessel in Algiers Harbour   (24)

(Des L. Carré. Eng J. Piel. Recess)

1939. *New York World's Fair.* P 13.

159	**23**	20 c. emerald-green	..	..	15	15
160		40 c. bright purple	..	..	15	15
161		90 c. sepia	..	..	5	5
162		1 f. 25, rose-carmine	..	..	55	25
163		2 f. 25, bright blue	..	..	20	20
159/163		*Set of 5*	..	..	1·00	70

1939–40. *Surch as T* **24**.

164	**3**	1 f. on 90 c. scarlet (bars 5¾ mm)	..	5	5
		a. Surch inverted	..	..	4·00	
		b. Surch double	..	..	8·00	
		c. Pair, one without surch	..	17·00	
165		1 f. on 90 c. scarlet (bars 7 mm) (1940)	40	5
		a. Surch inverted	..	..	4·00	
		b. Pair, one without surch	..		

25 Algerian Soldiers   **26** Algiers   +60ᶜ

                                                      (27)

(Des L. Carré. Photo)

1940 (Jan). *Soldiers' Dependents' Relief Fund.* Design surch as in T **25**. P 12.

166	**25**	1 f. + 1 f. blue (R.)	..	..	12	12
		a. Surch double	..	..	20·00	
167		1 f. + 2 f. brown-lake	..	..	12	12
168		1 f. + 4 f. green (R.)	..	..	15	15
169		1 f. + 9 f. brown (R.)	..	..	20	20
166/169		*Set of 4*	..	..	55	55

(Des and die eng J. Piel and A. Bodiniet. Typo)

1941. P 14 × 13½.
170 **26** 30 c. ultramarine 5 5
171   70 c. blackish brown 5 5
172   1 f. carmine 5 5
170/172 *Set of 3* 8 8
For 30 c. ultramarine, as No. 170, but without "RF" in bottom left-hand corner, see No. 177.

1941–42. (*a*) *Surch as T* **24.**
173 **3** 50 on 65 c. bright blue 5 5
      a. Surch inverted .. .. 4·00
      b. Pair, one without surch .. 12·00

(*b*) No. 124 *surch with T* **27**
173*c* **14** 90 c. + 60 c. scarlet (1942) 5 5
      a. Surch double .. .. 12·00

28 Marshal
Pétain

+4ᶠ
(29)

SECOURS
NATIONAL
+4ᶠ
(30)

(Eng J. Piel. Recess)

1941. P 13.
174 **28** 1 f. blue 5 5

1941. *National Relief Fund. As No. 174 but colour changed, surch with T* **29.**
175 **28** 1 f. + 4 f. black (R.) 5 5

1942. *National Relief Fund. No. 174 surch with T* **30.**
176 **28** 1 f. + 4 f. blue (R.) 5 5

1942. *Various modified types.*
(*a*) *Without "RF" in bottom left-hand corner*
177 **26** 30 c. ultramarine 5 5
(*b*) *Without "REPUBLIQUE FRANÇAISE"*
178 **5** 40 c. greenish grey (*p* 12) 5 5
179   50 c. red (*p* 14 × 13½) 5 5
      a. Perf 12 .. .. .. 5 5
(*c*) *Without "RF" in side panels*
180 **13** 1 f. 50, rose-carmine 5 5

1942. *POSTAGE DUE. Without "R F".*
D181 **D 1** 30 c. carmine 5 5
D182   2 f. magenta 5 5

31 Arms of
Constantine

32 Arms of Oran

33 Arms of
Algiers

1942–45. (*a*) *Local printing with "Berliot" imprint. Photo.* P 12.
181 **31** 40 c. violet (1943) 5 5
182 **32** 60 c. carmine (1943) 5 5
183 **31** 1 f. 20, yellow-green (1943) .. 5 5
184 **33** 1 f. 50, carmine 5 5
185 **32** 2 f. blue 5 5
186 **31** 2 f. 40, carmine (1943) 5 5
187 **33** 3 f. blue 5 5
188 **31** 4 f. blue (1943) 5 5
189 **32** 5 f. yellow-green (1943) .. 5 5
181/189 *Set of 9* 25 25
(*b*) *Paris printing without imprint. Typo.* P 14 × 13½
190 **33** 10 c. brown-lilac (1945) .. 5 5
191 **32** 30 c. blue-green (1945) .. 5 5

192 **31** 40 c. brown-lilac (1945) 5 5
193 **32** 60 c. carmine (1945) 5 5
194 **31** 70 c. blue (1945) 5 5
195 **33** 80 c. green 5 5
196 **31** 1 f. 20, blue-green (1945) .. 5 5
197 **33** 1 f. 50, carmine 5 5
198 **32** 2 f. blue (1945) 5 5
199 **31** 2 f. 40, carmine (1945) 5 5
200 **33** 3 f. blue (1945) 5 5
201 **32** 4 f. 50, plum 5 5
190/201 *Set of 12* 35 35

34 Marshal
Pétain

35 Allegories of Victory

36 Allegories
of Victory

(Des Bouguenec. Eng C. Mazelin. Recess)

1943. P 14 × 13.
202 **34** 1 f. 50, orange-red 5 5

(Des Fernez and Bodiniet (T **36**). Die eng C. Hervé. Litho)

1943. P 12.
203 **35** 1 f. 50, carmine 5 5
204 **36** 1 f. 50, blue 5 5

(37)

38 Summer Palace, Algiers

1943. *Surch with T* **37.**
205 **32** 2 f. on 5 f. red-orange 5 5
      a. Surch double .. .. 20·00
      b. Surch omitted .. .. 40·00

(Die eng C. Hervé. Litho)

1943 (1 Dec.). P 12.
206 **38** 15 f. grey 20 20
207   20 f. yellow-green 8 8
208   50 f. brown-lake 12 10
209   100 f. blue 25 20
210   200 f. olive-brown 45 30
206/210 *Set of 5* .. .. .. 1·00 80

39 Mother and
Children

40 "Marianne"

41 Gallic Cock

(Des L. Fernez. Die eng C. Hervé. Litho)

1943 (1 Dec.). *War Prisoners' Relief Fund.* P 12.
211 **39** 50 c. + 4 f. 50, pink 10 10
212   1 f. 50 + 8 f. 50, emerald-green .. 10 10
213   3 f. + 12 f. blue 10 10
214   5 f. + 15 f. brown-purple .. 10 10
211/214 *Set of 4* 35 35

(Des L. Fernez. Die eng C. Hervé. Litho)

1944. *P* 12.

215 **40**	10 c. grey	5	5
216	30 c. lilac	5	5
217	50 c. scarlet	5	5
218	80 c. emerald-green	5	5
219	1 f. 20, rose-lilac	5	5
220	1 f. 50, blue	5	5
221	2 f. 40, rose-red	5	5
222	3 f. violet	5	5
223	4 f. 50, olive-black	5	5
215/223	*Set of 9*	25	25

(Des "H.R." Die eng C. Hervé. Litho)

1944–45. *P* 12.

224 **41**	40 c. carmine (1945)	5	5
225	1 f. green	5	5
226	2 f. red	5	5
227	2 f. sepia (1945)	5	5
228	4 f. ultramarine	5	5
229	10 f. greenish black	10	5
224/229	*Set of 6*	20	15

TAXE P. C. V.
DOUANE

20 Fr.   **0ᶠ·30**   **0.50**

   (D 6)   (42)   (D 7)

1944. *POSTAGE DUE. No.* 208 *surch with Type* D 6.

D229 **38**	20 f. on 50 f. brown-lake	5	5
	a. Surch double	7·00	

1944. *No.* 39 *surch with T* **42.**

230 **4**	30 c. on 15 c. chestnut* ..	5	5
	a. Surch inverted	1·75	1·40
	b. Surch double	3·00	

*No. 230 pre-cancelled only. See note after No. 70.

1944. *POSTAGE DUE. No.* 42 *surch with Type* D **7.**

D231 **4**	50 c. on 20 c. yellow-green (R.) ..	5	5
	a. Surch inverted	65	
	b. Surch double	1·50	

1945–47. *Various types of France optd.* "ALGÉRIE", *as T* **1.**

(a) Shield and Broken Chains

231 **217**	40 c. magenta	5	5
232	50 c. violet-blue (R.)	5	5

(b) Ceres

233 **218**	60 c. ultramarine (R.)	5	5
234	1 f. carmine-red	5	5
235	1 f. 50, bright purple (1947) ..	5	5

(c) Iris

236 **136**	80 c. yellow-green	5	5
237	1 f. greenish blue	5	5
238	1 f. 20, violet	5	5
239	2 f. chocolate	5	5
240	2 f. 40, carmine	5	5
241	3 f. orange	5	5

(d) Marianne

242 **219**	2 f. blue-green (R.) (1946) ..	5	5
243	3 f. carmine	5	5
244	4 f. 50, blue (R.) (1947) ..	12	5
245	5 f. green (1946)	5	5
246	10 f. blue	8	5

(e) Arms of Corsica and Lorraine (1947)

247 **239**	5 c. black and ultramarine (R.) ..	5	5
248 –	50 c. brown, yellow and red (B.) ..	5	5
231/248	*Set of 18*	70	55

1945–47. *POSTAGE DUE. As Nos.* D34/44. *(a) Litho. P* 12.

D249 **D 1**	1 f. 50, magenta	5	5
D250	2 f. greenish blue	5	5
D251	5 f. carmine	5	5

(b) Typo. P 14×13½

D252 **D 1**	5 f. green (1947)	5	5
D249/252	*Set of 4*	12	12

0ᶠ50

R F   **RF**   **2ᶠ**
(43)   (44)   (45)

46 Aeroplane over Algiers

1945 (2 July). *Airmen and Dependents Fund. As No.* 742 *of France but colour changed, optd* "ALGÉRIE" *as T* **1,** *in black and further optd with T* **43** *and surch, in red.*

249 **169**	1 f. 50 + 3 f. 50, grey-blue	5	5
	a. "ALGÉRIE" omitted	55·00	
	b. "R F" omitted	75·00	

1945 (Sept). *Postal Employees War Victims' Fund. No.* 949 *of France optd* "ALGÉRIE" *as T* **1.**

250 **223**	4 f. + 6 f. purple-brown	5	5

1945 (15 Oct). *Stamp Day. As No.* 995 *of France but colour changed, optd* "ALGÉRIE" *as T* **1.**

251 **228**	2 f. + 3 f. brown-purple (B.) ..	5	5
	a. Opt omitted	80·00	

1946 (Jan). *No.* 197 *surch with T* **44.**

252 **33**	50 c. on 1 f. 50, carmine ..	5	5
	a. Surch inverted	5·00	

1946 (May). *Iris type of France optd* "ALGÉRIE" *as T* **1** *and surch with T* **45.**

253 **136**	2 f. on 1 f. 50, red-brown ..	5	5
	a. "2F" omitted	40·00	

I.

II.

Type I: Cross-bars of "F" of "RF" without serifs; "P" of "POSTES" 3½ mm. from end of coloured panel.
Type II: "F" with prominent sloping serifs; "P" 4½ mm. from end of panel.

(Eng Feltesse. Recess)

1946 (20 June). *AIR. P* 13.

254 **46**	5 f. scarlet	5	5
255	10 f. blue	5	5
256	15 f. green	8	5
257	20 f. brown (I)	10·00	9·00
	a. Type II	5	5
258	25 f. violet	8	5
259	40 f. black	12	5
254/259	*Set of 6*	35	20

1946 (29 June). *Stamp Day. As No.* 975 *of France (De la Varane), but colour changed, optd* "ALGÉRIE" *as T* **1.**

260 **241**	3 f. + 2 f. red (B.)	12	12

POSTES ALGERIE

47 Children at a Spring

SOLIDARITE ALGERIENNE

48 Boy gazing Skywards

(Des O. Ferru, F. Fauck (4 f., 8 f.) and A. Boutet. Eng Feltesse, Barlangue, Mazelin and C. P. Dufresne. Recess)

1946 (2 Oct). *National Fellowship. T 47/8 and similar designs inscr "SOLIDARITE ALGERIENNE". P 13.*

261	3 f. + 17 f. blue-green	..		25	25
262	4 f. + 21 f. rose-red			25	25
263	8 f. + 27 f. bright purple			80	80
264	10 f. + 35 f. blue ..	..		25	25
261/264	Set of 4			1·40	1·40

Designs: *Vert*—8 f. Laurel-crowned head. *Horiz*—10 f. Soldier looking at Algerian coastline.

1947 (18 Jan). *AIR. No. 254 surch "—10%".*

265	46	"—10%" on 5 f. scarlet	..	5	5

1947 (15 Mar). *Stamp Day. As No. 1008 of France (Louvois) but colour changed, optd "ALGÉRIE" as T 1.*

266	253	4 f. 50 + 5 f. 50, blue (R.)	..	8	8

49 Arms of Constantine   **50** Arms of Algiers   **51** Arms of Oran

1947–49. *Typo. P 14 × 13½.*

267	49	10 c. green and scarlet	..	5	5
268	50	50 c. black and orange		5	5
269	51	1 f. ultramarine and yellow ..		5	5
270	49	1 f. 30, black and greenish blue		8	8
271	50	1 f. 50, violet and yellow		5	5
272	51	2 f. black and emerald		5	5
273	49	2 f. 50, black and scarlet		5	5
274	50	3 f. carmine and emerald		5	5
275	51	3 f. 50, green and purple		5	5
276	49	4 f. brown and emerald	..	5	5
277	50	4 f. 50, ultramarine and scarlet		5	5
278		5 f. black and greenish (3.11.48)		5	5
279	51	6 f. brown and scarlet		5	5
280		8 f. brown and ultramarine (3.11.48)		5	5
281	49	10 f. rose and sepia (3.11.48)..	..	10	5
282	50	15 f. black and red (3.49)		10	5
267/282		Set of 16		75	70

For similar designs see Nos. 364/8 and 381/3.

1947. *POSTAGE DUE. Nos. D985/6 of France (inscr "TIMBRE TAXE"), optd "ALGÉRIE" as T 1.*

D283	D 10	10 c. blackish brown	..	5	5
D284		30 c. bright purple	..	5	5

18 Juin 1940 +10 Fr. (52)

1947 (18 June). *AIR. Seventh Anniv of De Gaulle's Call to Arms. No. 255 surch with T 52.*

283	46	10 f. + 10 f. blue (R.) ..	..	12	12

ALGÉRIE +10 f (53)

D 8 (53)   (54)

(Des M. Racim. Eng H. Cortot. Recess)

1947–55. *POSTAGE DUE. P 14 × 13.*

D285	D 8	20 c. red ..		5	5
D286		60 c. ultramarine ..		10	8
D287		1 f. brown		5	5
D288		1 f. 50, grey-olive	..	12	12
D289		2 f. carmine		5	5
D290		3 f. violet		5	5
D291		5 f. ultramarine ..		5	5
D292		6 f. black..		5	5
D293		10 f. bright purple		5	5
D294		15 f. bronze-green (22.8.55)	..	15	12
D295		20 f. emerald-green		5	5
D296		30 f. orange-red (1955)	..	12	12
D297		50 f. blue-black (1951)		20	20
D298		100 f. blue (15.6.53)	..	80	60
D285/298		Set of 14	..	1·75	1·50

1947 (13 Nov). *Resistance Movement. As No. 1019 of France but colour changed, surch with T 53.*

284	261	5 f. + 10 f. slate-grey (R.)	..	10	10

1948 (6 Mar). *Stamp Day. As No. 1027 of France (Arago), but colour changed, optd with T 54.*

285	267	6 f. + 4 f. blue-green (G.)	..	15	15

+4 f

ALGÉRIE (55)

1948 (May). *General Leclerc Memorial. As No. 1037 of France but colour changed, surch with T 55.*

286	270	6 f. + 4 f. red (B.)	..	8	8

18 JUIN 1940 +10 Fr. (56)

57 Battleship *Richelieu*

1948 (18 June). *AIR. Eighth Anniv of De Gaulle's Call to Arms. No. 254 surch with T 56.*

287	46	5 f. + 10 f. scarlet (B.) ..	..	12	12

(Des Berliot. Eng Dufresne (10 f.). T 57

1949 (15 Jan). *Naval Welfare Fund. T 57 and similar type inscr "ŒUVRES SOCIALES DE LA MARINE". P 13.*

288	10 f. + 15 f. deep blue	..	1·00	1·00
289	18 f. + 22 f. scarlet	..	1·00	1·00

Design:—18 f. Aircraft-carrier *Arromanches*.

58 Storks over Minaret   (59)   **60** French Colonials

(Des and eng Gandon. Recess)

1949–53. *AIR. T 58 and horizontal type. P 13.*

290	59	50 f. green (7.3.49)	..	50	5
291	–	100 f. brown-purple (7.2.49)	..	35	5
292	59	200 f. vermilion (16.11.49)	..	1·00	50
293	–	500 f. ultramarine (12.10.53)	..	3·25	2·50
290/293		Set of 4		4·75	1·90

Designs:—100 f., 500 f. Aeroplane over valley dwellings.

1949 (26 Mar). *Stamp Day. As No. 1954 of France (Choiseul), but colour changed, optd with* T 59.
294 **278** 15 f. + 5 f. magenta (B.) 20 25

(Des and eng Decaris. Recess)

1949 (24 Oct). *75th Anniv of U.P.U.* P 13.
295 **60** 5 f. green 25 25
296 15 f. scarlet 35 25
297 25 f. blue 65 50

61 Statue of   62 Grapes   63 Foreign
Duke of Orleans   Legionary

(Des Sayous. Eng Barlangue. Recess)

1949 (10 Nov). *AIR. 25th Anniv of First Algerian Stamp.* P 13.
298 **61** 15 f. + 20 f. purple-brown 80 80

1950 (25 Feb). *As* T **62** *(fruits). Recess.* P 13.
299 20 f. purple, green and deep purple .. 25 5
300 25 f. brown, green and black .. 30 8
301 40 f. orange, yellow, green and brown .. 40 15
Designs:—25 f. Dates; 40 f. Oranges and lemons.

1950 (11 Mar). *Stamp Day. As No. 1091 of France (Postman) but colour changed, optd with* T 54.
302 **292** 12 f. + 3 f. blackish brown (G.) .. 20 20

(Des Marin. Eng Barlangue. Recess)

1950 (30 Apr). *Foreign Legion Welfare Fund.* P 13.
303 **63** 15 f. + 5 f. deep green.. .. .. 20 20

64 R. P. de Foucauld and   65 Colonel C. d'Ornano
Gen. Laperrine

(Des M. Racim. Eng H. Cortot (25 f.), Dufresne (40 f.). Recess)

1950 (21 Aug). *50th Anniv of the French in the Sahara (25 f.) and Unveiling of Monument to Abd-el-Kader (40 f.).* T **64** *and similar horiz design.*
304 25 f. + 5 f. black and blackish olive .. 75 75
305 40 f. + 10 f. purple-brown and red-brn .. 75 75
Design:—40 f. Emir Abd-el-Kader and Marshal Bugeaud.

(Des R. Jeanne. Eng Dufresne. Recess)

1951 (11 Jan). *Colonel C. d'Ornano Monument Fund.* P 13.
306 **65** 15 f. + 5 f. purple, red-brown & black 15 15

1951 (10 Mar). *Stamp Day. As No. 1107 of France (Sorting Van), but colour changed, optd "ALGÉRIE" as* T 1.
307 **300** 12 f. + 3 f. red-brown 20 20

66 Apollo of   67 Algerian War   68 Médaille
Cherchel   Memorial   Militaire

(Des and eng J. Piel. Recess)

1952. T **66** *and similar vert designs.* P 14 × 13.
308 **66** 10 f. blackish brown (10.1) .. 5 5
309 – 12 f. orange-brown (10.3) .. 5 5
310 – 15 f. deep blue (8.2) 5 5
311 – 18 f. carmine (10.3) 8 5
312 – 20 f. green (10.3) 8 5
313 **66** 30 f. deep blue (10.3) 15 5
308/313 *Set of 6* 40 25
Statues:—15 f., 20 f. Boy and eagle, 12 f., 18 f. Isis of Cherchel.

1952 (8 Mar). *Stamp Day. As No. 1140 of France (Mail Coach), but colour changed, optd with* T 59.
314 **319** 12 f. + 3 f. indigo (B.) 25 25

(Des and eng Decaris. Recess)

1952 (11 Apr). *African Army Commemoration.* P 13.
315 **67** 12 f. deep green 12 8

(Des R. Louis. Eng J. Piel. Recess)

1952 (5 July). *Centenary of Médaille Militaire.* P 13.
316 **68** 15 f. + 5 f. dp brown, lemon & emer .. 30 30

69 Fossil (*Berbericeras sekikensis*)   (70)

1952 (11 Aug). *Nineteenth International Geological Congress, Algiers. Recess.* P 13.
317 **69** 15 f. carmine-red 10 8
318 – 30 f. bright blue 15 10
Design: *Horiz*—30 f. Phonolite Dyke Hogger (inscr as in T **69**).

1952 (15 Sept). *Tenth Anniv of Battle of Bir-Hakeim. As No. 1146 of France but colour changed, surch with* T 70.
319 30 f. + 5 f. ultramarine 30 30

72 Bou-Nara   73 Legionnaire,
                     Arab and Camel

(Des H. Razous. Eng Cottet (8 f.), Barlangue (12 f.). Recess)

1952 (15 Nov). *Red Cross.* T **72** *and similar horiz design.* P 13.
320 8 f. + 2 f. red and deep blue 30 30
321 12 f. + 3 f. red 40 40
Design:—8 f. El-Oued and Map of Algeria.

(Des R. Thiriet. Eng Dufresne. Recess)

1952 (30 Nov). *50th Anniv of Sahara Corps.* P 13.
322 **73** 12 f. orange-brown 12 12

1953 (14 Mar). *Stamp Day. As No. 1161 of France (Count D'Argenson), but colour changed, optd "ALGÉRIE" as* T 1.
323 **334** 12 f. + 3 f. reddish violet 10 10

A 43

74 "Victory" of Cirta **75 E. Millon**

(Des and eng Mazelin. Recess)

1953 (18 Dec). *Army Welfare Fund. P* 13.
324 **74** 15 f. + 5 f. red-brown & blackish brn . .   15   15

(Des and eng R. Serres. Recess)

1954 (4 Jan). *Military Health Service. T* **75** *and similar portraits. P* 13.
325   25 f. black-brown and deep bluish green   25   5
326   40 f. brown-lake and chestnut   35   8
327   50 f. indigo and ultramarine   35   5
Portraits: *Vert*—40 f. Dr. F. Maillot. *Horiz*—50 f. Dr. A. Laveran.

1954 (20 Mar). *Stamp Day. As No.* 1202 *of France (Lavalette), but colour changed, optd "ALGÉRIE" as T* 1.
328 **346** 12 f. + 3 f. scarlet   10   10

76 French and Algerian Soldiers   **77 Foreign Legionary**   **78**

1954 (27 Mar). *Old Soldiers' Welfare Fund. Recess. P* 13.
329 **76** 15 f. + 5 f. blackish brown   8   8

(Des Marin. Eng Dufresne. Recess)

1954 (30 Apr). *Foreign Legion Welfare Fund. P* 13.
330 **77** 15 f. + 5 f. deep emerald   20   20

(Des B. Sarraillon. Eng Pheulpin. Recess)

1954 (8 May). *Third International Congress of Mediterranean Citrus Fruit Culture. P* 13.
331 **78** 15 f. light blue and indigo   12   12

1954 (6 June). *Tenth Anniv of Liberation. As No.* 1204 *of France but colour changed, optd "ALGÉRIE" as T* 1.
332 **348** 15 f. carmine   10   10

79 Darguinah Hydro-electric Station   **80 Courtyard of Bardo Museum**

(Des H. Razous. Eng Dufresne. Recess)

1954 (19 June). *Inauguration of River Agrioun Hydro-electric Installations. P* 13.
333 **79** 15 f. bright purple   10   8

Two types of 12 f.
I. "POSTES" and "ALGERIE" in brown-orange.
II. Redrawn and inscriptions in white.

(Des B. Sarraillon. Typo)

1954–57. *P* 14 × 13½.
334 **80** 10 f. bistre-brown and pale brown
        (10.10.55)   5   5
335   12 f. brown-orange & red-brown (I)
        (15.11.54)   5   5
336   12 f. brown-orange & red-brown (II)
        (22.5.56)   5   5
337   15 f. blue and pale blue (1.7.54)   . .   5   5
338   18 f. carmine-red and red (1.9.57) . .   10   5
339   20 f. green and pale green (20.2.57) . .   5   5
340   25 f. deep reddish lilac and deep
        mauve (10.10.55)   8   5
334/340 *Set of* 7   35   35

1954 (17 Aug). *150th Anniv of First Presentation of Legion of Honour. As No.* 1223 *of France but colour changed, optd "ALGÉRIE" as T* 1.
341 **356** 12 f. deep green (R.)   15   12

81 Red Cross Nurses   **82 St. Augustine**

(Des A. Spitz (12 f.), J. Piel (15 f.). Eng J. Piel. Recess)

1954 (30 Oct). *Red Cross Fund. T* **81** *and similar horiz design. P* 13.
342   12 f. + 3 f. indigo and red   30   30
343   15 f. + 5 f. deep reddish violet and red . .   30   30
Design:—15 f. J. H. Dunant and ruins of Djemila.

(Des and eng Decaris. Recess)

1954 (12 Nov). *1600th Birth Anniv of St. Augustine. P* 13.
344 **82** 15 f. chocolate   10   10

83 Earthquake Victims and Ruins   **84 Statue of Aesculapius and Algiers**

(Des M. Racim. Eng Mazelin (12 f., 15 f.), Pheulpin (18 f., 20 f.), R. Serres (25 f., 30 f.). Recess)

1954 (5 Dec). *Orleansville Earthquake Victims' Relief Fund. T* **83** *and similar designs inscr "SEISME D'ORLEANSVILLE". P* 13.
345 **83** 12 f. + 4 f. chocolate   40   40
346   15 f. + 5 f. deep bright blue   40   40
347   18 f. + 6 f. bright reddish purple   . .   40   40
348   20 f. + 7 f. deep violet   40   40
349   25 f. + 8 f. lake   40   40
350   30 f. + 10 f. turquoise-blue   40   40
345/350 *Set of* 6   . .   . .   . .   2·10   2·10
Designs: *Horiz*—18 f., 20 f. Red Cross workers and injured; 25 f., 30 f. Stretcher-bearers.

1955 (19 Mar). *Stamp Day. As No. 1245 of France (Balloon Post), but colour changed, optd "ALGÉRIE" as T* **1**.
351 **364** 12 f. + 3 f. deep bright blue 8   8

(Des R. Sarraillon. Eng Pheulpin. Recess)

1955 (3 Apr). *30th French Medical Congress. P* 13.
352 **84** 15 f. scarlet 5   5

91 Marshal Leclerc and Memorial   **92** Oran

(Des and eng Serres. Recess)

1956 (29 Nov). *Marshal Leclerc Commemoration. P* 13.
363 **91** 15 f. red-brown and sepia 8   8

1956–58. *Various coats-of-arms as T* **49/51**. *Typo. P* 14 × 13½.
364   1 f. green and scarlet (12.56) 5   5
365   3 f. ultramarine and emerald (8.3.58) .. 10   5
366   5 f. bright blue and yellow (29.6.57) .. 5   5
367   6 f. green and orange-red (9.12.57) .. 15   8
368   12 f. ultramarine and vermilion (1.3.58) 15   10
364/368   Set of 5 45   25
Designs:—1 f. Bône; 3 f. Mostaganem; 5 f. Tlemcen; 6 f. Algiers; 12 f. Orleansville.
For similar designs see Nos. 381/3

85 Ruins of Tipasa   86 Widows and Children

(Des B. Sarraillon. Eng R. Serres. Recess)

1955 (31 May). *Bimillenary of Tipasa. P* 13.
353 **85** 50 f. lake-brown 12   5

(Des and eng H. Cheffer. Recess)

1956 (16 Dec)–**58**. *P* 13.
369 **92** 30 f. deep purple 10   5
370   35 f. rose-carmine (19.5.58) .. 20   10

1955 (13 June). *50th Anniv of Rotary International. As No. 1235 of France but colour changed, optd "ALGÉRIE" as T* **1**.
354   30 f. blue (R.) 12   12
   a. Pair, one without opt

1957 (16 Mar). *Stamp Day. As No. 1322 of France (Felucca), but colour changed, optd with T* **54**.
371 **403** 12 f. + 3 f. deep purple 15   15

1955 (3 Oct)–**57**. *As Nos. 1238 and 1238b of France ("France" type), but inscr "ALGÉRIE".*
355 **362** 15 f. carmine-rose 5   5
356   20 f. ultramarine (2.12.57) 5   5

(Des H. Racim. Eng Mazelin. Recess)

1955 (5 Nov). *War Victims' Welfare Fund. P* 13.
357 **86** 15 f. + 5 f. indigo and light blue .. 12   12

93 Electric Train crossing Viaduct   94 Fennec

(Des B. Sarraillon. Eng Pheulpin. Recess)

1957 (25 Mar). *Electrification of Bône-Tebessa Railway Line. P* 13.
372 **93** 40 f. deep bluish green and emerald 12   5

(Des and eng Mazelin. Recess)

1957 (6 Apr). *Red Cross Fund. T* **94** *and similar horiz design. P* 13.
373   12 f. + 3 f. reddish brown and red .. 70   70
374   15 f. + 5 f. sepia and red (Storks) .. 70   70

87 "Grande Kabylie"   88

(Des F. M. de Buzon. Eng Gandon. Recess)

1955 (17 Dec). *P* 13.
358 **87** 100 f. indigo and blue 40   5

(Des A. Boutet. Eng G. Barlangue. Recess)

1956 (3 Mar). *Anti-Cancer Fund. P* 13.
359 **88** 15 f. + 5 f. deep brown 10   10

1956 (17 Mar). *Stamp Day. As No. 1279 of France (Francis of Taxis), but colour changed, optd "ALGÉRIE" as T* **1**.
360 **383** 12 f. + 3 f. red 10   10

18 JUIN 1940
+ 5ᶠ
(95)

1957 (18 June). *Seventeenth Anniv of Gen. de Gaulle's Call to Arms. As No. 363 but colours changed and surch as T* **95**.
375 **91** 15 f. + 5 f. red and carmine-red (B.) .. 20   15

89 Foreign Legion Retirement Home, Sidi Bel Abbès   90 Marshal Franchet d'Esperey

(Des Pierre. Eng Pheulpin. Recess)

1956 (29 Apr). *Foreign Legion Welfare Fund. P* 13.
361 **89** 15 f. + 5 f. deep bluish green 10   10

(Des and eng J. Ebstein. Recess)

1956 (25 May). *Birth Centenary of Marshal Franchet d'Esperey. P* 13.
362 **90** 15 f. indigo and blue 8   8

96 Beni Bahdel Barrage, Tlemcen   97 "Horseman Crossing Ford" (after Delacroix)

(Des and eng Pheulpin. Recess)

1957 (29 June). *AIR.* P 13.
376 **96** 200 f. deep red .. .. .. 1·50 40

(Des and eng J. Piel. Recess)

1957 (30 Nov). *Army Welfare Fund. Designs as T* **97** *inscr* "MUSEE D'ALGER". P 13.
377 15 f. + 5 f. brown-red .. .. .. 1·00 1·00
378 20 f. + 5 f. green 65 65
379 35 f. + 10 f. blue 65 65
Designs: *Horiz*—20 f. "Lakeside view" (after Fromentin). *Vert*—35 f. "Arab dancer" (after Chasseriau).

1958 (15 Mar). *Stamp Day. As No.* 1375 (*Rural Posts*) *of France, but colour changed, optd with* **T 54.**
380 **421** 15 f. + 5 f. chestnut (B.) 10 10

1958. *Various coats-of-arms as T* **49/51**, *but inscr* "REPUBLIQUE FRANCAISE" *instead of* "R.F." *at foot. Typo. P* 14 × 13½.
381 2 f. orange-red and bright blue (5.6.58) 15 12
382 6 f. green and orange-red (7.58) .. 1·90 1·40
383 10 f. maroon and emerald (26.5.58) .. 20 10
Designs:—2 f. Tizi-Ouzou; 6 f. Algiers; 10 f. Sétif.

99 *Strelitzia Reginae* 100

(Des Mme. Garcin. Eng R. Cami. Recess)

1958 (14 June). *Algerian Child Welfare Fund.* P 13.
384 **99** 20 f. + 5 f. orange, violet and dp grn .. 50 50

1958 (20 July). *Marshal de Lattre Foundation.* P 13.
385 **100** 20 f. + 5 f. rose-red, emer & ultram .. 25 25

Stamps of France were used in Algeria from 22 July 1958 until Algeria became independent.
On 1 November 1954, an Algerian rising against French rule began; intervention by President De Gaulle led eventually to a cease-fire on 18 March 1962. An exodus of French settlers was followed by a referendum in favour of independence, which was recognised on 3 July 1962.

II. INDEPENDENT STATE

Postmasters throughout Algeria were instructed to overprint their stocks of the five postage and postage due stamps of France listed below with "E A" and to obliterate the words "REPUBLIQUE FRANCAISE". Such overprints, usually done with a handstamp, were made in very many towns and more than 250 different varieties of overprints have been recorded. In a few places the words "Etat Algerien" were used in full; in others the instructions were carried out with a ball-point pen. These instructions were issued on 27 June and the stamps were valid till 31 October 1962.
Though of great interest to specialists, we confine our listing to the postage stamps issued in Algiers and the postage due stamps issued in Tizi-Ouzou.

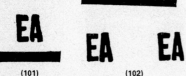

(101) (102)
(= "Etat Algérien")

1962 (4 July). *Various French stamps handstamped as T* **101** *or T* **102** (45 *c. to* 1 *f.*). *Issued in Algiers.*
386 **344** 10 c. emerald (Harvester) 15 12
387 **463** 25 c. grey and claret (Marianne) .. 12 8
388 – 45 c. reddish violet, purple and sepia
(1463) (Kerrata) .. .. 2·75 2·25
389 – 50 c. maroon & deep bronze-green
(1464) (Mosque) .. .. 2·75 2·25
390 – 1 f. brown, blue and blackish green
(1549) (Medea).. .. .. 85 60
386/390 *Set of* 5 .. .. 6·00 4·75
On No. 386 the obliterating bars occur at the top and left side. On Nos. 388/9 the handstamp is vertical reading up.

1962. *POSTAGE DUE. Nos. D1474/8 of France handstamped as T* **101**, *but with bar at top. Issued at Tizi-Ouzou.*
D391 **D 11** 5 c. cerise 40 40
D392 10 c. orange-red 40 40
D393 20 c. olive-brown 35 35
D394 50 c. deep slate-green 70 40
D395 1 f. green .. .. .. 1·10 1·10
D391/395 *Set of* 5 .. .. .. 2·50 2·40

(103) (D 9)

1962. *The same stamps of France but optd typographically as T* **103.**
391 **344** 10 c. emerald (18.8) 8 5
392 **463** 25 c. grey and claret (16.8) .. 5 5
393 – 45 c. reddish violet, pur & sep (8.8) .. 80 60
394 – 50 c. mar & dp bronze-grn (8.8) .. 90 60
395 – 1 f. brn, bl & blackish grn (20.8) .. 70 45
391/395 *Set of* 5 .. .. .. 2·25 1·60

1962. *POSTAGE DUE. Nos. D1474/8 of France optd typographically with Type* D **9.**
D396 **D 11** 5 c. cerise .. .. .. 1·50 1·50
D397 10 c. orange-red .. .. .. 1·25 1·25
D398 20 c. olive-brown 80 80
D399 50 c. deep slate-green .. .. 2·25 2·25
D400 1 f. green .. .. .. 2·75 2·75
D396/400 *Set of* 5 .. .. .. 8·00 8·00

(Litho Hussein Dey, Algiers)

1962 (1 Nov). *War Orphans' Fund. Vert design showing map of Africa with Algeria.* P 11½.
395a 1 f. + 9 f. green, black and red .. .. 22·00

1962 (1 Nov). *As pictorial types of France, but colours changed and inscr* "REPUBLIQUE ALGERIENNE."
396 5 c. deep blue-grn, emer & brn-pur .. 5 5
397 10 c. blue and blackish sepia .. 5 5
398 25 c. vermilion and deep slate .. 15 5
399 50 c. blue, buff and brown-black .. 35 12
400 1 f. brown-black and green 45 30
396/400 *Set of* 5 .. .. .. 95 50
Designs: *Vert*—5 c. Kerrata Gorges; 25 c. Tlemcen Mosque; 95 c. Oil derrick and pipeline at Hassi-Massaoud, Sahara. *Horiz*—10 c. Foum el Gherza Dam; 1 f. Medea.

104 Flag, Rifle and Olive   105 Campaign Emblem and
Branch   Globe

Algeria   1964

(Litho Govt Ptg Wks, Belgrade)

1963 (6 Jan). *"Return of Peace". T* **104** *and similar horiz design. Flag in green and red, inscription and background colours given. P* 12½.

401	104	5 c. bistre	..	..	..	5	5
402		10 c. blue	..	..	..	5	5
403		25 c. red	..	..	..	35	5
404		95 c. violet	..	..	..	25	20
405	–	1 f. green	..	..	..	20	8
406	–	2 f. brown	..	..	..	45	15
407	–	5 f. purple	..	..	..	90	35
408	–	10 f. black	..	..	..	2·40	1·90
401/408		*Set of* 8	..	..	..	4·25	2·50

Design:—1 f. to 10 f. As T **104** but with dove and broken chain added to design.

(Des Ferrer. Recess Govt Ptg Wks, Paris)

1963 (21 Mar). *Freedom from Hunger. P* 13.
409 **105** 25 c. yellow, blue-green and crimson   10   5

106 Clasped Hands   D **10** Scales of Justice   **107** Map and Emblems

(Des Bouzid and Ferrer. Recess Govt Ptg Wks, Paris)

1963 (27 May). *National Solidarity Fund. P* 13.
410 **106** 50 c. +20 c. red, green and black   ..   15   15

(Typo Govt Ptg Wks, Paris)

1963 (25 June). *POSTAGE DUE. P* 14×13½.

D411	D **10**	5 c. carmine and olive	..	5	5
D412		10 c. olive-brown and carmine	..	5	5
D413		20 c. blue and black	..	5	5
D414		50 c. yellow-brown and green	..	8	5
D415		1 f. light reddish violet & orange	15	8
D411/415		*Set of* 5	..	..	35	25

(Des Ali Khodja. Eng Combet. Recess Govt Ptg Wks, Paris)

1963 (5 July). *First Anniv of Independence. P* 13.
411 **107** 25 c. red, sepia, green and blue   ..   12   8

108 "Arab Physicians" (13th-century MS)   **109** Branch of Orange-tree

(Des Ali Khodja. Eng Combet. Recess Govt Ptg Wks, Paris)

1963 (29 July). *2nd Arab Physicians Union Congress. P* 13.
412 **108** 25 c. red-brown, green and bistre   ..   20   8

(Recess Govt Ptg Wks, Paris)

1963. *P* 14×13.

413	109	8 c. orange and bronze-green*	..	5	5
414		20 c. red-orange and slate-green*	..	5	5
415		40 c. orange and turquoise-green*	..	8	5
416		55 c. red-orange & dp yellow-grn*	..	10	8
413/416		*Set of* 4	..	..	..	25	20

*These stamps were only issued precancelled, the unused prices being for stamps with full gum.

110 "Constitution"   **111** "Freedom Fighters"

(Des Ali Khodja. Eng Fenneteaux. Recess Govt Ptg Wks, Paris)

1963 (13 Oct). *Promulgation of Constitution. P* 13.
417 **110** 25 c. red, emerald and deep sepia   ..   8   8

(Recess Govt Ptg Wks, Paris)

1963 (2 Nov). *Ninth Anniv of Revolution. P* 13.
418 **111** 25 c. carmine-red, yellow-grn & choc   12   8

112 Centenary Emblem   **113** Globe and Scales of Justice

(Des Ali Khodja. Photo Courvoisier)

1963 (8 Dec). *Red Cross Centenary. P* 11½.
419 **112** 25 c. violet-blue, crimson and yellow   12   8

(Photo Courvoisier)

1963 (16 Dec). *15th Anniv of Declaration of Human Rights. P* 11½.
420 **113** 25 c. black and light blue   12   5

New Currency

114 Labourers   **115** Map of Africa and Flags

(Recess Govt Ptg Wks, Paris)

1964 (1 May). *Labour Day. P* 13.
421 **114** 50 c. light blue, orge, maroon & red   12   8

(Des M. Choukri. Recess Govt Ptg Wks, Paris)

1964 (25 May). *Africa Day, and First Anniv of African Unity Charter. P* 13.
422 **115** 45 c. red, orange and blue   12   8

116 Tractors

117 Rameses II in War Chariot, Abu Simbel

(Typo Govt Ptg Wks, Paris)

1964–65. *T* **116** *and similar vert designs. P* 14×13½.

423	5 c. purple (16.10.64)	..	..	5	5
424	10 c. brown (21.9.64)	..	..	5	5
425	12 c. emerald (20.6.65)	..	..	5	5
426	15 c. deep ultramarine (27.2.65)		..	5	5
427	20 c. yellow (16.10.64)	..	..	5	5
428	25 c. vermilion (1.6.64)	..	..	5	5
429	30 c. reddish violet (18.4.65)	..	..	5	5
430	45 c. lake (1.1.65)	..	..	8	5
431	50 c. ultramarine (1.1.65)	..	..	8	5
432	65 c. orange (1.1.65)	..	..	12	5
433	85 c. green (1.1.65)	..	..	15	5
434	95 c. carmine (1.1.65)	..	..	15	5
423/434	*Set of* 12	..	..	80	55

Designs:—5 c., 25 c., 85 c. *T* 116; 10 c., 30 c., 65 c. Apprentices; 12 c., 15 c., 45 c. Research scientist; 20 c., 50 c., 95 c. Draughtsman and bricklayer.

(Des and eng P. Gandon (20 c.), R. Cottet (30 c.). Recess Govt Ptg Wks, Paris)

1964 (28 June). *Nubian Monuments Preservation. T* **117** *and similar horiz design. P* 13.

435	20 c. maroon, red and blue	..	..	8	5
436	30 c. ochre, turquoise-blue and red	..	12	8

Design:—30 c. Heads of Rameses II.

118 Hertzian-wave Radio Transmitting Pylon

119 Fair Emblems

(Des Ali Khodja. Recess Govt Ptg Wks, Paris)

1964 (30 Aug). *Inauguration of Algiers-Annaba Radio-Telephone Service. P* 13.

437	**118** 85 c. black, blue and chestnut	..	20	12

(Des A. Benyahia. Typo Govt Ptg Wks, Paris)

1964 (26 Sept). *Algiers Fair. P* 13½×14.

438	**119** 25 c. blue, yellow and red	..	..	8	5

120 Gas Plant

121 Planting Trees

122 Children

(Des M. Choukri. Typo Govt Ptg Wks, Paris)

1964 (27 Sept). *Inauguration of Natural Gas Plant, Arzew. P* 13½×14.

439	**120** 30 c. blue, yellow and bluish violet	..	10	8

(Des M. Choukri. Typo Govt Ptg Wks, Paris)

1964 (30 Nov). *Reafforestation Campaign. P* 13½×14.

440	**121** 25 c. deep bronze-green, red & yell	5	5

(Typo Govt Ptg Wks, Paris)

1964 (13 Dec). *Children's Charter. P* 13½×14.

441	**122** 15 c. ultramarine, yellow-grn & pink	5	5

123 Méhariste Saddle

124 Books Aflame

(Des S. Makous. Typo Govt Ptg Wks, Paris)

1965 (29 May). *Saharan Handicrafts. P* 13½×14.

442	**123** 20 c. red, green, brown and black	..	5	5

(Des M. Choukri. Recess Govt Ptg Wks, Paris)

1965 (7 June). *Burning of Algiers Library. P* 13.

443	**124** 20 c.+5 c. red, black & yellow-grn	..	5	5

125 I.C.Y. Emblem

126 I.T.U. Emblem and Symbols

(Des Ali Khodja. Recess Govt Ptg Wks, Paris)

1965 (29 Aug). *International Co-operation Year. P* 13.

444	**125** 30 c. black, turquoise-green & crim	8	5
445	60 c. black, turquoise-grn & new bl	..	10	8

(Des Ali Khodja. Recess Govt Ptg Wks, Paris)

1965 (19 Sept). *I.T.U. Centenary. P* 13.

446	**126** 60 c. reddish violet, ochre & emerald	10	8
447	95 c. chocolate, ochre and lake	..	12	8

127 Musicians playing Rebbah and Lute

128 Cattle

(Des M. Racim. Photo Courvoisier)

1965 (25 Dec). *Mohamed Racim's Miniatures* (1*st* Series). *T* **127** *and similar vert designs. Multicoloured. P* 11½.

448	30 c. Type **127**	..	..	15	8
449	60 c. Musicians Derbouka and Tarr	..	20	12
450	5 d. Algerian princess	..	..	1·10	70

See also Nos. 471/3.

(Des G. Le Poitevin. Photo Govt Ptg Wks, Paris)

1966 (29 Jan). *Rock-paintings of Tassili-N-Ajjer* (1*st Series*).
T **128** *and similar designs.* P 11½.

451	1 d. lake-brown, ochre & purple-brn	..	20	10
452	1 d. deep brown, yellow-ochre, yellow-orange, black and pale grey	..	20	10
453	2 d. red-brown, buff and chocolate	..	40	10
454	3 d. lake-brown, yellow-orange, black and pale cream	..	60	40
451/454	Set of 4	..	1·25	60

Designs: *Horiz*—No. 451, T **128**; 453, Ostriches. *Vert*—452,
Peuhl shepherd; 454, Peuhl girls.
See also Nos. 474/7.

129 Pottery   130 Meteorological Instruments

(Des Ali Khodja. Recess Govt Ptg Wks, Paris)

1966 (26 Feb). *Grand Kabylie Handicrafts.* T **129** *and similar designs.* P 13.

455	40 c. lake-brown, blackish brown and greenish blue	..	8	5
456	50 c. yellow-orange, olive-green and red	10	5
457	70 c. black, red and ultramarine	..	15	8

Designs: *Horiz*—50 c. Weaving. *Vert*—70 c. Jewellery.

(Des Ali Khodja. Recess Govt Ptg Wks, Paris)

1966 (23 Mar). *World Meteorological Day.* P 13.

458	**130** 1 d. brown-purple, emerald and blue	20	10

131 Open Book, Cogwheel and Ear of Corn   132 W.H.O. Building

(Des M. Kahlat (30 c.), M. Boutebba (60 c.). Typo)

1966 (30 Apr). *Literacy Campaign.* T **131** *and similar vert design embodying same features.* P 13 × 14.

459	30 c. black and ochre-yellow	..	8	5
460	60 c. red, black and light grey	..	10	8

(Des B. Azzouz. Recess Govt Ptg Wks, Paris)

1966 (28 May). *Inauguration of W.H.O. Headquarters, Geneva.* P 13 × 12½.

461	**132** 30 c. greenish blue, myrtle-green and brown-red	..	8	5
462	60 c. dp slate-bl, bl & brn-red	..	10	10

133 Mohammedan Scout Emblem and Banner   134 Soldiers and Battle Casualty

(Des M. Bouzid. Photo Delrieu)

1966 (23 July). *30th Anniv of Algerian Mohammedan Scouts, and 7th Arab Scouts Jamboree, Jedaid (Tripoli).* T **133** *and similar vert design. Multicoloured.* P 12 × 12½.

463	30 c. Type **133**	..	8	5
464	1 d. Jamboree emblem	..	20	8

(Des M. Racim. Photo Courvoisier)

1966 (20 Aug). *Freedom-Fighters' Day.* P 11½.

465	**134** 30 c. + 10 c. multicoloured	..	12	12
466	95 c. + 10 c. multicoloured	..	25	25

135 Massacre Victims   136 Emir Abd-el-Kader

(Des M. Choukri. Recess and typo Central Bank of Algeria)

1966 (24 Sept). *Deir Yasin Massacre* (1948). P 10½.

467	**135** 30 c. black and red	..	8	5

(Des M. Racim. Photo Courvoisier)

1966 (1 Nov). *Return of Emir Abd-el-Kader's Remains.* P 11½.

468	**136** 30 c. multicoloured	..	8	8
469	95 c. multicoloured	..	15	8

See also Nos. 495/502.

137 U.N.E.S.C.O. Emblems   138 Bardo Museum

(Des Ali Khodja. Typo)

1966 (19 Nov). *20th Anniv of U.N.E.S.C.O.* P 10½.

470	**137** 1 d. multicoloured	..	25	8

(Des M. Racim. Photo Courvoisier)

1966 (17 Dec). *Mohamed Racim's Miniatures* (2*nd Series*). *Designs as* T **127**. *Multicoloured.* P 11½.

471	1 d. Horseman	..	25	10
472	1 d. 50, Algerian bride	..	40	15
473	2 d. Barbarossa	..	60	20

(Des G. le Poitevin. Photo)

1967 (28 Jan). *Rock-paintings of Tassili-N-Ajjer (2nd Series). Designs as T 128. P 11½.*
474 1 d. dull violet, buff and purple-brown . .   25   8
475 2 d. chestnut, buff and purple-brown . .   45   15
476 2 d. chestnut, purple-brown & yell-buff   45   15
477 3 d. chestnut, yellow-buff and black   . .   70   25
474/477 *Set of 4* . .   . .   1·60   55
Designs: *Horiz*—No. 474, Cow; 475, Antelope; 476, Archers. *Vert*—477, Warrior.

(Des Ali Khodja (35 c., 95 c.), M. Racim (1 d. 30). Photo Courvoisier)

1967 (25 Feb). *"Musulman Art". T 138 and similar multicoloured designs. P 13.*
478   35 c. Type 138   8   5
479   95 c. La Kalaa minaret (*vert*)   . .   20   8
480   1 d. 30, Sedrata ruins   25   10

ALGERIE GHARDAIA · POSTE AERIENNE
139 Aircraft over Ghardaia

(Des and eng J. Combet. Recess Govt Ptg Wks, Paris)

1967 (25 Mar)—**68**. *AIR. T 139 and similar horiz designs. P 13.*
481   1 d. orange-brown, emerald and purple   20   10
482   2 d. orange-brown, emerald & new blue   40   20
483   5 d. orange-brown, emerald and new
          blue (20.1.68)   80   50
Designs:—2 d. Aircraft over El Oued (Souf); 5 d. Aircraft over Tipasa.

140 View of Moretti

(Des G. le Poitevin (70 c.). Litho De La Rue)

1967 (29 Apr). *International Tourist Year. T 140 and similar design. Multicoloured. P 14.*
484   40 c. Type 140   10   5
485   70 c. Cameleer, Tassili (*vert*)   . .   20   5

141 Boy and Girl, and Red   **142** Ostrich
          Crescent

(Litho De La Rue)

1967 (27 May). *Algerian Red Cross Organisation. P 14.*
486 **141** 30 c.+10 c. yellow-brown, red and
          bright emerald   10   5

(Des and photo Courvoisier)

1967 (24 June). *Sahara Fauna. T 142 and similar multicoloured designs. P 11½.*
487   5 c. Lizard (*horiz*)   5   5
488   20 c. Type 142   5   5
489   40 c. Gazelle   10   5
490   70 c. Fennecs (*horiz*)   20   8
487/490 *Set of 4*   35   20

143 Dancers with Tam-   **144** "Athletics"
          bourines

(Des Ali Khodja. Recess and typo Central Bank of Algeria)

1967 (4 July). *National Youth Festival. P 10½.*
491 **143** 50 c. black, yellow and chalky blue . .   10   5

(Des Ali Khodja. Typo)

1967 (2 Sept). *Mediterranean Games, Tunis. P 10½.*
492 **144** 30 c. black,   greenish   blue   and
          orange-red   5   5

145 Skiing   **146** Scouts supporting Jam-
                 boree Emblem

(Des B. Yelles (30 c.), P. Lambert (95 c.). Recess Govt Ptg Wks, Paris)

1967 (21 Oct). *Winter Olympic Games, Grenoble (1968). T 145 and similar design. P 13 (30 c.) or 13×12½ (95 c.).*
493   30 c. blue, bluish green and ultramarine   8   5
494   95 c. blue-green, reddish vio and chest   20   12
Design: *Horiz* (36×26 *mm*)—95 c. Olympic rings and competitors.

(Des M. Racim)

1967 (11 Nov)—**71**.

(a) Photo Courvoisier. P 11½
495 **136** 10 c. green   5   5
496   50 c. claret   8   5
497   70 c. deep blue   10   10

(b) As T 136, but redrawn with smaller, more open figures of value and different inscr at bottom right. Litho Central Bank of Algeria. P 14
498   5 c. bistre (4.7.68)   5   5
499   10 c. bronze-green (23.8.69)   5   5
500   25 c. yellow-orange (27.2.71)   . .   5   5
501   30 c. black (4.7.68)   5   5
502   30 c. light violet (9.68)   5   5
495/502 *Set of 8*   40   35

(Des P. Lambert. Eng J. Combet. Recess Govt Ptg Wks, Paris)

1967 (23 Dec). *World Scout Jamboree, Idaho. P 13.*
503 **146** 1 d. multicoloured   20   12

0,30
≡≡≡

(147)

1967 (28 Dec). *No. 428 surch with T 147.*
504 **116** 30 c. on 25 c. vermilion   5   5

≡
0.60

148 Kouitra (D 11) **149** Nememcha Carpet

(Des M. Temam. Photo Govt Ptg Wks, Paris)

1968 (17 Feb). *Musical Instruments. T* **148** *and similar vert designs. Multicoloured. P* 12½ × 13.
505	30 c. Type **148**	..	5	5
506	40 c. Lute	.. ..	8	5
507	1 d. 30, Rebbah	.. ..	20	8

1968 (28 Mar). *POSTAGE DUE. No.* D415 *surch with Type* **D 11**.
D508	**D 10** 60 c. on 1 f. lt reddish vio & orge	10	8

(Des B. Yelles. Photo Courvoisier)

1968 (13 Apr). *Algerian Carpets. T* **149** *and similar vert designs showing carpets. Multicoloured. P* 11½.
509	30 c. Type **149**	..	5	5
510	70 c. Guergour	.. ..	15	8
511	95 c. Djebel-Amour	.. ..	20	10
512	1 d. 30, Kalaa	.. ..	25	12
509/512	*Set of* 4	.. ..	60	30

150 Human Rights Emblem and Globe **151** W.H.O. Emblem

(Des Ali Khodja. Typo Central Bank of Algeria)

1968 (18 May). *Human Rights Year. P* 10½.
513	**150** 40 c. red, yellow and new blue	..	8	5

(Des B. Fares. Typo Central Bank of Algeria)

1968 (18 May). *20th Anniv of World Health Organisation. P* 10½.
514	**151** 70 c. yellow, black & light grey-blue	12	8

152 Emigrant **153** Scouts holding Jamboree Emblem **154** Torch and Athletes

(Des B. Yelles. Recess)

1968 (15 June). *Emigration of Algerians to Europe. P* 13.
515	**152** 30 c. brown, slate and bright blue	.. 5	5

(Des B. Yelles. Photo)

1968 (4 July). *Eighth Algerian Scout Jamboree. P* 13.
516	**153** 30 c. multicoloured	.. ..	5	5

(Des M. Temam (30 c., 50 c.), P. Lambert (1 d.). Photo Govt Ptg Wks, Paris)

1968 (4 July). *Olympic Games, Mexico. T* **154** *and similar multicoloured designs. P* 13 × 12½ (1 *d.) or* 12½ × 13 (*others*).
517	30 c. Type **154**	.. ..	8	5
518	50 c. Football	.. ..	10	5
519	1 d. Allegory of Games (*horiz*)	..	20	10

155 Moufflons **156** "Neptune's Chariot", Timgad

(Des and photo Courvoisier)

1968 (19 Oct). *Protected Animals. T* **155** *and similar vert design. Multicoloured. P* 11½.
520	40 c. Type **155**	.. ..	8	5
521	1 d. Red deer	.. ..	15	10

(Des M. Temam. Photo Govt Ptg Wks, Paris)

1968 (23 Nov). *Roman Mosaics. T* **156** *and similar multicoloured design. P* 12½ × 13 (40 *c.) or* 13 × 12½ (95 *c.*).
522	40 c. "Hunting Scene" (Djemila) (*vert*)	..	8	5
523	95 c. Type **156**	.. ..	20	10

157 Miner **158** Opuntia

(Des Courvoisier (No. 524), Sonatrach Bureau of Studies (others). Photo Courvoisier)

1968 (14 Dec). *"Industry, Energy and Mines". T* **157** *and other vert designs. P* 11½.
524	**157** 30 c. multicoloured	..	5	5
525	– 30 c. silver and orange-red	..	5	5
526	– 95 c. orange-red, black and silver	..	15	10

Designs:—30 c., Coiled spring ("Industry"); 95 c. Symbol of radiation ("Energy").

(Photo Courvoisier)

1969 (18 Jan). *Flowers. T* **158** *and similar vert designs. Multicoloured. P* 11½.
527	25 c. Type **158**	..	5	5
528	40 c. Dianthus	.. ..	8	5
529	70 c. Rose	.. ..	15	8
530	95 c. Strelitzia	.. ..	20	10
527/530	*Set of* 4	.. ..	45	25

159 Djorf Torba Dam, Oued Guir. **160** Desert Mail-coach of 1870

(Photo Courvoisier)

1969 (22 Jan). *Saharan Public Works. T* **159** *and similar horiz design. Multicoloured. P* 11½.
531	30 c. Type **159**	.. ..	5	5
532	1 d. 50, Route Nationale No. 51	..	25	20

(Photo Courvoisier)

1969 (22 Mar). *Stamp Day.* P 11½.
533 **160** 1 d. deep sep, yell-brn & lt bl .. 20 10

161 The Capitol, Tim-
gad

162 I.L.O. Emblem

(Des M. Temam. Photo Govt Ptg Wks, Paris)

1969 (5 Apr). *Roman Ruins in Algeria. T* **161** *and similar
multicoloured design.* P 12½×13 (30 c.) or 13×12½ (1 d.).
534 30 c. Type **161** 8 5
535 1 d. Septimien Temple, Djemila (*horiz*) 20 8

(Des and photo Courvoisier)

1969 (24 May). *50th Anniversary of International Labour
Organization.* P 11½.
536 **162** 95 c. carmine, yellow and black .. 20 10

0,20

(163)

164 Carved Bookcase

165 "Africa" Head

1969 (2 June). *No. 425 surch with T* **163**.
537 20 c. on 12 c. emerald 5 5
No. 537 was intended for use in automatic vending
machines.

(Des M. Temam. Photo Courvoisier)

1969 (28 June). *Handicrafts. T* **164** *and similar vert designs.
Multicoloured.* P 12×12½.
538 30 c. Type **164** 5 5
539 60 c. Copper tray 10 10
540 1 d. Arab saddle 15 15

(Des M. Issiakhem. Photo Delrieu)

1969 (19 July). *First Pan-African Cultural Festival, Algiers.*
P 12½.
541 **165** 30 c. multicoloured 5 5

166 Astronauts on
Moon

167 Bank Emblem

(Des and photo "Kultura" State Ptg Office, Budapest)

1969 (23 Aug). *First Man on the Moon.* P 12×11.
542 **166** 50 c. multicoloured 8 10

(Des B. Yelles. Typo Central Bank of Algeria)

1969 (23 Aug). *5th Anniversary of African Development
Bank.* P 10½.
543 **167** 30 c. black, yellow and light blue .. 5 5

168 Flood Victims

169 "Algerian Women" (Dinet)

(Des B. Yelles (30 c.), M. Temam (95 c.). Typo (30 c.), Litho
(45 c.) Central Bank of Algeria)

1969 (15 Nov). *Aid for 1969 Flood Victims. T* **168** *and similar
vert design.* P 10½.
544 30 c. + 10 c. black, flesh and dull blue .. 10 8
545 95 c. + 25 c. yellow-brown, violet-blue
and reddish purple 25 20
Design:—95 c. "Helping hand for flood victims".

(Photo Harrison)

1969 (29 Nov). *Paintings by E. Dinet. T* **169** *and similar horiz
design. Multicoloured.* P 14.
546 1 d. Type **169** 20 10
547 1 d. 50, "The Look-outs" 30 15

170 "Mother and Child"

171 "Agriculture"

(Des Baya. Photo Courvoisier)

1969 (27 Dec). *"Protection of Mother and Child".* P 11½.
548 **170** 30 c. multicoloured 5 5

(Des B. Yelles (50 c.). Litho De La Rue (30 c.), Photo Delrieu
(others))

1970 (31 Jan). *Four Year Plan. T* **171** *and similar horiz
designs.* P 14 (30 c.) or 12½×12 (*others*).
549 25 c. multicoloured 5 5
550 30 c. multicoloured 5 5
551 50 c. black and bright purple 8 8
Designs: *As T* **171**—50 c. "Industry". *Larger* (49×23
mm)—30 c. "Industry and Transport".

172 Postal Deliveries by
Donkey and Mail Van

173 Royal Prawn

(Des and photo Courvoisier)

1970 (28 Feb). *Stamp Day.* P 11½.
552 **172** 30 c. multicoloured 5 5

(Photo Courvoisier)

1970 (28 Mar). *Marine Life.* T **173** *and similar vert designs. Multicoloured.* P 11½.

553	30 c. Type **173** ..	..	..	..	5	5
554	40 c. Giant Pen ..	..	..	..	8	5
555	75 c. Neptune's Basket ..	..	..	..	15	8
556	1 d. Red coral ..	..	..	..	20	10
553/556	*Set of 4* ..	..	..	..	45	25

174 Oranges

175 Olives and Bottle of Olive-oil

(Des M. Temam (30, 70 c.). Photo Courvoisier)

1970 (25 Apr). *"Expo 70" World Fair, Osaka, Japan.* T **174** *and similar horiz designs. Multicoloured.* P 12½×12.

557	30 c. Type **174** ..	..	..	5	5
558	60 c. Algerian Pavilion ..	..	..	10	8
559	70 c. Bunches of grapes..	..	..	12	8

(Des M. Temam. Photo Courvoisier)

1970 (16 May). *World Olive-oil Year.* P 12½×12.
560 **175** 1 d. multicoloured 20 10

176 New U.P.U. Headquarters

178 Arab League Flag, Arms and Map

177 Crossed Muskets

(Des B. Yelles. Photo)

1970 (30 May). *Inaug of New U.P.U. Headquarters Building, Berne.* P 13.
561 **176** 75 c. multicoloured 12 8

(Des M. Temam. Photo)

1970 (27 June). *Algerian 18th-Century Weapons.* T **177** *and similar multicoloured designs.* P 12½.

562	40 c. Type **177** ..	..	..	8	5
563	75 c. Sabre (*vert*) ..	..	..	12	8
564	1 d. Pistol ..	..	..	15	10

(Des B. Yelles. Recess and typo Central Bank of Algeria)

1970 (25 July). *25th Anniversary of Arab League.* P 10½.
565 **178** 30 c. multicoloured 5 5

179 Lenin

180 Exhibition Palace

1970 (29 Aug). *Birth Centenary of Lenin. Photo.* P 11½.
566 **179** 30 c. bistre and yellow-ochre .. 5 5

(Des M. Adane. Recess De La Rue)

1970 (11 Sept). *7th International Fair, Algiers.* P 13½.
567 **180** 60 c. yellow-green 10 5

181 I.E.Y. and Education Emblems

182 Great Mosque, Tlemcen

(Des M. Racim (3 d.). Photo De La Rue)

1970 (24 Oct). *International Education Year.* T **181** *and similar multicoloured design.* P 13½.

568	30 c. Type **181** ..	..	5	5
569	3 d. Illuminated Koran (*vert*) ..	..	55	20

(Des B. Yelles. Litho Central Bank of Algeria)

1970 (28 Nov)–**71**. *Mosques.* T **182** *and similar designs.* P 14.

570	30 c. multicoloured ..	..	5	5
571	40 c. sepia and pale olive-bistre (26.6.71)		8	8
572	1 d. multicoloured ..	..	15	10

Designs: *Vert*—40 c. Ketchaoua Mosque, Algiers; 1 d. Sidi-Okba Mosque.

183 "Fine Arts"

184 G.P.O., Algiers

(Des Pupil of Fine Arts School, Algiers. Photo "Kultura" State Ptg Office, Budapest)

1970 (26 Dec). *Algerian Fine Arts.* P 13×12½.
573 **183** 1 d. yellow-orange, myrtle-green and apple-green 15 8

(Photo Courvoisier)

1971 (23 Jan). *Stamp Day.* P 11½.
574 **184** 30 c. multicoloured 5 5

185 Hurdling **186** "Racial Equality"

190 Aurès Costume **191** U.N.I.C.E.F. Emblem, Tree and Animals

(Photo Courvoisier)

1971 (6 Mar). *Mediterranean Games, Izmir, Turkey.* T **185** *and similar designs.* P 11½.

575	20 c. slate-grey and blue	..	5	5
576	40 c. slate-grey and olive-green	..	8	5
577	75 c. slate-grey and red-brown	..	12	8

Designs: *Vert*—40 c. Gymnastics; 75 c. Basketball

(Des I. Samsom. Photo)

1971 (27 Mar). *Racial Equality Year.* P 12½.

578	**186** 60 c. multicoloured	..	10	8

187 Symbols of Learning, and Students **188** Red Crescent Banner

(Des Ali Khodja. Photo)

1971 (24 Apr). *Inauguration of Technological Institutes.* P 12½ × 12.

579	**187** 70 c. multicoloured	..	12	5

(Des Boukendjakdji. Recess Central Bank of Algeria)

1971 (15 May). *Red Crescent Day.* P 10½.

580	**188** 30 c. + 10 c. red and myrtle-green	..	8	8

189 Casbah, Algiers

(Des I. Samsom. Photo Delrieu)

1971 (12 June)–**72.** AIR. T **189** *and similar horiz designs.* P 12½.

581	2 d. multicoloured	..	40	20
582	3 d. bright violet and black (26.2.72)	..	50	25
583	4 d. multicoloured (26.2.72)	..	60	35

Designs:—3 d. Port of Oran; 4 d. Rhumel Gorges.

(Des B. Yelles. Photo Courvoisier)

1971 (16 Oct). *Regional Costumes* (*1st series*). T **190** *and similar vert designs. Multicoloured.* P 11½.

584	50 c. Type **190**	..	8	5
585	70 c. Oran	..	12	8
586	80 c. Algiers	..	15	8
587	90 c. Djebel-Amour	..	15	8
584/587	*Set of 4*	..	45	25

See also Nos. 610/13.

(Des Baya. Photo Courvoisier)

1971 (4 Dec). *25th Anniversary of U.N.I.C.E.F.* P 11½.

588	**191** 60 c. multicoloured	..	10	8

192 Lion of St. Mark's

1972 (22 Jan). *U.N.E.S.C.O. "Save Venice" Campaign.* T **192** *and similar multicoloured design.* Litho. P 12.

589	80 c. Type **192**	..	12	8
590	1 d. 15, Bridge of Sighs, Venice (*vert*)	..	15	10

193 Cycling **194** Book and Book-mark

(Des K. Krim. Photo Courvoisier)

1972 (25 Mar). *Olympic Games, Munich.* T **193** *and similar multicoloured designs.* P 11½.

591	25 c. Type **193**	..	5	5
592	40 c. Throwing the javelin (*vert*)	..	8	5
593	60 c. Wrestling (*vert*)	..	10	8
594	1 d. Gymnastics (*vert*)	..	15	10
591/594	*Set of 4*	..	35	25

(Photo Courvoisier)

1972 (15 Apr). *International Book Year.* P 11½.

595	**194** 1 d. 15, vermilion, black & yell-brn	..	15	10

195 Algerian Postmen   **196** Jasmine

(Des I. Samsom. Photo Courvoisier)

1972 (22 Apr). *Stamp Day. P* 11½.
596 **195** 40 c. multicoloured 8 5

(Des M. Temam. Photo Courvoisier)

1972 (27 May). *Flowers. T* **196** *and similar vert designs. Multicoloured. P* 11½.
597 50 c. Type **196** 8 5
598 60 c. Violets 10 8
599 1 d. 15, Polyanthus 15 8

197 Olympic Stadium   **198** Festival Emblem

(Photo Courvoisier)

1972 (10 June). *Inauguration of Cheraga Olympic Stadium. P* 11½.
600 **197** 50 c. green, chocolate & pale violet 8 5

(Des A. Sahouli. Litho Central Bank of Algeria)

1972 (5 July). 1*st Festival of Arab Youth. P* 10½.
601 **198** 40 c. blackish brn, orge-yell & emer 8 8

199 Rejoicing Algerians   D **200** Ears of
                                     Corn

(Des M. Temam. Photo Courvoisier)

1972 (5 July). 10*th Anniversary of Independence. P* 11½.
602 **199** 1 d. multicoloured 15 10

(Des M. Teman. Litho Central Bank of Algeria)

1972 (21 Oct). *POSTAGE DUE. P* 13×14.
D603 D **200** 10 c. ochre 5 5
D604 20 c. chocolate 5 5
D605 40 c. yellow-orange 8 5
D606 50 c. deep blue 8 5
D607 80 c. deep olive-brown 12 8
D608 1 d. emerald 15 10
D609 2 d. greenish blue 40 20
D603/609 *Set of 7* 85 50

(Des B. Yelles. Photo Courvoisier)

1972 (18 Nov). *Regional Costumes* (2*nd series). Vert designs as T* **190**. *Multicoloured. P* 11½.
610 50 c. Hoggar 8 5
611 60 c. Kabylie 10 8
612 70 c. Mzab 12 8
613 90 c. Tlemcen 15 8
610/613 *Set of 4* 40 25

201 Child posting Letter

(Des I. Samson. Photo Courvoisier)

1973 (20 Jan). *Stamp Day. P* 11½.
614 **201** 40 c. multicoloured 8 8

Angola

1870. 1000 Reis = 1 Milreis
1913. 100 Centavos = 1 Escudo
1932. 100 Centavos = 1 Angolar
1954. 100 Centavos = 1 Escudo

The Portuguese conquest of Angola has been a gradual process since 1576, intensified in the 19th century. The present boundaries were fixed by treaties in the years 1886 to 1927. Angola was declared in 1935 to be an integral part of Portugal and on 11 June 1951 to be an overseas province.

PRINTERS. All the stamps of Angola were printed at the Mint, Lisbon, *unless otherwise stated.*

1	Plate 1	Plate 2

Both plates were used for the 50 r. blue perf 12½ of 1881. Two plates were also employed for the 10, 20, 25 and 40 r. values which differ in the figures of value. These are indicated but not illustrated as no stamps of the same colour, shade and perforation exist in both plates.

(Des and eng A. F. Gerard. Typo)

1870 (1 July). *Thick paper.* P 12½.

1	1	5 r. black	..	..	..	4·00	2·75
2		10 r. pale orange-yellow (Pl. 1)	..		..	5·00	4·25
3		20 r. bistre (Pl. 1)		..	..	6·00	5·25
4		25 r. red (Pl. 1)	..		..	3·25	2·50
		a. Rose (Pl. 1)	..		..	3·25	2·50
5		50 r. green (Pl. 1)		..	..	4·50	3·25
6		100 r. lilac	..		..	6·50	5·00
1/6		Set of 6	..	..	..	26·00	20·00

1875–77. *Medium paper varying in substance.*

(a) P 12½

7	1	5 r. black	..	..	..	45	30
		a. Grey-black	..		..	45	30
8		10 r. orange-yellow (Pl. 1)	..		..	1·90	1·25
		a. Pale orange (Pl. 1)	..		..	1·90	1·25
9		20 r. bistre (Pl. 1)	..		..	50	30
		a. Pale bistre (Pl. 1)		..	..	50	30
10		25 r. crimson (Pl. 1)	..		..	1·25	65
		a. Pale rose (Pl. 1)	..		..	1·25	65
		b. Vertically laid paper	..		..	65·00	35·00
11		40 r. deep blue (Pl. 1) (1.1.77)	..		18·00	13·00
		a. Pale blue (Pl. 1)	..		..	18·00	13·00
12		50 r. green (Pl. 1)	..		..	3·50	1·60
		a. Pale green (Pl. 1)	..		..	3·50	1·60
13		100 r. grey-lilac	..		..	1·50	1·25
		a. Dull purple	..		..	2·00	1·25
14		200 r. red-orange (1.1.77)	..		1·00	50
		a. Orange	..	..	..	80	50
		b. Pale orange	..		..	80	50
15		300 r. chocolate (1.1.77)	..		1·50	1·00
		a. Pale brown	..		..	1·00	80
7/15		Set of 9	..	..	..	27·00	17·00

(b) P 13½

16	1	5 r. black	..	..	..	75	55
		a. Grey-black	..		..	70	55
17		10 r. orange-yellow (Pl. 1)	..		2·40	1·75
		a. Pale yellow (Pl. 2)	..		..	2·40	1·90
18		20 r. bistre (Pl. 1)	..		..	8·00	4·50
19		25 r. crimson (Pl. 1)	..		..	4·50	2·00
		a. Pale rose (Pl. 1)	..		..	4·50	2·00
19b		40 r. deep blue (Pl. 2)	..		..	15·00	6·50
20		50 r. pale green (Pl. 1)	..		14·00	6·50
21		100 r. slate-lilac	..		..	1·00	70
		a. Dull purple	..		..	60	40

22	1	200 r. red-orange	..	..	..	65	40
		a. Orange	..	..	..	65	40
		b. Pale orange	..	..	..	65	40
23		300 r. chocolate	..	..	..	1·00	65
		a. Pale brown	..	..	..	65	65
16/23		Set of 9	..	..	..	40·00	20·00

(c) P 14

24	1	25 r. crimson	..	..	..	17·50	6·00

The stamps of 1875–77 were at first on thin hard paper, varying in substance; later printings on thick soft paper in paler shades.

All values were reprinted in 1885 and 1905, the 10, 20, 25, 40 and 50 r. being Plate 2.

1881–85. *Colours changed. Medium paper varying in substance.*

(a) P 12½

25	1	10 r. green (Pl. 1) (1883)	..		..	1·00	30
26		20 r. rosine (Pl. 2) (1885)	..		..	75	60
27		25 r. dull purple (Pl. 2) (1885)	..		25	20
28		40 r. yellow-buff (Pl. 1) (1882)	..		80	55
		a. Pale yellow (Pl. 1)	..		..	80	55
29		50 r. pale blue (Pl. 1)	..		..	2·00	30
		a. Deep blue (Pl. 1)	..		..	2·00	30
30		50 r. deep blue (Pl. 2)	..		..	1·75	30

(b) P 13½

31	1	10 r. green (Pl. 1)	..		..	50	30
32		25 r. dull purple (Pl. 2)	..		..	85	65
33		40 r. yellow-buff (Pl. 1)	..		..	70	55
34		50 r. pale blue (Pl. 1)	..		..	3·00	30

In the first printing of the 20 r. rosine a cliché of the 40 r. (No. 2 in the 2nd row) was inserted; this was found out before issue and the stamp was cancelled in indelible pencil, and is occasionally met with in this form. Sheets with the error were never issued.

Lithographed stamps perf 12½ are fraudulent.

All values were reprinted in 1885 and 1905, Plate 2.

2	**N 1**	**3**

(Des and eng F. A. de Campos. Typo and embossed)

1886 (1 June). *Chalk-surfaced paper.* (a) P 12½.

35	2	5 r. black	..	..	..	1·00	65
36		10 r. green	..	..	..	1·00	65
37		20 r. rosine	..	..	..	1·50	1·25
38		25 r. claret	..	..	..	1·25	30
39		25 r. bright mauve	..	..	..	1·25	30
40		40 r. chocolate	..	..	..	1·25	55
41		50 r. blue	..	..	..	1·25	30
		a. Pale blue	..	..	..	1·25	30
42		100 r. yellow-brown	..	..	..	1·25	1·00
43		200 r. lavender	..	..	..	2·25	1·25
44		300 r. orange	..	..	..	2·25	1·25
35/44		Set of 9	..	..	..	11·00	6·00

(b) P 13½

45	2	5 r. black	..	..	..	1·75	1·25
46		10 r. green	..	..	..	2·25	1·25
47		20 r. rosine	..	..	..	1·25	60
48		50 r. blue					

Stamps doubly printed or doubly embossed are met with in this issue and in the corresponding issues of other Portuguese Colonies.

The 5, 10 and 20 r. were reprinted in 1905.

(Des and eng E. C. Azedo Gneco. Typo)

1893 (3 July). *NEWSPAPER.*

N49	N **1**	2½ r. brown (*p* 11½)	30	20
N50		2½ r. brown (*p* 12½)	20	10
N51		2½ r. brown (*p* 13½)	12	8

Stamps of this type in this and other Colonies could be, and often were, used for franking ordinary correspondence.

(Des and eng M. D. Neto. Typo)

1894. *Chalk-surfaced paper or enamel-surfaced paper* (E).

(*a*) *P* 11½

49	**3**	5 r. pale orange (5 July)	20	12
50		5 r. pale orange (E)	30	20
		a. Pale yellow	30	15
51		10 r. rosy mauve (25 Sept)		
52		10 r. rosy mauve (E)	50	30
53		15 r. red-brown (25 Sept)	35	30
54		20 r. lavender (5 July)	40	30
55		25 r. green (5 July)	50	15
56		25 r. green (E)	55	25
57		50 r. pale blue (15 May)	50	20
58		75 r. rose (25 Sept)	2·25	1·25
59		75 r. rose (E)	1·60	1·00
60		100 r. brown/*buff* (25 Sept)	8·00	4·00
61		150 r. carmine/*rose* (25 Sept)	2·00	1·10
49/61		*Set of* 9	12·00	6·50

(*b*) *P* 12½

62	**3**	10 r. rosy mauve	25	15
63		15 r. red-brown	35	30
64		25 r. green (E)	65	15
65		50 r. pale blue	60	50
66		50 r. pale blue (E)	40	20
67		75 r. rose	90	70
68		80 r. pale green (25 Sept)	1·00	75
69		100 r. brown/*buff*	1·00	75
70		150 r. carmine/*rose*	2·00	1·25
71		200 r. blue/*blue* (25 Sept)	2·00	1·25
72		300 r. blue/*pale brown* (25 Sept)	2·00	1·25
62/72		*Set of* 10	9·00	5·50

(*c*) *P* 13½

73	**3**	5 r. pale orange (E)	20	12
74		25 r. green (E)	30	20
75		50 r. pale blue (E)	90	40
76		75 r. carmine (E)	1·60	1·10
77		200 r. blue/*blue*	2·00	1·25
78		300 r. blue/*pale brown*	2·00	1·25
73/78		*Set of* 6	6·00	3·75

(4)

5

1894 (Aug). *Newspaper stamp, Type* N **1**, *handstamped with T* **4**, *in dark blue for use on ordinary mail.*

79	N **1**	25 r. on 2½ r. brown (*p* 11½)	5·50	4·00
		a. Perf 12½	4·75	3·75
		b. Perf 13½	4·50	3·50

Stamps exist with the handstamp inverted and double.

(Des and eng E. Mouchon. Typo)

1898 (1 Aug)–**1901.** *Name and value in black, on* 500 *r. in carmine. P* 11½.

80	**5**	2½ r. pale grey	5	5
81		5 r. orange-red	5	5
82		10 r. green	5	5
83		15 r. chocolate	20	12
84		20 r. deep lilac	8	8
85		25 r. blue-green	20	10
86		50 r. blue	20	10
87		75 r. rose	65	35
88		80 r. mauve	60	35
89		100 r. blue/*blue*	15	10
90		150 r. brown/*buff*	55	45
91		200 r. purple/*pink*	35	15
92		300 r. blue/*pink*	45	35
93	**5**	500 r. black/*azure* (1901)	45	35
94		700 r. mauve/*yellow* (1901)	2·10	1·50
80/94		*Set of* 15	5·50	3·50

Sets may be made showing early, fine printings, and later, coarse printings. There are many shades.

(A)

(B)

In 1902 stamps of various colonies were surcharged as Types A and B, which it is unnecessary to repeat under each heading.

The perforation is given in brackets after each value. (E) denotes enamel-surfaced paper.

1902. *T* **2, 3** *and* N **1** *surch as Type* A.

95	**2**	65 r. on 40 r. (12½)	65	45
96		65 r. on 300 r. (12½)	75	55
97	**3**	65 r. on 5 r. (11½)	60	45
98		65 r. on 5 r. (E) (11½)	50	40
99		65 r. on 10 r. (E) (11½)	50	40
100		65 r. on 10 r. (12½)	55	45
101		65 r. on 20 r. (E) (11½)	1·10	80
102		65 r. on 20 r. (11½)	55	40
103		65 r. on 25 r. (11½)	1·60	1·10
104		65 r. on 25 r. (E) (12½)	60	45
105		65 r. on 25 r. (E) (13½)	65	45
106	**2**	115 r. on 10 r. (12½)	75	55
107		115 r. on 10 r. (13½)	3·50	2·25
108		115 r. on 200 r. (12½)	60	55
109	**3**	115 r. on 80 r. (12½)	1·00	75
110		115 r. on 100 r. (11½)	2·50	2·00
111		115 r. on 100 r. (12½)	1·10	90
112		115 r. on 100 r. (13½)	2·50	1·90
113		115 r. on 150 r. (11½)	1·00	80
114		115 r. on 150 r. (12½)	2·75	1·60
115		115 r. on 150 r. (13½)	2·75	1·60
116	**2**	130 r. on 50 r. blue (12½)	1·10	65
117		130 r. on 50 r. pale blue (12½)	1·10	85
118		130 r. on 100 r. (12½)	65	55
119	**3**	130 r. on 15 r. (11½)	45	35
120		130 r. on 15 r. (12½)	55	45
121		130 r. on 75 r. (11½)	4·00	3·50
122		130 r. on 75 r. (E) (11½)	90	65
123		130 r. on 75 r. (E) (13½)	4·00	3·50
124		130 r. on 75 r. (12½)	90	65
125		130 r. on 300 r. (12½)	1·75	1·40
126		130 r. on 300 r. (13½)	1·75	1·50
127	**2**	400 r. on 5 r. (12½) (R.)	1·75	1·50
128		400 r. on 20 r. (12½)	3·50	2·50
129		400 r. on 20 r. (13½)	5·00	4·00
130		400 r. on 25 r. (12½)	1·00	85
131	**3**	400 r. on 50 r. (E) (12½)	25	20
132		400 r. on 50 r. (12½)	1·10	75
133		400 r. on 200 r. (12½)	12	12
134		400 r. on 200 r. (13½)	4·00	2·50
135	N **1**	400 r. on 2½ r. (11½)	50	35
136		400 r. on 2½ r. (12½)	15	12
137		400 r. on 2½ r. (13½)	15	10

T **5** *optd with Type* B

138	**5**	15 r. chocolate	25	15
139		25 r. blue-green	15	10
140		50 r. blue	25	15
141		75 r. rose	50	40

The 130/50, 400/5, 400/20 and 400/25 r. values were reprinted in 1905.

1903. *Colours changed and new values. Name and value in black. P* 11½.

142	**5**	15 r. deep green	12	8
143		25 r. carmine	8	5
144		50 r. brown	55	30
145		65 r. dull blue	95	85
146		75 r. dull purple	20	12
147		115 r. orange-brown/*pink*	70	60
148		130 r. purple-brown/*straw*	70	60
149		400 r. dull blue/*straw*	45	30
142/149		*Set of* 8	3·25	2·50

50 RÉIS

D 1  (F)

(Des and eng J. S. de Carvalho e Silva. Typo)

1904. *POSTAGE DUE. Name and value in black. Typo.*
P 11½.

D150	D 1	5 r. yellow-green		5	5
D151		10 r. slate ..		5	5
D152		20 r. red-brown		10	8
D153		30 r. orange		10	8
D154		50 r. grey-brown		10	8
D155		60 r. pale-brown		45	30
D156		100 r. mauve		30	15
D157		130 r. blue		30	25
D158		200 r. carmine		55	40
D159		500 r. deep lilac		55	40
D150/159		*Set of 10*		2·25	1·60

1905. No. 145 *surch with Type F.*
150	5	50 reis on 65 r. dull blue		35	25

1911. *T 5 optd with T 50 of Portugal, in red or green* (G.).
151	5	2½ r. pale grey		5	5
152		5 r. orange-red		5	5
153		10 r. green		5	5
154		15 r. dull green		8	5
155		20 r. deep lilac		8	5
156		25 r. carmine (G.)		8	5
157		50 r. brown		25	20
158		75 r. dull purple		55	50
159		100 r. blue/*blue*		55	45
160		115 r. orange-brown/*pink*		20	15
161		130 r. purple-brown/*straw*		20	15
162		200 r. purple/*pink*		20	15
163		400 r. dull blue/*straw*		25	15
164		500 r. black/*azure*		25	15
165		700 r. mauve/*yellow*		25	20
151/165		*Set of 15*		2·75	2·00

1911. *POSTAGE DUE. Optd with T 50 of Portugal, in red or green* (G.).
D166	D 1	5 r. yellow-green		5	5
D167		10 r. slate ..		5	5
D168		20 r. red-brown		5	5
D169		30 r. orange		5	5
D170		50 r. grey-brown		5	5
D171		60 r. pale brown		10	5
D172		100 r. mauve		10	5
D173		130 r. blue ..		10	5
D174		200 r. carmine (G.) ..		10	5
D175		500 r. deep lilac		12	8
D166/175		*Set of 10*		55	35

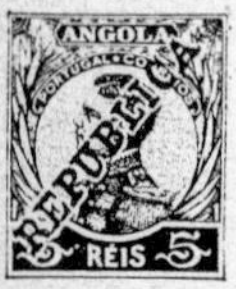

25 ■ **REPUBLICA**

6 (7)  (8)

(Des and eng D. A. do Rego. Typo)

1912. *T 6 optd with T 50 of Portugal, in red or green* (G.).
P 11½.
166	6	2½ r. lilac		5	5
167		5 r. black		10	8
168		10 r. grey-green		10	8
169		20 r. rose-red (G.)		10	8
170		25 r. chocolate		10	8
171		50 r. blue		15	12
172		75 r. yellow-brown		15	12
173		100 r. brown/*green*		20	15
174		200 r. deep green/*salmon*		20	15
175		300 r. black/*azure*		20	15
166/175		*Set of 10*		1·10	90

1912 (June). *Provisionais issued at Luanda.*

(a) No. 154 surch as T 7
176	5	2½ on 15 r. dull green			35	30
177		5 on 15 r. dull green			20	15
178		10 on 15 r. dull green			20	15

These stamps are each known with surcharge double, inverted and double and inverted.

(b) Optd with T 8, in violet, and surch with T 7, in black
179	5	25 on 75 r. rose (No. 141)		4·50	4·25
180		25 on 75 r. dull purple (No. 146)		20	15
		a. "REPUBLICA" ..		4·25	4·25
		b. "REPUBLICA" omitted ..		4·25	4·25

No. 180a occurs on the first stamp in the sheet.

REPUBLICA

ANGOLA

1 C.

(9)

10

1913. *New Currency. Vasco da Gama issues surch as T 9.*

(i) Africa (General Issues)
181		¼ c. on 2½ r. blue-green ..		15	12
		a. Name and value inverted ..			
182		½ c. on 5 r. vermilion ..		15	12
183		1 c. on 10 r. dull purple		15	12
184		2½ c. on 25 r. yellow-green		15	12
185		5 c. on 50 r. deep blue ..		15	12
186		7½ c. on 75 r. chocolate ..		50	50
187		10 c. on 100 r. bistre-brown		20	15
188		15 c. on 150 r. ochre		20	15
181/188		*Set of 8*		1·45	1·25

(ii) Macao
189		¼ c. on ½ a. blue-green ..		30	25
190		½ c. on 1 a. vermilion		30	25
191		1 c. on 2 a. dull purple ..		30	25
192		2½ c. on 4 a. yellow-green		25	20
193		5 c. on 8 a. deep blue		25	20
194		7½ c. on 12 a. chocolate ..		50	50
195		10 c. on 16 a. bistre-brown		35	25
196		15 c. on 24 a. ochre		35	25
189/196		*Set of 8*		2·25	1·90

(iii) Timor
197		¼ c. on ½ a. blue-green ..		30	25
198		½ c. on 1 a. vermilion		30	25
199		1 c. on 2 a. dull purple ..		30	25
200		2½ c. on 4 a. yellow-green		25	20
201		5 c. on 8 a. deep blue		25	20
202		7½ c. on 12 a. chocolate ..		50	50
203		10 c. on 16 a. bistre-brown		35	25
204		15 c. on 24 a. ochre		35	25
197/204		*Set of 8*		2·25	1·90

(Des C. Fernandes. Eng J. S. de Carvalho e Silva. Typo)

1914. *Name and value in black. Chalk-surfaced paper.*
P 15 × 14.
205	10	¼ c. brown-olive		15	10
206		½ c. black		15	10
207		1 c. deep green		25	10
208		1½ c. chocolate		40	30
209		2 c. carmine		40	30
210		2½ c. violet		12	5
211		5 c. blue		25	15
212		7½ c. yellow-brown		30	20
213		8 c. slate		35	20
214		10 c. brown-red		35	20
215		15 c. claret		35	25
216		20 c. yellow-green		15	10
217		30 c. chocolate/*green*		25	20
218		40 c. brown/*rose*		25	20
219		50 c. orange/*salmon* ..		65	55
220		1 E. deep green/*azure*		45	35
205/220		*Set of 16*		4·25	3·00

See also Nos. 276/329.

1914 (1 Oct). *Optd locally with T* **8**. (*a*) *Stamps of* 1898 *to* 1903.

221	**5**	10 r. green (R.)	55	40
222		15 r. deep green (R.)	55	40
223		20 r. deep lilac (G.)	10	8
224		75 r. dull purple (G.)	10	10
225		100 r. blue/*blue* (R.)	12	10
226		200 r. purple/*pink* (G.)	12	10
227		400 r. dull blue/*straw* (R.)	2·40	1·90
228		500 r. black/*azure* (R.)	30	20
229		700 r. mauve/*yellow* (G.)	1·25	1·10
221/229		*Set of* 9	5·00	3·75

The 130 r. (No. 161) with this overprint in red was not regularly issued (*Price* £50 *un*).

(*b*) *Provisional stamps of* 1902 *and* 1905

232	**5**	50 r. blue (No. 140) (R.)	10	8
233		50 r. on 65 r. dull blue (R.)	35	35
234		75 r. rose (No. 141) (G.)	30	25
235	**2**	115 r. on 10 r. (12½) (R.)	1·25	1·00
236		115 r. on 10 r. (13½) (R.)	2·50	2·40
237	**3**	115 r. on 80 r. (12½) (R.)	13·00	12·00
238		115 r. on 100 r. (11½) (R.)	19·00	18·00
239		115 r. on 100 r. (12½) (R.)	20·00	19·00
240		115 r. on 100 r. (13½) (R.)	35·00	30·00
241		115 r. on 150 r. (11½) (G.)	19·00	13·00
242		115 r. on 150 r. (12½) (R.)	19·00	14·00
243		115 r. on 150 r. (13½) (G.)	20·00	15·00
244	**2**	115 r. on 200 r. (12½) (R.)	1·25	1·00
245		130 r. on 50 r. blue (12½) (R.)	2·00	1·50
246		130 r. on 50 r. pale blue (12½) (R.)	2·00	1·50
247	**3**	130 r. on 75 r. (11½) (G.)	50	45
248		130 r. on 75 r. (E) (11½) (G.)	20	15
249		130 r. on 75 r. (12½) (G.)	75	50
250		130 r. on 300 r. (12½) (R.)	1·25	95
251		130 r. on 300 r. (13½) (R.)	60	50
252	N **1**	400 r. on 2½ r. (11½) (R.)	30	20
253		400 r. on 2½ r. (12½) (R.)	8	5
254		400 r. on 2½ r. (13½) (R.)	8	5

1915. *Provisionals of* 1902 *optd at Lisbon with T* **50** *of Portugal, in red.*

255	**2**	115 r. on 10 r. (12½)	30	25
256		115 r. on 10 r. (13½)	25	20
257	**3**	115 r. on 80 r. (12½)	30	25
258		115 r. on 80 r. (E) (11½)	15	12
260		115 r. on 100 r. (11½)	2·25	2·00
261		115 r. on 100 r. (12½)	20	15
262		115 r. on 100 r. (13½)	80	70
263		115 r. on 150 r. (11½)	15	12
264		115 r. on 150 r. (12½)	45	35
265		115 r. on 150 r. (13½)	30	25
266	**2**	115 r. on 200 r. (12½)	20	15
267	**3**	130 r. on 15 r. (11½)	15	12
268		130 r. on 15 r. (12½)	80	65
269		130 r. on 75 r. (11½)	25	12
270		130 r. on 75 r. (E) (11½)	35	30
271		130 r. on 75 r. (E) (13½)	60	50
272		130 r. on 75 r. (12½)	25	15
273	**2**	130 r. on 100 r. pale blue (12½)	12	10
274	**3**	130 r. on 300 r. (12½)	12	10
275		130 r. on 300 r. (13½)	45	35

1915–26. *Name and value in black.* (*a*) *Unsurfaced wove paper* (*thick, medium or thin*). *P* 15×14 (1915–21).

276	**10**	¼ c. brown-olive	5	5
		a. Thick carton paper	5	5
277		½ c. black	5	5
		a. Thick carton paper	5	5
278		1 c. green	5	5
		a. Deep green	5	5
		b. Pale yellow-green (1918)	5	5
279		1½ c. chocolate	5	5
		a. Thick carton paper	65	40
280		2 c. carmine	5	5
281		2½ c. deep violet	5	5
		a. Pale violet (1918)	5	5
282		3 c. orange (1921)	10	5
283		4 c. dull claret (1921)	5	5
284		5 c. deep blue	5	5
		a. Pale blue (1918)	5	5
285		6 c. mauve (1921)	5	5
286		7 c. cobalt (1921)	5	5
287		7½ c. yellow-brown (1920)	5	5
288		8 c. slate	5	5
289		10 c. brown-red (1918)	5	5
290		12 c. olive-brown (1921)	5	5
291		15 c. plum (1920)	5	5
		a. Dull rose (1921)	5	5
292	**10**	20 c. yellow-green (1918)	15	5
293		30 c. deep grey-green (1921)	5	5
294		80 c. carmine (1921)	8	5
		a. Bright rosine	8	5
295		2 E. deep purple (1921)	12	5
276/295		*Set of* 20	55	50

(*b*) *Unsurfaced paper. P* 12×11½ (1921–26)

296	**10**	¼ c. brown-olive (1924)	5	5
297		½ c. black	5	5
298		1 c. green (1924)	5	5
		a. Deep green	5	5
		b. Pale yellow-green	5	5
299		1½ c. chocolate (1924)	5	5
300		2 c. rose-scarlet (1924)	5	5
		a. Carmine-red	5	5
301		2 c. drab (1925)	5	5
302		2½ c. mauve (1924)	5	5
303		3 c. orange	5	5
304		4 c. dull claret	5	5
		a. Pink	5	5
305		4½ c. drab	5	5
306		5 c. deep blue (1924)	5	5
		a. Pale blue	5	5
307		6 c. mauve	5	5
308		7 c. cobalt	5	5
309		7½ c. yellow-brown (1924)	5	5
310		8 c. slate (1924)	5	5
311		10 c. brown-red (1924)	5	5
312		12 c. olive-brown	5	5
313		12 c. blue-green (1925)	5	5
314		15 c. dull rose (1924)	5	5
315		20 c. yellow-green (1924)	5	5
316		24 c. cobalt (1925)	10	8
317		25 c. chocolate (1925)	10	8
318		30 c. deep grey-green	5	5
		a. Dull blue-green	5	5
319		40 c. turquoise	5	5
320		50 c. purple (1925)	8	5
321		60 c. deep blue	5	5
322		60 c. carmine (1926)	5·00	5·00
322*a*		80 c. bright rosine	8	5
323		1 E. carmine-pink	8	5
296/323		*Set of* 29	5·50	5·50

(*c*) *Glazed paper. P* 12×11½ (1921–25)

324	**10**	1 E. carmine-pink	8	5
325		1 E. deep blue (1925)	12	10
326		2 E. deep purple	15	8
327		5 E. pale yellow-brown (1925)	40	30
328		10 E. pink (1925)	1·00	65
329		20 E. pale green (1925)	3·50	2·00
324/329		*Set of* 6	4·50	2·75

½ C.	1 cent	$00,5
(11)	(12)	(13)

1919–21. *Various stamps surch locally and with old values cancelled with two bars.*

(*a*) *Surch as T* **11** (1919)

330	**5**	½ c. on 75 r. dull purple (No. 158)	30	25
331	**6**	½ c. on 75 r. yellow-brown	12	10
332	**5**	½ c. on 75 r. dull purple (No. 224)	12	10
333		2½ c. on 100 r. blue/*blue* (No. 159)	25	20
334	**6**	2½ c. on 100 r. brown/*green*	12	10
335	**5**	2½ c. on 100 r. blue/*blue* (No. 225)	12	10

(*b*) *Surch as T* **12** *or* **13** (1921)

336	**6**	1 c. on 50 r. blue	10	8
337	**5**	4 c. on 130 r. purple-brown/*straw* (No. 161)	12	10
338		4 c. on 130 r. purple-brown/*straw**	20	20
339	**10**	$04 on 15 c. claret	12	10
340		$04 on 15 c. dull rose (No. 314)	2·25	
341	**6**	$00.5 on 75 r. yellow-brown	12	10
342	**10**	$00.5 on 7½ c. yellow-brown	12	10

*No. 338 was not issued without the surcharge; see note after No. 229.

1921. *POSTAGE DUE. Name and value ("centavos") in black. P* 11½.

D343	D **1**	½ c. pale yellow-green	5	5
D344		1 c. slate	5	5
D345		2 c. deep red-brown	5	5
D346		3 c. pale orange	5	5
D347		5 c. grey-brown	5	5
D348		6 c. pale brown	5	5
D349		10 c. mauve	5	5

D350	D 1	13 c. blue		5	5
D351		20 c. carmine		5	5
D352		50 c. lilac-grey		5	5
D343/352	Set of 10			25	25

Sets may be made on soft, smooth paper and thin coarse paper, the shades differing in the latter particularly in the 3 c., which is yellow.

CHARITY TAX STAMPS. Stamps bearing C numbers were for compulsory use on internal letters on certain days of the year as an additional postal tax for public charities. Other values in some of the types were for use on telegrams or for fiscal purposes.

1925 (8 May). *CHARITY TAX. Marquis de Pombal Commemoration. Types* C **6/8** *of Portugal,* (1925), *inscr* "ANGOLA".

C343	C 6	15 c. dull violet		5	5
C344	C 7	15 c. dull violet		5	5
C345	C 8	15 c. dull violet		5	5

Nos. C343/5 were in use from 8th to 13th May 1925 and from 5th to 15th May in 1926 and 1929.

1925 (8 May). *POSTAGE DUE. As Nos.* C343/5 *optd,* "MULTA".

D353	C 6	30 c. dull violet		5	5
D354	C 7	30 c. dull violet		5	5
D355	C 8	30 c. dull violet		5	5

República

40 C. (14)

C 1

50 C. (16)

1925 (July). *Provisionals of 1902 surch with* T **14.**

343	3	40 c. on 400 r. on 200 r. (12½)		10	8
344		40 c. on 400 r. on 200 r. (13½)		60	45
345	N 1	40 c. on 400 r. on 2½ r. (12½)		8	8
346		40 c. on 400 r. on 2½ r. (13½)		10	10

(Litho Imprensa Nacional de Luanda)

1929 (1 June). *CHARITY TAX.* P 10½×11.

C347	C 1	50 c. blue		30	12

In use from 1st to 30th June and from 8th December to 8th January in 1929 and 1930.

1931. *Surch as* T **16.** P 12×11½.

347	10	50 c. on 60 c. carmine		15	12
348		70 c. on 80 c. rosine		25	15
349		70 c. on 1 E. deep blue		25	15
350		1 E. 40 on 2 E. deep purple		20	15

17 Ceres

18

(Des C. Fernandes. Eng A. Fragoso. Typo)

1932–46. *New Currency.* W **18.** P 12×11½.

351	17	1 c. brown		5	5
352		5 c. sepia		5	5
353		10 c. mauve		5	5
354		15 c. black		5	5
355		20 c. grey		5	5
356		30 c. blue-green		5	5
357		35 c. emerald (1946)		10	5
358		40 c. vermilion		5	5
359		45 c. turquoise-blue		8	5
360		50 c. cinnamon		5	5
361		60 c. olive-green		5	5
362		70 c. red-brown		5	5

363	17	80 c. emerald		5	5
364		85 c. carmine		25	15
365		1 a. claret		5	5
366		1 a. 40, blue		40	15
367		1 a. 75, blue (1946)		20	5
368		2 a. mauve		20	5
369		5 a. yellow-green		40	8
370		10 a. bistre-brown		1·00	12
371		20 a. orange		2·00	20
351/371	Set of 21			4·50	70

Three copies of No. 369 are known on commercial mail postmarked from Lubito in 1938 with "5 A" omitted.

CORREIOS

≡ **5**

10 C. (19)

0,15 Cent. (21)

(20)

1934. *Surch locally as* T **19.**

372	17	10 c. on 45 c. turquoise		12	10
373		20 c. on 85 c. carmine		12	10
374		30 c. on 1 a. 40, blue		12	10
375		70 c. on 2 a. mauve		25	20
376		80 c. on 5 a. yellow-green		20	12

For similarly surcharged stamps see Nos. 413/8.

1935. *Surch locally as* T **20** *for ordinary mail.* P 11½.

377	D 1	5 c. on 6 c. pale brown		10	8
378		30 c. on 50 c. lilac-grey		10	8
379		40 c. on 50 c. lilac-grey		10	8
		a. Surch inverted		2·50	

1938. *Surch locally as* T **21.**

380	17	5 c. on 80 c. emerald		5	5
381		10 c. on 80 c. emerald		5	5
382		15 c. on 80 c. emerald		10	5

22 Vasco da Gama

24 "Fomento" (Symbolising Progress)

27 Aeroplane over Globe

23 Mousinho de Albuquerque
25 Prince Henry the Navigator
26 Afonso de Albuquerque

(Des A. R. Garcia. Recess Bradbury, Wilkinson)

1938 (26 July). *Various centres. Name and value in black.* P 13½×13.

(a) POSTAGE

383	22	1 c. grey-olive		5	5
384		5 c. orange-brown		5	5
385		10 c. carmine		5	5
386		15 c. brown-purple		5	5
387		20 c. slate		5	5
388	23	30 c. bright purple		8	5
389		35 c. emerald-green		10	5
390		40 c. brown		8	5
391		50 c. magenta		8	5
392	24	60 c. grey-black		8	5
393		70 c. slate-violet		8	5
394		80 c. orange		8	5
395		1 a. scarlet		8	5
396	25	1 a. 75, blue		12	5
397		2 a. lake		15	5
398		5 a. olive-green		60	5
399	26	10 a. ultramarine		1·10	15
400		20 a. red-brown		2·00	25
383/400	Set of 18			4·00	60

(b) AIR

401	27	10 c. scarlet		10	10
402		20 c. bright violet		10	10
403		50 c. orange		10	8
404		1 a. bright blue		15	5
405		2 a. brown-lake		15	8
406		3 a. blue-green		25	10
407		5 a. red-brown		45	10
408		9 a. carmine		85	20
409		10 a. magenta		1·00	20
401/409		Set of 9		2·75	80

28 Portuguese Colonial Column

C 2

(Recess Bradbury, Wilkinson)

1938 (29 July). *President's Colonial Tour.* P 12½.

410	28	80 c. blue-green		45	40
411		1 a. 75, blue		90	45
412		20 a. red-brown		4·75	2·00

(Litho Imprensa Nacional de Luanda)

1939 (1 Jan). *CHARITY TAX. No gum.* P 11.

C413	C 2	50 c. blue-green		20	5
C414		1 a. scarlet		40	5

A 1 a. 50 value also exists but was only used for fiscal purposes.

1942. *T 17 surch with new value and bars, as T 19, but distance between surch and bars increased to 8 mm.*

413	17	10 c. on 45 c. turquoise-blue		10	5
414		15 c. on 45 c. turquoise-blue		10	5
415		20 c. on 85 c. carmine		10	5
416		35 c. on 85 c. carmine		10	5
417		50 c. on 1 a. 40, blue		10	5
418		60 c. on 1 a. claret		25	20

50

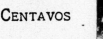

CENTAVOS

(29)

30 S. Miguel Fortress, Luanda

1945–46. *Surch locally with new value and bars, as T 29, or smaller surch on T 17, with bars above and "CENTAVOS" below the figure.*

419	17	5 c. on 80 c. emerald		8	8
420	24	5 c. on 80 c. orange		8	8
421		50 c. on 1 a. scarlet		8	8
422	25	50 c. on 1 a. 75, blue		8	8
423		50 c. on 1 a. 75, blue (R.)		8	8

(Des A. de Sousa. Litho Litografia Maia, Oporto)

1948 (May). *Tercentenary of Restoration of Angola. As T 30 (inscr "Tricentenario da Restauração de Angola 1648–1948").* P 14.

424		5 c. violet		5	5
425		10 c. chocolate		10	8
426		30 c. turquoise-green		5	5
427		50 c. purple		5	5
428		1 a. carmine		10	5
429		1 a. 75, blue		20	5
430		2 a. emerald-green		20	5
431		5 a. black		65	15
432		10 a. magenta		1·00	15
433		20 a. greenish blue		2·25	35
424/433		Set of 10		4·00	65

MS433*a* 162×225 mm. Nos. 424/33 (sold at 42 a. 50) ... ... 7·00
Designs: *Horiz*—10 c. Our Lady of Nazareth Hermitage, Luanda; 1 a. Surrender of Luanda; 5 a. Inscribed rocks at Yelala; 20 a. Massangano Fortress. *Vert (portraits)*—30 c. Don John IV; 50 c. Salvador Correia de Sa Benevides; 1 a. 75, Dioga Cao; 2 a. Manuel Cerveira Pereira; 10 a. Paulo Dias de Novais.

34 Our Lady of Fatima

PORTEADO
10
Centavos

(D 2)

(Des A. Negreiros. Litho Litografia Nacional, Oporto)

1948 (Dec). *Honouring the Statue of Our Lady of Fatima.* P 14.

434	34	50 c. carmine		35	30
435		3 a. ultramarine		1·00	55
436		6 a. orange		3·50	1·50
437		9 a. claret		7·50	1·50

1949 (Feb). *POSTAGE DUE. Optd as Type* D 2.

D438	17	10 c. on 20 c. grey		5	5
D439		20 c. on 30 c. blue-green		5	5
D440		30 c. on 50 c. cinnamon		5	5
D441		40 c. on 1 a. claret		5	5
D442		50 c. on 2 a. mauve		5	5
D443		1 a. on 5 a. yellow-green		12	10
D438/443		Set of 6		30	25

35 River Chiumbe

36 Pedras Negras

(Des M. Jorge (20 c., 40 c., 15 a.), A. de Sousa (others). Die eng Rosa (20 c., 15 a.), Fragoso (50 c., 3 a. 50), Americo (2 a. 50) and Norte (50 a.). Typo)

1949 (Feb). *Designs as T 35/6.* P 13½.

438		20 c. grey-blue		8	5
439		40 c. blackish brown		8	5
440		50 c. brown-lake		8	5
441		2 a. 50, bright blue		40	8
442		3 a. 50, slate		40	10
443		15 a. deep green		2·00	40
444		50 a. emerald-green		7·00	80
438/444		Set of 7		8·50	1·25

Designs: *Horiz*—50 c. View of Luanda; 2 a. 50, View of Bandeira; 3 a. 50, View of Moçâmedes; 15 a. River Cubal; 50 a. Braganza Falls.

37 Aeroplanes and Globe

38 Sailing Vessel

39 Letter and Globe

(Photo Courvoisier)

1949 (Feb). *AIR. P* 11½.
445	**37**	1 a. brown-orange	.. .. ..	12	5
446		2 a. red-brown	.. .. ..	20	5
447		3 a. magenta ..	.. ..	30	5
448		6 a. grey-green	.. .. ..	55	12
449		9 a. purple	.. .. ..	90	25
445/449		*Set of 5*	.. .. ..	1·75	45

Although intended for air mail use, the above issue was valid for all classes of mail.

(Des Malheiro. Litho Litografia Maia, Oporto)

1949 (Aug). *Centenary of Founding of Moçámedes. P* 14.
450	**38**	1 a. brown-purple	.. ..	8	5
451		4 a. blue-green	.. ..	20	5

(Des A. Negreiros. Litho Litografia Maia, Oporto)

1949 (Oct). *75th Anniv of U.P.U. P* 14.
452	**39**	4 a. blue-green	.. ..	75	20

40
Reproduction of
T **1**

41 Bells and Dove

42 Angel holding Candelabra

1950 (2 Apr). *Philatelic Exhibition and 80th Anniv of First Angolan Stamp. Litho. P* 11½ × 12.
453	**40**	50 c. yellow-green	.. ..	8	5
454		1 a. brown-red	.. ..	10	8
455		4 a. black	.. ..	25	15
MS455a		120×79 mm. Nos. 453/5 (sold at 6 a. 50)	.. ..	1·00	

(Des J. Araujo. Litho Litografia de Portugal, Lisbon)

1950 (May). *Holy Year. P* 13½.
456	**41**	1 a. violet	.. .. ..	8	5
457	**42**	4 a. black	.. .. ..	25	8

43 Angola dark chanting Goshawk

44 Our Lady of Fatima

D 3

(Photo Courvoisier)

1951 (23 Jan–27 Mar). *Birds as T* **43**. *Birds, etc. in natural colours. Colours of backgrounds and inscriptions given below. P* 11½.
458	5 c. grey-blue and black	.. ..	5	5
459	10 c. greenish blue and brown (27.3)	..	5	5
460	15 c. rose and black (22.3)	..	10	8
461	20 c. yellow and brown ..	..	15	12
462	50 c. slate-blue and black (22.3)..	..	12	5
463	1 a. grey-violet and black	..	12	5
464	1 a. 50, stone and black (27.3) ..	..	20	5
465	2 a. buff and black	..	20	5
466	2 a. 50, blue-grey and black	..	20	5
467	3 a. lemon and black (27.3)	..	12	8
468	3 a. 50, grey and black (22.3)	..	12	8
469	4 a. brown and black (22.3)	..	15	8
470	4 a. 50, lilac and black ..	..	20	15
471	5 a. green and blue	..	1·00	12
472	6 a. blue and black (27.3)	..	1·40	35

473	7 a. orange and black (22.3)	..	1·40	35
474	10 a. mauve and black (27.3)	..	3·50	55
475	12 a. 50, grey-green and black ..	..	2·00	1·25
476	15 a. yellow-green and black (27.1)	..	2·25	1·25
477	20 a. flesh and black (22.3)	..	15·00	2·00
478	25 a. pink and black (27.3)	..	5·00	1·75
479	30 a. salmon and black (27.3)	..	5·00	2·00
480	40 a. orange-yellow and black	..	7·50	2·50
481	50 a. turquoise and blue-green (27.3)	..	16·00	5·00
458/481	*Set of 24*	.. ..	55·00	16·00

Birds: *Horiz*—10 c. Racquet-tailed roller; 15 c. Bateleur; 20 c. Bee-eater; 2 a. 50, Scissor-billed tern or skimmer; 3 a. South African skira; 4 a. 50, Long-tailed shrike; 12 a. 50, White-crowned shrike; 30 a. Sulphur-breasted bush shrike. *Vert*—50 c. Giant kingfisher; 1 a. Yellow-headed barbet; 1 a. 50, African openbill; 2 a. Ground hornbill; 3 a. 50, Barrow's bustard; 4 a. African golden oriole; 5 a. Red glossy starling; 6 a. Wedge-tailed glossy starling; 7 a. Red-shouldered widow bird; 10 a. Half-collared kingfisher; 15 a. White-winged babbling starling; 20 a. Yellow-billed hornbill; 25 a. Violet-backed starling; 40 a. Secretary bird; 50 a. Rosy-faced love-bird.

(Litho Litografia Nacional, Oporto)

1951 (Oct). *Termination of Holy Year. P* 14.
482	**44**	4 a. orange and pale orange ..	..	25	15

To each of these stamps is attached a label of the same size inscribed with a Papal declaration which differs for each colony.

(Litho Litografia Nacional, Oporto)

1952. *POSTAGE DUE. Numerals in red, name in black. P* 14.
D483	**D 3**	10 c. red-brown and olive ..	..	5	5
D484		30 c. yellow-green and light blue ..		5	5
D485		50 c. brown and pale brown	..	5	5
D486		1 a. deep blue, green and orange	..	5	5
D487		2 a. red-brown and vermilion	..	5	5
D488		5 a. brown and light blue ..	..	10	5
D483/488		*Set of 6*	..	20	12

45 Laboratory

46 The Sacred Face

(Des A. de Sousa. Litho)

1952 (June). *First Tropical Medicine Congress, Lisbon. P* 13½.
483	**45**	1 a. grey and ultramarine	.. ..	5	5

1952 (Oct). *Missionary Art Exhibition. Litho. P* 13½.
484	**46**	10 c. deep blue and flesh	..	5	5
485		50 c. deep green and stone	..	5	5
486		2 a. purple and flesh	.. ..	10	5

47 Leopard

48 Stamp of 1853 and Colonial Arms

(Litho Litografia Maia, Oporto)

1953 (15 Aug). *As T 47 (Angolan fauna and surroundings in natural colours). Inscr in black. P 13.*

487	5 c. Leopard		5	5
488	10 c. Sable antelope		5	5
489	20 c. Elephant		5	5
490	30 c. Eland		5	5
491	40 c. Crocodile		5	5
492	50 c. Impala		5	5
493	1 a. Mountain zebra		8	5
494	1 a. 50, Situtunga		5	5
495	2 a. Black rhinoceros		8	5
496	2 a. 30, Gemsbuck		8	5
497	2 a. 50, Lion		10	5
498	3 a. Buffalo		8	5
499	3 a. 50, Gazelle		10	5
500	4 a. Gnu		1·75	8
501	5 a. Jungle cow		20	5
502	7 a. Warthog		30	10
503	10 a. Waterbuck		45	10
504	12 a. Hippopotamus		1·40	50
505	15 a. Greater Kudu antelope		1·50	55
506	20 a. Giraffe		2·00	35
487/506	*Set of 20*		7·50	1·60

Designs:—40 c., 2 a., 3 a. *horiz*, others *vert*.

(Litho Litografia Nacional, Oporto)

1953 (Nov). *Centenary of First Portuguese Postage Stamps. Stamps reproduced in T 48 and coat-of-arms in actual colours; inscr in black. P 13.*

507	**48** 50 c. grey and pale grey		12	10

Currency Reversion to Escudos

49 Father M. da Nobrega and São Paulo

50 Route of President's Tour

1954. *Fourth Centenary of São Paulo. Litho. P 13½.*

508	**49** 1 E. black, grey, ochre and buff		5	5

1954 (27 May). *Presidential Visit. Litho. P 13½.*

509	**50** 35 c. olive, red, green, pale blue-green and deep green		5	5
510	4 E. 50, deep blue, red, green, light blue and black		15	5

51 Map of Angola

C 3 Old Man

52 Colonel A. de Paiva

(Des J. de Moura. Litho)

1955 (Aug). *Map multicoloured; Angola territory in colour given below. P 13½.*

511	**51** 5 c. white		5	5
512	20 c. salmon		5	5
513	50 c. pale blue		5	5
514	1 E. orange-yellow		5	5
515	2 E. 30, greenish yellow		12	5
516	4 E. pale blue		15	5
517	10 E. apple-green		40	5
518	20 E. white		75	12
511/518	*Set of 8*		1·25	25

(Litho Foto-Lito E. G. A., Luanda)

1955. *CHARITY TAX. Type C 3 and similar vert designs. Heads in deep brown. Size 19½ × 26½ mm. Imprint at foot of design. P 13.*

C519	50 c. ochre-brown		5	5
C520	1 E. orange-red (Boy)		5	5
C521	1 E. 50, apple-green (Girl)		5	5
C522	2 E. 50, greenish blue (Old woman)		15	8

See also Nos. C544, C630/2 and C646/8.

1956 (9 Oct). *Birth Centenary of De Paiva. Litho. P 13½ × 12½.*

519	**52** 1 E. black, blue and yellow-orange		5	5

53 Quela Chief

54 Father J. M. Antunes

(Des Neves and Sousa. Photo Courvoisier)

1957 (1 Jan). *Native types as T 53. Multicoloured. P 11½.*

520	5 c. Type 53		5	5
521	10 c. Andulo flute player		5	5
522	15 c. Dembos man and woman		5	5
523	20 c. Quissama dancer (male)		5	5
524	30 c. Quibala family		5	5
525	40 c. Bocolo dancer (female)		5	5
526	50 c. Quissama woman		5	5
527	80 c. Cuanhama woman		5	5
528	1 E. 50, Luanda widow		45	5
529	2 E. 50, Bocolo dancer (male)		50	5
530	4 E. Muquixe man		15	5
531	10 E. Cabinda chief		25	10
520/531	*Set of 12*		1·40	30

(Des J. de Moura. Litho)

1957 (4 Jan). *Birth Centenary of Father Antunes. P 13½.*

532	**54** 1 E. deep brown, black, pale salmon and turquoise-green		12	8

(C 4) $30   (C 5) $10

1957. *CHARITY TAX. No. C519 surch as Type C 4.*

C533	10 c. on 50 c. ochre-brown (R.)		8	5
C534	30 c. on 50 c. ochre-brown		8	5

1958. *CHARITY TAX. No. C519 with smaller surch, Type C 5.*

C535	10 c. on 50 c. ochre-brown		5	5

55 Exhibition Emblem, Globe and Arms

56 Securidaca longipedunculata

(Des J. de Moura. Litho)

1958 (July). *Brussels International Exhibition. Multicoloured design; background colour below. P 12 × 11½.*

533	**55** 1 E. 50, grey-blue		8	5

(Des J. de Moura. Litho)

1958 (5 Sept). *Sixth International Congress of Tropical Medicine. P 13½.*

534	**56** 2 E. 50, multicoloured		30	20

57 Native Doctor and Patient

C 6 Mother and Child

(Des Neves and Sousa. Litho)

1958 (10 Oct). *75th Anniv of Maria Pia Hospital, Luanda. Various vert designs as T 57. P 11½ × 12.*
535	1 E. red-brown, black and pale blue			5	5
536	1 E. 50, multicoloured			5	5
537	2 E. 50, multicoloured			10	5

Designs:—1 E. 50, 17th-century doctor and patient; 2 E. 50, Present-day doctor, orderly and patients.

(Litho Foto-Lito E. G. A., Luanda)

1959. *CHARITY TAX. Type C 6 and similar vert design. P 13.*
C538	10 c. black and orange..		5	5
C539	30 c. black and slate (Boy and girl)		5	5

58 Welwitschia (plant)

59 Old Map of West Africa

(Des Neves and Sousa. Litho Litografia de Portugal, Oporto)

1959 (3 Sept). *Centenary of Discovery of Welwitschia. T 58 and similar horiz designs. P 14½ × 14½.*
538	1 E. 50, multicoloured			10	8
539	2 E. 50, multicoloured			20	8
540	5 E. multicoloured			25	10
541	10 E. multicoloured			80	30
538/541	*Set of 4*			1·10	50

Designs:—2 E. 50, 5 E., 10 E. Various types of Welwitschia (*Welwitschia mirabilis*).

(Des J. de Moura. Litho)

1960 (29 June). *Fifth Centenary of Death of Prince Henry the Navigator. P 13½ × 13.*
542	**59** 2 E. 50, multicoloured		8	5

60 "Agriculture" (distribution of seeds)

61

(Des Neves and Sousa. Litho Litografia Maia, Oporto)

1960 (Oct). *Tenth Anniv of African Technical Co-operation Commission. P 14½.*
543	**60** 2 E. 50, multicoloured		8	5

1961 (Nov). *CHARITY TAX. No. C520 redrawn with value in italics.*
C544	1 E. orange-red			5	5

1961 (30 Nov). *Angolan Women. T 61 and similar vert portraits. Litho. Portraits multicoloured; background colours below. P 13 × 13½.*
544	10 c. light yellow-green..				5	5
545	15 c. light blue				5	5
546	30 c. yellow				5	5
547	40 c. grey				5	5
548	60 c. orange-brown				5	5
549	1 E. 50, light greenish blue				8	5
550	2 E. lilac				20	5
551	2 E. 50, greenish yellow				20	5
552	3 E. pink				50	5
553	4 E. light olive-green				35	5
554	5 E. light blue				20	5
555	7 E. 50, light yellow				25	15
556	10 E. buff				30	12
557	15 E. pale brown				30	25
558	25 E. pale rose				75	30
559	50 E. light grey				1·50	65
544/559	*Set of 16*				4·00	1·50

62 Weightlifting

63 *A. fanestus* (mosquito)

(Des J. de Moura. Photo Litografia Nacional, Oporto)

1962 (18 Jan). *Sports. T 62 and similar designs. P 13.*
560	50 c. multicoloured			5	5
561	1 E. multicoloured			15	5
562	1 E. 50, multicoloured			5	5
563	2 E. 50, multicoloured			8	5
564	4 E. 50, multicoloured			15	5
565	15 E. multicoloured			45	20
560/565	*Set of 6*			80	30

Designs:—50 c. Flying; 1 E. Rowing four; 1 E. 50, Waterpolo; 2 E. 50, Putting the shot; 4 E. 50, High-jumping.

(Des J. de Moura. Litho)

1962 (Apr). *Malaria Eradication. P 13½.*
566	**63** 2 E. 50, multicoloured		10	5

64 Gen. Norton de Matos (statue)

C 7 Yellow, White and Black Men

(Litho Litografia Maia, Oporto)

1962 (8 Aug). *50th Anniv of New Lisbon. P 14½.*
567	**64** 2 E. 50, bluish green, black, red, blue and light ochre		8	5

(Litho Foto-Lito E. G. A., Luanda)

1962. *CHARITY TAX. Provincial Settlement Committee. No gum. P 10½.*
C568	C 7 50 c. multicoloured		5	5
	a. Perf 11½		5	5
C569	1 E. multicoloured		8	5

The tax was used to promote Portuguese settlement in Angola and to improve living standards of immigrants. Higher values were for fiscal use.

607	17 E. Quimbele				50	30
608	25 E. Noqui	..	..	..	75	40
609	35 E. Santa Cruz ..	..	..	..	1·00	45
610	50 E. General Freire	..	..	..	1·50	65
589/610	Set of 22			..	5·50	2·75

(Des J. de Moura. Litho Litografia Maia, Oporto)

1963 (5 Oct). *Tenth Anniv of T.A.P. Airline.* P 14½.

611	**69**	1 E. multicoloured	..	..	8	5

65 Locusts   **66** Arms of St. Paul of the
Assumption, Luanda

(Des J. de Moura. Litho Litografia Maia, Oporto)

1963 (17 June). *15th Anniv of International Locust Eradication Service.* P 14½.

568	**65**	2 E. 50, multicoloured	..	..	10	5

(Des J. de Moura. Litho)

1963 (15 Aug). *Angolan Civic Arms (First series). Various designs as T 66. Multicoloured.* P 13½.

569	5 c. Type **66**	..	..	..	5	5
570	10 c. Massangano	..	..	..	5	5
571	30 c. Muxima	..	..	..	5	5
572	50 c. Carmona	..	..	..	5	5
573	1 e. Salazar	..	..	..	5	5
574	1 E. 50, Malanje	..	..	..	8	5
575	2 E. Henry of Carvalho ..	..	..	8	5
576	2 E. 50, Moçâmedes	..	..	..	25	5
577	3 E. Novo Redondo	..	..	..	8	5
578	3 E. 50, St. Salvador (Congo) ..	..	10	5
579	5 E. Lusa	..	..	..	15	5
580	7 E. 50, St. Philip (Benguela) ..	..	20	12
581	10 E. Lobito	..	..	..	30	12
582	12 E. 50, Gabela ..	..	..	35	20
583	15 E. Sa da Bendeira	..	..	45	20
584	17 E. 50, Silva Porto	..	..	55	25
585	20 E. Nova Lisboa	..	..	..	60	25
586	22 E. 50, Cabinda	..	..	..	70	30
587	30 E. Serpa Pinto	..	..	..	90	35
569/587	Set of 19	..	..	..	4·50	1·75

67 Rear-Admiral   **68** Arms of   **69** Map of Africa
A. Tomás   Sanza-Pombo   and Airliners

1963 (16 Sept). *Presidential Visit. Litho.* P 13½.

588	**67**	2 E. 50, multicoloured	..	..	10	5

(Des J. de Moura. Litho)

1963 (5 Oct). *Angolan Civic Arms (Second series). Various designs as T 68. Multicoloured.* P 13½.

589	15 c. Type **68**	..	..	..	5	5
590	20 c. St. Antonio de Zaire	..	..	5	5
591	25 c. Ambriz	..	..	..	5	5
592	40 c. Ambrizete ..	..	..	5	5
593	60 c. Catete	..	..	..	5	5
594	70 c. Quibaxe	..	..	..	5	5
595	1 E. Maquela do Zombo	..	..	5	5
596	1 E. 20, Bembe ..	..	..	5	5
597	1 E. 50, Caxito ..	..	..	5	5
598	1 E. 80, Dondo	..	..	..	5	5
599	2 E. 50, Damba ..	..	..	20	5
600	4 E. Cuimba	..	..	..	12	5
601	6 E. 50, Negage	..	..	..	20	8
602	7 E. Quitexe	..	..	..	20	8
603	8 E. Mucaba	..	..	..	25	12
604	9 E. 31 de Janeiro	..	..	..	25	15
605	11 E. Novo Caipemba	..	..	30	20
606	14 E. Songo	..	..	..	40	25

70 Bandeira   **71** Dr. A. T. de Sousa
Cathedral

(Litho Litografia Nacional, Oporto)

1963 (1 Nov). *Angolan Churches. Various designs as T 70. Multicoloured.* P 14½ × 14 (vert) or 14 × 14½ (horiz).

612	10 c. Type **70**	..	..	..	5	5
613	20 c. Landana	..	..	..	5	5
614	30 c. Luanda (Cathedral)	..	..	5	5
615	40 c. Gabela	..	..	..	5	5
616	50 c. St. Martin, Bay of Tigers (Chapel)	5	5
617	1 E. Melange (Cathedral)	..	..	5	5
618	1 E. 50, St. Peter, Chibia	..	..	8	5
619	2 E. Bengulea ..	..	..	8	5
620	2 E. 50, Jesus, Luanda ..	..	..	8	5
621	3 E. Camabatela	..	..	..	8	5
622	3 E. 50, Cabinda Mission	..	..	10	5
623	4 E. Folgares Villa	..	..	..	12	5
624	4 E. 50, Arábida, Lobito	..	..	15	5
625	5 E. Cabinda	..	..	..	15	5
626	7 E. 50, Cacuso, Malange	..	..	20	8
627	10 E. Lubanga Mission	..	..	30	12
628	12 E. 50, Huila Mission	..	..	35	20
629	15 E. Island Cape, Luanda	..	..	45	20
612/629	Set of 18	..	..	..	2·10	75

The 1 E., 2 E., 3 E., 4 E., 4 E. 50, 7 E. 50, 12 E. 50 and 15 E. are horiz, the rest, vert.

1964 (Mar)–**65**. *CHARITY TAX. As Nos. C519/21 but redrawn, size 20 × 27 mm and without imprint. Typo.* P 11½.

C630	50 c. brown-orange	..	..	..	5	5
C631	1 E. orange-red (1965)	..	..	5	5
C632	1 E. 50, yellow-green (1965)	..	..	10	5

See also Nos. C646/8.

1964 (16 May). *Centenary of National Overseas Bank. Litho.* P 13½.

630	**71**	2 E. 50, multicoloured	..	..	10	5

72 Arms and Palace of   **73** I.T.U. Emblem and
Commerce, Luanda   St. Gabriel

1964 (13 Apr). *Centenary of Luanda Commercial Association. Litho.* P 12.

631	**72**	1 E. multicoloured	..	..	5	5

(Litho Litografia Nacional, Oporto)

1965 (17 May). *I.T.U. Centenary.* P 14½.

632	**73**	2 E. 50, multicoloured	..	..	12	5

74 Airliner over Petroleum Refinery   **C 8** "Full Employment"   **75** Aircraft over Luanda Airport

(Des I. Saslkovits (1 E. 50), C. Rocha (3 E., 4 E. 50, 5 E., 8 E.). Litho)

1965 (17 July). *AIR. T* **74** *and similar designs. Multi-coloured. P* $11\frac{1}{2} \times 12$ *(1 E. 50) or* $12 \times 11\frac{1}{2}$ *(others).*

633	1 E. 50, Type **74**	5	5
634	2 E. 50, Cambambe Dam	8	5
635	3 E. Salazar Dam	10	5
636	4 E. Capt. T. Duarte Dam	15	5
637	4 E. 50, Creveiro Lopes Dam	15	5
638	5 E. Cuango Dam	15	8
639	6 E. Quanza Bridge	20	8
	a. Ultramarine ("ANGOLA" and inscr) omitted		
640	7 E. Capt. T. Duarte Bridge	25	8
641	8 E. 50, Dr. Oliveira Salazar Bridge	25	10
642	12 E. 50, Capt. S. Carvalho Bridge	40	15
633/642	*Set of 10*	1·60	50

Nos. 634/42 are horiz and each design includes an airliner overhead.

(Des V. Santos. Litho Instituto Nacional de Assistencia)

1965 (1 Sept). *CHARITY TAX. Provincial Settlement Committee. P* 13.

C643	C **8** 5 c. multicoloured	5	5
C644	1 E. multicoloured	5	5
C645	2 E. multicoloured	10	5

(Litho Instituto Nacional de Assistencia)

1965. *CHARITY TAX. As Nos. C630/2 but smaller and with* "INA" *at foot. P* 13.

C646	50 c. brown-orange	5	5
C647	1 E. orange-red	5	5
C648	1 E. 50, yellow-green	8	5

(Litho Litografia Maia, Oporto)

1965 (1 Dec). *25th Anniv of Direcção dos Transportes Aéreos* (*Angolan airline*). *P* 13.
643 **75** 2 E. 50, multicoloured 8 5

76 Arquebusier, 1539   **77** St. Paul's Hospital, Luanda, and Sarmento Rodrigues Commercial and Industrial School

(Des A. Cutileiro. Litho Litografia Maia, Oporto)

1966 (25 Feb). *Portuguese Military Uniforms. Various vert designs as T* **76**. *Multicoloured. P* 14.

644	50 c. Type **76**	5	5
645	1 E. Arquebusier, 1640	5	5
646	1 E. 50, Infantry officer, 1777	5	5
647	2 E. Infantry standard-bearer, 1777	8	5
648	2 E. 50, Infantryman, 1777	8	5
649	3 E. Cavalry officer, 1783	8	5
650	4 E. Trooper, 1783	12	5
651	4 E. 50, Infantry officer, 1807	15	5
652	5 E. Infantryman 1807	15	8

653	6 E. Cavalry officer, 1807	15	8
654	8 E. Trooper, 1807	25	12
655	9 E. Infantryman, 1873	25	12
644/655	*Set of 12*	1·25	50

(Des A. Cutileiro. Litho)

1966 (28 May). *40th Anniv of National Revolution. P* $12 \times 11\frac{1}{2}$.
656 **77** 1 E. multicoloured 5 5

78 Emblem of Brotherhood   **79** M. Barata and Cruiser *Don Carlos I*

1966 (15 Aug). *Centenary of Brotherhood of the Holy Spirit. Litho. P* $13\frac{1}{2}$.
657 **78** 1 E. multicoloured 5 5

(Des A. Cutileiro. Litho Litografia Nacional, Oporto)

1967 (31 Jan). *Centenary of Military Naval Association. T* **79** *and similar horiz design. P* 13.

658	1 E. multicoloured	5	5
659	2 E. 50, multicoloured	8	5

Design:—2 E. 50, A. de Castilho and corvette *Mindelo*.

80 Basilica of Fatima   **81** 17th-century Map and M. C. Pereira (founder)

(Des J. de Moura. Litho)

1967 (13 May). *50th Anniv of Fatima Apparitions. P* $12\frac{1}{2} \times 13$.
660 **80** 50 c. multicoloured 5 5
  a. Black ("ANGOLA" and other inscr) omitted

1967 (15 Aug). *350th Anniv of Benguela. Litho. P* $12\frac{1}{2} \times 13$.
661 **81** 50 c. multicoloured 5 5

82 Town Hall, Uige-Carmona   **83** "The Three Orders"

1967 (12 Oct). *50th Anniv of Uige-Carmona. Litho. P* 12.
662 **82** 1 E. multicoloured 5 5

(Des J. de Moura. Litho Litografia Nacional, Oporto)

1967 (31 Oct). *Portuguese Civil and Military Orders. T 83 and similar vert designs. Multicoloured. P* 14.

663	50 c. Type **83**	5	5
664	1 E. "Tower and Sword"	5	5
665	1 E. 50, "Avis"	5	5
666	2 E. "Christ"	8	5
667	2 E. 50, "St. John"	8	5
668	3 E. "Empire"	8	5
669	4 E. "Infante Dom Henrique" ..	12	5
670	5 E. "Benemerencia"	15	8
671	10 E. "Public Instruction"	30	15
672	20 E. "Agricultural and Industrial Merit"	60	30
663/672	*Set of* 10	1·40	65

84 Belmonte Castle   85 Francisco Inocencio de Souza Coutinho

(Des J. de Moura. Litho Litografia Maia, Oporto)

1968 (22 Apr). *500th Birth Anniv of Pedro Cabral (explorer). T 84 and similar multicoloured designs. P* 14.

673	50 c. Our Lady of Hope	5	5
674	1 E. Type **84**	5	5
675	1 E. 50, St. Jeronimo's hermitage ..	8	5
676	2 E. 50, Cabral's fleet	12	5
673/676	*Set of* 4	25	12

The 50 c., 1 E. 50 and 2 E. 50 are vertical.

(Des J. de Moura. Litho Litografia Maia, Oporto)

1969 (7 Jan). *Bicentenary of Novo Redondo (Angolan city). P* 14.

677 **85** 2 E. multicoloured 8 5

86 Gunboat and Admiral Coutinho   87 Compass

(Des J. de Moura. Litho Litografia Nacional, Oporto)

1969 (17 Feb). *Birth Centenary of Admiral Gago Coutinho. P* 14.

678 **86** 2 E. 50, multicoloured 10 5

(Des J. de Moura. Litho Litografia Nacional, Oporto)

1969 (29 Aug). *500th Birth Anniv of Vasco da Gama (explorer). P* 14.

679 **87** 1 E. multicoloured 5 5

88 L. A. Rebello da Silva   89 Gate of Jerónimos

(Des J. de Moura. Litho Litografia Maia, Oporto)

1969 (25 Sept). *Centenary of Overseas Administrative Reforms. P* 14.

680 **88** 1 E. 50, multicoloured 5 5

(Des J. de Moura. Litho Litografia Nacional, Oporto)

1969 (1 Dec). *500th Birth Anniv of King Manoel I. P* 14.

681 **89** 3 E. multicoloured 8 5

90 *Angolasaurus bocagei*   91 Marshal Carmona

(Des J. de Moura. Litho Litografia Maia, Oporto)

1970 (31 Oct). *Fossils and Minerals. Diamond-shaped designs as T* **90**. *Multicoloured. P* 13½.

682	50 c. Type **90**	5	5
683	1 E. Ferro-meteorite	5	5
684	1 E. 50, Dioptase	8	5
685	2 E. *Gondwanidium validum* ..	8	5
686	2 E. 50, Diamonds	10	5
687	3 E. Estromatolitos	12	5
688	3 E. 50, *Procarcharodon megalodon* ..	15	5
689	4 E. *Microceratodus angolensis* ..	15	5
690	4 E. 50, Muscovite (mica)	20	8
691	5 E. Barytes	20	8
692	6 E. Nostoceras (helicinum) ..	20	8
693	10 E. *Rotula orbiculus angolensis* ..	40	10
682/693	*Set of* 12	1·75	50

(Des J. de Moura. Litho Litografia Nacional, Oporto)

1970 (15 Nov). *Birth Centenary of Marshal Carmona. P* 14.

694 **91** 2 E. 50, multicoloured 8 5

92 Cotton-picking   93 Mail-ships and 5 r. Stamp of 1870

1970 (20 Nov). *Centenary of Malanje Municipality. Litho. P* 13½ × 13.

695 **92** 2 E. 50, multicoloured 8 5

(Des J. de Moura. Litho Litografia Maia, Oporto)

1970 (1 Dec). *Stamp Centenary. T* **93** *and similar horiz designs. Multicoloured. P* 13½. (a) POSTAGE

696	1 E. 50, Type **93**	8	5
697	4 E. 50, Steam locomotive and 25 r. stamp of 1870 ..	20	10

(b) Air. Inscr "CORREIO AÉREO"

698	2 E. 50, Mail-planes and 10 r. stamp of 1870	12	8
MS699	150 × 105 mm. Nos. 696/8 (Sold at 15 E.)	1·00	

94 Map and Emblems   **95** Galleon at Mouth of Congo   **96** Planting Tree

(Des J. de Moura. Litho)

1971 (22 Aug). *5th Regional Soil and Foundation Engineering Conference, Luanda. P* 13.
700   **94**   2 E. 50, multicoloured   ..   8   5

(Des A. Cutileiro. Litho Litografia Maia, Oporto)

1972 (25 May). *400th Anniversary of Camoens' "Lusiad" (epic poem). P* 13.
701   **95**   1 E. multicoloured   5   5

1972. *CHARITY TAX. Provincial Settlement Committee. T* **96** *and similar vert designs. Litho. P* 13.
C702   50 c. red and drab   5   5
C703   1 E. black and green   5   5
C704   2 E. black and brown   5   5
Designs:—1 E. Agricultural workers; 2 E. Corncobs and flowers.

97 Sailing   **98** Seaplane "Santa Cruz" near Fernando de Noronha

(Des A. Cutileiro. Litho Litografia Nacional, Oporto)

1972 (20 June). *Olympic Games, Munich. P* 14 × 13½.
705   **97**   50 c. multicoloured   5   5

(Des A. Cutileiro. Litho Litografia Maia, Oporto)

1972 (20 Sept). *50th Anniversary of First Flight Lisbon–Rio de Janeiro. P* 13½.
706   **98**   1 E. multicoloured   5   5

PORTUGUESE CONGO

The northernmost district of Angola which had its own stamps from 1894 until 1920.

1894. 100 Reis=1 Milreis

1913. 100 Centavos=1 Escudo

PRINTERS. All stamps of Portuguese Congo were printed at the Mint, Lisbon, *unless otherwise stated.*

     1   N 1   2

(Des and eng M. D. Neto. Typo)

1894 (5 Aug). *Chalk-surfaced paper or enamel-surfaced paper* (E).

(a) P 11½

1	1	15 r. red-brown	..	..	..	85	65
2		20 r. lilac	..	..	..	85	65
3		25 r. green	..	..	..	55	12
4		50 r. pale blue ..		..	..	95	55
5		75 r. rose	..	..	..	65	55
6		80 r. pale green	..	..	90	80
7		100 r. brown/*yellow*	..	..	65	50

(b) P 12½

8	1	5 r. pale orange	..	..	15	10
9		10 r. rosy mauve	..	..	30	12
10		15 r. red-brown	..	..	45	35
11		20 r. lilac	..	..	..	45	35
12		20 r. lilac (E)	..	..	45	30
13		25 r. green	..	..	..	15	15
14		25 r. green (E) ..		..	..	45	30
15		75 r. rose (E)	..	..	2·50	2·00
16		80 r. pale green (E)	..	2·00	1·90
17		150 r. carmine/*rose*	..	1·10	1·00
18		200 r. blue/*blue* ..		..	1·10	1·00
19		300 r. blue/*pale brown*	..	1·40	1·25
8/19		*Set of* 10	..	..	8·50	7·00

(c) P 13½

20	1	5 r. pale orange	..	..	2·00	1·60
21		10 r. rosy mauve	..	..	3·00	2·25
22		50 r. pale blue (E)	..	..	45	30
23		100 r. brown/*buff*	..	..	4·00	2·00

(Des and eng E. C. Azedo Gneco. Typo)

1894 (5 Aug). *NEWSPAPER.*
N24   N 1   2½ r. brown (*perf* 13½)   ..   12   10
N25   2½ r. brown (*perf* 12½)   ..   12   10

(Des and eng E. Mouchon. Typo)

1898 (1 Aug)–**1901.** *Name and value in black or carmine* (500 *r.*). *P* 11½.

24	2	2½ r. pale grey ..		..	5	5
25		5 r. orange-red	..	..	5	5
26		10 r. green	..	..	..	8	5
27		15 r. chocolate ..		..	20	15
28		20 r. deep lilac	..	..	15	12
29		25 r. blue-green	..	..	20	15
30		50 r. blue	..	..	..	30	25
31		75 r. rose	..	..	..	50	40
32		80 r. mauve	..	..	..	50	40
33		100 r. blue/*blue* ..		..	30	30
34		150 r. purple-brown/*straw*	..	55	50
35		200 r. purple/*flesh*	..	..	60	60
36		300 r. blue/*pink* ..		..	50	45
		a. Error. On straw				
37		500 r. black/*azure* (1901)	..	1·25	1·00
38		700 r. mauve/*yellow* (1901)	..	2·10	1·75
24/38		*Set of* 15	..	..	6·50	5·00

1902. *(a) Surch as Type A of Angola.*

39	1	65 r. on 15 r. (11½)	..	..	.. 1·75 1·25
40		65 r. on 15 r. (12½)	..	..	.. 60 55
41		65 r. on 20 r. (12½)	..	..	.. 60 55
42		65 r. on 20 r. (E) (12½)	..		.. 1·25 1·10
43		65 r. on 25 r. (11½)	..	..	.. 2·00 1·50
44		65 r. on 25 r. (12½)	..	..	.. 55 40
45		65 r. on 25 r. (E) (12½)	..		.. 85 75
46		65 r. on 300 r. (12½)	..	..	.. 65 50
47		115 r. on 10 r. (12½)	..	..	.. 60 50
48		115 r. on 50 r. (11½)	..	..	.. 50 40
49		115 r. on 50 r. (E) (13½)	..		.. 55 50
50	N 1	115 r. on 2½ r. (12½)	..	..	.. 55 50
51		115 r. on 2½ r. (13½)	..	..	.. 55 50
		a. Surch inverted	..		.. 3·00 3·00
52	1	130 r. on 5 r. (12½)	..	..	.. 60 50
		a. Surch inverted	..		.. 3·00 3·00
53		130 r. on 5 r. (13½)	..	..	.. 55 50
54		130 r. on 75 r. (11½)	..	..	.. 60 45
55		130 r. on 75 r. (E) (12½)	..		.. 1·25 1·00
56		130 r. on 100 r. (11½)	..	..	.. 2·75 2·00
57		130 r. on 100 r. (13½)	..	..	.. 55 50
58		400 r. on 80 r. (11½)	..	..	.. 20 15
59		400 r. on 80 r. (E) (12½)	..		.. 75 75
60		400 r. on 150 r. (12½)	..	..	.. 20 15
61		400 r. on 200 r. (12½)	..	..	.. 20 15

(b) Optd with Type B of Angola

62	2	15 r. chocolate	..	..	20 15
63		25 r. blue-green	..	..	20 15
64		50 r. blue	..	..	25 20
65		75 r. rose	..	..	40 30

No. 64 is said to exist with a double overprint of Type B, the second impression being at the top of the stamp, but it was not put on sale in this condition.

1903. *Colours changed. Name and value in black. P 11½.*

66	2	15 r. deep green	..	..	12 10
67		25 r. carmine	..	..	15 8
68		50 r. brown	..	..	35 25
69		65 r. dull blue	..	..	1·00 85
70		75 r. dull purple	..	..	40 35
71		115 r. orange-brown/*pink*	..	..	75 65
72		130 r. purple-brown/*straw*	..	..	75 65
73		400 r. dull blue/*cream*	..	..	1·00 90
66/73		*Set of 8*	..	..	3·75 3·25

1905. *No. 54 surch with Type F of Angola.*

74	1	50 r. on 65 r. dull blue	..	..	50 35

CONGO   CONGO ▉

88	2	100 r. blue/*blue*	..		8 8
89		115 r. orange-brown/*pink*			12 10
90		130 r. purple-brown/*straw*			12 10
91		200 r. purple/*flesh*	..		25 15
92		400 r. dull blue/*cream*	..		20 20
93		500 r. black/*azure*	..		20 20
94		700 r. mauve/*yellow*	..		25 20
80/94		*Set of 15*	..		1·50 1·25

1913. *New Currency. Vasco da Gama issues surch as T 5.*

(i) Africa (General Issues)

95		¼ c. on 2½ r. blue-green	..		20 15
96		½ c. on 5 r. vermilion	..		20 15
97		1 c. on 10 r. dull purple	..		20 15
98		2½ c. on 25 r. yellow-green	..		20 15
99		5 c. on 50 r. deep blue	..		20 15
100		7½ c. on 75 r. chocolate	..		35 30
101		10 c. on 100 r. bistre-brown			20 15
		a. Surch inverted	..		3·00 3·00
102		15 c. on 150 r. ochre	..		20 15
95/102		*Set of 8*	..		1·50 1·10

(ii) Macao

103		¼ c. on ½ a. blue-green	..		25 20
104		½ c. on 1 a. vermilion	..		25 20
105		1 c. on 2 a. dull purple	..		25 20
106		2½ c. on 4 a. yellow-green			25 20
107		5 c. on 8 a. deep blue	..		25 20
108		7½ c. on 12 a. chocolate	..		35 30
109		10 c. on 16 a. bistre-brown			30 20
110		15 c. on 24 a. ochre	..		30 20
103/110		*Set of 8*	..		1·90 1·50

(iii) Timor

111		¼ c. on ½ a. blue-green	..		25 20
112		½ c. on 1 a. vermilion	..		25 20
113		1 c. on 2 a. dull purple	..		25 20
114		2½ c. on 4 a. yellow-green			25 20
115		5 c. on 8 a. deep blue	..		25 20
		a. Surch double	..		3·00 3·00
116		7½ c. on 12 a. chocolate	..		35 35
117		10 c. on 16 a. bistre-brown			30 20
118		15 c. on 25 a. ochre	..		30 20
111/118		*Set of 8*	..		1·90 1·50

6 Ceres

(7)

REPUBLICA

CONGO

▉ ▉**25** ¼ **C.**

(3)   (4)   (5)

1911. *Stamps of Angola, T 5, with local opt "REPUBLICA" in red, and*

(a) Optd with T 3, in black

75		2½ r. pale grey	..	..	12 8
		a. "CONGO" and bar as T 4			12 8
76		5 r. orange-red	..	..	15 15
		a. "REPUBLICA" inverted	..		2·25 2·25
77		10 r. green	..	..	15 15
		a. "REPUBLICA" inverted	..		2·25 2·25
78		15 r. deep green	..	..	20 15
		a. "REPUBLICA" inverted	..		2·25 2·25

(b) Surch with T 4, in black

79		25 r. on 200 r. purple/*flesh*			20 15
		a. "REPUBLICA" inverted	..		2·25 2·25
		b. "CONGO" double	..		2·00 2·00

1911. *Optd with T 50 of Portugal, in red or green (G.).*

80	2	2½ r. pale grey	..	..	5 5
81		5 r. orange	..	..	5 5
82		10 r. green	..	..	8 5
83		15 r. deep green	..	..	8 5
84		20 r. deep lilac	..	..	8 5
85		25 r. carmine (G.)	..	..	8 5
86		50 r. brown	..	..	8 5
87		75 r. dull purple	..	..	8 5

(Des C. Fernandes. Eng J. S. de Carvalho e Silva. Typo)

1914–20. *Name and value in black. P 15 × 14.*

(a) Chalk-surfaced paper (1914)

119	6	¼ c. brown-olive	..		12 10
120		½ c. black	..		12 12
121		1 c. deep green	..		30 25
122		1½ c. chocolate	..		20 15
123		2 c. carmine	..		30 20
124		2½ c. violet	..		8 8
125		5 c. blue	..		12 10
126		7½ c. yellow-brown	..		20 15
127		8 c. slate	..		20 15
128		10 c. brown-red	..		20 15
129		15 c. claret	..		25 20
130		20 c. yellow-green	..		25 20
131		30 c. chocolate/*green*			25 20
132		40 c. brown/*rose*	..		30 25
133		50 c. orange/*salmon*	..		30 30
134		1 E. deep green/*azure*	..		40 30
119/134		*Set of 16*	..		3·00 2·50

(b) Unsurfaced paper (1920)

135	6	¼ c. brown-olive	..		10 8
136		2 c. carmine	..		10 8

1914–18. *Optd locally with T 7.*

137	2	50 r. blue (No. 64) (R.)	..	..	8	8
138		50 r. brown (G.)	..	..	12	10
139	1	50 r. on 65 r. dull blue (No. 74) (R.)	..		12	10
140	2	75 r. rose (G.) ..	..	..	15	12
141		75 r. dull purple (G.) ..	..	..	15	15
142		100 r. blue/*blue* (R.)	..	..	10	8
143		200 r. purple/*flesh* (G.) ..	..	..	12	10
144		400 r. dull blue/*cream* (R.) (1918)	..	3·50	3·00
145		500 r. black/*azure* (R.) ..	..	..	3·00	2·75

1915. *Provisionals of 1902–05 optd with T 50 of Portugal, in red (reading down on Nos. 149/50).*

146	2	15 r. chocolate (No. 62)	..	..	5	5
147		50 r. blue (No. 64) ..	..	..	5	5
148	1	50 r. on 65 r. blue (No. 74) ..	..	..	5	5
149	N 1	115 r. on 2½ r. (12½)	..	..	12	8
150		115 r. on 2½ r. (13½) ..	..	..	5	5
151	1	115 r. on 10 r. (12½)	..	..	5	5
152		115 r. on 10 r. (13½) ..	..	2·25	1·75
153		115 r. on 50 r. (11½) ..	..	..	25	12
154		115 r. on 50 r. (E) (13½)	..	..	5	5
155		130 r. on 5 r. (12½)	..	..	20	12
156		130 r. on 5 r. (13½) ..	..	..	8	8
		a. Surch and opt inverted	..			
157		130 r. on 75 r. (11½) ..	..	..	20	12
158		130 r. on 75 r. (E) (12½)	..	..	20	12
159		130 r. on 100 r. (11½) ..	..	..	8	5
160		130 r. on 100 r. (13½) ..	..	..	25	15

From 1920 the stamps of Angola were again used in Portuguese Congo.

ANGRA. See Vol. 1 of Europe Catalogue.

ANJOUAN. See under Comoro Islands.

ANNAM & TONQUIN. See under Indo-China.

ANTIOQUIA. See Colombian States.

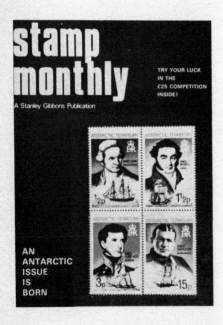

Argentine Republic

On 25 May 1810, a provisional junta in Buenos Aires assumed authority from the Spanish Viceroy of Rio de la Plata, which comprised the lands known as Argentina, Bolivia, Paraguay and Uruguay. Paraguay became independent in 1811 and on 9 July 1816, the independence of the United Provinces of Rio de la Plata was declared; Bolivia became an independent Republic in 1825 and Uruguay in 1828. The Argentine dictator Juan Manuel Rosas (1835–52) ordered that the country should be called the Argentine Confederation. Until 1862 there was an intermittent struggle between the Unitarians (or centralists) of Buenos Aires and the Federalists of the provinces; the first Argentine stamps were provincial issues, a consequence of this struggle.

I. PROVINCIAL ISSUES

A. BUENOS AIRES

On 11 September 1852 Buenos Aires seceded from the Argentine Confederation, and was independent until 1862.

8 Reales=1 Peso

For GREAT BRITAIN stamps used in Buenos Aires with obliteration "B32", see Great Britain Stamps Used Abroad in the *British Commonwealth Catalogue*.

CONDITION. The prices quoted for the stamps of Buenos Aires are for fine copies. Stamps in brilliant mint condition and exceptionally fine used copies are worth considerably more. Medium specimens can be supplied at from one-half the quoted prices and poor copies at very much less.

1 Steamship	**2** Head of Liberty

(Des Pablo Cataldi. Typo Mint, Buenos Aires)

1858 (29 Apr). *Imperf.*
P 1	**1** 2 p. (DOS Ps) blue	..	.. 20·00	15·00
P 2	2 p. (DOS Ps) dull blue..	..	.. 20·00	15·00
P 3	2 p. (DOS Ps) indigo	..	.. 35·00	30·00
P 4	3 p. (TRES Ps) green	..	.. £100	60·00
P 5	3 p. (TRES Ps) deep green	..	.. £150	90·00
P 6	3 p. (TRES Ps) yellow-green	..	.. £100	75·00
	a. "BUENOS AIPES"..	..	.. £250	£150
P 7	4 p. (CUATo Ps) red	..	.. £400	£300
P 8	4 p. (CUATo Ps) vermilion	..	.. £500	
P 9	5 p. (CINCo Ps) orange	..	.. £450	
P10	5 p. (CINCo Ps) yellow-ochre	..	.. £450	£300
P11	5 p. (CINCo Ps) olive-yellow	..	.. £500	£400
P12	5 p. (CINCo Ps) brownish yellow	..	£600	£450

The 2 and 4 pesos are known bisected and used for half their value.

Reprints were made in 1888 of the 2 and 3 pesos, in sheets of twenty, including a *tête-bêche* pair. They are on much thicker paper than the originals.

Reproductions from new plates made from original dies exist of all values, including the 4 r. and 1 p., 1858–9. They are on thick creamy wove paper, differing considerably from the originals.

Dangerous forgeries exist of the 3, 4 and 5 pesos.

1858 (26 Oct). *Imperf.*
P13	**1** 4 r. (CUATo rs) chestnut-brown	.. 25·00	15·00
P14	4 r. (CUATo rs) chocolate-brown	.. 25·00	15·00
P15	4 r. (CUATo rs) grey-brown ..	.. 25·00	15·00
P16	4 r. (CUATo rs) sepia ..	.. 30·00	15·00
	a. "CORRIOS"	.. 40·00	30·00
	b. "CUATo Cs"		
	c. "CUATo Ps"	.. 40·00	30·00
	d. Left argument above oval defective	—	35·00
P17	1 p. (:IN Ps), pale chestnut-brown	.. 25·00	20·00
P18	1 p. (:IN Ps), chestnut-brown ..	.. 25·00	20·00
P19	1 p. (:IN Ps), chocolate-brown..	.. 25·00	25·00
	a. "CORRLOS"	.. 50·00	35·00
	b. "CIN Ps"	.. 50·00	35·00

In the above issue the 4 r. was created by altering the plate of the 4 pesos by slightly erasing part of the "Ps" to read "rs" and the 1 p. was obtained by altering the plate of the 5 pesos by partly erasing the "C" at the beginning and the "Co" at the end.

1859 (Jan). *Colour changed. Imperf.*
P20	**1** 1 p. (:IN Ps), bright blue	.. 17·00	10·00
P21	1 p. (:IN Ps), blue ..	.. 17·00	10·00
P22	1 p. (:IN Ps), deep blue	.. 20·00	10·00
P23	1 p. (:IN Ps), indigo	.. 30·00	15·00
P24	1 p. (:IN Ps), slate-blue	.. 45·00	30·00
	a. "CIN Ps"	—	40·00
	b. Printed on both sides ..	£500	
	c. Tête-bêche (pair) ..	—£10000	
P25	1 p. (To rs), pale blue ..	.. 30·00	18·00
P26	1 p. (To rs), blue ..	.. 30·00	18·00
P27	1 p. (To rs), deep blue ..	.. 38·00	25·00
	a. "CUATo Ps" ..	.. 70·00	35·00
	b. "To Ps"	.. 80·00	30·00

Nos. P20/4 were printed from the same plate as Nos. P17/9 but for Nos. P25/27 the plate of the 4 reales brown was again altered by erasing the "CUA" of "CUATo".

The ":IN Ps" and "To rs" have been reprinted on thick paper, quite different from the originals.

(Des Jacob, Paris. Typo Mint, Buenos Aires)

1859 (3 Sept). *Imperf.*

(a) *First impressions from plate, with all lines clear and well defined*
P28	**2** 4 r. green/bluish	.. 25·00	15·00
P29	4 r. deep green/bluish..	.. 25·00	15·00
P30	1 p. pale blue ..	.. 4·00	2·50
P31	1 p. blue ..	.. 6·00	3·00
P32	1 p. deep blue ..	.. 6·00	3·50
	a. No stop after "1" ..	.. 7·00	5·00
P33	2 p. red.. ..	.. 25·00	15·00
P34	2 p. deep red ..	.. 25·00	15·00

(b) *Later impressions from worn plates, with lines blurred and indistinct*
P35	**2** 4 r. green/bluish	.. 20·00	12·00
P36	4 r. deep green/bluish..	.. 20·00	10·00
P37	4 r. yellow-green ..	.. 18·00	10·00
	a. No stop after "4" ..	.. 25·00	20·00
	b. "CORROOS"		
	c. Double impression		
	d. Yellowish paper		
P38	1 p. sky-blue ..	.. 2·50	2·00
P39	1 p. pale blue ..	.. 3·00	2·00
P40	1 p. blue ..	.. 2·50	2·00
P41	1 p. deep blue ..	.. 2·50	2·00
P42	1 p. indigo ..	.. 5·00	3·00
	a. No stop after "1" ..	.. 6·00	4·00
	b. Double print ..	.. 50·00	25·00
P43	2 p. red.. ..	.. 20·00	15·00
P44	2 p. deep red ..	.. 20·00	15·00

The 1 and 2 pesos are known bisected and used for half of their nominal value.

1862 (12 Nov). *Colours changed. Imperf.*
P45	**2** 1 p. pale rose ..	.. 5·00	3·00
P46	1 p. rose ..	.. 5·50	4·00
P47	1 p. carmine-rose ..	.. 8·00	4·50
	a. No stop after "1" ..	.. 7·00	5·00
P48	2 p. pale blue ..	.. 9·00	6·00

P49	**2**	2 p. blue	..	..	9·00	6·00
P50		2 p. greenish blue		10·00	6·00
P51		2 p. deep blue ..		15·00	7·00

The 2 p. exists with portions of papermaker's watermark, "LA CROIX FRÈRES".

B. CORDOBA

100 Centavos=1 Peso fuerte

3 Arms of Cordoba

(Litho Larsch, Buenos Aires)
1858 (28 Oct). *Laid paper. Imperf.*

P52	**3**	5 c. pale blue ..	..	..	..	8·00
P53		5 c. blue				8·00
P54		5 c. deep blue..				8·00
		a. Stop after "CEN." (No. 17)		..	12·00
		b. "C RDOBA" (No. 20)		..	12·00
		c. No top to "5" (No. 28)		..	12·00
P55		10 c. black	..	..	..	£250

The 5 c. was printed in sheets of 30 (10×3) and the 10 c. in sheets of 20 (5×4).
In the 10 c. all the stamps have a stop after "CEN.".
The paper on which these stamps are printed varies in the same sheet: generally it is *laid* or *strongly ribbed*; but stamps on the edge of some sheets appear to be on *wove* paper.
Stamps of 15 c., 20 c., 50 c. and 1 peso are bogus: there are also good forgeries of the 10 c.

C. CORRIENTES

Corrientes, a state in the remote northeast of Argentina, used its own stamps from 1856 to 1880.

1856. 1 Real M(oneda) C(orriente)=12½ Centimos M.C.
1860. 500 Centimos=100 Centavos fuerte=1 Peso fuerte

4   5

(Eng Matthew Pipet. Typo State Printing Works, Corrientes, in panes of eight types)
1856 (21 Aug). *Imperf.*

P56	**4**	1 real M.C. black/*blue* ..		..	10·00	25·00

1860 (8 Feb). *With value pen-cancelled.*

P57	**4**	(3 c.f.) black/*blue*	..	..	25·00	30·00

1860–71. *Value erased. Black on coloured paper.*

P58	**5**	(3 c.) *blue*	..	..	95	1·60
P59		(3 c.) *deep blue* (1871) ..		..	1·25	1·25

1864 (1 Jan). *Colour changed.*

P60	**5**	(2 c.) *yellow-green*	..	..	3·00	3·00
P61		(2 c.) *green*	..	..	3·00	3·00
P62		(2 c.) *blue-green*	..	..	4·25	4·25

From 1 Jan to 24 Feb 1864, No. P60 was used as a 5 centavos stamp.

1867. *Colour changed.*

P63	**5**	(2 c.) *lemon-yellow*	..	..	95	95
P64		(2 c.) *orange-yellow*	..	..	95	95

1873. *Colour changed.*

P65	**5**	(3 c.) *rose-lilac* ..	..	..	2·10	2·10

1875. *Colour changed.*

P66	**5**	(3 c.) *pale magenta*	..	..	2·75	2·10
P67		(3 c.) *lilac-rose* ..	..	..	2·75	2·10

1876. *Colour changed.*

P68	**5**	(3 c.) *rose-red* ..		..	4·25	2·75

1878. *Colour changed.*

P69	**5**	(3 c.) *lilac*	..	..	..	4·00	3·00
P70		(3 c.) *lilac-red* ..	..	..	5·50	3·50

The stamps of Corrientes were suppressed on 11 September 1880.
Forgeries of No. P56 have been made in sheets of eight stamps, but with the value quite different from the originals.

II. GENERAL ISSUES

100 Centavos=1 Peso
ARGENTINE CONFEDERATION

1   2

Argentine Confederation

(Printed from daguerreotype plates by Carlos Riviére, Rosario)
1858 (1 May). *Imperf.*

1	**1**	5 c. red ..	..	..	..	10	1·50
2		10 c. green (*shades*)	..	..	50	5·00
		a. *Pale green* (*thick paper*)	..	90	7·50
		b. *Deep green* ..	..	..	75	5·00
		c. Bisected (5 c.) (on cover)	..	—	30·00
3		15 c. blue ..	..	..	..	1·50	15·00
		a. *Deep blue* ..	..	..	2·50	18·00
		b. Trisected (5 c.) (on cover)	..	—	£400

Printed in sheets of 216 in two panes of 108 (9×12). There are various arrangements of the sheet.
Remainders of the 10 c. and 15 c. are on the market with fraudulent postmarks.

(Litho Carlos Riviére, Rosario)
1860 (Jan). *Large figure of value. Imperf.*

4	**2**	5 c. red ..	..	..	..	50	8·00
		a. First "A" of "ARGENTINA" inverted like inverted "V" (No. 2 in each group of 16 of Pl. A) ..	..	3·50	10·00
5		10 c. green	..	..	..	75
6		15 c. blue ..	..	..	..	2·50

The 10 c. and 15 c. were prepared but not issued.
Printed in sheets of 96 (8×12). There were two plates of the 5 c.: in Plate A the stamps are in groups of 16 varieties; in Plate B they are in strips of 8 varieties.
Beware of forged postmarks of the 5 c.

3   4

T **3.** Narrow "5" and broad "C" in "CENTAVOS".
T **4.** Large "5" and narrow "C".

(Litho R. Lange, Buenos Aires)

1862 (11 Jan). *Accent on "Ú" of "REPÚBLICA". Imperf.*

7	**3**	5 c. rose ..	..	..	5·00	5·00
		a. Red ..	..	..	7·00	6·00
8		10 c. yellow-green	..	..	20·00	12·00
		a. Deep green ..	..	..	25·00	15·00
		b. Bisected (5 c.) (on cover)	..			
9		15 c. blue ..	..	..	28·00	18·00
		a. Deep blue ..	..	..	35·00	30·00
		b. Ultramarine..	..	..	55·00	40·00
		c. No accent on "U"	..	..	£850	£450
		d. Tête-bêche (pair)	..	..	£12000	£6500

No. 9c comes on the second stamp in the eighth row and is often imitated by fakers painting out the accent. There are, however, methods by which experts can at once distinguish the stamp.

No. 9d. The inverted stamp is the first in the second row in the sheet.

Printed in sheets of 70 (7 × 10).

1863. *No accent on "U" of "REPUBLICA". Imperf.*

10	**3**	5 c. rose	..	..	3·50	2·50
		a. Rose-carmine	..	..	8·00	3·50
		b. Rose-lilac	..	..	12·00	12·00
		c. Rose (worn plate)	..	..	20·00	3·00
11		10 c. yellow-green	..	..	35·00	25·00

The stamps without accent were printed from new plates and the 10 c. always has an extra compartment line round each stamp.

In No. 10c the lines in the corners are almost worn away, giving the stamps the appearance of having blank corners.

1864 (Jan). *Imperf.*

12	**4**	5 c. brick-red	..	..	25·00	3·00
		a. Deep brick-red	..	..	30·00	3·50

Numerous imitations of this stamp were made in London about 1870, in shades of brick-red, red, and rose, usually on thicker paper; bogus varieties of the 10 c. and 15 c. with the narrow "c" were also made, but these never existed as originals.

5   6   7
B. Rivadavia

8

(Plates engraved on copper in London. Recess Casa de Correos, Buenos Aires)

1864–66. *W 8.*

(a) First printings. Medium paper. Imperf (17.4.64)

13	**5**	5 c. rose-red	..	..	£200	40·00
		a. Ribbed paper	..	..	£300	50·00
		b. Partial double impression..		..	—	60·00
14	**6**	10 c. green	..	..	£450	£250
15	**7**	15 c. blue	..	..	£850	£450

Beware of faked specimens of the 10 c. and 15 c. The originals have sharp and clear impressions and experts can recognise them by the shades and postmarks.

(b) P 11½ (1864–66)

16	**5**	5 c. rose-red (5 and 8.64)		..	5·00	2·00
		a. Ribbed paper	..	..	—	4·50
		b. Brown-red (1.65)	..	..	5·00	2·00
		ba. Ribbed paper	..	..	—	4·50
		c. Rose-carmine (11.65)	..	..	7·00	2·50
		ca. Complete double impression	..	—	25·00
		d. Deep carmine (29.8.66)	..	12·00	3·00
		da. Complete double impression	..	—	40·00
		e. Partial double impression (all shades)	From	14·00	7·00
17	**6**	10 c. green (shades)	..	..	12·00	4·50
		a. Ribbed paper	..	..	—	10·00
		b. Bisected (5 c.) (on cover)	..	—	30·00
		c. Partial double impression ..	..	—	25·00
		d. Complete double impression			
18	**7**	15 c. blue to deep blue ..	..	15·00	8·00
		a. Ribbed paper	..	..	—	30·00
		b. Partial double impression ..			
		c. Complete double impression	..	—	£100
		d. Slate-blue to indigo	..	25·00	14·00
		da. Ribbed paper	..	..	—	14·00
		e. Cobalt	..	..	—	25·00

There is considerable variation in the thickness of the paper.

1867 (25 Mar). *New plates. Fine impressions. Thick paper.*

(a) Imperf

19	**5**	5 c. red ..	..	..	—	20·00
		a. Partial double impression	..	..	—	28·00
		b. Orange-red ..	..	..	—	25·00

(b) P 11½

20	**5**	5 c. red ..	..	..	—	8·00
		a. Ribbed paper	..	..	—	10·00
		b. Partial double impression	..	..	—	10·00
		c. Complete double impression	..	—	20·00
		d. Orange-red ..	..	..	35·00	15·00
		da. Partial double impression	..	..	—	25·00

1867 (July). *Continuation of last printing but without wmk. Imperf. No gum.*

(a) Thick paper

21	**5**	5 c. rose-red	..	..	£500	£450

(b) Thinnish smooth paper

22	**6**	10 c. green	..	..	£750	£750
23	**7**	15 c. blue	..	..	£350	£350
		a. Slate-blue ..	..	..	£500	£500

1867. *No wmk. Thinnish smooth paper.*

(a) Imperf (15 July)

24	**5**	5 c. carmine-rose	..	..	35·00	15·00
		a. Partial double impression ..	..	—	20·00
		b. Complete double impression	..	75·00	35·00

(b) P 11½ (6 Aug)

25	**5**	5 c. carmine-rose	..	..	40·00	18·00
		a. Partial double impression	..	..	—	22·00
		b. Complete double impression	..	70·00	35·00

1872 (July–Aug). *Provisional issue printed from old plates. Smooth, thin white paper. Oily impression. Imperf.*

26	**5**	5 c. carmine	..	..	20·00	7·00
		a. Partial double impression	..	..	25·00	8·00
		b. Orange-red ..	..	..	25·00	10·00

Nos. 24, 25 and 26 exist with portions of papermaker's watermark, "LA CROIX FRÈRES".

The 5 c. *imperforate* was reprinted in 1888 in six different colours; there are also a number of colour proofs of the 5 c., mostly on thickish, coarse wove paper and on paper strongly ribbed.

9 B. Rivadavia   10 Gen. Belgrano   11 Gen. San Martin

Two types of 5 c.:

22 Sarsfield

23 San Martin

A Head on ground of horizontal lines   B Head on ground of crossed lines

Type A of the 5 c. has quite a different head from Type B, which was redrawn. Of the 15 c. there was only one plate, the differences being due to wearing and retouching.

(Recess American Bank Note Co, N.Y.)

1867 (1 Sept)–**74.** P 12.

27	9	5 c. vermilion (A)	..	..	10·00	65
28		5 c. vermilion (B) (1.1.68)	..	..	45	8
29	10	10 c. green	..	..	2·00	50
		a. Laid paper (1873)	..	..	12·00	1·50
30	11	15 c. blue (B)	..	..	4·00	1·25
		a. Worn plate. Horiz lines (1874)	..	4·50	1·25

12 Balcarce

13 Moreno

14 Alvear

15 Posadas

16 Saavedra

(18)

(Recess National Bank Note Co, N.Y.)

1873. P 12.

31	12	1 c. violet (15.3)	..	..	45	15
		a. Deep mauve	..	..	35	20
		b. Pale mauve	..	..	45	20
32	13	4 c. brown (15.3)	..	..	50	8
		a. Chestnut	..	..	2·25	75
33	14	30 c. orange (8.10)	..	..	10·00	1·25
34	15	60 c. black (8.10)	..	..	3·50	55
35	16	90 c. blue (8.10)	..	..	1·60	20

1876 (15 Sept). Rouletted.

36	9	5 c. vermilion (B)	..	..	15·00	5·00

Beware of faked roulettes.

1877 (Feb). Surch locally as T **18.** P 12.

37	9	1 on 5 c. vermilion (B)	..	..	3·25	1·25
		a. Surch inverted	..	..	25·00	16·00
38		2 on 5 c. vermilion (B)	..	..	7·00	4·50
		a. Surch inverted	..	..	50·00	45·00
39	10	8 on 10 c. green	..	..	5·00	1·50
		a. Surch inverted	..	..	45·00	30·00

Dangerous forgeries exist of all the above errors.
Double surcharges of Nos. 38/9 and No. 39 but on laid paper were of private origin.

20 Rivadavia

21 Belgrano

(Recess American Bank Note Co)

1877 (15 Mar)–**87.** (a) Rouletted.

40	20	8 c. lake	..	..	1·75	5
41	21	16 c. green	..	..	35	10
42	22	20 c. pale blue (15.3.78)	..	45	15
43	23	24 c. deep blue	..	..	2·25	30

(b) P 12

44	20	8 c. lake (1.9.80)	..	..	15	8
		a. Imperf horiz (vert pair)	..	14·00	
45	23	24 c. deep blue (6.87)	..	1·60	15

24 Lopez

25 Alvear

Two types of the 2 c.:—

A. National Bank Note Co. 19.9 × 24.9 mm. Side panels above value evenly shaded.
B. American Bank Note Co. 19.8 × 25.3 mm. Shading of side panels worn and uneven.

(Recess National Bank Note Co, N.Y.)

1877 (June)–**84.** P 12.

46	24	2 c. green (A)	..	..	30	12
		a. Yellow-green (B) (1884)	..	30	8
47	25	25 c. rosy lake (15.3.78)	..	2·00	65

½   ½

(PROVISORIO)   **(PROVISORIO)**
(26)   (27)

These types are two different printings. In T **26** the "P" has a small head, the "V" is narrow, and the "S" has a short top horizontal curve. The bracket is close to the "P".
In T **27** the "P" has a large head, the "V" is wide, the "S" has a longer top, and there is a wider space between the bracket and "P".

1882 (10 Feb). No 28 surch.

(i) Perforated horizontally across the centre of the stamp (10 Feb)

48	26	½ on 5 c. vermilion	..	..	15	15
		a. "PROVISORIQ". No. 47 on sheet	..	2·00	2·00
		b. Bracket to right of "PROVISORIO" omitted. Nos. 48 and 85 on sheet	1·40	1·40
		c. Vert pair, one without perforation across centre	..	3·00	
49	27	½ on 5 c. vermilion	..	..	90	1·00
		a. Surch inverted	..	..	5·00	
		b. Vert pair, one without perforation across centre	..	4·25	

(ii) Stamp not perforated across (27 Mar)

50	26	½ on 5 c. vermilion	..	..	12	12
		a. Surch inverted	..	..	2·25	
		b. Surch double	..	..	4·50	4·25
		c. Without "PROVISORIO"	..	3·25	
		d. Surch on back and on front	..	7·00	

51 **27**	½ on 5 c. vermilion	10	10
	a. Surch inverted	1·25	
	b. "½" inverted only, without "PROVI-		
	SORIO"	6·00	
	c. Without "PROVISORIO"	4·00	
	d. Error "PROVISOBIO"	2·00	2·00
	f. Surch diagonal	4·50	•
	g. Surch double	6·00	
	h. Horiz pair, one without surch	10·00	

The error "PROVISOBIO" is the fiftieth stamp on the sheet of the first printing of this type only and was corrected in the second printing. There are many minor varieties due to shifted surcharge.

29   OFICIAL   OFICIAL
                              (O 1)   **(O 2)**

(Typo Bradbury, Wilkinson, London)

1882 (13 July). (a) *P* 12.

52 **29**	½ c. brown	15	10
	a. Brown-red		
	b. No serif to foot of "2"	45	45
	c. Imperf (pair)	4·50	4·50
	d. Do. No serif to foot of "2"	10·00	
53	1 c. red	65	15
54	12 c. ultramarine	6·00	1·00
	a. No serif to foot of "2"	12·00	2·00

(b) *P* 14

55 **29**	1 c. red	15	12
56	12 c. ultramarine	8·00	1·10
	a. No serif to foot of "2"	15·00	3·00

(Recess Bradbury, Wilkinson)

1882 (Dec). *P* 14.

57 **29**	12 c. greenish blue	10·00	1·50

1883 (15 Dec). OFFICIAL. *Handstamped with Type* O **1**.

(a) *Horizontally*

O57 **29**	1 c. red (*p* 12)	20·00	20·00
O58	1 c. red (*p* 14)	10·00	6·00
O59 **24**	2 c. green (A)	30·00	25·00
	a. Yellow-green (B)	25·00	20·00
O60 **13**	4 c. brown	4·00	3·00
O61 **20**	8 c. lake	5·00	3·50
O62 **29**	12 c. ultramarine (*p* 12)	6·00	4·00
	a. No serif to foot of "2"	12·00	6·00

(b) *Diagonally*

O63 **24**	2 c. green (A)	20·00	
	a. Yellow-green (B)	4·00	3·00
O64 **23**	24 c. deep blue (*roul*)	4·50	3·50
O65 **15**	60 c. black	3·50	3·00

Being handstamped these are found double and inverted, etc.

1884 (From 1 Mar). OFFICIAL. *Optd litho with Type* O **2** *diagonally at various angles.*

(a) *In black*

O66 **33**	½ c. brown	1·50	1·50
	a. Opt inverted	1·50	1·50
O67 **29**	1 c. red (*p* 12)	5·00	5·00
	a. Opt inverted	2·00	2·00
O68	1 c. red (*p* 14)	40	25
	a. Opt inverted	2·25	2·25
O69 **33**	1 c. rose-red	5	5
	a. Opt inverted	12	15
	b. Opt double		
O70 **24**	2 c. yellow-green (B)	10	10
	a. Opt inverted	8·00	4·75
	b. Opt double	8·50	
O71 **13**	4 c. brown	8	10
	a. Opt inverted	4·50	4·00
	b. Chestnut	1·50	1·25
O72 **20**	8 c. lake (*p* 12)	8	8
	a. Opt inverted	9·00	7·00
O73 **10**	10 c. green	7·00	3·00
O74 **29**	12 c. ultramarine (*p* 12)	50	40
	a. No serif to foot of "2"	3·50	3·50
	b. Opt inverted	2·00	

O75	12 c. ultramarine (*p* 14)	30·00	5·00
	a. No serif to foot of "2"		
O76 **33**	12 c. blue	15	12
	a. Opt inverted	6·00	5·00
O77 **21**	16 c. green (*roul*)	20	15
	a. Opt inverted	7·00	
	b. Opt double	1·50	
	c. Opt treble	2·50	
O78 **22**	20 c. blue (*roul*)	75	65
	a. Opt inverted	4·00	
O79 **23**	24 c. deep blue (*roul*)	25	20
	a. Opt inverted	45	45
O80	24 c. deep blue (*p* 12)	20	20
	a. Opt inverted	50	50
O81 **25**	5 c. rosy lake	1·75	1·00
O82 **14**	30 c. orange	3·00	2·25
O83 **15**	60 c. black	2·00	1·50
	a. Opt inverted	7·00	4·00
O84 **16**	90 c. blue	1·50	1·10
	a. Opt inverted	4·00	3·00
	b. Opt double	5·00	

(b) *In red*

O85 **24**	2 c. green (A)	30	30
	a. Opt inverted	3·50	2·00
O86 **13**	4 c. brown	45	30
O87 **23**	24 c. deep blue (*roul*)	2·40	1·25
O88 **15**	60 c. black	2·75	2·00
O89 **16**	90 c. blue	40·00	20·00

Beware of forged overprints.

CUATRO
Centavos
1884

1884
½
(30)

1
c
1884
(31)

CUATRO
Centavos
1884
(32)

1884. *Surch with* T **30/2**.

(a) *On No.* 28 (1 May)

90 **9**	½ c. on 5 c. vermilion (B) (Bk.)	20	20
	a. "1884" omitted	7·00	
	b. Surch inverted	8·00	8·00
	c. Surch double	20·00	
	d. Surch diagonal	1·50	
	e. Pair, one without surch	20·00	

(b) *On No.* 30 (*ground of crossed lines*) (July)

91 **10**	½ c. on 15 c. blue (Bk.)	50	50
	a. Surch inverted	2·00	2·00
	b. Pair, one without surch	30·00	
92	½ c. on 15 c. blue (C.)	25	25
	a. "1884" omitted	6·00	
	b. "½" omitted	6·00	
	c. Surch inverted	1·25	1·25
	d. Pair, one without surch but		
	inserted in ink	35·00	
	e. Surch double	25·00	
	f. Surch on back only	20·00	
93	½ c. on 15 c. blue (Verm.)	—	1·50
94	1 c. on 15 c. blue (C.)	50	50
	a. No line under "1884"	1·40	1·25
	b. Surch double	2·75	
	c. Surch treble	4·00	
95	1 c. on 15 c. (Verm.)	1·75	1·75
	a. No line under "1884"	3·50	3·50
	b. Surch inverted	3·50	3·50

(c) *On No.* 30a (*ground of horiz lines*) (Aug)

96 **10**	½ c. on 15 c. blue (Bk.)	1·75	1·75
97	½ c. on 15 c. blue (C.)	5·00	5·00
98	1 c. on 15 c. blue (C.)	1·10	1·10
	a. No line under "1884"	3·50	3·25
99	1 c. on 15 c. blue (Verm.)	50	50
	a. No line under "1884"	1·40	1·25

(d) *On No.* 28 (Aug)

100 **9**	4 c. on 5 c. vermilion (B) (Bk.)	65	20
	a. "CUATRO" omitted	5·00	2·00
	b. "1884" omitted	5·00	2·00
	c. Surch inverted	1·50	1·50
	d. Surch double	15·00	15·00
	e. Surch diagonal	1·90	
	f. Pair, one surch diag, other omit-		
	ted with "4" inserted in ink	15·00	

33   T 1   T 2

A   B

(Recess American Bank Note Co)

1884 (Aug)–**85.** *P* 12.

101	**33**	½ c. brown	.. ..	8	8
102		1 c. rose-red ..	.. ..	20	5
		a. Bisected (½ c.) (on cover)	..	—	3·00
103		12 c. blue (12.9.85)	.. ..	2·00	15
		a. Greenish blue	.. ..	2·00	15

In Type T **2** the sun is closer to "NACIONAL" than in Type T **1**.

(Litho Juan H. Kidd & Co, Buenos Aires)

1887 (8 Dec). *TELEGRAPH STAMPS USED FOR POSTAGE.* *P* 11½–12.

T104	T **1**	10 c. rose-red	.. ..	10	5
T105	T **2**	10 c. rose-red	.. ..	15	5
T106	T **1**	40 c. blue ..	.. ..	15	8
T107	T **2**	40 c. blue ..	.. ..	15	5

Type T **1** is found with letters of papermaker's watermark "Apicer".

Two dies of 5 c.:—
A. Collar left of chin; cravatte not visible; chin 1½ mm from inner circle.
B. Collar extends under chin, cravatte visible; chin 2½ mm from inner circle.

(Litho Juan H. Kidd & Co, Buenos Aires)

1888 (1 Jan)–**90.** *P* 11½.

108	**34**	½ c. blue (15.1.88)	..	5	5
		a. Imperf (pair)	.. ..	3·50	3·50
		b. Indigo	.. ..	12	10
109	**35**	2 c. yellow-green (A) (20.2.88)	..	1·00	75
		a. Imperf (pair)	..	6·00	
110		2 c. green (B)	..	1·00	75
		a. Imperf between (vert pair)	..	5·00	
		b. Imperf between (horiz pair)	..	3·00	
		c. Imperf (pair)	.. ..	6·00	
111	**36**	2 c. blue-green (24.1.88)	..	15	10
		a. Deep green	.. ..	15	8
		b. Imperf between (vert pair)	..	5·00	
		c. Imperf between (horiz pair)	..	1·00	
112	**37**	5 c. dull rose-red (A)	..	75	20
		a. Imperf between (vert pair)	..	3·00	
113		5 c. bright rose-red (B) (2.88)	..	45	5
		a. Imperf between (vert pair)	..	10·00	
114	**38**	6 c. dull red ..	..		
		a. Imperf between (vert pair)	..	6·00	
		b. Perf 12 ..	.. ..	2·50	2·50
115	**39**	10 c. brown	.. ..	75	8
		a. Imperf (pair)	.. ..	3·00	
116	**40**	15 c. orange	.. ..	50	12
		a. Imperf between (vert pair)	..	25·00	
117	**41**	20 c. green (5.9.88)	..	40	10
		a. Blue-green	.. ..	40	12
118	**42**	25 c. violet (9.6.90)	..	65	12
119	**43**	30 c. brown (20.2.88) ..	..	75	15
		a. Imperf (pair)	.. ..	20·00	15·00
		b. Imperf between (horiz pair)	..		
		c. Reddish chocolate	..		
120	**44**	40 c. slate (20.2.88)	..	6·00	1·50
		a. Perf 12 ..	.. ..	2·75	50
		b. Do. Imperf between (horiz pair)	25·00		
121	**45**	50 c. blue (5.4.88)	..	4·00	50

34 Urquiza   **35** Lopez   **36** Celman

37 Rivadavia   **38** Sarmiento   **39** Avellaneda

40 San Martin   **41** Roca   **42** Belgrano

43 Dorrego   **44** Moreno   **45** Mitre

46 Urquiza   **47** Sarsfield   **48** Sarsfield

49 Derqui   **50** Celman   **51** Rivadavia

Two dies of the 2 c.:—
A. Collar is 1 mm from oval.
B. Collar is 2 mm from oval.

52 Rivadavia

53 Sarmiento

54 Avellaneda

55 Alberdi

56 Moreno

57 Mitre

58 Posadas

(59)

Two dies of 1 c.
T **47**. Wide space between ornament and "CORREOS"; Figures "1" with pronounced serifs.
T **48**. "CORREOS" closer to ornament; serifs almost missing from figures "1".

5 c. In T **51** the head and "CINCO CENTAVOS" are large and in T **52** they are much smaller.

(Recess South American Bank Note Co, Buenos Aires)

1888–91. *Inscr* "CORREOS Y TELEGRAFOS". P 11½×12 *(comb)* or 11½ *(line)*.

No.	T			
122	46	½ c. ultramarine (9.8.89)	5	5
		a. Prussian blue	5	5
		b. Imperf (pair)	1·50	1·50
123	47	1 c. brown (3.11.88)	5	5
		a. Sepia	8	5
		b. Imperf (pair)	80	70
		c. Imperf horiz (vert pair)	2·50	
		d. Imperf between (vert pair)	4·00	
124	48	1 c. brown (10.91)	5	5
125	49	2 c. violet (6.3.90)	5	5
		a. Purple	8	5
		b. Slate	20	8
		c. Imperf (pair)	5·00	
		d. Imperf between (horiz pair)	3·50	
126	50	3 c. blue-green (2.10.89)	8	8
127	51	5 c. rose (12.3.89)	15	5
		a. Imperf (pair)	3·50	3·50
		b. Imperf between (pair)	4·50	4·50
128	52	5 c. carmine-red (8.4.90)	12	5
		a. Dull scarlet	8	5
		b. Imperf (pair)	6·00	5·00
129	53	6 c. slate-blue (21.11.89)	12	8
		a. Greenish blue	50	25
		b. Indigo	1·50	75
		c. Imperf (pair)	10·00	10·00
130	54	10 c. yellowish brown (24.8.90)	15	5
		a. Deep brown	25	8
		b. Imperf between (vert pair)	4·50	
131	55	12 c. deep blue (3.9.90)	25	12
		a. Imperf (pair)	1·50	
		b. Bluish paper	45	15
132	56	40 c. olive-green (21.12.89)	45	5
		a. Imperf (pair)	4·00	
133	57	50 c. orange (3.7.90)	35	12
		a. Imperf (pair)	7·00	
134	58	60 c. blue-black (11.3.90)	90	35
		a. Imperf (pair)	8·00	8·00

No. 123 exists with portions of papermaker's watermark "SL" monogram and two globes inscribed "LA UNION" and Nos. 123 and 126 exist with portions of papermaker's watermark "STILLER & LAAS BUENOS AIRES".

1890 (31 May). (*a*) *Surch with* T **59**, *in black.*

135	**55**	¼ on 12 c. deep blue		5	5
		a. Surch double		3·00	
		b. Bluish paper		20	20

(*b*) *Surch as* T **59** *but with longer fraction bar and value above bars, in red*

136	**55**	¼ on 12 c. deep blue		5	5
		a. Surch double		5·00	5·00
		b. Bluish paper		20	20

Pairs with one stamp without surcharge are known but these were made in Montevideo on stamps which had been gummed on the face and so the surcharge could be washed off. They are without value.

60 Paz

61 Rivadavia

62 San Martin

63 La Madrid

64 G. Brown

(Recess South American Bank Note Co, Buenos Aires)

1890–91. *New values.* P 11½.

137	60	¼ c. green (12.90)		5	5
138	61	8 c. rose-carmine (1.5.91)		12	8
		a. Imperf (pair)		5·00	
139	62	1 p. deep blue (4.91)		3·00	75
140	63	5 p. ultramarine (3.91)		14·00	2·75
141	64	20 p. blue-green (4.91)		20·00	10·00

A 10 p. brown (V. López) and 50 p. vermilion (G. Funes) were prepared but not issued (*Price* £120 *each, un*).

65 Rivadavia

66 Belgrano

67 San Martin

68	**69**
4½ mm diameter	6 mm diameter

(Recess South American Bank Note Co)

1892–98. A. *Paper of local manufacture with impressed wmk,* T **68** (1892–95).

(*a*) P 11½

142	65	½ c. ultramarine (21.10.92)		5	5
		a. Slate-blue		5	5
		b. Imperf (pair)		2·50	
143		1 c. brown (21.10.92)		5	5
		a. Imperf (pair)		3·00	
		b. Imperf horiz (vert pair)		3·00	
		c. Imperf between (vert pair)		4·75	

144 **65**	2 c. yellow-green (10.9.92)	.. ..		5	5
	a. *Blue-green*			5	5
	b. Double impression	.. ..	20·00	20·00
	c. Imperf (pair)			1·50
	d. Imperf horiz (vert pair)	..		1·50
	e. Imperf vert (horiz pair)	..		1·50
145	3 c. orange (19.12.95)	..		5	5
	a. *Orange-yellow*	..		8	5
	b. Imperf between (vert pair)		8·00
146	5 c. rose-red (10.9.92)	..		12	5
	a. Imperf (pair)			2·50	2·00
	b. Double impression	..	20·00	20·00
	c. Imperf horiz (vert pair)	..		1·50
	d. Imperf vert (horiz pair)	..		1·50
	e. Green (error)			45·00	35·00
147 **66**	10 c. dull red (1.9.92)	..		50	5
	a. Imperf (pair)			3·00
	b. Imperf horiz (vert pair)	..		3·00
	c. Imperf vert (horiz pair)	..		3·00
148	12 c. deep blue (6.4.93)	..		30	5
	a. Imperf (pair)			3·00
	b. Imperf horiz (vert pair)	..		3·00
149	16 c. slate (1.9.92)	..		75	5
	a. Imperf (pair)			3·00
150	24 c. sepia (1.9.92)	..		65	5
	a. Imperf (pair)			3·00
151	50 c. deep green (1.9.92)	..		75	5
	a. Imperf (pair)			2·00
152 **67**	1 p. dull red (16.2.93)	..		1·00	75
	a. *Lake*			75	8
	b. Imperf (pair)			2·00
153	2 p. deep green (24.12.92)	..		2·00	25
154	5 p. indigo (24.12.92)	..		3·00	25
142/154	*Set of 13*	.. ..		

(b) P 12

155 **65**	½ c. ultramarine	.. ..		8	5
	a. *Slate-blue*	..		8	5
	b. Imperf horiz (vert pair)	..		5·00
156	1 c. brown	.. ..		15	8
	a. Imperf horiz (vert pair)	..		5·00
157	2 c. green	.. ..		45	10
	a. Imperf horiz (vert pair)	..		3·00
158	3 c. orange	.. ..		65	5
	a. Imperf horiz (vert pair)	..		10·00
159	5 c. rose-red	..		50	5
	a. Imperf horiz (vert pair)	..		3·00
160 **66**	10 c. dull red	..		1·10	8
161	12 c. deep blue	..		1·40	10
162	16 c. slate	..		1·40	8
163	24 c. sepia	..		1·75	25
164	50 c. deep green	..		1·75	25
165 **67**	2 p. deep green	..		5·00	1·00

(c) Perf compound of 11½ and 12

166 **65**	½ c. ultramarine	..		1·10	12
167	1 c. brown	..		65	5
	a. Imperf horiz (vert pair)	..		3·00
168	2 c. green	..		65	12
169	3 c. orange	..		65	30
170	5 c. rose-red	..		65	12
	a. Imperf horiz (vert pair)	..		3·00
171 **66**	10 c. dull red	..		75	12
	a. Imperf horiz (vert pair)	..		3·00
	b. Imperf vert (horiz pair)	..		3·00
172	12 c. deep blue	..		1·00	40
173	16 c. slate	..		1·50	40
174	50 c. deep green	..		1·50	10
175	1 p. dull red	..		3·00	20
176	2 p. deep green	..		

B. *German paper with true wmk T* **69** (Mar 1896–98)
(a) P 11½

177 **65**	½ c. ultramarine	..		5	5
	a. *Slate-blue*	..		5	5
	b. *Indigo* (1898)			5	5
	c. Imperf horiz (vert pair)	..		—	8·00
178	1 c. deep brown	..		5	5
	a. *Yellow-brown*	..		5	5
	b. Imperf horiz (vert pair)	..		5·00
	c. Imperf vert (horiz pair)	..		5·00
179	2 c. blue-green	..		5	5
	a. *Olive-green*	..		15	5
	b. Imperf horiz (vert pair)	..		5·00
	c. Imperf vert (horiz pair)	..		5·00
180	3 c. orange	..		45	20
	a. *Orange-yellow*	..		50	20
	b. Imperf horiz (vert pair)	..		8·00

181 **65**	5 c. rose-carmine	..		5	5
	a. Double impression	..		15·00	7·00
	b. Imperf (pair)			5·00
	c. Imperf horiz (vert pair)	..		5·00
182 **66**	10 c. carmine-red	..		50	5
183	12 c. deep blue	..		15	5
	a. *Slate-blue*	..		20	15
	b. Imperf (pair)			5·00
	c. Imperf horiz (vert pair)	..		5·00
	d. Imperf vert (horiz pair)	..		5·00
184	16 c. slate	..		45	5
185	24 c. sepia	..		50	5
	a. Imperf (pair)			5·00
186	50 c. deep green			65	5
187 **67**	1 p. lake	..		1·60	10
188	2 p. deep green	..		1·25	55
189	5 p. indigo	..		4·00	50

(b) P 12

190 **65**	½ c. slate-blue	..		5	5
	a. *Indigo* (1898)	..		5	5
191	1 c. deep brown	..		8	8
	a. *Yellow-brown*	..		5	5
	b. Imperf horiz (vert pair)	..		5·00
192	2 c. blue-green	..		8	5
	a. *Olive-green*	..		15	5
	b. Imperf horiz (vert pair)	..		5·00
193	3 c. orange	..		45	20
	a. *Orange-yellow*	..		50	20
194	5 c. rose-carmine	..		5	5
	a. Imperf horiz (vert pair)	..		5·00
	b. Imperf vert (horiz pair)	..		—	5·00
195 **66**	10 c. carmine-red	..		50	5
	a. Imperf vert (horiz pair)	..		5·00
196	12 c. deep blue	..		50	8
	a. *Slate-blue*	..		65	10
197	16 c. slate	..		1·00	12
198	24 c. sepia	..		1·00	25
199	50 c. deep green	..		1·60	30
200 **67**	1 p. lake	..		1·60	10
201	5 p. indigo	..		10·00	2·00

(c) Perf compound of 11½ and 12

202 **65**	½ c. slate-blue	..		60	10
	a. *Indigo* (1898)	..		—	65
203	1 c. brown	..		75	15
204	2 c. green	..		35	15
205	3 c. orange	..		45	15
206	5 c. rose-carmine	..		45	5
207 **66**	10 c. rose-red	..		65	15
208	12 c. deep blue	..		50	20
	a. *Slate-blue*	..		4·25	1·25
209	16 c. slate	..		90	40
210	50 c. deep green	..		—	50

70 Fleet of Columbus

(Des E. de Martino. Recess South American Bank Note Co)

1892 (12 Oct). *Fourth Centenary of Discovery of America.*
W **68**. *P* 11½.

211 **70**	2 c. pale blue	..		25	20
	a. Double impression	..		12·00
212	5 c. deep blue	..		35	25

1896–98. *New values.* W **69**. *(a) P* 11½.

213 **66**	30 c. orange (1.2.98)	..		75	10
214	80 c. dull lilac (1.4.96)	..		65	8
215 **67**	1 p. 20, black (25.7.97)	..		75	25

(b) P 12

216 **66**	30 c. orange	..		1·25	8
217	80 c. dull lilac	..		1·25	45
218 **67**	1 p. 20, black	..		1·25	45

(c) Perf compound of 11½ and 12

218 **66**	30 c. orange	..		—	50
219	80 c. dull lilac	..		—	50
220 **67**	1 p. 20, black	..		1·50	50

71   **72**

"Liberty" and Shield

(Des Bosco. Recess South American Bank Note Co)

1899 (12 Oct)–**1903**. *W* **69**. (*a*) *P* 11½.

221	**71**	½ c. brown		5	5
		a. Imperf (pair)	3·00		
		b. Imperf horiz (vert pair)		50	40
		c. Imperf vert (horiz pair)		1·00	80
222		1 c. green		5	5
		a. Imperf (pair)	4·00		
		b. Imperf horiz (vert pair)		75	75
		c. Imperf vert (horiz pair)	3·00		
223		2 c. slate		5	5
		a. Imperf (pair)		75	75
		b. Imperf horiz (vert pair)		15	20
		c. Imperf vert (horiz pair)		30	30
224		3 c. orange (1.2.01)		5	5
		a. Imperf (pair)	8·00	6·00	
		b. Imperf horiz (vert pair)	8·00	6·00	
		c. Imperf vert (horiz pair)	8·00		
225		4 c. yellow (23.12.03)		5	5
		a. Imperf horiz (vert pair)	15·00	12·00	
		b. Imperf vert (horiz pair)	12·00		
226		5 c. carmine		5	5
		a. Imperf (pair)		50	40
		b. Imperf horiz (vert pair)		25	30
		c. Imperf vert (horiz pair)		35	35
227		6 c. black (20.11.03)		5	5
		a. Imperf (pair)	3·00	3·00	
		b. Imperf horiz (vert pair)		50	
		c. Imperf vert (horiz pair)		50	
228		10 c. green		5	5
		a. Imperf (pair)	3·00		
		b. Imperf horiz (vert pair)	3·00	3·00	
		c. Imperf vert (horiz pair)	2·50	2·50	
229		12 c. sky-blue		35	30
		a. Slate-blue		15	8
230		12 c. olive-green (1.2.01)		8	8
		a. Imperf (pair)	3·00		
231		15 c. greenish blue (1.2.01)		8	5
		a. Slate-blue		15	5
		b. Imperf (pair)	3·50		
		c. Imperf horiz (vert pair)		50	
		d. Imperf vert (horiz pair)	1·50	1·50	
232		16 c. orange		75	75
233		20 c. lake		12	5
234		24 c. dull purple		15	10
		a. Deep lilac		15	8
235		30 c. carmine		40	5
236		30 c. pale vermilion (8.2.01)	1·25	12	
		a. Bright scarlet (18.6.01)	2·25	8	
237		50 c. bright blue		35	5
		a. Imperf vert (horiz pair)	7·00		
238	**72**	1 p. black and deep blue		90	8
		a. Imperf (pair)	25·00		
		b. Centre inverted	£150	80·00	
239		5 p. black and brown-orange	3·25	90	
		a. Imperf (pair)	25·00		
		b. Centre inverted	£150		
240		10 p. black and deep green	4·50	1·10	
		a. Imperf (pair)	25·00		
		b. Centre inverted	£700		
241		20 p. black and carmine	14·00	3·25	
		a. Imperf (pair)	25·00		
		b. Centre inverted	*		

*The 5 p. and 10 p. with centre inverted are only known unused and the 20 p. exists only perforated with the word "INUTILIZADO", these having been used on bundles of newspaper before the error was discovered (Price £250).

(*b*) *P* 12

242	**71**	½ c. brown		5	5
		a. Imperf horiz (vert pair)	1·50		
		b. Imperf vert (horiz pair)	1·75		
243	**71**	1 c. green		8	5
		a. Imperf horiz (vert pair)	1·50		
		b. Imperf vert (horiz pair)	2·00		
244		2 c. slate		5	5
		a. Imperf horiz (vert pair)		30	30
		b. Imperf vert (horiz pair)		45	
245		3 c. orange		8	5
246		4 c. yellow		45	10
247		5 c. carmine		15	5
		a. Imperf horiz (vert pair)		40	
		b. Imperf vert (horiz pair)		50	40
248		6 c. black		30	10
		a. Imperf horiz (vert pair)		75	40
		b. Imperf vert (horiz pair)	1·00		
249		10 c. green		15	5
250		12 c. sky-blue		25	10
		a. Slate-blue		35	10
251		12 c. olive-green		45	12
252		15 c. greenish blue		65	5
		a. Imperf horiz (vert pair)	1·40		
		b. Imperf vert (horiz pair)	2·00	1·75	
253		16 c. orange		75	75
254		20 c. lake		25	5
255		24 c. dull purple		25	10
		a. Deep lilac		25	10
256		30 c. carmine		50	5
257		30 c. pale vermilion	1·25	12	
		a. Bright scarlet	2·75	10	
258		50 c. bright blue		50	5
259	**72**	1 p. black and deep blue	5·00	75	

(*c*) *Perf compound of* 11½ *and* 12

260	**71**	½ c. brown		65	12
261		1 c. green		65	12
262		2 c. slate		15	10
263		3 c. orange		65	15
264		5 c. carmine		15	10
265		6 c. black		35	15
266		10 c. green		65	5
267		12 c. sky-blue		75	15
268		12 c. olive-green		45	12
269		15 c. greenish blue		60	5
270		20 c. lake		50	20
271		24 c. dull purple		50	20
		a. Deep lilac		30	15
272		30 c. carmine	1·00	15	
273		30 c. pale vermilion	1·25	15	
274		50 c. bright blue	1·10	15	

Stamps without watermark come from the outer rows of the sheet.

O 3   **73** Port Rosario

(Recess South American Bank Note Co)

1901 (1 Dec). OFFICIAL. *No wmk.* (*a*) *P* 11½.

O275	**O 3**	1 c. grey		5	5
		a. Imperf (pair)	1·00		
		b. Imperf horiz (vert pair)	1·25		
		c. Imperf vert (horiz pair)	1·00		
O276		2 c. brown		5	5
		a. Imperf (pair)	1·00		
		b. Imperf horiz (vert pair)	1·25		
O277		5 c. red		5	5
		a. Imperf (pair)	1·25		
O278		10 c. deep green		5	5
		a. Imperf (pair)	1·25		
O279		30 c. blue		15	12
		a. Imperf (pair)	1·25		
O280		50 c. orange		12	8
		a. Imperf (pair)	1·25		

(*b*) *P* 12

O281	**O 3**	1 c. grey		25	15
		a. Imperf horiz (vert pair)	1·25		
O282		2 c. brown		35	20
O283		5 c. red		40	20
O284		10 c. deep green		20	8
O285		50 c. orange		50	

(c) Perf compound of 11½ and 12

O286	O 3	1 c. grey	..	..	..	..	10	5
O287		2 c. brown					10	5
O288		5 c. red					15	5
O289		10 c. deep green	..	..	..		45	30

(Recess South American Bank Note Co)

1902 (26 Oct). *Completion of Port Rosario Docks.* W **69**. P 11½.

290	**73**	5 c. deep blue..	..	..	..	30	20
		a. Imperf (pair)	..	..	..	6·00	
		b. Imperf horiz (vert pair)	..	..	6·00	
		c. Imperf vert (horiz pair)	..	..	5·00	
		d. Perf 11½×12	..	..	..	30	20

74   **75**

General San Martin

(Typo Mint, Buenos Aires)

1908–9. W **69**. A. *P* 13½. B. *P* 13½×12½.

			A	B		
291	**74**	½ c. violet (3.10.09) ..	†	5	5
292		1 c. ochre (15.6.09) ..	†	5	5
293		2 c. choc (20.2.08) ..	5	5	5	5
294		3 c. green (8.1.09) ..	5	5	5	5
295		4 c. mauve (29.12.08)	5	5	5	5
296		5 c. pink (29.2.08) ..	5	5	5	5
		a. Rose-carmine ..	5	5	5	5
297		6 c. bistre (6.8.09) ..	†		5	5
298		10 c. slate-green				
		(20.1.09)	10	5	5	5
299		12 c. ochre (28.11.08)	5	5		†
300		12 c. blue (10.2.09) ..	10	5	5	5
301		15 c. yellow-green				
		(22.7.08) ..	5	5		†
302		20 c. ultram (1.10.09)		†	5	5
303		24 c. lake-brown				
		(29.11.09)	12	8	20	5
304		30 c. claret (11.1.09) ..	25	8	20	8
305		50 c. black (12.6.09) ..		†	20	5
306	**75**	1 p. rose and light				
		blue (10.12.09) ..	60	15		†
		a. Rose and indigo	12·00	4·00		†
293A/306A		Set of 11	..	1·00	55	
2291B/305B		Set of 13			1·00	60

The ½, 1, 5, 12 blue and 24 c. have watermark Type **69** and the remaining values have a similar watermark but with wavy sunrays. Stamps without watermark come from the outer rows of the sheets so that pairs, with and without watermark can be found.

The 1 c. in blue was prepared but not issued as it could be confused with the 12 c. which had to be blue to conform with the U.P.U. regulations. (*Price £45 un.*)

Nos. 307 to 365 are no longer used.

76 Pyramid of May   **77** Meeting at Peña's House

78 Azcuenaga and Alberti   **79** Fort of the Viceroys, Buenos Aires

80 Saavedra   **81** Congress Building

82 First National   **83** Crowds on 25   **84** Centenary
Council   May 1810   Monument

(Recess South American Bank Note Co)

1910 (1 May). *Centenary of Deposition of the Spanish Viceroy. Various designs inscr "1810–1910" as T* **76** *to* **84**. W **69**. *P* 11½.

366	**76**	½ c. bright and dull blue	..	..	5	5
		a. Centre inverted ..		..	60·00	
367	–	1 c. black and blue-green	..	..	10	5
		a. Centre inverted ..		..	60·00	
368	**77**	2 c. black and olive-green	..	..	10	5
		a. Centre inverted ..		..	35·00	
369	**78**	3 c. bright green	..	..	10	10
370	**79**	4 c. blue-green and blue	..	..	10	10
		a. Centre inverted ..		..	35·00	
371	**80**	5 c. carmine ..	..	..	10	5
372	–	10 c. black and brown	..	..	15	10
373	**81**	12 c. blue	..	..	..	15	10
		a. Centre inverted ..		..	60·00	
374	–	20 c. black and sepia ..		..	15	12
375	**82**	24 c. steel-blue and brown	..	..	20	15
376	–	30 c. black and lilac ..		..	20	10
377	**83**	50 c. black and rose ..		..	45	15
		a. Centre inverted ..		..	60·00	
378	–	1 p. deep blue	..	..	1·00	50
379	–	5 p. purple and orange	..	..	7·50	5·00
		a. Centre inverted ..		..	60·00	
380	**84**	10 p. black and orange	..	..	19·00	11·00
381	–	20 p. black and dull blue	..	..	20·00	20·00
366/381		Set of 16	..	..	..	50·00	35·00

Designs: *Vert*—20 p. San Martin. *Horiz*—1 c. Peña and Vieytes; 10 c. Distribution of badges; 20 c. Castelli and Matheu; 30 c. Belgrano and Larrea; 1 p. Moreno and Paso; 5 p. Oath of the Junta.

90   **91**   **92**

(Litho Mint, Buenos Aires)

1911 (15 May). *Birth Centenary of Pres. Sarmiento.* W **69**. *P* 13½.

382	**90**	5 c. black and brown ..	..	..	12	12

(Eng J. M. Lubary. Recess American Bank Note Co)

1911 (10 Nov). *Wmk as W* **69** *but with centre blank.*

383	**91**	5 c. rose	..	..	5	5
384		12 c. blue	..	..	15	5

PRINTERS. All the following were printed at the Mint, Buenos Aires, *unless otherwise stated.*

1911 (4 Dec)–**12.** *Typo. W* **69.** *P* 13½ × 12½.

385	**92**	½ c. violet	..	..	5	5
386		1 c. yellow-brown	..	..	5	5
387		2 c. brown	..	..	5	5
		a. Perf 13½	..	..	30	12
388		3 c. green	..	..	5	5
389		4 c. dull purple	..	..	5	5
390		10 c. sage-green	..	..	20	5
391		20 c. ultramarine	..	..	25	8
392		24 c. red-brown	..	..	40	15
393		30 c. claret	..	..	15	5
394		50 c. black	..	..	60	10
385/394		*Set of 10*	..	..	1·60	60

All values were issued with the wavy sunrays version of watermark Type **69** and all except the 2 c. also exist with the straight rays version (issued 14 March 1912). Stamps without watermark come from the outer rows.
See also Nos. 413/5.

93 (Vert)    **94**

1912 (26 July)–**15.** *Wmk Honeycomb, T* **93.** *P* 13½ × 12½.
I. *Vertical wmk.*   II. *Horizontal wmk*

					I.		II.	
395	**92**	½ c. violet	..	..	5	5	5	5
		a. Perf 13½	..	..	15	8		†
396		1 c. yellow-brown	..		5	5	5	5
		a. Perf 13½	..	..	15	5	15	8
397		2 c. brown	..	..	5	5	5	5
		a. Perf 13½	..	..	15	5	25	12
398		3 c. green	..	..	5	5	5	5
		a. Perf 13½	..	..	2·00	1·50		†
399		4 c. dull purple	..		5	5	5	5
		a. Perf 13½	..	..	35	20		†
400		5 c. rose	..	..	5	5	5	5
		a. Perf 13½	..	..	8	5		†
401		10 c. sage-green	..	..	8	5	15	8
402		12 c. blue	..	..	8	5	10	5
		a. Perf 13½	..	..	1·50	45	12	5
403		20 c. ultramarine	..	..	25	5		†
		a. Perf 13½	..	..	50	12		†
404		24 c. red-brown	..	..	35	8		†
405		30 c. claret	..	..	20	8		†
406		50 c. black	..	..	1·00	15		†

Owing to non-arrival of supplies of German paper, in 1915 these stamps were printed temporarily on Italian paper. In the former the watermark is blurred and indistinct, while in the latter it is sharp and clear.

1912–15. *W* **93.** *P* 13½.

(a) Horizontal wmk

408	**94**	1 p. rose and slate-blue (26.12.12)	..	60	15
409		5 p. green and slate-grey (7.3.13)	..	2·25	75
410		10 p. blue and violet (7.3.13)	..	10·00	2·25
411		20 p. dull claret and blue (7.3.13)	..	27·00	11·00

(b) Vertical wmk

412	**94**	20 p. dull claret and blue (10.15)	..	40·00

DEPARTMENTAL OFFICIAL STAMPS. Between 1913 and 1938 contemporary postage stamps were overprinted with initials for use in various Ministerial Offices and these Departmental Official stamps are listed in tabular form for convenience of reference at the end of the country. In 1938 stamps were overprinted "SERVICIO OFICIAL" for general official use and these are given in chronological order in the main list.

1915. *No wmk. P* 13½ × 12½.

413	**92**	1 c. yellow-brown	..	..	5	5
414		2 c. brown	..	..	5	5
416		5 c. rose	..	..	5	5

The paper of Nos. 413/6 was made in France. This printing precedes that on the Italian paper with watermark Type **93**. The ½ c. is also known, but only with overprint "AHORRO POSTAL" for fiscal use.

95 Dr. F. N.   **96** Declaration of   **97** San Martin
Laprida   Independence

1916 (9 July). *Independence Centenary. Litho. W* **93** (I. *Vert* II. *Horiz*).

(a) P 13½ × 12½

					I.		II.	
417	**95**	½ c. violet	..		5	5	5	5
		a. Perf 13½	..		5	5	5	5
418		1 c. buff	..		5	5	8	5
		a. Perf 13½	..		5	5	8	5
419		2 c. chocolate	..		5	5	5	5
420		3 c. green	..	..	5	5	5	5
421		4 c. purple	..	..	5	5	5	5

(b) P 13½

422	**96**	5 c. rose	..	5	5 14·00	35
423		10 c. grey-green	..	5	5	†
424	**97**	12 c. blue	..		5	5
425		20 c. ultramarine	..	†	10	5
426		24 c. red-brown	..	†	15	12
427		30 c. claret	..	†	15	12
428		50 c. grey-black	..	†	20	8
429		1 p. rose & slate-blue	†	1·00	50	
430		5 p. grn & slate-grey	†	15·00	8·50	
431		10 p. blue and violet	..	†	18·00	15·00
432		20 p. claret and slate		†	22·00	15·00
417/432		*Set of 16 (cheapest)*		50·00	35·00	

The peso values differ from T **97** in the frame design.

98 San Martin    **99** San Martin    **100** Dr. Juan
                                          Pujol

1917 (1 Jan)–**21.** *Litho. P* 13½. *W* **93** (I. *Vert,* II. *Horiz*).

					I		II	
433	**98**	½ c. violet	..		5	5	— 70·00	
		a. Deep lilac (1918)		5	5		†
		b. Perf 13½ × 12½	..	5	5		†
434		1 c. buff	..		5	5	5	5
		a. Perf 13½ × 12½		5	5	60	15
435		2 c. chocolate	..		5	5	8	5
		a. Perf 13½ × 12½		5	5	8	5
436		3 c. green	..		8	5	30	12
		a. Perf 13½ × 12½		8	5	12	8
437		4 c. purple-brown	..		8	5		†
		a. Perf 13½ × 12½	..	10	5		†
		b. Brown-pur (1918)		8	5		†
		ba. Perf 13½ × 12½	..	10	8		†
438		5 c. vermilion	..		8	5	8	5
		a. Perf 13½ × 12½		8	5	8	5
		b. Rosine (1918)		8	5	8	5
		ba. Perf 13½ × 12½		8	5	5	5
		c. Imperf (pair)	3·00	—	2·00	—
439		10 c. grey-green	..		15	5		†
		a. Perf 13½ × 12½		12	5		†

Horizontal wmk

440	**99**	12 c. blue	..	..	5	5
		a. Vertical wmk	..	..	9·00	4·50
441		20 c. ultramarine	..	..	8	5

442	**99**	24 c. red-brown	.. .. ..	30	20
443		30 c. claret	.. .. ..	30	12
444		50 c. grey-black	.. .. ..	35	12
445		1 p. rose & slate-bl ..	.. ..	25	5
		a. Verm & bl (1921)	.. ..	40	5
446		5 p. grn & slate-grey	.. ..	1·50	35
447		10 p. blue and violet ..	.. ..	4·50	1·10
448		20 p. claret and slate	.. ..	5·50	3·50
		a. Centre inverted	.. ..	75·00	
433/448		Set of 16 (cheapest)	.. ..	11·00	5·00

The peso values differ from T **99** in details of the frame design, etc.

1918 (15 June). *Birth Centenary of Dr. J. Pujol. Litho.* W **93** (horiz). P 13½.

449	**100**	5 c. grey and bistre ..	.. ..	8	8

1918 (July). *Litho. No wmk.* A. P 13½ × 12½. B. P 13½.

				A		B	
450	**98**	½ c. violet ..	..	5	5	5	5
		a. Dull mauve	..	5	5	5	5
451		1 c. buff	..	5	5	5	5
452		2 c. chocolate	..	5	5	5	5
		a. Grey-brown	..	5	5	5	5
453		3 c. green	..	5	5	5	5
454		4 c. purple ..	..	8	5	5	5
		a. Claret	..	8	5	5	5
455		5 c. red ..	..	5	5	5	5
		a. Vermilion	..	5	5	5	5
456		10 c. grey-green	..	8	5	5	5
457	**99**	12 c. dull blue	..	†		5	5
458		20 c. ultramarine	..	†		5	5
		a. Pale blue	..	†		8	5
459		24 c. red-brown	..	†		15	10
460		30 c. lilac-rose	..	†		10	5
		a. Claret	..	†		15	5
461		50 c. grey-black	..	†		30	5
450B/461B		Set of 12 ..				85	50

Stamps can be found with letters from later printings on papers bearing papermaker's watermarks "SERRA BOND" and "WHEATLEY BOND A&W CO HIC ET UBIQUE". Later printings were on paper completely without watermark.

101

1920 (Feb). *Litho. Wmk Mult Small Sun RA, T* **101**.

A. P 13½ × 12½. B. P 13½

				A		B	
462	**98**	½ c. dull mauve	..	5	5	5	5
463		1 c. buff ..	..	5	5	5	5
464		2 c. chocolate	..	5	5	8	5
465		3 c. green ..	..	5	5	10	5
466		4 c. purple ..	..	8	5		†
467		5 c. red ..	..	5	5	12	5
468		10 c. grey-green	..	12	5	1·00	40
469	**99**	12 c. dull blue	..	†		8	5
470		20 c. ultramarine	..	†		15	5
471		30 c. claret	..	†		30	8
472		50 c. black	..	†		35	8
462/472		Set of 11 (cheapest)				1·10	50

See also Nos. 481/7, 500/10 and 512.

102 Mausoleum of Belgrano  | **103** Creation of Argentine Flag  | **104** Gen. Belgrano

---

1920 (18 June). *Death Centenary of Gen: Belgrano. Litho.* W **101**. P 13½.

478	**102**	2 c. rose-red	..	8	8
		a. Perf 13½ × 12½ ..	.. ..	8	8
479	**103**	5 c. blue and rose-lake	..	12	8
480	**104**	12 c. blue and pale green	..	20	15

105

1920 (July–Aug). *Wmk Large Sun, T* **105**. *Litho.*

A. P 13½ × 12½. B. P 13½

				A		B	
481	**98**	½ c. violet ..	..	20	15	†	
482		1 c. buff	..	35	15	†	
483		2 c. chocolate	..	20	15	20	8
484		5 c. rose	..	20	5	1·25	25
485		10 c. grey-green	..	20	5	1·00	8
486	**99**	12 c. blue	..	†		95·00	10·00
487		20 c. ultramarine	..	†		85	15

This paper was intended to be used for fiscal stamps.

106 Gen. Urquiza    **107** Gen. Mitre

1920 (11 Nov). *Gen. Urquiza's Victory at Cepeda. Litho.* P 13½. (a) W **101**.

488	**106**	5 c. grey-blue	.. ..	8	5
		a. "PEPUBLICA"	..	2·50	1·50

(b) W **105**

489	**106**	5 c. grey-blue	..	40·00	30·00
		a. "PEPUBLICA"	..		

1921 (26 June). *Birth Centenary of Gen. Mitre. Litho. No wmk.* P 13½.

490	**107**	2 c. chocolate	.. ..	8	5
491		5 c. blue	.. ..	8	5

108    **109**    **110**

1921 (25 Aug). *First Pan-American Postal Congress. Litho. No wmk.* P 13½.

492	**108**	3 c. pale lilac	.. ..	8	8
493		5 c. blue	.. ..	8	5
494		10 c. chocolate	.. ..	12	8
495		12 c. carmine	.. ..	15	12
492/495		Set of 4	.. ..	40	30

1921. *Litho. No wmk.* A. P 13½ × 12½. B. P 13½.

				A		B	
496	**109**	5 c. rose (26.9)	..	8	5	10	5
497	**110**	5 c. rose (30.10)	..	10	5	10	5

No. 496 (inscribed "BUENOS AIRES—AGOSTO DE 1921") was issued as a temporary measure owing to the discovery that forgeries of the 5 c., Type **98**, were in circulation. All 5 c. stamps Type **98** were invalidated on 1 October 1921. The forgeries were perf 11½.

Litho   Typo

Differences

111

Vertical distance between suns is 20 mm. See also similar watermark Type **179**.

1921 (Dec). *Wmk Mult Large Sun RA, T* **111**. *Litho.*

A. *P* 13½ × 12½.   B. *P* 13½.

			A		B	
498	**109**	5 c. rose	8	5	15	8
499	**110**	5 c. rose	5	5	20	5

See also No. 511.

1922 (Feb). *Wmk Mult Large Sun RA, T* **111**. *Litho.*

A. *P* 13½ × 12½.   B *P* 13½.

			A		B	
500	**98**	½ c. violet	5	5	5	5
501		1 c. buff	5	5	8	5
502		2 c. chocolate	5	5	8	5
503		3 c. green	8	5	5	5
504		4 c. purple	60	40	8	5
505		10 c. grey-green	8	5	20	5
506	**99**	12 c. blue	†	5	5	5
507		20 c. ultramarine	†	8	5	
508		24 c. red-brown	†	65	5	
509		30 c. claret	†	50	5	
500/509		*Set of 10 (cheapest)*	†	1·40	55	

1923. *Mock wmk on face as T* **111**. *Litho.* A. *P* 13½ × 12½. B. *P* 13½.

			A		B	
510	**98**	2 c. chocolate (31.8)	20	10	20	10
511	**110**	5 c. rose (16.8)	8	5	25	5
512	**99**	20 c. ultramarine	†		80	15

This "watermark" shows clearly on the face of the stamp, but not when the stamp is looked through.

112   San Martin   **113**

1923 (May). *Litho. With stop below "c" of value. W* **111**.

A. *P* 13½ × 12½. B. *P* 13½.

			A		B	
513	**112**	½ c. purple	5	5	5	5
514		1 c. buff	5	5	8	5
515		2 c. deep brown	5	5	5	5
516		3 c. green	8	5	10	5
517		4 c. plum	5	5	8	5
518		5 c. scarlet	5	5	10	5
519		10 c. grey-green	25	5	20	8
520		12 c. blue	5	5	30	8
521		20 c. ultramarine	10	5	35	5
522		24 c. chocolate	20	10	60	15
523		30 c. claret	5	5	70	8
524		50 c. black	1·50	15	40	5

W **93** (*horiz*). *P* 13½

525	**113**	1 p. scarlet and blue		45	5
526		5 p. grn & grey-lilac		2·10	60
527		10 p. blue and claret		6·00	2·00
528		20 p. lake and slate		8·00	3·00
513/528		*Set of 16 (cheapest)*		16·00	5·00

The 2 c., 5 c., 20 c., 5 p., 10 p. and 20 p. were issued on the 11th May and the remainder on the 24th May.

Lithographed. Shading of face and whiskers is light and delicate; outer frame does not show in relief on back of unused stamps; small perforation holes.

Typographed. Shading is heavy and more extensive, leaving less white on forhead, cheek and chin; outer frame shows in relief on back of unused stamps; large perforation holes, Used for coil stamps only.

1924–31. *Litho. W* **111**. (*a*) *As T* **112** *but without stop below "c" of value. P* 13½ × 12½.

529	**112**	½ c. purple		5	5
		a. Vert pair, one without stop		15	8
		b. Perf 13½		60	25
530		1 c. buff		5	5
		a. Vert pair, one without stop		20	8
531		2 c. deep brown		5	5
		a. Vert pair, one without stop		15	8
532		3 c. green		5	5
		a. Vert pair, one without stop		20	10
		b. Typo (coil) (1931)		12	5
533		4 c. plum		5	5
		a. Vert pair, one without stop		20	10
534		5 c. scarlet		5	5
		a. Vert pair, one without stop		25	20
		b. Perf 13½		40	10
		c. Typo (coil) (1931)		20	5
535		10 c. grey-green		5	5
		a. Perf 13½		40	20
		b. Typo (coil) (1931)		55	5
536		12 c. blue		5	5
		a. Vert pair, one without stop		30	
		b. Typo (coil) (1931)		45	8
537		20 c. ultramarine		8	5
		a. Vert pair, one without stop		25	10
		b. Typo (coil) (1931)		2·25	20
538		24 c. chocolate		12	8
		a. Vert pair, one without stop		35	
		b. Perf 13½		40	10
		ba. Vert pair, one without stop		1·00	
539		25 c. bright violet		5	5
		a. Typo (coil) (1931)		95	8
540		30 c. claret		8	5
		a. Vert pair, one without stop		35	12
		b. Typo (coil) (1931)		80	5
541		50 c. black		10	5

(*b*) *T* **113**. *P* 13½

542	**113**	1 p. scarlet and blue		25	5
543		5 p. green and purple		1·60	15
544		10 p. blue and claret		3·75	60
545		20 p. lake and slate-blue		5·50	2·00
529/545		*Set of 17*		10·00	2·75

The peso values were issued in May and June 1924 and the remainder on 1 August 1924.

Between 1924 and 1930 printings were made on a wide range of papers and there were also variations in the watermark.

114 Bernardino Rivadavia    **115** Rivadavia    **116** San Martin

117 G.P.O., 1926   **118** G.P.O., 1826

1926 (8 Feb). *Rivadavia Centenary. Litho.* W **111**. *P* 13½.
546	**114**	5 c. rose	..	..	..	5	5

1926 (1 July). *Postal Centenary. Litho.* W **111**. *P* 13½ × 12½
(3 c., 5 c.) or 13½ (*others*).
547	**115**	3 c. green	..	..		5	5
548	**116**	5 c. red	..	..		5	5
549	**117**	12 c. blue	..	..		10	5
		a. "1925" for "1926"	..	..	1·10	60
550	**118**	25 c. brown	..	..		12	5
		a. "1326" for "1826" above view	40	25
		b. "LE CORREOS"	..	..	1·50	1·25
547/550		*Set of 4*	..	..	..	50	12

119 "Ahorro Postal" (*horiz*)

1927 (15 Sept)–**30**. *Litho. Postal Savings stamp paper.*
W **119** (*vert on* 5 c., 1 p.). *T* **112** (*no stop*) *or* **113**. *P* 13½
(1 p.) *or* 13½ × 12½ (*others*).
551	**112**	½ c. purple	..	..		5	5
		a. Pair, one with stop	..		80	50
		b. Very thin paper (1930)	..		12	8
552		1 c. buff	..	..		5	5
553		2 c. deep brown	..	..		5	5
		a. Very thin paper (1930)	..		5	5
554		5 c. scarlet	..	..		5	5
		a. Pair, one with stop	..		1·00	50
		b. Very thin paper (1930)	..		8	8
555		10 c. grey-green	..	..		25	8
		a. Pair, one with stop	..		1·50	1·00
556		20 c. ultramarine	..	..	1·25	30
557	**113**	1 p. scarlet and blue	..		2·25	80
551/557		*Set of 7*	..	..		3·50	1·10

120   **121**

122   **123**

1928 (28 Feb). *AIR. Litho.* W **111**. *P* 13 × 13½ (*vert*) *or*
13½ × 13 (*horiz*).
558	**120**	5 c. rose-red	..	..		20	15
		a. Double impression	..		25·00	
559		10 c. greenish blue	..	..		35	25
560	**121**	15 c. chocolate	..	..		35	25
561	**120**	18 c. slate-violet	..	..		85	85
		a. Deep slate-violet	..		85	85
		b. Double impression	..		25·00	
562	**121**	20 c. ultramarine	..	..		50	25
563		24 c. blue	..	..		65	25
564	**122**	25 c. violet	..	..		65	35
565		30 c. carmine-rose	..	..		60	30
566	**123**	35 c. pale claret	..	..		40	30
567	**120**	36 c. bistre	..	..		65	65
		a. Deep bistre	..		50	50
568	**123**	50 c. grey-black	..	..		60	20
569	**121**	54 c. maroon	..	..		65	60
570		72 c. yellow-green	..	..		60	50
		a. "SERVICIQ"	..			
		b. Double impression	..		25·00	
571	**122**	90 c. purple-brown	..	..	1·25	45
		a. "SOBPETASA"	..			
572		1 p. scarlet and blue	..		1·25	20
573		1 p. 08, blue and carmine	..	2·25	80
574	**123**	1 p. 26, green and violet	..	3·50	2·00
575		1 p. 60, claret and blue	..	3·00	2·25
576		3 p. 60, blue and grey	..	5·50	3·75
558/576		*Set of 19 (cheapest)*	..		21·00	12·00

124 Arms of Argentina and   **125** Torch
Brazil   illuminating New
                                     World

1928 (27 Aug). *Centenary of Peace Agreement with Brazil.*
Litho. W **111**. *P* 12½ × 13.
577	**124**	5 c. red	..	..	..	15	8
578		12 c. blue	..	..	..	20	10

1929 (12 Oct). *"Day of the Race." T* **125** *and horiz designs*
inscr "12 DE OCTUBRE". *Litho.* W **111**. *P* 13½.
579		2 c. chocolate	..	..		10	5
580		5 c. red	..	..		10	5
581		12 c. dull blue	..	..		12	8

Designs:—5 c. Symbolical figures, Spain and Argentina;
12 c. America offering laurels to Columbus.

(128)

(Optd by G. Kraft, Buenos Aires)

1930. *AIR. "Zeppelin" Europe Pan-American Flight. Optd*
with T **128**.

(a) Blue overprint (19.5.30)
582	**121**	20 c. ultramarine	..	..	2·75	2·25
583	**123**	50 c. grey-black	..	..	3·25	2·75
		a. Opt inverted	..	..	£100	
584	**122**	1 p. scarlet and blue	..	3·25	2·75
		a. Opt inverted	..	..	£120	
585	**123**	1 p. 80, claret and blue	..	9·00	9·00
586		3 p. 60, blue and grey	..	24·00	24·00
582/586		*Set of 5*	..	..	38·00	35·00

(b) Green overprint (21.5.30)
587	**121**	20 c. ultramarine	..	..	1·50	1·50
588	**123**	50 c. grey-black	..	..	1·90	1·90
589	**122**	90 c. purple-brown	..	1·90	1·90
590		1 p. scarlet and blue	..	3·00	3·00
591	**123**	1 p. 80, claret and blue	..	£120	£120
587/591		*Set of 5*	..	..	£120	£120

GRAF ZEPPELIN
1932
(133)

129 Soldier and Civilian Insurgents

130 The Victorious March, 6 Sept 1930

134 Refrigerating Plant

1930 (28 Nov)–**31**. *Revolution of 6 Sept. Litho. W* **111.**
P 13½×12½ **(129)** *or* 12½×13.

592	**129**	½ c. slate-violet	..	..	5	5
593		1 c. grey-green (16.3.31)	..	..	5	5
594	**130**	2 c. purple	..	..	5	5
595	**129**	3 c. green (16.12.30)	..	..	5	5
596		4 c. pale violet	..	..	8	5
597		5 c. scarlet ..	..	..	5	5
598		10 c. slate-black (16.12.30)	..	..	20	8
599	**130**	12 c. blue (7.12.30)	..	..	12	5
600		20 c. buff (7.12.30) ..	..	..	8	5
601		24 c. Venetian red (5.1.31)	..	..	35	25
602		25 c. green (16.12.30)	..	..	40	30
603		30 c. bright violet (16.12.30)	..	..	65	35
604		50 c. black (16.12.30)	..	1·00	50
605		1 p. carmine and blue (5.1.31)	..	2·00	1·50
606		2 p. orange and grey-black (5.1.31)	3·00	1·60
607		5 p. grey-black & dull green (5.1.31)	7·50	6·00
608		10 p. ultramarine and lake (12.1.31)	11·00	5·00
609		20 p. blue and yellow-green (12.1.31)	32·00	16·00
610		50 p. violet and blue-green (12.1.31)	£110	75·00
592/610	*Set of* 19	..	..	..	£150	95·00

1931 (16 Mar–11 July). *Type and colours changed. Litho.
W* **111.** *P* 12½×13.

611	**130**	½ c. purple ..	..	..	5	5
612		1 c. slate-black	..	..	8	8
613		3 c. green (11.7)	..	..	5	5
614		4 c. deep lake	..	..	8	5
615		5 c. scarlet ..	..	..	5	5
		a. Aeroplane missing in upper left corner	..	..	30	35
616		10 c. grey-green (11.7)	..	..	15	8
611/616	*Set of* 6	..	..	..	40	30

·6·   **6**
Septiembre   Septiembre
1930 · 1931   - 1931 -

(131)   (132)

1931 (6 Sept). *First Anniv of 1930 Revolution. Contemporary
types variously optd as T* **131** *and* **132.** *W* **111.**

(a) T **112** *(no stop) and* **113**

617	**112**	3 c. green (R.)	..	..	5	5
		a. Large "S"	..	..	5	5
618		10 c. grey-green (R.)	..	..	5	8
		a. Large "S"	..	..	8	5
619		30 c. claret (G.)	..	..	45	45
		a. Large "S"	..	..	20	15
620		50 c. black (R.)	..	..	60	60
		a. Large "S"	..	..	20	15
621	**113**	1 p. scarlet and blue (B.)	..	60	60
622		5 p. green and purple (B.)	..	3·00	1·75

(b) Revolution Issue

623	**130**	2 p. orange and grey-black (Bk.)	..	95	75

(c) AIR

624	**120**	18 c. slate-violet (R.)	..	..	1·00	1·00
625	**121**	72 c. green (R.)	..	..	1·00	1·00
626	**122**	90 c. purple-brown (R.)	..	1·25	1·00
		a. "SOBPETASA"	..	..		
627	**123**	1 p. 80, claret and blue (B.)	..	2·50	2·50
628		3 p. 60, blue and grey (R.) ..	..	5·00	5·00
617/628	*Set of* 12	..	..	13·00	13·00

No. 623 is overprinted in one line, Nos. 624/5 in four lines
and Nos. 626/8 in two. The "S" extends to well below the
rest of the line in the large "S" variety.

1932 (4 Aug). *AIR. "Zeppelin" stamps. Optd as T* **133.**

629	**120**	5 c. rose-red (B.)	..	..	1·40	1·25
630		18 c. slate-violet (R.)..	..	..	1·75	1·75
631	**122**	90 c. purple-brown (R.)	..	3·50	3·50
		a. "SOBPETASA"				

The words "GRAF ZEPPELIN" are extended in one line on
No. 631.

1932 (25 Aug). *Sixth International Refrigeration Congress.
Litho. W* **111.** *P* 13½×12½.

632	**134**	3 c. green ..	..	..	10	5
633		10 c. scarlet ..	..	..	10	5
634		12 c. blue	..	..	15	8

135 Port La Plata   **136** Pres. J. A. Roca

1933 (14 Jan). *50th Anniv of Founding of La Plata. T* **135/6**
and similar horiz designs inscr "CINCUENTENARIO DE LA
FUNDACION" *etc. Litho. W* **111.** *P* 13½×13 *or* 13×13½
(10 *c.*).

635		3 c. brown-purple and green	..	..	8	8
636		10 c. purple and orange ..	..	..	8	5
637		15 c. blue	..	..	45	35
638		20 c. brown and purple ..	..	30	20
639		30 c. claret and blue-green	..	1·40	1·10
635/639	*Set of* 5	..	..	2·10	1·60

Design:—15 c. Municipal buildings; 20 c. La Plata Cathedral; 30 c. Dr. Dardo Rocha.

139 Christ of the Andes   **140** Buenos Aires Cathedral

1934 (1 Oct). *32nd International Eucharistic Congress.
Buenos Aires. Litho. W* **111.** *P* 13×13½ *or* 13½×13 (15 *c.*).

640	**139**	10 c. pink and maroon	..	..	20	10
641	**140**	15 c. grey-blue and blue	..	..	20	10

141   **142** "Friendship"   **143** D. F. Sarmiento

1935 (15 May). *Visit of Brazilian President. Litho.* W **111.** P 13 × 13½.

642	**141**	10 c. red	..	5	5
643	**142**	15 c. dull blue	..	8	5

1935 (1 Oct)–**36.** *Various portraits as* T **143.** W **111.** (a) Litho. P 13½ × 13.

644		½ c. purple (Belgrano)		5	5
645		1 c. yellow-brown (Type **143**)..		5	5
646		2 c. grey-brown (Urquiza)		5	5
647		3 c. green (San Martin)		5	5
648		4 c. pearl-grey (Brown)		5	5
649		5 c. orange-brown (Moreno) ..		5	5
650		6 c. sage-green (Alberdi)		5	5
651		12 c. maroon (Mitre)		5	5
652		20 c. pale blue ("JUAN MARTIN GÜEMES")		10	5
653		20 c. pale blue ("MARTIN GÜEMES") (24.11.36) ..		5	5

(b) *Typo.* P 13½

653a	1 c. yellow-brown (Type **143**)..		5	5
653b	5 c. orange-brown (Urquiza)		5	5
	c. Tête-bêche (vert pair)		40	25
653d	10 c. scarlet (Rivadavia)		5	5
	e. Perf 13½ × 13		5	5
644/653d	Set of 13 ..		90	75

The 10 c. red lithographed, imperforate and without watermark is a forgery.

For other stamps as T **143** see Nos. 671, etc. W **111**; 701/16, W **179**; 747/64, no wmk, also Nos. 894/5b.

1935 (17 Oct). *Philatelic Exhibition, Buenos Aires* (EX. Fl. B.A.). T **112** (*without stop*) *in block of four, in sheet. Litho.* W **111.** *Imperf.*

MS654   83 × 100 mm. 10 c. grey-green (sold at 1 p.)   ..   ..   1·75   1·75

146 Prize Bull

147 Ploughman

148 Patagonien Ram

149 Sugar Cane and Factory

150 Petroleum Well

151 South America (with frontiers)

152 South America (without frontiers)

153 Fruit

154 Iguazu Falls   **155** Grapes

156 Cotton Plant

1936 (1 Jan)–**37.** *Litho.* W **111.** P 13½ × 13 (15 *c.*, 30 *c.*, 40 *c.*, 2 p.) *or* 13 × 13½ (*others*).

655	**146**	15 c. dull blue	..	5	5
656	**147**	25 c. carmine-red and pink	..	5	5
657	**148**	30 c. brown and yellow-brown		5	5
658	**149**	40 c. purple and mauve	..	5	5
659	**150**	50 c. vermilion and salmon		5	5
660	**151**	1 p. light blue and chocolate		90	15
660a	**152**	1 p. light blue & chocolate (3.2.37)		20	5
661	**153**	2 p. blue and maroon	..	20	5
662	**154**	5 p. sage-green and deep blue	..	35	5
663	**155**	10 p. black and maroon	..	1·00	15
664	**156**	20 p. chocolate and greenish blue		2·25	60
655/664		Set of 11	..	4·75	1·10

For stamps as T **146** see also Nos. 676, 677a, 678a and 678c, and for stamp similar to T **152**, see No. 826.

For stamps without wmk, see Nos. 740/9, or with larger wmk, see Nos. 802/8.

157

SERVICIO OFICIAL

(O **4.** 12 *mm* opt)

1936 (1 Dec). *Pan-American Peace Conference. Litho.* W **111.** P 13 × 13½.

665	**157**	10 c. scarlet ..	..	..	10	8

1938 (8 Feb)–**40.** *OFFICIAL. Optd with Type* O **4.** W **111.** (a) *Typo.* P 13½.

O666		5 c. orange-brown (653b)	..	5	5
O667		10 c. scarlet (653d)	..	5	5
		a. Perf 13½ × 13 (653e)	..	5	5

(b) *Litho.* P 13½ × 13 (15 c., 40 c.) *or* 13 × 13½ (*others*)

O668	**143**	1 c. yellow-brown (1940)..	..	5	5
O669	–	2 c. grey-brown (646) (1940)		5	5
O670	–	3 c. green (647) (1939)	..	5	5
O671	–	5 c. orange-brown (649) (1940)	..	5	5
O672	**146**	15 c. dull blue	..	5	5
O673	**147**	25 c. carmine-red and pink	..	5	5
O674	**149**	40 c. purple and mauve (658)	..	5	5
O675	**150**	50 c. vermilion and salmon	..	5	5
O676	**152**	1 p. light blue & chocolate (1939)		5	5
O666/676		Set of 10 ..	..	40	40

For 25 c., 50 c. and 2 p. with smaller overprint, see Nos. O813/5.

HAVE YOU READ THE NOTES AT THE BEGINNING OF THIS CATALOGUE?

These often provide answers to the enquiries we receive.

158 Pres. Sarmiento

159 Frigate *Pres. Sarmiento*

1938 (5 Sept). *50th Death Anniv. of Pres. Sarmiento. Litho. W 111. P 13 × 13½.*

666	**158**	.3 c. green ..	..	..	..	5	5
667		5 c. rose-carmine ..	..	..	..	5	5
668		15 c. blue ..	..	..	..	12	8
669		50 c. orange ..	..	..	..	20	15
666/669		*Set of 4*	..	..	..	35	25

1939 (16 Mar). *Last Voyage of Training-ship "Pres. Sarmiento". Litho. W 111. P 13 × 13½.*

670	**159**	5 c. deep and pale blue-green	..	10	8

1939 (20 Mar)–51. *T 146 and various portraits as T 143. W 111.*

(a) Litho. P 13½ × 13

671	2½ c. slate-black (Braille)	..	..	5	5
672	3 c. grey (San Martin)	..	..	5	5
672a	3 c. grey (Moreno) (23.2.46)	..		5	5
673	4 c. green (Brown)	..	..	5	5
674	8 c. orange (Avellaneda)	..		5	5
674a	10 c. maroon (Rivadavia) (1942)		5	5
675	12 c. scarlet (Mitre)	..	..	5	5
676	15 c. pale blue (T **146**)	..		5	5
677	20 c. blue (Martin Güemes)	..		8	5
677a	20 c. blue (T **146**) (7.5.51)	..		5	5

(b) Typo. P 13½

678	10 c. maroon (Rivadavia)	..		5	5
678a	20 c. blue (T **146**) (8.51)	..		5	5
671/678a	*Set of 12*	..	..	..	45	35

*(c) Designs interchanged. 15 c. as No. 653, 20 c. as T **146**, but larger. Litho (20.8.42)*

678b	15 c. blue-grey (p 13½ × 13)	..		1·90	20
678c	20 c. slate-blue and cobalt (p 13 × 13½)		10	5

Designs:—15 c. Martin Güemes (20½ × 26½ mm); 20 c. Prize bull (22 × 33 mm).

For similar stamps, but with different watermark, see Nos. 701/16 and without watermark, Nos. 747/64. For 5 c. Hernández and 20 c. Brown, see Nos. 894/5b.

1939–53. *OFFICIAL. Optd with Type O 4.*

(a) Litho. P 13½ × 13

O679	–	3 c. grey (672)	..	..	5	5
O680	–	10 c. maroon (674a)	..		5	5
O681	**146**	15 c. pale blue (676)	..		5	5
O682	–	15 c. blue-grey (678b) (1945)	..	5	5
O683	**146**	20 c. blue (677a) (1953)	..	5	5

(b) Typo. P 13½

O684	–	10 c. maroon (678)..	..	..	5	5
O679/684		*Set of 6*	..	..	20	15

For 25 c., 50 c., 1 p. and 2 p. with smaller overprint, see Nos. O813/6.

160 Allegory of the Post

161 Iguazu Falls

1939 (1 Apr). *11th U.P.U. Congress, Buenos Aires. T 160/1 and designs inscr "XI CONGRESO U.P.U.". Photo. W 111. P 13 × 13½ (vert) or 13½ × 13 (horiz).*

679	5 c. carmine	..		..	..	5	5
680	15 c. slate-blue	..	..	..	..	12	8
681	20 c. blue	..	..	..	..	10	8
682	25 c. green	..	·..	..	..	20	12
683	50 c. brown	..	..	..	..	30	20
684	1 p. purple	..	..	..	..	45	30
685	2 p. magenta	..	..	..	2·50	1·25
686	5 p. violet	..	..	..	6·00	3·00
679/686	*Set of 8*	..	..	..	8·50	4·25

Designs: *Horiz*—15 c. G.P.O., Buenos Aires; 50 c. Mt. Bonete; 5 p. Lake Frias, Nahuel Huapi Park. *Vert*—20 c. Seal of Argentina; 1 p. Symbols of Postal Communications; 2 p. Argentina "Land of Promise" (from a pioneer painting).

1939 (12 May). *International Philatelic Exhibition, Buenos Aires. Two sheets se-tenant horiz or vert, each comprising Nos. 679, 681/3 arranged differently. Imperf.*

MS686a 190 × 95 mm or 95 × 190 *2 sheets* .. 3·00 3·00
Also available as a block of four sheets arranged either with two the same vertically or two the same horizontally. Price for block of four un £6.50 us £6.50.

167 Working Class Family and New Home

RM **1** Winged Messenger

1939 (2 Oct). *First Pan-American Housing Congress. Litho. W 111. P 13½ × 13.*

687	**167**	5 c. pale blue-green ..		..	5	5

(Des A. B. Zurita (1 p. 18) F. Salender and A. S. Forno (1 p. 32), M. A. Segovia (1 p. 50). Photo)

1939 (11 Dec). *RECORDED MESSAGE. Type RM **1** and similar designs inscr "CORREOS FONOPOSTAL". W 111. P 13 × 13½ (vert) or 13½ × 13 (horiz).*

RM688	1 p. 18, steel blue	..	..	1·50	1·00
RM689	1 p. 32, pale blue	..	..	1·40	1·00
RM690	1 p. 50, red-brown	..	..	3·00	1·75

Designs: *Vert*—1 p. 32, Head of Liberty and Arms of Argentina. *Horiz*—1 p. 50, Record and winged letter.

The above stamps were for payment of special fees for postage on messages recorded on discs for transmission by post.

168 North and South America

168a Corrientes Type **5**

1940 (14 Apr). *50th Anniv of Pan-American Union. Photo. W 111. P 13 × 13½.*

688	**168**	15 c. bright blue	..	..	15	8

1940 (25 May). *Centenary of First Adhesive Postage Stamps and Philatelic Exhibition, Cordoba. Sheet 111 × 111 mm containing early Argentine issues as T 168a. Litho. W 111. Imperf.*

MS688a 5 c. blue (Type **168a**)
     5 c. blue (Cordoba T 3)
     5 c. red (Type 1) ..   } 1·75 1·75
     5 c. red (Type 3) ..
     10 c. blue (Buenos Aires T 1)

169 Aeroplane and Envelope   **170** "Mercury"

171 Aeroplane in Clouds   **172** Gen. French, Col. Beruti, and Rosette of the "Legion de Patricios"

(Des C. Rodriquez (**169**), G. D. Buccich (**170**), J. and A. Barbero Zurita (**171**). Photo)

1940 (23 Oct). *AIR. Size* 32½×22 *or* 22×32½ *mm.* W **111**. *P* 13½×13 *or* 13×13½ (*vert*).

689	**169**	30 c. red-orange	..	40	5
690	**170**	50 c. chocolate	..	45	5
691	**169**	1 p. carmine	..	15	5
692	**171**	1 p. 25, green	..	15	5
693	**169**	2 p. 50, blue	..	35	8
689/693		*Set of 4*	..	1·40	20

For lithographed stamps see Nos. 718/20 and 765/9.

1941 (20 Feb). *131st Anniv of Rising against Imperial Spanish Rule* (*May*, *1810*). *Litho.* W **111**. *P* 13½×13.

694	**172**	5 c. dark and light blue	..	5	5

173 Marco M. de Avellaneda   **174** Statue of Gen. J. A. Roca

1941 (3 Oct). *Death Centenary of Avellaneda* (*patriot*). *Litho.* W **111**. *P* 13½×13½.

695	**173**	5 c. slate-blue	..	5	5

1941 (19 Oct). *Dedication of Statue of Gen. J. A. Roca. Photo.* W **111**. *P* 13×13½.

696	**174**	5 c. grey-olive	..	5	5

175 C. Pelligrini (founder) and National Bank   **176** Gen. Juan Lavalle

1941 (26 Oct). *50th Anniv of National Bank. Photo.* W **111**. *P* 13½×13.

697	**175**	5 c. brown-lake	..	5	5

1941 (5 Dec). *Death Centenary of Gen. Lavalle. Photo.* W **111**. *P* 13×13½.

698	**176**	5 c. deep blue	..	5	5

177 New P.O. Savings Bank   **178** José Manuel Estrada

1942 (5 Apr). *Inauguration of Central P.O. Savings Bank. Litho.* W **111**. *P* 13½×13.

699	**177**	1 c. grey-green	..	5	5

1942 (13 July). *Birth Centenary of J. M. Estrada* (*patriot*). *Litho.* W **111**. *P* 13×13½.

700	**178**	5 c. purple	..	5	5

179

Vertical distance between suns is 25 mm. Rays connecting suns are long and straight

WATERMARK AND PAPER. This watermark when introduced in 1942 occurred on smooth white paper on which it was very indistinct.

There followed the stamps without watermark in 1945–47 but in 1948 the watermark was re-introduced, with suns slightly larger and on thinner translucent paper so that it is easily seen, but we do not list this separately. The 1942 watermark normally reads horizontally but the later version is found both horizontal and vertical.

The dates of issue are uncertain and we quote the earliest postmarks reported to us.

1942–50. *As earlier issues but* W **179**.

701	–	½ c. purple (644) (9.44)	..	75	12
702	143	1 c. yellow-brown (645) (7.50)	..	5	5
703	–	2 c. grey-brown (646) (12.50)	..	5	5
704	–	3 c. grey (San Martin) (672) (1.44)	..	1·50	8
705	–	3 c. grey (Moreno) (672a) (9.50)	..	5	5
706	–	10 c. maroon (674a) (7.49)	..	5	5
707	–	12 c. scarlet (675) (9.45)	..	5	5
708	–	15 c. blue-grey (678b) (8.42)	..	8	5
709	–	20 c. slate-blue and cobalt (678c) (12.42)	..	8	–
710	147	25 c. carm-red & pink (656) (9.49)	..	8	5
711	148	30 c. brown & yell-brn (657) (1.49)	..	10	5
712	149	40 c. purple and mauve (658) (6.49)	..	25	5
713	150	50 c. verm and salmon (659) (7.49)	..	25	5
714	152	1 p. light blue & choc (660a) (5.49)	..	45	5
715	153	2 p. blue and maroon (661) (8.49)	..	50	5
716	154	5 p. sage-green and deep blue (662) (1.50)	..	2·40	30
701/716		*Set of 16*	..	6·00	90

OFFICIAL. Optd with Type O **4**

O717	3 c. grey (Moreno) (705) (1950)	..	8	5
O718	5 c. brown (as 649) (11.44)	..	5	5
O719	10 c. maroon (706) (5.45)	..	5	5
O720	15 c. blue-grey (708) (6.45)	..	5	5
O717/720	*Set of 4*	..	15	10

The above are the earliest reported postmarks. The 5 c. was not issued watermarked Type **179** without the overprint. For 50 c. and 1 p. with smaller overprint, see Nos. O816/7.

180 G.P.O., Buenos Aires

1942 (5 Oct). *POSTAGE and EXPRESS. Inscr "CORREOS Y TELEGRAFOS". Litho. W 179. P 13½ × 13.*
717 **180** 35 c. ultramarine 8 5
For similar stamps inscr "CORREOS Y TELECOMUNICAC-IONES", see Nos. 745/6.

No. 689 Photo.   No. 718 Litho

No. 690 Photo No. 719 Litho

1942 (6 Oct)–**51**. *AIR. Litho. Redrawn: shading of lines instead of flat tints. Size 33½ × 22½ or 22½ × 33½ mm. W 111. P 13½ × 13 or 13 × 13½ (50 c.)*
718 **169** 30 c. red-orange 10 5
719 **170** 50 c. brown and buff (1943).. .. 10 5
720 **169** 1 p. carmine (1.10.51) 12 5
The 30 c. was issued on chalk-surfaced paper in 1944. The 50 c. first appeared on chalk-surfaced paper and came out on ordinary paper in lighter shades in 1944.
For lithographed stamps W **179** and without wmk see Nos. 765/9.

181 Proposed Columbus Lighthouse   182 Dr. José C. Paz

1942 (12 Oct). *450th Anniv of Discovery of America. Litho. P 13 × 13½. A. W 111. B. W 179.*

		A		B	
721 **181** 15 c. blue	3·25	70	8	5

1942 (15 Dec). *Birth Centenary of Dr. José C. Paz (founder of "La Prensa"). Litho. W 179. P 13 × 13½.*
722 **182** 5 c. slate-blue 5 5

183 Books   184 Arms of Argentina   185 National Independence House

1943 (1 Apr). *First National Book Fair. Litho. W 179. P 13½ × 13.*
723 **183** 5 c. blue 5 5

1943 (3 July). *Revolution of 4 June, 1943. Litho. P 13½ × 13 or 13 × 13½ (20 c.). A. W 111. B. W 179.*

			A		B	
724 **184**	5 c. red	5	5	8	5
725	15 c. green	8	5	†	
726	20 c. ultramarine (22×33 mm) ..	8	5	†	

1943 (24 Sept). *Restoration of Tucuman Museum. Litho. P 13½ × 13. A. W 111. B. W 179.*

			A		B	
727 **185** 5 c. green	12	5	5	5

186 Head of Liberty, Money-box and Laurels   187 Buenos Aires in 1800

1943 (25 Oct). *First National Savings Bank Conference. Litho. P 13½ × 13. A. W 111. B. W 179.*

		A		B	
728 **186** 5 c. chocolate ..	5	5	2·75	50

1943 (11 Dec). *Export Day. Litho. W 111. P 13 × 13½.*
729 **187** 5 c. grey-black 5 5

188 Postal Union of the Americas and Spain   189 Graham Bell   190 Columbus Landing in America

1944 (5 Jan). *Postmen's Benefit Fund. T 188, 189 (portraits inscr "PRO-CARTERO"), and T 190. Litho. W 111. P 13½ × 13.*
730 3 c. +2 c. black and violet 12 8
731 5 c. +5 c. black and scarlet 15 8
732 10 c. +5 c. black and orange 35 20
733 25 c. +15 c. black and brown 40 35
734 1 p. +50 c. black and green .. .. 1·40 1·25
730/734 *Set of 5* .. .. .. 2·10 1·75
Portraits:—3 c. Samuel Morse; 25 c. Rowland Hill.

191 Ships   192 Argentina   193 Arms of Argentina

1944 (31 Jan). *Naval Week. Litho. W 111. P 13½ × 13.*
735 **191** 5 c. blue 5 5

1944 (17 Feb). *San Juan Earthquake Relief Fund. Litho. W 111. P 13 × 13½.*
736 **192** 5 c. +10 c. black and olive-green .. 20 12
737 5 c. +50 c. black and brown-lake .. 45 30
738 5 c. +1 p. black and orange .. .. 1·50 1·25
739 5 c. +20 p. black and blue .. .. 2·75 2·25
736/739 *Set of 4* .. .. 4·50 3·50

1944 (4 June). *First Anniv of Revolution of 4 June 1943. Litho. W 111. P 13½ × 13.*
740 **193** 5 c. blue 5 5

193a National Flag

194 Archangel Gabriel

195 Cross of Palermo

1944 (17 July). *National Anthem and Aid for La Rioja and Catamarca Provinces. Two sheets each containing T* **193***a. Litho. W* **111.** *Imperf.*

MS740*a* Each 75×110 mm
5 c.+1 p. light blue and plum
5 c.+50 p. light blue and indigo } 35·00 35·00

1944 (11 Oct). *Fourth National Eucharistic Congress. Litho. W* **111.** *P* 13½×13.

741	**194**	3 c. yellow-green	5	5
742	**195**	5 c. carmine	5	5

196

197 Reservists

1944 (24 Oct). *Twentieth Anniv of Universal Savings Day. Litho. W* **111.** *P* 13½×13.

743	**196**	5 c. black	5	5

1944 (1 Dec). *Reservists' Day. Litho. W* **111.** *P* 13×13½.

744	**197**	5 c. blue	5	5

1945 (Mar)–**49**. *As T* **180**, *but inscr* "CORREOS Y TELECOMUNICACIONES". *Litho. P* 13½×13. A. *W* **111.** B. *No wmk.*

			A		B	
745	**180**	35 c. ultramarine	8	5	8	5

C. *W* **179**

746	**180**	35 c. ultram (10.49)	8	5

1945 (Mar)–**46**. *As earlier issues but without wmk. Litho.*

747	½ c. purple (644) (1946)	5	5
748	1 c. yellow-brown (645)	5	5
749	2 c. grey-brown (646)	5	5
750	3 c. brownish grey (San Martin) (672)	5	5
751	3 c. grey (Moreno) (672*a*) (23.2.46)	5	5
752	6 c. sage-green (650)	5	5
753	10 c. maroon (674*a*)	5	5
754	15 c. blue-grey (678*b*)	5	5
755	20 c. slate-blue and cobalt (678*c*)	5	5
756	25 c. carmine-red and pink (656)	5	5
757	30 c. brown and yellow-brown (657)	8	5
758	40 c. purple and mauve (658)	10	5
759	50 c. vermilion and salmon (659)	10	5
760	1 p. light blue and chocolate (660*a*)	20	5
761	2 p. blue and maroon (661)	40	5
762	5 p. sage-green & dp blue (662) (1946)	2·50	12
763	10 p. black and maroon (663)	85	20
764	20 p. choc & grnsh blue (664) (1946)	1·60	35
747/764	*Set of* 18	5·00	1·00

See also Nos. 894/5*b*.

1945–49. *AIR. As Nos.* 718/20 *and* 693. *Litho. Size* 33½×22½ *or* 22½×33½ *mm. P* 13½×13 *or* 13×13½ (50 *c.*).

(*a*) *No wmk*

765	**169**	30 c. red-orange	12	5
766	**170**	50 c. brown and olive-bistre (4.46)	20	5
767	**169**	1 p. carmine (8.47)	15	5
768		2 p. 50, blue (1947)	70	25

(*b*) *W* **179**

769	**170**	50 c. brown and olive-bistre (1949)	12	5
765/769		*Set of* 5	1·00	30

1945–48. *OFFICIAL. Stamps of* 1945–46 (*without wmk*), *optd with Type* O **4**.

O770	2 c. grey-brown (749)	12	10
O771	3 c. grey (Moreno) (751) (1946)	12	5
O772	5 c. brown (*as* 649)	8	5
O773	10 c. maroon (753) (1946)	5	5
O774	15 c. blue-grey (754) (1947)	5	5
O775	25 c. carmine-red & pink (756) (1947)	5	5
O776	50 c. vermilion & salmon (759) (1948)	10	5
O777	1 p. lt blue & choc (760) (1947)	8	5
O778	2 p. blue and maroon (761) (1946)	5	5
O779	5 p. sage-grn & dp bl (762) (1946)	8	5
O780	10 p. black and maroon (763) (1946)	15	8
O781	20 p. choc & greenish bl (764) (1946)	25	12
O770/81	*Set of* 12	90	45

No. O772 without watermark was not issued without the official overprint.

For 1 p. with smaller overprint, see No. O818.

198 B. Rivadavia

199 Rivadavia's Mausoleum

1945 (1 Sept). *Death Centenary of Rivadavia. T* **198** (*and another portrait of Rivadavia similarly inscr*) *and T* **199**. *Litho. P* 13½×13.

770	**198**	3 c. green	5	5
771	–	5 c. carmine	5	5
772	**199**	20 c. blue	5	5
770/772		*Set of* 3	8	8

200 San Martin

201 Memorial to Unknown Soldier of Independence

1945–48. *P* 13½. (i) *Typo.*

A. *W* **111** (22.11.45). B. *No wmk* (1946)

			A		B	
773	**200**	5 c. carmine-red	5	5	5	5

(ii) *Litho*
A. *No wmk* (1946). B. *W* **111** (1948)

			A		B	
774	**200**	5 c. carmine-red	5	5	5	5

C. *W* **179** (1948)

775	**200**	5 c. carmine-red	3·25	1·00

1946–48. *OFFICIAL. No.* 774 *optd with Type* O **4**.

			A		B	
O776	**200**	5 c. carmine-red	5	5	5	5

1946 (14 Jan). *Litho. P* 13½×13.

776	**201**	5 c. brown-purple	5	5

202 Pres. F. D. Roosevelt

203 "Affirmation"

204 Aeroplane over Iguazu Falls

1946 (12 Apr). *First Death Anniv of Pres. Franklin Roosevelt. Litho. P* 13 × 13½.
777 **202** 5 c. blue-grey 5 5

1946 (4 June). *Installation of Pres. Juan Perón. Litho. P* 13 × 13½.
778 **203** 5 c. light blue 5 5

1946 (10 June). *AIR. T* **204** *and similar design, inscr* "LINEAS AEREAS DEL ESTADO". *Litho. P* 13 × 13½. *A. No wmk.* B. W 111.

		A		B	
779	15 c. claret	5	5	5	5
780	25 c. grey-green	5	5	8	5

Design:—25 c. Aeroplane over the Andes.

205 "Flight"

206 Astrolabe

1946 (22 Sept). *AIR. Aeronautical Exhibition, Buenos Aires. Litho. P* 13½ × 13 (15 c.) *or* 13 × 13½ (60 c.).
781 **205** 15 c. deep green/*green* 15 12
782 **206** 60 c. purple/*buff* 30 20

207 "Argentina and Populace"

1946 (17 Oct). 1st *Anniv of Perón's Defeat of Counter-Revolution. Litho. P* 13½ × 13.
783 **207** 5 c. mauve 5 5
784 10 c. green 5 5
785 15 c. blue 8 5
786 50 c. purple-brown 12 8
787 1 p. carmine 30 20
783/787 *Set of 5* 50 30

208 Money-box and Map of the World

209 "Industry"

1946 (31 Oct). *Annual Savings Day. Litho. P* 13½ × 13.
788 **208** 30 c. carmine 8 5

1946 (6 Dec). *Industrial Exhibition. Litho. P* 13 × 13½.
789 **209** 5 c. brown-purple 5 5

210 International Bridge

211 South Pole

1947 (21 May). *Opening of Bridge between Argentina and Brazil. Litho. P* 13½ × 13.
790 **210** 5 c. green 5 5

1947 (25 May)–49. 43rd *Anniv of First Argentine Antarctic Mail. Litho. P* 13 × 13½.

(a) *No wmk*
791 **211** 5 c. violet and mauve 5 5
792 20 c. carmine and pink 8 5

(b) *W* 111
792a **211** 20 c. carmine and pink (1947) .. 8 5

(c) *W* 179
792b **211** 20 c. carmine and pink (2.49) .. 12 5

212 "Justice"

213 Icarus Falling

1947 (4 June). *First Anniv of Col. Juan Perón's Presidency. Litho. P* 13 × 13½.
793 **212** 5 c. purple and buff 5 5

1947 (25 Sept). "Week of the Wing". *Litho. P* 13½ × 13.
794 **213** 15 c. rose-lilac 5 5

214 Frigate, Pres. Sarmiento

215 Cervantes and "Don Quixote"

1947 (5 Oct). 50th *Anniv of Launching of Training Ship* "Pres. Sarmiento". *Litho. P* 13 × 13½.
795 **214** 5 c. blue and light blue 5 5

1947 (12 Oct). 400th *Birth Anniv of Cervantes. Photo. W* 111. *P* 13½ × 13.
796 **215** 5 c. grey-olive 5 5

216 Gen. San Martin and Urn

217 Young Crusaders

1947–49. *Arrival from Spain of Ashes of Gen. San Martin's Parents. Litho. P* 13½ × 13.
A. *No wmk* (24.11.47).   B. *W* 179 (1949)

		A		B	
797	**216** 5 c. green	5	5	5	5

1947 (24 Dec)–**49**. *Educational Crusade for Universal Peace.* 5 c. litho, 20 c. photo. P 13 × 13½.

A. *No wmk.* B. **W 111**

			A	B
798 **217**	5 c. green ..	..	5 5	— —
799	20 c. brown ..	..	15 10	5 5

C. **W 179** (1949)

| 800 **217** | 5 c. green .. | .. | 5 5 |

218 American Indian **219** Phrygian Cap and Sprig of Wheat **220** "Stop"

1948 (21 May). *American Indian Day. Photo.* **W 111**. P 13 × 13½.
801 **218** 25 c. yellow-brown 8 5

1948 (16 July). *Fifth Anniv of Revolution of 4 June. Photo.* **W 111**. P 13 × 13½.
802 **219** 5 c. ultramarine 5 5

1948 (22 July). *Safety First Campaign. Litho.* **W 111**. P 13 × 13½.
803 **220** 5 c. yellow and brown 5 5

221 Posthorn **222** Argentine Farmers **223** "Liberty and Plenty"

1948 (31 July). *Bicentenary of Postal Service in Rio de la Plata. Photo.* P 13 × 13½.
804 **221** 5 c. magenta.. .. .. .. 5 5

1948 (20 Sept). *Agriculture Day. Photo.* **W 179**. P 13 × 13½.
805 **222** 10 c. red-brown 5 5

224

1948 (23 Nov). *Re-election of Pres. Perón. Photo.* **W 224**. P 13 × 13½.
806 **223** 25 c. claret 5 5

225 Statue of Atlas **226** Map, Globe, and Compasses

1948–49. *AIR. Fourth Meeting of Pan-American Cartographers. Photo.* **W 179**. P 13½ × 13 (45 c.), or 13 × 13½ (70 c.).
807 **225** 45 c. deep brown (18.1.49) 10 5
808 **226** 70 c. green (27.11.48) 15 8

226a Buenos Aires (18th-Cent) **227** Winged Wheel

1948 (21 Dec). *Bicentenary of Regular Postal Services on the Plata River. Two sheets containing designs as T 226a. Photo. No wmk. Imperf.*
MS808a 144 × 103 mm (*horiz designs*)
　　15 c. deep green (Mail-coach, 1854)
　　45 c. orange-brown (Type **226a**)
　　55 c. red-brown (First train, 1857)
　　85 c. ultram. (Sailing ship 1867)
MS808b 103 × 144 mm (*vert designs*)
　　85 c. brown (Domingo de Basavilibaso)
　　1 p. 5, deep green (Postrider, 1748)
　　1 p. 20, indigo (Sailing ship, 1798)
　　1 p. 90, brown-purple (Courier in the Andes, 1772)
　　Price for two sheets .. .. 1·00 1·00

(Des A. Dell'Acqua. Photo)

1949 (1 Mar). *First Anniv of Nationalization of Argentine Railways.* **W 179**. P 13½ × 13.
809 **227** 10 c. blue 5 5

228 Head of Liberty **229** Trophy and Target

(Des Garrasi. Eng Baiardi. Recess)

1949 (20 June). *Constitution Day.* **W 111**. P 13½ × 13.
810 **228** 1 p. purple and red 12 5

1949 (4 Nov). *AIR. International Shooting Championship, Buenos Aires. Photo.* **W 179**. P 13 × 13½.
811 **229** 75 c. yellow-brown 40 12

SERVICIO
OFICIAL

230 "Intercommunication"   (O **5** 11 *mm* opt)

(Des Garrasi. Eng Baiardi. Recess)

1949 (19 Nov). *75th Anniv of U.P.U.* W **111**. *P* 13½×13.
812 **230** 25 c. blue-green and olive ..   8   5

1950–52. *OFFICIAL. Optd with smaller opt, Type O* **5**.

(a) W **111**
O813 **147** 25 c. carmine-red and pink (656) ..   5   5
O814 **150** 50 c. vermilion and salmon (659) ..   5   5
O815 **153** 2 p. blue and maroon (661) (1952)   8   5

(b) W **179**
O816 **150** 50 c. vermilion and salmon (713) ..   8   5
O817 **152** 1 p. light blue and chocolate (714)   10   5

(c) No wmk
O818 **152** 1 p. light blue and chocolate (760)   10   5

231 San Martin   **232** San Martin at Boulogne

(Portraits as T **231** recess; other designs photo)

1950 (17 Aug). *Death Centenary of Gen. San Martin. As T* **231**/2, *inscr* "1850 1950". W **111**. *P* 13½.
813   10 c. purple and blue ..   5   5
814   20 c. red-brown and lake ..   5   5
815   25 c. brown   5   5
816   50 c. blue and green ..   8   5
817   75 c. blue-green and brown ..   10   5
818   1 p. green   15   8
819   2 p. purple   25   10
813/819   *Set of 7*   65   30
MS819*a*   120×150 mm.   Nos. 813/4 and
   816/7. Imperf   40   40
Vert portraits of San Martin, as T **231**:—10 c. (1818) eng
Cerichelli after José Gil de Castro; 20 c. (1828) eng Baiardi;
50 c., 75 c. eng P. Nicastro; 50 c. after daguerreotype, Paris,
1848; 75 c. after portrait by his daughter, 1827; 2 p. Mausoleum in Buenos Aires Cathedral. *Horiz designs:*—25 c. San
Martin at Boulogne-sur-Mer, after Antonio Alice portrait; 1 p.
House at Grand-Bourg, France, where San Martin died.

(Des A. Dell'Acqua. Photo)

1950 (26 Aug). *International Philatelic Exhibition, Buenos
Aires. T* **233** *and similar designs inscr* "EXPOSICION
FILATELICA INTERNACIONAL". W **111**. *P* 13½×13.
      (a) POSTAGE. Inscr "CORREOS"
820 **233** 10 c. + 10 c. violet   5   5
      (b) AIR. Inscr "CORREO AEREO"
821   45 c. + 45 c. ultramarine ..   12   12
822   70 c. + 70 c. brown   20   20
823   1 p. + 1 p. carmine   65   50
824   2 p. 50 + 2 p. 50, brown-olive ..   2·75   2·75
825   5 p. + 5 p. blue-green ..   4·00   3·00
820/825   *Set of 6* ..   ..   6·00   5·50
MS825*a*   120×150 mm. Nos. 820/2. Imperf ..   1·00   1·00
  Designs:—45 c. Engraver; 70 c. Proofing; 1 p. Printer;
2 p. 50, Woman reading letter; 5 p. General San Martin.

1951 (21 May). *Litho.* W **111**. *P* 13×13½.
826 **234** 1 p. light blue and chocolate ..   10   5

1951. OFFICIAL. *(a) Optd with Type O* **4**.
O827 **234** 1 p. light blue and chocolate ..   5   5
      (b) Optd with Type O **5**
O828 **234** 1 p. light blue and chocolate ..   10   5

235 Aeroplane and Eagle

(Des A. Dell'Acqua. Photo)

1951 (20 June). *AIR. Tenth Anniv of State Airlines.* W **111**.
P 13×13½.
827 **235** 20 c. olive-green   5   5

236 Pegasus and Train

(Des R. Garrasi. Photo)

1951 (17 Oct). *Five Year Plan. T* **236** *and similar designs
inscr* "1947–1951". W **111**. *P* 13½. *(a) POSTAGE*.
828   5 c. brown-olive   5   5
829   25 c. blue-green   8   5
830   40 c. reddish purple   10   5
       (b) AIR
831   20 c. blue   5   5
  Designs: *Horiz*—25 c. Fish and ship. *Vert*—20 c. Eagle and
aeroplane; 40 c. Head of Mercury and telephone.

233 Stamp Designer   **234** South America
               and Antarctic

237 Woman Voter and   **238** "Piety"
   "Argentina"   (Michelangelo)

(T 237/8 des A. Dell'Acqua. Photo)

1951 (14 Dec). *Women's Suffrage in Argentina.* W **111**.
P 13½×13.
832 **237** 10 c. purple 5 5

1951 (22 Dec). *AIR. Eva Perón Foundation Fund.* W **111**.
P 13½×13.
833 **238** 2 p. 45+7 p. 55, blackish olive . . 4·50 3·00

239 **240**
Eva Perón

1952 (26 Aug). W **111**. (a) *Litho.* P 13½×13.
834 **239** 1 c. pale orange-brown 5 5
835 5 c. olive-grey 5 5
836 10 c. claret 5 5
837 20 c. rose-red 5 5
838 25 c. grey-green 5 5
839 40 c. purple 5 5
840 50 c. bistre-brown 5 5

(b) *Recess.* P 13½×13
841 **239** 45 c. deep blue 5 5

(c) *Photo.* P 13×13½
842 **240** 1 p. deep brown 8 5
843 1 p. 50, deep bluish green 20 5
844 2 p. crimson 15 5
845 3 p. indigo 20 5
834/845 *Set of 12* 80 35

1952 (Nov)–**53**. As T **239/240**, *but all inscr* "EVA PERON".
W **111**.

(a) *Photo. Size* 22×33 *mm.* P 13×13½
846 **240** 1 p. deep brown 5 5
847 1 p. 50, deep bluish green 8 5
848 2 p. crimson (1953). 15 5
849 3 p. indigo 25 5

(b) *Recess. Size* 30½×40 *mm.* P 13½×13
850 **240** 5 p. red-brown 25 10
851 **239** 10 p. red 60 20
852 **240** 20 p. green . . . . . . 1·40 60
853 **239** 50 p. blue . . . . . . 3·00 1·50
846/853 *Set of 8* . . . . . . 5·00 2·25

SERVICIO OFICIAL
(O 6)   (O 7)   (O 8)

1953. *OFFICIAL. Eva Perón stamps overprinted.*

(a) *Nos.* 835/41 *with Type* O **6**
O854 **239** 5 c. olive-grey 5 5
O855 10 c. claret 5 5
O856 20 c. rose-red 5 5
O857 25 c. grey-green 5 5
O858 40 c. purple 5 5
O859 45 c. deep blue 5 5
O860 50 c. bistre-brown 5 5

(b) *No.* 847 *with Type* O **7**, *in blue*
O861 **240** 1 p. 50, deep bluish green . . 10 5

(c) *Nos.* 846/52 *with Type* O **8**, *in blue*
O862 **240** 1 p. deep brown 5 5
O863 1 p. 50, deep bluish green . . 8 5
O864 2 p. crimson 12 5

O865 **240** 3 p. indigo 20 8
O866 5 p. red-brown 25 10
O867 **239** 10 p. red 80 50
O868 **240** 20 p. green. . . . . . 2·00 2·25
O854/868 *Set of 15* . . . . . . 3·25 2·75

241 Indian Funeral   **242** Rescue Ship *Uruguay*
Urn

(Des A. Dell'Acqua. Photo)

1953 (28 Aug). *Fourth Centenary of Santiago del Estero.*
W **111**. P 13×13½.
854 **241** 50 c. blue-green 5 5

(Des A. Dell'Acqua. Photo)

1953 (8 Oct). *50th Anniv of Rescue of the "Antarctic" by the
"Uruguay".* W **111**. P 13½.
855 **242** 50 c. ultramarine 10 5

243 Planting Flag in S.   **244** "Telegraphs"
Orkneys

(Des A. Dell'Acqua. Eng V. Cerichelli. Recess)

1954 (20 Jan). *50th Anniv of Argentine P.O. in South Orkneys.* W **111**. P 13½.
856 **243** 1 p. 45, blue 10 5

(Des A. Dell'Acqua. Photo)

1954 (30 Apr). *International Telecommunications Conference. T* **244** *and similar designs.* W **111**. P 13×13½ (vert)
or 13½ × 13 (horiz).
857 1 p. 50, slate purple 10 8
858 3 p. ultramarine 15 8
859 5 p. carmine-lake 35 15
Designs: *Vert*—3 p. "Radio". *Horiz*—5 p. "Television".

245 Pediment, Buenos   **246** Eva Perón
Aires Stock Exchange

(Des U. Zeppa. Photo)

1954 (13 July). *Centenary of Argentine Stock Exchange.*
W **111**. P 13½×13.
860 **245** 1 p. deep green 10 5

(Des A. Dell'Acqua. Photo)

1954 (26 July). *Second Death Anniv of Eva Perón.*
P 13½×13. A. **W 111.** B. **W 179.**

				A	B
861	**246**	3 p. carmine	..	25 10	9·50 3·75

247 San Martin   248 "Prosperity"

1954–59. **W 111.** (a) *Typo. P* 13½.

862	**247**	20 c. scarlet (18.8.54)	..	..	5	5
863		40 c. scarlet (28.8.56)	..	..	5	5
		a. Perf 13½×13 ..	..	..	5	5

(b) Litho. P 13½×13

864	**247**	20 c. scarlet (1955)..	..	..	5	5
865		40 c. scarlet (1956)..	..	..	5	5
866		40 c. carmine (1959)	..	..	5	5

OFFICIAL. Nos. 864/6 overprinted
(a) With Type O **6**

O867	**247**	20 c. scarlet (16.7.55)	..	..	5	5
O868		40 c. scarlet (1957)..	..	..	5	5
O869		40 c. carmine (1959)	..	..	5	5

(b) With Type O **4**

| O870 | **247** | 20 c. scarlet (1956).. | .. | .. | 5 | 5 |

Three types may be distinguished of No. 863: (a) Smooth
face; shaded with thin even lines; rough impression; yellowish rough paper; 26 mm high. (b) Smooth face; fine impression; white shiny paper; 26 mm high. (c) Shaded face; thick-
ened lines producing shadows under eyes, on cheek and
chin; rough impression; 25½ mm high.

(Des A. Dell'Acqua. Photo)

1954 (26 Aug). *Centenary of Argentine Corn Exchange.*
W 111. P 13½×13.

| 867 | **248** | 1 p. 50, slate-grey | .. | .. | 10 | 5 |

249 Wheat   249a Industrial Plant

250 Mt. Fitz Roy   250a San Martin

(50 c. recess and litho; 80 c. to 2 p. photo; 3 p. to 50 p.
recess. Des R. Garrasi (50 c., 2 p. to 20 p.), U. Zeppa (80 c.,
1 p.). Eng R. Izurieta (50 c.), V. Cerichelli (3 p., 5 p., 50 p.),
C. Sanchez (10 p.), P. Nicastro (20 p.))

1955–61. T **249/50a** *and similar designs.* **W 111.** P 13½ (50 c.,
1 p., 1 p. 50, 3 p. to 10 p.), 13×13½ (80 c.) or 13½×13
(others)

868	–	50 c. blue (*recess*) (12.3.56)	..	5	5
869	–	50 c. light blue (*litho*) (1959)		5	5
870	**249**	80 c. dp brn (*shades*) (12.1.55)	..	8	5
871	–	1 p. brown (7.4.58)	..	12	5
872	**249a**	1 p. 50, ultramarine (11.11.58)	..	8	5
873	–	2 p. carmine-lake (12.1.55)		12	5
874	–	3 p. dull purple (4.5.56)	..	12	5
875	–	5 p. deep blue-green (1.12.55)	..	10	5
		a. Perf 13½×13 . .	..	10	5
876	–	10 p. yellow-green & deep yellow-green (1.12.55)		55	5
877	**250**	20 p. slate-violet (12.1.55)	..	60	5
		a. Perf 13½		60	5
878	**250a**	50 p. slate-blue & dp blue (12.1.55)	1·10	15
		a. Perf 13½		1·10	15
868/878	*Set of 11*		..	2·40	45

Designs (As T **249**): *Horiz*—50 c. Port of Buenos Aires; 1 p.
Cattle; 2 p. Eva Perón Foundation; 3 p. El Nihuil Dam. (As
T **250**): *Vert*—5 p. Iguazu Falls. *Horiz*—10 p. Humahuaca Rav-
ine.

For other values in Type **249a**, see Nos. 1028, 1031/2 and
1039 and for 50 p. as Type **250a** but inscribed "REPUBLICA
ARGENTINA" and printed in photogravure, see Nos. 1033/4.
For 65 c. and 90 c. values as T **250a** see Nos. 1359/60 and
1405.

S. OFICIAL   **SERVICIO OFICIAL**
(O **9**)   (O **10**)

OFFICIAL. Nos. 868/78 overprinted (vert upwards on 50 p.)

O879	O **9**	50 c. blue (*recess*) (1958)..	..	5	5
O880	O **8**	1 p. brown (1959)	..	5	5
		a. Blue overprint (1959)		5	5
O881	O **10**	1 p. brown (1960)	..	8	5
O882		3 p. dull purple (1958)	..	5	5
O883		5 p. deep blue-green (1957)	..	8	5
O884	O **8**	10 p. yellow-green and deep yellow-green (1959?)	..	15	8
O885	O **10**	20 p. slate-violet (1958)	..	25	20
O886	O **7**	20 p. slate-violet (1959)	..	20	8
O887	O **8**	50 p. slate-blue & dp bl (1961)	..	55	25

251 Clasped Hands and   252
Emblem

1955 (21 Mar). *National Congress of Productivity and Social
Welfare. Photo.* **W 111.** P 13½×13.

| 879 | **251** | 3 p. chocolate | .. | .. | 20 | 8 |

(Des A. Dell'Acqua. Photo)

1955 (18 June). *Twenty-fifth Anniv of Commerical Air Services.* **W 111.** P 13½.

| 880 | **252** | 1 p. 50, grey-brown | .. | .. | 10 | 5 |

A regular new issue supplement to this
catalogue appears each month in

STAMP MONTHLY

—from your newsagent or by postal subscription
—details on request.

253 "Liberation"

254 Forces Emblem

1955 (16 Oct). *Anti-Perónist Revolution of 16 September 1955. Litho.* W **111**. P 13½.
881 **253** 1 p. 50, deep olive and pale olive .. 10 5

1955 (31 Dec). *Armed Forces Commemoration. Photo.* W **111**. P 13½×13.
882 **254** 3 p. blue 12 5

.255 Gen. Urquiza (after J. M. Blanes)

256 Detail from "Antiope" (Coreggio)

1956 (3 Feb). 104*th Anniv of Battle of Caseros. Photo.* W **111**. P 13½.
883 **255** 1 p..50, deep green 12 5

1956 (14 Apr). *Infantile Paralysis Relief Fund. Photo.* W **111**. P 13½×13.
884 **256** 20 c. + 30 c. deep grey 8 5

257 Coin and Die

1956 (28 July). 75*th Anniv of National Mint. Recess.* W **111**. P 13½×13.
885 **257** 2 p. chocolate and black-brown .. 10 5

258 Corrientes Stamp of 1856

259 Dr. J. G. Pujol

1956 (21 Aug). *Argentine Stamp Centenary (1st issue). Photo* (4 p. 40), *recess (others).* W **111**. P 13½×13.
886 **258** 40 c. Prussian bl & dp bluish green 5 5
887 2 p. 40, dp magenta & dp brown .. 12 5
888 **259** 4 p. 40, blue 20 10
Design:—40 c. 1 real Corrientes stamp of 1856.
For Nos. 886/8 in miniature sheet, see No. **MS**893*a*.

260 Cotton, Chaco

261 "Liberty"

(Des M. J. Bordino. Photo)

1956 (1 Sept). *New Provinces.* T **260** *and similar designs inscr* "NUEVA PROVINCIA", *etc.* W **111**. P 13½.
889 50 c. bright blue.. .. .. 5 5
890 1 p. lake 5 5
891 1 p. 50, green 10 5
Design: *Horiz*—50 c. Lumbering, La Pampa. *Vert*—1 p. 50, Yerba, Misiones.

1956 (15 Sept). *First Anniv of Revolution. Photo.* W **111**. P 13½.
892 **261** 2 p. 40, magenta 12 5

262 Detail from "Virgin of the Rocks" (Da Vinci)

263 José Hernandez

1956 (29 Sept). *AIR. Infantile Paralysis Victims Gratitude for Help. Photo.* W **111**. P 13½×13.
893 **262** 1 p. plum 8 5

1956 (12 Oct). *Argentine Stamp Centenary (2nd issue) and Corrientes Stamp Centenary Exhibition. Nos.* 886/7, *but in litho and* 2 *p.* 40 *colour changed, and No.* 888 *in sheet. Imperf.*
MS893*a* 147×169 mm 55 55

I.
GUILLERMO BROWN

II.

Two types of 20 c.
I. Bust touches upper frame line of name panel.
II. White line separates bust from frame line.

1956–60. *W* **111.** *Typo. Size* 16½ × 22½ *mm.* *P* 13½.
894 **263** 5 c. yellow-brown (28.10.57) .. 5 5

Portrait of G. Brown as No. 673. *Litho.* *P* 13
(a) Size 21 × 17 *mm*
895 – 20 c. dull lilac (I) (30.11.56) .. 5 5
    a. Redrawn. Type II 5 5

(b) Size 19½ × 25½ *mm*
895b – 20 c. dull purple (I) (1959) .. 5 5

OFFICIAL. Overprinted (vert upwards on 5 c.)
O896 O 9 5 c. yellow-brown (1957) 5 5
O897 O 6 20 c. dull lilac (II) (opt at top) (1957) 5 5
    a. Opt at foot (1960) 5 5

264 Esteban **265** F. Ameghino **266** Roque Saenz
Echeverria (poet) (anthropologist) Peña (statesman)

1956–57. *W* **111.** *Litho* (2 p. 40) *or photo* (*others*). *P* 13 × 13½
(2 p.) *or* 13½ (*others*).
896 **264** 2 p. reddish purple (2.9.57) .. 8 5
897 **265** 2 p. 40, bistre-brown (30.11.56) .. 10 5
898 **266** 4 p. 40, grey-olive (1.4.57) 15 5

OFFICIAL. Overprinted (vert up on 2 p.)
O899 O 9 2 p. reddish purple (1957) 5 5
O900 O 8 2 p. 40, bistre-brown (1957) .. 8 5
O901 O 4 4 p. 40, grey-olive (1957) 12 5

267 Franklin (after Duplessis)

1956 (22 Dec). 250th Anniv of Birth of Benjamin Franklin.
Photo. *W* **111.** *P* 13½.
899 **267** 40 c. deep greenish blue 10 5

268 Frigate **269** Admiral G. **270** Church of
Hercules Brown Santo Domingo

1957 (2 Mar). Death Centenary of Admiral Guillermo Brown.
T **268/9** *and similar designs.* Photo. *W* **111.** *P* 13½. (a)
POSTAGE.
900 **268** 40 c. blue 5 5
901 – 2 p. 40, blackish olive 12 5

(b) AIR. Inscr "CORREO AEREO"
902 – 60 c. slate-blue 8 5
903 – 1 p. magenta 8 5
904 **269** 2 p. sepia 10 5
900/904 Set of 5 .. .. .. 35 20
Designs: *Horiz*—60 c. Battle of Montevideo; 1 p. Leonardo
Rosales and Tomás Espora. *Vert*—2 p. 40. Admiral Brown in
later years.

1957 (6 July). 150th Anniv of Defence of Buenos Aires.
Photo. *W* **111** (*sideways*). *P* 13½.
905 **270** 40 c. turquoise-green 5 5

271 Map of the **272** "La Porteña"
Americas and Badge of (early locomotive)
Buenos Aires

1957 (16 Aug). AIR. Inter-American Economic Conference.
Photo. *W* **111.** *P* 13½.
906 **271** 2 p. plum 10 5

1957 (31 Aug). Centenary of Argentine Railways. *T* **272** and
similar horiz design. Photo. *W* **111.** *P* 13½. (a) POSTAGE.
907 40 c. deep brown 5 5

(b) AIR. Inscr "CORREO AEREO"
908 60 c. olive-grey 5 5
Design:—60 c. Diesel-electric locomotive.

273 Congress Symbol **274** Head of Liberty .

1957 (14 Sept). AIR. International Tourist Congress, Buenos
Aires. *T* **273** and similar vert design. Photo. *W* **111.** *P* 13½.
909 1 p. brown 5 5
910 2 p. turquoise-blue 10 5
Design:—2 p. Symbolic key of tourism.

1957 (28 Sept). Reform Convention. Photo. *W* **111.** *P* 13½.
911 **274** 40 c. carmine 5 5

275 **276** "Wealth in Oil"

1957 (6 Nov). AIR. International Correspondence Week.
Photo. *W* **111.** *P* 13½.
912 **275** 1 p. blue 5 5

1957 (21 Dec). 50th Anniv of Argentine Oil Industry. Photo.
W **111.** *P* 13½.
913 **276** 40 c. blue 5 5

277 La Plata Museum 278 Health Emblem and Flower

1958 (11 Jan). *75th Anniv of Founding of La Plata. Photo.* W **111.** *P* 13½.
914 277 40 c. black 5 5

1958 (15 Mar). *AIR. Child Welfare. Photo.* W **111.** *P* 13½.
915 278 1 p. +50 c. brown-purple 10 10

279 Stamp of 1858 and River Ferry 280 Stamp of 1858

1958 (4 Apr). *Centenary of Argentine Confederation Stamps, and Philatelic Exhibition, Buenos Aires. Designs as* T *279/80. Photo.* W **111.** *P* 13½. *(a) POSTAGE.*
916 40 c. + 20 c. deep slate-pur & emer .. 15 12
917 2 p. 40 + 1 p. 20, blue & olive-blk .. 20 15
918 4 p. 40 + 2 p. 20, maroon & pale bl 30 20

(b) AIR
919 280 1 p. +50 c. blue and olive 15 15
920 2 p. + 1 p. deep violet and crimson 20 20
921 3 p. + 1 p. 50, brown and emerald .. 25 25
922 5 p. + 2 p. 50, carmine & bronze-grn 45 45
923 10 p. + 5 p. sepia and olive 80 80
916/923 *Set of* 8 .. .. .. 2·00 1·90
Designs: *Horiz*—2 p. 40, Magnifier, stamp album and stamp of 1858; 4 p. 40, Post Office building of 1858.

281 Railway Locomotive and Arms of Argentina and Bolivia 282

1958 (19 Apr). *Argentine–Bolivian Friendship. Photo.* W **111.** *P* 13½. *(a) Inauguration of Yacuiba–Santa Cruz Railway.*
924 281 40 c. carmine-red and deep slate .. 5 5

(b) Exchange of Presidential Visits
925 282 1 p. sepia 5 5

283 "Liberty" and Flag 284 Farman-type Biplane

(Des M. Bordino. Eng G. Nicastro. Recess; flag and background litho)

1958 (30 Apr). *Transfer of Presidential Mandate. Head of "Liberty" and inscriptions greenish black; flag yellow and light blue; background colours given below.* W **111.** *P* 13½.
926 283 40 c. pale buff 5 5
927 1 p. pale red 5 5
928 2 p. pale green 8 5

1958 (31 May). *AIR. 50th Anniv of Argentine Aero Club. Photo.* W **111.** *P* 13½.
929 284 2 p. purple-brown 8 5

285 National Flag Monument 286 Map of Antarctica

1958 (21 June). *First Anniv of Inauguration of National Flag Monument, Rosario. Litho.* W **111.** *P* 13½.
930 285 40 c. grey-blue and pale blue .. 5 5

1958 (12 July). *International Geophysical Year. Litho.* W **111.** *P* 13½.
931 286 40 c. black and cerise 5 5

287 Confederation Stamp and "The Santa Fé Mail" (after lithograph by J. L. Palliére) 288 Aerial View of Flooded Town

1958. *Centenary of Argentine Confederation Stamps.* T **287** *and similar designs. Photo.* W **111.** *P* 13½. *(a) POSTAGE.*
932 40 c. grey-green and pale blue (18.10) .. 5 5

(b) AIR. Inscr "CORREO AEREO"
933 80 c. deep blue and pale yellow (18.10) 5 5
934 1 p. deep grey-blue and brn-orge (23.8) 8 5
Designs: *Horiz*—40 c., Cordoba 5 c. stamp of 1858 and mail-coach; 80 c., Buenos Aires 2 p. stamp of 1858 and "View of Buenos Aires" (after lithograph by Dercy).

1958 (4 Oct). *Flood Disaster Relief Fund. Various flood scenes as* T **288** *inscr* "PRO DAMNIFICADOS POR LA INUNDACION". *Photo.* W **111.** *P* 13½. *(a) POSTAGE.*
935 40 c. + 20 c. brown 5 5

(b) AIR. Inscr "CORREO AEREO"
936 1 p. + 50 c. plum 8 5
937 5 p. + 2 p. 50, slate-blue 35 25
Designs: *Horiz*—1 p. Different aerial view of flooded town; 5 p. Motor truck in flood-water, and garage.

289

290 U.N. Emblem and "The Slave" (after Michelangelo)

1958 (20 Dec). *Leukaemia Relief Campaign. Litho.* W **111**. P 13½.
938 289 1 p. +50 c. carmine and black   ..   5   5

(Des H. A. Viola. Eng G. Nicastro. Recess; background litho)

1959 (14 Mar). *Tenth Anniv of Declaration of Human Rights.* W **111**. P 13½.
939 290 40 c. olive-grey and chocolate   ..   5   5

291 Comet Airliner

292 Orchids and Globe

(Des E. Miliavaca. Litho)

1959 (16 May). *AIR. Inauguration of "Comet" Airliners by Argentine National Airlines.* W **111**. P 13½.
940 291 5 p. black and yellow-olive   ..   10   5

(Des S. Perez. Photo)

1959 (23 May). *First International Horticultural Exhibition, Buenos Aires.* W **111**. P 13½.
941 292 1 p. deep brown-purple   5   5

293 Pope Pius XII

294 William Harvey

(Des D. L. R. Vacek. Recess)

1959 (20 June). *Pope Pius XII Commemoration.* W **111**. P 13½.
942 293 1 p. black and yellow   5   5

1959 (8 Aug). *21st International Physiological Sciences Congress.* T **294** *and similar vert portraits. Litho.* W **111**. P 13½.
943   50 c. green   5   5
944   1 p. brown-red (C. Bernard)   ..   5   5
945   1 p. 50, sepia (I. P. Pavlov)   ..   5   5
943/945   *Set of 3*   8   8

295 Creole Horse

296 Tierra del Fuego

297 Inca Bridge, Mendoza

S. OFICIAL
(O 11)

S. OFICIAL

S. OFICIAL
(O 12)

S. OFICIAL
(O 13)

(10 c., 20 c. litho; 50 c. litho and typo; 1 p. typo; others photo)

1959–67. T **295/7** *and similar designs.* W **111**. P 13 × 13½ (10 c. to 50 c.), 13½ (*others*).
946 –   10 c. grey-green (9.9.59)   5   5
947 –   20 c. purple-brown (15.3.61)   ..   5   5
948 –   50 c. ochre (*litho*) (2.3.60)   ..   5   5
949 –   50 c. ochre (*typo, p* 13½) (1962?) ..   5   5
950 295   1 p. scarlet (19.8.59)   ..   5   5
951 –   3 p. blue (17.2.60)   ..   5   5
952 296   5 p. bistre-brown (4.10.59)   ..   8   5
953 297   10 p. red-brown (1.7.60)   ..   12   5
954 –   20 p. dp turq-green (17.12.60) ..   20   8
946/54   *Set of 9*   55   30
   Designs: As T **295**—10 c. Alligator; 20 c. Llama; 50 c. Puma. As T **296**—3 p. Zapata Hill, Catamarca. As T **297**—20 p. Lake Nahuel Huapi.

OFFICIAL. *Overprinted* (*vert upwards on Nos.* O963, O965)
O955 O 13 10 c. grey-green (1962)   5   5
O956   20 c. purple-brown (1962)   ..   5   5
          a. W **224** (1962)*   ..   5   5
O957 O 11 50 c. ochre (*litho*) (1960) ..   5   5
O958 O 8   3 p. blue (1960)   5   5
O959 O 13   3 p. blue (1967)   5   5
O960 O 8   5 p. bistre-brown (1960)..   8   5
          a. Blue overprint   ..   10   5
O961 O 13   5 p. bistre-brown (1966)..   5   5
O962 O 11 10 p. red-brown (1960)   ..   15   10
O963 O 13 10 p. red-brown (1966)   ..   5   5
O964 O 12 20 p. deep turquoise-green (1961)   20   15
O965 O 13 20 p. deep turquoise-green (1966)   10   8
   *No. O956a is not known without overprint.
   For 50 c. and 5 p. values in these designs with "CASA DE MONEDA" watermark, see Nos. 1298/9.
   For similar designs but without watermark, see Nos. 1331/9.
   For similar designs in revalued currency see Nos. 1349/62 and 1402/7.

298 Athletics

299

(Des H. Viola. Litho)

1959 (5 Sept). *Third Pan-American Games, Chicago.* T **298** *and similar designs bearing torch emblem.* W **111**. P 13½.

(a) POSTAGE

955	20 c. + 10 c. black and green	5	5
956	50 c. + 20 c. black and yellow	5	5
957	1 p. + 50 c. black and maroon	8	5

(b) AIR. Inscr "CORREO AEREO"

958	2 p. + 1 p. black and bright blue	20	12
959	3 p. + 1 p. 50, black and yellow-olive	25	15
955/959	*Set of 5*	50	40

Designs: *Vert*—50 c. Basketball; 1 p. Boxing. *Horiz*—2 p. Rowing; 3 p. High-diving.

(Des H. Viola. Litho)

1959 (3 Oct). *Red Cross Hygiene Campaign.* W **179**. P 13½.

960	**299** 1 p. red, blue and black	5	5

300 Child with Toys   **301** Buenos Aires 1 p. stamp of 1859

(Des H. Viola. Litho)

1959 (17 Oct). *Mothers' Day.* W **111**. P 13½.

961	**300** 1 p. carmine and black	5	5

(Des E. Miliavaca. Litho)

1959 (21 Nov). *Stamp Day.* W **111**. P 13½.

962	**301** 1 p. deep blue and grey	8	5

302 B. Mitre and J. J. de Úrquiza   **303** Andean Condor

(Des H. Alvarez Boero. Photo)

1959 (12 Dec). *Centenary of Pact of San José de Flores.* W **111**. P 13½.

963	**302** 1 p. deep lilac	5	5

(Des H. Alvarez Boero. Litho)

1960 (6 Feb). *Child Welfare. Various vert bird designs as* T **303**. W **111**. P 13½. *(a) POSTAGE.*

964	20 c. + 10 c. deep blue and slate-blue	5	5
965	50 c. + 20 c. bluish violet and lavender	5	5
966	1 p. + 50 c. red-brown and buff	5	5

(b) AIR. Inscr "CORREO AEREO"

967	2 p. + 1 p. magenta and pale salmon	12	8
968	3 p. + 1 p. 50, deep & pale grey-green	20	15
964/968	*Set of 5*	40	30

Birds:—50 c. Fork-tailed flycatcher; 1 p. Ivory-billed woodpecker; 2 p. Rufous tinamou; 3 p. Common rhea.

304 "Uprooted Tree"   **305** Abraham Lincoln

(Des E. Miliavaca. Litho)

1960 (7 Apr). *World Refugee Year.* W **111**. P 13½.

969	**304** 1 p. carmine-red and bistre-brown	5	5
970	4 p. 20, plum and light yellow-green	8	5
MS971	113×85 mm. No. 969/70 with premium added for aid to refugees 1 p. + 50 c. and 4 p. 20 + 2 p. 10. Imperf	55	55

(Des H. Alvarez Boero. Photo)

1960 (14 Apr). *150th Birth Anniv of Lincoln.* W **111**. P 13½.

972	**305** 5 p. ultramarine	10	5

306 Saavedra and Chapter Hall, Buenos Aires   **307** Dr. L. Drago

(Des E. Miliavaca and R. W. Grand. Photo)

1960 (28 May). *150th Anniv of May Revolution.* T **306** *and similar horiz designs inscr "25 DE MAYO 1860–1960".* W **111**. P 13½. *(a) POSTAGE.*

973	1 p. plum	5	5
974	2 p. bluish green	5	5
975	4 p. 20 green and grey-green	8	5
976	10 p. 70, ultramarine and slate	20	8

(b) AIR. Inscr "CORREO AEREO"

977	1 p. 80, reddish brown	5	5
978	5 p. maroon and light brown	10	5
973/978	*Set of 6*	45	20
MS979	2 sheets each 104×156 mm. Nos. 973/4, 977 in red-brown. Nos. 975/6, 978 in grey-green	75	75

Designs:—Chapter Hall, Buenos Aires, and: 1 p. 80, Moreno; 2 p. Paso; 4 p. 20, Alberti and Azcuénaga; 5 p. Belgrano and Castelli; 10 p. 70, Larrea and Matheu.

(Des H. Viola. Photo)

1960 (8 July). *Birth Centenary of Dr. Drago.* W **111**. P 13½.

980	**307** 4 p. 20, sepia	10	5

308 "Five Provinces"   **309** "Market Place, 1810". (Buenos Aires)

(Des H. Viola. Litho)

1960 (8 July). *AIR. New Argentine Provinces.* W **111**. P 13½.

981	**308** 1 p. 80, light blue and carmine-red	5	5

(Des H. R. Alvarez Boero. Photo)

1960 (20 Aug). *AIR. Inter-American Philatelic Exhibition, Buenos Aires ("EFIMAYO") and 150th Anniv of Revolution.* T **309** *and similar horiz designs inscr "EFIMAYO 1960".* W **111**. P 13½.

982	2 p. + 1 p. brown-lake	5	5
983	6 p. + 3 p. black	15	10
984	10 p. 70 + 5 p. 30, blue	25	20
985	20 p. + 10 p. blue-green	40	40
982/985	*Set of 4*	70	60

Designs:—6 p. "The Water Carrier"; 10 p. 70, "The Landing Place"; 20 p. "The Fort".

310 J. B. Alberdi   **311** Seibo (Argentine National Flower)   **312** Map of Argentina

1960 (10 Sept). *150th Birth Anniv of Alberdi (statesman).* Photo. *W* **111**. *P* 13½.
986 **310** 1 p. bronze-green   .   .   5   5

(Des H. Viola (6 p.), E. Miliavaca (10 p. 70). Photo)

1960 (10 Sept). *AIR. Chilean Earthquake Relief Fund. T* **311** *and similar vert design inscr "AYUDA CHILE". W* **111**. *P* 13½.
987   6 p. +3 p. carmine   10   10
988   10 p. 70+5 p. 30, red   15   15
Designs:—10 p. 70, Copihue (Chilean national flower).

(Des H. Viola. Litho)

1960 (24 Sept). *Census, 1960. W* **111**. *P* 13½.
989 **312** 5 p. deep lilac and black   . .   12   5

DIA DE LAS NACIONES UNIDAS
24 DE OCTUBRE

313 Galleon   **(314)**

(Des. E. Miliavaca. Photo)

1960 (1 Oct). *Eighth Spanish-American Postal Union Congress. W* **111**. *P* 13½. (a) *POSTAGE.*
990 **313** 1 p. bronze-green   5   5
991   5 p. sepia   12   5

(b) *AIR. Inscr "CORREO AEREO"*
992 **313** 1 p. 80, bright purple   5   5
993   10 p. 70, deep turquoise   15   12
990/993 *Set of 4*   35   20

1960 (24 Oct). *AIR. United Nations Day. Nos.* 982/5 *optd with T* **314**.
994   2 p. +1 p. brown-lake   10   10
995   6 p. +3 p. black.   15   15
996   10 p. 70+5 p. 30, blue   25   25
997   20 p. +10 p. blue-green   50   50
994/997 *Set of 4*   85   85

315 Blessed Virgin of Lujan   **316** Jacaranda

(Des H. Viola. Photo)

1960 (12 Nov). *First Inter-American Marian Congress. W* **111**. *P* 13½.
998 **315** 1 p. deep blue   5   5

(Des H. Viola. Photo)

1960 (3 Dec). *International Thematic Stamp Exhibition "TEMEX 61". T* **316** *and similar vert designs. W* **111**. *P* 13½.
999   50 c. +50 c. blue   5   5
1000   1 p. +1 p. grey-green   5   5
1001   3 p. +3 p. orange-brown   8   8
1002   5 p. +5 p. bistre-brown   15   12
999/1002 *Set of 4*   25   20
Designs:—1 p. Passion flowers (*Passiflora caerulea*); 3 p. Hibiscus (*Chorisia speciosa*); 5 p. Black lapacho (*Tabebuia ipe*).

317 Argentine Scout Badge   **318** "Shipment of Cereals" (after B. Q. Martin)

(Des H. Alvarez Boero. Litho)

1961 (17 Jan). *International Scout Jamboree. W* **111**. *P* 13½.
1003 **317** 1 p. carmine and black   5   5

1961 (11 Feb). *Export Campaign. Photo. W* **111**. *P* 13½.
1004 **318** 1 p. red-brown   5   5

319 Emperor Penguin and Chick   **320** Battle Scene

(T **319/20** des H. Alvarez Boero. Photo)

1961 (25 Feb). *Child Welfare. T* **319** *and similar vert design. W* **111**. *P* 13½. (a) *POSTAGE.*
1005   –   4 p. 20+2 p. 10, brown   . .   12   12

(b) *AIR. Inscr "CORREO AEREO"*
1006 **319** 1 p. 80+90 c. black.   8   8
Design:—4 p. 20, Blue-eyed shag.

1961 (2 Mar). *150th Anniv of Naval Battle of St. Nicholas. W* **111**. *P* 13½.
1007 **320** 2 p. black   5   5

321 Dr. M. Moreno   **322** Emperor Trajan

(Des H. Viola. Photo)

1961 (25 Mar). *150th Death Anniv of Moreno. W* **111**. *P* 13½.
1008 **321** 2 p. deep blue   5   5

(Des H. Alvarez Boero. Photo)

1961 (11 Apr). *Visit of President of Italy. W* **111**. *P* 13½.
1009 **322** 2 p. bronze-green   5   5

14 DE ABRIL
DIA DE LAS
AMERICAS
(323)

324 Tagore

1961 (15 Apr). *Americas Day. Nos. 999/1002 optd with T 323.*

1010	50 c. + 50 c. blue	5	5
1011	1 p. + 1 p. grey-green (Br.)	5	5
1012	3 p. + 3 p. orange-brown (B.)	12	10
1013	5 p. + 5 p. bistre-brown (R.)	20	15
1010/1013	Set of 4	35	30

(Des H. Alvarez Boero. Photo)

1961 (13 May). *Birth Centenary of Rabindranath Tagore (Indian poet). W 111. P 13½.*

1014	**324**	2 p. deep lilac/green	5	5

325 San Martin
Monument, Madrid

326 Belgrano (after
monument by Rocha)

1961 (24 May). *Inauguration of Spanish San Martin Monument. Photo. W 111. P 13½.*

1015	**325**	1 p. blackish olive	5	5

(Des H. Viola. Photo)

1961 (17 June). *Gen. M. Belgrano Commemoration. W 111. P 13½.*

1016	**326**	2 p. deep blue	5	5

327 San Martin

S. OFICIAL
(O 14)

1961–67. W 111.

(a) Typo. P 13½

1017	**327**	2 p. scarlet (19½ × 26 mm) (1961)	5	5
		a. Redrawn 19½ × 25 mm	5	5
1018		4 p. scarlet (1.9.62)	5	5
1019		8 p. scarlet (15.7.65)	5	5
1020		10 p. scarlet (1966)	5	5
1021		20 p. scarlet (1.6.67)	5	5

(b) Litho. P 13½ × 13 (2 p., 4 p.), 13½ (others)

1022	**327**	2 p. rose-red (19½ × 26 mm) ('61)	5	5
1023		4 p. scarlet (1.9.62)	5	5
1024		8 p. scarlet (15.7.65)	5	5
1025		10 p. scarlet (28.5.66)	5	5
1017/1025	Set of 9		35	35

The 2 p. and 4 p. lithographed stamps can also be distinguished from the typographed stamps in that they have more space between "ARGENTINA" and the upper and lower frame lines.

OFFICIAL. Overprinted horiz. Litho

O1026	O 13	2 p. rose-red (1962)	8	5
O1027		4 p. scarlet (1963)	5	5
O1028		8 p. scarlet (1965)	5	5
O1029		10 p. scarlet (1966)	5	5
O1030		20 p. scarlet (1967)*	10	8
O1031	O 14	20 p. scarlet (1967)*	5	5

*These are not known lithographed without overprint.
For 20 p. wmk "CASA DE MONEDA" and optd with Type O 13, see No. O1303.

328 Sunflowers

329 Quelracho Colorado

330 Ski-jumper

331 Mar del Plata

332 Stag

(Des H. Guimarans (1000 p.). Eng M. A. Cabrera (500 p., 1000 p.))

1961–68. W 111. P 13½.

(a) Photo

1026	**328**	1 p. bistre-brown (5.12.61)	5	5
1027	**329**	12 p. dull purple (31.10.62)	15	5
1028	**249a**	22 p. ultramarine (31.10.62)	25	8
1029	**329**	23 p. bronze-green (15.6.65)	15	8
1030		25 p. slate-lilac (27.7.66)	15	8
1031	**249a**	43 p. lake (15.6.65)	25	12
1032		45 p. red-brown (27.7.66)	25	8
1033	**250a**	50 p. chalky bl (29½ × 40 mm) (15.10.65)	30	5
1034		50 p. chalky bl (22½ × 33 mm) (1.6.67)	15	5
		a. Size 22 × 32½ mm (8.69)	12	5
1035	**330**	100 p. blue (12.6.61)	90	12
1036	**331**	300 p. violet (5.2.62)	2·50	85
1026/1036	Set of 11		4·50	1·25

(b) Litho

1037	**328**	1 p. bistre-brown (1968?)	5	5
1038	**329**	12 p. dull purple (7.64)	65	5
1039	**249a**	22 p. ultramarine (1964)	80	5
1040	**329**	25 p. purple (1967)	12	5
1041	**249a**	45 p. pale red-brown (1967)	20	8
1037/1041	Set of 5		1·60	25

(c) Recess

1042	**332**	500 p. yellow-green (20.5.66)	1·25	40
1043	–	1000 p. dp ultramarine (25.11.68)	2·50	60

Design: As T **332**—1000 p. Leaping fish.
The 50 p. stamps differ from Type **250a** in having the inscription "REPUBLICA ARGENTINA" instead of "ARGENTINA".
In the lithographed stamps the 12 p. and 25 p. have dotted background and the 22 p. and 45 p. have horizontal lines behind "INDUSTRIA".

For 100 p. with wmk "CASA DE MONEDA" see No. 1300.
For designs on paper without watermark, see Nos. 1331/9.
For similar designs in revalued currency see Nos. 1349/62 and 1402/7.

OFFICIAL. Overprinted
(a) Photo

O1044	O 12	1 p. bistre-brown (1962)	..	5	5
O1045	O 13	1 p. bistre-brn (vert up) ('63?)		5	5
O1046	O 14	12 p. dull purple (1963)	..	10	5
O1047		22 p. ultramarine (1963)	..	15	10
O1048	O 13	23 p. bronze-green (vert down) (1965)	..	15	10
O1049		25 p. slate-lilac (vert up) (R.) (1966)	..	12	5
O1050		43 p. lake (vert down) (1965)	..	20	10
O1051		45 p. red-brown (vert up) (1966)	..	10	10
O1052	O 9	50 p. chalky blue (vert up) (1966)*	..	25	10
O1053	O 13	50 p. chalky blue (vert up) (1967)	..	15	5
O1054	O 14	100 p. blue (1964)	..	90	35
O1055		100 p. blue (vert up) (1965)	..	65	35
O1056		300 p. violet (1967)	..	1·25	75

*Overprint is larger (21 mm long).

(b) Litho (1967)

O1057	O 13	25 p. purple (vert down) (R.)	..	8	5
O1058		45 p. pale red-brown (vert up)		20	5

(c) Recess

O1059	O 7	500 p. yellow-green (1967)	..	1·50	80

The overprint on No. O1059 is horizontal in two lines.

333 Antarctic Scene   334 Conquistador and Sword

1961 (19 Aug). *Tenth Anniv of San Martin Antarctic Base. Photo. W 111. P 13½.*
1044 333 2 p. black 5 5

(Des H. Alvarez Boero. Litho)

1961 (19 Aug). *Fourth Centenary of Jujuy. W 111. P 13½.*
1045 334 2 p. brown-red and black 5 5

335 Sarmiento Statue (Rodin)   336 Cordoba Cathedral

1961 (9 Sept). *150th Birth Anniv of D. F. Sarmiento (statesman). Photo. W 111. P 13½.*
1046 335 2 p. violet 5 5

(Des E. Miliavaca. Photo)

1961 (21 Oct). *"Argentina 62" International Philatelic Exhibition (First issue). T 336 and other designs. W 111. P 13½.*

1047	2 p. + 2 p. reddish purple	..	..	8	5
1048	3 p. + 3 p. blue-green	..	..	10	8
1049	10 p. + 10 p. blue	..	..	30	25
MS1050	86×86 mm. Nos. 1047/9 each indigo. Imperf	..	..	55	55

Designs: Horiz—10 p. Buenos Aires Cathedral. Vert—3 p. 10 c. stamp of 1862 (as T 343).

337   338 "The Flight into Egypt" (after Ana Maria Moncalvo)

(Des H. Viola. Litho)

1961 (25 Nov). *World Town-Planning Day. W 111. P 13½.*
1052 337 2 p. blue and greenish yellow .. 5 5

1961 (16 Dec). *Child Welfare. Litho. W 111. P 13½.*

1053	338	2 p. + 1 p. sepia and lilac	..	5	5
1054		10 p. + 5 p. brown-purple & mauve	25	20

339 Belgrano Statue   340 Mounted Grenadier

1962 (24 Feb). *150th Anniv of National Flag. Photo. W 111. P 13½.*
1055 339 2 p. Prussian blue 5 5

1962 (31 Mar). *150th Anniv of San Martin's Mounted Grenadiers. Photo. W 111. P 13½.*
1056 340 2 p. carmine 5 5

341 Mosquito and Emblem   342 Lujan Cathedral

(Des E. Miliavaca. Litho)

1962 (14 Apr). *Malaria Eradication. W 111. P 13½.*
1057 341 2 p. black and red 5 5

(Des H. Viola. Litho)

1962 (12 May). *75th Anniv of Coronation of Lujan Virgin. W 111. P 13½.*
1058 342 2 p. black and brown 5 5

343 15 c. Stamp of 1862   344 Juan Jufre (founder)

(Des E. Miliavaca. Litho)

1962 (19 May). *AIR. "Argentine 62" Philatelic Exhibition (Second issue).* W **111**. P 13½.

1059	**343**	6 p. 50 + 6 p. 50, deep blue and turquoise-green	..	..	20	15

See also No. 1048.

(Des H. Alvarez Boero. Photo)

1962 (23 June). *400th Anniv of San Juan.* W **111**. P 13½.

| 1060 | **344** | 2 p. greenish blue | .. | .. | .. | 5 | 5 |

345 U.N.E.S.C.O. Emblem　　**346** "Flight"

(Des E. Miliavaca. Litho)

1962 (14 July). *AIR. 15th Anniv of U.N.E.S.C.O.* W **111**. P 13½.

| 1061 | **345** | 13 p. brown and ochre | .. | .. | 20 | 15 |

(Des H. Viola. Litho)

1962 (18 Aug). *50th Anniv of Argentine Air Force.* W **111**. P 13½.

| 1062 | **346** | 2 p. lt blue, black and brown-purple | 5 | 5 |

347 Juan Vucetich (finger-prints pioneer)　　**348** 19th-century Mail-coach

(Des H. Alvarez Boero. Photo)

1962 (6 Oct). *Vucetich Commemoration.* W **111**. P 13½.

| 1063 | **347** | 2 p. deep bluish green | .. | .. | 5 | 5 |

(Des H. Viola. Litho)

1962 (6 Oct). *AIR. Postman's Day (14th September).* W **111**. P 13½.

| 1064 | **348** | 5 p. 60, black and grey-brown | .. | 8 | 5 |

(349)　　**350** U.P.A.E. Emblem　　**351** Pres. Sarmiento

1962 (31 Oct). *AIR.* (a) *No. 952 surch as T **349**, in deep green.*

| 1065 | **296** | 5 p. 60 on 5 p. bistre-brown | .. | 8 | 5 |

(b) *As No. 952, but printed on green paper, surch with T **349** in deep green*

| 1066 | **296** | 18 p. on 5 p. bistre-brown/green | .. | 20 | 12 |

1962 (24 Nov). *AIR. 50th Anniv of Postal Union of Americas and Spain.* Photo. W **111**. P 13½.

| 1067 | **350** | 5 p. 60, blue | .. | .. | .. | 8 | 5 |

Two types of 2 p. lithographed.
I. Lines of shading touch frame line at right.
II. Lines of shading stop short of frame line.

1962–69. *T **351** and similar portrait designs.* W **111**. P 13½.

(a) Photo

1068	2 p. deep green (14.12.62)	..	5	5
1069	4 p. brown-red (18.8.65)		5	5
1070	6 p. rose-red (23 × 32½ mm) ('68)		5	5
1071	6 p. brown　　(15 × 22　　mm)			
	(15.11.68)	..	5	5
1072	90 p. dp bistre　(22¼ × 31¾ mm)			
	(8.6.67)	..	30	15
	a. Yell-ol (22¾ × 32½ mm) (8.69)	20	12

(b) Litho

1073	2 p. green (I) (11.9.64)	..	..	5	5
	a. Type II	..	..	5	5
1074	4 p. rose-red (1966)	..	..	5	5
1075	6 p. rose-red (8.6.67)	..	..	5	5
1068/1075	*Set of 8*	..	..	40	30

Designs (*inscr* "ARGENTINA")—4 p. J. Hernández. (*Inscr* "REPUBLICA ARGENTINA")—6 p. J. Hernández; 90 p. G. Brown.

The 2 p. litho has shaded background and the 4 p. and 6 p. have dotted background.

For 6 p. and 90 p. on paper without watermark see Nos. 1334/5 and 1338.

For 1 p. 15, design as 90 p. see Nos. 1362 and 1407.

OFFICIAL. Overprinted
(a) Photo. Vert up (90 p.), down (others)

O1076	O **14**	2 p. deep green (1963)	..	5	5
O1077	O **13**	2 p. deep bluish green (1966)	..	5	5
O1078		90 p. deep bistre (1072) (1966)	..	25	15

(b) Litho. Vert down (1967)

O1079	O **13**	2 p. green (II)	..	..	5	5
O1080		4 p. rose-red	..	..	5	5
O1081		6 p. rose-red	..	..	5	5

352 Mocking-bird　　**353** "Skylark 3" Glider　　**354** "20 de Febrero" Monument, Salta

(Des H. Alvarez Boero. Litho)

1962 (29 Dec). *Child Welfare. T **352** and similar vert design inscr* "PRO INFANCIA". W **111**. P 13½.

1076	4 p. + 2 p. dp brn, turq-grn & yell-brn	12	10
1077	12 p. + 6 p. dp brown, yellow & slate	..	30	25

Bird:—12 p. Rufous-collared sparrow.

See also Nos. 1101/2, 1124/5, 1165/6, 1191/2, 1214/15, 1314/15, 1342/3 and 1408/9.

(Des E. Miliavaca. Litho)

1963 (9 Feb). *AIR. Ninth World Gliding Championships, Junin. T **353** and similar vert design.* W **111**. P 13½.

1078	5 p. 60, black and blue	..	..	8	5
1079	11 p. black, red and blue	..	20	12

Design:—11 p. "Super Albatross" glider.

1963 (23 Feb). *150th Anniv of Battle of Salta. Photo. W* **111.** *P* 13½.
1080 **354** 2 p. deep green 5 5

355 Cogwheels

356 National College

(Des H. Viola. Litho)

1963 (16 Mar). *75th Anniv of Industrial Union. W* **111.** *P* 13½.
1081 **355** 4 p. black, carmine and grey .. 5 5

(Des H. Viola. Litho)

1963 (16 Mar). *Centenary of National College, Buenos Aires. W* **111.** *P* 13½.
1082 **356** 4 p. black and brown-orange .. 5 5

357 Child drinking Milk   **358** "Flight"

(Des H. Viola after photo by P. Almasy. Litho)

1963 (6 Apr). *Freedom from Hunger. W* **111.** *P* 13½.
1083 **357** 4 p. ochre, black and red 5 5

Two types of 7 p.
I. "ARGENTINA" reads down. II. "ARGENTINA" reads up.

1963 (25 Apr)–**65.** *AIR. Litho. W* **111.** *P* 13½.
1084	**358**	5 p. 60, blue-green, mag & dp pur	5	5
1085		7 p. blk & ochre-yell (I) (22.10.64)	8	5
1086		7 p. blk & ochre-yell (II) (1965) ..	55	10
1087		11 p. purple, emerald and black	10	8
1088		18 p. ultramarine, red & dp maroon	20	5
1089		21 p. grey, red and red-brown ..	20	15
1084/1089		*Set of 6*	95	40

For other values inscribed "REPUBLICA ARGENTINA", see Nos. 1147/54.

359 Football   **360** Frigate *La Argentina* ·(after oil-painting by E. Biggeri)

(Des H. Alvarez Boero. Litho)

1963 (18 May). *Fourth Pan-American Games, São Paulo. T* **359** *and similar vert designs. W* **111.** *P* 13½.

(a) POSTAGE
1090 4 p. +2 p. blue-green, black and pink 10 5
1091 12 p. +6 p. lake, black and salmon .. 20 15
     a. Lake colour omitted .. ..

(b) AIR. Inscr "AEREO"
1092 11 p. +5 p. red, black and light green .. 20 15
Designs:—11 p. Cycling; 12 p. Show-jumping.

1963 (18 May). *Navy Day. Photo. W* **111.** *P* 13½.
1093 **360** 4 p. turquoise-blue 5 5

361 Assembly House and Seal   **362** Battle Scene

(Des E. Miliavaca. Litho)

1963 (13 July). *150th Anniv of the "1813" Assembly. W* **111.** *P* 13½.
1094 **361** 4 p. black and light blue 5 5

(Des H. Alvarez Boero. Litho)

1963 (24 Aug). *150th Anniv of Battle of San Lorenzo. W* **111.** *P* 13½.
1095 **362** 4 p. black and green/*emerald* .. 5 5

363 Queen Nefertari (bas-relief)   **364** Government House

(Des E. Miliavaca. Litho)

1963 (14 Sept). *U.N.E.S.C.O. Campaign for Preservation of Nubian Monuments. W* **111.** *P* 13½.
1096 **363** 4 p. black, turquoise-green and buff 5 5

(Des H. Alvarez Boero. Litho)

1963 (12 Oct). *Presidential Installation. W* **111.** *P* 13½.
1097 **364** 5 p. sepia and pink 5 5

365 "Science".   **366** Blackboards

(Des H. Viola. Litho)

1963 (16 Oct). *Tenth Latin-American Neurosurgery Congress. W* **111.** *P* 13½.
1098 **365** 4 p. light blue, black and chestnut .. 5 5

(Des E. Miliavaca. Litho)

1963 (23 Nov). *"Alliance for Progress". W* **111.** *P* 13½.
1099 **366** 5 p. red, black and blue 5 5

367 F. de las Carreras (President of Supreme Court)

368 Kemal Atatürk

369 "Payador" (after Castagnino)

374 U.P.U. Monument, Berne

375 Soldier of the Patricios Regiment

1963 (23 Nov). *Centenary of Judicial Power. Photo.* W **111**. P 13½.

1100 **367** 5 p. deep bluish green 5 5

(Des H. Alvarez Boero. Litho)

1963 (21 Dec). *Child Welfare. Designs as* T **352**, *but with* "ARGENTINA" *and values transposed.* W **111**. P 13½. *(a)* POSTAGE.

1101 4 p. + 2 p. multicoloured 10 8

(b) AIR. *Inscr* "CORREO AEREO"

1102 11 p. + 5 p. multicoloured 15 15

Birds:—4 p. Churrinche (Vermilion flycatcher); 11 p. Benteveo (Great kiskadee).

1963 (28 Dec). *25th Death Anniv of Kemal Atatürk. Photo.* W **111**. P 13½.

1103 **368** 12 p. brownish grey 10 5

1964 (25 Jan). *4th National Folklore Festival. Litho.* W **111**. P 13½.

1104 **369** 4 p. black, light blue and bright blue 5 5

370 Map of Antarctic Islands

371 Jorge Newbery in plane

1964 (22 Feb). *Antarctic Claims Issue.* T **370** *and similar designs. Litho.* W **111**. P 13½. *(a)* POSTAGE.

1105 2 p. light blue, deep blue and bistre .. 8 5
1106 4 p. light blue, deep blue and olive .. 12 5

(b) AIR. *Inscr* "AEREO"

1107 18 p. light blue, deep blue and olive .. 15 12

Designs: *Vert* (30 × 39½ *mm*)—4 p. Map of Argentina and Antarctica. *Horiz* (as T **370**)—18 p. Map of "Islas Malvinas" (Falkland Islands).

1964 (29 Feb). *50th Death Anniv of Jorge Newbery* (aviator). *Photo.* W **111**. P 13½.

1108 **371** 4 p. green 5 5

372 Pres. Kennedy

373 Father Brochero

1964 (14 Apr). *President Kennedy Memorial Issue. Recess.* W **111**. P 13½.

1109 **372** 4 p. deep blue and magenta 5 5

1964 (9 May). *50th Death Anniv of Father J. G. Brochero. Photo.* W **111**. P 13½.

1110 **373** 4 p. bistre-brown 5 5

376 Pope John XXIII

377 Olympic Stadium

1964 (23 May). *AIR. 15th U.P.U. Congress, Vienna.* W **111**. P 13½.

1111 **374** 18 p. dull purple and red 15 12

(Des E. Marenco. Litho)

1964 (30 May). *Army Day* (29 *May*). W **111**. P 13½.

1112 **375** 4 p. multicoloured 5 5
    a. Yellow (trousers, etc) omitted 5·00

1964 (27 June). *Pope John Commemoration. Recess.* W **111**. P 13½.

1113 **376** 4 p. black and orange 5 5

1964 (18 July). *Olympic Games, Tokyo.* T **377** *and similar designs. Litho.* W **111**. P 13½. *(a)* POSTAGE.

1114 4 p. + 2 p. brown, yellow and red .. 8 15
1115 12 p. + 6 p. black and green 15 15

(b) AIR. *Inscr* "AEREO"

1116 11 p. + 5 p. black and blue 20 20

Designs: *Vert*—11 p. Sailing; 12 p. Fencing.

378 University Arms

379 Olympic Flame and Crutch

380 "The Discovery of America" (Florentine woodcut)

1964 (22 Aug). *350th Anniv of Cordoba University. Litho.* W **111**. P 13½.

1117 **378** 4 p. olive-yellow, ultramarine & blk 5 5

(Des E. Miliavaca. Litho)

1964 (19 Sept). *AIR. Invalids Olympic Games, Tokyo.* W **111**. P 13½.

1118 **379** 18 p. + 9 p. multicoloured 20 20

1964 (10 Oct). *AIR. "Columbus Day"* (or *"Day of the Race"*). *Litho.* W **111**. P 13½.

1119 **380** 13 p. black and light drab 12 8

381 Pigeons and U.N. Headquarters

382 J. V. Gonzalez (medallion)

383 Gen. J. Roca

(Des Silvia Cristina Z. Martinez. Litho)

1964 (24 Oct). *United Nations Day.* W **111**. *P* 13½.
1120 **381** 4 p. ultramarine and light blue .. 5 5

1964 (14 Nov). *Birth Centenary of J. V. Gonzalez.* *Photo.* W **111**. *P* 13½.
1121 **382** 4 p. carmine .., ... 5 5

1964 (12 Dec). 50th *Death Anniv of General Julio Roca.* *Photo.* W **111**. *P* 13½.
1122 **383** 4 p. ultramarine 5 5

384 "Market Place, Montserrat Square" (after C. Morel)

385 Icebreaker *General San Martin*

1964 (19 Dec). *"Argentine Painters".* *Photo.* W **111**. *P* 13½.
1123 **384** 4 p. sepia 8 5

(Des H. Alvarez Boero. Photo)

1964 (23 Dec). *Child Welfare. Designs as T* **352** *but with "ARGENTINA" and values transposed. Multicoloured.* W **111**. *P* 13½. (*a*) *POSTAGE.*
1124 4 p. + 2 p, Cardinal 5 5

(*b*) *AIR. Inscr "CORREO AEREO"*
1125 18 p. + 9 p. Argentine swallow 20 20

1965 (27 Feb–5 June). *"National Territory of Tierra del Fuego, Antarctic and South Atlantic Isles". T* **385** *and other horiz designs inscr "ANTARTIDA ARGENTINA", etc. Photo.* W **111**. *P* 13½. (*a*) *POSTAGE.*
1126 2 p. dull purple (5.6) 5 5
1127 4 p. ultramarine 5 5

(*b*) *AIR. Inscr "CORREO AEREO"*
1128 11 p. light vermilion 10 5
Designs:—2 p. General Belgrano Base; 11 p. Teniente Matienzo Joint Antarctic Base.

PRIMERAS JORNADAS FILATELICAS RIOPLATENSES
(386)

387 Young Saver

1965 (17 Mar). *AIR. First Rio Plata Philatelists' Day. No.* 1086 *optd with T* **386**, *in silver.*
1129 **383** 7 p. black and ochre-yellow (II) .. 5 5

1965 (3 Apr). 50th *Anniv of National Postal Savings Bank. Litho.* W **111**. *P* 13½.
1130 **387** 4 p. black and orange-red 5 5

388 I.T.U. Emblem

389 I.Q.S.Y. Emblem

(Des E. Miliavaca. Litho)

1965 (11 May). *AIR. I.T.U. Centenary.* W **111**. *P* 13½.
1131 **388** 18 p. multicoloured 15 10

1965 (22 May). *International Quiet Sun Year and Space Research. T* **389** *and similar designs (inscr "INVESTIGACIONES ESPACIALES"). Litho (4 p.) or photo (others).* W **111**. *P* 13½. (*a*) *POSTAGE.*
1132 4 p. black, red-orange and blue .. 5 5

(*b*) *AIR. Inscr "CORREO AEREO"*
1133 18 p. vermilion 15 12
1134 50 p. ultramarine 40 25
Designs: *Vert*—18 p. Rocket launching. *Horiz*—50 p. Earth, trajectories and space phenomena.

390 Soldier of the Pueyrredon Hussars

391 Ricardo Güiraldes

(Des E. Marenco. Litho)

1965 (5 June). *Army Day (29 May).* W **111**. *P* 13½.
1135 **390** 8 p. multicoloured 5 5
See also Nos. 1170, 1201, 1223, 1296, 1367, 1387 and 1413.

(Des H. Alvarez Boero. Photo)

1965 (26 June). *Argentine Writers (1st series). T* **391** *and similar portrait designs. Each bistre-brown.* W **111**. *P* 13½.
1136 8 p. Type **391** 5 5
1137 8 p. E. Larreta 5 5
1138 8 p. L. Lugones.. .. .. .. 5 5
1139 8 p. R. J. Payró 5 5
1140 8 p. R. Rojas 5 5
1136/1140 *Set of* 5 .. .. 20 15
Nos. 1136/40 were arranged together in two horizontal rows of each design within the sheet.
See also Nos. 1174/8.

392 H. Yrigoyen (statesman)

393 "Children looking through a Window"

(Des A. J. Jaro. Litho)

1965 (3 July). *Hipolito Yrigoyen Commemoration.* W **111**. *P* 13½.
1141 **392** 8 p. black and rose.. .. .. 5 5

(Des S. Mendaro, from photograph by S. Facio. Centre photo, frame litho)

1965 (24 July). *International Mental Health Seminar.* W **111.** P 13½.
1142 **393** 8 p. black and cinnamon 5 5

394 Ancient Map and Funeral Urn   **395** Msgr. Dr. J. Cagliero

(Des E. Miliavaca. Litho)

1965 (7 Aug). *400th Anniv of San Miguel de Tucuman.* W **111.** P 13½.
1143 **394** 8 p. red, yellow, brown and lt green 5 5

1965 (21 Aug). *Cagliero Commemoration. Photo.* W **111.** P 13½.
1144 **395** 8 p. violet 5 5

396 Dante (statue in Church of Holy Cross, Florence)   **397** Clipper *Mimosa*

(Des H. Guimarans. Photo)

1965 (16 Sept). *700th Anniv of Dante's Birth.* W **111.** P 13½.
1145 **396** 8 p. grey-blue 5 5

(Des H. Guimarans. Litho)

1965 (25 Sept). *Centenary of Welsh Colonisation of Chubut and of Foundation of Rawson.* W **111.** P 13½.
1146 **397** 8 p. black and vermilion .. 5 5

1965 (15 Oct)–**67.** AIR. As T 358 but inscr "REPUBLICA ARGENTINA", *reading downwards. Litho.* W **111.** P 13½.
1147   12 p. brown-lake and brown 10 5
1148   15 p. ultramarine and brown-red .. 12 5
1149   26 p. deep ochre (20.12.67) 8 5
1150   27 p. 50, deep bluish green and black .. 20 12
1151   30 p. 50, brown and blue 20 15
1152   40 p. slate-lilac (20.12.67) 12 10
1153   68 p. blue-green (20.12.67) 20 15
1154   78 p. ultramarine (20.12.67) 25 15
1147/1154   *Set of 8* .. .. 1·10 70
For values with "CASA DE MONEDA" watermark, see Nos. 1301/2.
For stamps on paper without watermark see Nos. 1340/1.
For designs in revalued currency see Nos. 1363/4.

398 Police Emblem   **399** Schoolchildren

(Des H. Viola. Photo)

1965 (30 Oct). *Federal Police Day.* W **111.** P 13½.
1155 **398** 8 p. carmine 5 5

1965 (6 Nov). *81st Anniv of Law* 1420 *(Public Education). Litho.* W **111.** P 13½.
1156 **399** 8 p. black and yellow-green 5 5

400 St. Francis' Church, Catamarca   **401** R. Dario (Nicaraguan poet)

(Des H. Alvarez Boero. Litho)

1965 (8 Dec). *Brother Mamerto Esquiu Commemoration.* W **111.** P 13½.
1157 **400** 8 p. brown-red and orange-yellow 5 5

(Des H. Alvarez Boero. Litho)

1965 (22 Dec). *50th Death Anniv of Ruben Dario.* W **111.** P 13½.
1158 **401** 15 p. bluish violet/*pale grey* .. 8 5

402 "The Orange-seller" (detail)   **403** Rocket "Centaur" and Antarctic Map

1966 (29 Jan). *Prilidiano Pueyrredon's Paintings.* T **402** and similar horiz designs showing details from the original works, each printed in deep bluish green. *Photo.* W **111.** P 13½.
1159   8 p. Type **402** 5 5
1160   8 p. "A Halt at the Village Grocer's Shop" 5 5
1161   8 p. "San Fernando Landscape" .. 5 5
1162   8 p. "Bathing Horses on the Banks of the River Plate" 5 5
1159/1162   *Set of* 4 .. .. 15 15
Nos. 1159/62 were issued together in blocks of 4 within the sheets consisting of 40 stamps and 20 labels, also arranged in blocks of 4, each bearing the title of one of the paintings and the inscr "PINTORES ARGENTINOS" ("ARGENTINE PAINTERS").

(Des E. Miliavaca. Litho)

1966 (19 Feb). *AIR. Rocket Launches in Antarctica.* W **111.** P 13½.
1163 **403** 27 p. 50, orange-red, black and blue 12 8

404 Dr. Sun Yat-sen   **405** "Rivadavia" 5 c. Stamp of 1864

(Des H. Guimarans. Photo)

1966 (12 Mar). *Birth Centenary of Dr. Sun Yat-sen.* W **111.** P 13½.
1164 **404** 8 p. red-brown 5 5

(Des H. Alvarez Boero. Litho)

1966 (26 Mar). *Child Welfare. Designs as T* **352** *but differently arranged and inscr "R. ARGENTINA". Multicoloured. W* **111.** *P* 13½. *(a) POSTAGE.*
1165   8 p. +4 p. Cayenne lapwing   8   8

(b) AIR. Inscr "AEREO"
1166   27 p. 50+12 p. 50, Rufous ovenbird   ..   25   25

(Des E. Miliavaca. Litho)

1966 (20 Apr). *2nd Rio Plata Philatelists' Days and Exhibition. Miniature sheet containing designs as T* **405.** *W* **111.** *Imperf.*
MS1167   141×100 mm ..   ..   ..
   4 p. brown-red and grey (T **405**) ..
   5 p. green and grey (10 c. stamp) ..   }   15
   8 p. deep blue and grey (15 c. stamp) ..   ..

406 "Human Races"

(Des H. Guimarans. Litho)

1966 (23 Apr). *Inauguration of W.H.O. Headquarters, Geneva. W* **111.** *P* 13½.
1168 **406**   8 p. black and deep yellow-brown   5   5

407 Seagull

(Des H. Viola. Litho)

1966 (14 May). *AIR. 50th Anniv of Naval Aviation School, Puerto Militar. W* **111.** *P* 13½.
1169 **407**   12 p. multicoloured   8   5

(Des E. Marenco. Litho)

1966 (28 May). *Army Day (29 May). Design similar to T* **390.** *W* **111.** *P* 13½.
1170   8 p. multicoloured   5   5
Design:—8 p. Militiaman of Guemes "Infernals".

408   **409** Arms of Argentina

1966 (25 June). *AIR. "Argentina '66" Philatelic Exhibition, Buenos Aires. Litho. W* **111.** *P* 13½.
1171 **408**   10 p. +10 p. multicoloured..   15   15
The above stamp was only issued in small sheets of four.

1966 (30 July). *150th Anniv of Independence. Sheet of 25 (5×5) comprising different 10 p. designs—national, federal and provincial arms and maps, as T* **404.** *Inscr "1816–1966". Multicoloured. Litho. W* **111.** *P* 13½.
MS1172   Sheet of 25 stamps..   ..   1·90

410 "Charity" Emblem   **411** Anchor

1966 (10 Sept). *Argentine Charities. Litho. W* **111.** *P* 13½.
1173 **410**   10 p. light blue, black & olive-grn ..   5   5

(Des H. Alvarez Boero. Photo)

1966 (17 Sept). *Argentine Writers (2nd series). Portraits as T* **391.** *Each deep bluish green. W* **111.** *P* 13½.
1174   10 p. H. Ascasubi   5   5
1175   10 p. Estanislao del Campo   ..   5   5
1176   10 p. M. Cane   5   5
1177   10 p. Lucio V. Lopez   5   5
1178   10 p. R. Obligado   5   5
1174/1178   *Set of 5*   20   15
Nos. 1174/8 were arranged together in two horizontal rows of each design within the sheet.

(Des H. Guimarans. Litho)

1966 (8 Oct). *25th Anniv of Argentine Mercantile Marine. W* **111.** *P* 13½.
1179 **411**   4 p. multicoloured   5   5

412 L. Agote   **413** Map and Flags of the American States

(Des H. Guimarans. Photo)

1966 (22 Oct). *Argentine Scientists. T* **412** *and similar portrait designs. Each bluish violet. W* **111.** *P* 13½.
1180   10 p. Type **412**   5   5
1181   10 p. J. B. Ambrosetti   5   5
1182   10 p. M. I. Lillo   5   5
1183   10 p. F. P. Moreno   5   5
1184   10 p. F. J. Muniz   5   5
1180/1184   *Set of 5*   20   15
Nos. 1180/4 were arranged together in horizontal rows of each design within the sheet.

(Des H. Guimarans. Litho)

1966 (29 Oct). *7th American Armies' Conference, Buenos Aires. W* **111.** *P* 13½.
1185 **413**   10 p. multicoloured   5   5

414 Bank Façade   **415** La Salle Statue and College

(Des H. Guimarans. Photo)

1966 (5 Nov). *75th Anniv of Argentine National Bank. W* **111.** *P* 13½.
1186 **414**   10 p. bluish green   5   5

(Des C. Gomez. Litho)

1966 (26 Nov). *75th Anniv of La Salle College, Buenos Aires. W* **111**. *P* 13½.
1187 **415** 10 p. black and yellow-brown .. 5 5

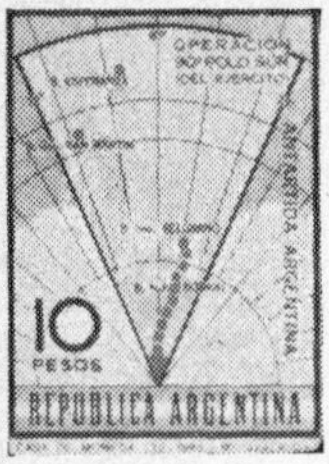

416 Antarctic Map

417 Gen. J. M. de Pueyrredon

(Des E. Miliavaca. Litho)

1966 (10 Dec). *Argentine South Pole Expedition*, 1965–66. *W* **111**. *P* 13½.
1188 **416** 10 p. multicoloured 8 5

(Design from oil by Prilidiano Pueyrredon. Photo)

1966 (17 Dec). *Gen. Juan Martin de Pueyrredon Commemoration. W* **111**. *P* 13½.
1189 **417** 10 p. lake-brown 5 5

418 Gen. J. G. de Las Heras

419 Ancient Pot

(Eng G. Nicastro. Recess)

1966 (17 Dec). *Gen. Juan G. de Las Heras Commemoration. W* **111**. *P* 13½.
1190 **418** 10 p. black 5 5

(Des H. Alvarez Boero. Litho)

1967 (14 Jan). *Child Welfare. Designs as T* **352** *but differently arranged and inscr* "R. ARGENTINA". *Multicoloured. W* **111**. *P* 13½. (a) *POSTAGE*.
1191 10 p.+5 p. Scarlet-headed marsh bird (*horiz*) 10 10

(b) *AIR. Inscr* "CORREO AEREO"
1192 15 p.+7 p. Blue and yellow tanager (*vert*) 15 15

(Des H. Viola. Litho)

1967 (18 Feb). *20th Anniv of U.N.E.S.C.O. W* **111**. *P* 13½.
1193 **419** 10 p. multicoloured 5 5

420 "The Meal" (after F. Fader)

1967 (25 Feb). *Fernando Fader (painter). Photo. W* **111**. *P* 13½.
1194 **420** 10 p. red-brown 8 5

421 J. Azurduy de Padilla

422 Schooner *Invincible*

(Des H. Viola. Litho)

1967 (13 May). *Famous Argentine Women. T* **421** *and similar portrait designs. Each sepia. W* **111**. *P* 13½.
1195 6 p. Type **421** 5 5
1196 6 p. J. M. Gorriti 5 5
1197 6 p. C. Grierson 5 5
1198 6 p. J. P. Manso 5 5
1199 6 p. A. Storni 5 5
1195/1199 *Set of* 5 .. .. 15 12

Nos. 1195/9 were arranged together in horizontal rows of each design within the sheet.

(Des E. Biggeri. Litho)

1967 (20 May). *Navy Day. W* **111**. *P* 13½.
1200 **422** 20 p. multicoloured 8 5
a. Yellow omitted .. .. 5·00

(Des J. J. Saracho. Litho)

1967 (27 May). *Army Day* (29 *May*). *Design similar to T* **390**. *W* **111**. *P* 13½.
1201 20 p. multicoloured 8 5
Design:—20 p. Soldier of the Highlanders' Corps.

423 M. Belgrano (6 p.) and J. G. de Artigas (22 p.)

(Des H. Alvarez Boero. Photo)

1967 (22 June). *3rd Rio Plata Philatelist Days and Exhibition. Sheet* (57×43 *mm*) *comprising designs as T* **423**. *W* **111**. *Imperf*.
MS1202 6 p. and 22 p. each yellow-brown and olive-grey 10 10

424 Suitcase and Dove

425 PADELAI Emblem and Sun

(Des H. Viola. Litho)

1967 (5 Aug). *International Tourist Year. W* **111**. *P* 13½.
1203 **424** 20 p. multicoloured 5 5

(Des H. Guimarans. Litho)

1967 (12 Aug). *75th Anniv of PADELAI (Argentine Children's Welfare Association).* W **111**. *P* 13½.
1204 **425** 20 p. multicoloured 5 5

426 Fels' Blériot Aircraft

(Des H. Guimarans. Litho)

1967 (2 Sept). *AIR. 50th Anniv of first Argentine–Uruguay Airmail Flight.* W **111**. *P* 13½.
1205 **426** 26 p. blackish brn, yell-olive & lt bl 8 5

427 Ferreyra's Oxwagon and Skyscrapers

(Des H. Guimarans. Litho)

1967 (23 Sept). *Centenary of Villa Maria.* W **111**. *P* 13½.
1206 **427** 20 p. multicoloured 8 5

428 "General San Martin" (from statue by M. P. Nuñez de Ibarra) **429** Interior of Museum

(20 p. litho. 40 p. eng M. A. Cabrera; recess)

1967 (30 Sept). *150th Anniv of Battle of Chacabuco.* T **428** and similar design. W **111**. *P* 13½.
1207 20 p. blackish brown & pale grnsh yell 8 5
1208 40 p. indigo 15 8
Design: *Horiz* (48×31 *mm*)—40 p. "Battle of Chacabuco" (from painting by P. Subercaseaux)

1967 (11 Oct). *Tenth Anniv of Government House Museum.* Photo. W **111**. *P* 13½.
1209 **429** 20 p. slate-blue 5 5

430 Pedro Zanni and Fokker Biplane
431 Training Ship *General Brown* (from painting by E. Biggeri)

(Des H. Viola. Litho)

1967 (21 Oct). *Aeronautics Week.* W **111**. *P* 13½.
1210 **430** 20 p. multicoloured 8 5

1967 (28 Oct). *"Temex 67" Stamp Exhibition and 95th Anniv of Naval Military School.* Litho. W **111**. *P* 13½.
1211 **431** 20 p. multicoloured 10 5

432 Ovidio Lagos and Front Page of *La Capital*
433 St. Barbara

1967 (11 Nov). *Centenary of "La Capital" (newspaper).* Photo. W **111**. *P* 13½.
1212 **432** 20 p. blackish brown 8 5

1967 (2 Dec). *Artillery Day (4 Dec).* Photo. W **111**. *P* 13½.
1213 **433** 20 p. rose 8 5

(Des Alvarez Boero. Litho)

1967 (23 Dec). *Child Welfare. Designs as T 352, but differently arranged and inscr "R. ARGENTINA". Multicoloured.* W **111**. *P* 13½. *(a) POSTAGE.*
1214 20 p. + 10 p. Amazon kingfisher .. 10 10
(b) AIR. Inscr "AEREO"
1215 26 p. + 13 p. Toco toucan 15 15

434 "Sivori's Wife"
435 "Almirante Brown" Scientific Station

1968 (27 Jan). *50th Death Anniv of Eduardo Sivori (painter).* Photo. W **111**. *P* 13½.
1216 **434** 20 p. blue-green 8 5

(Des E. Miliavaca. Litho)

1968 (17 Feb). *"Antarctic Territories". T* **435** and similar designs. W **111**. *P* 13½.
1217 6 p. multicoloured 5 5
1218 20 p. multicoloured 8 5
1219 40 p. multicoloured 15 8
Designs: *Vert* (22½×32 *mm*)—6 p. Map of Antarctic radiopostal stations. *Horiz (as T* **435***)*—40 p. Aircraft over South Pole ("Trans-Polar Round Flight").

436 Man in Wheelchair
437 "St. Gabriel" (detail from "The Annunciation" by Leonardo da Vinci)
438 Children and W.H.O. Emblem

(Des H. Alvarez Boero. Litho)

1968 (23 Mar). *Rehabilitation Day for the Handicapped.* W **111**. P 13½.
1220 **436** 20 p. black and light emerald   .. 5 5

1968 (23 Mar). *St. Gabriel (patron saint of army communications). Photo.* W **111**. P 13½.
1221 **437** 20 p. magenta 5 5

(Des H. Guimarans. Litho)

1968 (11 May). *20th Anniv of World Health Organisation.* W **111**. P 13½.
1222 **438** 20 p. chalky blue and vermilion .. 5 5

1968 (8 June). *Army Day (29 May). Design similar to T **390**. Multicoloured. Litho.* W **111**. P 13½.
1223 20 p. Iriarte's artilleryman 5 5

439 Frigate *Libertad* (E. Biggeri)

440 G. Rawson and Hospital

1968 (15 June). *Navy Day. Litho.* W **111**. P 13½.
1224 **439** 20 p. multicoloured 8 5

(Des P. Mettke. Photo)

1968 (20 July). *Centenary of Guillermo Rawson Hospital.* W **111**. P 13½.
1225 **440** 6 p. deep bistre 5 5

441 Vito Dumas and *Legh II*

442 Children crossing "Zebra"

(Des H. Alvarez Boero. Litho)

1968 (27 July). *AIR. Vito Dumas' World Voyage in Yacht 'Legh II'.* W **111**. P 13½.
1226 **441** 68 p. multicoloured 20 15

(Des E. Miliavaca. Litho)

1968 (10 Aug). *Road Safety.* W **111** (*sideways*). P 13½.
1227 **442** 20 p. multicoloured 5 5

443 "Maipo's Embrace" (P. Subercaseaux)

444 Dr. O. Magnasco (lawyer)

(Des from painting. Eng G. Nicastro. Recess)

1968 (15 Aug). *150th Anniv of Battle of the Maipo.* W **111**. P 13½.
1228 **443** 40 p. indigo 15 8

(Des H. Alvarez Boero. Photo)

1968 (7 Sept). *Magnasco Commemoration.* W **111**. P 13½.
1229 **444** 20 p. brown 5 5

445 "The Sea" (E. Gomez)   **446** "Grandmother's Birthday Anniversary" (P. Lynch)

(Des by children (named in captions above). Litho)

1968 (21 Sept). *Children's Stamp Design Competition.* W **111**. P 13½.
1230 **445** 20 p. multicoloured 5 5
1231 **446** 20 p. multicoloured 5 5

447 Mar del Plata at Night   **448** Mounted Gendarme

1968 (19 Oct). *Fourth Plenary Assembly of International Telegraph and Telephone Consultative Committee, Mar del Plata.* T **447** *and similar horiz designs inscr* "MAR DEL PLATA". *Litho.* W **111**. P 13½. (a) *POSTAGE.*
1282 20 p. black, yellow and new blue   .. 5 5

(b) *AIR. Inscr* "AEREO"
1283 40 p. black, magenta and light blue .. 12 8
1284 68 p. black, gold, new and light blue .. 20 15
Designs: (As T **447**)—40 p. South America in Southern hemisphere. *Larger* (40×30 *mm*)—68 p. Assembly emblem.

(Des H. Guimarans. Litho)

1968 (26 Oct). *National Gendarmerie.* W **111**. P 13½.
1285 **448** 20 p. black, yellow, green & brown 5 5

449 Coastguard Cutter   **450** A. de Anchorens and "Pampero"

(Des H. Alvarez Boero. Litho)

1968 (26 Oct). *National Maritime Prefecture (Coastguard).* W **111**. P 13½.
1286 **449** 20 p. black, grey, bright & light blue 5 5

(Des E. Miliavaca. Photo)

1968 (2 Nov). *Aeronautics Week.* W **111**. P 13½.
1287 **450** 20 p. multicoloured 5 5

451 St. Martin of Tours (A. Guido) **452** Bank Emblem

457
Illustration from Schmidl's book, *Journey to the River Plate and Paraguay*

1968 (9 Nov). *St. Martin of Tours (patron saint of Buenos Aires). Litho.* W **111**. P 13½.
1288 **451** 20 p. blackish brown & reddish lilac   5   5

(Des E. Miliavaca. Litho)

1968 (16 Nov). *Municipal Bank of Buenos Aires.* W **111**. P 13½.
1289 **452** 20 p. black, green, yellow and blue   5   5

1969 (8 Feb). *Ulrich Schmidl Commemoration. Litho.* W **111**. P 13½.
1295 **457** 20 p. black, yellow and red   5   5

458

(Des E. Marenco. Litho)

1969 (31 May). *Army Day (29 May). Vert design similar to* T **390**. *Multicoloured.* W **458**. P 13½.
1296 20 p. Sapper, Buenos Aires, 1856   8   5

453 Anniversary and A.L.P.I. Emblems   **454** "The Anniversary of My Grandmother" (Patricia Lynch)

1968 (14 Dec). *25th Anniv of "Fight Against Polio Association" (A.L.P.I.). Litho.* W **111**. P 13½.
1290 **453** 20 p. bluish green and cerise   ..   5   5

(Des from child's drawing. Litho)

1968 (14 Dec). *First "Solidarity" Philatelic Exhibition, Buenos Aires.* W **111**. P 12½ × 13½.
1291 **454** 40 p. + 20 p. multicoloured   15   15

459 Frigate *Hercules*   **460** "Freedom and Equality" (poster by S. Zagorski)

455 "The Potter Woman" (Ramon Gaz y Cornet)   **456** Emblem of State Coalfields

(Des E. Biggeri. Litho)

1969 (31 May). *Navy Day.* W **458**. P 13½.
1297 **459** 20 p. multicoloured   8   5

1969–70. *As previous issues, but* W **458**. P 13½.

(a) POSTAGE
1298	–	50 c. brown-ochre (as No. 948) (litho) (1970) ..		5	5
1299	**296**	5 p. brown (photo) (28.6.69)		5	5
1300	**330**	100 p. blue (photo) (28.6.69) ..		30	15

(b) AIR. Litho. As Nos. 1152/3
1301	40 p. slate-lilac (8.69)	12	10
1302	68 p. blue-green (2.70) ..	20	15

(c) OFFICIAL. Litho. As No. O1030 (optd with Type O **13**)
O1303 **327** 20 p. scarlet   5   5
This stamp was not issued without the overprint.

1968 (21 Dec). *Centenary of Witcomb Gallery, Buenos Aires. Photo.* W **111**. P 13½.
1292 **455** 20 p. cerise   5   5

(Des H. Viola (1293), E. Miliavaca (1294). Litho)

1968 (21 Dec). *Coal and Steel Industries.* T **456** *and similar vert design.* W **111**. P 13½.
1293 20 p. multicoloured   5   5
1294 20 p. multicoloured   5   5
Design:—No. 1294, Ladle and emblem of Military Steel-manufacturing Agency ("FM").

1969 (28 June). *Human Rights Year. Litho.* W **111**. P 13½.
1304 **460** 20 p. black and yellow   5   5

461 I.L.O. Emblem
within Honeycomb

462 P. N. Arata
(biologist)

(Des H. Viola. Litho)

1969 (28 June). *50th Anniversary of International Labour Organization.* W **458**. P 13½.
1305 **461** 20 p. multicoloured   5   5

(Des H. Alvarez Boero. Litho)

1969 (9 Aug). *Argentine Scientists.* T **462** and similar vert portraits, each brown and yellow. W **458**. P 13½.
1306 6 p. Type **462**   5   5
1307 6 p. M. Fernandez (zoologist) ..   5   5
1308 6 p. A. Gallardo (biologist) ..   5   5
1309 6 p. C. Hicken (botanist)   5   5
1310 6 p. E. Holmberg (botanist)   5   5
1306/1310 Set of 5 ..   15   12
Nos. 1306/10 were issued together *se-tenant* in sheets of 100, each design appearing on two adjoining horiz rows.

463 Dish Aerial and
Satellite

464 Nieuport "28" Fighter
and Route-map

(Des E. Miliavaca (20 p.), H. Alvarez Boero (40 p.). Litho (20 p.) or photo (40 p.))

1969 (23 Aug). *Satellite Communications.* T **463** and similar design. W **111**. P 13½. (a) POSTAGE.
1311 20 p. black, yellow and buff ..   5   5

(b) AIR. Inscr "AEREO"
1312 40 p. Prussian blue ..   12   8
Design: Horiz—40 p. Balcarce earth station and dish aerial.

(Des E. Miliavaca. Litho)

1969 (13 Sept). *50th Anniversary of 1st Argentine Airmail Service.* W **111**. P 13½.
1313 **464** 20 p. multicoloured ..   5   5

(Des H. Alvarez Boero. Photo)

1969 (20 Sept). *Child Welfare. Vert designs as* T **352**. Multi-coloured. W **111**. P 13½. (a) POSTAGE.
1314 20 p.+10 p. Widow duck ..   8   8

(b) AIR. Inscr "AEREO"
1315 26 p.+13 p. Red-headed striped wood-pecker ..   12   12

465 College Entrance

(Des H. Viola. Litho)

1969 (4 Oct). *Centenary of Argentine Military College.* W **458**. P 13½.
1316 **465** 20 p. multicoloured   5   5

466 General Pacheco
(from painting by R.
Giudice)

467 B. Mitre (founder) and
Logotypes of *La Nacion*

1969 (8 Nov). *Death Centenary of General Angel Pacheco.* Photo. W **458**. P 13½.
1317 **466** 20 p. deep green ..   5   5

(Des H. Viola. Litho)

1969 (8 Nov). *Centenary of "La Nacion" and "La Prensa" Newspapers.* T **467** and similar vert design. W **458**. P 13½.
1318 **467** 20 p. black, emerald and pale green   5   5
1319 – 20 p. black, orge-yell & pale yellow   5   5
Design:—No. 1319, "The Lantern" (mast-head) and logo-types of La Prensa.

468 J. Aguirre

469 Chocon-Cerros Colorados
Hydro-electric Project

(Des H. Alvarez Boero. Litho)

1969 (6 Dec). *Argentine Musicians.* T **468** and similar vert portraits, each myrtle-green and pale blue. W **458**. P 13½.
1320 6 p. Type **468** ..   5   5
1321 6 p. F. Boero ..   5   5
1322 6 p. C. Gaito ..   5   5
1323 6 p. C. L. Buchardo ..   5   5
1324 6 p. A. Williams ..   5   5
1320/1324 Set of 5 ..   15   12
Nos. 1320/4 were issued together *se-tenant* in sheets of 60.

(Des E. Miliavaca. Litho)

1969 (13 Dec). *National Development Projects.* T **469** and similar horiz designs. Multicoloured. W **458**. P 13½. (a) POSTAGE.
1325 6 p. Type **469** ..   5   5
1326 20 p. Parana-Santa Fé river tunnel ..   8   5

(b) AIR. Inscr "AEREO"
1327 26 p. Atomic power plant, Atucha ..   12   5

470 Lieut. B. Matienzo and Nieuport Aircraft

(Des E. Miliavaca. Litho)

1969 (13 Dec). *Aeronautics Week.* W **458**. P 13½.
1328 **470** 20 p. multicoloured ..   5   5

471 Capital "L" and Lions' Emblem

472 "Madonna and Child" (R. Soldi)

(Des H. Viola. Litho)

1969 (20 Dec). *50th Anniversary of Lions' International.* W **458**. P 13½.
1329 **471** 20 p. blackish olive, orge & brt grn   5   5

1969 (27 Dec). *Christmas. Litho.* W **458**. P 13½.
1330 **472** 20 p. multicoloured   8   5

1970–71. *As previous issues, but without watermark.* P 13½.

(a) POSTAGE
1331 **328** 1 p. sepia (*photo*) (8.70) ..   5   5
1332 – 3 p. deep blue (*as No. 951, litho*) (30.4.71)   5   5
1333 **296** 5 p. bistre-brown (*photo*) (7.70) ..   5   5
1334 – 6 p. rose-red (*as No. 1070, photo*) (1970)   5   5
1335 – 6 p. red-brown (*as No. 1071, photo*) (1970)   5   5
1336 **297** 10 p. brown-red (*litho*) (30.4.71) ..   5   5
1337 – 50 p. chalky blue (*as No. 1034a, photo*) (1970)   15   15
1338 – 90 p. olive-brown (*as No. 1072a, photo*) (1970) ..   20   10
1339 **330** 100 p. blue (*photo*) (5.71) ..   30   15

(b) AIR. Litho. As Nos. 1149 and 1162
1340 – 26 p. deep ochre (30.4.71)   ..   8   5
1341 – 40 p. slate-lilac (30.4.71)   15   10
1331/1341 *Set of 11*   90   55

Currency Revaluation. 100 (old) Pesos=1 (new) Peso

473 Hummingbird

474 "General Belgrano" (lithograph by Gericault)

(Des H. Alvarez Boero. Litho)
1970 (9 May). *Child Welfare. As earlier bird designs in this series, but with face values in new currency as T **473**. Multicoloured.* W **458**. P 13½. (a) POSTAGE.
1342   20 c. + 10 c. Type **473**   8   5

(b) AIR. Inscr "CORREO AEREO"
1343   40 c. + 20 c. Flamingo   15   10

1970 (4 July). *Birth Bicentenary of General Manuel Belgrano. T **474** and similar designs. Photo (20 c.) or litho (50 c.). P 13½ (20 c.), 12½ (50 c.).*
1344   20 c. brown   5   5
1345   50 c. black, flesh and light blue   ..   15   10
Design: *Horiz* (56 × 15 mm)—50 c. "Monument to the Flag" (bas-relief by J. Fioravanti).
No. 1345 was issued *se-tenant* with a small label inscr "LA CREACION DE LA BANDERA" etc.

475 Early Fire Engine

(Des H. Viola. Litho)

1970 (8 Aug). *AIR. Centenary of Buenos Aires Fire Brigade.* P 13½.
1346 **475** 40 c. multicoloured   12   8

476 Schooner *Juliet*, 1814

(Des E. Biggeri. Litho)

1970 (8 Aug). *Navy Day.* P 13½.
1347 **476** 20 c. multicoloured   5   5

477 San José Palace

(Des E. Miliavaca. Litho)

1970 (8 Aug). *Death Centenary of General Justo de Urquiza.* P 13½.
1348 **477** 20 c. multicoloured   5   5

478 Sunflowers

479 Gen. Belgrano

480 Ski-jumper

1970–73. *As previous issues, and some new designs as T **479**, with face values in revalued currency as T **478/80**. No wmk. P 13½. (a) POSTAGE. Litho (Nos. 1354/5) or photo (others).*
1349 **478** 1 c. green (17.6.71)   ..   5   5
1350 – 3 c. carm (*as No. 951*) (30.6.71) ..   5   5
1351 **296** 5 c. greenish blue (30.6.71)   ..   5   5
1352 **479** 6 c. blue (10.8.70)   ..   5   5
1353 – 8 c. green (22.2.72)   ..   5   5
1354 **297** 10 c. yellow-brown (*litho*) (30.6.71)   5   5
1355 – 10 c. brown-red (*litho*) (1971)   5   5
1356 – 10 c. yellow-brown (1971)   ..   5   5
1357 – 25 c. bistre-brown (30.4.71)   ..   5   5
1358 – 50 c. carmine (29.1.73)   ..   12   8
1359 **250a** 65 c. yellow-brown (22 × 32½ mm) (17.6.71)   15   10
1360 – 90 c. yellowish grn (22 × 32½ mm) (29.1.73)   20   12

```
1361  480  1 p. yellow-brown (1.10.71)    ..     25    15
1362   -   1 p. 15, steel-blue (as No. 1072a)
       -         (17.6.71)      ..    ..    ..   25    15
           (b) AIR. Litho. As Nos. 1147/54
1363   -   45 c. brown (19.11.71)   ..    ..    10    10
1364   -   68 c. red (2.11.71)..    ..    ..    15    10
1349/1364  Set of 16   ..    ..    ..    ..  1·25    90
```
New design: Vert (as 479)—25 c., 50 c. General San Martin.
For these stamps wmkd "CASA DE MONEDA" see Nos.
1402/7.

Nos. 1350, 1353, 1357/8 and 1363/4 are printed on fluorescent paper which reacts with a greenish yellow glow under U.V. light. The 3 c. also comes on ordinary paper.

481 Wireless Set of 1920 and Radio "Waves"

482 Education Year Emblem

(Des E. Miliavaca. Litho)

1970 (29 Aug). 50th Anniversary of First Radio Outside Broadcast. P 13½.
```
1365  481  20 c. multicoloured     ..    ..     5     5
```

(Des V. Vassarely. Litho)

1970 (29 Aug). AIR. International Education Year. P 13½.
```
1366  482  68 c. black and new blue   ..    20    12
```

483 Military Courier, 1879

484 "Liberation Fleet leaving Valparaiso" (A. Abel)

(Des E. Marenco. Litho)

1970 (17 Oct). Military Uniforms. As previous Army Day issues, but with face value in revalued currency. P 13½.
```
1367  483  20 c. multicoloured     ..    ..     5     5
```

1970 (17 Oct). AIR. 150th Anniversary of Peruvian Liberation. Litho. P 13½.
```
1368  484  26 c. multicoloured     ..    ..     5     5
```

485 "United Nations"

486 Cordoba Cathedral

(Des H. Viola. Litho)

1970 (7 Nov). 25th Anniversary of United Nations. P 13½.
```
1369  485  20 c. multicoloured     ..    ..     5     5
```

(Des E. Miliavaca (50 c.). Photo (50 c.) or litho (40 c.))

1970 (7 Nov). 400th Anniversary of Tucuman Diocese. T 486 and similar design. P 13½. (a) POSTAGE.
```
1370  50 c. black and grey    ..    ..    ..    15    10
```
           (b) AIR. Inscr "AEREO"
```
1371  40 c. multicoloured     ..    ..    ..    12    10
```
Design: Horiz—40 c. Chapel, Sumampa.

487 Planetarium

1970 (28 Nov). AIR. Buenos Aires Planetarium. Litho. P 13½.
```
1372  487  40 c. multicoloured     ..    ..    12    10
```

488 "Liberty" and Mint Building

1970 (28 Nov). 25th Anniversary of State Mint Building, Buenos Aires. Litho. P 13½.
```
1373  488  20 c. black, blue-green and gold  ..    5     5
```

489 "The Manger" (H. G. Gutierrez)

1970 (19 Dec). Christmas. Litho. P 13½.
```
1374  489  20 c. multicoloured     ..    ..     5     5
```

490 Jorge Newbery and "Morane Saulnier" Aircraft

(Des H. Alvarez Boero. Litho)

1970 (19 Dec). AIR. Aeronautics Week. P 13½.
```
1375  490  26 c. multicoloured     ..    ..     8     5
```

491 St. John Bosco and Mission Building

492 "Planting the Flag"

(Des H. Alvarez Boero. Photo)

1970 (19 Dec). *Salesian Mission in Patagonia.* P 13½.
1376 **491** 20 c. black and yellow-olive .. 5 5

1971 (20 Feb). *5th Anniversary of Argentine Expedition to South Pole. Litho.* P 13½.
1377 **492** 20 c. multicoloured .. 5 5

493 Dorado

(Des E. Miliavaca. Litho)

1971 (20 Feb). *Child Welfare. T 493 and similar vert fish design. Multicoloured.* P 12½. (a) POSTAGE.
1378 20 c. + 10 c. Type **493** 10 8

(b) AIR. Inscr "AEREO"
1379 40 c. + 20 c. Pejerrey 15 12

494 Einstein and Scanners

495 Elias Alippi

(Des H. Alvarez Boero. Litho)

1971 (30 Apr). *Electronics in the Postal Service. "Greenish yellow" fluorescent paper.* P 13½.
1380 **494** 25 c. multicoloured 5 5

(Des H. Alvarez Boero. Litho)

1971 (29 May). *Argentine Actors and Actress. T 495 and similar vert portraits, each black and pink.* W 458. P 13½.
1381 15 c. Type **495** 5 5
1382 15 c. Juan Casacuberta 5 5
1383 15 c. Roberto Casaux 5 5
1384 15 c. Angelina Pagano 5 5
1385 15 c. Florencio Parravicini 5 5
1381/1385 *Set of 5* 20 15
Nos. 1381/5 were issued together *se-tenant* within the sheet of 100.

496 Federation Emblem

1971 (29 May). *Inter-American Regional Meeting of International Roads Federation, Buenos Aires. Litho.* W 458. P 13½.
1386 **496** 25 c. black and light blue 5 5

(Des E. Marenco. Litho)

1971 (3 July). *Army Day (29 May). Vert design similar to T 390 and 483. Multicoloured.* P 13½.
1387 25 c. Artilleryman, 1826 .. .. 5 5

497 Sloop *Carmen*

(Des E. Biggeri. Litho)

1971 (3 July). *Navy Day.* P 13½.
1388 **497** 25 c. multicoloured 5 5

498 "General Güemes" (L. Gigli)

1971 (28 Aug). *150th Death Anniv of General Martin Güemes. T 498 and similar horiz design. Multicoloured. Litho.* P 13½.
1389 25 c. Type **498** 5 5
1390 25 c. "Death of Güemes" (A. Alice) (84×29 mm) 5 5

499 Order of Peruvian Sun

500 Stylised Tulip

(Des H. Viola. Litho)

1971 (28 Aug). *150th Anniversary of Peruvian Independence.* P 13½.
1391 **499** 31 c. yellow, black and red 8 5

1971 (18 Sept). *3rd International and 8th National Horticultural Exhibition. Litho.* P 13½.
1392 **500** 25 c. multicoloured 5 5

501 "Dr. Antonio Saenz"   **502** Arsenal Emblem
(founder) (J. Gut)

1971 (18 Sept). *150th Anniversary of Buenos Aires University. Litho.* P 13½.
1393 **501** 25 c. multicoloured   ..   5   5

(Des E. Miliavaca. Litho)
1971 (16 Oct). *30th Anniversary of Fabricaciones Militares (Arsenals).* P 13½.
1394 **502** 25 c. multicoloured   ..   5   5

503 Road Transport

(Des H. Viola. Litho)
1971 (16 Oct). *Nationalised Industries.* T **503** *and similar horiz designs.* P 13½. (a) POSTAGE.
1395   25 c. multicoloured   5   5
1396   65 c. multicoloured   15   10

(b) AIR. *Inscr* "AEREO"
1397   31 c. lemon, black and dull vermilion ..   8   5
Designs:—31 c. Refinery and formula ("Petro-chemicals");
65 c. Tree and paper roll ("Paper and Cellulose").

504 Constellation and Telescope

(Des H. Alvarez Boero. Litho)
1971 (27 Nov). *Centenary of Cordoba Observatory.* P 13½.
1398 **504** 25 c. multicoloured   5   5

505 Capt. L. Candelaria and   **506** "Stamps" (M. Lydis)
"Morane-Saulnier" Aircraft

(Des E. Miliavaca. Litho)
1971 (27 Nov). *25th Aeronautics Week.* P 13½.
1399 **505** 25 c. multicoloured   ..   5   5

1971 (18 Dec). *2nd Charity Philatelic Exhibition. Litho.* P 13½.
1400 **506** 1 p. + 50 c. multicoloured ..   35   30

507 "Christ in Majesty"   **508** "Maternity" (J.
(tapestry, H. Butler)   Castagnino)

1971 (18 Dec). *Christmas. Litho.* P 13½.
1401 **507** 25 c. multicoloured   5   5

1972. *As 1970–72 issue, face values in revalued currency, but* W **458.** *Photo* (1 c., 1 p.), *litho* (others). P 13½.
1402 **478**   1 c. green (22.5)   5   5
1403 **296**   5 c. steel-blue (17.4)   ..   5   5
1404 **297**   10 c. yellow-brown (18.4)..   5   5
1405 **250**a 65 c. ol-brn (22½ × 33½ mm) (3.5) ..   15   10
1406 **480**   1 p. yellow-brown (16.6)..   25   15
1407   **–**   1 p. 15, grey-blue (as No. 1072a)
       (8.6)   25   15
1402/1407   Set of 6   70   45

(Des H. Alvarez Boero. Litho)
1972 (6 May). *Child Welfare. Multicoloured bird designs similar to* T **352** *and* **473.** P 13½.
1408   25 c. + 10 c. Saffron finch (vert)   8   5
1409   65 c. + 30 c. Chocolate tyrant (horiz)   25   15

1972 (6 May). *25th Anniversary of U.N.I.C.E.F. Photo.* P 13½.
1410 **508** 25 c. black and chestnut   ..   5   5

509 Treaty Emblem and "Almirante Brown" Base

1972 (2 Sept). *10th Anniversary of Antarctic Treaty. Litho.* P 13½.
1411 **509** 25 c. multicoloured   5   5

510 Postman's Mail Pouch

(Des H. Viola. Litho)
1972 (2 Sept). *Bicentenary of Appointment of First Buenos Aires Postman.* P 13½.
1412 **510** 25 c. multicoloured   5   5

FLUORESCENT PAPER. From No. 1413 all issues were printed on fluorescent paper which reacts with a greenish yellow glow under U.V. light, *unless otherwise stated.* This paper was introduced in connection with an electronic sorting system.

(Des E. Marenco. Litho)

1972 (23 Sept). *Army Day (29 May). Vert design similar to T* **390** *and* **483***. Multicoloured. P* 13½.
1413 25 c. Sergeant, Negro and Mulatto Battalion (1806–7) 5 5

511 Brigantine *Santisima Trinidad* **512** Sonic Balloon

(Des E. Biggeri. Litho)

1972 (23 Sept). *Navy Day. P* 13½.
1414 **511** 25 c. multicoloured 5 5

(Des A. Gutierrez. Litho)

1972 (30 Sept). *Centenary of National Meteorological Service. P* 13½.
1415 **512** 25 c. multicoloured 5 5

513 Oil Pump

(Des H. Viola. Litho)

1972 (30 Sept). *50th Anniversary of State Oilfields (YPF). P* 13½.
1416 **513** 45 c. black, light blue and gold .. 12 10

514 Forest of Trees

(Des H. Viola. Litho)

1972 (14 Oct). *7th World Forestry Congress, Buenos Aires. P* 13.
1417 **514** 25 c. black, new blue and light blue 5 5

515 Arms and Frigate *Presidente Sarmiento*

(Des E. Biggeri. Litho)

1972 (14 Oct). *Centenary of Naval School. P* 13.
1418 **515** 25 c. multicoloured 5 5

516 Baron A. de Marchi, **517** Bartolomé Mitre
Balloon and Aeroplane

(Des E. Miliavaca. Litho)

1972 (4 Nov). *Aeronautics Week. P* 13½.
1419 **516** 25 c. multicoloured 5 5

(Eng M. A. Cabrera. Recess)

1972 (4 Nov). *150th Birth Anniv of General Bartolomé Mitre* (1971). *P* 13½.
1420 **517** 25 c. deep ultramarine 5 5

518 Heart and Flower **519** "Martin Fierro" (J. C. Castagnino)

(Des H. Viola. Litho)

1972 (2 Dec). *World Health Day. P* 13½.
1421 **518** 90 c. black, violet-blue and pale greenish blue 20 15

1972 (2 Dec). *International Book Year and Centenary of "Martin Fierro" (poem by José Hernández). T* **519** *and similar vert design. Multicoloured. Litho. P* 13½.
1422 50 c. Type **519** 12 10
1423 90 c. "Spirit of the Gaucho" (V. Forte) 20 15

520 "Wise Man on **522** Cockerel Emblem
Horseback" (18th-century
wood-carving)

521 Iguazu Falls

1972 (16 Dec). *Christmas. Litho.* P 13½.
1424 **520** 50 c. multicoloured   12   10

1972 (16 Dec). *American Tourist Year. Litho.* P 13.
1425 **521** 45 c. multicoloured   12   10

(Des H. Viola. Litho)

1973 (3 Feb). *150th Anniv of Federal Police Force.* P 13½.
1426 **522** 50 c. multicoloured   12   10

523 Bank Emblem and First Coin

A regular new issue supplement to this catalogue appears each month in

STAMP MONTHLY

—from your newsagent or by postal subscription
—details on request.

(Des H. Alvarez Boero. Litho)

1973 (3 Feb). *150th Anniv of Buenos Aires Provincial Bank.* P 13½.
1427 **523** 50 c. multicoloured   12   10

PHILATELIC TERMS ILLUSTRATED

This successful STAMP MONTHLY series has now been brought together in a snappy black and yellow binding and published as the latest addition to Stanley Gibbons range of essential handbooks for keen stamp collectors. Within its 192 pages this handy limp-bound volume houses a veritable mine of useful information, on the words and phrases used in philately. It describes and illustrates printing processes and watermarks, papers and perforations, errors and varieties ... and it does all this IN COLOUR. Indeed, there are 92 full page plates in colour, plus many black and white illustrations, making it

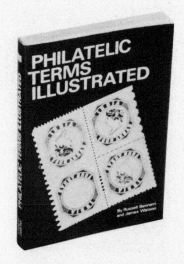

FANTASTIC VALUE AT ONLY A £1!

DEPARTMENTAL OFFICIAL STAMPS

M. A.
I Sans-Serif

M. A.
II Seriffed

A = **M.A.** Ministry of Agriculture.   E = **M.J.I.** Ministry of Justice and Instruction.
B = **M.G.** Ministry of War.   F = **M.M.** Ministry of Marine.
C = **M.H.** Ministry of Finance.   G = **M.O.P.** Ministry of Public Works.
D = **M.I.** Ministry of the Interior.   H = **M.R.C.** Ministry of Foreign Affairs and Religion.

1913–38. *Postage stamps overprinted in black for use in various Ministerial Offices.*
    I. *Overprints with sans-serif capitals (vert on T* **99** *and* **101***) (1913–26)*

1913. *W* **69** *(Sun).* *P* $13\frac{1}{2} \times 12\frac{1}{2}$.

			A.M.A.		B.M.G.		C.M.H.		D.M.I.	
OD 1	**92**	2 c. brown	387	5 5	5 5	5 5	8 5
				E.M.J.I.		F.M.M.		G.M.O.P.		H.M.R.C.	
OD 1	**92**	2 c. brown	387	12 5	5 5	5 5	1·50 25
		a. Perf $13\frac{1}{2}$	387a	†	3·00 60	10 5	†

1913. *W* **93** *(Honeycomb, vert).* *P* $13\frac{1}{2} \times 12\frac{1}{2}$.

				A. M.A.	B. M.G.	C. M.H.	D. M.I.
OD 2	**92**	1 c. yellow-brown	396I	5 5	5 5	5 5	5 5
		a. Wmk horiz	396II	†	20 5	†	†
OD 3		2 c. brown	397I	5 5	8 5	5 5	5 5
		a. Perf $13\frac{1}{2}$	397aI	†	20 5	†	†
		b. Wmk horiz	397II	†	5 5	†	†
		ba. Perf $13\frac{1}{2}$	397aII	†	10 5	†	†
OD 4		5 c. rose	400I	5 5	5 5	5 5	5 5
		a. Opt inverted		†	— 1·25	†	†
		b. Perf $13\frac{1}{2}$	400aI	5 5	†	†	†
OD 5		12 c. blue	402I	5 5	5 5	5 5	5 5
		a. Perf $13\frac{1}{2}$	402aI	5 5	8 5	5 5	8 5
		b. Wmk horiz	402II	5 5	5 5	5 5	5 5
				E.M.J.I.	F.M.M.	G.M.O.P.	H.M.R.C.
OD 2	**92**	1 c. yellow-brown	396I	5 5	5 5	†	5 5
		a. Wmk horiz	396II	5 5	8 5	†	†
OD 3		2 c. brown	397I	5 5	15 5	†	5 5
		b. Wmk horiz	397II	5 5	†	†	†
		ba. Perf $13\frac{1}{2}$	397aII	20 5	†	†	†
OD 4		5 c. rose	400I	5 5	5 5	5 5	5 5
		a. Opt inverted		— 1·25	— 1·25	†	†
		b. Perf $13\frac{1}{2}$	400aI	†	40 8	†	†
OD 5		12 c. blue	402II	5 5	5 5	8 5	5 5
		a. Perf $13\frac{1}{2}$	402aI	5 5	8 5	30 5	75 15
		b. Wmk horiz	402II	5 5	†	†	20 8
		b. Perf $13\frac{1}{2}$	402aII	†	†	†	— 65

1915. *No wmk.* *P* $13\frac{1}{2} \times 12\frac{1}{2}$.

				A.M.A.	B.M.G.	C.M.H.	D.M.I.
OD 6	**92**	1 c. yellow-brown	413	5 5	35 12	†	†
OD 7		2 c. brown	414	5 5	8 5	5 5	10 5
OD 8		5 c. rose	416	5 5	8 5	5 5	5 5
				E.M.J.I.	F.M.M.	G.M.O.P.	H.M.R.C
OD 6	**92**	1 c. yellow-brown	413	5 5	†	†	†
OD 7		2 c. brown	414	5 5	8 5	†	†
OD 8		5 c. rose	416	10 5	5 5	†	5 5

1916. *Independence Centenary.*

				A.M.A.	B.M.G.	C.M.H.	D.M.I.
OD 9	**96**	5 c. rose	422	5 5	8 5	5 5	8 5
OD10	**97**	12 c. blue	424	†	8 5	†	†
				E.M.J.I.	F.M.M.	G.M.O.P.	H.M.R.C.
OD 9	**96**	5 c. rose	422	5 5	†	1·00 10	5 5
OD10	**97**	12 c. blue	424	5 5	†	†	†

1918. *W* **93** *(Honeycomb, vert).* *P* $13\frac{1}{2}$.

				A. M.A.	B. M.G	C. M.H.	D. M.I.
OD11	**98**	1 c. buff	434I	†	5 5	†	†
		a. Perf $13\frac{1}{2} \times 12\frac{1}{2}$	434aI	†	12 5	†	†
OD12		2 c. chocolate	435I	†	8 5	†	†
		a. Perf $13\frac{1}{2} \times 12\frac{1}{2}$	435aI	†	5 5	5 5	†
OD13		5 c. vermilion	438I	†	†	8 5	†
		a. Perf $13\frac{1}{2} \times 12\frac{1}{2}$	438aI	†	3·50 1·00	†	15 5
		b. Do. Wmk horiz	438aII	†	†	†	†
OD14	**99**	12 c. blue (*wmk horiz*)	440	5 5	8 5	5 5	†
				E.M.J.I.	F.M.M.	G.M.O.P.	H.M.R.C.
OD11	**98**	1 c. buff	434I	5 5	†	†	†
		a. Perf $13\frac{1}{2} \times 12\frac{1}{2}$	434aI	5 5	5 5	†	†
OD12		2 c. chocolate	435I	12 5	†	50 8	†
		a. Perf $13\frac{1}{2} \times 12\frac{1}{2}$	435aI	8 5	5 5	†	†
OD13		5 c. vermilion	438I	25 5	5 5	8 5	†
		a. Perf $13\frac{1}{2} \times 12\frac{1}{2}$	438aI	5 5	5 5	†	†
OD14	**99**	12 c. blue (*wmk horiz*)	438aII	1·75 40	†	†	†

1918. *No wmk.* P 13½.

				A. M.A.		B. M.G.		C. M.H.		D. M.I.	
OD15	98	1 c. buff..	451B	5	5	5	5	†		†	
		a. Perf 13½×12½	451A	†		5	5	†			
OD16		2 c. chocolate	452B	5	5	5	5	—	1·50	5	5
		a. Perf 13½×12½	452A	†		5	5	†			
OD17		5 c. red ..	455B	5	5	5	5	5	5	5	5
		a. Perf 13½×12½	455A	†		5	5	5	5	5	5
OD18	99	12 c. dull blue	457B	5	5	5	5	5	5		
OD19		20 c. ultramarine	458B	5	5	8	5	5	5	†	

				E.M.J.I.		F.M.M.		G.M.O.P.		H.M.R.C.	
OD15	98	1 c. buff..	451B	5	5	5	5	†		†	
		a. Perf 13½×12½	451A	40	10	†		†		†	
OD16		2 c. chocolate	452B	5	5	5	5	†		†	
		a. Perf 13½×12½	452A	5	5	5	5	†		†	
OD17		5 c. red ..	455B	5	5	5	5	†		†	
		a. Perf 13½×12½	455A	5	5	5	5	†		†	
OD18	99	12 c. dull blue	457B	5*	5*	5	5	†		†	
OD19		20 c. ultramarine	458B	5	5	20	5	†		20	8

*On this stamp the overprint exists 10 mm and 11½ mm long (*same prices for either*).

1920. *W 101 (Multiple Small Sun RA).* P 13½.

				A. M.A.		B. M.G.		C. M.H.		D. M.I.	
OD20	98	1 c. buff (p 13½×12½)	463A	5	5	†		8	5	20	8
OD21		2 c. chocolate	464B	8	5	8	5	†		†	
		a. Perf 13½×12½	464A	†		5	5	10	5	†	
OD22		5 c. red ..	467B	5	5	5	5	5	5	8	5
		a. Perf 13½×12½	467A	5	5	5	5	12	5	†	
OD23	99	12 c. dull blue	469B	†		5	5	8	5	†	

				E.M.J.I.		F.M.M.		G.M.O.P.		H.M.R.C.	
OD20	98	1 c. buff (p 13½×12½)	463A	5	5	5	5	†		5	5
OD21		2 c. chocolate	464B	5	5	5	5	60	10	†	
		a. Perf 13½×12½	464A	5	5	5	5	†		†	
OD22		5 c. red ..	467B	12	5	5	5	10	5	5	5
		a. Perf 13½×12½	467A	5	5	5	†	†		†	
OD23	99	12 c. dull blue	469B	5	5	5	†	†		†	

1921. *W 105 (Large Sun).* P 13½.

				A. M.A.		B. M.G.		C. M.H.		D. M.I.	
OD24	99	12 c. blue	486 B	†		10	5	†		†	

1922. *W 111 (Multiple Large Sun RA).* P 13½.

				A. M.A.		B. M.G.		C. M.H.		D. M.I.	
OD27	110	5 c. rose	499B	†		8	5	†		10	5
OD28	99	12 a. blue	506B	8	5	†		†		8	5
OD29		20 c. ultramarine	507B	†		†		75	10	8	5

				E.M.J.I.		F.M.M.		G.M.O.P.		H.M.R.C.	
OD25	98	1 c. buff	501B	8	5	†		†		†	
		a. Perf 13½×12½	501A	5	5	†		†		†	
OD26		2 c. chocolate	502B	†		†		†		†	
		a. Perf 13½×12½	502A	5	5	†		†		40	12
OD27	110	5 c. rose	499B	5	5	10	5	†		†	
		a. Perf 13½×12½	499A	5	5	5	5	†		†	
OD28	99	12 c. blue	506B	5	5	50	8	†		†	
OD29		20 c. ultramarine	507B	12	5	90	8	†		†	

1922. *Mock wmk on face as T 111.* P 13½×12½.

				A. M.A.		B. M.G.		C. M.H.		D. M.I.	
OD30	98	2 c. chocolate	510A	†		15	5	†		†	

				E.M.J.I.		F.M.M.		G.M.O.P.		H.M.R.C.	
OD30	98	2 c. chocolate	510A	5	5	†		†		†	

1923. *T 112 (with stop). Litho.* W 111. P 13½×12½.

				A. M.A.		B. M.G.		C. M.H.		D. M.I.	
OD31	112	1 c. buff	514A	5	5	5	5	20	10	5	5
		a. Perf 13½	514B	8	5	10	5	8	5	5	5
		b. Do. Opt inverted		†		25	5				
OD32		2 c. deep brown	515A	5	5	5	5	5	5	5	5
		a. Opt inverted		50	20	†		—	30	†	
		b. Perf 13½	515B	5	5	5	5	15	5	60	10
OD33		5 c. scarlet	518A	5	5	5	5	5	5	5	5
		a. Opt inverted		†		25	10	†		†	
		b. Perf 13½	518B	†		5	5	5	5	8	5
OD34		12 c. blue	520A	5	5	5	5	8	5	12	5
		a. Perf 13½	520B	†		†		†		50	8
OD35		20 c. ultramarine	521A	5	5	8	5	5	5	15	5
		a. Perf 13½	521B	10	5	8	5	8	5	12	5
		b. Do. Opt inverted		—	1·00	2·00	1·00	†		†	

				E.M.J.I.		F.M.M.		G.M.O.P.		H.M.R.C.	
OD31	112	1 c. buff	514A	5	5	5	5	5	5	5	5
		a. Perf 13½	514B	5	5	—	75	60	12	35	12
OD32		2 c. deep brown	515A	5	5	5	5	5	5	5	5
		a. Opt inverted			†	—	1·25		†		†
		b. Perf 13½	515B	5	5	5	5	5	5	10	5
		c. Do. Opt inverted		40	20		†		†		†
OD33		5 c. scarlet	518A	5	5	8	5	5	5	5	5
		a. Opt inverted			†	—	1·25		†		†
		b. Perf 13½	518B	5	5	30	5	5	5	8	5
		c. Do. Opt inverted			†	—	1·25		†		†
OD34		12 c. blue	520A	5	5	5	5	5	5	5	5
		a. Perf 13½	520B		†	15	5	5	5	5	5
OD35		20 c. ultramarine	521A	5	5	8	5	8	5	5	5
		a. Perf 13½	521B	5	5	10	5	8	5		†

1924. *T* **112** *(without stop).* *Litho.* *W* **111.** *P* 13½×12½.

				A.M.A.		B.M.G.		C.M.H.		D.M.I	
OD36	112	1 c. buff	530	5	5	10	5		†	5	5
		a. Opt inverted		25	—		†		†		†
OD37		2 c. deep brown	531	5	5	5	5	—	1·25	5	5
		a. Pair, one without stop		15	10	15	10		†	12	—
OD38		3 c. green	532		†	5	5		†	8	5
OD39		5 c. scarlet	534	5	5	5	5	5	5	5	5
		a. Pair, one without stop		35	15	20	—		†		†
OD40		10 c. grey-green	535	5	5	5	5		†		†
OD41		12 c. blue	536	5	5		†	75	30	5	5
OD42		20 c. ultramarine	537	5	5	5	5	5	5	8	5
		a. Opt inverted		1·25	1·00		†		†		†
		b. Pair, one without stop		—	2·50	25	12		†		†
OD43		30 c. claret	540		†	8	5		†		†

				E.M.J.I.		F.M.M.		G.M.O.P.		H.M.R.C.	
OD36	112	1 c. buff	530	5	5	8	5	5	5	5	5
OD37		2 c. deep brown	531	5	5	5	5	5	5	5	5
		a. Pair, one without stop		15	10	20	10	15	10	15	10
OD38		3 c. green	532	5	5		†		†	5	5
OD39		5 c. scarlet	534	5	5	5	5	5	5	5	5
		a. Pair, one without stop		20	10	35	12		†	25	10
OD40		10 c. grey-green	535	5	5		†		†	12	5
OD41		12 c. blue	536	5	5		†	50	8	5	5
OD42		20 c. ultramarine	537	5	5	8	5	5	5	5	5
OD43		30 c. claret	540		†		†		†	5	5

1926. *Postal Centenary.*

				A. M.A.		B. M.G.		C. M.H.		D. M.I.	
OD44	116	5 c. red	548		†	5	5		†		†
OD45	117	12 c. blue	549	5	5		†	75	40		†

				E.M.J.I.		F.M.M.		G.M.O.P.		H.M.R.C.	
OD44	116	5 c. red	548	5	5	8	5	8	5		†
		a. Opt inverted		1·00	60		†		†		†
OD45	117	12 c. blue	549	5	5		†		†	5	5

II. Overprints with seriffed capitals (1931–38)

1931–36. *T* **112** *(without stop) and* **113.** *W* **111.** *P* 13½×12½.

				A.M.A.		B.M.G.		C.M.H.		D.M.I.	
OD48	112	2 c. deep brown	531	12	8		†		†		†
OD49		3 c. green	532	5	5	5	5	35	8	5	5
OD50		5 c. scarlet	534	5	5	5	5		†	5	5
		a. Opt inverted			†	—	1·25		†		†
OD51		10 c. grey-green	535	5	5	5	5	5	5	5	5
		a. Typo (coil)	535b	5	5	5	5	5	5	5	5
OD53		20 c. ultramarine	537	5	5	12	5	5	5	5	5
		a. Typo (coil)	537b	5	5	5	5	5	5		†
OD54		30 c. claret	540	5	5	5	5	8	5	10	5
		a. Typo (coil)	540b	5	5	5	5	8	5	5	5
OD55	113	1 p. scarlet and blue	542		†	15	5	5	5		†

				E.M.J.I.		F.M.M.		G.M.O.P.		H.M.R.C.	
OD46	112	½ c. purple	529	12	5		†		†	8	5
OD47		1 c. buff	530	5	5		†		†		†
		a. Pair, one without stop		20	10		†		†		†
OD49		3 c. green	532	5	5	8	5	5	5		†
		a. Typo (coil)	532b	5	5		†	50	12		†
OD50		5 c. scarlet	534	5	5	5	5	5	5		†
OD51		10 c. grey-green	535	5	5	8	5	5	5		†
		a. Typo (coil)	535b	5	5	5	5	10	5	5	5
OD52		12 c. blue	536	5	5		†		†		†
OD53		20 c. ultramarine	537	5	5	12	5		†		†
		a. Typo (coil)	537b	5	5	5	5	25	5	5	5
OD54		30 c. claret	540	5	5	8	5	5	5		†
		a. Typo (coil)	540b	5	5		†		†	5	5
OD55	113	1 p. scarlet and blue	542	5	5	75	25	1·40	40	5	5

1936–38. *Types of 1935–37.* W 111. *(a) Litho.* P 13×13½ (25 c., 50 c., 1 p.) or 13½×13 (*others*).

					A.M.A.		B.M.G.		C.M.H.		D.M.I.	
OD56	143	1 c. yellow-brown	.. ..	645	5	5	5	5	5	5	5	5
OD57	–	2 c. grey-brown	.. .. ..	646	5	5	5	5	5	5	5	5
OD58	–	3 c. green	.. ..	647	5	5	5	5	5	5	5	5
OD59	–	5 c. orange-brown	.. ..	649	5	5	5	5	5	5	5	5
OD60	146	15 c. dull blue ..	.. .. ..	655	5	5	5	5	5	5	5	5
		a. Opt inverted	..			†		†	—	1·50		†
OD61	–	20 c. pale blue (J.M.G.)	..	652	8	5	12	5	5	5	8	5
OD62	–	20 c. pale blue (M.G.) ..	..	653	5	5	5	5	5	5	5	5
OD63	147	25 c. carmine-red and pink	..	656	5	5	5	5		†		†
OD64	148	30 c. brown and yellow-brown	..	657	5	5	5	5	5	5	5	5
OD65	150	50 c. vermilion and salmon	..	659		†	5	5		†		†
OD66	151	1 p. blue and chocolate	..	660	20	8	8	5	15	5	12	5
OD67	152	1 p. blue and chocolate	..	660a	5	5	5	5	5	5	5	5
(b) Typo. P 13½												
OD68	–	5 c. orange-brown	.. ..	653b	5	5	5	5	5	5	5	5
		a. Opt inverted	..			†		†	—	1·25	—	1·50
OD69	–	10 c. scarlet ..	..	653d	5	5	5	5	5	5	5	5
		a. Opt inverted	..			†	1·25	60		†		†
		b. Perf 13½×13	.. ..	653e	5	5	5	5	5	5	5	5

(a) Litho. Perfs as before

					E.M.J.I.		F.M.M.		G.M.O.P.		H.M.R.C.	
OD56	143	1 c. yellow-brown	.. ..	645	5	5	5	5	5	5	5	5
OD57	–	2 c. grey-green	.. ..	646	5	5	5	5	5	5	5	5
OD58	–	3 c. green ..	..	647	5	5	5	5	5	5	5	5
OD59	–	5 c. orange-brown	.. ..	649	5	5	5	5	5	5	5	5
OD60	146	15 c. dull blue ..	..	655	5	5	5	5	5	5	5	5
OD61	–	20 c. pale blue (J.M.G.)	..	652	5	5	5	5	5	5	5	5
OD62	–	20 c. pale blue (M.G.)	..	653	5	5	5	5	5	5	5	5
OD63	147	25 c. carmine-red and pink	..	656	5	5		†		†		†
OD64	148	30 c. brown and yellow-brown	..	657	5	5	5	5	5	5	5	5
OD65	150	50 c. vermilion and salmon	..	659		†		†	5	5		†
OD66	151	1 p. blue and chocolate	..	660	8	5	25	8	12	5	12	5
OD67	152	1 p. blue and chocolate	..	660a	5	5	8	5	5	5	5	5
(b) Typo. P 13½												
OD68	–	5 c. orange-brown	.. ..	653b	5	5	5	5	5	5	5	5
		a. Opt inverted	..			†	50	—	75	50		†
OD69	–	10 c. scarlet	..	653d	5	5	5	5	5	5	5	5
		b. Perf 13½×13	..	653e	5	5	5	5	5	5	5	5

AZORES. See Vol. 1 of Europe Catalogue.

Bahrain

1000 Fils = 1 Dinar

Bahrain consists of a group of islands in the Persian Gulf, an Arab Shaikhdom in treaty relations with the United Kingdom since 1820. It has had an independent postal administration since 1966. Full independence was declared on 15 August 1971.

Indian and British stamps overprinted "BAHRAIN" issued by the earlier postal administrations are listed in the British Commonwealth Catalogue.

21 Shaikh Isa bin Sulman al-Khalifa   **22** Ruler and Bahrain Airport

(Photo Harrison)

1966 (21 Jan). *T* **21/2** *and various designs. P* 14 (30, 40, 50, 75 f.), 14½ (1 d.) or 14½ × 14 (*others*).

139	**21**	5 f. blue-green	..	..	5	5
140		10 f. brown-red	..	..	5	5
141		15 f. bright blue	..	..	5	5
142		20 f. bright purple	..	..	5	5
143	**22**	30 f. black and myrtle-green	..	5	5
144		40 f. black and blue ..	..	..	8	8
145		50 f. black and magenta	..	8	8
146		75 f. black and bluish violet	..	15	15
147		100 f. deep blue and greenish yellow	15	15
148		200 f. deep green and orange	..	30	30
149		500 f. lake-brown and light yellow	..	85	85
150	–	1 d. multicoloured ..	..	..	1·75	1·75
139/150		*Set of* 12	..	..	3·25	3·25

Designs: As T **22**—50 f., 75 f. Ruler and Mina Sulman deepwater harbour. *Vert* (26½×42½ *mm*)—100 f. Pearl-diving; 200 f. Falconry and horse-racing; 500 f. Serving coffee, and Ruler's Palace. *Larger* (37×52½ *mm*)—1 d. Ruler, crest, datepalm, horse, dhow, pearl necklace, mosque, coffee-pot and Bab-al-Bahrain (gateway).

23 Produce   **24** W.H.O. Emblem and Map of Bahrain

(Litho De La Rue)

1966 (27 Mar). *Trade Fair and Agricultural Show. P* 13 × 13½.

151	**23**	10 f. turquoise-green & carmine-red	5	5
152		20 f. lilac and myrtle-green	..	..	5	5
153		40 f. light blue and bistre-brown	..	12	12
154		200 f. rose and royal blue	..	..	30	30
151/154		*Set of* 4	..	..	..	45	45

(Litho De La Rue)

1968 (1 June). 20*th Anniv of World Health Organisation. P* 13½ × 14.

155	**24**	20 f. black and grey ..	..	..	5	5
156		40 f. black and bright turq-green	..	8	8
157		150 f. black and rosine	..	..	25	25

25 View of Isa Town

(Des L. Morland. Photo Harrison)

1968 (13 Nov). *Inauguration of Isa New Town. T* **25** *and similar horiz designs. Multicoloured. P* 14½.

158		50 f. Type **25**	..	..	..	10	10
159		80 f. Shopping centre	..	..	15	15
160		120 f. Stadium	..	..	..	20	20
161		150 f. Mosque	..	..	..	25	25
158/161		*Set of* 4	..	..	..	60	60

26 Symbol of Learning

1969 (26 Apr). 50*th Anniversary of School Education in Bahrain. Litho. P* 13.

162	**26**	40 f. multicoloured	..	..	..	8	8
163		60 f. multicoloured	..	..	..	12	12
164		150 f. multicoloured	..	..	6	30	30

27 Dish Aerial and Map

(Des A. Larkins. Litho De La Rue)

1969 (14 July). *Opening of Satellite Earth Station, Ras Abu Jarjour. T* **27** *and similar multicoloured design. P* 14.

165		20 f. Type **27**	..	..	..	5	5
166		40 f. Dish aerial and palms (*vert*)	..	8	8
167		100 f. Type **27**	..	..	..	15	15
168		150 f. As 40 f.	..	..	..	25	25
165/168		*Set of* 4	..	..	..	45	45

28 Arms, Map and Manama Municipality Building

(Des A. Muharraqi. Litho De La Rue)

1970 (23 Feb). 2*nd Arab Cities Organization Conference. P* 12½.

169	**28**	30 f. multicoloured	..	..	5	5
170		150 f. multicoloured	..	..	25	25

29 Copper Bull's Head, Barbar

(Photo Harrison)

1970 (1 Mar). *3rd International Asian Archaeology Confer-*
ence, Bahrain. T **29** *and similar horiz designs. Multicol-*
oured. P 14½.
171	60 f. Type **29**	..	..	10	10
172	80 f. Palace of Dilmun excavations	..		10	10
173	120 f. Desert gravemounds	..	..	20	20
174	150 f. Dilmun seal	..	..	25	25
171/174	*Set of 4*	..	..	55	55

30 "VC-10", Big Ben, London, and Bahrain Minaret

(Des L. Morland. Litho Harrison)

1970 (5 Apr). *1st "Gulf Aviation" "VC-10" Flight to London.*
P 14½ × 14.
175	**30**	30 f. multicoloured	..	..	5	5
176		60 f. multicoloured	..	..	10	10
177		120 f. multicoloured	..	..	20	20

31 I.E.Y. Emblem and Open Book

32 Allegory of Independence

(Litho Harrison)

1970 (1 Nov). *International Education Year.* T **31** *and similar*
horiz design. Multicoloured. P 14½ × 14.
178	60 f. Type **31**	..	..	..	10	8
179	120 f. Emblem and Bahraini children	..	20	15

(Photo Harrison)

1971 (12 Dec). *Independence Day and 12th Anniv of Ruler's*
Accession. T **32** *and similar vert designs. Multicoloured.*
P 14½ × 14.
180	30 f. Type **32**	..	..	5	5
181	60 f. Government House	..	10	8
182	120 f. Arms of Bahrain	..	..	20	15
183	150 f. As 120 f., but gold background	..	25	20
180/183	*Set of 4*	..	..	55	40

33 Arab Dhow   **34** Human Heart

(Litho Harrison)

1972 (1 Feb). *Bahrain's Membership of Arab League and*
United Nations. T **33** *and similar multicoloured design.*
P 14 × 14½ *(horiz)* or 14½ × 14 *(vert).*
184	30 f. Type **33**	..	..	..	5	5
185	60 f. Type **33**	..	..	10	8
186	120 f. Dhow sails *(vert)*	..	..	20	15
187	150 f. As 120 f.	..	..	..	25	20
184/187	*Set of 4*	..	..	..	55	40

1972 (8 Apr). *World Health Day. Litho.* P 14½ × 14.
188	**34**	30 f. multicoloured	..	..	5	5
189		60 f. multicoloured	..	..	10	8

BELGIAN CONGO. This will be found under Zaire Republic.

BENADIR. See Somalia, 1903.

BENGHAZI. See Turkish Empire (Italian Post Offices) in Europe Vol. 3.

BENIN. See Dahomey.

Bhutan

1954. 16 Annas = 1 Rupee
1967. 100 Chetrum = 1 Ngultrum

Bhutan is a kingdom in the eastern Himalayas guided by India in external affairs under a treaty of August 1949. Joined the U.P.U. on 7 March 1969.

King Jigme Dorji Wangchuk

March 1952–October 1972

F 1 "Dorje" (Thunderbolt)

1955 (1 Jan). *POSTAL FISCAL. Offset-litho. No wmk.* P 12½.

F1	F 1	¼ r. blue	15	1·00
F2		½ r. carmine-red	30	1·50
F3		1 r. green	60	1·50
F4		5 r. orange	3·00	1·75
F1/4		*Set of 4*	3·50	5·00

On 1 January 1955 the Bhutan Government decreed that these fiscal stamps could be used for postage on domestic mail.

DATES OF ISSUE. Wherever possible we have quoted the dates when the stamps were placed on sale in Bhutan but these sometimes differ considerably from the dates of release by the agency in Bahamas.

1 Postal Runner

2 "Uprooted Tree" Emblem and Crest of Bhutan

(Litho Harrison & Sons, London)

1962 (10 Oct). *T 1 and similar designs.* P 14 × 14½ (2 ch., 33 ch.) or 14½ × 14 (*others*).

1	2 ch. brown-red and grey		5	5
2	3 ch. rose-red and violet-blue		5	5
3	5 ch. sepia and blue-green		15	15
4	15 ch. yellow, black and brown-red		5	5
5	33 ch. blue-green and reddish violet		10	10
6	70 ch. ultramarine and light blue		20	20
7	1 n. 30, black and blue		40	40
1/7	*Set of 6*		90	90

Designs: *Vert*—2 ch., 33 ch. T 1. *Horiz*—3 ch., 70 ch. Archer; 5 ch., 1 n. 30, Wild Yak; 15 ch. Map of Bhutan, Maharaja Druk Gyalpo and Paro Dzong (fortress and monastery).

(Litho Harrison)

1962 (10 Oct). *World Refugee Year.* P 14½ × 14.

8	2	1 n. carmine and dull ultramarine	30	30
9		2 n. reddish violet and apple-green	55	55

3 Accoutrements of Ancient Warrior

4 "Boy filling box" (with grain)

(Litho Harrison)

1962 (5 Dec). *Membership of Colombo Plan.* P 14 × 14½.

10	3	33 ch. red, sepia, yellow and green	10	10
11		70 ch. red, sepia, yellow and slate-blue	15	15
12		1 n. 30, red, sepia and yellow	30	30

(Litho De La Rue)

1963 (15 July). *Freedom from Hunger.* P 13½ × 14.

13	4	20 ch. red-brown, light blue & grnsh yell	10	10
14		1 n. 50, bright purple, red-brown & lt bl	40	40

(5)

6 Dancer with upraised Hands

1966 (7 Apr). *Winter Olympic Games, Innsbruck, and Bhutanese Winter Sports Committee Fund. Nos.* 10/12 *surch as T* 5.

15	3	33 ch. +50 ch.			1·25	1·25
16		70 ch. +50 ch.			1·25	1·25
17		1 n. 30 +50 ch.			1·25	1·25
15/17		*Set of 3*			3·25	3·25

(Photo Harrison)

1964 (16 Apr). *Bhutanese Dancers. Designs as T* 6. *Multicoloured.* P 14½ × 14 (*vert*) or 14 × 14½ (*horiz*).

18	2 ch. Standing on one leg		5	5
19	3 ch. Type 6		5	5
20	5 ch. With "tambourine"		5	5
21	20 ch. Standing on one leg		5	5
22	33 ch. Type 6		8	8
23	70 ch. With sword		15	15
24	1 n. With tasselled hat		15	20
25	1 n. 30, With "tambourine"		25	30
26	1 n. With sword		30	35
18/26	*Set of 9*		1·00	1·10

The 2 ch., 5 ch., 20 ch., 1 n. and 1 n. 30 are vertical designs.

IMPERF STAMPS. This and many later issues exist imperforate from limited printings but most of these were not on sale in Bhutan.

7 Bhutanese Athlete

1964 (10 Oct). *Olympic Games, Tokyo. T **7** and similar vert designs. Multicoloured. Litho. P 14½.*

27	2 ch. Type **7**		5	5
28	5 ch. Boxing		5	5
29	15 ch. Type **7**		5	5
30	33 ch. Boxing		8	8
31	1 n. Archery		20	25
32	2 n. Football		50	45
33	3 n. Archery		70	70
27/33	*Set of 7*		1·40	1·40
MS33*a*	85×118 mm. Nos. 31/2		4·50	4·50

8 Flags at Half-mast

1964 (22 Nov). *President Kennedy Commemoration. Litho. P 14½.*

34	**8** 33 ch. multicoloured		8	8
35	1 n. multicoloured		15	20
36	3 n. multicoloured		55	60
MS36*a*	82×119 mm. Nos. 35/6		2·75	2·75

WINSTON CHURCHILL
1874   1965

9 Primula   **(10)**

(Des F. Ludlow. Litho De La Rue)

1965 (6 Jan). *Bhutan Flowers. T **9** and similar vert designs. Multicoloured. P 13.*

37	2 ch. Type **9**		5	5
38	5 ch. Gentian		5	5
39	15 ch. Type **9**		5	5
40	33 ch. Gentian		8	8
41	50 ch. Rhododendron		10	10
42	75 ch. Peony		15	15
43	1 n. Rhododendron		20	20
44	2 n. Peony		40	40
37/44	*Set of 8*		1·00	1·00

1965 (27 Feb). *Churchill Commemoration. Nos. 5, 35/6 and 43/4 optd as T **10**.*

45	– 33 ch. blue-green and reddish lilac		12	15
46	**8** 1 n. multicoloured		25	25
47	– 1 n. multicoloured (No. 43)		25	25
48	– 2 n. multicoloured (No. 44)		50	50
49	**8** 3 n. multicoloured		80	80
45/49	*Set of 5*		1·75	1·75

The overprint on Nos. 45, 47/8 is in smaller sans-serif type, set in three lines.

It is understood that Nos. 46 and 49 were not issued in Bhutan.

11 Pavilion and Skyscrapers

1965 (21 Apr). *New York World's Fair. T **11** and similar horiz designs. Multicoloured. Litho. P 14½.*

50	1 ch. Type **11**		5	5
51	10 ch. Buddha and Michelangelo's "Pieta"		5	5
52	20 ch. Bhutan houses and New York sky-line		5	5
53	33 ch. Bhutan and New York bridges		8	8
54	1 n. 50, Type **11**		30	30
55	2 n. As 10 ch.		45	45
50/55	*Set of 6*		90	90
MS55*a*	120×86 mm. Nos. 54/5		1·75	1·75

(12)

1965–67. *Various stamps surch as T **12**.*

56	**2** 5 ch. on 1 n. (No. 8) (1967)		1·00	1·00
57	5 ch. on 2 n. (No. 9)		1·00	1·00
58	– 10 ch. on 70 ch. (No. 23) (1967)		50	50
59	– 10 ch. on 2 n. (No. 26)		45	45
60	– 15 ch. on 70 ch. (No. 6)		35	35
61	– 15 ch. on 1 n. 30 (No. 7)		35	35
62	– 20 ch. on 1 n. (No. 24) (1967)		45	45
63	– 20 ch. on 1 n. 30 (No. 25)		45	45
56/63	*Set of 8*		4·00	4·00

13 "Telstar" and Portable Transmitter

1966 (2 Mar). *I.T.U. Centenary. T **13** and similar horiz designs. Multicoloured. Photo. P 14½.*

64	35 ch. Type **13**		8	8
65	2 n. "Telstar" and morse key		40	40
66	3 n. "Relay" and ear-phones		60	60
MS67	118×78 mm. Nos. 65/6		2·50	2·50

14 Bear   **15** Simtoka Dzong (fortress)

1966 (24 Mar). *Animals. T* **14** *and similar vert designs. Multicoloured. Litho. P* 13½.

68	1 ch. Type **14**			5	5
69	2 ch. Leopard			5	5
70	4 ch. Wild boar			5	5
71	8 ch. Tiger			5	5
72	10 ch. Wild dog			5	5
73	75 ch. Tiger			15	12
74	1 n. Buffalo			20	15
75	1 n. 50, Wild dog			35	25
76	2 n. Wild boar			45	30
77	3 n. Leopard			55	40
78	4 n. Type **14**			70	50
79	5 n. Buffalo			1·00	65
68/79	*Set of 12*			3·00	2·25

(Photo Security Printing Press, Nasik (India))

1966 (2 May)–**67**. *T* **15** *and similar horiz design. P* 14½ × 14.

80	–	5 ch. chestnut (2.5.67)		5	5
81	**15**	15 ch. brown		5	5
82		20 ch. yellow-green		5	5
80/82	*Set of 3*			8	8

Design:—5 ch. Rinpung Dzong (fortress).

16 King Jigme Dorji Wangchuk (obverse of 50 n.p. coin)

(Des and embossed Walsall Lithographic Co, Ltd)

1966 (8 July). *40th Anniv of King Jigme Dorji Wangchuk's Accession. Circular designs, embossed on gold foil, backed with multicoloured patterned paper. Imperf. Sizes:—*
(*a*) *Diameter* 1½ *in.;* (*b*) *Diameter* 1⅝ *in.;* (*c*) *Diameter* 2½ *in.*

(i) 50 *n.p. Coin*

83	10 ch. emerald (*a*)			5	5

(ii) 1 *r. Coin*

84	25 ch. emerald (*b*)			5	5

(iii) 3 *r. Coin*

85	50 ch. emerald (*c*)			10	10

(iv) 1 *sertum Coin*

86	1 n. carmine (*a*)			15	15
87	1 n. 30, carmine (*a*)			20	20

(v) 2 *sertum Coin*

88	2 n. carmine (*b*)			40	40
89	3 n. carmine (*b*)			55	55

(vi) 5 *sertum Coin*

90	4 n. carmine (*c*)			70	70
91	5 n. carmine (*c*)			95	95
83/91	*Set of 9*			2·75	2·75

The 10, 25, 50 ch., 1, 2, 4 n. each show the obverse side of the coins as T **16**. The remainder show the reverse side of the coins (Symbol).

17 "Abominable Snowman"

(Photo Heraclio Fournier, Vitoria, Spain)

1966 (10 Oct)–**67**. *"Abominable Snowman". Various triangular designs as T* **17**. *P* 13.

92	1 ch. multicoloured			5	5
93	2 ch. multicoloured			5	5
94	3 ch. multicoloured			5	5
95	4 ch. multicoloured			5	5
96	5 ch. multicoloured			5	5
97	15 ch. multicoloured			5	5
98	30 ch. multicoloured (15.11.66)			5	5
99	40 ch. multicoloured			5	5
100	50 ch. multicoloured			8	8
101	1 n. 25, multicoloured (15.11.66)			15	15
102	2 n. 50, multicoloured (15.11.66)			35	35
103	3 n. multicoloured (15.11.66)			40	40
104	5 n. multicoloured (15.11.66)			65	65
105	6 n. multicoloured (4.3.67)			80	80
106	7 n. multicoloured (4.3.67)			1·00	1·00
92/106	*Set of 15*			3·25	3·25

(18)   AIR MAIL (19)

1967 (10 Jan). *AIR. Various stamps overprinted.*

				A. *T* **18**		B. *T* **19**	
107	**6**	33 ch. (No. 22)		5	5	5	5
108	–	50 ch. (No. 41)		8	8	8	8
109	–	70 ch. (No. 23)		10	10	10	10
		a. Opt inverted		20·00	20·00	—	—
110	–	75 ch. (No. 42)		10	10	10	10
111	–	1 n. (No. 24)		15	15	15	15
112	–	1 n. 50 (No. 75)		20	20	20	20
113	–	2 n. (No. 76)		25	25	25	25
114	–	3 n. (No. 77)		40	40	40	40
115	**14**	4 n. (No. 78)		55	55	55	55
116	–	5 n. (No. 79)		65	65	65	65
107/116	*Set of 10*			1·50	1·50	1·50	1·50

All values exist in *se-tenant* pairs showing both types of overprint.

20 *Lilium sherriffiae*

(Designs from watercolours selected by F. Ludlow, Natural History Museum, London. Litho)

1967 (9 Feb). *Bhutan Flowers. T* **20** *and similar multicoloured designs. P* 13½.

117	3 ch. Type **20**			5	5
118	5 ch. *Meconopsis*			5	5
119	7 ch. *Rhododendron dhwoju*			5	5
120	10 ch. *Pleione hookeriana*			5	5
121	50 ch. Type **20**			8	8
122	1 n. *Meconopsis*			20	20
123	2 n. 50, *Rhododendron dhwoju*			40	40
124	4 n. *Pleione hookeriana*			60	60
125	5 n. *Rhododendrons giganteum*			70	70
117/125	*Set of 9*			1·90	1·90

HAVE YOU READ THE NOTES AT THE BEGINNING OF THIS CATALOGUE?

These often provide answers to the enquiries we receive.

21 Scouts tending Camp-fire

1967 (28 Mar). *Bhutanese Boy Scouts. T***21** *and similar multi-coloured designs. Photo. P* 13½.
126	5 ch. Type **21**	..	..	5	5
127	10 ch. Scouts preparing meal	..		5	5
128	15 ch. Scout mountaineering	..		5	5
129	50 ch. Type **21**	..	..	8	8
130	1 n. 25, As 10 ch.	..	..	15	15
131	4 n. As 15 ch.	..	..	55	55
126/131	*Set of* 6	..	..	80	80
MS132	93×93 mm. Nos. 130/1	..	..	1·00	1·00

(22)

1967 (15 May). *World Fair, Montreal. Nos.* 53/5 *and* **MS**55*a optd with T* **22**.
133	33 ch. multicoloured	..	..	5	5
134	1 n. 50, multicoloured	..	..	20	20
135	2 n. multicoloured	..	..	25	25
MS136	120×86 mm. Nos. 134/5	..	..	75	75

23 "Lancaster" Bomber

1967 (25 July). *Churchill and Battle of Britain Commemoration. T* **23** *and similar horiz designs. Multicoloured. Litho. P* 13½.
137	45 ch. Type **23**	..	..	10	10
138	2 n. "Spitfire" fighter	..	..	25	25
139	4 n. "Hurricane" fighter	..	..	55	55
MS140	118×75 mm. Nos. 138/9	..	..	1·25	1·25

It is understood that the miniature sheet was not issued in Bhutan.

**WORLD JAMBOREE
IDAHO, U.S.A.
AUG. 1-9/67**

(24)

1967 (8 Aug). *World Scout Jamboree, Idaho. Nos.* 126/31 *and* **MS**132 *optd with T* **24**.
141	5 ch. multicoloured	..	..	..	5	5
142	10 ch. multicoloured	..	..	..	5	5
143	15 ch. multicoloured	..	..	..	5	5
144	50 ch. multicoloured	..	..	..	8	8
145	1 n. 25, multicoloured	..	..		15	15
146	4 n. multicoloured	..	..	..	55	55
141/146	*Set of* 6	..	..		80	80
MS147	93×93 mm. Nos. 145/6	..	..	1·00	1·00

A second setting of the overprint is known with the "I" of "IDAHO" below "OR" of "WORLD".

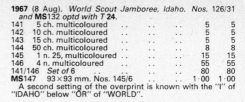

25 Painting

1967 (28 Sept). *Bhutan Girl Scouts. T* **25** *and similar multicoloured designs. Photo. P* 13½.
148	5 ch. Type **25**	..	..	5	5
149	10 ch. Playing musical instrument	..	5	5
150	15 ch. Picking fruit	..	..	5	5
151	1 n. 50, Type **25**	..	..	20	20
152	2 n. 50, Playing musical instrument	..	35	35
153	5 n. Picking fruit	..	..	65	65
148/153	*Set of* 6	..	..	1·25	1·25
MS154	93×93 mm. Nos. 152/3	..	..	1·50	1·50

26 Astronaut in Space

1967 (30 Oct). *Space Achievements. T* **26** *and similar horiz designs. Multicoloured. Litho with laminated prismatic-ribbed plastic surface. Imperf.* (a) POSTAGE.
155	3 ch. Type **26**	..	..	8	8
156	5 ch. Space vehicle and astronaut	..	8	8
157	7 ch. Astronaut and landing vehicle	..	8	8
158	10 ch. Three astronauts in space	..	10	10
159	15 ch. Type **26**	..	..	10	10
160	30 ch. As 5 ch	..	..	12	12
161	50 ch. As 7 ch.	..	..	15	15
162	1 n. 25, As 10 ch.	..	..	30	30

(b) AIR
163	2 n. 50, Type **26**	..	..	35	35
164	4 n. As 5 ch.	..	..	55	55
165	5 n. As 7 ch.	..	..	65	65
166	9 n. As 10 ch.	..	..	1·25	1·25
155/166	*Set of* 12	..	..	3·25	3·25
MS167	Three sheets, each 130×111 mm.				

Nos. 155/8, 159/62 and 163/6 Imperf .. 3·50 3·50
The laminated plastic surface gives the stamp a three-dimensional effect.

27 Tashichho Dzong

(Des from photos by L. Wangchuck. Photo Security Printing Press, Nasik (India))

1968 (29 Feb). P 13.
168 **27** 10 ch. purple and bronze-green .. 5 5

APPENDIX. Further commemorative issues will be found recorded in the Appendix to this volume.

28 Tongsa Dzong

(Photo Security Ptg Press, Nasik (India))

1968 (30 Oct)–**70.** T **28** and similar horiz designs. P 13½×13.
169   50 ch. deep bluish green 8 8
170   75 ch. olive-brown & dp ultram (2.5.70) 10 10
171   1 n. ultramarine and violet (2.5.70) 12 12
Designs:—75 ch. Daga Dzong; 1 n. Lhuntsi Dzong.

29 Mahatma Gandhi

(Photo Security Ptg Press, Nasik, India)

1969 (2 Oct). Birth Centenary of Mahatma Gandhi. P 13×13½.
172 **29** 20 ch. sepia and light new blue .. 5 5
173   2 n. olive-brown and olive-yellow .. 40 40

(30)   **31** Wangdiphodrang
        Dzong and Bridge

(Surch by Security Ptg Press, Nasik, India)

1970 (June). Provisionals. Various stamps surch as T **30**.
  I. 1966 Animals issue (Nos. 77/9)
174 – 20 ch. on 3 n. multicoloured .. 35 35
175 **14** 20 ch. on 4 n. multicoloured 35 35
176 – 20 ch. on 5 n. multicoloured 35 35
  II. 1966–67 Abominable Snowmen issue (Nos. 103/6)
177 – 20 ch. on 3 n. multicoloured 50 50
178 – 20 ch. on 4 n. multicoloured 50 50
179 – 20 ch. on 6 n. multicoloured 50 50
180 – 20 ch. on 7 n. multicoloured 50 50
  III. 1967 Flowers issue (Nos. 124/5)
181 – 20 ch. on 4 n. multicoloured 50 50
182 – 20 ch. on 5 n. multicoloured 50 50

  IV. 1967 Boy Scouts issue (No. 131)
183 – 20 ch. on 4 n. multicoloured 30 30
  V. 1968 Pheasants issue (Appendix)
184 – 20 ch. on 4 n. multicoloured 50 50
  VI. 1968 Mythological Creatures issue (Appendix)
        (a) POSTAGE
185 – 20 ch. on 2 n. multicoloured 50 50
        (b) AIR
186 – 20 ch. on 5 n. multicoloured 50 50
187 – 20 ch. on 10 n. multicoloured .. 50 50
  VII. 1968–69 Rare Birds issue (Appendix). (a) POSTAGE
188 – 20 ch. on 2 n. multicoloured 25 25
        (b) AIR
189 – 20 ch. on 2 n. 50, multicoloured .. 50 50
190 – 20 ch. on 4 n. multicoloured 50 50
191 – 20 ch. on 5 n. multicoloured 40 40
192 – 20 ch. on 10 n. multicoloured .. 40 40
174/192 Set of 19 .. .. .. 7·50 7·50
See also Nos. 193/215 and 223/35.

(Surch by Security Ptg Press, Nasik, India)

1970 (2 Nov). Provisionals. Various stamps surch similar to T **30**.
  I. 1963 Freedom from Hunger issue (No. 14)
193 **4** 20 ch. on 1 n. 50, bright purple, red-
      brown and light blue 30 30
  II. 1965 Animals issue (Nos. 75/6)
194 – 20 ch. on 1 n. 50, multicoloured .. 35 35
195 – 20 ch. on 2 n. multicoloured .. 35 35
  III. 1966–67 Abominable Snowmen issue (Nos. 101/2)
196 – 20 ch. on 1 n. 25, multicoloured .. 90 90
197 **17** 20 ch. on 2 n. 50, multicoloured .. 50 50
  IV. 1967 Boy Scouts issue (No. 130)
198 – 20 ch. on 1 n. 25, multicoloured .. 35 35
  V. 1967 Churchill issue (Nos. 138/9)
199 – 20 ch. on 2 n. multicoloured 90 90
200 – 20 ch. on 4 n. multicoloured 90 90
  VI. 1968 Pheasants issue (Appendix)
201 – 20 ch. on 2 n. multicoloured 50 50
202 – 20 ch. on 7 n. multicoloured 50 50
  VII. 1968 Mythological Creatures issue (Appendix)
        (a) POSTAGE
203 – 5 ch. on 30 ch. multicoloured .. 40 40
204 – 5 ch. on 50 ch. multicoloured .. 35 35
205 – 5 ch. on 1 n. 25, multicoloured .. 20 20
206 – 5 ch. on 2 n. multicoloured .. 25 25
        (b) AIR
207 – 5 ch. on 1 n. 50, multicoloured .. 30 30
208 – 5 ch. on 2 n. 50, multicoloured .. 40 40
  VIII. 1968–69 Rare Birds issue (Appendix). (a) POSTAGE
209 – 20 ch. on 30 ch. multicoloured .. 25 25
210 – 20 ch. on 50 ch. multicoloured .. 25 25
211 – 20 ch. on 1 n. 25, multicoloured .. 25 25
        (b) AIR
212 – 20 ch. on 1 n. 50, multicoloured .. 50 50
  IX. 1969 U.P.U. issue (Appendix)
213 – 20 ch. on 1 n. 05, multicoloured .. 2·00 2·00
214 – 20 ch. on 1 n. 40, multicoloured .. 2·00 2·00
215 – 20 ch. on 4 n. multicoloured .. 2·00 2·00
193/215 Set of 23 .. .. .. 13·00 13·00

(Photo Security Ptg Press, Nasik, India)

1971 (22 Feb)–**72.** P 14×13½.
216 **31** 2 ch. grey (1972) 5 5
217   3 ch. deep mauve (1972) 5 5
218   4 ch. bluish violet (1972) 5 5
219   5 ch. yellow-green 5 5
220   10 ch. orange-brown 5 5
221   15 ch. blue 5 5
222   20 ch. reddish purple 5 5
216/222 Set of 7 .. .. .. 25 25

1971 (1 July). *Provisionals. Various stamps surch similar to T 30* (*No.* 235 *handstamped*).

I. 1964 *Dancers issue* (*Nos.* 25/6)
223	–	55 ch. on 1 n. 30, multicoloured ..	40	40
224	–	90 ch. on 2 n. multicoloured ..	50	50

II. 1966 *Animals issue* (*Nos.* 77/8)
225	–	55 ch. on 3 n. multicoloured	40	40
226	**14**	90 ch. on 4 n. multicoloured ..	50	50

III. 1967 *Boy Scouts issue* (*No.* 131)
227	–	90 ch. on 4 n. multicoloured ..	35	35

IV. 1968 *Pheasants issue* (*Appendix*)
228	–	55 ch. on 5 n. multicoloured ..	40	40
229	–	90 ch. on 9 n. multicoloured ..	50	50

V. 1968 *Mythological Creatures issue* (*Appendix*). *AIR*
230	–	55 ch. on 4 n. multicoloured ..	35	35

VI. 1968 *Mexico Olympics issue* (*Appendix*)
231	–	90 ch. on 1 n. 05, multicoloured ..	40	40

VII. 1968–69 *Rare Birds issue* (*Appendix*)
232	–	90 ch. on 2 n. multicoloured	50	50

VIII. 1969 *U.P.U. issue* (*Appendix*)
233	–	55 ch. on 60 ch. multicoloured ..	2·00	2·00

IX. 1970 *New U.P.U. Headquarters issue* (*Appendix*)
234	–	90 ch. on 2 n. 50, gold and lake ..	50	50

X. 1971 *Moon Vehicles* (*plastic-surfaced*) *issue* (*Appendix*)
235	–	90 ch. on 1 n. 70, multicoloured (Y.) ..	2·40	2·40
223/235		*Set of 13*	8·00	8·00

32 Book Year Emblem

1972 (15 May). *International Book Year. Photo. P* 13½ × 13.
236	**32**	2 ch. dp grn, pale turq-grn & turq-bl	5	5
237		3 ch. brn-pur, pale yell & yell-ochre	5	5
238		5 ch. blackish brn, sal & red-orge ..	5	5
239		20 ch. multicoloured	5	5
236/239		*Set of 4*	12	12

BOLIVAR. See Colombian States.

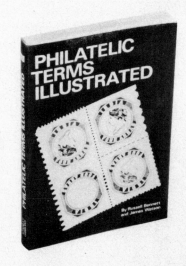

Bolivia

1866. 100 Centavos = 1 Boliviano
1963. 100 Centavos = 1 Peso Boliviano ($b)

Bolivia, known as Upper Peru in the Spanish colonial period, became an independent republic on 6 August 1825, and was given its name in honour of the liberator Simon Bolivar.

> For GREAT BRITAIN stamps used in Cobija (then in Bolivia) with obliteration "C39", see British Stamps Used Abroad in the British Commonwealth Catalogue.

On 21 February 1863 the Government issued a Decree offering a contract for carrying the mails to the highest bidder, and a Decree of 18 March granted the contract to Justiniano Garcia who prepared stamps which were to be issued on 1 June. In the event the contract was suspended by an Order of 29 April. Thus the stamps were officially authorised but never brought into use. Some are known on covers but their authenticity has not been established.

The stamps are all in the design illustrated above and all values were printed in the same sheet which comprised 30 ½ r., 50 1 r., 20 2 r. and 10 4 r. They were printed first in black and then in blue, all imperforate.

(Eng Estruch, La Paz. Recess at Cochabamba)

1866–68. *Imperf.*

					Un	Us	Pen-c
1	1	5 c. yellow-green (a)	..	..	20·00	20·00	3·00
		a. Olive-green	..	..	6·00	8·00	30
		b. Grass-green	..	..	2·25	4·00	30
		c. Green	..	..	75	1·00	5
		d. Blue-green ..	..	..	75	1·00	5
2		5 c. yellow-green (b)	..	..	18·00	15·00	
		a. Grass-green	..	..	2·75	4·00	
		b. Green	..	..	65	1·50	10
		c. Blue-green ..	..	..	50	1·00	8
3		5 c. green (c)	..	..	1·25	2·50	15
4		5 c. pale green (d)	..	..	30	50	5
		a. Deep green	..	..	25	50	5
5		5 c. pale green (e)	..	..	25	50	5
		a. Deep green	..	..	25	50	5
6		5 c. pale green (f)	..	..	35	75	10
		a. Deep green	..	..	35	75	10
7	2	10 c. brown (1868)	..	..	22·00	25·00	
		a. Deep brown	..	..	22·00	25·00	1·00
		b. Black-brown	..	..	22·00	25·00	
		c. Grey-brown	..	..	25·00	28·00	
8	3	50 c. yellow (1867)	..	..	2·00	5·00	
		a. Orange-yellow	..	..	2·00	5·00	50
		b. Lemon-yellow	..	..	2·25	5·00	50
9	2	100 c. blue (1867) ..	..	..	4·50	10·00	50
		a. Deep blue ..	..	..	4·25	12·00	50

1868. *Colours changed. Imperf.*

					Un	Us	Pen-c
10	1	5 c. mauve (f) ..	..	..	20·00	20·00	4·00
		a. Grey-lilac ..	..	..	20·00	20·00	4·00
		b. Violet	..	..	25·00	25·00	4·00
11	3	50 c. pale blue ..	..	..	50·00	50·00	12·00
		a. Deep blue ..	..	..	50·00	50·00	12·00
12	2	100 c. deep green	..	..	18·00	20·00	3·00
		a. Pale green	..	..	18·00	20·00	3·00

PRINTERS. Issues of 1868 to 1891 were recess printed by the American Bank Note Co, New York.

1 Condor

2

3

10 c. and 100 c. have values as T **2**, 50 c. as T **3**

This issue also served for fiscal use and prices for pen cancellations are given in the third column.

The plate of the 5 c. was entirely re-engraved four times, and more or less retouched at least six times, making possible eleven clearly defined states of the plate. There are 72 varieties on this plate. There was only one plate each for the other values containing 78 varieties of the 10 c. and 50 varieties each of the 50 c. and 100 c.

General types of the 5 c. are distinguished by the lines on the globe although these may not be typical of all the stamps on the sheet.

(a) Vertical and diagonal lines
(b) Diagonal lines only
(c) Diagonal and horizontal lines with faint traces of vertical lines
(d) Diagonal and horizontal lines
(e) Horizontal lines only
(f) No lines except the curved lines forming the shape of the globe

In addition there are other varieties peculiar to certain stamps only on the plate, mostly consisting in the absence or presence of lines other than those usually to be found. Amongst these are varieties in which the "A" in "CENTAVOS", "CONTRATOS" or "BOLIVIA" has no bar.

4 (9 Stars)

F **1** Figure of Justice

5 (11 Stars)

1868 (April). *P* 12.

32	4	5 c. green	..	..	..	1·30	45
33		10 c. red	..	..	..	1·50	50
34		50 c. blue	..	..	..	1·50	1·25
35		100 c. orange	..	..	..	1·75	1·75
36		500 c. black	..	..	..	75·00	75·00

1870. *POSTAL FISCAL. P* 12.

F37	F **1**	5 c. black ..	..	..	..	5	8
F38		10 c. green ..	..	..	..	15	10
F39		50 c. brown ..	..	..	..	1·50	1·75
F40		100 c. red	..	..	..	3·50	3·50
F41		500 c. blue	..	..	..	15·00	25·00

Used prices are for postally used copies.

1871. *P* 12.

37	5	5 c. green	..	..	..	30	20
38		10 c. red	..	..	..	75	35
39		50 c. blue	..	..	..	1·25	1·10
40		100 c. orange	..	..	..	1·25	90
41		500 c. black	..	..	..	£150	£150

6	F 2

1878. *Various frames.* P 12.

42	6	5 c. ultramarine	..	..	..	65	30
43		10 c. orange	..	..	..	65	15
		a. Bisected (5 c.) on cover	..	..	—	3·50
44		20 c. green	..	..	..	1·25	15
45		50 c. carmine	..	..	..	25·00	1·50

On 14 February 1879 Chilean troops seized the Bolivian port of Antofagasta and on 1 March Bolivia declared war; Peru joined in the war against Chile from 5 April 1879 to 20 October 1883. On 11 December 1883, Bolivia made peace with Chile and by the treaty lost all her sea-coast.

The stamps of Chile used in Bolivia were the 1867 issue (T **9**), the 1877–78 issue (T **10/12**) and the 1 c. to 10 c. values of the 1881–86 issue (T **13/14**).

Amongst the places in Bolivia where Chilean stamps are known to have been used with special postmarks during the period of the war are Antofagasta, Calama, Caracoles, Carmen Alto, Cobija, Mejillones, Pampa Alto, Puquios, Salinas, San Antonio de Atacamba and Tocopilla.

1884. *POSTAL FISCAL. Fiscal stamps of 1883 used for postage. Various frames.* P 12.

					Un	Postally us
						1884 1883
F46	F 2	5 c. blue	..	..	60	70 50
F47		10 c. blue	..	..	90	80 60
F48		50 c. blue	..	..	5·00	6·00 4·00

These are inscribed respectively "1 CLASE", "2 CLASE" and "4 CLASE". In 1884 they were issued for postal use only in the province of Chuquisaca but in 1893 they were again brought into general use.

See also Nos. F68/9.

1887. *Numerals upright. Rouletted.*

46	5	1 c. carmine	..	..	..	15	8
47		2 c. slate-violet	..	..	..	15	8
48		5 c. blue	..	..	..	1·00	12
49		10 c. orange	..	..	..	1·00	12

1890 (1 Nov)–**91.** *Numerals upright.* P 12.

50	4	1 c. carmine (1891)	..	..	15	12
51		2 c. slate-violet (1891)	..	..	35	25
52		5 c. blue	..	..	..	15	8
53		10 c. orange (1891)	..	..	55	15
54		20 c. green (1891)	..	..	1·50	20
55		50 c. red	..	..	..	35	20
56		100 c. yellow	..	..	..	1·25	50

The 50 c. and 100 c. were reissued in 1908.

(Litho Litografia Boliviana, La Paz)

1893. *Numerals upright.* P 11.

57	4	1 c. rose	..	..	..	20	15
		a. Imperf (pair)	..	..	2·50	
58		2 c. slate-violet	..	..	20	15
59	5	5 c. pale blue	..	..	15	12
60	4	10 c. orange	..	..	1·25	20
61		20 c. blue-green	..	..	3·50	2·75

(F 3)	(F 4)

1893. *POSTAL FISCAL. Optd with Type* F **3.**

F62	5	1 c. carmine (B.) (No. 46)	..	..	25	30
F63	4	1 c. carmine (B.) (No. 50)	..	..	85	60
		a. Violet opt	..	..	1·50	
F64	5	2 c. slate-violet (R.) (No. 47)	..	..	25	25
F65	4	2 c. slate-violet (R.) (No. 51)	..	..	60	60

No. 57 also exists with this overprint but it is believed that it was not used postally.

1893. *POSTAL FISCAL. Stamps similar to Type* F **2** *optd with Type* F **4** *and with "1893" added by hand.*

F66	5 c. blue (R.)	..	..	..	..	2·00	1·50
	a. Opt inverted	..	..	..	—	10·00
	b. Black opt	..	..	..	3·50	3·50
F67	10 c. blue	..	..	..	3·50	3·50

(Recess American Bank Note Co)

1893. *POSTAL FISCAL.* P 12.

F68	F **2**	1 c. blue	..	..	..	20	15
F69		c. blue	..	..	..	1·50	1·00

The used quotations for Nos. F62/69 are for postally used copies; fiscal cancellations are worthless.

8

(Recess Bradbury, Wilkinson & Co)

1894 (Apr). *Thin paper.* P 14 to 14½.

63	8	1 c. ochre	..	..	..	10	20
64		2 c. orange-vermilion	..	..	10	25
65		5 c. green	..	..	..	10	10
66		10 c. yellow-brown	..	..	10	10
67		20 c. deep blue	..	..	40	1·00
68		50 c. claret	..	..	..	75	2·00
69		100 c. rose-red	..	..	1·00	5·00

(Recess Eudes & Chassepot, Paris)

1895. *Thicker paper.* P 13 to 13½.

70	8	1 c. pale ochre	..	..	..	—	35
71		2 c. orange-vermilion	..	..	—	35
72		5 c. green	..	..	..	—	35
73		10 c. bistre-brown	..	..	—	10
74		20 c. dull blue	..	..	—	50
75		50 c. dull claret	..	..	—	50
76		100 c. carmine-red	..	..	—	2·00

The circumstances surrounding the issue of these stamps are complicated. A substantial part of the London printing was delivered to Bolivia and then, without authority, the Secretary of the Bolivian Legation in Paris instructed the printers to deliver to him the rest of the stamps together with the plates. These plates were used to print much larger quantities in Paris, these being distinguishable by the perforation and paper.

It was the Paris printing which was substituted for the rest of the London printing and sent to Bolivia and these were put on sale there about the middle of 1895 according to the earliest genuine postmarks, and remained in use until 1898. In fact the Bolivian authorities withdrew their stocks of the London printing and these were later used for Nos. 85/91.

Meanwhile stereos were made from the original plates and used to make many more printings by various printers in a wide range of shades and these were marketed as "reprints".

The situation is that the London and Eudes & Chassepot printings exist with both genuine postmarks and faked cancellations since the latter were also applied to the balance of the London printing, but the later "reprints" only exist with faked cancellations.

Under the circumstances we now list the Eudes & Chassepot stamps but only price them postally used since it is difficult to distinguish unused copies from the later "reprints" as there were so many shades of each. The used prices for the London printing are also for postally used. The spurious cancellations are easily recognisable as they bear no wording and consist either of bars or circles made up of variously shaped blobs.

9 Frias 10

(Litho J. M. Gamarra, La Paz)

1897 (15 Mar–15 April). *T 9 (portraits) and* **10**. *P* 12.

77	1 c. olive-green (15.4)	..	..	..	20	15
78	2 c. vermilion		..	..	40	30
79	5 c. blue-green (15.4)		..	..	15	8
80	10 c. brownish purple		..	..	20	12
81	20 c. black and lake		..	..	25	15
	a. Imperf (pair)		..	..	2·00	
82	50 c. orange (15.4)		..	..	40	25
83	1 b. blue (15.4)	..		..	60	40
84	2 b. black, red, yellow and green			..	2·75	3·25
77/84	*Set of 8*		..	..	4·50	4·25

Portraits:—2 c. Linares; 5 c. Murillo; 10 c. Monteagudo;
20 c. J. Ballivian; 50 c. Sucre; 1 b. Bolívar.
Beware of forgeries of No. 84.

(17) 18 Sucre

(T 17 shows a forged overprint; originals differ in the shape
of the numerals)

1899. *Nos. 63/9 handstamped as T* 17, *in violet*.

85	8	1 c. ochre	..	..	1·50	1·50
86		2 c. orange-vermilion..	..		1·90	1·90
87		5 c. green	..	..	1·10	1·10
88		10 c. yellow-brown	..	..	1·50	1·50
89		20 c. deep blue..	..	..	2·50	2·50
85/89		*Set of 5*	..	..	7·50	7·50

Prepared for use, but not issued

90		50 c. claret	..	..	50·00	
91		100 c. rose-red ..	..	..	50·00	

These stamps were used in the northern part of Bolivia
during the civil war caused by La Paz revolting against a
proposal to make Sucre the permanent capital. The letters
"E.F." stand for "Estado Federal".
It is believed that the 50 c. and 100 c. were never officially
overprinted, but they are known with genuine postal cancellations.

(Recess South American Bank Note Co, Buenos Aires)

1899–1901. *Thin paper. P* 11½, 12.

92	18	1 c. dull blue ..	..	..	..	12	12
93		2 c. red	..	..	..	12	8
94		5 c. deep green	..	..	..	35	15
95		5 c. red (1.1.01)	..	..	..	20	15
96		10 c. orange	..	..	..	15	10
97		20 c. rose	..	..	..	25	10
98		50 c. bistre-brown	..	..	..	40	15
		a. Thick paper	..	..	..	50	15
99		1 b. dull lilac ..	..	..	..	20	15
		a. Thick paper	..	..	..	25	30
92/99		*Set of 8*	..	..	..	1·60	90

19 A. Ballivian   20 Camacho   21 Campero

22 J. Ballivian   23 Santa Cruz   24

(Recess American Bank Note Co, N.Y.)

1901–04. *P* 11½, 12.

100	19	1 c. claret	..	..	..	5	5
101	20	2 c. green	..	..	..	5	5
102	21	5 c. scarlet	..	..	..	5	5
		a. Vermilion				5	5
103	22	10 c. blue (1904)	..	..	15	5
104	23	20 c. black and purple		..	8	5
105	24	2 b. brown	..	..	..	75	50
100/105		*Set of 6*	..	..	..	1·00	65

See also Nos. 133/41.

1904. *T 19, redrawn. Litho. The shading above the word
"CENTAVO" consists of dots instead of lines.*

106	19	1 c. claret	..	..	..	40	15

25   26 Murillo

1909 (16 July). *Centenary of Revolution (La Paz issue). T 25
and* **26** *(portraits dated "1809–1909"). Litho. P* 11½.

110	5	c. black and blue	..	..	1·25	90
		b. Tête-bêche (pair) ..		..	3·00	
111	10	c. black and green	..	..	1·25	90
		a. Centre inverted	..	..	2·50	3·00
		b. Tête-bêche (pair)	..	..	3·00	
112	20	c. black and pale orange (Lanza)	..	1·25	1·00
		a. Centre inverted	..	..	2·50	3·00
		b. Tête-bêche (pair)	..	..	3·00	
113	2	b. black and red (Montes)	..	1·75	1·10
		a. Centre inverted	..	..	2·50	3·00
		b. Tête-bêche (pair) ..		..	3·00	
110/113		*Set of 4*	..	..	5·00	3·50

29   37

1909 (Dec?). *Centenary of Beginning of War of Independence, 1809–25 (Sucre issue). As T 29 (portraits dated
"1809–1825"). Litho. Centres in black. P* 11½.

115	1 c. chocolate (M. Betanzos)	..	..	15	8
116	2 c. green (I. Warnes) ..		..	15	12
117	5 c. red (P. D. Murillo)	..	..	15	5
118	10 c. Prussian blue (B. Monteagudo)	..	15	5
119	20 c. violet (E. Arze)	..	..	20	12
120	50 c. bistre (A. J. Sucre)..		..	20	20
121	1 b. brown (S. Bolívar) ..		..	25	20
122	2 b. chocolate (M. Belgrano)	..	30	30
115/122	*Set of 8*	..	..	1·40	1·00

(Litho Soc Imp y Lit Universo, Chile)

1910. *Centenary of Liberation of Santa Cruz, Potosi and
Cochabamba. As T 37 (portraits dated "1910–1825"). Centres in black. P* 13×13½.

123	5 c. green (I. Warnes)	..	..	8	5
124	10 c. carmine (M. Betanzos)	..	..	8	5
125	20 c. slate (E. Arze)	..	..	15	10

Correos
10
Centavos

CORREOS

5 Centavos
1911

1912

1912.

(40)

(41)

(42)

1911 (Aug). *Surch with T* **40**.
126	**20**	5 c. on 2 c. green	..	..	10	8
		a. Surch inverted	..	..	3·25	3·25
		b. Stop after date	..	..	1·60	1·00
127	**23**	5 c. on 20 c. black and lilac	..	..	2·50	2·50
		a. Surch inverted	..	..	7·00	7·00

1912 (Mar). *Surch with T* **41**.
129	F **5**	10 c. on 1 c. blue (R.)..	..	..	10	10
		a. Black surch	..	..	30·00	30·00

1912 (June–July). *Fiscal stamps as Type* F **5** *optd with T* **42**.
130		2 c. green (Bk.)..	..	..	10	10
131		5 c. orange (R.)..	..	..	10	10
		a. Opt inverted	..	..	3·25	3·25
		b. Black opt	..	..	10·00	
132		10 c. vermilion (B.)	..	..	20	12

43 Frias

44 Sucre

45 Bolivar

1913. *Various types.* P 11½, 12.
133	**19**	1 c. carmine-pink	..	..	5	5
134	**20**	2 c. red	..	..	5	5
135	**21**	5 c. green	..	..	8	5
136	**43**	8 c. yellow	..	..	15	10
137	**22**	10 c. grey-lilac	..	..	12	5
138	**23**	20 c. black and dull violet	..	..	20	8
139	**44**	50 c. purple	..	..	25	12
140	**45**	1 b. slate-blue	..	..	35	25
141	**24**	2 b. black	..	..	80	60
133/141		Set of 9	..	..	1·75	1·10

This 20 c. is a re-issue, deeper in colour than No. 104 and having the shading under the numerals and the word "centavos" accentuated.

46 Monolith

47 El Potosi

48 Lake Titicaca

49 Illimani

50 Parliament Building, La Paz

Two types of 5 c.
I. Numerals have background of coloured lines.
II. Numerals on white ground.

Two types of 10 c.
I. "PALACIO LEGISLATIVO" in large letters, with stop.
II. Smaller letters, no stop. Also differences in the design.

(Litho J. Böttger, La Paz)

1916–18. P 11½.
142	**46**	½ c. brown (1917)	..	..	..	5	5
143	**47**	1 c. green (1917)	..	..	..	5	5
		a. Imperf (pair)	..	..		1·00	
144	**48**	2 c. black and rose (1918)	..	..	5	5
		a. Imperf (pair)	..	..		1·00	
		b. Centre inverted	..	..	8·00	8·00
145	**49**	5 c. blue (I) (2.16)	..	..	10	5
		a. Imperf (pair)	..	..		1·00	
		b. Dull blue				10	5
146		5 c. dull blue (II) (1918)	..	..	10	5
		a. Imperf (pair)	..	..		1·50	
147	**50**	10 c. blue and orange (I) (1917)	..	15	5
		a. Imperf (pair)	..	..		1·75	
148		10 c. blue and orange (II)	..	..	15	5
		a. Centre inverted	..	..	19·00	19·00
142/148		Set of 7	..	..	..	55	25

51

51a

(Recess American Bank Note Co, N.Y.)

1919–20. P 12.
149	**51**	1 c. lake	..	..	..	5	5
150		2 c. violet	..	..	..	60	50
151		5 c. green	..	..	..	5	5
152		10 c. vermilion	..	..	..	5	5
153		20 c. deep blue	..	..	..	20	5
154		22 c. pale blue	..	..	..	10	10
155		24 c. bright violet	..	..	..	15	8
156		50 c. orange ..	..	..	..	80	12
157	**51a**	1 b. red-brown (1920)	..	..	1·10	30
158		2 b. brown (1920)	..	..	1·90	1·00
149/158		Set of 10	..	..	..	4·50	2·00

There are numerous minor differences between the design of this issue and those of the Perkins Bacon and Waterlow (engraved and lithographed) issues which follow, but these can be readily distinguished by the perforation or colours.

(Recess Perkins, Bacon & Co, London)

1923–27. T **51** *and* **51a**, *redrawn.* P 13½.
158a	**51**	1 c. lake (1927)	..	..	..	5	5
158b		2 c. deep purple (1926)	..	..	8	5
159		5 c. green..	..	..	..	20	5
160		10 c. vermilion	..	..	..	4·00	2·75
161		20 c. deep blue	..	..	..	25	8
162		50 c. orange	..	..	..	85	15
163	**51a**	1 b. red-brown	..	..	..	25	5
164		2 b. brown	..	..	..	15	8
158a/164		Set of 8	..	..	..	5·00	3·00

See also Nos. 178/80 and 194/206.

Habilitada

Habilitada

15 cts.

15 cts.

(52)

(53)

1923–24. *Stamps of 1919–23 surch as T* **52**.
165	**51**	5 c. on 1 c. lake (B.) (149)	..	12	8
		a. Surch inverted	..	..	3·00	3·00
166		15 c. on 10 c. vermilion (152)..		30	10
167		15 c. on 10 c. vermilion (160)..		20	8
		a. Surch inverted	..	..	3·50	3·50
168		15 c. on 22 c. pale blue (154) ..		20	5
		a. Surch inverted	..	..	3·25	3·50

Surch with T **53**
169	**51**	15 c. on 10 c. vermilion (152)..		20	8

54

54a

(Recess Perkins, Bacon)

1924 (Dec). *AIR. Establishment of National Aviation School. P 14.*

170	**54**	10 c. black and red	..	..	8	8
		a. Centre inverted	..	..	£300	
171		15 c. black and lake ..	..	..	55	45
172		25 c. black and blue ..	..	..	20	20
173		50 c. black and orange	..	..	55	30
174	**54a**	1 b. black and red-brown	..	..	65	50
175		2 b. black and brown	..	..	1·40	1·40
176		5 b. black and violet	..	..	1·50	1·50
170/176		*Set of 7*	..	..	4·25	4·00

(Recess Waterlow & Sons, London)

1925. *T 51 again redrawn. P 12½.*

178	**51**	5 c. green	..	..	..	15	5
179		15 c. blue	..	..	..	15	5
180		20 c. deep blue	..	..	..	12	5

| 55 Torch of Freedom | 56 President B. Saavedra | 58 Archer |

57 Condor

(Recess Perkins, Bacon)

1925. *Independence Centenary. T 55/7 and similar designs. P 14.*

184		5 c. red/green ..	..	..	..	15	12
185		10 c. red/yellow ..	..	..	..	55	30
186		15 c. carmine	..	..	..	15	8
187		25 c. blue	..	..	..	40	20
188		50 c. purple	..	..	..	15	8
189		1 b. vermilion ..	..	..	..	25	25
190		2 b. orange-yellow	..	..	..	30	30
191		5 b. sepia	..	..	..	40	40
184/191		*Set of 8*	..	..	..	2·10	1·50

Designs: As T **55**—10 c. Immortelle blooms. As T **56**—50 c. Head of Liberty; 5 b. Marshal Sucre. As T **57**—2 b. Hermes.

1 c. and 2 c. stamps in types typical of Labour also exist, but these were not on sale at post offices.

(Surch by Imprentas y Litografia Unidas, La Paz)

1927 (Sept). *T 51 surch as T 63.*

192		5 c. on 1 c. lake (B.) (No. 158a) ..	..	45	40
		a. Surch inverted	..	..	2·25	2·25
193		10 c. on 24 c. bright violet (No. 155)	..	45	40
		a. Surch inverted	..	..	18·00	18·00
		b. Surch in red	..	..	12·00	12·00

(Litho Waterlow)

1928. *T 51 and 51a (redrawn). P 13½.*

194	**51**	2 c. dull yellow	..	..	..	5	5
195		3 c. carmine-pink	..	..	..	10	8
196		4 c. claret	..	..	..	8	5
197		20 c. olive-green	..	..	..	12	5
198		25 c. blue	..	..	..	10	5
199		30 c. violet	..	..	..	10	8
200		40 c. orange ..	..	..	..	20	10
201		50 c. chocolate	..	..	..	20	8
202	**51a**	1 b. scarlet ..	..	..	..	25	8
203		2 b. purple ..	..	..	..	35	10
204		3 b. sage-green	..	..	..	35	25
205		4 b. lake	..	..	..	50	30
206		5 b. brown ..	..	..	..	60	25
194/206		*Set of 13*	..	..	..	2·75	1·25

(Opt litho Imprentas y Litografia Unidas, La Paz)

1928. *As last, optd with T 64.*

207	**51**	5 c. green	..	..	..	5	5
208		10 c. grey	..	..	..	10	8
209		15 c. carmine	..	..	..	10	5

This overprint was applied to prevent the use of stocks of these values which were stolen before issue.

(Surch at Rinacimiento Ptg Wks)

1928. *T 51 surch as T 65.*

210		15 c. on 20 c. deep blue (R.) (No. 153)	..	3·25	2·75
211		15 c. on 20 c. deep blue (R.) (No. 161)	..	2·50	2·50
		a. Black surch	..	..	30·00	
212		15 c. on 20 c. deep blue (R.) (No. 180)	..	28·00	28·00
213		15 c. on 24 c. bright violet (No. 155)	..	40	15
		a. Surch inverted	..	..	2·75	2·75
		b. Blue surch	..	..	30·00	
215		15 c. on 50 c. orange (No. 156) ..	..	7·00	6·00
216		15 c. on 50 c. orange (No. 162) ..	..	40	20

66 "L. A. B." (= Lloyd Aereo Boliviano)

(Litho Imprentas y Litografia Unidas, La Paz)

1928 (13 June). *AIR. P 11½.*

217	**66**	15 c. green	..	..	..	30	25
218		20 c. blue	..	..	..	10	8
219		35 c. brown-red	..	..	..	20	20

| 68 Condor | 70 Map of Bolivia |

O.01
Centavos

R. S. 21-4
1930
(71)

(Recess Perkins, Bacon)

1928. *P 13½.*

221	**68**	5 c. green	..	..	..	35	5
222	—	10 c. slate-blue (Pres. Siles)	..	..	5	5
223	**70**	15 c. carmine ..	..	..	..	20	5

1930. *Stamps of 1913 and 1916 surch as T 71.*

224	**20**	0.01 c. on 2 c. red (B.)..	..	..	20	20
225	**48**	0.03 c. on 2 c. black and rose (Br.)	..	30	30
226	**46**	25 c. on ½ c. brown ..	..	..	20	20
		a. Surch inverted				
227	**48**	25 c. on 2 c. black and rose (V.)	..	20	20

CORREO AEREO   **CORREO AEREO**

R. S. 6-V-1930   R. S.

5 Cts.   6-V- 1930
(72)   (73)

1930 (6 May). *AIR. Nos. 170/4 surch or optd as T **72** or **73**.*

(a) Surch in ordinary inks

228	**72**	5 c. on 10 c. black and red (G.)		1·00	1·00
229	**73**	10 c. black and red (B.)	.. ..	1·00	1·00
		a. Brown opt	.. ..	£100	£110
231		15 c. black and lake (V.)	..	1·00	1·00
232		25 c. black and blue (R.)	..	1·00	1·00
233		50 c. black and orange (Br.)	..	1·00	1·00
		a. Red opt	..	£125	£125
235		1 b. black and red-brown (Gold)		28·00	28·00
228/235		Set of 6	..	30·00	30·00

(b) Surch in metallic ink

236	**72**	5 c. on 10 c. black and red (G.)		19·00	19·00
237	**73**	10 c. black and red (B.)	..	15·00	15·00
238		15 c. black and lake (V.)	..	19·00	15·00
239		25 c. black and blue (R.)	..	19·00	15·00
240		1 b. black and red-brown (Gold)		30·00	30·00
236/240		Set of 5 ..	..	90·00	90·00

The overprint on No. 235 is a light gilt colour and that on No. 240 reddish gold.

Z 1930

Bs. 6.—

(74)

1930 (6 May). *AIR. "Graf Zeppelin" stamps. Surch as T **74**.*

241	**66**	1 b. 50 on 15 c. green ..	..	5·00	5·00
		a. Surch inverted ..	..	10·00	
242		3 b. on 20 c. blue	..	5·00	5·00
		a. Surch inverted ..	..	10·00	
243		6 b. on 35 c. brown-red	..	7·50	7·50
		a. Surch inverted ..	..	10·00	

75 Bullock cart   **76** 'Plane over River Boat

(Litho Perkins, Bacon)

1930 (24 July). *AIR. P 14.*

244	**75**	5 c. deep purple	..	..	12	10
245	**76**	15 c. scarlet ..	..	..	12	10
246		20 c. yellow	..	..	12	10
247	**75**	35 c. yellow-green	..	..	10	10
248	**76**	50 c. grey-blue	..	..	10	10
249	**75**	1 b. brown ..	..	..	12	10
250	**76**	2 b. carmine ..	..	..	15	15
251	**75**	3 b. blue-grey	..	..	1·25	75
244/251		Set of 8	..	..	1·90	1·40

Nos. 244/51 exist imperforate. *Price per set in un pairs,* £45.

77 President Siles   **77a** El Potosi   **78** Map of Bolivia

---

79 Marshal Sucre   **80**

(Recess Perkins, Bacon)

1930–37. *T **77**/9 and similar types. P 14 × 13½ or 14 (T **79**).*

252	**77**	1 c. yellow-brown (1937)		..	5	5
253	**77a**	2 c. green	..	..	8	5
254	–	5 c. light blue	..	..	5	5
255	–	10 c. vermilion (24.12.30)	..		5	5
256	**78**	15 c. violet (24.12.30)		..	8	5
257		35 c. carmine (24.12.30)		..	20	12
258		45 c. orange ..	..	..	20	15
259	**79**	50 c. slate	..	..	10	5
260	–	1 b. chocolate	..	..	25	30
252/260		Set of 9	..	..	95	75

Designs: As T **77a**—5 c. El Illimani. As T **77**—10 c. A. Abaroa. As T **79**—1 b. Bolivar.
See also No. 272.

1931. *First Anniv of Revolution of 25 June 1930. Litho. P 11.*

263	**80**	15 c. scarlet	..	25	12
264		50 c. bright magenta ..	..	20	20

D 1   **81**

(Recess Perkins, Bacon)

1931. *POSTAGE DUE. P 14.*

D265	**D 1**	5 c. ultramarine	..	..	12	12
D266		10 c. scarlet	..	..	12	12
D267		15 c. yellow	..	..	12	12
D268		30 c. green ..	..	..	12	12
D269		40 c. purple	..	..	12	12
D270		50 c. sepia ..	..	..	12	12
D265/270		Set of 6	..	..	60	60

(Litho Imprentas y Litografia Unidas, La Paz)

1932 (16 Sept). *AIR. P 11.*

265	**81**	5 c. ultramarine	..	..	25	15
266		10 c. grey	..	..	10	8
267		15 c. carmine ..	..	..	30	20
268		25 c. orange ..	..	..	35	20
269		30 c. green ..	..	..	15	15
270		50 c. mauve ..	..	..	20	15
271		1 b. chocolate	..	..	25	15
265/271		Set of 7	..	..	1·40	90

(Litho Imprentas y Litografia Unidas, La Paz)

1932. *As T **78** but without printer's imprint. P 11.*

272	**78**	15 c. bright violet	..	..	25	10

Habilitada
A 15 Cts.

D. S. 13-7 1933

(82)

83

1933. *Surch as T 82.*

273	**51**	5 c. on 1 b. scarlet (202)	..	..	12	5
		a. No stop after "Cts"	..	..	40	35
274	**78**	15 c. on 35 c. carmine (257)	..	..	5	5
275		15 c. on 45 c. orange (258)	..	..	5	5
		a. Surch inverted	..	..	1·75	1·75
276	**51**	15 c. on 50 c. chocolate (201)..		..	12	5
277		25 c. on 40 c. orange (200)	..	..	12	5
273/277		*Set of 5*	..	..	40	20

(Recess Bradbury, Wilkinson)

1933. *P 12.*

278	**83**	2 c. green	..	..	5	5
279		5 c. dull blue..	..	..	5	5
280		10 c. scarlet	..	..	12	8
281		15 c. purple	..	..	5	5
282		25 c. indigo	..	..	15	12
278/282		*Set of 5*	..	..	35	25

84 Mariano Baptista   **85** Map of Bolivia   **86** Aeroplane over Bolivia

(Recess American Bank Note Co)

1935. *Ex-President Baptista Commemoration. P 12.*

283	**84**	15 c. violet	..	..	..	10	5

(Recess American Bank Note Co)

1935 (1 Feb). *P 12. (a) POSTAGE.*

284	**85**	2 c. blue	..	..	5	5
285		3 c. orange-yellow	..	..	5	5
286		5 c. grey-green	..	..	5	5
287		5 c. red	..	..	5	5
288		10 c. black-brown	..	..	5	5
289		15 c. ultramarine	..	..	5	5
290		15 c. crimson	..	..	5	5
291		20 c. deep green	..	..	5	5
292		25 c. light blue	..	..	5	5
293		30 c. carmine ..	..	..	12	5
294		40 c. orange-vermilion	..	..	10	5
295		50 c. deep violet	..	..	10	5
296		1 b. orange-yellow	..	..	15	10
297		2 b. brown	..	..	25	15
284/297		*Set of 14*	..	..	1·00	70

(b) AIR

298	**86**	5 c. red-brown	..	..	5	5
299		10 c. deep green	..	..	5	5
300		20 c. violet	..	..	5	5
301		30 c. ultramarine	..	..	5	5
302		50 c. orange	..	..	5	5
303		1 b. yellow-brown	..	..	8	5
304		1½ b. orange-yellow	..	..	20	5
305		2 b. carmine-red	..	..	20	5
306		5 b. green	..	..	40	10
307		10 b. chocolate	..	..	60	15
298/307		*Set of 10*	..	..	1·50	55

Comuni-
caciones

D. S.
25-2-37
0.05
(87)

Correo Aéreo
D. S. 25-2-37
0.05
(88)

1937. *Surch as T 87 (but diagonally downwards with "Co-municaciones" in one line on T 80).*

308	**83**	5 c. on 2 c. green (278)	..	..	5	5
310		15 c. on 25 c. indigo (282)	..	..	5	5
311		30 c. on 25 c. indigo (282)	..	..	8	8
312	**51a**	45 c. on 1 b. red-brown (163)	..	..	10	10
313		1 b. on 2 b. purple (203)	..	..	12	12
		a. "1" omitted	..	..	2·00	2·00
314	**83**	2 b. on 25 c. indigo (282)	..	..	15	15
315	**80**	3 b. on 50 c. bright magenta (264)	..	..	20	20
		a. "3" omitted	..	..	2·00	2·00
316		5 b. on 50 c. bright magenta (264)	..	..	50	50
308/316		*Set of 8*	..	..	1·10	1·10

1937 (25 Feb). *AIR. Nos. 188/91 surch in five lines as T 87, but with "Correo Aéreo" instead of "Comunicaciones", in green.*

317		3 b. on 50 c. purple	..	..	45	40
318		4 b. on 1 b. vermilion	..	..	60	45
319		5 b. on 2 b. orange-yellow	..	..	80	55
320		10 b. on 5 b. sepia	..	..	1·50	1·10
317/320		*Set of 4*	..	..	3·00	2·25

1937 (6 Oct). *AIR. Surch as T 88.*

321	**75**	5 c. on 35 c. yellow-green (R.)	..	8	5
322	**66**	20 c. on 35 c. brown-red (R.) ..	..	12	8
323		50 c. on 35 c. brown-red (R.)	..	15	12
324		1 b. on 35 c. brown-red (R.) ..	..	15	12
325	**54**	2 b. on 50 c. black and orange (G.) ..	..	40	20
326		12 b. on 10 c. black and red (G.)	..	1·60	1·25
327		15 b. on 10 c. black and red (G.)	..	1·60	1·25
321/327		*Set of 7*	..	..	3·50	2·50

89 Native School   **90** Indian and Eagle   **91** Mint, Potosi

92 Aeroplane over Cornfield   **D 2**

(Litho Guillermo Kraft Ltd, Buenos Aires)

1938 (May). *Various designs. P 10½.*

(a) POSTAGE. As T 89/90

328		2 c. brown-red	..	..	5	5
329		10 c. vermilion..	..	..	5	5
330		15 c. green	..	..	8	5
331		30 c. yellow	..	..	12	5
332		45 c. carmine	..	..	15	5
333		60 c. violet	..	..	15	5
334		75 c. deep blue	..	..	20	5
335		1 b. pale brown	..	..	20	5
336		2 b. buff	..	..	25	8
328/336		*Set of 9*	..	..	1·10	40

Designs: *Vert*—2 c. Oil Wells; 15 c. Industrial buildings; 30 c. Pincers and torch. *Horiz*—45 c. Sucre-Camiri Railway map; 60 c. Natives and book; 1 b. Machinery; 2 b. Agriculture.

(b) AIR. As T 91/2

337		20 c. carmine	..	..	..	5	5
338		30 c. grey	..	..	..	5	5
339		40 c. yellow	..	..	..	8	5
340		50 c. green	..	..	..	8	5
341		60 c. deep blue	..	..	..	8	5
342		1 b. brown-red	..	..	..	10	5
343		2 b. buff	..	..	..	30	5
344		3 b. pale brown	..	..	..	45	5
345		5 b. violet	..	..	..	65	5
337/345		*Set of 9*	..	..	1·60	40

Designs: *Vert*—30 c. Miner; 40 c. "Women's Suffrage"; 1 b. Pincers, torch and slogan; 3 b. New Government

emblem; 5 b. Aeroplanes over Bolivia. *Horiz*—50 c. Aeroplane over cornfield; 60 c. Aeroplanes and Cochabamba natives monument; 2 b. Aeroplane over river.

(c) POSTAGE DUE. As Type D 2

D346	5 c. carmine	..	..	..	12	12
D347	10 c. green	..	..	..	12	12
D348	30 c. light blue. .	..	..	..	12	12
D346/348	*Set of 3*	..	..	..	30	30

Designs:—10 c. Torch of Knowledge: 30 c. Date and symbol of 17 May 1936 Revolution.

102 Llamas

103 Arms

104 Herons

105 Jaguar

(Litho Guillermo Kraft,Ltd, Buenos Aires)

1939 (21 Jan). *T* 102/5 *and similar designs.* P 11 *or* 11½×10½ *(horiz); or* 10½×11 *or* 11½ *(vert).*

346	102	2 c. green ..	..	..	..	25	8
347	–	4 c. cinnamon	..	..	..	25	8
348	–	5 c. mauve ..	..	..	..	25	8
349	–	10 c. black	..	..	..	25	8
350	–	15 c. emerald-green..	..	..	25	8
351	–	20 c. grey-green	..	..	..	25	8
352	103	25 c. lemon-yellow ..	..	..	8	8
353	–	30 c. blue ..	..	..	..	8	8
354	104	40 c. scarlet ..	..	..	..	25	10
355	–	45 c. grey-black	..	..	..	25	10
356	–	60 c. carmine	..	..	..	30	12
357	–	75 c. blue-slate	..	..	..	30	12
358	–	90 c. orange ..	..	..	..	50	20
359	–	1 b. light blue	..	..	..	50	20
360	–	2 b. claret ..	..	..	..	1·00	25
361	–	3 b. slate-violet ..	..	..	1·50	25
362	105	4 b. chestnut	..	..	..	2·00	30
363	–	5 b. brown-purple ..	..	..	2·50	35
346/363	*Set of 18*	..	..	..	..	9·50	2·40

Designs (*Zoological types*): *Horiz*—10 c., 15 c., 20 c. Vicuña; 60 c., 75 c. Chinchilla; 90 c., 1 b. Toucan; 2 b., 3 b. Condor.

106 Chalice

107 Virgin of Copacabana

108 The Sacred Heart

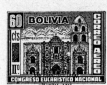

109 St. Francis Church, La Paz

110 St. Anthony of Padua

(Litho Lito-Unidas, La Paz)

1939 (19 Aug). *AIR. Second National Eucharistic Congress.* P 13½ (5 *c.*, 60 *c.*, 75 *c.*, 10 *b.*) *or* 10½ *(others).*

364	106	5 c. violet ..	..	..	..	10	5
365	107	30 c. emerald-green..	..	..	10	5
366	108	45 c. ultramarine	..	..	..	10	5
367	109	60 c. carmine	..	..	..	10	5
368	110	75 c. scarlet ..	..	..	..	12	8
369	–	90 c. blue	..	..	..	12	5
370	109	2 b. brown ..	..	..	..	20	5
371	108	4 b. magenta	..	..	..	30	8
372	107	5 b. light blue	..	..	..	65	5
373	106	10 b. yellow ..	..	..	..	2·00	5
364/373	*Set of 10*	..	..	..	..	3·50	45

111 Workman

112 Flags of 21 American Republics

1939–40. *OBLIGATORY TAX. Workers' Home Building Fund. Litho.* (a) *Imprint* "LITO. UNIDAS. LA PAZ".

374	111	5 c. dull violet (*perf* 10½)	..	5	5
		a. Perf 13½×10½	..	..	5	5

(b) *Imprint* "TALL. OFFSET LA PAZ" (1940)

374b	111	5 c. bright violet (*p* 10½)	..	5	5
		c. Perf 12×11	..	..	5	5

(Litho Imprentas y Litografia Unidas, La Paz)

1940 (Apr). *50th Anniv of Pan-American Union. Flags in national colours.* P 10½.

375	112	9 b. scarlet, blue, pale blue & yellow	60	25

113 Statue of Murillo

114 Urns of Murillo and Sagarnaga

(Litho Litografia Unidas, La Paz)

1941 (16 July). *130th Death Anniv of P. D. Murillo (patriot). T* 113/4 *and designs inscr* "1810 1940". P 10½.

376	–	10 c. brown-purple	..	..	5	5
377	–	15 c. green	..	..	..	5	5
378	–	45 c. carmine	..	..	..	5	5
379	–	1 b. 05, blue	..	..	..	8	5
376/379	*Set of 4*	..	..	..	20	15

Designs: *Horiz*—45 c. Murillo dreaming in prison. *Vert*—1 b. 05, Murillo.

117 Shadow of Aeroplane on Lake Titicaca

118 Condor over Mt Illimani

(Litho Litografia Unidas, La Paz)

1941 (Aug). *AIR. P* 13½.

380	**117**	10 b. slate-green	..	65	10
381		20 b. bright blue	.. 1·00		15
382	**118**	50 b. magenta	.. 2·40		30
383		100 b. olive-brown	.. 6·50		1·00
380/383		*Set of 4*	.. 9·50		1·40

119 Early and Late Issues

120 "Union is Strength"

(Litho Litografia Unidas, La Paz)

1942 (Oct). *First Students' Philatelic Exhibition, La Paz. P* 13½.

384	**119**	5 c. magenta	..	12	10
385		10 c. orange..	..	12	10
386		20 c. green	..	20	15
387		40 c. carmine	..	30	20
388		90 c. ultramarine	..	60	25
389		1 b. violet	.. 1·00		60
390		10 b. olive-brown	.. 5·00	2·50	
384/390		*Set of 7*	.. 6·50	3·50	

(Litho Litografia Unidas, La Paz)

1942 (12 Nov). *AIR. First Chancellors' Meeting, Rio de Janeiro. P* 13½.

391	**120**	40 c. claret	..	10	5
392		50 c. ultramarine	..	10	5
393		1 b. chestnut	..	20	8
394		5 b. magenta	..	60	10
395		10 b. purple	.. 1·25		80
391/395		*Set of 5*	.. 2·00	1·00	

121 Mt Potosi

122 Chaquiri Dam

(Recess Waterlow)

1943. *Mining Industry. T* **121/2** *and similar designs. P* 12½.

396	15 c. reddish brown	..	8	5
397	45 c. violet-blue..	..	8	5
398	1 b. 25, bright purple	..	12	·10
399	1 b. 50, emerald-green..	..	12	10
400	2 b. sepia	..	15	12
401	*2 b. 10, pale blue	..	15	15
402	3 b. red-orange..	..	25	20
396/402	*Set of 7*	..	85	70

Designs: *Vert*—45 c. Quechisla (at the foot of Mt. Choroloque); 1 b. 25, Miner drilling. *Horiz*—1 b. 50, Dam; 2 b. Truck convoy; 3 b. Entrance to Pulacayo Mine.

125 Gen. Ballivian leading Cavalry Charge

126 Gen. Ballivian and Trinidad Cathedral

(Photo Waterlow)

1943. *Centenary of Battle of Ingavi. P* 12½.

403	**125**	2 c. blue-green	..	5	5
404		3 c. orange..	..	5	5
405		25 c. maroon	..	5	5
406		45 c. blue	..	5	5
407		3 b. scarlet ..	..	20	12
408		4 b. purple ..	..	25	20
409		5 b. black-brown	..	30	25
403/409		*Set of 7*	..	85	70

MS409a Two sheets each 139×100 mm. Nos. 403/6 and Nos. 407/9 .. .. 1·90 1·90

(Recess Waterlow)

1943. *Centenary of Founding of El Beni. T* **126** *and similar type. P* 12½. *(a) POSTAGE.*

410	**126**	5 c. brown and blue-green..	..	5	5
411		10 c. brown and purple	..	5	5
412		30 c. brown and scarlet	..	8	5
413		45 c. brown and ultramarine	..	10	8
414		2 b. 10, brown and orange..	..	20	20

(b) AIR. Inscr "AEREO"

415	10 c. brown and violet ..	..	5	5
416	20 c. brown and emerald-green..	..	5	5
417	30 c. brown and carmine	..	8*	5
418	3 b. brown and light blue	..	12	8
419	5 b. brown and black	..	25	15
410/419	*Set of 10*	..	90	70

Design:—Nos. 415/9. Gen. Ballivian, and mule convoy crossing bridge below aeroplane.

127 *Trans.* "Honour-Work-Law/ All for the Country"

128 Clasped Hands and Flag

129 Allegory of "Flight"

130 Aeroplane and Sun

(Litho Litografia Unidas, La Paz)

1944 (20 Sept)–**45**. *Revolution of 20 December, 1943. P* 13½.

(a) POSTAGE

420	**127**	20 c. orange ..	..	5	5
421		20 c. green (1945)	..	5	5
422		90 c. ultramarine	..	5	5
423		90 c. carmine (1945)..	..	5	5
424	**128**	1 b. bright purple	..	5	5
425		2 b. 40, brown	..	10	8

(b) AIR. Inscr "CORREO AEREO"

426	**129**	40 c. magenta	..	5	5
427		1 b. violet	..	5	5
428	**130**	1 b. 50, emerald-green	..	5	5
429		2 b. 50, grey-blue ..	..	10	8
420/429		*Set of 10*	..	55	40

131 Posthorn and Envelope **132** National Airways Route Map

(Litho Litografia Unidas, La Paz)

1944–45. OBLIGATORY TAX. Communications Employees. P 10½.

430	**131**	10 c. red	..	.. .. ..	5	5
432		10 c. blue (1945)	..	.. .. ..	5	5

See also Nos. 469/72.

(Litho Taller Offset, La Paz)

1945 (2 June). AIR. Panagra Airways. Tenth Anniv of First La Paz–Tacna Flight. P 11.

433	**132**	10 c. carmine	..	..	5	5
434		50 c. orange ..	..	..	5	5
435		90 c. green	..	..	5	5
436		5 b. blue	..	..	8	5
437		20 b. chocolate	..	..	45	15
433/437		Set of 5	..	..	60	20

133 Lloyd Aereo Boliviano Air Routes **134** Composers of National Anthem

(Litho Litografia Unidas, La Paz)

1945 (15 Sept). AIR. 20th Anniv of Establishment of First National Air Service. P 14×13½.

438	**133**	20 c. blue, orange and violet	..	5	5
439		30 c. blue, orange and red-brown	..	5	5
440		50 c. blue, orange & emerald-green		5	5
441		90 c. blue, orange and purple	..	5	5
442		2 b. blue, orange and blue ..	..	5	5
443		3 b. blue, orange and claret	..	8	5
444		4 b. blue, orange and olive-bistre	..	10	5
438/444		Set of 7	..	..	35	25

(Litho Taller Offset, La Paz)

1946 (Sept). Centenary of Adoption of National Anthem. P 11.

445	**134**	5 c. black and mauve	..	..	5	5
446		10 c. black and ultramarine ..	..	5	5
447		15 c. black and green	..	..	5	5
448		30 c. chocolate and vermilion	..	8	5
449		90 c. chocolate and blue	..	8	5
450		2 b. chocolate and black	..	10	5
445/450		Set of 6	..	..	35	25

MS450a Two sheets each 86×131 mm. (a) No. 448; (b) No. 450. Imperf. Each sold at 4 b. 75 75

(135)

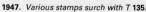

1947. Various stamps surch with T **135**.

(a) POSTAGE

451	1 b. 40 on 75 c. deep blue (R.) (334)	..		8	5
452	1 b. 40 on 75 c. blue-slate (Bk.) (357)			8	5
453	1 b. 40 on 75 c. blue-slate (R.) (357)	..		8	5
454	1 b. 40 on 75 c. blue-slate (O.) (357)			8	5

(c) AIR

455	**110**	1 b. 40 on 75 c. scarlet (Bk.) ..		..	8	5

136 Seizure of Government Palace **137** Mt Illimani

(Litho Litografia Unidas (T **136**), Taller Offset (T **137**))

1947. First Anniv of Popular Revolution of 21 July 1946.

(a) POSTAGE. P 13½ (20 Sept)

456	**136**	20 c. green ..	..	..	5	5
457		50 c. magenta	..	..	5	5
458		1 b. 40, greenish blue	..	..	5	5
459		3 b. 70, orange	..	..	8	5
460		4 b. violet	..	..	10	5
461		10 b. olive-bistre	..	..	25	15

(b) AIR. P 11½ (15 Sept)

462	**137**	1 b. carmine	..	..	5	5
463		1 b. 40, emerald-green	..	..	5	5
464		2 b. 50, blue	..	..	5	5
465		3 b. orange ..	..	..	5	5
466		4 b. purple	..	..	8	5
456/466		Set of 11	..	..	75	50

138 Arms of Bolivia and Argentina **139** Posthorn and Envelope

(Litho Litografia Unidas, La Paz)

1947 (23 Oct). Meeting of Presidents of Bolivia and Argentina. P 13½. (a) POSTAGE.

467	**138**	1 b. 40, red-orange	..	..	5	5

(b) AIR. Inscr "AEREO"

468	**138**	2 b. 90, blue ..	..	..	12	10

(Litho Litografia Unidas, La Paz)

1947–48. OBLIGATORY TAX. Communications Employees. As T **131** but posthorn and envelope reduced in size. P 10½.

469	**139**	10 c. carmine	..	..	5	5
470		10 c. yellow (1948)	..	..	5	5
471		10 c. emerald-green (1948)	..	..	5	5
472		10 c. bistre-brown (1948)	..	..	5	5
469/472		Set of 4	..	..	15	15

140 Cross and Child **141** Map of S. America and Bolivian Auto Club Badge **142** Posthorn, Globe and Pres. G. Pacheco

(Litho Don Bosco Ptg Wks, La Paz)

1948 (24 Sept). *Third Inter-American Catholic Education Congress. T* **140** *and similar designs. P* 11½. *(a) POSTAGE.*

473	1 b. 40, light blue and yellow	..		5	5
474	2 b. yellow-green and yellow	..	..	8	5
475	3 b. grey-green and light blue	..	..	10	8
476	5 b. violet and orange	..	..	25	12
477	5 b. brown and green	..	..	25	12

(b) AIR. Inscr "AEREA"

478	2 b. 50, red-orange and yellow			10	5
479	3 b. 70, carmine and buff	..	..	12	8
480	4 b. magenta and blue ..	..	..	15	10
481	4 b. ultramarine and orange	..		15	10
482	13 b. 60, ultramarine and green..			40	15
473/482	*Set of 10*	..	..	1·40	75

Designs:—1 b. 40, 2 b. 50, Christ the Redeemer, Monument; 2 b., 3 b. 70, T **140**; 3 b., 4 b. (No. 480), Don Bosco; 5 b. (476), 4 b. (481), Virgin of Copacabana; 5 b. (477), 13 b. 60, Pope Pius XII.

(Litho Don Bosco Ptg Wks, La Paz)

1948 (23 Oct). *Pan-American Motor Race. P* 11½.

(a) POSTAGE

483	**141**	5 b. blackish blue and pink..	..	70	12

(b) AIR. Inscr "AEREA"

484	**141**	10 b. emerald and cream	..	80	15

(Litho La Papelera, S.A., La Paz)

1950 (2 Jan). *75th Anniv of U.P.U. P* 11½. *(a) POSTAGE.*

485	**142**	1 b. 40, blue ..			5	5
486		4 b. 20, vermilion	..	..	5	5

(b) AIR. Inscr "AEREO"

487	**142**	1 b. 40, brown	..	..	5	5
488		2 b. 50, orange	..	..	5	5
489		3 b. 30, purple	..	..	5	5
485/489	*Set of 5*	..	..	..	20	20

(143)

(144)

1950 (1 June). *AIR. Fifteenth Anniv of Panagra Service. Nos.* 433 *and* 437 *surch as T* **143**.

490	**132**	4 b. on 10 c. carmine	..	5	5
491		10 b. on 20 b. chocolate	..	15	10
		a. Surch inverted..	..	10·00	

1950 (6 July). *No.* 379 *surch with T* **144**.

492	2 b. on 1 b. 05, blue	..	..	8	5

145 Apparition at Potosi

146 Aeroplane

(Litho La Papelera, S.A., La Paz)

1950 (Sept). *Fourth Centenary of Apparition at Potosi. P* 11½.

493	**145**	20 c. violet ..	..	..	5	5
494		30 c. orange..	..	..	5	5
495		50 c. bright purple	..	..	5	5
496		1 b. carmine	..	..	5	5
497		2 b. turquoise-blue..	..	..	8	5
498		6 b. brown	..	..	10	5
493/498	*Set of 6*	..	..	..	35	25

(Litho Litografia Unidas, La Paz)

1950 (24 Sept). *AIR. 25th Anniv of Lloyd–Aereo Boliviano. P* 13½.

499	**146**	20 c. red-orange	..	..	5	5
500		30 c. violet	..	..	5	5
501		50 c. green	..	..	5	5
502		1 b. yellow-orange ..		..	5	5
503		3 b. ultramarine	..	..	5	5
504		15 b. carmine	..	..	15	5
505		50 b. brown	..	..	40	10
499/505	*Set of 7*	..	..	..	70	30

Triunfo de la Democracia 24 de Sept. 49
Bs. 1.40

(147)

148 United Nations Emblem and Globe

1950 (24 Sept). *AIR. First Anniv of 1949 Revolution. No.* 465 *surch with T* **147**.

506	**137**	1 b. 40 on 3 b. orange	..	..	5	5

(Litho La Papelera, S.A., La Paz)

1950 (24 Oct). *Fifth Anniv of U.N.O. P* 11½. *(a) POSTAGE. Inscr "CORREOS".*

507	**148**	60 c. ultramarine	..	..	50	5
508		2 b. green	..	..	75	12

(b) AIR

509	**148**	3 b. 60, scarlet	..	..	30	10
510		4 b. 70, sepia	..	..	60	15
507/510	*Set of 4*	..	..	..	1·90	35

149 Sun Gate

150 St. Francis Gate

(Recess Security Bank Note Co, N.Y.)

1951 (1 Mar). *Fourth Centenary of Founding of La Paz. Various designs as T* **149/50** *dated "1548 1948". P* 12½. *(a) POSTAGE.*

511	**149**	20 c. black and yellow-green	..	10	5
512	**150**	30 c. black and orange	..	5	5
513	–	40 c. black and yellow-brown	..	5	5
514	–	50 c. black and scarlet	..	5	5
515	–	1 b. black and slate-purple ..		5	5
516	–	1 b. 40, black and violet-blue		5	5
517	–	2 b. black and slate-purple ..		5	5
518	–	3 b. black and reddish purple		8	5
519	–	5 b. black and scarlet		12	5
520	–	10 b. black and sepia	..	15	8
MS520a		Three sheets each 150×100 mm.			
		Nos. 511/2, 520; 513, 516, 519; 514/5, 517/8		1·10	1·10

(b) AIR

521	**149**	20 c. black and carmine	..	5	5
522	**150**	30 c. black and violet-blue	..	5	5
523	–	40 c. black and grey-blue	..	5	5
524	–	50 c. black and blue-green	..	5	5
525	–	1 b. black and scarlet	..	5	5
526	–	2 b. black and red-orange	..	8	5
527	–	3 b. black and blue ..	..	10	5
528	–	4 b. black and vermilion	..	10	5
529	–	5 b. black and green	..	12	10
530	–	10 b. black and red-brown	..	20	15
511/530	*Set of 20*	..	..	1·35	1·00

MS530*a* Three sheets each 150×100 mm.
Nos. 521/2, 530; 523, 527, 529; 524/5, 526,
528 .. .. 1·25 1·25
Designs: *Horiz*—40 c. (2) Camacho Avenue; 50 c. (2) Consistorial Palace; 1 b. (2) Legislative building; 1 b. 40, 2 b. (No. 526) G.P.O.; 2 b. (517), 3 b. (527), Arms of La Paz in 1548 and 1948; 3 b. (518), 4 b. Planning La Paz; 5 b. (2) Mendoza founding La Paz: 10 b. (2) Arms and Mendoza.

151 Tennis

152 Condor and Flag

(Recess Security Bank Note Co, N.Y.)

1951 (1 July). *T* **151** *and similar sporting designs, variously
inscribed. P* 12½. *(a) POSTAGE.*
531 20 c. black and blue 5 5
532 50 c. black and scarlet 5 5
533 1 b. black and reddish purple .. 8 5
534 1 b. 40, black and yellow .. 8 5
535 2 b. black and carmine 10 5
536 3 b. black and yellow-brown .. 25 15
537 4 b. black and violet-blue .. 30 25
MS537*a* Two sheets each 150×100 mm.
Nos. 531/2, 535/6; 533/4, 537 .. 1·50 1·50

(b) AIR
538 20 c. black and slate-violet .. 8 5
539 30 c. black and purple 12 5
540 50 c. black and red-orange .. 20 5
541 1 b. black and brown 20 5
542 2 b. 50, black and orange .. 25 15
543 3 b. black and sepia 35 20
544 5 b. black and scarlet 70 40
531/544 *Set of* 14 .. .. .. 2·50 1·50
MS544*a* Two sheets each 150×100 mm.
Nos. 538/40, 544; 541/3 .. .. 3·50 3·50
Designs: *Horiz—Postage*: 20 c. Boxing; 1 b. Diving; 1 b. 40,
Football; 2 b. Skiing; 3 b. Pelota; 4 b. Cycling. *Air*: 20 c.
Horse-jumping; 30 c. Basket-ball; 50 c. Fencing; 1 b. Hurdling; 2 b. 50, Javelin throwing; 3 b. Relay racing; 5 b. La Paz
Stadium.

(Litho La Papelera S.A., La Paz)

1951 (5 Nov). *Centenary of National Flag. Flag in red, yellow
and green. P* 11½.
545 **152** 2 b. turquoise-green 5 5
546 3 b. 50, ultramarine 5 5
547 5 b. reddish violet 5 5
548 7 b. 50, grey 8 8
549 15 b. pale claret 15 8
550 30 b. blackish brown 30 20
545/550 *Set of* 6 .. .. .. 60 40

153 Posthorn and
Envelope

154 E. Abaroa

155 Isabella the
Catholic

(Litho La Papelera, S.A., La Paz)

1951–55. *OBLIGATORY TAX. T* **153** *and similar horiz design
inscr* "PRO CAJA DE JUBILACIONES" *etc. P* 10½ (No. 553
also P 13½).
551 – 20 c. orange 5 5
551*a* – 20 c. green (1962) 5 5
552 – 20 c. blue (1952) 5 5
553 **153** 50 c. green (1952) 5 5
553*a* 50 c. carmine-red (1953) .. 5 5
553*b* 3 b. green (3.10.54) 5 5
553*c* 3 b. bistre (4.55) 25 25
553*d* 3 b. bright violet (1953) .. 5 5
551/553*d* *Set of* 8 .. .. .. 50 50
Design:—20 c. (3), Condor over posthorn and envelope.

(Litho La Papelera S.A., La Paz)

1952 (24 Mar). *73rd Death Anniv of Abaroa (patriot). P* 11½.
(a) POSTAGE
554 **154** 80 c. claret 5 5
555 1 b. orange 5 5
556 2 b. emerald-green 5 5
557 5 b. ultramarine 5 5
558 10 b. magenta 12 5
559 20 b. chocolate 25 12

(b) AIR. Inscr "AEREO"
560 **154** 70 c. vermilion 5 5
561 2 b. orange-yellow 5 5
562 3 b. apple-green 5 5
563 5 b. light blue 5 5
564 50 b. bright purple 35 15
565 100 b. black 75 45
554/565 *Set of* 12 .. .. .. 1·60 1·00

(Litho Litografia Unidas, La Paz)

1952 (18 July). *Fifth Birth Centenary of Isabella the Catholic.
P* 13½. *(a) POSTAGE.*
566 **155** 2 b. violet-blue 5 5
567 6 b. 30, rose-red 8 5

(b) AIR. Inscr "AEREO"
568 **155** 50 b. pale emerald 20 10
569 100 b. brown 35 15
566/569 *Set of* 4 .. .. .. 60 30

156 Columbus Lighthouse

157 Miner

(Litho Litografia Unidas, La Paz)

1952 (18 July). *Columbus Memorial Lighthouse Fund.
P* 13½. *(a) POSTAGE.*
570 **156** 2 b. ultramarine/*blue* 5 5
571 5 b. carmine-red/*salmon* .. 10 8
572 9 b. emerald/*greenish* 15 12

(b) AIR. Inscr "AEREO"
573 **156** 2 b. bright purple/*salmon* .. 5 5
574 3 b. 70, greenish blue/*blue* .. 5 5
575 4 b. 40, orange/*salmon* .. 8 5
576 20 b. deep brown/*cream* .. 25 8
570/576 *Set of* 7 .. .. .. 60 40

(Litho Litografia Unidas, La Paz)

1953 (9 Apr). *Nationalization of Mining Industry. P* 13½.
577 **157** 2 b. 50, pale vermilion 5 5
578 8 b. violet 5 5

158 Villarroel, Paz Estenssoro
and Siles Zuazo

159 Revolutionaries

(Litho La Papelera, S.A. (T **158**), Litografia Unidas (T **159**))

1953. *First Anniv of Revolution of 9 April 1952.*

(a) POSTAGE. P 11½ (9 April)
579 **158** 50 c. mauve 5 5
580 1 b. rose 5 5
581 2 b. violet-blue 5 5
582 3 b. green 5 5
583 4 b. yellow 5 5
584 5 b. bluish violet 5 5

(b) AIR. Inscr "AEREA". *P* 11½ (9 April–1 Sept)
585 **158** 3 b. 70, chocolate 5 5
586 9 b. rose-carmine (1.9) 5 5

587	158	10 b. turquoise (1.9) ..	.. ..	5	5
588		16 b. red-orange (1.9)		5	5
589		40 b. grey-black (1.9)	.. ..	5	5

(c) AIR. P 13½ (1 Sept)

590	159	6 b. bright mauve	.. ..	5	5
591		22 b. 50, bistre-brown	.. ..	8	5
579/591		Set of 13 ..	.. ..	60	45

50cts

(160)

161

1953 (Sept). *OBLIGATORY TAX. No. 551a and similar stamp surch as T 160.*

592		50 c. on 20 c. bright mauve		5	5
593		50 c. on 20 c. green	.. ..	5	5

(Litho Litografia Unidas, La Paz)

1954–55. *OBLIGATORY TAX. P 10½.*

594	161	1 b. brown	..	5	5
595		1 b. carmine-lake (1955)	.. ..	5	5

PRINTERS. Except where otherwise stated all the following were printed by La Papelera S.A., La Paz.

162 Ear of Wheat and Map

163 President Paz embracing Indian

Bs. 5.—

D. S. 21-IV-55

(165)

1954 (2 Aug). *First National Agronomical Congress. Litho. P 12.*

596	162	25 b. blue	.. ..	5	5
597		85 b. sepia ..	.. ..	15	12

1954 (2 Aug). *AIR. Third Inter-American Indigenous Congress. Litho. P 12.*

598	163	20 b. chestnut	.. ..	5	5
599		100 b. turquoise-green	.. ..	20	8

1954 (2 Aug). *First Anniv of Agrarian Reform. As T 162, but inscr "REFORMA AGRARIA". Litho. P 12. (a) POSTAGE.*

600		5 b. bright carmine-red	.. ..	5	5
601		17 b. turquoise ..	.. ..	5	5

(b) AIR. Inscr "AEREO"

602		27 b. bright magenta	.. ..	5	5
603		30 b. red-orange	.. ..	5	5
604		45 b. purple-brown	.. ..	8	5
605		300 b. bright green	.. ..	50	12
600/605		Set of 6	.. ..	70	30

Designs:—5 b., 17 b. Cow's head and map. 27 b. to 300 b. Indian peasant woman.

1955. *OBLIGATORY TAX. Postal Workers' Pension Fund. Nos. 553b/c surch with T 165.*

606	153	5 b. on 3 b. green	.. ..	5	5
607		5 b. on 3 b. bistre	.. ..	5	5

166 Refinery

167 Derrick

(Litho T **166**, La Papelera S.A., La Paz; T **167**, Litografia Unidas, La Paz)

1955 (9 Oct). *Development of Petroleum Industry.*

(a) POSTAGE. P 12

608	166	10 b. ultramarine and cobalt	..	5	5
609		35 b. carmine and pink	.. ..	5	5
610		40 b. green and pale green	..	5	5
611		50 b. reddish purple & pale mag		5	5
612		80 b. bistre-brown & yellow-brn ..		5	5

(b) AIR. P 10½

613	167	55 b. greenish blue and pale greenish blue	.. ..	5	5
614		70 b. black and grey	.. ..	5	5
615		90 b. bluish green and pale green		5	5
616		500 b. bright purple and mauve	..	30	20
617		1,000 b. olive-brown and pale brown		60	40
608/617		Set of 10 ..	.. .. ..	1·10	85

168 Control Tower

169 Aeroplanes

(Litho T **168** Litografia Unidas, La Paz; T **169** La Papelera S.A., La Paz)

1955 (20 Oct). *OBLIGATORY TAX. Airport Building Fund. P 13½ (5 b.), 12 (10 b.).*

618	168	5 b. deep blue	.. ..	5	5
619	169	10 b. dull green	.. ..	5	5
618/619		Set of 2	.. .. ..	8	8

169a Aeroplane

169b Aeroplane

1956. *OBLIGATORY TAX. Airport Building Fund. Litho.*

620	169a	5 b. scarlet (p 10½)	.. ..	5	5
620a	169b	20 b. deep brown (p 12) ..		5	5
620/620a		Set of 2	.. ..	8	8

Bs. 50

(170)

Bs. 100.—

(171)

1957 (14 Feb). *(a) POSTAGE. Nos. 511/20 surch as T 170, in blue.*

621		50 b. on 3 b. ..	.. ..	5	5
622		100 b. on 2 b. ..	.. ..	5	5
623		200 b. on 1 b. ..	.. ..	5	5
624		300 b. on 1 b. 40	.. ..	5	5
625		350 b. on 20 c. ..	.. ..	8	5
626		400 b. on 40 c. ..	.. ..	8	5
627		600 b. on 30 c. ..	.. ..	10	5
628		800 b. on 50 c. ..	.. ..	12	5
629		1,000 b. on 10 b. ..	.. ..	15	10
630		2,000 b. on 5 b. ..	.. ..	30	15

(b) AIR. Nos. 521/30 surch as T 171

631		100 b. on 3 b. (R.)	.. ..	5	5
632		200 b. on 2 b. ..	.. ..	5	5
633		500 b. on 4 b. ..	.. ..	5	5
634		600 b. on 1 b. ..	.. ..	5	5
635		700 b. on 20 c. ..	.. ..	8	5
636		800 b. on 40 c. (R.)	.. ..	10	8
637		900 b. on 30 c. (R.)	.. ..	10	5
638		1,800 b. on 50 c. (R.)	.. ..	25	12

639	3,000 b. on 5 b. (R.)	.. .. ..	40	25
640	5,000 b. on 10 b. (R.)	.. .. ..	1·00	45
621/640	Set of 20	.. .. ..	2·75	1·60

172 Congress Buildings **173** "Latin America" on Globe

1957 (22 May). *Seventh Latin-American Economic Congress, La Paz. Litho. P 12. (a) POSTAGE.*

641	**172**	150 b. ultramarine and grey	5	5
642		350 b. black and bistre-brown	5	5
643		550 b. deep brown and grey-blue	8	5
644		750 b. grey-green and carmine-red	12	8
645		900 b. sepia & deep yellow-green	20	12

(b) AIR

646	**173**	700 b. violet and reddish lilac	15	10
647		1,200 b. bistre-brown & light brown	20	15
648		1,350 b. claret and rose-carmine	30	20
649		2,700 b. bronze-green & light bl-grn	50	25
650		4,000 b. violet-blue & pale ultram	80	35
641/650		Set of 10	2·10	1·25

174 Railway Train and Presidents of Bolivia and Argentina **175** Presidents and Flags of Bolivia and Mexico

1957 (15 Dec). *Inauguration of Yacuiba-Santa Cruz Railway and Exchange of Presidential Visits. Litho. P 12.*

(a) POSTAGE

651	**174**	50 b. red-orange and pale orange	5	5
652		350 b. blue and pale blue	5	5
653		1,000 b. dp brown & pale cinnamon	15	5

(b) AIR. Inscr "AEREO"

654	**174**	600 b. reddish purple and pink	8	5
655		700 b. bluish violet and blue	12	5
656		900 b. green and pale green	15	5
651/656		Set of 6	50	20

1960 (30 Jan). *Visit of Mexican President to Bolivia. Litho. P 11½. (a) POSTAGE.*

657	**175**	350 b. yellow-olive	5	5
658		600 b. orange-brown	8	5
659		1,500 b. sepia	20	12

(b) AIR. Inscr "AEREO"

660	**175**	400 b. claret	12	5
661		800 b. slate-blue	12	10
662		2,000 b. slate-green	30	20
657/662		Set of 6	80	50

This visit did not take place.

176 Indians and Mt Illimani **177** "Gate of the Sun", Tiahuanacu

1960 (26 Mar). *Tourist Publicity. Litho. P 11½. (a) POSTAGE.*

663	**176**	500 b. bistre	5	5
664		1,000 b. light blue	12	5
665		2,000 b. sepia	20	12
666		4,000 b. green	40	20

(b) AIR

667	**177**	3,000 b. grey	35	25
668		5,000 b. brown-orange	50	40
669		10,000 b. reddish purple	95	75
670		15,000 b. bluish violet	1·50	1·25
663/670		Set of 8	3·75	2·75

178 Refugees **179** "Uprooted Tree"

1960 (7 Apr). *World Refugee Year. Litho. P 11½.*

(a) POSTAGE

671	**178**	50 b. bistre-brown	5	5
672		350 b. brown-purple	5	5
673		400 b. slate-blue	8	5
674		1,000 b. brownish black	20	15
675		3,000 b. bronze-green	60	40

(b) AIR

676	**179**	600 b. ultramarine	10	8
677		700 b. chestnut	12	10
678		900 b. deep bluish green	12	15
679		1,800 b. deep bluish violet	30	20
680		2,000 b. grey-black	35	20
671/680		Set of 10	1·75	1·25

180 **181**
Jaime Laredo (violinist)

1960 (Aug). *Jaime Laredo Commemoration. Photo. P 11½.*

(a) POSTAGE

681	**180**	100 b. olive-green	8	5
682		350 b. carmine-lake	8	5
683		500 b. slate-blue	8	5
684		1,000 b. bistre-brown	12	8
685		1,500 b. bluish violet	20	10
686		5,000 b. grey-black	60	35

(b) AIR

687	**181**	600 b. plum	8	5
688		700 b. brown-olive	10	5
689		800 b. chocolate	12	5
690		900 b. deep blue	15	8
691		1,800 b. deep bluish green	25	20
692		4,000 b. violet-grey	45	35
681/692		Set of 12	2·00	1·25

182 Rotary Emblem and Nurse with Children **183**

1960 (19 Nov). *Founding of Children's Hospital by La Paz Rotary Club. Litho. P 11½.* (a) POSTAGE.

693	182	350 b. ultramarine, yell & dp grn ..	5	5
694		500 b. ultramarine, yellow & sep ..	8	5
695		600 b. ultramarine, yellow & vio ..	8	5
696		1,000 b. ultramarine, yell & grey ..	12	8

(b) AIR. Inscr "CORREO AEREO"

697	182	600 b. ultramarine, yell & orge-brn	10	8
698		1,000 b. ultramarine, yellow & ol-grn	12	10
699		1,800 b. ultram, yellow & reddish pur	20	15
700		5,000 b. ultram, yell & brownish blk	60	50
693/700		Set of 8	1·25	95

1960 (14 Dec). *Unissued stamp, surch as in T 183. Litho. P 11½.*

701	183	1,200 b. on 10 b. orange	12	10

184

185 Flags of Argentina and Bolivia

1960 (17 Dec). *Unissued Tiahuanacu Excavations stamps surch as in T 184. Various designs with gold backgrounds. Litho. P 11×13½ (719), 11 (718), 13×12 (702/6) or 12×13 (others).*

702		50 b. on ½ c. red	10	10
703		100 b. on 1 c. red	5	5
704		200 b. on 2 c. black	12	10
705		300 b. on 5 c. green (R.) ..	8	5
706		350 b. on 10 c. green	10	25
707		400 b. on 15 c. indigo	10	8
708		500 b. on 20 c. red	12	10
709		500 b. on 50 c. red	12	10
710		600 b. on 22½ c. green	15	12
711		600 b. on 60 c. violet	15	12
712		700 b. on 25 c. violet	20	20
713		700 b. on 1 b. green	20	20
714		800 b. on 30 c. red	20	20
715		900 b. on 40 c. green	25	20
716		1,000 b. on 2 b. blue	25	20
717		1,800 b. on 3 b. grey	70	50
718		4,000 b. on 4 b. grey	5·50	4·75
719		5,000 b. on 5 b. grey	1·25	1·25
702/719		Set of 18	8·50	7·50

Designs: Various gods, motifs and ornaments. Sizes as T 184—*Vert* Nos. 707/17. *Horiz* Nos. 702/6. Size 49×23 mm—No. 718. Size 50×52½ mm—No. 719.

According to the official decree Nos. 709, 711, 713 and 716/9 were intended as air stamps but "Aereo" was not included in the surcharge.

1961 (23 May). *AIR. Visit of President Frondizi of Argentina. T 185 and similar horiz design. Litho. P 11.*

720		4,000 b. red, yellow, green, pale bl & sep	40	30
721		6,000 b. sepia and deep bluish green ..	50	40

Design:—6,000 b. Portraits of Argentine and Bolivian Presidents.

186 Miguel de Cervantes (First Mayor of La Paz)

187 "United in Christ"

(Photo Govt Ptg Wks, Madrid)

1961 (Nov). *Cervantes Commemoration and Fourth Centenary of Santa Cruz de la Sierra (1500 b.). T 186 and similar designs.* (a) POSTAGE. P 13×12½.

722		600 b. violet and ochre	10	5
723		1,500 b. deep blue and salmon ..	20	12

(b) AIR. Inscr "CORREO AEREO". P 13.

724		1,400 b. olive-brown and green	20	12

Designs: *Diamond* (30½×30½ mm)—1,400 b. Cervantes as T 186. *Vert*—1,500 b. Nuflo de Chaves.

See also Nos. 755/6.

1962 (21 Mar). *Fourth National Eucharistic Congress, Santa Cruz. T 187 and similar vert design. Litho. P 11.*

(a) POSTAGE

725	187	1,000 b. yellow, red & deep green ..	15	12

(b) AIR. Inscr "CORREO AEREO"

726	–	1,400 b. yellow, pink & deep brown	20	15

Design:—1,400 b. Virgin of Cotoca.

Bs. 600.—

(188)

189 Hibiscus

1962 (7 June). *Nos. 671/80 surch as T 188.* (a) POSTAGE.

727	178	600 b. on 50 b. bistre-brown ..	8	5
728		900 b. on 350 b. brown-purple ..	12	8
729		1,000 b. on 400 b. slate-blue ..	12	8
730		2,000 b. on 1,000 b. brownish black	20	15
731		3,500 b. on 3,000 b. bronze-green ..	40	25

(b) AIR. Inscr "CORREO AEREO"

732	179	1,200 b. on 600 b. ultramarine	20	15
733		1,300 b. on 700 b. chestnut ..	15	15
734		1,400 b. on 900 b. deep bluish green	20	15
735		2,800 b. on 1,800 b. dp bluish violet.	25	20
736		3,000 b. on 2,000 b. grey-black ..	35	25
727/736		Set of 10	1·90	1·25

The surcharge on Nos. 732/36 reads upwards.

1962 (2 July). *Flowers. T 189 and similar vert designs (flowers in actual colours: backgrounds below). Litho. P 11.* (a) POSTAGE.

737		200 b. slate-green	5	5
738		400 b. brown	8	5
739		600 b. deep blue	12	8
740		1,000 b. deep violet	20	10

(b) AIR. Inscr "CORREO AEREO"

741		100 b. blue	5	5
742		800 b. bronze-green	12	8
743		1,800 b. deep violet	40	15
744		10,000 b. deep blue	1·25	1·00
737/744		Set of 8	2·00	1·25
MS744a		130×80 mm. Nos. 741/3. Imperf (20.8.62)	1·25	1·25

Designs:—Nos. 738, 740, orchids; No. 739, St. James' lily; Nos. 741/4 various types of kantuta (national flower).

190 Infantry

191 Campaign Emblem

1962 (5 Sept). *Armed Forces Commemoration.* T **190** and *similar vert designs. Multicoloured. Litho.* P 11.

(a) POSTAGE

745	400 b. Type **190**	..	..	..	5	5
746	500 b. Cavalry ..	..	..	..	5	5
747	600 b. Artillery ..	..	..	..	8	5
748	2,000 b. Engineers	..	..	..	20	10

(b) AIR. Inscr "AEREO"

749	600 b. Parachutists and 'planes	..	5	5
750	1,200 b. 'Plane over oxen-cart	..	10	8
751	2,000 b. 'Plane photographing ground	..	20	10
752	5,000 b. 'Plane over oxen-cart	..	50	30
745/752	Set of 8	.. ..	1·10	70

1962 (4 Oct). *Malaria Eradication.* T **191** and *similar vert design.* P 11½. *Litho. (a) POSTAGE.*

753	**191**	600 b. yellow, violet & deep violet	10	10

(b) AIR. Inscr "AEREO"

754	–	2,000 b. yellow, emerald and indigo	25	20

Design:—2,000 b. Laurel wreath and inscription encircling emblem.

(Photo Govt Ptg Wks, Madrid)

1962 (20 Oct). *Spanish Discoverers. Portraits as* T **186** but *inscr "1548–1962".* P 13 × 12½. *(a) POSTAGE.*

755	600 b. magenta/azure (Á. de Mendoza)	8	5

(b) AIR. Inscr "CORREO AEREO"

756	1,200 b. brown/cream (P. de la Gasca) ..	12	10

Currency Revaluation

1000 old Bolivianos = 1 Peso Boliviano

192 Goal-keeper diving to save Ball **193** Globe and Emblem

1963 (22 Apr). *21st South American Football Championships, La Paz.* T **192** and *similar designs but vert. Multicoloured. Litho.* P 11½. *(a) POSTAGE.*

757	60 c. Type **192** ..	..	..	8	5
758	1 p. Goal-keeper saving ball	..	..	12	10

(b) AIR. Inscr "AEREO"

759	1 p. 40, Eagle on football	..	..	20	15
760	1 p. 80, Ball in corner of net	..	25	20
757/760	Set of 4	..	..	..	60	45

1963 (Aug). *Freedom from Hunger.* T **193** and *similar horiz design. Litho.* P 11½. *(a) POSTAGE.*

761	60 c. yellow, light blue and deep blue ..	5	5

(b) AIR. Inscr "AEREO"

762	1 p. yellow, light blue and black-green	15	12

Design:—1 p. 20, Ear of wheat across Globe.

194 Alliance Emblem **195** Oil Derrick

1963 (16 Nov). *AIR. "Alliance for Progress". Litho.* P 11½.

763	**194**	1 p. 20, light green, blue & bistre-yell	15	12

1963 (21 Dec). *10th Anniv of Revolution* (1962). T **195** and *similar vert designs dated "1952–1962". Litho.* P 11½. *(a) POSTAGE.*

764	10 c. yellow-green and brown ..	..	5	5
765	60 c. deep brown & lt orange-brown	..	8	5
766	1 p. pale yellow, deep violet & lt green	8	5

(b) AIR. Inscr "AEREO"

767	1 p. rose, deep brown and grey	..	10	8
768	1 p. 40, dp bluish green & yell-ochre	..	15	10
769	2 p. 80, buff and deep greenish slate	..	25	20
764/769	Set of 6	..	..	..	65	45

Designs:—60 c. Map of Bolivia; 1 p. Students; 1 p. 20, Ballot box and voters; 1 p. 40, Peasant breaking chain; 2 p. 80, Miners.

196 Flags of Argentina and Bolivia **197** Marshal Santa Cruz

(Photo Mint, Buenos Aires)

1966 (12 Aug). *Death Centenary of Marshal Santa Cruz.* W **111** *of Argentine Republic.* P 13½. *(a) POSTAGE.*

770	**196**	10 c. multicoloured ..	..	5	5
771		60 c. multicoloured ..	..	5	5
772		1 p. multicoloured ..	..	8	5
773		2 p. multicoloured ..	..	15	10

(b) AIR

774	**197**	20 c. blue ..	..	..	5	5
775		60 c. deep bluish green	..	5	5
776		1 p. 20, lake-brown ..	..	10	5
777		2 p. 80, black ..	..	25	15
770/777	Set of 8	..	..	..	70	50

198 Generals Barrientos and Ovando, Bolivian Map and Flag **199** Needy Children

1966 (16 Dec). *Co-Presidents Commemoration. Litho.* P 13½. *(a) POSTAGE. Inscr "CORREOS".*

778	**198**	60 c. multicoloured ..	..	5	5
779		1 p. multicoloured ..	..	10	8

(b) AIR

780	**198**	2 p. 80, multicoloured	..	..	40	35
781		10 p. multicoloured ..	..	90	60
778/781	Set of 4	..	..	..	1·25	1·00
MS782	136 × 83 mm. Nos. 778/81. Imperf	..	1·50	1·50

1966 (16 Dec). *Aid for Poor Children.* T **199** and *similar vert design. Litho.* P 13½. *(a) POSTAGE.*

783	**199**	30 c. blackish brown, sepia & ochre	5	5

(b) AIR. Inscr "AEREO"

784	–	1 p. 40, black and grey-blue	..	20	15

Design:—1 p. 40, Mother and needy children.

Centenario de la
Cruz Roja
Internacional

$b. 0.20

(200)

1966 (21 Dec). *Commemorative Issues. Various stamps surch with inscription (as given below) and value as T* **200.**

(i) *Red Cross Centenary. Surch as T* **200**
(a) POSTAGE
785 **172** 20 c. on 150 b. (No. 641) 5 5

(b) AIR
786 **173** 4 p. on 4,000 b. (No. 650) 35 25

(ii) *General Azurduy de Padilla. Surch "Homenaje a la Generala J. Azurduy de Padilla"*
787 **172** 30 c. on 550 b. (No. 643) 5 5
788 2 p. 80 on 750 b. (No. 644) 25 20

(iii) *AIR. Tupiza Centenary. Surch "Centenario de Tupiza"*
789 **173** 60 c. on 1,350 b. (No. 648) 5 5

(iv) *AIR. 25th Anniv of Bolivian Motor Club. Surch "XXV Aniversario Automovil Club Boliviano"*
790 **173** 2 p. 80 on 2,700 b. (No. 649) .. 45 40

(v) *AIR. Cochabamba Philatelic Society Anniversary. Surch "Aniversario Centro Filatelico Cochabamba"*
791 – 1 p. 20 on 800 b. (No. 742) 10 8
792 – 1 p. 20 on 1,800 b. (No. 743) .. 10 8

(vi) *Rotary Help for Children's Hospital. Surch with value only.* (a) POSTAGE
793 **182** 1 p. 60 on 350 b. (No. 693) 15 12
794 2 p. 40 on 500 b. (No. 694) 20 12

(b) AIR
795 **182** 1 p. 40 on 1,000 b. (No. 698) .. 12 10
796 1 p. 40 on 1,800 b. (No. 699) .. 12 10
793/796 *Set of 4* 55 40

(vii) *150th Anniv of the Coronilla Heroines. Surch "CL Aniversario Heroinas Coronilla".* (a) POSTAGE
797 **18u** 60 c. on 350 b. (No. 682) 5 5

(b) AIR
798 **181** 1 p. 20 on 800 b. (No. 689) 10 8

(viii) *AIR. Centenary of Hymn La Paz. Surch "Centenario Himno Paceno"*
799 **181** 1 p. 40 on 4,000 b. (No. 692) .. 12 10

(ix) *AIR. 12th Anniv of Agrarian Reform. Surch "XII Aniversario Reforma Agraria"*
800 – 10 c. on 27 b. (No. 602) 5 5
a. "Agraria Agraria" for "Reforma Agraria" .. .. .. 4·00 4·00

(x) *AIR. 25th Anniv of Chaco Peace Settlement. Surch "XXV Aniversario Paz del Chaco"*
801 **167** 10 c. on 55 b. (No. 613) 5 5

All the following are surcharged on Revenue stamps. The design shows a beach scene with palms, size 27 × 21½ mm.

(xi) *Centenary of Rurrenabaque. Surch "Centenario de Rurrenabaque"*
802 1 p. on 10 b. brown 10 8

(xii) *25th Anniv of Busch Government. Surch "XXV Aniversario Gobierno Busch"*
803 20 c. on 5 b. red 5 5
a. "Gobierno Busch XXV Aniversario" (lines transposed) .. 1·00 1·00

(xiii) *20th Anniv of Villarroel Government. Surch "XX Aniversario Gob. Villarroel"*
804 60 c. on 2 b. green 8 8
a. Error. "Aniversrio" 50 50

(xiv) *25th Anniv of Pando Department. Surch "XXV Aniversario Dpto Pando"* (a) POSTAGE
805 1 p. 60 on 50 c. violet 15 12

(b) AIR. Surch "Aereo" also
806 1 p. 20 on 1 b. deep blue 10 8

201 Sower   **202** "Macheteros"

(Des Gil Imana. Litho)

1967 (20 Sept). *50th Anniv of Lions International. T* **20** *and similar design. Multicoloured.* (a) POSTAGE. *P* 13½ × 13.
807 70 c. Type **201** 8 5

(b) AIR. *Inscr* "Aereo". *P* 13 × 13½
808 2 p. Lions emblem and Inca obelisks (horiz) 15 12
MS809 129 × 80 mm. Nos. 807/8. Imperf .. 75 75

(Des Gil Imana. Litho)

1968 (24 June). *Ninth Congress of the U.P.A.E. (Postal Union of the Americas and Spain). Bolivian Folklore. T* **202** *and similar vert designs showing costumed figures. Multicoloured. P* 13½. (a) POSTAGE.
810 30 c. Type **202** 5 5
811 60 c. "Chunchos" 5 5
812 1 p. "Wiphala" 8 8
813 2 p. "Diablada" 15 15

(b) AIR. *Inscr* "AEREO"
814 1 p. 20, "Pujllay" 10 10
815 1 p. 40, "Ujusiris" 12 12
816 2 p. "Morenada" 15 15
817 3 p. "Auki-aukis" 25 25
810/817 *Set of 8* 85 85
MS818 Two sheets each 132 × 80 mm. Nos. 810/13 and 814/17. Imperf .. .. 2·50

203 Arms of Tarija   **204** President G. Villarroel

1968 (1 Nov). *150th Anniv of Battle of the Tablada (1817). T* **203** *and similar vert design. Litho. P* 13½ × 13.

(a) POSTAGE
819 **203** 20 c. multicoloured 5 5
820 30 c. multicoloured 5 5
821 40 c. multicoloured 5 5
822 60 c. multicoloured 5 5

(b) AIR. *Inscr* "AEREO"
823 – 1 p. multicoloured 8 5
824 – 1 p. 20, multicoloured 10 8
825 – 2 p. multicoloured 20 15
826 – 4 p. multicoloured 35 25
819/826 *Set of 8* 80 65
Design:—Nos. 823/6, Moto Mendez.

1968 (6 Nov). *400th Anniv of Cochabamba. T* **204** *and similar design. Litho.* (a) POSTAGE. *P* 13½ × 13.
827 **204** 20 c. blackish brown & yellow-orge 5 5
828 30 c. blackish brown & turq-green .. 5 5
829 40 c. blackish brn & lt brn-pur .. 5 5
830 50 c. blackish brown and light green 5 5
831 1 p. blackish brown and bistre .. 8 5

(b) AIR. *Inscr* "AEREO". *P* 13 × 13½
832 – 1 p. 40, black and light orange-red 12 10
833 3 p. black and light blue .. 25 15
834 4 p. black and rose-red .. 35 25
835 5 p. black and light bluish green 40 30
836 – 10 p. black and light slate-violet 80 60
827/836 *Set of 10* .. .. 2·00 1·50
Design: Horiz—Nos. 832/6, Pres. G. Villarroel.

205 I.T.U. Emblem   206 Copper Urn

1968 (6 Nov). *I.T.U. Centenary* (1965). *Litho.* P 13½.

(a) POSTAGE
837	205	10 c. black, grey and light yellow	5	5
838		60 c. black, yellow-orange & lt bistre	5	5

(b) AIR. Inscr "AEREO"
839	205	1 p. 20, black, greenish grey and light yellow	10	8
840		1 p. 40, black, light blue & lt ol-brn	12	10
837/840		Set of 4	30	25

1968 (14 Nov). *20th Anniv of U.N.E.S.C.O.* (1966). *T 206 and similar vert design. Litho.* P 13½. *(a) POSTAGE.*
841	206	20 c. multicoloured	5	5
842		60 c. multicoloured	5	5

(b) AIR. Inscr "AEREO"
843	–	1 p. 20, black and light violet-blue	10	8
844	–	2 p. 80, black and light sage-green	25	20
841/844		Set of 4	40	35
Design:—Nos. 843/4, U.N.E.S.C.O. emblem.

207 President J. F. Kennedy   208 Tennis Player

1968 (22 Nov). *Kennedy Commemoration. Litho.* P 13½. *(a) POSTAGE.*
845	207	10 c. brownish black & light ol-grn	5	5
846		4 p. brownish black & bluish violet	35	25

(b) AIR. Inscr "AEREO"
847	207	1 p. brownish black & deep bl-grn	8	5
848		10 p. brownish black and red	80	60
845/848		Set of 4	1·10	85
MS849		Two sheets each 131×80 mm. (a) No. 846; (b) No. 847. Imperf	50	

1968 (10 Dec). *South American Tennis Championships, La Paz. Litho.* P 13½. *(a) POSTAGE.*
850	208	10 c. black, light brown and grey	5	5
851		20 c. black, light brown and yellow	5	5
852		30 c. black, light brown & violet-blue	5	5

(b) AIR. Inscr. "AEREO"
853	208	1 p. black, light brown & lt orange	12	10
854		2 p. 80, black, light brown and light greenish blue	25	15
850/854		Set of 5	45	35
MS855		Two sheets each 132×81 mm. (a) Nos. 850/2; (b) No. 853. Imperf	1·25	

209 Unofficial 1 r. Stamp of 1867   210 Rifle-shooting

1968 (22 Dec). *Stamp Centenary. T 209 and similar horiz design inscr "1867–1967". Litho.* P 13½. *(a) POSTAGE.*
856	209	10 c. bistre-brown, black and light yellow-green	5	5
857		30 c. bistre-brown, black & light blue	5	5
858		2 p. bistre-brown, black & light drab	20	15

(b) AIR. Inscr "AEREO"
859	–	1 p. 40, olive-green, black and orange-yellow	12	10
860	–	2 p. 80, olive-green, blk & light pink	25	20
861	–	3 p. olive-green, black and lilac	30	25
856/861		Set of 6	85	70
MS862		Two sheets each 132×83 mm. (a) Nos. 856/8; (b) Nos. 859/61. Imperf	1·75	1·75
Design:—Nos. 859/61, First Bolivian stamp.

1969 (29 Oct). *Olympic Games, Mexico* (1968). *T 210 and similar designs.* P 13×13½ *(horiz)* or 13½×13 *(vert). (a) POSTAGE.*
863		40 c. black, brown-red & yellow-orange	5	5
864		50 c. black, red and bright green	5	5
865		60 c. black, light blue and yellow-green	5	5

(b) AIR. Inscr "AEREO"
866		1 p. black, yellow-green and ochre	12	8
867		2 p. black, red and yellow	25	15
868		5 p. multicoloured	50	35
863/868		Set of 6	90	65
MS869		Two sheets each 131×81 mm. (a) Nos. 863/5; (b) Nos. 866/8. Imperf (10.4.70)	1·10	1·10
Designs: Horiz—50 c. Horse-jumping; 60 c. Canoeing; 5 p. Hurdling. Vert—1 p. 20, Running; 2 p. 80, Throwing the discus.

211 F. D. Roosevelt   212 Temensis laothoe violetta

1969 (29 Oct). *AIR. Franklin D. Roosevelt Commemoration. Litho.* P 13½×13.
870	211	5 p. black, pale orange & orange-brn	50	40

(Des T. Herzenberg. Litho)

1970 (24 Apr). *Butterflies. T 212 and similar horiz designs. Multicoloured.* P 13×13½. *(a) POSTAGE.*
871		5 c. Type 212	5	5
872		10 c. Papilio crassus	5	5
873		20 c. Catagramma cynosura	5	5
874		30 c. Eunica eurota flora	5	5
875		80 c. Ituna phenarete	10	8

(b) AIR. Inscr "AEREO"
876		1 p. Metamorpha dido wernichei	10	5
877		1 p. 80, Heliconius felix	15	10
878		2 p. 80, Morpho casica	25	12
879		3 p. Papilio yurucares	25	15
880		4 p. Heliconsus melitus	35	25
871/880		Set of 10	1·25	85
MS881		Two sheets each 132×80 mm. (a) Nos. 871/3; (b) Nos. 876/8. Imperf	1·00	1·00

213 Scout mountaineering   214 Pres. A. Ovando and Revolutionaries

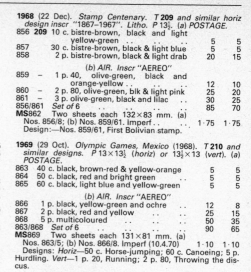

(Des Gil Imana. Litho)

1970 (17 June). *Bolivian Scout Movement. T 213 and similar vert designs. Multicoloured. P 13½×13. (a) POSTAGE.*
882   5 c. Type 213   5   5
883   10 c. Girl-scout planting shrub   5   5

(b) AIR. Inscr "AEREO"
884   50 c. Scout laying bricks   5   5
885   1 p. 20, Bolivian scout badge   15   8
882/885 Set of 4   25   15

1970 (26 Sept). *OBLIGATORY TAX. T 214 and similar horiz design. Litho. P 13½. (a) POSTAGE. Revolution Day.*
886   20 c. black and red   5   5

(b) AIR. Inscr "AEREO". National Day
887   30 c. black and emerald   5   5
Designs:—30 c. Pres. Ovando, oil derricks and laurel sprig.
During shortages these Obligatory Tax stamps were used as postal issues.

(215)   (216)

1970 (6 Dec). *"Exfilca 70" Stamp Exhibition, Caracas, Venezuela. No. 706 further surch with T 215.*
888   30 c. on 350 b. on 10 c. green (R.)   ..   5   5

1970 (18 Dec). *Provisionals. Various stamps surch as T 216.*

(a) POSTAGE
889 **178** 60 c. on 900 b. on 350 b. brown-purple (No. 728)   ..   5   5
890 – 1 p. 20 on 1,500 b. deep blue and salmon (No. 723) (R.)   12   5

(b) AIR. Inscr "CORREO AEREO"
891 **185** 1 p. 20 on 4,000 b. mult (No. 720) ..   12   8

217 Pres. G. Busch and Oil Derrick   **218** Amaryllis escobar uriae

1971 (May). *OBLIGATORY TAX. Presidential Annivs. T 217 and similar horiz design. Litho. P 13×13½.*

(a) POSTAGE. 32nd Death Anniv of Pres. G. Busch
892   20 c. black and bright lilac (13.5)   ..   5   5

(a) AIR. Inscr "AEREO". 25th Death Anniv of Pres. G. Villarroel
893   30 c. black and light blue (25.5)   5   5
Design:—30 c. Pres. Villarroel and oil refinery.
During shortages these Obligatory Tax stamps were used as postal issues.

(Des from photographs by Dr. M. Cardenas. Litho)

1971 (9 Aug). *Bolivian Flora. T 218 and similar multicoloured designs. P 13×13½ (horiz) or 13½×13 (vert). (a) POSTAGE.*
894   30 c. Type 218   5   5
895   40 c. Amaryllis evansae   5   5
896   50 c. Amaryllis yungacensis (vert)   ..   5   5
897   2 p. Gymnocalycium chiquitanumum (vert)   20   10

(b) AIR. Inscr "AEREO"
898   1 p. 20, Amaryllis pseudopardina   ..   12   8
899   1 p. 40, Rebutia kruegeri (vert)..   ..   15   10
900   2 p. 80, Lobivia pentlandii   ..   30   12
901   4 p. Rebutia tunariensis (vert)   40   25
894/901 Set of 8   ..   ..   ..   1·25   70
MS902 Two sheets each 130×80 mm. (a) Nos. 894/5, 898 and 900; (b) Nos. 896/7, 899 and 901. Imperf   ..   ..   1·40   1·40

219 Sica Sica Cathedral   **220** Pres. H. Banzer

(Des F. Avila. Litho)

1971 (6 Nov). *"Exfilima" Stamp Exhibition, Lima, Peru. P 13½.*
903 **219** 20 c. multicoloured   5   5

1972 (24 Jan). *"Bolivia's Development". Litho. P 13½.*
904 **220** 1 p. 20, multicoloured   12   8

221 Chiriwano de Achocalla Dance   **222** "Virgin and Child" (B. Bitti)

(Des F. Avila. Litho)

1972 (23 Mar). *Folk Dances. T 221 and similar vert designs. Multicoloured. P 13½×13. (a) POSTAGE.*
905   20 c. Type 221   5   5
906   40 c. Rueda Chapaca   5   5
907   60 c. Kena-Kena..   5   5
908   1 p. Waca Thokori   10   8

(b) AIR. Inscr "AEREO"
909   1 p. 20, Kusillo   12   8
910   1 p. 40, Taquirari   15   10
905/910 Set of 6   50   35
These stamps also exist in two imperf miniature sheets, each 80×130 mm, one containing Nos. 905/6 and 910, the other No. 907/9, each sheet also including the Winter Olympic Games, Sapporo emblem. Supplies of these sheets are severely restricted.

1972 (17 Aug–4 Dec). *Bolivian Paintings. T 222 and similar vert designs. Multicoloured. Litho. P 13½. (a) POSTAGE.*
911   10 c. "The Nativity" (M. P. Holguin) (4.12)   5   5
912   50 c. "Coronation of the Virgin" (G. M. Berrio) (4.12)   5   5
913   70 c. "Arquebusier" (anon) (4.12)   ..   8   5
914   80 c. "St. Peter of Alcantara" (M. P. Holguin) (4.12)   8   5
915   1 p. Type 222   10   8

(b) AIR. Inscr "AEREO"
916   1 p. 40, "Chola Pacena" (G. de Rojas) (4.12)   15   10
917   1 p. 50, "Adoration of the Kings" (G. Gamarra)   15   10
918   1 p. 60, "Pachamama Vision" (A. Borda)   15   10
919   2 p. "Idol's Kiss" (G. de Rojas)..   ..   20   10
911/919 Set of 9   90   60
Nos. 915 and 918, 917 and 919 also exist in imperf miniature sheets with Olympic Games, Munich emblem, similar to those noted below No. 910.

223 Tarija Cathedral **224** National Arms

1972 (26 Aug). *"EXFILIBRA 72" Stamp Exhibition, Rio de Janeiro. Litho. P 13½.*
920 **223** 30 c. multicoloured 5 5

1972 (4 Dec). *AIR. Litho. P 13½.*
921 **224** 4 b. multicoloured 40 25

BOYACA. See Colombian States.

PHILATELIC TERMS ILLUSTRATED

This successful STAMP MONTHLY series has now been brought together in a snappy black and yellow binding and published as the latest addition to Stanley Gibbons range of essential handbooks for keen stamp collectors.
Within its 192 pages this handy limp-bound volume houses a veritable mine of useful information, on the words and phrases used in philately. It describes and illustrates printing processes and watermarks, papers and perforations, errors and varieties ... and it does all this IN COLOUR. Indeed, there are 92 full page plates in colour, plus many black and white illustrations, making it

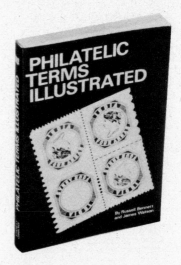

FANTASTIC VALUE AT ONLY A £1!

Brazil

1843. 1000 Reis = 1 Milreis
1942. 100 Centavos = 1 Cruzeiro

EMPIRE

Brazil was established on 7 September 1822 as an Empire, independent of Portugal, of whose dominions it had formed part since it was discovered in 1500.

Emperor Pedro II

7 April 1831–15 November 1889

For GREAT BRITAIN stamps used in Brazil with obliterations C 81/3, see Great Britain Stamps Used Abroad in the *British Commonwealth Catalogue*.

PRINTERS.—All the stamps of Brazil were printed at The Mint, Rio de Janeiro (later called the National Printing Works), *except where otherwise stated.*

CONDITION. Prices for Nos. 1 to 16 are for fine copies. Medium specimens can be supplied at much lower rates.

1 "Bull's Eye"

(Eng C. C. de Azevedo and Q. J. de Faria. Recess The Mint, Rio de Janeiro)

1843 (1 Aug). *Imperf.*

I. *Clear impressions. Background sharp and distinct. Thin to thick yellowish paper or greyish paper*

1	1	30 (r.) black	..	..	£100 50·00
2		60 (r.) black	..	..	70·00 38·00
3		90 (r.) black	..	..	£250 £150

II. *Worn impressions. Background worn and blurred. Yellowish or greyish paper*

4	1	30 (r.) grey-black	..	..	75·00 35·00
5		60 (r.) grey-black	..	..	50·00 30·00
6		90 (r.) grey-black	..	..	£200 80·00

2   3   4

(T **2/4** eng and recess Mint)

1844 (1 July). *Imperf. Thick yellowish paper.*

7	2	30 (r.) black	..	..	35·00 15·00
8		60 (r.) black	..	..	18·00 8·00
9		90 (r.) black	..	..	40·00 25·00

1845–46. *Imperf. Thin paper.*

A. *Yellowish paper.*   B. *Greyish paper*

					A		B	
10	2	10 (r.) black	..	..	3·25	2·00	3·25	2·00
11		30 (r.) black	..	..	6·00	2·50	6·00	3·00
12		60 (r.) black	..	..	3·00	1·50	3·00	1·75
13		90 (r.) black	..	..	25·00	25·00	25·00	20·00
14		180 (r.) black	..	..	£250	£180	£250	£180
15		300 (r.) black	..	..	£350	£250	£350	£250
16		600 (r.) black	..	..	£350	£250	£350	£250

Dates of issue on yellowish paper:—23.5.45—30, 60 and 90 (r.); 26.9.46—remainder.
The 10, 30, 60 and 90 (r.) are found showing early and worn impressions.

1850 (1 Jan–23 Aug). *Imperf.*

A. *Yellowish paper.*   B. *Greyish paper*

					A		B	
17	3	10 (r.) black	..	..	1·50	75	1·50	60
18		20 (r.) black (23.8)	..	..	6·00	6·00	8·00	6·00
19		30 (r.) black	..	..	50	20	50	20
20		60 (r.) black	..	..	50	20	50	20
21		90 (r.) black	..	..	2·00	1·00	2·00	1·00
22		180 (r.) black	..	..	7·00	3·50	9·00	3·50
23		300 (r.) black	..	..	25·00	7·00	30·00	8·00
24		600 (r.) black	..	..	30·00	15·00	32·00	12·00

The 30 and 60 r. especially, vary very much in colour from *pale grey* to *jet-black*.
In January, 1910, the old plates were cleaned up, and a single sheet of each value (except the 90 r.) was printed in black on very thick paper.

1854–61. *Imperf.* (*a*) *Yellowish paper.*

25	3	10 (r.) pale blue (17.2.54)	..	..	1·00	75
		a. Blue	..	..	1·00	85
		b. Deep blue	..	..	1·25	1·00
26		30 (r.) pale blue (17.2.54)	..	..	2·50	2·50
		a. Blue	..	..	2·50	2·50
		b. Deep blue	..	..	3·00	3·00
27	4	280 (r.) vermilion (2.6.61)	..	..	18·00	10·00
		a. Scarlet-vermilion	..	..	18·00	10·00
28		430 (r.) yellow (2.6.61)	..	..	25·00	18·00

(*b*) *Greyish paper*

29	3	10 (r.) pale blue	..	..	1·00	75
		a. Blue	..	..	1·50	90
		b. Deep blue	..	..	1·50	90
30		30 (r.) pale blue	..	..	2·50	2·50
		a. Blue	..	..	2·50	2·50

In 1884, the 280 r. was reprinted in *carmine* on *thin yellow* paper, and in January 1910, one sheet each of the 280 r. and 430 r. were pulled off on *thick paper* in original colours. Proofs are known on laid paper.

1866. P 13½ in the Post Office at Rio de Janeiro, as required.

31	3	10 (r.) black	..	..	7·00	5·00
32		20 (r.) black	..	..	12·00	10·00
33		30 (r.) black	..	..	2·50	1·50
34		60 (r.) black	..	..	2·50	2·00
35		90 (r.) black	..	..	6·00	3·00
36		180 (r.) black	..	..	15·00	9·00
37		300 (r.) black	..	..	30·00	12·00
38		600 (r.) black	..	..	40·00	25·00
39		10 (r.) pale blue	..	..	3·00	2·25
		a. Deep blue	..	..	3·00	2·25
40		30 (r.) pale blue	..	..	8·00	8·00
		a. Deep blue	..	..	8·00	8·00
41	4	280 (r.) vermilion	..	..	35·00	30·00
42		430 (r.) yellow	..	..	40·00	32·00

5   **6**

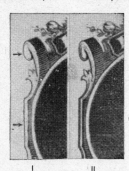

7   **8**   **9**

10   **11**

(T **5** to **24** all show portraits of the Emperor Pedro II)

I   **II**

100 r.

Type I. Very faint weak outer frame line.
Type II. Clear double outer frame lines.

(Eng and recess American Bank Note Co., N.Y.)

1866 (1 July)**–68.** *P* 12.

43	5	10 r. vermilion	..	..	1·25	25
		a. Blued paper (1868)	..	..	30·00	25·00
		b. Orange-vermilion	..	..	3·50	60
		c. Carmine-vermilion	..	..	1·50	30
44	6	20 r. dull purple	..	..	7·00	80
		a. Rosy brown (shades)	..	..	1·25	30
		aa. Blued paper (1868)	..	..	8·00	4·00
45	7	50 r. blue	..	..	1·00	20
		a. Blued paper (1868)	..	..	3·25	1·00
		b. Deep blue	..	..	1·75	35
46	8	80 r. purple-brown	..	..	2·50	35
		a. Purple-grey	..	..	2·00	25
		aa. Blued paper (1868)	..	..	6·00	3·00
47	9	100 r. green (shades) (I)	..	..	2·25	25
		a. Type II	..	..	1·00	10
		b. Blued paper (1868)	..	..	20·00	4·00
48	10	200 r. black	..	..	2·50	25
		a. Grey	..	..	2·75	20
49	11	500 r. orange	..	..	12·00	2·00
		a. Orange-yellow	..	..	10·00	2·00

The 200 r. is often found bisected and used for 100 r.

The 10 and 20 r. *imperf* on *white* paper, and the 10, 20 and 50 r. *imperf* on *blue* paper are known, but are supposed to be proofs and not used in this form.

1876–77. *Rouletted.*

50	5	10 r. vermilion (1.77)	..	..	3·25	1·75
51	6	20 r. rosy-brown (1.77)	..	..	3·00	1·00
52	7	50 r. blue (1.77)	..	..	3·00	40
		a. Deep blue	..	..	3·00	40
53	8	80 r. slate-violet (1.77)	..	..	10·00	1·00
54	9	100 r. green (I) (7.76)	..	..	2·00	10
		a. Type II	..	..	1·50	10
55	10	200 r. black (1.77)	..	..	3·00	35
		a. Grey-black	..	..	3·50	40
56	11	500 r. orange (6.77)	..	..	14·00	2·25
		a. Orange-yellow	..	..	15·00	2·50

The 20 r. and 200 r. are known bisected and used for 10 r. and 100 r. respectively. The 10 r. and 20 r. are known *imperf,* but unused only, and are probably proofs.

12

(Eng and recess Continental Bank Note Co., N.Y.)

1878 (21 Aug). *Opaque paper. P* 12.

57	12	300 r. dark green and orange	..	..	4·00	1·25

This was also printed in myrtle-green and deep orange on *thin transparent paper* but was not issued thus. (*Price* £2.50 *un.*)

13   **14**   **15**

16   **17**

(Eng and recess A.B.N. Co, N.Y.)

1878–79. *T* **13** *to* **17** *and similar types with white beard.* *Rouletted.*

58	13	10 r. vermilion (15.1.78)	..	..	35	15
		a. Carmine-vermilion	..	..	45	20
59	14	20 r. mauve (shades) (29.5.78)	..	..	35	12
		a. Lilac	..	..	65	12
60	15	50 r. blue (28.8.79)	..	..	50	15
		a. Deep blue	..	..	65	15
61	—	80 r. rose-lake (18.8.79)	..	..	1·50	75
		a. Lake	..	..	1·50	90
62	16	100 r. green (4.7.78)	..	..	1·00	8
63	—	200 r. black (12.9.79)	..	..	8·00	1·00
64	17	260 r. sepia (21.8.78)	..	..	4·50	1·10
65	—	300 r. bistre-brown (12.9.79)	..	..	30	35
66	—	700 r. brown-red (1.9.79)	..	..	18·00	9·00
67	—	1000 r. purple-slate (1.9.79)	..	..	18·00	3·00

The 200 r. is known bisected and used for 100 r.

18   **19**   **20**

(T **18** to **24** eng and recess from copper plates, Mint)

1881 (15 July). *Small heads. Laid paper. P* 12½–14.

68	18	50 r. dull blue..	..	..	..	4·75	90
		a. *Bright blue*	..	..	..	5·00	90
69	19	100 r. olive-green	..	..	..	9·00	90
		a. *Deep olive-green*	..	..	..	9·00	90
70	20	200 r. pale brown (I)	..	..	..	30·00	7·00
		a. *Brown-rose*	..	..	..	30·00	7·00

21   **22**   **23**

50 r. T **18**, Small head. T **22**, Large head.
100 r. T **19**, Value tablets do not cut into circle of pearls.
  T **23**, Value tablets cut into circle of pearls.

100 r. Type **23**. Three types

I	II
Background of crossed diagonal, vertical and horizontal lines	Background of crossed diagonal and horizontal lines

III
Background of crossed diagonal and vertical lines

200 r. Type **20**. Three types

I	II
Bulge in forehead; lock of white hair above ear; space between beard and neck	Long, straight forehead; lock of hair shaded; space between beard and neck nearly filled in. Background of crossed diagonal and horizontal lines

III
Similar to Type II but background of crossed diagonal lines only

1882–85. *Larger heads. New value and redrawn types. Laid paper. P* 12½ to 14.

71	21	10 r. grey (*shades*) (7.9.82)	..	..	25	25
		a. *Black*	..	..	30	25
72		10 r. pale orange-vermilion (7.9.82)	..		15	15
		a. *Deep orange-vermilion*	..	..	20	20
		b. Wove paper	..	..	12·00	12·00
73	22	50 r. pale blue (10.3.85)	..	..	1·90	20
		a. *Blue*	..	..	2·10	20
74	23	100 r. olive-green (I) (8.5.82)	..	..	2·25	20
		a. *Myrtle-green*	..	..	2·25	20
		b. Type II (either shade)	..		3·00	90
		c. Type III (either shade) (17.3.83)	..		4·00	75
75	20	200 r. pale brown (II) (9.82)	..		8·00	1·00
		a. *Brown-rose*	..	..	4·50	20
		b. Type III. *Brown-rose* (1884)	..		8·00	1·25
		ba. *Mauve-pink*	..	..	8·00	75

The 10 r. grey has background of crossed diagonal, vertical and horizontal lines and the 10 r. orange-vermilion has background of horizontal lines only.

24 Inscr "CORREIO"

I. Background of horizontal and diagonal lines which usually form solid background (stamps with clear lines are scarce).
II. Background of horizontal lines.

1883. *Laid paper. P* 13–14.

76	24	100 r. lilac (I) (17.3.83)	..	..	..	22·00	2·00
		a. *Lilac-brown*	..	..	..	20·00	2·00
77		100 r. lilac (II) (23.4.83)	..	..	..	3·75	30
		a. *Mauve*	..	..	..	4·00	35

ALBUM LISTS
Write for our latest lists of albums and accessories.
These will be sent free on request.

25   **26**   **27** Pedro II

28

29

30 Southern Cross

31

32

33 Entrance to Bay of Rio de Janeiro

1884–88. *Recess. Laid paper.* P 12–14.

78	25	20 r. olive-green (*shades*) (1.1.84)	..		40	15
79		20 r. myrtle-green	..	..	50	15
80	26	50 r. blue (pale to deep) (8.2.87)	..		1·50	20
81	27	100 r. pale lilac (*shades*) (16.6.84)	..		11·00	50
82	28	100 r. pale lilac (3.10.85)	..		3·25	35
		a. Imperf (pair)	..		15·00	15·00
83	29	100 r. lilac (3.3.88)	..		3·00	35
		a. Imperf (pair)	..		10·00	10·00
84	30	300 r. dull blue (3.1.87)	..		9·00	80
85	31	500 r. olive-green (3.1.87)	..		8·00	1·00
		a. Olive-yellow	..		7·00	70
86	32	700 r. lilac (*shades*) (28.10.88)	..		1·90	2·10
87	33	1000 r. blue (*shades*) (3.3.88)	..		24·00	4·25

In No. 78 there is a small dot in the "R" near its centre. No. 79 was printed from new plates in which the dot was removed.

N 1

D 1

(Litho A.B.N. Co, N.Y.)

1889 (1 Feb). *NEWSPAPER. Rouletted.*

N88	N 1	10 r. orange-yellow	..	..	35	25
		a. Imperf between (vert pair)	..		9·00	9·00
N89		20 r. orange-yellow	..	..	95	60
N90		50 r. orange-yellow	..	..	2·00	1·40
N91		100 r. orange-yellow	..	..	80	65
N92		200 r. orange-yellow	..	..	50	35
N93		300 r. orange-yellow	..	..	50	35
N94		500 r. orange-yellow	..	..	3·00	2·40
N95		700 r. orange-yellow	..	..	65	65
N96		1000 r. orange-yellow	..	..	1·25	1·25
N88/96		*Set of 9*	..	..	9·00	7·00

See also Nos. N97/105.

(Typo A.B.N. Co, N.Y.)

1889 (1 Feb). *POSTAGE DUE. Rouletted.*

D88	D 1	10 r. scarlet	..	..	12	10
D89		20 r. scarlet	..	..	15	12
D90		50 r. scarlet	..	..	25	20
D91		100 r. scarlet	..	..	12	8
D92		200 r. scarlet	..	..	4·00	2·25
D93		300 r. scarlet	..	..	80	55
D94		500 r. scarlet	..	..	40	35
D95		500 r. scarlet	..	..	40	35
D96		1000 r. scarlet	..	..	95	55
D88/96		*Set of 9*	..	..	6·50	4·00

See also Nos. D97/104.

1889 (21 May)–**90.** *NEWSPAPER. Colours changed. Roul.*

N 97	N 1	10 r. slate-green	..	..	10	10
N 98		20 r. apple-green	..	..	10	10
N 99		50 r. dull orange (1890)	..		15	10
N100		100 r. lilac (1890)	..		15	12
		a. Reddish violet	..	..	12	10
N101		200 r. black	..	..	25	25
N102		300 r. rose-red	..	..	80	70
N103		500 r. dull green (1890)	..		6·00	5·00
N104		700 r. pale violet-blue	..		6·00	5·00
N105		1000 r. red-brown (1890)	..		1·75	1·50
N97/105		*Set of 9*	..	..	13·00	11·00

34 Inscr "BRAZIL"

On 14 November, 1889 a 100 r. red-lilac stamp, T **34**, perf 12½ to 14, was issued by the Mint to the P.O. but withdrawn on the fall of the Monarchy the following day and not issued to the public although a few are known postmarked. (*Price* £35 *un*). A reprint was made in January 1910, on thick paper. (*Price* £12 *un*).

REPUBLIC OF THE UNITED STATES OF BRAZIL

On 15 November 1889, the Emperor was deposed after a military rising and a federal republic was decreed, with the title of the United States of Brazil.

1890 (10 Jan). *POSTAGE DUE. Colours changed. Roul.*

D 97	D 1	10 r. orange	..	..	5	5
D 98		20 r. dull blue	..	..	5	5
D 99		50 r. yellow-olive	..	..	5	5
D100		200 r. purple	..	..	30	12
D101		300 r. dull green	..	..	30	15
D102		500 r. drab	..	..	40	20
D103		700 r. violet	..	..	45	25
D104		1000 r. slate-purple	..	..	70	45
D97/104		*Set of 8*	..	..	2·00	1·10

35

36

Southern Cross

Die I

Die II

Die III

100 r. Type **35**. Three Dies

Die I has a small tongue of white between the outer band of the oval and the left top ornament. The base and upstroke of the figure "1" are thin.

Die II has a tongue of white as in Die I. Base and upstroke of figure "1" thicker.

Die III. The tongue over left top ornament is shaded. Figure "1" is shorter, and the upstroke is hollowed. Traces of a horizontal line of colour project to the right and left of the stamp.

100 r. Type **36**. Redrawn

In the redrawn 100 r. the figures are smaller, the curved lines of shading on the left side of the central oval are omitted, and the corner ornaments are smaller. The pearls under the second "R" of "CORREIO" and above the "S" of "REIS" are out of position. Varieties may be found with coloured dots in the centre of one or more of the stars; these occur in the top row of the sheet.

1890 (20 Jan)–91. *Recess.* (a) P 12½–14.

88	**35**	20 r. turquoise-green	.. ..	25	20
		a. Dull green ..	.. ..	25	20
89		50 r. grey-green (shades)	..	30	15
		a. Turquoise-blue	.. ..	70	30
		b. Dull green	.. ..	40	12
		c. Sage-green ..	.. ..	40	12
90		100 r. rose-pink (Die I)	..	30·00	5·00
		a. Mauve (shades)	.. ..	10·00	2·00
		b. Die II. Mauve ..	..	10·00	90
		c. Die III. Mauve ..	..	10·00	90
91		200 r. violet ..	.. ..	60	12
92		300 r. slate-blue	.. ..	2·00	50
		a. Prussian blue ..	..	4·25	1·50
		b. Slate ..	.. ..	2·50	65
93		500 r. olive-buff	.. ..	1·90	65
		a. Olive-grey	.. ..	1·90	65
94		500 r. slate ..	.. ..	2·25	1·00
95		700 r. chestnut	.. ..	2·10	1·50
96		1000 r. yellow-ochre (shades) (1891)	2·25	30

(b) P 11–11½

97	**35**	20 r. turquoise-green	..	35	20
		a. Dull green	.. ..	25	12
98		50 r. dull green	.. ..	50	20
99		200 r. violet ..	.. ..	1·25	20
100		300 r. slate	.. ..	2·25	50
101		500 r. olive-buff	.. ..	1·90	65
102		700 r. pale brown	.. ..	2·25	1·25
103		1000 r. yellow-ochre ..	..	2·25	30

(c) Perf compound 12½–14 × 11–11½

104	**35**	20 r. pale turquoise-green ..	1·10	40
		a. Dull green	.. ..	1·10	40
105		50 r. dull green	.. ..	3·00	1·25
		a. Olive-green	.. ..	3·50	1·90
106		200 r. violet ..	.. ..	1·25	45
107		300 r. slate-blue	.. ..	7·00	1·50
108		500 r. olive-buff	.. ..	3·75	1·10
109		700 r. pale brown	.. ..	4·50	2·50
110		1000 r. yellow-ochre ..	..	10·00	2·00

For these stamps, three kinds of paper were used: (1) Thin, poor paper, brownish to white. (2) Medium to very thick white paper showing a very distinct and regular mesh when held up to the light. (3) Medium to very thick hard toned hand-made paper.

1890 (16 Aug). *Redrawn. Typo.* P 12½–14.

110a	**36**	100 r. pale mauve ..	..	5·00	10
		b. Perf 11 to 11½	.. ..	12·00	8·00
		c. Comp perf 12½–14 × 11–11½	7·50	85
		d. Tête-bêche (pair)	..	£1250	£1000

N 2

N 3 Southern Cross and Sugar Loaf Mountain

1890 (20 Jan–30 Aug). *NEWSPAPER. Typo. Thin to thick paper.*

(a) P 12½ × 14

N111	N **2**	10 r. dull blue (5.7.90)	..	95	60
		a. Deep blue ..	.. ..	95	60
N112		20 r. pale bluish green (20.1.90) ..	1·25	75
		a. Turquoise-green	.. ..	1·25	60
N113		100 r. reddish purple (30.8.90) ..	1·40	1·10
		a. Dull pink ..	.. ..	6·00	5·50

(b) P 11–11½

N114	N **2**	10 r. deep blue ..	..	2·50	1·40
N115		20 r. turquoise-green	..	4·50	3·25
N116		100 r. reddish purple	..	10·00	5·00

(c) Perf compound 12½–14 × 11–11½

N117	N **2**	20 r. pale bluish green	..	1·40	1·25
N118		100 r. reddish purple	..	1·25	95

1890 (11 Sept)–91. *NEWSPAPER. Typo.* (i) Thin buff tinted paper. P 12½–14.

N119	N **3**	10 r. dull ultramarine (11.9.90) ..	10	8
		a. Perf 11–11½ ..	..	20	20
		b. Perf comp 12½–14 × 11–11½ ..	60	50

(ii) Thin to thick white paper. (a) P 12½–14

N120	N **3**	10 r. blue (1891) ..	..	12	10
		a. Slate-blue	.. ..	20	20
		b. Ultramarine ..	.. ..	15	12
N121		20 r. turquoise-green (1891) ..	30	30
		a. Yellowish green	.. ..	30	30
		b. Emerald-green	.. ..	40	30

(b) P 11–11½

N122	N **3**	10 r. blue ..	..	20	12
		a. Slate-blue	.. ..	40	20
		b. Ultramarine ..	.. ..	40	20
N123		20 r. turquoise	.. ..	20	20
		a. Bluish green	.. ..	20	12
		b. Emerald-green	.. ..	20	12
N124		50 r. yellow-green (24.7.93)	..	95	95

(c) Perf compound 12½–14 × 11–11½

N125	N **3**	10 r. blue ..	..	40	40
		a. Slate-blue	.. ..	50	60
		b. Ultramarine ..	.. ..	80	80
N126		20 r. pale bluish green	..	55	40
		a. Emerald-green	.. ..	50	50
N127		50 r. yellow-green ..	..	65	65

37    38

Head of Liberty

1891 (1 May). *Typo.* (a) P 12½–14.

111	**37**	100 r. vermilion and dull blue	..	2·25	12
		a. Tête-bêche (pair)	..	£110	£100
		b. No stop after "U"	..	4·50	2·25
		c. Vermilion and sky-blue	..	2·00	20
		ca. Frame inverted ..	..	25·00	22·00
		d. Vermilion and ultramarine	..	2·00	12
		da. Frame inverted ..	..	25·00	22·00
		db. Head reversed on back	..	5·00	3·50
		dc. Frame reversed on back	..	5·00	3·50
		dd. No stop after "U"	..	4·50	2·25
		de. No stops after "E" & "U"	..	5·50	2·25

(b) P 11–11½

112	**37**	100 r. vermilion and dull blue	..	3·50	15
		a. Tête-bêche (pair)	..	£110	£100
		b. Frame inverted ..	..	25·00	22·00
		c. Head reversed on back			
		d. Frame reversed on back	..	5·00	5·00
		e. Vermilion and ultramarine	..	3·00	25
		ea. Frame inverted ..	..	25·00	22·00
		eb. No stop after "U"	..	5·00	2·25

(c) Perf compound 12½–14 × 11–11½

113	**37**	100 r. vermilion and dull blue	..	4·25	55
		a. Tête-bêche (pair)	..	£130	£110
		b. Vermilion and ultramarine	..	4·75	40
		ba. Frame inverted..	..	50·00	

1893 (18 Jan). *Litho. P* 12½–14.
114 **38** 100 r. rose (*shades*) .. .. .. 2·25 12
 a. Perf 11–11½ .. .. .. 2·25 20
 b. Perf comp 12½–14×11–11½ .. 4·00 40
The 10, 20 and 50 r. values in this type were not issued.

39   **40**
Sugar-loaf Mountain

41   **42**
Head of Liberty

43   **44**
Head of Mercury

I   II

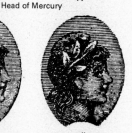

III   IV

HAVE YOU READ THE NOTES AT THE BEGINNING OF THIS CATALOGUE?

These often provide answers to the enquiries we receive.

V
Five types of 100 r.

 I. Head of 100 r. Leaf above ear long and pointed. Small ear. Hair behind neck lacking detail.
 II. Head of 700 r. Leaf above ear broad and stubby. Ear indistinct. Long, wavy, pointed lock of hair on shoulder.
 III. Head over ear broad with straight top, which is distinct and concave. Distinct horizontal band confining hair at back of head.
 IV. Head of 500 r. Leaf above ear long, with blunt end. Three lines shading broken on nostril. Heavy line separates neck from jaw.
 V. Head of 100 r. redrawn. Snub nose. White vertical line down side of nose, where it joins cheek, and in front of chin.

1894 (20 Aug)–**97**. *Typo.*
 A. *Thin to medium hard toned paper* (1894–97)
 (*a*) *P* 12½–14
115 **39** 10 r. blue and rose 40 10
116 **40** 20 r. blue and yellow-orange .. 1·25 50
117 50 r. blue (1895) 65 8
118 **41** 100 r. black and rose (I) .. .. — 15
 a. Type II.. .. .. ..
 b. Type III .. .. ..
 c. Type IV .. .. ..
119 **42** 200 r. black and orange .. .. 3·00 65
120 300 r. black and pale green (1895) .. 2·25 30
121 500 r. black and blue (1895).. .. 6·50
122 700 r. black & pale mauve (1895) .. 1·60 10
123 **43** 1000 r. mauve and green (1895) .. 6·50 10
 (*b*) *P* 11–11½
124 **39** 10 r. blue and rose 5 5
125 **40** 20 r. blue and yellow-orange .. 8 5
 a. *Blue and orange* 8 5
 b. *Blue and yellow* 12 5
126 50 r. blue 8 5
 a. *Deep blue* 20 5
127 **41** 100 r. black and rose (I) 12 5
 a. Type II.. .. .. .. — 85
 b. Type III .. .. .. — 2·50
 c. Type IV .. .. .. — 3·00
 d. Type V (1897) 50 5
 da. Imperf between (vert pair) .. 20·00
128 **42** 200 r. black and orange 12 5
 a. Imp between (vert pair) .. 15·00 12·00
 b. *Black and yellow* 20 5
129 300 r. black and pale green 12 5
 a. *Black and emerald* 20 5
130 500 r. black and blue 65 5
131 700 r. black and pale mauve .. 70 5
 a. *Black and mauve* 60 5
132 **43** 1000 r. mauve and green .. .. 2·50 5
133 **44** 2000 r. purple and grey .. .. 10·00 3·00
 (*c*) *Perf compound* 12½–14×11–11½
134 **39** 10 r. blue and rose 65 30
135 **40** 20 r. blue and orange .. .. 1·25 20
136 50 r. blue 65 15
137 **41** 100 r. black and rose (I) .. .. 2·40 8
 a. Type II.. .. .. .. — 2·75
 b. Type III .. .. .. — 7·00
138 **42** 200 r. black and orange 12 12
139 300 r. black and pale green .. .. 2·25 20
 a. *Black and emerald* .. .. 2·25 20
140 500 r. black and blue .. .. 2·75 20
141 700 r. black and mauve .. .. 2·00 1·25
142 **43** 1000 r. mauve and green .. .. 2·00 1·25

B. *Thick opaque white wove paper* (1895)
(a) *P* 12½–14

143	40	50 r. blue	..	.. 1·90	1·10
144	41	100 r. black and rose (I)	..	2·75	15
145	42	200 r. black and orange	..	2·25	12
146		500 r. black and blue	..	.. 4·00	10

(b) *P* 11–11½

147	39	10 r. blue and rose	..	40	5
148	40	20 r. blue and yellow-orange		50	10
149		50 r. blue	..	.. 4·00	2·75
150	41	100 r. black and rose (I)	..	2·00	5
151	42	200 r. black and pale orange		1·50	5
152		300 r. black and pale green	..	5·00	2·00
153		500 r. black and blue	..	15	5
154		700 r. black and mauve	..	—	1·75
155	43	1000 r. mauve and green	..	4·75	1·75
156	44	2000 r. purple and grey	..	22·00	1·50

(c) *Perf compound* 12½–14 × 11–11½

157	39	10 r. blue and rose	..	5·50	2·75
158	40	20 r. blue and orange	..		2·50
159		50 r. blue	..	.. 12·00	2·75
160	41	100 r. black and rose	..		2·50
161	42	500 r. black and blue	..	4·00	1·50

In 1900 the 20 r., 50 r. and 700 r. appeared on a white paper similar to the above, but not so thick. It is easily distinguished by the stamps themselves, the 20 r. being orange-yellow, the 50 r. being printed from a single plate, and the 700 r. being in the *deep* mauve shade.

C. *Medium to thick paper showing very distinct mesh.*
P 11–11½ (1896)

162	39	10 r. blue and rose	..	4·00	2·50
163	40	20 r. blue and orange	..	2·00	65
164	41	100 r. black and rose (I)	..	—	2·75
		a. Type II..	..		
		b. Type III	..	—	6·50
		c. Type IV	..	—	6·50

For other perforations, see Nos. 203 etc.

D 2

45 Sugar-loaf Mountain

(46)

1895–1901. *POSTAGE DUE. Typo. Medium to thick paper. No wmk.*

(a) *P* 12½–14

D165	D 2	10 r. deep blue	..	2·00	2·00
		a. Blue	..	2·75	2·75
D166		20 r. yellow-green	..	30	20
D167		50 r. yellow-green	..	50	20
D168		100 r. red	..	70	50
D169		200 r. slate-violet	..	70	50
D170		300 r. grey-blue	..		
D171		2000 r. red-brown	..	4·75	4·25

(b) *P* 11–11½

D172	D 2	10 r. deep blue	..	20	15
		a. Blue	..	20	20
D173		20 r. yellow-green	..	30	20
D174		50 r. yellow-green	..	40	20
D175		100 r. red	..	20	5
D176		200 r. deep lilac	..	30	15
		a. Pale slate-lilac	..	25	20
		b. Violet (1897)	..	25	8
D177		300 r. grey-blue	..	70	25
		a. Blue	..	50	20
D178		2000 r. red-brown	..	4·00	2·75

(c) *Perf compound* 12½–14 × 11–11½

D179	D 2	10 r. deep blue	..	1·40	1·40
		a. Blue	..	1·40	1·40
D180		20 r. yellow-green	..	1·10	85
D181		50 r. yellow-green	..	1·00	85
D182		100 r. red	..	1·40	1·00
D183		200 r. slate-blue	..	1·40	1·00
D184		300 r. blue	..	2·75	2·50
D185		2000 r. red-brown	..	4·75	3·25

Dates of issue: 10 r. 1901, 200 r. 1896, others 1895.

The 10, 20, 100 and 200 r. values exist with the variety no stop after "E" of "E. U DO BRASIL". These occur on the same sheets as the stamps with stops. Prices about double the value of the normals.

1897. *Inscr "REIS REIS". Typo. Thin to thick paper.*

(a) *Perf* 11–11½

165	45	10 r. blue and rose	..	8	5
		a. Deep blue and carmine	..	5	5

(b) *Perf* 12½–14

166	45	10 r. blue and rose	..	—	2·00

(c) *Perf compound* 11–11½ × 12½–14

167	45	10 r. blue and carmine	..	16·00	2·00

See also Nos. 202, etc.

(Surch at National Printing Works, Rio de Janeiro)

1898 (29 Oct). *Newspaper stamps surch as T 46. Roul.*

(a) *Typographical surcharge*

168	N 1	100 on 50 r. dull orange (V.)	..	15	20
169		200 on 100 r. lilac	..	20	20
		a. Reddish violet	..	20	20
		aa. Surch double	..	16·00	16·00
		ab. Surch inverted	..	22·00	20·00
170		300 on 200 r. black (V.)	..	25	12
		a. Blue surch	..	20·00	20·00
171		500 on 300 r., rose-red	..	35	12
		a. Blue surch	..	1·25	1·00
		b. Violet surch..	..	16·00	16·00
172	N 2	700 on 500 r. orange-yellow (G.)	..	1·60	1·10
		a. Surch double	..	11·00	11·00
173		700 on 500 r. dull green	..	85	35
174		1000 on 700 r. orange-yellow (G.)	..	2·25	1·90
		a. Error "700" for "1000"	..	£100	90·00
175		1000 on 700 r. pale violet-blue (R.)	..	2·50	2·00
		a. Surch inverted	..	35·00	32·00
176		2000 on 1000 r. orange-yellow (G.)	..	2·25	1·10
177		2000 on 1000 r. red-brown (G.)	..	1·90	1·10

(b) *Handstamped surcharge*

178	N 1	100 on 50 r. dull orange (V.)	..	3·25	3·25

The figures in the handstamped surcharges are blurred and the date is taller and wider. There are dangerous forgeries of this surcharge and forgeries of the rare error 700 on 700 r. exist.

(47) 200 1898

(48) 1898 50 RÉIS 50

(49) 1899 50 RÉIS

1898 (28 Nov). *Newspaper stamp surch with T 47. Thin to thick paper.*

(a) *P* 12½–14

179	N 2	200 on 100 r. reddish purple (B.)	..	9·00	9·00
		a. Black surch	..	2·50	2·00
		aa. Surch double	..		
		ab. Dull pink	..	12·00	

(b) *P* 11–11½

180	N 2	200 on 100 r. reddish purple (B.)	..	2·00	1·10

(c) *Perf compound* 12½–14 × 11–11½

181	N 2	200 on 100 r. reddish purple (B.)	..	2·75	1·25
		a. Black surch	..		

1899 (30 Jan). *Newspaper stamps surch as T 48. White paper.*

(a) *P* 11–11½

182	N 3	20 r. on 10 r. dull blue	..	35	25
		a. Slate-blue	..	35	25
183		50 r. on 20 r. yellowish green (B.)	..	25	15
		a. Emerald-green	..	40	40
184		100 r. on 50 r. yellow-green (R.)	..	1·25	1·40
		a. Blue surch	..	6·00	6·00

(b) *P* 12½–14

185	N 3	50 r. on 20 r. emerald-green (R.)	..	18·00	11·00

(c) *Perf compound* 11–11½ × 12½–14

186	N 3	20 r. on 10 r. dull blue	..	4·50	
187		50 r. on 20 r. emerald-green (B.)	..	1·75	
188		100 r. on 50 r. yellow-green (R.)	..	1·25	1·25
		a. Blue surch	..	4·25	4·25

1899 (25 June). *Surch as T 49, in magenta. Thin to medium hard toned paper.*

(a) P 12½–14

189	35	50 r. on 20 r. dull green	25	30
190		500 r. on 300 r. slate-blue ..	1·10	1·10
		a. Pair, one without surch	30·00	
		b. Slate	30	35
		ba. Pair, one without surch		
191		700 r. on 500 r. olive-buff ..	80	45
192		1000 r. on 700 r. chestnut ..	1·10	70
		a. Pale brown	95	70
		aa. Pair, one without surch	40·00	
193		2000 r. on 1000 r. yellow-ochre	1·50	50

(b) P 11–11½

194	35	50 r. on 20 r. dull green	20	20
195		100 r. on 50 r. dull green ..	15	15
		a. Surch double	6·00	
196		300 r. on 200 r. violet ..	90	75
		a. Pair, one without surch	40·00	
197		500 r. on 300 r. slate	5·00	
		a. Pair, one without surch	40·00	
198		700 r. on 500 r. olive-buff ..	1·25	1·10
		a. Pair, one without surch		
199		1000 r. on 700 r. pale brown ..	2·25	45
200		2000 r. on 1000 r. yellow-ochre	1·75	50

(c) Perf compound 12½–14 × 11–11½

200a	35	700 r. on 500 r. olive-buff ..	—	20·00
201		2000 r. on 1000 r. yellow-ochre	12·00	3·50

1899. *As 1894–97. Perforations changed.*

(a) P 5½–7

202	45	10 r. blue and rose ..	75	40
203	40	20 r. blue and yellow-orange	85	40
		a. Blue and yellow	90	40
204		50 r. deep blue	75	60
205	41	100 r. black and rose (V)	75	20
206	42	200 r. black and orange	75	20
207		300 r. black and emerald	2·25	45

(b) Perf compound 11–11½ × 5½–7

208	45	10 r. blue and carmine	9·00	
209	40	20 r. blue and yellow-orange	—	7·00
210		50 r. deep blue ..		
211	41	100 r. black and rose (V)	9·00	
212	42	200 r. black and orange	8·00	
213		300 r. black and emerald	—	4·00

(c) P 8½–9½

214	45	10 r. blue and rose ..	75	15
215	40	20 r. blue and yellow-orange	80	15
		a. Blue and yellow	1·00	60
216		50 r. deep blue ..	10·00	8·00
217	41	100 r. black and rose (V)	80	30
218	42	200 r. black and orange	80	30
		a. Black and yellow	2·50	30
219		300 r. black and pale green ..	3·00	40
		a. Black and emerald	2·75	30
220	43	1000 r. mauve and green	5·50	45

(d) Perf compound 8½–9½ × 11–11½

221	40	20 r. blue and yellow-orange	7·00	1·25
222		50 r. deep blue	—	5·00
223	41	100 r. black and rose (V)	—	4·50
224	42	200 r. black and orange	20·00	1·25
		a. Black and yellow	24·00	2·00

(e) Perf compound 5½–7 and 14

225	41	100 r. black and rose (V)	22·00	14·00

52 Emancipation of Slaves **53** Brazil as a Republic

(Litho Paulo Robin and Pinho, Rio)

1900 (1 Jan). *400th Anniv of Discovery of Brazil. P 13.*

226	50	100 r. scarlet ..	60	65
		a. Imperf (pair)	25·00	
227	51	200 r. deep blue-green and yellow	60	65
228	52	500 r. blue	60	65
229	53	700 r. pale blue-green	60	65
226/229		Set of 4 ..	2·10	2·25

100 r. Die A 100 r. Die B

200 r. Die A 200 r. Die B

200 r. Die C

100 r.
Die A. Coloured line round oval of background.
Die B. No coloured line round oval.

200 r.
Die A. Long neck to head of Liberty. Horiz background lines overlap inner oval line of frame.
Die B. Short neck; white space between lines of background and inner oval line.
Die C. Figures shaded inside with lines and dots; corner triangles above "REIS" both recut with white vertical lines.

50 Discovery of Brazil

51 Declaration of Independence

1900–6. *Some colours changed. Typo. Thin paper.*

I. *Stamps printed close together, about ½ mm apart (1.2.1900)*
100 r. and 200 r. both Die A and printed from double plates, with centre frequently misplaced.
(a) P 12½–14

230	40	50 r. dull green	..	.. ..	2·00	60
		a. Thick paper	..	.. ..	4·75	1·90
231	42	200 r. blue ..	..	..	2·00	60
		a. Thick paper	..	.. ..	4·75	1·75

(b) P 11–11½

232	40	50 r. green ..	..	..	12	5
		a. Thick paper	.·	.. ..	1·00	12
233	41	100 r. pale carmine	..	..	2·75	20
234	42	200 r. blue	..	.. ..	65	5
		a. Deep blue	..	.. ..	1·00	5
		aa. Thick paper	..	..	1·90	40

(c) Perf compound 12½–14 × 11–11½

235	40	50 r. dull green	..	..	1·50	35
		a. Thick paper	..	..	2·75	95
236	42	200 r. blue	..	.. ..	1·90	12
		a. Deep blue	..	.. ..	1·90	12
		aa. Thick paper	..	..	5·00	1·75

II. *Printed from new single plates (Die B) with stamps about 1½ mm apart (1901)*
(a) P 12½–14

237	41	100 r. pale carmine	..	..	—	80
238	42	200 r. blue	..	.. ..	—	20

(b) P 11–11½

239	41	100 r. pale carmine	..	..	50	5
		a. Thick paper	..	..	1·00	12
		b. Carmine	..	.. ..	65	8
		ba. Thick paper	..	..	1·40	10
240	42	200 r. blue	..	.. ..	80	5
		a. Deep blue	..	.. ..	80	5
		aa. Thick paper	..	..	1·75	30

(c) Perf compound 12½–14 × 11–11½

241	41	100 r. carmine	..	..	95	12
242	42	200 r. blue ..	..	..	3·75	60

III. *Printed from new plates with stamps 2 mm apart vert and from 1¾ to 2 mm apart horiz (100 r. 3 mm apart) (1904–6)*
(a) P 11–11½

243	45	10 r. blue and rose	..	..	20	5
		a. Blue and rose-red	..	..	25	5
244	40	20 r. blue and orange	..	..	15	5
245		50 r. dull green	..	..	25	5
246	41	100 r. rose-red (Die B)	..	..	80	8
		a. Thick paper	..	..	1·40	25
247	42	200 r. pale blue (Die C)	..	..	1·00	5
		a. Deep blue	..	.. ..	95	5
		aa. Thick paper	..	..	2·50	30
248		300 r. black and green	..	..	2·75	5
		a. Black and emerald	..	..	1·60	
249		500 r. black and blue	..	..	2·00	5
250	43	1000 r. mauve and green	..	..	11·00	30

(b) P 12½–14

251	41	100 r. rose-red (Die B)	..	..	2·40	80

(c) Perf compound 11–11½ × 12½–14

252	41	100 r. rose-red (Die B)	..	..	2·75	80

54 ("REPUBLICA DOS ESTADOS UNIDOS DO BRAZIL
CORREIO FEDERAL")

55 ("REPUBLICA DOS ESTADOS UNIDOS DO BRAZIL
IMPOSTO DE CONSUMO")

1905. *As Nos. 243, etc, but wmkd. P 11–11½.*
I. Indistinct wmk. II. W **54**. III. W **55**

			I		II		III	
253	45	10 r.	25	15	1·25	40	2·00	1·10
254	40	20 r.	40	10	1·40	40	3·00	65
255		50 r.	65	10	1·50	40	3·00	65
256	41	100 r.	1·00	5	2·50	35	3·00	25
257	42	200 r.	1·25	5	2·40	25	6·50	40
258		300 r.	2·50	25	6·00	3·50	10·00	3·25
259	43	1000 r.	14·00	3·50	14·00	3·75		†

1905 (22 June). *POSTAGE DUE. As Nos. D175/6, but wmkd as above. P 11–11½.*

			I		II		III	
D260	D 2	100 r.	80	40	90	35		†
D261		200 r.	2·00	20	4·00	1·60	2·50	1·10

No. D261III was issued on 3 July.
Both watermarks, occur eight times vertically in the sheet.
Stamps which do not clearly show some portions of the letters "CORREIO FEDERAL" (W 54) or "IMPOSTO DE CONSUMO" (W 55) are valued at the prices given in the first price column.

56 Pan-American Congress

(Des H. Bernardelli. Typo)

1906 (23 July). *3rd Pan-American Congress, Rio de Janeiro. P 11–11½.*

259a	56	100 r. carmine-rose ..	..	..	4·50	2·50
259b		200 r. blue	..	..	6·00	1·25

57 A. Lobo   58 C. Constant   59 A. Cabral   60 B. do Rio Branco

61 Liberty   62 Liberty   63 N. Pecanha

(Recess A. B. N. Co, N.Y.)

1906 (10 Nov)–**17**. *T 57/63 and similar portraits. Yellowish white or (1910) bluish grey paper. P 12.*

260	57	10 r. slate ..	..	..	5	5
261	58	20 r. violet..	..	..	5	5
		a. Bright violet (1910)	..	..	5	5
262	59	50 r. grey-green	..	..	5	5
263		50 r. bluish green (1915)	..	..	5	5
		a. Yellow-green	..	..	5	5
264	—	100 r. rose-carmine	..	..	12	5
		a. Perf 12 × imperf (10.2.16)	..		75	10
		b. Scarlet (1910)	..	..	15	5
		c. Bright carmine (aniline)	..	..	15	5

265	–	200 r. dull blue	..	12	5
266	–	200 r. bright ultramarine (1915)	..	15	5
		a. Perf 12×imperf (10.2.16)	..	75	15
267	–	300 r. sepia.. ..	..	55	5
268	–'	400 r. olive-green ..	..	45	5
269	–	500 r. deep violet (30.11.06)	..	55	5
270	–	500 r. deep lilac (1915)	..	60	5
271	–	600 r. olive-brown (15.11.10)	..	20	5
272	–	600 r. olive-green (1915) ..	..	20	5
273	–	700 r. red-brown (10.11.06)	..	30	10
274	–	1000 r. orange-vermilion (21.12.06)		2·75	10
275	60	1000 r. deep green (20.4.13)..	..	25	12
276	–	1000 r. slate (1.11.15)	..	80	8
277	61	2000 r. yellowish green (30.11.06)	..	95	8
		a. Deep green (1910)	..	90	8
278	–	2000 r. turquoise-blue (1.11.15)	..	1·60	10
279	62	5000 r. carm-rose (shades) (21.12.06)		80	25
280	–	5000 r. red-brown (31.8.17) ..	..	4·00	1·25
281	63	10000 r. brown (15.11.10)	..	60	15
260/281		Set of 22 (cheapest)..	..	13·00	2·50

Portraits:—100 r. Wandenkolk; 200 r. Deodoro da Fonseca; 300 r. Floriano Peixoto; 400 r., 600 r. Prudente de Moraes; 500 r. Campos Salles; 700 r., 5000 r. (No. 280), Rodrigues Alves; 1000 r. (No. 274), Liberty.

50 r., 100 r. and 200 r. stamps imperf on one side or on two adjacent sides come from booklets. Nos. 264a and 266a are from coils and are also found imperf on three sides.

D 3

D 4

O 1 President Affonso Penna

(Recess A.B.N. Co, N.Y.)

1906 (10 Nov)–**10.** POSTAGE DUE. P 12.

D282	D 3	10 r. blue-grey ..	..	..	5	5
D283		20 r. violet (30.11.06)	..	..	5	5
D284		50 r. grey-green ..	..	..	5	5
D285	D 4	100 r. rose-red	..	..	5	5
D286		200 r. blue	..	..	8	5
D287		300 r. sepia	..	..	5	5
D288		400 r. olive-green ..	..	..	10	8
D289		500 r. slate-purple (30.11.06)	..	7·00	7·00
D290		600 r. purple (15.11.10)	..	..	12	8
D291		700 r. red-brown (10.11.10)	..	6·00	5·50
D292		1000 r. orange-red (30.11.06)	..	12	8
D293		2000 r. green (30.11.06)	..	20	8
D294		5000 r. chocolate (15.11.10)	..	40	25
D282/294		Set of 13 ..	..	..	12·00	11·00

(Recess A.B.N. Co, N.Y.)

1906 (15 Nov). OFFICIAL. As Type O **1** (various frames). P 12.

O282		10 r. green and orange	..	..	5	5
O283		20 r. green and orange	..	..	5	5
O284		50 r. green and orange	..	..	5	5
O285		100 r. green and orange	..	..	5	5
O286		200 r. green and orange	..	..	5	5
O287		300 r. green and orange	..	..	5	5
O288		400 r. green and orange	..	..	15	5
O289		500 r. green and orange	..	..	15	5
O290		700 r. green and orange	..	..	35	12
O291		1000 r. green and orange	..	..	25	5
O292		2000 r. green and orange	..	..	30	15
O293		5000 r. green and orange	..	..	80	35
O294		10000 r. green and orange	..	..	25	12
O282/294		Set of 13 ..	..	..	2·25	1·00

64 King Carlos and Affonso Penna and Emblems of Portuguese-Brazilian Amity

65 Emblems of Peace, Commerce and Industry

(T **64/5** des H. Bernardelli. Recess A.B.N. Co, N.Y.)

1908 (14 July). Cent of Opening of Brazilian Ports to Foreign Commerce. P 12.

282	64	100 r. scarlet ..	..	..	90	15

1908 (14 July). National Exhibition, Rio de Janeiro. P 12.

283	65	100 r. rose-carmine	..	..	1·90	20

66 Bonifacio, San Martin, Hidalgo, Washington, O'Higgins, Bolivar

O 2 President Hermes de Fonseca

(Des H. Bernardelli. Recess A.B.N. Co, N.Y.)

1909 (7 Sept). Pan-American Congress, Rio de Janeiro. P 12.

284	66	200 r. blue ..	..	..	70	12

(Recess A.B.N. Co, N.Y.)

1913 (15 Nov). OFFICIAL. As Type O **2** (various frames). P 12.

O295	10 r. black and slate	..	..	5	5
O296	20 r. black and olive	..	..	5	5
O297	50 r. black and slate	..	..	5	5
O298	100 r. black and red	..	..	5	5
O299	200 r. black and blue	..	..	5	5
O300	500 r. black and yellow-orange	..	8	5
O301	600 r. black and reddish violet	...	10	5
O302	1000 r. black and grey-brown	..	10	5
O303	2000 r. black and chestnut..	..	20	8
O304	5000 r. black and bistre-brown	..	35	20
O305	10000 r. black	..	..	60	35
O306	20000 r. black and blue	..	2·40	80
O307	50000 r. black and green	..	6·00	3·50
O308	100000 r. black and vermilion	..	16·00	11·00
O309	500000 r. black and brown	..	32·00	32·00
O310	1000000 r. black and sepia	..	40·00	40·00
O295/310	Set of 16 ..	..	..	90·00	80·00

67 Cape Frio

69 Bay of Guajara

68 ("CORREIO" repeated diagonally)

(Des F. H. T. da Silva. Litho)

1915 (13 Nov). *300th Anniv of Discovery of Cape Frio.* W **68**.
P 11½.
285 **67** 100 r. blue-green/*yellow* 40 20

1916 (5 Jan). *300th Anniv of City of Belem. Litho.* W **68**.
P 11½.
286 **69** 100 r. carmine 70 30

70 Revolutionary Flag

1917 (6 Mar). *Centenary of Revolution of Pernambuco.
Litho.* W **68**. P 11½.
287 **70** 100 r. blue .. .. 2·75 1·00

71 Liberty   72 Liberty

73 ("CASA DA MOEDA" in sheet)

In this watermark, there is a space between "MOEDA" and
"CASA" resulting in some stamps in each sheet being
without watermark. These "No wmk" varieties are only listed
in cases where the particular stamps were not issued in
sheets without watermark. Otherwise they are usually indistinguishable.

(Des A. Chaves. Typo)

1918–20. *Thin to thick paper.* P 12½ to 13½.
I. *No wmk.* II. W **73**.

			I		II	
288	**71**	10 r. chestnut ..	5	5	12	5
289		20 r. indigo ..	5	5	12	5
290		25 r. olive-grey ('20)	5	5	12	5
291		50 r. dull green ..	55	10	12	5
292	**72**	100 r. carmine ..	8	5	1·00	5
		a. *Rose-red* ..	8	5	1·00	5
293		200 r. blue ..	†		15	5
		a. No wmk ..	†		90	30
294		300 r. yellow-orange ..	95	5	1·10	8
		a. *Salmon* ..	95	5	1·25	8
295		500 r. purple ..	95	8	1·40	8
		a. *Slate-violet* ..	1·10	8	†	
296		600 r. orange	†		20	10
		a. No wmk ..	†		75	25

CHANGES OF WATERMARK. In the following lists we have
not attempted arrangements by strict chronological order,
either of issue or of the appearance of the various watermarks. Instead we have taken each design or set of designs
in order of issue and followed them with their watermark
changes in sequence.

74 Inscr "BRAZIL"

1918–38. T **74**, *inscr* "BRAZIL". *Recess.*
(*a*) W **73**. P 11 (11.6.18)
297	**74**	1000 r. blue	30	8
		a. No wmk	1·00	20
298		2000 r. chestnut-brown ..	1·90	35
		a. No wmk	5·50	50
299		5000 r. violet (*shades*) ..	80	40
		a. No wmk	1·50	95

75 Arms of Brazil

W **75** is reduced. The actual size of the Arms wmk is about
5½″×7⅞″. It is only found on a portion of the stamps in each
sheet, the remainder being without wmk. All are on thick laid
paper. Some wmks are dated "1909" at foot instead of
"1905".

(*b*) *Thick laid paper.* W **75** (1934)
300	**74**	10000 r. claret (*p* 11)	1·40	10
		a. Perf 12	1·50	15
		b. Perf 12×11	1·25	5

76 ("BRAZIL CORREIO" repeated in vert columns)

(*c*) W **76** (23.3.38)
301	**74**	10000 r. claret (*p* 11)	50	5
		a. Perf 12	70	8
		b. Perf 12×11	85	8

O **3** President   D **5**
Wenceslao Braz

1919 (11 Apr). *OFFICIAL. Recess.* W **73**. P 11×11½.

O311	O **3**	10 r. olive-brown ..	.. .. ..	8	8
		a. No wmk	.. .. ..	25	20
O312		50 r. green	.. .. ..	8	8
		a. No wmk	.. .. ..	25	20
O313		100 r. rose-red	.. .. ..	10	8
		a. No wmk	.. .. ..	30	20
O314		200 r. blue ..	.. .. ..	10	8
		a. No wmk	.. .. ..	35	20
O315		500 r. orange	.. .. ..	65	65
		a. No wmk	.. .. ..	1·90	1·25
O311/315		*Set of 5*	.. .. ..	90	85

The use of official stamps was abolished as from 1 January 1920.

(Des A. de Moura. Typo)

1919 (15 Apr)–**22**. *POSTAGE DUE. No wmk. Thin to thick paper.*

			I. P 12½		II. P 10½	
D302	D **5**	5 r. chestnut ..	5	5	5	5
D303		10 r. lilac ..	5	5		†
D304		20 r. olive.. ..	15	15	5	5
D305		50 r. bluish green	5	5	5	5
		a. Emerald-grn	5	5		†
D306		100 r. rose-red ..	75	40	12	8
D307		200 r. blue	1·50	50	30	20
D308		400 r. brn (18.12.22)		†	20	5

77 Locomotive   **78** "Industry"

79 "Agriculture"   **80** "Aviation"   **81** Mercury

82 "Shipping"   **83** Inscr "BRASIL"

(T **77** des Z. Nogueria. Typo (T **77/81**). Recess (T **82/3**))

1920–40. *Various papers from pelure to carton.*

A. *No wmk.* P 12½×13½ *(vert) or* 13½×12½ *(horiz)* (12.5.20–1922)

302	**77**	10 r. purple ..	.. ..	5	5
303		20 r. olive-grey	.. ..	5	5
304	**78**	25 r. purple ..	.. ..	5	5
305	**79**	40 r. yellow-brown (9.8.22) ..		5	5
306	**78**	50 r. blue-green	.. ..	5	5
307		50 r. chestnut (27.9.22)	..	5	5
308	**79**	80 r. blue-green (9.8.22) ..		5	5
309	**80**	100 r. rose-red	.. ..	12	5
310		100 r. orange (27.9.22) ..		35	5
311		150 r. violet (11.2.21) ..		12	5
312		200 r. blue ..	.. ..	20	5
313		200 r. rose-red (2.5.22)	..	20	5
314	**81**	300 r. olive-grey	.. ..	55	5
315		400 r. blue (2.5.22) ..	..	1·00	5
316		500 r. red-brown	.. ..	65	5
302/316		*Set of 15*	.. ..	3·25	55

B. W **73** ("CASA DA MOEDA")
(a) P 12½×13½ *or* 13½×12½ (1921–28)

317	**77**	10 r. purple ..	.. ..	5	5
318		20 r. olive-grey	.. ..	5	5
319	**80**	20 r. slate-violet (1928)	..	5	5
		a. No wmk	.. ..	40	20
320	**78**	25 r. purple ..	.. ..	5	5
321	**79**	40 r. yellow-brown (1926) ..		5	5
322	**78**	50 r. blue-green	.. ..	35	25
323		50 r. chestnut (1922)	..	5	5
324	**80**	50 r. claret (*error*) (1928)	..	30·00	28·00
		a. No wmk	.. ..	50·00	40·00
325		100 r. rose-red	.. ..	50	5
326		100 r. orange (1922) ..		15	5
327		100 r. turquoise-green (1928)		5	5
		a. No wmk	.. ..	35	25
328		150 r. violet ..	.. ..	20	5
329		200 r. blue ..	.. ..	22·00	80
330		200 r. rose-red (1922)	..	5	5
		a. Vermilion (1928)	..	5	5
331		200 r. grey-olive (1928)	..	20	8
		a. No wmk	.. ..	1·40	35
332	**81**	300 r. olive-grey	.. ..	12	5
333		300 r. rose-red (1928)	..	5	5
		a. No wmk	.. ..	45	20
334		400 r. blue (1922)	.. ..	8	5
335		400 r. orange-yellow (1928) ..		5	5
		a. No wmk	.. ..	40	20
336		500 r. red-brown	.. ..	8	5
337		500 r. ultramarine (1928)	..	8	5
		a. No wmk	.. ..	1·40	25
338		600 r. orange-brown (1928) ..		20	5
		a. No wmk	.. ..	85	30
339		700 r. reddish violet (1928) ..		20	5
		a. No wmk	.. ..	1·00	20
340		1000 r. turquoise-blue (1928)..		20	5
		a. No wmk	.. ..	1·25	20

(b) P 11½ (12.5.20)

341	**82**	600 r. red-orange	.. ..	40	5
		a. No wmk	.. ..	1·25	25
342		1000 r. purple ..	.. ..	25	5
		a. No wmk	.. ..	1·25	20
		b. Perf 8½ ..	.. ..	2·25	20
		ba. No wmk	.. ..	5·00	50
343	**83**	2000 r. violet ..	.. ..	65	5
		a. No wmk	.. ..	3·25	65
344		5000 r. brown ..	.. ..	1·00	12
		a. No wmk	.. ..	2·25	40

Many stamps in this and succeeding issues are found with horizontal or vertical watermark. There are also many shades.

POSTAGE DUE. P 12½–13½ (1920–34)

D345	D **5**	5 r. chestnut (15.12.20)	..	5	5
		a. No wmk	.. ..	20	20
D346		100 r. carmine-red (15.6.28)	..	5	5
		a. No wmk	.. ..	25	15
D347		200 r. blue (15.6.28)	..	5	5
		a. No wmk	.. ..	50	20
D348		400 r. red-brown (15.6.28) ..		8	5
		a. No wmk	.. ..	60	25
D349		600 r. violet (15.6.28)	..	12	5
		a. No wmk	.. ..	1·00	50
D350		600 r. yellow-orange (9.11.34)	..	10	5
		a. No wmk	.. ..	90	25
D345/350		*Set of 6*	.. ..	40	25

Nos. D346a, D347a and D348a coming from watermarked sheets can only be distinguished from Nos. D306/8 by differences in shade or perf.

84 ("ESTADOS UNIDOS DO BRASIL")

C. W **84**. P 12½×13½ *(vert) or* 13½×12½ *(horiz)* (1923)

345	**77**	10 r. purple ..	.. ..	30	12
346		20 r. olive-grey	.. ..	35	12
347	**79**	40 r. yellow-brown	..	30	12
348	**78**	50 r. chestnut	.. ..	40	20
349	**80**	100 r. orange ..	.. ..	30	12
350		200 r. rose-red	.. ..	30	12
351	**81**	400 r. blue ..	.. ..	30	12
345/351		*Set of 7*	.. ..	2·00	70

POSTAGE DUE. P 11×10½ (28.12.23)

D352	D **5**	100 r. rose-red	.. ..	2·75	1·90
D353		200 r. slate-blue	.. ..	1·00	60

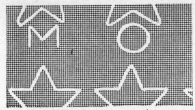

85 ("CASA DA MOEDA" between rows of stars repeated in vert columns)

D. *W* **85** (1924–28)
(a) P 12½ × 13½ *(vert) or* 13½ × 12½ *(horiz)*

352	**77**	10 r. purple	..	..	5	5
353		20 r. olive-grey	..	..	5	5
354	**79**	40 r. yellow-brown	..	..	5	5
355	**78**	50 r. chestnut	..	..	5	5
356	**80**	100 r. orange	..	..	10	5
357		200 r. rose-red	..	..	10	5
358	**81**	300 r. olive-grey	..	..	30	5
359		400 r. blue ..	..	..	15	5
360		500 r. red-brown	..	..	25	5

(b) P 11

361	**82**	600 r. orange	..	..	20	8
362	**83**	2000 r. violet-blue	..	..	65	5
		a. Perf 9 (1926)..	..	..	50	5
		b. Perf 9 × 11 (1926)	..	2·00	25
		c.`Perf 12	..	..	35	5
		d. Perf 12 × 11	..	..	35	8
363		5000 r. brown	..	..	1·00	12
		a. Perf 9	..	..	75	12
364		10000 r. claret (1928) ..	..	65	12
		a. Perf 9	..	..	85	12
		b. Perf 9 × 11	..	3·00	1·10

352/364 *Set of 13 (cheapest)*.. .. .. 2·75 65
The 10000 r. stamps have single-lined numerals as in T **74**.

POSTAGE DUE
(a) P 11 × 10½ (18.8.25)

D365	D **5**	20 r. olive-grey	..	..	5	5
D366		200 r. pale blue	..	..	12	5
D367		400 r. red-brown	..	..	15	5
D368		600 r. violet	..	..	40	12

(b) P 12½ × 13½ (1926–27)

D369	D **5**	100 r. rose-red	..	..	5	5
D370		200 r. pale blue	..	..	12	5

D365/370 *Set of 6* 80 30

86 ("EUBRASIL" repeated in vert columns)

E. *W* **86**. P 13 × 12½ (1929)

365	**80**	20 r. slate-violet	..	..	5	5
366		50 r. claret ..	..	..	5	5
367		100 r. turquoise-green	..	..	5	5
368		200 r. grey-olive	..	..	40	8
369	**81**	300 r. rose-red	..	..	5	5
370		400 r. orange	..	..	8	5
371		500 r. ultramarine	..	..	15	5
372		600 r. orange-brown	..	..	20	5
373		700 r. reddish violet ..	..	15	5
374		1000 r. turquoise-blue	..	..	25	5

365/374 *Set of 10* .. .. .. 1·25 40

POSTAGE DUE. P 12½ × 13½ (12.9.29)

D375	D **5**	100 r. pale red	..	..	5	5
D376		200 r. deep blue	..	..	5	5
D377		400 r. red-brown	..	..	10	5
D378		1000 r. deep bluish green ..	..	30	10

D375/378 *Set of 4* 45 20

87 ("EUBRASIL" repeated in echelon)

F. *W* **87**. P 13½ × 12½, 13 *or* 13 × 12½ (1929)

375	**80**	20 r. slate-violet	..	..	5	5
376		50 r. claret ..	..	5·00	2·50
377	**81**	300 r. rose-red	..	..	8	5
378		500 r. ultramarine	..	..	15·00	1·50
379		1000 r. turquoise-blue	..	1·10	70

375/379 *Set of 5* .. .. .. 19·00 4·25

88 ("ESTADOSUNIDOSDOBRASIL" in one word, repeated in vert columns)

G. *W* **88**. P 13 × 12½ (1930)

380	**80**	20 r. slate-violet	..	..	5	5
381		50 r. claret ..	..	,.	5	5
382		100 r. turquoise-green	..	..	8	5
383		200 r. grey-olive	..	..	15	5
384	**81**	300 r. rose-red	..	..	5	5
385		500 r. ultramarine	..	..	8	5
386		1000 r. turquoise-blue	..	..	65	5

380/386 *Set of 7* .. .. .. 1·00 25

89 (Southern Cross)

H. *W* **89**. I. P 13 × 12½ (1931). II. P 11 (1933–34)

				I		II	
387	**80**	10 r. red-brown	..	5	5	5	5
388		20 r. slate-violet	..	5	5	5	5
389	**78**	25 r. dull purple	..	†	5	5	5
390	**80**	50 r. claret ..	..	5	5	†	
391		50 r. turq-green	..	5	5	5	5
392		100 r. orange	..	5	5	†	
393		200 r. rose	..	5	5	5	5
394	**81**	300 r. grey-olive	..	5	5	5	5
395		400 r. ultramarine	..	5	5	5	5
396		500 r. red-brown	..	5	5	5	5
397		600 r. yellow-brown	..	5	5	5	5
398		700 r. reddish violet	..	8	5	8	5
399		1000 r. turquoise-blue	..	30	5	25	5

387/399 *Set of 13 (cheapest)* 70 50

POSTAGE DUE
(a) P 12½×13 (1931–33)

D400	D 5	20 r. black (1933)	..	5	5
D401		600 r. reddish violet (9.2.31)	..	8	5
D402		1000 r. bluish green (9.2.31)	..	15	8

(b) P 11 (1935–36)

D403	D 5	10 r. lilac (27.8.35)	..	5	5
D404		20 r. black (28.8.35)	..	5	5
D405		50 r. bluish green (28.8.35)	..	5	5
D406		100 r. carmine-red (28.8.35)	..	5	5
D407		200 r. bluish slate (20.8.35)	..	5	5
D408		400 r. sepia (19.8.35)	..	8	5
D409		1000 r. slate-green (1936)	..	12	5
D410		2000 r. chocolate (1936)	..	50	20
D411		5000 r. indigo (1936)	..	65	35
D400/411		Set of 12	..	1·60	90

I. *Thick laid paper.* W 75 (*Arms*) (1934)

400	83	2000 r. violet-blue (p 11)	..	20	5
		a. Perf 12	..	40	5
		b. Perf 12×11	..	25	5

J. W 76 ("BRASIL CORREIO"). P 11 (1936–38)

401	80	10 r. red-brown	..	5	5
402		20 r. slate-violet	..	5	5
403		50 r. turquoise-green	..	5	5
404		100 r. yellow-orange	..	5	5
405	81	300 r. drab	..	5	5
406		400 r. blue	..	5	5
407		500 r. brown	..	8	5
408		600 r. orange-brown (1937)	..	8	5
409		700 r. reddish violet	..	12	5
410		1000 r. turquoise-blue	..	40	5
411	83	2000 r. violet (1938)	..	20	5
		a. Perf 12	..	20	5
		b. Perf 12×11	..	20	5
401/411		Set of 11	..	1·00	40

POSTAGE DUE. P 11 (19.4.38)

D412	D 5	200 r. bluish slate	..	15	5

90 ("CASA+DA+MOEDA+DO+BRASIL" and Maltese Crosses, repeated in vert columns)

K. W 90. P 11 (1936–38)

412	80	50 r. turquoise-green	..	5	5
413		100 r. yellow-orange	..	5	5
414	81	300 r. drab	..	5	5
415		400 r. blue (1938)	..	7·00	2·50
416		500 r. brown (1938)	..	12	12
412/416		Set of 5	..	6·50	2·50

91 ("CASA+DA+MOEDA+DO+BRASIL" and plain crosses repeated in echelon). Letters 7 mm high

L. W 91. P 11 (1939)

417	80	10 r. red-brown	..	5	5
418		20 r. slate-purple	..	5	5
419		50 r. turquoise-green	..	5	5
420		100 r. yellow	..	5	5
421	81	400 r. blue	..	5	5
422		600 r. yellow-orange	..	5	5
423		1000 r. turquoise-blue	..	12	5
417/423		Set of 7	..	30	25

POSTAGE DUE. P 11 (1940)

D424	D 5	10 r. mauve	..	8	5
D425		20 r. grey-black	..	10	5
D426		100 r. carmine-red	..	10	5
D427		200 r. slate-green	..	10	5
D424/427		Set of 4	..	30	10

92 ("BRASIL CORREIO" and stars, repeated in echelon).
Letters 7 mm high

M. W 92. P 11 (1940)

424	80	10 r. chestnut	..	5	5
425		20 r. slate-purple	..	5	5
426		50 r. turquoise-green	..	10	5
427		100 r. yellow	..	5	5
428	81	400 r. blue	..	8	5
429		600 r. yellow-orange	..	10	5
430		1000 r. turquoise-blue	..	25	5
424/430		Set of 7	..	60	25

POSTAGE DUE. P 11 (1942)

D431	D 5	10 r. mauve	..	8	5
D432		20 r. olive-brown	..	8	5
D433		50 r. pale bluish green	..	8	5
D434		100 r. rose-red	..	5	5
D435		200 r. grey-blue	..	15	5
D436		400 r. red-brown	..	12	5
D437		600 r. dull purple	..	20	15
D438		1000 r. deep bluish green	..	20	12
D439		2000 r. chocolate	..	40	15
D440		5000 r. deep blue	..	80	40
D431/440		Set of 10	..	1·90	90

See also Nos. D665/6.

93 King Albert and President
Pessoa

94 Declaration of
Ypiranga, from painting
by Pedro Americo

95 Emperor Pedro I. and J.
Bonifacio

96 National Exhibition
and President Pessoa

(Des and eng O. Reim. Recess)

1920 (19 Sept). *Visit of King of Belgium.* W 73 ("CASA DA MOEDA" *in sheet*). P 11.

431	93	100 r. scarlet	..	25	15
		a. No wmk	..	2·50	1·75

(T **94/5** des The Mint, Rio de Janeiro. T **96** des and all recess Waterlow & Sons, London)

1922 (7 Sept). *Independence Centenary.* P 14.

432	94	100 r. deep blue	..	25	10
433	95	200 r. red	..	25	10
434	96	300 r. grey-green	..	45	10

97 Brazilian Army
entering Bahia

98 Arms of the
Confederation

99 Ruy
Barbosa

1923 (12 July). *Centenary of Capture of Bahia from the Portuguese.* Typo. P 13.

435	97	200 r. rose-red	..	1·25	50

1924 (2 July). *Centenary of the Confederation of the Equator. Litho. Frame and inscriptions in black. P* 11.

436	98	200 r. blue, red and yellow	..	45	20

The Confederation of the Equator resulted from a short-lived republican movement in the northern provinces.

A. Original die. 21½ mm high. Collar very lightly shaded at left. Coat at right lightly shaded.
B. Retouched die. 20¾ mm high. Collar heavily shaded at left. Coat heavily shaded at right.
C. New die. 21 mm high. V-shaped opening to collar. Bold lines of shading on forehead.

1925–27. *Thin to thick paper. Recess. P* 11.

(a) W **73** ("CASA DA MOEDA" *in sheet*)

437	99	1000 r. claret (A) (28.1.25)	..	30	5
		a. No wmk	.. ..	1·00	25

(b) W **85** ("CASA DA MOEDA" *between stars*)

438	99	1000 r. claret (A)	.. ..	75	10
		a. Type B (1926)	..	20	5
		b. Type C (1927)	.. ..	25	5

100 "Justice"

101 Scales of Justice and Map

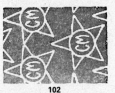

SERVICO AEREO

50 Rs.

102　**(103)**

(Des P. Moraes and O. Campifioriti. Typo)

1927 (11 Aug). *Centenary of Foundation of Law Courses. W* **102**. *P* 13.

439	100	100 r. blue	.. .. ..	25	12
440	101	200 r. carmine	.. ..	25	15

1927 (28 Dec). *AIR. Official stamps as Type O* **2** *surch as T* **103**.

441	50 r. on 10 r. black and slate	..	5	5
442	200 r. on 1000 r. black & grey-brown	12	8
443	200 r. on 2000 r. black and chestnut ..	40	25
444	200 r. on 5000 r. black & bistre-brown	15	15
445	300 r. on 500 r. black & yellow-orge ..	20	15
446	300 r. on 600 r. black & reddish violet	15	15
447	500 r. on 50 r. black and slate	20	15
448	1000 r. on 20 r. black and olive	12	5
449	2000 r. on 100 r. black and red ..	30	20
450	2000 r. on 200 r. black and blue	45	30
451	2000 r. on 10000 r. black	35	20
452	5000 r. on 20000 r. black and blue ..	65	40
453	5000 r. on 50000 r. black and green ..	80	65
454	5000 r. on 100000 r. black & vermilion	7·00	6·00
455	10000 r. on 500000 r. black and brown ..	5·50	4·25
456	10000 r. on 1000000 r. black and sepia ..	5·50	4·25
441/456	*Set of 16*	19·00	15·00

The lozenge-shaped obliterations shown in T **103** only occur on Nos. 441 and 447/9.

104 Liberty holding Coffee Leaves

700 Réis

(105)

 (note: actually stamp 106)

106 Ruy Barbosa

(Des L. Campos. Typo)

1928 (5 Feb). *Bicentenary of Introduction of the Coffee plant into Brazil. W* **102**. *P* 13.

457	104	100 r. bluish green	.. .. ..	25	20
458		200 r. carmine	.. ..	20	10
459		300 r. black	.. ..	1·00	25

1928 (22 Feb). *Nos. O302/6 surch as T* **105** *for use as postage stamps.*

460	O 3	700 r. on 500 r. orange (R.)	..	35	15
		a. No wmk	.. ..	50	20
461		1000 r. on 100 r. rose-red	..	20	10
		a. No wmk	..	35	8
462		2000 r. on 200 r. blue (R.)	..	20	10
		a. No wmk	..	45	8
463		5000 r. on 50 r. green (R.)	..	40	12
		a. No wmk	..	75	25
464		10000 r. on 10 r. olive-brown (R.)	..	1·40	30
		a. No wmk	..	2·00	60
460/464	*Set of 5*	.. .. ..	2·25	70

(Des and eng O. Reim. Recess)

1929–38. (a) W **85** ("CASA DA MOEDA" *between rows of stars*) (1929).

465	106	5000 r. violet-blue (*p* 11)	..	60	5
		a. Perf 9	.. ..	90	5
		b. Perf 9×11	..	2·50	1·40

(b) W **88** ("ESTADOSUNIDOSDOBRASIL" *in one word*) (1930)

466	106	5000 r. violet-blue (*p* 11)	..	60·00

(c) W **75** (*Arms*) (1934)

467	106	5000 r. violet-blue (*p* 11)	..	75	5
		a. Perf 12	.. ..	90	5
		b. Perf 12×11	..	65	5

(d) W **76** ("BRASIL CORREIO") (3.3.38)

468	106	5000 r. violet-blue (*p* 11)	..	20	5
		a. Perf 12	.. ..	30	8
		b. Perf 12×11	..	20	5

107 De Gusmao's Monument

108 Santos Dumont's Airship

109 Santos Dumont

(Des Dr. G. Barroso)

1929–40. *AIR. T* **107/9** *and similar vert types. Typo.*

(a) W **102** ("CM" *in star, multiple*)

			I. *P* 13		II. *P* 11	
469		50 r. deep blue-green	5	5	5	5
470		200 r. carmine ..	5	5	5	5
471		300 r. light blue	5	5	15	5
472		500 r. purple ..	15	5	5	5
473		1000 r. red-brown	55	5	45	5

(b) W **89** (*Southern Cross*). *P* 11 (1934)

474		50 r. deep blue-green	.. ..	5
475		200 r. carmine ..	.. ..	8	5
476		300 r. light blue	.. ..	10	5
477		500 r. purple ..	.. ..	12	5
478		1000 r. red-brown	.. ..	50	5

Recess. (a) W **85** ("CASA DA MOEDA" *between rows of stars*). *P* 11 (1929–30)

479		2000 r. green	.. ..	50	5
		a. Perf 9	.. ..	70	5
		c. Perf 12 ..	.. ..	1·10	5
		d. Perf 12×11	..	2·75	55
480		5000 r. carmine-red	..	80	8
		a. Perf 9	.. ..	1·60	8
		b. Perf 9×11	..	3·25	30
		c. Perf 12 ..	.. ..	1·00	10
		d. Perf 12×11	..	3·50	35
481		10000 r. olive-brown	..	1·90	8
		a. Perf 9	.. ..	2·50	15
		b. Perf 9×11	..	5·50	30

(b) *Thick laid paper. W 75 (Arms). P 11 (14.6.34)*
482   2000 r. green   40   8
  a. Perf 12   50   15
  b. Perf 12×11   50   15

(c) *W 76 ("BRASIL CORREIO" repeated in columns). P 11*
(21.6.40)
483   5000 r. carmine-red   ..   ..   1·00   15
  a. Perf 12 ..   ..   ..   1·25   15
  b. Perf 12×11   ..   ..   1·25   25
Designs:—300 r. A. Severo's airship "Pax"; 500 r. S. Dumont's biplane "14 bis"; 1000 r. R. de Barros' seaplane "Jahu"; 2000 r. Friar Bartholomeo de Gusmao; 5000 r. Portrait of Augusto Severo.
Dates of issue. Perf 13—1929, 28 Oct, 200, 300, 500 r.; 20 Nov, 50 and 1000 r. Perf 11—1929, 18 Dec, 10000 r.; 27 Dec, 5000 r.; 1930, 12 Mar, 2000 r.

110

1930–39. AIR. Typo.

(a) *W 102 ("CM" in star, multiple). P 11 (20.2.30)*
484   110   3000 r. bright violet   80   8
  a. Perf 9   ..   ..   ..   1·00   12
  b. Perf 11×9   90   15

(b) *W 76 ("BRASIL CORREIO"). P 11 (10.6.37)*
485   110   3000 r. bright violet ..   ..   1·25   40
  a. Perf 12   ..   ..   ..   1·90   50

(c) *W 91 ("CASA + DA + MOEDA + DO + BRASIL", and plain crosses repeated in echelon, letters 7 mm high). P 11½×11*
(1939)
486   110   3000 r. bright violet   50   8
  a. Perf 12   60   8
  b. Perf 11½×12   55   8

111   112

1000
REIS
EXPRESSO
(E 1)

(Des N. do Figuerdo (300 r.), P. Pires (others). Typo)

1930 (20 June). *Fourth Pan-American Architectural Congress. T 111/2 and similar vert type, inscr "IV CONGRESSO PAN-AMERICANO DE ARCHITECTOS". W 102. P 13.*
487   100 r. turquoise-green   25   12
488   200 r. drab   30   15
489   300 r. rosine   80   25

1930 (21 Oct). *EXPRESS LETTER. No. 284 surch with Type E 1.*
E490   66   1000 r. on 200 r. blue   50   25

113 G. Vargas and J. Pessoa—"Redemption of Brazil"   114 O. Aranha—"What is the matter?"

115 Vargas—"Rio Grande stands by Brazil" and Pessoa—"I say, No!"   116 A. Carlos—"We make the revolution rather than that the people do so"

(Litho Officinas Graphicas da Livraria do Globo, Porto Alegre)

1931 (29 Apr). *Revolution of 3 October, 1930. T 113/6 (and similar types). P 13½.*
490   113   10 r. + 10 r. light blue   5   5
491   20 r. + 20 r. brown   5   5
492   114   50 r. + 50 r. green, scarlet & yellow   5   5
  a. Scarlet missing from left side.
  In block with 3 normals   ..   25   30
493   113   100 r. + 50 r. orange   5   5
494   200 r. + 100 r. green   8   5
495   115   300 r. + 150 r. blk, grn, yell & scar   10   5
496   113   400 r. + 200 r. carmine   ..   12   10
497   500 r. + 250 r. deep blue   ..   15   10
498   600 r. + 300 r. purple   ..   20   15
499   115   700 r. + 350 r. blk, grn, yell & scar   20   10
500   —   1 $ + 500 r. green, scarlet & yellow   40   8
501   116   2 $ + 1$ grey and scarlet ..   1·50   15
502   —   5 $ + 2$500, black and scarlet   ..   5·00   1·50
503   —   10 $ + 5$ green and yellow   ..   6·50   3·00
490/503   *Set of 14*   ..   ..   13·00   4·75
Designs:—1$ as T 114 but different background; 5$ as T 116 but portrait of Pessoa, inscr "NEGO" ("I say, No!"); 10$ as T 114 but portrait of Vargas, inscr as at left in T 115.
The above were intended for use as charity stamps but were put on sale at face value without premium.

A revolt caused by discontent in the provinces of Rio Grande do Sul, Minas Geraes and Paralyba was successful after troops in Rio de Janeiro joined the rebels; Getulio Vargas became acting President. On 20 July 1934 he became President, and after a *coup d'état* on 10 November 1937 became virtual dictator, until another *coup* on 30 October 1945 forced him to give up his powers.

1931   ZEPPELIN

200 Réis   **2$500**
(117)   (118)

1931 (20 July). *Surch with T 117. P 13½×12½.*

(a) *W 73 ("CASA DA MOEDA" in sheet)*
504   81   200 r. on 300 r. rose-red   ..   3·50   3·50
  a. No wmk   ..   ..   8·00   8·00

(b) *W 86 ("EUBRASIL" in vert columns)*
505   81   200 r. on 300 r. rose-red   ..   12   5
  a. Surch inverted ..   ..   5·00

(c) *W 87 ("EUBRASIL" in echelon)*
506   81   200 r. on 300 r. rose-red   ..   80   45

(d) *W 88 ("ESTADOSUNIDOSDOBRASIL")*
507   81   200 r. on 300 r. rose-red   ..   20   5
  a. Surch inverted ..   ..   4·50

1931 (16 Aug). *AIR. Zeppelin stamps. Nos. 470I and 471I surch as T 118.*
508   "2$500" on 200 r. carmine (B.)..   ..   2·00   1·75
509   "5$000" on 300 r. light blue (R.)   ..   2·00   1·75

2.500 REIS   **ZEPPELIN**
7$000
(119)   (120)

1931 (23 Sept). *AIR. No. 484 surch with T 119.*
510   110   2500 r. on 3000 r. bright violet   ..   1·50   1·50
  a. Surch inverted   ..   ..   13·00

1932 (4 May). *AIR. Zeppelin stamps. Nos.* 465 *and* 364
surch as T **120**.

511	**106**	"3$500" on 5000 r. violet-blue ..	1·75	1·50
512	**83**	"7$000" on 10000 r. claret	1·75	1·50

121 Brazil

122 King John III of Portugal **123** Founding of São Vicente

(Des L. Campos. Dies eng M. d'Oglio)

1932 (3 June). *Fourth Centenary of the Colonization of Brazil
and Foundation of São Vicente.* T **121/2** (*and similar horiz
portrait types) and* **123**.

(a) Typo. W **89**. *P* 13×12½

513	**121**	20 r. purple ..	.. ..	5	5
514	–	100 r. olive-black ..	..	10	8
515	–	200 r. reddish violet ..	..	25	5
516	**122**	600 r. maroon ..	..	40	15

(b) Recess. W **85**. *P* 11

517	**123**	700 r. ultramarine ..	..	40	25
		a. Perf 9 ..	..	40	25
		b. Perf comp of 9 and 11	..	50	25
513/517		*Set of 5* ..	..	1·00	50

Designs:—100 r. J. Ramalho and Kazike Tibiriçá; 200 r.
Martim Afonso de Souza.

124 Map of   **125** Soldier and Flag   **126**
Brazil   "Freedom,
                                               Justice,
                                               Equality"

127 "Tin Helmet"   **128** "LEX" and Sword

129 "Law and Order"   **130** "Justice"

(Litho Litografia Ipiranga, São Paulo)

1932 (13 Sept). *Issue of São Paulo Provisional Government.*
P 11½.

518	**124**	100 r. orange-brown	.. ..	20	20
519	**125**	200 r. carmine	.. ..	20	20
520	**126**	300 r. dull green	.. ..	30	35
521	**127**	400 r. blue..	.. ..	30	35
522	**124**	500 r. sepia	.. ..	40	45
523	**126**	600 r. scarlet	.. ..	55	60
524	**125**	700 r. purple	.. ..	55	60
525	**127**	1000 r. orange	.. ..	55	60
526	**128**	2000 r. red-brown ..	..	6·50	7·00
527	**129**	5000 r. yellow-green	..	8·00	8·50
528	**130**	10000 r. purple	..	9·00	10·00
518/528		*Set of 11*	..	24·00	26·00

A revolt broke out in the state of São Paulo on 9 July 1932
and a Provisional Government was set up. Action by Federal
troops led to the fall of this government on 2 October.

131 Campo Bello Square and   **132** Flag and Aeroplane
Memorial, Vassouras

(Des J. B. Paiva. Typo)

1933 (15 Jan). *Centenary of Founding of Vassouras. W* **89**.
P 11½.

529	**131**	200 r. carmine-rose ..	.. ..	20	12

1933–40. *AIR. Typo. P* 11.

(a) W **89** (*Southern Cross*)

530	**132**	3500 r. blue, green & yellow (7.6.33)	60	20

(b) W **76** ("BRASIL CORREIO")

531	**132**	3500 r. blue, green and yellow (1937)	40	20

(c) W **91** ("CASA+DA+MOEDA+DO+BRASIL" *and plain
crosses in echelon, letters 7 mm high*)

532	**132**	3500 r. blue, green and yellow (1940)	30	12

200
RÉIS
(133)

134 Flag of the Race

1933 (25 July). *Surch with T* **133**. *P* 13½×12½.

(a) W **73** ("CASA DA MOEDA" *in sheet*)

533	**81**	200 r. on 300 r. rose-red	.. ..	9·00	7·00
		a. No wmk	.. ..	18·00	18·00

(b) W **86** ("EUBRASIL" *in columns*)

534	**81**	200 r. on 300 r. rose-red	15	5

(c) W **87** ("EUBRASIL" *in echelon*)

535	**81**	200 r. on 300 r. rose-red	2·00	1·00

(d) W **88** ("ESTADOSUNIDOSDOBRASIL")

536	**81**	200 r. on 300 r. rose-red	12	5

(Des and die eng B. Lancetta. Typo)

1933 (18 Aug). *441st Anniv of Columbus's Departure from
Palos. W* **89**. *P* 13×12½.

537	**134**	200 r. scarlet..	.. ..	15	12

135	136 From Santos Dumont Statue, St. Cloud	137 Faith and Energy

(Des O. C. Pereira. Typo)

1933 (3 Sept). *First National Eucharistic Congress.* W **89**. P 12½ × 13.

538	**135**	200 r. scarlet..	..	..	15	12

1933 (1 Oct). *OBLIGATORY TAX. Airport Fund.* Typo. W **89**. P 13½ × 12½.

539	**136**	100 r. red-brown	..	..	..	5	5
		a. Perf 11	..	..	..	20	5

1933–40. Typo. P 11.

*(a) W **89** (Southern Cross)*

540	**137**	200 r. scarlet (30.10.33)	..	..	5	5
541		200 r. violet (14.11.33)	..	..	5	5

*(b) W **76** ("BRASIL CORREIO")*

542	**137**	200 r. violet (12.36)	..	..	5	5

*(c) W **91** ("CASA+DA+MOEDA+DO+BRASIL" and plain crosses in echelon, letters 7 mm high)*

543	**137**	200 r. violet (1939)	..	..	..	5	5

*(d) W **92** ("BRASIL CORREIO" and stars in echelon, letters 7 mm high)*

544	**137**	200 r. violet (1940)	..	..	5	5

138 "Republic and Flags"	139 Santos Dumont Statue, St. Cloud

(T **138/9** des L. Campos. Eng M. d'Oglio. Recess)

1933. *Visit of President Justo of Argentina.* P 11, 12 or compound.

*(a) W **85** ("CASA DA MOEDA" between stars)*

545	**138**	200 r. blue (7.10.33)	..	..	15	10

*(b) Thick laid paper. W **75** (Arms)*

546	**138**	400 r. green (14.12.33)	..	..	25	12
547		600 r. carmine (14.12.33)	..	..	85	50
548		1000 r. reddish violet (5.12.33)	..	1·25	70
545/548		Set of 4	..	..	..	2·25	1·25

1934 (15 Apr). *First National Aviation Congress, São Paulo.* Thick laid paper. W **75**. P 12.

549	**139**	200 r. blue	..	..	25	12

140 Exhibition Building	141

(Des B. Lancetta. Typo)

1934 (12 May). *7th International Exhibition, Rio de Janeiro.* W **89**. P 11.

550	**140**	200 r. olive-brown	..	..	..	20	12
551		400 r. red	..	..	..	50	25
552		700 r. ultramarine	..	..	..	50	25
553		1000 r. yellow-orange	..	..	1·00	35
550/553		Set of 4	..	..	..	2·00	90

(Des and eng M. d'Oglio. Recess)

1934 (16 Sept). *National Philatelic Exhibition, Rio.* Thick laid paper. W **75**. Imperf.

555	**141**	200 r. + 100 r. claret	..	..	20	20
556		300 r. + 100 r. vermilion	..	..	20	20
557		700 r. + 100 r. blue	..	..	2·25	2·25
558		1000 r. + 100 r. black..	..	..	2·25	2·25
555/558		Set of 4	..	..	..	4·50	4·50

142 Christ of Mt Corcovado	143 José de Anchieta

(Des P. Landowsky and S. Costa. Recess)

1934 (20 Oct). *Visit of Cardinal Pacelli.* W **89**. P 11.

559	**142**	300 r. scarlet..	..	..	1·50	1·25
560		700 r. ultramarine	..	..	2·00	1·25

These stamps were printed in sheets of 32 (8×4), the two lower rows being inverted in relation to the two upper rows. The two middle rows thus form eight vertical *tête-bêche* pairs (*Price £6 for pair, un*).

1934 (8 Nov). *400th Anniv of Founding of São Paulo by Anchieta. Recess. Thick laid paper.* W **75**. P 11, 12 or compound.

561	**143**	200 r. buff	..	..	40	12
562		300 r. reddish violet	..	..	20	12
563		700 r. blue	..	..	80	50
564		1000 r. green	..	..	1·00	55
561/564		Set of 4	..	..	2·10	1·10

144	145

"Brazil" and "Uruguay"

(Dies eng O. P. Borges (T **144**), A. M. Barbosa (T **145**). Typo)

1935 (8 Jan). *Visit of Pres. Terra of Uruguay.* W **89**. P 11.

565	**144**	200 r. orange	..	..	25	10
566	**145**	300 r. yellow	..	..	30	10
567		700 r. ultramarine	..	..	80	50
568	**144**	1000 r. violet..	..	..	1·50	80
565/568		Set of 4	..	..	2·50	1·40

146 Town of Igarassu	147 Nurse and Patient

1935 (2 July). *Fourth Centenary of Foundation of Pernambuco. Typo. W* **89**. *P* 11.
569	**146**	200 r. brown and claret	..	..	35	20
570		300 r. olive and violet	..	..	35	20

1935 (19 Sept). *Third Pan-American Red Cross Conference. Typo. Cross in scarlet. W* **89**. *P* 11.
571	**147**	200 r. + 100 r. violet ..	..	..	50	35
572		300 r. + 100 r. olive-brown	..	..	50	35
573		700 r. + 100 r. turquoise-blue	..	2·50	1·50

148 Mounted Gaucho   **149** Gen. da Silva

150 Marshal Caxias

(Des L. Campos. Eng M. d'Oglio. Recess)

1935–36. *Centenary of Farroupilha "Ragged" Revolution. Thick laid paper. W* **75**. *P* 11, 12 *or compound.*
574	**148**	200 r. black (30.10.35)	..	..	20	15
575		300 r. claret (13.1.36)	..	..	20	15
576	**149**	700 r. blue (20.9.35)	..	..	1·00	65
577	**150**	1000 r. violet (20.12.36)	..	..	1·00	65
574/577		Set of 4	..	..	..	2·10	1·40

151 Gavea

(Des J. de Lima. Typo)

1935 (12 Oct). *Child Welfare. W* **90**. *P* 11.
578	**151**	300 r. reddish violet.& chocolate	..	55	35
579		300 r. turquoise-blue and black	..	55	35
580		300 r. ultramarine & greenish blue	..	55	35
581		300 r. black and scarlet	..	..	55	35
578/581		Set of 4	..	..	..	2·00	1·25

152 Federal District Coat-of-Arms

1935 (19 Oct). *8th International Sample Fair, Rio. Typo. W* **89**. *P* 11.
582	**152**	200 r. ultramarine	..	..	..	50	30

See also No. 594.

153 Coutinho's Ship   **154** Arms of Fernando Coutinho

1935 (25 Oct). *Fourth Centenary of Colonization of State of Espirito Santo. Typo. W* **89**. *P* 11.
583	**153**	300 r. bright purple ..	..	..	30	12
584	**154**	700 r. turquoise-blue	..	..	60	40

154a Viscount Cairu   **155** Cametá

1936 (20 Jan). *Death Centenary of Cairu. Recess. Thick laid paper. W* **75**. *P* 11, 12 *or compound.*
585	**154a**	1200 r. bright violet	..	..	2·25	1·00

1936 (26 Feb). *Tercentenary of Foundation of Cametá. Recess. Thick laid paper. W* **75**. *P* 11, 12 *or compound.*
586	**155**	200 r. buff	..	..	..	..	40	20
587		300 r. light green	..	..	..	40	20

156 Coin Press   **157** Scales of Justice

(Des B. Lancetta. Eng M. d'Oglio. Recess)

1936 (24 Mar). *Numismatic Congress, São Paulo. Thick laid paper. W* **75**. *P* 11, 12 *or compound.*
588	**156**	300 r. chocolate	..	..	..	20	12

(Des L. Campos. Eng O. P. Borges. Typo)

1936 (4 July). *First National Juridical Congress, Rio. W* **89**. *P* 11.
589	**157**	300 r. carmine	..	..	..	20	10

158 Carlos Gomes

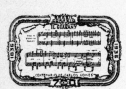

159 "Il Guarany" **160** Congress Seal

165 Botanical Gardens, Rio de Janeiro **166** Iguazu Falls

(T **158** des L. Campos, eng M. d'Oglio.; T **159** des B. Lancetta, eng W. B. de Freitas. Recess)

1936. *Centenary of Birth of Carlos Gomes (composer). Thick laid paper.* W **75.** P 11, 12 *or compound.*

590	**158**	300 r. rose-carmine (28.7.36)	..	30	20
591		300 r. sepia (28.7.36)	..	30	20
592	**159**	700 r. blue (10.7.36) ..	..	1·10	50
593		700 r. buff (28.7.36) ..	..	1·10	50
590/593		*Set of 4*	..	2·50	1·25

1936 (13 Nov). *9th International Sample Fair, Rio. As T* **152** *(inscr and date altered).* W **76.** P 11.

594	**152**	200 r. carmine	..	25	15

1936 (17 Dec). *Second National Eucharistic Congress, Belo Horizonte. Litho.* W **90.** P 11.

595	**160**	300 r. blue, yellow, green and black		20	12

167 Monroe Palace, Rio de Janeiro **168** J. Da Silva Paes

(Recess Waterlow, London)

1937–38. *Tourist Propaganda.* P 12½.

602	**167**	200 r. blue and brown	..	12	8
603	**165**	300 r. green and red-orange	..	15	8
604	**166**	1000 r. brown and sepia	.:	40	15
605	**167**	2000 r. carmine and blue-green	..	80	40
606	**166**	5000 r. emerald and olive-black	..	4·00	1·50
607	**165**	10000 r. deep blue and lake ..	..	10·00	4·00
602/607		*Set of 6*	..	14·00	5·50

Dates of issue:—10 Jan 1938, 1000 r., 5000 r.; 30 Sept 1937, remainder.

1937 (11 Oct). *Bicentenary of Foundation of Rio Grande do Sul. Recess.* W **76.** P 11, 12 *or compound.*

608	**168**	300 r. blue	..	15	10

161 Botafogo Bay **162** Esperanto Star and National Flags

1937 (2 Jan). *Birth Centenary of Dr. Francisco Pereira Passos. Recess. Thick laid paper.* W **75.** P 11, 12 *or compound.*

596	**161**	700 r. light blue	..	30	15
597		700 r. black ..	..	30	15

(Des L. Campos. Die eng B. Lancetta. Typo)

1937 (19 Jan). *Ninth Brazilian Esperanto Congress, Rio de Janeiro.* W **76.** P 11, 12 *or compound.*

598	**162**	300 r. emerald-green	..	25	15

169 Eagle and Shield **170** Coffee

(Des L. Campos. Die eng W. B. de Freitas. Typo)

1937 (2 Dec). *150th Anniv of U.S. Constitution.* W **76.** P 11.

609	**169**	400 r. blue	..	20	12

(Centre offset. Frame recess; Waterlow, London)

1938 (17 Jan). *Coffee Propaganda.* P 12½.

610	**170**	1200 r. multicoloured	..	60	40

163 Bay of Rio de Janeiro **164** Globe

(Recess Waterlow, London)

1937 (June). *2nd South American Radio Conference.* P 12½.

599	**163**	300 r. black and orange (9.6)	..	12	10
600		700 r. chocolate and blue (12.6)	..	30	20

1937 (4 Sept). *Golden Jubilee of Esperanto. Recess.* W **76.** P 11, 12 *or compound.*

601	**164**	300 r. emerald-green	..	20	10

171 "Grito" Memorial **172** Arms of Olinda

(Des M. F. Pinheiro. Die eng O. P. Borges. Typo)

1938 (24 Jan). *Proclamation of Republic Commemoration.* W **76.** P 11.

611	**171**	400 r. olive-brown ..	..	40	12

(Des L. Campos. Eng W. B. de Freitas. Recess)

1938 (24 Jan). *Fourth Centenary of Founding of Olinda.* W **76.** P 11, 12 *or compound.*

612	**172**	400 r. violet ..	..	12	8

173 Couto de Magalhães

174 National Archives

(Des L. Campos. Eng M. d'Oglio. Recess)

1938 (17 Mar). *Birth Centenary of Couto de Magalhães.* W **76**. P 11.
613 **173** 400 r. bluish green 12 8
For similar type see No. 636.

(Des B. Lancetta. Eng V. F. da Silva. Recess)

1938 (20 May). *Centenary of Foundation of National Archives.* W **76**. P 11.
614 **174** 400 r. red-brown 12 8

174a Rowland Hill

174b President Vargas

(Des A. Bueno, Junior. Eng M. d'Oglio. Recess)

1938 (22 Oct). *Brazilian International Philatelic Exhibition (BRAPEX), Rio de Janeiro.* T **174a** *repeated ten times in sheet together with exhibition emblem.* W **76**. *Imperf.*
MS614a 117×118 mm. 400 r. blue-green .. 2·25 2·25

(Des L. Campos. Eng M. d'Oglio. Recess)

1938 (10 Nov). *First Anniv of Constitution issued by President Vargas.* T **174b** *repeated ten times in sheet together with star emblem. No gum.* W **76**. P 11.
MS614b 115×138 mm. 400 r. steel-blue .. 1·50 1·50

175 Rio de Janeiro

176 Santos

1939 (14 June). *Recess.* W **76**. P 11.
615 **175** 1200 r. purple 30 5

1939 (23 Aug). *Centenary of City of Santos. Recess.* W **76**. P 11.
616 **176** 400 r. light blue 20 8

177 Chalice-vine and Cup-of-gold Blossoms

178 Seal

1939 (23 Aug). *First South American Botanical Congress, Rio. Recess.* W **76**. P 11.
617 **177** 400 r. green 30 15

1939 (3 Sept). *3rd National Eucharistic Congress, Recife. Recess.* W **76**. P 11.
618 **178** 400 r. rose-carmine 12 8

179 Duke of Caxias

(Photo Lito-Tipo Guanabara, Rio de Janeiro)

1939 (12 Sept). *Soldiers' Day.* W **76**. *Roul.*
619 **179** 400 r. bright ultramarine 12 10

180 Washington

181 Emperor Pedro II

182 Grover Cleveland

183 Statue of Liberty, Rio de Janeiro

(Recess A.B.N. Co, N.Y.)

1939 (7 Oct). *New York World's Fair* (1*st issue*). P 12.
620 **180** 400 r. yellow-orange 20 8
621 **181** 800 r. bluish green 15 5
622 **182** 1200 r. carmine 25 8
623 **183** 1600 r. blue 25 10
620/623 *Set of 4* 70 25

184 Benjamin Constant

185 Marshal da Fonseca

186 Marshal da Fonseca and Pres. Vargas

(T **184** and **186** photo Lito-Tipo Guanabara, Rio. T **185** recess)

1939 (15 Nov). *50th Anniv of Constitution.* W **76**. T **184** and **186**, rouletted. T **185**, P 11.
624 **184** 400 r. green 12 5
625 **185** 800 r. black.. .. .. .. 20 12
626 **186** 1200 r. purple-brown 20 12

187 The Three Wise Men   **188** Child and Southern Cross

1939 (20 Dec). *Child Welfare.* T **187/8** and similar vert designs inscr "PRO JUVENTUDE". Litho. W **76**. P 11.
627 100 r. + 100 r. violet-blue and indigo .. 15 15
628 200 r. + 100 r. greenish and pale blue .. · 35 25
629 400 r. + 200 r. olive and pale green .. 35 12
630 1200 r. + 400 r. scarlet and pink .. .. 1·40 50
627/630 Set of 4 .. .. 2·00 90
Designs:—200 r. Angel and child; 1200 r. Mother and child. These stamps are printed on adhesive paper and have no apparent gum.

189 Roosevelt, Vargas and the Americas   **190** Map of Brazil

1940 (14 Apr). *50th Anniv of Pan-American Union.* Recess. W **76**. P 11.
631 **189** 400 r. blue 45 20

1940 (7 Sept). *Ninth National Geographical Congress, Florianopolis.* Recess. W **92**. P 11.
632 **190** 400 r. carmine 12 8

191 Water Lily   **192** Map of Brazil   **193** Two Workers

(Des L. Campos. Recess)

1940 (30 Oct). *New York World's Fair (2nd issue).* T **191/2** and vert design similarly inscr. No gum. W **76**. P 11.
633 **191** 1 m. dull violet 60 20
634 ~ 5 m. red (Pres. Vargas) 80 30
635 **192** 10 m. slate-blue 90 20
MS635a Three sheets each 127 × 147 mm.
Nos. 633/5 each in block of ten .. .. 20·00 16·00

1940 (1 Nov). *Birth Centenary of Machado de Assis (poet and novelist). Portrait as T **173** but of Machado de Assis, dated "1839–1939".* Recess. W **76**. P 11.
636 **173** 400 r. grey-black 12 8

1940 (2 Nov). *Bicentenary of Colonization of Porto Alegre.* Recess. W **92**. P 11.
637 **193** 400 r. green 12 8

194 Acclaiming King John IV of Portugal   **195** Brazilian Flags and Head of Liberty

1940 (1 Dec). *Centenaries of Portugal (1140–1640–1940).* Recess. W **76**. P 11.
638 **194** 1200 r. blue-grey 25 10
This commemorates the eighth centenary of the Independence of Portugal and the Tercentenary of the Resurrection of the Monarchy under King John IV.
See also Nos. 642/5.

1940 (18 Dec). *Tenth Anniv of Govt of Pres Vargas.* Recess. P 11. Wmk "CASA + DA + MOEDA + DO + BRASIL".

I. W **90** (with Maltese Crosses, repeated in columns)
II. W **91** (with plain crosses, repeated in echelon, letters 7 mm high)

			I	II
639 **195** 400 r. purple	..	3·75	2·50	15	8

196 Date of Fifth Census   **197** Globe showing Spotlight on Brazil

1941 (14 Jan). *Fifth General Census.* P 11.

(a) POSTAGE. Typo
		I W **90**	II W **91**
640 **196** 400 r. blue & scar ..		30 20	10 8

(b) AIR. Recess
641 **197** 1200 r. brown .. † ~45 8

198 Alfonso Henriques   **199** Father Antonio Vieira   **200** Governor-General Benevides

201 Presidents of Portugal and Brazil

202 Father José de Anchieta

(Photo Lito-Tipo Guanabara, Rio de Janeiro)
1941 (20 July). *Centenaries of Portugal (2nd issue). Roul 9.*
I. *W* **76** ("BRASIL CORREIO" *repeated in columns*)
II. *W* **92** ("BRASIL CORREIO" *and stars repeated in echelon, letters 7 mm high*)

				I		II	
642	198	200 r. pink ..	..	30	12	10	8
643	199	400 r. ultramarine ..	2·75	85		12	8
644	200	800 r. violet ..	..	†		12	8
645	201	5400 r. grey-green ..	50		25	35	15
642/645ll		*Set of 4* ..	..			60	40

(Des L. Campos. Eng M. d'Oglio. Recess)
1941 (1 Aug). *400th Anniv of Order of Jesuits. W* **92.** *P* 11.
| 646 | 202 | 1 m. violet .. | .. | .. | .. | 25 | 12 |

203 ("BRASIL CORREIO" and stars, repeated in echelon). Letters 5 mm high

204 ("CASA + DA + MOEDA + DO + BRASIL" and plain crosses repeated in echelon). Letters 5 mm high

205 Oil Wells

206 Harvesting Machinery

207 Smelting Works

208 "Commerce"

209 Marshal Peixoto

210 Count of Porto Alegre

210a Admiral Maurity

211 "Armed Forces"

212 President Vargas

(Des L. Campos (**209, 210a**), A. Veiga (**210**). Eng B. Lancetta (**205**), J. B. Paiva (**206**), O. P. Borges (**207**), A. M. Barbosa (**208**), M. d'Oglio (**209, 210a**), V. F. da Silva (**210**). Typo (**205/8**); Recess (**209/12**))

1941–49. *P* 11.

A. *W* **92** ("BRASIL CORREIO" *and stars repeated in echelon). Letters 7 mm high* (1941)
B. *W* **203** (*Wmk as W* **92,** *but letters only 5 mm high*) (1942–44)
C. *W* **90** ("CASA + DA + MOEDA + DO + BRASIL" *and Maltese Crosses, repeated in vert columns*) (1942)
D. *W* **204** ("CASA + DA + MOEDA + DO + BRASIL" *and plain Crosses, repeated in echelon. Letters 5 mm high*) (1944–46)

							A		B		C		D	
647	205	10 r. yellow-brown	..	..	..	..	5	5	†		†		†	
648		20 r. sage-green ..	..	..	..	..	5	5	5	5	5	5	5	5
649		50 r. olive-brown ..	..	..	..	..	5	5	5	5	5	5	5	5
650		100 r. turquoise-blue	..	..	..	..	5	5	5	5	5	5	5	5
		a. *W* **76** (1942) ..	..	..	..	..	50	20	†		†		†	
651	206	200 r. brown-orange	..	..	..	..	5	5	5	5	5	5	5	5
652		300 r. claret	..	..	..	..	5	5	†		†		5	5
653		400 r. light blue	..	..	..	..	15	5	5	5	5	5	5	5
654		500 r. red ..	..	..	..	..	5	5	2·50	1·10	†		5	5
655	207	600 r. violet ..	..	..	..	..	8	5	50	25	15	5	10	5
		a. *W* **76** (1942)	..	..	..	..	40	15	†		†		†	
656		700 r. bright rose ..	..	..	..	..	8	5	30	25	20	5	12	5
657		1000 r. grey ..	..	..	..	..	10	5	12	5	†		8	5
658		1200 r. dull blue ..	..	..	..	..	20	5	15	5	40	5	8	5
659	208	2000 r. slate-purple ..	..	..	..	..	20	5	25	5	70	5	10	5
660	209	5000 r. pale blue ..	..	..	..	..	75	5	30	5	1·00	5	25	5
661	210	10000 r. carmine-red ..	..	..	..	..	60	5	50	5	80	5	2·00	5
662	210a	20000 r. pale chocolate	..	..	..	..	80	15	1·10	10	70	10	1·10	8
663	211	50 m. scarlet ..	..	..	..	..	2·75	15	2·00	40	†		1·60	25
664	212	100 m. blue ..	..	..	..	..	15	15	†		7·00	1·00	30	25
647/664		*Set of 18 (cheapest)*	..	..	..	..	3·50	90						

POSTAGE DUE (1949)

D665	D 5	10 r. mauve	.. ..	†	†	†	60 50
D666		20 r. black		†	†	†	9·00 7·50

Many of the watermark varieties listed above are also to be found upright or sideways on thick and thin papers, with or without three parallel green lines on the back.

Stamps which only show portions of "BRASIL" in letters 5 mm high repeated in echelon and no cross or star may be either W 203 or W 204.

For stamps with values in centavos and cruzeiros, see Nos. 751/68.

213 Amador Bueno

214 Brazilian Air Force Emblem

(Des R. Pinheiro. Eng V. F. da Silva. Recess)

1941 (20 Oct). *300th Anniv of Acclamation of Amador Bueno as King of São Paulo. W 92. P 11.*

665	213	400 r. black	..	.. ..	15	5
		a. Perf 12	..	.. ..	15	5

1941 (20 Oct). *Aviation Week. Recess. W 92. P 11.*

666	214	5400 r. slate-green	.. .. ..	50	30

AÉREO "10 Nov." 937-941

(214a)

215 Indo-Brazilian Cattle

1941 (10 Nov). *AIR. 4th Anniv of Constitution issued by Pres. Vargas. No. 645 optd with T 214a.*

			I. W 76	II. W 92
667	201	5400 r. grey-grn (R.)	10·00 10·00	40 25

(Des B. Lancetta. Eng W. B. de Freitas. Recess)

1942 (1 May). *2nd Agriculture and Cattle Show, Uberaba. P 12. Wmk "BRASIL CORREIO" and stars repeated in echelon. I. W 92 (letters 7 mm high). II. W 203 (letters 5 mm high).*

					I		II
668	215	200 r. blue	..	..	15	5	†
		a. Perf 11	..	..	12	5	†
669		400 r. chestnut	..	..	15	5 6·50 6·50
		a. Perf 11	..	..	12	5	†

216 Bernardino de Campos

217 Torch of Learning

218 Map of Brazil showing Goiania

(Des R. W. Pinto. Eng M. d'Oglio (1000 r.), W. B. de Freitas (1200 r.). Recess)

1942 (25 May). *Birth Centenaries of B. de Campos and of P. de Morais (lawyers and statesmen). T 216 and similar type. W 92. P 11.*

670		1000 r. red	.. ..	50	12
671		1200 r. blue (Prudente de Morais)	..	65	15

1942 (5 July). *8th National Education Congress, Goiania. Typo. W 92. P 11.*

672	217	400 r. chestnut	.. ..	10	5

1942 (5 July). *Founding of Goiania City. Typo. W 92. P 11.*

673	218	400 r. reddish violet ..	..	..	10	5

AÉREO "10 Nov." 937-942

Cr.$ 5,40

219 Congressional Seal (220)

1942 (30 Sept). *4th National Eucharistic Congress, São Paulo. P 11. Wmk "BRASIL CORREIO" and stars, repeated in echelon. I. W 92 (letters 7 mm high). II. W 203 (letters 5 mm high).*

			I		II
674	219	400 r. bistre-brown ..	12	5	2·25 2·00

New Currency

1942 (10 Nov). *AIR. 5th Anniv of Constitution issued by Pres. Vargas. No. 645 surch with T 220.*

			I W 76	II W 92
675	210	5 cr. 40, on 5400 r.		
		grey-green ..	6·00 6·00	35 15

221 Tributaries of R. Amazon

222 Early Brazilian Stamp

(Des R. Pinheiro. Die eng V. F. da Silva. Typo)

1943 (19 Mar). *400th Anniv of Discovery of R. Amazon. W 203. P 11.*

676	221	40 c. chestnut	.. .. ..	10	5

1943 (28 Mar). *Centenary of Petropolis. Typo. P 11. I. W 203 ("BRASIL CORREIO" and stars, repeated in echelon, letters 5 mm high). II. W 204 ("CASA+DA+MOE-DA+DO+BRASIL" and plain crosses, repeated in echelon, letters 5 mm high).*

			I		II
677	222	40 c. violet ..	..	20	8 38·00 —

223 Memorial Tablet

224 Map of S. America showing Brazil and Bolivia

1943 (11 May). *AIR. Visit of Pres. Higinio Morinigo of Paraguay. Litho. Wmk Wavy lines and "SECURITY" in circle. P 12½.*
678 **223** 1 cr. 20, blue 20 12

1943 (30 June). *AIR. Visit of Pres. Penaranda of Bolivia. Litho. W 165 of El Salvador ("wavy lines"). P 12½.*
679 **224** 1 cr. 20, black, green, red and yellow 20 15

225 "Bull's-eye"   **226**

1943 (1 Aug). *Centenary of First Brazilian Postage Stamps. T 225 and similar types. Recess. W 203. Imperf.*
680 **225** 30 c. black 20 12
681   60 c. black 20 12
682   90 c. black 20 15
MS682*a* 127×95 mm. Nos. 680/2. Wmk Wavy lines. No gum. Imperf .. .. 2·00 2·00

1943 (7 Aug). *AIR. Brazilian Stamp Centenary. Litho. W 165 of El Salvador ("wavy lines"). P 12½.*
683 **226** 1 cr. black and yellow .. .. 1·00 60
684   2 cr. black and bluish green .. .. 1·50 60
685   5 cr. black and dull rose .. .. 2·40 60
MS685*a* 155×155 mm. Nos 683/5. Imperf.
No gum .. .. 7·00 7·00
No. **MS**685*a* was printed in panes of six (3×2) and subdivided perf 12½. Each sheet is therefore perforated on two or three sides.

227 Book of the Law

228 Ubaldino do Amaral

1943 (13 Aug). *AIR. Inter-American Advocates Conference. Litho. W 165 of El Salvador ("wavy lines"). P 12½.*
686 **227** 1 cr. 20, carmine and red-brown .. 10 5

1943 (27 Aug). *Birth Centenary of Ubaldino do Amaral. Typo. P 11. Wmk "BRASIL CORREIO" and stars, repeated in echelon.* I. *W 92 (letters 7 mm high).* II. *W 203 (letters 5 mm high).*

		I		II	
687	**228** 40 c. grey	10	8	3·00	1·90

229 Indo-Brazilian Cattle   **230** Justice and Seal

1943 (30 Aug). *9th Cattle Show, Bahia. Recess. W 203. P 11.*
688 **229** 40 c. red-brown .. .. .. 15 8·

1943 (30 Aug). *Centenary of Institute of Brazilian Lawyers. Typo. W 203. P 11 or 11½.*
689 **230** 2 cr. rose-carmine 20 12

231 Santa Casa de Misericordia Hospital

232 J. Barbosa Rodrigues

1943 (7 Nov). *4th Centenary of Santa Casa de Misericordia de Santos. Recess. W 203. P 11.*
690 **231** 1 cr. light blue 12 5

(Des R. Trompovski. Typo)

1943 (13 Nov). *Birth Centenary of Barbosa Rodrigues (botanist). W 203. P 11.*
691 **232** 40 c. bluish green 10 5

233 Pedro Americo   **AÉREO**

40 Cts.

(234)

1943 (16 Dec). *Birth Centenary of Americo (artist and author). Typo. W 203. P 11.*
692 **233** 40 c. orange-brown 10 5

1944 (3 Jan). *AIR. No. 629 surch as T 234.*
693 **188** 20 c. on 400 r.+200 r. (R.) 15 5
694   40 c. on 400 r.+200 r. 15 5
695   60 c. on 400 r.+200 r. (R.) 25 15
696   1 cr. on 400 r.+200 r. 35 15
         a. Black ptg omitted .. ..
697   1 cr. 20 on 400 r.+200 r. (R.) .. 40 15
693/697 *Set of 5* .. .. .. 1·10 50

235 Gen. Carneiro and Defenders of Lapa

236 Baron do Rio Branco

1944 (9 Feb). *50th Anniv of Siege of Lapa. Recess.* W **203**.
 P 11.
698 **235** 1 cr. 20, carmine 12 8

1944 (13 May). *Inauguration of Monument to Baron do Rio
Branco. Typo.* W **203**. P 11.
699 **236** 1 cr. blue 12 5

243 Woman and Map   244 L. L. Zamenhof

1945 (16 Apr). *Tenth Brazilian Esperanto Congress, Rio de
Janeiro. Litho.* W **204**. P 11. (a) *POSTAGE.*
706 **243** 40 c. turquoise-green 8 8
 (b) *AIR*
707 **244** 1 cr. 20, chocolate 12 8

237 Duke of Caxias   238 Emblem of
                          Y.M.C.A.

1944 (13 May). *Centenary of Pacification of Revolutionary
Uprising of 1842. Litho. No wmk.* P 11½ × 12.
700 **237** 1 cr. 20, blue-green & orge-yell . . 15 8

1944 (7 June). *Centenary of Young Men's Christian Association. Litho. No wmk.* P 11.
701 **238** 40 c. blue, scarlet and yellow . . 8 5

245 Bookplate   246 S. America   247 Baron do Rio
                                      Branco

1945 (20 Apr). *Birth Centenary of Baron do Rio Branco
(statesman). Litho.* W **204**. P 11. (a) *POSTAGE.*
708 **245** 40 c. lavender 8 5
 (b) *AIR*
709 **246** 1 cr. 20, brown-purple 10 5
710 **247** 5 cr. reddish purple 25 12

239 Rio Grande Chamber of   240 "Bartolomeo de
      Commerce   Gusmao and the
                              Aerostat" by
                              Bernardino de Souza
                              Pereira

1944 (25 Sept). *Centenary of Founding of Rio Grande Chamber of Commerce. Recess.* W **204**. P 11.
702 **239** 40 c. yellow-brown 8 5

1944 (23 Oct). *AIR. Air Week. Recess.* W **204**. P 11.
703 **240** 1 cr. 20, carmine 10 5

248 "Glory"   249 "Victory"

250 "Co-operation"

241 Martim F. R. de   242 Meeting between
    Andrada   Caxias and Canabarro

1945 (30 Jan). *Death Centenary of Martim de Andrada
(statesman). Recess.* W **204**. P 11.
704 **241** 40 c. blue 8 5

1945 (18 Mar). *Centenary of Pacification of Rio Grande do
Sul. Litho.* W **204**. P 11.
705 **242** 40 c. ultramarine 8 5

1945 (8 May). *Victory of the United Nations. As* T **248/50**
(symbolic designs). Recess. W **204**. *Roul.*
711   20 c. reddish violet 5 5
712   40 c. carmine 8 5
713   1 cr. orange 10 5
714   2 cr. greenish blue 15 5
715   5 cr. dull green 40 15
711/715 *Set of 5* 70 25
 Designs: *Vert*—20 c. "Tranquillity" (*inscr* "SAUDADE").
Horiz—2 cr. "Peace" (*inscr* "PAZ").

251 F. M. da Silva   252 Bahia Institute

1945 (30 May). *150th Birth Anniv of Francisco Manoel da Silva (composer of Brazilian National Anthem). Typo. P 11½–12. Wmk "CASA+DA+MOEDA+DO+BRASIL".*
I. *W 90 (with Maltese Crosses, repeated in vert columns).*
II. *W 204 (with plain crosses, repeated in echelon).*

		I		II	
716 251	40 c. carmine	8	5	50	50

1945 (30 May). *50th Anniv of Founding of Bahia Institute of Geography and History. Typo. W 204. P 11.*
717 **252** 40 c. blue   8   5

253 Shoulder Flash   255 "V" Sign and Flashes

254 U.S. Flag and Flashes   256 Wireless Mast and Map

1945 (18 July). *Return of Brazilian Expeditionary Force. T 253/5 and similar designs. Litho. W 204. P 11.*
718	20 c. blue, red and green	..	5	5
719	40 c. green, yellow, blue and red	..	5	5
720	1 cr. blue, red, green and yellow	..	20	10
721	2 cr. blue, yellow, green and red	..	25	12
722	5 cr. blue, red, green and yellow	..	50	25
718/722	Set of 5	.. ..	75	50

Designs:—40 c. (24×28½ mm) B.E.F., "smoking snake" shoulder flash; 2 cr. (37×24 mm) Brazilian flag and shoulder flashes.

1945 (3 Sept). *Third Inter-American Radio-Communication Conference. Litho. W 204. P 11.*
723 **256** 1 cr. 20, black 20   8
     a. "1245" for "1945" ..   1·75   1·75

A 40 c. grey-lilac stamp showing Presidents Justo and Vargas and the bridge was prepared in 1945 to commemorate the opening of the international bridge between Argentina and Brazil. It was not issued but was later sold without franking value.

257 Admiral Saldanha da Gama   258 Princess Isabel d'Orleans-Braganza

1946 (7 Apr). *Birth Centenary of Admiral da Gama. Litho. W 204. P 11.*
724 **257** 40 c. grey-black   5   5

(Des L. Campos. Eng M. d'Oglio. Recess)

1946 (29 July). *Birth Centenary of Princess Isabel d'Orleans-Braganza. No wmk. P 11.*
725 **258** 40 c. black   8   5

259 Posthorn, V and Envelope   261 P.O., Rio de Janeiro

260 Aeroplane over Bay of Rio de Janeiro   262 Proposed Columbus Lighthouse

(T **259**, litho Mint; T **260/1**, recess Waterlow)

1946 (2 Sept). *5th Postal Union Congress of the Americas and Spain.* (a) *W 204. P 11.*
726 **259** 40 c. salmon and black 5   5

          (b) *No wmk. P 12½*
727	**260**	1 cr. 30, orange and green ..	..	8	5
728		1 cr. 70, orange and carmine	..	10	5
729	**261**	2 cr. blue and slate ..	..	10	5
730	**260**	2 cr. 20, orange and ultramarine	..	12	5
731	**261**	5 cr. blue and red-brown	..	35	25
732		10 cr. blue and violet	..	45	25
726/732	Set of 7	.. ..	..	1·10	65

(Des B. Lancetta. Litho)

1946 (14 Sept). *Construction of Columbus Lighthouse, Dominican Republic. W 204. P 11.*
733 **262** 5 cr. greenish blue   45   30

263 "Liberty"   264 Orchid   265 Gen. A. E. Gomes Carneiro

1946 (17 Sept). *New Constitution. Litho. W 204. P 11½×12.*
734 **263** 40 c. grey   5   5
     a. No wmk ..   ..   5·50

1946 (8 Nov). *4th National Exhibition of Orchids, Rio de Janeiro. Litho. W 204. P 11.*
735 **264** 40 c. ultramarine, red and yellow ..   12   5

(Des L. Campos. Eng W. B. Freitas. Recess)

1946 (6 Dec). *Birth Centenary of General A. E. Gomes Carneiro. No wmk. P 11×12.*
736 **265** 40 c. bluish green   5   5

266 Academy of Letters

267 Antonio de Castro Alves

(Eng M. d'Oglio. Recess)

1946 (14 Dec). *50th Anniv of Brazilian Academy of Letters. No wmk. P* 11.
737 **266** 40 c. blue 5 5

(Des L. Campos. Litho)

1947 (14 Mar). *Birth Centenary of Castro Alves (poet). W* **203**. *P* 11.
738 **267** 40 c. turquoise-green 5 5

268 Pres. González

(Des B. Lancetta. Die eng O. P. Borges. Typo)

1947 (26 June). *Visit of Chilean President. No wmk. P* 12×11.
739 **268** 40 c. chestnut 5 5

269 "Peace and Security"

270 "Dove of Peace"

(Des M. F. Pinheiro. Eng M. d'Oglio and O. P. Borges. Recess)

1947 (15 Aug). *Inter-American Defence Conference, Petropolis. No wmk.*
(a) POSTAGE. *P* 11×12
740 **269** 1 cr. 20, blue 10 5
(b) AIR. *P* 12×11
741 **270** 2 cr. 20, deep bluish green 12 8

271 Pres. Truman, Map of S. America and Statue of Liberty

(Des B. Lancetta. Die eng O. P. Borges. Typo)

1947 (1 Sept). *Visit of President Truman. No wmk. P* 12×11.
742 **271** 40 c. ultramarine 8 5

272 Pres. Eurico Gaspar Dutra

273 Woman and Child

(Des and eng W. B. de Freitas. Recess)

1947 (Sept)–**48**. *Pres. Dutra Commemoration. P* 11.
(a) W **204**
743 **272** 20 c. green (18.9) 5 5
744 40 c. carmine (18.9) 5 5
745 1 cr. 20, pale ultramarine (7.9) .. 10 5
(b) W **203**
746 **272** 20 c. green 30 15
(c) AIR. *Miniature sheet. No gum. Imperf*
MS746a 130×75 mm. Nos. 743/5 but inscr "AEREO" (14.12.48) .. .. 8·00 8·00

(Des M. F. Pinheiro. Die eng A. M. Barbosa. Typo)

1947 (10 Oct). *Children's Week. First Brazilian Convention of Infant Welfare and Pediatrics. No wmk. P* 11.
747 **273** 40 c. ultramarine 5 5

274 Icarus

1947 (15 Nov). OBLIGATORY TAX. *"Week of the Wing" Aviation Fund. Typo. W* **203**. *P* 11.
748 **274** 40 c. +10 c. red-orange 8 5

275 Santos Dumont Monument, St. Cloud, France

276 Arms of Minas Geraes

277 Rio de Janeiro and Rotary Symbol

(Des B. Lancetta. Die eng O. P. Borges. Typo)

1947 (15 Nov). AIR. *Homage to Santos Dumont. No wmk. P* 11×12.
749 **275** 1 cr. 20, chestnut and yellow-green 12 5

(Des Hugo de Castro. Eng A. J. Smith. Recess)

1947 (12 Dec). *50th Anniv of Founding of City of Belo Horizonte. W* **203**. *P* 11.
750 **276** 1 cr. 20, carmine 8 5

1947–54. *Types of 1941–46, but values in centavos or cruzeiro.* P 11.

(a) W 203 ("BRASIL CORREIO" and stars, repeated in echelon, letters 5 mm high)

751	205	2 c. sage-green (1949)	.. ..	5	5
752		5 c. drab (1950?)	.. ..	5	5
753		10 c. turquoise-green (1948)	..	5	5
754	206	20 c. chestnut	..	5	5
755		30 c. claret (1949)	.. ..	5	5
756		40 c. light blue	..	5	5
757		50 c. red (1949)	..	5	5
758	207	60 c. reddish violet (1948)	..	5	5
759		70 c. pale rose-red (1954)	..	5	5
760		1 cr. grey	.. ..	5	5
761		1 cr. 20, dull blue (1948)	..	5	5
762	208	2 cr. slate-purple (1948)	..	8	5
763	209	5 cr. pale blue (1949)	..	15	5
764	210	10 cr. carmine (1950?)	..	20	5
765	–	20 cr. brown (1950)	..	40	5
		a. Perf 13½		50	8
766	211	50 cr. brown-red (1951)	..	1·75	15
		a. Perf 13½	..	1·75	20
751/766		*Set of 16*	..	2·75	75

(b) W 204 ("CASA + DA + MOEDA + DO + BRASIL" and plain crosses repeated in echelon)

767	206	40 c. light blue (1947)	.. ..	10·00	3·75
768	207	1 cr. 20, dull blue (1947)	..	1·25	80

As with the 1941–46 issues, some values are to be found with three parallel green lines on the back. This practice was discontinued in 1949.

(Des B. Lancetta. Eng R. da Fonseca. Recess)

1948 (16 May). *AIR. Rotary Congress.* P 11.

769	277	1 cr. claret	.. ..	12	10
770		3 cr. 80, slate-violet	..	25	15

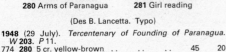

278 Globe   279 Quitandinha Hotel

(Des Arnau. Litho)

1948 (10 July). *International Industrial and Commercial Exhibition, Petropolis.* W 203. P 11. (a) POSTAGE.

771	278	40 c. green and mauve	.. ..	5	5

(b) AIR

772	279	1 cr. 20, reddish brown & chestnut	10	5
773		3 cr. 80, lilac and slate-violet	..	20	10

280 Arms of Paranagua   281 Girl reading

(Des B. Lancetta. Typo)

1948 (29 July). *Tercentenary of Founding of Paranagua.* W 203. P 11.

774	280	5 cr. yellow-brown	.. ..	45	20

(Des V. F. da Silva. Litho)

1948 (1 Aug). *National Children's Campaign.* W 203. P 11.

775	281	40 c. green	.. ..	8	5

282 The Three Muses (after   283 President Berres
Henrique Bernardelli)

1948 (13 Aug). *AIR. National School of Music Centenary. Recess.* P 11.

776	282	1 cr. 20, blue..	.. ..	10	5

(Des B. Lancetta. Typo)

1948 (2 Sept). *AIR. Visit of President of Uruguay.* P 11.

777	283	1 cr. 70, light blue	.. ..	10	5

284 Ram   285 Congress Seal

(Des B. Lancetta. Typo)

1948 (10 Oct). *AIR. International Cattle Show, Bagé.* W 203. P 12×11.

778	284	1 cr. 20, orange	.. ..	20	5

(Des J. Heitgen. Eng R. A. da Silva. Recess)

1948 (28 Oct). *AIR. 5th National Eucharistic Congress, Porto Alegre.* P 11.

779	285	1 cr. 20, red-purple ..	.. ..	10	5

286 "Tiradentes"   287 Crab and Globe
(*trans.* "Tooth-drawer")

(Des R. Pinheiro. Typo)

1948 (12 Nov). *Birth Bicentenary of A. J. J. da Silva Xavier (patriot).* W 203. P 11.

780	286	40 c. orange-brown ..	.. ..	5	5

(Des J. Graça. Litho)

1948 (14 Dec). *Anti-Cancer Campaign.* W 203. P 11.

781	287	40 c. reddish purple ..	.. ..	5	5

288 Teacher

(Des B. Lancetta. Litho)

1949 (3 Jan). *Campaign for Adult Education.* W 203. P 12×11.

782	288	60 c. reddish purple and mauve	..	8	5

289 Battle of Guararapes   290 St. Francis of Paula Church

294 Aeroplane and Air Force Badge   295 Joaquim Nabuco

(Des B. Lancetta. Litho)

1949 (15 Feb). *300th Anniv of Second Battle of Guararapes.* T 289 *and similar type.* W 203. P 12×11½. (a) *POSTAGE.*

783	289	60 c. light blue	.. .. ..	15	8

(b) AIR. *View of Guararapes, inscr "AEREO"*

784	–	1 cr. 20, pink	.. .. ..	25	10

(Des B. Lancetta. Eng R. A. da Silva. Recess)

1949 (8 Mar). *Bicentenary of Ouro Fino.* P 11×12.

785	290	60 c. brown ..	.. .. ..	5	5
MS785a		70×89 mm. No. 785. Imperf	..	4·00	4·00

(Des B. Lancetta. Eng B. R. Fonseca. Recess)

1949 (18 June). *Homage to the Brazilian Air Force. Imperf.*

789	294	60 c. bluish violet	.. .. ..	5	5

(Des and eng W. G. de Freitas. Recess)

1949 (30 Aug). AIR. *Birth Centenary of Joaquim Nabuco (lawyer and author).* P 12.

790	295	3 cr. 80, purple	.. .. ..	20	12

291 Father Nobrega   292 De Souza and Indians

(T 291 des J. Campos, eng A. Faria. T 292 des E. P. Merdes, eng A. J. Smith. Recess)

1949 (29 Mar). *400th Anniv of Founding of Bahia.*

(a) POSTAGE. *Imperf*

786	291	60 c. violet ..	.. .. ..	5	5

(b) AIR. P 11×12

787	292	1 cr. 20, blue	.. .. ..	10	5

296 "Revelation"   297 Globe

(Des A. S. Lopes. Litho)

1949 (22 Oct). *First Sacerdotal Vocational Congress, Bahia.* W 203. P 11×12.

791	296	60 c. magenta	.. .. ..	5	5

(Des M. F. Pinheiro. Typo)

1949 (30 Oct). *75th Anniv of Universal Postal Union.* W 203. P 12×11.

792	297	1 cr. 50, blue..	.. .. ..	12	8

298 Ruy Barbosa   299 Cardinal Arcoverde

293 Franklin D. Roosevelt

(Des and eng W. B. de Freitas. Recess)

1949 (20 May). AIR. *Homage to Franklin D. Roosevelt. No wmk. Imperf.*

788	293	3 cr. 80, blue..	.. .. ..	25	15
MS788a		85×110 mm. No. 788	.. ..	1·75	1·75
MS788b		As above but W 203	.. ..	2·75	2·75

(Des B. Lancetta. Eng M. d'Oglio. Recess)

1949 (14 Dec). *Birth Centenary of Ruy Barbosa (statesman).* P 12.

793	298	1 cr. 20, carmine-red	.. ..	12	5

(Des M. F. Pinheiro. Litho)

1950 (27 Feb). *Birth Centenary of Cardinal Joaquim Arcoverde.* W 203. P 11×12.

794	299	60 c. rose	.. .. ..	5	5

300 "Agriculture and Industry"

301 "Sister of Mercy"

(Des D. Ratti and A. S. Lopes. Typo)

1950 (15 Mar). *75th Anniv of Arrival of Italian Immigrants.* W **203**. P 12×11.
795 **300** 60 c. claret 5 5

(Des B. Lancetta. Litho)

1950 (31 May). *Centenary of Establishment of "Sisters of Mercy".* W **203**. P 11×12.
796 **301** 60 c. turquoise-blue and black .. 5 5

302 Globe and Footballers

303 Stadium

(Des B. Lancetta and M. F. Pinheiro (797) and M. F. Pinheiro (others). Litho)

1950 (24 June). *4th World Football Championship, Rio de Janeiro. T* **302/3** *and similar type.* W **203**. P 11×12 (*vert*), 12×11 (*horiz*).

(*a*) POSTAGE
797 60 c. grey, light blue and ultramarine .. 15 8

(*b*) AIR. *Inscr* "CORREIO AEREO"
798 1 cr. 20, pale orange and ultramarine .. 30 8
799 5 cr. 80, yellow, green and light blue .. 55 15
Design: (*Vert*)—5 cr. 80, Linesman and flag.

304 Three Heads, Map and Graph

305 Line of People and Map

1950 (10 July). *National Survey, 1950.* W **203**.

(*a*) POSTAGE. Typo. P 12×11
800 **304** 60 c. claret 5 5

(*b*) AIR. Litho. P 11×12
801 **305** 1 cr. 20, red-brown 8 5

306 Oswaldo Cruz

307 Blumenau and Itajaí River

1950 (23 Aug). *5th International Microbiological Congress.* Litho. W **203**. P 11×12.
802 **306** 60 c. orange-brown 5 5

(Des W. Puntar and W. Granado. Litho)

1950 (9 Sept). *Centenary of Founding of Blumenau.* W **203**. P 12×11.
803 **307** 60 c. pink 5 5

308 Government Offices

309 Arms

(Des W. Puntar. Litho)

1950 (27 Sept). *Centenary of Amazon Province.* W **203**. P 12×11.
804 **308** 60 c. red 5 5

(Des A. S. Lopes. Litho)

1950 (24 Oct). *Centenary of Juiz de Fora City.* W **203**. P 11×12.
805 **309** 60 c. carmine-red 5 5

310 Post Office, Pernambuco

311 Arms of Joinville

1951 (Jan). *Inauguration of Post Office, Pernambuco.* Typo. W **203**. P 12×11.
806 **310** 60 c. carmine (30.1) 5 5
807 1 cr. 20, carmine (10.1) 8 5

(Des A. S. Lopes. Litho)

1951 (9 Mar). *Centenary of Founding of Joinville.* W **203**. P 11×12.
808 **311** 60 c. pale chestnut 5 5

312 S. Romero

313 De La Salle

1951 (21 Apr). *Birth Centenary of Sylvio Romero (poet).* Litho. **W 203.** P 11×12.
809 312 60 c. purple-brown 5 5

1951 (30 Apr). *Birth Tercentenary of Jean-Baptiste de la Salle (educational reformer).* Litho. **W 203.** P 11×12.
810 313 60 c. blue 5 5

314 Hearts and Flowers   **315** J. Caetano and Stage

1951 (13 May). *Mothers' Day.* Recess. **W 230.** P 11×12.
811 314 60 c. reddish purple 5 5

1951 (9 July). *First Brazilian Theatrical Congress.* Litho. **W 203.** P 12×11.
812 315 60 c. turquoise 5 5

316 O. A. Derby   **317** Crucifix and Congregation

1951 (23 July). *Birth Centenary of Derby (geologist).* Litho. **W 203.** P 11×12.
813 316 2 cr. slate 10 5

1951 (25 July). *Fourth Inter-American Catholic Education Congress.* Litho. **W 203.** P 11×12.
814 317 60 c. brown and buff .. 5 5

318 E. P. Martins and Map   **319** Penha Convent

1951 (16 Aug). *29th Anniv of First Rio de Janeiro–New York Flight.* Litho. **W 203.** P 12×11.
815 318 3 cr. 80, brown and pale green .. 25 10

1951 (8 Sept). *Fourth Centenary of Founding of Vitoria.* Litho. **W 203.** P 12×11.
816 319 60 c. brown and buff 5 5

320 Santos Dumont and Boys with Model Aeroplanes   **321** Wheat Harvesters

1951 (19 Oct). *"Week of the Wing" and 50th Anniv of Dumont's Flight over Paris.* **T 320** and another vert type inscr "1901–1951". P 11×12. (a) Litho. **W 203.**
817 60 c. purple-brown and orange .. 10 5

  (b) Recess. No wmk
818 3 cr. 80, slate-purple 20 8
Design:—3 cr. 80, Airship over Eiffel Tower, Paris.

1951 (10 Nov). *Wheat Festival, Bagé.* Litho. **W 203.** P 11×12.
819 321 60 c. bluish green and grey 8 5

322 Bible and Map   **323** Isabella the Catholic

(T **322/3** des B. Lancetta. Litho)

1951 (9 Dec). *Bible Day.* **W 203.** P 12×11.
820 322 1 cr, 20, orange-brown 10 5

1952 (10 Mar). *Fifth Birth Centenary of Isabella the Catholic.* **W 203.** P 11×12.
821 323 3 cr. 80, blue and pale blue 15 10

324 Henrique Oswald   **325** Map and Symbol of Labour

(Des B. Lancetta. Litho)

1952 (22 Apr). *Birth Centenary of Oswald (composer).* **W 203.** P 11×12.
822 324 60 c. brown 5 5

(Des A. S. Lopes. Litho)

1952 (30 Apr). *Fifth Conference of American Members of International Labour Organization.* **W 203.** P 11×12.
823 325 1 cr. 50, claret 10 5

326 Dr. L. Cardoso   **327** Gen. da Fonseca

(Des B. Lancetta. Litho)

1952 (2 May). *Birth Centenary of Cardoso (scientist) and 4th Brazilian Homoeopathic Congress, Porto Alegre.* **W 203.** P 11×12.
824 326 60 c. deep grey-blue.. .. 5 5

(Des B. Lancetta. Recess)

1952 (11 May). *Centenary of Telegraphs in Brazil. T 327 and similar vert portraits inscr "1852–1952". No wmk. P 11.*
825	2 cr. 40, rose-carmine	..	..	..	15	5
826	5 cr. blue	..	..	..	30	8
827	10 cr. deep blue-green	..	..	60	15

Portraits:—5 cr. Baron de Capanema; 10 cr. E. de Queiros.

328 L. de Albuquerque

329 Olympic Flame and Athletes

1952 (8 June). *Bicentenary of Mato Grosso City. Litho. W 203. P 11×12.*
| 828 | **328** | 1 cr. 20, bluish violet | .. | .. | 5 | 5 |

1952 (21 July). *50th Anniv of Fluminense Football Club. Litho. W 203. P 12×11.*
| 829 | **329** | 1 cr. 20, blue and light blue | .. | .. | 12 | 5 |

330 Councillor J. A. Saraiva

331 Emperor Pedro II

1952 (16 Aug). *Centenary of City of Terezina. Litho. W 203. P 11×12.*
| 830 | **330** | 60 c. mauve | .. | .. | .. | 5 | 5 |

1952 (3 Sept). *Stamp Day and Second Philatelic Exhibition, São Paulo. Litho. W 203. P 11×12.*
| 831 | **331** | 60 c. black and blue | .. | .. | 5 | 5 |

332 Globe, Staff and Bay of Rio de Janeiro

333 Dove, Globe and Flags

1952 (20 Sept). *Second American Congress of Industrial Medicine. Litho. W 203. P 12×11.*
| 832 | **332** | 3 cr. 80, dull green and purple-brown | 20 | 5 |

(Des M. F. Pinheiro. Litho)

1952 (24 Oct). *United Nations Day. W 203. P 12×11.*
| 833 | **333** | 3 cr. 80, blue | .. | .. | .. | 45 | 8 |

334 Compasses and Modern Buildings

335 D. A. Feijo (statesman)

1952 (8 Nov). *City Planning Day. Litho. W 203. P 12×11.*
| 834 | **334** | 60 c. yellow, green and blue | .. | 5 | 5 |

1952 (9 Nov). *Homage to D. A. Feijo. Litho. W 203. P 11×12.*
| 835 | **335** | 60 c. pale red-brown | .. | 5 | 5 |

336 Father Damien

337 R. Bernardelli

1952 (24 Nov)–53. *OBLIGATORY TAX. Leprosy Research Fund. Litho. W 203. P 12×11.*
| 836 | **336** | 10 c. orange-brown | .. | .. | 5 | 5 |
| 837 | | 10 c. pale yellow-green (30.11.53) | .. | 5 | 5 |

1952 (18 Dec). *Birth Centenary of Bernardelli (sculptor). Litho. W 203. P 12×11.*
| 838 | **337** | 60 c. deep grey-blue | .. | .. | 5 | 5 |

338 Arms of São Paulo and Settler

339 "Expansion"

(Des Koetz (1 cr. 20), Baldassari (2 cr. 80), Di Pretti (others). Litho)

1953 (25 Jan). *Fourth Centenary of São Paulo. T 338 and vert designs as T 339. W 203. P 11.*
839	**338**	1 cr. 20, black and olive-brown	..	8	5
840	–	2 cr. bronze-green and pale yellow	..	75	15
841	–	2 cr. 80, red-brown and orange	..	15	5
842	**339**	3 cr. 80, brown and apple-green	..	15	8
843		5 cr. 80, deep blue and pale green	..	20	8
839/843		Set of 5	..	..	1·10	35

Designs:—2 cr. Coffee blossom and berries; 2 cr. 80, Monk planting tree.

340

341 J. Ramalho

(Des B. Lancetta. Litho)

1953 (22 Feb). *Sixth Brazilian Accountancy Congress, Porto Alegre.* W **203**. P 12×11.
844 **340** 1 cr. 20, brown and pale chestnut .. 8 5

(Des A. S. Lopes. Eng R. A. da Silva. Recess)

1953 (8 Apr). *Fourth Centenary of Santo André.* W **92**. P 11½.
845 **341** 60 c. blue 5 5

342 A. Reis and Plan of Bello Horizonte

343 Admiral Saldanha

(Des W. Puntar. Photo)

1953 (6 May). *Birth Centenary of Reis (engineer).* W **92**. P 11½.
846 **342** 1 cr. 20, deep chestnut 5 5

(Des B. Lancetta. Photo)

1953 (16 May). *Fourth Voyage of Circumnavigation by Training Ship "Admiral Saldanha".* W **92**. P 11½.
847 **343** 1 cr. 50, ultramarine 10 5

344 Viscount de Itaborahy

345 Lamp and Rio–Petropolis Highway

(Des W. Puntar. Photo)

1953 (5 July). *Centenary of Bank of Brazil. Photo.* W **92**. P 11½.
848 **344** 1 cr. 20, bluish violet .. 8 5

(Des W. Puntar. Photo)

1953 (14 July). *Tenth International Nursing Congress, Petropolis.* W **92**. P 11½.
849 **345** 1 cr. 20, grey-olive 8 5

346 Bay of Rio de Janeiro

347 Ministry of Health & Education, Rio de Janeiro

(Des B. Lancetta. Photo)

1953 (15 July). *Fourth World Conference of Young Baptists.* W **92**. P 11½.
850 **346** 3 cr. 80, deep bluish green 15 8

(Des and eng R. A. da Silva. Recess)

1953 (1 Aug). *Stamp Day and First National Philatelic Exhibition of Education.* W **92**. P 11½.
851 **347** 1 cr. 20, deep turquoise-green .. 8 5

348 Arms and Map

349 Maria Quiteria de Jesus

(Des W. Puntar. Photo)

1953 (15 Aug). *Centenary of City of Jaú.* W **92**. P 11½.
852 **348** 1 cr. 20, violet 8 5

(Des M. F. Pinheiro and J. R. da Silva. Photo)

1953 (21 Aug). *Death Centenary of Maria Quiteria de Jesus.* W **92**. P 11½.
853 **349** 60 c. ultramarine 5 5

350 President Odria

351 Caxias leading Troops

352 Quill-pen and Map

(Des B. Lancetta. Photo)

1953 (25 Aug). *Visit of President Odria of Peru.* W **92**. P 11½.
854 **350** 1 cr. 40, brown-lake 8 5

(60 c., 5 cr. 80 des and eng M. d'Oglio and A. J. Smith; recess. Others des W. Granado; photo)

1953 (25 Aug). *150th Birth Anniv of Duke of Caxias.* T **351** and similar vert designs inscr "1803–1953". W **92**. P 11½.
855 60 c. deep bluish green 5 5
856 1 cr. 20, reddish purple 5 5
857 1 cr. 70, deep turquoise 10 5
858 3 cr. 80, brown-lake 15 8
859 5 cr. 80, blackish violet 25 8
Designs:—1 cr. 20, Tomb; 1 cr. 70, 5 cr. 80, Portrait of Caxais; 3 cr. 80, Coat-of-arms.

(Des W. Puntar. Photo)

1953 (12 Sept). *Fifth National Congress of Journalists, Curitiba.* W **92**. P 11½.
860 **352** 60 c. ultramarine 5 5

353 H. Hora

354 President Somoza

355 A. de Saint-Hilaire

(Des W. Granado. Litho)

1953 (17 Sept). *Birth Centenary of Hora (painter).* W **203**. P 11×12.
861 **353** 60 c. reddish purple & yellow-orge .. 5 5

(Des B. Lancetta. Photo)

1953 (24 Sept). *Visit of President Somoza of Nicaragua.*
W **92**. P 11½.
862 354 1 cr. 40, brown-purple 8 5

(Des W. Puntar. Photo)

1953 (30 Sept). *Death Centenary of A. de Saint-Hilaire (explorer and botanist).* W **92**. P 11½.
863 355 1 cr. 20, lake 8 5

356 J. do Patrocinio and "Spirit of Emancipation"

357 Clock Tower, Crato

358 C. de Abreu

(Des P. Amenta. Photo)

1953 (9 Oct). *Death Centenary of J. do Patrocinio (slavery abolitionist).* P 11½.
864 356 60 c. deep slate 5 5

(Des W. Puntar. Photo)

1953 (17 Oct). *Centenary of Crato City.* W **92**. P 11½.
865 357 60 c. deep blue-green 5 5

(Des B. Lancetta. Photo)

1953 (23 Oct). *Birth Centenary of Abreu (historian).* W **92**. P 11½.
866 358 60 c. bright blue 5 5
867 5 cr. bluish violet 15 8

359 "Justice"

360 Harvesting

(Des O. Maia. Photo)

1953 (17 Nov). *50th Anniv of Treaty of Petropolis.* W **92**. P 11½.
868 359 60 c. indigo 5 5
869 1 cr. 20, reddish purple 10 5

(Des O. Maia. Photo)

1953 (29 Nov). *Third National Wheat Festival, Erechim.* W **92**. P 11½.
870 360 60 c. deep bluish green 5 5

361 Teacher and Pupils

362 Porters with Trays of Coffee Beans

363 A. de Gusmão

(Des O. Maia. Photo)

1953 (14 Dec). *First National Congress of Elementary School-teachers.* W **92**. P 11½.
871 361 60 c. vermilion 5 5

(Des W. Puntar. Photo)

1953 (19 Dec)–**54**. *Centenary of State of Parana.* Inscr "CENTENARIO DO PARANA". W **92**. P 11½.
872 – 2 cr. orange-brown & black (18.1.54) 25 10
  a. On buff paper (23.12.54) .. 15 10
873 362 5 cr. orange and black 25 5
Portrait : *Vert*—2 cr. Z. de Góis e Vasconellos.
In No. 872 "BRASIL CORREIO" in the wmk measures 21 mm and in No. 872a it measures 24 mm.

1954 (13 Jan). *Death Bicentenary of Gusmão (statesman).* Photo. W **92**. P 11½.
874 363 1 cr. 20, purple 5 5

364 Growth of São Paulo

365 São Paulo and Arms

1954 (25 Jan–25 Feb). *Fourth Centenary of São Paulo (Second issue).* T **364/5** and other designs similarly inscr. Photo (1 cr. 20), recess (others). W **92**. P 11½×11 (vert) or 11×11½ (horiz).
875 364 1 cr. 20, chocolate (25.2) 15 5
876 – 2 cr. magenta (25.2) 25 5
877 – 2 cr. 80, slate-violet 15 5
878 365 3 cr. 80, myrtle-green 20 5
879 5 cr. 80, red 20 5
875/879 *Set of 5* 85 20
Designs: *Vert*—2 cr. Priest, pioneer and Indian; 2 cr. 80, J. de Anchieta.

366 J. F. Vieira, A. V. de Negreiros, A. F. Camarao and H. Dias

367 São Paulo and Allegorical Figure

(Des W. Puntar. Photo)

1954 (18 Feb). *Third Centenary of Restoration of Pernambuco. Granite paper. No wmk.* P 11×11½.
880 366 1 cr. 20, bright blue 8 5

1954 (24 Feb). *Tenth International Congress of Scientific Organization, São Paulo. Photo. Granite paper. No wmk.* P 11×11½.
881 367 1 cr. 50, reddish purple 8 5

368 Grapes and Winejar

369 Immigrants' Monument

1954 (27 Feb). *Grape Festival, Rio Grande do Sul. Photo. Granite paper. No wmk. P 11½×11.*
882 368 40 c. lake 5 5

1954 (28 Feb). *Immigrants' Monument, Caxias do Sul. Photo. Granite paper. No wmk. P 11½×11.*
883 369 60 c. violet 5 5

370 First Locomotive used in Brazil

VISITA DO PRESIDENTE DA REPÚBLICA LIBANESA · 1954

371 President Chamoun

1954 (30 Apr). *Centenary of Brazilian Railways. Photo. Granite paper. No wmk. P 11×11½.*
884 370 40 c. scarlet 5 5

1954 (12 May). *Visit of President of Lebanon. Photo. Granite paper. No wmk. P 11½×11.*
885 371 1 cr. 50, brown-purple 8 5

372 Marist School

373 Vel Marcelino Champagnat

1954 (6 June). *50th Anniv of Marist Schools. Photo. Granite paper. No wmk. P 11×11½ (60 c.) or 11½×11 (1 cr. 20).*
886 372 60 c. bluish violet 5 5
887 373 1 cr. 20, bright blue 8 5

374 Apolonia Pinto

375 Admiral Tamandare

1954 (21 June). *Birth Centenary of Apolonia Pinto (actress). Photo. Granite paper. No wmk. P 11½×11.*
888 374 1 cr. 20, emerald 5 5

1954–61. *Various portraits as T 375. Photo. P 11×11½.*

(a) W 203

889	375	2 c. violet-blue (5.8.54) ..	5	5
890		5 c. oranged-red (5.8.54) ..	5	5
891		10 c. emerald (5.8.54) ..	5	5
892	–	20 c. claret (2.7.54) ..	5	5
893	–	30 c. deep bluish green (1.8.54) ..	5	5
894	–	40 c. deep rose-red (2.7.54) ..	5	5
895	–	50 c. deep lilac (1.10.54) ..	5	5
896	–	60 c. dull blue-green (1.8.54)	5	5
897	–	90 c. red-orange (4.1.55) ..	25	5
898	–	1 cr. red-brown (20.10.54)	12	5
899	–	1 cr. 50, pale blue (1.10.54) ..	5	5
		a. W 92	1·75	40
900	–	2 cr. deep bluish green (25.4.56) ..	15	5
901	–	5 cr. bright purple (19.5.56)	5	5
902	–	10 cr. emerald (13.4.60) ..	8	5
903	–	20 cr. scarlet (23.9.59) ..	12	5
904	–	50 cr. bright blue (20.10.59)	25	5

(b) W 204

904a	–	1 cr. brown (23.8.61) ..	10	5
904b	–	2 cr. deep bluish green (23.8.61) ..	15	5
904c	–	5 cr. bright purple (22.8.61)	35	5
904d	–	10 cr. emerald (22.8.61) ..	55	5
889/904		Set of 16	1·20	60

Portraits:—20 c., 30 c., 40 c. O. Cruz; 50 c., 60 c., 90 c. J. Murtinho, 1 cr., 1 cr. 50, 2 cr. Duke of Caxias; 5 cr., 10 cr. R. Barbosa; 20 cr., 50 cr. J. Bonifacio.

376 Boy Scout 377 B. Fernandes 378 Cardinal Piazza

(Des O. Maia. Photo)

1954 (2 Aug). *International Scout Encampment. São Paulo. Granite paper. No wmk. P 11½×11.*
905 376 1 cr. 20, ultramarine 12 5

1954 (15 Aug). *Third Centenary of City of Sorocaba. Photo. Granite paper. No wmk. P 11½×11.*
906 377 60 c. deep orange-red 5 5

1954 (2 Sept). *Visit of Cardinal Piazza (Papal Legate). Photo. Granite paper. No wmk. P 11½×11.*
907 378 4 cr. 20, orange-red 12 5

379 Virgin and Map

380 Benjamin Constant and Braille Book

1954 (Sept). *Marian Year. T 379 and another design inscr "ANO MARIANO". Photo. Granite paper. No wmk. P 11½×11.*
908 60 c. carmine-lake (6.9) 15 5
909 1 cr. 20, ultramarine (8.9) .. 15 5
Design: *Vert*—1 cr. 20, Virgin and globe.
No. 909 also commemorates the Centenary of the Proclamation of the Dogma of the Immaculate Conception.

1954 (27 Sept). *Centenary of Education for the Blind in Brazil. Photo. Granite paper. No wmk. P 11×11½.*
910 380 60 c. deep turquoise-green 5 5

381 Battle Scene   382 Admiral Barroso

1954 (6 Oct). *150th Birth Anniv of Admiral Barroso. Photo. Granite paper. No wmk.* P 11×11½ (40 c.) *or* 11½×11 (60 c.).
911 **381** 40 c. purple-brown 5 5
912 **382** 60 c. violet 5 5

383 S. Hahnemann (physician)   384 Nisia Floresta   385 Ears of Wheat

1954 (8 Oct). *First World Congress of Homoeopathy. Photo. Granite paper.* P 11½×11.
913 **383** 2 cr. 70, deep turquoise-green .. 8 5

1954 (12 Oct). *Removal from France to Brazil of Ashes of Nisia Floresta (suffragist). Photo. Granite paper. No wmk.* P 11½×11.
914 **384** 60 c. dull magenta 5 5

1954 (22 Oct). *Fourth Wheat Festival, Carazinho. Photo. Granite paper. No wmk.* P 11½×11.
915 **385** 60 c. brown-olive 5 5

386 Globe and Basketball Player   387 Girl, Torch and Spring Flowers   388 Father Bento

1954 (23 Oct). *Second World Basketball Championship. Photo. Granite paper. No wmk.* P 11½×11.
916 **386** 1 cr. 40, deep orange-red 10 5

(Des M. F. Pinheiro. Photo)

1954 (6 Nov). *Sixth Spring Games.* W **203.** P 11½×11.
917 **387** 60 c. chocolate 8 5

(Des W. Puntar. Photo)

1954 (22 Nov)–**66.** *OBLIGATORY TAX. Leprosy Research Fund.* W **203.** P 11½.
918 **388** 10 c. ultramarine 5 5
919   10 c. magenta (24.11.55) 5 5
919a   10 c. orange-red (24.11.57) .. 5 5
919b   10 c. green (24.11.58) 5 5
919c   10 c. reddish lilac (24.11.61) .. 5 5
919d   10 c. red-brown (24.11.62) 5 5
919e   10 c. deep slate (24.11.63) 5 5
919f   2 cr. carmine-lake (24.11.64) .. 5 5
919g   2 cr. slate-lilac (24.11.65) 5 5
919h   2 cr. orange (24.11.66) 5 5
918/919h *Set of 10* 35 25
Nos. 919f/h are inscribed "Correios do Brasil".
For 5 c. value in T **388**, see No. 1238.

389 S. Francisco Power Station   390 Itutinga Power Plant

1955 (15 Jan). *Inauguration of São Francisco Hydro-Electric Station. Photo.* W **203.** P 11×11½.
920 **389** 60 c. deep brown-orange .. 5 5

1955 (3 Feb). *Inauguration of Itutinga Hydro-Electric Station. Photo.* W **203.** P 11×11½.
921 **390** 40 c. blue 5 5

391 Rotary Symbol and Rio Bay   392 Aviation Symbols

(Des W. Puntar. Photo)

1955 (23 Feb). *50th Anniv of Rotary International.* W **203.** P 11½.
922 **391** 2 cr. 70, blackish blue-green .. 8 5

(Des W. Granado. Photo)

1955 (13 Mar). *Third Aeronautical Congress, São Paulo.* W **203.** P 11½.
923 **392** 60 c. deep bluish green 5 5

393 Fausto Cardoso Palace   394 Arms of Botucatú

1955 (17 Mar). *Centenary of Aracajú. Photo.* W **203.** P 11×11½.
924 **393** 40 c. chestnut 5 5

(Des B. de Miranda. Photo)

1955. *Centenary of Botucatú.* W **203.** P 11½.
925 **394** 60 c. deep chestnut (11.5) 5 5
926   1 cr. 20, emerald (14.4) 5 5

395 Young Athletes

396 Marshal da Fonseca

(Des W. Puntar. Photo)

1955 (30 Apr). *Fifth Children's Games, Rio de Janeiro. Granite paper. No wmk. P 11½.*
927 **395** 60 c. deep chestnut 10 5

1955 (12 May). *Birth Centenary of Marshal da Fonseca. Photo. W 203. P 11½.*
928 **396** 60 c. deep violet 5 5

397

398 Cardinal Masella

1955 (17 July). *Thirty-sixth International Eucharistic Congress. T 397 and similar vert design. Recess (1 cr. 40) or photo (2 cr. 70). Granite paper. No wmk. P 11½.*
929 **397** 1 cr. 40, deep green 5 5
930 — 2 cr. 70, lake (St Pascoal) 5 5

1955 (17 July). *Visit of Cardinal Masella (Papal Legate) to Eucharistic Congress. Recess. Granite paper. No wmk. P 11½.*
931 **398** 4 cr. 20, blue 12 5

399 Gymnasts

(Des W. Puntar. Eng G. de Souza Ferreira and N. M. dos Santos. Recess)

1955 (12 Nov). *Seventh Spring Games. Granite paper. No wmk. P 11½.*
932 **399** 60 c. reddish purple 10 5

400 Monteiro Lobato

401 A. Lutz

(T **400/1** des B. Lancetta. Eng G. de Souza Ferreira and N. M. dos Santos. Recess)

1955 (8 Dec). *Honouring M. Lobato (author). Granite paper. No wmk. P 11½.*
933 **400** 40 c. myrtle-green 5 5

1955 (18 Dec). *Birth Centenary of Lutz. Granite paper. No wmk. P 11½.*
934 **401** 60 c. myrtle-green 5 5

402 T. C. Vilagran Cabrita

403 Salto Grande Dam

(Des M. F. Pinheiro. Photo)

1955 (22 Dec). *Centenary of 1st Battalion of Engineers. W 203. P 11½.*
935 **402** 60 c. ultramarine 5 5

1956 (15 Jan). *Salto Grande Dam. Photo. Granite paper. No wmk. P 11½.*
936 **403** 60 c. orange-red 5 5

404

405 Arms of Mococa

1956 (14 Apr). *Eighteenth International Geographical Congress, Rio de Janeiro. Photo. Granite paper. No wmk. P 11½.*
937 **404** 1 cr. 20, ultramarine 5 5

(Des M. Dracxler. Photo)

1956 (17 Apr). *Centenary of Mococa, São Paulo. W 204. P 11½.*
938 **405** 60 c. deep orange-red 5 5

406 Girls Running

407 Aeroplane and Map

1956 (28 Apr). *Children's Games. Photo. Granite paper. No wmk. P 11½.*
939 **406** 2 cr. 50, blue 10 5

(Des J. F. da Silva. Photo)

1956 (12 June). *25th Anniv of National Air Mail. W 203. P 11½.*
940 **407** 3 cr. 30, ultramarine 8 5

408 Rescue Work

409 Franca Cathedral

413 Baron da Bocaina and Express Letter

414 Commemorative Stamp from Panama

1956 (2 July). *Centenary of Firemen's Corps of Rio de Janeiro. Photo. W 92. P 11½.*
941 408 2 cr. 50, rose-red 5 5
a. On buff paper 10 5

(Des W. Granado. Eng G. de Souza Ferreira and N. M. dos Santos. Recess)

1956 (7 Sept). *Centenary of City of Franca. W 203. P 11½.*
942 409 2 cr. 50, deep blue 5 5

1956 (8 Oct). *Birth Centenary of Baron da Bocaina. Recess. W 204. P 11½.*
947 413 2 cr. 50, red-brown 5 5

(Des W. Puntar and B. Lancetta. Photo)

1956 (12 Oct). *Pan-American Congress, Panama. W 203. P 11½.*
948 414 3 cr. 30, black and green 10 5

410 Open Book with Inscription and Map

410a Father J. B. Marcelino Champagna

415 Dumont's Aeroplane

416 Volta Redonda Steel Mill, and Molten Steel

(Des G. de Souza Ferreira. Photo)

(2 cr. 50 des W. Granado. Photo. 3 cr. 30 des B. Lancetta, eng G. Souza Ferreira and N. M. dos Santos. Recess)

1956 (8 Sept). *50th Anniv of Arrival of Marist Brothers in North Brazil. W 203. P 11½.* (a) POSTAGE.
943 410 2 cr. 50, ultramarine 5 5

(b) AIR
944 410a 3 cr. 30, reddish purple 8 5

1956 (14 Oct). *AIR. 50th Anniv of Dumont's First Heavier than Air Flight. W 203. P 11½.*
MS948a 125×156 mm. 415 3 cr. brown-red (in block of four) 45 45

1956 (16 Oct). *AIR. Santos Dumont Commemoration. W 203. P 11½.*
949 415 3 cr. blackish blue-green 15 10
950　　 3 cr. 30, ultramarine 10 5
951　　 4 cr. brown-purple 10 5
952　　 6 cr. 50, reddish brown 15 5
953　　 11 cr. 50, brown-orange 30 15
949/953 *Set of 5* 70 30

1957 (31 Jan). *National Steel Company's Expansion Campaign. Photo. W 203. P 11½.*
955 416 2 cr. 50, brown 5 5

411 Hurdler

412

(Des B. Lancetta. Photo)

1956 (22 Sept). *Eighth Spring Games. Granite paper. No wmk. P 11½.*
945 411 2 cr. 50, deep rose-red 10 5

1956 (30 Sept). *Afforestation Campaign. Photo. W 203. P 11½.*
946 412 2 cr. 50, blackish blue-green .. 5 5

417 J. E. Gomes da Silva

418 Allan Kardec, Code and Globe

1957 (1 Mar). *Birth Centenary of Gomes da Silva (civil engineer). Photo. Granite paper. No wmk. P 11½.*
956 417 2 cr. 50, blackish green 5 5

1957 (18 Apr). *Centenary of Spiritualism Code. Recess. W 204. P 11½.*
957 418 2 cr. 50, chocolate-brown 5 5

419 Young Gymnast   **420** General Craveiro
Lopes

425 Basketball   **426** U.N. Emblem, Map of Suez
Canal and Soldier

(Des Portinari. Photo)

1957 (27 Apr). *Children's Games. Granite paper. No wmk.*
P 11½.
958 419 2 cr. 50, lake-brown 8 5

(Des B. Lancetta. Eng G. de Souza Ferreira and N. M. dos
Santos. Recess)

1957 (7 June). *Visit of President of Portugal. W 203. P 11½.*
959 420 6 cr. 50, dull blue 12 5

(Des B. Lancetta. Photo)

1957 (12 Oct). *Second Women's World Basketball Cham-*
pionships. No wmk. P 11½.
964 425 3 cr. 30, emerald and orange-brown 15 5

1957 (24 Oct). *AIR. United Nations Day. Recess. W 203.*
P 11½.
965 426 3 cr. 30, deep blue 15 5

421 Commemorative
Stamp of 1932
422 Lord Baden-Powell

427 Count of Pinhal (founder),   **428** Auguste Comte
Arms and Locomotive

(Des J. L. de Barros Pimental. Photo)

1957 (9 July). *25th Anniv of São Paulo Revolutionary*
Government. W 203 (sideways). P 11½.
960 421 2 cr. 50, rose-red 5 5

(Des L. Almeida and W. Puntar. Photo)

1957 (1 Aug). *AIR. Birth Centenary of Lord Baden-Powell.*
Granite paper. No wmk. P 11½.
961 422 3 cr. 30, carmine-lake 8 5

(Des B. Lancetta. Photo)

1957 (4 Nov). *Centenary of City of San Carlos. W 203. P 11½.*
966 427 2 cr. 50, dull carmine-red 5 5

1957 (15 Nov). *Death Centenary of Comte (philosopher).*
Photo. W 203. P 11½.
967 428 2 cr. 50, deep red-brown 8 5

429 Sarapui Radio Station

(Des M. F. Pinheiro. Photo)

1957 (10 Dec). *Inauguration of Sarapui Radio Station.*
W 204. P 11½.
968 429 2 cr. 50, slate-green 5 5

423 Convent of San Antonio   **424** Volleyball

(Eng G. de Souza Ferreira. Recess)

1957 (24 Aug). *Third Centenary of Emancipation of San*
Antonio Province. W 203. P 11½.
962 423 2 cr. 50, crimson 5 5

1957 (28 Sept). *Ninth Spring Games. Photo. No wmk.*
P 11½.
963 424 2 cr. 50, chestnut 15 5

430 Admiral Tamandaré
(founder) and Cruiser
Tamandaré
431 Coffee Beans and
Emblem

(No. 969 des W. Puntar. Photo. No. 970 des B. Lancetta. Eng
G. de Souza Ferreira. Recess)

1957 (13 Dec)–**58**. *150th Anniv of Brazilian Navy. T* **430** *and
similar design.* W **204**. P 11½.
969 2 cr. 50, blue   8   5
970 3 cr. 30, deep green (7.3.58)   8   5
Design: *Horiz*—3 cr. 30, Aircraft-carrier *Minas Gerais*.

(Des B. Lancetta. Photo)

1957 (28 Dec)–**58**. *Centenary of City of Ribeirao Preto.* P 11½.
I. W **203**. II. *No wmk* (1958).

		I		II	
971 **431**	2 cr. 50, claret ..	5	5	5	5

432 King John VI of Portugal   **433** Bugler
and Sailing Ship

(Des B. Lancetta. Photo)

1958 (28 Jan). *150th Anniv of Freedom of Ports.* W **204**.
P 11½.
972 **432** 2 cr. 50, crimson   5   5

(Des B. Lancetta. Photo)

1958 (18 Mar). *150th Anniv of Brazilian Marine Corps.*
W **203**. P 11½.
973 **433** 2 cr. 50, red   5   5

434 Early Locomotive   **435** High Court Building
and Skyscraper

(Des W. Puntar. Photo)

1958 (29 Mar). *Centenary of Central Brazil Railway.* W **203**.
P 11½.
974 **434** 2 cr. 50, red-brown   5   5

(Des W. Puntar. Eng G. de Souza Ferreira. Recess)

1958 (1 Apr). *150th Anniv of Military High Court.* W **204**.
P 11½.
975 **435** 2 cr. 50, deep green   5   5

436 Brazilian Pavilion   **437** Marshal C. M. da Silva
Rondon

(Des B. Lancetta. Photo)

1958 (17 Apr). *Brussels International Exhibition.* W **203**.
P 11½.
976 **436** 2 cr. 50, deep blue   5   5

(Des B. Lancetta. Eng G. de Souza Ferreira. Recess)

1958 (19 Apr). *Rondon Commemoration and "Day of the
Indian".* W **203**. P 11½.
977 **437** 2 cr. 50, crimson   5   5

438 Jumping   **439**

(Des W. Granado. Photo)

1958 (20 Apr). *Children's Games, Rio de Janeiro. Granite
paper. No wmk.* P 11½.
978 **438** 2 cr. 50, rose-red   10   5

(Des W. Puntar. Eng G. de Souza Ferreira. Recess)

1958 (28 Apr). *Inauguration of Salto Grande Hydro-Electric
Station.* W **203**. P 11½.
979 **439** 2 cr. 50, crimson   5   5

440 National Printing Works   **441** Marshal Osorio

(Des B. Lancetta. Photo)

1958 (22 May). *150th Anniv of National Printing Works.*
W **203**. P 11½.
980 **440** 2 cr. 50, red-brown   5   5

(Des W. Puntar. Photo)

1958 (24 May). *150th Birth Anniv of Marshal Osorio.* W **203**.
P 11½.
981 **441** 2 cr. 50, violet   5   5

442 Pres. Morales   **443** Botanical   **444** Hoe, Rice and
of Honduras   Gardens, Rio de   Cotton
     Janeiro

(Des B. Lancetta. Eng G. de Souza Ferreira. Recess)

1958 (7 June). *Visit of President of Honduras.* W **203**. P 11½.
982 **442** 6 cr. 50, deep green   8   5
     a. W **204**   60   20

1958 (13 June). *150th Anniv of Botanical Gardens, Rio de
Janeiro. Recess.* W **203**. P 11½.
983 **443** 2 cr. 50, deep green   8   5

(Des C. Tan Yamamato. Photo)

1958 (18 June). *50th Anniv of Japanese Immigration.*
W **203**. P 11½.
984 **444** 2 cr. 50, crimson   5   5

445 Prophet Joel   **446** Brazil on Globe

(Des B. Lancetta. Eng G. de Souza Ferreira. Recess)

1958 (21 June). *Bicentenary of Basilica of the Good Jesus, Matosinhos.* W **203**. P 11½.
985 **445** 2 cr. 50, deep blue 5 5

1958 (10 July). *International Investments Conference. Belo Horizonte. Photo.* W **203**. P 11½.
986 **446** 2 cr. 50, chocolate-brown 5 5

447 Tiradentes Palace, Rio de Janeiro   **448** J. B. Brandão

1958 (24 July). *47th Inter-Parliamentary Union Conference. Recess.* W **204**. P 11½.
987 **447** 2 cr. 50, chocolate 5 5

1958 (1 Aug). *Centenary of Brandão* (*statesman*). *Photo.* W **204**. P 11½.
988 **448** 2 cr. 50, chestnut (*shades*) 5 5

449 Dawn Palace, Brasilia   **450** Merchant Ships

(Des B. Lancetta. Photo)

1958 (8 Aug). *Construction of Presidential Palace.* W **203**. P 11½.
989 **449** 2 cr. 50, blue.. .. .. 5 5

(Des M. F. Pinheiro. Photo)

1958 (22 Aug). *Government Aid for Brazilian Merchant Marine.* W **203**. P 11½.
990 **450** 2 cr. 50, blue.. .. .. 5 5

451 J. C. da Silva   **452** Pres. Gronchi

(Des W. Granado. Photo)

1958 (2 Sept). *Birth Centenary of Da Silva* (*author*). *No wmk.* P 11½.
991 **451** 2 cr. 50, red-brown 5 5

(Des B. Lancetta. Eng G. de Souza Ferreira. Recess)

1958 (4 Sept). *Visit of President of Italy.* W **204**. P 11½.
992 **452** 7 cr. deep blue 10 5

453 Archers   **454** Old People within Hour-glass

(T **453**/4 des W. Granado. Photo)

1958 (21 Sept). *Tenth Spring Games, Rio de Janeiro. Granite paper. No wmk.* P 11½.
993 **453** 2 cr. 50, orange-red 8 5

1958 (27 Sept). *Old People's Day.* W **203**. P 11½.
994 **454** 2 cr. 50, crimson 5 5

455 Machado de Assis   **456** Pres. Vargas with Oily Hand

(Des M. F. Pinheiro. Photo)

1958 (28 Sept). *50th Death Anniv of Machado de Assis* (*writer*). *No wmk.* P 11½.
995 **455** 2 cr. 50, light brown 5 5

(Des Miranda, Jun. Photo)

1958 (6 Oct). *Fifth Anniv of State Petroleum Law.* W **204**. P 11½.
996 **456** 2 cr. 50, blue.. .. .. 5 5

457 Globe showing Brazil and the Americas   **458** Gen. L. Sodré   **459** U.N. Emblem

1958 (14 Nov). *Seventh Inter-American Municipalities Congress, Rio de Janeiro. Photo.* W **203**. P 11½.
997 **457** 2 cr. 50, blue.. .. .. 5 5

1958 (15 Nov). *Birth Centenary of Sodré. Recess.* W **203**. P 11½.
998 **458** 3 cr. 30, deep green 5 5

(Des B. Lancetta. Photo)

1958 (26 Dec). *Tenth Anniv of Declaration of Human Rights.* W **203** (*sideways*). P 11½.
999 **459** 2 cr. 50, blue.. .. .. 5 5

460 Footballer **461** Map and Railway Line **462** Pres. Sukarno

(Des B. Lancetta. Photo)

1959 (20 Jan). *World Football Cup Victory, 1958.* W **203**. P 11½.
1000 **460** 3 cr. 30, brown-red and green .. 10 5

1959 (24 Apr). *Centenary of Opening of Patos–Campina Grande Railway. Photo.* W **203** (*sideways*). P 11½.
1001 **461** 2 cr. 50, orange-red 5 5

(Des B. Lancetta. Photo)

1959 (20 May). *Visit of President of Indonesia.* W **203** (*sideways*). P 11½.
1002 **462** 2 cr. 50, blue 5 5

463 Basketball Player **464** King John VI of Portugal **465** Polo Players

(Des B. Lancetta. Photo)

1959 (30 May). *AIR. World Basketball Championships, 1959.* W **203**. P 11½.
1003 **463** 3 cr. 30, chestnut and blue 8 5

1959 (12 June). *Photo.* W **203**. P 11 × 11½.
1004 **464** 2 cr. 50, rose-red 5 5

(Des W. Granado. Photo)

1959 (13 June). *Children's Games.* W **203**. P 11½.
1005 **465** 2 cr. 50, chestnut 5 5

466 Dockside Scene **467** Church Organ, Diamantina **468** Dom J. S. de Souza (first Archbishop of Diamantina)

(Des W. Granado. Photo)

1959 (10 July). *Rehabilitation of National Ports Law.* W **203**. P 11½.
1006 **466** 2 cr. 50, slate-green 5 5

(Des W. Puntar. Photo)

1959 (16 July). *Bicentenary of Carmelite Order in Diamantina.* W **203**. P 11½.
1007 **467** 3 cr. 30, crimson 5 5

(Des W. Puntar. Photo)

1959 (20 July). *Centenary of Archbishopric of Diamantina.* W **203**. P 11½.
1008 **468** 2 cr. 50, red-brown 5 5

469 **470**

1959 (20 Sept). *11th International Roads Congress. Photo.* W **203**. P 11½.
1009 **469** 3 cr. 30, ultramarine and blue-green 5 5

(Des W. Granado. Photo)

1959 (27 Sept). *25th Anniv of Londrina.* W **203**. P 11½.
1010 **470** 2 cr. 50, slate-green 5 5

471 **472** Daedalus

(Des B. Lancetta. Photo)

1959 (4 Oct). *Spring Games. No wmk.* P 11½.
1011 **471** 2 cr. 50, magenta 10 5

1959 (21 Oct). *AIR. Aviation Week. Photo.* W **203**. P 11½.
1012 **472** 3 cr. 30, ultramarine 5 5

473 Globe and "Snipe" Class Yachts **474**

(Des A. A. Kower. Photo)

1959 (22 Oct). *World Sailing Championships, Porto Alegre. Photo.* W **203**. P 11½.
1013 **473** 6 cr. 50, slate-green 12 5

(Des Brother Paul O. F. M. Eng G. de Souza Ferreira. Recess)

1959 (24 Oct). *Fourth International Brazilian-Portuguese Study Conference, Bahia University.* W **203**. P 11½.
1014 **474** 6 cr. 50, deep blue 8 5

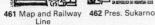

475 Gunpowder Factory

476

(Des W. Puntar. Photo)

1959 (19 Nov). *50th Anniv of President Vargas Gunpowder Factory. W* **203.** *P* 11½.
1015 **475** 3 cr. 30, chestnut 5 5

(Des M. F. Pinheiro. Photo)

1959 (26 Nov). *Thanksgiving Day. W* **203.** *P* 11½.
1016 **476** 2 cr. 50, blue 5 5

477 *Caravelle* Airliner

478

(Des VARIG. Photo)

1959 (18 Dec). *AIR. Inauguration of "Caravelle" Airliners by Brazilian National Airlines. W* **203.** *P* 11½.
1017 **477** 6 cr. 50, bright blue 8 5

(Des A. Lima. Photo)

1959 (24 Dec). *Centenary of Presbyterian Work in Brazil. W* **203.** *P* 11½.
1018 **478** 3 cr. 30, emerald-green 5 5

479 P. da Silva and Schistosoma Mansoni

480 L. de Matos and Church

1959 (28 Dec). *50th Anniv of Discovery and Identification of "Schistosoma Mansoni" (Fluke). Photo. W* **203.** *P* 11½.
1019 **479** 2 cr. 50, purple 5 5

1960 (3 Jan). *Birth Centenary of Luiz de Matos (evangelist). Photo. W* **203.** *P* 11½.
1020 **480** 3 cr. 30, deep orange-brown .. 5 5

481 Pres. Lopez Mateos of Mexico

482 Pres. Eisenhower

(T **481/2** des B. Lancetta. Photo)

1960 (19 Jan). *AIR. Visit of Mexican President. W* **203.** *P* 11½.
1021 **481** 6 cr. 50, yellow-brown 8 5

1960 (23 Feb). *AIR. Visit of United States President. No wmk. P* 11½.
1022 **482** 6 cr. 50, brown-orange 8 5

483 Dr. L. Zamenhof

484 Adél Pinto

485 "Care of Refugees"

(Des C. Gandini. Photo)

1960 (10 Mar). *Birth Centenary of Zamenhof (inventor of Esperanto). W* **203.** *P* 11½.
1023 **483** 6 cr. 50, emerald-green 8 5

(Des B. Lancetta. Eng G. de Souza Ferreira. Recess)

1960 (19 Mar). *Birth Centenary of Adél Pinto (engineer). W* **204.** *P* 11½.
1024 **484** 11 cr. 50, rose-red 12 5

1960 (7 Apr). *AIR. World Refugee Year. Photo. W* **204.** *P* 11½.
1025 **485** 6 cr. 50, blue 5 5

486 Plan of Brasilia

(Des Arthur P. and Aloysio Guimarães. Photo)

1960 (21 Apr). *Inauguration of Brasilia as Capital. T* **486** *and similar designs. W* **203.** *P* 11½×11 (6 *cr.* 50), *Imperf** (27 *cr.*) *or P* 11×11½ (*others*).

(*a*) POSTAGE. Inscr "Correio"
1026 2 cr. 50, bright blue-green 5 5

(*b*) AIR
1027 3 cr. 30, violet 5 5
1028 4 cr. blue 5 5
1029 6 cr. 50, magenta 8 5
1030 11 cr. 50, brown 12 8
1026/1030 Set of 5 .. .. 30 20

(*c*) Miniature Sheet. POSTAGE. Birthday of Pres. Kubitschek (12.9.60)
MS1031 110×52 mm. 27 cr. brown-orange 25 15
Designs:—Outlines representing: *Horiz*—2 cr: 50, President's Palace of the Plateau; 3 cr. 30 Parliament Buildings; 4 cr. Cathedral; 11 cr. 50, 27 cr. T **486.** *Vert*—6 cr. 50, Tower.
*No. **MS**1031 was printed in panes of four and and subdivided by perf 11×11½, the stamp itself being imperf.

487

(Des A. Lobato. Photo)

1960 (16 June). *AIR. Seventh National Eucharistic Congress, Curitiba. W* **203.** *P* 11×11½.
1032 **487** 3 cr. 30, magenta 5 5

488

489 Boy Scout

496 Maria Bueno in Play   497 Exhibition Emblem

(Des W. Granado. Photo)

1960 (15 Dec). *AIR. Maria Bueno's Wimbledon Tennis Victories*, 1959–60. *W* **204**. *P* 11×11½.
1041 **496** 6 cr. light brown   10   5

(T 488/9 des B. Lancetta. Photo)

1960 (1 July). *AIR. Tenth World Baptist Alliance Congress, Rio de Janeiro*. *W* **203**. *P* 11×11½.
1033 **488** 6 cr. 50, blue   8   5

1960 (23 July). *AIR. 50th Anniv of Scouting in Brazil*. *W* **203**. *P* 11½×11.
1034 **489** 3 cr. 30, orange-red   5   5

(Des B. Lancetta. Photo)

1960 (16 Dec). *International Industrial and Commercial Exhibition, Rio de Janeiro*. *W* **204**. *P* 11½.
1042 **497** 2 cr. 50, chocolate and yellow   5   5

490 "Agriculture"   491 Caravel   492 P. de Frontin

498 War Memorial, Rio de Janeiro   499 Pylon and Map

(Des W. Granado. Photo)

1960 (28 July). *Centenary of Brazilian Ministry of Agriculture*. Photo. *W* **203**. *P* 11½×11.
1035 **490** 2 cr. 50, brown   5   5

(Des B. Lancetta. Eng G. de Souza Ferreira. Recess)

1960 (5 Aug). *AIR. Fifth Death Centenary of Prince Henry the Navigator*. *W* **204**. *P* 11½×11.
1036 **491** 6 cr. 50, black   8   5

(Des W. Puntar. Photo)

1960 (12 Oct). *Birth Centenary of Paulo de Frontin (engineer)*. *W* **204**. *P* 11½×11.
1037 **492** 2 cr. 50, orange-red   5   5

1960 (22 Dec). *AIR. Return of Ashes of World War II Heroes from Italy*. *W* **204**. *P* 11×11½.
1043 **498** 3 cr. 30, crimson   5   5

(Des W. dos Santos. Photo)

1961 (20 Jan). *AIR. Inauguration of Tres Marias Hydro-Electric Station*. *W* **204** (sideways). *P* 11½×11.
1044 **499** 3 cr. 30, crimson   5   5

493 Locomotive Piston Gear   494 Athlete   495

500 Haile Selassie   501 Sacred Book and Map of Brazil

(Des B. Lancetta. Photo)

1960 (15 Oct). *Tenth Pan-American Railways Congress*. *W* **204**. *P* 11½×11.
1038 **493** 2 cr. 50, ultramarine   5   5

(Des W. Granado. Photo)

1960 (18 Oct). *Twelfth Spring Games*. *W* **204**. *P* 11½×11.
1039 **494** 2 cr. 50, blue-green   5   5

(Des W. Granado. Photo)

1960 (11 Nov). *World Volleyball Championships*. *W* **203**. *P* 11½×11.
1040 **495** 11 cr. blue   12   5

(Des W. Puntar. Photo)

1961 (31 Jan). *Visit of Emperor of Ethiopia*. *W* **204** (sideways). *P* 11½×11.
1045 **500** 2 cr. 50, chocolate   5   5

(Des B. Lancetta. Photo)

1961 (13 Mar). *50th Anniv of College of Sacré Coeur de Marie*. *W* **204**. *P* 11×11½.
1046 **501** 2 cr. 50, blue   5   5

502 Map of Guanabara State

503 Arms of Academy

508 Tagore

509 280 r. Stamp and Map of France

(Des B. Lancetta. Photo)

1961 (27 Mar). *Promulgation of Guanabara Constitution.* W 203. P 11×11½.
1047 **502** 7 cr. 50, chestnut 8 5

(Des L. F. de Almeida and W. Puntar. Photo)

1961 (28 July). *Birth Centenary of Rabindranath Tagore.* W 203. P 11½×11.
1054 **508** 10 cr. crimson 8 5

(Des W. Puntar and M. F. Pinheiro. Photo)

1961 (23 Apr). *150th Anniv of Agulhas Negras Military Academy.* T 503 and similar vert design inscr "1811–1961". W 203. P 11½×11.
1048 2 cr. 50, emerald 5 5
1049 3 cr. 30, crimson (Military cap and sabre) 5 5

(Des B. Lancetta. Photo)

1961 (1 Aug). *Centenary of 1861 "Goat's Eye" stamps.* T 509 and similar horiz design. W 203. P 11×11½.
1055 10 cr. rose-red 20 5
1056 20 cr. red-orange 25 5
Design:—20 cr. 430 r. stamp and map of the Netherlands.

504 "Spanning the Atlantic Ocean"

505 Ouro Preto

510 Cloudburst

511 Pinnacle, Rope and Haversack

(Des A. Magalhães and N. Pontual. Photo)

1961 (28 Apr). *Visit of Foreign Minister to Senegal.* W 203. P 11½×11.
1050 **504** 27 cr. bright blue 8 5

(Des B. Mazzeo. Photo)

1961 (6 June). *250th Anniv of Ouro Preto.* W 203. P 11×11½.
1051 **505** 1 cr. orange-red 5 5

(Des W. Puntar and J. F. da Silva. Photo)

1962 (23 Mar). *World Meteorological Day.* W 203. P 11½×11.
1057 **510** 10 cr. red-brown 8 5

(Des W. Granado and J. F. da Silva. Photo)

1962 (14 Apr). *50th Anniv of First Ascent of "Finger of God" Mountain.* W 203. P 11½×11.
1058 **511** 8 cr. emerald 5 5

506 Arsenal, Rio de Janeiro

507 Coffee Plant

512 Dr. G. Vianna and Parasites

513 Campaign Emblem

(Des W. Puntar. Photo)

1961 (20 June). *150th Anniv of Rio de Janeiro Arsenal.* W 204. P 11×11½.
1052 **506** 5 cr. red-brown 5 5

(Des A. Magalhães and N. Pontual. Photo)

1961 (30 June). *International Coffee Convention, Rio de Janeiro.* W 204. P 11½×11.
1053 **507** 20 cr. red-brown 15 8

(Des M. F. Pinheiro and F. J. da Silva. Photo)

1962 (24 Apr). *50th Anniv of Vianna's Cure for Leishman's Disease.* W 203. P 11×11½.
1059 **512** 8 cr. blue 5 5

(Des W. Puntar and F. J. da Silva. Eng G. de Souza Ferreira. Recess)

1962 (24 May). *AIR. Malaria Eradication.* W 203. P 11½×11.
1060 **513** 21 cr. deep blue 5 5

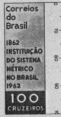

514 Henrique Dias

515 Metric Measure

(Des L. F. de Almeida. Photo)

1962 (18 June). *300th Death Anniv of Dias (patriot).* W **203**. P 11×11½.
1061 **514** 10 cr. deep maroon 5 5

(Des M. F. Pinheiro. Photo)

1962 (26 June). *Centenary of Brazil's Adoption of Metric System.* W **203**. P 11½×11.
1062 **515** 100 cr. carmine 45 20

520 Foundry Ladle

521 U.P.A.E. Emblem

(Des K. Saito and I. Tanaka. Photo)

1962 (26 Oct). *Inauguration of "Usiminas" (national iron and steel foundry).* W **203**. P 11½×11.
1067 **520** 8 cr. orange 5 5

(Des M. F. Pinheiro. Photo)

1962 (19 Nov). *50th Anniv of Postal Union of the Americas and Spain.* W **203**. P 11×11½.
1068 **521** 8 cr. magenta 5 5

516 "Snipe" Sailing-boats

517 J. Mesquita and Newspaper *O Estado de São Paulo*

(Des E. de Araújo Jorge. Photo)

1962 (21 July). *13th "Snipe" Class Sailing Championships, Rio de Janeiro.* W **203**. P 11½×11.
1063 **516** 8 cr. deep turquoise 5 5

(Des M. F. Pinheiro. Photo)

1962 (18 Aug). *Birth Centenary of Mesquita (journalist and founder of "O Estado de São Paulo").* W **203**. P 11×11½.
1064 **517** 8 cr. bistre-brown 5 5

522 Emblems of Industry

523 Q. Bocaiura

524 Footballer

(Des A. Alves. Photo)

1962 (26 Nov). *Tenth Anniv of National Bank.* W **203** (sideways). P 11½×11.
1069 **522** 10 cr. turquoise-green 5 5

(Des L. F. de Almeida. Photo)

1962 (27 Dec). *50th Death Anniv of Bocaiura (journalist and patriot).* W **203** (sideways). P 11½×11.
1070 **523** 8 cr. orange-brown.. .. .. 5 5

(Des W. Granado. Photo)

1963 (14 Jan). *Brazil's Victory in World Football Championships, 1962.* W **203** (sideways). P 11½×11.
1071 **524** 10 cr. turquoise 5 5

518 Empress Leopoldina

519 Brasilia

(Des W. Granado. Photo)

1962 (7 Sept). *140th Anniv of Independence.* W **203**. P 11½×11.
1065 **518** 8 cr. deep magenta 5 5

(Des W. Granado. Photo)

1962 (24 Oct). *51st Interparliamentary Conference, Brasilia.* W **203**. P 11×11.
1066 **519** 10 cr. orange 5 5

525 Carrier Pigeon

526 Dr. S. Neva (First Brazilian P.M.G.)

(Des Di Cavalcanti. Litho De La Rue, Rio de Janeiro)

1963 (25 Jan). *Third Centenary of Brazilian Posts.* P 14.
1072 **525** 8 cr. deep blue, red, green & yellow 5 5
MS1072a 145×58 mm. **525** 100 cr. deep blue, red, green and yellow (31 Jan) .. 20 20

(Des M. F. Pinheiro (30 cr., 200 cr.), W. Granado (50 cr.), W. Puntar (100 cr.), L. F. de Almeida (500 cr.), E. de Araújo Jorge (1000 cr.). Photo)

1963 (31 Jan)–**66**. *T* **526** *and similar vert designs.* W **203**. *P* 11×11½.

1073	8 cr. violet..	5	5
1073a	30 cr. turquoise (20.1.66)	12	5
1073b	50 cr. bistre-brown (1.8.66)	10	5
1073c	100 cr. light blue (10.2.65)	10	5
1073d	200 cr. orange-red (24.2.65)..	15	8
1073e	500 cr. red-brown (29.1.65)	40	15
1073f	1000 cr. slate-blue (1.7.66)	40	15
1073/1073f	Set of 7	1·10	50

Portraits:—30 cr. Euclides da Cunha; 50 cr. Prof. A. Moreira da Costa Lima; 100 cr. G. Dias; 200 cr. Tiradentes; 500 cr. Emperor Pedro I; 1000 cr. Emperor Pedro II.

527 Rockets and Dish Aerial 21,00

528 Cross 8,00

529 "abc" Symbol 8,00

(Des L. F. de Almeida. Photo)

1963 (15 Mar). *International Aeronautics and Space Exhibition, São Paulo.* W **204** (*sideways*). *P* 11½×11.
1074 **527** 21 cr. blue 5 5

(Des E. de Araújo Jorge. Photo)

1963 (19 Apr). *Ecumenical Council, Vatican City.* W **203** (*sideways*). *P* 11½×11.
1075 **528** 8 cr. purple.. .. .. 5 5

(Des W. Puntar. Photo)

1963 (25 Apr). *National Education Week.* W **203** (*sideways*). *P* 11½×11.
1076 **529** 8 cr. blue 5 5

530 Basketball 8,00

531 Torch Emblem 10,00

532 "OEA" and Map

(Des W. Granado. Photo)

1963 (15 May). *Fourth World Basketball Championships.* W **203** (*sideways*). *P* 11½×11.
1077 **530** 8 cr. bright reddish purple .. 5 5

(Des M. F. Pinheiro. Photo)

1963 (22 May). *Fourth Pan-American Games, São Paulo.* W **203** (*sideways*). *P* 11½×11.
1078 **531** 10 cr. carmine 5 5

(Des W. Granado. Photo)

1963 (6 June). *15th Anniv of O.E.A. (Organization of American States) Charter.* W **203** (*sideways*). *P* 11½×11.
1079 **532** 10 cr. yellow-orange .. 5 5

533 J. B. de A. é Silva 8,00

534 Campaign Emblem 10,00

(Des W. Puntar. Photo)

1963 (13 June). *Birth Bicentenary of José B. de Andrade é Silva ("Father of Independence").* W **203** (*sideways*). *P* 11½×11.
1080 **533** 8 cr. bistre-brown 5 5

(Des A. Zaluar. Photo)

1963 (18 June). *Freedom from Hunger.* W **203**. *P* 11×11½.
1081 **534** 10 cr. blue 5 5

535 Centenary Emblem 8,00

536 J. Caetano 8,00

537 "Atomic Development"

(Des W. Puntar. Photo)

1963 (19 Aug). *Red Cross Centenary.* W **203** (*sideways*). *P* 11½×11.
1082 **535** 8 cr. red and yellow .. 5 5

(Des M. F. Pinheiro. Photo)

1963 (24 Aug). *Death Centenary of João Caetano (actor).* W **203** (*sideways*). *P* 11½×11.
1083 **536** 8 cr. black 5 5

(Des B. Lancetta. Photo)

1963 (28 Aug). *First Anniv of National Nuclear Energy Commission.* W **203** (*sideways*). *P* 11½×11.
1084 **537** 10 cr. magenta 5 5

538 Throwing the Hammer 10,00

539 Pres. Tito 80,00

540 Cross and Map 8,00

(Des N. Pinheiro and W. Granado. Photo)

1963 (3 Sept). *International Students' Games, Porto Alegre.* W **203** (*sideways*). *P* 11½×11.
1085 **538** 10 cr. black and grey .. 5 5

(Des M. F. Pinheiro. Photo)

1963 (19 Sept). *Visit of Pres. Tito of Yugoslavia.* W **203** (*sideways*). *P* 11½×11.
1086 **539** 80 cr. bistre-brown.. .. 20 8

(Des W. Granado. Photo)

1963 (20 Sept). *Eighth International Leprology Congress, Rio de Janeiro.* W **203** (*sideways*). P 11½×11.
1087 **540** 8 cr. turquoise 5 5

541 Petroleum Installations

(Des R. Amenta. Photo)

1963 (3 Oct). *Tenth Anniv of National Petroleum Industry.* W **203**. P 11×11½.
1088 **541** 8 cr. deep grey-green 5 5

542 "Jogos da Primavera"
(Des W. Granado. Photo)

1963 (5 Nov). *Spring Games. Photo.* W **203**. P 11×11½.
1089 **542** 8 cr. orange-yellow 5 5

543 A. Borges de Medeiros

544 Bridge of São João del Rey

(Des W. Puntar. Photo)

1963 (29 Nov). *Birth Centenary of A. Borges de Medeiros (politician).* P 11×11½ (*sideways*). P 11½×11.
1090 **543** 8 cr. red-brown 5 5

(Des W. Puntar. Photo)

1963 (8 Dec). *250th Anniv of São João del Rey.* W **203**. P 11×11½.
1091 **544** 8 cr. ultramarine 5 5

545 Dr. A. Alvim

546 Viscount de Mauá

(Des A. Pacheco. Photo)

1963 (19 Dec). *Birth Centenary of Dr. Alvaro Alvim (scientist).* W **203**. P 11×11½.
1092 **545** 8 cr. slate-black 5 5

(Des W. Granado. Photo)

1963 (28 Dec). *150th Birth Anniv of Viscount de Mauá (founder of Brazilian railway).* W **203** (*sideways*). P 11½×11.
1093 **546** 8 cr. magenta 5 5

547 Cactus **548** C. Netto **549** L. Müller

(Des A. Pacheco. Photo)

1964 (25 Jan). *Tenth Anniv of Brazilian North-East Bank.* W **203** (*sideways*). P 11½×11.
1094 **547** 8 cr. grey-green 5 5

(Des L. F. de Almeida. Photo)

1964 (21 Feb). *Birth Centenary of Coelho Netto (author).* W **203** (*sideways*). P 11½×11.
1095 **548** 8 cr. violet 5 5

(Des W. Puntar. Photo)

1964 (9 Mar). *Birth Centenary of Lauro Müller (patriot).* W **203** (*sideways*). P 11½×11.
1096 **549** 8 cr. orange-red 5 5

550 Child with Spoon **551** "Chalice" (carved rock), Vila Velha, Paraná

(Des W. Granado. Photo)

1964 (23 Mar). *Schoolchildren's Nourishment Week.* W **203**. P 11×11½.
1097 **550** 8 cr. yellow and orange-brown .. 5 5

(Des W. Granado. Photo)

1964 (9 Apr). *Tourism.* W **203** (*sideways*). P 11½×11.
1098 **551** 80 cr. orange-red 10 5

552 A. Kardec (author) **553** Pres. Lübke

(Des B. Lancetta. Photo)

1964 (18 Apr). *Centenary of Spiritual Code, "O Evangelho".* W **203** (*sideways*). P 11½×11.
1099 **552** 30 cr. deep grey-green 5 5

(Des E. de Araújo Jorge. Photo)

1964 (6 May). *Visit of President Lübke of West Germany.* W 203 (*sideways*). P 11½ × 11.
1100 **553** 100 cr. deep chestnut 20 5

554 Pope John XXIII   **555** Pres. Senghor

1964 (3 July). *Pope John Commemoration.* W 203 (*sideways*). P 11½ × 11.
1101 **554** 20 cr. lake 5 5

(Des W. Puntar. Photo)

1964 (19 Sept). *Visit of President Senghor of Senegal.* W 203 (*sideways*). P 11 × 11½.
1102 **555** 20 cr. sepia 5 5

556 "Visit Rio de Janeiro"   **557** Statue of St. Sebastian

(Des E. de Araújo Jorge (1105), W. Granado (others). Photo)

1964 (30 Sept)—65. *400th Anniv of Rio de Janeiro* (1965). T **556** *and similar designs* (*inscr* "IV CENTENARIO", *etc*) *and* T **557**. W 203 (*sideways on* 30 cr. (1104), 35 cr., 100 cr.). P 11½ (1104) *or* 11 × 11½ (*others*).
1103　　15 cr. blue and orange 5 5
1104　　30 cr. rose-red and cobalt (5.3.65) .. 5 5
1105　　30 cr. black and blue (30.11.65) .. 5 5
1106　　35 cr. black and orange (28.7.65) .. 5 5
1107　　100 cr. brown & blue-green/*light yellow* (18.12.64) .. 10 5
1108　　200 cr. rose-red & black-grn (6.11.64) .. 20 5
1103/1108　　*Set of 6* .. 45 25
MS1109　Two sheets, 129 × 76 mm containing stamps similar to Nos. 1103, 1107/8 each in brown (sold at 320 cr.) and 132 × 78 mm containing stamps similar to Nos. 1104/6 each in red-orange (sold at 100 cr.). No gum. Imperf (30.12.65). *Price for two sheets* 40 40
Designs: *Horiz*—30 cr. (No. 1105), Tramway viaduct; 200 cr. Copacabana Beach. *Vert*—35 cr. Estácio de Sa's statue; 100 cr. Church of Our Lady of the Rock.

(Des W. Granado. Photo)

1964 (13 Oct). *Visit of President De Gaulle.* W 203 (*sideways*). P 11½ × 11.
1110 **558** 100 cr. orange-brown 12 5

(Des W. Granado. Photo)

1964 (24 Oct). *President Kennedy Commemoration.* W 203 (*sideways*). P 11½ × 11.
1111 **559** 100 cr. black 12 5

(Des M. F. Pinheiro. Photo)

1964 (18 Nov). *150th Death Anniv of A. F. Lisboa* (*sculptor*). W 203 (*sideways*). P 11½ × 11.
1112 **560** 10 cr. black 5 5

561 Cross and Sword   **562** Vital Brazil

(Des W. Granado. Photo)

1965 (15 Apr). *First Anniv of Democratic Revolution.* W 203 (*sideways*). P 11½.
1113 **561** 120 cr. grey 10 5

(Des M. F. Pinheiro. Photo)

1965 (28 Apr). *Birth Centenary of Vital Brazil* (*scientist*). W 203 (*sideways*). P 11½.
1114 **562** 120 cr. red-orange 10 5

563 Shah of Persia   **564** Marshal Rondon and Map

(Des W. Granado. Photo)

1965 (5 May). *Visit of Shah of Persia.* W 203 (*sideways*). P 11½.
1115 **563** 120 cr. carmine 10 5

(Des B. Mazzeo. Eng L. A. da Fonseca. Recess)

1965 (7 May). *Birth Centenary of Marshal C. M. da S. Rondon.* W 203 (*sideways*). P 11½.
1116 **564** 30 cr. maroon 5 5

558 Pres. De Gaulle

559 Pres. Kennedy

560 Nahum (statue)

565 Lions Emblem

566 I.T.U. Emblem and Symbols

(Des A. Fagundes. Photo)

1965 (14 May). *Brazilian Lions Clubs National Convention, Rio de Janeiro. W 203 (sideways). P 11½.*
1117 **565** 35 cr. black and lilac 5 5

(Des W. Puntar. Photo)

1965 (20 May). *I.T.U. Centenary. W 203. P 11½.*
1118 **566** 120 cr. green and yellow 10 5

567 E. Pessoa

568 Barroso's Statue

(Des M. F. Pinheiro. Photo)

1965 (23 May). *Birth Centenary of Epitácio Pessoa. W 203 (sideways). P 11½.*
1119 **567** 35 cr. deep bluish slate 5 5

(Des E. de Araújo Jorge. Photo)

1965 (11 June). *Centenary of Naval Battle of Riachuelo. W 203 (sideways). P 11½.*
1120 **568** 30 cr. light blue 5 5

569 Author and Heroine

570 Sir Winston Churchill

(Des A. Ipisajá. Photo)

1965 (24 June). *Centenary of Publication of José de Alencar's "Iracema". W 203 (sideways). P 11½.*
1121 **569** 30 cr. maroon 5 5

(Des W. Puntar. Photo)

1965 (25 June). *Churchill Commemoration. W 203. P 11½.*
1122 **570** 200 cr. slate 25 15

571 Scout Badge and Emblem of Rio's 400th Anniv

572 I.C.Y. Emblem

(Des B. Lancetta. Photo)

1965 (17 July). *1st Pan-American Scout Jamboree, Rio de Janeiro. W 203 (sideways). P 11½.*
1123 **571** 30 cr. deep bluish green 5 5

(Des W. Puntar. Photo)

1965 (25 Aug). *International Co-operation Year. W 203. P 11½.*
1124 **572** 120 cr. black and blue 12 5

573 L. Correia

574 Exhibition Emblem

(Des A. Lima. Photo)

1965 (1 Sept). *Birth Centenary of Leoncia Correia (poet). W 203 (sideways). P 11½ × 11.*
1125 **573** 35 cr. slate-green 5 5

(Des A. Magalhães. Photo)

1965 (4 Sept). *São Paulo Biennale (Art Exhibition). W 203 (sideways). P 11½ × 11.*
1126 **574** 30 cr. rose 5 5

575 President Saragat

576 Grand Duke and Duchess of Luxembourg

(Des W. Granado. Photo)

1965 (11 Sept). *Visit of President of Italy. W 203 (sideways). P 11½ × 11.*
1127 **575** 100 cr. slate-green/pale pink .. 10 5

(Des W. Puntar. Photo)

1965 (17 Sept). *Visit of Grand Duke and Duchess of Luxembourg. W 203. P 11 × 11½.*
1128 **576** 100 cr. bistre-brown 10 5

577 Biplane on Map

578 O.E.A. Emblem

(Des Air Ministry. Photo)

1965 (8 Oct). *Aviation Week and 3rd Philatelic Exhibition. W 203 (sideways). P 11½ × 11.*
1129 **577** 35 cr. blue 5 5

(Des A. Fagundes. Photo)

1965 (17 Nov). *Inter-American Conference, Rio de Janeiro. W 203. P 11 × 11½.*
1130 **578** 100 cr. black and blue 8 5

579 King Baudouin and Queen Fabiola

580 Coffee Beans

585 "Steel"

586 Prof. Rocha Lima

(Des W. Granado. Photo)

1965 (18 Nov). *Visit of King and Queen of the Belgians.* W **203**. P 11×11½.
1131 579 100 cr. slate-grey   10   5

(Des W. Granado. Photo)

1965 (21 Dec). *Brazilian Coffee.* W **203** (*sideways*). P 11½×11.
1132 580 30 cr. brown/*cream*   5   5

1966 (16 Apr). *Silver Jubilee of National Steel Company.* Photo. W **203** (*sideways*). P 11½×11.
1137 585 30 cr. black/*orange*..   5   5

(Des B. Lancetta. Photo)

1966 (26 Apr). *50th Anniv of Professor Lima's Discovery of the Characteristics of "Rickettsia prowazeki" (cause of typhus fever).* W **203** (*sideways*). P 11½×11.
1138 586 30 cr. turquoise   5   5

581 F. A. Varnhagen

582 Emblem and Map

587 Battle Scene

588 "The Sacred Face"

(Des A. Lima and W. Puntar. Photo)

1966 (24 May). *Centenary of Battle of Tuiuti.* W **203**. P 11×11½.
1139 587 30 cr. bronze-green   5   5

(Des W. Puntar. Photo)

1966 (17 Feb). *AIR. 150th Birth Anniv of Francisco Varnhagen (historian).* W **203** (*sideways*). P 11½×11.
1133 581 45 cr. red-brown   5   5

(Des E. de Araújo Jorge. Photo)

1966 (14 Mar). *AIR. Fifth Anniv of Alliance for Progress.* W **203**. P 11×11½.
1134 582 120 cr. ultramarine and turquoise ..   10   5

(Des W. Granado. Photo)

1966 (3 June). *AIR. 2nd Vatican Council.* W **203** (*sideways*). P 11½×11.
1140 588 45 cr. orange-brown   5   5

583 Sister and Globe

584 Loading Ore at Quayside

589 M. e Barros

590 Decade Symbol

591 Pres. Shazar

(Des W. Puntar. Photo)

1966 (13 June). *AIR. Death Centenary of Commander Mariz e Barros.* W **203** (*sideways*). P 11½×11.
1141 589 35 cr. chestnut   5   5

(Des J. W. P. Moraes. Photo)

1966 (1 July). *International Hydrological Decade.* W **203** (*sideways*). P 11½×11.
1142 590 100 cr. new blue and brown   ..   8   5

(Des M. F. Pinheiro. Photo)

1966 (18 July). *Visit of President Shazar of Israel.* W **203** (*sideways*). P 11½×11.
1143 591 100 cr. ultramarine..   8   5

(Des W. Granado. Photo)

1966 (25 Mar). *AIR. Centenary of Dorothean Sisters Educational Work in Brazil.* W **203** (*sideways*). P 11½×11.
1135 583 35 cr. violet..   5   5

1966 (1 Apr). *Inauguration of Rio Doce Iron-ore Terminal, Tubarão, Espirito Santo.* Photo. W **203**. P 11×11½.
1136 584 110 cr. black and pale bistre   ..   10   5

592 "Youth"   **593** Imperial Academy of Fine Arts

(Des W. Granado. Photo)

1966 (31 July). *AIR. Birth Centenary of Eliseu Visconti (painter). W 203 (sideways). P 11½ × 11.*
1144 **592** 120 cr. chestnut 10 5

(Des E. de Araújo Jorge. Eng J. Rodrigues. Recess)

1966 (12 Aug). *150th Anniv of French Art Mission's Arrival in Brazil. W 203. P 11 × 11½.*
1145 **593** 100 cr. chestnut 8 5

594 Military Service Emblem   **595** R. Dario

(Des W. Granado. Photo)

1966 (6 Sept). *New Military Service Law. W 203. P 11 × 11½ or imperf* (No. MS1147).*
1146 **594** 30 cr. bright blue & greenish yell .. 5 5
MS1147 111 × 53 mm. No. 1146. No gum
(sold at 100 cr.) 8 8
*No. **MS**1147 was printed in panes of four and subdivided by perf 11 × 11½, the stamp itself being imperf.

(Des E. de Araújo Jorge. Photo)

1966 (20 Sept). *50th Death Anniv of Ruben Dario (Nicaraguan poet). W 203 (sideways). P 11½ × 11.*
1148 **595** 100 cr. bright purple 8 5

596 Santarem Candlestick   **597** Arms of Santa Cruz

(T **596/7** des M. F. Pinheiro. Photo)

1966 (6 Oct). *Centenary of Goeldi Museum. No wmk. P 11 × 11½.*
1149 **596** 30 cr. deep brown/salmon 5 5

1966 (15 Oct). *First National Tobacco Exhibition, Santa Cruz. W 203 (sideways). P 11½ × 11.*
1150 **597** 30 cr. grey-green 5 5

598 U.N.E.S.C.O. Emblem

(Des M. F. Pinheiro. Eng J. Rodrigues. Recess)

1966 (24 Oct). *20th Anniv of U.N.E.S.C.O. W 203. P 11½ or imperf* (No. MS1152).*
1151 **598** 120 cr. black 10 5
MS1152 110 × 52 mm. No. 1151. No gum
(sold at 150 cr.) 40 20
*No. **MS**1152 was printed in panes of four and subdivided by perf 11 × 11½, the stamp itself being imperf.

599 Capt. A. C. Pinto   **600** Maltese Cross and
and Map   Southern Cross

(Des E. de Araújo Jorge. Photo)

1966 (22 Nov). *Arrival Bicentenary of Captain A. C. Pinto. W 203 (sideways). P 11½ × 11.*
1153▴**599** 30 cr. rose-red 5 5

(Des W. Puntar. Photo)

1966 (4 Dec). *"Lubrapex 1966" Stamp Exhibition, Rio de Janeiro. No wmk. P 11½.*
1154 **600** 100 cr. blue-green 8 5

601 Madonna and   **601a**
Child

(Des B. Mazzeo (30 cr.), W. Granado (others). Photo)

1966 (Dec). *Christmas. T **601**, **601a** and similar design. W 203 (sideways on 30 cr.) or no wmk (150 cr.). P 11½ × 11 (30 cr., 150 cr.) or 11½ (35 cr.).*
1155 **601** 30 cr. blue-green (8.12) 5 5
1156 **601a** 35 cr. ultram & salmon (22.12) .. 5 5
1157 — 150 cr. salmon and ultramarine
(no gum) (28.12) 45 35
Design: *Vert (23 × 51 mm)*—150 cr. As 35 cr. *inscr* "Pax Hominibus" *but not* "Brasil Correio".

602 Arms of Laguna **603** Railway Bridge

(Des W. Puntar. Eng L. Ạ. da Fonseca. Recess)

1967 (4 Jan). *Centenary of Laguna Postal and Telegraphic Agency. No wmk.* P 11 × 11½.
1158 **602** 60 cr. sepia   5   5

(Des W. Puntar. Photo)

1967 (16 Feb). *Centenary of Santos–Jundiai Railway.* W **203**. P 11 × 11½.
1159 **603** 50 cr. deep orange   5   5

604 Polish Cross and "Black Madonna" **605** Research Rocket

(Des E. Kubiczek. Photo)

1967 (12 Mar). *Polish Millennium. No wmk.* P 11 × 11½.
1160 **604** 50 cr. red, blue and yellow   10   5

(Des W. Puntar. Photo)

1967 (23 Mar). *World Meteorological Day.* W **203** (*sideways*). P 11½ × 11.
1161 **605** 50 cr. black and blue   8   5

Currency Revaluation

1000 (old) Cruzeiros = 1 (new) Cruzeiro

606 Anita Garibaldi

(Des W. Puntar. Photo)

1967–69. T **606** *and similar vert portrait designs.* W **203** (*sideways*). P 11 × 11½.
1162	1 c. deep ultramarine (3.5.67)	5	5
1163	2 c. deep orange-red (11.8.67)	5	5
1164	3 c. bright green (7.6.67)	5	5
1165	5 c. black (14.4.67)	5	5
1166	6 c. brown (12.5.67)	5	5
1167	10 c. slate-green (18.6.69)	5	5
1162/1167	*Set of* 6	20	20

Portraits:—1 c. Mother Angelica; 2 c. Marilia de Dirceu; 3 c. Dr. R. Lobato; 6 c. Ana Neri; 10 c. Darci Vargas.

607 "VARIG 40 Years" **608** Lions Emblem and Globes

(Des W. Puntar. Photo)

1967 (8 May). *40th Anniv of Varig Airlines. No wmk.* P 11½ × 11.
1171 **607** 6 c. black and new blue   ..   5   5

(Des W. Puntar. Eng J. Rodrigues. Recess)

1967 (9 May). *50th Anniv of Lions International.* W **203**. P 11½ × 11½.
1172 **608** 6 c. dull green   5   5
MS1173 130 × 80 mm. No. 1172. Imperf (sold at 15 c.)   15   10

609 "Madonna and Child" **610** Prince Akihito and Princess Michiko

(Des E. de Araújo Jorge. Photo)

1967 (14 May). *Mothers' Day. No wmk.* P 11½ × 11.
1174 **609** 5 c. violet   5   5
MS1175 130 × 76 mm. **609** 15 c. violet. Imperf   15   10

(Des W. Puntar. Photo)

1967 (25 May). *Visit of Crown Prince and Princess of Japan. No wmk.* P 11 × 11½.
1176 **610** 10 c. black and rose-red   ..   5   5

611 Radar Aerial and Pigeon **612** Brother Vincente do Salvador

(Des W. Puntar. Photo)

1967 (20 June). *Inauguration of Communications Ministry, Brasilia.* W **203** (*sideways*). P 11½ × 11.
1177 **611** 10 c. black and light magenta   ..   5   5

(Des W. Granado. Eng J. Rodrigues. Recess)

1967 (28 June). *400th Birth Anniv of Brother Vicente do Salvador (founder of Franciscan Brotherhood, Rio de Janeiro).* W **203** (*sideways*). P 11½ × 11.
1178 **612** 5 c. brown   5   5

613 Emblem and Members   **614** Mobius Symbol

620 N. Pecanha   **621** Our Lady of the Apparition and Basilica   **622** "Song Bird"

(Des W. Granado. Photo)

1967 (14 July). *National 4-S ("4-H") Clubs Day. No wmk. P 11½.*
1179 **613** 5 c. emerald-green and black   .. 5   5

(Des F. J. da Silva. Photo)

1967 (2 Oct). *Birth Centenary of Nilo Pecanha (statesman). W 203 (sideways). P 11½×11.*
1186 **620** 5 c. dull purple   5   5

(Des E. de Araújo Jorge. Photo)

1967 (21 July). *Sixth Brazilian Mathematical Congress, Rio de Janeiro. W 203 (sideways). P 11½×11½.*
1180 **614** 5 c. black and new blue   5   5
"impa"=Instituto de Matemática Pura e Aplicada.

(Des W. Puntar. Photo)

1967 (12 Oct–Dec). *250th Anniv of Discovery of Statue of Our Lady of the Apparition. W 203 (sideways). P 11½.*
1187 **621** 5 c. bright blue and ochre   5   5
MS1188   80×130 mm. **621** 5 c. and 10 c. each bright blue and ochre. Imperf (27.12)   ..   15   8
No. **MS**1188 was issued for Christmas.

(Des E. de Araújo Jorge. Recess and photo)

1967 (16 Oct). *International Song Festival. W 203 (sideways). P 11½×11.*
1189 **622** 20 c. multicoloured   10   5

615 Fish and "Waves"   **616** Papal Arms and "Golden Rose"

623 Balloon, Rocket and Aircraft   **624** Pres. Wenceslau Braz

(Des R. Wagner. Photo)

1967 (1 Aug). *Bicentenary of Piracicaba. No wmk. P 11½.*
1181 **615** 5 c. black and deep slate-blue   ..   5   5

(Des E. de Araújo Jorge. Photo (10, 20 c.) or recess (others))

1967. *Aviation Week. W 203. P 11×11½.*
1190 **623** 10 c. blue (18 Oct)   5   5
MS1191   131×76 mm. **623** 15 c. blue. Imperf (23 Oct)   15   8

(Des W. Granado. Photo)

1967 (15 Aug). *Pope Paul's "Golden Rose" Offering to Our Lady of Fatima. W 203. P 11½.*
1182 **616** 20 c. deep magenta and yellow   ..   10   5

(Des W. Puntar. Photo (10, 20 c.) or recess (others))

1967–68. *T 624 and similar vert portrait designs. W 203 (sideways). P 11×11½.*
1192   10 c. blue (16.11.67)   5   5
1193   20 c. deep red-brown (16.11.67)   ..   8   5
1195   50 c. black (19.3.68)   15   5
1198   1 cr. bright purple (19.3.68)   ..   30   10
1199   2 cr. bright green (18.7.68)   ..   60   15
1192/1199   *Set of 5*   ..   ..   ..   1·00   45
Portraits of Brazilian Presidents:—10 c. Arthur Bernardes; 20 c. Campos Salles; 1 cr. Washington Luiz; 2 cr. Castello Branco.

617 General A. de Sampaio   **618** King Olav of Norway   **619** Sun and Rio de Janeiro

625 Rio Carnival   **626** Sailor, Anchor and Ships

(Des W. Puntar. Eng A. S. Lopes. Recess)

1967 (24 Aug). *General Sampaio Commemoration. W 203 (sideways). P 11½×11.*
1183 **617** 5 c. blue   5   5

(Des W. Granado. Photo)

1967 (6 Sept). *Visit of King Olav. W 203 (sideways). P 11½×11.*
1184 **618** 10 c. orange-brown   5   5

1967 (25 Sept). *Meeting of International Monetary Fund, Rio de Janeiro. Photo. W 203 (sideways). P 11½.*
1185 **619** 10 c. black and orange-red..   ..   5   5

(Des W. Granado. Photo)

1967 (Nov). *International Tourist Year.* W **203** (*sideways*).
P 11½ × 11.
1200 **625** 10 c. multicoloured (22.11)..   5   5
MS1201 76 × 130 mm. **625** 15 c. multicoloured. Imperf (24.11)   15   5

(Des W. N. de Oliveira. Photo)

1967 (6 Dec). *Navy Week.* W **203** (*sideways*). P 11½ × 11.
1202 **626** 10 c. ultramarine   5   5

627 Christmas Decorations

628 O. Bilac (poet), Aircraft, Tank and Aircraft Carrier

(Des W. Granado. Photo)

1967 (8 Dec). *Christmas.* W **203**. P 11½.
1203 **627** 5 c. multicoloured ..   5   5

(Des W. Granado. Photo)

1967 (16 Dec). *Reservists' Day.* W **203**. P 11 × 11½.
1204 **628** 5 c. blue and lemon   5   5

629 J. Rodrigues de Carvalho

630 O. Rangel

(Des J. R. da Silva. Recess)

1967 (18 Dec). *Birth Centenary of José Rodrigues de Carvalho (jurist and writer).* W **203** (*sideways*). P 11½ × 11.
1205 **629** 10 c. bluish green ..   5   5

(Des W. Puntar. Photo)

1968 (29 Feb). *Birth Centenary of Orlando Rangel (pioneer pharmaceutist).* W **203**. P 11½ × 11½.
1206 **630** 5 c. black and turquoise-blue ..   5   5

631 Madonna and Diver

632 Map of Free Zone

633 Human Rights Emblem

(Des B. Mazzeo. Photo)

1968 (9 Mar). *250th Anniv of Paranagua Underwater Exploration.* W **203** (*sideways*). P 11½ × 11.
1207 **631** 10 c. yellow-green and slate-green   5   5

(Des W. Puntar. Photo)

1968 (13 Mar). *Manaus Free Zone.* W **203** (*sideways*). P 11½ × 11.
1208 **632** 10 c. carmine, myrtle-grn & yell ..   5   5

(Des E. de Araújo Jorge. Photo)

1968 (21 Mar). *20th Anniv of Declaration of Human Rights.* W **203** (*sideways*). P 11½ × 11.
1209 **633** 10 c. orange-red and blue ..   5   5

GUM. All the following issues are *without* gum, except where otherwise stated.

634 Paul Harris

635 College Arms

(Des B. Lancetta. Litho)

1968 (19 Apr). *Birth Centenary of Paul Harris.* P 11½ × 11.
1210 **634** 20 c. chestnut and emerald ..   8   5

(Des E. de Araújo Jorge. Photo)

1968 (22 Apr). *Centenary of St. Luiz College.* W **203**. With gum. P 11½.
1211 **635** 10 c. gold, ultramarine and red ..   5   5

636 Cabral and Ships

(Des W. N. de Oliveira (10 c.). Litho)

1968 (22 Apr–11 July). *500th Birth Anniv of Pedro Cabral (explorer).* T **636** *and similar horiz design. Multicoloured.* P 11½.
1212   10 c. Type **636** ..   5   5
    a. Grey (value and inscr) omitted ..   6·00
1213   20 c. "The First Mass" (11.7) ..   8   5

637 "Maternity" (after H. Bernardelli)

638 Harpy Eagle

(Des W. Granado. Litho)

1968 (12 May). *Mothers' Day.* P 11½.
1214 **637** 5 c. multicoloured 5 5

1968 (30 May). *150th Anniv of National Museum. Recess and photo.* W **203**. *With gum.* P 11½.
1215 **638** 20 c. black and new blue 8 5

639 Women of Brazil and Japan

(Des E. de Araújo Jorge. Litho)

1968 (26 June). *Inauguration of "VARIG" Brazil–Japan Air Service.* P 11½.
1216 **639** 10 c. multicoloured 5 5

640 Horse-racing

1968 (14 July). *Centenary of Brazilian Jockey Club. Litho.* P 11 × 11½.
1217 **640** 10 c. multicoloured 5 5

641 Wren (*Leucolepis modulator*)

(Des E. de Araújo Jorge (10 c.), W. Granado (others). Recess)

1968–69. *Birds.* T **641** *and similar designs.* P 11 × 11½ (20 c.) or 11½ × 11 (others).
1218 10 c. multicoloured (20.8.69) 5 5
1219 20 c. yellow-brown, grn & bl (19.7.68) 8 5
1220 50 c. sep, carm, emer & ultram (2.8.68) 20 12
Design: *Vert*—10 c. Cardinal; 50 c. Swainson's Royal Fly-catcher.
Some stamps show part of the paper-maker's watermark: "WESTERPOST INDUSTRIA CIP BRASILEIRA" in two lines with diamond-shaped emblem.

642 Ancient Post-box

643 Marshal E. Luiz Mallet

(Des J. P. Guimarães. Photo)

1968 (1 Aug). *Stamp Day.* W **203**. *With gum.* P 11 × 11½.
1221 **642** 5 c. black, bronze-green & olive-yell 5 5

(Des A. Lima. Recess)

1968 (25 Aug). *Mallet Commemoration.* W **203** (*sideways*). *With gum.* P 11½ × 11.
1222 **643** 10 c. reddish lilac 5 5

644 Map of South America   **645** Lyceum Badge

(Des A. Magalhães. Photo)

1968 (5 Sept). *Visit of Chilean President.* W **203** (*sideways*). *With gum.* P 11½ × 11.
1223 **644** 10 c. red-orange 5 5

(Des E. de Araújo Jorge. Recess and photo)

1968 (10 Sept). *Centenary of Portuguese Literacy Lyceum (High School).* W **203** (*sideways*). *With gum.* P 11½.
1224 **645** 5 c. yellow-green and pink 5 5

646 Map and Telex Tape   **647** Soldiers on Medallion

1968 (18 Sept). *"Telex Service for 25th City (Curitiba)". Photo.* W **203**. *With gum.* P 11 × 11½.
1225 **646** 20 c. emerald and olive-yellow .. 8 5

1968 (23 Sept). *Eighth American Armed Forces Conference. Litho.* P 11½ × 11.
1226 **647** 5 c. black and greenish blue .. 5 5

.648 "Cock" shaped as Treble Clef   **649** "Petrobas" Refinery

(Des E. de Araújo Jorge. Litho)

1968 (30 Sept). *Third International Song Festival, Rio de Janeiro.* P 11½.
1227 **648** 6 c. multicoloured 5 5

1968 (3 Oct). *15th Anniv of National Petroleum Industry. Litho.* P 11½.
1228 **649** 6 c. multicoloured 5 5

650 Boy walking towards Rising Sun

651 Children with Books

656 F. Braga and part of "Hymn of National Flag"

657 Clasped Hands

(Des J. P. Guimarães. Litho)

1968 (16 Oct). *U.N.I.C.E.F.* **T 650** *and similar designs. P* 11×11½ *(10 c.) or* 11½×11 *(others).*

1229	5 c. black and pale blue	5	5
1230	10 c. black, carm-red, new & light blue	5	5
1231	20 c. black, grey, red, pink & yellow-ol	8	5

Designs: *Horiz*—10 c. Hand protecting child. *Vert*—20 c. Young girl in plaits.

(Des B. Mazzeo. Litho)

1968 (23 Oct). *Book Week. P* 11×11½.

1232	**651** 5 c. multicoloured	5	5

652 W.H.O. Emblem and Flags

1968 (24 Oct). *20th Anniv of World Health Organization. Litho. P* 11½.

1233	**652** 20 c. multicoloured	8	5

653 J. B. Debret

(Des W. Granado. Litho)

1968 (30 Oct). *Birth Bicentenary of Jean Baptiste Debret (painter) (1st issue). P* 11×11½.

1234	**653** 10 c. black and yellow	5	5

See also Nos. 1273/4.

1968 (19 Nov). *Birth Centenary of Francisco Braga (composer). W* **203** *(sideways). With gum. P* 11½×11.

1237	**656** 5 c. purple-brown	5	5

1968 (25 Nov). *Blood Donors' Day. Typo. P* 11×11½.

1238	**657** 5 c. scarlet, black and new blue	5	5

1968 (25 Nov)–**69**. *OBLIGATORY TAX. Leprosy Research Fund. Revalued currency. Photo. W* **203**. *With gum. P* 11½.

1239	**388** 5 c. green	5	5
1240	5 c. deep carmine (28.11.69)	5	5

658 Steam Locomotive of 1868

659 Angelus Bell

(Des E. de Araújo Jorge. Litho)

1968 (28 Nov). *Centenary of São Paulo Railway. P* 11½.

1241	**658** 5 c. multicoloured	5	5

(Des J. P. Guimarães (5 c.), W. Puntar (6 c.). Litho)

1968 (Dec). *Christmas. T* **659** *and similar vert design. Multicoloured. P* 11½×11.

1242	5 c. Type **659** (12.12)	5	5
1243	6 c. Father Christmas giving present (20.12)	5	5

654 Queen Elizabeth II

655 Brazilian Flag

1968 (4 Nov). *State Visit of Queen Elizabeth II. Litho. P* 11½.

1235	**654** 70 c. multicoloured	25	25

(Des W. Puntar. Litho)

1968 (19 Nov). *Brazilian Flag Day. P* 11½.

1236	**655** 10 c. blue, yellow, green & black	5	5

660 F. A. V. Caldas, Jr.

661 Reservists' Emblem and Memorial

(Des Cecilia de Melo Tavares. Litho)

1968 (13 Dec). *Birth Centenary of Francisco Caldas, Junior (founder of "Correio do Povo" newspaper). P* 11½×11.

1244	**660** 10 c. black, pale pink and red	5	5

(Des W. N. de Oliveira. Photo)

1968 (16 Dec). *Reservists' Day. W* **203**. *With gum. P* 11×11½.

1245	**661** 5 c. turquoise-green & yell-brn	5	5

662 Dish Aerial

663 Viscount do Rio Branco

668 Mint and Banknote Pattern

(Des J. H. da Rocha. Litho)

1969 (28 Feb). *Inauguration of Satellite Communications System.* P 11½×11.
1246 **662** 30 c. black, blue and light blue . . 10 5

(Des W. Granado. Litho)

1969 (16 Mar). *150th Birth Anniv of Viscount do Rio Branco.* P 11½×11.
1247 **663** 5 c. deep sepia and pale drab . . 5 5

(Des W. Puntar. Litho)

1969 (14 Apr). *Opening of New State Mint Printing Works.* P 11½.
1252 **668** 5 c. bistre and yellow-orange . . 5 5

664 St. Gabriel

665 Shoemaker's Last and Globe

669 Society Emblem and Stamps

670 "Our Lady of Santana" (statue)

(Des W. Granado. Litho)

1969 (24 Mar). *St. Gabriel's Day (Patron Saint of Telecommunications).* P 11½×11.
1248 **664** 5 c. multicoloured 5 5

(Des W. Puntar. Litho)

1969 (29 Mar). *4th International Shoe Fair, Novo Hamburgo.* P 11×11½.
1249 **665** 5 c. multicoloured 5 5

(Des W. Granado. Litho)

1969 (30 Apr). *50th Anniversary of São Paulo Philatelic Society.* P 11×11½.
1253 **669** 5 c. multicoloured 5 5

(Des W. Granado. Litho)

1969 (8 May). *Mothers' Day.* P 11½.
1254 **670** 5 c. multicoloured 5 5

666 Kardec and Monument

(Des B. Lancetta. Photo)

1969 (31 Mar). *Death Centenary of "Allan Kardec" (Prof. H. Rivail) (French educationalist and spiritualist).* W **203.** With gum. P 11×11½.
1250 **666** 5 c. orange-brown and bluish green 5 5

667 Men of Three Races and Arms of Cuiaba

(Des B. Mazzeo. Litho)

1969 (8 Apr). *250th Anniversary of Cuiaba (capital of Mato Grosso state).* P 11×11½.
1251 **667** 5 c. multicoloured 5 5

671 I.L.O. Emblem

672 Diving Platform and Swimming Pool

(Des E. de Araújo Jorge. Photo)

1969 (13 May). *50th Anniversary of International Labour Organization.* W **203.** With gum. P 11×11½.
1255 **671** 5 c. gold and carmine-red 5 5

(Des F. J. Avila. Litho)

1969 (13 June). *40th Anniversary of Cearense Water Sports Club, Fortaleza.* P 11½×11.
1256 **672** 20 c. black, turq-grn & lt orge-brn . . 8 5

673 "Mother and Child at Window" (Di Cavalcanti)

674 Angelfish

1969. 10th Biennial Art Exhibition, São Paulo. T **673** and similar multicoloured designs. Litho. P 11½.
1257   10 c. Type 673 (30.6) 5   5
1258   20 c. Modern sculpture (F. Leirner) (33×33 mm) (27.9) 8   5
1259   50 c. "The Sun is Brasilia" (D. di Prete) (33×53 mm) (27.9) 15   10
1260   1 cr. "Angelfish" (A. Martins) (33×53 mm) (7.11) 30   15
1257/1260   Set of 4   50   25

(Des W. Puntar. Litho)

1969 (July). A.C.A.P.I. Fish Preservation and Development Campaign. T **674** and similar multicoloured designs. P 11½.
1261   20 c. Type 674 (21.7) 8   5
MS1262   134×100 mm. Four designs, each 38×22 mm. 10 c. Tetra; 15 c. Piranha; 20 c. Megalamphodus megalopterus; 30 c. Black tetra. Imperf (24.7) 35   35

675 I.O. Teles de Menezes (founder)

676 Postman delivering Letter

(Des B. Lancetta. Photo)

1969 (26 July). Centenary of Spiritualist Press. W **203** (sideways). With gum. P 11½×11.
1263   675   50 c. blue-green and orange .. 15   8

(Des E. de Araújo Jorge. Photo)

1969 (1 Aug). Stamp Day. W **203** (sideways). With gum. P 11½×11.
1264   676   30 c. new blue 10   5

677 General T. Fragoso

678 Map of Army Bases

(Des E. de Araújo Jorge. Eng J. R. da Silva. Recess)

1969 (25 Aug). Birth Centenary of General Tasso Fragoso. W **203** (sideways). With gum. P 11½×11.
1265   677   20 c. dull green 8   5

(Des A. Lima (10 c.), J. P. Guimarães (20 c.). Litho)

1969 (25 Aug). Army Week. T **678** and similar multicoloured design. P 11½ (10 c.) or 11×11½ (20 c.).
1266   10 c. Type 678 5   5
1267   20 c. Monument and railway bridge (horiz, 39×22 mm) 8   5

679 Jupia Dam

680 Gandhi and Spinning-wheel

(Des D. Ippolito. Litho)

1969 (10 Sept). Inauguration of Jupia Dam. P 11½.
1268   679   20 c. multicoloured 8   5

(Des W. Granado. Litho)

1969 (2 Oct). Birth Centenary of Mahatma Gandhi. P 11×11½.
1269   680   20 c. black and lemon 8   5

681 Santos Dumont, Eiffel Tower and Moon Landing

(Des E. de Araújo Jorge. Litho)

1969 (17 Oct). 1st Man on the Moon and Santos Dumont's Flight (1906) Commemoration. P 11½.
1270   681   50 c. multicoloured 15   5

682 Smelting Plant

683 Steel Furnace

(Des W. Puntar. Litho)

1969 (26 Oct). *Expansion of USIMINAS Steel Consortium.*
P 11½.
1271 **682** 20 c. multicoloured 8 5

(Des ACESITA staff. Litho)

1969 (31 Oct). *25th Anniversary of ACESITA Steel Works.*
P 11½.
1272 **683** 10 c. multicoloured 5 5

684 "The Water Cart" (Debret)

(Des W. Granado. Litho)

1969 (5 Nov)-**70**. *Birth Bicenenary of Jean Baptiste Debret
(painter) (2nd issue). T* **684** *and similar horiz design Multicoloured.* P11½.
1273 20 c. Type **684** 8 5
1274 30 c. "Street Scene" (19.5.70) .. 10 8

685 Exhibition
Emblem

687 Pele scoring Goal

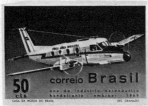

686 "Bandeirante" Aircraft

(Des B. Mazzeo. Litho)

1969 (15 Nov). *"Abuexpo 69" Stamp Exhibition.* P 11½×11.
1275 **685** 10 c. multicoloured 5 5

(Des W. Granado. Litho)

1969 (23 Nov). *Brazilian Aeronautical Industry Expansion
Year.* P 11½.
1276 **686** 50 c. multicoloured 15 5

(Des E. de Araújo Jorge. Litho)

1969 (28 Nov)-**70**. *Footballer Pele's 1000th Goal.* P 11½.
1277 **687** 10 c. multicoloured 12 5
MS1278 81×120 mm. **687** 75 c. multicoloured. Imperf (23.1.70) 25 25

688 "Madonna and Child" 689 Destroyer and Submarine
(painted panel)

(Des W. Puntar. Litho)

1969 (Dec). *Christmas.* P 11½.
1279 **688** 10 c. multicoloured (8.12) .. 5 5
MS1280 137×102 mm. **688** 75 c. multicoloured. Imperf (18.12) 25 25

(Des and eng A. S. Lopes. Recess)

1969 (9 Dec). *Navy Day.* W 203. *With gum.* P 11×11½.
1281 **689** 5 c. grey-blue 5 5

690 Dr. Herman Blumenau 691 Carnival Dancers

(Des and eng J. R. da Silva. Recess)

1969 (26 Dec). *150th Birth Anniv of Dr. Herman Blumenau
(German immigrant leader).* W 203 *(sideways). With
gum.* P 11½.
1282 **690** 20 c. grey-green 8 5

(Des W. Puntar (30 c.). B. Lancetta (50 c.), W. Granado
(others). Litho)

1969 (29 Dec)-**70**. *Carioca Carnival, Rio de Janeiro* (1970).
T **691** *and similar multicoloured designs.* P 11½.
1283 5 c. Type **691** 5 5
1284 10 c. Samba dancers (*horiz*) .. 5 5
1285 20 c. Clowns (*horiz*) 8 5
1286 30 c. Confetti and mask (5.2.70) .. 8 5
1287 50 c. Tambourine-player (5.2.70) .. 15 10
1283/1287 Set of 5 .. .. 35 25

692 Gomes conducting

693 Monastery

(Des W. Puntar. Litho)

1970 (19 Mar). *Centenary of Opera "O Guarani" by Antonio
Gomes.* P 11½.
1288 **692** 20 c. multicoloured 8 5

(Des J. P. Guimarães. Litho)

1970 (6 Apr). *400th Anniversary of Penha Monastery, Vilha Velha.* P 11½.
1289 **693** 20 c. multicoloured 8 5

694 National Assembly Building   **695** Emblem on Map

(Des B. Lancetta. Litho)

1970 (21 Apr). *10th Anniversary of Brasilia.* T **694** and similar horiz designs. Multicoloured. P 11½.
1290 20 c. Type **694** 8 5
1291 50 c. Reflecting pool 15 10
1292 1 cr. Presidential Palace .. 30 20

(Des Elizabeth S. de Paiva. Litho)

1970 (5 May). *Rondon Project (student's practical training scheme).* P 11½.
1293 **695** 50 c. multicoloured 15 10

696 Marshal Osorio and Arms

(Des W. Puntar. Litho)

1970 (8 May). *Opening of Marshal Osorio Historical Park.* P 11½.
1294 **696** 20 c. multicoloured 8 5

697 "Madonna and Child"   **698** Brasilia Cathedral
(San Antonio Monastery)   (stylised)

(Des W. Granado. Litho)

1970 (10 May). *Mother's Day.* P 11½.
1295 **697** 20 c. multicoloured 8 5

1970 (27 May). *8th National Eucharistic Congress, Brasilia.* Recess. W **203** (sideways). With gum. P 11½.
1296 **698** 20 c. yellow-green 8 5

699 Census Symbol   **700** Jules Rimet Cup and Map

(Des Marilena P. da Silva. Litho)

1970 (22 June). *8th National Census.* P 11½.
1297 **699** 20 c. yellow and dull green .. 8 5

(Des Ferrari Publicity. Litho)

1970 (24 June). *World Cup Football Championship, Mexico.* P 11½.
1298 **700** 50 c. black, gold and greenish blue 15 10

701 Statue of Christ   **703** Pandia Calogeras

702 Bellini and Swedish Flag (1958)

(Des B. Lancetta. Litho)

1970 (18 July). *6th World Congress of Marist Students.* P 11½.
1299 **701** 50 c. multicoloured 15 10

(Des W. Puntar (1 cr.), W. Granado (others). Litho)

1970 (4 Aug). *Brazil's Third Victory in World Cup Football Championships.* T **702** and similar horiz designs. Multicoloured. P 11½.
1300 1 cr. Type **702** 25 15
1301 2 cr. Garrincha and Chilean flag (1962) 50 30
1302 3 cr. Pele and Mexican flag (1970) .. 75 50

(Des E. de Araújo Jorge. Photo)

1970 (25 Aug). *Birth Centenary of Pandia Calogeras (author and politician).* W **203** (sideways). With gum. P 11½ × 11.
1303 **703** 20 c. blue-green 8 5

ALBUM LISTS
Write for our latest lists of albums and accessories.
These will be sent free on request.

709 "The Holy Family" (C. Portinari)

710 Warship

704 Brazilian Forces' Badges and Map

705 "The Annunciation" (Cassio M'Boy)

(Des W. Granado. Litho)

1970 (Dec). *Christmas. P* 11½.
1312 **709** 50 c. multicoloured (1.12) 12 8
MS1313 107×52 mm. **709** 1 cr. multicoloured. Imperf (8.12) 25 25

(Des J. P. Guimarães. Litho)

1970 (14 Sept). *25th Anniversary of Victory in Second World War. P* 11×11½.
1304 **704** 20 c. multicoloured 8 5

(Des W. Granado. Litho)

1970 (11 Dec). *Navy Day. P* 11½.
1314 **710** 20 c. multicoloured 8 5

(Des W. Granado. Litho)

1970 (29 Sept). *St. Gabriel's Day* (*Patron Saint of Telecommunications*). *P* 11½.
1305 **705** 20 c. multicoloured 8 5

706 Boy in Library

707 U.N. Emblem

711 Congress Emblem

712 Links and Globe

(Des National Housing Bank staff. Litho)

1971 (28 Mar). *3rd Inter-American Housing Congress, Rio de Janeiro. P* 11½.
1315 **711** 50 c. red and black 12 8

(Des E. de Araújo Jorge. Litho)

1970 (23 Oct). *Book Week. P* 11½.
1306 **706** 20 c. multicoloured 8 5

(Des E. de Araújo Jorge. Litho)

1970 (24 Oct). *25th Anniversary of United Nations. P* 11½.
1307 **707** 50 c. ultramarine, silver & pale blue 12 8

(Des W. Granado. Litho)

1971 (31 Mar). *Racial Equality Year. P* 11½×11.
1316 **712** 20 c. multicoloured 5 5

708 "Rio de Janeiro" (*c* 1820)

713 *Morpho melacheilus*

714 Madonna and Child

(Des W. Puntar (20 c., 1 cr.), E. Rodrigues (50 c.), W. Puntar and W. Granado (**MS**1311). Litho)

1970 (Oct). *3rd Brasilian-Portuguese Stamp Exhibition "LUBRAPEX 70", Rio de Janeiro. T* **708** *and similar horiz designs. P* 11½.
1308 20 c. multicoloured (27.10) 8 5
1309 50 c. yellow-brown and black (27.10) .. 12 8
1310 1 cr. multicoloured (27.10) 25 12
MS1311 60×80 mm. **708** 1 cr. multicoloured. Imperf (28.10) 25 25
Designs:—50 c. Exhibition emblem; 1 cr. Rio de Janeiro (modern view).

(Des W. Granado. Litho)

1971 (28 Apr). *Butterflies. T* **713** *and similar horiz design. Multicoloured. P* 11×11½.
1317 20 c. Type **713** 5 5
1318 1 cr. *Papilio thoas brasiliensis* .. 25 12

(Des W. Granado. Litho)

1971 (9 May). *Mothers' Day. P* 11½.
1319 **714** 20 c. multicoloured 5 5

715 Hands reaching for Ball   **716** Eastern Part of Highway Map

(Des C. B. B. Agency. Litho)

1971 (19 May). *6th Women's Basketball World Championships.* P 11½.
1320 **715** 70 c. multicoloured 15 8

(Des W. Puntar. Litho)

1971 (1 July). *Trans-Amazon Highway Project.* T **716** *and similar square design.* P 11½.
1321 40 c. Type **716** 8 5
1322 1 cr. Western part of Highway Map .. 20 12
Nos. 1321/2 form a composite design. Issued in sheets of 28, each horiz line containing two *se-tenant* pairs of Nos. 1321/2; the pairs separated by an inscribed stamp-sized label.

717 "Head of a Man" (V. M. Lima)   **718** Gen. Caxias and Map

1971 (1 Aug). *Stamp Day.* T **717** *and similar vert painting. Multicoloured. Litho.* P 11½.
1323 40 c. Type **717** 8 5
1324 1 cr "Arab Violinist" (P. Americo) .. 20 12

(Des W. Puntar. Photo)

1971 (25 Aug). *Army Week. With gum.* P 11½.
1325 **.718** 20 c. brown-red and apple-green .. 5 5

719 Anita Garibaldi   **721** Flags of Central American Republics

720 "Xavante" Jet Fighter and Early Aircraft

(Des B. Mazzeo. Litho)

1971 (30 Aug). *150th Birth Anniv of Anita Garibaldi.* P 11½.
1326 **719** 20 c. multicoloured 5 5

(Des EMBRAER staff. Litho)

1971 (6 Sept). *1st Flight of "Xavante" Jet Fighter.* P 11½.
1327 **720** 40 c. multicoloured 8 5

(Des W. Puntar. Litho)

1971 (15 Sept). *150th Anniversary of Central American Republics' Independence.* P 11½.
1328 **721** 40 c. multicoloured 8 5

722 Exhibition Emblem   **723** "Black Mother" (L. de Albuquerque)

(Des French Embassy. Litho)

1971 (17 Sept). *"Franca 71" Industrial, Technical and Scientific Exhibition, São Paulo.* P 11½.
1329 **722** 1 cr. 30, multicoloured 25 12

(Des W. Granado. Litho)

1971 (28 Sept). *Centenary of Slaves Emancipation Law.* P 11½.
1330 **723** 40 c. multicoloured 8 5

724 Archangel Gabriel   **725** "Couple on Bridge" (Marisa da S. Marques)

(Des W. Granado. Litho)

1971 (29 Sept). *St. Gabriel's Day (Patron Saint of Telecommunications).* P 11½×11.
1331 **724** 40 c. multicoloured 8 5

(Des from Children's Drawings. Litho)

1971 (15 Oct). *Children's Day.* T **725** *and similar square designs. Multicoloured.* P 11½.
1332 35 c. Type **725** 8 5
1333 45 c. "Couple on River-bank" (Mary R. e Silva) 8 5
1334 60 c. "Girl in Hat" (Teresa A. P. Ferreira) 12 8

726 *Werkhauserii superba*   727 Eunice Weaver

732 Pres. Lanusse

1971 (16 Nov). *Brazilian Orchids. Litho.* P 11½.
1335 **726** 40 c. multicoloured 8 5

1971 (24 Nov). *OBLIGATORY TAX. Leprosy Research Fund. Photo.* W 203 (*sideways*). *With gum.* P 11½.
1336 **727** 10 c. grey-green 5 5

(Des E. de Araújo Jorge. Litho)

1972 (13 Mar). *Visit of President Lanusse of Argentina.* P 11×11½.
1347 **732** 40 c. multicoloured 8 5

728 "25 SENAC"   729 Patrolboat

733 Presidents Castel Branco, Costa e Silva and Medici   734 Post Office Symbol

(Des R. Coachman, A. Bosisio and E. Serman. Litho)

1971 (3 Dec). *25th Anniversaries of SENAC (apprenticeship scheme) and SESC (workers social service).* T 728 and similar vert design. P 11½.
1337 20 c. new blue and black 5 5
1338 40 c. yellow-orange and black .. 8 5
Design:—40 c. "25 SESC".
Nos. 1337/8 were issued together *se-tenant* within the sheet.

(Des W. Granado. Litho)

1971 (8 Dec). *Navy Day.* P 11×11½.
1339 **729** 20 c. multicoloured 5 5

(Des M. Popp. Litho)

1972 (29 Mar). *8th Anniversary of 1964 Revolution.* P 11×11½.
1348 **733** 20 c. multicoloured 5 5

FLUORESCENT PAPER. From No. 1349 certain stamps were only issued with a fluorescent coating on the face. This reacts as a pale green colour under U.V. light. The coating was introduced in connection with electronic sorting equipment. In the listings references to fluorescent paper are to this "green" coating and not to the normal "white" fluorescence found in some Brazilian stamp paper.

1972 (10 Apr). *Photo. Fluorescent paper.* P 11½×11.
1349 **734** 20 c. red-brown 5 5

735 Pres. Tomas   736 Exploratory Borehole (CPRM)

(Des W. Puntar. Litho)

1972 (22 Apr). *Visit of Pres. Tomas of Portugal.* P 11×11½.
1350 **735** 75 c. multicoloured 15 8

730 Cruciform Symbol   731 Washing Bonfim Church

(Des J. Rodrigues. Litho)

1971 (11 Dec). *Christmas.* P 11½.
1340 **730** 20 c. lilac, magenta and light blue .. 5 5
1341 75 c. black and silver 15 8
1342 1 cr. 30, multicoloured 25 12

(Des E. Gato (20 c.), R. Tissot (40 c.), W. Granado (others). Litho)

1972 (18 Feb). *Tourism.* T 731 and similar vert designs. *Multicoloured.* P 11½×11.
1343 20 c. Type **731** 5 5
1344 40 c. Cogwheel and grapes (Grape Festival, Rio Grande do Sul) 8 5
1345 75 c. Nazareth Festival procession, Belem 15 8
1346 1 cr. 30, Street scene (Winter Festival, Ouro Preto) 25 12
1343/1346 *Set of 4* 45 25

(Des G. Calvi (20 c.), R. Vieira (40 c.), P. Simoes (75 c.), D. Cardoso (1 cr. 30). Litho)

1972 (3 May). *Mineral Resources.* T 736 and similar multicoloured designs. P 11½.
1351 20 c. Type **736** 5 5
1352 40 c. Drilling rig (PETROBRAS) (*vert*) .. 8 5
1353 75 c. Power station and dam (ELETROBRAS) 15 8
1354 1 cr. 30, Iron ore production (Vale do Rio Doce Co.) 25 12
1351/1354 *Set of 4* 45 25

737 "Female Nude" (1922 Catalogue cover by Di Cavalcanti)

738 Postman and Map (Post Office)

(Des G. Calvi. Photo)

1972 (5 May). *50th Anniversary of 1st Modern Art Week, São Paulo. Sheet* 79×111 *mm. With gum.* P 11½.

MS1355	**737** 1 cr. black and carmine..	20	12

(Des A. Carvão. Litho)

1972 (26 May). *Communications.* T **738** *and similar multicoloured designs.* P 11½.

1356	35 c. Type **738** ..	5	5
1357	45 c. Microwave transmitter (Telecommunications) (*vert*)	8	5
1358	60 c. Symbol and diagram of Amazon microwave system	8	5
1359	70 c. Worker and route map (Amazon Basin development)	12	8
1356/1359	*Set of 4* ..	30	20

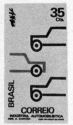

739 Motor Cars

740 Footballer (Independence Cup Championships)

(Des G. Calvi (70 c.), A. Carvão (others). Photo (35 c.), Litho (others))

1972 (21 June). *Major Industries.* T **739** *and similar designs. Fluorescent paper* (35 c.) P 11½×11 (35 c.) or 11×11½ (*others*).

1360	35 c. red-orange, cerise and black	5	5
1361	45 c. multicoloured	8	5
1362	70 c. multicoloured	12	8

Designs: *Horiz*—45 c. Three hulls (Shipbuilding); 70 c. Metal blocks (Iron and Steel Industry).

(Des J. Machado. Photo)

1972 (7 July). *"Sports and Pastimes".* T **740** *and similar vert designs. Fluorescent paper.* P 11½×11.

1363	20 c. black and yellow-ochre ..	5	5
1364	75 c. black and red ..	12	8
1365	1 cr. 30, black and new blue ..	25	12

Designs:—75 c. Treble clef in open mouth ("Popular Music"); 1 cr. 30, Hand grasping plastic ("Plastic Arts").

741 Diego Homem's Map of Brazil, 1568

742 Figurehead, Sao Francisco River

(Des G. Calvi. Litho)

1972. *"EXFILBRA 72" 4th International Stamp Exhibition, Rio de Janeiro.* T **741** *and similar multicoloured designs.* P 11½.

1366	70 c. Type **741** (26.8) ..	12	8
1367	1 cr. Nicolau Visscher's Map of the Americas, c 1652 (26.8) ..	20	12
1368	2 cr. Lopo Homem's World Map, 1519 (26.8)	40	25
MS1369	125×89 mm. 1 cr. "Declaration of Ypiranga" (Pedro Americo) (*horiz*) (19.7) ..	20	20

(Des N. B. Faerdrich (60 c.), G. Calvi (1 cr. 15), E. Gatto (others). Litho)

1972 (6 Aug). *Brazilian Folklore.* T **742** *and similar square designs. Multicoloured.* P 11½.

1370	45 c. Type **742** ..	8	5
1371	60 c. Fandango, Rio Grande do Sul	8	5
1372	75 c. Capoeira (game), Bahia	12	8
1373	1 cr. 15, Karaja statuette	20	10
1374	1 cr. 30, "Bumba-Meu-Boi" (folk play)	25	12
1370/1374	*Set of 5* ..	65	35

743 "Institution of Brazilian Flag" (E. de Sá)

744

(Des B. Lancetta (1, 2 cr.), A. Martins (others). Litho)

1972 (4 Sept). *150th Anniversary of Independence.* T **743** *and similar designs.* P 11½×11.

1375	30 c. myrtle-green and pale yellow ..	5	5
1376	70 c. mauve and pale pink ..	12	8
1377	1 cr. Venetian red and pale brown ..	20	12
1378	2 cr. black and pale buff ..	40	25
1379	3 cr. 50, black and pale grey ..	70	45
1375/1379	*Set of 5* ..	1·40	90

Designs: *Horiz*—70 c. "Proclamation of Emperor Pedro I" (lithograph after Debret); 2 cr. Commemorative gold coin of Pedro I; 3 cr. 50, Declaration of Ypiranga monument. *Vert*—1 cr. "Emperor Pedro I" (H. J. da Silva).

1972 (16 Sept). *Photo. Fluorescent paper* (20, 30 c.). P 11½×10½.

1380	**744** 5 c. orange ..	5	5
1381	10 c. olive-brown ..	5	5
1382	20 c. ultramarine ..	5	5
1383	30 c. carmine-red ..	5	5
1380/1383	*Set of 4* ..	10	8

Nos. 1382/3 have matt, almost invisible, gum. The 10 c. value is on very thick paper.

745 Fittipaldi in Racing Car

(Des G. Calvi. Litho)

1972 (14 Nov). *Emerson Fittipaldi's Victory in Formula 1 World Motor-racing Championship. Sheet 122×87 mm. P* 11½.
MS1384 **745** 2 cr. multicoloured 40 25

748 Pottery Crib   **749** Farm-worker and
Pension Book (Rural
Social Security
Scheme)

(Des G. Calvi. Photo)

1972 (13 Dec). *Christmas. Fluorescent paper. P* 11½×11.
1390 **748** 20 c. black and brown-ochre .. 5 5

(Des J. Carlos (No. 1392), G. Calvi (others). Litho)

1972 (20 Dec). *Government Services. T* **749** *and similar designs. P* 11½×11 (*vert*) *or* 11×11½ (*horiz*).
1391   10 c. black, yell-orge & greenish blue .. 5 5
1392   10 c. multicoloured 5 5
1393   70 c. black, yellow-brown and scarlet .. 12 8
1394   2 cr. multicoloured 40 25
1391/1394 *Set of 4* 65 35
Designs: *Vert*—10 c. (No. 1391), T **749**; 70 c. Dr. Oswald Cruz, public health pioneer (birth centenary). *Horiz*—10 c. (No. 1392), Children and traffic lights (Transport system development); 2 cr. Bull, fish and produce (Agricultural exports).

750 Brazilian Expeditionary Force Monument

(Des G. Calvi. Recess and litho)

1972 (28 Dec). *Armed Forces' Day. T* **750** *and similar horiz designs. P* 11×11½.
1395   10 c. black, brn-purple & orge-brown .. 5 5
1396   30 c. multicoloured 5 5
1397   30 c. multicoloured 5 5
1398   30 c. blk, red-brown & bright lilac .. 5 5
1395/1398 *Set of 4* 15 10
Designs:—No. 1396, Sailing-ship (Navy); No. 1397, Trooper (Army); No. 1398, "Mirage III" jet-fighter (Air Force).
Nos. 1395/8 were issued together *se-tenant* in blocks of four within the sheet, the blocks being separated by labels 17×48 mm in the vertical margins, showing insignia.

BUENOS AIRES. See beginning of Argentine Republic.

746 Writing Hand, and   **747** Legislative Building,
People (MOBRAL Literacy   Brasilia
Campaign)

(Des G. Calvi. Litho)

1972 (28 Nov). *Social Development. T* **746** *and similar square designs. Multicoloured. P* 11½.
1385   10 c. Type **746** 5 5
1386   20 c. Graph and people (National Census centenary) 5 5
1387   1 cr. House in hand (Pension Fund system) 20 12
1388   2 cr. Workers and factory (Gross National Product) 40 25
1385/1388 *Set of 4* .. .. .. ·65 35

(Des G. Calvi. Litho)

1972 (4 Dec). *National Congress Building, Brasilia. P* 11×11½.
1389 **747** 1 cr. black, orange and new blue .. 20 12

Burma

1948. 12 Pies=1 Anna; 16 Annas=1 Rupee
1953. 100 Pyas=1 Kyat

REPUBLIC OF THE UNION OF BURMA

By the Burma Independence Act, 1947, Burma became an independent state, outside the British Commonwealth and Empire, at 4.20 a.m., the time chosen by astrologers, on 4 January 1948.

Earlier issues as well as those of the Japanese Occupation in 1942–45, are listed in the *British Commonwealth Catalogue*.

20 Gen. Aung San, Chinthe and Map of Burma

21 Martyrs' Memorial

(Des A. G. I. McGeogh. Litho De La Rue)

1948 (6 Jan). *Independence Day.* P 12½×12.

83	**20**	½ a. yellow-green	..	..	5	5
84	–	1 a. rose	..	..	5	5
85	–	2 a. scarlet	..	..	5	5
86	–	3½ a. blue	..	..	5	5
87	–	8 a. brown	..	..	8	8
83/87		*Set of 5*	..	..	20	20

(Recess De La Rue)

1948 (19 July). *First Anniv of Murder of Aung San and his Ministers.* P 14½×13½.

88	**21**	3 p. ultramarine	..	..	5	5
89	–	6 p. yellow-green	..	..	5	5
90	–	9 p. carmine	..	..	5	5
91	–	1 a. violet	..	..	5	5
92	–	2 a. magenta	..	..	5	5
93	–	3½ a. grey-green	..	..	5	5
94	–	4 a. brown	..	..	5	5
95	–	8 a. red	..	..	8	5
96	–	12 a. purple	..	..	8	5
97	–	1 r. blue-green	..	..	12	8
98	–	2 r. blue	..	..	20	15
99	–	5 r. purple-brown	..	..	60	45
88/99		*Set of 12*	..	..	1·25	1·00

22 Boys playing

25 Bell

26 Legendary Bird

STAMP MONTHLY

—finest and most informative magazine for all collectors. Obtainable from your newsagent or by postal subscription—details on request.

27 Planting Rice

28 Royal Throne

(Recess De La Rue)

1949 (4 Jan). *First Anniv of Independence.* T **22/28** and similar designs. P 12×12½ (105/7 and 109), 12½ (100/4 and 108), or 13 (T **28**).

100	**22**	3 p. ultramarine	..	..	8	8
101	–	6 p. green	..	..	5	5
102	–	9 p. carmine	..	..	5	5
103	**25**	1 a. vermilion	..	..	5	5
104	**26**	2 a. yellow-orange	..	..	8	5
105	**27**	2 a. 6 p. magenta	..	..	5	5
106	–	3 a. violet	..	..	5	5
107	–	3 a. 6 p. slate-green	..	..	5	5
108	–	4 a. brown	..	..	5	5
109	–	8 a. red	..	..	5	5
110	**28**	1 r. blue-green	..	..	15	5
		a. Perf 14	..	..	—	1·00
111	–	2 r. indigo	..	..	25	15
112	–	5 r. brown	..	..	60	40
113	–	10 r. red-orange	..	..	1·25	60
100/113		*Set of 14*	..	..	2·50	1·40

Designs: as T **22**—6 p. Dancer. 9 p. Girl musician. As T **25**—4 a. Elephant hauling log. As T **27**—3 a. Girl weaving. 3 a. 6 p. Royal Palace. 8 a. Ploughing.

See also Nos. 120/133 and 137/150.

အသိုးရက်စ္စ

(O **4**) 13 mm

29 U.P.U. Monument, Berne

30 Monument and Map

1949 (4 Jan). *OFFICIAL. First Anniv of Independence. Nos. 100/104 and 107/113 optd as Type O* **4** *(3 p. to 2 a. and 4 a.) or larger, 14½ mm long (others).*

O114	**22**	3 p. ultramarine (R.)	..	..	12	5
O115	–	6 p. green (R.)	..	..	5	5
O116	–	9 p. carmine	..	..	5	5
O117	**25**	1 a. vermilion	..	..	5	5
O118	**26**	2 a. yellow-orange	..	..	5	5
O119	–	3 a. 6 p. slate-green (R.)	..	..	5	5
O120	–	4 a. brown	..	..	5	5
O121	–	8 a. red	..	..	5	5
O122	**28**	1 r. blue-green (R.)	..	..	12	10
O123	–	2 r. indigo (R.)	..	..	25	20
O124	–	5 r. brown	..	..	60	55
O125	–	10 r. red-orange	..	..	1·50	1·25
O114/125		*Set of 12*	..	..	2·50	2·10

(Recess De La Rue)

1949 (9 Oct). *75th Anniv of Universal Postal Union.* P 13.

114	**29**	2 a. orange	..	..	5	5
115		3½ a. olive-green	..	..	5	5
116		6 a. violet	..	..	8	10
117		8 a. scarlet	..	..	12	10
118		12½ a. ultramarine	..	..	20	15
119		1 r. blue-green	..	..	25	20
114/119		*Set of 6*	..	..	65	60

1952–53. *As Nos. 100/113, but litho. Colours changed.* W **10.** P 13 (*Nos. 125/7 and 129*) or 14 (*others*).

120	**22**	3 p. red-orange	..	..	12	5
121	–	6 p. purple	..	..	5	5
122	–	9 p. light blue	..	..	5	5
123	**25**	1 a. ultramarine	..	..	5	5
124	**26**	2 a. green (1.7.52)	..	..	8	5
125	**27**	2 a. 6 p. green	..	..	5	5
126	–	3 a. vermilion (1.9.52)	..	..	5	5
127	–	3 a. 6 p. red-orange	..	..	5	5
128	–	4 a. vermilion	..	..	5	5
129	–	8 a. light blue (1.9.52)	..	..	8	5
130	**28**	1 r. reddish violet	..	..	12	20
131		2 r. green	..	..	25	30
132		5 r. ultramarine	..	..	90	1·00
133		10 r. light blue	..	..	1·75	2·00
120/133		*Set of 14*	..	..	3·25	3·50

See also Nos. 137/150.

New Currency

(Litho Security Ptg Press, Nasik, India)

1953 (4 Jan). *Fifth Anniv of Independence.* W **10** (*sideways*).
(a) Size 22×18 mm. P 14.

134	**30**	14 p. green	..	..	5	5

(b) Size 36½×26½ mm. P 13

135	**30**	20 p. rose-red	..	..	5	5
136		25 p. ultramarine	..	..	8	5

1954 (4 Jan). *New Currency. As Nos. 120/133, but values in pyas and kyats.*

137	**22**	1 p. red-orange	..	..	10	5
138	–	2 p. purple	..	..	5	5
139	–	3 p. light blue	..	..	5	5
140	**25**	5 p. ultramarine	..	..	5	5
141	**27**	10 p. green	..	..	5	5
142	**26**	15 p. green	..	..	5	5
143	–	20 p. vermilion	..	..	5	5
144	–	25 p. red-orange	..	..	5	5
145	–	30 p. vermilion	..	..	8	5
146	–	50 p. light blue	..	..	10	5
147	**28**	1 k. reddish violet	..	..	20	10
148		2 k. green	..	..	45	12
149		5 k. ultramarine	..	..	1·10	45
150		10 k. light blue	..	..	2·10	40
137/150		*Set of 14*	..	..	4·00	1·25

1954–57. *OFFICIAL. Nos. 137/40 and 142/50 optd as Type* O **4** (*1 p. to 15 p. and 30 p.*) *or larger, 15½ mm long* (*25 p., 50 p.*) *or 14½ mm long* (*others*).

O151	**22**	1 p. red-orange	..	..	15	5
O152		2 p. purple	..	..	5	5
O153	–	3 p. light blue	..	..	5	5
O154	**25**	5 p. ultramarine	..	..	5	5
O155	**26**	15 p. green	..	..	5	5
O156	–	20 p. vermilion (1957)	..	..	5	5
O157	–	25 p. red-orange	..	..	5	5
O158	–	30 p. vermilion	..	..	8	5
O159	–	50 p. light blue	..	..	10	5
O160	**28**	1 k. reddish violet	..	..	20	8
O161		2 k. green	..	..	35	20
O162		5 k. ultramarine	..	..	80	45
O163		10 k. light blue	..	..	1·50	1·00
O151/O163		*Set of 13*	..	..	3·00	1·90

31 "Kaba-Aye" Rock Cave and Monuments

32 Fifth Buddhist Council Monuments

(Litho Security Ptg Press, Nasik, India)

1954 (17 May–15 Nov). *Sixth Buddhist Council, Rangoon. Various designs as* T **31.** W **10.** P 13.

151		10 p. ultramarine	..	..	5	5
152		15 p. maroon	..	..	5	5
153		35 p. olive-brown (17.5)	..	..	8	5
154		50 p. green	..	..	12	8
155		1 k. carmine-red	..	..	25	12
156		2 k. bright violet	..	..	50	25
151/156		*Set of 6*	..	..	95	50

Designs:—10 p. Sangha of Cambodia; 15 p. Buddhist priests and temples; 50 p. Sangha of Thailand; 1 k. Sangha of Ceylon; 2 k. Sangha of Laos.

(Photo Enschedé & Sons, Netherlands)

1956 (24 May). *Buddha Jayanti.* T **32** *and similar horiz designs inscr* "2500TH BUDDHIST ERA". No wmk. P 11×11½.

157		20 p. bronze-green and blue	..	..	5	5
158		40 p. apple-green and pale blue	..	..	10	8
159		60 p. lemon and deep green	..	..	12	10
160		1 k. 25, slate-blue and yellow	..	..	30	25
157/160		*Set of 4*	..	..	50	40

Designs:—4 p. Pagoda; 60 p. Shwedagon Pagoda; 1 k. 25, Site of Sixth Buddhist Council.

မြန်မာလှလ—နှစ်တရာ

၁၂၂၁–၁၃၂၁

15 P   ၁၅ P

(33) "Mandalay Town—100 Years/1221–1321"   **(34)**

1959 (9 Nov). *Centenary of Mandalay. No. 144 surch with* T **33** *and Nos. 147/8 with two-line opt only.*

161	–	15 p. on 25 p. red-orange	..	..	5	5
162	**28**	1 k. reddish violet	..	..	25	20
163		2 k. green	..	..	40	25

1961 (June). *No. 134 surch with* T **34.**

164	**30**	15 p. on 14 p. green	..	..	8	5
		a. Surch inverted	..	..	4·50	

35 Torch-bearer in Rangoon   **36** Children at Play

(Photo Enschedé)

1961 (11 Dec). *Second S.E.A.P. Games.* T **35** *and similar designs.* P 14×13 (*horiz*) or 13×14 (*vert*).

165		15 p. blue and scarlet	..	..	5	5
166		25 p. orange-brown and deep green	..	..	5	5
167		50 p. cerise and deep violet-blue	..	..	12	8
168		1 k. yellow and emerald	..	..	25	20
165/168		*Set of 4*	..	..	40	35

Designs: *Vert*—25 p. Contestants; 50 p. Women sprinting in Aung San Stadium, Rangoon. *Horiz*—1 k. Contestants.

(Litho De La Rue)

1961 (11 Dec). *15th Anniv of U.N.I.C.E.F.* P 13.

169	**36**	15 p. crimson and pink	..	..	5	5

37 Flag and Map   **FREEDOM FROM HUNGER**   **(38)**

1963 (2 Mar). *First Anniv of Military Coup by General Ne Win. Recess.* P 13×13½.

170	**37**	15 p. scarlet	..	..	5	5

1963 (21 Mar). *Freedom from Hunger. Nos. 141, 146 optd with T 38.*
171	**27**	10 p. green (V.)	..	..	..	10 8
172	–	50 p. light blue (R.)	..	..	20 15
		a. Opt inverted	..	..	

အလုပ်သမားနေ့

၁၉၆၃

Service

(39)　　　(O 5)　　　(O 6) 11½ mm

1963 (1 May). *Labour Day. No. 143 optd with T 39.*
173	20 p. vermilion	..	8	5

1964. OFFICIAL. *No. 139 optd locally with Type O 5.*
O174	3 p. light blue	..	1·75	1·10

1964. OFFICIAL. *Nos. 137, 139, 140 and 142 optd locally with Type O 6.*
O175	**22**	1 p. red-orange	..	5	5
O176	–	3 p. light blue	..	5	5
O177	**25**	5 p. ultramarine	..	5	5
O178	**26**	15 p. green	..	5	5
O175/178	Set of 4	..		15	15

40 Fantailed Flycatcher

41 I.T.U. Emblem and Symbols

(Photo Govt Ptg Wks, Tokyo)

1964 (16 Apr). *Burmese Birds (1st Series). T 40 and similar designs. P 13½ (T 40), 13 (20 p.) or 13½ × 13 (others).*
174	**40**	1 p. black	..	..	5	5
175		2 p. carmine	..	..	5	5
176		3 p. turquoise			5	5
177	–	5 p. bluish violet			5	5
178	–	10 p. orange-brown			5	5
179	–	15 p. yellow-olive			5	5
180	–	20 p. brown and rose-red			5	5
181	–	25 p. brown and greenish yellow			5	5
182	–	50 p. grey-blue, black and red			15	5
183	–	1 k. deep blue, yellow and grey			25	12
184	–	2 k. dp blue, red and light yell-olive			60	20
185	–	5 k. multicoloured			1·25	50
174/185		Set of 12			2·40	1·10

Birds: *Vert (22 × 26 mm)*—5 p. to 15 p. Roller; *(27 × 37 mm)*—25 p. Crested serpent-eagle; 50 p. Sarus crane; 1 k. Pied hornbill; 5 k. Peafowl. *Horiz (35½ × 25 mm)*—20 p. Red-whiskered bulbul; *(37 × 27 mm)*—2 k. Silver pheasant.
See also Nos. 195/206.

1965. OFFICIAL. *Nos. 175/7, 179 and 181 optd locally with Type O 6.*
O186	**40**	2 p. carmine	..	5	5
O187		3 p. turquoise	..	5	5
		a. Opt inverted	..	—	3·50
O188	–	5 p. bluish violet	..	5	5
O189	–	15 p. yellow-olive	..	5	5
O190	–	25 p. brown and greenish yellow		5	5
O186/190	Set of 5	..		20	20

1965 (17 May). *I.T.U. Centenary. Litho. P 15 (20 p.) or 13 (50 p.).*
186	**41**	20 p. magenta		5	5
187		50 p. green (*larger, 34 × 24½ mm*)	..	10	10

42 I.C.Y. Emblem

43 Harvesting

1965 (1 July). *International Co-operation Year. Litho. P 13.*
188	**42**	5 p. ultramarine	..	5	5
189		10 p. orange-brown	..	5	5
190		15 p. yellow-olive	..	5	5
188/190	Set of 3	..		10	10

(Litho German Bank Note Ptg Co, Leipzig)

1966 (2 Mar). *Peasants' Day. P 13½ × 13.*
191	**43**	15 p. multicoloured	..	..	5	5

အစိုးရကိစ္စ　　　အစိုးရကိစ္စ　　　အစိုးရကိစ္စ

(O 7) 15 mm　　　(O 8) 12 mm　　　(O 9) 14½ mm

1966. OFFICIAL. *Nos. 174/6 optd locally with Type O 7, and No. 179 optd with Type O 8.*
O192	**40**	1 p. black		5	5
O193		2 p. carmine		5	5
O194		3 p. turquoise		5	5
O195	–	15 p. yellow-olive		5	5
O192/195	Set of 4			15	15

1966. OFFICIAL. *Nos. 174/7 and 179/85 optd with Type O 9 by Govt Ptg Wks, Tokyo.*
O196	**40**	1 p. black		5	5
O197		2 p. carmine		5	5
O198		3 p. turquoise		5	5
O199	–	5 p. bluish violet		5	5
O200	–	15 p. yellow-olive		5	5
O201	–	20 p. brown and rose-red		5	5
O202	–	25 p. brown & greenish yellow (R.)		5	5
O203	–	50 p. grey-blue, black and red		10	10
O204	–	1 k. deep blue, yellow and grey (R.)		20	15
O205	–	2 k. deep blue, red and light yellow-olive (R.)		45	25
O206	–	5 k. multicoloured (R.)	..	1·25	50
O196/206	Set of 11	..		2·10	1·25

44 Cogwheel and Hammer

45 Bogyoke Aung San and Agricultural Cultivation

(Litho German Bank Note Ptg Co, Leipzig)

1967 (1 May). *May Day. P 13½ × 13.*
192	**44**	15 p. yellow, black and greenish blue		5	5

(Litho German Bank Note Ptg Co, Leipzig)

1968 (4 Jan). *20th Anniv of Independence. P 13½.*
193	**45**	15 p. multicoloured	..	5	5

46 Burma Pearls

47 Spike of Paddy

(Litho German Bank Note Ptg Co, Leipzig)

1968 (4 Mar). *Burmese Gems, Jades and Pearls Emporium, Rangoon. P 13½.*
194	**46**	15 p. ultram, new blue & pale yellow		5	5

(Photo German Bank Note Ptg Co, Leipzig)

1968 (1 July). *Burmese Birds (2nd Series). Designs and colours as Nos. 174/85 but formats, sizes and printers changed.* P 14.

195	1 p. black			5	5
196	2 p. carmine			5	5
197	3 p. turquoise			5	5
198	5 p. bluish violet			5	5
199	10 p. orange-brown			5	5
200	15 p. yellow-olive			5	5
201	20 p. brown and rose-red			5	5
202	25 p. brown and greenish yellow			5	5
203	50 p. grey-blue, black and red			10	5
204	1 k. deep blue, yellow and grey			20	5
205	2 k. dp blue, red & lt yellow-olive			45	12
206	5 k. multicoloured			1·10	30
195/206	*Set of 12*			2·00	80

New sizes: *Horiz* (21×17 *mm*)—1, 2, 3 p.; (39×21 *mm*) —20 p., 2 k. *Vert* (23×28 *mm*)—5, 10, 15 p.; (21×39 *mm*)—25, 50 p., 1 k., 5 k.

1968 (1 July). *OFFICIAL. Nos. 195/8 and 200/6 optd as Type O 9, but 13 mm long (1, 2 p.), 15 mm long (5, 15 p.) or 14 mm long (others), by German Bank Note Ptg Co, Leipzig.*

O207	1 p. black			5	5
O208	2 p. carmine			5	5
O209	3 p. turquoise			5	5
O210	5 p. bluish violet			5	5
O211	15 p. yellow-olive			5	5
O212	20 p. brown and rose-red			5	5
O213	25 p. brown and greenish yellow (R.)			5	5
O214	50 p. grey-blue, black and red			10	8
O215	1 k. deep blue, yellow and grey (R.)			20	12
O216	2 k. dp blue, red & lt yell-ol (R.)			40	30
O217	5 k. multicoloured (R.)			1·10	80
O207/217	*Set of 11*			1·90	1·50

(Litho Pakistan Security Ptg Corp, Ltd)

1969 (2 Mar). *Peasants' Day.* P 13.

218	**47**	15 p. greenish yellow, blue & lt emer	5	5

48 I.L.O. Emblem   **49** Football

(Photo Pakistan Security Ptg Corp Ltd)

1969 (29 Oct). *50th Anniversary of International Labour Organization.* P 13.

219	**48**	15 p. gold and bluish green		5	5
220		50 p. gold and carmine		10	8

(Litho German Bank Note Ptg Co, Leipzig)

1969 (1 Dec). *5th South East Asian Peninsular Games, Rangoon. T 49 and similar designs.* P 13×12½ (25 p.) or 12½×13 (others).

221	15 p. multicoloured			5	5
222	25 p. multicoloured			5	5
223	50 p. multicoloured			10	8
224	1 k. black, apple-grn & greenish blue			20	12
221/224	*Set of 4*			35	25

Designs: *Horiz*—25 p. Running. *Vert*—50 p. Weightlifting; 1 k. Volleyball.

STAMP MONTHLY

—finest and most informative magazine for all collectors. Obtainable from your newsagent or by postal subscription—details on request.

50 Marchers with Independence, Resistance and Union Flags

(Litho Pakistan Security Ptg Corp Ltd)

1970 (27 Mar). *25th Anniversary of Burmese Armed Forces.* P 13.

225	**50**	15 p. multicoloured		5	5

51 "Peace and Progress"

(Des U Ba Moe. Photo Govt Ptg Wks, Tokyo)

1970 (26 June). *25th Anniversary of United Nations.* P 13.

226	**51**	15 p. multicoloured		5	5

52 Boycott Declaration and Marchers

(Des U Myint Thein (50 p.), U Ba Lon Gale (others). Litho German Bank Note Ptg Co, Leipzig)

1970 (23 Nov). *National Day and 50th Anniversary of University Boycott. T 52 and similar horiz designs. Multicoloured.* P 13.

227	15 p. Type **52**			5	5
228	25 p. Students on Boycott march			5	5
229	50 p. Banner and demonstrators			10	5

53 Burmese Workers   **54** Child drinking Milk

(Des U Ba Moe (5, 50 p.), U San Toe (15, 25 p.). Litho Bradbury, Wilkinson)

1971 (28 June). *1st Burmese Socialist Programme Party Congress. T 53 and similar horiz designs. Multicoloured.* P 13½.

230	5 p. Type **53**			5	5
231	15 p. Burmese races and flags			5	5
232	25 p. Hands holding scroll			5	5
233	50 p. Party flag			10	5
230/233	*Set of 4*			20	15
MS234	179×127 mm. Nos. 230/3. Imperf			35	35

(Des Thin Thin Aye. Litho Harrison)

1971 (11 Dec). *25th Anniversary of U.N.I.C.E.F. T 54 and similar square design. Multicoloured.* P 14½.

235	15 p. Type **54**			5	5
236	50 p. Marionettes			10	5

55 Aung San and Independence Monument, Panglong

1972 (12 Feb). *25th Anniversary of Independence. T 55 and similar multicoloured designs.* P 14.

237	15 p. Type **55**	..	..	5	5
238	50 p. Aung San and Burmese in national costumes	..	..	10	5
239	1 k. Flag and map (*vert*)	..	..	20	5

56 Burmese and Stars

57 Human Heart

(Des Sai Yee Leik. Litho Harrison)

1972 (2 Mar). *10th Anniversary of Revolutionary Council.* P 14.

240	**56**	15 p. multicoloured	..	..	5	5

(Des U Ba Thit. Litho Harrison)

1972 (7 Apr). *World Health Day.* P 14 × 14½.

241	**57**	15 p. carmine, black & greenish yell ..		5	5

58 Burmese Races

(Des U. Min Naing. Litho Harrison)

1973 (12 Feb). *National Census.* P 14.

242	**58**	15 p. multicoloured	..	..	5	5

Burundi

100 Centimes = 1 Franc

Burundi (formerly Urundi), in eastern equatorial Africa, became an independent kingdom on 1 July 1962.

As part of Ruanda-Urundi (see that heading), it had been under Belgian administration as a mandated territory of the League of Nations from 1924 to 1946 and as a trust territory of the United Nations from 1946 to 1960.

KINGDOM
King Mwambutsa IV
1 July 1962–8 July 1966

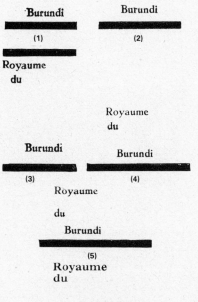

(1)
(2)
(3)
(4)
(5)
(6)
(7)
(8)

(9)

T **5** differs from T **4** in the vertical position of the "du", and in the length of the bar.

T **9** has continuous bars but in the varieties listed they do not extend more than 45 mm, these being from different plates.

1962 (1 July)–**63**. *Stamps of Ruanda-Urundi optd or surch.*

(a) Flower stamps of 1953 optd with T **1**

1	**1**	25 c. yellow-orange and green	..	5	5
2		40 c. salmon and green	..	5	5
3		60 c. purple and green..	..	8	8
4		1 f. 25, light green and green	..	4·25	4·25
5		1 f. 50, pale green and violet..	..	15	15
6		5 f. blue-green and purple	..	20	20
7		7 f. pale brown-pur & bronze-green ..		45	45
8		10 f. pale olive and plum	..	70	70
1/8		*Set of 8*	..	5·50	5·50

(b) Animal stamps of 1959 optd or surch with T **2/9**

9	**2**	10 c. black, brown-red and brown	..	5	5
10	**4**	20 c. black and yellow-green	..	5	5
11	**2**	40 c. blue-black, olive-black & dp mag		5	5
11a	**3**	40 c. blue-black, olive-black & dp mag		5	5
12	**4**	50 c. brown, yellow and green	..	5	5
		a. Optd "Royaume du Royaume"	..	4·00	1·75
12b	**5**	50 c. brown, yellow and green (11.63)		5	5
12c	**6**	50 c. brown, yellow & green (19.12.63)		5	5
13	**2**	1 f. black, blue and brown	..	5	5
13a	**3**	1 f. black, blue and brown	..	5	5
14	**4**	1 f. 50, black and orange (B.)..	..	5	5
		a. Black opt	..		
15	**2**	2 f. blue-black, brown and turq-blue		5	5
16	**4**	3 f. blue-black, red and brown	..	8	5
16a	**5**	3 f. blue-black, red and brown (11.63)		8	5
17	**4**	3 f. 50 on 3 f. blue-black, red & brn	..	10	8
18	**7**	4 f. on 10 f. brown, black, mag & yell		25	25
18a	**8**	4 f. on 10 f. brown, black, mag & yell		8	8
19	**4**	5 f. brown, black, green & yell (Bk.) ..		8	8
		a. Blue opt	..		
20		6 f. 50, brown, yellow and red	..	15	10
		a. Optd "Royaume du Royaume"	..	4·00	1·75
21		8 f. blue-black, magenta & blue (Bk.)		20	20
22		8 f. blue-black, magenta & blue (B.) ..		35	35
23		10 f. brown, black, magenta & yellow		20	20
24	**9**	20 f. yellow, black, red & blue-green ..		40	35
		a. Bars 45×4 mm	..		
25		50 f. bistre-brown, black, brt bl & verm		75	75
		a. Bars 45×4 mm	..	..	2·00	2·00
		b. Bars 45×2 mm	..	..	3·00	3·00
9/25		*Set of 16 (one of each value)*	..	2·10	2·00

Genuine copies of Nos. 12a and 20a have the second "Ro" under "du"; copies with the word to the right of "du" are forgeries.

In all values with Type **4** there is a constant variety on Row 1 No. 5 with "du" spaced as Type **5**. Various other varieties occur in the setting, such as "Burundi" starting under "du" but they are only known on some values and are not constant. An italic "o" is found on the 50 c. and 3 f. Type **5** (thirteen copies in the sheet). Inverted overprints are known.

IMPERF STAMPS. Many Burundi stamps from No. 26 onwards exist imperf from limited printings.

10 King Mwambutsa IV and Royal Drummers

(Des O. Adler. Photo Govt Printer, Israel)

1962 (27 Sept). *Independence. T 2 and similar designs.*
P 14.

26	**10**	50 c. sepia and lake		5	5
27	–	1 f. green, red and deep green	..	5	5
28	–	2 f. sepia and brown-olive ..	..	5	5
29	**10**	3 f. sepia and red		8	5
30	–	4 f. green, red and greenish blue	..	8	5
31	–	8 f. sepia and violet		15	5
32	**10**	10 f. sepia and blue-green ..		20	8
33	–	20 f. green, red and sepia ..		45	10
34	–	50 f. sepia and magenta ..	..	1·00	25
26/34		Set of 9		1·90	60

Designs: *Vert*—1 f., 4 f., 20 f. Burundi flag and arms.
Horiz—2 f., 8 f., 50 f. King Mwambutsa IV and outline map of
Burundi.

HOMMAGE A
DAG HAMMARSKJÖLD

3⁵⁰F

ROYAUME DU BURUNDI

(11)

1962 (31 Oct). *Dag Hammarskjoeld Commemoration. 1960*
Technical Co-operation stamp of Ruanda-Urundi surch as
T 11. Inscr in French (I) or Flemish (II).

			I		II	
35		3 f. 50 on 3 f. orange-red				
		and ultramarine ..	8	8	8	8
36		6 f. 50 on 3 f. orange-red				
		and ultramarine ..	12	12	12	12
37		10 f. on 3 f. orange-red				
		and ultramarine ..	20	20	20	20

1962 (10 Dec). *Malaria Eradication. As Nos. 31, 34 but with*
colours changed and campaign emblem superimposed on
map.

38		8 f. blk-brn, greenish bl & yell-bistre ..	20	10
39		50 f. blk-brn, greenish bl & sage-grn ..	95	25

12 Prince Louis Rwagasore   **13** Sowing

(T **12/13** des O. Adler. Photo Govt Printer, Israel)

1963 (15 Feb). *Prince Rwagasore Memorial and Stadium*
Fund. T 12 and similar designs. P 14×13 (50 c., 3 f. 50) or
13×14 (others).

40		50 c. + 25 c. violet.. ..	..	5	5
41		1 f. + 50 c. blue and orange-red..	..	5	5
42		1 f. 50 + 75 c. dull purple and bistre	..	5	5
43		3 f. 50 + 1 f. 50 magenta.. ..		5	5
44		5 f. + 2 f. blue and rose		10	5
45		6 f. 50 + 3 f. dull purple and olive ..		15	5
40/45		Set of 6	..	40	25

Designs: *Horiz*—1 f., 5 f. Prince Rwagasore and stadium;
1 f. 50, 6 f. 50, Prince Rwagasore and memorial. *Vert*—50 c.,
3 f. 50, T **12**.

1963 (21 Mar). *Freedom from Hunger. P 14×13.*

46	**13**	4 f. purple and yellow-olive	..	..	8	5
47		8 f. purple and orange	..	..	12	8
48		15 f. purple and green ..	..	..	20	10

Premier
Anniversaire

(14)   (15)

1963 (17 June). *"Peaceful Uses of Space". Nos. 28 and 34*
with map superimposed with T 14, in green.

49		2 f. sepia and brown-olive	..	1·00	1·00
50		50 f. sepia and magenta ..	..	1·25	1·25

1963 (1 July). *First Anniv of Independence. Nos. 30/33 with*
colours changed and optd with T 15.

51		4 f. green, red and olive (R.)	..	5	5
52		8 f. sepia, orange and red (P.)	..	12	5
53		10 f. sepia and mauve (R.) ..	..	15	8
54		20 f. green, red and deep brown-grey (R.)	40	15
51/54		Set of 4	..	65	30

6,50 F

(16)

1963 (24 Sept). *Nos. 27 and 33 surch as T 16, in brown.*

55		6 f. 50 on 1 f. green, red and deep green	20	5
56		15 f. on 20 f. green, red and sepia ..	40	20

17 Globe and Red   **18** "1962" and U.N.E.S.C.O.
Cross Flag   Emblem

(Photo Govt Printer, Israel)

1963 (26 Sept). *Red Cross Centenary. P 14×13.*

57	**17**	4 f. green, carmine and grey ..		8	5
58		8 f. olive-brown, carmine and grey	..	15	5
59		10 f. blue, carmine and grey ..	..	20	8
60		20 f. reddish violet, carmine and grey	45	15
57/60		Set of 4	..	80	30

MS60a 90×140 mm. Nos. 57/60 in new colours, each with +2 f. surcharge in black.
Imperf .. .. 1·40 1·40

(Photo Govt Printer, Israel)

1963 (4 Nov). *First Anniv of Admission to U.N.O. T 18 and*
similar designs. Emblems and values in black. P 14.

61		4 f. yellow-olive and yellow ..	..	8	5
62		8 f. blue and lilac	..	12	5
63		10 f. reddish violet and light blue	..	15	5
64		20 f. green and light yellow-green	..	30	10
65		50 f. red-brown and ochre ..	..	80	25
61/65		Set of 5	..	1·25	40

MS65a 111×74 mm. Nos. 64/5 but with
emblems changed. Imperf .. .. 2·00 2·00
Designs: As T **18** but with emblems of—8 f. I.T.U.; 10 f.
W.M.O.; 20 f. U.P.U.; 50 f. F.A.O. **MS**65a: 20 f. F.A.O.; 50 f.
W.M.O.

19 U.N.E.S.C.O. Emblem and Scales of Justice

(Litho Govt Printer, Israel)

1963 (10 Dec). *15th Anniv of Declaration of Human Rights.*
T **19** *and similar designs. P* 13½ × 14.

66	50 c. black, light blue and pink	..		5	5
67	1 f. black, light blue and yellow-orange			5	5
68	3 f. 50, black, lt green & Venetian red	..		5	5
69	6 f. 50, black, light green and lilac			10	5
70	10 f. black, yellow-bistre, blue & lt blue	..		15	8
71	20 f. blk, yellow-bistre, blue and yell-brn			30	12
66/71	*Set of 6*	..	..	60	35

Designs: 50 c., 1 f. 50, *T* **19**; 3 f. 50, 6 f. 50, Scroll; 10 f., 20 f.
Abraham Lincoln.

20 Ice-hockey

22 Burundi Dancer

21 Hippopotamus

(Photo Govt Printer, Israel)

1964 (25 Jan). *Winter Olympic Games, Innsbruck. Vert
designs as T* **20**. *P* 14½ × 14.

72	50 c. black, gold and light yellow-olive	..		5	5
73	3 f. 50, black, gold and cinnamon			8	5
74	6 f. 50, black, gold & light greenish grey			15	5
75	10 f. black, gold and light grey	..		25	8
76	20 f. black, gold and yellow-bistre	..		45	15
72/76	*Set of 5*			90	35

MS76*a* 122×85 mm. 10 f. + 5 f. and 20 f. + 5 f.
(as Nos. 75/6 but in new colours). Perf or
imperf .. .. .. 3·75 3·75
Designs:—3 f. 50, Figure-skating; 6 f. 50, Olympic flame;
10 f. Speed skating; 20 f. Skiing (slalom).

1964. *Burundi Animals. T* **21** *and similar types. Multicoloured. Litho.* (i) *POSTAGE.*

(*a*) *Size as T* **21**. *P* 14 × 14½ (*vert*) *or* 14½ × 14 (*horiz*) (10 Feb)

77	50 c. Impala	..	..	..	5	5
78	1 f. Type **21**	..	..	..	5	5
79	1 f. 50, Giraffe	..	.:	..	5	5
80	2 f. Buffalo	..	..	..	5	5
81	3 f. Zebra	..	..	..	5	5
82	3 f. 50. Defassa waterbuck		..		8	5

(*b*) *Size* 26×42½ *mm or vice versa. P* 14½ × 13 (*vert*) *or*
13 × 14½ (*horiz*) (28 Feb)

83	4 f. Impala				8	5
84	5 f. Hippopotamus	..	..		8	5
85	6 f. 50, Zebra	..	..		10	5
86	8 f. Buffalo	..	..		12	5
87	10 f. Giraffe	..	..		15	5
88	15 f. Defassa waterbuck		..		25	8

(*c*) *Size* 53½ × 33½ *mm. P* 14½ (20 Mar)

89	20 f. Spotted leopard	..	..		30	10
90	50 f. Elephant	..	..		75	20
91	100 f. Lion	..	..		1·50	40

(ii) *AIR. Inscr* "POSTE AERIENNE" *and optd gold border*
(2 July)

(*a*) *Size* 26×42½ *mm or vice versa. P* 14

92	6 f. Zebra	..	..	..	10	5
93	8 f. Buffalo	..	..	..	12	5
94	10 f. Impala	..	..	..	15	5
95	14 f. Hippopotamus	..	..	..	25	5
96	15 f. Defassa waterbuck	..	..		25	5

(*b*) *Size* 53½ × 33½ *mm. P* 14

97	20 f. Spotted leopard	..	..		35	10
98	50 f. Elephant	..	..		1·00	20
77/98	*Set of 22*	..	..	..	5·50	1·75

The impala, giraffe and waterbuck stamps are all vert
designs and the remainder are horiz.

1964 (27 Aug). *World's Fair, New York* (1st series). *T* **22** *and
similar vert designs on gold backgrounds. Litho. P* 14½.

99	50 c. multicoloured	..	..	5	5
100	1 f. multicoloured	..	..	5	5
101	4 f. multicoloured	..	..	8	5
102	6 f. 50, multicoloured	..	..	10	5
103	10 f. multicoloured	..	..	20	5
104	15 f. multicoloured	..	..	30	8
105	20 f. multicoloured	..	..	40	10
99/105	*Set of 7*	..	..	1·00	35

MS105*a* 120×100 mm. Nos. 103/5. Perf or
imperf .. .. .. 2·00 2·00
Designs:—1 f. to 20 f. Various dancers and drummers as
T **22**.
See also Nos. 175/81.

23 Pope Paul and King
Mwambutsa IV

24 Putting the Shot

1964 (12 Nov). *Canonisation of 22 African Martyrs. T* **23** *and
similar designs. Inscriptions in gold. Photo. P* 12.

106	**23** 50 c. Venetian red and blue	..			5	5
107	— 1 f. indigo and bright purple				5	5
108	— 4 f. sepia and mauve	..			5	5
109	— 8 f. bistre-brown and red	..			12	5
110	— 14 f. brown and light turq-green				25	8
111	**23** 20 f. green and brown-red				40	15
106/111	*Set of 6*	..	..		80	35

Designs: *Vert*—1 f., 8 f. Group of martyrs. *Horiz*—4 f., 14 f.
Pope John XXIII and King Mwambutsa IV.

1964 (18 Nov). *Olympic Games, Tokyo. T 24 and similar designs inscr "TOKYO 1964". Multicoloured. Litho. P 14½.*

112	50 c. Type 24	..	..	5	5
113	1 f. Throwing the discus	..	..	5	5
114	3 f. Swimming (*horiz*) ..	..	..	5	5
115	4 f. Relay-racing	..	..	5	5
116	6 f. 50, Throwing the javelin	..	..	8	5
117	8 f. Hurdling (*horiz*)	..	..	10	5
118	10 f. Long-jumping (*horiz*)	..	..	15	8
119	14 f. High-diving	..	..	20	12
120	18 f. High-jumping (*horiz*)	..	..	25	15
121	20 f. Gymnastics (*horiz*)..	..	..	30	20
112/121	*Set of 10*	..	..	1·10	75

MS121a 115×71 mm. 18 f.+2 f. and 20 f.+5 f. (as Nos. 120/1). Perf or imperf .. 20 20

25 Scientist, Map and Emblem

26 African Gallinule

(Photo and litho Govt Printer, Israel)

1965 (28 Jan). *Anti-T.B. Campaign. Country name, values and Lorraine Cross, in red. P 14½.*

122	**25**	2 f. +50 c. sepia and pale drab	..	5	5
123		4 f. +1 f. 50, deep green and pink	..	8	5
124		5 f. +2 f. 50, violet and buff ..	..	10	5
125		8 f. +3 f. ultramarine and light grey	15	8
126		10 f. +5 f. brown-red & lt grey-green	25	10
122/126		*Set of 5*	55	30

MS126a 100×71 mm. **25** 10 f.+10 f. sepia and pale olive. Perf or imperf 75 75

1965. *Birds. T 26 and similar vert designs. Multicoloured. Litho. P 14×14½.*

(a) *POSTAGE.* (i) *Size as* T **26** (31 Mar)

127	50 c. Type **26**	..	..	5	5
128	1 f. Little bee-eater	..	..	5	5
129	1 f. 50, Secretary bird	..	..	5	5
130	2 f. Wood ibis	..	..	5	5
131	3 f. Congolese peacock	..	..	5	5
132	3 f. 50, African darter ..	..	..	5	5

(ii) *Size* 26×42½ *mm* (16 Apr)

133	4 f. Type **26**	..	..	5	5
134	5 f. Little bee-eater	..	..	5	5
135	6 f. 50, Secretary bird	..	..	8	5
136	8 f. Wood ibis..	..	..	8	5
137	10 f. Congolese peacock	..	..	10	8
138	15 f. African darter	..	..	15	10

(iii) *Size* 33½×53 *mm* (30 Apr)

139	20 f. Saddle-billed stork, or jabiru	..	20	12
140	50 f. Abyssinian ground hornbill	..	50	25
141	100 f. Crowned crane	..	..	1·10	50

(b) *AIR. Inscr* "POSTE AERIENNE" (10 June)

(i) *Size* 26×42½ *mm* (*excluding gold borders*)

142	6 f. Secretary bird	..	..	5	5
143	8 f. African darter	..	..	8	5
144	10 f. Congolese peacock	..	..	10	5
145	14 f. Little bee-eater	..	..	12	8
146	15 f. Wood ibis..	..	..	15	8

(ii) *Size* 33½×53 *mm* (*excluding gold borders*)

147	20 f. Saddle-billed stork, or jabiru	..	20	10
148	50 f. Abyssinian ground hornbill	..	50	25
149	75 f. Martial eagle	..	..	75	50
150	130 f. Lesser flamingo	..	..	1·10	75
127/150	*Set of 24*	..	..	5·00	3·00

27 "Relay" Satellite and Telegraph Key   28 Arms (Reverse of 10 f. Coin)

1965 (3 July). *I.T.U. Centenary. T 27 and similar vert designs. Multicoloured. Litho. P 13½.*

151	1 f. Type **27**	..	..	5	5
152	3 f. "Telstar 1" and hand telephone	..	5	5
153	4 f. "Lunik 3" and wall telephone	..	5	5
154	6 f. 50, Weather satellite and tracking station	..	5	5
155	8 f. "Telstar 2" and headphones	..	8	5
156	10 f. "Sputnik" and radar scanner	..	10	5
157	14 f. "Syncom" and aerial	..	12	8
158	20 f. "Pioneer 5" space probe and radio aerial	..	20	10
151/158	*Set of 8*	..	..	65	45

MS158a 121×85 mm. Nos. 156 and 158. Perf or imperf .. .. .. 2·25 2·25

(Des and embossed Walsall Lithographic Co Ltd)

1965. *First Independence Anniversary Gold Coinage Commemoration. Circular designs as T 28, embossed on gold foil, backed with multicoloured patterned paper. Imperf.*

(i) *POSTAGE* (9 Aug)

(a) *10 f. coin. Diameter* 1½ *in.*

159	2 f. +50 c. carmine & yellow-orange ..	5	5
160	4 f. +50 c. blue and vermilion	5	5

(b) *25 f. coin. Diameter* 1¾ *in.*

161	6 f. +50 c. red-orange and light grey ..	8	8
162	8 f. +50 c. greenish blue and maroon	10	10

(c) *50 f. coin. Diameter* 2⅛ *in.*

163	12 f. +50 c. light green & bright purple	15	15
164	15 f. +50 c. light emerald and lilac	..	20	20

(d) *100 f. coin. Diameter* 2⅝ *in.*

165	25 f. +50 c. royal blue and flesh	..	35	35
166	40 f. +50 c. mauve and red-brown	..	50	50

(ii) *AIR* (10 Nov)

(a) *10 f. coin. Diameter* 1½ *in.*

167	3 f. +1 f. royal blue and violet	..	5	5
168	5 f. +1 f. vermilion & light grey-green	..	5	5

(b) *25 f. coin. Diameter* 1¾ *in.*

169	11 f. +1 f. purple and yellow-orange	..	12	12
170	14 f. +1 f. emerald and carmine-red	..	15	15

(c) *50 f. coin. Diameter* 2⅛ *in.*

171	20 f. +1 f. black and blue	..	20	20
172	30 f. +1 f. brown-purple & red-orange	..	30	30

(d) *100 f. coin. Diameter* 2⅝ *in.*

173	50 f. +1 f. violet and greenish blue	..	50	50
174	100 f. +1 f. maroon and rose	..	95	95
159/174	*Set of 16*	..	..	3·50	3·50

The 2, 3, 6, 11, 12, 20, 25 and 50 f. each show the reverse side of the coins, as T **28**. The remainder show the obverse side of the coins (King Mwambutsa IV).

1965 (10 Sept). *World's Fair, New York (2nd series). Designs as Nos. 99/105, but with silver backgrounds.*

175	50 c. multicoloured	..	..	5	5
176	1 f. multicoloured	..	..	5	5
177	4 f. multicoloured	..	..	5	5
178	6 f. 50, multicoloured	..	..	8	8
179	10 f. multicoloured	..	..	12	10
180	15 f. multicoloured	..	..	20	15
181	20 f. multicoloured	..	..	25	20

175/181	Set of 7	..	..	70	60
MS181a	120×100 mm. Nos. 179/81. Perf or imperf	.. .. ..	..	1·25	1·25

29 Globe and I.C.Y. Emblem

1965 (5 Nov). *International Co-operation Year. T **29** and similar multicoloured designs. Litho. P 13½.*

182	1 f. Type **29**	..	..	5	5
183	4 f. Map of Africa and cogwheel emblem of U.N. Science and Technology Conference	..	..	5	5
184	8 f. Map of South-East Asia and Colombo Plan emblem	..	..	8	5
185	10 f. Globe and U.N. emblem	..	..	10	5
186	18 f. Map of Americas and Alliance for Progress emblem	..	..	20	8
187	25 f. Map of Europe and C.E.P.T. emblems	..	..	30	12
188	40 f. Space map and satellite (U.N.—"Peaceful Uses of Outer Space")	..	..	45	20
182/188	Set of 7	..	..	1·10	55
MS188a	100×100 mm. 18 f. (Map of Africa and UN emblem), 25 f. and 40 f. (similar to Nos. 187/8). Perf or imperf	..	..	2·00	2·00

30 Prince Rwagasore and Memorial

31 Protea

1966 (21 Jan). *Prince Rwagasore and President Kennedy Commemoration. T **30** and similar designs. Photo. P 13½.*

189	4 f. + 1 f. deep brown and slate-blue	..	..	5	5
190	10 f. + 1 f. Prussian blue, brown and light grey-green	..	..	10	5
191	20 f. + 2 f. green and lilac	..	..	20	10
192	40 f. + 2 f. deep brown and grey-green	..	..	40	20
189/192	Set of 4	..	..	65	35
MS193	75×90 mm. 20 f. + 5 f. and 40 f. + 5 f. (as Nos. 189 and 191). Perf or imperf	..	..	1·75	1·75

Designs: *Horiz*—10 f. Prince Rwagasore and Pres. Kennedy; 20 f. Pres. Kennedy and memorial library. *Vert*—40 f. King Mwambutsa at Pres. Kennedy's grave.

1966. *Flowers. T **31** and similar multicoloured designs. Litho. P 13½.*

(a) POSTAGE. On white backgrounds
*(i) Size as T **31***

194	50 c. Type **31**	..	..	5	5
195	1 f. Crossandra	..	..	5	5
196	1 f. 50, Ansellia	..	..	5	5
197	2 f. Thunbergia	..	..	5	5
198	3 f. Schizoglossum	..	..	5	5
199	3 f. 50, Dissotis	..	..	5	5

(ii) Size 41×41 mm

200	4 f. Type **31**	..	..	5	5
201	5 f. Crossandra	..	..	5	5
202	6 f. 50, Ansellia	..	..	8	5

203	8 f. Thunbergia	..	..	10	5
204	10 f. Schizoglossum	..	..	10	5
205	15 f. Dissotis	..	..	15	5

(iii) Size 50×50 mm

206	20 f. Type **31**	..	..	20	8
207	50 f. Gazania	..	..	50	30
208	100 f. Hibiscus	..	..	1·00	60
209	150 f. Markhamia	..	..	1·25	80

(b) AIR. On gold backgrounds
(i) Size 41×41 mm

210	6 f. Dissotis	..	..	5	5
211	8 f. Crossandra	..	..	10	5
212	10 f. Ansellia	..	..	12	5
213	14 f. Thunbergia	..	..	15	5
214	15 f. Schizoglossum	..	..	15	5

(ii) Size 50×50 mm

215	20 f. Gazania	..	..	20	8
216	50 f. Type **31**	..	..	60	20
217	75 f. Hibiscus	..	..	75	25
218	130 f. Markhamia	..	..	1·25	60
194/218	Set of 25	..	..	6·50	3·25

Dates of issue: 28 Feb—Nos. 194/200; 18 May—Nos. 201/6; 15 June—Nos. 207/9; 10 Oct—Nos. 210/18.

King Ntare V
1 September–28 November 1966

32 U.N.E.S.C.O. Emblem **33**

1966 (4 Nov). *20th Anniv of U.N.E.S.C.O. Litho. P 13½.*
MS219 Three sheets each 201×127 mm each containing single stamp (Type **32**) with se-tenant label inscribed in English or French and an adjoining block of six stamps (3×2), as Type **33**, forming a composite design of the mural tapestry hanging in the U.N. General Assembly building, New York. (a) Postage: Two sheets 1 f. 50×7 and 4 f.×7. (b) Air. Inscr "POSTE AERIENNE". One sheet 14 f.×7. Multicoloured. *Price for three sheets un £2.*

REPUBLIC
28 November 1966

1967 (6 Feb). *Fourth Anniv of Independence (in 1966). Litho. P 13½.*
MS220 Four unissued sheets, diamond-shaped, 200×200 mm, each containing eight "Flower" stamps as Type **31**, but with values and corresponding designs changed, and centre *se-tenant* label showing "Flag", "Map", "Arms" or "Flower" emblem. Values: 6, 7, 8, 10, 14, 15, 20 and 50 f. Multicoloured. Stamps and sheet margins have the original inscriptions obliterated by the overprint "REPUBLIQUE DU BURUNDI" in black on gold panels.
Price for four sheets un £5.50.

REPUBLIQUE
DU
BURUNDI

(34)

35 Sir Winston Churchill and St. Paul's Cathedral

1967 (Feb). *Various stamps optd.*

(i) *Nos. 127, etc (Birds) optd as T* **34**
(a) *POSTAGE*

221	50 c. multicoloured	..	..	30	30
222	1 f. 50, multicoloured..	..	..	5	5
223	3 f. 50, multicoloured..	..	..	5	5
224	5 f. multicoloured	..	..	5	5
225	6 f. 50, multicoloured..	..	..	5	5
226	8 f. multicoloured	..	..	5	5
227	10 f. multicoloured	..	..	8	5
228	15 f. multicoloured	..	..	20	10
229	20 f. multicoloured	..	..	30	15
230	50 f. multicoloured	..	..	80	80
231	100 f. multicoloured	..	..	1·75	1·60

(b) *AIR. Inscr "POSTE AERIENNE"*

232	6 f. multicoloured	..	..	12	12
233	8 f. multicoloured	..	..	15	15
234	10 f. multicoloured	..	..	15	15
235	14 f. multicoloured	..	..	25	25
236	15 f. multicoloured	..	..	25	25
237	20 f. multicoloured	..	..	40	40
238	50 f. multicoloured	..	..	1·00	80
239	75 f. multicoloured	..	..	1·40	1·25
240	130 f. multicoloured	..	..	2·25	2·00
221/240	*Set of 20*	..	..	8·50	7·50

(ii) *Nos. 194, etc (Flowers) optd as T* **34** *but with two obliterating bars.* (a) *POSTAGE*

241	50 c. multicoloured	..	..	5	5
242	1 f. multicoloured	..	..	5	5
243	1 f. 50, multicoloured..	..	..	5	5
244	2 f. multicoloured	..	..	5	5
245	3 f. multicoloured	..	..	5	5
246	3 f. 50, multicoloured..	..	..	5	5
247	4 f. multicoloured	..	..	25	25
248	5 f. multicoloured	..	..	5	5
249	6 f. 50, multicoloured..	..	..	5	5
250	8 f. multicoloured	..	..	5	5
251	10 f. multicoloured	..	..	8	8
252	15 f. multicoloured	..	..	12	12
253	50 f. multicoloured	..	..	75	60
254	100 f. multicoloured	..	..	2·00	1·90
255	150 f. multicoloured	..	..	2·25	2·00

(b) *AIR. Inscr "POSTE AERIENNE"*

256	6 f. multicoloured	..	..	8	8
257	8 f. multicoloured	..	..	10	10
258	10 f. multicoloured	..	..	12	10
259	14 f. multicoloured	..	..	15	12
260	15 f. multicoloured	..	..	15	12
261	20 f. multicoloured	..	..	20	15
262	50 f. multicoloured	..	..	60	35
263	75 f. multicoloured	..	..	95	50
264	130 f. multicoloured	..	..	1·60	1·00
241/264	*Set of 24*	..	..	9·50	7·00

1967 (23 Mar). *Churchill Commemoration. T* **35** *and similar multicoloured designs. Photo. P 13½.* (a) *POSTAGE. As T* **35.**

265	4 f. + 1 f. Type **35**	..	..	5	5
266	15 f. + 2 f. Churchill and Tower of London	..	..	20	15
267	20 f. + 3 f. Big Ben and Boadicea Statue, Westminster		..	25	20

(b) *AIR. Inscr "POSTE AERIENNE". Diamond* (57×57 *mm*)
MS268 80×80 *mm.* 50 f. + 5 f. Sir Winston Churchill. Perf or imperf 90 90

1967. *Fishes. T* **36** *and similar horiz designs. Multicoloured. Photo. P 13½.*

(a) *POSTAGE.* (i) *Size as T* **36** (4 Apr)

269	50 c. Type **36**	..	..	5	5
270	1 f. Spotted Climbing Perch	..	..	5	5
271	1 f. 50, Six Banded Panchax	..	..	5	5
272	2 f. Congo Tetra	..	..	5	5
273	3 f. Red Jewel Fish	..	..	5	5
274	3 f. 50, White Spotted Cichlid	..	..	5	5

(ii) *Size* 53½ × 27 *mm* (28 Apr)

275	4 f. Type **36**	..	..	5	5
276	5 f. As 1 f.	..	..	5	5
277	6 f. 50, As 1 f. 50	..	..	8	5
278	8 f. As 2 f.	..	..	10	5
279	10 f. As 3 f.	..	..	15	5
280	15 f. As 3 f. 50	..	..	15	8

(iii) *Size* 63½ × 31½ *mm* (18 May)

281	20 f. Type **36**	..	..	20	10
282	50 f. Snakehead	..	..	55	20
283	100 f. Tooth Carp	..	..	1·10	30
284	150 f. African Tetra	..	..	1·60	50

(b) *AIR* (8 Sept). (i) *Size* 50×23 *mm*

285	6 f. Type **36**	..	..	8	5
286	8 f. As 1 f.	..	..	8	5
287	10 f. As 1 f. 50	..	..	12	5
288	14 f. As 2 f.	..	..	12	5
289	15 f. As 3 f.	..	..	15	5

(ii) *Size* 59×27 *mm*

290	20 f. As 3 f. 50	..	..	20	8
291	50 f. As 50 f. (*postage*)..		..	50	20
292	75 f. As 100 f.	..	..	70	30
293	130 f. As 150 f.	..	..	1·25	40
269/293	*Set of 25*	..	..	6·50	2·75

1967 (5 June). *"African Art". T* **37** *and similar vert designs. Multicoloured. Photo. P 13½.* (a) *POSTAGE.*

294	50 c. Type **37**	..	..	5	5
295	1 f. "Master of Buli's" carved seat		..	5	5
296	1 f. 50, Karumba antelope's head		..	5	5
297	2 f. Bobo buffalo's head	..	..	5	5
298	4 f. Guma-Goffa funeral figures		..	5	5

(b) *AIR. Inscr "POSTE AERIENNE"*

299	10 f. Bakoutou "spirit" (carving)		..	10	5
300	14 f. Bamum sultan's throne	..		15	5
301	17 f. Benin bronze head..		..	15	5
302	24 f. Statue of 109th Bakouba king		..	25	10
303	26 f. Burundi basketwork and lances		..	25	10
294/303	*Set of 10*	..	..	1·00	45

1917 ——— 1967

(38)

36 Egyptian Mouthbreeder

37 Baule Ancestral Figures

39 Lord Baden-Powell (founder)

1967 (14 July). *50th Anniv of Lions International.*

    (*a*) *POSTAGE. Nos. 265/7 optd with T* **38**
304	4 f. +1 f. multicoloured	..	..	5	5
305	15 f. +2 f. multicoloured	..	..	15	10
306	20 f. +3 f. multicoloured	..	..	25	15

(*b*) *AIR. Sheet No.* **MS**268 *optd with T* **38** *in sheet margin and stamp optd "LIONS INTERNATIONAL", etc.*
MS307   80×80   mm.   50   f.+5   f.   multicoloured. Perf or imperf   75   75

1967 (9 Aug). *60th Anniv of Scout Movement and World Scout Jamboree, Idaho. T* **39** *and similar multicoloured designs. Photo. P* 13½. (*a*) *POSTAGE.*
308	50 c. Scouts climbing	..	..	5	5
309	1 f. Scouts preparing meal	..	..	5	5
310	1 f. 50, Type **39**	..	..	5	5
311	2 f. Two Scouts	..	..	5	5
312	4 f. Giving first aid	..	..	5	5

    (*b*) *AIR. Inscr* "POSTE AERIENNE"
313	10 f. As 50 c.	..	..	10	5
314	14 f. As 1 f.	..	..	15	5
315	17 f. Type **39**	..	..	15	5
316	24 f. As 2 f.	..	..	25	10
317	26 f. As 4 f.	..	..	25	10
308/317	*Set of 10*	..	..	1·00	45

40 "The Gleaners" (Millet)

1967 (12 Oct). *World Fair, Montreal. T* **40** *and similar vert designs showing paintings. Multicoloured. Photo. P* 13½.
318	4 f. Type **40**	..	5	5
319	8 f. "The Water-carrier of Seville" (Velazquez) ..	..	10	5
320	14 f. "The Triumph of Neptune and Amphitrite" (Poussin)	..	20	8
321	18 f. "Acrobat with a ball" (Picasso)	..	25	8
322	25 f. "Margaret van Eyck" (Van Eyck)	..	30	10
323	40 f. "St. Peter denying Christ" (Rembrandt)	..	50	12
318/323	*Set of 6*	..	1·25	45
MS324	105×105 mm. Nos. 322/3. Perf or imperf	..	1·00	1·00

41 Boeing "707"

1967 (3 Nov). *AIR. Opening of Bujumbura Airport. T* **41** *and similar horiz designs. Aircraft and inscr in black and silver. Photo. P* 13½.
325	10 f. yellow-green	..	12	5
326	14 f. orange-yellow	..	15	8
327	17 f. greenish blue	..	20	10
328	26 f. bright purple	..	30	12
325/328	*Set of 4*	..	70	30

Aircraft:—14 f. Boeing "727" over lakes; 17 f. "VC–10" over lake; 26 f. Boeing "727" over Bujumbura Airport.

42 Pres. Micombero and Flag

1967 (23 Nov). *First Anniv of Republic. T* **42** *and similar horiz designs. Multicoloured. Photo. P* 13½.
329	5 f. Type **42**	..	8	5
330	14 f. Memorial and Arms	..	15	8
331	20 f. View of Bujumbura and Arms	..	20	10
332	30 f. "Place de la Revolution" and President Micombero ..	..	35	15
329/332	*Set of 4*	..	70	35

43 "The Adoration of the Shepherds" (J. B. Mayno)

1967 (7 Dec). *Christmas Religious Paintings. T* **43** *and similar vert designs. Multicoloured. Photo. P* 13½.
333	1 f. Type **43**	..	5	5
334	4 f. "The Holy Family" (A. van Dyck)	..	8	5
335	14 f. "The Nativity" (Maitre de Moulins)	15	12
336	26 f. "Madonna and Child" (C. Crivelli) ..		30	15
333/336	*Set of 4*	..	55	35
MS337	120×120 mm. Nos. 333/6. Perf or imperf	..	1·25	1·25

44 Burundi Scouts

1968 (19 Jan). *AIR. 20th Anniv of Burundi Scouts and 60th Anniv of Scout Movement. Diamond-shaped sheet containing T* **44** *and similar design. Multicoloured. Photo. P* 13½ *or imperf.*
MS338   142×142 mm. 24 f. and 26 f. with two *se-tenant* labels depicting Lord Baden-Powell and scouting activities   ..   65   65
Design:—26 f. Burundi scouts practising first-aid.

45 Downhill Skiing **46** "Portrait of a Young Man" (Botticelli)

1968 (16 Feb). *Winter Olympic Games, Grenoble.* **T 45** *and similar vert designs. Multicoloured. Photo.* P 13.

339	5 f. Type **45**	..	5	5
340	10 f. Ice-hockey ..	..	8	5
341	14 f. Figure-skating	..	15	5
342	17 f. Bobsleighing	..	20	5
343	26 f. Ski-jumping	..	30	10
344	40 f. Speed-skating	..	35	15
345	60 f. Olympic torch	..	55	20
339/345	*Set of 7*	..	1·50	60

MS346 129×82 mm. Nos. 344/5. Perf or imperf .. .. 1·25 1·25
Nos. 339/45 were each issued in sheets of 10 stamps and one *se-tenant* label.

1968 (29 Mar). *Famous Paintings.* **T 46** *and similar multicoloured designs. Photo.* P 13½. (a) POSTAGE.

347	1 f. 50, Type **46** ..	..	5	5
348	2 f. "La Maja Vestida" (Goya) (*horiz*) ..		5	5
349	4 f. "The Lacemaker" (Vermeer)	..	5	5

(b) AIR. *Inscr* "POSTE AERIENNE"

350	17 f. "Woman and Cat" (Renoir)	..	20	5
351	24 f. "The Jewish Bride" (Rembrandt) (*horiz*)	..	25	10
352	26 f. "Pope Innocent X" (Velasquez)	..	30	10
347/352	*Set of 6*	..	80	35

47 Module landing on Moon **48** Salamis aethiops

1968 (15 May). *Space Exploration.* **T 47** *and similar square designs. Multicoloured. Photo.* P 13. (a) POSTAGE. *Size as* **T 47**.

353	4 f. Type **47**	..	5	5
354	6 f. Russian cosmonaut in Space	..	8	5
355	8 f. Weather satellite ..	..	8	5
356	10 f. American astronaut in Space	..	10	5

(b) AIR. *Inscr* "POSTE AERIENNE". *Larger designs,* 41×41 mm

357	14 f. Type **47**	..	15	8
358	18 f. As 6 f.	..	20	8
359	25 f. As 8 f.	..	25	10
360	40 f. As 10 f.	..	35	15
353/360	*Set of 8*	..	1·10	55

MS361 109×82 mm. 25 f. Type **47**; 40 f. Weather satellite. Perf or imperf .. 1·00 1·00

1968. *Butterflies.* **T 48** *and similar multicoloured designs. Photo.* P 13½.

(a) POSTAGE. (i) *Size as* **T 48** (7 June)

362	50 c. Type **48** ..	.. ..	5	5
363	1 f. *Graphium ridleyanus*	.. ..	5	5
364	1 f. 50, *Cymothoe*	.. ..	5	5
365	2 f. *Charaxes eupale* ..		5	5
366	3 f. *Papilio bromius*	.. ..	5	5
367	3 f. 50, *Teracolus annae*	..	5	5

(ii) *Size* 34×38 *mm* (28 June)

368	4 f. Type **48**	..	5	5
369	5 f. As 1 f. ..	..	5	5
370	6 f. 50, As 1 f. 50	..	8	5
371	8 f. As 2 f.	..	8	5
372	10 f. As 3 f.	..	10	5
373	15 f. As 3 f. 50 ..		15	5

(iii) *Size* 41×46 *mm* (19 July)

374	20 f. Type **48**	..	25	8
375	50 f. *Papilio zenobia*	..	60	15
376	100 f. *Danais chrysippus*	..	1·25	25
377	150 f. *Salamis temora* ..	..	1·75	40

(b) AIR. *With gold frames* (9 Sept)
(i) *Size* 33×37 *mm*

378	6 f. As 3 f. 50 ..	..	8	5
379	8 f. As 1 f.	..	8	5
380	10 f. As 1 f. 50	..	10	5
381	14 f. As 2 f.	..	15	5
382	15 f. As 3 f.	..	15	5

(ii) *Size* 39×44 *mm*

383	20 f. As 50 f. (No. 375) ..		25	8
384	50 f. Type **48**	..	60	15
385	75 f. As 100 f. ..	..	85	20
386	130 f. As 150 f. ..	..	1·40	35
362/386	*Set of 25*	..	7·50	2·25

49 "Women on the Manzanares" (Goya) **50** Football

1968 (30 Sept). *International Letter-writing Week.* **T 49** *and similar vert paintings. Multicoloured. Photo.* P 13. (a) POSTAGE.

387	4 f. Type **49**	..	5	5
388	7 f. "Reading a Letter" (De Hooch)	..	8	5
389	11 f. "Woman reading a Letter" (Terborch)	..	10	5
390	14 f. "Man writing a Letter" (Metsu)	..	15	8

(b) AIR. *Inscr* "POSTE AERIENNE"

391	17 f. "The Letter" (Fragonard) ..	..	20	8
392	26 f. "Young Woman reading a Letter" (Vermeer)	..	25	10
393	40 f. "Folding a Letter" (Vigée-Lebrun) ..		35	15
394	50 f. "Mademoiselle Lavergne" (Liotard)	..	40	20
387/394	*Set of 8*	..	1·40	70

MS395 103×120 mm. Nos. 393/4 (without "POSTE AERIENNE" inscr). Perf or imperf .. 1·00 1·00
Nos. 387/94 were each issued in sheets of 8 stamps and a se-tenant label.

1968 (24 Oct). *Olympic Games, Mexico.* **T 50** *and similar vert designs. Multicoloured. Photo.* P 13. (a) POSTAGE.

396	4 f. Type **50**	..	5	5
397	7 f. Basketball ..	..	8	5
398	13 f. High-jumping	..	12	5
399	24 f. Relay-racing	..	20	8
400	40 f. Throwing the javelin	..	40	20

(b) AIR. Inscr "POSTE AERIENNE"

401	10 f. Putting the shot	..	..	..	8	5
402	17 f. Running	..	..	..	15	5
403	26 f. Throwing the hammer	..	..	25	8
404	50 f. Hurdling	..	..	..	45	15
405	75 f. Long-jumping	..	..	..	60	20
396/405	*Set of 10*	..	..	..	2·10	85

MS406 95×85 mm. Nos. 404/5 (without "POSTE AERIENNE" inscr). Perf or imperf .. 1·50 1·50
Issued in sheets of 20 with *se-tenant* stamp-size labels.

51 "Virgin and Child" (Lippi)

53 Hand holding Flame

52 W.H.O. Emblem and Map

1968 (26 Nov). *Christmas. Paintings. T 51 and similar vert designs. Multicoloured. Photo. P 13. (a) POSTAGE.*

407	3 f. Type **51**			5	5
408	5 f. "The Magnificat" (Botticelli)		..	5	5
409	6 f. "Virgin and Child" (Dürer) ..		8	5
410	11 f. "Virgin and Child" (Correggio)	..	12	5

(b) AIR. Inscr "POSTE AERIENNE"

411	10 f. "Madonna" (Raphael)	..	..	8	5
412	14 f. "The Nativity" (Baroccio) ..		..	12	8
413	17 f. "The Holy Family" (El Greco)	..	15	8
414	26 f. "Adoration of the Magi" (Maino) ..		25	10
407/414	*Set of 8*	..	..	..	80	45

MS415 Two sheets each 120×120 mm. (a) Nos. 407/10; (b) Nos. 411/14. Perf or imperf .. 1·25 1·25
Issued in sheets of ten stamps and two *se-tenant* labels.

1969 (22 Jan). *20th Anniversary of World Health Organisation Operations in Africa. Photo. P 13.*

416	**52**	5 f. multicoloured	..	..	..	5	5
417		6 f. multicoloured	..	..	..	8	5
418		11 f. multicoloured	..	..	..	12	5

1969 (22 Jan). *AIR. Human Rights Year. Photo. P 13.*

419	**53**	10 f. multicoloured	..	..	..	10	5
420		14 f. multicoloured	..	..	..	12	8
421		26 f. multicoloured	..	..	..	25	10

(54)

55 Map showing African Members

1969 (17 Feb). *Space Flight of "Apollo 8". Nos. 407/14 optd with T 54 in silver. (a) POSTAGE.*

422	3 f. multicoloured	..	..	..	5	5
423	5 f. multicoloured	..	..	..	5	5
424	6 f. multicoloured	..	..	..	8	5
425	11 f. multicoloured	..	..	..	12	5

(b) AIR. Inscr "POSTE AERIENNE"

426	10 f. multicoloured	..	..	..	8	5
427	14 f. multicoloured	..	..	..	12	8
428	17 f. multicoloured	..	..	..	15	8
429	26 f. multicoloured	..	..	..	25	10
422/429	*Set of 8*	..	..	..	80	45

1969 (12 Mar). *5th Anniversary of Yaoundé Agreement between Common Market Countries and African-Malagasy Economic Community. T 55 and similar multicoloured designs. Photo. P 13.*

430	5 f. Type **55**	..	..	..	5	5
431	14 f. Ploughing with tractor	..	..	12	8
432	17 f. Teacher and pupil	..	..	20	8
433	26 f. Maps of Africa and Europe (*horiz*)	30	15
430/433	*Set of 4*	..	..	..	60	30

56 "Resurrection" (Isenmann)

57 Potter

1969 (24 Mar). *Easter. T 56 and similar vert paintings. Multicoloured. Photo. P 13.*

434	11 f. Type **56**	..	..	..	12	5
435	14 f. "Resurrection" (Caron)	..	..	15	8
436	17 f. "Noli me Tangere" (Schongauer) ..		20	12
437	26 f. "Resurrection" (El Greco) ..		..	30	15
434/437	*Set of 4*	..	..	..	70	35

MS438 102×125 mm. Nos. 434/7. Perf or imperf .. 75 75
Issued in sheets of ten stamps and two *se-tenant* labels.

1969 (6 May). *50th Anniversary of International Labour Organization. T 57 and similar vert designs. Multicoloured. Photo. P 13.*

439	3 f. Type **57**	..	..	..	5	5
440	5 f. Farm workers	..	..	..	5	5
441	7 f. Foundry worker	..	..	..	8	5
442	10 f. Harvester ..	..	..	..	10	5
439/442	*Set of 4*	..	..	..	25	15

58 Nurse and Patient

1969 (26 June). *50th Anniversary of League of Red Cross Societies.* T **58** *and similar horiz designs. Multicoloured. Photo. P 13.* (a) *POSTAGE.*

443	4 f. +1 f. Type **58**	..	5	5
444	7 f. +1 f. Stretcher bearers	..	10	5
445	11 f. +1 f. Operating theatre	..	12	8
446	17 f. +1 f. Blood bank	..	15	10

(b) *AIR. Inscr* "POSTE AERIENNE"

447	26 f. +3 f. Laboratory	..	30	12
448	40 f. +3 f. Red Cross truck in African village	..	40	15
449	50 f. +3 f. Nurse and woman patient	..	45	20
443/449	Set of 7	..	1·40	70
MS450	90×97 mm. Nos. 447/9 (without "POSTE AERIENNE" inscr). Perf or imperf	..	1·25	1·25

59 Steel Works   60 Pope Paul VI

1969 (29 July). *5th Anniversary of African Development Bank.* T **59** *and similar vert designs. Multicoloured. Photo. P 13.*

451	10 f. Type **59**	..	8	5
452	17 f. Broadcaster	..	15	5
453	30 f. Language laboratory	..	30	10
454	50 f. Tractor and harrow	..	40	15
451/454	Set of 4	..	85	30
MS455	103×125 mm. Nos. 451/4. Perf or imperf	..	90	90

1969 (12 Sept). *1st Papal Visit to Africa.* T **60** *and similar multicoloured designs. Photo. P 13.*

456	3 f. +2 f. Type **60**	..	5	5
457	5 f. +2 f. Pope Paul and map of Africa (horiz)	..	8	5
458	10 f. +2 f. Pope Paul and African flags (horiz)	..	12	5
459	14 f. +2 f. Pope Paul and the Vatican (horiz)	..	15	8
460	17 f. +2 f. Type **60**	..	15	8
461	40 f. +2 f. Pope Paul and Uganda Martyrs (horiz)	..	40	15
462	50 f. +2 f. Pope Paul enthroned (horiz)	..	45	20
456/462	Set of 7	..	1·25	60
MS463	80×103 mm. As Nos. 461/2, but face values 40 f. +5 f. and 50 f. +5 f. Perf or imperf	..	1·40	1·40

ALBUM LISTS

Write for our latest lists of albums and accessories.
These will be sent free on request.

61 "Girl reading Letter" (Vermeer)   62 Blast-off

1969 (24 Oct). *International Letter-writing Week.* T **61** *and similar vert paintings. Multicoloured. Photo. P 13.*

464	4 f. Type **61**	..	5	5
465	7 f. "Graziella" (Renoir)	..	5	5
466	14 f. "Woman writing a Letter" (Terborch)	..	15	8
467	26 f. "Galileo" (unknown painter)	..	25	10
468	40 f. "Beethoven" (unknown painter)	..	35	15
464/468	Set of 5	..	75	40
MS469	133×75 mm. Nos. 467/8. Perf or imperf	..	80	80

1969 (6 Nov). *1st Man on the Moon.* T **62** *and similar vert designs. Multicoloured. Photo. P 13.* (a) *POSTAGE.*

470	4 f. Type **62**	..	5	5
471	6 f. 50, Rocket in Space	..	8	5
472	7 f. Separation of Lunar module	..	8	5
473	14 f. Module landing on Moon	..	12	5
474	17 f. Command module in orbit	..	15	8

(b) *AIR. Inscr* "POSTE AERIENNE"

475	26 f. Astronaut descending ladder	..	25	8
476	40 f. Astronaut on Moon's surface	..	35	12
477	50 f. Module in sea	..	40	15
470/477	Set of 8	..	1·40	55
MS478	140×90 mm. 26 f. As 14 f.; 40 f. As 26 f.; 50 f. As 40 f. Perf or imperf	..	1·60	1·60

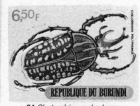

63 "Adoration of the Magi" (detail, Rubens)   64 Chelorrhina polyphemus

1969 (2 Dec). *Christmas.* T **63** *and similar multicoloured paintings. Photo. P 13.* (a) *POSTAGE.*

479	5 f. Type **63**	..	5	5
480	6 f. "Virgin and Child with St. John" (Romano)	..	5	5
481	10 f. "Madonna of the Magnificat" (Botticelli)	..	10	5

(b) *AIR. Inscr* "POSTE AERIENNE"

482	17 f. "Virgin and Child" (Garofalo) (horiz)	..	15	8
483	26 f. "Madonna and Child" (Negretti) (horiz)	..	25	8
484	50 f. "Virgin and Child" (Barbarelli) (horiz)	..	40	15
479/484	Set of 6	..	90	40

MS485 Two sheets (a) 110×85 mm. Nos. 479/81; (b) 85×110 mm. Nos. 482/4. Perf or imperf .. .. 1·10 1·10
Issued in sheets with *se-tenant* stamp-size labels.

1970 (6 Jan–Apr). *Beetles. T 64 and similar horiz designs. Multicoloured. Photo.* P 13. (a) *POSTAGE.*

(i) *Size 39×28 mm* (6 Jan)

486	50 c. Sternotomis bohemani	..	5	5
487	1 f. Tetralobus flabellicornis	..	5	5
488	1 f. 50, Type **64**	..	5	5
489	2 f. Brachytritus hieroglyphicus	..	5	5
490	3 f. Goliathus goliathus	..	5	5
491	3 f. 50, Homoderus mellyi	..	5	5

(ii) *Size 46×32 mm*

492	4 f. As 50 c. (6.1)	..	5	5
493	5 f. As 1 f. (6.1)	..	5	5
494	6 f. 50, Type **64** (17.2)..	..	5	5
495	8 f. As 2 f. (17.2)	..	8	5
496	10 f. As 3 f. (17.2)	..	10	5
497	15 f. As 3 f. 50 (17.2)	..	12	5

(iii) *Size 62×36 mm*

498	20 f. As 50 c. (17.2)	..	20	8
499	50 f. Stephanorrhina guttata (4.4)		50	20
500	100 f. Phyllocnema viridicostata (4.4)	..	1·00	35
501	150 f. Mecynorrhina oberthueri (4.4)	..	1·50	50

(b) *AIR. Inscr* "POSTE AERIENNE". (i) *Size 46×32 mm* (20 Jan)

502	6 f. As 3 f. 50	..	5	5
503	8 f. As 1 f.	..	5	5
504	10 f. Type **64**	..	8	5
505	14 f. As 2 f.	..	12	5
506	15 f. As 3 f.	..	12	5

(ii) *Size 52×36 mm*

507	20 f. As 50 f. (No. 499) (20.1)	..	15	8
508	50 f. As 50 c. (27.2)	..	40	12
509	75 f. As 100 f. (27.2)	..	60	15
510	130 f. As 150 f. (27.2)	..	80	25
486/510	Set of 25	..	5·50	2·25

65 "Jesus Condemned to Death"

67 Burundi Cow

66 Japanese Parade

1970 (16 Mar). *Easter. "The Stations of the Cross" (Carredano). T 65 and similar vert designs. Multicoloured. Photo.* P 13. (a) *POSTAGE.*

511	1 f. Type **65**	..	5	5
512	1 f. 50, "Carrying the Cross"	..	5	5
513	2 f. "Jesus falls for the First Time"	..	5	5
514	3 f. "Christ meets His Mother"	..	5	5
515	3 f. 50, "Simon of Cyrene takes the Cross"	..	5	5
516	4 f. "Veronica wipes the face of Christ"		5	5
517	5 f. "Jesus falls for the Second Time"		5	5

(b) *AIR. Inscr* "POSTE AERIENNE"

518	8 f. "The Women of Jerusalem"	..	8	5
519	10 f. "Jesus falls for the Third Time"		10·	5
520	14 f. "Christ stripped"	..	12	8
521	15 f. "Jesus nailed to the Cross"	..	12	8
522	18 f. "The Crucifixion"	..	15	8
523	20 f. "Descent from the Cross"	..	20	10
524	50 f. "Christ laid in the Tomb"	..	50	20
511/524	Set of 14	..	1·40	90

MS525 Two sheets each 155×125 mm. (a) Nos. 511/17; (b) Nos. 518/24. Perf or imperf 1·50 1·50

1970 (5 May). *World Fair, Osaka, Japan (EXPO '70). T 66 and similar multicoloured designs. Photo.* P 13. (a) *POSTAGE.*

526	4 f. Type **66**	..	5	5
527	6 f. 50, Exhibition site from the air	..	5	5
528	7 f. African pavilions	..	5	5
529	14 f. Pagoda (vert)	..	12	8
530	26 f. Recording pavilion and pool	..	25	12
531	40 f. Tower of the Sun (vert)	..	40	20
532	50 f. National flags (vert)	..	45	20
526/532	Set of 7	..	1·25	65

(b) *AIR. Inscr* "POSTE AERIENNE"

MS533 105×80 mm. As Nos. 531/2 with additional "POSTE AERIENNE" inscr. Perf or imperf 90 90

1970 (8 July). *Sources of the Nile. Small sheet containing 18 different se-tenant designs as T 67, showing map sections, animals and birds. Together these form a map of the Nile from Cairo to Burundi. Multicoloured. Photo.* P 13. (a) *POSTAGE.*

534	7 f. Any design ..	..	8	5
	a. Complete sheet of 18	..	1·25	75

(b) *AIR. As above, but inscr* "POSTE AERIENNE"

535	14 f. Any design ..	..	15	5
	a. Complete sheet of 18	..	2·40	90

68 European Redstart

1970 (30 Sept)–**71**. *Birds. T 68 and similar multicoloured designs. Photo.* P 13. (a) *POSTAGE. Size 44×33 or 33×44 mm.*

536	2 f. Northern shrike (vert)	..	5	5
537	2 f. European starling (vert)	..	5	5
538	2 f. Yellow wagtail (vert)	..	5	5
539	2 f. Bank swallow (vert)	..	5	5
540	3 f. Wren	..	5	5
541	3 f. Firecrest	..	5	5
542	3 f. Skylark	..	5	5
543	3 f. Crested lark	..	5	5
544	3 f. 50, Wood shrike (vert)	..	5	5
545	3 f. 50, Rock thrush (vert)	..	5	5
546	3 f. 50, Black redstart (vert)	..	5	5
547	3 f. 50, Ring ouzel (vert)	..	5	5
548	4 f. Type **68**	..	5	5
549	4 f. Hedge-sparrow	..	5	5
550	4 f. Grey wagtail	..	5	5
551	4 f. Meadow pipit	..	5	5
552	5 f. Eurasian hoopoe (vert)	..	5	5
553	5 f. Flycatcher (vert)	..	5	5
554	5 f. Great reed warbler (vert)	..	5	5
555	5 f. Kingfisher (vert)	..	5	5
556	6 f. 50, House martin	..	5	5
557	6 f. 50, Sedge-warbler	..	5	5
558	6 f. 50, Fieldfare	..	5	5
559	6 f. 50, Golden oriole	..	5	5

(b) *AIR. Inscr* "POSTE AERIENNE". *Size 52×44 mm or 44×52 mm*

560	8 f. As No. 536 (16.11.70)	..	8	5
561	8 f. As No. 537 (16.11.70)	..	8	5
562	8 f. As No. 538 (16.11.70)	..	8	5
563	8 f. As No. 539 (16.11.70)	..	8	5

564	10 f. As No. 540 (16.11.70)	.. ..	10	8
565	10 f. As No. 541 (16.11.70)	.. ..	10	8
566	10 f. As No. 542 (16.11.70)	.. ..	10	8
567	10 f. As No. 543 (16.11.70)	.. ..	10	8
568	14 f. As No. 544 (16.11.70)	.. ..	15	10
569	14 f. As No. 545 (16.11.70)	.. ..	15	10
570	14 f. As No. 546 (16.11.70)	.. ..	15	10
571	14 f. As No. 547 (16.11.70)	.. ..	15	10
572	20 f. Type **68** (29.1.71)	..	20	12
573	20 f. As No. 549 (29.1.71)	..	20	12
574	20 f. As No. 550 (29.1.71)	..	20	12
575	20 f. As No. 551 (29.1.71)	..	20	12
576	30 f. As No. 552 (29.1.71)	..	30	15
577	30 f. As No. 553 (29.1.71)	..	30	15
578	30 f. As No. 554 (29.1.71)	..	30	15
579	30 f. As No. 555 (29.1.71)	..	30	15
580	50 f. As No. 556 (18.2.71)	..	45	25
581	50 f. As No. 557 (18.2.71)	..	45	25
582	50 f. As No. 558 (18.2.71)	..	45	25
583	50 f. As No. 559 (18.2.71)	..	45	25
536/583	*Set of 48*	.. ..	5·50	3·75

The four designs of each value were issued in *se-tenant* blocks of four within the sheet of 16, each block forming a composite design.

69 Library

1970 (23 Oct). *International Education Year. T* **69** *and similar horiz designs. Multicoloured. Photo. P* 13.

584	3 f. Type **69**	.. ..	5	5
585	5 f. Examination	.. ..	5	5
586	7 f. Experiments in the laboratory		5	5
587	10 f. Students with electro-microscope		10	8
584/587	*Set of 4*	.. ..	20	15

70 United Nations Building, New York

72 King Baudouin and Queen Fabiola

71 Pres. Micombero and Wife

1970 (23 Oct). *AIR. 25th Anniversary of United Nations. T* **70** *and similar vert designs. Multicoloured. Photo. P* 13.

588	7 f. Type **70**	.. ..	5	5
589	11 f. Security Council in session	..	12	5
590	26 f. Pope Paul VI and U Thant	..	25	15
591	40 f. U.N. and National flags	..	40	20
588/591	*Set of 4*	.. ..	75	40
MS592	125×80 mm. As Nos. 590/1, but without "POSTE AERIENNE" inscr. Perf or imperf	.. ..	65	65

1970 (28 Nov). *4th Anniversary of Republic. T* **71** *and similar vert designs. P* 13. (*a*) POSTAGE.

593	4 f. Type **71**	.. ..	5	5
594	7 f. Pres. Micombero and flag	..	5	5
595	11 f. Revolution Memorial	..	12	5

(*b*) AIR. *Inscr* "POSTE AERIENNE"

MS596	125×142 mm. Nos. 593/5. Perf or imperf	.. ..	25	25

1970 (28 Nov). *AIR. Visit of King and Queen of the Belgians. T* **72** *and similar horiz designs. Each sepia, deep reddish purple and gold. Photo. P* 13.

597	6 f. Type **72**	.. ..	5	5
598	20 f. Pres. Micombero and King Baudouin	..	20	10
599	40 f. Pres. Micombero in evening dress		40	20
MS600	143×117 mm. As Nos. 597/9, but with "POSTE AERIENNE" inscr omitted. Perf or imperf	.. ..	65	65

73 "Adoration of the Magi" (Dürer)   **74** Lenin in Discussion

1970 (14 Dec). *Christmas. T* **73** *and similar vert paintings. Multicoloured. Photo. P* 13. (*a*) POSTAGE.

601	6 f. 50+1 f. Type **73**	.. ..	5	5
602	11 f. +1 f. "The Virgin of the Eucharist" (Botticelli)	.. ..	12	5
603	20 f. +1 f. "The Holy Family" (El Greco)		20	12

(*b*) AIR. *Inscr* "POSTE AERIENNE"

604	14 f. +3 f. "The Adoration of the Magi" (Velasquez)	..	15	5
605	26 f. +3 f. "The Holy Family" (Van Cleve)		25	12
606	40 f. +3 f. "Virgin and Child" (Van der Weyden)	.. ..	40	20
601/606	*Set of 6*	.. ..	1·00	55
MS607	Two sheets each 135×75 mm. (a) Nos. 601/3; (b) Nos. 604/6. Perf or imperf	..	1·25	1·25

1970 (31 Dec). *Birth Centenary of Lenin. T* **74** *and similar vert designs. Each purple-brown and gold. Photo. P* 13.

608	3 f. 50, Type **74**	.. ..	5	5
609	5 f. Lenin addressing Soviet	..	5	5
610	6 f. 50, Lenin with soldier and sailor	..	5	5
611	15 f. Lenin speaking to crowd	..	15	12
612	50 f. Lenin	.. ..	50	25
608/612	*Set of 5*	.. ..	80	45

75 Lion   **76** "The Resurrection"
(Il Sodoma)

1971 (19 Mar–June). *African Animals. T* **75** *and similar square designs. Multicoloured. Photo. P* 13.

(a) POSTAGE. *Size* 38 × 38 *mm*

613	1 f. Type **75**	..	..	5	5
614	1 f. Water buffalo	..	..	5	5
615	1 f. Hippopotamus	..	..	5	5
616	1 f. Giraffe	..	..	5	5
617	2 f. Damas antelope	..	..	5	5
618	2 f. Rhinoceros ..	..	..	5	5
619	2 f. Zebra	..	..	5	5
620	2 f. Leopard	..	..	5	5
621	3 f. Grant's gazelle	..	..	5	5
622	3 f. Cheetah	..	..	5	5
623	3 f. Vultures	..	..	5	5
624	3 f. Okapi	..	..	5	5
625	5 f. Chimpanzee	..	..	5	5
626	5 f. Elephant	..	..	5	5
627	5 f. Spotted hyena	..	..	5	5
628	5 f. Oryx	..	..	5	5
629	6 f. Gorilla	..	..	5	5
630	6 f. Gnu..	..	..	5	5
631	6 f. Warthog	..	..	5	5
632	6 f. Wild dog	..	..	5	5
633	11 f. Sable antelope	..	..	12	5
634	11 f. Caracal lynx	..	..	12	5
635	11 f. Ostriches	..	..	12	5
636	11 f. Bongo	..	..	12	5

(b) *AIR. Inscr* "POSTE AERIENNE". *Size* 44 × 44 *mm*

637	10 f. Type **75** (30.4)	..	..	10	5
638	10 f. As No. 614 (30.4)	..	..	10	5
639	10 f. As No. 615 (30.4)	..	..	10	5
640	10 f. As No. 616 (30.4)	..	..	10	5
641	14 f. As No. 617 (30.4)	..	..	15	8
642	14 f. As No. 618 (30.4)	..	..	15	8
643	14 f. As No. 619 (30.4)	..	..	15	8
644	14 f. As No. 620 (30.4)	..	..	15	8
645	17 f. As No. 621 (30.4)	..	..	15	8
646	17 f. As No. 622 (30.4)	..	..	15	8
647	17 f. As No. 623 (30.4)	..	..	15	8
648	17 f. As No. 624 (30.4)	..	..	15	8
649	24 f. As No. 625 (17.5)	..	..	25	12
650	24 f. As No. 626 (17.5)	..	..	25	12
651	24 f. As No. 627 (17.5)	..	..	25	12
652	24 f. As No. 628 (17.5)	..	..	25	12
653	26 f. As No. 629 (17.5)	..	..	25	12
654	26 f. As No. 630 (17.5)	..	..	25	12
655	26 f. As No. 631 (17.5)	..	..	25	12
656	26 f. As No. 632 (17.5)	..	..	25	12
657	31 f. As No. 633 (14.6)	..	..	30	15
658	31 f. As No. 634 (14.6)	..	..	30	15
659	31 f. As No. 635 (14.6)	..	..	30	15
660	31 f. As No. 636 (14.6)	..	..	30	15
613/660	*Set of* 48	..	..	5·50	3·25

The four designs of each value were issued *se-tenant* in horiz strips of four within the sheet, forming composite designs.

1971 (2 Apr). *Easter. T* **76** *and similar vert paintings. Multicoloured. Photo. P* 13. (*a*) *POSTAGE.*

661	3 f. Type **76**	..	..	5	5
662	6 f. "The Resurrection" (Del Castagno)		..	5	5
663	11 f. "Noli me Tangere" (Correggio)	..		12	5

(b) *AIR. Inscr* "POSTE AERIENNE"

664	14 f. "The Resurrection" (Borrassi)	..	15	8
665	17 f. "The Resurrection" (Della Francesca)	..	15	8
666	26 f. "The Resurrection" (Pleydenwyurff)		25	12
661/666	*Set of* 6		70	40
MS667	Two sheets each 117 × 84 mm. (a) Nos. 661/3; (b) Nos. 664/6. Colours changed. Perf or imperf	..	75	75

LUTTE CONTRE LE RACISME ET LA DISCRIMINATION RACIALE

(**77** Racial Equality Year)

1971 (20 July). *AIR. United Nations Campaigns. Nos.* 637/48 *optd or surch with T* **77** *and similar types in black and gold.*

(a) Optd with T **77**

668	10 f. multicoloured	..	10	5
669	10 f. multicoloured	..	10	5
670	10 f. multicoloured	..	10	5
671	10 f. multicoloured	..	10	5

(*b*) Surch "LUTTE CONTRE L'ANALPHABETISME", U.N.E.S.C.O. *emblem and premium* (*Campaign against Illiteracy*)

672	14 f. + 2 f. multicoloured		15	8
673	14 f. + 2 f. multicoloured		15	8
674	14 f. + 2 f. multicoloured		15	8
675	14 f. + 2 f. multicoloured		15	8

(*c*) Surch "AIDE INTERNATIONALE AUX REFUGIES", *emblem and premium* (*Int Help for Refugees*)

676	17 f. + 1 f. multicoloured	..	15	8
677	17 f. + 1 f. multicoloured	..	15	8
678	17 f. + 1 f. multicoloured	..	15	8
679	17 f. + 1 f. multicoloured	..	15	8
668/679	*Set of* 12	..	1·40	75

République du Burundi

(**78** 75th Anniv of Modern Olympic Games)   **79** "Venetian Girl"

1971 (28 July). *AIR. Olympic Commemorations. Nos.* 653/60 *surch with T* **78** *and similar type in black and gold.*

(a) Surch with T **78**

680	26 f. + 1 f. multicoloured	..	30	15
681	26 f. + 1 f. multicoloured	..	30	15
682	26 f. + 1 f. multicoloured	..	30	15
683	26 f. + 1 f. multicoloured	..	30	15

(*b*) Surch "JEUX PRE-OLYMPIQUES MUNICH 1972", *rings and premium* (*Olympic Games, Munich* (1972))

684	31 f. + 1 f. multicoloured	..	35	20
685	31 f. + 1 f. multicoloured	..	35	20
686	31 f. + 1 f. multicoloured	..	35	20
687	31 f. + 1 f. multicoloured	..	35	20
680/687	*Set of* 8	..	2·40	1·25

Burundi

1971 (20 Sept). *International Letter-writing Week. Paintings by Dürer. T* **79** *and similar vert designs. Multicoloured. Photo. P* 13. (*a*) *POSTAGE.*

688	6 f. Type **79**	.. ..	5	5
689	11 f. "Jerome Holzschuhers"	.. ..	12	5
690	14 f. "Emperor Maximilian"	.. ..	15	8
691	17 f. Altar painting, Paumgartner	..	15	8
692	26 f. "The Halle Madonna"	.. ..	25	12
693	31 f. Self-portrait	.. ..	30	15
688/693	*Set of 6*	.. .. ..	95	45

(*b*) *AIR. Inscr* "POSTE AERIENNE"

MS694	137×80 mm. As Nos. 692/3. Perf or imperf	.. ..	60	60

(80)

81 "The Virgin and Child" (Il Perugino)

1971 (8 Oct). *6th Congress of International Institute of French Law, Bujumbura. Nos.* 688/**MS**694 *optd with T* **80** *in black and gold.* (*a*) *POSTAGE.*

695	6 f. multicoloured	.. ..	5	5
696	11 f. multicoloured	.. ..	12	5
697	14 f. multicoloured	.. ..	15	8
698	17 f. multicoloured	.. ..	15	8
699	26 f. multicoloured	.. ..	25	12
700	31 f. multicoloured	.. ..	30	15
695/700	*Set of 6*	.. ..	95	45

(*b*) *AIR. Inscr* "POSTE AERIENNE"

MS701	137×80 mm. No. **MS**694 optd. Perf or imperf	.. .. ..	60	60

1971 (2 Nov). *Christmas. Paintings of "Virgin and Child" by following artists. Multicoloured. Photo. P* 13. (*a*) *POSTAGE*

702	3 f. Type **81**	.. ..	5	5
703	5 f. Del Sarto	.. ..	5	5
704	6 f. Morales	.. ..	5	5

(*b*) *AIR. Inscr* "POSTE AERIENNE"

705	14 f. Da Conegliano	.. ..	15	8
706	17 f. Lippi	.. ..	15	8
707	31 f. Leonardo da Vinci	..	30	15
702/707	*Set of 6*	.. ..	70	40
MS708	Two sheets each 125×80 mm. (*a*) Nos. 702/4; (*b*) Nos. 705/7	..	90	90

(82)

83 "Archangel Michael" (icon, St. Mark's)

1971 (27 Nov). *25th Anniversary of U.N.I.C.E.F. Nos.* 702/**MS**708 *surch with T* **82** *in black and gold.* (*a*) *POSTAGE*

709	3 f. +1 f. multicoloured	.. ..	5	5
710	5 f. +1 f. multicoloured	.. ..	5	5
711	6 f. +1 f. multicoloured	.. ..	8	5

(*b*) *AIR. Inscr* "POSTE AERIENNE"

712	14 f. +1 f. multicoloured	.. ..	15	8
713	17 f. +1 f. multicoloured	.. ..	15	8
714	31 f. +1 f. multicoloured	.. ..	35	20
709/714	*Set of 6*	.. ..	75	50
MS715	Two sheets each 125×80 mm. No. **MS**708 surch with 2 f. premium on each stamp in the sheets	..	95	95

1971 (27 Dec). *U.N.E.S.C.O. "Save Venice" Campaign. T* **83** *and similar horiz designs. Multicoloured. Photo. P* 13.

(*a*) *POSTAGE*

716	3 f. +1 f. Type **83**	.. ..	5	5
717	5 f. +1 f. "La Polenta" (Longhi)	..	5	5
718	6 f. +1 f. "Gossip" (Longhi)	..	8	5
719	11 f. +1 f. "Diana's Bath" (Pittoni)	..	12	5

(*b*) *AIR. Inscr* "POSTE AERIENNE"

720	10 f. +1 f. Casa d'Oro	.. ..	10	5
721	17 f. +1 f. Doge's Palace	..	15	8
722	24 f. +1 f. St. John and St. Paul Church		25	10
723	31 f. +1 f. "Doge's Palace and Piazzetta" (Canaletto)	.. ..	30	15
716/723	*Set of 8*	.. ..	1·00	85
MS724	Two sheets each 115×132 mm. (*a*) Nos. 716/19; (*b*) Nos. 720/3. Each design in the sheets has a 2 f. premium. Perf or imperf	.. .. ..	1·25	1·25

84 "Lunar Orbiter"   86 "Ecce Homo" (Metzys)

85 Slalom skiing

1972 (15 Jan). *Conquest of Space. T* **84** *and similar vert designs. Multicoloured. Photo. P* 13. (*a*) *POSTAGE.*

725	6 f. Type **84**	.. ..	5	5
726	11 f. "Vostok" spaceship	.. ..	12	5
727	14 f. "Luna 1"	.. ..	15	8
728	17 f. First Man on the Moon	.. ..	20	8
729	26 f. "Soyuz 11" space flight	..	25	10
730	40 f. "Lunar Rover"	.. ..	40	15
725/730	*Set of 6*	.. ..	1·10	45

(*b*) *AIR. Inscr* "POSTE AERIENNE"

MS731	135×135 mm. Nos. 725/30 with additional inscr	.. ..	1·10	1·10

1972 (Feb). *Winter Olympic Games, Sapporo, Japan. T* **85** *and similar horiz designs. Multicoloured. Photo. P* 13. (*a*) *POSTAGE.*

732	5 f. Type **85** (3.2)	.. ..	5	5
733	6 f. Pair skating (3.2)	.. ..	5	5
734	11 f. Figure-skating (3.2)	..	12	5
735	14 f. Ski-jumping (3.2)	.. ..	15	8
736	17 f. Ice-hockey (3.2)	.. ..	20	8
737	24 f. Speed skating (3.2)	..	25	10
738	26 f. Snow scooting (21.2)	..	25	10

739	31 f. Downhill skiing (21.2)	..	..	·35	15
740	50 f. Bobsleighing (21.2)	..	..	50	25
732/740	Set of 9	..	..	1·75	80

(b) AIR. Inscr "POSTE AERIENNE"
MS741 107×127 mm. As Nos. 738/40. Perf
or imperf (3.2)   ..   ..   ..   1·10   1·10

1972 (20 Mar). *Easter. T* **86** *and similar vert paintings. Multicoloured. Photo.* P 13.

742	3 f. 50, Type **86** ..	..	..	5	5
743	6 f. 50, "The Crucifixion" (Rubens)	..	..	5	5
744	10 f. "The Descent from the Cross" (Portormo)	..	..	12	5
745	18 f. "Pieta" (Gallegos) ..	..	..	20	8
746	27 f. "The Trinity" (El Greco)	..	..	25	.10
742/746	Set of 5	..	..	60	30

MS747 111×160 mm. Nos. 742/6. Perf or
imperf   60   60

87 Gymnastics   **88** Prince Rwagasore, Pres.
                           Micombero and Drummers

1972. *Olympic Games, Munich. T* **87** *and similar vert designs. Multicoloured. Photo.* P 13. *(a) POSTAGE (19 May).*

748	5 f. Type **87**	..	..	5	5
749	6 f. Throwing the javelin	..	..	5	5
750	11 f. Fencing	..	..	12	5
751	14 f. Cycling	..	..	15	8
752	17 f. Pole-vaulting	..	..	20	8

(b) AIR. Inscr "POSTE AERIENNE" (24 July)

753	24 f. Weightlifting	..	..	25	10
754	26 f. Hurdling	..	..	25	10
755	31 f. Throwing the discus	..	..	35	15
756	40 f. Football	..	..	40	15
748/756	Set of 9	..	..	1·75	70

MS757 123×75 mm. Nos. 755/6 without
"POSTE AERIENNE" inscr (19.5)   ..   75   75

1972 (24 Aug). *10th Anniv of Independence. T* **88** *and similar vert designs. Multicoloured. Photo.* P 13. *(a) POSTAGE.*

758	5 f. Type **88**	..	..	5	5
759	7 f. Rwagasore, Micombero and map ..	..	..	5	5
760	13 f. Pres. Micombero and Burundi flag	..	..	15	8

(b) AIR. Inscr "POSTE AERIENNE"

761	15 f. Type **88**	..	..	15	8
762	18 f. As 7 f.	..	..	20	8
763	27 f. As 13 f.	..	..	25	10
758/763	Set of 6	..	..	80	40

MS764 Two sheets each 147×80 mm. (a)
Nos. 758/60; (b) Nos. 761/3   80   80

89 "Madonna and Child" (A. Solario)

1972 (2 Nov). *Christmas. Vert paintings as T* **89** *showing "Madonna and Child" by artists given below. Multicoloured. Photo.* P 13. *(a) POSTAGE.*

765	5 f. Type **89**	..	..	5	5
766	10 f. Raphael	..	..	12	5
767	15 f. Botticelli	..	..	15	8

(b) AIR. Inscr "POSTE AERIENNE"

768	18 f. S. Mainardi..	..	..	20	8
769	27 f. H. Memling..	..	..	25	10
770	40 f. L. Lotto	..	..	40	15
765/770	Set of 6	..	..	1·10	45

MS771 Two sheets each 128×82 mm. (a)
Nos. 765/7; (b) Nos. 768/70 ..   ..   1·10   1·10

90 *Platycoryne crocea*   **(91)**

1972 (6 Nov)–73. *Orchids. T* **90** *and similar diamond-shaped designs. Photo.* P 13. *(a) POSTAGE.*

(i) Size as T **90**

772	50 c. Type **90**	..	..	5	5
773	1 f. Cattleya trianaei	..	..	5	5
774	2 f. Eulophia cucullata ..	..	..	5	5
775	3 f. Cymbidium hamsey	..	..	5	5
776	4 f. Thelymitra pauciflora	..	..	5	5
777	5 f. Miltassia	..	..	5	5
778	6 f. Miltonia	..	..	5	5

(ii) Size 54×54 mm (29.11.72)

779	7 f. Type **90**	..	..	5	5
780	8 f. As 1 f.	..	..	8	5
781	9 f. As 2 f.	..	..	10	5
782	10 f. As 3 f.	..	..	12	5

(b) AIR. Inscr "POSTE AERIENNE" (18.1.73)

783	13 f. As 4 f.	..	..	15	8
784	14 f. As 5 f.	..	..	15	8
785	15 f. As 6 f.	..	..	15	8
786	18 f. Type **90**	..	..	20	8
787	20 f. As 1 f.	..	..	25	10
788	27 f. As 2 f.	..	..	25	10
789	36 f. As 3 f.	..	..	40	15
772/789	Set of 18	..	..	2·00	1·00

1972 (12 Dec). *Christmas Charity. Nos.* 765/**MS**771 *surch with premiums as T* **91** *in silver. (a) POSTAGE.*

790	5 f. + 1 f. multicoloured	..	..	5	5
791	10 f. + 1 f. multicoloured	..	..	12	5
792	15 f. + 1 f. multicoloured	..	..	15	8

(b) AIR. Inscr "POSTE AERIENNE"

793	18 f. + 1 f. multicoloured	..	..	25	10
794	27 f. + 1 f. multicoloured	..	..	25	10
795	40 f. + 1 f. multicoloured	..	..	40	15
790/795	Set of 6	..	..	1·10	45

MS796 Two sheets as **MS**771 with 2 f. premium surch on each stamp ..   ..   1·25   1·25

CABO. See after Nicaragua.

CAMBODIA. See Khmer Republic.

Cameroun

GERMAN COLONIAL KEY TYPES

Types as below representing the ex-Kaiser's yacht *Hohenzollern* were in use throughout the German Colonies, inscribed with the name of the particular colony for which they were issued.

A (P 14) *Pfennig*
values

B (P 14½, 14 or compound)
Mark values

Frame Type I

Centre Type I

Frame Type II

Centre Type II

Plates.
There are two types of design according to the length of name of the Colony—Type I with plain scroll and Type II with folded scroll at the top.

The top value of each Colony (5 m., 3 r. or 2½ d.) is printed in two colours and therefore has two plates; there are two types of the centre plates to fit the two types of frame plates and it sometimes happened that centre plates were used with frame plates for which they were not intended.

Where this occurred either the lines of shading from the sky run across the protruding folds (Centre Type I) or there are two clear spaces in the sky below the top scroll (Centre Type II).

In the lists which follow "(I)" means that both plates are Type I and "(II)" means that both are Type II. Combinations of plates are listed separately.

Perforations.
In Type B there are three types of perforation, all measuring about 14½. They are distinguishable by the number of holes along the horizontal and down the vertical sides of the stamps thus:—

    (a) 26×17 holes
    (b) 25×17 holes
    (c) 25×16 holes

Some values listed on paper wmkd Lozenges were prepared for use and sold in Berlin, but owing to the war of 1914–18 were not issued in the colonies.

I. KAMERUN

GERMAN PROTECTORATE
100 Pfennige=1 Mark

On 14 July 1884, by agreement between Dr. Gustav Nachtigal and local rulers, the coastal area round Douala became the German Protectorate of Kamerun. The protectorate was extended inland to Lake Chad in 1894 and in 1911 territory giving access to the Congo and Ubangi rivers was acquired from France in return for German recognition of a French protectorate in Morocco.

ERRORS. Errors such as double and inverted overprints were never issued but come from waste sheets which later leaked out of the printers.

Kamerun

(1)

1897–98. *Stamps of Germany, 1889, optd with* **T 1.**

K1	**8**	3 pf. grey-brown	..	..	2·50	6·00
		a. Yellow-brown (1898)	..	..	75	1·25
		b. Reddish brown (1898)	..	..	4·00	6·00
K2		5 pf. green	..	..	70	50
K3	**9**	10 pf. carmine	..	..	40	45
K4		20 pf. ultramarine	..	..	60	90
K5		25 pf. orange	..	..	2·25	4·75
K6		50 pf. red-brown	..	..	1·75	4·50
		a. Chocolate..	..	..	1·75	4·50

1900 (Nov). *No wmk.*					
K 7	A	3 pf. brown	..	15	15
K 8		5 pf. green	..	2·00	15
K 9		10 pf. carmine..	..	6·50	25
K10		20 pf. ultramarine	..	3·50	40
K11		25 pf. black and red/*yellow*	..	15	1·25
K12		30 pf. black and orange/*buff* ..		25	85
K13		40 pf. black and carmine	..	25	1·10
K14		50 pf. black and purple/*buff*	..	30	1·25
K15		80 pf. black and carmine/*rose*..		45	1·60
K16	B	1 m. carmine (*a*)	..	9·00	9·00
K17		2 m. blue (*a*)	..	1·25	9·00
K18		3 m. violet-black (*a*)	..	1·40	16·00
K19		5 m. carmine and black (II) (*a*)	..	25·00	70·00

1905–19. *Wmk Lozenges.*					
K20	A	3 pf. brown (1918)	..	8	
K21		5 pf. green (1905)	..	8	25
K22		10 pf. carmine (1906)	..	8	15
K23		20 pf. ultramarine (*shades*) (1914)	..	35	25·00
K24	B	1 m. carmine (*a*) (1915)	..	75	
		a. 25×17 holes (1919)	..	45	
K25		5 m. carmine and black (II) (*a*) (1913)		7·00	£275
		a. 25×17 holes (1919)	..	4·50	
		b. Frame II, Centre I (*b*)	..		

In 1914–16 Kamerun was occupied by British and French forces and on 4 March 1916 was provisionally divided between France and Britain, the latter receiving a strip of territory along the Nigerian border. This arrangement was recognised by the peace settlement of 1919, with the proviso that what had been the German protectorate before 1911 was to be administered by the two powers under League of Nations mandates (after 1946 U.N. trusteeships).

The stamps issued in the British area are listed in the *British Commonwealth Catalogue*.

II. CAMEROUN

100 Centimes=1 Franc

PRINTERS. All the stamps of Cameroun were printed at the Government Printing Works, Paris, *unless otherwise stated.*

IMPERFORATE STAMPS. Many stamps exist imperforate in their issued colours but were not valid for postage. Imperforate stamps in other colours are colour trials.

A. FRENCH OCCUPATION

September 1914–20 July 1922

Corps Expéditionnaire Franco-Anglais CAMEROUN
(1)

1915 (10 Nov). *Stamps of Gabon of 1910–17 (except 10 c., which is No. 37), optd as T 1, reading up on vert stamps.*				
1	1 c. brown and orange ..	..	7·00	2·75
2	2 c. black and chocolate..	..	14·00	12·00
3	4 c. violet and dull blue ..	..	15·00	12·00
4	5 c. olive-grey and emerald	..	1·80	85
	a. Opt double ..	..	£475	
5	10 c. red and rose-lake	..	1·80	65
	a. Error. On Gabon No. 53	..	£1000	£1000
6	20 c. chocolate and violet	..	15·00	12·00
7	25 c. chocolate and dull blue	..	4·75	1·25
8	30 c. scarlet and grey	..	12·00	11·00
9	35 c. green and violet	..	2·50	1·10
	a. Opt double ..	..	£100	£100
10	40 c. ultramarine and brown	..	15·00	12·00
	a. "Franco-Anglais" omitted ..			
11	45 c. violet and carmine	..	15·00	12·00
12	50 c. grey and blue-green	..	12·00	11·00
13	75 c. chocolate and orange-vermilion	..	12·00	11·00
14	1 f. bistre and brown	..	15·00	12·00
15	2 f. brown and carmine..	..	16·00	12·00

Inverted "s" in "Corps" exists on all values.

Occupation Française du Cameroun
(2)

CAMEROUN Occupation Française.
(3)

1916 (Jan). *Stamps of Congo optd locally as T 2 (vert on 20 c. to 2 f.).*					
		(a) On stamps of Middle Congo, 1907–17			
16		1 c. olive and brown	..	6·00	6·00
17		2 c. violet and brown	..	6·00	6·00
18		4 c. blue and brown	..	6·00	6·00
19		5 c. green and blue	..	2·50	1·75
20		35 c. chocolate and blue ..		9·00	7·00
21		45 c. violet and salmon	..	4·50	3·50
		(b) On stamps of French Congo, 1900–4			
22		15 c. dull violet and olive-green ..		3·50	3·50
		a. Opt inverted..	..	8·00	8·00
23		20 c. green and pale red ..		15·00	6·00
24		30 c. carmine and yellow..		6·00	4·75
25		40 c. chestnut and green ..		4·00	4·00
26		50 c. deep violet and lilac	..	7·00	4·50
27		75 c. claret and orange	..	7·00	6·00
28		1 f. drab and slate	..	10·00	6·00
29		2 f. carmine and grey-brown	..	10·00	6·00
16/29		*Set of 14*	..	85·00	60·00

The overprint reads down on Nos. 20/21. On Nos. 23/29 it reads up or down (same prices) but pairs with overprint *tête-bêche* are rare.

1916–17. *Stamps of Congo (Middle Congo issue of 1907–17), optd in Paris with T 3 (1 c. to 20 c.) or with first two lines 7 mm apart (others).*					
30	1	1 c. olive and brown ..	..	5	5
		a. No stop ..	..	25	25
31		2 c. violet and brown ..	..	5	5
		a. No stop ..	..	25	25
32		4 c. blue and brown ..	..	5	5
33		5 c. green and blue ..	..	5	5
34		10 c. carmine and blue ..	..	8	5
34a		15 c. purple and carmine (1917)	..	5	5
35		20 c. pale brown and blue	..	5	5
36	2	25 c. blue and grey-green ..		5	5
		a. Surch triple	..	25·00	
		b. Inverted "s"	..	45	45
		c. No stop	..	50	50
37		30 c. salmon-pink and green	..	5	5
		a. Surch double	..	8·00	
		b. Inverted "s"	..	45	45
		c. No stop	..	50	50
38		35 c. chocolate and blue	..	5	5
		a. Inverted "s"	..	45	45
		b. No stop	..	50	50
39		40 c. dull green and pale brown	..	8	5
		a. Inverted "s"	..	50	50
		b. No stop	..	65	65
40		45 c. violet and salmon	..	10	5
		a. Inverted "s"	..	50	50
		b. No stop	..	65	65
41		50 c. green and salmon	..	8	5
		a. Inverted "s"	..	50	50
		b. No stop	..	65	65
42		75 c. brown and blue	..	10	5
		a. Inverted "s"	..	30	30
43	3	1 f. deep green and pale violet	..	10	5
		a. Inverted "s"	..	45	45
		b. No stop	..	1·00	1·00
44		2 f. violet and grey-green	..	70	65
		a. Inverted "s"	..	3·25	3·25
45		5 f. blue and pink	..	75	70
		a. Inverted "s"	..	3·25	3·25
		b. No stop	..		
30/45		*Set of 17*	..	2·00	1·75

All values except the 15 c. exist on chalk-surfaced paper (same prices).

CAMEROUN
(4)

1921 (15 July). *Stamps of Congo (Middle Congo types of 1907–17) but colours changed, optd in Paris with T 4.*					
46		1 c. orange and olive-green	..	5	5
47		2 c. carmine and brown..	..	5	5
		a. Opt "CAMEROUN" omitted	..	14·00	

48	4 c. green and grey	..	..	5	5
	a. Opt "CAMEROUN" omitted		.. 14·00		
49	5 c. orange and red	..	..	5	5
	a. Opt double ..	..	.. 45·00		
50	10 c. pale green and green	..		5	5
51	15 c. orange and blue	..	..	5	5
	a. Opt "CAMEROUN" omitted		.. 30·00		
52	20 c. grey and dull purple	..		5	5
53	25 c. orange and slate	..		5	5
	a. Opt "CAMEROUN" omitted		.. 35·00		
54	30 c. red and carmine	..		5	5
55	35 c. ultramarine and grey	..		5	5
56	40 c. orange and olive-green	..		5	5
57	45 c. carmine and brown ..			5	5
58	50 c. ultramarine and blue	..		5	5
	a. Opt "CAMEROUN" omitted		.. 18·00		
59	75 c. green and claret	..		5	5
60	1 f. orange and slate	..		12	12
61	2 f. carmine and olive-green	..		55	45
62	5 f. grey and vermilion ..	..		55	45
46/62	*Set of 17*	..		1·60	1·40

No. 47a differs from No. 2a of Chad in that the centre is carmine instead of pink.

B. FRENCH MANDATED TERRITORY
20 July 1922–12 December 1946

1924 (June)–**25.** *Stamps* of 1921 *surch with new value, and bars obliterating original value.*

63	25 c. on 15 c. orange and blue (1.2.25) ..		5	5
64	25 c. on 2 f. carmine and olive-green	..	5	5
65	25 c. on 5 f. grey and vermilion ..	..	5	5
66	"65" on 45 c. carmine and brown (1.2.25)		15	15
67	"85" on 75 c. green and claret (1.2.25)		15	15
63/67	*Set of 5*	..	40	40

5 Cattle fording River

6 Tapping Rubber-trees

7 Liana Suspension Bridge

D 1 Felling Mahogany Tree

(Des J. Kerhor. Eng G. Daussy. Typo)
1925 (1 May)–**26.** *P* 14×13½ (*horiz*) or 13½×14 (*vert*).

68	**5** 1 c. magenta and yellow-olive..	..	5	5
69	2 c. green and carmine/*greenish*		5	5
70	4 c. black and pale blue	..	5	5
71	5 c. bright violet and yellow	..	5	5
72	10 c. orange and purple/*yellow* ..		5	5
73	15 c. yellow-green and green	..	5	5
74	**6** 20 c. chestnut and olive ..		5	5
75	25 c. black and yellow-green	..	5	5
76	30 c. scarlet and pale green	..	5	5
77	35 c. black and brown	..	5	5
78	40 c. bright violet and orange	..	8	5
79	45 c. carmine and rose-red	..	5	5
80	50 c. carmine and yellow-green	..	5	5
81	60 c. black and mauve	..	5	5
82	65 c. brown and deep blue	..	5	5
83	75 c. bright and deep blue	..	5	5
84	85 c. light blue and rose-red	..	5	5
85	**7** 1 f. brown and deep blue	..	5	5
86	2 f. red-orange and olive-green	..	20	5
	a. Error. Black and brown/*azure*	.. £175		
	b. Value omitted	.. 10·00		
	c. Value double	.. 6·00		
87	5 f. black and brown/*azure*	..	25	12
68/87	*Set of 20*	..	1·10	85

(Des J. Kerhor. Eng G. Daussy. Typo)

1925 (20 May)–**27.** *POSTAGE DUE.* P 14×13½.

D 88	**D 1** 2 c. black and light blue	..		5	5
D 89	4 c. purple and yellow-olive	..		5	5
D 90	5 c. black and lilac	..		5	5
D 91	10 c. black and red ..			5	5
D 92	15 c. black and drab	..		5	5
D 93	20 c. black and olive-green	..		5	5
D 94	25 c. black and yellow	..		5	5
D 95	30 c. orange and blue	..		12	12
D 96	50 c. black and brown	..		12	12
D 97	60 c. carmine and green	..		15	15
D 98	1 f. green and red/*greenish*	..		15	15
D 99	2 f. mauve and red (10.10.27)	..		15	15
D100	3 f. brt blue & red-brn (10.10.27) ..			15	15
D88/100	*Set of 13*	..		1·00	1·00

1927–38. *New values and colours.* P 14×13½ or 13½×14.

88	**5** 15 c. red and black (14.11.27) ..			10	10
89	**6** 20 c. green (1.3.26)	..		5	5
90	20 c. brown and lake (28.2.27)	..		5	5
91	30 c. green and deep olive (14.11.27)			5	5
91a	35 c. yellow-green & green (1938)	..		10	5
92	45 c. chestnut and mauve (14.11.27)	..		15	15
93	55 c. carmine and bright blue (1938)	..		8	8
	a. Value omitted	..		7·50	
94	60 c. carmine (1.3.26)..	..		5	5
95	75 c. magenta and chestnut (5.9.27) ..			5	5
95a	80 c. brown and carmine (1938)	..		8	8
96	90 c. rose-red and carmine (28.2.27)	..		12	10
97	**7** 1 f. blue (1.3.26)	..		5	5
98	1 f. magenta and carmine (14.11.27) ..			5	5
99	1 f. brown and green (25.3.29)	..		12	8
100	1 f. 10, brown and carmine (25.9.28)	..		40	35
100a	1 f. 25, blue and brown (25.9.33)	..		25	20
101	1 f. 50, blue (28.2.27)	..		5	5
101a	1 f. 75, orange and brown (25.9.33)	..		8	5
101b	1 f. 75, blue and deep blue (1938)	..		8	5
102	3 f. magenta and brown (19.12.27)	..		65	15
103	10 f. mauve and orange (20.12.26)	..		65	40
	a. Value omitted			15·00	
104	20 f. green and carmine (20.12.26)	..		1·75	35
88/104	*Set of 22*			4·50	2·40

=

1ᶠ25

(8)

1926 (14 June). *Surch with T* **8.**

105	**7** 1 f. 25 on 1 f. blue (R.) ..	.. ..	5	5

9 French Colonial Races

10 Native Women

11 "France the Civiliser"

12 French Colonial Commerce

(Des J. de la Nézière, Mme Cayon-Rouan, A. Parent and G. François resp. Recess)

1931 (13 Apr). *International Colonial Exhibition, Paris. Inscr "CAMEROUN" in black. P 12½.*

106	**9**	40 c. green	..	..	25	25
		a. "CAMEROUN" omitted	..	..	1·50	
107	**10**	50 c. mauve	..	..	45	45
		a. "CAMEROUN" omitted	..	12·00	
108	**11**	90 c. vermilion	..	..	40	40
		a. "CAMEROUN" omitted	..	1·50	
109	**12**	1 f. 50, blue	..	..	45	45
		a. "CAMEROUN" omitted	..	1·50	
106/109		Set of 4	..	..	1·40	1·40

13 Commerce ·

14 Sailing Ships

15 Berber, Negress and Annamite

16 Agriculture

17 France extends Torch of Civilisation

18 Diane de Poitiers

(Des Jean Goujon (**13**), Robichon (**14**), Mme Cayon-Rouan (**15**), Decaris (**16, 18**) and Barlangue (**17**). Eng Cottet (**13**), Feltesse (**14**), Munier (**15**), Decaris (**16, 18**) and Delzers (**17**). Recess)

1937 (15 Apr). *International Exhibition, Paris. Inscr "CAMEROUN". P 13.*

110	**13**	20 c. bright violet	..	..	10	5
111	**14**	30 c. green	..	..	10	5
112	**15**	40 c. carmine	..	..	10	· 5
113	**16**	50 c. brown	..	..	5	5
114	**17**	90 c. scarlet	..	..	10	10
115	**18**	1 f. 50, blue	..	..	10	10
110/115		Set of 6	..	..	50	35
MS115a		120×100 mm. 3 f. orange-red and black (T **16**). Imperf	..	50	55

19 Pierre and Marie Curie

20

(Des J. de la Nézière. Eng J. Piel. Recess)

1938 (24 Oct). *International Anti-Cancer Fund. P 13.*

116	**19**	1 f. 75+50 c. ultramarine	..	..	90	80

(Des and eng Decaris. Recess Institut de Gravure, Paris)

1939 (10 May). *New York World's Fair. P 12½.*

117	**20**	1 f. 25, lake	..	..	5	5
118		2 f. 25, ultramarine	..	..	5	5

21 Lamido Woman

22 Banyo Waterfall

23 Elephants

24 African Boatman

D **2** African Idols

(Eng Degorce (**21, 24**), H. Cheffer (**22**) and Decaris (**23**). Recess)

1939 (12 June)–**40**. *P 13.*

119	**21**	2 c. black-brown	..	..	5	5
120		3 c. magenta	..	..	5	5
121		4 c. ultramarine	..	..	5	5
122		5 c. brown-lake	..	..	5	5
123		10 c. green	..	..	5	5
124		15 c. scarlet	..	..	5	5
125		20 c. purple	..	..	5	5
126	**22**	25 c. black-brown	..	..	5	5
127		30 c. red-orange	..	..	5	5
128		40 c. ultramarine	..	..	5	5
129		45 c. myrtle-green	..	..	12	12
130		50 c. brown-lake	..	..	5	5
131		60 c. turquoise-blue	..	..	5	5
132		70 c. purple	..	..	20	20
133	**23**	80 c. turquoise-blue	..	..	15	15
134		90 c. turquoise-blue	..	..	5	5
135		1 f. carmine	..	..	10	10
135a		1 f. chocolate (15.4.40)	..	..	5	5
136		1 f. 25, carmine	..	..	20	20
137		1 f. 40, red-orange	..	..	10	10
138		1 f. 50, chocolate	..	..	5	5
139		1 f. 60, black-brown	..	..	20	20
140		1 f. 75, blue	..	..	5	5
141		2 f. green	..	..	5	5
142		2 f. 25, blue	..	..	5	5
143		2 f. 50, bright purple	..	..	10	10
144		3 f. deep violet	..	..	5	5
145	**24**	5 f. black-brown	..	..	5	5
146		10 f. bright purple	..	..	10	10
147		20 f. green	..	..	15	15
119/147		Set of 30	..	..	2·00	2·00

(Eng Decaris. Recess)

1939 (12 June). *POSTAGE DUE.* P 14 × 13.

D148	**D 2**	5 c. bright purple ..	5	5
D149		10 c. turquoise-blue	5	5
D150		15 c. carmine	5	5
D151		20 c. black-brown	5	5
D152		30 c. ultramarine	5	5
D153		50 c. green ..	5	5
D154		60 c. deep purple	5	5
D155		1 f. deep violet	5	5
D156		2 f. red-orange	12	12
D157		3 f. blue	12	12
D148/157		Set of 10 ..	50	50

25 Storming the Bastille

(Des and eng Ouvré. Design photo, remainder typo Vaugirard, Paris)

1939 (5 July). *150th Anniv of French Revolution. Name and value in black.* P 13½ × 13.

148	**25**	45 c. + 25 c. green ..	65	65
149		70 c. + 30 c. brown	65	65
150		90 c. + 35 c. red-orange	65	65
151		1 f. 25 + 1 f. carmine..	65	65
152		2 f. 25 + 2 f. blue	65	65
148/152		Set of 5 ..	3·00	3·00

CAMEROUN FRANCAIS

CAMEROUN FRANCAIS

27-8-40	27.8.40
(26)	(27)

1940 (2–26 Oct). *Adherence to General de Gaulle. Variously optd as T* **26.**

153	**21**	2 c. black-brown (R.)	5	5
		a. Black opt	£130	
154		3 c. magenta..	5	5
155		4 c. ultramarine (R.) ..	5	5
		a. Black opt	£130	
156		5 c. brown-lake	15	15
157		10 c. green (R.)	5	5
158		15 c. scarlet	5	5
159		20 c. purple (R.)	50	35
160	**22**	25 c. black-brown	5	5
		a. Opt inverted	16·00	
161		30 c. red-orange	60	50
162		40 c. ultramarine	15	15
163		45 c. myrtle-green	8	8
164	**6**	50 c. carmine and yellow-green	5	5
		a. Opt inverted	20·00	
165	**22**	60 c. turquoise-blue	25	25
166		70 c. purple	8	8
167	**23**	80 c. turquoise-blue (R.)	35	35
168		90 c. turquoise-blue (R.)	8	5
169	**20**	1 f. 25, lake ..	15	15
170	**23**	1 f. 25, carmine	5	5
171		1 f. 40, red-orange	20	20
172		1 f. 50, chocolate	8	8
173		1 f. 60, black-brown (R.)	10	10
174		1 f. 75, blue (R.)	12	12
		a. Opt inverted	14·00	
175	**20**	2 f. 25, ultramarine	15	15
176	**23**	2 f. 25, blue (R.)	5	5
177		2 f. 50, bright purple	5	5
178	**7**	5 f. black and brown/*azure* ..	65	65
179	**24**	5 f. black-brown	1·40	1·25
180	**7**	10 f. mauve and orange	1·50	1·25
181	**24**	10 f. bright purple	3·50	2·75
182	**7**	20 f. green and carmine	2·75	2·50
183	**24**	20 f. green	16·00	15·00
153/183		Set of 31 ..	26·00	24·00

The overprint settings consisted of mixed type and many varieties exist, including mixed numerals, closed "4", wrong fount "C" in "CAMEROUN", broken "B" for "R", etc.

OEUVRES DE GUERRE

+ 3 frs.	+ 5 Frs.
	SPITFIRE
(28)	(29)

1940 (21 Oct). *War Relief Fund. Optd as T* **28.**

184	**7**	1 f. 25 + 2 f. blue and brown ..	75	75
185		1 f. 75 + 3 f. orange and brown	75	75
186		2 f. + 5 f. red-orange and olive-green ..	75	75

Exist without "S" in "OEUVRES". (*Price each £2 un or us.*)

1940 (28 Nov). *Spitfire Fund. Surch with T* **29.**

187	**22**	25 c. + 5 f. black-brown	8·00	5·00
188		45 c. + 5 f. myrtle-green	8·00	5·00
189		60 c. + 5 f. turquoise-blue	8·00	5·00
190		70 c. + 5 f. purple ..	8·00	5·00
187/190		Set of 4 ..	30·00	18·00

SPITFIRE 10 fr. Général de GAULLE

(29a)

1941 (25 Feb). *Spitfire Fund. Surch with T* **29a.**

190a	**20**	1 f. 25 + 10 f. lake ..	6·00	5·00
190b		2 f. 25 + 10 f. ultramarine	6·00	5·00

Nos. 190a/b exist with "a" of "Géneral" inverted and also with "e" of "de" inverted (*Price each £30 un or us*).

29b 'Plane over Map

29c Seaplane

29d 'Plane over Harbour

+ 10 Frs.
AMBULANCE
LAQUINTINIE
(30)

(T **29**b/c des J. Douy. T **29**d des Ouvré. Photo Vaugirard)

1941 (17 Mar). *AIR. Vichy Govt issue.* P 13½.

190c	**29b**	25 c. brown-red	5	5
190d		50 c. green	5	5
190e		1 f. purple	5	5
190f	**29c**	2 f. olive-green	5	5
190g		3 f. brown	5	5
190h		4 f. deep blue	5	5
190i		6 f. myrtle-green..	5	5
190j		7 f. purple	5	5
190k		12 f. yellow-orange	40	40
190l		20 f. rose-red	10	10
190m	**29d**	50 f. ultramarine-blue	15	15
190c/190m		Set of 11 ..	95	95

1941 (3 June). *Laquintinie Hospital Fund. Surch with T* **30.**

191	**20**	1 f. 25 + 10 f. lake (B.) ..	1·00	90
192		2 f. 25 + 10 f. ultramarine	1·00	90

31 Cross of Lorraine, Sword and Shield

32 Modern Aeroplane

35 "Victory"

(Des and eng Decaris. Recess Institut de Gravure)

1946 (8 May). *AIR. Victory. P* 12½.
225 **35** 8 f. brown-purple   5   5

(Des Edmund Dulac. Photo Harrison & Sons)

1942. *Free French Issue.* (a) *POSTAGE. P* 14×14½.
193	**31**	5 c. brown	..	..	5	5
194		10 c. blue	..	..	5	5
195		25 c. emerald-green	..	..	5	5
196		30 c. red-orange	..	..	5	5
197		40 c. slate-green	..	..	5	5
198		80 c. maroon	..	..	5	5
199		1 f. magenta	..	..	5	5
200		1 f. 50, scarlet	..	..	5	5
201		2 f. grey-black	..	..	5	
		a. Error. Deep green	..	..	25·00	
202		2 f. 50, ultramarine	..	..	5	5
203		4 f. violet	..	..	5	5
204		5 f. yellow-bistre	..	..	8	8
		a. Error. Carmine	..	..	25·00	
205		10 f. red-brown	..	..	5	5
206		20 f. blue-green	..	..	15	8
		a. Error. Blue	..	..	20·00	
		b. Error. Carmine	..	..	20·00	
		c. Error. Orange	..	..	20·00	

(b) *AIR. P* 14½×14.
207	**32**	1 f. red-orange	..	..	5	5
208		1 f. 50, scarlet	..	..	5	5
209		5 f. maroon	..	..	5	5
210		10 f. black	..	..	5	5
211		25 f. ultramarine	..	..	8	8
212		50 f. green	..	..	10	10
213		100 f. claret	..	..	15	12
193/213		*Set of 21*	..	..	1·25	1·10

36 Chad

(Des and eng Decaris. Recess Institut de Gravure)

1946 (6 June). *AIR. From Chad to the Rhine. As T* **36** (*inscr* "DU TCHAD AU RHIN"). *P* 12½.
226		5 f. greenish blue (T **36**)	..	..	5	5
227		10 f. purple (Koufra)	..	..	8	8
228		15 f. rose-red (Mareth)	..	..	8	8
229		20 f. ultramarine (Normandy)	..	..	10	10
230		25 f. brown-red (Paris)	..	..	12	12
231		50 f. blackish olive (Strasbourg)	..	..	15	15
226/231		*Set of 6*	..	..	50	50

33

34 Félix Eboué

37 Zebu and Herdsman   **38** Tikar Women
39 Africans carrying Bananas (23×37 *mm*)
40 Bowman (23×37 *mm*)

(Des Edmund Dulac. Photo Harrison)

1944 (Dec). *Mutual Aid and Red Cross Funds. P* 14½×14.
214 **33** 5 f. + 20 f. rose   15   15

1945. *Surch with new values and bars.*
215	**31**	50 c. on 5 c. brown (R.)	..	..	5	5
216		60 c. on 5 c. brown (R.)	..	..	5	5
		a. Surch inverted	..	..	8·00	
217		70 c. on 5 c. brown (R.)	..	..	5	5
218		1 f. 20 on 5 c. brown (R.)	..	..	5	5
219		2 f. 40 on 25 c. emerald-green	..	..	5	5
220		3 f. on 25 c. emerald-green	..	..	5	5
221		4 f. 50 on 25 c. emerald-green	..	..	8	8
222		15 f. on 2 f. 50, ultramarine (R.)	..	..	10	10
215/222		*Set of 8*	..	..	45	45

1945. *Recess. P* 13.
223	**34**	2 f. black	..	..	5	5
224		25 f. blue-green	..	..	5	8

41 Lamido Horsemen

45 Aeroplane, African and Mask

42 Native Head (23×37 *mm*)

43 Birds in Flight over Mountain Ranges

44 African Horsemen and Aeroplane (49×27 *mm*)
45a Aeroplane over Piton d'Humsiki (27×48 *mm*)

(Des and eng G. Barlangue (**37, 38, 43**), Decaris (**39/41, 44**), G. Bétemps (**42, 45**), P. Gandon (**45a**). Recess Institut de Gravure, Paris)

1946–53. *P* 12½. (*a*) POSTAGE.

232	37	10 c. blue-green	..		5	5
233		30 c. brown-orange	..	..	5	5
234		40 c. ultramarine	..		5	5
235	38	50 c. olive-brown	..	..	5	5
236		60 c. purple	..	..	5	5
237		80 c. chestnut	..	..	5	5
238	39	1 f. red-orange	..	..	5	5
239		1 f. 20, bright green	..	..	5	5
240		1 f. 50, lake	..	..	12	12
241	40	2 f. black	..	..	5	5
242		3 f. carmine	..	..	5	5
243		3 f. 60, brown-red	..	..	5	5
244		4 f. blue	..	..	5	5
245	41	5 f. lake	..	..	5	5
246		6 f. ultramarine	..	..	5	5
247		10 f. greenish slate	..	..	5	5
248	42	15 f. greenish blue	..	..	15	5
249		20 f. dull green	..	..	15	5
250		25 f. black	..	..	20	5

(*b*) AIR

251	43	50 f. greenish grey	..	..	25	15
252	44	100 f. red-brown	..	..	45	5
253	45	200 f. blackish olive	..	..	90	20
253a	45a	500 f. indigo, deep ultramarine and deep lilac (16.2.53)	..	..	2·25	45
232/253a		*Set of 23*	..	..	4·50	1·60

C. FRENCH TRUST TERRITORY

13 December 1946–31 December 1959

D 3   **46** Africans, Globe and Aeroplane

(Recess Institut de Gravure)

1947. *POSTAGE DUE. P* 13.

D254	D 3	10 c. scarlet	..	..	5	5
D255		30 c. orange	..	..	5	5
D256		50 c. black	..	..	5	5
D257		1 f. carmine	..	..	5	5
D258		2 f. emerald-green	..	..	5	5
D259		3 f. magenta	..	..	5	5
D260		4 f. ultramarine	..	..	5	5
D261		5 f. red-brown	..	..	5	5
D262		10 f. greenish blue	..	..	5	5
D263		20 f. sepia	..	..	8	8
D254/263		*Set of 10*	..	..	40	40

(Des and eng R. Serres. Recess)

1949 (4 July). *AIR. 75th Anniv of U.P.U. As T* **46** *but inscr* "CAMEROUN". *P* 13.

254	46	25 f. red, purple, green and blue	..	60	60

47 Doctor and Patient   **48**

(Des and eng R. Serres. Recess)

1950 (15 May). *Colonial Welfare Fund. P* 13.

255	47	10 f. + 2 f. green and blue-green	..	25	25

(Des R. Serres. Recess)

1952 (1 Dec). *Centenary of Médaille Militaire. Name and value typo, in black. P* 13.

256	48	15 f. carmine-lake, yellow and green	40	30

49 Edéa Barrage

(Des and eng Hertenberger. Recess)

1953 (18 Nov). *AIR. Opening of Edéa Barrage. P* 13.

257	49	15 f. blue, brown-lake & blk-brown	..	30	12

50 "D-Day"

(Des and eng R. Serres. Recess)

1954 (6 June). *AIR. Tenth Anniv of Liberation. P* 13.

258	50	15 f. emerald and deep turquoise	..	40	40

51 Dr. Jamot and Students

(Des and eng Pheulpin. Recess)

1954 (29 Nov). *AIR. 75th Birthday of Dr. Jamot (physician). P* 13.

259	51	15 f. blackish brown, ind & dp bl-grn	..	50	50

52 Porters   **53** Transporting Logs
Carrying Bananas

(Des Mazelin. Eng Serres (40 f.). Des and eng Cami (8 f., 15 f.), Pheulpin (50 f.), Hertenberger (100 f.), Cheffer (200 f.). Recess)

1954–55. *Various designs.* P 13. (a) POSTAGE. As T **52** (29.11.54).

260	8 f. bluish violet, orange & bright pur	5	5
261	15 f. black-brown, yellow and red ..	10	5
262	40 f. orange-brown, magenta and blackish brown	15	5

(b) AIR. As T **53** *(24.1.55)*

263	50 f. olive-green, brown & blackish brn	20	5
264	100 f. blackish brown, brown & turq ..	60	8
265	200 f. chocolate, dp blue & slate-green ..	90	12
260/265	Set of 6	1·75	35

Designs: *Vert*—8 f., as T **52**. 40 f. Woman gathering coffee. *Horiz*—100 f. Aeroplane over giraffes; 200 f. Douala Port.

54 Native Cattle   **55** Coffee

(Des and eng Cottet. Recess)

1956 (4 June). *Economic and Social Development Fund.* T **54** *and similar horiz designs inscr* "F.I.D.E.S." P 13.

266	5 f. orange-brown and blackish brown	5	5
267	15 f. turquoise-blue, violet-grey & blk ..	8	5
268	20 f. turquoise-blue and deep blue ..	8	5
269	25 f. deep bright blue	10	5
266/269	Set of 4	25	15

Designs:—15 f. R. Wouri bridge; 20 f. Technical education; 25 f. Mobile medical unit.

(Des and eng R. Serres. Recess)

1956 (22 Oct). P 13.

270	**55** 15 f. vermilion and carmine-red ..	5	5

56 Woman, Child and Flag   **57** "Human Rights"

(Des and eng Cottet. Recess)

1958 (10 May). *Anniv of First Cameroun Government.* P 13.

271	**56** 20 f. brown, green, red, yell & ultram	12	5

(Des and eng Cami. Recess)

1958 (10 Dec). *Tenth Anniv of Declaration of Human Rights.* P 13.

272	**57** 20 f. chocolate and brown-red ..	15	12

58 *Randia malleifera*   **59** Loading Bananas on Ship

(Des M. Rolland. Photo)

1959 (5 Jan). *Tropical Flora.* P 12½.

273	**58** 20 f. multicoloured	12	5

(Des and eng Durrens. Recess)

1959 (23 Mar). T **59** *and a similar design.* P 13.

274	20 f. orange, brown, bl & dp bluish-grn	12	5
275	25 f. grey-grn, red-brown and pur-brown	15	5

Design: *Vert*—25 f. Bunch of bananas, and Africans on jungle path.

D. CAMEROUN REPUBLIC

A National Assembly was elected in 1959 and the French trust territory of Cameroun became an independent republic on 1 January 1960.

60 Prime Minister A. Ahidjo   **61** "Uprooted Tree"

(Des and eng Decaris (20 f.), Pheulpin (25 f.). Recess)

1960 (1 Jan). *Proclamation of Independence.* T **60** *and similar vert design inscr* "1ER JANVIER 1960". P 12½ × 13.

276	20 f. carmine-red, yellow and blue-green	12	5
277	25 f. blue-green, pale bistre and black ..	15	5

Design:—20 f. Cameroun flag and map.

(Des and eng Decaris. Recess)

1960 (7 Apr). *World Refugee Year.* P 13.

278	**61** 30 f. yellow-green, ultram & red-brn ..	20	20

62 C.C.T.A. Emblem   **63** Map and Flag

(Des and eng Cami. Recess)

1960 (16 May). *Tenth Anniv of African Technical Co-operation Commission (C.C.T.A.).* P 13.

279	**62** 50 f. black and maroon	25	20

(Des and eng Mazelin. Recess)

1961 (25 Mar). *Red Cross Fund. Flag green, red and yellow; cross red; background colours below.* P 13.

280	**63** 20 f. +5 f. bluish green and red ..	20	15
281	25 f. +10 f. red, green, yellow & blk ..	20	20
282	30 f. +15 f. carmine-red & bluish grn	30	30

64 U.N. Headquarters, Emblem and Cameroun Flag

(Des and eng Pheulpin. Recess)

1961 (20 May). *Admission to U.N. Flag green, red and yellow.* P 13.

283	**64** 15 f. chocolate, blue and green ..	15	10
284	25 f. green and blue	15	15
285	85 f. brown-purple, blue and red ..	45	45

E. CAMEROUN FEDERAL REPUBLIC

On 11 February 1961 a plebiscite was held in the British trust territory of the Cameroons, the strip of the former German protectorate which had been administered with Nigeria. The Northern Cameroons voted for union with Nigeria and the Southern Cameroons voted for union with Cameroun. For overprinted Nigerian stamps issued during the plebiscite period, see under Southern Cameroons in the *British Commonwealth Catalogue.*

The Southern Cameroons, which became West Cameroon, united with the Cameroun Republic, which became East Cameroon, on 1 October 1961 to form the Cameroun Federal Republic.

REPUBLIQUE FEDERALE
(65)

1961 (1 Oct). *Various issues optd "REPUBLIQUE FEDERALE" and surch in sterling currency as T* **65.** (a) *POSTAGE.*

286	**39**	½ d. on 1 f. (No. 238) red-orge (R.)	8	5
287	**40**	1 d. on 2 f. (No. 241) black (R.)	8	5
288	**54**	1½ d. on 5 f. (No. 266) orange-brown and black-brown (R.)	10	5
289	**41**	2 d. on 10 f. (No. 247) greenish slate (R.)	10	5
290	–	3 d. on 15 f. (No. 267) turquoise-blue, violet-green & black (R.)	12	8
291	**55**	4 d. on 15 f. (No. 270) vermilion & carmine-red	20	12
292	**59**	6 d. on 20 f. (No. 274) orange, brn, bl & dp bluish grn (R.)	20	12
293	**60**	1 s. on 25 f. (No. 277) blue-green, pale bistre and black (R.)	35	35
294	**61**	2 s. 6d. on 30 f. (No. 278) yellow-green, ultram & red-brn (R.)	65	65
		a. Small "2/6" surch	2·25	2·25
		(b) *AIR. Inscr "POSTE AERIENNE"*		
295	–	5 s. on 100 f. (No. 264) black-brown, brown & turquoise (R.)	1·40	1·40
		a. Small "5/-" surch	4·00	4·00
296	–	10 s. on 200 f. (No. 265) chocolate, deep blue & slate-green (R.)	2·50	2·50
		a. Small "10/-" surch	15·00	15·00
297	**45**a	£1 on 500 f. (No. 253a) indigo, dp ultramarine & dp lilac (R.)	5·00	5·00
		a. Wide "REPUBLIQUE FEDERALE" (22½ mm)	8·00	8·00
286/297		*Set of 12*	9·50	9·00

Nos. 286/297 were sold in sterling currency and used in the former Southern Cameroons pending the introduction of the Cameroun franc.

66 Pres. Ahidjo and Prime Minister Foncha

6 d
(67)

(Des A. Decaris. Recess)

1962 (1 Jan). *Reunification. P* 13.

298	**66**	20 f. choclate and violet		
299		25 f. chocolate & deep bronze-green		
300		60 f. bluish green and carmine		
298/300		*Set of 3*	10·00	8·00

Surch in sterling currency as T **67**

301	**66**	3 d. on 20 f. chocolate and violet		
302		6 d. on 25 f. choc & dp bronze-green		
303		2 s. 6d. on 50 f. deep bluish green and carmine		
301/303		*Set of 3*	60·00	55·00

68 Lions International Badge, Doctor and Leper

(Des and eng Decaris. Recess)

1962 (28 Jan). *World Leprosy Day. Lions International Relief Fund. P* 13.

304	**68**	20 f. + 5 f. lake, maroon and sepia	12	12
305		25 f. + 10 f. lake, plum and blue	15	15
306		50 f. + 15 f. lake, maroon & blue-grn	35	35

69 Airliners and Africans

70 Campaign Emblem

(Des and eng Decaris. Recess)

1962 (17 Feb). *AIR. Foundation of "Air Afrique" Airline. P* 13.

307	**69**	25 f. lake, reddish violet and green	15	15

(Eng Bétemps. Recess Chaix)

1962 (7 Apr). *Malaria Eradication. P* 12½ × 12.

308	**70**	25 f. + 5 f. reddish purple	15	12

71 Giraffes and Waza Camp

72 Union Flag

(Des and eng Durrens (1, 1.50, 2, 3, 4, 5, 10, 25, 100 and 500 f.). Des François; eng Hertenberger (200 f.). Des and eng Combet (others). Recess Chaix)

1962 (15 June–10 Aug). *Various designs as T* **71.** *P* 13. (a) *POSTAGE.*

309		50 c. sepia, blue and blue-green	5	5
310		1 f. black, turquoise-green & orange	5	5
311		1 f. 50, brn, sage-grn & ol-blk (10.8)	5	5
312		2 f. blk, turq-blue & turq-grn (10.8)	5	5
313		3 f. brown, orange and dull pur (10.8)	5	5
314		4 f. sepia, bright green & turq-green	5	5
315		5 f. purple-blk, grn & cinnamon (10.8)	5	5
316		6 f. sepia, blue and lemon	5	5
317		8 f. deep blue, brown-red & grn (10.8)	5	5
318		10 f. black, red-orange and blue (10.8)	5	5
319		15 f. brown, blue & turquoise-blue	8	5
320		20 f. chocolate and grey	8	5
321		25 f. red-brown, yellow & dp grn (10.8)	10	5
322		30 f. black, bright bl & brn-orge (10.8)	12	5
323		40 f. lake and apple-green	15	8
		(b) *AIR. Inscr "POSTE AERIENNE"*		
324		50 f. red-brown, grey-green & dp blue	20	10
325		100 f. red, brown, olive and blue	40	15
326		200 f. black, yellow-brown & blue-grn	85	30
327		500 f. buff, brown-purple & pale blue	2·00	80
309/327		*Set of 19*	4·00	2·00

Designs: *Vert*—20 f., 40 f. T **71**. *Horiz (as* T **71**)—50 c., 6 f., 15 f. Moustac monkey; 1 f., 4 f. Elephant and Ntem Falls; 1 f. 50, 3 f. Buffon's cob, Dschang; 2 f., 5 f. Hippopotamus, Hippo Camp; 8 f., 30 f. Manatee, Lake Ossa; 10 f., 25 f. Native Ox, Batouri Region. (48×27 *mm*)—50 f. Cocotiers Hotel, Douala; 100 f. *Cymothoe sangaris* (butterfly); 200 f. Ostriches; 500 f. Kapsikis, Mokolo (landscape).

(Des Decaris. Photo Delrieu)

1962 (8 Sept). *First Anniv of Union of African and Malagasy States. P* 12½×12.
328 **72** 30 f. blue-green, red, gold and choc ..   15   12

D **4** *Hibiscus rosa sinensis*

77 VHF Station, Mt. Bankolo, Yaoundé

(Des and eng Bétemps. Recess Chaix)

1963 (10 Apr). *POSTAGE DUE. Flower designs as Type* D **4**. *Multicoloured. P* 11.

D342	50 c. Type D **4** ..	..	..	5	5
D343	50 c. *Erythrine* ..		..	5	5
D344	1 f. *Plumeria lutea*	..	..	5	5
D345	1 f. *Ipomœa sp*	..	..	5	5
D346	1 f. 50, *Grinum sp*	..	..	5	5
D347	1 f. 50, *Hoodia gordonii*	..	..	5	5
D348	2 f. *Ochna*	..	..	5	5
D349	2 f. *Gloriosa* ..	..	..	5	5
D350	5 f. *Costus spectabilis*	..	..	5	5
D351	5 f. *Bougainvillea spectabilis*		..	5	5
D352	10 f. *Delonix regia*	..	..	5	5
D353	10 f. *Haemanthus*	..	..	5	5
D354	20 f. *Titanopsis*	..	..	8	8
D355	20 f. *Ophthalmophyllum*	..	..	8	8
D356	40 f. *Zingiberacee*	..	..	12	12
D357	40 f. *Amorphophalus*	..	..	12	15
D342/357	*Set of 16* ..	..	..	80	80

The two designs in each value are arranged *se-tenant* in *tête-bêche* pairs throughout the sheet.

(Des Combet. Photo Delrieu)

1963 (11 May). *Inauguration of Douala-Yaoundé VHF Radio Service.* T **77** *and similar vert designs. Multicoloured. P* 12×13 (100 f.) *or* 12×12½ *(others).* (a) *POSTAGE.*
342   15 f. Type **77**   10   5
343   20 f. Aerials and control panel   12   10

        (b) *AIR. Inscr* "POSTE AERIENNE"
344   100 f. Edea relay station (26×44 *mm*) ..   55   40

73 Map and View

74 "The School Under the Tree"

(Des and eng Decaris. Recess)

1962 (1 Oct). *First Anniv of Reunification.* T **73** *and similar horiz designs. P* 13.
329   9 f. bistre, violet and chocolate   ..   5   5
330   18 f. brown-red, green and blue   ..   12   8
331   20 f. bistre, indigo and bright purple   12   8
332   25 f. orange, sepia and blue   ..   12   8
333   50 f. blue, sepia and scarlet   ..   25   20
329/333   *Set of 5*   60   45
Designs:—18 f. As T **73**; 20 f., 25 f. Sunrise over Cameroun; 50 f. Commemorative scroll.

(Des P. Munier. Photo Delrieu)

1962 (5 Nov). *Literacy and Popular Education Campaign. P* 12×12½.
334 **74** 20 f. red, yellow and emerald   ..   12   5

M **1** Arms and Crossed Swords

78 "Centre régional..."

(Des and eng Aufschneider. Typo)

1963 (1 July). *MILITARY FRANK. P* 13½×14.
M1 M **1** (–) Lake   25   25

(Photo Delrieu)

1964 (10 Aug). *Inauguration of U.N.E.S.C.O. Regional Schoolbooks Production Centre, Yaoundé. P* 12½.
345 **78** 20 f. red, black and green   ..   10   8
346   25 f. red, black and yellow-orange   12   8
347   100 f. red, black and gold   ..   35   30

75 Globe and "Telstar"

76 Globe and Emblem

(Des and eng Durrens. Recess)

1963 (9 Feb). *First Trans-Atlantic Television Satellite Link. P* 13. (a) *POSTAGE.*
335 **75** 1 f. blue, olive and violet   ..   5   5
336   2 f. blue, lake and blue-green   ..   5   5
337   3 f. slate-green, olive & brown-pur   5   5
338   25 f. blue-green, brown-pur & blue ..   20   15

        (b) *AIR. Inscr* "POSTE AERIENNE" (size 48×27 *mm*)
339 **75** 100 f. deep green, red-brn & slate-grn   60   40
335/339   *Set of 5*   85   60

(Des and eng Durrens. Recess)

1963 (21 Mar). *Freedom from Hunger. P* 13.
340 **76** 18 f. +5 f. ultramarine, red-brn & grn   12   10
341   25 f. +5 f. blue-green and red-brown   15   12

HAVE YOU READ THE NOTES AT THE BEGINNING OF THIS CATALOGUE?

These often provide answers to the enquiries we receive.

79 "Posts and Telecommunications"

80 Pres. Ahidjo

(Des P. Béquet. Photo Delrieu)

1963 (8 Sept). *AIR. African and Malagasy Posts and Telecommunications Union.* P 12½.
348 **79** 85 f. red, buff, light blue & ultram .. 45 25

(Des Ringard. Photo Delrieu)

1963 (1 Oct). *Second Anniv of Reunification.* T **80** *and similar vert design.* Multicoloured. P 12×12½.
349 9 f. Type **80** 5 5
350 18 f. Map and flag 10 5
351 20 f. Type **80** 12 12

81 Airline Emblem

(Des R. Baudry. Photo Delrieu)

1963 (19 Nov). *AIR. First Anniv of "Air Afrique" and Inauguration of "DC-8" Service.* P 13×12.
352 **81** 50 f. black, green, light grey and pink 25 20

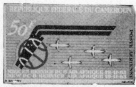

82 Globe and Scales of Justice

83 Lion

(Photo Delrieu)

1963 (10 Dec). *15th Anniv of Declaration of Human Rights.* P 12½×12.
353 **82** 9 f. light orange-brown, black & bl .. 5 5
354 18 f. red, black and yellow-green .. 10 8
355 25 f. yellow-green, black and red .. 12 8
356 75 f. blue, black and yellow .. 30 20
353/356 *Set of 4* 50 35

(Des and eng Bétemps. Recess)

1964 (20 June). *Waza National Park.* P 13.
357 **83** 10 f. bistre-brown, green & red-brown 5 5
358 25 f. bistre-brown and yellow-green .. 12 8

84 Football Stadium, Yaoundé

(Des and eng Decaris. Recess)

1964 (11 July). *Tropics Cup.* T **84** *and similar horiz designs.* P 13.
359 10 f. chestnut, turquoise-blue & yell-grn 5 5
360 18 f. green, red and violet .. 10 5
361 30 f. blue, orange-brown and black .. 15 8
Designs:—18 f. Sports Equipment; 30 f. Stadium entrance, Yaoundé.

85 Palace of Justice, Yaoundé

(Des Béquet. Photo Delrieu)

1964 (20 July). *First Anniv of European-African Economic Convention.* T **85** *and similar design.* P 13×12 (15 f.) or 12×13 (40 f.).
362 15 f. yellow-brown, grey, red & dp green 10 8
363 40 f. orange-red, green, black and slate 20 15
Design: *Vert*—40 f. Sun, Moon and various emblems of agriculture, industry and science.

86 Olympic Flame and Hurdling

87 Ntem Falls

(Des and eng Bétemps. Recess)

1964 (10 Oct). *Olympic Games, Tokyo.* T **86** *and similar designs.* P 13. (a) *POSTAGE.*
364 9 f. red, black and yellow-green .. 10 5
365 10 f. brown-olive, violet and red .. 10 5

(b) *AIR. Inscr "POSTE AERIENNE"*
366 300 f. deep bluish green, choc and red .. 1·50 1·25
MS366a 168×100 mm. Nos. 364/66 .. 1·90 1·90
Designs: *Vert*—10 f. Running. *Horiz*—300 f. Wrestling.

(Des and eng Béquet (25 f.), Decaris (250 f.), Forget (others). Recess)

1964. *Folklore and Tourism.* T **87** *and similar designs.* P 13. (a) *POSTAGE.*
367 9 f. red, blue and yellow-green (26.11) 5 5
368 18 f. blue, bistre-brown & red (26.11) .. 8 5
369 20 f. drab, green & crimson (26.10) .. 8 5
370 25 f. red, choc & yell-orange (26.11) .. 10 8

(b) *AIR. Inscr "POSTE AERIENNE"*
371 50 f. red-brown, green & blue (26.10) .. 20 15
372 250 f. sepia, green and chestnut (15.12) 1·10 60
367/372 *Set of 6* .. .. 1·40 90
Designs: As T **87**—*Vert*—9 f. Bamiléké dance costume; 18 f. Bamenda dance mask. *Horiz*—25 f. Fulani horseman. *Larger*—(43×27½ mm), 50 f. View of Kribi and Longji; 250 f. Rhinoceros.

88 "Co-operation"

89 President Kennedy

(Des and eng Decaris. Recess)

1964 (7 Nov). *French, African and Malagasy Co-operation.* P 13.
373 **88** 18 f. chocolate, yellow-green & blue .. 10 8
374 30 f. chocolate, turq-blue & chestnut 15 10

(Photo Delrieu)

1964 (8 Dec). *AIR. President Kennedy Commemoration.* P 13 × 12.
375 **89** 100 f. sepia, green & apple-green .. 45 45
MS375*a* **89** 129 × 90 mm. Block of four .. 2·00 2·00

90 Inscription recording laying of First Rail

91 Abraham Lincoln

(12 f. des and eng Gandon; recess. 20 f. des M. Biais, die eng G. Aufschneider; typo)

1965 (1 Jan). *Opening of Mbanga-Kumba Railway.* T **90** and another design. P 13 (12 f.) or 14 × 13½ (20 f.).
376 12 f. indigo, green and blue 8 5
377 20 f. lemon, yellow-green & brown-red 12 8
Design: *Horiz* (26 × 22 *mm*)—20 f. Diesel engine.

(Des P. Lambert. Photo So.Ge.Im)

1965 (20 Apr). *AIR. Death Centenary of Abraham Lincoln.* P 13.
378 **91** 100 f. multicoloured 45 35

92 Ambulance and First Aid Post

(Des P. Lambert. Eng A. Frères (25 f.), R. Fenneteaux (50 f.). Recess)

1965 (8 May). *Cameroun Red Cross.* T **92** and similar design. P 13.
379 25 f. yellow, dp bluish grn & carmine .. 12 8
380 50 f. orange-brown, red and grey .. 20 12
Design: *Vert*—50 f. Nurse and child.

93 "Syncom" and I.T.U. Emblem

94 Churchill giving "V" Sign

(Des and eng C. Haley. Recess)

1965 (17 May). *AIR. I.T.U. Centenary.* P 13.
381 **93** 70 f. black, deep blue and red .. 35 25

(Des J. Combet. Photo Delrieu)

1965 (28 May). *AIR. Churchill Commemoration.* T **94** and similar vert design. Multicoloured. P 12½.
382 12 f. Type **94** 30 25
383 18 f. Churchill, oak spray and battleship 30 25
Nos. 382/3 were issued together in sheets with a *se-tenant* stamp-size label inscr "SIR WINSTON CHURCHILL 1874–1965".

95 "Map" Savings Bank

96 Africa Cup and Players

(Des and eng J. Combet from schools design competition. Recess)

1965 (10 June). *Federal Postal Savings Bank.* T **95** and similar designs. P 13.
384 9 f. orange-yellow, rose-carm & green 5 5
385 15 f. chocolate, emerald and blue .. 8 5
386 20 f. brown, orange-brown & turq-grn .. 10 8
Designs: *Horiz* (48 × 27 *mm*)—15 f. Savings Bank building. *Vert* (27 × 48 *mm*)—20 f. "Cocoa-bean" savings bank.

(Des and eng J. Combet. Recess)

1965 (26 June). *Winning of Africa Cup by Oryx Football Club.* P 13.
387 **96** 9 f. chocolate, yellow and carmine .. 5 5
388 20 f. slate-blue, yellow and carmine .. 12 10

97 Map of Europe and Africa

98 U.P.U. Monument, Berne, and Doves

(Des Durrens. Photo Delrieu)

1965 (20 July). *"Europafrique".* T **97** and similar vert designs. P 12 × 13.
389 5 f. carmine-red, reddish lilac and black 5 5
390 40 f. multicoloured 20 15
Design:—40 f. Yaoundé Conference of 20.7.63.

(Des and eng C. Haley. Recess)

1965 (26 July). *Fifth Anniv of Admission to U.P.U.* P 13.
391 **98** 30 f. slate-purple and red 15 12

99 I.C.Y. Emblem

(Des and eng J. Combet. Recess)

1965 (11 Sept). *International Co-operation Year.* P 13. (*a*) POSTAGE.

392	**99**	10 f. carmine and blue	5	5

(*b*) AIR. Inscr "POSTE AERIENNE"

393	**99**	100 f. blue and carmine-red	45	35

100 Pres. Ahidjo and Government House   **101** Musgum Huts, Pouss

(Des H. Biais. Photo Delrieu)

1965 (1 Oct). *Re-election of President Ahidjo. T* **100** *and similar multicoloured design.* P 12×12½ (*vert*) or 12½×12 (*horiz*).

394	9 f. Pres. Ahidjo wearing hat, and Government House (*vert*)			5	5
395	18 f. Type **100**		8	5
396	20 f. As 9 f.		10	8
397	25 f. Type **100**		12	8
394/397	*Set of 4*		30	20

(Des and eng Decaris. Recess)

1965. *Folklore and Tourism. T* **101** *and similar designs.* P 13. (*a*) POSTAGE.

398	9 f. myrtle-green, red-brown and red (27.11)		5	5
399	18 f. red-brown, deep green and new blue (27.11)		8	5
400	40 f. red-brown, yell-brn & bl (27.11)		10	8
401	25 f. grey, lake and emerald (27.10)		12	8

(*b*) AIR. Inscr "POSTE AERIENNE"

402	50 f. red-brn, ind & myrtle-grn (27.10)		30	20
398/402	*Set of 5*		60	40

Designs: *Horiz*—18 f. Great Calao's dance (N. Cameroun); 25 f. National Tourist Office, Foumban. *Vert*—20 f. Sultan's palace gate, Foumban. *Larger* (48×27 *mm*)—50 f. Racing pirogue on Sanaga River, Edéa.

102 "Vostok 6"

(Des and eng C. Haley. Recess)

1966 (30 Mar). *AIR. Spacecraft. T* **102** *and similar horiz designs.* P 13.

403	50 f. deep myrtle-green and lake		25	15
404	100 f. deep ultramarine and purple		50	30
405	200 f. dp reddish violet & ultramarine		1·00	60
406	500 f. new blue and indigo		2·40	1·50
403/406	*Set of 4*		3·75	2·25

Designs:—100 f. "Gemini 4", and White in space; 200 f. "Gemini 5"; 500 f. "Gemini 6" and "Gemini 7" making rendezvous.

103 Mountains Hotel, Buea

(Des and eng A. Decaris. Recess)

1966 (6 Apr–4 June). *Cameroun Hotels. T* **103** *and similar designs.* P 13. (*a*) POSTAGE.

407	9 f. bistre, deep bluish green and crimson (6.4)		5	5
408	20 f. black, myrtle-green and blue (6.4)		10	5
409	35 f. crimson, choc & myrtle-green		15	8

(*b*) AIR. Inscr "POSTE AERIENNE"

410	18 f. blk, dp bluish grn & new bl (6.4)		10	5
411	25 f. slate-blue, red & bright blue (6.4)		12	8
412	50 f. choc, yell-orge & myrtle-green		20	15
413	60 f. chocolate, myrtle-green & new bl		30	15
414	85 f. greenish blue, crimson and myrtle-green		40	20
415	100 f. dull purple, indigo & myrtle-grn		45	30
416	150 f. yell-orge, red-brn & greenish blue		70	40
407/416	*Set of 10*		2·25	1·25

Hotels: *Horiz*—18 f. Type **103**; 20 f. Deputies, Yaoundé; 25 f. Akwa Palace, Douala; 35 f. Dschang; 50 f. Terminus, Yaoundé; 60 f. Imperial, Yaoundé; 85 f. Independence, Yaoundé; 150 f. Huts, Waza Camp. *Vert*—100 f. Hunting Lodge, Mora.

104 Foumban Bas-relief   **105** W.H.O. Headquarters, Geneva

(Des and eng P. Béquet (9 f., 25 f.). Des P. Béquet. Eng J. Derrey (18 f.), J. Piel (20 f.). Recess)

1966 (15 Apr). *World Festival of Negro Arts, Dakar. T* **104** *and similar designs.* P 13.

417	9 f. black and red		5	5
418	18 f. purple-brn, brn-orange & emer		10	5
419	20 f. chestnut, blue and reddish violet		10	5
420	25 f. chocolate and plum		12	8
417/420	*Set of 4*		35	15

Designs: *Vert*—18 f. Ekoi mask; 20 f. Bamileke statue. *Horiz*—25 f. Bamoun stool.

(Des H. Biais. Photo So.Ge.lm.)

1966 (3 May). *U.N. Agency Buildings. T* **105** *and similar horiz design.* P 12½×13.

421	**105**	50 f. lake-brown, blue and yellow	25	15
422	–	50 f. yellow, blue and olive-green	25	15

Design:—No. 422, I.T.U. Headquarters, Geneva.

106 Phaeomeria magnifica

(Des P. Lambert. Photo Delrieu)

1966 (20 May)–**67**. *Flowers. T* **106** *and similar vert designs.* Multicoloured.

(*a*) POSTAGE. Size as T **106**. P 12×12½

423	9 f. Type **106**		5	5
424	15 f. Strelitzia reginae (22.6.67)		5	5
425	18 f. Hibiscus schizopetalus X, rosa sinensis		5	5
426	20 f. Antigonon leptopus		8	5

(*b*) AIR. Size 26×45½ mm. Inscr "POSTE AERIENNE". P 12½

427	25 f. Hibiscus mutabilis ("Caprice des dames")		10	5
428	50 f. Delonix regia		20	8
429	100 f. Bougainvillea glabra		40	10
430	200 f. Thevetia peruviana (22.6.67)		70	30
431	250 f. Hippeastrum equestre (22.6.67)		90	35
423/431	*Set of 9*		2·25	1·00

For stamps as T **106**, but showing fruits, see Nos. 463/71.

107 Mobile Gendarmerie

(Des C. Haley. Eng C. Haley (20 f.), R. Cami (25 f.), G. Auf-schneider (60 f.), P. Gandon (100 f.). Recess)

1966 (21 June). *AIR. Cameroun Armed Forces.* T **107** *and similar horiz designs.* P 13.

432	20 f. ultramarine, orange-brn & plum	..	10	5
433	25 f. myrtle-green, violet & light brn		12	8
434	60 f. slate-blue, turq-grn & new blue	..	30	12
435	100 f. greenish blue, crim & pur-brn	..	50	25
432/435	Set of 4	.. .. ..	90	45

Designs:—25 f. Paratrooper; 60 f. Gunboat *Vigilant*; 100 f. Transport aircraft.

108 Wembley Stadium

(Des and eng J. Combet. Recess)

1966 (20 July). *AIR. World Cup Football Championships.* T **108** *and similar horiz design.* P 13.

436	50 f. green, indigo and red	..	25	15
437•	200 f. red, new blue and emerald (Foot-ballers)	.. .. ..	1·00	55

109 Aircraft and "Air Afrique" Emblem

(Des Dessirier. Photo Delrieu)

1966 (31 Aug). *AIR. Inauguration of "DC-8" Air Services.* P 12½.

438	**109** 25 f. light olive-grey, black & brt pur		12	8

110 U.N. General Assembly

(Des and eng C. Haley. Recess)

1966 (20 Sept). *Sixth Anniv of Admission to U.N.* T **110** *and similar design.* P 13.

439	50 f. purple, green and blue	..	20	5
440	100 f. ultramarine, lake-brown & green		45	25

Design: *Vert*—100 f. Africans encircling U.N. emblem within figure "6".

111 First Minister's Residency, Buea (side view)

(Des G. Aufschneider. Photo So.Ge.Im.)

1966 (1 Oct). *Fifth Anniv of Reunification.* T **111** *and similar horiz designs showing Ministerial Residencies. Multicoloured.* P 13.

441	9 f. Type **111**	.. .. ..	5	5
442	18 f. Prime Minister's Residency, Yaoundé (front view)		8	5
443	20 f. As 18 f. but side view	..	8	5
444	25 f. As T **111** but front view	..	12	5
441/444	Set of 4	.. .. ..	30	15

112 Learning to Write

(Des and eng J. Pheulpin. Recess)

1966 (14 Nov). *20th Anniv of U.N.E.S.C.O. and U.N.I.C.E.F.* T **112** *and similar horiz design.* P 13.

445	**112** 50 f. bistre-brn, brt pur & new bl	..	25	15
446	– 50 f. black, blue & bright purple (Cameroun children)	..	25	15

113 Buea Cathedral

(Des Hanniquet. Eng Miermont (18 f.), Mazelin (25 f.), Velly (30 f.), Forget (60 f.). Recess)

1966 (19 Dec). *AIR. Religious Buildings.* T **113** *and similar horiz designs.* P 13.

447	18 f. brown-purple, blue & myrtle-grn	..	10	5
448	25 f. reddish violet, brn & myrtle-grn	..	12	8
449	30 f. brn-lake, myrtle-grn & bright pur	..	15	10
450	60 f. myrtle-green, brn-lake & turq-grn	..	25	15
447/450	Set of 4	.. .. ..	55	35

Buildings:—25 f. Yaoundé Cathedral; 30 f. Orthodox Church, Yaoundé; 60 f. Garoua Mosque.

114 Proclamation

115 Map of Africa, Railway Lines and Signals

(Des and eng J. Combet. Recess)

1967 (1 Jan). *Seventh Anniv of Independence.* P 13.
451 **114** 20 f. red, emerald and yellow   12   8

(Des C. Haley. Photo So.Ge.lm.)

1967 (21 Feb). *Fifth African and Malagasy Railway Technicians Conference, Yaoundé.* T **115** *and similar multicoloured design.* P 13.
452 20 f. Type **115**   10   5
453 25 f. Map of Africa and diesel train   12   8

116 Lions Emblem and Jungle   **117** Aircraft and I.C.A.O. Emblem

(Des J. Gauthier. Photo So.Ge.lm.)

1967 (3 Mar). *50th Anniv of Lions International.* T **116** *and similar horiz design. Multicoloured.* P 13.
454 50 f. Type **116**   20   12
455 100 f. Lions emblem and palms..   45   25

(Des C. Haley. Photo So.Ge.lm.)

1967 (15 Mar). *International Civil Aviation Organization.* P 13×12½.
456 **117** 50 f. multicoloured ..   20   12

118 Dove and I.A.E.A. Emblem   **119** Rotary Banner and Emblem

(Des N. Hanniquet. Photo So.Ge.lm.)

1967 (15 Mar). *International Atomic Energy Agency.* P 12½×13.
457 **118** 50 f. blue and light emerald ..   20   15

(Photo Delrieu)

1967 (17 Apr). *Tenth Anniv of Cameroun Branch, Rotary International.* P 12½.
458 **119** 25 f. red, gold and deep ultramarine   12   8

120 "Pioneer A"   **121** Grapefruit

(Des and eng A. Decaris. Recess)

1967 (30 Apr). *AIR. "Conquest of the Moon".* T **120** *and similar horiz designs.* P 13.
459 25 f. myrtle-green, yell-brown & blue ..   12   8
460 50 f. deep reddish violet, dull purple and deep green ..   25   12
461 100 f. reddish purple, lake-brn & blue ..   50   25
462 250 f. pur-brn, grnsh grey & lake-brn   1·10   50
459/462 *Set of 4* .. ..   1·75   85
Designs:—50 f. "Ranger 6"; 100 f. "Luna 9"; 250 f. "Luna 10".

(Des P. Lambert. Photo Delrieu)

1967 (10 May). *Fruits.* T **121** *and similar vert designs. Multicoloured.* P 12×12½.
463 1 f. Type **121**   5   5
464 2 f. Papaw   5   5
465 3 f. Custard-apple   5   5
466 4 f. Breadfruit   5   5
467 5 f. Coconut   5   5
468 6 f. Mango   5   5
469 8 f. Avocado pear   5   5
470 10 f. Pineapple   5   5
471 30 f. Bananas   15   10
463/471 *Set of 9*   40   35

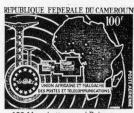

122 Sanaga Waterfalls   **123** Map, Letters and Pylons

(Des C. Haley. Photo So.Ge.lm.)

1967 (14 Aug). *International Tourist Year.* P 13×12½.
472 **122** 30 f. green, greenish blue, brown and black   12   5

(Des and eng Monvoisin. Recess)

1967 (9 Sept). *AIR. Fifth Anniv of African and Malagasy Posts and Telecommunications Union (U.A.M.P.T.).* P 13.
473 **123** 100 f. light purple, lake and deep turquoise-blue   40   20

HAVE YOU READ THE NOTES AT THE BEGINNING OF THIS CATALOGUE?

These often provide answers to the enquiries we receive.

124 Harvesting Coconuts (carved box)

125 Crossed Skis

127 Chancellor Adenauer and Cologne Cathedral

128 Arms of the Republic

(Des C. Guillame. Photo So.Ge.Im)

1967 (22 Sept). *Cameroun Art.* T **124** *and similar horiz designs.* P 12½ × 13.

474	10 f. brown, carmine and new blue	..	5	5
475	20 f. brown, myrtle-green and yellow	..	10	5
476	30 f. brown, carmine and yellow-green		12	5
477	100 f. brown, vermilion and light green		40	20
474/477	*Set of 4*	.. ..	60	30

Designs: (carved boxes)—20 f. Lion-hunting; 30 f. Harvesting coconuts (*different*); 100 f. Carved chest.

(Des and eng G. Bétemps. Recess)

1967 (11 Oct). *AIR. Winter Olympic Games, Grenoble.* P 13.

478	**125**	30 f. chocolate and bright blue	..	15	8

(Des O. Bonnevalle. Photo Delrieu)

1967 (1 Dec). *AIR. Adenauer Commemoration.* T **127** *and similar vert design. Multicoloured.* P 12½.

482	30 f. Type **127**	..	..	15	8
483	70 f. Adenauer and Chancellor's residence, Bonn	..	..	35	15

Nos. 482/3 were issued together with an intervening *se-tenant* label showing the C.E.P.T. emblem.

(Des S. Gauthier. Photo Se.Ge.Im.)

1968 (1 Jan). *8th Anniv of Independence.* P 12½ × 13.

484	**128**	30 f. multicoloured	..	..	..	12	5

126 Cameroon Exhibit

(Des and eng J. Combet. Recess)

1967 (18 Oct). *AIR. World Fair, Montreal.* T **126** *and similar vert designs.* P 13.

479	50 f. lake-brown, olive-brown & brt pur		20	10
480	100 f. chocolate, brn-pur & black-grn	∴	40	15
481	200 f. black-green, brt purple & dp brn	..	·80	30

Designs:—100 f. Totem poles; 200 f. African pavilion.
For No. 481 optd "PREMIER HOMME SUR LA LUNE 20 JUILLET 1969/FIRST MAN LANDING ON MOON 20 JULY 1969" see note below No. **MS**518.

129 Pres. Ahidjo and King Faisal of Saudi Arabia

(Des J. Combet. Photo Delrieu)

1968 (18 Feb). *AIR. President Ahidjo's Pilgrimage to Mecca and Visit to the Vatican.* T **129** *and similar horiz design. Multicoloured.* P 12½.

485	30 f. Type **129**	..	..	12	5
486	60 f. Pope Paul VI greeting President Ahidjo	..	..	..	25	12

130 "Explorer 6" (televised picture of Earth)

(Des and eng A. Decaris. Recess)

1968 (20 Apr). *AIR. Telecommunications Satellites.* T **130** *and similar horiz designs.* P 13.

487	20 f. grey, brown-red and greenish blue	12	5
488	30 f. greenish blue, indigo and carmine	15	8
489	40 f. myrtle-green, carmine and plum	..	20	12

Satellites:—30 f. "Molnya"; 40 f. "Molnya" (televised picture of Earth)

131 Douala Port

(Des and eng M. Monvoisin. Recess)

1968 (5 June). *AIR. Five-Year Development Plan.* T **131** and similar designs. P 13.

490	20 f. slate-blue, brown-red & myrtle-grn	8	5
491	30 f. slate-blue, myrtle-green & lt brown	12	5
492	30 f. bright blue, choc & myrtle-green ..	12	5
493	40 f. bistre-brn, blkish grn & turq-grn	15	8
494	60 f. purple-brown, indigo and blue ..	20	12
490/494	*Set of 5*	60	30

Designs: *Vert*—20 f. Steel forge; 30 f. (No. 491), "Transcamerounais" express train leaving tunnel; 30 f. (No. 492), Tea-harvesting; 40 f. Rubber-tapping.

132 Spiny Lobster

(Des and eng C. Haley. Recess)

1968 (28 June). *Fishes and Crustaceans.* T **132** and similar designs. P 13.

495	5 f. deep bluish green, bistre-brown and bluish violet	5	5
496	10 f. slate, olive-brown & bright blue	5	5
497	15 f. bistre-brown, orange-brn & brt pur	5	5
498	20 f. bistre-brown and blue ..	5	5
499	25 f. slate-blue, yellow-brown & brt grn	5	5
500	30 f. chocolate, dp ultram & carmine	8	5
501	40 f. slate-blue, orge-brn & red-orge	10	5
502	50 f. cerise, slate and emerald ..	12	8
503	55 f. purple-brown, orge-brn & grnsh bl	12	10
504	60 f. slate-blue, maroon & blue-green ..	15	10
495/504	*Set of 10*	70	50

Designs: *Horiz*—10 f. Freshwater crayfish; 15 f. Nile mouthbreeder; 20 f. Sole; 25 f. Pike; 30 f. Swimming crab; 55 f. Snakehead; 60 f. Threadfin. *Vert*—40 f. Sickle fish; 50 f. Prawn.

133 Refinery and Tanker

134 Boxing

(Des C. Haley. Photo Delrieu)

1968 (30 July). *Inauguration of Petroleum Refinery, Port Gentil, Gabon.* P 12½.

505	**133** 30 f. new blue, red, green, chestnut and bright purple	10	5

(Des and eng C. Durrens. Recess)

1968 (19 Aug). *AIR. Olympic Games, Mexico.* T **134** and similar vert designs. P 13.

506	30 f. chocolate, blackish green & lt emer	12	8
507	50 f. chocolate, brown-red & lt emerald	20	10
508	60 f. chocolate, ultramarine & light emer	20	15
MS509	131×101 mm. Nos. 506/8	60	60

Designs:—50 f. Long-jumping; 60 f. Gymnastics.

135 Human Rights Emblem

136 Mahatma Gandhi and Map of India

(Photo So.Ge.Im.)

1968 (14 Sept). *Human Rights Year.* P 12½×13.

(a) POSTAGE

510	**135** 15 f. blue and light salmon-red ..	5	5

(b) AIR. Inscr "POSTE AERIENNE"

511	**135** 30 f. emerald and light bright purple	12	5

(Photo Delrieu)

1968 (5 Dec). *AIR. "Apostles of Peace".* T **136** and similar vert designs. P 12½.

512	30 f. black, orange-yellow & light blue ..	12	5
513	30 f. black and light greenish blue ..	12	5
514	60 f. black and pink	15	8
515	60 f. black and lilac	20	12
516	70 f. black, blue and light buff ..	25	15
517	70 f. black and light olive-green.. ..	25	15
512/517	*Set of 6*	95	55
MS518	122×162 mm. Nos. 512, 514/5 and 517	80	80

Portraits:—Nos. 512, T **136**; 513, Martin Luther King; 514, J. F. Kennedy; 515, R. F. Kennedy; 516, Gandhi (full-face); 517, Martin Luther King (half-length).

Nos. 512 and 516, 513 and 517, and 514/5 were respectively issued together in sheets *se-tenant* with stamp-size labels bearing commemorative inscriptions.

During October, 1969, Nos. 512/MS518, together with No. 481, were issued with a red opt "PREMIER HOMME SUR LA LUNE 20 JUILLET 1969/FIRST MAN LANDING ON MOON 20 JULY 1969" in very limited quantities.

137 "The Letter" (A. Cambon)

139 President Ahidjo

138 Wouri Bridge and 1 f. Stamp of 1925

(Photo Delrieu)

1968 (10 Dec). *AIR. "Philexafrique" Stamp Exhibition, Abidjan (in 1969). P* 12½.
519 **137** 100 f. multicoloured 50 40
No. 519 was issued in sheets with a *se-tenant* stamp-size label inscribed "PHILEXAFRIQUE ABIDJAN 14–23 FEVRIER 1969" and showing the U.A.M.P.T. posthorn emblem.

(Des and eng J. Combet. Recess)

1969 (14 Feb). *AIR. "Philexafrique" Stamp Exhibition, Abidjan, Ivory Coast. P* 13.
520 **138** 50 f. greenish blue, yellow-olive and
blackish green 25 20

(Photo Delrieu)

1969 (10 Apr). *Ninth Anniv of Independence. P* 12½.
521 **139** 30 f. multicoloured 12 5

140 Vat of Chocolate   **141** *Caladium bicolor*

(Des and eng M. Monvoisin. Recess)

1969 (24 Apr). *Chocolate Industry Development. T* **140** *and similar designs. P* 13.
522 15 f. indigo, chocolate and brown-red .. 5 5
523 30 f. blackish brown, choc & turq-green 12 5
524 50 f. red, bluish green and bistre-brown 15 12
Designs: *Horiz*—30 f. Chocolate factory. *Vert*—50 f. Making confectionery.

(Des S. Gauthier. Photo Delrieu)

1969 (14 May). *AIR. 3rd International Flower Show, Paris. T* **141** *and similar vert designs. Multicoloured. P* 12½.
525 30 f. Type **141** 10 8
526 50 f. *Aristolochia elegans* 20 12
527 100 f. *Gloriosa simplex* 40 25

142 Reproduction Symbol   **143** Post Office, Douala

(Des and eng J. Gauthier. Recess)

1969 (30 May). *Abbia Art and Folklore. T* **142** *and similar designs. P* 13.
528 5 f. bright purple, turq-blue & bright bl 5 5
529 10 f. yellow-orge, brn-olive & bright blue 5 5
530 15 f. indigo, red and bright blue .. 5 5
531 30 f. turq-green, bistre & bright blue .. 10 5
532 70 f. red, blackish green and bright blue 25 12
528/532 *Set of* 5 .. .. .. 45 25
Designs: *Horiz*—10 f. "Two Toucans"; 30 f. "Vulture attacking Monkey". *Vert*—10 f. Forest symbol; 70 f. Oliphant player.

(Des and eng N. Hanniquet. Recess)

1969 (19 June). *AIR. New Post Office Buildings. T* **143** *and similar horiz designs. P* 13.
533 30 f. brown, ultramarine & myrtle-grn 12 5
534 50 f. brown-red, slate & light blue-grn 20 10
535 100 f. brown, purple-brn & blue-green .. 40 20
Post Offices:—50 f. Buea; 100 f. Bafoussam.

144 "Coronation of Napoleon" (David)

(Photo Delrieu (30 f.), Embossed on foil Societé Pierre Mariotte (1000 f.))

1969 (4 July). *AIR. Birth Bicentenary of Napoleon Bonaparte. T* **144** *and similar horiz design. P* 12 × 12½ (30 f.) *or* 10 (1000 f.).
536 30 f. multicoloured 12 10
537 1000 f. gold .. .. .. 4·00
Designs—1000 f. "Napoleon crossing the Alps" (detail, David).

145 Kumba Station   **146** Bank Emblem

(Des H. Biais. Photo So.Ge.Im.)

1969 (11 July). *Opening of Mbanga-Kumba Railway. T* **145** *and similar multicoloured design. P* 12½ × 13 (30 f.) *or* 13 × 12½ (50 f.).
538 30 f. Type **145** 12 5
539 50 f. Diesel train on bridge (*vert*) .. 20 12

(Des and eng C. Haley. Recess)

1969 (10 Sept). *5th Anniversary of African Development Bank. P* 13.
540 **146** 30 f. orge-brn, emerald & bluish vio 12 5

147 Dr. P. Mars (Haiti)

(Photo Delrieu)

1969 (25 Sept). *AIR. Negro Writers. T* **147** *and similar vert portraits. P* 12½.

541	15 f. blackish brown & light turq-blue	..	5	5
542	30 f. blackish brown & light brown-pur		12	5
543	30 f. blackish brown and olive-yellow	..	12	5
544	50 f. blackish brown and light emerald		20	8
545	50 f. blackish brown and light agate	..	20	8
546	100 f. blackish brown and greenish yell		40	15
541/546	*Set of 6*	.. ..	1·00	40
MS547	115×125 mm. Nos 541/6	.. ..	90	90

Designs:—No. 542, W. Dubois (U.S.A.); No. 543, A. Césaire (Martinique);` No. 544, M. Garvey (Jamaica); No. 545, L. Hughes (U.S.A.); No. 546, R. Maran (Martinique).

148 I.L.O. Emblem

(Photo So.Ge.Im.)

1969 (29 Oct). *AIR. 50th Anniversary of International Labour Organization. P* 13.

548	**148**	30 f. black and turquoise	.. ..	12	5
549		50 f. black and bright magenta	..	20	8

149 Astronauts and "Apollo 11" in Sea

(Des P. Riou. Photo Delrieu)

1969 (29 Nov). *AIR. 1st Man on the Moon. T* **149** *and similar horiz design. Multicoloured. P* 12½.

550	200 f. Type **149**	.. ..	60	·40
ʾ551	500 f. Astronaut and module on Moon	..	1·50	90

150 Aircraft, Map and Airport

(Des and eng J. Combet. Recess)

1969 (12 Dec). *10th Anniversary of Aerial Navigation Security Agency for Africa and Madagascar (Agence pour la Sécurité de la Navigation Aérienne=ASECNA). P* 13.

552	**150**	100 f. myrtle-green	.. .. ..	35	20

151 Pres. Ahidjo, Arms and Map

(Embossed and typo on foil Societé Pierre Mariotte)

1970 (1 Jan). *AIR. 10th Anniversary of Independence. P* 10.

553	**151**	1000 f. multicoloured on gold foil	..	3·00	

152 Mont Fébé Hotel, Yaoundé

(Des and eng A. Decaris. Recess)

1970 (15 Jan). *AIR. Tourism. P* 13.

554	**152**	30 f. grey, myrtle-green & yell-brn	..	10	5

153 Lenin   **154** *Lantana camara*

(Photo Delrieu)

1970 (25 Jan). *AIR. Birth Centenary of Lenin. P* 12½.

555	**153**	50 f. blackish brown & orge-yellow	..	15	10

(Des P. Lambert. Photo Delrieu)

1970 (24 Mar). *African Climbing Plants. T* **154** *and similar vert designs. Multicoloured. (a) POSTAGE. Size as T* **154.** *P* 12×12½.

556	15 f. Type **154**	.. ..	..	5	5
557	30 f. *Passiflora quadrangularis*	..	10	5

(b) *AIR. Inscr* "POSTE AERIENNE". *Size 26×46 mm. P* 12½

558	50 f. *Cleome speciosa*	..	..	15	12
559	100 f. *Mussaenda erythrophylla*	..	30	20
556/559	*Set of 4*	.. .. ..	55	35

155 Lions' Emblem and Map of Africa

(Des J. Combet. Photo Delrieu)

1970 (2 May). *AIR. 13th Congress of Lions' International District 403, Yaoundé.* P 12½.
560 **155** 100 f. multicoloured   35   20

156 New U.P.U. Headquarters   158 Fermenting Vats

157 U.N. Emblem and Stylised Doves

(Des and eng J. Gauthier. Recess)

1970 (20 May). *New U.P.U. Headquarters Building, Berne.* P 13.
561 **156** 30 f. slate-grn, dp reddish vio & blue   12   5
562   50 f. greenish blue, red and grey   ..   20   8

(Des and eng J. Combet. Recess)

1970 (26 June). *AIR. 25th Anniversary of United Nations.* T **157** *and similar design.* P 13.
563   30 f. brown and yellow-orange   12   5
564   50 f. indigo and turquoise-blue   20   8
Design: *Vert*—50 f. U.N. emblem and stylised dove.

(Des and eng A. Decaris. Recess)

1970 (9 July). *Brewing Industry.* T **158** *and similar horiz design.* P 13×12½.
565   15 f. yellow-brown, myrtle-green & slate   5   5
566   30 f. brown-red, chocolate and turq-blue   12   5
Design:—30 f. Storage tanks.

159 Japanese Pavilion

(Des M. Monvoisin. Eng C. Guillame (100 f.). Des and eng M. Monvoisin (others). Recess)

1970 (1 Aug). *AIR. World Fair "EXPO 70", Osaka, Japan.* T **159** *and similar designs.* P 13.
567   50 f. indigo, red and emerald   20   8
568   100 f. red, blue and emerald   40   12
569   150 f. chocolate, slate and blue   60   20
Designs: *Vert*—100 f. EXPO emblem and map of Japan.
Horiz—150 f. Australian Pavilion.

160 Gen. De Gaulle in Tropical Kit

162 Dancers

161 Aztec Stadium, Mexico City

(Des and eng C. Haley. Recess)

1970 (27 Aug). *AIR. 30th Anniversary of De Gaulle's "Free French" Organization.* T **160** *and similar vert design.* P 13.
570   100 f. bistre-brown, ultram & blue-green   40   20
571   200 f. ultram, blue-green & bistre-brown   70   35
Design:—200 f. De Gaulle in military uniform.
Nos. 570/1 were issued together as a triptych, separated by a stamp-size label showing maps of France and Cameroun.

(Des J. Combet. Photo Delrieu)

1970 (14 Oct). *AIR. World Cup Football Championships, Mexico.* T **161** *and similar multicoloured designs.* P 12½.
572   50 f. Type **161**   20   8
573   100 f. Mexican team   40   15
574   200 f. Pele and Brazilian team with Cup (*vert*)   60   30

(Des and eng D. Guillame. Recess)

1970 (19 Oct). *Ozila Dancers.* T **162** *and similar vert design.* P 13.
575   30 f. maroon, yellow-orange & emerald   10   5
576   50 f. maroon, orange-brown & scarlet   ..   15   8
Design:—50 f. Musicians.

163 Doll in National Costume

164 Beethoven (after Stieler)

(Des and eng J. Derrey. Recess)

1970 (2 Nov). *Cameroun Dolls.* T **163** *and similar vert designs, showing dolls in regional costumes.* P 12½×13.
577   10 f. blue-green, black and carmine   ..   5   5
578   15 f. brown-red, myrtle-grn & orge-yell   5   5
579   30 f. brown-lake, myrtle-green & black ..   10   5

(Des and eng J. Combet. Recess)

1970 (23 Nov). *AIR. Birth Bicentenary of Beethoven.* P 13.
580 **164** 250 f. multicoloured   70   45

165 "Christ at Emmaus" (Rembrandt)

(Photo Delrieu)

1970 (5 Dec). *AIR. Paintings by Rembrandt.* T **165** and similar horiz design. Multicoloured. P 12½.
581 70 f. Type **165**   25   10
582 150 f. "The Anatomy Lesson"   45   20

166 "Industry and Agriculture"   167 Bust of Dickens

(Des M. Monvoisin. Photo)

1970 (9 Dec). *"Europafrique" Economic Community.* P 13.
583 **166** 30 f. multicoloured   8   5

(Des P. Lambert. Photo)

1970 (22 Dec). *AIR. Death Centenary of Charles Dickens.* T **167** and similar vert designs. P 13.
584 40 f. blackish brown and carmine   ..   15   5
585 50 f. multicoloured   20   8
586 100 f. multicoloured   35   15
   a. Horiz strip of 3. Nos. 584/6   ..   75   40
   Designs:—50 f. Characters from *David Copperfield;* 100 f. Dickens writing.
   Nos. 584/6 were issued together *se-tenant* within the sheet, forming the triptych No. 586a.

IN MEMORIAM 1890-1970

(168)   169 University Buildings

For similar designs inscr "United Republic of Cameroon" etc, see Nos. 648/52.

1971 (15 Jan). *AIR. Gen. De Gaulle, Memorial Issue.* Nos. 570/1 *optd with* T **168** *or similar opt.*
587 100 f. bistre-brown, ultram & blue-green   30   15
588 200 f. ultramarine, blue-grn & bistre-brn   60   30

(Des A. Decaris. Recess)

1971 (19 Jan). *Inauguration of Federal University, Yaoundé.* P 13.
589 **169** 50 f. myrtle-grn, bright bl & orge-brn   15   8

170 Presidents Ahidjo and Pompidou

(Des R. Quillivic. Photo Delrieu)

1971 (9 Feb). *Visit of French President.* P 13.
590 **170** 30 f. multicoloured   10   5

171 "Cameroun Youth"   173 Gerbera hybrida

REPUBLIQUE FEDERALE DU CAMEROUN

172 Timber Yard, Douala

(Des P. Lambert. Photo Delrieu)

1971 (11 Feb). *5th National Youth Festival.* P 13.
591 **171** 30 f. multicoloured   10   5

(Des and eng J. Combet. Recess)

1971 (14 Feb). *AIR. Industrial Expansion.* T **172** and similar designs. P 13.
592 40 f. bistre-brown, turq-grn & brn-red   12   5
593 70 f. bistre-brn, myrtle-grn & grnsh bl   20   10
594 100 f. brown-red, greenish bl & brt grn   25   12
   Designs: *Vert*—70 f. "Alucam" aluminium plant, Edéa. *Horiz*—100 f. Mbakaou Dam.

(Des "Lacroix" (H. Ouin). Photo Delrieu)

1971 (14 Mar). *Flowers.* T **173** and similar vert designs. Multicoloured. P 13.
595 20 f. Type **173**   5   5
596 40 f. *Opuntia polyantha*   12   5
597 50 f. *Hemerocallis hybrida*   15   8

178 Peace Palace, The Hague **180** Rope Bridge

174 "World Races" **175** Crested Cranes, Waza Camp

(Des C. Haley. Photo Delrieu)

1971 (21 Mar). *Racial Equality Year. T* **174** *and similar vert design. Multicoloured. P* 12½.
598 20 f. Type **174** 5 5
599 30 f. Hand of four races clasping globe 8 5

(Des and eng C. Durrens. Recess)

1971 (9 Apr). *Landscapes. T* **175** *and similar horiz designs. P* 13×12½.
600 10 f. indigo, red and emerald 5 5
601 20 f. red, brown and myrtle-green .. 5 5
602 30 f. myrtle-green, new blue & chestnut 8 5
Designs:—20 f. African pirogue; 30 f. Sanaga River.

179 1916 French Occupation 20 c., and 1914–18 War Memorial, Yaoundé

(Des and eng J. Gauthier. Recess)

1971 (14 June). *25th Anniversary of International Court of Justice, The Hague. P* 13×12½.
610 **178** 50 f. orge-brn, ultram & myrtle-grn .. 15 8

(Des C. Jumelet. Eng J. Miermont (20 f.), R. Fenneteaux (25 f.) R. Quillivic (40 f.), C. Jumelet (50 f.) G. Aufschneider (100 f.). Recess)

1971 (1 Aug). *AIR. "PHILATECAM '71" Stamp Exhib, Yaoundé (1st issue). T* **179** *and similar horiz designs. P* 13.
611 20 f. chocolate, ochre and emerald .. 8 5
612 25 f. chocolate, slate-green & ultram .. 10 5
613 40 f. emerald, deep slate & brown-lake 15 8
614 50 f. black, vermilion, sepia & brown .. 20 10
615 100 f. slate-green, brn-lake & yell-orge .. 40 20
611/615 *Set of 5* 85 45
Designs:—25 f. 1954 15 f. Jamot stamp, and memorial; 40 f. 1965 25 f. Tourist Office stamp, and public buildings, Yaoundé; 50 f. German Kamerun 5 m. "Yacht" stamp, and Imperial German postal emblem; 100 f. 1915 Expeditionary Force opt error, No. 5a, and Expeditionary Force memorial.
See also No. 620.

176 Relay-racing

(Des and eng G. Bétemps. Recess)

1971 (24 Apr). *AIR. 75th Anniversary of Modern Olympic Games. T* **176** *and similar designs. P* 13.
603 30 f. indigo, vermilion and chocolate .. 10 5
604 50 f. maroon, new blue and indigo .. 15 10
605 100 f. black, emerald and red .. 30 20
Designs: *Vert*—50 f. Runner with Olympic torch. *Horiz*—100 f. Throwing the discus.

(Des M. Monvoisin. Photo Delrieu)

1971 (16 Aug). *"Rural Life". T* **180** *and similar multicoloured design. P* 13×12½ (40 f.) *or* 12½×13 (45 f.).
616 40 f. Type **180** 15 8
617 45 f. Local market (*horiz*) 15 8

177 Deep-sea Trawler

(Des P. Béquet. Eng J. Miermont (30 f.). Des and eng P. Béquet (others). Recess)

1971 (14 May). *AIR. Fishing Industry. T* **177** *and similar horiz designs. P* 13.
606 30 f. brown, dp bluish green & new bl 10 5
607 40 f. maroon, new blue & blackish grn 12 8
608 70 f. purple-brn, orge-red & new blue .. 20 12
609 150 f. purple-brown, orange-yellow, new blue and bluish green 45 25
606/609 *Set of 4* 80 45
Designs:—40 f. Traditional fishing method, Northern Cameroun; 70 f. Fish quay, Douala; 150 f. Shrimp-boats, Douala.

181 Bamoun Horseman (carving) **183** Satellite and Globe

182 Pres. Ahidjo, Flag and "Reunification" Road

(Des "Lacroix" (H. Ouin). Photo Delrieu)

1971 (18 Sept). *Cameroun Carvings. T 181 and similar vert design.* P 13×12½.
618   10 f. brown and greenish yellow   ..   5   5
619   15 f. chocolate and yellow   5   5
Design:—15 f. Fetish statuette.

(Des Martimor. Typo and embossed on gold foil Societé Pierre Mariotte)

1971 (1 Oct). *AIR. "PHILATECAM 71" Stamp Exhib, Yaoundé (2nd issue).* P 12½.
620   **182**   250 f. multicoloured   80

(Des C. Guillame. Photo)

1971 (14 Oct). *Pan-African Telecommunications Network.* P 13×12½.
621   **183**   40 f. multicoloured   12   5

184 U.A.M.P.T. Headquarters, Brazzaville, and Carved Stool

(Des R. Quillivic. Photo Delrieu)

1971 (13 Nov). *AIR. 10th Anniversary of African and Malagasy Posts and Telecommunications Union.* P 13×13½.
622   **184**   100 f. multicoloured   35   12

185 Children acclaiming Emblem

(Des A. Peyrié. Eng C. Jumelet. Recess)

1971 (11 Dec). *25th Anniversary of U.N.I.C.E.F. T 185 and similar design.* P 13.
623   40 f. purple, turquoise-blue and slate   ..   12   5
624   50 f. red, bright green and bright blue   ..   15   8
Design: *Vert*—50 f. Ear of wheat and emblem.

186 "The Annunciation" (Fra Angelico)

(Photo Delrieu)

1971 (19 Dec). *AIR. Christmas. T 186 and similar paintings. Multicoloured.* P 13.
625   40 f. Type **186**   12   5
626   45 f. "Virgin and Child" (Del Sarto)   ..   12   8
627   150 f. "The Holy Family with the Lamb" (detail, Raphael) (*vert*)   45   20

187 Cabin, South-Central Region

(Des G. Umlauft. Photo Delrieu)

1972 (15 Jan). *Traditional Cameroun Houses. T 187 and similar horiz design. Multicoloured.* P 13.
628   10 f. Type **187**   5   5
629   15 f. Adamaoua round house   5   5

188 Airline Emblem   **189** Giraffe and Palm Tree

(Des Baillais. Photo Delrieu)

1972 (2 Feb). *AIR. Cameroun Airways' Inaugural Flight.* P 12½×12.
630   **188**   50 f. multicoloured   15   8

(Des from Children's Drawings. Litho De La Rue)

1972 (18 Feb). *Youth Festival. T 189 and similar multicoloured designs.* P 13.
631   2 f. Type **189**   5   5
632   5 f. Domestic scene   5   5
633   10 f. Blacksmith (*horiz*)   5   5
634   15 f. Women   5   5
631/634   *Set of 4*   10   10

190 Africa Cup   **191** "St. Mark's Square and Doge's Palace" (detail, Caffi)

(Des G. Bétemps. Photo Delrieu)

1972 (22 Feb). *Africa Cup Football Championships, Cameroun. T 190 and similar multicoloured designs.* P 13.
635   20 f. Type **190**   5   5
636   40 f. Players with ball (*horiz*)   ..   12   5
637   45 f. Team captains   15   8

(Photo Delrieu)

1972 (19 Mar). *AIR. U.N.E.S.C.O. "Save Venice" Campaign.*
T **191** *and similar vert paintings. Multicoloured. P* 13.
638	40 f. Type **191**	..	12	5
639	100 f. "Regatta on the Grand Canal" (detail, Canaletto) ..		30	15
640	200 f. "Regatta on the Grand Canal" (different detail, Canaletto)		60	25

192 Assembly Building, Yaoundé

(Des P. Sampoux. Photo Delrieu)

1972 (6 Apr). *110th Inter-Parliamentary Council Session,*
Yaoundé. P 12½×12.
641	**192** 40 f. multicoloured ..	..	12	5

193 Horseman, North Cameroun

(Des P. Lambert. Photo)

1972 (24 Apr). *Traditional Life and Folklore. T* **193** *and*
similar multicoloured designs. P 12½×13 (20 f.) *or* 13×12½
(others).
642	15 f. Type **193**	..	5	5
643	20 f. Bororo woman (*vert*)	..	5	5
644	40 f. Wouri River and Mt Cameroun	..	12	5

194 Pataiev, Dobrovolsky and Volkov

(Des Delfaut. Photo Delrieu)

1972 (1 May). *AIR. "Soyuz 11" Cosmonauts Memorial*
Issue. P 13.
645	**194** 50 f. multicoloured ..	..	15	8

195 U.N. Building, New York; Gate of Heavenly Peace,
Peking, and Chinese Flag

(Des P. Sampoux. Photo)

1972 (15 May). *AIR. Admission of Chinese People's Republic*
to United Nations. P 13.
646	**195** 50 f. multicoloured ..	..	15	8

196 Chemistry Laboratory, Federal University

(Des and eng J. Combet. Recess)

1972 (19 May). *President Ahidjo Prize. P* 13×12½.
647	**196** 40 f. red, blue-green and purple ..		12	5

E. UNITED REPUBLIC OF CAMEROUN

The above name was adopted in June 1972 following a
plebiscite held on 21 May.

(Des "Lacroix" (H. Ouin). Photo Delrieu)

1972. *Flowers. Vert designs similar to T* **173***, but inscr*
"UNITED REPUBLIC OF CAMEROON" *etc. Multicoloured.*
P 13.
648	40 f. Solanum macranthum (20.7)	..	12	5
649	40 f. Kaempferia aethiopica (16.9)	..	12	5
650	45 f. Hoya carnosa (20.7)	..	15	8
651	45 f. Cassia alata (16.9) ..	..	15	8
652	50 f. Crinum sanderianum (16.9)	..	15	8
648/652	Set of 5	..	60	30

197 Swimming   **198** Charaxes ameliae

(Des and eng J. Combet. Recess)

1972 (1 Aug). *AIR. Olympic Games, Munich. T* **197** *and*
similar designs. P 13.
653	50 f. myrtle-green, blackish brown and lake-brown	..	15	8
654	50 f. brown, slate-blue & blackish brn ..		15	8
655	200 f. brown-lake, slate & reddish purple ,		60	30
MS656	140×100 mm. As Nos. 653/5, but colours changed; 50 f. red-brn, reddish vio & turq-bl; 50 f. red-brn, turq-bl & bright pur; 200 f. red-brn & turq-bl	..	1·00	1·00

Designs: *Horiz*—No. 653, T **197**; No. 655, Horse-jumping.
Vert—No. 654, Boxing.

(Des M. Louis. Photo)

1972 (20 Aug). *Butterflies. T* **198** *and similar horiz design.*
Multicoloured. P 13.
657	40 f. Type **198**	..	12	5
658	45 f. Papilio tynderaeus ..	..	15	8

40 F	NATATION MARK SPITZ 7 MEDAILLES D'OR
(199)	(200)

1972 (30 Aug). *No. 471 surch with T* **199**.
659	40 f. on 30 f. multicoloured (Bananas) ..		12	5

1972 (23 Oct). *AIR. Olympic Gold Medal Winners. Nos.*
653/5 *optd with T* **200** *or similar types in red* (No. 660) *or*
black.
660	50 f. myrtle-green, blackish brown and lake-brown ..		15	8
661	50 f. brown, slate-blue & blackish brn ..		15	8
662	200 f. brown-lake, slate & reddish purple		60	30

Overprints:—No. 660, T **200**; No. 661, "SUPER-WELTER
KOTTYSCH MEDAILLE D'OR"; No. 662, "CONCOURS COM-
PLET MEADE MEDAILLE D'OR".

201 Giant (Great Blue) Turacos

202 "The Virgin with Angels" (Cimabue)

(Des G. Umlauft. Litho and typo Edila)

1972 (20 Nov). *Birds.* T **201** *and similar multicoloured design. No gum.* P 13.
663	10 f. Type **201**	..	..	5	5
664	45 f. Red-headed lovebirds (*horiz*)	..	15	8

(Photo Delrieu)

1972 (21 Dec). *AIR. Christmas.* T **202** *and similar vert painting. Multicoloured.* P 13.
665	45 f. Type **202**	..	..	15	8
666	140 f. "Madonna of the Rose Arbour" (S. Lochner)	..	..	40	20

203 St. Theresa

204 Emperor Haile Selassie and "Africa Hall", Addis Ababa

(Des C. Jumelet. Recess)

1973 (2 Jan). *AIR. Birth Centenary of St. Theresa of Lisieux.* T **203** *and similar vert design.* P 13.
667	45 f. ultram, brn-lake & reddish vio	..	15	8
668	100 f. magenta, chocolate and blue	..	30	15

Design:—100 f. Lisieux Basilica.

(Des P. Sampoux. Photo Delrieu)

1973 (14 Mar). *AIR. 80th Birthday of Emperor Haile Selassie of Ethiopia.* P 13.
669	**204** 45 f. multicoloured	..	..	..	15	8

205 Cotton Cultivation, North Cameroon

(Des P. Lambert. Photo)

1973 (26 Mar). *3rd Five Year Plan.* T **205** *and similar vert designs. Multicoloured.* P 12½×13.
670	5 f. Type **205**	..	..	5	5
671	10 f. Cacao seeds, South-central region	5	5
672	15 f. Forestry, South-eastern area	..	5	5
673	20 f. Coffee plant, West Cameroun	..	5	5
674	45 f. Tea-picking, West Cameroun	..	15	8
670/674	*Set of 5*	..	..	..	25	15

CANTON. See under China (Indo-Chinese Post Offices).

Canal Zone

1904. 100 Centavos = 1 Peso
1906. 100 Centesimos = 1 Balboa
1924. 100 Cents = 1 Dollar (U.S.)

On 18 November 1903 the newly-established Republic of Panama granted to the U.S.A. the use, occupation and control in perpetuity of a strip of territory to a depth of 5 miles along either side of the proposed canal across the isthmus of Panama. The cities of Panama and Colón at either end of the canal remain under the jurisdiction of Panama. The canal was opened to traffic on 15 August 1914.

Until April 1914, the civil administration of the Zone was performed by the Isthmian Canal Commission; it was then handed over to an independent Government Agency, called The Panama Canal. On 1 July 1951 the civil government functions of this agency were renamed the Canal Zone Government, the Governor being appointed by the President of the United States, subject to confirmation by the Senate.

The Canal Zone list follows the same style as has been adopted in the United States List:—

SHADES are given equal status being numbered A, B, C, etc. following the same number of the first listed shade.

VARIETIES are given va, vb, vc numbers, etc. to avoid any confusion with shade numbers and they are placed immediately after the *first* listed shade. *Such varieties may exist in any or all of the shades and not necessarily in the first listed shade.*

Types of Panama Republic

62 Hurtado   63 Obaldia

65 Balboa reaches the Pacific (1915 Types)

66 Balboa Docks   69 Vallarino Dated   75
(1918–20 Types)   "1821 1921"

D 1 San Geronimo Castle Gate, Portobelo (*wrongly inscr* "CASTILLO DE SAN LORENZO CHAGRES")

(Postage Due Types)

CANAL ZONE   CANAL ZONE   PANAMA

(1)   (2)

---

4   47   51 Fernandez de Cordoba

53 Justo Arosemena   54 Manuel J. Hurtado   55 José de Obaldia

58 Balboa   59 De Cordoba   61 Arosemena

PUZZLED?

Then you need
PHILATELIC TERMS ILLUSTRATED
to tell you all you need to know about printing methods, papers, errors, varieties, watermarks, perforations, etc. 192 pages, almost half in full colour, soft cover. £1 post paid.

FOR WELL CENTRED COPIES ADD 50%
(Nos. 1/24)

1904 (24 June). *Stamps of Panama Republic (T 4) optd "PANAMA", about 13 mm long (on 5 c. and 10 c. about 15 mm long), at left and right, and with bar across top of stamp, all in carmine, handstamped with T 1, in grey-blue.*

1	**4**	2 c. carmine	..	25·00	25·00
		va. "CANAL ZONE" inverted	..	50·00	50·00
		vb. "CANAL ZONE" double	..	£100	
		vc. Do., both inverted	..	£250	
		vd. "PANAMA" reading up or down	..	40·00	40·00
		ve. Do., "CANAL ZONE" inverted	..	—	£300
		vf. "PANAMA" 15 to 16 mm	..	32·00	32·00
		vg. "PANAMA" about 13 mm one side and 15 to 16 mm the other	..		
		vh. As vd with "CANAL ZONE" inverted			
2		5 c. blue	..	15·00	12·00
		va. "CANAL ZONE" inverted	..	50·00	50·00
		vb. "CANAL ZONE" double	..	60·00	60·00
		vc. Pair, one without "CANAL ZONE"	..	£275	
		vd. "CANAL ZONE" diagonal	..	30·00	30·00
3		10 c. orange	..	20·00	18·00
		va. "CANAL ZONE" inverted	..	40·00	40·00
		vb. "CANAL ZONE" double	..	—	£375
		vc. Pair, one without "CANAL ZONE"	..	£250	£250

On No. 1 the "PANAMA" opt normally reads up or down both sides; on Nos. 2 and 3 it reads up at left and down at right.

There are numerous forgeries of this set. The illustration differs from the genuine type.

1904 (18 July). *Stamps of the United States, 1902–3, optd in Washington with T 2. W 87. P 12.*

4	**103**	1 c. blue-green	..	..	1·50	1·40
5	**117**	2 c. scarlet	..	..	2·00	2·00
5A		2 c. carmine	..	..	1·40	1·00
6	**107**	5 c. blue	..	..	4·50	4·50
7	**109**	8 c. grey-violet	..	..	7·50	7·50
8	**110**	10 c. brown	..	..	8·00	8·00

C A N A L   **CANAL**

Z O N E.   **ZONE**

   (3)   **(4)** (Antique type)

1904 (12 Dec). *Stamps of Panama Republic (T 47), optd locally with T 3.*

9	**47**	1 c. green	..	25	20
		va. "CANAL" in antique type	..	7·50	7·50
		vb. "ZONE" in antique type	..	3·00	3·00
		vc. Opt inverted	..	—	£160
		vd. Opt double	..	£300	£190
10		2 c. carmine	..	30	25
		va. Opt inverted	..	9·00	9·00
		vb. "L" sideways	..	50·00	50·00

1904 (12 Dec)–**06**. *Stamps of Panama Republic (T 4 optd "PANAMA" twice and bar across top of stamps, in carmine), optd locally with T 3, in black.*

"PANAMA" 15 mm long, reading up at left and down at right

11	**4**	2 c. carmine (9 Dec 1905)	..	50	40
		va. "ZONE" in antique type	..	5·00	5·00
		vb. "PANAMA" opt inverted, bar at bottom	..	15·00	15·00
12		5 c. blue	..	35	25
		va. "CANAL" in antique type	..	2·50	2·50
		vb. "ZONE" in antique type	..	2·50	2·50
		vc. "CANAL ZONE" double	..	27·00	27·00
		vd. "PANAMA" opt double	..	27·00	27·00
		ve. "PANAMA" opt inverted, bar at bottom	..		9·00
13		10 c. orange	..	1·00	85
		va. "CANAL" in antique type	..	7·50	7·50
		vb. "ZONE" in antique type	..	4·00	4·00
		vc. "PANAMA" opt double	..	35·00	35·00
		vd. "PANAMA" opt in red-brown	..	3·00	3·00

8 cts   **8 cts.**   **8 cts**

   (5)   **(6)**   **(7)**

Surch with T 5 in red

14	**4**	8 c. on 50 c. bistre-brown	..		1·25	1·00
		va. "ZONE" in antique type	..		35·00	35·00
		vb. "CANAL ZONE" inverted	..		21·00	21·00
		vc. Surch in rose-brown	..		2·10	2·10
		vd. Do. "CANAL" in antique type	..		55·00	
		ve. Do. "ZONE" in antique type	..		55·00	
		vf. Do. "8 cts" double	..		50·00	

Surch with T 5 in red on stamp with "PANAMA" 13 mm long, both reading up

15	**4**	8 c. on 50 c. bistre-brown	..		£140	£140
		va. "PANAMA" reading up and down	..		£180	£180

Stamp as last but surch with T 6, in red

16	**4**	8 c. on 50 c. bistre-brown (Nov 1905)	..		3·75	3·75
		va. "ZONE" in antique type	..		9·00	9·00
		vb. "PANAMA" reading up and down	..		6·00	6·00

Stamp as last but surch with T 7, in red

17	**4**	8 c. on 50 c. bistre-brown (23 Apr 1906)	..		3·00	3·00
		va. "CANAL" in antique type	..		7·00	7·00
		vb. "ZONE" in antique type	..		7·00	7·00
		vc. "8 cts" double	..		—	£200
		vd. "PANAMA" reading up and down	..		5·00	5·00

Surch as T 7 but with stop after "cts.", in red on stamp with "PANAMA" reading up and down

18	**4**	8 c. on 50 c. bistre-brown (Sept 1906)	..		1·40	1·25
		va. "CANAL" in antique type	..		7·00	7·00
		vb. "ZONE" in antique type	..		7·00	7·00
		vc. "8 cts." double	..			
		vd. "8 cts." omitted	..		50·00	50·00

(8)

(9)

(10)

(11)

(12)

(13)

There were three printings of this issue producing three types for each value differing in the relative position of the various parts of the surcharges.

1906. *Stamps of Panama Republic (T 4), surch with T 8/13, by Isthmian Canal Commission Press.*

19	**8**	1 c. on 20 c. slate-violet (Apr)	..	..	8	8
20	**9**	1 c. on 20 c. slate-violet (May)	..		8	8
21	**10**	1 c. on 20 c. slate-violet (Sept)	..		8	8
22	**11**	2 c. on 1 p. lake (Apr)	..		15	10
23	**12**	2 c. on 1 p. lake (May)	..		15	15
24	**13**	2 c. on 1 p. lake (Sept)	..		25	20

(14)

FOR WELL CENTRED COPIES ADD 40%
(Nos. 25/73)

(Recess Hamilton Bank Note Co, N.Y. Optd by Isthmian
Canal Commission Press)
1906–07. *Stamps of Panama Republic, optd with T* **14.**

(a) Opt reading up

25	**51**	2 c. black and scarlet (29 Oct 1906) ..		1·10	1·00

(b) Opt reading down

26	**50**	1 c. green and black (14 Jan 1907) ..		15	12
		va. Imperf horiz (vert pair) ..	..	35·00	35·00
		vb. Opt reading up ..	..	30·00	30·00
		vc. Opt double	..	11·00	11·00
		vd. Opt double, one reading up	..	45·00	45·00
		ve. Centre inverted, opt reading up		90·00	90·00
27	**51**	2 c. black and scarlet (25 Nov 1906)		20	15
		va. Vert pair, one without opt	..	85·00	85·00
		vb. Opt double ..	..	18·00	18·00
		vc. Opt double, one diagonal	..	30·00	30·00
27A		2 c. black and carmine (9 Sept 1907)		50	25
		vd. Centre inverted, opt reading up		—	£650
		ve. Opt double, one "ZONE CANAL"..	..		
28	**53**	5 c. black & ultramarine (Dec 1906)		35	15
		va. Opt double ..	..	30·00	24·00
		vb. "ZONE" omitted ..	..	65·00	65·00
		vc. Optd "ZONE CANAL" ..	..		
28A		5 c. black and blue (16 Sept 1907) ..		35	15
28B		5 c. black and dull blue ..	..	40	15
29	**54**	8 c. black and plum (Dec 1906) ..		1·00	40
30	**55**	10 c. black and violet (Dec 1906) ..		1·00	40
		va. Opt double, one reading up	..	42·00	
		vb. Opt reading up ..			

(Recess American Bank Note Co, N.Y. Optd by Isthmian
Canal Commission Press)
1909. *Stamps of Panama Republic, optd with T* **14,** *reading down.*

31	**59**	2 c. black and vermilion (11 May)	..	1·00	40
		va. Pair, one without opt ..	..	40·00	40·00
32	**61**	5 c. black and steel-blue (28 May)	..	2·40	50
33	**62**	8 c. black and purple (25 May)	..	1·75	60
34	**63**	10 c. black and purple (19 Jan)	..	2·00	60
		va. Pair, one without opt ..	..	£150	

(15)

Five types of T **15**

Type I   Type II

Type III   Type IV

Type V

*The illustrations of Types I to V are considerably enlarged
to show the differences and therefore do not show the actual
spacing between the lines of overprint.*

Type I. "C" with serifs both top and bottom; "L", "Z" and
"E" with slanting serifs.
Type II. "C" with serifs at top only; "L" and "E" with vertical
serifs; inner oval of "O" tilts to left.
Type III. Similar to Type I but letters appear thinner, particu-
larly lower bar of "L", "Z" and "E". Impressions usually
light, rough and irregular.
Type IV. "C" thick at bottom; "E" with centre bar same
length as top and bottom bars.
Type V. Smaller, 1¾ mm high; "A" with flat top.

1909–21. *Stamps of Panama Republic, optd as T* **15.**

(a) As Type I by American Bank Note Co

35	**58**	1 c. black and green (8 Nov 1909) ..		15	10
		va. Centre inverted, opt reading down	..	—	£1000
		vb. "ZONE" omitted	..	50·00	
36	**59**	2 c. black and vermilion (8 Nov 1909)		20	10
		va. Imperf horiz (vert pair) ..	..	35·00	35·00
		vb. "CANAL" double..	..	42·00	42·00
37	**61**	5 c. black and steel-blue (8 Nov 1909)		25	15
		va. Opt double ..	..	29·00	29·00
38	**62**	8 c. black and purple (18 Mar 1910) ..		40	25
		va. Pair, one without opt ..	..	80·00	
39	**63**	10 c. black and purple (8 Nov 1909) ..		1·50	50

(b) As Type II by American Bank Note Co

40	**58**	1 c. black and green (July 1913) ..		25	15
		a. Booklet pane of six ..	..	17·00	
		va. Pair, one without opt ..	..	30·00	
41	**59**	2 c. black and vermilion (Dec 1912) ..		25	12
		a. Booklet pane of six ..	..	15·00	
		va. Pair, one without opt ..	..	20·00	
		vb. "ZONE" omitted ..	..	28·00	
		vc. Opt reading down ..	..	6·00	
		vd. Centre inverted, opt reading down	..	15·00	13·00
42	**61**	5 c. black and steel-blue (Dec 1912) ..		50	12
		va. With portrait of 2 c. ..	..	—	£750
43	**63**	10 c. black and purple (Feb 1916) ..		2·00	40

(c) As Type III by Panama Canal Press

44	**58**	1 c. black and green (Dec 1915) ..		11·00	10·00
		va. Opt reading down ..	..	13·00	13·00
		vb. Opt double ..	..	13·00	13·00
		vc. "ZONE" double ..	..	40·00	40·00
		vd. Opt double, one reading "ZONE CANAL"	..	30·00	
		ve. "CANAL" double ..	..	30·00	
45	**59**	2 c. black and vermilion (Aug 1920) ..		40·00	8·00
46	**61**	5 c. black and steel-blue (Dec 1915) ..		32·00	10·00

(d) As Type IV by American Bank Note Co

47	**58**	1 c. black and green (Jan 1918) ..		50	25
		va. Opt reading down ..	..	10·00	
		vb. Pair, one without opt ..	..	90·00	
		c. Booklet pane of six ..	..	17·00	
		vc. Do. Left three without opt ..	..	£110	
		vd. Do. Right three without opt ..	..	£140	

48	59	2 c. black and vermilion (Nov 1918)	..	75	15
		va. Opt reading down	..	3·75	3·75
		vb. Pair, one without opt	..	25·00	
		c. Booklet pane of six	..	18·00	
		vc. Do. Left three without opt	..		
49	61	5 c. black and steel-blue (Apr 1920)	..	3·00	1·10

(e) As Type V by American Bank Note Co

50	58	1 c. black and green (Apr 1921)	..	35	12
		a. Booklet pane of six	..	21·00	
		va. Opt reading down	..	3·00	3·00
		vb. Horiz pair, one without opt	..	42·00	
		vc. Vert pair, one without opt	..		
		vd. "CANAL" double	..	30·00	
		ve. "CANAL" omitted	..	32·00	
51	59	2 c. black and vermilion (Sept 1920)	..	25	12
		a. Booklet pane of six	..	15·00	
		va. Opt double	..	10·00	
		vb. Opt double, one reading down	..	15·00	
		vc. Pair, one without opt	..	30·00	
		vd. "CANAL" double	..	20·00	
		ve. "ZONE" double	..	20·00	
		vf. "ZONE" omitted	..	£100	
52	61	5 c. black and steel-blue (Apr 1921)	..	3·50	60
		va. Pair, one without opt	..	65·00	

CANAL **10 cts.** ZONE

(16)

1911 (14 Jan). *Type of Panama Republic (As T 47 but with value in "CENTÉSIMOS DE BALBOA" and printer's imprint at foot), surch with T 16.*

53	10 c. on 13 c. grey	..	..	35	15
	va. "10 cts." inverted	..		15·00	8·00
	vb. "10 cts." omitted	..	..	15·00	

The overprint was applied by the American Bank Note Co and the stamps were then surcharged by the Isthmian Canal Commission Press.

1914 (6 Jan). *Type as No. 53 but optd "CANAL ZONE" only, as in T 16.*

54	10 c. grey	..	..	..	..	2·00	50

CANAL ZONE CANAL **2** ZONE

(D 1) **(D 2)**

FOR WELL CENTRED COPIES ADD 50%

1914 (11 or 12 Mar). *POSTAGE DUE. Nos. D45/6 and D49 of United States optd in Washington with Type D 1, diagonally.*

D55	D 2	1 c. lake	..	..	..	1·75	75
D56		2 c. lake	..	..	..	4·50	2·00
D57		10 c. lake	..	..	..	18·00	2·25

FOR WELL CENTRED COPIES ADD 40%

1915 (1 Mar). *Stamps of 1915 of Panama Republic (as T 65), optd by American Bank Note Co, as T 15 but more widely spaced (Type II).*

55	1 c. black and deep green (B.)	..	..	60	30
56	2 c. black and carmine (B.)	..	..	40	20
57	5 c. black and deep blue (B.)	..	..	60	40
58	10 c. black and orange (B.)	..	..	1·10	90

ALBUM LISTS

Write for our latest lists of albums
and accessories.
These will be sent free on request.

FOR WELL CENTRED COPIES ADD 20%
(Nos. D59/66)

1915 (Mar). *POSTAGE DUE. Postage Due stamps of Panama Republic, optd by American Bank Note Co, with T 15, Type II, in blue.*

D59	1 c. brown (No. D21)	..	..	60	25
	va. Opt Type V, reading up	..	2·25	
	vb. Opt Type V, reading down	..	2·25	
D60	2 c. brown (No. D22)	..	..	3·75	1·00
D61	10 c. brown (No. D24)	..	..	1·75	75

1915–19. *POSTAGE DUE. Postage Due stamps of Panama Republic surch as Type D 2.*

(a) In red (Nov 1915)

D62	1 c. on 1 c. brown (No. D21)	..	3·25	75
D63	2 c. on 2 c. brown (No. D22)	..	85	35
D64	10 c. on 10 c. brown (No. D24)	..	75	30

(b) In carmine by Panama Canal Press (Dec 1919)

D65	2 c. on 2 c. brown (No. D22)	..	1·25	40
D66	4 c. on 4 c. brown (No. D23)	..	2·00	90
	va. "ZONE" omitted	..	..	50·00	
	vb. "4" omitted	..	..	40·00	

FOR WELL CENTRED COPIES ADD 40%
(Nos. 59/73)

1917 (Jan)–**20**. *Stamps of 1918–20 of Panama Republic (as T 66), optd by American Bank Note Co, as T 15 but more widely spaced, Type II (12 c. to 24 c.) or Type V (others).*

59	12 c. black and bright violet (B.)	..	65	30
60	15 c. black and blue (B.)	..	1·50	85
61	24 c. black and brown (B.)	..	1·50	50
62	50 c. black and orange (4 Sept 1920)	18·00	12·00
63	1 b. black and indigo-violet (4 Sept 1920)	10·00	4·50

1921 (13 Nov). *Independence Centenary issue of Panama Republic (as T 69, dated "1821 1921"), optd by American Bank Note Co, as T 15, Type V, except 5 c. which is larger (2 mm high × 10 mm).*

64	69	1 c. green	..	..	20	10
		a. Booklet pane of six	..	23·00	
		va. "CANAL" double	..	60·00	
65	70	2 c. carmine	..	..	20	8
		a. Booklet pane of six	..	60·00	
		va. Opt reading down	..	4·00	
		vb. Opt double	..	30·00	
		vc. Pair, one without opt	..	30·00	
		vd. "CANAL" double	..	28·00	
		ve. "CANAL" omitted	..	28·00	
66	71a	5 c. indigo (R.)	..	..	60	30
		va. Opt reading down	..	2·75	
		vb. Opt Type V (R.)	..	7·00	
		vc. Opt Type V (Bk.)	..	3·75	
67	72	10 c. violet	..	..	90	30
		va. Opt reading down	..	4·50	
68	–	15 c. pale blue (No. 341)	..	1·40	60
69	–	24 c. sepia (No. 343)	..	2·75	1·40
70	–	50 c. black (No. 344)	..	8·00	4·00

1924 (28 Jan). *Optd with T 15, Type III by the Panama Canal Press.*

71	69	1 c. green	..	..	28·00	7·00
		va. "ZONE CANAL" reading down	..	50·00	
		vb. "ZONE" only, reading down	..	90·00	

1924 (Feb). *Arms type of Panama Republic optd by American Bank Note Co, as T 15.*

72	75	1 c. green	..	..	50	35
73		2 c. carmine	..	..	35	25

CANAL CANAL

ZONE ZONE

(17) "A" with flat tops **(18)** "A" with pointed tops

(T **17/18** optd by U.S. Bureau of Engraving and Printing)
1924 (1 July)–**25**. *Stamps of the United States, optd as T* **17**. *Flat plate printings. P* 11.

74	**143**	c. sepia (R.) (15 Apr 1925) ..		5	5
75	**144**	1 c. green	..	8	5
		a. Booklet pane of six	..	3·00	
		va. Opt inverted ..	..	30·00	30·00
		vb. "ZONE" inverted ..	..	15·00	15·00
		vc. "ZONE" omitted ..	..	30·00	
		vd. Optd "ZONE CANAL" ..		16·00	
76	**145**	1 c. yellow-brown (15 Apr 1925)	..	5	5
77	**146**	2 c. carmine	..	30	5
		a. Booklet pane of six ..	..	4·00	
78	**149**	5 c. deep blue	..	85	60
79	**154**	10 c. orange	..	3·00	1·75
80	**156**	12 c. plum	..	1·60	1·40
		va. "ZONE" inverted ..	..	£350	£200
81	**157**	14 c. indigo (17 June 1925) ..		1·10	95
82	**158**	15 c. grey	..	3·00	2·25
83	**161**	30 c. olive-brown ..	..	1·50	1·25
84	**162**	50 c. lilac	..	2·00	1·75
85	**163**	$1 purple-brown ..	..	12·00	7·00

1924 (1 July). *POSTAGE DUE. Postage Due stamps of United States, optd with T* **17** ("A" *with flat tops). No wmk. P* 11.

D86	D **2**	1 c. carmine ..	..	5·00	2·25
D87		2 c. deep claret ..	..	2·50	1·00
D88		10 c. deep claret ..	..	9·50	3·75

POSTAGE
DUE
(D 3)

1925 (Feb). *POSTAGE DUE. Nos.* 75, 77 *and* 79 *optd with Type D* **3**.

D89	**144**	1 c. green (R.) ..	..	3·75	90
D90	**146**	2 c. carmine (B.) ..	..	65	35
D91	**154**	10 c. orange (R.) ..	..	2·00	75
		va. Type D **3** double ..	..	21·00	
		vb. "E" of "POSTAGE" omitted ..		14·00	
		vc. Ditto and Type D **3** double ..		85·00	

1925 (24 June). *POSTAGE DUE. Postage Due stamps of United States, optd with T* **18** ("A" *with pointed tops). No wmk. P* 11.

D92	D **2**	1 c. carmine ..	..	30	20
		va. Optd "ZONE ZONE" ..	..	50·00	
D93		2 c. carmine ..	..	1·00	25
		va. Optd "ZONE ZONE" ..	..	£100	
D94		10 c. carmine ..	..	3·50	70
		va. Pair, one without opt ..	..	60·00	
		vb. Opt double ..	..	25·00	

1925–28. *Stamps of the United States, optd as T* **18**.
(i) *Flat plate printings. Perf* 11

86	**146**	2 c. carmine (26 May 1926) ..		1·25	50
		a. Booklet pane of six ..		9·00	
		va. "ZONE" omitted ..	..	42·00	30·00
		vb. Optd "ZONE CANAL" ..		12·00	
		vc. Pair, one without opt ..		60·00	
87	**147**	3 c. violet (27 June 1925) ..		20	15
		va. Optd "ZONE ZONE" ..		35·00	
88	**149**	5 c. deep blue (7 Jan 1926) ..		20	15
		va. Opt inverted		20·00	
		vb. "CANAL" inverted ..	..	15·00	
		vc. Optd "ZONE CANAL" ..		11·00	
		vd. Optd "ZONE ZONE" ..		38·00	
		ve. "CANAL" omitted ..	..	35·00	
		vf. "ZONE" omitted ..	..	40·00	
		vg. Horiz pair, one without opt ..		50·00	
		vh. Vert pair, one without opt, other opt inverted ..	..	£100	

89	**154**	10 c. orange (Aug 1925) ..		1·90	30
		va. Optd "ZONE ZONE" ..	..	£350	
		vb. "CANAL" omitted ..	..	90·00	
90	**156**	12 c. plum (Feb 1926) ..		1·00	90
		va. Optd "ZONE ZONE" ..		£350	
91	**157**	14 c. indigo (Dec 1928) ..		1·10	1·00
92	**158**	15 c. grey (Jan 1926) ..		30	25
		va. Optd "ZONE ZONE" ..		£350	
		vb. "CANAL" omitted ..	..	90·00	
93	**176**	17 c. black (R.) (5 Apr 1926) ..		25	20
		va. Optd "ZONE ZONE" ..		7·00	
		vb. "CANAL" omitted ..	..	16·00	
		vc. "ZONE" omitted ..	..	16·00	
94	**159**	20 c. carmine (5 Apr 1926) ..		30	25
		va. Optd "ZONE CANAL" ..		£600	
		vb. "CANAL" inverted ..	..	£600	
		vc. "ZONE" inverted ..	..	£600	
95	**161**	30 c. olive-brown (Dec 1926) ..		35	25
96	**162**	50 c. lilac (July 1928) ..		12·00	8·00
97	**163**	$1 purple-brown (Apr 1926) ..		5·00	2·50

(ii) *Rotary press printings. Perf* 10

98	**146**	2 c. carmine (Jan 1927) ..		1·60	60
		a. Booklet pane of six ..		15·00	
		va. "CANAL" omitted ..	..	40·00	
		vb. "ZONE" omitted ..	..	40·00	
		vc. Pair, one without opt ..		95·00	
99	**147**	3 c. violet (9 May 1927) ..		35	30
100	**154**	10 c. orange (9 May 1927) ..		85	70

1926 (4 July). *Liberty Bell issue of the United States, optd as T* **18**.

101	**177**	2 c. carmine ..	..	35	30

1927–31. *Stamps of the United States, optd as T* **18**. *Rotary press printings. Perf* 11 × 10½.

102	**144**	1 c. yellow-green (28 June 1927) ..		10	10
		va. Pair, one without opt ..		80·00	
103	**146**	2 c. carmine (I) (28 June 1927) ..		8	5
		a. Booklet pane of six ..		5·00	
		vb. Do. "CANAL" double on two bottom stamps ..		70·00	
104	**147**	3 c. violet (Feb 1931) ..		40	15
105	**149**	5 c. dark blue (13 Dec 1927) ..		75	70
106	**154**	10 c. orange (July 1930) ..		85	60

19 Gen. Gorgas

20 Gen. Goethals

21 Panama Canal under Construction

22 H. F. Hodges

23 Col. Gaillard

24 Gen. Sibert

25 Jackson Smith

26 Admiral
Rousseau

27 Col. S. B. Williamson

28 Governor
Blackburn

A 4 Panama Canal

D 5 Canal Zone
Shield

PRINTERS. This and subsequent issues were recess-printed at the Bureau of Engraving and Printing, Washington.

1928–40. *Flat plate printings. Perf* 11.

107	19	1 c. green (3 Oct 1928)	..	5	5
108	20	2 c. carmine (1 Oct 1928)	..	5	5
		a. Booklet pane of six		70	40
109	21	5 c. blue (25 June 1929)	..	15	5
110	22	10 c. orange (11 Jan 1932)	..	8	5
111	23	12 c. plum (1 July 1929)	..	15	8
112	24	14 c. blue (27 Sept 1937)	..	15	12
113	25	15 c. grey (11 Jan 1932)	..	10	5
114	26	20 c. sepia (11 Jan 1932)	..	15	5
115	27	30 c. black (15 Apr 1940)	..	20	15
116	28	50 c. mauve (1 July 1929)	..	35	8
107/116		*Set of 10*	..	1·25	65

AIR MAIL

AIR MAIL

15 CENTS 15   15   15   25 CENTS 25

(A 1)   I   II   (A 2)

FOR WELL CENTRED COPIES ADD 25%

1929–31. *AIR. Nos.* 107/8 *surch as Types* A 1/2, *in blue.*

117	19	15 c. on 1 c. green (I) (1 Apr 1929)	..	90	65
118		15 c. on 1 c. green (II) (Mar 1931)	..	7·50	4·50
119	20	25 c. on 2 c. carmine (11 Jan 1929)	..	30	25

AIR MAIL

POSTAGE DUE

-1-   10 c

(D 4)   (A 3)

FOR WELL CENTRED COPIES ADD 20%

1929–30. *POSTAGE DUE. T* 21 *surch as Type* D 4. *P* 11.

D120	1 c. on 5 c. blue (20 Mar 1930)	..	10	10
	va. "POSTAGE DUE" omitted	..	95·00	
D121	2 c. on 5 c. blue (18 Oct 1930)	..	25	12
D122	5 c. on 5 c. blue (1 Dec 1930)	..	25	20
D123	10 c. on 5 c. blue (16 Dec 1929)	..	30	20
D120/123	*Set of 4*	..	80	55

In No. D122 the bars in corners are omitted.

FOR WELL CENTRED COPIES ADD 25%

1929 (31 Dec). *AIR. Surch as Type* A 3.

124	28	10 c. on 50 c. mauve	..	1·00	75
125	20	20 c. on 2 c. carmine	..	55	15

FOR WELL CENTRED COPIES ADD 20%
(Nos. 126/166)

1931 (18 Nov)**–49.** *AIR. P* 11.

126	A 4	4 c. bright purple (3 Jan 1949)	..	8	5
127		5 c. green	..	5	5
128		6 c. brown (15 Feb 1946)	..	8	5
129		10 c. orange	..	15	5
130		15 c. blue	..	15	5
131		20 c. violet	..	20	5
132		30 c. rosy lake (15 July 1941)	..	30	12
133		40 c. yellow	..	50	15
134		$1 black	..	1·10	35
126/134		*Set of 9*	..	2·40	75

1932 (2 Jan)**–41.** *POSTAGE DUE. Flat plate printings. P* 11.

D135	D 5	1 c. claret	..	5	5
D136		2 c. claret	..	5	5
D137		5 c. claret	..	5	5
D138		10 c. claret	..	10	10
D139		15 c. claret (21 Apr 1941)	..	15	15
D135/139		*Set of 5*	..	30	30

The use of postage due stamps was discontinued in 1967.

1933 (14 Jan). *Stamps of the United States optd as T* 18. *Rotary press printings. Perf* 11 × 10½.

140	220	3 c. deep violet (No. 720)	..	25	5
		va. "CANAL" omitted	..	75·00	
		vb. "ZONE" omitted	..		
141	157	14 c. dark blue (No. 695)	..	30	15
		va. Optd "ZONE CANAL"	..	55·00	

29 Gen. Goethals

CANAL ZONE

(30)

1934 (15 Aug). *20th Anniv of Opening of Panama Canal. Flat plate printing. Perf* 11.

142	29	3 c. violet	..	5	5
		a. Booklet pane of six	..	60	50

For coil stamp, see No. 218.

1939 (1 Sept). *Stamps of the United States optd with T* 30. *Rotary press printings. Perf* 11 × 10½.

143	276	c. orange (No. 799)	..	5	5
144	278	1½ c. brown (No. 801)	..	5	5

31 Balboa (before construction)

32 Balboa (after construction)

33 Gaillard Cut (before construction)

34 Gaillard Cut (after construction)

35 Bas Obispo (before construction)

36 Bas Obispo (after construction)

A **5** Douglas Plane over Sosa Hill

A **6** Planes and Map of Central America

37 Gatun Locks (before construction)

38 Gatun Locks (after construction)

A **7** Seaplane and Scene near Fort Amador

A **8** Seaplane at Cristobal Harbour, Manzanillo Island

39 Canal Channel (before construction)

40 Canal Channel (after construction)

A **9** Seaplane over Culebra Cut

A **10** Seaplane and Palm Trees

41 Gamboa (before construction)

42 Gamboa (after construction)

(Des V. D. Westbrook)

1939 (15 July). *AIR. 10th Anniv of Canal Zone Airmail Service and 25th Anniv of Opening of Panama Canal.* P 11.

161	A 5	5 c. black	..	..	..	30	30
162	A 6	10 c. violet	..	..	..	40	30
163	A 7	15 c. brown	..	..	..	40	15
164	A 8	25 c. blue	..	..	..	1·75	1·25
165	A 9	30 c. carmine-rose	..	..	..	1·25	1·00
166	A 10	$1 green	..	..	..	4·00	3·00
161/166	*Set of 6*		..	..	..	7·00	5·50

43 Pedro Miguel Locks (before construction)

44 Pedro Miguel Locks (after construction)

OFFICIAL	**OFFICIAL**
PANAMA CANAL	**PANAMA**
	CANAL
(AO 1)	(O 1)

45 Gatun Spillway (before construction)

46 Gatun Spillway (after construction)

FOR WELL CENTRED COPIES ADD 20%

(Des V. D. Westbrook)

1939 (15 July). *25th Anniv of Opening of Panama Canal.* P 11.

145	31	1 c. yellow-green	..	..	..	8	5
146	32	2 c. carmine-rose	..	..	..	8	5
147	33	3 c. bright violet	..	..	..	8	5
148	34	5 c. blue	..	..	..	20	15
149	35	6 c. red-orange	..	..	..	30	30
150	36	7 c. black	..	..	..	30	30
151	37	8 c. green	..	..	..	45	45
152	38	10 c. bright ultramarine	..	..	..	50	35
153	39	11 c. blue-green	..	..	..	85	85
154	40	12 c. maroon	..	..	..	85	75
155	41	14 c. violet	..	..	..	1·00	1·00
156	42	15 c. olive-green	..	..	..	1·25	40
157	43	18 c. bright carmine	..	..	..	1·00	1·00
158	44	20 c. sepia	..	..	..	1·25	50
159	45	25 c. red-orange	..	..	..	2·00	1·50
160	46	50 c. brown-purple	..	..	..	2·75	50
145/160	*Set of 16*		..	..	..	11·00	7·50

1941 (31 Mar)–**47**. *AIR OFFICIAL. Optd as Type AO* **1**.
(a) Opt 19–20½ mm long

O167	A 4	5 c. green	..	..	..	40	15
O168		6 c. brown (Nov 1947)	..	..	..	65	30
		va. Optd inverted	..	..	..	£180	
O169		10 c. orange	..	..	..	60	20
O170		15 c. blue	..	..	..	75	30
O171		20 c. violet	..	..	..	95	60
O172		30 c. rosy lake (25 Mar 1942)	..	..	1·00	60
O173		40 c. yellow	..	..	..	1·50	60
O174		$1 black	..	..	..	1·75	1·00
O167/174	*Set of 8*		..	..	..	7·00	3·25

(b) Opt 17 mm long (22 Sept 1941)

O175	A 4	5 c. green	..	..	..	—	10·00
O176		10 c. orange	..	..	..	—	11·00
O177		20 c. violet	..	..	..	—	12·00
O178		30 c. rosy lake	..	..	..	—	4·50
O179		40 c. yellow	..	..	..	—	12·00

The note below No. O188 also applies here, except that Nos. O175/9 were not put on sale in unused condition.

THE WORLD CENTRE FOR FINE STAMPS IS 391 STRAND

FOR WELL CENTRED COPIES ADD 25%
(Nos. O180/8)

1941 (31 Mar). *OFFICIAL.* 5 c. optd with Type AO **1**. *Others optd as Type* O **1**.

(a) "PANAMA" 10 mm long

O180	**19**	1 c. green	..	..	..	5	5
O181	**29**	3 c. violet	..	..	..	10	5
O182	**21**	5 c. blue	..	..	..	—	2·00
O183	**22**	10 c. orange..	..	..	..	25	15
O184	**25**	15 c. grey	..	..	..	45	20
O185	**26**	20 c. sepia	..	..	..	50	25
O186	**28**	50 c. mauve..	..	..	..	1·25	60

(b) "PANAMA" 9 mm long

O187	**28**	50 c. rose-lilac	..	..	—	28·00

1947 (Feb). *Optd with Type* O **1**.

O188	**50**	5 c. blue	..	..	..	40	25

During their currency Nos. O180/8 were not on sale in unused condition and could only be obtained cancelled "Balboa Heights, Canal Zone" between two wavy lines. On 2nd Jan 1952 they were put on sale unused at face value for three months (except Nos. O182 and O187). The above used prices are for cancelled-to-order specimens, postally used copies being worth more.

47 Maj-Gen. G. W. Davis

48 Governor C. E. Magoon

49 Theodore Roosevelt

50 John F. Stevens

51 J. F. Wallace

1946–49. *P* 11.

189	**47**	c. vermilion (16 Aug 1948)	..	5	5
190	**48**	1 c. reddish brown (16 Aug 1948)	..	5	5
191	**49**	2 c. carmine (27 Oct 1949)	..	5	5
192	**50**	5 c. blue (25 Apr 1946)	..	5	5
193	**51**	25 c. yellow-green (16 Aug 1948)	..	20	12
189/193		*Set of 5*	..	..	35	25

For 5 c. coil stamp, see No. 219.

52 Coati-mundi and Barro Colorado Island

53 "Arriving at Chagres on the Atlantic Side"

54 "Up the Chagres River to Las Cruces"

55 "Las Cruces Trail to Panama"

56 "Leaving Panama for San Francisco"

1948 (17 Apr). *25th Anniv of Establishment of Canal Zone Biological Area.* P 11.

194	**52**	10 c. black	..	..	60	25

1949 (1 June). *Centenary of the Gold Rush.* P 11.

195	**53**	3 c. blue	..	..	8	5
196	**54**	6 c. violet	..	..	8	5
197	**55**	12 c. green	..	..	15	10
198	**56**	18 c. magenta..	..	..	20	15
195/198		*Set of 4*	..	..	45	30

A 11 Western Hemisphere

57 Labourers at Gaillard Cut

58 Early Train

1951 (16 July)–**63.** *AIR.*

(a) Flat plate printings. Perf 11

199	A **11**	4 c. bright purple	..	..	5	5
200		5 c. light green (16 Aug 1958)	..	8	5
201		6 c. brown .	..	..	8	5
202		7 c. yellow-olive (16 Aug 1958)	..	8	5
203		10 c. orange	..	..	12	5
204		15 c. maroon (16 Aug 1958)	..	35	20
205		21 c. pale blue	..	..	55	30
206		25 c. orange-yellow (16 Aug 1958)	..	50	15
207		31 c. carmine-lake	..	..	60	25
		va. Imperf vert (horiz pair)	..	£120	
208		35 c. deep blue (16 Aug 1958)	..	65	25
209		80 c. black	..	..	75	30

(b) Rotary press printing. Perf 10½ × 11

210	A **11**	8 c. carmine-red (7 Jan 1963)	..	8	5
199/210		*Set of 12*	..	..	3·50	1·50

1951 (15 Aug). *West Indian Panama Canal Labourers.* P 11.

211	**57**	10 c. carmine ..	..	..	25	20

1955 (28 Jan). *Centenary of Panama Railway.* P 11.

212	**58**	3 c. deep violet	..	..	8	5

59 Gorgas Hospital

60 S.S. *Ancon*

1957 (17 Nov). *75th Anniv of Gorgas Hospital.* P 11.

213	**59**	3 c. black/*bluish green*	..	..	5	5

1958 (30 Aug). *P* 11.

214	**60**	4 c. turquoise-blue	..	..	5	5

61 Roosevelt Medal and Map of Canal Zone

62 "First Class" Scout Badge

1958 (15 Nov). *Birth Centenary of Theodore Roosevelt.* P 11.

215	**61**	4 c. brown	..	..	5	5

1960 (8 Feb). *50th Anniv of American Boy Scout Movement.* P 11.

216	**62**	4 c. ochre, scarlet and deep blue	..	10	8

63
Administration
Building, Balboa

A 12 U.S. Army Caribbean
School Crest

1960 (1 Nov). *P* 11.
217 **63** 4 c. reddish purple 5 5

1960–62. *Coil stamps.* (a) *Imperf × perf* 10.
218 **29** 3 c. violet (1 Nov 1960) 5 5
219 **50** 5 c. blue (10 Feb 1962) 5 5

(b) *Perf* 10 × *imperf*
220 **63** 4 c. reddish purple (1 Nov 1960) .. 5 5

1961 (21 Nov). *AIR. P* 11.
221 A **12** 15 c. deep blue and scarlet 20 12

64 Girl Scout Badge and
Camp on Lake Gatun

A 13 Campaign Emblem and
Mosquito

1962 (12 Mar). *50th Anniv of U.S. Girl Scout Movement.*
P 11.
222 **64** 4 c. ochre, deep green & turquoise-bl 5 5

1962 (24 Sept). *AIR. Malaria Eradication. P* 11.
223 A **13** 7 c. black/yellow 10 5

65 Thatcher Ferry Bridge

A 14 Torch of Progress

1962 (12 Oct). *Opening of Thatcher Ferry Bridge. P* 11.
224 **65** 4 c. black and silver 5 5
      va. Silver (bridge) omitted £400

1963 (17 Aug). *AIR. "Alliance for Progress". P* 11.
225 A **14** 15 c. ultramarine, green and black 20 15

A 15 Cristobal

A 16 Gatun Locks

A 17 Madden Dam

A 18 Gaillard Cut

A 19 Miraflores Locks

A 20 Balboa

1964 (15 Aug). *AIR. 50th Anniv of Panama Canal. P* 11.
226 A **15** 6 c. black and emerald 8 5
227 A **16** 8 c. black and carmine-red .. 8 8
228 A **17** 15 c. black and blue 15 10
229 A **18** 20 c. black and reddish purple .. 20 15
230 A **19** 30 c. black and brown 30 20
231 A **20** 80 c. black and bistre 80 45
226/231 *Set of* 6 .. .. .. 1·40 90

A 21 Seal and Jetliner

1965 (15 July)–**71.** *AIR. P* 11.
232 A **21** 6 c. black and green 5 5
233   8 c. black and rose-red 5 5
234   10 c. black & orange (15 Mar 1968) 8 5
            a. Booklet pane of four (1970) .. 30 30
235   11 c. black & yell-ol (24 Sept 1971) 10 5
            a. Booklet pane of four 40 40
236   15 c. black and blue 10 8
237   20 c. black and reddish violet .. 15 8
238   25 c. black and light yellow-green
                 (15 Mar 1968) 20 10
239   30 c. black and light brown .. 20 12
240   80 c. black and yellow-ochre .. 60 35
232/240 *Set of* 9 .. .. .. 1·40 80

66 Goethals
Memorial, Balboa

67 Fort San Lorenzo

1968 (15 Mar)–**71.** *P* 11.
241 **66** 6 c. ultramarine and green .. 5 5
242 **67** 8 c. multicoloured (14 July 1971) .. 5 5

CAPE JUBY. See after Spanish Sahara.

Cape Verde Islands

1877. 1000 Reis = 1 Milreis
1913. 100 Centavos = 1 Escudo

The ten islands of the Cape Verde Archipelago, off the west coast of Africa, were discovered in 1456 or 1460 and became part of the Portuguese royal dominions in 1495. On 11 June 1951 they became a Portuguese Overseas Province and on 6 September 1961 their inhabitants were given full Portuguese citizenship.

PRINTERS. All the stamps of Cape Verde Islands were printed at the Mint, Lisbon, *unless otherwise stated*.

1   2   N 1

(Des and eng A. F. Gerard. Typo)

1877 (1 Jan). (a) P 12½.

1	1	5 r. black	..	70	40
2		10 r. pale orange	..	1·80	1·40
		a. Yellow	..	1·80	1·40
3		20 r. deep bistre	..	40	25
		a. Pale bistre	..	40	25
4		25 r. deep rose ..	..	40	20
		a. Pale rose ..	..	40	20
5		40 r. blue	..	7·00	5·00
		a. "MOÇAMBIQUE" (in pair)	..	£150	£150
6		50 r. green	..	8·00	4·00
		a. Yellow-green	..	8·00	4·00
7		100 r. grey-lilac	..	1·25	50
		a. Lilac	..	1·25	50
		b. Dull purple	..	1·00	45
8		200 r. deep orange	..	90	70
		a. Orange	..	85	65
9		300 r. chocolate ..	..	1·25	85
		a. Lake-brown	..	1·25	85
		b. Pale brown	..	1·00	70

(b) P 13½.

10	1	5 r. black	..	70	50
11		10 r. yellow	..	1·75	1·40
12		20 r. pale bistre	..	35	30
13		25 r. pale rose	..	1·50	85
14		40 r. blue	..	7·00	5·00
		a. "MOÇAMBIQUE" (in pair)	..	£250	£250
15		50 r. yellow-green	..	7·00	4·00
16		100 r. slate-lilac ..	..	1·00	45
17		200 r. orange	..	2·25	1·50

All values were reprinted perf 13½ in 1885 and 1905 and the 25, 40 and 50 r. were also reprinted in 1885 imperf. No. 14a also exists in the 1885 reprint.

1881–85. Colours changed. A. P 12½. B. P 13½.

				A		B	
18	1	10 r. yellow-grn (shades)		45	35	45	35
19		20 r. rosine (1885)	..	60	40	5·00	4·50
20		25 r. deep lilac (1885)	..	45	35	†	
21		40 r. orange-yellow	..	35	30	1·00	55
		a. "MOÇAMBIQUE"					
		(in pair)	..	10·00	10·00	17·00	15·00
22		50 r. blue	..	1·00	50	1·00	75
		a. Deep blue ..	..	1·00	70	1·00	75

Nos. 5a, 14a and 21a with inscription "MOÇAMBIQUE" occur on the second stamp, fifth row. To identify them as the errors, they must be se-tenant with normal stamp.

All values were reprinted in 1885 and 1905.

(Des and eng F. A. de Campos. Typo and embossed)

1886. Chalk-surfaced paper. (a) P 12½.

23	2	5 r. black	..	..	55	35
24		10 r. green	..	..	55	35
25		20 r. rosine	..	..	65	50
26		25 r. bright mauve	..		65	40
		a. Reddish violet	..		55	40
		b. Claret	..		65	40
27		40 r. chocolate ..		..	60	50
28		50 r. blue	..	..	65	50
		a. Pale blue ..	..		75	50
29		100 r. yellow-brown	..		70	45
30		200 r. lavender ..	..		1·50	1·25
31		300 r. red-orange	..		1·75	1·25
32		300 r. orange	..		1·75	1·25
23/32		Set of 9	..		6·50	5·00

(b) P 13½

33	2	5 r. black	..	..	45	30
34		10 r. green	..	..	45	30
35		20 r. rosine	..	..	75	60
36		40 r. chocolate ..	..		1·25	70

The 25, 50 and 100 r. were reprinted in 1905.

(Des and eng E. C. Azedo Gneco. Typo)

1893 (3 July). NEWSPAPER.

N37	N 1	2½ r. brown (perf 11½)	..	..	12	10
N38		2½ r. brown (perf 12½)	..	..	30	15
N39		2½ r. brown (perf 13½)	..	..	85	40

3   4

(Des and eng M. D. Neto. Typo)

1894–95. Chalk-surfaced paper, or enamel-surfaced paper (E).

(a) P 11½

37	3	5 r. pale orange (5.9.94)	..	..	20	15
38		10 r. rosy mauve (5.9.94)	..	..	25	20
39		15 r. red-brown (5.9.94)	..	..	45	35
40		20 r. lilac (5.9.94)	..	..	45	35
41		25 r. green	..	..	45	35
42		50 r. pale blue ..	..	..	45	35
43		80 r. pale green (E) (6.5.95)	..		1·25	1·10
44		100 r. brown/buff (6.5.95)	..		85	45
45		150 r. carmine/rose (6.5.95)	..		5·00	3·00
46		300 r. blue/bright buff (6.5.95)	..		2·25	1·25
37/46		Set of 10	..		10·00	6·50

(b) P 12½

47	3	15 r. red-brown	..	..	15·00	9·00
48		25 r. green	..	..	65	50
49		50 r. pale blue ..	..			
50		50 r. pale blue (E)	..			
51		75 r. carmine (6.5.95)	..		1·00	85
52		100 r. brown/buff	..		2·75	1·75
53		150 r. carmine/rose	..		20·00	15·00
54		200 r. blue/blue ..	..		15·00	10·00

(c) P 13½

55	3	50 r. pale blue (E)	..		75	30
56		75 r. carmine	..		3·50	2·25
57		80 r. pale green (E)	..		3·00	1·75
58		150 r. carmine/rose	..		2·40	1·75
59		200 r. blue/blue ..	..		2·00	1·50

(Des and eng E. Mouchon. Typo)

1898 (1 July)–**1901.** *Name and numerals in black; on 500 r. in carmine. P* 11½.

60	4	2½ r. pale grey . .	. .	. .	5	5
61		5 r. orange-yellow	. .	. .	5	5
		a. Orange-red	. .	. .	5	5
62		10 r. green . .	. .	. .	5	5
63		15 r. chocolate . .	. .	. .	40	20
64		20 r. deep lilac . .	. .	. .	15	10
65		25 r. blue-green	. .	. .	35	20
		a. Perf 12½	. .	. .	7·00	2·50
66		50 r. blue	. .	. .	35	20
67		75 r. carmine	. .	. .	70	50
68		80 r. mauve	. .	. .	75	45
69		100 r. blue/blue . .	. .	. .	30	20
70		150 r. purple-brown/straw		. .	70	50
71		200 r. purple/flesh	. .	. .	40	30
72		300 r. blue/pink . .	. .	. .	75	50
73		500 r. black/azure (1901)		. .	75	50
74		700 r. mauve/yellow (1901)		. .	2·00	1·50
60/74		Set of 15	. .	. .	7·00	4·75

1902 (1 Dec). *T* **2, 3** *and* N **1** *surch as Type A of Angola.*

75	2	65 r. on 5 r. (12½)	. .	. .	70	60
76		65 r. on 200 r. (12½) . .		. .	70	60
77		65 r. on 300 r. (12½) . .		. .	70	60
78	3	65 r. on 10 r. (11½)	. .	. .	70	55
79		65 r. on 20 r. (11½)	. .	. .	70	60
80		65 r. on 100 r. (11½)	. .	. .	1·10	75
81		65 r. on 100 r. (12½)	. .	. .	2·40	1·90
82	2	115 r. on 10 r. (12½)	. .	. .	60	50
83		115 r. on 20 r. (12½)	. .	. .	60	50
84		115 r. on 20 r. (13½)	. .	. .	4·00	3·50
85	3	115 r. on 5 r. (11½)	. .	. .	55	45
86		115 r. on 25 r. (11½)	. .	. .	2·25	1·10
87		115 r. on 25 r. (12½)	. .	. .	50	40
88		115 r. on 150 r. (11½)	. .	. .	1·00	80
89		115 r. on 150 r. (13½)	. .	. .	3·00	2·50
90	2	130 r. on 50 r. blue (12½)		. .	60	50
91		130 r. on 50 r. pale blue (12½)		. .	60	50
92		130 r. on 100 r. (12½)	. .	. .	60	50
93	3	130 r. on 75 r. (12½)	. .	. .	50	40
94		130 r. on 75 r. (13½)	. .	. .	6·00	4·00
95		130 r. on 80 r. (E) (11½)		. .	55	50
96		130 r. on 80 r. (E) (13½)		. .	55	50
97		130 r. on 200 r. (13½)	. .	. .	55	50
98	2	400 r. on 25 r. (12½)	. .	. .	45	40
99		400 r. on 40 r. (12½)	. .	. .	55	50
100		400 r. on 40 r. (13½)	. .	. .	4·00	3·50
101	3	400 r. on 50 r. (11½)	. .	. .	70	55
102		400 r. on 50 r. (13½)	. .	. .	8·00	6·00
103		400 r. on 300 r. (11½)	. .	. .	25	20
104	N 1	400 r. on 2½ r. (11½)	. .	. .	25	20
105		400 r. on 2½ r. (12½)	. .	. .	7·00	5·00
106		400 r. on 2½ r. (13½)	. .	. .	25	20

The 65/5, 400/25, 400/40 and 400/50 r. were reprinted in 1905.

1902 (1 Dec)–**03.** *T* **4** *opt with Type B of Angola.*

107	4	15 r. chocolate . .	. .	. .	20	20
108		25 r. blue-green (11½)	. .	. .	20	20
109		50 r. blue (1.1.03)	. .	. .	20	20
110		75 r. carmine (1.1.03)	. .	. .	40	35
107/110		Set of 4	. .	. .	90	85

1903 (1 Jan–Oct). *Colours changed. Name and value in black. P* 11½.

111	4	15 r. dull green (15.1) . .		. .	20	12
112		25 r. carmine (15.10)	. .	. .	12	8
113		50 r. brown (15.6)	. .	. .	40	30
114		65 r. dull blue . .	. .	. .	1·25	1·10
115		75 r. dull purple (15.6)	. .	. .	30	25
116		115 r. orange-brown/pink		. .	75	65
117		130 r. sepia/cream	. .	. .	75	65
118		400 r. dull blue/straw	. .	. .	75	65
111/118		Set of 8	. .	. .	4·00	3·25

(Des and eng J. S. de Carvalho e Silva. Typo)

1904 (1 Aug). *POSTAGE DUE. Name and value in black. P* 11½.

D119	D 1	5 r. yellow-green	. .	. .	5	5
D120		10 r. slate . .	. .	. .	5	5
D121		20 r. brown	. .	. .	8	5
D122		30 r. orange	. .	. .	8	5
D123		50 r. deep brown . .	. .	. .	8	5
D124		60 r. pale red-brown	. .	. .	20	15
D125		100 r. mauve	. .	. .	12	10
D126		130 r. blue . .	. .	. .	12	10
D127		200 r. carmine	. .	. .	12	10
D128		500 r. deep lilac	. .	. .	30	25
D119/128		Set of 10	. .	. .	1·00	85

1905 (1 July). *No. 114 surch with Type F of Angola.*

119	4	50 r. on 65 r. dull blue . .		. .	40	35

1911 (20 Aug). *T* **4** *optd with T* **50** *of Portugal, in red or green (G.).*

120	4	2½ r. pale grey	. .	. .	8	8
121		5 r. orange-red	. .	. .	8	8
122		10 r. green	. .	. .	15	10
123		15 r. dull green	. .	. .	10	8
124		20 r. deep lilac	. .	. .	15	10
125		25 r. carmine (G.)	. .	. .	15	10
126		50 r. brown	. .	. .	65	55
127		75 r. dull purple	. .	. .	20	10
128		100 r. blue/blue	. .	. .	20	10
129		115 r. orange-brown/pink		. .	12	10
		a. Orange-brown/buff	. .	. .	4·00	4·00
130		130 r. sepia/cream	. .	. .	12	10
131		200 r. purple/flesh	. .	. .	60	40
132		400 r. dull blue/straw	. .	. .	25	12
133		500 r. black/azure	. .	. .	25	12
134		700 r. mauve/yellow	. .	. .	25	15
120/134		Set of 15	. .	. .	3·00	2·00

1911. *POSTAGE DUE. Optd with T* **50** *of Portugal, in red or green (G.).*

D135	D 1	5 r. yellow-green	. .	. .	5	5
		a. Chalk-surfaced paper		. .	5	5
D136		10 r. slate . .	. .	. .	5	5
D137		20 r. brown	. .	. .	5	5
D138		30 r. orange	. .	. .	5	5
D139		50 r. deep brown	. .	. .	5	5
D140		60 r. pale red-brown	. .	. .	5	5
D141		100 r. mauve	. .	. .	5	5
D142		130 r. blue . .	. .	. .	5	5
D143		200 r. carmine (G.)	. .	. .	5	5
D144		500 r. deep lilac	. .	. .	8	5
D135/144		Set of 10	. .	. .	30	25

(Des and eng D. A. do Rego. Typo)

1912. *T* **5** *optd with T* **50** *of Portugal, in red or green (G.).*

(a) P 11½

135	5	2½ r. lilac	. .	. .	5	5
136		5 r. black	. .	. .	5	5
137		10 r. grey-green	. .	. .	8	8
138		20 r. rose-red (G.)	. .	. .	25	20
139		25 r. chocolate (13 Feb)		. .	12	8
140		50 r. indigo-blue (13 Feb)		. .	50	40
141		75 r. yellow-brown	. .	. .	12	10
142		100 r. brown/green	. .	. .	12	10
143		200 r. deep green/salmon		. .	15	10
144		300 r. black/azure	. .	. .	15	10

(b) P 14×15

145	5	400 r. blue and black	. .	. .	30	25
146		500 r. chocolate and olive		. .	30	25
135/146		Set of 12	. .	. .	1·90	1·50

D 1	5	(6)	(7)

PORTEADO
CABO VERDE
5
REIS
RECEBER

CABO VERDE
5 REIS 5

REPUBLICA
CABO VERDE
¼   C.

REPUBLICA

1913 (13 Feb). *New Currency. Vasco da Gama issues surch as T 6.*

(i) Africa (General Issues)

147	¼ c. on 2½ r. blue-green..		..	..	20	15
148	½ c. on 5 r. vermilion	..	..	..	20	15
149	1 c. on 10 r. dull purple		..	..	20	15
150	2½ c. on 25 r. yellow-green		..	..	20	15
151	5 c. on 50 r. deep blue ..		..	..	30	20
152	7½ c. on 75 r. chocolate ..		..	..	40	30
153	10 c. on 100 r. bistre-brown		..	..	30	20
154	15 c. on 150 r. ochre		..	..	40	30
147/154	*Set of 8*	..	..	..	2·00	1·40

(ii) Macao

155	¼ c. on ½ a. blue-green		..	..	25	20
156	½ c. on 1 a. vermilion	..	..	..	25	20
157	1 c. on 2 a. dull purple ..		..	..	25	20
158	2½ c. on 4 a. yellow-green		..	..	25	20
159	5 c. on 8 a. deep blue ..		..	..	70	60
160	7½ c. on 12 a. chocolate ..		..	..	55	35
161	10 c. on 16 a. bistre-brown		..	..	30	25
162	15 c. on 24 a. ochre		..	..	50	40
155/162	*Set of 8*	..	..	..	2·75	2·10

(iii) Timor

163	¼ c. on ½ a. blue-green ..		..	..	25	15
164	½ c. on 1 a. vermilion ..		..	..	25	15
165	1 c. on 2 a. dull purple ..		..	..	25	15
166	2½ c. on 4 a. yellow-green		..	..	25	15
167	5 c. on 8 a. deep blue ..		..	..	60	45
168	7½ c. on 12 a. chocolate ..		..	..	60	45
169	10 c. on 16 a. bistre-brown		..	..	30	25
170	15 c. on 24 a. ochre		..	..	40	30
163/170	*Set of 8*	..	..	..	2·50	1·75

1913 (3 Nov)**–14**. *Nos. 110 and 95/6 optd locally with T 7.*

171	**4**	75 r. carmine (G.) (14.1.14)	..	40	35
		a. Opt double (G.+R.)	..	7·00	6·00
172	**3**	130 r. on 80 r. (E) (11½) (R.) (3.11.13)		35	30
173		130 r. on 80 r. (E) (13½) (R.)	..	35	30

The 115 r. on 150 r. and 130 r. on 200 r. were never issued.

8 Ceres

(Des C. Fernandes. Eng J. S. de Carvalho e Silva. Typo)

1914 (1 Sept)**–16**. *Name and value in black. Chalk-surfaced paper or enamel-surfaced paper (E). P 15×14.*

174	**8**	¼ c. brown-olive	..	..	12	8
175		¼ c. brown-olive (E) (1916)	..	..	5	5
176		½ c. black	..	..	12	8
177		1 c. deep green	..	..	12	8
178		1½ c. chocolate..	..	..	12	8
179		2 c. carmine	..	..	12	8
180		2½ c. violet	..	..	8	5
181		5 c. deep blue	..	..	12	10
182		5 c. deep blue (E) (1916)	..	..	10	8
183		7½ c. yellow-brown	..	..	12	10
184		8 c. slate	..	..	15	12
185		10 c. brown-red	..	..	25	15
186		15 c. claret	..	..	65	55
187		20 c. yellow-green	..	..	20	10
188		30 c. chocolate/green ..		..	50	40
189		40 c. brown/rose	..	..	45	30
190		50 c. orange/salmon ..		..	35	30
191		1 E. deep green/azure	..	..	35	30
174/191	*Set of 16*	..	..	..	3·25	2·50

See also Nos. 209/51.

1915. *Provisionals of 1902 optd with T 50 of Portugal, in red.*

192	**3**	115 r. on 5 r. (11½)	..	15	12
		a. Surch and opt inverted ..		9·00	9·00
193	**2**	115 r. on 10 r. (12½)	..	40	35
194		115 r. on 10 r. (13½)	..	3·50	3·00
195		115 r. on 20 r. (12½)	..	45	30
196		115 r. on 20 r. (13½)	..	3·50	3·00
197	**3**	115 r. on 25 r. (11½)	..	3·75	3·25
198		115 r. on 25 r. (12½)	..	35	35
199		115 r. on 150 r. (11½)	..	30	20
200		115 r. on 150 r. (13½)	..	15	12

201	**2**	130 r. on 50 r. (12½)	..	..	35	30
202	**3**	130 r. on 75 r. (12½)	..	..	30	25
203		130 r. on 75 r. (13½)	..	..	25	20
204		130 r. on 80 r. (E) (11½)	..	..	25	15
205		130 r. on 80 r. (E) (13½)	..	..	30	25
206	**2**	130 r. on 100 r. (12½)	..	..	20	15
207	**3**	130 r. on 200 r. (12½)	..	..	10·00	6·00
208		130 r. on 200 r. (13½)	..	..	20	15

1920–26. *Name and value in black.*

(a) *Unsurfaced paper (thick, medium or thin). P 15×14 (1920–22)*

209	**8**	¼ c. brown-olive	..	..	5	5
210		½ c. black	..	..	5	5
211		1 c. deep blue-green	..	..	30	25
		a. Pale yellow-green (1921)..		..	5	5
212		1½ c. chocolate..	..	..	5	5
213		2 c. carmine	..	..	5	5
214		2½ c. mauve	..	..	5	5
215		3 c. orange (1922)	..	..	5	5
216		4 c. carmine (1922)	..	..	5	5
217		12 c. blue-green (1922)	..	..	10	8
218		15 c. dull rose (1921)	..	..	20	15

(b) *Unsurfaced paper. P 12×11½ (1921–26)*

219	**8**	¼ c. brown-olive	..	..	5	5
220		½ c. black	..	..	5	5
221		1 c. yellow-green	..	..	5	5
222		1½ c. chocolate..	..	..	5	5
223		2 c. carmine	..	..	5	5
224		2 c. drab (1926)	..	..	5	5
225		2½ c. mauve	..	..	5	5
226		3 c. orange (1922)	..	..	8	8
227		4 c. carmine (1922)	..	..	5	5
228		4½ c. drab (1922)	..	..	5	5
229		5 c. pale dull blue	..	..	5	5
230		6 c. mauve (1922)	..	..	5	5
231		7 c. pale blue (1922)	..	..	5	5
232		7½ c. yellow-brown	..	..	5	5
233		8 c. slate	..	..	5	5
234		10 c. brown-red	..	..	5	5
235		12 c. blue-green (1922)	..	..	8	8
236		15 c. dull rose ..		..	5	5
237		20 c. yellow-green	..	..	5	5
238		24 c. ultramarine (1926)	..	..	12	10
239		25 c. chocolate (1926)	..	..	12	10
240		30 c. deep grey-green (1922)	..	..	8	8
241		40 c. turquoise (1922)	..	..	8	5
242		50 c. mauve (1926)	..	..	12	10
243		60 c. deep blue (1922)	..	..	10	10
244		60 c. carmine (1926)	..	..	12	10
245		80 c. bright rosine (1922)	..	..	30	12

(c) *Glazed paper. P 12×11½ (1922–26)*

246	**8**	1 E. carmine-pink	..	..	50	30
247		1 E. blue (1926)	..	..	30	15
248		2 E. deep purple	..	..	40	30
249		5 E. buff (1926)	..	..	60	55
250		10 E. pink (1926)	..	..	1·25	1·00
251		20 E. emerald-green (1926)	..	..	2·75	2·25
219/51	*Set of 33*	..	..	..	6·50	5·00

1921. *POSTAGE DUE. Value in centavos. P 11½.*

D252	D 1	½ c. pale yellow-green	..	..	5	5
D253		1 c. slate	..	..	5	5
D254		2 c. deep red-brown	..	..	5	5
D255		3 c. pale orange	..	..	5	5
D256		5 c. grey-brown	..	..	5	5
D257		6 c. pale brown	..	..	5	5
D258		10 c. mauve	..	..	5	5
D259		13 c. blue	..	..	5	5
D260		20 c. carmine	..	..	5	5
D261		50 c. lilac-grey	..	..	5	5
D252/261	*Set of 10*	..	..	..	25	20

Sets may be made on soft smooth paper and thin coarse paper, the shades differing in the latter, particularly in the 3 c., which is yellow.

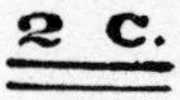

(9)

(10)

1921 (3 Feb). (a) Nos. 153/4 surch locally as T **9**.

252	2 c. on 15 c. on 150 r. bistre-brown	..	25	20
253	4 c. on 10 c. on 100 r. ochre	..	25	25
	a. Error. Surch on No. 161	..	..	12·00	12·00

(b) No. 69 surch locally with T **10**

254	**4**	6 c. on 100 r. blue/*blue*	..	20	15

CABO VERDE

CORREIOS

(12)	**(13)**

1921 (3 Feb). Type C **1** of Portuguese Colonies (General Issues) surch locally as T **12**, or optd only.

A. P 15×14. B. P 11½

				A		B	
255	C **1**	¼ c. on 1 c. green	..	8	5	15	15
256		½ c. on 1 c. green	..	8	8	15	15
257		1 c. green	..	8	8	15	15

Nos. 255/7B also exist on enamel-surfaced paper (same prices).

1922 (Apr). Surch locally with T **13** and bars cancelling previous surch. (a) Nos. 172/3.

258	**3**	4 c. on 130 r. on 80 r. (E) (11½) ..	..	20	15
259		4 c. on 130 r. on 80 r. (E) (13½) ..	..	30	30

(b) Nos. 202/5 and 207/8

260	**3**	4 c. on 130 r. on 75 r. (12½)	..	15	12
261		4 c. on 130 r. on 75 r. (13½)	..	60	60
262		4 c. on 130 r. on 80 r. (E) (11½)	..	20	15
263		4 c. on 130 r. on 80 r. (E) (13½)	..	30	30
264		4 c. on 130 r. on 200 r. (12½)	..	3·00	2·75
265		4 c. on 130 r. on 200 r. (13½)	..	12	12

One stamp in each sheet has "$" sign smaller.

CHARITY TAX STAMPS. The notes above No. C343 of Angola also apply to Charity Tax stamps of Cape Verde Islands.

1925 (8 May). CHARITY TAX. Marquis de Pombal issue of Portugal inscr "CABO VERDE".

C266	C **6**	15 c. violet ..	..	10	8
C267	C **7**	15 c. violet ..	..	10	8
C268	C **8**	15 c. violet ..	..	10	8

Nos. C266/8 were in use from 8th to 13th October, 1925 and from 5th to 15th May of 1926 to 1929.

1925 (8 May). POSTAGE DUE. As Nos. C266/8 optd "MULTA".

D266	C **6**	30 c. dull violet	..	8	8
D267	C **7**	30 c. dull violet	..	8	8
D268	C **8**	30 c. dull violet	..	8	8

1925 (17 June). Provisionals of 1902 surch as T **14** of Angola.

266	N **1**	40 c. on 400 r. on 2½ r. (11½)	..	15	12
267		40 c. on 400 r. on 2½ r. (13½)	..	12	10
268	**3**	40 c. on 400 r. on 300 r. (11½)	..	12	10

1931 (Nov). No. 245 surch as T **16** of Angola.

269	**8**	70 c. on 80 c. bright rosine	..	20	15

1934 (1 May). Ceres type of Angola but inscr "CABO VERDE". W **18** of Angola. P 12×11½.

270	**17**	1 c. brown ..	..	5	5
271		5 c. sepia ..	..	5	5
272		10 c. mauve ..	..	5	5
273		15 c. black ..	..	5	5
274		20 c. grey ..	..	5	5
275		30 c. blue-green ..	..	5	5
276		40 c. vermilion ..	..	5	5
277		45 c. turquoise ..	..	10	10
278		50 c. cinnamon ..	..	10	8
279		60 c. olive-green ..	..	10	8
280		70 c. red-brown ..	..	10	8
281		80 c. emerald ..	..	10	8
282		85 c. carmine ..	..	25	20
283		1 E. claret ..	..	20	5
284		1 E. 40, blue ..	..	20	20
285		2 E. mauve ..	..	20	15
286		5 E. yellow-green ..	..	65	40
287		10 E. bistre-brown ..	..	1·25	70
288		20 E. orange ..	..	2·25	1·75
270/288		Set of 19	..	5·00	3·50

1938. 1938 pictorial issue of Angola, but inscr "CABO VERDE". Name and value in black. P 13½×13.

(a) POSTAGE

289	**22**	1 c. grey-olive	..	..	5	5
290		5 c. orange-brown	..	..	5	5
291		10 c. carmine ..	..	..	5	5
292		15 c. brown-purple	..	..	15	10
293		20 c. slate	..	..	10	8
294	**23**	30 c. bright purple	..	..	10	8
295		35 c. emerald-green	..	..	10	8
296		40 c. brown ..	..	..	10	8
297		50 c. magenta	..	..	5	8
298	**24**	60 c. grey-black	..	..	10	8
299		70 c. slate-violet	..	..	10	8
300		80 c. orange	..	..	10	8
301		1 E. scarlet	..	..	10	8
302	**25**	1 E. 75, blue ..	..	..	20	12
303		2 E. blue-green	..	..	20	12
304		5 E. olive-green	..	..	50	20
305	**26**	10 E. ultramarine	..	..	80	35
306		20 E. red-brown	..	..	2·10	55
289/306		Set of 18	..	..	4·50	2·00

(b) AIR

307	**27**	10 c. scarlet	..	..	12	10
308		20 c. bright violet	..	..	12	10
309		50 c. orange	..	..	12	15
310		1 E. bright blue	..	..	12	10
311		2 E. brown-lake	..	..	25	15
312		3 E. blue-green	..	..	30	20
313		5 E. red-brown	..	..	45	25
314		9 E. carmine ..	..	..	90	55
315		10 E. magenta	..	..	1·10	55
307/315		Set of 9	..	..	3·00	1·90

14 Route of President's Tour	**(15)**	C **1** St. Isabel

(Des Zimbarra. Litho)

1939 (23 June). Pres. Carmona's Second Colonial Tour. P 11½×12.

316	**14**	80 c. violet/*mauve* ..	..	60	40
317		1 E. 75, blue/*pale blue*	..	1·10	80
318		20 E. chocolate/*cream*	..	8·00	3·50

1948. Nos. 276 and 294 surch locally as T **15**.

319	**23**	10 c. on 30 c. bright purple	..	15	12
		a. Surch inverted ..	..	4·00	4·00
320	**17**	25 c. on 40 c. vermilion	..	15	12

(Des A. de Sousa. Litho Litografia Nacional, Oporto)

1948. CHARITY TAX. P 11, 11½.

C321	C **1**	50 c. deep bluish green	..	30	25
C322		1 E. brown-red	..	35	30

See also Nos. C369/70.

16 Machado Point, St. Vincent	**17** Ribeira Brava, St. Nicholas

(Des M. Jorge (5 c., 20 E.), A. de Sousa (others). Litho Litografia Nacional, Oporto)

1948 (1 Oct). *As T* **16/17** *(views).* P 14.
321	5 c. brown-purple and bistre	..	..	10	8
322	10 c. blackish green and pale green	..	10	8
323	50 c. magenta and lilac ..		..	15	10
324	1 E. reddish purple	..	..	55	15
325	1 E. 75, ultramarine and turquoise	..	60	35
326	2 E. purple-brown and ochre	..	..	1·25	50
327	5 E. olive-green and lemon	..	..	2·50	1·25
328	10 E. scarlet and orange	..	..	4·25	2·75
329	20 E. dull violet and buff	..	..	7·00	4·00
321/329	*Set of 9*	..	..	15·00	8·00

Designs: *Vert*—10 c. Town of Ribeira Grande. *Horiz*—1 E. Port, St. Vincent; 1 E. 75, Mindelo; 2 E. João de Evora beach, St. Vincent; 5 E. St. Vincent, Mindelo; 10 E. Volcano, Fire Island; 20 E. Paul.

1948 (Oct). *Honouring the Statue of Our Lady of Fatima. As T* **34** *of Angola.*
330   50 c. deep blue ..   ..   ..   2·25   1·75

1949 (Oct). *75th Anniv of U.P.U. As T* **39** *of Angola.*
331   1 E. bright magenta ..   ..   ..   1·50   85

1950 (May). *Holy Year. As T* **41/2** *of Angola.*
332   1 E. red-brown   10   8
333   2 E. greenish blue   45   40

$10

$10

═
(18)

✖
(19)

1951 (21 May). *Surch as T* **18.**
334	23	10 c. on 35 c. emerald-green ..	..	10	10
335	24	20 c. on 70 c. slate-violet	..	..	15	12
336		40 c. on 70 c. slate-violet	..	..	15	12
337		50 c. on 80 c. orange ..	..	..	15	12
338	25	1 E. on 1 E. 75, blue ..	..	15	12
339	26	2 E. on 10 E. ultramarine	..	..	45	35
		a. Error. 1 E. on 10 E.	..	..	15·00	7·00

1951 (Oct). *Termination of Holy Year. As T* **44** *of Angola.*
340   2 E. deep violet and mauve   20   15
See note after No. 482 of Angola.

1952 (25 Jan). *No. 302 surch locally as T* **19.**
341	25	10 c. on 1 E. 75 blue ..	..	..	30	25
342		20 c. on 1 E. 75 blue ..	..	..	30	25
343		50 c. on 1 E. 75 blue ..	..	..	80	80
344		1 E. on 1 E. 75 blue ..	..	..	5	5
345		1 E. 50 on 1 E. 75 blue	..	..	5	5

20 Map, *c.* 1471   **21** V. Dias and G. de Cintra

(Des R. Preto Pacheco. Litho Litografia Nacional, Oporto)

1952 (9 May). *Portuguese Navigators. T* **20/21** *and similar horiz designs. Multicoloured.* P 14.
346	5 c. Type **20**	..	..	..	5	5
	a. Green (islands etc) omitted	..		
347	10 c. Type **21**	..	..	..	5	5
348	30 c. D. Afonso and A. Fernandes	..	5	5
349	50 c. Lançarote and S. da Costa	..	5	5
350	1 E. D. Gomes and A. da Nola ..	..	5	5
351	2 E. Prince Fernando and Prince Henry		
	the Navigator	..	..	..	25	5
352	3 E. A. Gonçalves and D. Dias ..	..	60	12
353	5 E. A. Gonçalves Baldaia & J. Fernandes	..	..	..	50	12

354	10 E. D. Eanes da Grã and A. de Freitas	1·10	40
355	20 E. Map, 1502 ..	..	..	..	2·10	50
346/355	*Set of 10*	..	..	..	4·25	1·25

1952. *POSTAGE DUE. As* 1952 *issue of Angola.*
D356	10 c. brown and olive-grey	..	..	5	5
D357	30 c. black, blue and mauve	..	5	5
D358	50 c. slate-blue, green and yellow	..	5	5
D359	1 E. deep blue and pale blue ..	..	5	5
D360	2 E. red-brown and yellow-orange	..	8	5
D361	5 E. olive-green and olive-grey	..	15	15
D356/361	*Set of 6*	..	..	..	30	25

22 Doctor giving Injection   **23** Façade of Monastery

(Des A. de Sousa. Litho)

1952 (June). *First Tropical Medicine Congress, Lisbon.* P 13½.
356   **22**   20 c. black and grey-green   8   5

1953 (Jan). *Missionary Art Exhibition. Litho.* P 13½.
357   **23**   10 c. brown and yellow-olive   ..   5   5
358   50 c. violet and salmon   5   5
359   1 E. deep green and orange   8   5

1953 (Oct). *Centenary of First Portuguese Postage Stamps. As T* **48** *of Angola.*
360   50 c. grey and pale reddish purple   ..   20   15

1954. *Fourth Centenary of São Paulo. As T* **49** *of Angola.*
361   1 E. black, grey, green and buff   5   5

24 Arms of Cape Verde Islands and Portuguese Guinea   **25** Arms of Praia

(Des J. de Moura. Litho)

1955 (14 Apr). *Presidential Visit.* P 13½.
362   **24**   1 E. multicoloured   5   5
363   1 E. 60, multicoloured   5   5

1958 (14 June). *Centenary of City of Praia. Litho.* P 11½×12.
364   **25**   1 E. multicoloured/*pale yellow*   ..   5   5
365   2 E. 50, multicoloured/*pale salmon* ..   10   5

1958 (July). *Brussels International Exhibition. As T* **55** *of Angola. Multicoloured design; background colour given.*
366   2 E. blue   10   5

1958 (5 Sept). *Sixth International Congress of Tropical Medicine. As T* **56** *of Angola.*
367   3 E. yellow, green, red, brn & pale lilac   60   30
Design:—*Aloë vera* (plant).

1959. *CHARITY TAX. No. C322, surch.*
C368   C 1   50 c. on 1 E. brown-red   20   15

1959. *CHARITY TAX. Colours changed.* P 14.
C369   C 1   50 c. cerise   12   10
C370   1 E. blue   12   10

26 Prince Henry the Navigator

27 Antonio da Nola

30 Militia Regiment Drummer, 1806

C 2 St. Isabel

C 3

(Des J. de Moura. Litho)

1960 (29 June). *Fifth Centenary of Death of Prince Henry the Navigator. P* 13×13½.
368 **26** 2 E. multicoloured 8 5

(Des J. de Moura. Litho Litografia Nacional, Oporto)

1960 (30 Sept). *Fifth Centenary of Colonisation of Cape Verde Islands. T* **27** *and similar vert design. P* 14½.
369 1 E. multicoloured 5 5
370 2 E. 50, multicoloured (Diogo Gomes) .. 10 8

28 "Education"

29 Arms of Praia

(Des Neves and Sousa. Litho Litografia Maia, Oporto)

1960 (Oct). *Tenth Anniv of African Technical Co-operation Commission. P* 14½.
371 **28** 2 E. 50, multicoloured 10 5

(Des J. de Moura. Photo)

1961 (July). *Urban Arms. Various vert designs as T* **29**. *Arms multicoloured; inscriptions red and green; background colours given. P* 13½.
372 5 c. orange-buff 5 5
373 15 c. light blue (Nova Sintra) 5 5
374 20 c. light yellow (Riberia Brava) .. 5 5
375 30 c. lilac (Assomada) 5 5
376 1 E. light green (Maio) 10 5
377 2 E. pale greenish yellow (Mindelo) .. 10 5
378 2 E. 50, pink (Santa Maria) 10 5
379 3 E. light brown (Pombas) 20 5
380 5 E. cobalt (Sal-Rei) 15 5
381 7 E. 50, pale yellow-olive (Tarrafal) .. 20 12
382 15 E. pale reddish lilac (Maria Pia) .. 45 20
383 30 E. pale yellow (San Felipe) 85 40
372/383 *Set of 12* .. .. 2·10 1·00

1962 (18 Jan). *Sports. As T* **62** *of Angola. Multicoloured. P* 13.
384 50 c. Throwing the javelin 5 5
385 1 E. Discus thrower 5 5
386 1 E. 50, Batsman (cricket) 5 5
387 2 E. 50, Boxing 8 5
388 4 E. 50, Hurdler.. .. .. .. 8 8
389 12 E. 50, Golfers.. .. .. .. 20 15
384/389 *Set of 6* 45 35

1962. *Malaria Eradication. As T* **63** *of Angola.*
390 2 E. 50, multicoloured (*A. pretoriensis*) .. 12 5

1963 (8 Oct). *Tenth Anniv of T.A.P. Airline. As T* **69** *of Angola.*
391 2 E. 50, multicoloured 10 5

1964 (16 May). *Centenary of National Overseas Bank. As T* **71** *of Angola but with portrait of J. da S. M. Leal.*
392 1 E. 50, multicoloured 8 5

1965 (17 May). *I.T.U. Centenary. As T* **73** *of Angola.*
393 2 E. 50, multicoloured 25 15

(Des A. Cutileiro. Litho Litografia Nacional, Oporto)

1965 (1 Dec). *Portuguese Military Uniforms. T* **30** *and similar vert designs. Multicoloured. P* 13½.
394 50 c. Type **30** 5 5
395 1 E. Militiaman, 1806 .. .. .. 8 5
396 1 E. 50, Infantry grenadiers officer, 1833 .. .. 10 5
397 2 E. 50, Infantry grenadier, 1833 .. 12 5
398 3 E. Cavalry officer, 1834 .. .. 12 8
399 4 E. Infantry grenadier, 1835 .. .. 20 10
400 5 E. Artillery officer, 1848 .. .. 20 12
401 10 E. Infantry drum-major, 1856 .. 40 30
394/401 *Set of 8* .. .. 1·10 70

1966 (28 May). *40th Anniv of National Revolution. As T* **77** *of Angola but design shows local buildings.*
402 1 E. Dr. A. Moreira's Academy and Public Assistance Building 5 5

1967 (31 Jan). *Centenary of Military Naval Association. As T* **79** *of Angola but different designs.*
403 1 E. F. da Costa and gunboat *Mandovy* 5 5
404 1 E. 50, C. Araujo and minesweeper *Augusto Castilho* 8 5

1967 (13 May). *50th Anniv of the Fatima Apparitions. Vert design as T* **80** *of Angola.*
405 1 E. Image of Virgin Mary 5 5

(Des A. de Sousa. Litho Litografia Nacional, Oporto)

1967–72. *CHARITY TAX. P* 14½.
C406 **C 2** 30 c. multicoloured 5 5
C407 50 c. mult (bright purple panel) .. 10 10
C408 50 c. mult (red panel) (1972) .. 5 5
C409 1 E. multicoloured (brown panel) 15 15
C410 1 E. mult (purple panel) (1972) .. 5 5
C406/410 *Set of 5* 35 35
Nos. C408 and C410 are in different colour combinations from the 1967 issue, the most noticeable difference being the "ASSISTENCIA" panel at the foot of the design.

(Background litho. Opt typo by José Santos, Cape Verde)

1968–71. *CHARITY TAX. Pharmaceutical Tax stamps surch as in Type* **C 3**. *P* 12.
C411 **C 3** 50 c. on 1 c. black, yellow-orange and pale blue-green (1969) .. 70 40
  a. Blue surch (1970) 10 8
  b. Green surch (1971) 5 5
C412 50 c. on 2 c. black, yellow-orange and pale blue-green (1969) .. 70 40
  a. Surch inverted .. .. .. 3·00 3·00
  b. Blue surch (1970) 10 8
  c. Green surch (1971) 5 5
C413 50 c. on 3 c. black, yellow-orange and pale blue-green (G.) (1971) 5 5
C414 50 c. on 5 c. black, yellow-orange and pale blue-green (G.) (1971) 5 5
C415 50 c. on 10 c. black, yellow-orange and pale blue-green (G.) (1971) 5 5
C416 1 E. on 1 c. black, yellow-orange and pale blue-green 35 30
C417 1 E. on 2 c. black, yellow-orange and pale blue-green 35 30
  a. Blue surch (1970) 5 5
  b. Green surch (1971) 5 5
C411/417 *Set of 7* 60 55

31 President Tomás   **32** Port of Sao Vicente

1968 (2 Feb). *Visit of President Tomás of Portugal. Litho.*
P 13½.
406 **31** 1 E. multicoloured   5   5

(Des J. de Moura (No. 408). Litho)

1968 (22 Apr). *500th Birth Anniv of Pedro Cabral (explorer).*
*Designs as T **84** of Angola.*
407   1 E. Cantino's map, 1502 (*horiz*)   ..   8   5
408   1 E. 50, Pedro Alvares Cabral (*vert*)   ..   10   5
     a. Red ("CORREIOS" and value)
      omited   ..   ..

(Des J. de Moura. Litho)

1968 (15 Oct). *"Produce of Cape Verde Islands". T **32** and*
similar multicoloured designs. P 14.
409   50 c. Type **32**   5   5
410   1 E. "Purgueira" (*Tatrophus curcus*) ..   5   5
411   1 E. 50, Groundnuts   5   5
412   2 E. 50, Caster-oil plant   ..   8   5
413   3 E. 50, "Inhame" (*Dioscorea alata*) ..   12   5
414   4 E. Date palm   15   5
415   4 E. 50, "Goiabeira" (*Psidium guajava*)   20   5
416   5 E. Tamarind   20   5
417   10 E. Manioc   35   12
418   30 E. "Girl of Cape Verde"   ..   1·00   40
409/418   *Set of 10*   ..   ..   ..   2·00   70
   The 1 E. to 30 E. values are vertical. Nos. 410/17 show
agricultural produce.

(Des J. de Moura. Litho)

1969 (17 Feb). *Birth Centenary of Admiral Gago Coutinho.*
*Multicoloured design as T **86** of Angola.*
419   30 c. Seaplane and map of Lisbon–Rio
     flight (*vert*)   5   5

1969 (29 Aug). *500th Birth Anniv of Vasco da Gama (ex-*
*plorer). Multicoloured design as T **87** of Angola.*
420   1 E. 50, Vasco da Gama   5   5

1969 (25 Sept). *Centenary of Overseas Administrative*
*Reforms. As T **88** of Angola.*
421   2 E. multicoloured   8   5

1969 (1 Dec). *500th Birth Anniv of King Manoel I. Multicol-*
*oured design as T **89** of Angola.*
422   3 E. Manoel I   8   5

1970 (15 Nov). *Birth Centenary of Marshal Carmona. Multi-*
*coloured design as T **91** of Angola.*
423   2 E. 50, Half-length portrait   ..   8   5

33 Desalination Installation

(Des J. de Moura. Litho)

1971 (1 Dec). *Inauguration of Desalination Plant, Mindelo.*
P 13.
424   **33** 4 E. multicoloured   15   5

1972 (25 May). *400th Anniversary of Camoens' "Lusiad"*
*(epic poem). Multicoloured design as T **95** of Angola.*
425   5 E. Galleons at Cape Verde   ..   20   5

1972 (20 June). *Olympic Games, Munich. Multicoloured*
*design as T **97** of Angola.*
426   4 E. Basketball and boxing   ..   15   5

1972 (20 Sept). *50th Anniversary of First Flight Lisbon–Rio*
*de Janeiro. Multicoloured design as T **98** of Angola.*
427   3 E. 50, Seaplane "Lusitania" near Sao
     Vicente   12   5

Caroline Islands

100 Pfennige = 1 Mark

GERMAN PROTECTORATE

The Caroline Islands in the Western Pacific Ocean were discovered in 1526 and claimed by Spain in 1875. The claim was contested by Germany, but arbitration by the Pope awarded the islands to Spain. Germany purchased rights to a protectorate from Spain in 1899.

ERRORS. Errors such as double and inverted overprints were never issued but come from waste sheets which later leaked out of the printers.

(1)   (2)

1899–1900. *Stamps of Germany, 1889, optd.*

(a) Overprint sloping as T 1 (48°). (12.10.99)

1	8	3 pf. grey-brown	..	..	30·00	35·00
2		5 pf. green	..	..	38·00	35·00
3	9	10 pf. carmine ..	..	..	3·50	5·50
4		20 pf. ultramarine	..	..	3·50	5·50
5		25 pf. orange ..	..	..	£160	£190
6		50 pf. chocolate ..	..	..	50·00	85·00

(b) Overprint sloping as T 2 (56°). (5.00)

7	8	3 pf. grey-brown	..	..	1·25	1·50
8		5 pf. green ..	..	..	1·60	1·50
9	9	10 pf. carmine ..	..	..	2·50	2·50
10		20 pf. ultramarine	..	..	2·50	4·00
11		25 pf. orange ..	..	..	7·00	8·00
12		50 pf. chocolate ..	..	..	8·00	9·00

For illustrations and notes about German Colonial Types A and B, see under Cameroun.

1901. *No wmk.*

13	A	3 pf. brown ..	..	..	10	20
14		5 pf. green ..	..	..	12	40
15		10 pf. carmine ..	..	..	10	1·10
16		20 pf. ultramarine	..	..	20	1·75
17		25 pf. black and red/*yellow*	..		20	3·25
18		30 pf. black and orange/*buff*	..		20	3·25
19		40 pf. black and carmine	..		25	3·50
20		50 pf. black and purple/*buff*	..		30	4·00
21		80 pf. black and carmine/*rose* ..			40	5·00
22	B	1 m. carmine (*a*)	..	..	60	9·00
23		2 m. blue (*a*) ..	..	..	1·00	12·00
24		3 m. violet-black (*a*)	..	..	1·40	22·00
25		5 m. carmine and black (II) (*a*) ..			20·00	70·00
		a. Frame II, Centre I (*a*)	..			

On 1 July, 1905, 10 pf. stamps (No. 15) were bisected and used as 5 pf. In such cases half-stamps were cancelled with a special postmark as above. These bisected stamps are known as the "typhoon" provisionals, from the fact that the stock of 5 pf. stamps was destroyed during a typhoon. (*Price on cover* £50.)

1910 (12 July). *Surch* "**5 Pf**", *in black.*

26	5 pf. on 3 pf. brown (No. 13)	..	..	—	£400
	a. Surch inverted	..	..	—	£450 ·

1915–19. *Wmk Lozenges.*

27	A	3 pf. brown (1919)	..	..	..	10
28		5 pf. green ..	..	..	..	2·00
29	B	5 m. carmine and black (II) (*a*) ..		..	5·00
		a. Frame II, Centre I (*a*)				
		b. 25×17 holes (1919)	..	..	4·25

The islands were occupied by Japan in October 1914 and from 17 December 1920 were a Japanese mandated territory. From 18 July 1947 they have been a United States trust territory.

CAUCA. See under Colombian States.

Central African Republic

100 Centimes = 1 Franc

The country which is now the Central African Republic was from 1903 to 1958 the French colony of Ubangi-Shari. The explorer Savorgnan de Brazza extended French influence north of the Ubangi river in 1887 and the town of Bangui was founded in 1889. The French territory of Upper Bangui was formed in 1894 and the Shari area was occupied in 1898. After the failure of the French expedition to Fashoda on the Nile in 1898 the frontier with Sudan was fixed on 21 March 1899.

Ubangi-Shari, at first part of the French Congo, became a colony as from 1 July 1904 by a decree of 29 December 1903. Until 1915 the stamps of French Congo were used there; from 1915 to 1922 it shared a postal administration with Chad.

PRINTERS. All stamps, except for those in lithography, were printed at the Government Printing Works, Paris, *unless otherwise stated.*

IMPERFORATE STAMPS. Stamps exist imperforate in their issued colours but they were not valid for postage. Imperforate stamps in other colours are colour trials.

A. UBANGI-SHARI-CHAD

OUBANGUI-CHARI-TCHAD
(1)

1915–18. *Stamps of Middle Congo, 1907–17, optd as T 1 (1 c. to 20 c.) or in two lines (others).*

1	**1**	1 c. olive and brown ..	..	5	5
		a. Opt double ..	..	8·00	
2		2 c. violet and brown ..	..	5	5
3		4 c. blue and brown ..	..	5	5
4		5 c. green and blue ..	..	5	5
5		10 c. carmine and blue ..	..	5	5
5a		15 c. dull purple and pink (1918)	..	10	10
6		20 c. pale brown and blue	..	15	15
7	**2**	25 c. blue and grey-green	..	5	5
8		30 c. red and green ..	..	5	5
9		35 c. chocolate and blue	..	30	30
10		40 c. dull green and pale brown	..	40	40
11		45 c. violet and salmon	..	40	40
12		50 c. green and salmon	..	8	8
13		75 c. blue and brown ..	..	55	55
14	**3**	1 f. deep green and pale violet	..	65	65
15		2 f. violet and grey-green	..	1·00	1·00
16		5 f. blue and pink ..	..	3·25	3·25
1/16		*Set of 17* ..	..	6·50	6·50

The 15 c. is on ordinary paper and the rest on chalk-surfaced paper; however, the 1 c. to 10 c., 20 c., 45 c. and 50 c. also exist on ordinary paper.

(2)   **(3)**   **(4)**   OUBANGUI-CHARI

1916 (4 Jan). *No. 5 surch with T 2. Chalk-surfaced paper.*

17	10 c. + 5 c. carmine and blue	..	15	15
	a. Surch inverted	..	4·00	4·00
	b. Surch double	..	4·00	4·00
	c. Surch double, one inverted ..	..	5·00	5·00
	d. Surch vert	..	6·50	6·50
	e. No stop below "c"	..	70	70

1916 (July). *No. 5 surch with T 3.*

18	10 c. + 5 c. carmine and blue (R.) ..	..	5	5

1922 (1 Jan). *As 1915–18. New colours.*

19	**1**	5 c. yellow and blue	..	5	5
20		10 c. green and blue-green	..	5	5
21	**2**	25 c. green and black	..	5	5
22		30 c. carmine	..	5	5
23		50 c. blue and green	..	5	5
19/23		*Set of 5*	..	20	20

From 1922 to 1936 separate issues of stamps were made for Ubangi-Shari and for Chad.

B. UBANGI-SHARI

1922 (Nov). *Stamps of Middle Congo, new colours, optd with T 4 (1 c. to 20 c.) or in two lines (others).*

24	1 c. violet and green	..	..	5	5
	a. Opt omitted ..		..	8·00	
25	2 c. green and rose	..	..	5	5
26	4 c. brown and purple	..	..	5	5
	a. Opt omitted ..		..	8·50	
27	5 c. deep blue and rose ..		..	8	8
28	10 c. green and blue-green	..	..	12	12
29	15 c. bright rose and blue	..	..	20	20
30	20 c. brown and rose	..	..	45	45
31	25 c. violet and rose	..	..	35	35
32	30 c. carmine ..	..	..	25	25
33	35 c. violet and green	..	..	45	45
34	40 c. slate-blue and mauve (R.)	..	..	45	45
35	45 c. brown and mauve	..	..	45	45
36	50 c. blue and pale blue	..	..	25	25
37	60 on 75 c. violet/*rose*	..	..	25	25
38	75 c. brown and rose	..	..	25	25
39	1 f. green and blue (R.) ..		..	35	35
40	2 f. green and rose	..	..	60	60
41	5 f. green and brown	..	..	70	70
24/41	*Set of 18*	..	..	4·75	4·75

AFRIQUE ÉQUATORIALE FRANÇAISE	AFRIQUE ÉQUATORIALE FRANÇAISE
(5)	**(6)**

1924 (27 Oct)–*33. Stamps of 1922 and similar stamps additionally optd with T 5 (1 c. to 20 c.) or 6 (others).*

42	1 c. violet and green (B.)	..	..	5	5
	a. T 4 opt omitted ..		..	8·00	
43	2 c. green and rose (B.)	..	..	5	5
	a. T 4 opt omitted	..	..	8·00	
	b. T 5 opt double	..	..	6·50	
44	4 c. brown and chocolate (B.) ..		..	5	5
	a. T 5 opt double (Bk. + B.)	..	..	6·00	
	b. T 5 opt omitted	..	..	10·00	
44c	4 c. brown (B.) ..	..	..	12	12
45	5 c. deep blue and rose	..	..	5	5
	a. T 4 opt omitted	..	..	8·00	
46	10 c. green and blue-green	..	..	5	5
47	10 c. orange-vermilion and blue (1.12.25)		..	5	5
	a. T 5 opt double	..	..	7·00	
48	15 c. bright rose and blue	..	..	5	5
	a. T 5 opt in blue (6.26)	..	..	5	5
49	20 c. brown and rose (B.)	..	..	5	5
50	25 c. violet and rose (B.)..		..	5	5
51	30 c. carmine (B.)	..	..	5	5
52	30 c. chocolate and rose (1.12.25)		..	5	5
	a. "OUBANGUI-CHARI" opt omitted		..	8·00	
53	30 c. olive-green and green (14.11.27)		..	5	5
54	35 c. violet and green (B.)	..	..	5	5
55	40 c. deep blue and mauve (B.)*		..	5	5
56	45 c. brown and mauve (B.)	..	..	5	5
57	50 c. blue and pale blue (R.)	..	..	5	5
58	50 c. grey and ultramarine (R.) (1.12.25)		..	10	8
59	60 on 75 c. violet/*rose* (R.)	..	..	5	5
	a. "60" omitted	..	..	12·00	
	b. Surch double (R. + Bk.)	..	..	8·00	
60	65 c. red-brown and blue (2.4.28)	..	..	12	12

61	75 c. brown and rose (B.)	5	5
62	75 c. blue and pale blue (R.) (1.6.25)	5	5
	a. "OUBANGUI-CHARI" opt omitted †	8·00	
63	75 c. claret and brown (25.9.28)	12	12
64	90 c. bright rose and scarlet (22.3.30)	45	45
65	1 f. green and blue (B.)*	5	5
	a. "OUBANGUI-CHARI" in black (B.) (1.2.25)	5	5
66	1 f. 10 yellow-brn & ultram (25.9.28)	15	15
67	1 f. 25, magenta & green (25.9.33)	50	50
68	1 f. 50, ultramarine and blue (22.3.30)	55	55
69	1 f. 75, chocolate and orange (25.9.33)	75	75
70	2 f. green and rose	5	5
	a. "OUBANGUI-CHARI" opt omitted	55·00	24·00
71	3 f. magenta/rose (22.3.30)	55	55
72	5 f. green and brown (B.)	20	20
42/72	Set of 31	4·00	4·00

†On No. 62a the top line of Type **6** is 10 mm from the top of the stamp but is 13 mm from the top on No. 39a of Chad.
*Nos. 55 and 65 have Type **4** in red. No. 65a was not issued without Type **6** overprint.

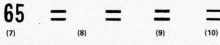

65	=	=	=	=
(7)	(8)	(9)	(10)

1925–27. Stamps as 1924–33 but colours changed, with "OUBANGUI-CHARI" opt in black and opt T **6** in black or colours shown, further surch in black as T **7/10**.

(a) In figures only (1.2.25)

73	65 on 1 f. violet and grey-brown (R.)	8	8
	a. "65" omitted	5·50	
74	85 on 1 f. violet and grey-brown (R.)	8	8
	a. Opt T **6** omitted	6·00	
	b. Opt T **6** double	8·00	

(b) In figures with bars over old values

75	90 on 75 c. bright rose & scarlet (11.4.27)	8	8
76	1 f. 25 on 1 f. blue and ultramarine (B. + R.) (14.6.26)	5	5
	a. "1 f. 25" omitted	8·00	
77	1 f. 50 on 1 f. ultramarine and greenish blue (11.4.27)	8	8
78	3 f. on 5 f. red-brn & carm (19.12.27)	15	15
	a. No stop after "F"	75	75
79	10 f. on 5 f. vermilion & mag (21.3.27)	1·00	1·00
80	20 f. on 5 f. magenta and grey (21.3.27)	1·25	1·25
	a. No stop after "F"	4·00	4·00
73/80	Set of 8	2·50	2·50

On No. 76 the Type **6** overprint is in blue and the surcharge in red.

OUBANGUI-CHARI

A. E. F.
(D **1**)

1928 (4 Apr). POSTAGE DUE. Type D **3** of France, optd with Type D **1**. P 14 × 13½.

D81	5 c. light blue	5	5
D82	10 c. brown	5	5
D83	20 c. olive-green	10	10
D84	25 c. rosine	10	10
D85	30 c. rose	10	10
D86	45 c. green	10	10
D87	50 c. claret	10	10
	a. No stop after "F"	80	80
D88	60 c. yellow-brown/cream	15	15
D89	1 f. maroon/cream	20	20
D90	2 f. rose-red	20	20
D91	3 f. bright violet	25	25
D81/91	Set of 11	1·25	1·25

D 2 Mobaye	D 3 E. Gentil

(Des and eng G. Hourriez (D **2**), A. Delzers (D **3**). Typo)

1930 (17 Feb). POSTAGE DUE. P 14 × 13½ (D **2**) or 13½ × 14 (D **3**).

D 92	D **2**	5 c. olive and deep blue	5	5
D 93		10 c. chocolate and scarlet	8	8
D 94		20 c. chocolate and green	12	12
D 95		25 c. chocolate and light blue	10	10
D 96		30 c. blue-green and yellow-brown	20	20
D 97		45 c. olive and blue-green	30	30
D 98		50 c. chocolate and magenta	45	45
D 99		60 c. black and lilac-blue	45	45
D100	D **3**	1 f. slate-black & yellow-brown	20	20
D101		2 f. chocolate and mauve	30	30
D102		3 f. chocolate and scarlet	35	35
D92/102		Set of 11	2·25	2·25

1931 (13 Apr). International Colonial Exhibition, Paris. As T **9/12** of Cameroun.

103	40 c. green	35	35
104	50 c. mauve	35	35
105	90 c. vermilion	35	35
106	1 f. 50, blue	35	35
103/106	Set of 4	1·25	1·25

From 16 March 1936 to 1960, stamps of French Equatorial Africa were used in Ubangi-Shari.

C. CENTRAL AFRICAN REPUBLIC

The Central African Republic, formerly Ubangi-Shari, was created as an autonomous state on 1 December 1958, and became independent, within the French Community, on 13 August 1960.

1 President Boganda	2 C.C.T.A. Emblem

(Des Gandon. Eng Gandon (15 f.), Piel (25 f.). Recess)

1959 (1 Dec). First Anniv of Republic. T **1** and similar design. Multicoloured centres; frame colours given below. P 13.

1	15 f. blue	10	8
2	25 f. carmine-red	12	8

Design: Horiz—25 f. As T **1** but flag behind portrait.

(Des and eng R. Cami. Recess)

1960 (21 May). Tenth Anniv of African Technical Co-operation Commission. P 13.

3	**2**	50 f. blue and emerald	40	30

3 Dactyloceras widenmanni

4 Abyssinian Roller

(Des and eng Mazelin (5 f. to 85 f.). Des G. Prestat. Eng P. Béquet (50 f., 250 f.), Mazelin (100 f.), Gandon (200 f.), Cottet (500 f.). Recess)

1960 (3 Sept)–**63.** *T 3/4 and similar horiz designs.* P 13. *(a) POSTAGE. Butterflies as T 3.*

4	50 c. brown, red & turq-grn (10.6.61)		5	5
5	1 f. black-grn, orge-brn & vio (10.6.61)		5	5
6	2 f. blk-grn, brn & slate-green (10.6.61)		5	5
7	3 f. brown, red & olive-green (10.6.61)		5	5
8	5 f. bistre-brown and yellow-green	..	5	5
9	10 f. bright blue, black and dull green		5	5
10	20 f. crimson, black and dull green	..	12	5
11	85 f. crimson, black and dull green	..	45	20

(b) AIR. Birds as T 4

12	50 f. turquoise-blue, orange-red and black-green (15.11.62)	..	25	12
13	100 f. violet, orange-brown and green	..	45	20
14	200 f. green, violet, carmine & turq-blue		95	45
15	250 f. red, bright green, ultramarine and purple-brown (11.3.63)	..	1·25	70
16	500 f. red-brown, indigo and green	..	2·25	1·10
4/16	*Set of* 13	..	5·50	2·75

Designs: (As T 3)—50 c., 3 f. *Cymothoe sangaris;* 1 f., 2 f. *Charaxe mobilis;* 10 f. *Charaxes ameliae;* 20 f. *Charaxes zingha;* 85 f. *Drurya antimachus.* (As T 4)—50 f. Great touraco; 200 f. Persian touraco; 250 f. Red-headed love-birds; 500 f. Fish eagle.
See also Nos. 42/5.

XVII° OLYMPIADE 1960   REPUBLIQUE CENTRAFRICAINE
(5)

1960 (15 Dec). *AIR. Olympic Games. No. 257 of French Equatorial Africa surch with T 5, in red.*
17   250 f. on 500 f. dp blue, blk & dp bl-grn ..   2·10   2·10

FETE NATIONALE 1-12-1960
(6)

1960 (1 Dec). *National Festival. No. 2 optd with T 6.*
18   25 f. multicoloured   35   35

7 Pasteur Institute, Bangui   **8** U.N. Emblem, Map and Flag

(Des and eng Gandon. Recess)

1961 (25 Feb). *Opening of Pasteur Institute, Bangui.* P 13.
19 **7** 20 f. multicoloured   25   20

(Des Combet. Eng Pheulpin. Recess)

1961 (4 Mar). *Admission of Central African Republic into U.N.O.* P 13.

20	**8** 15 f. multicoloured	.. .. ..	10	8
21	25 f. multicoloured	.. .. ..	15	12
22	85 f. multicoloured	.. .. ..	55	40

FÊTE NATIONALE 1-12-61
(9)

U. A. M.
CONFERENCE DE BANGUI
25-27 MARS 1962   50F
(10)

1961 (1 Dec). *National Festival. Optd with T 9.*
23 **8** 25 f. multicoloured (G.)   50   50

1962 (17 Feb). *AIR. Foundation of "Air Afrique" Airline. As T 69 of Cameroun.*
24   50 f. violet, red-brown and green ..   25   25

1962 (25 Mar). *Union of African States and Madagascar Conference, Bangui. Surch with T 10.*
25 **8** 50 f. on 85 f. multicoloured (Br.) ..   45   45

11 Campaign Emblem   **12** Hurdling

(Eng Bétemps. Recess Chaix)

1962 (7 Apr). *Malaria Eradication.* P 12½×12.
26 **11** 25 f. +5 f. slate-blue   25   20

(Des Ringard. Photo Delrieu)

1962 (21 July). *Sports. T 12 and similar designs.* P 12×13 (100 f.) *or* 12½×12. *(a) POSTAGE.*

27	20 f. brown, yellow-green and black	..	12	10
28	50 f. brown, yellow-green and black	..	25	20

(b) AIR. Inscr "POSTE AERIENNE"
29 100 f. brown, yellow-green and black ..   55   40
Designs: *Horiz*—50 f. Cycling. *Vert* (26×47 *mm*)—100 f. Pole-Vaulting.

13 President Dacko   **14** Union Flag

(Photo Delrieu)

1962. P 12×12½.

30	**13** 20 f. multicoloured (13.8)	.. ..	10	5
31	25 f. multicoloured (1.12)	.. ..	12	5

(Des Decaris. Photo Delrieu)

1962 (8 Sept). *First Anniv of Union of African and Malagasy States.* P 12½×12.
32 **14** 30 f. blue-green, red, gold & yellow-grn   20   15

D **1** *Sternotomis gama* (beetle)

(Des R. Serres. Eng G. Bétemps. Recess)

1962 (15 Oct). *POSTAGE DUE. Various designs showing beetles, as Type* D **1**. *P* 11.

D33	50 c. yellow-orange, blue-grn & dp grn	5	5
D34	50 c. green, yellow-orange & dp green	5	5
D35	1 f. black, brown and light green ..	5	5
D36	1 f. light green, black and brown ..	5	5
D37	2 f. orange-red and black	5	5
D38	2 f. yellow-green, black & orange-red	5	5
D39	5 f. olive-green, orange-red and brown	5	5
D40	5 f. olive-green, orange-red and brown	5	5
D41	10 f. green, yellow-brown and black ..	5	5
D42	10 f. yellow-brown and black	5	5
D43	25 f. yellow-brown, black and emerald	8	8
D44	25 f. yellow-brown, emerald and black	8	8
D33/44	*Set of* 12	45	45

Designs:—Nos. D33, Type D **1**; D34, *Sternotomis virescens*; D35, *Augosoma centaurus*; D36, *Phosphorus virescens* and *ceroplesis carabarica*; D37, *Ceroplesis S.P.*; D38, *Cetoine scaraboidae*; D39, *Cetoine scaraboidae* (different colours); D40, *Macrorhina S.P.*; D41, *Taurina longiceps*; D42, *Phryneta leprosa*; D43, *Monohamus griseoplagiatus*; D44, *Jambonus trifasciatus*.

The two designs in each value are arranged in *tête-bêche* pairs throughout the sheet.

15 Athlete

16 Globe and Emblem

(Des and eng J. Combet. Recess)

1962 (24 Dec). *AIR. "Coupe des Tropiques" Games, Bangui. P* 13.

33	**15** 100 f. choc, dp bluish green & carm-red	55	40

(Des and eng Durens. Recess)

1963 (21 Mar). *Freedom from Hunger. P* 13.

34	**16** 25 f. + 5 f. deep bluish green, red-brown and bistre	20	20

17 "National Army"

18 "Posts and Telecommunications"

(M **1**) (M **2**)

1963. *MILITARY FRANK. No.* 1 *optd.*

M35	M **1** (–) multicoloured	80	
M36	M **2** 15 f. multicoloured	1·00	

(Des P. Béquet. Photo Delrieu)

1963 (13 Aug). *Third Anniv of Proclamation of Republic. P* 12 × 12½.

35	**17** 20 f. multicoloured	10	5

(Des P. Béquet. Photo Delrieu)

1963 (8 Sept). *AIR. African and Malagasy Posts and Tele-communications Union. P* 12½.

36	**18** 85 f. red, buff, blue-green and green ..	40	30

19 "Telecommunications"

20 "Young Pioneers"

(Des Durrens. Photo Delrieu)

1963 (19 Sept). *Space Telecommunications. T* **19** *and similar design. P* 12½.

37	25 f. green and purple	15	15
38	100 f. dp bluish green, yellow-orange & bl	60	60

Design:—100 f. Radio waves and globe.

(Des P. Béquet. Recess and litho Chaix)

1963 (14 Oct). *Young Pioneers. P* 12½.

39	**20** 50 f. brown, violet-blue & greenish bl ..	20	15

21 Boali Falls

22 Map of Africa and Sun

(Des and eng C. Mazelin. Recess)

1963 (28 Oct). *P* 13.

40	**21** 30 f. brown-purple, deep green & blue	12	10

(Des Durrens. Photo Delrieu)

1963 (9 Nov). *AIR. "African Unity". P* 13 × 12.

41	**22** 25 f. ultramarine, yellow and blue ..	12	8

23 *Colotis evippe*

24 "Europafrique"

(Des Gandon. Photo So.Ge.Im)

1963 (18 Nov). *Butterflies. T* **23** *and similar horiz designs. Multicoloured. P* 12½ × 13.

42	1 f. Type **23**	5	5
43	3 f. *Papilio dardanus*	5	5
44	4 f. *Papilio lormieri*	5	5
45	60 f. *Papilio zalmoxis*	25	20
42/45	*Set of* 4	35	30

(Des P. Béquet. Photo Delrieu)

1963 (30 Nov). *AIR. European-African Economic Convention.* P 12×13.
46 **24** 50 f. deep brown, yellow, ochre & blue   30   20

25 Diesel Train

26 UNESCO Emblem. Scales of Justice and Tree

(Des and eng Decaris. Recess)

1963 (1 Dec). *AIR. Bangui-Douala Railway Project.* T **25** and similar designs. P 13.
47   20 f. myrtle, brown-purple & lt brown ..   12   8
48   25 f. chocolate, blue and light brown ..   15   10
49   50 f. violet, bright purple & light brown   25   20
50 100 f. brown-purple, blue-green & lt brn   55   35
47/50   Set of 4   95   65
MS50*a* 190×98 mm. Nos. 47/50   1·00 1·00
  Designs:—Diesel rolling stock. *Horiz*—20 f. Rail-car; 100 f. Locomotive. *Vert*—50 f. Shunter.

(Des Bétemps. Eng Durrens. Recess)

1963 (10 Dec). *15th Anniv of Declaration of Human Rights.* P 13.
51 **26** 25 f. bistre, blue-green and brown ..   15   12

27 Bangui Cathedral

28 Cleopatra, Temple of Kalabsha

(Des and eng A. Decaris. Recess)

1964 (21 Jan). *AIR.* P 13.
52 **27** 100 f. chestnut, green and blue ..   45   30

(Des and eng J. Combet. Recess)

1964 (7 Mar). *AIR. Nubian Monuments Preservation Fund.* P 13.
53 **28** 25 f. + 10 f. mag, brt bl & bronze-grn   20   20
54   50 f. + 10 f. red-brown, yellow-olive and deep bluish green ..   40   40
55 100 f. + 10 f. brown-purple, reddish violet and bronze-green ..   60   60

29 Radar Scanner

(Des and eng C. Haley. Recess)

1964 (23 Mar). *AIR. World Meteorological Day.* P 13.
56 **29** 50 f. reddish violet, chestnut and blue   25   20

30 "Tree" and Sun Emblem

31 Map and African Heads of State

(Des C. Durrens. Eng A. Frères. Recess)

1964 (20 Apr). *International Quiet Sun Years.* P 13.
57 **30** 25 f. red-orange, ochre & dp bluish grn   20   15

(Photo Delrieu)

1964 (23 June). *AIR. 5th Anniv of Equatorial African Heads of State Conference.* P 12½.
58 **31** 100 f. multicoloured   55   40

32 Throwing the Javelin

33 President Kennedy

(Des and eng Gandon (25 f., 250 f.). Des Gandon. Eng Forget (others). Recess)

1964 (23 June). *AIR. Olympic Games, Tokyo.* T **32** and similar horiz designs. P 12½.
59   25 f. chocolate, emerald and blue ..   12   8
60   50 f. red, black and green ..   25   15
61 100 f. chocolate, ultramarine and green .   45   30
62 250 f. black, green and red ..   1·00   85
59/62   Set of 4 ..   ..   1·60 1·25
MS62*a* 130×100 mm. Nos. 59/62 ..   2·00 2·00
  Designs:—50 f. Basketball; 100 f. Running; 250 f. Diving and swimming.

(Photo Delrieu)

1964 (4 July). *AIR. President Kennedy Memorial Issue.* P 12½.
63 **33** 100 f. red-brown, black & lt reddish vio   50   40
MS63*a* 90×130 mm. No. 63 in block of four   2·40 2·40

34 African Child

35 Silhouettes of European and African

(Des and eng J. Combet. Recess)

1964 (13 Aug). *Child Welfare. Vert portraits of children as T 34.* P 13.

64	20 f. brown, yellow-green & bright purple		12	8
65	25 f. brown, light blue and red	..	15	10
66	40 f. brown, bright purple & yellow-green		20	15
67	50 f. brown, yellow-green & reddish pur		25	15
64/67	Set of 4		65	40
MS67a	144×100 mm. Nos. 64/7		75	75

1964 (7 Nov). *French, African and Malagasy Co-operation. As T 547 of France.*

68	25 f. chocolate, crimson and green	..	15	10

(Des G. Prestat. Litho So.Ge.Im)

1964 (1 Dec). *National Unity.* P 13×12½.

69 **35**	25 f. multicoloured	..	..	12	8

36 "Economic Co-operation"

(Des H. Biais. Photo Delrieu)

1964 (19 Dec). *AIR. "Europafrique".* P 13×12.

70 **36**	50 f. green, red and yellow	..	..	25	20

37 Handclasp

(Photo So.Ge.Im)

1965 (2 Jan). *AIR. International Co-operation Year.* P 13.

71 **37**	100 f. brown, flesh, blue and yellow	..	50	30

38 Weather Satellite

(Des Gauthier. Eng J. Miermont. Recess)

1965 (23 Mar). *AIR. World Meteorological Day.* P 13.

72 **38**	100 f. ultramarine and orange-brown	..	55	30

39 Abraham Lincoln

(Des P. Lambert. Photo So.Ge.Im)

1965 (15 Apr). *AIR. Death Centenary of Abraham Lincoln.* P 13.

73 **39**	100 f. flesh, indigo and bluish green	..	55	30

40 Team of Oxen ⬥ **O 1** Arms

(Des J. Pheulpin. Eng J. Pheulpin (25 f., 100 f.), J. Miermont (50 f.), R. Fenneteaux (85 f.). Recess)

1965 (28 Apr). *Harnessed Animals in Agriculture. T 40 and similar horiz designs.* P 13.

74	25 f. rose-red, bistre-brown & bluish grn		12	8
75	50 f. brown-purple, bluish green & lt bl		20	15
76	85 f. brown, yellow-green and light blue		40	25
77	100 f. multicoloured		45	30
74/77	Set of 4		1·00	70

Designs:—50 f. Ploughing with bullock; 85 f. Ploughing with oxen; 100 f. Oxen with hay cart.

(Des G. Richer. Litho So.Ge.Im)

1965 (1 May)–**69**. OFFICIAL. P 13×12½.

O78 **O 1**	1 f. multicoloured	..	5	5
O79	2 f. multicoloured	..	5	5
O80	5 f. multicoloured	..	5	5
O81	10 f. multicoloured	..	5	5
O82	20 f. multicoloured	..	8	8
O83	30 f. multicoloured (1.69)	..	10	10
O84	50 f. multicoloured	..	15	15
O85	100 f. multicoloured	..	40	40
O86	130 f. multicoloured (1.69)	..	40	40
O87	200 f. multicoloured	..	65	65
O78/87	Set of 10	..	1·75	1·75

For similar design printed in photogravure by Delrieu, see Nos. O238/43.

41 Pouget-Maisonneuve ⬥ **42** Women and Loom ("To
Telegraph Instrument ⬥ Clothe")

(Des and eng C. Haley (100 f.), C. Durrens (others). Recess)

1965 (17 May). *I.T.U. Centenary.* P 13.

(a) POSTAGE. T 41 and similar designs

78	25 f. blue, carmine-red and green	..	12	8
79	30 f. lake and emerald-green	..	12	10
80	50 f. carmine-red and bluish violet	..	20	15
81	85 f. indigo and bright purple	..	40	20

(b) AIR. Larger (48½×27 mm). Inscr "POSTE AERIENNE"

82	100 f. brown, violet-blue & bronze-green		50	35
78/82	Set of 5		1·10	80

Designs: *Vert*—30 f. Chappe's telegraph instrument; 50 f. Doignon regulator for Hughes telegraph. *Horiz*—85 f. Pouillet's telegraph apparatus; 100 f. "Relay" satellite and I.T.U. emblem.

(Des O. Adler. Eng Hertenberger (25 f., 60 f.), Bétemps (50 f.), Monvoisin (85 f., 100 f.). Recess)

1965 (10 June). *"M.E.S.A.N." Welfare Campaign. T 42 and similar horiz designs depicting "Five Aims".* P 13. *(a) POSTAGE.*

83	25 f. emerald, chocolate & bright blue	..	12	8
84	50 f. chocolate, brt blue & dp bluish grn		20	15
85	60 f. chocolate, bright blue & emerald	..	25	20
86	85 f. multicoloured		35	25

(b) AIR. Inscr "POSTE AERIENNE"

87	100 f. bright blue, chocolate & dull green		45	35
83/87	Set of 5		1·25	90

Designs:—50 f. Doctor examining child, and hospital ("To care for"); 60 f. Student and school ("To instruct"); 85 f. Woman and child, and harvesting scene ("To nourish").

(48×27mm)—100 f. Village huses ("To house"). "M.E.S.A.N." —"Mouvement Evolution Social Afrique Noire".

43 Coffee Plant, Hammer Grubs and Moth   **(44)**   **5**F

(Des G. Prestat. Eng J. Combet. Recess)

1965 (25 Aug). *Plant Protection.* **T 43** *and similar designs.* P 13.

88	2 f. purple, orange-red and myrtle-green		5	5
89	3 f. carmine, myrtle-green and black	..	5	5
90	30 f. bright purple, myrtle-green and red		15	10

Designs: *Horiz*—3 f. Coffee plant, caterpillar and hawk-moth. *Vert*—30 f. Cotton plant, caterpillar and rose-moth.

1965 (26 Aug)–**66**. *Various stamps surch as T* **44**.

91	–	2 f. on 3 f. (No. 43)		..	60	
92	**1**	5 f. on 15 f. (No. 1)	..	..	60	
93	–	5 f. on 85 f. (No. 76) (15.4.66)	..		8	8
94	**13**	10 f. on 20 f. (No. 30) (Br.)		..	60	
95	–	10 f. on 100 f. (No. 77) (15.4.66)			12	12

45 Camp Fire   **46** U.N. and Campaign Emblems

(Des and eng C. Haley. Recess)

1965 (27 Sept). *Scouting.* **T 45** *and similar horiz design.* P 13.

96	25 f. brown-red, purple and blue	..	12	8
97	50 f. brown & dp turq-blue (Boy Scout)	..	25	15

(Des and eng P. Béquet. Recess)

1965 (16 Oct). *Freedom from Hunger.* P 13.

98	**46**	50 f. orange-brn, blue & blackish grn	..	25	15

47 "Industry and Agriculture"   **48** Mercury (statue after Coysevox)

(Des H. Ouin (Lacroix). Photo Delrieu)

1965 (7 Nov). *AIR. "Europafrique".* P 12×13.

99	**47**	50 f. multicoloured	..	25	20

(Des and eng G. Aufschneider. Recess)

1965 (5 Dec). *AIR. Fifth Anniv of Admission to U.P.U.* P 13.

100	**48**	100 f. black, brown-red and blue.	..	50	35

49 Father and Child   **50** Grading Diamonds

(Des and eng C. Haley. Recess)

1965 (12 Dec). *AIR. Red Cross.* **T 49** *and similar vert design.* P 13.

101	50 f. black, blue and carmine-red	..	25	15
102	100 f. red-brown, green and vermilion	..	45	35

Design:—100 f. Mother and child.

(Des and eng A. Decaris. Recess)

1966 (14 Mar). *National Diamond Industry.* P 13.

103	**50**	25 f. bistre-brown, dp vio & crimson	12	5

51 Mbaka Porter   **52** W.H.O. Building   **53** *Eulophia cucullata*

(Des J. Combet. Photo So.Ge.Im)

1966 (9 Apr). *World Festival of Negro Arts, Dakar.* P 13×12½.

104	**51**	25 f. multicoloured	..	12	5

(Des H. Biais. Photo So.Ge.Im)

1966 (3 May). *Inauguration of W.H.O. Headquarters, Geneva.* P 13×12½.

105	**52**	25 f. reddish violet, new blue & yellow	12	5

(Des P. Lambert, after Prestat. Photo Delrieu)

1966 (16 May). *Flowers.* **T 53** *and similar vert designs.* Multicoloured. P 12×12½.

106	2 f. Type **53**	..		5	5
107	5 f. Lissochilus horsfalii			5	5
108	10 f. Tridactyle bicaudata		..	5	5
109	15 f. Polystachya			5	5
110	20 f. Eulophia alta	..	..	10	5
111	25 f. Microcelia macrorrhynchium		..	12	5
106/111	Set of 6		..	35	20

54 Aircraft and "Air Afrique" Emblem

(Des Dessirier. Photo Delrieu)

1966 (31 Aug). *AIR. Inauguration of "DC–8" Air Services.* P 12½.

112	**54**	25 f. yellow, green, black & new blue	12	5

55 *Deomys ferrugineus*

(Des P. Martial and F. Berille (5 f.), Berille (10 f.), Martial (20 f.). Photo Delrieu)

1966 (15 Sept). *Rodents. T* **55** *and similar designs. Multicoloured. P* 12×12½ (20 f.) *or* 12½×12 (*others*).
113	5 f. Type **55**	..	5	5
114	10 f. *Hybomis univittatus*	.. ..	5	5
115	20 f. *Prionomys batesi* (*vert*)	.. ..	10	5

XX

10 F

(62)

60 Symbols of Industry and Agriculture

61 Pres. Bokassa

(Des J. Gauthier. Photo Delrieu)

1966 (5 Dec). *AIR. Europafrique. P* 12×13.
124	**60**	50 f. multicoloured	..	.. ..	20	12

(Photo Delrieu)

1967 (1 Jan). *P* 12×12½.
125	**61**	30 f. black, yellow-ochre & brt green	12	8

1967 (8 May). *Provisional Issue.* (a) POSTAGE. No. 111 surch with T **62**.
126	10 f. on 25 f. multicoloured	..	5	5

(b) *AIR. No.* 112 *with face value altered by obliteration of figure* "2" *in* "25".
127	**54**	5 f. yellow, green, black & new blue	5	5

56 "Luna 9"

57 Cernan

(Des P. Béquet. Photo Delrieu)

1966 (24 Oct). *AIR. "Conquest of the Moon". T* **56** *and similar horiz designs, each in orange-brown, reddish violet, black and blue. P* 12½.
116	130 f. Type **56**	.. ..	..	55	40
117	130 f. "Surveyor"	..	..	55	40
118	200 f. "From the Earth to the Moon" (Jules Verne)	.. ..	85	60
MS119	132×160 mm. Nos. 116/8	..	2·00	2·00

(Des P. Lambert. Photo So.Ge.Im)

1966 (14 Nov). *AIR. Astronauts. T* **57** *and similar vert design. Multicoloured. P* 13.
120	50 f. Type **57**	..	..	..	25	12
121	50 f. Popovich	..	..	..	25	12

63 Bangui M'Poko Airport

(Des and eng C. Guillame. Recess)

1967 (3 July). *AIR. P* 13.
128	**63**	100 f. indigo, myrtle-green & choc	..	45	15

64 Aerial View of Fair

(Des and eng J. Combet. Recess)

1967 (17 July). *AIR. World Fair, Montreal. P* 13.
129	**64**	100 f. chocolate, ultram & turq-blue	..	45	15

58 Satellite "D1" and Rocket "Diamant"

59 U.N.E.S.C.O. Emblem

(Des and eng J. Combet. Recess)

1966 (14 Nov). *AIR. Launching of Satellite "D1". P* 13.
122	**58**	100 f. purple, bright purple & choc	..	50	25

(Photo So.Ge.Im)

1966 (5 Dec). *20th Anniv of U.N.E.S.C.O. P* 13.
123	**59**	30 f. multicoloured	.. ..	12	8

65 Central Market, Bangui

(Des G. Aufschneider. Photo So.Ge.Im)

1967. *T* **65** *and similar horiz design. Multicoloured. P* 12½×13.
130	30 f. Type **65** (8.8)	..	..	12	5
131	30 f. Safari Hotel, Bangui (26.9)	..	..	12	5

66 Map, Letters and Pylons

67 *Leucocoprinus africanus*

(Des and eng Monvoisin. Recess)

1967 (9 Sept). *AIR. Fifth Anniv of African and Malagasy Posts and Telecommunications Union (U.A.M.P.T.).* P 13.
132 **66** 100 f. purple, blue-green and carmine   45   15

(Des Gandon, after M. Bory. Photo So.Ge.lm)

1967 (3 Oct). *Mushrooms. T 67 and similar vert designs. Multicoloured.* P 13×12½.
133	5 f. Type **67**	..	..	5	5
134	10 f. *Synpodia arborescens*	..	..	5	5
135	15 f. *Phlebopus sudanicus*	..	..	5	5
136	30 f. *Termitomyces schimperi*	..	..	15	5
137	50 f. *Psalliota sebedulis* ..		..	25	10
133/137	*Set of 5*	..	..	50	25

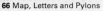

68 Projector, Africans and Map

69 Coiffure

(Des Igot-Cochinard. Eng M. Monvoisin. Recess)

1967 (31 Oct). *"Radiovision" Service.* P 13.
138 **68** 30 f. slate-blue, lt emer & orge-brown   12   8

(Des and eng P. Béquet (after Mme Bonnet). Recess)

1967 (7 Nov). *Female Coiffures. T 69 and similar vert designs showing different hairstyles. Heads in yellow-brown and chocolate.* P 13.
139	5 f. bright blue ..	..	..	5	5
140	10 f. carmine	..	..	5	5
141	15 f. blue-green ..	..	..	5	5
142	20 f. red-orange ..	..	..	10	5
143	30 f. bright purple	..	..	15	5
139/143	*Set of 5* ..	..	..	35	20

70 Inoculation Session

71 Douglas "DC-3"

(Des and eng J. Combet. Recess)

1967 (14 Nov). *Vaccination Programme, 1967–70.* P 13.
144 **70** 30 f. red-brown, blue-green & lake-brn   12   5

(Des and eng Gauthier (1 f., 2 f., 5 f.), Miermont (others). Recess)

1967 (24 Nov). *Aircraft. T 71 and similar horiz designs.* P 13. (a) POSTAGE.
145	1 f. slate-blue, blue-green & lake-brn	5	5
146	2 f. black, new blue & bright purple ..	5	5
147	5 f. black, emerald & greenish blue ..	5	5

(b) AIR. Inscr "POSTE AERIENNE"
148	100 f. brown, myrtle-green and new blue		45	20
149	200 f. ultramarine, chocolate & bl-green		90	45
150	500 f. slate-blue, brown-red and light greenish blue	..	1·90	1·00
145/150	*Set of 6*	..	3·00	1·60

Designs:—2 f. Beechcraft "Baron"; 5 f. Douglas "DC-4". (48×27 mm)—100 f. Potez "25-TOE"; 200 f. Junker "52"; 500 f. Caravelle "11-R".

72 Presidents Boganda and Bokassa

(Photo Delrieu)

1967 (1 Dec). *AIR. Ninth Anniv of Republic.* P 12½.
151 **72** 130 f. multicoloured   45   30

73 Primitive Shelter, Toulou   **74** Pres. Bokassa

(Des and eng C. Haley. Recess)

1967 (26 Dec). *Sixth Pan-African Prehistory Congress, Dakar. T 73 and similar designs.* P 13.
152	30 f. indigo, brown-purple and scarlet		12	8
153	50 f. bistre-brown, yellow-ochre and blackish green	..	20	10
154	100 f. maroon, yellow-brown & new bl ..		45	20
155	130 f. brown-red, blackish green & brn ..		50	25
152/155	*Set of 4*	..	1·10	55

Designs: Vert—50 f. Kwe perforated stone; 100 f. Megaliths, Bouar. Horiz—130 f. Rock drawings, Toulou.

(Photo Delrieu)

1968 (1 Jan). *AIR.* P 12½.
156 **74** 30 f. multicoloured   12   8

75 Human Rights Emblem, Human Figures and Globe

(Des H. Bétemps. Photo So.Ge.lm.)

1968 (26 Mar). *AIR. Human Rights Year.* P 13.
157 **75** 200 f. vermilion, emerald and violet ..   70   40

76 Human Figure and W.H.O. Emblem

77 Downhill Skiing

(Des and eng P. Béquet. Recess)

1968 (8 Apr). *AIR. 20th Anniv of World Health Organization.* P 13.
158 **76** 200 f. carmine, new blue & yellow-brn .. 70 40

(Des and eng A. Decaris. Recess)

1968 (16 Apr). *AIR. Olympic Games, Grenoble and Mexico.* T **77** *and similar vert design.* P 13.
159 200 f. chocolate, greenish blue & carm .. 80 40
160 200 f. chocolate, greenish blue & carm .. 80 40
Designs:—No. 159, T **77**; No. 160, Throwing the javelin.

78 Parachute-landing on Venus

79 Marie Curie and impaled Crab (of Cancer)

(Des and eng J. Gauthier. Recess)

1968 (23 Apr). *AIR. Venus 4. Exploration of the planet Venus.* P 13.
161 **78** 100 f. bright, blue, turquoise-green and myrtle-green 40 20

(Des and eng P. Gandon. Recess)

1968 (30 Apr). *AIR. Marie Curie Commemoration.* P 13.
162 **79** 100 f. chocolate, violet and blue .. 40 20

80 Refinery and Tanker **(81)**

(Des C. Haley. Photo Delrieu)

1968 (30 July). *Inauguration of Petroleum Refinery, Port Gentil, Gabon.* P 12½.
163 **80** 30 f. new blue, red, green & chestnut 12 5

1968 (16 Sept). *AIR. Various stamps surch as T* **81** *or with digits obliterated (Nos. 165/6).*
164 **56** 5 f. on 130 f. (No. 116) 5 5
165 – 10 f. (100 f. No. 148) 5 5
166 – 20 f. (200 f. No. 149) 8 5
167 – 50 f. on 130 f. (No. 117) 20 15
164/167 *Set of 4* 35 25

82 "CD-8" Bulldozer **83** Bangui Mosque

(Des Bétemps. Eng Fenneteaux (No. 171), Bétemps (others). Recess)

1968 (1 Oct). *Bokassa Project.* T **82** *and similar horiz designs.* P 13.
168 5 f. red-brown, black and myrtle-green 5 5
169 10 f. black, yellow-brown & lt emerald .. 5 5
170 20 f. emerald, yellow and brown 8 5
171 30 f. bright blue, olive-drab & pur-brown 10 5
172 30 f. brown-red, grey-blue & myrtle-grn 10 5
168/172 *Set of 5* 35 20
Designs:—10 f. Baoulé cattle; 20 f. Spinning-machine; 30 f. (No. 171), Automatic looms; 30 f. (No. 172), "D4-C" bull-dozer.

1968 (14 Oct). *Second Anniv of Bangui Mosque.* P 13.
173 **83** 30 f. flesh, emerald and blue 12 5

84 Za Throwing-knife **85** *Ville de Bangui* (1958)

(Des and eng J. Gauthier. Recess)

1968 (19 Nov). *Hunting Weapons.* T **84** *and similar horiz designs.* P 13.
174 10 f. greenish blue, yellow-bistre & blue 5 5
175 20 f. myrtle-green, olive-brown and blue 8 5
176 30 f. myrtle-green, brown-orange & blue 12 5
Designs:—20 f. Kpinga-Gbengue throwing-knife; 30 f. Mbano cross-bow.

(Des R. Chapelet. Eng G. Aufschneider (10 f.), P. Forget (30 f.), M. Monvoisin (50 f.), J. Miermont (100 f., 130 f.). Recess)

1968 (10 Dec). *River Craft. Horiz designs as T* **85**. P 13. (a) *POSTAGE.*
177 10 f. ultramarine, blue-green & brt pur 5 5
178 30 f. chocolate, new bl & myrtle-grn .. 12 5
179 50 f. slate-blue, light brown & ol-grn .. 20 10

(b) *AIR. Inscr* "POSTE AERIENNE"
180 100 f. chocolate, olive-green & new blue 40 20
181 130 f. slate-blue, myrtle-green & brt pur 45 25
177/181 *Set of 5* .. .. .. 1 · 10 55
Designs: (*As* T **85**)—30 f. *J. B. Gouandjia* (1968); 50 f. *Lamblin* (1944). (48×27 *mm*)—100 f. *Pie X* (Bangui, 1894); 130 f. *Ballay* (Bangui, 1891).

86 "Madame de Sévigné" (French School, 17th century)

Central African Republic

(Photo Delrieu)

1968 (17 Dec). *AIR. "Philexafrique" Stamp Exhibition, Abidjan (1969). P 12½.*
182 **86** 100 f. multicoloured 45 45
No. 182 was issued in sheets with *se-tenant* stamp-size label inscr "PHILEXAFRIQUE".

87 President Bokassa, Cotton Plantation, and Ubangui-Shari Stamp of 1930

(Des and eng J. Gauthier. Recess)

1969 (14 Feb). *AIR. "Philexafrique" Stamp Exhibition, Abidjan, Ivory Coast (2nd Issue). P 13.*
183 **87** 50 f. black, myrtle-green & orange-brn 25 20

88 *Holocerina angulata*   **89** Throwing the Javelin

(Des H. Crouzet. Photo So.Ge.Im.)

1969 (25 Feb). *AIR. Butterflies. T 88 and similar multicoloured designs. P 13.*
184 10 f. Type **88** 5 5
185 20 f. *Nudaurelia dione* 5 5
186 30 f. *Eustera troglophylla* (*vert*) .. 10 5
187 50 f. *Aurivillius aratus* 15 10
188 100 f. *Epiphora albida* 30 20
184/188 *Set of 5* 60 40

(Des P. Lambert. Photo So.Ge.Im.)

1969 (18 Mar). *Sports. T 89 and similar multicoloured designs.* (a) *POSTAGE. Vert designs size as T 89. P 13×12½.*
189 5 f. Type **89** 5 5
190 10 f. Start of race 5 5
191 15 f. Football 5 5
(b) *AIR. Inscr "POSTE AERIENNE". Horiz designs size 48×28 mm. P 13*
192 50 f. Boxing 15 8
193 100 f. Basketball 30 15
189/193 *Set of 5* 55 35

90 Miner and Emblems

(Des J. Derrey. Photo So.Ge.Im.)

1969 (20 May). *50th Anniversary of International Labour Organization. P 12½×13.*
194 **90** 30 f. multicoloured 8 8
195 50 f. multicoloured 15 8

91 "Apollo 8" over Moon's Surface

(Des C. Guillame. Photo So.Ge.Im.)

1969 (27 May). *AIR. Flight of "Apollo 8" around the Moon. P 13.*
196 **91** 200 f. multicoloured 60 35

92 Nuremberg Spire and Toys

(Des H. Biais. Photo So.Ge.Im.)

1969 (3 June). *AIR. International Toy Fair, Nuremberg. P 13.*
197 **92** 100 f. black, bright purple & emerald 30 20

(Photo Delrieu)

1969 (4 Nov). *AIR. Birth Bicentenary of Napoleon Bonaparte. Multicoloured paintings similar to T 144 of Cameroun. P 12½×12 (100 f.) or 12×12½ (others).*
198 100 f. "Napoleon as First Consul" (Girodet-Trioson) (*vert*) .. 40 20
199 130 f. "Meeting of Napoleon and Francis II of Austria" (Gros) .. 50 30
200 200 f. "Marriage of Napoleon and Marie-Louise" (Rouget) 80 50

93 Pres. Bokassa in Military Uniform   **94** Pres. Bokassa, Flag and Map

(Litho De La Rue)

1969 (1 Dec). *P 13×13½.*
201 **93** 30 f. multicoloured 10 5

1969 (12 Dec). *10th Anniversary of ASECNA. As T 150 of Cameroun.*
202 100 f. blue 30 15

(Die-stamped on foil Societé Pierre Mariotte)

1970 (1 Jan). *AIR. P 10½.*
203 **94** 2000 f. gold .. .. .. 5·50

95 Garayah

97 F. D. Roosevelt (25th Death Anniv)

96 Flour Storage Depot

(Des A. Peyrié. Eng Hanniquet (10 f.), Fenneteaux (15 f.), Guillame (30 f.), Braquemond (50 f.), Lacaque (130 f.). Recess)

1970 (6 Jan). *Musical Instruments. Designs as T* **95**. *P* 13.

204	10 f. orge-brn, sepia, yell-grn & dp grn				5	5
205	15 f. pur-brown, yell-brn & turq-green				5	5
206	30 f. pur-brown, brn-lake & yell-brown				8	5
207	50 f. indigo and carmine	..	..		15	10
208	130 f. brown, olive and new blue				40	25
204/208	*Set of* 5	..	..	..	65	40

Designs: *Horiz*—15 f. Ngombi; 30 f. Xylophone; 50 f. Ndala. *Vert*—130 f. Gatta and Babyon.

(Litho De La Rue)

1970 (24 Feb). *SICPAD Project (Sociétié Industrielle Centra-africaine des Produits Alimentaires et Dérivés). T* **96** *and similar horiz designs. Multicoloured. P* 14.

209	25 f. Type **96**	..	..	..	12	5
210	50 f. Mill machinery	..	..	..	30	20
211	100 f. View of flour mill	..	..	..	55	30

(Litho De La Rue)

1970 (Apr). *AIR. World Leaders. T* **97** *and similar vert portrait. Multicoloured. P* 14.

212	100 f. Lenin (birth cent) (22.4)	..	..	30	20
213	100 f. Type **97** (29.4)	..	..	30	20

1970 (20 May). *New U.P.U. Headquarters Building, Berne. Design as T* **156** *of Cameroun.*

214	100 f. brown-red, vermilion and blue	..	30	15

ATTERRISSAGE
d'APOLLO 12
19 novembre 1969

(98)

99 Pres. Bokassa

1970 (1 June). *AIR. Moon Landing of "Apollo 12". No.* 196 *optd with T* **98**, *in red.*

215	**91**	200 f. multicoloured	..	..	60	40

(Litho De La Rue)

1970 (13 Aug). *P* 14.

216	**99**	30 f. multicoloured	..	..	..	12	5
217		40 f. multicoloured	..	..	..	15	8

100 Cheese Factory, Sarki   **101** Silkworm

(Des Frank. Litho)

1970 (15 Sept). *"Operation Bokassa" Development Projects. T* **100**/1 *and similar multicoloured designs as T* **100**. *No gum.* (*a*) *POSTAGE. P* 13½ × 13 (20 f.) *or* 13 × 13½ (*others*).

218	5 f. Type **100**	..	..	..	5	5
219	10 f. M'Bali Ranch	..	..	..	5	5
220	20 f. Zebu bull and herdsman (*vert*)	..	5	5
221	40 f. Type **101**	..	..	..	12	5

(*b*) *AIR. Inscr* "POSTE AERIENNE". *P* 10

222	140 f. Type **101**	..	..	..	40	20
218/222	*Set of* 5	..	..	..	60	35

102 African Dancer

1970 (15 Sept). *AIR. "Knokphila 70" Stamp Exhibition, Knokke, Belgium. T* **102** *and similar horiz design. Multicoloured. Litho. No gum. P* 10.

223	100 f. Type **102**	..	..	..	30	20
224	100 f. African produce	..	..	..	30	20
	a. Triptych. Nos. 223/4 and inscr label				70	50

Nos. 223/4 were issued together in the same sheet separated by an inscr label, each triptych being imperf between vertically.

103 Footballer

(Des Frank. Litho)

1970 (8 Dec). *AIR. World Cup Football Championships, Mexico. No gum. P* 13 × 13½.

225	**103**	200 f. multicoloured	..	..	60	35

104 Central African Republic's Pavilion

1970 (18 Dec). *AIR. World Fair "EXPO 70". Osaka, Japan. Litho. No gum. P* 13½×13.
226 **104** 200 f. multicoloured.. .. .. 60 35

105 Dove and Cogwheel

(Des Frank. Litho Dereume)

1970 (31 Dec). *AIR. 25th Anniversary of United Nations. No gum. P* 13×13½.
227 **105** 200 f. black, yellow and light blue .. 60 35

106 Presidents Mobutu, Bokassa and Tombalbaye

(Des Frank. Litho Dereume)

1971 (10 Jan). *AIR. Reconciliation with Chad and Zaire. No gum. P* 13×13½.
228 **106** 140 f. multicoloured.. .. .. 40 25

107 Guineafowl and Partridge   **108** Lengue Dancer

(Des H. Crouzet. Photo Delrieu)

1971 (9 Feb). *Wildlife. T* **107** *and similar horiz designs. Multicoloured. P* 12½×12.
229   5 f. +5 Type **107** 5   5
230   10 f. +5 f. Duiker and snails 5   5
231   20 f. +5 f. Hippopotamus, elephant and tortoise in tug-of-war 10   8
232   30 f. +10 f. Tortoise and cuckoo .. 15 12
233   50 f. +20 f. Monkey and leopard .. 25 20
229/233 *Set of 5* 55 45

1971 (9 Feb). *Traditional Dances. T* **108** *and similar vert designs, showing female dancers. Multicoloured. Litho. No gum. P* 13½×13.
234   20 f. +5 f. Type **108** 8   5
235   40 f. +10 f. Lengue (*different*) 20   12
236   100 f. +40 f. Teke 50 30
237   140 f. +40 f. Englabolo 65 40
234/237 *Set of 4* .. .. .. 1·25 80

O **109** Arms   **110** *Gnathonemus monteiri*

(Des G. Richer. Photo Delrieu)

1971 (1 Apr). *OFFICIAL. Type* O **1** *redrawn Type* O **109**. *P* 12×12½.
O238   5 f. multicoloured 5   5
O239   30 f. multicoloured 10   8
O240   40 f. multicoloured 15 10
O241   100 f. multicoloured 35 25
O242   140 f. multicoloured 50 30
O243   200 f. multicoloured 70 50
O238/243 *Set of 6* .. .. .. 1·60 1·10

(Des H. Crouzet. Photo Delrieu)

1971 (6 Apr). *Fishes. T* **110** *and similar horiz designs. Multicoloured. P* 12½.
244   10 f. Type **110** 5   5
245   20 f. *Mormyrus proboscirostris* 8   5
246   30 f. *Marcusenius wilverthi* 10   8
247   40 f. *Gnathonemus elephas* 15 10
248   50 f. *Gnathonemus curvirostris* 20 12
244/248 *Set of 5* 50 35

111 Satellite and Globe

(Des P. Lambert. Photo Delrieu)

1971 (17 May). *AIR. World Telecommunications Day. P* 12½.
249 **111** 100 f. multicoloured.. .. .. 35 20

PUZZLED?

Then you need
PHILATELIC TERMS ILLUSTRATED
to tell you all you need to know about printing methods, papers, errors, varieties, watermarks, perforations, etc. 192 pages, almost half in full colour, soft cover. £1 post paid.

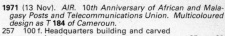

112 Berberati Cathedral

113 Gen. de Gaulle

1971 (20 July). *Consecration of Roman Catholic Cathedral, Berberati. Litho. No gum. P* 13½ × 13.
250 **112** 5 f. multicoloured 5 5

(Litho De La Rue)

1971 (20 Aug). 1st *Death Anniversary of Gen. Charles de Gaulle. P* 13.
251 **113** 100 f. multicoloured 35 20

114 Grey Galago

116 Crab Emblem

115 Shepard in Capsule

(Des H. Crouzet. Photo)

1971 (25 Oct). *Monkeys and Lemurs. T* **114** *and similar multicoloured designs. P* 13.
252 30 f. Type **114** 10 5
253 40 f. Elegant galago 15 8
254 100 f. Calabar potto (*horiz*) 35 20
255 150 f. Bosman's potto (*horiz*) 50 25
256 200 f. Oustalet's colobus monkey (*horiz*) 70 30
252/256 *Set of 5* .. .. 1·60 80

1971 (13 Nov). *AIR.* 10th *Anniversary of African and Malagasy Posts and Telecommunications Union. Multicoloured design as T* **184** *of Cameroun.*
257 100 f. Headquarters building and carved head 35 20

1971 (19 Nov). *Space Achievements. T* **115** *and similar diamond-shaped designs. Multicoloured. Litho. P* 14.
258 40 f. Type **115** 15 8
259 40 f. Gagarin in helmet 15 8
260 100 f. Aldrin in Space 35 20
261 100 f. Leonov in Space 35 20
262 200 f. Armstrong on Moon 70 40
263 200 f. "Lunokhod 1" on Moon 70 40
258/263 *Set of 6* .. .. .. 2·10 1·25

(Des P. Lambert. Photo Delrieu)

1971 (20 Nov). *AIR. Anti-Cancer Campaign. P* 12½.
264 **116** 100 f. multicoloured 35 20

117 "Operation Bokassa"

(Des P. Lambert. Photo Delrieu)

1971 (1 Dec). 12th *Year of Independence. P* 13.
265 **117** 40 f. multicoloured 15 8

118 Racial Equality Year Emblem

1971 (6 Dec). *Racial Equality Year. Litho. P* 13.
266 **118** 50 f. multicoloured 20 8

119 I.E.Y. Emblem and Child with Toy Bricks

(Des Frank. Litho)

1971 (11 Dec). *AIR.* 25th *Anniversary of U.N.E.S.C.O. No gum. P* 13 × 13½.
267 **119** 140 f. multicoloured 40 20

120 African Children

(Des Frank. Litho Dereume)

1971 (11 Dec). *AIR. 25th Anniversary of U.N.I.C.E.F. No gum.* P 13×13½.
268 **120** 140 f.+50 f. multicoloured 60 50

121 Arms and Parade   **122** Pres. Gamal Nasser

(Des P. Lambert. Photo Delrieu)

1972 (1 Jan). *Pres. Bokassa Military School.* P 13.
269 **121** 30 f. multicoloured 10 5

(Des P. Lambert. Photo Delrieu)

1972 (15 Jan). *AIR. Pres. Gamal Nasser Commemoration.* P 12½.
270 **122** 100 f. yellow-ochre, blackish brown and carmine-red 35 20

123 Book Year Emblem   **124** Heart Emblem

(Des P. Sampoux. Photo)

1972 (11 Mar). *International Book Year.* P 12½×13.
271 **123** 100 f. gold, yellow and lake-brown .. 35 20

(Des Krumenacker. Photo)

1972 (7 Apr). *World Heart Month.* P 13×12½.
272 **124** 100 f. red, black and yellow 35 20

125 First-Aid Post   **126** Global Emblem

(Des P. Lambert. Photo Delrieu)

1972 (8 May). *Red Cross Day.* P 13.
273 **125** 150 f. multicoloured 50 25

(Photo Delrieu)

1972 (17 May). *World Telecommunications Day.* P 13.
274 **126** 50 f. black, lemon and orange-red .. 20 8

127 Boxing

(Des and eng G. Bétemps. Recess)

1972 (26 May). *AIR. Olympic Games, Munich.* T **127** and similar design. P 13.
275 100 f. bistre-brown and orange-brown .. 35 20
276 100 f. reddish violet and emerald .. 35 20
MS277 130×100 mm. Designs as Nos. 275/6, but colours changed: 100 f. emerald & bright pur; 100 f. bright purple & orge-brn .. 70 70
Designs: *Horiz*—No. 275, T **127**. *Vert*—No. 276 Long-jumping.

128 Pres. Bokassa and Family   **129** Pres. Bokassa planting Cotton Bush

(Litho De La Rue)

1972 (28 May). *Mothers' Day.* P 14.
278 **128** 30 f. multicoloured 10 5

(Des Frank. Photo Delrieu)

1972 (5 June). *"Operation Bokassa" Cotton Development.* P 13.
279 **129** 40 f. multicoloured 15 8

130 Savings Bank Building

(Des Krumenacker. Photo)

1972 (21 June). *Opening of New Postal Cheques and Savings Bank Building.* P 13×12½.
280 **130** 30 f. multicoloured 10 5

131 "Le Pacifique" Hotel   **132** Hunting Scene

(Des and eng A. Decaris. Recess)

1972 (27 June). *"Operation Bokassa" Completion of "Le Pacifique" Hotel.* P 13×12½.
281 **131** 30 f. slate-blue, rosine and emerald 10 5

(Des Chesnot. Photo Delrieu)

1972 (31 July). *Clock-faces from Central African HORCEN Factory. T 132 and similar square designs. Multicoloured.* P 12½.

282	5 f. Type **132**	..	..	..	5	5
283	10 f. Camp fire and warriors	..	..	5	5
284	20 f. Fishermen	..	..	..	8	5
285	30 f. Giraffe and monkeys	..	..	10	5
286	40 f. Warriors fighting	..	..	15	8
282/286	*Set of 5*	..	..	..	40	25

133 Postal Runner

135 University Buildings

134 Tiling's Postal Rocket, 1931

(Des P. Lambert. Photo Delrieu (10, 20 f.). Des and eng J. Gauthier. Recess (others))

1972 (12 Aug). *"CENTRAPHILEX" Stamp Exhibition, Bangui.*
(a) *POSTAGE. T 133 and similar multicoloured design.* P 13.

287	10 f. Type **133**	..	..	5	5
288	20 f. Protestant Youth Centre (*horiz*)	..	8	5

(b) *AIR. T 134 and similar designs*

289	40 f. red-orange, new blue & slate-blue	15	8
290	50 f. slate-blue, new blue & red-orange	20	8
291	150 f. slate, red-orange and brown	..	50	25
292	200 f. new blue, red-orange and brown	70	40
287/292	*Set of 6*	..	..	..	1·50	80
MS293	201×100 mm. Nos. 289/92 ..		1·50	1·50

Designs: *Vert*—50 f. "DC-3" aircraft and camel postman; 150 f. "Sirio" satellite and rocket. *Horiz*—200 f. "Intelsat 4" satellite and rocket.

(Des and eng A. Decaris. Recess)

1972 (26 Aug). *Inauguration of Bokassa University.* P 13×12½.

294	**135** 40 f. grey, greenish bl & brown-red	15	8

136 Mail Van

138 Four Linked Arrows

137 Paddy Field

(Des P. Lambert. Photo Delrieu)

1972 (23 Oct). *World U.P.U. Day.* P 13.

295	**136**	100 f. multicoloured ..	..	..	35	20

(Litho De La Rue)

1972 (10 Nov). *Bokassa Plan. State Farms. T 137 and similar horiz design. Multicoloured.* P 13.

296	5 f. Type **137**	..	..	5	5
297	25 f. Rice cultivation	..	..	10	5

(Des "Lacroix" (H. Ouin). Typo Edila)

1972 (17 Nov). *AIR. "Europafrique".* P 13.

298	**138**	100 f. multicoloured ..	..	35	20

POIDS-MOYEN LEMECHEV MEDAILLE D'OR

(139)

140 Hotel Swimming Pool

1972 (24 Nov). *AIR. Munich Olympics Gold-medal Winners.* Nos. 275/**MS**277 optd with T **139** or similar inscr.

299	**127**	100 f. bistre-brown & orange-brown	35	20
300	–	100 f. reddish violet and emerald	..	35	20
MS301		130×100 mm. **MS**277 with opts as Nos. 299/300			
		..	..	..	70	70

Overprints:—No. 299, T **139**; No. 300, "LONGUEUR WILLIAMS MEDAILLE D'OR".

(Des and eng A. Decaris. Recess)

1972 (9 Dec). *Opening of Hotel St. Sylvestre. T 140 and similar horiz design.* P 13×12½.

302	30 f. chocolate, blue-grn & blackish grn	10	5
303	40 f. brn-purple, blackish grn & brt bl	..	15	8

Design:—40 f. Hotel façade.

141 Landing Module and Lunar Rover on Moon

(Des and eng C. Guillame. Recess)

1972 (18 Dec). *AIR. Moon Flight of "Apollo 16". P* 13.
304 **141** 100 f. deep bluish green, blue & slate   35   20

142 "Virgin and Child" (F. Pesellino)

143 Learning to Write

(Photo Delrieu)

1972 (25 Dec). *AIR. Christmas. T* **142** *and similar vert painting. Multicoloured. P* 13.
305   100 f. Type **142** ..   35   20
306   150 f. "Adoration of the Child" (F. Lippi)   50   25

(Litho De La Rue)

1972 (27 Dec). *"Central African Mothers". T* **143** *and similar vert designs. Multicoloured. P* 13.
307   5 f. Type **143**   5   5
308   10 f. Baby-care   5   5
309   15 f. Dressing hair   5   5
310   20 f. Learning to read   8   5
311   180 f. Suckling baby   65   35
312   190 f. Learning to walk   65   35
307/312   Set of 6   ..   ..   1·40   75

144 Louys (marathon), Athens, 1896

(Des and eng C. Haley. Recess)

1972 (28 Dec). *AIR. 75th Anniv of Revival of Olympic Games. T* **144** *and similar horiz designs. P* 13.
313   30 f. magenta, brown and turq-green ..   10   5
314   40 f. emerald, ultramarine & purple-brn   15   8
315   50 f. bluish violet, turq-blue & carmine   20   8
316   100 f. bright pur, purple-brown & slate ..   35   20
317   150 f. black, turq-blue & bright purple ..   50   25
313/317   Set of 5   ..   ..   1·25   60
    Designs:—40 f. Barrelet (sculling), Paris, 1900; 50 f. Prinstein (triple-jump), St. Louis, U.S.A., 1904; 100 f. Taylor (400 m. freestyle swimming), London, 1908; 150 f. Johansson (Graeco–Roman wrestling), Stockholm, 1912.

145 W.H.O. Emblem, Doctor and Nurse

(Des Baillais. Photo Delrieu)

1973 (7 Apr). *AIR. 25th Anniv of World Health Organization. P* 13.
318 **145** 100 f. multicoloured   35   20

Chad

100 Centimes = 1 Franc

A. FRENCH POSSESSION

Lake Chad was first explored by British explorers in 1823, but French influence reached there with the expeditions of Paul Crampel in 1890–91 and Emile Gentil in 1896–97. It was then within the empire of the Sudanese military adventurer and slave-dealer Rabah. After his defeat and death at the hands of a French expedition, Chad became a French military territory on 5 September 1900.

Chad became part of the French Congo and was integrated with Ubangi-Shari in 1906. The stamps of French Congo were used until 1915 and those of Ubangi-Shari-Chad (see under Central African Republic), from 1915 to 1922. Chad became a separate Colony on 17 March 1920.

PRINTERS. All the stamps of Chad, other than those in lithography, were printed at the Government Printing Works, Paris, *unless otherwise stated.*

IMPERFORATE STAMPS. Many stamps exist imperforate in their issued colours but they were not valid for postage. Imperforate stamps in other colours are colour trials.

TCHAD
(1)

1922 (Nov). *Types of Middle Congo, colours changed, optd with* T 1.

1	1 c. bright rose and violet	..	5	5
	a. Opt omitted ..	..	8·00	
2	2 c. brown and pink	..	5	5
	a. Opt omitted†	..	20·00	
3	4 c. slate-blue and violet	..	5	5
4	5 c. brown and green	..	8	8
5	10 c. green and blue-green	..	10	12
6	15 c. violet and rose	..	12	12
7	20 c. green and violet	..	15	15
8	25 c. brown and chocolate	..	50	50
9	30 c. carmine	..	10	10
10	35 c. slate-blue and pink	..	20	20
11	40 c. purple-brown and green	..	20	20
12	45 c. violet and green	..	20	20
13	50 c. blue and pale blue	..	20	20
14	60 on 75 c. violet/*rose*	..	30	30
	a. Opt omitted	..	10·00	
	b. "60" omitted	..	10·00	
15	75 c. brown rose and violet	..	12	12
16	1 f. slate-blue and rose ..	..	80	80
17	2 f. slate-blue and violet..	..	1·00	1·00
18	5 f. slate-blue and brown	..	80	80
1/18	*Set of 18*	..	4·50	4·50

†See footnote relating to No. 47a of Cameroun.

1924 (Sept)-**33**. *Stamps of 1922 and similar stamps optd with Ubangi-Shari (Central African Republic)* T 5 (1 *c. to* 20 *c.*) *or* 6 *(others).*

19	1 c. bright rose and violet	..	5	5
	a. T 1 opt omitted	..	8·00	
	b. T 1 opt double	..	6·00	
	c. Violet (background) omitted	..	6·00	
20	2 c. brown and pink	..	5	5
	a. T 1 opt omitted	..	8·00	
	b. T 1 opt double	..	6·00	
21	4 c. slate-blue and violet	..	5	5
22	5 c. brown and green	..	5	5
	a. T 1 opt omitted	..	8·00	
	b. T 5 opt in blue	..	5	5
	c. Do. T 1 opt omitted ..	..	6·00	
23	10 c. green and blue-green	..	5	5
	a. T 5 opt in blue	..	5	5
24	10 c. orange-vermilion and grey (1.12.25)	..	5	5
	a. T 1 opt omitted	..	7·00	
	b. T 5 opt omitted	..	7·00	
25	15 c. violet and rose	..	5	5
26	20 c. green and violet	..	5	5
	a. T 1 opt omitted	..	8·00	

27	25 c. brown and chocolate	..	5	5
	a. T 6 opt double	..	4·00	
28	30 c. carmine	..	5	5
29	30 c. grey and blue (R.) (1.12.25)	..	5	5
30	30 c. olive-green and green (14.11.27)	..	5	5
	a. T 6 opt omitted	..	9·00	
31	35 c. slate-blue and pink ..	..	5	5
32	40 c. purple-brown and green	..	10	10
	a. T 6 opt double (Bk. + R.)	..	15·00	
33	45 c. violet and green	..	5	5
	a. T 6 opt double (Bk. + B.)	..	16·00	
34	50 c. blue and pale blue (R.)	..	5	5
	a. T 6 opt inverted	..	7·00	
35	50 c. green and purple (1.12.25)	..	8	8
36	60 on 75 violet/*rose*	..	5	5
	a. "60" omitted	..	8·00	
37	65 c. red-brown and blue (2.4.28)	..	12	12
	a. T 6 opt omitted	..	8·00	
38	75 c. bright rose and violet (B.)	..	5	5
39	75 c. blue and pale blue (R.) (1.6.25)	..	5	5
	a. T 1 opt omitted†	..	8·00	
40	75 c. claret and brown (25.9.28)	..	15	15
41	90 c. carmine and rose-red (22.3.30)	..	50	50
42	1 f. slate-blue and rose (B.)	..	8	8
43	1 f. 10, green and ultramarine (25.9.28)	..	15	15
44	1 f. 25, red-brown & ultram (25.9.33)	..	50	50
45	1 f. 50, ultramarine and blue (22.3.30)	..	45	45
46	1 f. 75, chocolate and magenta (25.9.33)	..	4·50	4·50
47	2 f. slate-blue and violet (B.)	..	15	15
48	3 f. magenta/*rose* (22.3.30)	..	50	50
49	5 f. slate-blue and brown (B.)	..	15	15
19/49	*Set of 31*	..	7·50	7·50

†See footnote relating to No. 62a of Ubangi-Shari (Central African Republic).

1925–27. *Stamps as 1924–33 but colours changed, with opt* T 1 *in black and opt Ubangi-Shari* T 6 *in black or colours shown, further surch as Ubangi-Shari* T 7/10, *in black.*

(a) In figures only (1.2.25)

50	65 on 1 f. chocolate and olive-green (R.)		10	10
51	85 on 1 f. chocolate and olive-green (R.)		10	10

(b) In figures with bars over old values

52	90 on 75 c. carmine and rose-red (11.4.27)		8	8
53	1 f. 25 on 1 f. blue and ultramarine (B. + R.) (14.6.26)	..	5	5
	a. T 6 opt omitted	..	8·00	
54	1 f. 50 on 1 f. ultramarine and greenish blue (11.4.27)		15	15
55	3 f. on 5 f. chestnut & carm (19.12.27)	..	40	40
	a. No stop after "F"	..	1·10	1·10
56	10 f. on 5 f. green and rose (21.3.27)	..	90	90
	a. "10 F" omitted	..	20·00	
57	20 f. on 5 f. violet and vermilion (21.3.27)	..	1·25	1·25
	a. No stop after "F"	..	2·75	2·75
50/57	*Set of 8*	..	2·75	2·75

On No. 53 the Type 6 overprint is in blue and the surcharge in red.

1931 (13 Apr). *International Colonial Exhibition, Paris. As* T 9/12 *of Cameroun.*

58	40 c. green	..	40	40
59	50 c. mauve	..	40	40
60	90 c. vermilion	..	40	40
61	1 f. 50, blue	..	40	40
58/61	*Set of 4*	..	1·40	1·40

TCHAD

A. E. F.
(D 1)

1928 (4 Apr). *POSTAGE DUE. Type* D **3** *of France, optd with Type* D **1**. *P* 14 × 13½.

D62	5 c. light blue	..	..	..	..	5	5
D63	10 c. brown		..	..	..	5	5
D64	20 c. olive-green		..	..	..	5	5
D65	25 c. rosine	..		..	..	5	5
D66	30 c. rose	..		..	..	5	5
D67	45 c. green	..		..	..	8	8
D68	50 c. claret	..	..		..	8	8
	a. No stop after "F"			..	..	50	50
D69	60 c. yellow-brown/*cream*		..	..	12	12
D70	1 f. maroon/*cream*			..	..	12	12
D71	2 f. rose-red	..		..	..	35	35
D72	3 f. bright violet		..	..	..	15	15
D62/72	*Set of* 11	..		..	..	1·00	1·00

D **2** Village of Straw-huts   D **3** Pirogue on Lake Chad

(Des J. Kerhor. Eng G. Daussy. Typo)

1930 (17 Feb). *POSTAGE DUE. P* 14 × 13½ (D **2**) *or* 13½ × 14 (D **3**).

D73	D **2**	5 c. drab and deep blue		..	5	5
D74		10 c. chocolate and scarlet	..	..	5	5
D75		20 c. chocolate and green	..		12	12
D76		25 c. chocolate and light blue		..	12	12
D77		30 c. blue-green and yellow-brown		12	12
D78		45 c. drab and blue-green	..		12	12
D79		50 c. chocolate and magenta		..	12	12
D80		60 c. black and lilac-blue	..		15	15
D81	D **3**	1 f. slate-black and yellow-brown	..	15	15
D82		2 f. chocolate and mauve	..	..	20	20
D83		3 f. chocolate and scarlet	..		2·50	2·50
D73/83		*Set of* 11	..	..	3·25	3·25

From 16 March 1936 to 1959, stamps of French Equatorial Africa were used in Chad.

B. CHAD REPUBLIC

The Chad Republic was created as an autonomous state on 28 November 1958, and became independent, within the French Community, on 11 August 1960.

2 "Birth of the Republic"   3 Flag, Map and U.N. Emblem

(Des and eng Combet. Recess)

1959 (28 Nov). *First Anniv of Republic. T* **2** *and similar vert design. P* 13.

62	15 f. lake, green, yellow and bright blue	..	8	5
63	25 f. lake and blackish green	..	..	15	5

Design:—25 f. Map and birds.

1960 (21 May). *Tenth Anniv of African Technical Co-operation Commission. As No.* 3 *of Central African Republic.*

64	50 f. violet and bright purple	..	..	40	40

1960 (15 Dec). *AIR. Olympic Games. No.* 257 *of French Equatorial Africa surch as* T **5** *of Central African Republic in red, but inscr* "REPUBLIQUE DU TCHAD".

65	250 f. on 500 f. deep bl, blk & dp bl-grn ..	2·25	2·25

(Des and eng Combet. Recess)

1961 (11 Jan). *Admission into U.N. P* 13.

66	**3**	15 f. multicoloured	..	..	12	5
67		25 f. multicoloured		..	15	12
68		85 f. multicoloured	..	..	50	40

4 Shari Bridge and Hippopotamus   5 *Euplectes oryx*

(Des Hervigo. Eng Aufschneider (50 c., 1 f., 5 f.), Barre (2 f., 4 f., 15 f., 25 f.), Miermont (3 f., 60 f., 85 f.), Fenneteaux (10 f., 30 f.), Frères (20 f.). Typo)

1961–62. *T* **4** *and similar designs including animal silhouettes. P* 14 × 13½ (5 f.) *or* 13½ × 14 (*others*).

69	50 c. yellow-green and black (11.1.62)		5	5
70	1 f. green and black (11.1.62)		5	5
71	2 f. red-brown and black (11.1.62)		5	5
72	3 f. yellow-orange & dull grn (25.5.62)		5	5
73	4 f. carmine-red and black (11.1.62)		5	5
74	5 f. lemon and black (11.8.61)		5	5
75	10 f. pink and black (11.8.61)		5	5
76	15 f. light reddish violet & blk (25.5.62)		8	5
77	20 f. scarlet and black (11.8.61)	..	·12	5
78	25 f. greenish blue and black (25.5.62)		12	5
79	30 f. bright blue and black (25.5.62)		15	8
80	60 f. yellow and black (11.1.62)	..	15	8
81	85 f. orange and black (11.8.61)	..	35	15
69/81	*Set of* 13		..	1·10	70

Designs: *Vert*—50 c. Biltine and Dorcas gazelle; 1 f. Logone and elephant; 2 f. Batha and lion; 3 f. Salamal and buffalo; 4 f. Ouaddai and greater kudu; 10 f. Abtouyour and bullock; 15 f. Bessada and Derby's eland; 20 f. Tibesti and moufflon; 25 f. Tikem Rocks and hartebeest; 30 f. Kanem and cheetah; 60 f. Borkou and oryx; 85 f. Guelta D'Archei and addax.

(Des P. Lambert. Eng Bétemps (50 f., 200 f.), Cottet (100 f.), Durrens (500 f.). Recess)

1961 (27 Oct)–**63.** *AIR. T* **5** *and similar vert designs. P* 13.

82	50 f. black, crimson and green	..	30	12
83	100 f. indigo, red, green and maroon	..	50	25
84	200 f. orange-red, blue, violet & pur-brn	1·00	50
85	250 f. blue, orange and green (6.2.63)	..	1·25	60
86	500 f. orange-red, emerald, brown & blue	2·25	1·25
82/86	*Set of* 5	..	4·75	2·40

Birds:—100 f. *Chalcomitra senegalensis*; 200 f. *Tchitrea viridis*; 250 f. *Corythornis cristata*; 500 f. *Merops nubicus*.

1962 (17 Feb). *AIR. Foundation of "Air Afrique" Airline. As T* **69** *of Cameroun.*

87	25 f. light blue, orange-brown and black	15	12

1962 (7 Apr). *Malaria Eradication. As T* **11** *of Central African Republic.*

88	25 f. + 5 f. yellow-orange ..	..	..	20	15

D **4** Gonoa Hippopotamus

(Des and eng P. Munier (Nos. D89/94). Des P. Munier. Eng P. Béquet (others). Recess)

1962 (20 Apr). *POSTAGE DUE. Various triangular designs as Type D 4. P 11.*

D 89	50 c. yellow-bistre				5	5
D 90	50 c. red-brown				5	5
D 91	1 f. turquoise-blue				5	5
D 92	1 f. bluish green				5	5
D 93	2 f. vermilion..				5	5
D 94	2 f. deep claret				5	5
D 95	5 f. deep greenish blue				5	5
D 96	5 f. bluish violet				5	5
D 97	10 f. chocolate..			·.	5	5
D 98	10 f. chestnut ..				5	5
D 99	25 f. bright purple				10	10
D100	25 f. violet				10	10
D89/100	*Set of 12*				50	50

Designs (Rock-paintings):—No. D90, Gonoa kudu; D91, Two Gonoa antelopes; D92, Three Gonoa antelopes; D93, Gonoa antelope; D94, Tibesti ram; D95, Tibesti ox; D96, Oudingueur boar; D97, Gonoa elephant; D98, Gira-Gira rhinoceros; D99, Bardai warrior; D100, Gonoa masked archer.
The two designs in each value are arranged in *tête-bêche* pairs throughout the sheet.

(Des Ringard. Photo Delrieu)

1962 (21 July). *Sports. Designs as T 12 of Central African Republic inscr "JEUX SPORTIFS". P 12×13 (100 f.) or 12½×12. (a) POSTAGE.*

89	20 f. brown, red-brown, green & black ..	12	8
90	50 f. brown, red-brown, green & black ..	25	20

(b) AIR. Inscr "POSTE AERIENNE"

91	100 f. brown, red-brown, green and black	55	35

Designs: *Horiz*—20 f. Relay-racing; 50 f. High-jumping. *Vert* (26×47 mm)—100 f. Throwing the discus.

1962 (8 Sept). *First Anniv of Union of African and Malagasy States. As T 14 of Central African Republic.*

92	30 f. blue-green, red, gold & deep blue ..	20	15

1963 (21 Mar). *Freedom from Hunger. As T 16 of Central African Republic.*

93	25 f. + 5 f. deep blue, red-brown and deep bluish green ..				20	20

6 Pres. Tombalbaye

7 Carved Thread-weight

(Photo Delrieu)

1963 (22 Apr). *P 12×12½.*

94	**6**	20 f. deep sepia, yellow, green and blue	12	5
95		85 f. dp sepia, lt green, yell, grn & red ..	30	15

1963 (8 Sept). *AIR. African and Malagasy Posts and Telecommunications Union. As T 18 of Central African Republic.*

96	85 f. red, buff, light blue and blue		..	40	30

1963 (19 Sept). *Space Telecommunications. As Nos. 37/8 of Central African Republic.*

97	25 f. violet, deep emerald and green	..	12	12
98	100 f. blue and pink	..	55	45

1963 (19 Nov). *AIR. First Anniv of "Air Afrique", and Inauguration of "DC-8" Service. As T 81 of Cameroun.*

99	50 f. black, green, grey and chestnut	..	40	30

1963 (30 Nov). *AIR. European-African Economic Convention. As T 24 of Central African Republic.*

100	50 f. deep brown, yell, ochre & dp grn ..	25	20

(Des R. Cottet. Eng Béquet (5 f.), Cottet (15 f.), Gauthier (25 f.), Bétemps (60 f.) and Forget (80 f.). Recess)

1963 (2 Dec). *Sao Art. T 7 and similar vert designs. P 13.*

101	5 f. orange-red and blue-green	..	5	5
102	15 f. brown-purple, slate and red	..	8	5
103	25 f. orange-brown and deep blue	..	12	5
104	60 f. bronze-green and orange-brown ..		25	12
105	80 f. bronze-green and chestnut	..	35	15
101/105	*Set of 5*	..	..	..	75	35

Designs:—15 f. Ancestral mask; 25 f. Ancestral statuette; 60 f. Gazelle's-head pendant; 80 f. Pectoral.

1963 (10 Dec). *15th Anniv of Declaration of Human Rights. As T 26 of Central African Republic.*

106	25 f. maroon and blue-green	..	..	12	10

8 Broussard Monoplane

(Des and eng C. Haley. Recess)

1963 (16 Dec). *AIR. P 13.*

107	**8**	100 f. lt bl, deep green, chest & brt bl ..	45	30

9 Pottery

(Des and eng G. Bétemps. Recess Chaix)

1964 (5 Feb). *Sao Handicrafts. T 9 and similar horiz designs. P 12½.*

108	10 f. black, yellow-orange and blue	..	5	5
109	30 f. red, black and yellow	..	..	12	5
110	50 f. black, red and green	..	..	20	10
111	85 f. black, yellow and purple	..	..	35	15
108/111	*Set of 4*	..	..	..	..	65	30

Designs:—30 f. Canoe-building; 50 f. Carpet-weaving; 85 f. Blacksmith working iron.

10 Rameses II in War Chariot, Abu Simbel

(Des and eng C. Haley. Recess)

1964 (9 Mar). *AIR. Nubian Monuments Preservation Fund. P 13.*

112	**10**	10 f. + 5 f. violet, green and red	..	10	10
113		25 f. + 5 f. purple-brown, green & red		15	15
114		50 f. + 5 f. dp bluish green, grn & red		30	30

1964 (23 Mar). *World Meteorological Day. As Congo T 14.*

115	50 f. deep reddish vio, ultram & brt pur	30	15

11 Cotton

(Photo So.Ge.Im.)

1964. *T* **11** *and similar horiz design. P* 12½×13.
116   20 f. blue, yellow, red and black (6.4)   10   5
117   25 f. red, brown, green and blue (8.6)   10   8
     Design:—25 f. Flamboyant tree.

1964 (23 June). *AIR. 5th Anniv of Equatorial African Heads of State Conference. As T* **31** *of Central African Republic.*
118   100 f. multicoloured   45   30

12 Globe, Chimneys and Ears of Wheat

(Des J. Combet. Photo Delrieu)

1964 (20 July). *AIR. "Europafrique". P* 13×12.
119 **12** 50 f. orange-red, purple and brown 20   15

13 Football   **14** Pres. Kennedy

(Des and eng C. Durrens. Recess)

1964 (12 Aug). *AIR. Olympic Games, Tokyo. T* **13** *and similar designs. P* 13.
120   25 f. deep bluish green, yellow-green
       and orange-brown   12   10
121   50 f. orange-brown, indigo & light blue 25   15
122   100 f. black, blue-green and red   50   40
123   200 f. black, bistre and carmine-red 1·00   60
120/123   *Set of 4*   1·75 1·10
MS123*a* 191×100 mm. Nos. 120/3   2·00 2·00
    Designs: *Vert*—50 f. Throwing the javelin; 100 f. High-jumping. *Horiz*—200 f. Running.

1964 (2 Nov). *AIR. Pan-African and Malagasy Posts and Telecommunications Congress, Cairo. As T* **23** *of Congo.*
124   25 f. sepia, Venetian red and mauve 12   8

1964 (7 Nov). *French, African and Malagasy Co-operation. As T* **547** *of France.*
125   25 f. chocolate, blue and vermilion 12   10

(Des R. Aubry. Photo Delrieu)

1964 (23 Nov). *AIR. President Kennedy Commemoration. P* 12½.
126 **14** 100 f. sepia, brt purple, black & lt blue 55   35
MS126*a* 90×129 mm. No. 126 (×4)..   2·00 2·00

15 National Guard   **16** Moufflon

(Des P. Lambert. Photo So.Ge.Im.)

1964 (11 Dec). *Chad Army. T* **15** *and similar design. P* 12½×13 (20 f.) *or* 13×12½ (25 f.).
127   20 f. multicoloured   10   8
128   25 f. multicoloured   10   8
    Design: *Vert*—25 f. Standard-bearer and troops of Land Forces.

(Des M. Fievet. Photo Delrieu)

1965 (11 Jan). *Fauna Protection. T* **16** *and similar designs. Multicoloured.* ⋆*P* 12½×12 (*horiz*) *or* 12×12½ (*vert*).
129   5 f. Type **16**   5   5
130   10 f. Addax   5   5
131   20 f. Oryx   8   5
132   25 f. Derby's Eland (*vert*)   10   5
133   30 f. Giraffe, buffalo and lion (Zakouma
       Park) (*vert*)..   12   8
134   85 f. Great Kudu (*vert*)   30   20
129/134 *Set of 6*   60   40

17 Perforator of Olsen's   **18** Badge and Mobile
Telegraph Apparatus   Gendarmes

(Des Derrey. Eng Fenneteaux (30 f.), Miermont (60 f.), Derrey (100 f.). Recess)

1965 (17 May). *I.T.U. Centenary. T* **17** *and similar designs. P* 13.
135   30 f. chocolate, red and dp bluish green 15   10
136   60 f. deep bluish green, red & choc   25   20
137   100 f. deep bluish green, choc & red 50   30
    Designs: *Vert*—60 f. Mildé's telephone. *Horiz*—100 f. Distributor of Baudot's telegraph apparatus.

(Des P. Lambert. Photo Delrieu)

1965 (22 June). *National Gendarmerie. P* 12½×12.
138 **18** 25 f. multicoloured   12   8

19 I.C.Y. Emblem

(Photo So.Ge.Im.)

1965 (5 July). *AIR. International Co-operation Year. P* 13.
139 **19** 100 f. multicoloured   45   30

20 Abraham Lincoln

(Des P. Lambert. Photo So.Ge.Im.)

1965 (7 Sept). *AIR. Death Centenary of Abraham Lincoln. P* 13.
140 **20** 100 f. multicoloured   45   30
Issued in sheets of ten.

25ᶠ

MF 1 Soldier   24 Mask in Mortar   (25)
with Standard

21 Guitar   **22** Sir Winston
Churchill

(Des J. Gauthier. Eng P. Gandon (60 f.), J. Gauthier (others).
Recess)

1965 (26 Oct). *Native Musical Instruments. T* **21** *and similar
designs. P* 13. (*a*) POSTAGE.
141   1 f. chocolate and bright green   ..   5   5
142   2 f. red-brown, brt purple & brn-rèd ..   5   5
143   3 f. brown-lake, black & bistre-brown   5   5
144   15 f. myrtle-green, yell-orge & brn-red   8   5
145   60 f. myrtle-green and lake   ..   25   15

(*b*) AIR. Inscr "POSTE AERIENNE"
146   100 f. deep ultramarine, orange-brown
and greenish blue   40   30
141/146   *Set of 6*   80   60
Designs: *Vert*—1 f. Drum and seat; 3 f. Shoulder drum;
60 f. Harp. *Horiz*—15 f. Viol. *Larger* (48½×27 mm)—100 f.
Xylophone.

(Des A. Spitz. Eng C. Mazelin. Recess)

1965 (23 Nov). *AIR. Churchill Commemoration. P* 13.
147   **22**   50 f. black and blackish green   ..   20   15

1965. *MILITARY FRANK. No.* 77 *optd* "F.M.".
MF148   20 f. scarlet and black   ..   ..

O **1** Flag and Map   **23** Dr. Schweitzer and "Helping
Hands"

(Des Roy. Die eng A. Barre. Typo)

1966 (1 Jan)–**71.** *OFFICIAL. Flag in blue, orange-yellow and
red. P* 13½×14.
O148   O **1**   1 f. light blue   5   5
O149   2 f. grey   5   5
O150   5 f. black..   5   5
O151   10 f. ultramarine   5   5
O152   25 f. orange   8   8
O153   30 f. turquoise-green   10   10
O154   40 f. carmine (1971)   15   15
O155   50 f. reddish violet   15   15
O156   85 f. blue-green   25   25
O157   100 f. brown   30   30
O158   200 f. red   65   65
O148/158   *Set of 11*   ..   ..   ..   1·75   1·75

(Des J. Gauthier. Photo Delrieu)

1966 (15 Feb). *AIR. Schweitzer Commemoration. P* 12½.
148   **23**   100 f. multicoloured   45   30

(Des J. Combet. Litho So.Ge.Im.)

1966. *MILITARY FRANK. No value indicated. P* 13×12½.
MF149   MF **1**   (–) multicoloured   10   10

(Des Cottet. Eng Forget (15 f., 20 f.), Cottet (others). Recess)

1966 (1 Apr). *World Festival of Negro Arts, Dakar. T* **24** *and
similar vert designs. P* 13.
149   15 f. maroon, bistre and blue   8   5
150   20 f. bistre-brown, deep red & blue-grn   10   5
151   60 f. purple-brown, new blue & verm   ..   25   15
152   80 f. deep bluish green, yell-brn & vio   ..   35   20
149/152   *Set of 4*   70   40
Designs: Sao Art. From J. Courtin's excavations at Bouta
Kebira—15 f. T **24**; 20 f. Mask; 60 f. Mask (different). From
I.N.T.S.H. excavations, Gawi—80 f. Armband.

1966 (15 Apr). *No.* 94 *surch with T* **25**, *in red.*
153   **6**   25 f. on 20 f. sepia, yellow, grn & blue   12   5

26 W.H.O. Building   **27** Caduceus and Map of Africa

(Des H. Biais. Photo So.Ge.Im.)

1966 (3 May). *Inauguration of W.H.O. Headquarters,
Geneva. P* 13×12½.
154   **26**   25 f. blue, yellow and red   12   10
155   32 f. blue, yellow and green   15   12

(Des J. Derrey. Photo Delrieu)

1966 (24 May). *Central African Customs and Economic
Union. P* 12½×12.
156   **27**   30 f. multicoloured   12   8

28 Footballer   **29** Youths, Flag and Arms

(Des Durrens. Eng Durrens (30 f.), Aufschneider (60 f.).
Recess)

1966 (12 July). *World Cup Football Championships. T* **28**
and similar vert design showing a footballer. P 13.
157   30 f. claret, turquoise-green and emerald   12   8
158   60 f. rose-red, black and blue   ..   25   15

(Des P. Lambert. Photo So.Ge.Im.)

1966 (11 Aug). *Youth Movement. P* 12½×13.
159   **29**   25 f. multicoloured   12   5

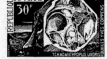

30 Columns   **31** Skull of Lake Chad Man (*Tchadanthropus uxoris*)

(Des and eng J. Derrey. Recess)

1966 (23 Aug). *20th Anniv of U.N.E.S.C.O.* P 13.
160   **30** f. Prussian blue, violet and carmine   15   8

1966 (31 Aug). *AIR. Inauguration of "DC-8" Air Services. As T 54 of Central African Republic.*
161   30 f. light olive-grey, black & yellow-grn   12   8

(Des and eng M. Monvoisin. Recess)

1966 (20 Sept). *Archaeological Excavation.* P 13.
162   **31** 30 f. slate, yellow-orange and red   15   8

32 White-throated Bee-eater

(Des P. Lambert. Photo So.Ge.Im.)

1966 (18 Oct)–**67**. *AIR. Birds. T 32 and similar horiz designs. Multicoloured.* P 13.
163   50 f. Hartlaub's glossy starling (21.3.67)   15   8
164   100 f. Type **32** ..   30   15
165   200 f. Pigmy Kingfisher ..   60   35
166   250 f. Red-throated bee-eater (21.3.67)   80   40
167   500 f. Little green bee-eater ..   1·50   80
163/167   *Set of 5* ..   ..   3·00   1·60

33 Battle-axe

(Des and eng P. Gandon. Recess)

1966 (11 Dec). *Prehistoric Implements. T 33 and similar horiz designs.* P 13.
168   25 f. bistre-brown, blue and red   8   5
169   30 f. black, yellow-brown and blue ..   12   5
170   85 f. bistre-brown, scarlet and blue ..   25   15
171   100 f. yellow-brown, greenish bl & sepia   30   20
168/171   *Set of 4* ..   70   40
MS172   129×99 mm. Nos. 168/71 ..   1·00   1·00
    Designs:—30 f. Arrowhead; 85 f. Harpoon; 100 f. Sandstone grindstone and pounder. From Chad National Museum.

34 Congress Palace

(Des M. Monvoisin. Photo Delrieu)

1967 (5 Jan). *AIR.* P 12½.,
173   **34** 25 f. multicoloured   12   5

35 Sportsmen and Dais on Map   **36** *Colotis protomedia klug*

(Des Gérin. Photo Delrieu)

1967 (10 Apr). *Sports Day.* P 12×12½.
174   **35** 25 f. multicoloured ..   10   5

(Des S. Gauthier. Photo Delrieu)

1967 (23 May). *Butterflies. T 36 and similar horiz designs. Multicoloured.* P 12½×12.
175   5 f. Type **36**   ..   5   5
176   10 f. *Charaxes jasius epijasius* L. ..   5   5
177   20 f. *Junonia cebrene trim* ..   8   5
178   130 f. *Danaida petiverana H.D.* ..   45   30
175/178   *Set of 4*   ..   55   40

37 Lions Emblem   **38** Dagnaux's Bréguet "19" Aircraft

(Des Roy. Photo So.Ge.Im.)

1967 (5 July). *AIR. 50th Anniv of Lions International.* P 13.
179   **37** 50 f. + 10 f. multicoloured ..   20   15

(Des and eng Monvoisin. Recess)

1967 (1 Aug). *AIR. First Anniv of Air Chad Airline. T 38 and similar horiz designs showing aircraft.* P 13.
180   25 f. myrtle-green, lt greenish bl & brn   12   5
181   30 f. slate-blue, emerald & lt grnsh blue   15   8
182   50 f. bistre-brown, myrtle-green and light greenish blue   ..   20   12
183   100 f. red, blue and myrtle-green ..   45   25
180/183   *Set of 4*   85   45
    Designs:—30 f. Latecoere "631" flying-boat; 50 f. Douglas "DC-3"; 100 f. Piper Cherokee "6".

1967 (9 Sept). *AIR. Fifth Anniv of U.A.M.P.T. Horiz design as T 66 of Central African Republic.*
184   100 f. chestnut, bistre and magenta ..   45   30

39 H.Q. Building   **40** Scouts and Jamboree Emblem

(Des H. Biais. Photo So.Ge.Im.)

1967 (23 Sept). *Opening of W.H.O. Regional Headquarters, Brazzaville. P* 12½×13.
185 **39** 30 f. multicoloured 10 5

(Des Monvoisin. Photo So.Ge.Im.)

1967 (17 Oct). *World Scout Jamboree, Idaho. T* **40** *and similar horiz design. Multicoloured. P* 12½×13.
186 25 f. Type **40** 8 5
187 32 f. Scout and Jamboree emblem .. 10 5

41 Flour Mills   **42** Woman and Harpist

(Des and eng P. Béquet. Recess)

1967 (14 Nov). *Economic Development. T* **41** *and similar horiz design. P* 13.
188 25 f. slate, bistre-brown and blue .. 8 5
189 30 f. bright blue, bistre-brown & brt grn 10 8
Design:—30 f. Land reclamation, Lake Bol.

(Des and eng J. Pheulpin. Recess)

1967 (19 Dec)–**68**. *Bailloud Mission in the Ennedi. Rock Paintings. T* **42** *and similar horiz designs. P* 13.

(a) POSTAGE
190 2 f. choc, yell-brn & red (19.11.68) .. 5 5
191 10 f. red, yellow-brn & vio (19.11.68) .. 5 5
192 15 f. brown-lake, orange-brn & new bl 5 5
193 20 f. red, yellow-brn & emer (19.11.68) 8 5
194 25 f. red, yellow-brown & bl (19.11.68) 12 8
195 30 f. brown-lake, orange-brn & lt blue 12 8
196 50 f. brown-lake, orange-brn & lt emer 20 12
(b) AIR. Inscr "POSTE AERIENNE"
197 100 f. brown-lake, orange-brown & emer 40 20
198 125 f. brown-lake, orange-brown & brt bl 50 30
190/198 *Set of 9* .. .. .. 1·40 90
Designs:—2 f. Archers; 10 f. Male and female costumes; 20 f. Funeral vigil; 25 f. "Dispute"; 30 f. Giraffes; 50 f. Cameleer pursuing ostrich. (48×27 *mm*)—100 f. Masked dancers; 125 f Hunters and hare.

43 Emblem of   **44** Downhill Skiing
    Rotary
 International

(Des Mme. Netter. Photo So.Ge.Im.)

1968 (9 Jan). *Tenth Anniv of Rotary Club, Fort Lamy. P* 13×12½.
199 **43** 50 f. multicoloured 15 10

(Des and eng Forget. Recess)

1968 (5 Feb). *AIR. Winter Olympic Games, Grenoble. T* **44** *and similar design. P* 13.
200 30 f. olive-brown, turq-green & brt pur 15 8
201 100 f. royal blue, myrtle-grn & lt grnsh bl 45 30
Design: *Vert*—100 f. Ski-jumping.

45 Chancellor Adenauer   **46** "Health Services"

(Photo Delrieu)

1968 (19 Mar). *AIR. Adenauer Commemoration. P* 12½.
202 **45** 52 f. blackish brown, lilac and deep
       bluish green 20 12
MS203 120×170 mm. No. 202×4 .. .. 1·00 1·00

(Des Baille. Photo So.Ge.Im.)

1968 (6 Apr). *20th Anniv of World Health Organization. P* 13×12½.
204 **46** 25 f. multicoloured 10 5
205 32 f. multicoloured 12 8

47 Allegory of Irrigation   **48** "The Snake-charmer"

(Des and eng A. Decaris. Recess)

1968 (23 Apr). *International Hydrological Decade. P* 13.
206 **47** 50 f. greenish blue, chocolate & emer 15 10

(Litho (values and border inscriptions) and photo Delrieu)

1968 (14 May). *AIR. Paintings by Henri Rousseau. T* **48** *and similar design. Multicoloured. P* 13½ (100 *f.*) or 12½ (130 *f.*).
207 100 f. Type **48** 40 25
208 130 f. "The War" (*horiz*—49×35 *mm*) .. 45 35

49 College Building, Student   **50** Child writing and
    and Emblem   Blackboard

(Des Mariscalchi. Eng Hanniquet. Recess)

1968 (20 Aug). *National College of Administration. P* 13.
209 **49** 25 f. purple, indigo and brown-red .. 8 5

(Des and eng C. Haley. Recess)

1968 (10 Sept). *Literacy Day. P* 13.
210 **50** 60 f. black, new blue and chocolate .. 20 10

51 Harvesting Cotton

52 *Utetheisa pulchella*

(Des and eng Forget. Recess)

1968 (24 Sept). *Cotton Industry.* T **51** *and similar design.*
P 13.
211   25 f. purple-brown, dp grn & greenish bl   8   5
212   30 f. olive-brown, new blue and bl-grn ..   10   5
Design: *Vert*—30 f. Loom, Fort Archambault Mill.

(Des P. Lambert. Photo)

1968 (1 Oct). *Butterflies and Moths.* T **52** *and similar vert
designs. Multicoloured.* P 13.
213   25 f. Type **52**   8   5
214   30 f. *Ophideres materna*   10   5
215   50 f. *Gynanisa maja*   15   8
216 100 f. *Epiphora bauhiniae*   30   15
213/216   Set of 4   55   30

53 Hurdling

(Des P. Forget. Eng M. Monvoisin. Recess)

1968 (15 Oct). *AIR. Olympic Games, Mexico.* T **53** *and
similar horiz design.* P 13.
217   32 f. chocolate, emerald and lake-brown   12   10
218   80 f. purple-brown, blue and cerise   ..   25   20
Design:—80 f. Relay-racing.

54 Human Rights
Emblem within
Man

55 G. Nachtigal and Tibesti
Landscape, 1869

(Des and eng Durrens. Recess)

1968 (10 Dec). *Human Rights Year.* P 13.
219 **54** 32 f. vermilion, blue-green and blue ..   12   8

(No. 220 photo Delrieu. No. 221 des and eng G. Bétemps.
Recess)

1969. *Air. "Philexafrique" Stamp Exhibition, Abidjan, Ivory
Coast. Multicoloured.*
   (a) *Vert design as* T **86** *of Central African Republic.*
P 12½ (15 Jan)
220   100 f. "The actor Wolf, called Bernard"
            (J. L. David)   50   50
   Issued in sheets with *se-tenant* "PHILEXAFRIQUE" stamp-
size label.
   (b) *Horiz design similar to* T **87** *of Central African Republic.*
P 13 (14 Feb)
221   50 f. Moundangs dancers and Chad
            postage due stamp of 1930   ..   25   25

(Des P. Béquet. Eng P. Forget (No. 233), M. Monvoisin (No.
224). Recess)

1969 (17 Feb). *AIR. Chad Explorers.* T **55** *and similar horiz
design.* P 13.
222   –   100 f. violet, myrtle-green & new blue   40   25
223 **55** 100 f. purple-brn, dp ultram & chest ..   40   25
Designs:—No. 222, H. Barth (portrait) and in canoe, Lake
Region, 1851.

56 "Apollo 8" circling Moon

(Des M. Monvoisin. Photo So.Ge.Im.)

1969 (10 Apr). *AIR. Flight of "Apollo 8" around the Moon.*
P 13.
224 **56** 100 f. black, blue and yellow-orange   40   25

57 St. Bartholomew   **58** Mahatma Gandhi

1969 (6 May). *Jubilee Year of Catholic Church.* T **57** *and
similar vert designs. Multicoloured. Litho. No gum.*
P 12½ × 13.
225   50 c. St. Paul   ..   ..
226   1 f. St. Peter   ..   ..
227   2 f. St. Thomas   ..   ..   ..
228   5 f. St. John the Evangelist   ..   ..
229   10 f. Type **57**   ..   ..
230   20 f. St. Matthew   ..   ..
231   25 f. St. James the Less   ..   ..   ..
232   30 f. St. Andrew   ..   ..
233   40 f. St. Jude   ..   ..
234   50 f. St. James the Greater   ..   ..
235   85 f. St. Philip   ..   ..
236 100 f. St. Simon ..   ..
225/236   Set of 12   ..   ..   1·00   1·00
   Nos. 225/36 were only issued printed together in sheets,
149 × 169 mm.

(Photo Delrieu)

1969 (20 May). *AIR. "Apostles of Peace". T* **58** *and similar vert designs. P* 12½.

237	50 f. blackish brown and light green	..	20	12
238	50 f. blackish brown and light agate	..	20	12
239	50 f. blackish brown and light pink	..	20	12
240	50 f. blackish brown and light blue	..	20	12
237/240	*Set of 4*	..	70	40
MS241	120×160 mm. Nos. 237/40 ..	..	1·10	1·10

Designs:—No. 237, T **58**; No. 238, Pres. John Kennedy; No. 239, Martin Luther King; No. 240, Robert Kennedy.

59 Motor Vehicles and I.L.O. Emblem

(Des and eng M. Monvoisin. Recess)

1969 (19 June). *50th Anniversary of International Labour Organization. P* 13.

242	**59** 32 f. steel-blue, brown-purple & emer		10	5

60 Cipolla, Baran and Sambo (pair with cox)   **61** "African Woman" (Bezombes)

1969 (30 June). *"World Solidarity". Multicoloured designs as T* **60**/1. *Litho.* (a) *Gold Medal Winners, Mexico Olympics. Vert designs as T* **60**. *P* 12½×13.

243	1 f. Type **60**	5	5
244	1 f. D. Beamon (long-jump) ..	5	5
245	1 f. I. Becker (women's pentathlon) ..	5	5
246	1 f. C. Besson (women's 400 metres) ..	5	5
247	1 f. W. Davenport (110 metres hurdles)	5	5
248	1 f. K. Dibiasi (diving) ..	5	5
249	1 f. R. Fosbury (high-jump) ..	5	5
250	1 f. M. Gamoudi (5000 metres) ..	5	5
251	1 f. Great Britain (sailing) ..	5	5
252	1 f. J. Guyon (cross-country riding) ..	5	5
253	1 f. D. Hemery (200 metres hurdles) ..	5	5
254	1 f. S. Kato (gymnastics) ..	5	5
255	1 f. B. Klinger (small bore rifle-shooting)	5	5
256	1 f. R. Matson (shot put) ..	5	5
257	1 f. R. Matthes (100 metres backstroke)	5	5
258	1 f. D. Meyer (women's 200 metres freestyle) ..	5	5
259	1 f. Morelon and Trentin (tandem cycle)	5	5
260	1 f. D. Rebillard (4000 m cycle pursuit)	5	5
261	1 f. T. Smith (200 metres)	5	5
262	1 f. P. Trentin (1000 metres cycle)	5	5
263	1 f. F. Vianelli (196 kilometre cycle race)	5	5
264	1 f. West Germany (dressage) ..	5	5
265	1 f. M. Wolke (welterweight boxing) ..	5	5
266	1 f. Zimmermann and Esser (women's kayak pair) ..	5	5

(b) *Paintings. Designs as T* **61**. *P* 13×12½ (*No.* 269) *or* 12½×13 (*others*)

267	1 f. Type **61**	5	5
268	1 f. "Mother and Child" (Gauguin) ..	5	5
269	1 f. "Holy Family" (Murillo) (*horiz*)	5	5
270	1 f. "Adoration of the Kings" (Rubens) ..	5	5
271	1 f. "Three Negroes" (Rubens) ..	5	5

272	1 f. "Woman with Flowers" (Veneto) ..		5	5
243/272	*Set of 30* ..	..	75	75

62 Presidents Tombalbaye and Mobutu

(Embossed on gold foil, flags enamelled Société Pierre Mariotte)

1969 (July). *AIR. 1st Anniversary of Central African States Union. P* 13½×12½.

273	**62** 1000 f. red, blue and gold ..	..	3·75

63 *Cochlospermum tinctorium*

(Des P. Lambert. Photo So.Ge.Im.)

1969 (8 July). *Flowers. T* **63** *and similar horiz designs. Multicoloured. P* 13.

274	1 f. Type **63**		5	5
275	4 f. *Parkia biglobosa* ..		5	5
276	10 f. *Pancratium trianthum* ..		5	5
277	15 f. *Ipomoea aquatica* ..		5	5
274/277	*Set of 4* ..	..	12	12

1969 (23 July). *AIR. Birth Bicentenary of Napoleon Bonaparte. Multicoloured designs as T* **144** *of Cameroun. P* 12×12½.

278	30 f. "Napoleon at Les Invalides Hospital" (Veron-Bellecourt) ..	..	12	8
279	85 f. "Battle of Wagram" (Vernet) ..	30	20
280	130 f. "Battle of Austerlitz" (Gerard) ..	50	35

64 Frozen Carcases   D **65** Kanem Puppet

(Des C. Guillame. Eng C. Guillame (25 f.), M. Monvoisin (30 f.). Recess)

1969 (19 Aug). *Frozen Meat Industry. T* **64** *and similar horiz design. P* 13.

281	25 f. brown-red, myrtle-grn & yell-orge	8	5
282	30 f. lake-brown, slate & myrtle-green ..	10	5

Design:—30 f. Cattle and refrigerated abattoir, Farcha.

1969 (10 Sept). *5th Anniversary of African Development Bank. Vert design as T* **146** *of Cameroun.*

283	30 f. orange-brown, emerald and scarlet	10	5

(Des and eng J. Combet. Recess)

1969 (19 Sept). *POSTAGE DUE. Chad Dolls. Type D* **65** *and similar vert designs. P* 14×13.

D284	1 f. bistre-brown, vermilion & emer ..	5	5
D285	2 f. purple-brown, bright grn & verm	5	5
D286	5 f. myrtle-green, brown & blue-green	5	5
D287	10 f. purple-brown, bright pur & emer	5	5
D288	25 f. purple-brn, new blue & bright pur	5	5
D284/288	*Set of 5* ..	15	15

Designs:—2 f. Kotoko doll; 5 f. Copper doll; 10 f. Kotoko doll (*different*); 25 f. Guera doll.

66 Astronaut and Lunar Module

(Des Martimor. Embossed on gold foil Societé Pierre Mariotte)

1969 (17 Oct). *AIR. First Man on the Moon.* P 10.
289 **66** 1000 f. gold .. .. 3·75

70 Lenin   **71** Class and Torchbearers

(Photo State Security Printers, Moscow)

1970 (22 Apr). *Birth Centenary of Lenin.* P 11½.
299 **70** 150 f. black, cream and gold 45 30

1970 (20 May). *New U.P.U. Headquarters Building, Berne.
Design as T 156 of Cameroun.*
300 30 f. brown, reddish violet and carmine 10 5

(Des A. Mendandi. Litho De La Rue)

1970 (16 June). *International Education Year.* P 14.
301 **71** 100 f. multicoloured 30 20

67 Nile Mouth Breeder   **68** President
Tombalbaye

(Des and eng C. Haley. Recess)

1969 (25 Nov). *Fishes. T 67 and similar horiz designs.* P 13.
290   2 f. maroon, slate and blue-green .. 5 5
291   3 f. slate, red and light blue 5 5
292   5 f. indigo, lemon and ochre 5 5
293   20 f. indigo, emerald and red 5 5
290/293 *Set of 4* 12 12
    Fishes:—3 f. Moonfish; 5 f. Puffer fish; 20 f. Tiger fish.

1969 (12 Dec). *10th Anniversary of ASECNA. As T 150 of
Cameroun.*
294   30 f. yellow-orange 10 5

(Litho De La Rue)

1970 (11 Jan). P 13½.
295 **68** 25 f. multicoloured 8 5

72 Osaka Print   **74** Meteorological
Equipment and
"Agriculture"

**APOLLO XI
1ᵉʳ débarquement sur la lune
20 juillet 1969**

(**73** "Apollo 11")

(Des and eng M. Monvoisin. Recess)

1970 (30 June). *AIR. World Fair "EXPO 70", Osaka, Japan.
T 72 and similar vert designs.* P 13.
302   50 f. myrtle-green, new blue & brn-red 15 12
303   100 f. turquoise-blue, yell-grn & scarlet 30 20
304   125 f. slate, yellow-brown & carmine .. 40 30
    Designs:—100 f. Tower of the Sun; 125 f. Osaka print (*different*).

1970 (8 July). *AIR. "Apollo" Moon Flights. Nos. 164/6 surch
with T 73 and similar types, in red.*
305 **32**   50 f. on 100 f. (Type **73**) 15 10
306   –   100 f. on 200 f. ("Apollo 12") 30 20
307   –   125 f. on 250 f. ("Apollo 13") 40 25

(Des and eng P. Forget. Recess)

1970 (22 July). *World Meteorological Day.* P 13.
308 **74** 50 f. grey, emerald and yellow-orange 15 10

69 "Village Life" (G. Narcisse)

(Photo Delrieu)

1970. *AIR. African Paintings. T 69 and similar multicoloured
designs.* P 12½ × 12 (No. 298) or 12 × 12½ (*others*).
296   100 f. Type **69** (17.3) 30 25
297   250 f. "Market Woman" (I. N'Diaye)
    (28.8) 80 50
298   250 f. "Flower-seller" (I. N'Diaye) (*vert*)
    (28.8) 80 50

75 "DC 8–63" over Airport

(Des J. Combet. Photo Delrieu)

1970 (5 Aug). *AIR. "Air Afrique" DC-8 "Fort Lamy". P 12½.*
309 **75** 30 f. multicoloured 8 5

76 Ahmed Mangue   **77** Tanning
(Minister of Education)

(Recess and litho De La Rue)

1970 (15 Sept). *Ahmed Mangue (air crash victim) Commemoration. P 12½×13.*
310 **76** 100 f. black, carmine and gold .. 30 20

(Des C. Durrens. Eng C. Jumelet (4 f.), G. Aufschneider (5 f.),
C. Durrens (others). Recess)

1970 (10 Oct). *Trades and Handicrafts. T 77 and similar
designs. P 13×12½ (horiz) or 12½×13 (vert).*
311   1 f. bistre-brown, chestnut and new blue   5   5
312   2 f. deep chocolate, slate-blue & olive ..   5   5
313   3 f. reddish violet, ol-brn & magenta   5   5
314   4 f. chocolate, bistre and blue-green   5   5
315   5 f. chocolate, olive-green and rosine   5   5
311/315   *Set of 5*   15   15
   Designs: *Vert*—2 f. Dyeing; 4 f. Water-carrying. *Horiz*—3 f.
Milling palm nuts for oil; 5 f. Copper-founding.

78 U.N. Emblem   **79** "The Visitation" (Venetian
and Dove   School, 15th cent)

(Des P. Lambert. Photo Delrieu)

1970 (24 Oct). *25th Anniversary of United Nations.
P 12×12½.*
316 **78** 32 f. multicoloured 10 5

(Photo Delrieu)

1970 (15 Dec). *AIR. Christmas. T 79 and similar vert paintings. Multicoloured. P 12½×12.*
317   20 f. Type **79**   5   5
318   25 f. "The Nativity" (Venetian School,
       15th cent) 8 5
319   30 f. "Virgin and Child" (Veneziano) .. 10 5

80 Map and O.C.A.M. Building, Yaoundé

(Des P. Lambert. Photo Delrieu)

1971 (23 Jan). *O.C.A.M. (Organisation Commune Africaine et
Malgache) Conference, Fort Lamy. P 12½×12.*
320 **80** 30 f. multicoloured 8 5

81 Mauritius "Post Office" 2d.   **82** Pres. Gamal Nasser
of 1847

(Des and eng P. Forget. Recess)

1971 (23 Jan). *AIR. "PHILEXOCAM '71" Stamp Exhibition,
Fort Lamy. T 81 and similar square designs, showing classic stamps. P 13.*
321   10 f. indigo, ochre and turquoise-green   5   5
322   20 f. ochre, indigo and turquoise-green   5   5
323   30 f. orange-brown, black and scarlet .. 10 10
324   60 f. black, orange-brown & brn-pur .. 15 15
325   80 f. slate-blue, orange-brown & blue .. 20 20
326   100 f. chestnut, slate-blue and blue   25 25
321/326   *Set of 6*   70   70
MS327   160×130 mm. Nos. 321/6 ..   1·00 1·00
   Designs:—20 f. Tuscany 3 lire of 1860; 30 f. France 1 f.
orange-vermilion of 1849; 60 f. U.S.A. 10 c. black of 1847;
80 f. Japan 5 sen of 1872; 100 f. Saxony 3 pf. of 1850.

(Photo Delrieu)

1971 (19 Feb). *AIR. 1st Death Anniv of Pres. Nasser (Egypt).
P 12½.*
328 **82** 75 f. multicoloured 20 12

83 "Racial Harmony"   **84** Map and Dish Aerial
Tree

(Des and eng M. Monvoisin. Recess)

1971 (21 Mar). *Racial Equality Year. P 12½×13.*
329 **83** 40 f. scarlet, turquoise-grn & lt blue .. 12 5

(Photo Delrieu)

1971 (28 Apr). *AIR. Reconciliation with Central African Republic and Zaire. Design as T* **105** *of Central African Republic. P* 13.

330	100 f. multicoloured	..	..	35	20

(Des and eng C. Haley. Recess)

1971 (17 May). *World Telecommunications Day. T* **84** *and similar horiz designs. P* 13. (*a*) *POSTAGE. Size as T* **84.**

331	5 f. orange, red and blue		..	5	5
332	40 f. emerald, chocolate and purple	..	15	5
333	50 f. black, chocolate and red	..	15	8

(*b*) *AIR. Inscr* "POSTE AERIENNE". *Design* 48×27 *mm*

334	125 f. brown-red, slate-green & ultram	..	45	30
331/334	*Set of 4*		..	70	40

Designs:—40 f. Map and Communications tower; 50 f. Map and satellite; 125 f. Map and telecommunications symbols.

85 Scouts by Camp-fire

(Des Baillais. Photo Delrieu)

1971 (24 Aug). *AIR. World Scout Jamboree, Asagiri, Japan. P* 12½.

335	**85**	250 f. multicoloured	..		90	55

86 Great White Heron

(Des P. Lambert. Photo)

1971 (28 Sept). *AIR. P* 13.

336	**86**	1000 f. multicoloured	..	..	3·50	2·00

87 Ancient Marathon Race   **88** Sidney Bechet

(Des J. Combet. Photo Delrieu)

1971 (5 Oct). *AIR. 75th Anniversary of Modern Olympic Games. T* **87** *and similar horiz designs. Multicoloured. P* 12½.

337	40 f. Type **87**	..		15	5
338	45 f. Ancient stadium, Olympia	..	15	10
339	75 f. Ancient wrestling	..		25	12
340	130 f. Athens stadium, 1896 Games	..	45	30
337/340	*Set of 4*	..	..	90	50

(Litho De La Rue)

1971 (20 Oct). *AIR. Famous American Black Musicians. T* **88** *and similar vert portraits. Multicoloured. P* 13×13½.

341	50 f. Type **88**	..	..	15	10
342	75 f. Duke Ellington	..	..	25	15
343	100 f. Louis Armstrong	..	..	35	20

89 Gen. de Gaulle   **90** Children's Heads

(Des P. Forget. Litho, portraits embossed on gold foil Societé Pierre Mariotte)

1971 (9 Nov). *AIR. First Death Anniv of General De Gaulle. T* **89** *and similar vert portrait. P* 12½.

344	200 f. gold, blue and light blue	..	..	70	
345	200 f. gold, emerald & pale greenish yell		70	
MS346	110×70 mm. Nos. 344/5 and central stamp-sized label with inscr	..	1·50	

Designs:—No. 344, Governor-General Félix Eboué; No. 345, T **89.**

1971 (13 Nov). *AIR. 10th Anniversary of African and Malagasy Posts and Telecommunications Union. Multicoloured design as T* **184** *of Cameroun.*

347	100 f. Headquarters building and Sao carved animal head	..	..	35	20

(Des and eng P. Forget. Recess)

1971 (11 Dec). *25th Anniversary of U.N.I.C.E.F. P* 12½×13.

348	**90**	50 f. greenish bl, yell-grn & bright pur		15	10

On No. 348 the inscr "24e" has been obliterated and replaced by an overprint reading "25e".

APPENDIX. Further commemorative issues are recorded in the Appendix at the end of this volume.

91 Gorane Nangara Dancers   M **92** Shoulder Flash of 1st Regiment

(Litho De La Rue)

1971 (18 Dec). *Chad Dances. T* **91** *and similar multicoloured designs. P* 13½×13 (*horiz*) *or* 13×13½ (*vert*).

349	10 f. Type **91**	..	..	5	5
350	15 f. Yondo initiates	..	..	5	5
351	30 f. M'Boum (*vert*)	..	..	10	5
352	40 f. Sara Kaba (*vert*)	..	..	15	5
349/352	*Set of 4*	..	..	30	15

(Des M. Louis. Photo Delrieu)

1972 (21 Jan). *MILITARY FRANK. No value indicated. P* 13.

M353	M **92**	(–) multicoloured	..	..	12	12

93 Presidents Pompidou and Tombalbaye

(Des P. Lambert. Photo Delrieu)

1972 (25 Jan). *Visit of French President.* P 13.
354 **93** 40 f. multicoloured 15 8

94 Bob-sleighing   **95** Human Heart

(Des and eng G. Bétemps (100 f. after Tohaku). Recess)

1972 (24 Feb). *AIR. Winter Olympic Games, Sapporo, Japan.* T **94** *and similar horiz design.* P 13.
355 50 f. red and greenish blue 15 10
356 100 f. slate-green and bright purple .. 35 20
Design:—100 f. Downhill skiing.

(Des and eng C. Haley. Recess)

1972 (25 Apr). *World Heart Month.* P 13.
357 **95** 100 f. carmine, light bl & reddish vio 35 20

96 *Gorrizia dubiosa*   **97** Hurdling

(Des P. Lambert. Photo)

1972 (6 May). *Insects.* T **96** *and similar vert designs. Multicoloured.* P 13.
358 1 f. Type **96** 5 5
359 2 f. *Argiope sector* 5 5
360 3 f. *Nephila senegalense* 5 5
361 4 f. *Oryctes boas* 5 5
362 5 f. *Hemistigma albipunctata* 5 5
358/362 Set of 5 .. .. 15 15

1972 (23 May). *AIR. U.N.E.S.C.O. "Save Venice" Campaign. Multicoloured paintings as T **191** of Cameroun.* P 13.
363 40 f. "Harbour Panorama" (detail, Caffi) 15 5
364 45 f. "Venice Panorama" (detail, Caffi)
      (horiz) 15 10
365 140 f. "Grand Canal" (detail, Caffi) .. 50 30

(Litho De La Rue)

1972 (9 June). *Olympic Games, Munich.* T **97** *and similar horiz designs. Multicoloured.* P 13½×13.
366 40 f. Type **97** 15 10
367 130 f. Gymnastics 45 25
368 150 f. Swimming 55 35
MS369 102×86 mm. 300 f. Cycling .. .. 1·00 1·00

98 Alphonse Daudet and "Tartarin de Tarascon"

(Des and eng P. Béquet. Recess)

1972 (22 July). *AIR. International Book Year.* P 13.
370 **98** 100 f. choc, carmine-red & bright pur 35 20

99 Dromedary   **100** "Luna 16" and Moon Probe

(Des and eng G. Bétemps. Recess)

1972 (29 Aug). *Domestic Animals.* T **99** *and similar horiz designs.* P 13.
371 25 f. yellow-brown and violet 8 5
372 30 f. slate-blue and magenta 10 5
373 40 f. yellow-brown and emerald .. 15 8
374 45 f. brown and greenish blue 15 10
371/374 Set of 4 .. .. 45 25
Designs:—30 f. Horse; 40 f. Saluki hound; 45 f. Goat.

(Des and eng J. Pheulpin. Recess)

1972 (19 Sept). *AIR. Russian Moon Exploration.* T **100** *and similar design.* P 13.
375 100 f. violet, bistre-brown and deep blue 35 20
376 150 f. brown, slate-blue and purple .. 55 35
Design: *Horiz*—150 f. "Lunokhod 1" Moon vehicle.

101 Tobacco Production

(Des and eng C. Haley (40 f.). Des R. Roy. Eng E. Lacaque (50 f.). Recess)

1972 (24 Oct). *Economic Development.* T **101** *and similar horiz design.* P 13×12½.
377 40 f. blackish grn, carmine & purple-brn 15 8
378 50 f. brown, myrtle-green & bright blue 15 10
Design:—50 f. Ploughing with oxen.

HAVE YOU READ THE NOTES AT THE BEGINNING OF THIS CATALOGUE?

These often provide answers to the enquiries we receive.

102 Microscope, Cattle and Laboratory   **103** Massa Warrior

(Photo Delrieu)

1972 (11 Nov). *AIR. 20th Anniversary of Farcha Veterinary Laboratory.* P 13.
379 **102** 75 f. multicoloured 25 12

(Des M. & G. Shamir. Photo Govt Printer, Jerusalem)

1972 (15 Nov). *Chad Warriors.* T **103** *and similar vert design. Multicoloured.* P 14×13.
380 15 f. Type **103** 5 5
381 20 f. Moundang archer 5 5

104 King Faisal and Pres. Tombalbaye

(Litho De La Rue (No. 382). Des M. Roy. Photo Delrieu (No. 383)

1972 (17 Nov). *Visit of King Faisal of Saudi Arabia.* T **104** *and similar horiz design. Multicoloured.* (a) POSTAGE. P 13×13½.
382 100 f. Type **104** 35 20

(b) AIR. Inscr "POSTE AERIENNE". P 13
383 75 f. King Faisal and Kaaba, Mecca . . 25 12

105 Gen. Gowon, Pres. Tombalbaye and Map

(Des M. Roy. Photo Delrieu)

1972 (7 Dec). *Visit of Gen. Gowon, Nigerian Head-of-State.* P 13.
384 **105** 70 f. multicoloured 25 12

106 "Madonna and Child" (G. Bellini)   **107** Commemorative Scroll

(Photo Delrieu)

1972 (15 Dec). *AIR. Christmas.* T **106** *and similar multicoloured designs, showing paintings.* P 13.
385 40 f. Type **106** 15 8
386 75 f. "Virgin and Child" (bas-relief, Da Santivo, Dall' Occhio) . . 25 12
387 80 f. "Nativity" (B. Angelico) (*horiz*) . . 30 15
388 95 f. "Adoration of the Magi" (P. Perugino) 35 20
385/388 *Set of 4* 95 50

(Litho State Security Printers, Moscow)

1972 (30 Dec). *50th Anniv of U.S.S.R.* P 12.
389 **107** 150 f. multicoloured 55 35

108 High-jumping

(Litho De La Rue)

1973 (17 Jan). *2nd African Games, Lagos.* T **108** *and similar horiz designs. Multicoloured.* P 13½×13.
390 50 f. Type **108** 15 10
391 125 f. Running 40 25
392 200 f. Putting the shot 70 40
MS393 103×86 mm. 250 f. Throwing the discus 85 85

109 Copernicus and Planetary System Diagram

(Des and eng C. Guillame. Recess)

1973 (31 Mar). *AIR. 500th Birth Anniv of Nicholas Copernicus.* P 13.
394 **109** 250 f. slate, chocolate & dp magenta 85 50

Chile

1853. 100 Centavos = 1 Peso.
1960. 1000 Milesimos = 100 Centesimos = 1 Escudo

On 18 September 1810 leading men in Santiago took a first step towards independence of Spain by forcing the resignation of the President-Governor, appointed by the usurper Joseph Bonaparte in Madrid. Attempts to reassert the authority of Spain in 1813–18 were finally defeated at the battle of the Maipo, two months after the independence of Chile was declared on 12 February 1818.

For GREAT BRITAIN stamps used in Chile with obliterations "C30", "C37" or "C40", see Great Britain Stamps Used Abroad in the *British Commonwealth Catalogue*.

PORTRAITS. The head on all postage stamps of Chile issued prior to 1910 is that of Christopher Columbus.

| 1 | 2 | 3 |

(Eng and recess Perkins, Bacon & Co, London)

1853 (1 July). *W* **2** (5 *c.*) or **3** (10 *c.*). *Imperf.*

1	1	5 c. brown-red/*blued*	..	..	£100 10·00
		a. Ivory head	..	..	— 25·00
		b. Paper with no trace of blueing			— 35·00
2		10 c. deep bright blue	..	..	£150 25·00
		a. On bluish	..	..	— £150
		b. Bisected (5 c.) on cover	..	..	

This first "5" watermark is about 9 mm high and 7 mm wide, and has the neck slanting. See *W* **4** for second type.

(Printed at Santiago)

1854. *W* **2** (5 *c.*) or **3** (10 *c.*). *Imperf.*

(a) *Recess by N. Desmadryl from Perkins, Bacon plates* (from Feb)

3	1	5 c. chestnut-brown	..	..	£200 35·00
		a. Doubly printed	..	..	
4		5 c. pale reddish brown	..	..	£120 12·00
5		5 c. deep reddish brown	..	..	£150 9·00

The above are generally fine impressions.

Printings by recess are known to have been made by Desmadryl in Jan, Feb and Sept 1854 and it is believed that more were printed in Feb 1855. Owing to the wide range of shades it is not possible to ascribe them to particular printings with any degree of certainty.

(b) *Litho by transfer from Perkins, Bacon plates by N. Desmadryl* (from July)

6	1	5 c. brown (*shades*)	..	..	£500 60·00
7		5 c. dull brown (*shades*)	..	..	£500 60·00
7a		5 c. yellow-brown (*shades*)	..	..	— £100
8		5 c. red-brown (*shades*)	..	..	£600 60·00
9		5 c. chestnut-brown (*shades*)	..	..	£650 65·00

In transferring the design to the litho stone, several transfer papers were creased, producing some interesting varieties, such as narrow "5", letters "AVOS" or "ILE" squeezed up and shorter than usual, etc.

(c) *Recess by H. C. Gillett from Perkins, Bacon plates* (from Aug)

10	1	5 c. burnt sienna	..	..	£350 50·00
11		5 c. deep chocolate	..	..	£500 £150

(d) *Recess by N. Desmadryl from Perkins, Bacon plates with lines on face clear and distinct* (from Oct)

12	1	10 c. greenish blue	..	..	— 60·00
13		10 c. deep blue	..	..	— 45·00
14		10 c. slate-blue	..	..	— 40·00
15		10 c. blue	..	..	— 30·00
16		10 c. pale blue	..	..	— 35·00
		a. Bisected (5 c.) on cover (*shades*)			
				from	— 30·00

4

(Recess Perkins, Bacon from new plate)

1855 (Apr). *W* **4.** *Imperf.*

17	1	5 c. brown-red/*blued*	..	..	40·00 2·00
		a. Ivory head	..	..	— 4·50
		b. Paper with no trace of blueing			

This second type of the "5" wmk is about 10 mm high and 8 mm wide, and has a straight neck to the "5".

(Recess at the Post Office, Santiago from Perkins, Bacon plates)

1856–62. *W* **2** (5 *c.*) or **3** (10 *c.*). *Imperf.*

18	1	5 c. dull reddish brown (11.57)	..	75·00 6·00
19		5 c. red (1858)	..	..	10·00 1·00
20		5 c. rose-red (1858)	..	..	10·00 1·00
		a. Printed on both sides	..	..	— £200
		b. Coloured lines on face			
21		5 c. vermilion (*shades*) (1861)	..	60·00 30·00
22		5 c. carmine-red (1862)	..	..	35·00 4·00

(a) *Lines on head clear and sharp*

23	1	10 c. indigo-blue (6.56)	..	..	70·00 10·00
24		10 c. slate-blue (5.57)	..	..	75·00 5·00
		a. Bisected (5 c.) on cover (*shades*)			
				from	— 25·00

(b) *Worn impressions*

25	1	10 c. sky-blue (12.57)	..	..	65·00 5·00
26		10 c. greenish blue (8.58)	..	..	75·00 9·00
27		10 c. grey-blue (11.58)	..	..	68·00 5·50
28		10 c. deep blue (3.61)	..	..	65·00 5·00
		a. Doubly printed			
		b. Bisected (5 c.) on cover (*shades*)			
				from	— 20·00

| 5 | 6 |

7   8

12   13   14

(Recess Perkins, Bacon & Co)

1861–62. *W 5 to 7. Imperf.*

29	1	1 c. chrome-yellow (1.1.62)	..	..	5·00	8·00
		a. Doubly printed, one inverted	..		—	£300
30		1 c. lemon-yellow	..	..	6·00	8·00
31		10 c. blue (10.61)	..	..	10·00	1·25
		a. On blued paper	..	..	9·00	5·00
32		10 c. deep blue	..	..	10·00	1·50
		a. On blued paper	..	..	25·00	5·00
		b. Error with narrow wmk, T **3**	..			
		c. Error, wmk "20"	..	..	£1500	£600
		d. Bisected (5 c.) on cover (*shades*)				
				from	—	25·00
33		20 c. green (1.1.62)	..	..	15·00	12·00
34		20 c. yellowish green	..	..	25·00	13·00
35		20 c. intense green	..	..	£250	£150

15

(Recess at the Post Office, Santiago from Perkins, Bacon plates)

1866. *W 8. Imperf.*

36	1	5 c. rose-red	..	..	3·50	1·25
		a. Printed on both sides	..	..	£350	£100
		b. Coloured lines on face	..	..	6·00	1·75
37		5 c. red	..	..	3·00	1·25
		a. Doubly printed	..	..	£350	£100
		b. Laid paper	..	..	£350	£100
38		5 c. carmine-red	..	..	10·00	1·50
39		5 c. vermilion	..	..	5·00	1·25

(a)   (b)   (c)   (d)

Scrolls on either side o figures   Scrolls removed

(Eng and recess A.B.N. Co, N.Y.)

All these 5 c. stamps are known on a thin silky paper.
Proofs of the 5 c. are known in rose-red, pale red, and deep red, and these come on ribbed paper, thick wove paper, and paper with the arms of Chile watermarked in the sheet. These are quite common. Rare proofs of the 1 c., 5 c., and 20 c. are also known in correct colours on thick paper and without watermark, and proofs of all values are known in black.

1879–99. *Rouletted.*

54	12	1 c. green (a) (8.8.81)	..		15	5
55		1 c. green (c) (1894)	..		8	5
56		2 c. pale carmine (b) (5.2.81)	..		25	5
		a. Bright carmine	..		30	5
57		2 c. crimson-lake (d) (1894)	..		8	5
58	13	5 c. dull rose (1.81)	..		80	10
59		5 c. bright ultramarine (10.7.83)			30	5
		a. Dull ultramarine (1892)	..		25	5
		b. Thick carton paper	..		1·50	
60		10 c. yellow (4.85)	..		2·50	10
		a. Orange (1892)	..		35	5
61		15 c. greenish slate (1892)	..		15	10
62		20 c. slate-grey (1886)	..		35	5
63		25 c. red-brown (1892)	..		25	10
64		30 c. pale rose (5.99)	..		50	25
		a. Rose-carmine	..		50	25
65	14	50 c. mauve (1878)	..		9·00	1·75
		a. Violet (1890)	..		15	10
66	15	1 p. black and brown (1892)	..		1·50	10
		a. Thick carton paper	..		5·00	1·00
		b. Imperf horiz (vert pair)	..		13·00	10·00
		c. Imperf vert (horiz pair)	..		13·00	10·00

9   10   11

(Eng and recess American Bank Note Co, N.Y.)

1867. *P 12.*

40	9	1 c. orange-yellow (Aug)	..	..	1·90	45
41		1 c. orange	..	..	1·60	45
42		2 c. grey-black (May)	..	..	2·75	80
43		2 c. black	..	..	2·40	60
44		5 c. pale red (Sept)	..	..	1·90	12
45		5 c. deep red	..	..	1·90	12
46		10 c. blue (May)	..	..	1·90	15
47		10 c. deep blue	..	..	2·10	15
48		20 c. green (June)	..	..	2·25	45

CHILEAN STAMPS USED IN PERU. Stamps of Types 10/14 were used by Chileans in Peru without overprints during the war between 1 December 1881 and 11 October 1883. Such stamps with Peruvian postmarks are listed under Peru.

(Eng and recess A.B.N. Co, N.Y.)

1877–78. *Thin to thick paper. Rouletted.*

49	10	1 c. slate	..	..	30	10
50		2 c. orange	..	..	1·75	30
51	11	5 c. lake	..	..	1·75	8
52	10	10 c. blue	..	..	1·90	10
53		20 c. green	..	..	1·90	30

F 1   T 1

(Recess A.B.N. Co, N.Y.)

1880 (27 Nov)**–81.** *POSTAL FISCAL. As Type* F **1** (*various frames*). *P 12.*

F67		1 c. red	..	..	15	5
F68		2 c. brown	..	..	15	5
F69		5 c. blue (3.7.80)	..	..	15	5
F70		10 c. green (21.4.81)	..	..	50	30
F71		20 c. orange (21.4.81)	..	..	1·00	75
F72		1 p. orange (21.4.81)	..	..	1·75	1·50
F67/72		Set of 6	..	..	3·25	2·40

These are the only values that were legitimately used.

The STANLEY GIBBONS Stamp Service

 offer you the complete stamp service!

Gibbons stay-at-home services

The collector can make use of virtually all the Stanley Gibbons facilities without ever coming to London! Apart from the albums and accessories which he can get from us by mail-order, the stay-at-home collector can use our Approval and New Issue services to build up his entire collection if he wishes! Stanley Gibbons introduced the Approval Service to Britain, and every week hundreds of "books" of stamps required by distant customers are made up and posted off, with each stamp or set priced. All the customer has to do is detach the stamps he wants, send us a cheque to cover them and return those he doesn't want!

The New Issue service is all-world; collectors' requirements are posted to them automatically against their Standing Order.

We welcome the opportunity of helping you to build your collection, and suggest you complete this form and return it to us today.

Please Write in Block Letters

Approval Books

Please send me approval selections of stamps from the following group of countries:

Great Britain ☐ Commonwealth ☐ Foreign ☐

I am particularly interested in the following

Countries or Reigns..........................

....

....

....

I collect Unused ☐ Used ☐

I should be pleased to see on approval items from the groups mentioned above.
I am over 18 years of age.

Signature ....

Name ....

Address ....

....

....

Business or Banker's Reference..............

....

Rare Stamps

Please inform me of any unusual material you have available from the following Countries:

....

....

....

Overseas 1

New Issues
Please send me the New Issues Selective Service brochure ☐

Publications
Please send me a copy of your latest list. I am particularly interested in

Catalogues ☐   Albums ☐   Accessories ☐

Auctions
Please send me your brochure giving details of the auction services ☐

Stamp Monthly
Please send me a specimen copy ☐

Stamps as an Investment
Please send me your investment brochure ☐

Please tick items which are of interest and return this slip when completed to:
Stanley Gibbons Limited
391 Strand, London, WC2R 0LX

Tel: 01-836 9707

Use this part for the advertisement opposite only
Please send me the following

......Philatector(s) at £3·85 each

......Colour Key(s) at £1·10 each

......Instanta(s) at 33p each

I enclose cheque/P.O. to the value £..........

Name . . . .

Address . . . .

. . . .

. . . .

. . . . Post Code. . . . .

London 348043

ii

We also buy stamps
Our buyers search the world for stamps to maintain our stocks against the enormous demands of collectors. Every day individuals walk in casually to offer us their stamps, and collections are posted to us for sale, or for valuation for insurance or probate. If we do buy, immediate cash payment is given no matter what the figure. Please write in the first instance, giving general particulars, before sending stamps or asking our valuer to make a visit.

Rare stamps
We retain a large "bank" of rare and elusive philatelic material at Romano House. Serious collectors have their wants recorded on our Specialist Register, or send us lists of their "rare stamp" wants. Investment advice and assistance in building up valuable collections is given here, and collectors appreciate the luxurious, quiet atmosphere of the viewing rooms.

Auctions
The auction is the culmination of many weeks of expert cataloguing and organisation, and of the dissemination well in advance to enquirers throughout the world of fine, illustrated catalogues. Thanks to these catalogues, much of the bidding is by post, but the auction itself is always an occasion of excitement for collectors present.

"The Shop" itself
If you do come to London, "the Shop" at 391 Strand is the Philatelist's Mecca, with the latest and most complete range of albums, catalogues and accessories; the sales counters for new issues and for a wide selection of stamps of all countries. There's always an interesting window display on some topical aspect of philately. And there's always a welcome for stamp collectors, new and old.

Stamp Publications
Stanley Gibbons Stamp Catalogues (the first was in 1865) are the world's most authoritative and best-known reference guides. They are supported by *Stamp Monthly* the popular Gibbons magazine with its record circulation, fully detailed Catalogue Supplement, regular Stamp Market and Trends features and articles on all stamp topics. And there are Gibbons albums and accessories which cater for all the needs of the enthusiast no matter how long he collects.

Want to know more?
This is only an introduction to the complete service offered by Stanley Gibbons to the collector. If you'd like detailed information about any of the services mentioned here just fill in the coupon and send it off today.

YOU NEED THESE ESSENTIAL AIDS

Colour Key

200 colours, including all those formerly found in our standard colour guide. More comprehensive and simple to use—it opens out like a fan and shades can be matched with stamps still on cover or mounted in albums.

£1·10

The Instanta Perforation Gauge

The finest, most accurate and most practicable of perforation gauges. Indicates a definite and unmistakable gauge for every stamp. For the average collector, gives Gibbons Catalogue Standard Descriptions, and for the Specialist requiring great accuracy, gives decimal reading. Is very quick and simple to use. Printed on strong transparent material.

33p

The Philatector

The New Philatector is a scientifically designed instrument which will effectively assist in the detection of watermarks on postage stamps without the use of benzine or other fluids. Stamps are held in slides and illuminated through colour filters to help you with identification. No risk of damage to stamps. No fluids. No smell. Batteries included.

£3·85

Currency Conversion Tables

These tables were calculated in March 1973 when the pound and other currencies were floating, and for this reason we have not attempted to include European currencies.

The tables are based on the following rates of exchange for the pound sterling but when using them it is advisable to check the current ruling rates. They should not be used for the purposes of paying for purchases and foreign remittances will be sold and the proceeds credited.

Australian Dollars and South African Rands	1·74
New Zealand Dollars	1·86
U.S. and Canadian Dollars	2·46

Sterling	Australian S. African	New Zealand	U.S. and Canadian	Sterling	Australian S. African	New Zealand	U.S. and Canadian
5	9	9	12	9·50	16·53	17·67	23·37
8	14	15	20	10·00	17·40	18·60	24·60
10	17	19	25	11·00	19·14	20·46	27·06
12	21	23	31	12·00	20·88	22·32	29·52
15	26	28	37	13·00	22·62	24·08	31·98
20	35	37	49	14·00	24·36	26·04	34·44
25	44	47	62	15·00	26·10	27·90	36·90
30	52	56	74	16·00	27·84	29·76	39·36
35	61	65	86	17·00	29·58	31·62	41·82
40	70	74	98	18·00	31·32	33·48	44·28
45	78	84	1·11	19·00	33·06	35·34	46·74
50	87	93	1·23	20·00	34·80	37·20	49·20
55	96	1·02	1·35	21·00	36·54	39·06	51·66
60	1·04	1·12	1·48	22·00	38·28	40·92	54·12
65	1·13	1·21	1·60	23·00	40·02	42·78	56·58
70	1·22	1·30	1·72	24·00	41·76	44·64	59·04
75	1·31	1·40	1·85	25·00	43·50	46·50	61·50
80	1·39	1·49	1·97	26·00	45·24	48·36	63·96
85	1·48	1·58	2·09	27·00	46·98	50·22	66·42
90	1·57	1·67	2·21	28·00	48·72	52·08	68·88
95	1·65	1·77	2·34	29·00	50·46	53·94	71·34
1·00	1·74	1·86	2·46	30·00	52·20	55·80	73·80
1·10	1·91	2·05	2·70	32·00	55·68	59·52	78·72
1·25	2·18	2·33	3·08	35·00	60·90	65·10	86·10
1·40	2·44	2·60	3·44	38·00	66·12	70·68	93·48
1·50	2·61	2·79	3·69	40·00	69·60	74·40	98·40
1·60	2·78	2·98	3·94	42·00	73·08	78·12	$103
1·75	3·05	3·25	4·31	45·00	78·30	83·70	$111
1·90	3·31	3·53	4·67	48·00	83·52	89·28	$118
2·00	3·48	3·72	4·92	50·00	87·00	93·00	$123
2·10	3·66	3·91	5·17	55·00	95·70	$102	$135
2·25	3·92	4·00	5·53	60·00	R104	$112	$148
2·40	4·18	4·46	5·90	65·00	R113	$121	$160
2·50	4·35	4·65	6·15	70·00	R122	$130	$172
2·75	4·79	5·12	6·76	75·00	R130	$140	$185
3·00	5·22	5·58	7·38	80·00	R139	$149	$197
3·25	5·66	6·05	8·00	85·00	R148	$158	$209
3·50	6·09	6·51	8·61	90·00	R157	$167	$221
3·75	6·53	6·98	9·23	95·00	R165	$177	$234
4·00	6·96	7·44	9·84	£100	R174	$186	$246
4·25	7·40	7·91	10·45	£150	R261	$279	$369
4·50	7·83	8·37	11·07	£200	R348	$372	$492
4·75	8·27	8·84	11·69	£250	R435	$465	$615
5·00	8·70	9·30	12·30	£300	R522	$558	$738
5·50	9·57	10·23	13·53	£400	R696	$744	$984
6·00	10·44	11·16	14·76	£500	R870	$930	$1230
6·50	11·31	12·09	15·99	£600	R1044	$1196	$1476
7·00	12·18	13·02	17·22	£700	R1218	$1302	$1722
7·50	13·05	13·95	18·45	£750	R1305	$1395	$1845
8·00	13·92	14·88	19·68	£800	R1392	$1488	$1968
8·50	14·79	15·81	20·91	£900	R1566	$1674	$2214
9·00	15·66	16·74	22·14	£1000	R1740	$1860	$2460

(Recess Bradbury, Wilkinson & Co, London)

1891 (21 Apr). *POSTAL TELEGRAPH. P* 12.

T73	T **1**	2 c. yellow-brown	..	..	..	90	10
T74		10 c. olive-green	..	..	..	15	10
T75		20 c. blue	..	..	..	1·40	25
T76		1 p. brown	..	..	..	5	40
T73/76		*Set of 4*		..	..	2·25	75

AR 1   D 1   D 2

(Litho, probably by H. C. Gillett)

1894. *ACKNOWLEDGMENT OF RECEIPT. P* 11½.

AR77	AR **1**	5 c. chocolate	..	..	..	30	30
		a. Imperf (pair)	..	..	..	2·00	2·00

This was also printed in black but not issued.

1894 (12 Oct). *POSTAGE DUE. Issue for Valparaiso. Hand-stamped on coloured paper. P* 13.

A. *On buff paper.*   B. *On yellow paper*

					A		B	
D77	D **1**	2 c. black	..	..	1·10	1·00	20·00	18·00
D78		4 c. black	..	..	1·10	1·00	10·00	8·00
D79		6 c. black	..	..	1·10	1·00	6·50	5·50
D80		8 c. black	..	..	1·10	1·00	3·25	3·25
D81	D **2**	10 c. black	..	..	1·10	1·00	3·25	3·25
D82	D **1**	16 c. black	..	..	1·10	1·00	3·25	3·25
D83		20 c. black	..	..	1·10	1·00	3·25	3·25
D84		30 c. black	..	..	1·10	1·00	3·25	3·25
D85		40 c. black	..	..	1·10	1·00	3·25	3·25
D77/85		*Set of 9*		..	9·00	8·00	50·00	45·00

The first issue on the buff paper was on upright paper and these are worth very much more than the prices quoted above which are for stamps printed oblong in shape and which appeared on both papers in December 1894.

D 3   D 4

(Litho H. C. Gillett, Valparaiso)

1895 (Jan). *POSTAGE DUE. P* 11.

D86	D **3**	1 c. rose/*yellow*	..	..	..	1·50	20
D87		2 c. rose/*yellow*	..	..	..	1·50	20
D88		4 c. rose/*yellow*	..	..	..	1·50	20
D89		6 c. rose/*yellow*	..	..	..	1·50	20
D90		8 c. rose/*yellow*	..	..	..	90	20
D91		10 c. rose/*yellow*	..	..	..	90	20
D92		20 c. rose/*yellow*	..	..	..	15	15
D93		40 c. rose/*yellow*	..	..	..	15	15
D94		50 c. rose/*yellow*	..	..	..	25	25
D95		60 c. rose/*yellow*	..	..	..	50	50
D96		80 c. rose/*yellow*	..	..	..	85	85
D97		1 p. rose/*yellow*	..	..	..	90	90
D86/97		*Set of 12*		..	..	9·50	3·50

The 1 peso is known surcharged "10 c." in a circle in black; this is an essay and was never issued.

1896 (Dec). *POSTAGE DUE. P* 13½.

D 98	D **3**	1 c. carmine/*straw*	..	..	..	10	8
D 99		2 c. carmine/*straw*	..	..	..	10	8
D100		4 c. carmine/*straw*	..	..	..	10	8
D101		6 c. carmine/*straw*	..	..	..	10	8
D102		8 c. carmine/*straw*	..	..	..	10	8
D103		10 c. carmine/*straw*	..	..	..	10	8
D104		20 c. carmine/*straw*	..	..	..	10	8
D105		40 c. carmine/*straw*	..	..	..	1·75	1·75
D106		50 c. carmine/*straw*	..	..	..	2·25	1·90
D107		60 c. carmine/*straw*	..	..	..	2·25	1·90

D108	D **3**	80 c. carmine/*straw*	..	..	..	5·50	3·75
D109		100 c. carmine/*straw*	..	..	..	5·50	3·75
D98/109		*Set of 12*		..	..	16·00	12·00

The 1, 2, 4, 6, 8, 10 and 20 c. in rose on white paper, gummed and perforated were prepared but it is believed that they were not issued.

(Litho H. C. Gillett, Valparaiso)

1898 (Jan). *POSTAGE DUE. P* 13.

D110	D **4**	1 c. rose	..	..	..	5	5
D111		2 c. rose	..	..	..	10	10
D112		4 c. rose	..	..	..	5	5
D113		10 c. rose	..	..	..	5	5
D114		20 c. rose	..	..	..	5	5
D110/114		*Set of 5*		..	..	20	20

The 6 c. and 8 c. were also prepared but not issued.

16   F 2   (17)

A Shadow above head

B Shadow removed

(Eng and recess Waterlow & Sons, London)

1900–01. *Rouletted.* (a) *Die A.*

75	**16**	1 c. green (7.3.00)	..	..	..	10	5
		a. *Emerald-green*	..	..	..	50	20
76		2 c. lake (7.3.00)	..	..	..	20	10
77		5 c. blue (24.3.00)	..	..	..	60	10
78		10 c. deep lilac (17.4.00)	..	..	70	8
		a. *Mauve*	..	..	..	70	8
79		20 c. grey (18.7.01)	..	..	..	35	12
80		30 c. orange-red (7.01)	..	..	50	12
81		50 c. red-brown (7.01)	..	..	50	12

(b) *Die B*

82	**16**	1 c. green (3.01)	..	..	..	5	5
83		2 c. lake (4.01)	..	..	..	5	5
84		5 c. pale blue (3.01)	..	..	50	12
		a. *Deep blue*	..	..	..	40	10
85		10 c. dull lilac (7.01)	..	..	1·00	15

(Recess Waterlow)

1900–13. *POSTAL FISCAL. P* 14.

F86	F **2**	1 c. vermilion (25.10.00)	..	..	5	5
F87		2 c. brown (1913)	..	..	..	5	5
F88		5 c. blue (6.12.00)	..	..	..	30	5

The 1 c. and 5 c. were the only values to be authorised for use in 1900, although others are known to have been used without authority. The 2 c. was not authorised until 1913.

1900 (28 Dec). *No. 64a surch with T* **17**, *by G. Schäfer, Santiago.*

86	**13**	5 on 30 c. rose-carmine	..	..	8	5
		a. Surch inverted	..	..	..	2·00	2·00
		b. Surch double	..	..	..	6·00	6·00
		c. Surch double, one inverted	..	6·00	6·00

Dangerous forgeries of the errors exist.

18

(19)

24 Pedro Valdivia

(25)

(Recess Waterlow (5 c.); A.B.N. Co (20 c.))

(Des H. A. Arias. Eng and recess A.B.N. Co, N.Y.)

1901–04. *P* 12.

87	18	1 c. green (2.02)				5	5
88		2 c. carmine (15.4.02)				5	5
89		5 c. ultramarine (21.10.01)				5	5
		a. Deep ultramarine (1904)				8	5
90		10 c. black and red (9.02)				15	8
91		30 c. black and deep violet (8.7.02)			60	8
92		50 c. black and red (18.7.02)				60	15
87/92		*Set of 6*				1·40	40

1903 (27 Nov). *No.* 80 *surch with* T **19**, *by Barros & Balcells, Santiago.*

93	16	10 c. on 30 c. orange-red (B.)			15	5
		a. Surch inverted			3·50	3·50
		b. Surch double			7·00	7·00
		c. Surch double, one inverted		7·00	7·00

There are two types of this surcharge: In Type I the "T" and "V" of "CENTAVOS" are higher than the "A"; in Type II they are the same height (*same prices*).

20 Huemul without Mane and Tail

21 Huemul with Mane and Tail

(22)

(23)

(Recess A.B.N. Co (T **20**); Bradbury, Wilkinson (T **21**))

1904 (26 May). *Telegraph stamps surch or optd for postal use.*

A. *Optd with* T **22.** *P* 12

94	20	2 c. pale brown				5	5
		a. Opt inverted				3·00	3·00
95		5 c. red				10	5
		a. Opt inverted				3·00	3·00
96		10 c. olive-green				25	10
		a. Opt inverted				12·00	12·00

B. *Optd with* T **22** *or surch with* T **23.** *P* 14

97	21	2 c. pale brown				80	80
98		3 c. on 1 p. deep brown				5	5
		a. Surch double				16·00	16·00
		b. Inverted "V" for "A"			1·00	1·00
99		5 c. red				1·40	1·40
100		10 c. olive-green				2·00	2·00

Nos. 94 to 100 exist with variety "no centre bar to 'E' of 'CORREOS'". Other varieties are known due to surcharge being misplaced.

C. *Surch as* T **23** (3 c.) *or* **25** (*others*)

(*a*) *P* 12. (*b*) *P* 12½ *to* 16 *and compound*

101	24	1 c. on 20 c. blue (*a*)				5	5
		a. Surch inverted				8·00	8·00
		b. Inverted "V" for "A"				3·00	1·25
		c. Imperf between (vert pair)			10·00	
102		3 c. on 5 c. red (*b*)				7·00	7·00
		a. Surch inverted					
103		12 c. on 5 c. red (*b*)				15	8
		a. Surch inverted				10·00	10·00
		b. No star left of "CENTAVOS"			30	30
		c. Surch double				18·00	

The "no centre bar to 'E'" variety also exists on Nos. 101–103.

26

27

28

(Eng and recess A.B.N. Co, N.Y.)

1905–9. *P* 12.

104	26	1 c. green				5	5
105		2 c. carmine				5	5
106		3 c. brown				5	5
107		5 c. blue				5	5
108	27	10 c. black and grey				10	5
109		12 c. black and lake				20	20
110		15 c. black and lilac				12	5
111		20 c. black and orange-brown			20	5
112		30 c. black and blue-green			20	8
113		50 c. black and blue				20	8
114	28	1 p. grey and bronze-green			1·50	1·50
104/114		*Set of 11*				2·40	2·00

Differences in height in stamps of T **27** are attributable to shrinkage of the paper.

A 20 c. in black and dull red was prepared but not issued.

Nos. 105/7 overprinted "MARINA OFICIAL" had no official status.

O **1**

(O **2**)

OFFICIAL STAMPS FOR MINISTRY OF MARINE

A. For Inland Use

1906 (1 Jan). *Single-lined frame. Small control numerals in violet. Imperf.*

O115	O **1**	(—) Blue, "CARTA" in yellow		20·00	15·00
O116		(—) Red, "OFICIO" in blue		22·00	17·00
		a. "OFICIO" omitted			30·00	20·00
O117		(—) Violet, "PAQUETE" in red		20·00	17·00
		a. "PAQUETE" inverted			25·00	20·00
O118		(—) Brown/*blue*, "EP" in violet		20·00	15·00
		a. "EP" inverted			30·00	20·00

1906 (29 Jan). *Double-lined frame. Large control numerals in black. P* 11.

O119	O **1**	(–) Blue, "CARTA" in yellow	3·75	3·00
		a. "CARTA" double	5·00	4·00
		b. "CARTA" inverted	5·00	4·00
O120		(–) Red, "OFICIO" in blue	6·50	3·75
		a. "OFICIO" double	8·50	5·00
		b. "OFICIO" inverted	13·00	5·50
		c. "OFICIO" omitted	—	5·00
O121		(–) Brown, "PAQUETE" in green	7·00	3·75
		a. Stamps printed tête-bêche		
		b. "PAQUETE" double	8·00	5·00
		c. "PAQUETE" inverted	8·00	5·00
		d. "PAQUETE" omitted	13·00	5·00
		e. Numerals and black frame omitted		
O122		(–) Green, large "C" in red	65·00	40·00
		a. Numerals omitted		

The inscriptions denote type of usage: "CARTA" for letters of ordinary weight; "OFICIO" for heavy letters up to 100 grams; "PAQUETE" for parcels to 100 grams; "EP" (Encomienda Postal) for heavier parcels; "C" (Certificado) for registration, including postage.

B. For External Use

1907 (1 Jan). *Contemporary stamps optd with Type O* **2**, *in red.*

O123	**26**	1 c. green	4·00	4·00
		a. Opt inverted		
O124	**21**	3 c. on 1 p., deep brown	15·00	15·00
O125	**26**	5 c. blue	6·00	4·75
		a. Opt inverted	15·00	15·00
O126	**27**	10 c. black and grey	11·00	7·00
O127		15 c. black and lilac	16·00	14·00
O128		20 c. black and orange-brown	16·00	14·00
O129		50 c. black and blue	35·00	35·00
O130	**15**	1 p. black and brown	40·00	40·00

These normally bear a rubber handstamp on the back reading "Ministerio de Marina—Conforme—Sub Secretaria" in violet-blue but this was not applied at the start of the issue.

Forgeries exist.

ISLAS DE JUAN FERNANDEZ

5

(29)

ISLAS DE JUAN FERNANDEZ

10 Cts.

(30)

1910 (1 Aug). *Surch as T* 29/30 *or optd only.*

115	**27**	5 c. on 12 c. black and lake (B.)	5	5
116	**28**	10 c. on 1 p. grey & bronze-grn (R.)	10	10
117		20 c. on 1 p. grey & bronze-grn (R.)	10	10
118		1 p. grey and bronze-green (R.)	40	40
115/118		*Set of 4*	60	60

These stamps although overprinted "Islas de Juan Fernandez" were authorised for use throughout Chile.

31 Battle of Chacabuco

32 *Lautaro* and *Esmeralda*

33 San Martin Monument

34 Admiral Cochrane

(Eng and recess A.B.N. Co, N.Y.)

1910. *Centenary of Independence. As T* **31/2** (*historic scenes*), **33** (*monuments*) *and* **34** (*portraits*). *P* 12.

119	1 c. black and deep green	5	5
	a. Centre inverted	†	£1000
120	2 c. black and rose-lake	5	5
121	3 c. black and chestnut	5	5
122	5 c. black and dull blue	5	5
123	10 c. black and brown	12	10
124	12 c. black and red	25	20
125	15 c. black and slate	15	15
126	20 c. black and orange	20	20
127	25 c. black and blue	45	30
128	30 c. black and mauve	40	20
129	50 c. black and olive-green	50	25
130	1 p. black and yellow	1·50	1·00
131	2 p. black and red	1·25	55
132	5 p. black and green	8·00	6·00
133	10 p. black and purple	6·00	5·00
119/133	*Set of 15*	17·00	12·00

Designs: *Horiz*—1 c. Oath of Independence; 3 c. Battle of Roble; 5 c. Battle of the Maipo; 12 c. Capture of the *Maria Isabella*; 15 c. First sortie of the liberating forces; 20 c. Abdication of O'Higgins; 25 c. First Chilean Congress. *Vert*—30 c. O'Higgins Monument; 50 c. Carrera Monument; 2 p. General Blanco; 5 p. General Zenteno.

Dates of issue: 18 Sept, 2 c., 5 c.; 30 Sept, 10 c., 20 c., 1 p.; 1 Oct, remainder.

46 Columbus

47 Valdivia

48 M. de Toro Zambrano

49 O'Higgins

50 Freire

51 F. A. Pinto

52 Prieto

53 Bulnes

54 Montt

55 Perez

56 F. E. Zañartu

57 A. Pinto

58 Santa Maria

59 Balmaceda

60 F. E. Echaurren

(Eng and recess A.B.N. Co, N.Y.)

1911 (1 Sept). *Whole stamp recess-printed. Background outside oval composed of horizontal and diagonal lines. No wmk. P 12.*

135	**46**	1 c. green	..	5	5
136	**47**	2 c. scarlet	..	5	5
137	**48**	3 c. sepia	..	5	5
138	**49**	5 c. blue	..	5	5
139	**50**	10 c. black and grey	..	5	5
		a. Centre inverted	..	£140	£110
		b. Black and greenish grey	..	10	5
140	**51**	12 c. black and rose	..	5	5
141	**52**	15 c. black and purple	..	5	5
		a. Centre inverted	..	†	£850
142	**53**	20 c. black and orange-brown	..	10	5
		a. Centre inverted	..	7·00	7·00
143	**54**	25 c. black and pale blue	..	10	10
144	**55**	30 c. black and bistre-brown	..	20	5
145	**56**	50 c. black and myrtle	..	20	5
146	**57**	1 p. black and emerald	..	30	5
147	**58**	2 p. black and red	..	1·00	15
148	**59**	5 p. black and olive-green	..	3·50	45
149	**60**	10 p. black and yellow	..	2·00	·35
135/149		*Set of 15*	..	7·00	1·40

See also Nos. 157/75, 185/90a and 204/12.

(a)	(b)

Two types of 8 c.

(a) Openings of "8" circular.
(b) Openings of "8" oval, and top of head further from oval.

1912 (Sept)–**13**. *Whole stamp recess-printed. Changes of colour and type and new values. Background outside oval of horizontal and diagonal lines. No wmk. P 12.*

150	**46**	2 c. scarlet	..	5	5
151	**48**	4 c. sepia	..	5	5
152	**50**	8 c. grey (a)	..	5	5
153	**49**	10 c. black and blue	..	8	5
		a. Centre inverted	..	£130	£100
154	**51**	14 c. black and carmine (1913)	..	5	5
155	**52**	40 c. black and purple (1913)	..	15	5
156	**54**	60 c. black and pale blue (1913)	..	25	15
150/156		*Set of 7*	..	60	40

PRINTERS. All the following stamps were printed at the Chilean Mint, *unless otherwise stated.*

61 Columbus (Small Head)

62 Valdivia

63 Columbus (Large Head)

64 Admiral Cochrane

65 M. Rengifo

66 Admiral Latorre

1915–27. *Inscr "CHILE CORREOS". No wmk. P 13½ × 14 or 14 (peso values).*

(a) *Whole stamp typo. Background outside oval of horiz lines only*

157	**61**	1 c. dull green (10.14)	..	8	5
		a. Re-engraved. *Grey-green* (1920)	5	5
158	**62**	2 c. scarlet (2.9.15)	..	5	5
159	**63**	4 c. brown (8.16)	..	10	5
160	**61**	4 c. brown (1918)	..	5	5

No. 157a has much finer and clearer lines of shading and the white shirt front is less shaded.

(b) *Whole stamp recess*

161	**64**	5 c. slate-blue (5.16)	..	5	5
		a. Imperf (pair)	..	50	
162	**50**	8 c. slate (b) (6.16)	..	35	10
		a. *Grey (worn plate)* (1921)	2·75	75

No. 162a has no diagonal lines in the frame and shorter ones above the shoulders.

(c) *Head litho, frame typo*

163	**49**	10 c. black and blue (1916)	..	8	5

(d) *Head recess, frame litho*

164	**49**	10 c. black and blue (1920)	..	15	5
		a. Centre inverted	..	60·00	
165	**52**	15 c. black and violet (3.17)	..	10	5
166	**53**	20 c. black and orange-red (1916)	..	10	5
		a. *Black and brown-orange* (1920)	10	5
167	**54**	25 c. black and blue (1918)	..	5	5
168	**55**	30 c. black and bistre (1916)	..	8	5
169	**65**	40 c. black and violet (1921)	..	5	5
170	**56**	50 c. black and green (1916)	..	12	5
171	**66**	80 c. black and sepia (1927)	..	15	10
172	**57**	1 p. black and bright green (1918)	..	50	5
173	**58**	2 p. black and scarlet (1918)	..	40	5
174	**59**	5 p. black and olive-green (1921)	..	60	5
175	**60**	10 p. black and orange (1925)	..	75	30

Nos. 163/4 are both from a re-engraved die. Both can be distinguished from No. 153 by plain horizontal lines across the top of the frame instead of cross-hatching. This characteristic also enables Nos. 167, 170 and 172 to be distinguished from Nos. 143 and 145/6. No. 163 can generally be recognized by solid strips of colour in the four outer panels, whereas on No. 164 these panels are formed of quadrillé lines.

The perforation also provides a clear distinction between the above issue and Nos. 135/56.

A 4 c. brown with portrait of Balmaceda was prepared but not issued (*price £25 un.*) and also a 14 c. black and carmine with portrait of Manuel de Salas (*price £4 un.*).

See also Nos. 185/90a and 204/12.

67 Chilean Congress Building

D 5

(O 3)

OFICIAL

(Centre recess; frame typo)

1923 (15 Apr). *Pan-American Conference. P 14½ × 14.*

176	**67**	2 c. red	..	5	5
177		4 c. brown	..	5	5
178		10 c. black and blue	..	8	5
179		20 c. black and orange	..	8	5
180		40 c. black and mauve	..	10	5
181		1 p. black and green	..	20	8
182		2 p. black and scarlet	..	45	10
183		5 p. black and deep green	..	1·25	35
176/183		*Set of 8*	..	2·00	70

The above issue overprinted "Libre de Porte Servicio del ESTADO" were not officially issued.

(Litho Imprenta Universo)

1924 (Feb). *POSTAGE DUE. P 12½.*

D184	**D 5**	2 c. scarlet and blue	..	10	10
D185		4 c. scarlet and blue	..	10	10
D186		8 c. scarlet and blue	..	10	10
D187		10 c. scarlet and blue	..	5	5
D188		20 c. scarlet and blue	..	5	5
D189		40 c. scarlet and blue	..	5	5

D190	D 5	60 c. scarlet and blue	.. ..	12	12
D191		80 c. scarlet and blue	.. ..	12	12
D192		1 p. scarlet and blue	.. ..	20	20
D193		2 p. scarlet and blue	.. ..	65	65
D194		5 p. scarlet and blue	.. ..	1·00	1·00
D184/194		Set of 11	.. ..	2·25	2·25

There were two printings of the above. The first, in scarlet and blue, was in sheets of 150 containing all values in the following proportions: 14×2, 4 and 40 c.; 20×8 c.; 27×10 and 20 c.; 12×60 c.; 8×80 c.; 6×1 p.; 4×2 and 5 p.

The second printing, in carmine and blue, comprised values to 20 c. printed in sheets of 50 as follows: 5×2 c.; 10×4, 8 and 10 c.; 15×20 c. This printing has wider gutters between the stamps which are thus larger.

Because of these sheet arrangements, various values are to be found *se-tenant*.

1926 (May). *OFFICIAL. For use at National Library. Stamps of 1915–27 optd with Type O 3.*

(a) Reading diagonally upwards

O184	64	5 c. slate-blue (R.) ..	..	30	8
O185	49	10 c. black and blue (164)	..	50	8
O186	53	20 c. black and orange-red (B.)	..	15	5
O187	56	50 c. black and green (B.)	..	20	5

(b) Vert up at left and down at right

O188	57	1 p. black and green (R.)	..	35	10
O189	58	2 p. black and scarlet (B.) ..	..	45	15
O184/189		Set of 6	..	1·75	45

Servicio del

ESTADO

67a   (O 4)

(Centre recess; frame litho)

1927 (3 May). *AIR. Unissued stamp surch as in T 67a. P 13½×14.*

184	67a	40 c. on 10 c. blue & black-brown ..		45·00	7·00
184a		80 c. on 10 c. blue & black-brown ..		55·00	10·00
184b		1 p. 20 on 10 c. blue & black-brn ..		55·00	10·00
184c		1 p. 60 on 10 c. blue & black-brown ..		55·00	10·00
184d		2 p. on 10 c. blue & black-brown ..		55·00	10·00
184/184d		Set of 5		£250	40·00

Used on air mail service operated by Luis Testart between Santiago and Valparaiso.

1928. *OFFICIAL. For External use at the Ministry of Foreign Affairs. Stamps of 1915–27 optd as Type O 4, in red.*

O190	49	10 c. black and blue (164) ..	..	1·25	15
O191	53	20 c. black and orange-red ..	..	1·25	15
O192	54	25 c. black and blue	..	1·25	15
O193	56	50 c. black and green	..	1·40	20
O194	57	1 p. black and bright green	..	1·60	20
O190/194		Set of 5	..	6·00	75

The spacing between the lines of overprints on No. O194 is larger and measures 16 mm against 14 mm on Nos. O223/a.

68

This watermark also occurs inverted, sideways and sideways inverted as well as in different sizes.

(5 c. recess; remainder, centre recess, frame litho)

1928–35. *W 68. Inscr "CHILE CORREOS". P 13½×14 or 14 (peso values).*

185	64	5 c. slate-blue (11.28)	..	5	5
185a	52	15 c. black and violet	..	—	45·00
186	65	40 c. black and violet (12.29)	..	10	5
187	56	50 c. black and green	..	15	5
188	57	1 p. black and green (12.29)	..	12	5
		a. Black & yellow-green (1932)	..	2·50	10
189	58	2 p. black and scarlet (9.34)	..	30	5
190	59	5 p. black and olive-green (1.34)	..	55	8
190a	60	10 p. black and orange (9.35)	..	65	15

Stamps on thin paper are worth more.
See also Nos. 204/12.

(69)   (70)

1928–32. *AIR. Stamps inscr "CHILE CORREOS" optd as T 69 (larger on peso values), or surch in addition as T 70.*

(a) No wmk

191	53	20 c. black & orange-brown (8.7.28)		10	10
192	65	40 c. black and violet (R.) (6.8.28)	..	15	15
193	57	1 p. black and green (B.) (6.8.28)	..	45	15
194	58	2 p. black and scarlet (B.) (6.8.28)	..	50	12
		a. Black and vermilion (1931)	..	40·00	10·00
195	59	5 p. black & ol-green (B.) (6.8.29)	..	1·00	20
196	49	6 p. on 10 c. black and blue (R.) (163) (30.6.28) ..	..	10·00	10·00
197	60	10 p. black and orange (B.) (8.7.28) ..		10·00	10·00
198		10 p. black and orange (Bk.) (16.8.29)		1·25	55

(b) W 68

199	65	40 c. black and violet (R.) (4.30)	..	8	5
200	57	1 p. black and green (B.) (11.29)	..	12	5
		a. Thin paper	..	60	15
		b. Black and yellow-green	..	30	10
200c		1 p. black & yell-green (Bk.) (8.32) ..		50	45
200d	58	2 p. black and scarlet (B.) (9.32)	..	2·00	15
201	64	3 p. on 5 c. slate-blue (R.) (30.6.28)		10·00	10·00
202	59	5 p. black and olive-green (B.) (12.32)	..	1·00	30
203	60	10 p. black and orange (Bk.) (1.31)	..	2·25	25

1928–30. *Inscr altered to "CORREOS DE CHILE". P 13½×14.*

(a) No wmk. Head litho, frame typo

204	49	10 c. black and blue (10.29) ..	..	8	5

(b) W 68

(i) Whole stamp recess

205	64	5 c. blue (12.28)	..	5	5

(ii) Whole stamp litho

206	64	5 c. green (4.29)	..	5	5
207	49	10 c. black and blue (10.29)	..	12	5
208	52	15 c. black and violet (8.29)	..	12	5

(iii) Head recess, frame litho

209	53	20 c. black and orange-red (12.28)	..	50	5
		a. Shaded background (5.30)	..	60	5
210	54	25 c. black and light blue (12.28)	..	8	5
211	55	30 c. black and bistre (3.29)	..	8	5
212	56	50 c. black and green (12.28) ..	..	10	5
204/212		Set of 9	..	1·00	35

No. 204, thick unwatermarked paper, shoulders shaded; No. 207, thin watermarked paper, shoulders shaded.
Nos. 209a and 213a have the central oval shaded all over; in Nos. 209 and 213 the shading is only partial and forms an irregularly shaped ground for the portrait.

1928 (July)–**30.** *AIR. Nos. 209/12 optd with T 69.*

213	53	20 c. black and orange-red (29.7.29) ..		50	30
		a. Shaded background (1.30)	..	8	5
214	54	25 c. black and blue (R.)	..	5	5
215	55	30 c. black and bistre ..	..	8	5
		a. Opt double, one inverted	..	55·00	55·00
216	56	50 c. black and green (R.)	..	8	5

Servicio del

ESTADO

(O 5)

1930–36. OFFICIAL. Optd as Type O **5**, in red.

(a) No wmk. Inscr "CORREOS DE CHILE"

O217	49	10 c. black and blue (1931) ..	..		25	15

(b) W 68
(i) Inscr "CORREOS DE CHILE"

O218	49	10 c. black and blue	..	..	45	35
O219	53	20 c. black and orange-red	..	..	12	8
O220	54	25 c. black and light blue	..	..	15	5
O221	56	50 c. black and green	..	..	20	8

(ii) Inscr "CHILE CORREOS"

O222	56	50 c. black and green	..	..	20	5
O223	57	1 p. black and green	..	..	15	8
		a. Black & yellow-green (1936)	..	1·25		15
O217/223		Set of 7 ..	..	..	1·40	90

71 Winged Wheel

71a Girl Harvester

72 Sower

1930 (21–30 July). Centenary of First Export of Chilean Nitrate. Litho. W **68**.

(a) Size 20 × 25 mm. P 13½ × 14

217	71	5 c. green (25.7)	..	..	5	5
218		10 c. red-brown (30.7)	..	..	5	5
219		15 c. violet (22.7)	..	..	8	5
220	71a	25 c. slate-grey	..	..	20	10
221	72	70 c. blue	..	..	35	12

(b) Size 24½ × 30 mm. P 14

222	72	1 p. deep sage-green	..	..	35	5
217/222		Set of 6 ..	..	..	1·00	35

73

74

75 Los Cerrillos Airport

1931 (1 May). AIR (Inland). Litho. W **68**. P 13½ × 14 or 14½ × 14 (T **75**).

223	73	5 c. yellow-green	..	..	5	5
224		10 c. yellow-brown	..	..	5	5
		a. Thick paper	..	..	5	5
225		20 c. carmine ..	..	..	5	5
		a. Thick paper	..	..	5	5
226	74	50 c. sepia	..	..	20	5
		a. Thick paper	..	..	5	5
227	75	50 c. deep blue	..	..	25	20
228	74	1 p. bright violet	..	..	15	5
229		2 p. blue-black	..	..	25	8
		a. Slate	..	..	50	45
230	75	5 p. scarlet	..	..	35	12
223/230		Set of 8 (cheapest)	..	..	1·10	60

76 O'Higgins

77 Bulnes

78 J. J. Perez

1931–34. Litho. W **68**. P 13½ × 14.

231	76	10 c. blue (26.4.32)	..	..	5	5
232	77	20 c. purple-brown (1931)	..	..	5	5
		a. Thin paper	..	..	50	5
233	78	30 c. magenta (1934) ..	..	..	5	5

1932–34. OFFICIAL. Optd with Type O **5**. W **68**.

O234	76	10 c. blue (1934)	..	..	8	5
O235	77	20 c. purple-brown	..	..	8	5

1934–38. OFFICIAL. Optd diagonally upwards as Type O **3**. W **68**.

(a) Inscr "CORREO DE CHILE"

O236	64	5 c. green (R.)	..	..	10	8
O237	76	10 c. blue (R.) (1935)	..	..	10	8
O238	77	20 c. purple-brown (1936)	..	3·00		10

(b) Inscr "CHILE CORREOS"

O239	57	1 p. black and green (R.) (1938)	..	60		30

79 Mariano Egaña

80 Joaquin Tocornal

1934. Centenary of the Constitution of 1833. Litho. W **68**. P 13½ × 14 (30 c.) or 14 (1 p. 20).

234	79	30 c. magenta	..	..	5	5
235	80	1 p. 20, greenish blue	..	..	10	5

81 Aeroplane over Santiago

82 Condor in Flight

83 Aeroplanes above Globe

(Des J. Moreno. Recess)

1934–52. AIR (Foreign). T **81** to **83** and similar types. W **68**. P 13½ × 14 or 14 (pesos values).

236	81	10 c. yellow-green (1935)	..	..	5	5
237		15 c. blue-green (11.35)	..	..	5	5
238		20 c. blue (1936)	..	..	5	5
239	–	30 c. black-brown (1935)	..	..	5	5
239a	–	40 c. indigo (11.4.38)	..	..	5	5
240	–	50 c. sepia (3.36)	..	..	5	5
241	82	60 c. violet-black (11.35)	..	..	5	5
242	–	70 c. light blue (11.35)	..	..	5	5
243	–	80 c. blackish olive (1935)	..	..	5	5
244	83	1 p. bluish slate	..	..	5	5
245	–	2 p. light blue (26.2.34)	..	..	5	5
246	–	3 p. red-brown (26.5.35)	..	..	5	5
247	–	4 p. brown. (1935) ..	..	..	5	5
248	–	5 p. orange-red (4.34)	..	..	5	5
249	–	6 p. yellow-brown (1935)	..	..	8	5
		a. Red-brown (12.38)	..	..	50	25
250	–	8 p. green (9.35)	..	..	8	5
251	–	10 p. claret (9.5.34)	..	..	12	5
252	–	20 p. brown-olive	..	..	20	5
253	–	30 p. grey-black	..	..	35	5
254	–	40 p. violet ..	..	..	45	5

255	–	50 p. purple	75	5
		a. Slate-purple (1952)	40	5
236/255*a*		*Set of* 21 (*cheapest*)	2·10	75

Designs: As T **81/2**—30 c., 40 c., 50 c. Aeroplane over landscape; 70 c. Aeroplane and star; 80 c. Condor and statue of Caupolican. As T **83**—3 p., 4 p., 5 p. Seaplane in flight; 6 p., 8 p., 10 p. Aeroplane and rainbow; 20 p., 30 p. Flying boat and compass; 40 p., 50 p. Aeroplane riding a storm.

For stamps without watermark, see Nos. 351*a*/66*e*.

84 Atacama Desert

85 Coal Mines

86 Ships at Valparaiso

87 Diego de Almagro

(Peso values eng J. Moreno, recess. Others litho)

1936 (1 Mar). *400th Anniv of Discovery of Chile. As T* **84** *to* **87** (*agricultural and industrial types*), *all, except* 2 p. *inscr* "1536–1936". *Network backgrounds of* 40 c. *and* 50 c. *in brackets.* W **68**. P 14.

256	5 c. vermilion	5	5
257	10 c. bright violet	5	5
258	20 c. bright magenta	5	5
259	25 c. greenish blue	12	12
260	30 c. pale green	5	5
261	40 c. black (*cream*)	15	15
262	50 c. bright blue (*bluish*)	8	8
263	1 p. deep green	25	8
264	1 p. 20, deep blue	25	8
265	2 p. sepia	45	20
266	5 p. lake-red	55	45
267	10 p. purple	2·00	1·25
256/267	*Set of* 12	3·50	2·40

Designs:—10 c. Fishing boats; 20 c. Coquito Palms; 25 c. Sheep; 40 c. Lonquimay forests; 50 c. Lota coal port; 1 p. 20, Mt Puntiagudo; 5 p. Cattle; 10 p. Shovelling nitrate.

88 Laja Waterfall

89 Copper Mine

90 Fishing Smack

91 Lake Villarrica

1938–40. *T* **88/91** *and similar designs.* W **68**.

(*a*) *Litho.* P $13\frac{1}{2} \times 14$

268	5 c. claret (1939)	5	5
269	10 c. vermilion (*shades*) (1939)	5	5
269*a*	15 c. brown-orange (1940)	5	5
270	20 c. light blue (1938)	5	5
271	30 c. carmine-pink (11.38)	5	5
272	40 c. emerald-green (1939)	5	5
273	50 c. violet (8.38)	5	5

(*b*) *Recess.* P 14

274	1 p. orange-brown (4.38)	8	5
275	1 p. 80, blue (8.38)	10	5
276	2 p. lake (1939)	8	5
277	5 p. myrtle-green (*shades*) (1939)	12	5
278	10 p. purple (*shades*) (6.40)	15	5
268/278	*Set of* 12	80	40

Designs: *As T* **88/9**—10 c. Rural landscape; 15 c. Boldo tree; 20 c. Nitrate works; 30 c. Mineral spas; 50 c. Petroleum tanks. *As T* **90/91**—1 p. 80, Osorno Volcano; 2 p. Mercantile Marine; 10 p. Railway train.

For stamps without watermark, see Nos. 338*a*/*j*.

1939. *OFFICIAL. Nos.* 273/4 *optd with Type* O **5**.

O279	50 c. violet	65	60
O280	1 p. orange-brown	90	30

1940–45. *OFFICIAL. Nos.* 269/76 *optd as Type* O **3**.

O281	10 c. vermilion (1945)	50	40
O282	15 c. brown-orange	15	5
O283	20 c. light blue (R.) (1942)	20	5
O284	30 c. carmine-pink (B.)	20	5
O285	40 c. emerald-green	20	5
O286	50 c. violet (1945)	55	45
O287	1 p. orange-brown (1942)	1·75	25
O288	1 p. 80, blue (R.) (1945)	2·50	1·75
O289	2 p. lake (1942)	1·25	25
O281/289	*Set of* 9	6·50	3·00

For 1 p. and 2 p. without watermark, see Nos. O339/40.

92 *Abtao* and Policarpo Toro

93 Western Hemisphere

1940 (1 Mar). *50th Anniv of Occupation of Easter Island and Local Hospital Fund. T* **92** *and similar type. Recess.* P $14\frac{1}{2}$.

279	80 c.+2 p. 20, carmine and green	15	15
280	3 p. 60+6 p. 40, green and carmine	20	15

Design:—3 p. 60 *Abtao* and Eugenio Eyraud.

Nos. 279/80 were printed together in sheets of 30 (5×6), arranged as follows:—

No. 279. Nos. 1 to 5, 8 to 15, 21 to 22.

No. 280. Nos. 6 and 7. 16 to 20 and 23 to 30.

This provides nine *se-tenant* pairs.

1940 (11 Sept). *50th Anniv of Pan-American Union. Litho.* P 14.

281	**93**	40 c. dull green and yellow-green	15	8

LAN **Cts.80** (94)

LAN **$ 1.60** (95)

("LAN"=Linea Aerea Nacional)

1940. *AIR. Nos.* 225 *and* 229/30 *surch as T* **94** ("Cts. 80" *and* "$5.10") *and T* **95**.

282	**73**	80 c. on 20 c. carmine	8	5
		a. Surch in deep blue	90·00	
283	**75**	1 p. 60 on 5 p. scarlet	30	15
284	**74**	5 p. 10 on 2 p. slate (R.)	40	35

96 Fray Camilo Henriquez

97 Founding of Santiago

(Des J. Moreno. Recess)

1941 (23 Jan). *Fourth Centenary of Santiago. As T **96** (portraits) and T **97**. W **68**. P 14×14½.*

285	10 c. carmine	..	8	8
286	40 c. green (Pedro Valdivia)	..	8	5
287	1 p. 10, scarlet (B. V. MacKenna)	..	10	8
288	1 p. 80, bright blue	..	15	10
289	3 p. 60, indigo (D. B. Arana)	..	45	30
285/289	*Set of 5*	..	75	55

98 Aeroplane and Globe

99 Seaplane and Galleon

(Des E. Matthey. Litho)

1941–50. *AIR. (Inland). Designs as T **98/9**. P 14. (a) W **68**.*

290	10 c. grey-olive (20.8.41)	..	5	5
291	10 c. mauve (8.47)	..	5	5
292	20 c. carmine (20.8.41)..	..	5	5
293	20 c. green (8.47)	..	5	5
294	20 c. orange-brown (5.48)	..	5	5
295	30 c. slate-violet (11.41)	..	5	5
295a	30 c. blackish olive (1948)	..	5	5
296	40 c. brown-lake (11.41)	..	5	5
297	40 c. ultramarine (6.48)	..	5	5
298	50 c. red-orange (2.42)..	..	5	5
299	60 c. deep green (20.8.41)	..	5	5
299a	60 c. olive-green (1948)	..	5	5
300	70 c. rose-carmine (11.41)	..	5	5
301	80 c. ultramarine (3.42)	..	55	20
302	80 c. blackish olive (1948)	..	5	5
303	90 c. brown (11.41)	..	8	5
303a	90 c. chocolate (1948)	..	5	5
304	1 p. bright blue (1941)	..	8	5
304a	1 p. green and light blue (12.48)	..	5	5
305	1 p. 60, reddish violet (1946)	..	5	5
306	1 p. 80, reddish violet (1948)	..	5	5
307	2 p. carmine-lake (11.41)	..	12	8
308	2 p. Venetian red (1946)	..	8	5
309	3 p. blue-green & yellow-grn (11.41)	..	20	15
310	3 p. violet and orange (1947)	..	20	5
	a. Violet and yellow (1950)	..	20	5
311	4 p. violet and buff (11.41)	..	25	25
311a	4 p. blue-green and green (1948)	..	8	5
312	5 p. reddish brown (2.42)	..	1·75	1·25
313	5 p. rose-carmine (8.47)	..	8	5
314	10 p. green and light blue (11.41)	..	1·00	65
315	10 p. deep blue (1947)	..	20	10
290/315	*Set of 31*	..	5·00	3·50

(b) No wmk

316	10 c. ultramarine (1943)	..	5	5
317	10 c. mauve (8.45)	..	5	5
318	20 c. dull green (1943)	..	5	5
319	20 c. orange-brown (2.45)	..	5	5
320	30 c. slate-violet (1944)	..	5	5
321	30 c. brown-olive (1.45)	..	5	5
322	40 c. brown-lake (6.44)..	..	8	5
323	40 c. ultramarine (1.45)	..	5	5
324	50 c. carmine (7.43)	..	5	5
325	50 c. orange-red (6.45)..	..	5	5
326	60 c. red-orange (28.9.42)	..	5	5
327	60 c. deep green (11.46)	..	5	5
328	70 c. rose (5.45)	..	5	5
329	80 c. blackish olive (28.9.42)	..	5	5

330	90 c. brown (8.45)	..	..	5	5
331	1 p. greenish and light blue (11.3.43)			5	5
332	1 p. 60, reddish violet (4.8.45)		..	5	5
333	2 p. Venetian red (28.9.42)		..	10	5
334	3 p. violet and orange (27.8.43)		..	8	5
335	4 p. blue-green and green (30.7.43)		..	8	5
336	5 p. rose-carmine (7.43)		..	15	5
336a	5 p. brown-red (10.44)		..	8	5
337	10 p. deep blue (1943)	..	..	15	10
316/337	*Set of 23*	..	..	1·25	90

Designs (each incorporating a different type of aeroplane):—10 c. Steeple; 30 c. Flag; 40 c. Stars; 50 c. Mountains; 60 c. Tree; 70 c. Estuary; 80 c. Shore; 90 c. Sun rays; 1 p. T **99** (No. 304 commemorates the 4th Centenary of Santiago and is dated "1541 1941"; Nos. 304a and 331 are undated); 1 p. 60, 1 p. 80, Wireless mast; 2 p. Compass; 3 p. Telegraph wires; 4 p. Rainbow; 5 p. Factory; 10 p. Snowcapped mountain.

Nos. 290/337. There are numerous minor paper, gum and shade varieties.

For issues in similar designs, see Nos. 395/404j and 478/83.

100 Arms of Talca

1942–49. *OBLIGATORY TAX. Bicentenary of Talca. Litho. P 14. I. No wmk (2.7.42). II. W **68** ('49).*

				I		II
T338	**100** 10 c. blue	..	..	5	5	5

This stamp was on sale at Talca only. Its use, at first, was obligatory on all correspondence from Talca to Chilean addresses, to provide funds for the celebration of the bicentenary.

1942–45. *As Nos. 269, etc. but without wmk.*

338a	10 c. vermilion (1942)	..	5	5
338b	15 c. brown-orange (1943)	..	5	5
338c	20 c. light blue (1943)	..	5	5
338d	30 c. carmine-pink (1942)	..	5	5
338e	40 c. emerald-green (10.42)	..	5	5
338f	50 c. violet (1943)	..	5	5
338g	1 p. orange-brown (6.42)	..	8	5
338h	2 p. lake (1.43)	..	5	5
338i	5 p. myrtle-green (3.43)	..	5	5
338j	10 p. purple (*shades*) (1945)	..	10	5
338a/j	*Set of 10*	..	45	30

1942–46. *OFFICIAL. Nos. 338g/h optd as Type O **3**.*

O339	1 p. orange-brown	..	65	25
O340	2 p. lake (1946)	..	1·10	25

101 V. Letelier

102 National University

103 Coat of Arms and Aeroplane

(Eng J. Moreno. Recess)

1942 (1–5 Nov). *Centenary of University of Santiago de Chile. T 101 and similar portrait types and T 102/3. No wmk.*

(a) POSTAGE. P 14 (1 *p.*) *or* 14 × 14½ *(others)* (1 Nov)

339	101	30 c. scarlet	..	5	5
340	–	40 c. blue-green (A. Bello) ..	..	5	5
341	–	90 c. violet (M. Bulnes)	..	8	5
342	102	1 p. brown	..	10	5
343	–	1 p. 80, blue (M. Montt)	..	20	15

(b) AIR. P 15 (5 Nov)

344	103	100 p. carmine	..	14·00	7·00
339/344		Set of 6	..	13·00	6·50

104 M. Bulnes

105 Straits of Magellan

106 "Lamp of Life"

1944 (2 Mar). *Centenary of Occupation of Straits of Magellan. Litho. P* 14.

345	104	15 c. black ..	..	5	5
346	–	30 c. carmine	..	5	5
347	–	40 c. yellow-green ..	..	5	5
348	–	1 p. purple-brown ..	..	5	5
349	105	1 p. 80, ultramarine	..	15	8
345/349		Set of 5	..	30	25

Portraits: As T **104**—30 c. J. W. Wilson; 40 c. D. D. Almeida; 1 p. J. de los Santos Mardones.

1944 (18 Oct). *80th Anniv of International Red Cross. T* **106** *and similar type. Litho. P* 14.

350		40 c. black, scarlet and yellow-green	..	8	5
351		1 p. 80, scarlet and ultramarine	..	15	5

Design:—1 p. 80, Serpent and Chalice, symbol of Hygiene.

1944–55. *AIR. As Nos. 236/55a but without wmk.*

351a	81	10 c. yellow-green (1955)	..	5	5
352		20 c. blue (20.5.44)	..	5	5
353		30 c. black-brown (1944)	..	5	5
354	–	40 c. indigo (7.44)	..	5	5
355	–	50 c. sepia (1947)	..	5	5
356	82	60 c. violet-black (1944)	..	5	5
356a	–	70 c. light blue (1948)	..	5	5
357	–	80 c. slate-green (1944)	..	5	5
358	83	1 p. bluish slate (1944)	..	5	5
359		2 p. light blue (1944)	..	5	5
360	–	3 p. red-brown (1945)	..	5	5
361	–	4 p. brown (7.44)	..	5	5
362	–	5 p. orange-red (1944)	..	8	5
363	–	6 p. yellow-brown (1946)	..	8	5
364	–	8 p. green (1944)	..	8	5
365	–	10 p. claret (1944)	..	10	5
366	–	20 p. brown-olive (1945)	..	12	5
		a. Grey-olive (3.52)	..	8	5
366b	–	30 p. brownish grey (1953)	..	15	8
366c	–	40 p. violet (1951)	..	20	10
366d	–	50 p. purple (1950)	..	45	15
		e. Slate-purple (1951)	..	25	8
351a/366e		Set of 20	..	1·25	85

107 O'Higgins

108 Battle of Rancagua

(Eng J. Moreno. Recess)

1945. *Death Centenary of Bernardo O'Higgins. P* 14 (15 *c.*) *or* 14½ *(others).*

367	107	15 c. black and scarlet	..	..	5	5
368	–	30 c. black and brown	..	..	5	5
369	–	40 c. black and green	..	..	5	5
370	108	1 p. 80, black and blue	..	..	12	10
367/370		Set of 4	..	..	25	20

Designs (As T **107**):—30 c. Battle of the Maipo; 40 c. Abdication of O'Higgins.

109 Columbus Lighthouse

110 Andres Bello

1945 (10 Sept). *450th Anniv of Discovery of America. Litho. W* **68.** *P* 14.

371	109	40 c. emerald-green ..	..	..	5	5

1946. *80th Death Anniv of Andres Bello (educationist). Recess. W* **68.** *P* 14.

372	110	30 c. green ..	..	..	5	5
373		1 p. 80, blue	..	..	5	5

111 Antarctic Territory

112 E. Lillo and R. Carnicer

1947 (12 May). *Litho. W* **68.** *P* 14.

374	111	40 c. carmine	..	..	5	5
375		2 p. 50, blue	..	..	15	5

(Des and eng J. Moreno. Recess)

1947 (18 Sept). *Centenary of National Anthem. W* **68.** *P* 14½.

376	112	40 c. blue-green	..	..	5	5

113 Miguel de Cervantes

114 Arturo Prat

(Des and eng J. Moreno. Recess)

1947 (11 Oct). *400th Birth Anniv of Cervantes. W* **68.** *P* 14½.

377	113	40 c. carmine-lake ..	..	..	5	5

1948 (24 Dec). *Birth Centenary of Arturo Prat. W* **68.** *Recess. P* 14½.

378	114	40 c. blue	..	..	5	5

OFICIAL

(O 6)

1948–54. *OFFICIAL. Optd diagonally with Type O* **6.**

(a) W **68.** *Nos. 271/2, 274, 276/7*

O379	30 c. carmine-pink (1954)	..	..	1·90	1·25
O380	40 c. emerald-green (1954)	..	..	1·90	1·10
O381	1 p. orange-brown	..	..	1·25	25
O382	2 p. lake (1954)	..	..	2·00	20
O383	5 p. myrtle-green (1951)	..	..	2·25	40

(b) No wmk. Nos. 338c, 338f

O384	20 c. light blue	..	..	80	20
O385	50 c. violet	..	..	80	20
O379/385	*Set of 7*	..	..	10·00	4·25

For Nos. O382/3 with horizontal overprint, see Nos. O442/3.

115 O'Higgins

116 M. de Toro y Zambrano

117 O'Higgins

1948–54. *Litho. P* 13½ × 14. *(a)* W **68.**

379	**115**	60 c. black (1948)	..	..	5	5
379a	**116**	80 c. green (13.3.53)	..	..	5	5
379b	**117**	1 p. blue-green (10.53)	..	..	5	5

(b) No wmk

379c	**115**	60 c. black (1950)	..	..	5	5
379d	**116**	80 c. green (6.11.54)	..	..	5	5
379e	**117**	1 p. blue-green (7.52)	..	..	5	5
379/379e	*Set of 6*		..	..	20	20

OFFICIAL. Optd diagonally with Type O **6.**
(a) No wmk

O380	**117**	1 p. blue-green (R.) (30.11.52)	..	65	25
	a. Black opt (1955)	..	..	75	10

(b) W **68**

O381	**117**	1 p. blue-green (R.) (1955)	..	80	15

VEINTE

CTS.

(118)

119 *Chiasognathus Grantii*

1948. *No. 272 surch with T* **118.**

380	20 c. on 40 c. emerald-green	..	..	5	5

(Des R. Thenct and A. Matthey. Litho)

1948 (6 Dec). *Centenary of Claude Gay's Book on Chilean Flora and Fauna. As T* **119** *(inscr* "CENTENARIO DEL LIBRO DE GAY 1844–1944"*).* W **68.** *P* 14. *(a) POSTAGE.*

381	60 c. ultramarine	..	..	15	5
382	2 p. 60, green	..	..	20	10

(b) AIR

383	3 p. carmine	..	..	20	20
381/3 × 25	*Set of 75*	..	..	18·00	

The above were each printed in 25 different botanical and zoological designs repeated four times in the sheet of 100 stamps.

120 Airline Badge

121 B. V. Mackenna

122 Wheel and Lamp

1949 (15 Mar). *AIR. 20th Anniv of National Airline. Litho.* W **68.** *P* 14.

384	**120**	2 p. pale ultramarine	..	8	5

1949 (22 Mar). *Benjamin Vicuña Mackenna Museum. Recess.* W **68.** *P* 13½ × 14. *(a) POSTAGE.*

385	**121**	60 c. deep blue	..	5	5

(b) AIR. Inscr "CORREO AEREO"

386	**121**	3 p. carmine-lake	..	8	8

1949 (11 Nov). *Centenary of School of Arts and Crafts, Santiago. T* **122** *and similar types. Litho. No wmk. P* 14. *(a) POSTAGE.*

387	60 c. magenta	..	..	5	5
388	2 p. 60, blue	..	..	5	5

(b) AIR. Inscr "CORREO AEREO"

389	5 p. green	..	..	8	5
390	10 p. brown	..	..	15	8
387/390	*Set of 4*	..	..	30	20

Designs:—2 p. 60, Shield and book; 5 p. Shield, book and factory; 10 p. Wheel and pillar.

123 Heinrich von Stephan

124 Aeroplane and Globe

(T **123** *eng J. Moreno. Anniv recess)*

1950 (6 Jan). *75th Anniv of U.P.U. P* 14. *(a) POSTAGE.*

391	**123**	60 c. carmine	..	5	5
392	2 p. 50, blue	..	..	8	5

(b) AIR

393	**124**	5 p. green	..	10	5
394	10 p. brown	..	..	15	8
391/394	*Set of 4*	..	..	35	20

1950–55. *AIR (Inland). As T* **98/99** *but new designs. Imprint* "ESPECIES VALORADAS". *Litho. P* 14.

(a) W **68**

395	20 c. bistre-brown (19.1.54)	..	..	5	5
396	40 c. reddish violet (11.8.52)	..	..	5	5
397	60 c. pale blue (13.3.53)	..	..	5	5
398	1 p. blue-green (3.7.50)	..	..	5	5
399	2 p. red-brown (2.7.50)	..	..	5	5
400	3 p. blue (3.7.50)	..	..	5	5
401	4 p. red-orange (19.1.54)	..	..	5	5
402	5 p. violet (3.7.50)	..	..	5	5
403	10 p. emerald-green (13.3.53)	..	..	8	5
404	20 p. chocolate (*shades*) (5.12.53)	..	20	5
395/404	*Set of 10*	..	..	60	40

(b) No wmk

404a	20 c. bistre-brown (2.12.53)	..	..	5	5
404b	40 c. reddish violet (14.11.51)	..	..	5	5
404c	60 c. pale blue (13.3.53)	..	..	5	5
404d	1 p. blue-green (19.9.54)	..	..	5	5
404e	2 p. red-brown (1951)	..	..	5	5
404f	3 p. blue (1951)	..	..	5	5
404g	4 p. red-orange (15.11.52)	..	..	5	5
404h	5 p. violet (1951)	..	..	8	5
404i	10 p. emerald-green (1951)	..	..	8	5
404j	20 p. chocolate (*shades*) (1951)	..	12	5
404a/404j	*Set of 10*	..	..	55	40

Designs (each incorporating a different type of aeroplane):—20 c. Mountains; 40 c. Coastline; 60 c. Fishing vessel; 1 p. Araucanian pine tree; 2 p. Chilean flag; 3 p. Dock crane; 4 p. River; 5 p. Industrial plant; 10 p. Landscape; 20 p. Aerial railway.

For similar stamps, but with imprint "CASA DE MONEDA DE CHILE", see Nos. 478/83.

125 San Martin **126** Crossing the Andes

(T **126** eng J. Moreno. Both recess)

1951 (16 Mar). *Death Centenary of General San Martin.* W **68**. (a) POSTAGE. P 14.
405 **125** 60 c. blue 5 5

(b) AIR. P 14½
406 **126** 5 p. purple 12 10

UN PESO
(127)   **128** Isabella the Catholic

1951 (Nov). AIR. No. 303a surch with T **127**.
407 1 p. on 90 c. chocolate 5 5

(Eng J. Moreno. Recess)

1952 (20 Mar). *Fifth Birth Centenary of Isabella the Catholic.* W **68**. P 14. (a) POSTAGE.
408 **128** 60 c. bright blue 5 5

(b) AIR. Inscr "CORREO AEREO"
409 **128** 10 p. carmine 12 10
A souvenir sheet containing Nos. 408/9, but colours changed, imperf and without gum, was issued in Dec 1969 for a Chilean-Spanish Philatelic Exhibition. This sheet had no franking value (*Price 75p un*).

40   **40**
Ctvs.   **Centavos**
(129)   (130)

1952 (Sept). *Nos. 379 and 379c surch with T **129**, in red.*
                    A. W 68   B. No wmk
410 **115** 40 c. on 60 c. black .. 5 5 5 5

1952 (Sept). AIR. *Nos. 302 and 329 surch with T **130**, in red.*
                    A. W 68   B. No wmk
411 40 c. on 80 c. blackish olive .. .. 5 5 1·90 1·90

131 Arms of Valdivia   **132** Old Spanish Watch-tower

1953 (May). *Fourth Centenary of Valdivia. T **131** and various horiz designs as T **132**. Litho. W **68**. P 14. (a) POSTAGE.*
414 **131** 1 p. ultramarine 5 5
415 – 2 p. reddish violet 5 5
416 – 3 p. blue-green 5 5
417 – 5 p. deep brown .. ' .. 8 5

(b) AIR
418 **132** 10 p. brown-red 10 10
414/418 *Set of 5* 30 25
Designs:—2 p. Ancient cannon, Corral Fort; 3 p. View of Valdivia from river; 5 p. Street scene (after old engraving).

133 J. Toribio Medina   **134** Stamp of 1853

1953 (June). *Birth Centenary of Toribio Medina. Recess. W **68**. P 14½.*
419 **133** 1 p. brown 5 5
420 2 p. 50, deep blue 5 5

1953 (15 Oct). *Chilean Stamp Centenary. Recess. W **68**. P 14½. (a) POSTAGE.*
421 **134** 1 p. red-brown 5 5

(b) AIR. Inscr "CORREO AEREO"
422 **134** 100 p. deep turquoise-blue .. .. 1·25 70
Nos. 421/2, but imperforate, exist in a miniature sheet (178×230 mm), but it was not valid for postage (*Price un* £60).

135 Map and Graph   **136** Aeroplanes of 1929 and 1954

1953 (5 Nov). *Twelfth National Census. Litho. W **68**. P 13½×14.*
423 **135** 1 p. deep blue-green 5 5
424 2 p. 50, ultramarine 5 5
425 3 p. brown 5 5
426 4 p. carmine-red 5 5

1954 (26 May). AIR. *25th Anniv of National Air Line. Recess. No wmk. P 14.*
427 **136** 3 p. deep blue 5 5

137 Arms of Angol   **138** I. Domeyko

1954 (28 May). *Fourth Centenary of Angol City. Litho. No wmk. P 14.*
428 **137** 2 p. deep carmine-red 5 5

1954 (16 Aug). *150th Birth Anniv of Domeyko (educationist and mineralogist). Recess. No wmk. P 14. (a) POSTAGE.*
429 **138** 1 p. deep turquoise-blue 5 5

(b) AIR. Inscr "CORREO AEREO"
430 **138** 5 p. red-brown 5 5

A 325

139 Early Locomotive   **140** Arturo Prat

1954 (10 Sept). *Chilean Railway Centenary. Recess.* W **68**. P 14½. (*a*) *POSTAGE.*
431 **139** 1 p. deep rose-red 5 5

(*b*) *AIR. Inscr "CORREO AEREO"*
432 **139** 10 p. slate-purple 12 5
Nos. 431/2, but imperforate, exist in a miniature sheet (174×232 mm), but it was not valid for postage (*Price un £45*).

1954. *75th Anniv of Naval Battle of Iquique. Litho.* P 14.
433 **140** 2 p. blue-violet 5 5

141 Arms of Viña del Mar   **142** Dr. A. del Rio

1955 (5 Mar). *International Philatelic Exhibition, Viña del Mar.* T **141** *and similar vert design. Litho.* W **68**. P 14.
434 **141** 1 p. deep violet-blue 5 5
435 2 p. red (Arms of Valparaiso) 5 5

1955 (24 May). *Fourteenth Pan-American Sanitary Conference. Litho.* W **68**. P 14.
436 **142** 2 p. ultramarine 5 5

143 Christ of the Andes   **144** *Comet* Airliner

1955. *Exchange of Visits between Argentine and Chilean Presidents.* P 14½.

(*a*) *POSTAGE. Litho. No wmk.. Inscr "CORREOS DE CHILE"*
437 **143** 1 p. violet-blue (31.8) 5 5

(*b*) *AIR. Recess.* W **68**
438 **143** 100 p. deep rose-red (24.5) 60 60

1955 (3 Oct)–**60.** *AIR (Foreign).* T **144** *and similar horiz designs.* P 14.

(*a*) *Recess.* W **68** (3.10.55)
439 100 p. deep myrtle-green 15 5
440 200 p. deep ultramarine 35 5
441 500 p. scarlet 75 15

(*b*) *Recess. No wmk*
441*a* 100 p. deep myrtle-green (17.8.57) .. 10 5
441*b* 200 p. deep ultramarine (28.2.58) .. 25 5
441*c* 500 p. scarlet (15.4.58) 55 10

(*c*) *Litho. No wmk*
441*d* 100 p. deep myrtle-green (2.60) .. 15 5
439/441*d Set of 7* .. .. .. 2·00 40
Designs:—200 p. *Beechcraft* monoplane; 500 p. Four-engined airliner.
See also Nos. 516/8.

1955–56. *OFFICIAL. Nos. 276 and 278 optd horiz as Type O **6**.*
O442 2 p. lake (1956) .. .. .. 1·25 50
O443 10 p. purple (B.) .. .. .. 2·00 75

145 M. Rengifo   **146** J. M. Carrera   **147** Helicopter and Bridge

1955–57. *Death Centenary of President Prieto.* T **145** *and similar portraits. Litho. No wmk.*

(*a*) *POSTAGE.* P 14×14½
442 3 p. violet-blue (22.10.55) 5 5
443 5 p. carmine (11.55) 5 5
444 50 p. reddish purple (1.1.56) 10 5
Portraits:—5 p. M. Egaña; 50 p. D. Portales.

(*b*) *COMPULSORY TAX.* P 14
T445 15 p. green (Pres. Prieto) (8.4.57) .. 5 5
This was for compulsory use on parcels entering or leaving Chile to raise a tax for the Prieto Foundation.

Two types of the 5 p.:—

Type A. Size 19½×23 mm; hair almost solid colour with no outline around back of head; "A"s in imprint have cross-bars centred.
Type B. Size 19×22½ mm; hair composed of clear-cut lines of shading, with strong outline behind back of head; "A"s have lower cross-bars leaving triangular white space instead of small dot.

1956–58. T **146** *and similar portraits. Litho.* P 14×14½.

(*a*) *W **68***
446 2 p. deep lilac 5 5
447 3 p. violet-blue (9.7.56) 5 5

(*b*) *No wmk*
447*a* 2 p. deep lilac 5 5
447*b* 4 p. violet-blue (1957) 5 5
448 5 p. sepia (A) 5 5
  a. Type B 5 5
449 10 p. violet 5 5
  a. Perf 13½×14½ (1958) .. 5 5
450 50 p. rose-red 8 5
446/450 *Set of 7* 30 25
Portraits:—3 p. R. Freire; 5 p. M. Bulnes; 10 p. F. A. Pinto; 50 p. M. Montt.

1956–58. *OFFICIAL. As above, optd horiz as Type O **6**. No wmk.* P 14×14½.
O451 2 p. deep lilac 75 50
O452 3 p. violet-blue (R.) .. .. 3·00 3·00
O453 5 p. sepia 75 50
O454 10 p. violet (R.) .. .. .. 2·00 60
  a. Perf 13½×14½ (19½×23½ mm) (1958) .. .. .. 1·50 30
O455 50 p. rose-red .. .. .. 7·50 1·75
O451/455 *Set of 5* .. .. .. 12·00 5·50

1956–57. *AIR (Foreign).* T **147** *and similar horiz designs. Litho.* P 14½×14.

(*a*) *W **68***
451 1 p. claret (30.7.56) 5 5
452 2 p. sepia (10.7.56) 5 5
453 10 p. deep bluish green (9.7.56) .. 5 5
454 50 p. rose-red (30.7.56) 8 5

(*b*) *No wmk*
455 5 p. violet (9.7.56) 5 5
456 10 p. deep bluish green (5.57) .. 5 5
456*a* 20 p. ultramarine (10.8.56) .. 5 5
456*b* 50 p. rose-red (12.57) 8 5
451/456*b Set of 8* 40 30
Designs:—1 p. Jet 'plane; 5 p. Locomotive and 'plane; 10 p. Oil derricks and 'plane; 20 p. Jet 'plane and monolith; 50 p. 'Plane and control tower.
See also Nos. 512/5.

148 F. Santa Maria

149 Atomic Symbol and Cogwheels

(5 p. des J. Moreno. All recess)

1956 (15 Dec)–57. *25th Anniv of Santa Maria Technical University, Valparaiso. No wmk. P 14 (5 p). or 14½ (others).* (a) *POSTAGE.*

457	148	5 p. red-brown (31.1.57)	..	5	5

(b) *AIR*

458	149	20 p. deep green	..	8	5
459	–	100 p. deep slate-violet	..	15	10

Design:—*As T* **149**—100 p. Aerial view of University.
A souvenir sheet exists containing Nos. 457/9 imperforate and without gum (*Price £7.50 un*).

SOUVENIR SHEETS. The souvenir sheets issued in 1957–62 which are recorded in footnotes were issued in very limited quantities and we understand they were not valid for postage, although some are known in used condition. The miniature sheets issued after 1966 were printed in much larger quantities and usually bear the imprint of the Chilean Mint and some of these are listed.

150 Gabriela Mistral

151 Arms of Osorno

1958 (10 ....). *Gabriela Mistral (poet) Commemoration. Recess. No wmk. P 14.*

(a) *POSTAGE. Inscr "CORREOS"*

460	150	10 p. reddish brown	..	5	5

(b) *AIR*

461	150	100 p. deep green	..	12	5

1958 (23 Mar). *Fourth Centenary of Osorno. T* **151** *and vert portrait designs. Litho (T* **151**) *or recess (others). No wmk. P 14.* (a) *POSTAGE.*

462		10 p. red	..	5	5
463		50 p. deep green	..	8	5

(b) *AIR. Inscr "CORREO AEREO"*

464		100 p. Prussian blue	..	12	5

Portraits:—50 p. G. H. de Mendoza; 100 p. O'Higgins.
A souvenir sheet exists containing Nos. 463/4 but in red-brown, imperforate and without gum (*Price £6 un*).

152 "La Araucana" (poem) and Antarctic Map

153 Arms of Santiago de Chile

1958–59. *Antarctic Issue. T* **152** *and similar vert design. Litho (T* **152**), *recess (others). No wmk. P 14.*

(a) *POSTAGE*

465	152	10 p. ultramarine (10.7.58) ..		5	5
466	–	200 p. deep purple (1959)	..	25	15

(b) *Air. Inscr "CORREO AEREO"*

467	152	20 p. violet (10.7.58)	..	5	5
468	–	500 p. deep blue (26.12.58) ..		75	25
465/468		Set of 4	..	1·00	45

Design:—200 p., 500 p. Chilean Map of 1588.

1958. *OFFICIAL. No. 465 optd vert as Type O* **6.**

O469	152	10 p. ultramarine (R.)	..	60·00	5·50

1958 (18 Oct). *National Philatelic Exhibition, Santiago. Recess. No wmk. P 14.* (a) *POSTAGE.*

469	153	10 p. deep purple	..	5	5

(b) *AIR. Inscr "CORREO AEREO"*

470	153	50 p. deep green	..	10	5

A souvenir sheet exists containing Nos. 469/70 but in carmine, imperforate and without gum (*Price £6 un*).

154

155 Antarctic Territory

1958 (18 Dec). *Chilean Civil Servants' Savings Bank Centenary. Recess. No wmk. P 14.* (a) *POSTAGE.*

471	154	10 p. deep blue	..	5	5

(b) *AIR. Inscr "CORREO AEREO"*

472	154	50 p. red-brown	..	10	5

A souvenir sheet exists containing Nos. 471/2 but in lilac-grey, imperforate and without gum (*Price £4.50 un*).

1958–59. *International Geophysical Year. Recess. No wmk. P 14.* (a) *POSTAGE.*

473	155	40 p. carmine	..	12	5

(b) *AIR. Inscr "CORREO AEREO"*

474	155	50 p. green (27.8.59) ..		10	5

156 Religious Emblems

157 Bridge, Valdivia

1959 (22 Jan). *AIR. Human Rights Day. Recess. No wmk. P 15 × 14½.*

475	156	50 p. carmine	..	15	8

1959. *Centenary of German School, Valdivia, and Philatelic Exhibition. T* **157** *and vert portrait inscr "INSTITUTO ALEMAN C. ANWANDTER VALDIVIA 1858–1958". Recess. No wmk. P 14.* (a) *POSTAGE.*

476	157	40 p. green	..	5	5

(b) *AIR. Inscr "CORREO AEREO"*

477	–	20 p. carmine (18.6.59)	..	5	5

Portrait:—20 p. C. Anwandter (founder).
A souvenir sheet exists containing Nos. 476/7, imperforate and without gum (*Price £9 un*).

1959–60. *AIR (Inland). As Nos. 398 and 403/4 and new designs as T* **98/9**. *Imprint "CASA DE MONEDA DE CHILE". Litho. No wmk. P* 14.

478	1 p. blue-green (1960)	..	..		40	20
	a. W **68**				8·00	
479	10 p. emerald-green	..			5	5
480	20 p. chocolate	..	..		5	5
481	50 p. light green (10.59)	..			8	5
482	100 p. carmine (10.59)	..	..		15	10
483	200 p. blue (10.59)	..	..		25	12
478/483	*Set of 6*	..			90	50

Designs (each incorporating an aircraft) :—50 p. Mountainous coastline; 100 p. Antarctic map; 200 p. Rock "bridge" in sea.

158 Expedition Map

159 D. Barros-Arana

1959 (27 Aug). *400th Anniv of Juan Ladrillero's 1557 Expedition. Litho. P* 14. (*a*) *POSTAGE.*

484	**158**	10 p. blackish violet ..	..	..	5	5

(*b*) *AIR. Inscr "CORREO AEREO"*

485	**158**	50 p. deep green	..	..	8	5

1959 (27 Aug). *50th Death Anniv of Barros-Arana (historian). Litho. P* 14. (*a*) *POSTAGE.*

486	**159**	40 p. bright blue	..	..	8	5

(*b*) *AIR. Inscr "CORREO AEREO"*

487	**159**	100 p. deep lilac	..	..	12	10

160 J. H. Dunant

1959 (6 Oct). *Red Cross Commemoration. Litho. No wmk. P* 14. (*a*) *POSTAGE.*

488	**160**	20 p. brown-lake and red	..	..	5	5

(*b*) *AIR. Inscr "CORREO AEREO"*

489	**160**	50 p. black and red	..	..	8	5
		a. Red ptg double, also negative impression of black portrait on back	..	..		

New Currency

161 F. A. Pinto

162 Choshuenco Volcano

163 Plane and Dock Crane

164 Refugee Family

1960–67. *Litho. No wmk. P* 14×13½ (*No.* 492a), 13½×14½ (5 *m.,* 1 *c.,* 5 *c.*) *or* 14 (*others*).

(*a*) *POSTAGE.* T **161/2** *and similar designs*

490	5 m. turquoise-green (4.60)	..	..		5	5
491	1 c. lake-red (5.2.60)	..			5	5
492	2 c. bright blue (29×25 *mm*) (5.8.61)				5	5
492*a*	2 c. bright blue (23½×18 *mm*) (1962)				5	5
493	5 c. deep ultramarine (5.11.60)		..		5	5
494	10 c. green (27.9.62)	..	..		5	5
495	20 c. blue (1962)	..	..		5	5
496	1 E. deep turquoise-green (29.12.67)				12	5
490/496	*Set of 8*	..	..		35	25

Designs: *Vert*—5 m. M. Bulnes; 5 c. M. Montt. *Horiz*—10 c. R. Maule Valley; 20 c. 1 E. Inca Lake.

(*b*) *AIR (Inland).* T **163** *and similar horiz designs*

497	1 m. red-orange (12.60)	..	..		5	5
498	2 m. yellow-green (12.60)	..	..		5	5
499	3 m. violet (3.3.60)	..	..		5	5
500	4 m. olive (12.60)	..	..		5	5
501	5 m. turquoise-green (25.9.60)		..		5	5
502	1 c. ultramarine (5.2.60)	..			5	5
503	2 c. red-brown (8.61)	..			5	5
504	5 c. green (1961)	..	..		5	5
505	10 c. carmine (1962)	..	..		8	5
506	20 c. blue (1962)	..	..		12	10
497/506	*Set of 10*	..	..		50	35

Designs: Plane over—1 m. Araucanian pine; 2 m. Chilean flag; 4 m. River; 5 m. Industrial plant; 1 c. Landscape; 2 c. Aerial railway; 5 c. Mountainous coastline; 10 c. Antarctic map; 20 c. Rock "bridge" in sea.

(*c*) *OFFICIAL. No.* 493 *optd horiz as Type* O **6**

O507	5 c. deep ultramarine (1960)	..	..	2·10	70

1960 (7 Apr). *World Refugee Year. Litho. P* 15×14½. (*a*) *POSTAGE.*

507	**164**	1 c. green	..	..	5	5

(*b*) *AIR. Inscr "CORREO AEREO"*

508	**164**	10 c. violet	..	..	8	5

A souvenir sheet exists containing No. 507 in blue and No. 508 in red-brown, imperforate and without gum (*Price* £25 *un*).

165 Arms of Chile

166 Rotary Emblem and Map

1960. *150th Anniv of First National Government (1st issue). Recess. W* **68**. *P* 14½×15.

(*a*) *POSTAGE*

509	**165**	1 c. olive-brown & brown-lake (8.6)		5	5

(*b*) *AIR. Inscr "CORREO AEREO"*

510	**165**	10 c. chestnut & dp red-brown (25.8)		5	5

See also Nos. 519/30.

1960 (1 Dec). *AIR. Rotary International South American Regional Conference, Santiago. Litho. No wmk. P* 14.

511	**166**	10 c. blue	..	..	8	5

A souvenir sheet exists containing No. 511 in red-brown, imperforate (*Price* £9 *un*).

1960–67. AIR (Foreign). Horiz designs as T 147 and 144, with values in new currency. Litho. No wmk. P 14½ × 13½.

512	5 m. red-brown (1964) ..	5	5
513	1 c. greenish blue (1962)	5	5
514	2 c. ultramarine (1961) ..	5	5
515	5 c. rose-red (1964)	5	5
516	10 c. ultramarine (2.3.67)	5	5
517	20 c. carmine-red (4.62) ..	10	8
518	50 c. blue-green (12.62) ..	12	8
512/518	Set of 7	40	30

Designs: As T 147—5 m. Locomotive and 'plane; 1 c. Oil derricks and 'plane; 2 c. 'plane over Easter Island; 5 c. Plane and control tower. 10 c. T 144. As T 144—20 c. Beechcraft monoplane; 50 c. Four-engined airliner.

167 J. M. Carrera

168 "Population"

1960–65. 150th Anniv of First National Government (later issues). T 167 and similar designs inscr "SESQUICENTENARIO DEL PRIMER GOBIERNO NACIONAL". Recess. W 68 (No. 524); no wmk (others). P 15 × 14½ (vert) or 14½ × 15 (horiz). (a) POSTAGE.

519	1 c. lake and brown (12.4.62) ..	5	5
520	5 c. turquoise-blue & green (13.4.61) ..	5	5
521	10 c. purple-brn and yellow-brn (1964) ..	5	5
522	20 c. deep bluish green & indigo (1965)	5	5
523	50 c. lake and red-brown (1965)	12	5
524	1 E. bistre-brown & bronze-grn (12.60)	45	30
519/524	Set of 6	70	50

Designs: Horiz—1 c. Tribunal del Consulado; 10 c. M. de Toro y Zambrano and M. de Rozas; 20 c. M. de Salas and Juan Egana; 50 c. M. Rodriguez and J. Mackenna. Vert—5 c. Temple of the National Vow.

(b) AIR. Inscr "CORREO AEREO"

525	2 c. slate-purple and lake (1962)	5	5
526	5 c. purple and violet-blue (13.4.61) ..	5	5
527	10 c. bistre-brown and chocolate (1964)	5	5
528	20 c. reddish violet and deep ultramarine (20.3.64) ..	5	5
529	50 c. blue & deep bluish green (1965) ..	12	8
530	1 E. orange-brown & brn-lake (17.6.63)	25	15
525/530	Set of 6	50	35

Designs: Horiz—2 c. Tribunal del Consulado; 10 c. J. G. Marin and J. G. Argomedo; 20 c. J. A. Eyzaguirre and J. M. Infante; 50 c. Bishop J. I. Cienfuegos and Fray C. Henriquez. Vert—5 c. Temple of the National Vow; 1 E. O'Higgins.

A souvenir sheet exists containing No. 526 in brown and No. 510 in blue-green, imperforate (Price £10 un).

1961 (18 Jan). National Census of Population (5 c.) and Housing (10 c.). T 168 and similar vert design. Litho. No wmk. P 14.

531	5 c. green	5	5
532	10 c. violet (Buildings) ..	8	5

169 Pedro de Valdivia

170 Congress Building

(Photo State Ptg Wks, Madrid)

1961 (29 Apr). Earthquake Relief Fund. T 169 and similar vert portrait designs inscr "ESPANA A CHILE". No wmk. P 13 × 12½. (a) POSTAGE.

533	5 c. + 5 c. black-green and flesh ..	12	5
534	10 c. + 10 c. black-violet and buff	8	8

(b) AIR. Inscr "CORREO AEREO"

535	10 c. + 10 c. red-brown and light salmon	10	10
536	20 c. + 20 c. lake and pale blue ..	20	20
533/536	Set of 4	45	35

Portraits:—No. 534, José Toribio Medina; No. 535, Alonso de Ercilla; No. 536, Gabriela Mistral.

1961. 150th Anniv of First National Congress. Litho. W 68. P 14½ × 15. (a) POSTAGE.

537	**170**	2 c. purple-brown (14.8) ..	5	5

(b) AIR. Inscr "CORREO AEREO"

538	**170**	10 c. bronze-green (5.10) ..	8	5

171 Footballers and Globe

172 Mother and Child

(Des J. Moreno. Recess)

1962. World Football Championships, Chile. T 171 and similar design. No wmk. P 14½. (a) POSTAGE. Inscr "CORREOS".

539	**171**	2 c. blue (30.5) ..	5	5
540	–	5 c. green (30.5) ..	5	5

(b) AIR

541	–	5 c. dull purple (30.5) ..	5	5
542	**171**	10 c. lake-red (12.4) ..	8	5
539/542	Set of 4	20	15

Design: Vert—5 c. (2), Goalkeeper and stadium.

A souvenir sheet exists containing Nos. 539/42, but all in orange-brown, imperforate and sold at 7 E. 50 (Price £1.90 un).

1963 (21 Mar). Freedom from Hunger. T 172 and similar design. Litho. P 14. (a) POSTAGE.

543	**172**	3 c. brown-purple ..	5	5

(b) AIR. Inscr "LINEA AEREA NACIONAL"

544	–	20 c. olive-green ..	10	8

Design: Horiz—20 c. Mother holding out food bowl.

173 Centenary Emblem

174 Fire Brigade Monument

1963 (23 Aug). Red Cross Centenary. T 173 and similar design. Litho. P 14. (a) POSTAGE.

545	3 c. red and grey-blue ..	5	5

(b) AIR. Inscr "LAN"

546	20 c. red and slate-violet ..	8	5

Design: Horiz—20 c. Centenary emblem and silhouette of aircraft.

1963 (20 Dec). Santiago Fire Brigade Centenary. T 174 and similar design. Litho. P 14 (3 c.) or 14½ × 15 (30 c.). (a) POSTAGE.

547	3 c. violet ..	5	5

(b) AIR. Inscr "LINEA AEREA NACIONAL"

548	30 c. carmine-red ..	15	10

Design: Horiz (39 × 30 mm)—30 c. Fire engine of 1863.

175 Band encircling Globe   **176** Enrique Molina

1964 (9 Apr). *AIR. "Alliance for Progress" and Pres. Kennedy Commemoration. Litho. P 15 × 14½.*
549 **175** 4 c. blue   5   5

1964 (Nov)–**65**. *Molina Commemoration (founder of Concepcion University). Litho. P 14. (a) POSTAGE.*
550 **176** 4 c. light bistre-brown   ..   5   5

     (b) *AIR. Inscr "LINEA AEREA NACIONAL"*
551 **176** 60 c. bright violet (6.65)   ..   15   12

1965. *Casanueva Commemoration. Design as T* **176** *but with portrait of Msgr. Carlos Casanueva, Rector of Catholic University. Litho. P 14. (a) POSTAGE.*
552   4 c. reddish purple   5   5

     (b) *AIR. Inscr "LINEA AEREA NACIONAL"*
553   60 c. deep bluish green   15   12

177 Battle Scene   **178** Monolith

1965 (7 May). *AIR. 150th Anniv of Battle of Rancagua. Recess. P 14½ × 15.*
554 **177** 5 c. brown and deep bluish green ..   5   5

1965 (May)–**68**. *Easter Island Discoveries. Litho. P 14 × 14½.*
555 **178** 6 c. reddish purple   5   5
556   10 c. magenta (1.10.68)   5   5

179 I.T.U. Emblem and Symbols   **180** Skier descending Slope

1965 (17 May). *AIR. I.T.U. Centenary. Litho. P 14½ × 14.*
557 **179** 40 c. brown-purple and rose-red   ..   10   8

1965 (30 Aug). *World Skiing Championships. T* **180** *and similar designs. Litho. P 14. (a) POSTAGE.*
558 **180** 4 c. deep bluish green   ..   5   5

     (b) *AIR. Inscr "LINEA AEREA NACIONAL"*
559   – 20 c. ultramarine   5   5
   Design: *Horiz*—20 c. Skier crossing slope.

181 Crusoe on Juan Fernandez   **182** Angelmo Harbour   **183** Aviators' Monument

1965 (Aug). *Robinson Crusoe Commemoration. Litho. P 14 × 14½.*
560 **181** 30 c. claret   8   5

1965 (31 Oct). *AIR. Litho. P 14 or 14 × 14½ (1 E.).*
561 **182** 40 c. light bistre-brown   ..   8   5
562 **183** 1 E. carmine   15   12

184 Copihue (National Flower)   **185** A. Bello   **186** Dr. L. Sazie

1965 (17 Nov)–**69**. *Litho. P 14.*
563 **184** 15 c. carmine-red and green   ..   5   5
563a   20 c. carmine-red and grn (20.4.69)   5   5

1965 (29 Nov). *AIR. Death Centenary of Andres Bello (poet). Recess. P 14 × 14½.*
564 **185** 10 c. carmine-lake   5   5

1966 (9 Feb). *Death Centenary of Dr. Lorenzo Sazie. Litho. P 14 × 14½.*
565 **186** 1 E. myrtle-green   15   8

186a Skier in Slalom Race   **187** Skiers

1966. *AIR. World Skiing Championship, Partillo. Litho.*

     (a) *P* 15 (20 July)
566 **186a** 75 c. claret and pale lilac   15   10
567   3 E. ultramarine and pale blue   ..   60   30

     (b) *P* 14 (6 April)
568 **187** 4 E. lake-brown and blue   65   50
MS568a   110 × 140   mm. Nos. 566/7 Imperf.
   No gum (20 July)   90

188 Ball and Basket   **189** J. Montt

1966 (28 Apr). *AIR. World Basketball Championships. Litho. P 14.*
569 **188** 13 c. carmine   5   5

1966. *T* **189** *and similar vert design. Litho.* P 13½×14½.
570 30 c. reddish violet (Aug) 5 5
571 50 c. brown (G. Riesco) (20 July) .. 8 5

190 W. Wheelwright and Paddle-steamer *Chile*

191 "Learning"

1966 (2 Aug). *125th Anniv* (*in* 1965) *of Arrival of Paddle-steamers "Chile" and "Peru". Litho.* P 14½. (a) POSTAGE.
572 **190** 10 c. ultramarine and pale blue .. 5 5

(b) AIR. Inscr "LINEA AEREA NACIONAL"
573 **190** 70 c. greenish blue & pale yell-grn .. 12 8

1966. *Education Campaign. Litho.* P 14.
574 **191** 10 c. brown-purple 5 5

192 I.C.Y. Emblem

193 Chilean Flag and Ships

1966 (28 Oct). *International Co-operation Year* (1965). *Litho.* P 14½×15. (a) POSTAGE.
575 **192** 1 E. bistre-brown and emerald .. 15 10

(b) AIR. Inscr "LINEA AEREA NACIONAL"
576 **192** 3 E. carmine-red and new blue .. 45 40
MS576a 111×140 mm. Nos. 575/6 Imperf. No gum (9 Dec) .. 65

1966 (21 Nov). *AIR. Antofagasta Centenary. Litho.* P 14.
577 **193** 13 c. brown-purple 5 5

194 Capt. Pardo and Rescue Vessel

195 Chilean Family

1967 (6 Jan). *50th Anniv of Pardo's Rescue of Shackleton Expedition.* *T* **194** *and similar horiz design. Litho.* P 14½×15. (a) POSTAGE.
578 **194** 20 c. deep turquoise.. .. .. 5 5

(b) AIR. Inscr "LAN-CHILE"
579 – 40 c. ultramarine 10 8
Design:—40 c. Capt. Pardo and Antarctic sectoral map.

1967 (13 Apr). *8th International Family Planning Congress. Litho.* P 14. (a) POSTAGE.
580 **195** 10 c. black and bright purple .. 5 5

(b) AIR. Inscr "LAN CHILE"
581 **195** 80 c. black and new blue 12 10

196 R. Dario

197 Pine Forest

(Des J. Moreno. Recess)

1967 (15 May). *AIR. Birth Centenary of Ruben Dario* (*Nicaraguan poet*). P 14½×15.
582 **196** 10 c. deep ultramarine 5 5

(Des J. Moreno. Litho)

1967 (9 June). *National Afforestation Campaign.* P 15×14½. (a) POSTAGE.
583 **197** 10 c. bluish green and pale blue .. 5 5

(b) AIR. Inscr "LAN-CHILE"
584 **197** 75 c. lt grey-green & lt orge-brown .. 12 10

198 Lions Emblem

199 Chilean Flag

(Des J. Moreno. Litho)

1967. *50th Anniv of Lions International.* P 14. (a) POSTAGE.
585 **198** 20 c. turquoise-blue and yell (12.7) .. 5 5

(b) AIR. Inscr "CORREO AEREO"
586 **198** 1 E. bluish violet and yellow (12.7) 15 12
587 – 5 E. ultramarine and yellow (11.8) .. 75 55
A souvenir sheet containing Nos. 585/7 had no franking value.

1967 (20 Oct). *150th Anniv of National Flag. Litho.* P 14½×15. (a) POSTAGE.
588 **199** 80 c. rosine and bright blue .. 12 8

(b) AIR. Inscr "CORREO AEREO"
589 **199** 50 c. rosine and bright blue .. 8 5
A souvenir sheet containing No. 589, imperf and without gum, exists, issued in connection with a Chilean-Austrian Philatelic Exhibition during April 1971 (*Price* £4.75 un).

200 I.T.Y. Emblem

201 Cardinal Caro

(Des J. Moreno. Litho)

1967 (22 Nov). *AIR. International Tourist Year.* P 14½×15.
590 **200** 30 c. black and blue 5 5

(Des J. Moreno. Recess)

1967 (4 Dec). *Birth Centenary of Cardinal Caro.* P 14½. (a) POSTAGE.

591	**201**	20 c. brown-lake	.. .. ..	5	5

(b) AIR. *Inscr* "CORREO AEREO"

592	**201**	40 c. violet	.. ..	8	5

202 San Martin and O'Higgins   203 Farmer and Wife

(Des J. Moreno. Litho)

1968 (5 Apr). *150th Anniv of Battles of Chacabuco and the Maipo.* P 14½×15. (a) POSTAGE.

593	**202**	3 E. new blue	.. ..	25	15

(b) AIR. *Inscr* "CORREO AEREO"

594	**202**	2 E. violet	.. .. ..	20	15
MS594a		140×109 mm. Nos. 593/4 Imperf		1·25	

A souvenir sheet also exists containing No. 593 in brown and No. 594 in green, imperforate.

(Des J. Moreno. Litho)

1968 (18 June). *Agrarian Reform.* P 15×14½. (a) POSTAGE.

595	**203**	20 c. black, green and yellow-orange		5	5

(b) AIR. *Inscr* "CORREO AEREO"

596	**203**	50 c. black, green and yellow-orange		8	5

204 Juan I. Molina (scientist)   205 Hand
and "Lamp of Learning"   supporting
    Cogwheel

(Des J. Moreno. Litho)

1968 (27 Aug). *Molina Commemoration.* T **204** *and similar horiz design.* P 14½×15. (a) POSTAGE.

597	**204**	2 E. bright purple	.. ..	12	8

(b) AIR. *Inscr* "CORREO AEREO"

598	–	1 E. emerald-green (Molina and books)	.. ..	8	5

1968 (1 Oct). *Fourth Manufacturing Census.* Litho. P 14×14½.

599	**205**	30 c. carmine	.. ..	5	5

206 Map, Galleon and   207 Club Emblem
Ferry-boat

1968 (7 Oct). *"Five Towns" Centenary.* T **206** *and similar design.* Litho.

(a) POSTAGE. P 14½×15

600	**206**	30 c. ultramarine	.. ..	5	5

(b) AIR. *Inscr* "CORREO AEREO". P 15×14½

601	–	1 E. reddish purple..	.. ..	8	5

Design: *Vert*—1 E. Map of Chiloe Province.

(Des and eng J. Moreno. Recess)

1968 (4 Nov). *40th Anniv of Chilean Automobile Club.* P 14½×14. (a) POSTAGE.

602	**207**	1 E. carmine-red	.. ..	8	5

(b) AIR. *Inscr* "CORREO AEREO"

603	**207**	5 E. ultramarine	.. ..	45	25

208 Chilean Arms   209 Don Francisco Garcia
    Huidobro (founder)

(5 E. eng J. Moreno, recess. Others litho)

1968 (12 Nov). AIR. *State Visit of Queen Elizabeth II.* T **208** *and similar designs.* P 15×14½ (5 E.) or 14½×15 (*others*).

604		50 c. light bistre-brown & myrtle-green	5	5
605		3 E. light orange-brown and deep blue	25	15
606		5 E. bright purple and plum	..	45	25
MS607		124×189 mm. Nos. 604/6. Imperf. No gum	.. .. ..	1·25	

Designs: *Horiz*—3 E. Royal arms of Great Britain. *Vert*—5 E. St. Edward's Crown on map of South America.

(Des J. Moreno. Litho)

1968 (31 Dec)–**69**. *225th Anniv of Chilean Mint.* T **209** *and similar horiz designs.* P 14½×15. (a) POSTAGE.

608		2 E. violet-blue and light brown-red	..	15	10
609		5 E. brown and light yellow-green	..	45	25

(b) AIR. *Inscr* "CORREO AEREO"

610		50 c. maroon and yellow	.. ..	5	5
611		1 E. orange-red and light new blue	..	10	8
608/611		*Set of 4*	.. ..	65	45
MS612		150×120 mm. Nos. 608/11. Imperf. No gum (Sold at 12 E.) (30.10.69)		70	

Designs:—50 c. First Chilean coin and press; 1 E. First Chilean stamp printed by the Mint (1915); 5 E. Philip V of Spain.

210 Satellite and Dish Aerial

1969 (20 May). *Inauguration of "ENTEL-CHILE" Satellite Communications Ground Station, Longovilo (1st issue).* Litho. P 14½×15. (a) POSTAGE.

613	**210**	30 c. blue	.. .. ..	5	5

(b) AIR. *Inscr* "CORREO AEREO"

614	**210**	2 E. reddish purple..	.. ..	15	8

For a similar design, but with different inscription see Nos. 668/9.

211 Red Cross Symbols   212 Rapel Dam

1969 (5 Sept). *50th Anniversary of League of Red Cross Societies. Litho. P 14½×15. (a) POSTAGE.*
615 **211** 2 E. red and bluish violet 12 8

(b) AIR. Inscr "CORREO AEREO"
616 **211** 5 E. red and black 40 20
A souvenir sheet containing designs as Nos. 615/16 was issued in May, 1970, imperf without gum (*Price 80p. un*).

1969 (18 Nov). *Rapel Hydro-electric Project. Litho. P 14½×15. (a) POSTAGE.*
617 **212** 40 c. green 5 5

(b) AIR. Inscr "CORREO AEREO"
618 **212** 3 E. blue 30 15

213 Rodriguez Memorial

1969 (24 Nov). *150th Death Anniversary of Col. Manuel Rodriguez. Litho. P 14½×15. (a) POSTAGE.*
619 **213** 2 E. crimson 12 8

(b) AIR. Inscr "CORREO AEREO"
620 **213** 30 c. brown 5 5

214 Open Bible

1969 (3 Dec). *400th Anniversary of Spanish Translation of the Bible. Litho. P 14½×15. (a) POSTAGE.*
621 **214** 40 c. red-brown 5 5

(b) AIR. Inscr "CORREO AEREO"
622 **214** 1 E. emerald 8 5

215 Hemispheres and I.L.O. Emblem

1969 (17 Dec). *50th Anniversary of International Labour Organization. Litho. P 14½×15. (a) POSTAGE.*
623 **215** 1 E. blue-green and black 10 5

(b) AIR. Inscr "CORREO AEREO"
624 **215** 2 E. purple and black 20 10

216 Human Rights Emblem   **217** "EXPO" Emblem

1969 (18 Dec). *Human Rights Year* (1968). *Litho. P 14½×15. (a) POSTAGE.*
625 **216** 4 E. red and greenish blue 35 25

(b) AIR. Inscr "CORREO AEREO"
626 **216** 4 E. red and chocolate 35 25
MS627 119×140 mm. Nos. 635/6. Imperf. No gum (Sold at 12 E.) .. .. 1·00

1969 (22 Dec). *World Fair "EXPO 70", Osaka, Japan. Litho. P 14. (a) POSTAGE.*
628 **217** 3 E. blue 30 15

(b) AIR. Inscr "CORREO AEREO"
629 **217** 5 E. vermilion 45 35

218 Mint, Valparaiso (18th century)

1970 (Jan–Apr). *Spanish Colonization of Chile. T 218 and similar designs. Recess. P 14½×15 (horiz) or 15×14½ (vert).*
630 2 E. maroon (30.4) 12 8
631 3 E. red (30.4) 15 12
632 4 E. steel-blue (30.4) 25 15
633 5 E. brown (30.4) 35 25
634 10 E. myrtle-green (30.4) 65 40
630/634 *Set of 5* .. .. .. 1·40 90
MS635 110×140 mm. Nos. 631, 633/4. Imperf. No gum (Sold at 25 E.) (Jan) .. 1·90
Designs: *Vert*—3 E. Pedro de Valdivia; 4 E. Santo Domingo Church, Santiago; 10 E. Ambrosio O'Higgins. *Horiz*—5 E. Cal y Canto Bridge.
No. **MS**635 was issued in connection with a Chilean-Spanish Philatelic Exhibition to commemorate the 80th anniversary of the Chilean Philatelic Society.

219 Policarpo Toro and Map

1970 (26 Jan). *80th Anniversary of Easter Island Annexation. Litho. P 14½×15. (a) POSTAGE.*
636 **219** 5 E. reddish violet 45 35

(b) AIR. Inscr "CORREO AEREO"
637 **219** 50 c. turquoise 5 5

 E° 0,10
Art. 77
LEY
17272

(220)

221 Chilean Schooner and Arms

1970 (1 Feb–July). *COMPULSORY TAX. Postal Modernisation. Nos. 492a and 555 surch with T 220 or similar type.*
T638 **162** 10 c. on 2 c. bright blue 5 5
T639 **178** 10 c. on 6 c. reddish purple (July) .. 5 5

1970 (4 Feb). *150th Anniversary of Capture of Valdivia by Lord Cochrane. Litho. P 14½×15. (a) POSTAGE.*
640 **221** 40 c. lake 5 5

(b) AIR. Inscr "CORREO AEREO"
641 **221** 2 E. ultramarine 15 12

222 Paul Harris
223 Mahatma Gandhi

1970 (18 Mar). *Birth Centenary of Paul Harris (founder of Rotary International). Litho. P* 14. (*a*) *POSTAGE.*
642 **222** 10 E. ultramarine 85 70
   (*b*) *AIR. Inscr* "CORREO AEREO"
643 **222** 1 E. claret 8 5

1970 (1 Apr). *Birth Centenary of Mahatma Gandhi. Litho. P* 15×14½. (*a*) *POSTAGE.*
644 **223** 40 c. blue-green 5 5
   (*b*) *AIR. Inscr* "CORREO AEREO"
645 **223** 1 E. red-brown 8 5

224 Chilean Arms
225 Education Year Emblem
226 Virgin and Child

1970 (23 Apr)–72. *COMPULSORY TAX. Postal Modernization. Litho. P* 14½×14.
T646 **224** 10 c. blue 5 5
T647   15 c. red (7.72) 5 5

1970 (17 July). *International Education Year. Litho. P* 15×14½. (*a*) *POSTAGE.*
648 **225** 2 E. claret 12 8
   (*b*) *AIR. Inscr* "CORREO AEREO"
649 **225** 4 E. lake-brown 35 20

1970 (28 July). *O'Higgins National Shrine, Maipo. Litho. P* 15×14½. (*a*) *POSTAGE.*
650 **226** 40 c. blue-green 5 5
   (*b*) *AIR. Inscr* "CORREO AEREO"
651 **226** 1 E. violet-blue 8 5

227 Snake and Torch Emblem
228 Chilean Arms and Copper Symbol

1970 (11 Aug). *10th International Cancer Congress, Houston, U.S.A. Litho. P* 15×14½. (*a*) *POSTAGE.*
652 **227** 40 c. reddish purple and light blue .. 5 5
   (*b*) *AIR. Inscr* "CORREO AEREO"
653 **227** 2 E. brown and light olive 15 10

1970 (21 Oct). *Nationalization of Copper Mines. Litho. P* 15×14½. (*a*) *POSTAGE.*
654 **228** 40 c. rose and light red-brown .. 5 5
   (*b*) *AIR. Inscr* "CORREO AEREO"
655 **228** 3 E. blue-green and light red-brown 25 15

229 Globe, Dove and Cogwheel
52 CTS
(230)

1970 (22 Oct). *25th Anniversary of United Nations. Litho. P* 14½×15. (*a*) *POSTAGE.*
656 **229** 3 E. reddish violet and claret .. 25 12
   (*b*) *AIR. Inscr* "CORREO AEREO"
657 **229** 5 E. green and lake 45 20

1970 (24 Dec)–71. *Nos.* 613/14 *surch with T* 230 *in red.* (*a*) *POSTAGE.*
658 **210** 52 c. on 30 c. blue 5 5
   (*b*) *AIR. Inscr* "CORREO AEREO"
659 **210** 52 c. on 2 E. reddish purple ((21.1.71) 5 5

231 Bow of Freighter and Ship's Wheel
232 Bernardo O'Higgins and Fleet

1971 (18 Jan). *State Maritime Corporation. Litho. P* 14. (*a*) *POSTAGE.*
660 **231** 52 c. claret 5 5
   (*b*) *AIR. Inscr* "CORREO AEREO"
661 **231** 5 E. light red-brown 30 20

1971 (3 Feb). *150th Anniversary of Peruvian Liberation Expedition. Litho. P* 14½×15. (*a*) *POSTAGE.*
662 **232** 5 E. deep bluish green and light blue 30 20
   (*b*) *AIR. Inscr* "CORREO AEREO"
663 **232** 1 E. dull purple and cobalt .. 8 5

233 Scout Badge
234 Young People and U.N. Emblem

1971 (10 Feb). *60th Anniversary of Chilean Boy Scouts Association. Litho. P* 14. (*a*) *POSTAGE.*
664 **233** 1 E. light chocolate and green .. 8 5
   (*b*) *AIR. Inscr* "CORREO AEREO"
665 **233** 5 c. light yellow-olive and lake .. 5 5

1971 (11 Feb). *1st Latin-American Meeting of U.N.I.C.E.F. Executive Council, Santiago* (1969). *Litho. P* 14½×15. (*a*) *POSTAGE.*
666 **234** 52 c. brown and deep blue 5 5
   (*b*) *AIR. Inscr* "CORREO AEREO"
667 **234** 2 E. bright green and Prussian blue 12 10

1971 (25 May). *Longovilo Satellite Communications Ground Station (2nd issue).* As **T 210,** *but with "LONGOVILO" added to centre inscr and wording at foot of design changed to "PRIMERA ESTACION LATINOAMERICANA".* Litho. *P* 14½ × 15. (a) *POSTAGE.*
668   40 c. deep bluish green   5   5

    (b) *AIR. Inscr "CORREO AEREO"*
669   2 E. brown   12   10

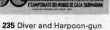

235 Diver and Harpoon-gun   **(236)**   **(237)**

1971 (1 Sept). *10th World Underwater Fishing Championships, Iquique.* Litho. *P* 14½ × 15.
670 **235** 1 E. 15, myrtle-green & light green ..   5   5
671   2 E. 35, deep ultram & lt grey-blue ..   8   5

1971 (Sept). *COMPULSORY TAX. Postal Modernization. No.* T646 *surch with* **T 236** *or* **237,** *in red.*
T672 **236** 15 c. on 10 c. blue   5   5
T673 **237** 15 c. on 10 c. blue   5   5
    On No. T673 the obliterating bar is continuous across each horiz row of the sheet.

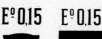

238 Magellan and Caravel

1971 (3 Nov). *450th Anniversary of Discovery of Magellan Straits.* Litho. *P* 14½.
674 **238** 35 c. plum and violet-blue   5   5

239 D. Godoy, and Plane over Andes   **240** Statue of the Virgin, San Cristobal

1971 (4 Nov). *1st Trans-Andes Flight* (1918) *Commemoration.* Litho. *P* 14½.
675 **239** 1 E. 15, light grey-green and blue ..   5   5

1971 (Nov). *10th Spanish-American Postal Union Congress, Santiago.* **T 240** *and similar designs.* Litho. *P* 15 × 14½ (vert) *or* 14½ × 15 (horiz).
676   1 E. 15, deep blue (11.11)   5   5
677   2 E. 35, ultramarine and red (5.11)   ..   12   8
678   4 E. 35, brown-red (5.11)   25   15
679   9 E. 35, slate-lilac (18.11)   55   45
680   18 E. 35, magenta (19.11)   ..   ..   1·10   85
676/680   *Set of 5*   ..   ..   ..   1·75   1·40
    Designs: *Horiz*—2 E. 35, U.P.A.E. emblem; 9 E. 35, Central Post Office, Santiago; 18 E. 35, Corregidor Inn. *Vert*—4 E. 35, St. Francis' Church, Santiago.
    A souvenir sheet containing these stamps imperf had no franking value.

241 Cerro el Tololo Observatory

1971 (18 Dec). *Inauguration of Astronomical Observatory, Cerro el Tololo.* Litho. *P* 14½.
681 **241** 1 E. 95, deep blue and new blue   ..   5   5

242 Boeing "707" over Easter Island   **243** Alonso de Ercilla y Zuniga

1971 (18 Dec). *First Air Service Santiago–Easter Island–Tahiti.* Litho. P 14½.
682 **242** 2 E. 35, reddish purple & light ochre   8   5

1972 (20 Mar). *400th Anniversary of "La Araucana"* (*epic poem by de Ercilla y Zuniga*) (1969). Recess. *P* 14. (a) *POSTAGE.*
683 **243** 1 E. brown-lake   5   5

    (b) *AIR. Inscr "CORREO AEREO"*
684 **243** 2 E. greenish blue   5   5

244 Antarctic Map and Dog-sledge   **245** Human Heart

1972 (20 Mar). *10th Anniversary of Antarctic Treaty.* Litho. *P* 14½ × 15.
685 **244** 1 E. 15, black and violet-blue   ..   5   5
686   3 E. 50, turquoise-blue & blue-green   20   12

1972 (2 Apr). *World Heart Month.* Litho. *P* 15 × 14½.
687 **245** 1 E. 15, carmine and black   5   5

246 Text of Speech by Pres. Allende

1972 (13 Apr). *3rd United Nations Conference on Trade and Development, Santiago.* *T 246 and similar horiz design. Litho.* P 14½×15.

688	**246**	35 c. bluish green and buff ..	5	5
689	–	1 E. 15, reddish violet & bright blue	5	5
690	**246**	4 E. deep violet and pale pink ..	25	15
691	–	6 E. deep blue and yellow-orange ..	35	25
688/691		*Set of 4*	65	45

Design:—1 E. 15, 6 E. Conference Hall, Santiago.

Nos. 688 and 690 were issued in sheets with *se-tenant* stamp-size labels showing Chilean workers and inscr "CORREOS DE CHILE". These two values were only valid for postage with the *se-tenant* label attached.

247 Soldier and Crest   **248** Copper Miner

1972 (9 June). *150th Anniversary of O'Higgins Military Academy. Litho.* P 14½×15.

692	**247**	1 E. 15, yellow and blue	5	5

1972 (11 July). *Copper Mines Nationalization Law (1971). Litho.* P 15×14½.

693	**248**	1 E. 15, blue and rose-red	5	5
694	–	5 E. black, blue and rose-red ..	30	20

A souvenir sheet containing Nos. 693/4 imperf on thin card with copper medallion exists (*Price 30p. un*).

249 Training Ship *Esmeralda*   **250** Observatory and Telescope

1972 (4 Aug). *150th Anniversary of Arturo Prat Naval College. Litho.* P 15×14½.

695	**249**	1 E. 15, maroon	5	5

1972 (31 Aug). *Inauguration of Cerro Calan Observatory. Litho.* P 14½×15.

696	**250**	50 c. ultramarine	5	5

(251)   **252** Dove with Letter

1972 (Sept). *COMPULSORY TAX. Postal Modernization.* No. T647 *surch with* T 251, *in blue.*

T697	**224**	20 c. on 15 c. red	5	5

1972 (9 Oct). *International Correspondence Week. Litho.* P 15×14½.

698	**252**	1 E. 15, bluish violet & bright mauve	5	5

253 Gen. Schneider, Flag and Quotation

1972 (25 Oct). *2nd Death Anniv of General Rene Schneider. Litho.* P 14.

699	**253**	2 E. 30, multicoloured ..	8	5

No. 699 has a vertical line of perforations through the centre of the stamp.

254 Book and Students

1972 (31 Oct). *International Book Year. Litho.* P 14½×15.

700	**254**	50 c. black and orange-red	5	5

255 "Folklore and Handicrafts"   **256** Carrera in Prison

1972 (20 Nov). *American Tourist Year.* T 255 *and similar designs. Litho.* P 15×14½ (3 E. 50) or 14½×15 (others).

701		1 E. 15, black and red	5	5
702		2 E. 65, reddish purple & dp ultramarine	10	8
703		3 E. 50, red-brown and red	20	12

Designs: *Horiz*—2 E. 65, Natural produce. *Vert*—3 E. 50, Stove and rug.

1973 (1 Feb). *150th Death Anniv of General J. M. Carrera. Litho.* P 15×14½.

704	**256**	2 E. 30, blue	8	5

257 Antarctic Map

1973 (8 Feb). *25th Anniv of General O'Higgins Antarctic Base. Litho.* P 15×14½.

705	**257**	10 E. red and blue	60	40

TIERRA DEL FUEGO. This will be found in alphabetical order under "T".

China

The Chinese Imperial Government had a courier service, the I Chan, supervised by the Board of War, for the delivery of official correspondence; it is believed that this was started under the Chou Dynasty (1122–255 B.C.). Unofficial mail was carried by private postal agencies, the Min Chu.

The first postage stamps issued in China were those of the Municipality of Shanghai, in 1865. Shanghai was opened up as a foreign port in 1843 and the Shanghai Municipality was created in July 1854. Foreign traders in the city became dissatisfied with the high charges of the Min Chu and in 1864 organised a postal system under the Municipal Council.

Agencies of the Shanghai Local Post Office were opened in 16 cities of China. In the 1893–96 period many of these agencies became part of the postal services opened by municipal councils, and local stamps for these services were issued at Amoy, Chefoo, Chinkiang, Chungking, Foochow, Hankow, Ichang, Kewkiang, Nanking and Wuhu. We confine our listing of these "Treaty Port" local stamps to those issued at Shanghai.

SHANGHAI

LOCAL POST

1865. 16 Cash=1 Candareen
100 Candareens=1 Tael
1890. 100 Cents=1 Dollar

1 Dragon

Characters at left of stamp

2 c.		4 c.		8 c.	
兩 分 銀	二 分 銀	四 分 銀	四 錢 銀	八 分 銀	八 錢 銀
I.	II.	III.	IV.	V.	VI.

Numerals of value

A	R	M
1	**I**	**1**

A	M	A	M
2	**2**	**3**	**3**

(A=Antique; R=Roman; M=Modern)

1865. *Type-set. Antique numerals. Imperf.*

A. "CANDAREENS" *in the plural* (Aug–Nov)
Wove paper. Roman "I" in "16"

1	1	2 c. black (I)	..	..	..	14·00	30·00
		a. Pelure paper	..	..	20·00	
2		2 c. black (II)	..	..	..	15·00	
		a. Pelure paper	..	..	12·00	
3		4 c. yellow (III) ..	..	..	10·00	30·00
		a. Pelure paper	..	..	16·00	
4		8 c. olive-green (V)	..	..	14·00	
		a. Bright yellow-green	..	..	12·00	
5		16 c. red ..	..	..	..	10·00	
		a. Scarlet	..	..	..	10·00	

Error. Chinese value "mace" for candareens. Pelure paper

6	1	4 c. yellow (IV) ..	..	..	15·00
7		8 c. grey-green (VI)	..	..	15·00

B. "CANDAREEN" *in the singular* (Dec)
(*a*) *Laid paper*

8	1	1 c. blue	..	..	..	15·00
		a. Deep blue ..	..	..	18·00
9		2 c. black (I)	..	..	..	£160
10		4 c. yellow (III) ..	..	..	50·00

(*b*) *Wove paper*

11	1	1 c. dull blue	..	..	..	12·00
12		2 c. black (I)	..	..	..	14·00
13		4 c. yellow (III)	..	..	..	12·00
14		8 c. dark olive-green	..	..	14·00
15		16 c. dull scarlet..	..	..	10·00
		a. "1" of "16" omitted	..	..	£1000

1866. *Colours changed and new values. Antique numerals. "CANDAREENS" in the plural (except 1 c.). Imperf.*

(*a*) *Wove paper*

16	1	1 c. indigo	..	..	..	16·00
		a. Blue	..	..	..	16·00
		b. Pelure paper	..	..	15·00
17		3 c. red-brown ..	..	..	8·00
		a. Pelure paper	..	..	15·00
18		6 c. red-brown ..	..	..	8·00
19		6 c. terra-cotta ..	..	..	50·00
20		6 c. scarlet	..	..	..	12·00
21		12 c. red-brown	..	..	..	9·00
22		16 c. scarlet	..	..	..	9·00
		a. "1" of "16" omitted	..	..	24·00

Roman Numeral "I"

23	1	1 c. blue	..	..	..	28·00
24		12 c. terra-cotta ..	..	..	15·00
		a. Chocolate ..	..	..	20·00

(*b*) *Laid paper. Roman "I" in 1 c.*

25	1	1 c. blue	..	..	..	£2500
26		2 c. black (II) ..	..	..	£200
27		3 c. terra-cotta ..	..	..	£1500

The inscriptions and frames of these stamps are type-set, and there are many settings of nearly all the varieties. One setting of the 16 c. shows only a slight trace of the figure "1", but specimens from which it is entirely absent have been tampered with.

1866. *Modern numerals. Wove paper. Imperf.*

A. "CANDAREEN" *in the singular*

28	1	1 c. dull blue	..	..	..	10·00
		a. Slate-blue	..	..	..	10·00
29		3 c. red-brown	..	..	..	10·00

B. "CANDAREENS" *in the plural*

30	1	2 c. black (II)	..	..	..	8·00
		a. Grey ..	..	..	..	8·00
31		3 c. red-brown	..	..	..	7·00

STAMPS IN USED CONDITION. Most of the above are unpriced used because they are either extremely rare or not known in this condition. Genuine used stamps have the margins cut into.

2   3

4   5

(Des and litho Nissen & Parker, London)

1866 (Mar)–**72.** *Value in cents.* (*a*) *P* 12.

32	2	2 c. carmine					75	75
		a. Imperf horiz (vert pair)				10·00		
33	3	4 c. grey-lilac					1·75	2·00
		a. Lilac					1·75	2·00
34	4	8 c. grey-blue					2·00	2·25
		a. Defective "8" like "3"				10·00	12·00
35	5	16 c. green					4·50	5·00

(*b*) *P* 15 (1872)

36	2	2 c. carmine					6·00	6·00

6   7

8   9

(Litho Nissen & Parker, London)

1867. *Value in candareens. P* 15.

37	6	1 c. brown					40	50
		a. "CANDS" for "CAND"				5·50	5·50
38	7	3 c. orange-yellow					1·75	2·00
		a. Defective "3" like "6"				20·00	20·00
39	8	6 c. slate					2·00	4·00
40	9	12 c. grey-brown					4·50	7·00

(10)   (11)

1873–75. *Stamps of 1866–72 surch as T* **10.**

(*a*) *On cents issue* (1.73–1.75)

41	2	1 c. on 2 c. carmine (B.) (*p* 12)			2·50	1·75
42		1 c. on 2 c. carmine (B.) (*p* 15)			3·00	2·00
43	3	1 c. on 4 c. grey-lilac (Bk.)			2·50	1·75
		a. Surch inverted				
44		1 c. on 4 c. grey-lilac (B.)			2·50	2·00
		a. Lilac			2·50	1·50
		b. Surch inverted			10·00	
		c. Surch double			10·00	
45		1 c. on 4 c. grey-lilac (R.)			£250	£200
		a. Surch double (R. + B.)				
46	4	1 c. on 8 c. grey-blue (B.)			3·00	2·50
		a. Surch double				
47		1 c. on 8 c. grey-blue (R.)			£600	£450
		a. Defective "8" like "3"			18·00	
48	5	1 c. on 16 c. green (B.)			£150	£130
		a. Surch double				
49		1 c. on 16 c. green (R.)			£650	£450
50	2	3 c. on 2 c. carmine (B.) (*p* 12) (1.75)		11·00	9·00
51		3 c. on 2 c. carmine (B.) (*p* 15) (1.75)		35·00	35·00
52	5	3 c. on 16 c. green (B.) (1.75)		£250	£250

(*b*) *On candareens issue* (Jan 1875)

53	7	1 c. on 3 c. orange-yellow (B.)			£650	£500
54	8	1 c. on 6 c. slate (B.)			32·00	22·00
55		1 c. on 6 c. slate (R.)			£400	£350
56	9	1 c. on 12 c. grey-brown (B.)			40·00	30·00
57		1 c. on 12 c. grey-brown (R.)			£375	£350
58		3 c. on 12 c. grey-brown (B.)			£240	£200

1875 (July). *Colours changed and on coloured paper.*

(*a*) *P* 15

59	6	1 c. yellow/yellow				2·00	2·00
60	7	3 c. rose/*rose*				2·00	2·00

(*b*) *P* 11½

61	6	1 c. yellow/yellow				30·00	25·00

1876 (Feb). *Colours changed and new value. Litho. P* 15.

62	6	1 c. yellow				50	75
63	7	3 c. carmine				5·00	6·00
64	8	6 c. green				9·00	
65	9	9 c. blue-grey				9·00	
66		12 c. brown				14·00	

1877 (Feb). *Stamps of 1875–76 surch with T* **10.**

67	7	1 c. on 3 c. carmine (B.)			6·00	4·50
		a. Surch double				
68		1 c. on 3 c. rose/*rose* (B.)			35·00	30·00
69	8	1 c. on 6 c. green (B.)			8·00	7·00
70	9	1 c. on 9 c. blue-grey (B.)			35·00	30·00
71		1 c. on 12 c. brown (B.)			£150	£130
72		1 c. on 12 c. brown (R.)			£550	£450

1877 (June). *Recess locally. Thick paper. P* 12½.

73	6	1 c. carmine				90·00	£140

1877 (June)–**80.** *Values in cash.* (*a*) *P* 15.

74	6	20 c. grey-blue				40	50
75		20 c. lilac				40	50
		a. Reddish lilac				40	50
76	7	40 c. rose				65	75
77	8	60 c. green				90	90
78	9	80 c. blue				1·50	1·75
79		100 c. brown				1·50	1·75

(*b*) *P* 11½ (June 1880)

80	6	20 c. lilac				75	75
		a. Reddish lilac				75	75
		b. Imperf between (horiz pair)			25·00	
		c. Imperf horiz (vert pair)			25·00	
81	7	40 c. rose				45	50
		a. Imperf between (horiz pair)			25·00	
82	8	60 c. green				45	45
83	9	80 c. blue				90	1·00
84		100 c. brown				90	1·00

(*c*) *P* 15 × 11½

85	6	20 c. reddish lilac				4·00	3·50

1879 (July)–**84.** *Values in cash. Surch as T* **11,** *in blue.*

(*a*) *P* 15

86	7	20 c. on 40 c. rose				1·40	1·40
		a. Surch inverted				
87	9	60 c. on 80 c. blue				2·00	2·00
88		60 c. on 100 c. brown				2·00	2·00

(*b*) *P* 11½ (1884)

89	7	20 c. on 40 c. rose				90	1·00
		a. Surch double				

90	**9**	60 c. on 80 c. blue	.. .. ..	1·75	2·00
91		60 c. on 100 c. brown	.. .. ..	2·00	2·25

1884–86. *Values in cash. Colours changed.*

(a) P 11½ (1884)

92	**6**	20 c. green	.. ..	40	40

(b) P 15 (1885–86)

93	**6**	20 c. green (10.2.85)	.. ..	30	30
		a. Perf comp 11½ and 15	..	2·50	
94	**7**	40 c. brown (28.3.86)	..	50	50
95	**8**	60 c. violet (2.3.85)	..	55	55
		a. Reddish lilac	..	55	55
		b. Imperf between (vert pair)	..		
96	**9**	80 c. reddish buff (9.85)	..	55	55
		a. Imperf between (horiz pair)	..		
97		100 c. yellow (9.85)	..	55	55

(c) P 11½ × 15 (1885)

98	**6**	20 c. green	..	50	70
99	**8**	60 c. reddish lilac	..	80	80

1886 (1 Jan)–**88.** *Nos. 96/7 surch as T 11, in blue.*

100	**9**	40 c. on 80 c. reddish buff	..	40	50
		a. Surch inverted	..	2·50	
		b. Surch in red	..	15·00	
101		40 c. on 100 c. yellow (6.88)	..	50	50
		a. Surch inverted	..	1·75	
		b. Surch double	..	2·50	
		c. Surch in red	..	65	65
102		60 c. on 100 c. yellow	..	55	65
		a. Surch inverted	..	4·00	4·00
		b. Surch double	..		
		c. Surch in red	..	3·50	

20 CASH.

文十二

(12)

(13)　　**(14)**

1888 (Jan). *Nos. 94 and 96 surch in greenish blue.*

103	**12**	20 c. on 40 c. brown	.. ..	1·40	1·40
		a. Surch inverted	..	4·00	4·00
		b. Surch double	..		
		c. Surch in red	..		
104	**13**	20 c. on 40 c. brown	..	1·40	1·40
		a. Surch inverted	..	6·00	6·50
105	**12**	20 c. on 80 c. reddish buff	..	40	40
		a. Surch inverted	..	4·00	4·00
		b. Surch double	..		
		c. Surch in red	..		

1888 (Mar–July). *Values in cash. Colours changed. No wmk. P 15.*

106	**6**	20 c. grey	..	25	25
107	**7**	40 c. black (July)	..	40	40
108	**8**	60 c. carmine	..	40	40
		a. Without dot over lowest character on left	..	90	90
109	**9**	80 c. green (July)	..	50	50
110		100 c. blue (July)	..	75	75

1889 (Apr). *Nos. 109/110 surch with T 12, in red.*

111	**9**	20 c. on 80 c. green	..	65	65
		a. Surch inverted	..		
112		20 c. on 100 c. blue	..	65	65

1889 (6 Apr). *No. 97 surch as T 14, "20 CASH" in black, and "100 CASH" in red. Frame in black.*

113	**9**	100 c. yellow	.. ..	3·00	3·00
		a. Frame in blue	..		

15

The watermark consists of the Chinese characters for "Kung" (Labour) "Pu" (a Board), being an abbreviation for *Kung pu chu*, Office of the Labour Board, or Board of Works Office, the title adopted by the Shanghai Municipal Council, the authority issuing the stamps.

1889. W 15 (*"Kung Pu"*). *(a) P 15.*

114	**6**	20 c. grey (10.5)	.. ..	20	20
115	**7**	40 c. black (18.7)	..	30	40
116	**8**	60 c. carmine (9.12)	..	40	50
		a. Without dot over lowest character on left	..	1·00	2·00

(b) P 12

117	**9**	80 c. green (14.8)	..	50	75
		a. Imperf between (horiz pair)	..		
118		100 c. blue (14.8)	..	90	1·00

16　　　　　**(D 1)**　　　　**(17)**

(Litho Nissen & Arnold, London)

1890 (1 Jan). *Value in cents. P 15.*

(a) No wmk

119	**16**	2 c. brown	.. ..	15	15
120		5 c. carmine-pink	..	45	45
		a. On buff	..	45	45
121		15 c. blue	..	50	50

(b) W 15 (sideways)

122	**16**	10 c. black	..	35	35
		a. Perf 12	..	15·00	15·00
123		15 c. blue	..	1·40	1·40
		a. On buff	..	1·40	90
124		20 c. mauve	..	50	50
		a. On buff	..	50	50

Nos. 122/4 without watermark come from sheets with the watermark misplaced.

1891 (May). W 15 (*upright*). P 12.

125	**16**	2 c. brown	..	25	30
		a. On buff	..	20	20
126		5 c. carmine-pink	..	50	50

1892–93. *POSTAGE DUE. Stamps of 1890–92 optd with Type D 1.*

(a) P 15 (7.1.92)

(i) No wmk

D127	**16**	2 c. brown	..	20·00	
D128		5 c. carmine-pink	..	40	40
		a. Opt inverted	..	35	35
		b. On buff	..		
D129		15 c. blue	..	1·75	1·75
		a. Opt inverted	..	15·00	
		b. Opt in blue	..		

(ii) W 15 (sideways)

D130	**16**	10 c. black (R.)	..	90	90
D131		15 c. blue	..	65	65
		a. Opt inverted	..		
		b. Opt double	..		
		c. Pair, one without opt	..		
D132		20 c. mauve	..	35	35

(b) P 12. W 15 (upright) (9.92–3.93)

D133	**16**	2 c. brown	..	8	10
		a. On buff	..	8	10
		b. Opt inverted	..	3·00	3·00
		c. Opt double	..		
		d. Pair, one without opt	..		
D134		2 c. brown (B.)	..	5	8
D135		5 c. carmine-pink (B.)	..	25	30
		a. Opt inverted	..		
D136		5 c. carmine-pink (Bl–blk.)	..	30	40
D137		10 c. orange (9.92)	..	7·00	7·00
D138		10 c. orange (B.)	..	25	30
		a. Opt inverted	..		
D139		15 c. mauve (R.)	..	70	70
D140		20 c. brown (R.)	..	70	70

1892 (3 Aug). *No. 120 surch with T 17, in blue.*

141	**16**	2 c. on 5 c. carmine-pink	..	2·75	2·25
		a. Surch inverted	..	15·00	12·00

1892. *Colours changed.* W **15** *(upright).* P 12.

142	**16**	2 c. green (11.11)	..	12	12
143		5 c. vermilion (11.11)	..	20	20
144		10 c. orange (6.9)	..	30	30
145		15 c. mauve (11.11)	..	50	50
146		20 c. brown (11.11)	..	55	55
		a. Imperf between (vert pair)			
142/146		Set of 5	..	1·50	1·50

銀分半   鑀分壹

HALF   ONE

CENT.   CENT.

(18)   (19)

1893 (Mar). *Nos. 145/6 surch with T* **18/19,** *in blue.*

147	**16**	½ c. on 15 c. mauve	..	45	45
		a. Surch double ..			
		b. Imperf between (vert pair)	..	10·00	10·00
148		1 c. on 20 c. brown	..	50	50
		a. Error. ½ c. on 20 c.	..	£550	

Nos. 148/a with surcharge in black are from a trial printing.

½Ct.   ½Ct.   ½Ct.   1Ct.   1Ct.

(20)   (21)   (22)   (23)   (24)

The ½ c. on half 5 c. surcharges were from settings of 20 (2×10), comprising 11 T **20,** 8 T **21** and 1 T **22.** The top ten, corresponding to the upper pane of the sheet, all have raised stops as in T **22** and the bottom ten have normal stops as shown. T **22** only exists with raised stop.

In the setting of 20 of the 1 c. on half 2 c. vermilion surcharge T **24** occurs twice.

1893 (Apr). *Half stamps surcharged.*

(a) No. 126 *surch with T* **20/22,** *in blue.*

149	**20**	½ c. on half 5 c. carmine-pink..	..	75	20
		a. Surch inverted ..			
		b. Surch double, one inverted			
150	**21**	½ c. on half 5 c. carmine-pink..	..	75	30
		a. Surch inverted ..			
		b. Surch double, one inverted			
151	**22**	½ c. on half 5 c. carmine-pink..	..	7·50	
		a. Surch inverted ..			
		b. Surch double, one inverted			

(b) No. 143 *surch with T* **20/22,** *in blue.*

152	**20**	½ c. on half 5 c. vermilion	..	75	25
		a. Surch inverted ..			
153	**21**	½ c. on half 5 c. vermilion	..	75	25
		a. Surch inverted ..		—	1·75
154	**22**	½ c. on half 5 c. vermilion	..	7·50	
		a. Surch inverted ..			

(c) No. 125 *surch with T* **23,** *in blue.*

155	**23**	1 c. on half 2 c. brown	..	12	12
		a. Surch double, one inverted	..	8·00	
		b. Surch double (B.+G.)	..	45·00	
		c. Surch double (B.+Bk.)	..	45·00	
		d. Surch inverted ..	..	10·00	

(d) No. 142 *surch with T* **23/24,** *in vermilion.*

156	**23**	1 c. on half 2 c. green..	..	1·50	1·50
		a. Surch double (Verm. over B.)			
157	**24**	1 c. on half 2 c. green..	..	10·00	10·00
		a. Surch double (Verm. over B.)			

No. 155c exists with both surcharges in black but is believed to be from a trial printing.

             Litho   Typo

25   No dot   Dot

(Des R. A. de Villard. Printed by Barclay & Fry, London)

1893 (May–Dec). *Inscriptions in outer frame in black.* W **15.** P 13½×14.

(a) Whole stamp litho

158	**25**	½ c. orange	..	50	60
		a. Imperf vert (horiz pair)	..	6·00	
159		1 c. brown	..	50	25
160		2 c. orange-vermilion	..	40	40
		a. Imperf (pair)	..		
161		5 c. blue	..	5	5
		a. Inscriptions inverted	..	85·00	
		b. Inscriptions double	..		
162		10 c. green	..	40	50
163		15 c. yellow	..	10	10
164		20 c. mauve	..	50	75

(b) Whole stamp typo

165	**25**	½ c. orange	..	5	5
166		1 c. brown	..	5	5

(b) Stamp typo, inscriptions litho

167	**25**	10 c. green	..	5	5
168		20 c. mauve	..	10	10

See also Nos. 187/9.

D 2    26   (27)

1893 (July–Sept). POSTAGE DUE. *Litho.* W **15.** P 13½×14.

D169	**D 2**	½ c. orange and black	..	5	5
D170		1 c. brown and black	..	5	5
		a. Imperf vert (horiz pair)	..		
D171		2 c. red and black	..	5	5
		a. Imperf vert (horiz pair)	..		
D172		5 c. blue and black	..	5	5
D173		10 c. green and black	..	5	5
D174		15 c. yellow and bluish black	..	5	5
		a. Yellow and grey-black	..	1·00	
D175		20 c. mauve and black	..	5	5
D169/175		Set of 7	..	20	25

1893 (11 Nov). *Jubilee of First Settlement. Litho.* W **15.** P 13½.

176	**26**	2 c. rose-red and black	..	8	8
		a. Carmine and black	..	8	8

1893 (14 Dec). *Jubilee of First Settlement (2nd issue). Optd with T* **27.**

177	**25**	½ c. orange (165)	..	5	5
178		1 c. brown (166)	..	8	8
		a. Opt double	..	3·00	3·00
179		2 c. orange-vermilion	..	8	8
		a. Opt inverted	..		
180		5 c. blue	..	25	30
		a. Opt inverted	..		
181		10 c. green (167)	..	40	40
182		15 c. yellow	..	45	45
183		20 c. mauve (164)	..	50	50
177/183		Set of 7	..	1·60	1·60

FOUR CENTS

肆四

(28)

1896 (11 Apr). *Surch as T* **28.**

184	**25**	4 c. on 15 c. yellow	..	45	45
		a. Surch inverted	..	7·00	3·50
185		6 c. on 20 c. mauve (168)	..	45	40
		a. Surch inverted	..	7·00	3·50
186		6 c. on 20 c. mauve (164)	..	7·00	7·00
		a. Surch inverted	..		

1896 (Oct). *Colours changed and new values. Inscriptions in outer frame in black. W* **15.** *P* 13½ × 14.

187	**25**	2 c. brownish red	..	..	..	5	5
		a. Inscriptions inverted	..	..	20·00	
		b. Inscriptions double	..			
188		4 c. orange/*yellow*	..	..	..	5	5
189		6 c. carmine/*rose*	..	..	..	10	10

No. 187 can also be distinguished by its larger sized water-mark.

In 1898 the postal services of Shanghai were amalgamated with those of the Chinese Empire.

CHINESE EMPIRE

1878. 100 Candarins = 1 Tael

1897. 100 Cents = 1 Dollar or Yuan

Chinese Characters

| Simple | Formal | Simple | Formal |

半	半	= ½	七	柴	= 7
一	壹	= 1	八	捌	= 8
二	貳	= 2	九	玖	= 9
三	叄	= 3	十	拾	= 10
四	肆	= 4	百	佰	= 100
五	伍	= 5	千	仟	= 1,000
六	陸	= 6	萬	萬	= 10,000
	分	= cent	圓	圓	= dollar

Examples

十 五 = 15

五 十 = 50

叄 佰 圓 = 300 dollars

伍 仟 圓 = 5,000 dollars

Emperor Kwang-Su

12 January 1875–14 November 1908

(Dowager Empress T'zu-Hsi was Regent until 1889)

Robert Hart was appointed Inspector-General of the Imperial Customs Service in 1863. To this Service he entrusted the delivery of mail-bags for foreign legations and despatches for members of the Service. The Customs Post grew rapidly and stamps, in imitation of those of Shanghai, were issued in 1878.

IMPERIAL CUSTOMS POST

| 1 Dragon | 2 Dragon | 3 Symbol of "Yin Yang" |

(T **1/2** typo Customs Statistical Dept, Shanghai)

1878–83. *No wmk. P* 12½.

(a) *Thin paper. Stamps printed about* 2½ *mm apart* (Oct 1878)

1	**1**	1 c. green	..	..	..	6·00	3·50
		a. *Yellow-green*	..	..	6·00	4·50
		b. *Deep green*	..	..	6·00	4·50
		c. Imperf (pair)	..	..	40·00	
2		3 c. brown-red	..	..	..	3·00	1·50
		a. *Vermilion*	..	..	6·00	1·50
		b. Imperf (pair)	..	..	40·00	
3		5 c. orange	..	..	..	4·00	2·00
		a. *Yellow*	..	..	5·00	2·00
		b. Imperf (pair)	..	..	75·00	

(b) *Thin to pelure* (5 *c.*) *paper. Stamps printed* 4½ *mm apart* (June 1882)

4	**1**	1 c. green	..	..	10·00	6·00
		a. *Deep green*	..	..	12·00	10·00
		b. Thicker paper	..	..	12·00	10·00
5		3 c. brown-red (*shades*)	..	..	30·00	2·50
6		5 c. yellow-ochre	..	..	£180	30·00

The 1 c. and 3 c. exist on paper bearing portions of paper-maker's watermark "ORIGINAL TURKEY MILL, KENT" in double-lined capitals.

(c) *Thicker, more opaque paper. Stamps printed about* 2½ *mm apart* (Mar 1883)

7	**1**	1 c. green	..	..	8·00	3·50
		a. *Bright sage-green*	..	..	8·00	2·75
		b. Imperf between (vert pair)	..	£180	
8		3 c. brown-red	..	..	12·00	2·00
		a. *Pale red*	..	..	10·00	2·00
		b. *Vermilion*	..	..	15·00	2·00
		c. *Deep Venetian red*	..	..	25·00	12·00
		d. Imperf between (vert pair)	..	—	£250
9		5 c. chrome-yellow	..	..	15·00	2·00

1885–88. *W* **3.**

(a) *P* 12½ (25.11.85)

10	**2**	1 c. bright green	..	..	1·00	60
		a. *Dull green*	..	..	1·10	1·00
		b. Imperf between (vert pair)	..	90·00	
11		3 c. mauve	..	..	1·50	1·00
		a. Imperf between (horiz pair)	..	50·00	40·00
12		5 c. olive-yellow	..	..	1·50	90
		a. *Bistre*	..	..	4·00	1·75
		b. *Bistre-brown*	..		
		c. Imperf between (horiz pair)	..	—	55·00
		d. Imperf between (vert pair)	..	65·00	

(b) *P* 11½, 12 (1888)

13	**2**	1 c. bright green	..	..	40	30
		a. *Dull green*	..	..	50	25
		b. Imperf (pair)	..	..	50·00	
14		3 c. mauve	..	..	60	15
		a. Imperf (pair)	..	..	35·00	
		b. Double impression	..	—	25·00
15		5 c. olive-yellow	..	..	55	25
		a. Imperf (pair)	..	..	40·00	
		b. Imperf vert (horiz pair)	..	—	65·00
		c. Double impression	..	30·00	25·00

WARNING. As the above were printed in fugitive ink, the colours run when the stamps are exposed to moisture.

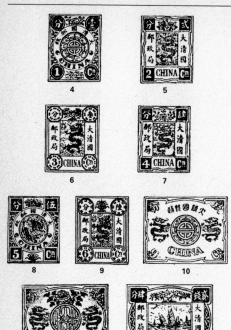

4   5

6   7

8   9   10

11   12

(Des R. A. de Villard. Litho Shanghai by transfers from stereotyped plates made by Tokyo Tsukiji Type Foundry, Japan)

1894 (17 Nov). *60th Birthday of the Dowager Empress (first printing).* W **3**. P 11½.

16	**4**	1 c. reddish orange	..	50	50
		a. Imperf between (horiz pair)	..	45·00	45·00
		b. Imperf between (vert pair)	..	45·00	45·00
17	**5**	2 c. green	..	50	50
		a. Imperf between (horiz pair)	..	45·00	
18	**6**	3 c. orange-yellow ..	..	35	30
		a. Brownish yellow ..	..	1·60	1·10
		b. Imperf between (horiz pair)	..	25·00	25·00
		c. Imperf between (vert pair)	..	25·00	25·00
19	**7**	4 c. rose-pink ..	..	2·00	2·00
		a. Imperf between (horiz pair)	..	50·00	
20	**8**	5 c. dull orange	..	2·00	2·00
		a. Imperf between (horiz pair)	..	60·00	55·00
21	**9**	6 c. brown	..	75	75
		a. Chocolate	..	75	75
		b. Reddish brown ..	..	2·00	2·25
		c. Imperf between (horiz pair)	..	45·00	
		d. Imperf between (vert pair)	..	45·00	
22	**10**	9 c. dull green ..	..	1·50	1·00
		a. Imperf vert (horiz pair)	..	40·00	
		b. Imperf horiz (vert pair)	..	40·00	35·00
		c. Imperf between (vert pair)	..	35·00	40·00
		d. Tête-bêche (pair) ..	..	22·00	24·00
		da. Do. Imperf vert (horiz pair)	..	£150	£100
		db. Do. Imperf horiz (vert pair)	..	£150	£120
23	**11**	12 c. brown-orange ..	..	2·50	1·75
24	**12**	24 c. rose-carmine ..	..	3·50	2·50
		a. Imperf between (vert pair)	..	80·00	
16/24		*Set of 9*	..	12·00	10·00

CHINESE IMPERIAL POST

Sir Robert Hart, knighted in 1882, organised an Imperial Postal Service, and the Chinese Imperial Post Office was established by a decree of 20 March 1896; it competed with the Min Chu, which it put out of business.

1897. *60th Birthday of the Dowager Empress (second printing from new stones).* W **3**. P 11½, 12.

Shades differ from first printing

25	**4**	1 c. salmon-red	..	..	12·00
26	**5**	2 c. dull yellow-green..	..	..	24·00
27	**6**	3 c. yellow	..	..	12·00
28	**7**	4 c. pale rose ..	..	..	20·00
29	**8**	5 c. yellow ..	..	..	27·00
30	**9**	6 c. red-brown	..	..	40·00
31	**10**	9 c. yellow-green	..	..	40·00
32	**11**	12 c. orange-yellow	..	..	55·00
33	**12**	24 c. deep rose-red	..	..	40·00

This printing was made for surcharging in the new currency, and genuinely used copies are unknown. The inverted stamp in the sheet of the 9 c. was corrected.

There was also a special printing of 5,000 sets on thick, unwatermarked paper made for presentation purposes.

貳洋暫
分銀作
2
cents.
(13)

貳洋暫
分銀作
2
cents.
(14)

貳洋暫
分銀作
2
cents.
(15)

T **13**. Small figures, 3 mm below characters
T **14**. Large figures, 2½ mm below characters
T **15**. Large figures, 1½ mm below characters

(T **13/15** surch by Customs Statistical Dept, Shanghai)

New Currency Surcharges

1897. *Surch as T* **13**.

    (a) On T **2**. P 11½, 12 (early 1897)

34	**2**	1 c. on 1 c. dull green..	..	75	50
		a. Figure 4 mm below characters	..	1·50	1·50
35		2 c. on 3 c. mauve	..	1·75	75
		a. Surch double	..	£200	
36		5 c. on 5 c. olive-yellow	..	60	50

    (b) On Nos. 16/24 (2.1.97)

37	**6**	½ c. on 3 c. orange-yellow	..	20	20
		a. Yellow-brown	..	50	40
		b. Imperf horiz (vert pair)	..	45·00	
		c. Imperf between (horiz pair)	..	40·00	
		d. Surch double	..	60·00	70·00
		e. "2" and fraction bar omitted	..	16·00	18·00
		f. Figure 4 mm below characters	..	60	50
38	**4**	1 c. on 1 c. vermilion	..	40	40
		a. Surch inverted	..	£125	85·00
		b. Figure 4 mm below characters	..	1·10	1·00
39	**5**	2 c. on 2 c. green	..	45	40
		a. Imperf vert (horiz pair)	..		
		b. Imperf between (horiz pair)	..	30·00	
		c. Imperf between (vert pair)	..	35·00	
		d. Surch inverted	..	90·00	90·00
		e. Surch double	..	60·00	60·00
		f. Figure 4 mm below characters	..	1·25	1·10
40	**7**	4 c. on 4 c. rose-pink	..	35	35
		a. Imperf between (horiz pair)	..	55·00	55·00
		b. Imperf between (vert pair)	..	55·00	55·00
		c. Surch double	..	70·00	70·00
		d. Figure 4 mm below characters	..	1·40	1·40
41	**8**	5 c. on 5 c. dull orange	..	30	30
		a. Imperf between (vert pair)	..	60·00	60·00
		b. Figure 4 mm below characters	..	1·25	1·00
42	**9**	8 c. on 6 c. brown	..	45	35
		a. Reddish brown	..	55	40
		b. Imperf horiz (vert pair)	..	25·00	25·00
		c. Imperf between (horiz pair)	..	45·00	45·00
		d. Imperf between (vert pair)	..	30·00	30·00
		e. Figure 4 mm below characters	..	1·00	1·00
43		10 c. on 6 c. brown	..	1·25	1·50
		a. Reddish brown	..	1·75	1·50
		b. Imperf vert (horiz pair)	..	35·00	
		c. Imperf between (vert pair)	..	32·00	32·00
		d. Figures 4 mm below characters	..	4·00	4·00
44	**10**	10 c. on 9 c. dull green..	..	2·00	1·75
		a. Imperf between (vert pair)	..		
		b. Surch inverted	..	£150	£150
		c. Surch double	..	£100	90·00
		d. Figures 4 mm below characters	..	4·50	4·50
45	**11**	10 c. on 12 c. brown-orange	..	3·00	2·50
		a. Imperf horiz (vert pair)	..	30·00	
		b. Figures 4 mm below characters	..	7·00	6·00

46 12 30 c. on 24 c. rose-carmine .. .. 3·50 2·75
  a. Figures 4 mm below characters .. 9·00 7·00

1897 (Mar). *Surch as T* **14.**

(a) On Nos. 16/24

48 6 ½ c. on 3 c. orange-yellow .. .. 45·00 18·00
  a. Surch inverted .. .. — 95·00
49 4 1 c. on 1 c. reddish orange .. .. 10·00 10·00
50 5 2 c. on 2 c. green .. .. 12·00 10·00
51 7 4 c. on 4 c. rose-pink.. .. .. 12·00 8·00
  a. Imperf between (horiz pair) .. £500
52 8 5 c. on 5 c. dull orange .. .. 2·00 2·75
53 9 8 c. on 6 c. reddish brown .. .. 55·00 80·00
  a. Chocolate.. .. .. 80·00 80·00
54 10 10 c. on 9 c. dull green.. .. 22·00 15·00
55 11 10 c. on 12 c. brown-orange .. £150 38·00
56 12 30 c. on 24 c. rose-carmine .. 30·00 30·00
  a. "30" 2 mm above "cents." instead of 1 mm £225 £140

(b) On Nos. 25/33

57 6 ½ c. on 3 c. yellow 20 20
  a. Vert pair imperf horiz .. 12·00 12·00
  b. "cen" for "cent." .. .. 25·00 25·00
  c. Do. in vert pair, imperf horiz .. £100 £100
58 4 1 c. on 1 c. salmon-red 35 25
  a. Imperf between (horiz pair) .. £100
  b. No stop after "cent" .. 3·00
59 5 2 c. on 2 c. dull yellow-green .. 25 25
  a. No stop after "cents" .. 3·00 3·00
60 7 4 c. on 4 c. pale rose 45 45
  a. Imperf between (horiz pair) .. 30·00 30·00
61 8 5 c. on 5 c. yellow 65 65
62 9 8 c. on 6 c. red-brown .. .. 2·50 2·00
63 10 10 c. on 9 c. yellow-green .. 2·00 1·50
  a. Emerald .. .. 2·50 2·00
64 11 10 c. on 12 c. orange-yellow .. 2·50 1·50
65 12 30 c. on 24 c. deep rose-red .. 4·00 2·75
  a. Imperf between (vert pair) .. £180
  b. "30" 2 mm above "cents." instead of 1 mm .. 27·00 23·00
  c. No stop after "cents" .. 10·00 5·00

This surcharge is known to exist on No. 12, in a block of four. This is considered by experts to be part of a trial printing which was not issued.

1897 (May). *Surch as T* **15.**

(a) On T **2.** *P* 11½, 12

66 2 1 c. on 1 c. dull green .. .. 12·00
67 2 c. on 3 c. mauve .. .. 16·00
68 2 c. on 5 c. olive-yellow .. .. 5·00

(b) On Nos. 16/24

69 6 ½ c. on 3 c. orange-yellow .. 3·50 2·50
70 4 1 c. on 1 c. reddish orange .. 10·00 10·00
71 5 2 c. on 2 c. green .. .. £750 12·00
72 7 4 c. on 4 c. rose-pink .. .. 3·50 3·00
73 8 5 c. on 5 c. dull orange .. .. 3·75 3·25
74 9 8 c. on 6 c. chocolate .. .. 22·00 23·00
75 10 10 c. on 9 c. dull green .. .. 3·00 3·00
76 11 10 c. on 12 c. brown-orange .. 18·00 20·00
77 12 30 c. on 24 c. rose-carmine .. £185

(c) On third printing of Dowager Empress issue

78 6 ½ c. on 3 c. buff 10 15
  a. Dull yellow 8 12
  b. Surch omitted .. .. 70·00
  c. Surch inverted .. .. 25·00 25·00
  d. "½" ½ mm below Chinese characters .. £125
79 4 1 c. on 1 c. salmon 20 20
80 5 2 c. on 2 c. dull yellow-green .. 40 40
  a. Surch inverted £100 £110
81 7 4 c. on 4 c. pink .. .. 4·25 3·00
  a. Surch inverted .. .. 18·00 20·00
82 8 5 c. on 5 c. chrome-yellow .. 4·75 3·00
83 10 10 c. on 9 c. grey-green .. .. 3·00 2·00
  a. Surch inverted .. .. 16·00 16·00
84 11 10 c. on 12 c. orange-yellow .. 6·00 2·50
85 12 30 c. on 24 c. pale rose-red .. £130 55·00

The third printing was made specially for the above surcharges.

In Type A the "3" is larger and the symbols surrounding the characters in the corners are clearer.

1897. *T* **6** *and* **5** *redrawn as Types A and B and surch as T* **15.**

86 A ½ c. on 3 c. bright orange-yellow .. 3·50 3·00
  a. "½" ½ mm below Chinese characters 50·00 40·00
87 B 2 c. on 2 c. pale green .. .. 1·00 35
  a. Imperf between (horiz pair) .. 45·00

one cent. (18)

2 cents. (19)

1 dollar (20)

(A)   (B)

Translation of top line: Ching Dynasty Postal Administration

(T **17** recess Waterlow. Surch in Shanghai)

1897 (Feb). *Revenue stamps surch for postal use (a) as T* **18/20.** *No wmk. P* 12 *to* 16 *and compound.*

88 17 1 c. on 3 c. deep red (A) 70 30
  a. Central character as B .. 2·00 2·00
  b. No stop after "cent" .. 5·00 5·00
  c. Value 3 mm below Chinese characters instead of 4 mm .. 2·00
89 2 c. on 3 c. deep red .. .. 1·00 75
90 4 c. on 3 c. deep red .. .. 3·00 2·00
91 $1 on 3 c. deep red .. .. 20·00 10·00
92 $5 on 3 c. deep red £150 £130
  a. Surch inverted £190 £170

2 cents. (21)

cents (22)

1 dollar. (23)

(b) Surch as T **21/23**

93 17 2 c. on 3 c. deep red .. .. 2·50 1·40
  a. Surch inverted .. .. 40·00 40·00
  b. Surch double £150
  c. Surch double, both inverted .. £275
  d. "s" in "cents." inverted .. 5·00 5·00
  e. No stop after "cents." .. 5·00 5·00
  f. Comma for stop .. 5·00 5·00
94 4 c. on 3 c. deep red £160 £150
  a. Surch double (Bk.+V.) .. £400 £300
95 $1 on 3 c. deep red £1000 £1200
  a. No stop after "dollar." .. £1800

A   B

24   25

26   27   28

29   30   31

(Des R. A. de Villard. Typo Tokyo Tsukiji Type Foundry, Japan)

1897 (16 Aug). *Inscr "IMPERIAL CHINESE POST". W 3. P 11–12.*

96	24	½ c. dull purple		20	15
		a. Rosy lake		20	20
		b. Imperf between (horiz pair)		25·00	
97	25	1 c. orange-yellow		20	12
		a. Chrome-yellow		70	50
98	26	2 c. deep orange		10	8
		a. Orange-buff		15	15
		b. Imperf horiz (vert pair)		30·00	25·00
99	27	4 c. bistre-brown		30	15
		a. Deep brown		35	15
		b. Imperf between (horiz pair)		60·00	
100	28	5 c. rose-red		40	15
101	29	10 c. deep green		50	15
102	30	20 c. deep maroon		1·10	65
103		30 c. rose		1·40	1·25
104		50 c. bright yellow-green		2·00	1·75
		a. Error. Blue-green		60·00	
		b. Error. Deep green		27·00	35·00
105	31	$1 deep and pale red		4·75	3·75
		a. Imperf vert (horiz pair)		£125	
106		$2 orange and yellow		30·00	35·00
		a. Imperf vert (horiz pair)		£225	
107		$5 yellow-green and rose		16·00	22·00
		a. Deep yellow-green and rose		40·00	30·00
96/107		Set of 12		50·00	60·00

Nos. 104a/b were printed in the colour of the 10 c., the blue-green being from a batch printed when the ink was not properly mixed.

32   33   34

(Des R. A. de Villard. Recess Waterlow)

1898 (28 Jan). *Inscr "CHINESE IMPERIAL POST". W 3. P 12 to 16.*

108	32	½ c. brown		5	5
		a. Chocolate		5	5
		b. Imperf between (vert pair)		27·00	35·00
109		1 c. ochre-buff		5	5
		a. Imperf between (vert pair)		8·00	10·00
		b. Imperf between (horiz pair)		18·00	18·00
110		2 c. deep red		5	8
		a. Scarlet		5	5
		b. Imperf between (vert pair)		8·00	8·00
		c. Imperf vert (horiz pair)		8·00	8·00
111		4 c. deep chestnut		15	15
		a. Imperf between (vert pair)		16·00	18·00
		b. Imperf vert (horiz pair)		12·00	12·00
112		5 c. salmon		45	15
		a. Flesh		40	25
		b. Imperf between (vert pair)		12·00	14·00
		c. Imperf between (horiz pair)		14·00	14·00
		d. Imperf horiz (vert pair)		18·00	18·00

113	32	10 c. deep green		20	5
		a. Imperf between (vert pair)		20·00	22·00
		b. Imperf between (horiz pair)		20·00	24·00
114	33	20 c. claret		65	20
		a. Imperf between (horiz pair)		25·00	
		b. Imperf horiz (vert pair)		20·00	
115		30 c. rose		65	30
		a. Imperf between (horiz pair)		35·00	
		b. Imperf between (vert pair)		35·00	
		c. Imperf horiz (vert pair)		35·00	
116		50 c. green		1·10	50
		a. Imperf between (vert pair)		40·00	
117	34	$1 deep red and salmon		2·00	75
118		$2 claret and yellow		4·50	1·25
119		$5 deep green and salmon		8·00	4·00
		a. Imperf between (horiz pair)		£120	
		b. Imperf between (vert pair)		£190	
108/119		Set of 12		16·00	6·50

Owing to an irregularity in the perforating machine, these stamps may be found perf 12 to 13 on one or more sides in conjunction with 14 regular on the other sides.

The stock of watermarked paper, 110 reams, enough to print about 13,000,000 stamps, was forwarded to Messrs. Waterlow & Sons to print on without regard to the stamps fitting the watermark; after exhaustion of this paper the stamps were to be printed on plain paper (Nos. 121/33). The two classes of stamps are difficult to separate, the watermark not showing very clearly, but the plain paper is slightly thicker and far more opaque.

See also Nos. 121/33 and 151/7.

B.R.A.
5
Five Cents
(BR **1**)

1901 (20 Apr). *BRITISH RAILWAY ADMINISTRATION (Peking-Taku Railway). No. 108 surch with Type BR **1**.*

BR120	32	5 c. on ½ c. brown (Bk.)		8·00	8·00
		a. Surch inverted		70·00	50·00
		b. Small "5"		35·00	
		c. Surch in green		12·00	10·00

Price used on cover (black or green surch) £15.

"B.R.A." stamps were used for the collection of a late letter fee on letters posted in a railway postal van. The stamps were affixed to correspondence by the postal officials and cancelled by a special circular postmark with "RAILWAY POST OFFICE" at top and the name of the town (PEKING, TIENTSIN, TONGKU, TONGSHAN or SHANHAIKWAN) below. The official period of use was from 20 April to 20 May, though covers with later dates are known.

1902–03. *As Nos. 108/119 but without wmk. P 12 to 16.*

121	32	½ c. brown		5	5
		a. Chocolate		5	5
		b. Imperf between (vert pair)		12·00	14·00
		c. Imperf between (horiz pair)		12·00	14·00
122		1 c. ochre		5	5
		a. Brownish orange		10	5
		b. Imperf between (vert pair)		8·00	10·00
		c. Imperf between (horiz pair)		8·00	12·00
		d. Imperf horiz (vert pair)		10·00	10·00
123		2 c. deep red		10	5
		a. Scarlet		10	5
		b. Imperf between (vert pair)		6·00	8·00
		c. Imperf between (horiz pair)		6·00	8·00
		d. Imperf vert (horiz pair)		6·00	8·00
124		4 c. deep chestnut		15	5
		a. Imperf between (vert pair)		9·00	12·00
		b. Imperf between (horiz pair)		9·00	12·00
125		5 c. rose		65	25
		a. Flesh		75	35
		b. Imperf between (vert pair)		12·00	
		c. Imperf horiz (vert pair)		12·00	
126		5 c. reddish orange		75	25
		a. Orange		75	30
		b. Imperf between (vert pair)		10·00	
		c. Imperf between (horiz pair)		12·00	
		d. Imperf horiz (vert pair)			
127		10 c. deep green		25	5
		a. Imperf between (vert pair)		8·50	
		b. Imperf between (horiz pair)		10·00	
		c. Imperf horiz (vert pair)		8·00	
128	33	20 c. maroon		50	12
		a. Imperf between (vert pair)		15·00	20·00
		b. Imperf between (horiz pair)		16·00	20·00
		c. Imperf vert (horiz pair)		14·00	

129 **33**	30	c. red	70	15
		a. Vermilion	1·25	45
		b. Imperf between (vert pair)	35·00	
130	50	c. green	65	15
		a. Imperf between (horiz pair)	50·00	
		b. Imperf horiz (vert pair)		
131 **34**	$1	red and flesh	2·25	30
132	$2	claret and bright yellow	6·00	1·00
133	$5	myrtle and salmon	9·00	4·50
121/133	*Set of 13*		19·00	6·00

The note after No. 119b about perforations also applies here.
See also Nos. 151/7.

POSTAGE DUE
資 欠

(35)   (D 1)

1903 (22–24 Oct). *Provisional issued at Foochow. No.* 123 *bisected diagonally and surch "Postage 1 Cent Paid", as in* T **35**.

			Used Piece Cover
134 **32**	1 c. on half 2 c. deep red		12·00 40·00

The above provisional was authorised by the Foochow postmaster during a temporary shortage of 1 c. stamps. Forgeries are numerous. It is understood that the bisecting and surcharging were done by the postal authorities after the mail matter needing a 1 c. stamp had been handed in for despatch.

Provisional issues. Stamps bisected and used without surch at Chungking (Aug 1904)

			Piece Cover
135 **32**	Half of 2 c. deep red		6·00 26·00

The above was duly authorised. It is understood that the 4 c. deep chestnut was bisected and used at Kweifu in February 1905 and the 2 c. deep red was bisected and used at Changsha in April 1906 but they were not authorised (*Prices: Kweifu on cover £30, on piece £5: Changsha on cover £45, on piece £12).*

1904 (16 Mar). *POSTAGE DUE. Stamps of 1902–03 optd with Type* D **1**.

D137 **32**	½ c. brown		25	8
D138	1 c. ochre		25	8
D139	2 deep red		25	10
	a. Scarlet		25	8
D140	4 c. deep chestnut		30	15
D141	5 c. rose		40	15
D142	10 c. deep green		40	15
	a. Imperf between (vert pair)		15·00	50·00
D137/142	*Set of 6*		1·60	60

D **2**

(Recess Waterlow)

1904 (10 Nov). *POSTAGE DUE. Numeral to left on* 10 c. *to* 30 c. *P* 14 *to* 15.

D143 D **2**	½ c. blue		5	5
	a. Imperf between (horiz pair)		26·00	25·00
D144	1 c. blue		5	5
D145	2 c. blue		5	5
	a. Imperf between (horiz pair)		26·00	25·00
D146	4 c. blue		10	8
D147	5 c. blue		15	10
D148	10 c. blue		15	12
D149	20 c. blue		50	30
D150	30 c. blue		75	35
D143/150	*Set of 8*		1·60	1·00

See also Nos. D168/71.

1905–10. *Colours changed and new values. No wmk. P* 13½ *to* 15.

151 **32**	2 c. deep green (20.10.08)		5	5
	a. Imperf between (horiz pair)		10·00	10·00
	b. Imperf between (vert pair)		10·00	10·00
	c. Imperf vert (horiz pair)		12·00	
152	3 c. grey-green (1909)		8	5
	a. Blue-green		8	5
	b. Imperf between (horiz pair)		10·00	14·00
	c. Imperf between (vert pair)		12·00	
153	4 c. scarlet (1909)		10	5
	a. Vermilion		10	5
154	5 c. mauve (10.7.05)		15	5
	a. Deep purple		20	5
	b. Deep violet (1909)		20	5
	c. Imperf between (horiz pair)		10·00	12·00
	d. Imperf between (vert pair)		10·00	12·00
	e. Imperf horiz (vert pair)		8·00	
155	7 c. crimson-lake (1909)		30	15
156	10 c. sky-blue (1908)		35	5
	a. Dull blue (1910)		45	5
	b. Ultramarine		45	5
	c. Imperf between (horiz pair)		14·00	16·00
	d. Imperf between (vert pair)		14·00	16·00
	e. Imperf horiz (vert pair)		14·00	18·00
157 **33**	16 c. olive-green (1906)		1·00	30
151/157	*Set of 7*		1·75	60

The 3 c. and 7 c. have background of value tablets crosshatched instead of solid, as in the other values in Type **32**. The 16 c. has the value-labels framed on all four sides instead of as in Type **33**.

E **1** (*Actual size* 8¼ × 2½ *in*)

1905–12. *EXPRESS LETTER. Large Dragon design as Type* E **1**, *divided into four parts by serrated roulette, in black. Borders imperf.*

Unused prices are for complete stamp, used for a single part

A. *"Chinese Imperial Post Office" repeated horiz to form background. Serial number of 3 digits*

(a) Dragon's head facing downwards

E158	10 c. olive-green (4.11.05)	20·00	10·00

Perf 11 instead of roulette

E159	10 c. grass-green (1906, May?)	£250	20·00

(b) Dragon's head facing upwards
(i) No date in background

E160	10 c. lt green & yellow-green (1907)	25·00	4·00

(ii) Date in second lowest line of background

E161	10 c. light green and yellow-green (dated "Feb 1909")	15·00	4·00
E162	10 c. green and yellow-green (dated "Jan 1911")	40·00	4·00
	a. Serial number of 4 digits		

B. *"Imperial Post Office" in background. Serial number of 4 digits*

E163	10 c. light green & yellow-green (1911)	15·00	2·00

C. *Central medallion with background of Chinese characters. Coloured border*

E164	10 c. light green & yellow-green (1912)	15·00	3·50

Nos. E161/4 may be found with overprints reading "Republic of China" applied by local postmasters.

The above were printed in booklets. The first part at left remained in the booklet for control purposes; the last part was given as a receipt; the 2nd part (dragon's head) was signed by the addressee and returned to the post office by the postman, who was paid for his services against delivery of the third part (dragon's body).

Emperor Hsuan T'ung
14 November 1908–12 February 1912

(Prince Ch'un was regent until 6 December 1911)

36 Temple of Heaven

(Des and eng L. J. Hatch. Recess Waterlow)

1909 (8 Sept). *First Year of Reign of Emperor Hsuan T'ung.*
P 13 *to* 15.

165	**36**	2 c. green and orange		..	10	10
166		3 c. greenish blue and orange		..	12	12
167		7 c. purple and orange		..	12	12
165/167		*Set of 3*	..	..	30	30

1911 (22 Feb). *POSTAGE DUE. Colour changed.* P 14–15.

D168	D **2**	1 c. brown	..	..	12	10
D169		2 c. brown	..	..	20	15
D170		4 c. brown	..	..	£180	
D171		5 c. brown	..	..	80·00	

The ½ c. and 20 c. also exist in this type without overprint, but were not issued.

CHINESE REPUBLIC

On 10 October 1911 a revolution began in Wuchang (then Wuhan); whilst awaiting the course of events, post offices in some cities overprinted imperial stamps with "Provisional Neutrality". On 15 February 1912, Yuan Shih-kai was elected provisional president of the Chinese Republic. On 11 December 1915 he was elected Emperor, but in face of revolts he revoked the monarchy on 22 March 1916.

China fell into the hands of local warlords and the ruling Kuomintang party under Sun Yat-sen at Canton accepted Russian advisers. In 1925 Sun Yat-sen died and in 1927 Chiang Kai-shek broke with the communists. In his northern campaign of 1928 he defeated the warlords and achieved a temporary unity.

中華   中華民國

立中時臨   中華民國   中華民國   中華民國

立中時臨
(37)   (37a)   (38)   (39)   (40)

1912. T 32/4 (*without wmk*) *and Type* D **2** *variously overprinted.*

(i) *With* T **37** ("Provisional Neutrality") *for use in Foochow*
      (a) *POSTAGE* (30 Jan)

172	**32**	3 c. blue-green (R.)		..	4·00	4·00
173	**34**	$1 red and flesh..		..	70·00	£120
174		$2 claret and yellow		..	£100	£100
175		$5 myrtle and salmon		..	75·00	£110

      (b) *POSTAGE DUE* (2 Feb)

D176	D **2**	½ c. blue	..	..	30·00	30·00
D177		1 c. brown	..	..	£300	£300
D178		2 c. brown		..	£300	
D179		4 c. blue	..	..	50·00	50·00
D180		5 c. blue	..	..	55·00	55·00
D181		10 c. blue	..	..	55·00	55·00
D182		20 c. blue	..	..	£200	£275
D183		30 c. blue	..	..	£200	

(ii) *With* T **37a** ("Republic of China Provisional Neutrality") *for use in Hankow, Nanking and Changsha* (20 Mar)

184	**32**	1 c. brownish orange (R.)		..	3·50	3·50
185		3 c. blue-green (R.)		..	3·50	3·50
186		7 c. crimson-lake..		..	15·00	15·00
187	**33**	16 c. olive-green (R.)		..	45·00	45·00

188	**33**	50 c. green (R.)	..	..	90·00	90·00
189	**34**	$1 red and flesh..	..	..	75·00	70·00
190		$2 claret and yellow	..	..	£140	£140
191		$5 myrtle and salmon	..	..	£225	£250

(iii) *Optd at Statistical Dept. of Customs, Shanghai with* T **38** ("Republic of China") (Mar)
      (a) *POSTAGE*

192	**32**	½ c. brown	..	..	5	5
		a. Chocolate	..	..	5	5
		b. Opt inverted	..	..	35	40
		c. Opt double	..	..	8·00	
193		1 c. ochre (R.)	..	..	5	5
		a. Brownish orange	..	..	5	5
		b. Opt inverted	..	..	6·00	6·00
		c. Opt double	..	..	8·00	8·00
		d. Pair, one without opt		..	10·00	
		e. Imperf between (horiz pair)	..		15·00	10·00
		f. Imperf horiz (vert pair)		..	20·00	20·00
		g. Imperf vert (horiz pair)		..	15·00	
194		2 c. deep green (R.)	..	..	5	5
		a. Imperf between (horiz pair)	..		10·00	
		b. Imperf between (vert pair)	..		10·00	
195		3 c. grey-green (R.)	..	..	20	5
		a. Blue-green	..	..	5	5
		b. Opt inverted	..	..	8·00	4·00
		c. Imperf between (horiz pair)	..		10·00	10·00
		d. Imperf between (vert pair)	..		12·00	
		e. Imperf vert (horiz pair)		..	15·00	
196		4 c. scarlet	..	..	8	5
		a. Vermilion	..	..	8	5
		b. Imperf between (vert pair)	..		75·00	
197		5 c. mauve (R.)	..	..	8	5
		a. Deep violet	..	..	25	15
		b. Imperf between (horiz pair)	..			
198		7 c. crimson-lake..	..	..	20	5
199		10 c. blue (R.)	..	..	15	5
		a. Ultramarine	..	..	15	5
		b. Opt inverted	..	..	20·00	20·00
		c. Opt double	..	..	16·00	
		d. Pair, one without opt		..	85·00	
		e. Opt in brownish red	..		1·00	65
200	**33**	16 c. olive-green (R.)	..	..	30	10
201		20 c. maroon	..	..	20	5
		a. Imperf between (vert pair)	..		12·00	
202		30 c. vermilion	..	..	75	15
203		50 c. green (R.)	..	..	75	8
204	**34**	$1 red and flesh..	..	..	2·00	25
		a. Opt inverted	..	..	—	£400
205		$2 claret and yellow	..	..	2·00	75
		a. Opt inverted	..	..	15·00	16·00
206		$5 myrtle and salmon	..	..	9·00	9·00
192/206		*Set of 15*	..	..	14·00	14·00

No. 199e resulted from the use of red ink on type from which the black ink had not been properly cleaned.

      (b) *POSTAGE DUE. Optd in red*

D207	D **2**	½ c. blue	..	..	5	5
D208		1 c. brown	..	..	5	5
		a. Opt inverted	..	..	20·00	20·00
		b. Imperf between (horiz pair)	..		25·00	20·00
D209		2 c. brown	..	..	5	5
D210		4 c. blue	..	..	8	8
D211		5 c. blue	..	..	4·00	4·00
D212		5 c. brown	..	..	15	8
		a. Opt inverted	..	..	18·00	12·00
D213		10 c. blue	..	..	15	15
D214		20 c. blue	..	..	40	20
D215		30 c. blue	..	..	85	45
D207/215		*Set of 9*	..	..	5·00	4·50

(iv) *Optd by Shanghai Commercial Press with* T **39** ("Republic of China"), *in red* (Mar)

216	**32**	1 c. ochre..	..	..	12	5
		a. Opt inverted	..	..	10·00	10·00
		b. Opt double		..		
		c. Imperf between (vert pair)	..		13·00	13·00
217		2 c. deep green	..	..	1·00	8
		a. Opt inverted	..	..	—	65·00
		b. Imperf between (horiz pair)	..		16·00	
		c. Imperf between (vert pair)	..		15·00	15·00

(v) *Optd in London by Waterlow with* T **40** ("Republic of China") (mid 1912)

218	**32**	½ c. brown (B.)	..	..	5	5
		a. Chocolate	..	..	5	5
		b. Imperf between (vert pair)	..		50·00	50·00
219		1 c. ochre (R.)	..	..	5	5
		a. Brownish orange	..	..	5	5
		b. Imperf between (horiz pair)	..		10·00	

220	**32**	2 c. deep green (R.)	..	..	5	5
221		3 c. grey-green (R.)	..	..	5	5
		a. Blue-green	..	..	5	5
		b. Opt inverted ..	..	..	—	60·00
		c. Imperf between (vert pair)	..	15·00	
222		4 c. vermilion	..	..	8	5
223		5 c. mauve (R.)	..	..	8	5
		a. Deep purple ..	..	..	15	5
224		7 c. crimson-lake..	..	..	40	20
225		10 c. blue (R.)	..	..	20	5
		a. Imperf between (vert pair)	..	30·00	25·00
226	**33**	16 c. olive-green (R.)	..	..	35	25
227		20 c. maroon	..	..	35	15
228		30 c. vermilion	..	..	60	20
229		50 c. green (R.)	..	..	90	25
230	**34**	$1 red and flesh..	..	..	1·50	30
231		$2 claret and yellow	..	..	4·50	3·50
232		$5 myrtle and salmon (R.)	..	8·00	9·00
218/232		Set of 15	..	..	15·00	12·00

A number of overprints in similar characters were made by local postmasters; they were unauthorised, but many did postal service.

(D 3)

41 Dr. Sun Yat-sen   **42** President Yuan Shih-kai

1912 (Sept). POSTAGE DUE. Optd by Waterlow with Type D 3.

D233	**D 2**	½ c. blue (5 Sept)	..	..	15	15
D234		½ c. brown	..	..	5	5
D235		1 c. brown	..	..	5	5
		a. Opt inverted	..	..	20·00	
D236		2 c. brown	..	..	5	5
D237		4 c. blue ..	..	..	10	10
D238		5 c. brown	..	..	20	15
		a. Imperf between (horiz pair)	..	30·00	25·00
D239		10 c. blue	..	..	25	25
D240		20 c. brown	..	..	30	30
D241		30 c. blue ..	..	..	50	75
D233/241		Set of 9	..	..	1·50	1·60

(Eng L. J. Hatch and W. A. Grant. Recess Chinese Bureau of Engraving and Printing, Peking)

1912 (14 Dec). P 14½.

(a) Commemorating the Revolution

242	**41**	1 c. orange	..	..	8	8
243		2 c. yellow-green	..	..	10	10
244		3 c. blue-green	..	..	10	10
245		5 c. mauve	..	..	10	10
246		8 c. sepia	..	..	15	15
247		10 c. blue	..	..	12	12
248		16 c. olive-green	..	..	30	30
249		20 c. lake	..	..	40	30
250		50 c. deep green	..	..	1·40	1·25
251		$1 carmine..	..	..	3·00	2·00
252		$2 brown	..	..	16·00	16·00
253		$5 slate	..	..	6·00	6·00
242/253		Set of 12	..	..	25·00	24·00

(b) Commemorating the Republic

254	**42**	1 c. orange	..	..	10	10
255		2 c. yellow-green	..	..	12	10
256		3 c. blue-green	..	..	12	10
257		5 c. mauve	..	..	10	10
258		8 c. sepia	..	..	35	20
259		10 c. blue	..	..	20	12
260		16 c. olive-green	..	..	35	25
261		20 c. lake	..	..	30	20
262		50 c. deep green	..	..	1·75	75
263		$1 carmine..	..	..	2·50	1·50
264		$2 brown	..	..	3·00	2·00
265		$5 slate	..	..	9·00	9·00
254/265		Set of 12	..	..	16·00	12·00

E 2 (Actual size 9¾ × 2¾ in)

1913–14. EXPRESS LETTER. Large design as Type E **2** divided into five parts by roulette, with flying goose design on two parts.

Unused prices are for complete stamps, used for a single part

(a) "Chinese Post Office" in background in unseriffed letters. Coloured border. Serial number and rouletting in black (Jan 1913)

E266	10 c. green, light green & yellow-green	2·50	1·00

(b) "Chinese Post Office" in background in seriffed letters. No border. Serial number and rouletting in green (Feb 1914)

E267	10 c. green, light green & yellow-green	1·50	30

In February 1916, the Express Letter stamps were demonetised, and became merely receipts without franking value. To show this, four of the five sections were handstamped or overprinted with the letters A, B, C, D.

43 Junk   **44** Reaper   **45** Gateway, Imperial Academy, Peking

Differences between the printings

Type **43**

London Printing

Pearls at top are shaded; vertical lines of shading below tablet are thin and short; left banner on masthead appears longer and is not broken. Also (not illustrated) rudder consists of three clear lines of shading.

First Peking Printing

Pearls at top are shaded; vertical lines of shading are thick and longer; banner appears shorter and is broken. The lines of shading forming the rudder are thick and run together.

Second Peking Printing

Pearls at top are unshaded and there is no vertical shading below the tablet. Two vertical lines of shading on either side also removed. Stops below "t" or "ts" are square instead of round.

Type **44**

London Printing
Vertical fringe above
columns at both sides;
sickle touches grain;
reaper's left foot touches
the shadow.

First Peking Printing
Vertical fringe above
columns at both sides;
sickle does not touch grain
and foot clear of shadow.

Second Peking Printing
Pearls replace the vertical fringe at both sides; also the
stops below "ts" are square instead of round.

Type **45**

London Printing
Thin double curved lines below panel at top; large top left
Chinese character is straight at top and at right side.

First Peking Printing
Curved lines as before; character is curved at top, coming
to a point in top left corner and is thinner at bottom right
side.

Second Peking Printing
Curved lines replaced by a single thick curved line.

(Eng and recess Waterlow)

1913–33. (a) *London printing.* P 14 to 15 (May 1913).

268	**43**	½ c. sepia	..	..	5	5
		a. Imperf between (horiz pair)	..	22·00		
		b. Imperf between (vert pair)	..	24·00		
269		1 c. yellow-orange..	..	..	5	5
		a. Imperf between (horiz pair)	..	15·00	10·00	
270		2 c. yellow-green ..	..	..	5	5
		a. Imperf between (horiz pair)	..	15·00	15·00	
271		3 c. deep blue-green	..	..	5	5
		a. Imperf between (horiz pair)	..	15·00	16·00	
		b. Imperf between (vert pair)	..	20·00	24·00	
272		4 c. scarlet..	..	..	15	5
273		5 c. rosy mauve	..	..	20	5
274		6 c. grey	..	..	20	5
275		7 c. violet	..	..	25	12
276		8 c. brown-orange..	..	..	25	5
277	**43**	10 c. deep blue	..	..	25	5
		a. Imperf between (horiz pair)	..	38·00	42·00	
		b. Imperf between (vert pair)	..	38·00	40·00	
278	**44**	15 c. brown ..	..	..	1·25	15
279		16 c. olive	..	..	25	5
280		20 c. brown-lake	..	..	35	5
281		30 c. plum	..	..	60	5
		a. Imperf between (horiz pair)	..	50·00	30·00	
282		50 c. green	..	..	60	5
283	**45**	$1 black and ochre	..	..	2·00	15
284		$2 black and blue	..	..	3·50	15
285		$5 black and scarlet	..	..	8·00	2·50
286		$10 black and green	..	..	35·00	35·00
268/286		*Set of 19*	..	..	48·00	35·00

(Eng William A. Grant. Recess Chinese Bureau of Engraving
and Printing, Peking)

(b) *First Peking Printings. Re-engraved.* P 14 (Dec 1914–19)

287	**43**	½ c. sepia	..	..	5	5
288		1 c. bright yellow-orange	..	..	5	5
289		1½ c. purple (1919) ..	..	..	5	5
290		2 c. yellow-green	..	..	5	5
291		3 c. blue-green	..	..	5	5
292		4 c. bright scarlet ..	..	..	8	5
293		5 c. rosy mauve	..	..	8	5
294		6 c. grey	..	..	8	5
295		7 c. violet ..	..	..	12	5
296		8 c. brown-orange..	..	..	5	5
297		10 c. deep blue	..	..	8	5
298	**44**	13 c. brown (1919)	..	..	8	5
299		15 c. brown ..	..	..	70	15
300		16 c. olive	..	..	12	5
301		20 c. brown-lake	..	..	20	5
302		30 c. deep brownish purple	..	..	15	5
		a. Imperf between (horiz pair)	..	20·00		
303		50 c. deep green	..	..	40	5
304	**45**	$1 black and orange-yellow	..	..	1·25	5
305		$2 black and blue	..	..	2·00	20
		a. Centre inverted	..	£650		
306		$5 black and scarlet	..	..	3·50	1·50
307		$10 black and green	..	..	12·00	5·50
308		$20 black and orange (1919)	..	..	80·00	80·00
287/308		*Set of 22*	..	..	90·00	80·00

The dollar values of this and later issues are found
machine and handstamped with the names of post offices to
prevent speculation in stamps between provinces where the
dollar differed in value.

(c) *Second Peking printings. Redrawn.* P 13 (1923–33)

309	**43**	½ c. sepia	..	..	5	5
		a. Imperf between (horiz pair)	..	15·00	18·00	
310		1 c. bright yellow-orange ..	..	..	5	5
		a. Imperf (pair)	..	12·00	12·00	
		b. Imperf between (horiz pair)	..	15·00		
311		1½ c. violet	..	..	5	5
312		2 c. yellow-green	..	..	5	5
313		3 c. blue-green	..	..	5	5
314		4 c. slate-grey	..	..	25	5
		a. Imperf between (horiz pair)	..	10·00		
		b. Imperf vert (horiz pair)	..	8·00		
315		4 c. olive-green (1926)	..	..	5	5
		a. Imperf between (horiz pair)	..	15·00	12·00	
		b. Imperf vert (horiz pair)	..	12·00		
316		5 c. rosy mauve	..	..	5	5
317		6 c. bright scarlet	..	..	5	5
318		6 c. yellow-brown (1933) ..	..	..	30	5
319		7 c. violet	..	..	8	5
320		8 c. orange	..	..	5	5
321		10 c. deep blue	..	..	8	5
322	**44**	13 c. yellow-brown ..	..	..	60	5
323		15 c. deep blue	..	..	8	5
324		16 c. olive-green	..	..	25	5
325		20 c. red-brown	..	..	20	5
326		30 c. purple ..	..	..	25	5
		a. Imperf between (horiz pair)	..	25·00	28·00	
327		50 c. green	..	..	25	5
328	**45**	$1 sepia and brown-orange	..	..	1·00	5
329		$2 red-brown and deep blue	..	..	1·50	5
330		$5 grey-green and scarlet	..	..	3·50	12
331		$10 rosy mauve and green	..	..	7·50	2·00
332		$20 blue and plum	..	..	16·00	3·00
309/332		*Set of 24*	..	..	29·00	5·00

D 4   London Printing   Peking Printing

In the London printing the upper straight line of spandrel at top is unbroken. In the Peking printing it is broken by the lower left-hand barb of the ornament.

(Eng and recess Waterlow)

1913. *POSTAGE DUE. London printing.* P 14 to 15.

D333	D 4	½ c. blue	..	..	..	5	5
		a. Imperf between (horiz pair)	..	20·00	20·00
D334		1 c. blue	..	..	..	8	5
		a. Imperf between (horiz pair)	..	15·00
D335		2 c. blue	..	..	..	10	5
D336		4 c. blue	..	..	..	15	5
D337		5 c. blue	..	..	..	20	5
D338		10 c. blue	..	..	..	30	15
D339		20 c. blue	..	..	..	50	20
D340		30 c. blue	..	..	..	60	25
D333/340		*Set of 8*	..	..	..	1·75	70

(Eng William A. Grant. Recess Chinese Bureau of Engraving and Printing, Peking)

1915. *POSTAGE DUE. Peking printing.* P 14.

D341	D 4	½ c. blue	..	..	..	5	5
D342		1 c. blue	..	..	..	5	5
D343		2 c. blue	..	..	..	5	5
D344		4 c. blue	..	..	..	5	5
D345		5 c. blue	..	..	..	5	5
D346		10 c. blue	..	..	..	5	5
D347		20 c. blue	..	..	..	20	5
D348		30 c. blue	..	..	..	45	8
D341/348		*Set of 8*	..	..	..	80	30

PRINTERS. The following stamps up to No. 456 were engraved and recess-printed by the Chinese Bureau of Printing and Engraving, Peking, *unless otherwise stated.*

(46)   47 Aeroplane over Great Wall of China

1920 (1 Dec). *Flood Relief Fund. Stamps of 1914 surch as T 46.*

349	43	1 c. on 2 c. yellow-green (R.) ..	..	..	20	10
350		3 c. on 4 c. bright scarlet (B.) ..	..	..	40	15
351		5 c. on 6 c. grey (R.) ..	..	..	65	25

The surcharge represented the actual franking value, the difference of 1 c. being for victims of the Yellow River floods. Pictorial stamps inscribed "FAMINE RELIEF" had no postal validity.

1921 (1 July). *AIR.* P 14.

352	47	15 c. black and blue-green	..	..	2·25	1·75
353		30 c. black and scarlet	..	..	1·50	1·00
354		45 c. black and purple	..	..	1·50	1·00
355		60 c. black and blue	..	..	2·25	1·10
356		90 c. black and olive-green	..	..	2·50	1·75
352/356		*Set of 5*	..	..	9·00	6·00

See also Nos. 384/8.

48 Yeh Kung-cho, Pres. Hsu Shih-chang, and Chin Yung-peng

(49)

1921 (10 Oct). *25th Anniv of Chinese National Postal Service.* P 14.

357	48	1 c. orange	..	..	25	15
358		3 c. blue-green	..	..	25	15
359		6 c. grey	..	..	65	45
360		10 c. blue	..	..	55	40
357/360		*Set of 4*	..	..	1·50	1·00

1923 (12 Feb). *No. 313 surch with T 49, in red.*

361	43	2 c. on 3 c. blue-green	..	20	5
		a. Surch inverted	..	£200	£150

53 Temple of Heaven   (54)

1923 (17 Oct). *Adoption of the Constitution.* P 14.

362	53	1 c. orange	..		15	12
363		3 c. blue-green	..		20	15
364		4 c. scarlet	..		30	15
365		10 c. blue	..		90	35
362/365		*Set of 4*	..		1·40	70

1925–35. *Surch as T 54.*

(a) On Second Peking printings

366	43	1 c. on 2 c. yellow-green (R.) (1.5.35)	5	5
367		1 c. on 3 c. blue-green (R.) (20.3.30)	5	5
		a. No stop after "Ct"	1·50	1·25
368		1 c. on 3 c. blue-green (Bk.) (7.32)	5	5
369		1 c. on 4 c. olive-green (R.) (1933)	5	5
		a. No stop after "Ct"	8·00	8·00
370		3 c. on 4 c. slate-grey (R.) (31.1.25)	5	5
		a. Surch inverted	£225	£100

(b) On First Peking printing

371	43	1 c. on 3 c. blue-green (R.) (10.30)	10	5
366/371		*Set of 6*	30	20

For 5 c. surcharges, see Nos. 452/3.

55 Marshal Chang Tso-lin   56 General Chiang Kai-shek

1928 (1 Mar). *Assumption of Title of Marshal of the Army and Navy by Chang Tso-lin.* P 14.

372	**55**	1 c. orange		10	10
373		4 c. olive-green		10	10
374		10 c. blue		30	20
375		$1 scarlet		3·50	2·75
372/375		*Set of 4*		3·50	2·75

These stamps were valid in the provinces of Chihli (now Hopeh) and Shantung, then under the control of the Manchurian warlord Chang Tso-lin, but were withdrawn when the forces of Chiang Kai-shek reached Peking in June, 1928.

1929 (16 Apr). *Unification of China under Gen. Chiang Kai-shek.* P 14.

376	**56**	1 c. orange		20	5
377		4 c. olive-green		30	5
378		10 c. blue		50	15
379		$1 scarlet		5·50	3·50
376/379		*Set of 4*		6·00	3·50

57 Mausoleum at Nanking  (I)  (II)

1929 (30 May). *State Burial of Dr. Sun Yat-sen.* P 14.

380	**57**	1 c. orange		10	5
381		4 c. olive-green		15	10
382		10 c. blue		40	15
383		$1 scarlet		4·50	2·25
380/383		*Set of 4*		4·50	2·25

The Republican emblem (I) seen in T **47** on the tail of the aeroplane in the air stamps of 1921 was replaced by the badge of the Nationalist Government (II) in the redrawn type.

1929 (8 July). *AIR. T* **47** *redrawn as* II. P 14.

384		15 c. black and blue-green		30	8
		a. Black and green		30	5
385		30 c. black and scarlet		60	15
386		45 c. black and purple		70	50
387		60 c. black and blue		1·00	50
388		90 c. black and olive-green		1·50	1·25
384/388		*Set of 5*		4·00	2·25

58 Dr. Sun Yat-sen  / A. First issue  / B. Second issue

Stamps in Type A were printed first with the emblem incorrectly drawn. The master die was then altered to produce the thick inner circle, Type B. The first stamps to be issued were the 4 c. and 5 c. Type B and it appears that these were followed early in 1932 by Type A stamps and the Type B stamps were released as and when supplies were received.

(Recess De La Rue)

1931–37. P 12½, 13.

(a) First issue. Emblem with double circles (Type A) (2.32)

389	**58**	1 c. red-orange		5	5
390		2 c. olive-green		5	5
391		4 c. green		5	5
392		20 c. ultramarine		5	5
393		$1 sepia and red-brown		12	5
394		$2 red-brown and blue		50	5
395		$5 black and scarlet		55	5
389/95		*Set of 7*		1·25	25

(b) Second issue. Emblem with thick inner circle (Type B) (1931–37)

396	**58**	2 c. olive-green (12.11.31)		5	5
397		4 c. green (12.11.31)		5	5
398		5 c. yellow-green (1933)		5	5
399		15 c. blue-green (1932)		10	5

400	**58**	15 c. scarlet (1933)		5	5
401		20 c. ultramarine (1937)		5	5
402		25 c. ultramarine (1932)		5	5
403		$1 sepia and red-brown (1932)		65	5
		a. Perf 11½ × 12½ (1936)		20	5
404		$2 red-brown and blue (1932)		1·00	5
		a. Perf 11½ × 12½ (1937)		45	5
405		$5 black and scarlet (1932)		90	12
		a. Perf 11½ × 12½ (1937)		80	5
396/405a		*Set of 10*		1·60	30

In the thick-circle issue the use of wet or dry printing leads to differing paper shrinkages and so to "wide" or "narrow" stamps according to whether the width is greater or less than 19½ mm. All stamps exist in both widths except the 15 c. blue-green (narrow only) and the 15 c. scarlet, 20 c. and the dollar values perf 11½ × 12½ (wide only).

Specialists distinguish three types of the 2 c., two of the 4 c. and four of the 5 c.

For other dollar values in this design, see Nos. 735/9.

59 "Nomads of the Desert" (A.D. 300)  | **60** General Teng Keng

1932 (3 June). *North-West Scientific Expedition.* P 14.

406	**59**	1 c. orange		1·50	2·50
407		4 c. bronze-green		1·50	2·50
408		5 c. claret		1·50	2·50
409		10 c. deep blue		1·50	2·50
406/409		*Set of 4*		5·50	9·00

Of 25,000 sets printed, 20,500 were sold at $5 each to finance the expedition of Dr. Sven Hedin.

(Eng De La Rue. Recess Bureau of Engraving and Printing, Peking.)

1932 (13 Aug)–**34.** *Martyrs of the Revolution.* T **60** *and similar portrait designs.* P 14.

410		½ c. sepia (10.32)		5	5
411		1 c. yellow-orange (1934)		5	5
412		2½ c. claret (1933)		5	5
413		3 c. brown (1933)		5	5
414		8 c. orange-red		5	5
415		10 c. purple		5	5
416		13 c. blue-green (10.32)		5	5
417		17 c. bronze-green (10.32)		5	5
418		20 c. brown-lake		5	5
419		30 c. maroon		5	5
420		40 c. orange		5	5
421		50 c. green (1934)		5	5
410/421		*Set of 12*		40	25

Designs:—½ c., 2½ c. Gen. Teng Keng; 1 c., 50 c. Chen Ying-shih; 8 c., 13 c. Chu Chih-hsing; 10 c., 17 c. Chung Chiao-jen; 20 c., 40 c. Gen. Huang Hsing; 3 c., 30 c. Liao Chung-kai.

The design of all the above stamps is normally 22½ mm in height, the so-called "high" types. The ½, 1, 3, 10 and 50 c. also occur in "low" types, 21½ mm in height. Of these the ½ c. and 1 c. come in two settings, with stamps either 2½ or 3½ mm apart.

For the 8 c. in redrawn and wider design see Japanese Occupation of North China, No. 1.

For plain or watermarked issues, perf 12, 12½, 13 or compound, see Nos. 507/44.

61 Aeroplane over Great Wall    D 5

1932 (29 Aug)–37. *AIR.* P 14.

422	**61**	15 c. blue-green	..	..	5	5
423		25 c. orange (13.5.33)	..	..	5	5
424		30 c. scarlet	..	..	5	5
425		45 c. purple	..	..	5	5
426		50 c. chocolate (13.5.33)	..	..	5	5
427		60 c. blue	..	..	5	5
428		90 c. bronze-green	..	..	8	8
429		$1 yellow-green (13.5.33)	..		8	8
430		$2 brown (9.6.37)	..	..	8	10
431		$5 carmine (9.6.37)	..	..	30	35
422/431		*Set of 10*	..	..	75	80

Early printings were narrow (41×22½ mm) and later printings wide (41½×22 mm). The 45 c., 60 c. and 90 c. exist narrow only. The $2 and $5 exist wide only. Other values exist in both widths.

For plain or watermarked issues, perf 12, 12½, 13 or compound, see Nos. 545/64.

(Recess Waterlow)

1932. *POSTAGE DUE.* P 14.

D432	D **5**	½ c. orange	..	..	5	5
D433		1 c. orange	..	..	5	5
D434		2 c. orange	..	..	5	5
D435		4 c. orange	..	..	5	5
D436		5 c. orange	..	..	5	5
D437		10 c. orange	..	..	5	5
D438		20 c. orange	..	..	5	5
D439		30 c. orange	..	..	5	5
D432/439		*Set of 8*	..	..	25	25

For stamps perf 12, 12½, 13 or compound, see Nos. D565/75.

62 Tan Yen-kai

1933 (9 Jan). *Tan Yen-kai Memorial.* P 14.

440	**62**	2 c. olive-green	..	..	12	12
441		5 c. green	..	..	15	12
442		25 c. blue	..	..	40	20
443		$1 scarlet	..	..	5·00	2·50
440/443		*Set of 4*	..	..	5·25	2·50

63 Emblems of "New Life" Movement   64 Emblems of "New Life" Movement   65 Lighthouse

1936 (1 Jan). *"New Life" Movement.* P 14.

444	**63**	2 c. olive-green	..	..	12	8
445		5 c. green	..	..	12	8
446	**64**	20 c. blue	..	..	50	10
447	**65**	$1 scarlet	..	..	2·40	75
444/447		*Set of 4*	..	..	2·75	90

66 "Postal Communications"   67 The Bund, Shanghai

68 G.P.O., Shanghai   69 Ministry of Communications, Nanking

1936 (10 Oct). *40th Anniv of Chinese National Postal Service.* P 14.

448	**66**	2 c. orange	..	..	..	10	8
449	**67**	5 c. green	..	..	..	10	8
450	**68**	25 c. blue	..	..	..	50	12
451	**69**	100 c. scarlet	..	..	2·00	75
448/451		*Set of 4*	..	..	2·40	90

A miniature sheet in the design of the 2 c. but denominated "100" is bogus.

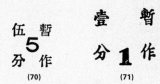

(70)   (71)

1936 (11 Oct). Nos. 323/4 surch with T **70**, in red.

452	**44**	5 c. on 15 c. deep blue	..	..	8	5
453		5 c. on 16 c. olive-green	..	..	8	5

1937–38. Nos. 397, 420 and 402 surch as T **71**.

454	**58**	1 c. on 4 c. green (R.) (3.37)	..	5	5
455	–	8 c. on 40 c. orange (7.38) ..	..	8	5
456	**58**	10 c. on 25 c. ultramarine (R.) (7.38) ..		8	5

THE WAR AGAINST JAPAN

Japan had seized Manchuria in 1931 and Jehol in 1933. On 7 July 1937 the Japanese attacked in North China and from then until the surrender of Japan in 1945, they occupied much of North and Central China and areas round Canton and Foochow. In March 1940 they established a puppet Chinese government at Nanking, headed by Wang Ching-wei, a former rival of Chiang Kai-shek.

The stamps listed below were current in areas not occupied by the Japanese or by Communist forces who were fighting against Japan.

72 Dr. Sun Yat-sen   73

Die I   Button = ⌒

II   Button = ○

III   Button = ○

A   2 c.   B

C   8 c.   D

Die I. Top border shaded only in centre; coat button a semi-circle.
Die II. Same, but coat button a circle.
Die III. Top border completely shaded; coat button a circle. (Nos. 478/82 also exist with coat button an incomplete circle.)

1938–41. *Sun Yat-sen (Third issue).* T **72.** *Emblem as B of* T **58.** *Recess.*

(i) *P* 12½. *Printed and perforated by Chung Hwa Book Co, Hong Kong. No wmk.*

(a) *Die* I (11.11.1938)

457	$1 sepia and red-brown	..	2·50	30
458	$2 red-brown and blue	..	1·50	30
459	$5 deep green and scarlet	..	4·00	1·50

(b) *Die* II (1938)

460	$1 sepia and red-brown	..	30	8
461	$2 red-brown and blue	..	45	10

(c) *Die* III (Nov 1938–41)

462	2 c. olive-green (A)	..	5	5
463	2 c. olive-green (B)	..	5	5
464	3 c. brown-lake	..	5	5
465	5 c. green	..	5	5
466	5 c. olive-green	..	5	5
467	8 c. sage-green (C)	..	5	5
468	8 c. sage-green (D)	..	12	5
469	10 c. green	..	5	5
470	15 c. scarlet	..	5	5
471	16 c. olive-brown	..	15	5
472	25 c. violet-blue	..	5	5
473	$1 sepia and red-brown	..	12	5
474	$2 red-brown and blue	..	15	5
	a. Imperf (pair)	..	35·00	
475	$5 deep green and scarlet	..	20	8
476	$10 violet and green	..	35	15
477	$20 ultramarine and purple	..	1·00	50
462/477	*Set of 16*	..	2·25	1·10

(d) *W* **73.** *Die* III (16.8.1941)

478	$1 sepia and red-brown	..	10	5
479	$2 red-brown and blue	..	15	5
480	$5 deep green and scarlet	..	15	8
481	$10 violet and green	..	25	12
482	$20 ultramarine and purple	..	45	25
478/482	*Set of 5*	..	1·00	50

The 15 c. brown in this design was issued in Shanghai under Japanese occupation (see Japanese Occupation of Nanking and Shanghai).

Collectors are warned against imperforate, ungummed copies of No. 475 and other values in the same design. Sheets of these, in an unfinished state, were looted from the printing works in Hong Kong. The stamps were never issued in this state.

8 c.   Dollar values

E   F   G   H

Plain (button) ("Dah" in button)

(ii) *P* 14. *No wmk. Die* III. *Printed by Chung Hwa Book Co, Hong Kong, and perforated by Dah Tung Book Co, Hong Kong* (6 Dec 1939–40)

483	2 c. olive (A)	..	10	8
484	5 c. green (F)	..	15	10
485	$1 sepia and red-brown (G)	..	2·25	55
486	$2 red-brown and blue (G)	..	75	20
487	$5 deep green and scarlet (G)	..	1·00	20
488	$10 violet and green (G)	..	1·10	20
483/488	*Set of 6*	..	4·75	1·10

(iii) *P* 14. *Die* III. *Printed and perforated by Dah Tung Book Co, Hong Kong*
A. *No wmk* (6 Dec 1939–41). B. *W* **73** (1940–July 1941)

		A		B	
489	5 c. green (F)	5	5	5	5
490	5 c. olive (F)	5	5	†	
491	8 c. sage-green (E)	15	5	†	
492	8 c. sage-green (F)	5	5	†	
493	10 c. green	5	5	5	5
494	30 c. scarlet	5	5	5	5
495	50 c. blue	5	5	5	5
496	$1 sep & red-brn (H)	10	5	10	5
497	$2 red-brn & bl (H)	15	5	15	5
498	$5 dp grn & scar (H)	15	5	15	5
499	$10 violet & green (H)	20	8	25	10
500	$20 ultram & pur (H)	30	15	50	20
489A/500A	*Set of 12*	1·25	60		

See also Nos. 656/74 for redrawn dollar values in single colours.

74 Chinese and U.S. Flags and Map of China

(D **6** "Temporary Use Postage Due")

(Recess American Bank Note Co, N.Y.)

1939 (4 July). *150th Anniv of U.S. Constitution. Flags in scarlet and blue. P* 12.

501	**74**	5 c. green	..	15	12
502		25 c. blue	..	30	30
503		50 c. brown	..	40	35
504		$1 carmine	..	80	75
501/504		*Set of 4*	..	1·50	1·40

1940 (1 Mar). *POSTAGE DUE. Nos.* 496/7A *optd with Type* D **6.**

505	**72**	$1 sepia and red-brown	..	5	5
506		$2 red-brown and blue (R.)	..	10	8

(a)   (b)

This issue differs in design from Nos. 410/21 in that it has a secret mark, Type (a), in the first character of the bottom inscription. In Nos. 410/21 and 508b this character is as Type (b).

(Recess Commercial Press, Hong Kong)

1940–41. T **60** *and similar portraits of Martyrs of the Revolution. P* 12, 12½, 13 *or compound.*

(a) *No wmk*

507	½ c. sepia (20.6.40)	..	5	5
508	1 c. yellow-orange (20.6.40)	..	5	5
	a. Imperf vert (horiz pair)	..	2·00	
	b. Without secret mark (b)	..	15	5
509	2 c. blue (21.4.41)	..	5	5
	a. Imperf vert (horiz pair)	..	17·00	
	b. Imperf horiz (vert pair)	..	75	
510	2½ c. claret (25.12.40)	..	5	5
511	3 c. brown (3.12.40)	..	5	5
512	4 c. lilac (26.6.41)	..	5	5
513	5 c. red-orange (26.6.41)	..	5	5
514	8 c. brown-orange (25.12.40)	..	5	5
515	10 c. dull purple (20.6.40)	..	5	5
516	13 c. blue-green (25.12.40)	..	5	5
517	15 c. maroon (3.2.41)	..	5	5
518	17 c. bronze-green (25.12.40)	..	5	5
519	20 c. light blue (3.12.40)	..	5	5
	a. Imperf vert (horiz pair)	..	15·00	
	b. Imperf horiz (vert pair)	..	15·00	
520	21 c. sepia (26.6.41)	..	5	5
521	25 c. purple (23.5.41)	..	5	5
522	28 c. olive (26.6.41)	..	5	5
523	30 c. maroon (10.10.41)	..	5	5
524	40 c. orange (22.2.41)	..	5	5
525	50 c. green (20.6.40)	..	5	5
507/525	*Set of 19*	..	70	70

(b) *W* **73**

526	½ c. sepia (3.12.40)	..	5	5
527	1 c. yellow-orange (20.6.40)	..	5	5
528	2 c. blue (23.5.41)	..	5	5
529	2½ c. claret (3.12.40)	..	5	5
530	3 c. brown (3.12.40)	..	5	5
531	4 c. lilac (26.6.41)	..	5	5
532	5 c. red-orange (16.8.41)	..	5	5
533	8 c. brown-orange (20.6.40)	..	5	5
534	10 c. dull purple (20.6.40)	..	5	5
535	13 c. blue-green (3.12.40)	..	5	5
536	15 c. maroon (3.2.41)	..	5	5
537	17 c. bronze-green (25.12.40)	..	5	5
538	20 c. light blue (25.12.40)	..	5	5

539	21 c. sepia (16.8.41)	..	..	5	5
540	25 c. purple (23.5.41)	..	..	5	5
541	28 c. olive (16.8.41)	..	..	5	5
542	30 c. maroon (20.6.40)	..	..	5	5
	a. Imperf vert (horiz pair)	..	12·00		
543	40 c. orange (3.12.40)	..	..	5	5
544	50 c. green (20.6.40)	..	..	5	5
526/544	Set of 19			70	70

Designs: ½ c., 2½ c., 4 c. Gen. Teng Keng; 1 c., 25 c., 50 c. Chen Ying-shih; 2 c., 10 c., 17 c., 28 c. Chung Chiao-jen; 3 c., 5 c., 15 c., 30 c. Liao Chung-kai; 8 c., 13 c., 21 c. Chu Chih-hsing; 20 c., 40 c. Gen. Huang Hsing.

(a)   (b)

These Hong Kong prints bear a secret mark in that the first character of the inscription at bottom is as Type (a). In Nos. 422/31 the character is as Type (b).

(Recess Commercial Press, Hong Kong)

1940–41. *AIR.* P 12, 12½, 13 *or compound.*

(a) W 73

545	61	15 c. blue-green (20.6.40)	..	..	5	8
546		25 c. orange (20.6.40)	..	..	5	8
547		30 c. scarlet (20.6.40)	..	..	5	8
		a. Imperf between (vert pair)	..	22·00		
548		45 c. purple (23.5.41)	..	..	5	8
549		50 c. chocolate (3.12.40)	..	..	5	12
550		60 c. blue (23.6.41)	..	..	5	8
551		90 c. olive (23.5.41)	..	..	5	8
552		$1 apple-green (23.5.41)	..	..	5	10
553		$2 brown (26.6.41)	..	..	5	10
554		$5 lake (20.6.40)	..	..	5	10
545/554		Set of 10	..	..	40	80

(b) No wmk

555	61	15 c. blue-green (1941)	..	..	5	5
556		25 c. orange (21.4.41)	..	..	5	5
557		30 c. scarlet (21.4.41)	..	..	5	5
558		45 c. purple (23.5.41)	..	..	5	5
559		50 c. chocolate (3.12.40)	..	..	5	5
560		60 c. blue (23.5.41)	..	..	5	5
561		90 c. olive (23.5.41)	..	..	5	5
562		$1 apple-green (23.5.41)	..	..	5	5
563		$2 brown (23.5.41)	..	..	5	5
564		$5 lake (23.5.41)	..	..	5	5
555/564		Set of 10	..	..	40	40

These stamps were issued with or without gum. The 30, 45, 60 and 90 c. values exist with and without lower frameline. There are variations of size in all values.

(a)   (b)

These Hong Kong prints bear a secret mark in that the third character of the inscription at top is as Type (a). In Nos. D432/9 the character is as Type (b).

(Recess Commercial Press, Hong Kong)

1940 (23 Oct)**–41.** *POSTAGE DUE.* P 12, 12½, 13 *or compound. No wmk.*

D565	D 5	½ c. orange	..	..	5	5
D566		1 c. orange	..	..	5	5
D567		2 c. orange	..	..	5	5
D568		4 c. orange	..	..	5	5
D569		5 c. orange	..	..	5	5
D570		10 c. orange	..	..	5	5
D571		20 c. orange	..	..	5	5
D572		30 c. orange	..	..	5	5
D573		50 c. orange	..	..	5	5
D574		$1 orange	..	..	5	5
D575		$2 orange	..	..	5	5
D565/575		Set of 11	..	..	45	45

PROVINCIAL SURCHARGES. Alterations in postal rates during the war made surcharging necessary. As it was impracticable to collect local stocks and surcharge them centrally, the surcharges were made by provincial authorities; they naturally differ in each province.

The provinces involved are identified by key letters as follows:—

A.	Anhwei	L.	Kiangsi
B.	Chekiang	M.	Kiangsu
C.	Chungking G.P.O.	N.	Kwangsi
D.	Fukien	P.	Kwangtung
E.	Fukien-Chekiang	Q.	Kweichow
F.	Honan	R.	Shensi
G.	Hunan	S.	Szechwan
H.	Hunan-Kwangtung	T.	East Szechwan
J.	Hupeh	U.	West Szechwan
K.	Kansu	W.	Yunnan

叁 暫 分 **3** 作   叁 暫 分 **3** 作   叁 暫 **分3**作

B Chekiang   **G** Hunan   **K** Kansu

叁 暫 分 **3** 作   叁 暫 分 **3** 作   叁 暫 分 3 作

L Kiangsi   **M** Kiangsu (Shanghai)   **T** East Szechwan

(G surch litho; K handstamped; rest typo)

1940 (21 Oct)**–41.** *PROVINCIAL SURCHARGES.* 5 c. stamps of T 72 surch "3 c." as above.

(a) Chung Hwa. Die III (Nos. 465/6)

576	M	On 5 c. green (Kiangsu) (3.12.40)	..		10	8
577	G	On 5 c. olive-green (Hunan) (9.11.40)			5	5
		a. Type K Kansu (20.12.40)	..		15	15

(b) Dah Tung. No wmk (Nos. 489/90A)

578	M	On 5 c. green (Kiangsu) (3.12.40)	..		8	5
579		On 5 c. olive (Kiangsu) (3.12.40)	..		8	5
		a. Type L Kiangsi (10.11.40)			5	5
		aa. Bottom left character repeated at right			3·00	3·00
		b. Type T E. Szechwan (28.11.40)			5	5
		ba. Surch double	..		35	
		bb. Smaller "3"	..		25	20
		bc. Top right character omitted	..		40	40

(c) Dah Tung. W 73 (Nos. 489/90B)

580	M	On 5 c. green (Kiangsu) (3.12.40)			8	5
		a. Type B Chekiang (R.) (21.10.40)			10	8
		b. Type G Hunan (17.12.40)			5	5
		c. Type L Kiangsi (10.11.40)			5	5
		ca. Bottom left character repeated at right			2·00	2·00
581		On 5 c. olive (Kiangsu) (3.12.40)			10	5
		a. Type B Chekiang (R.) (21.10.40)			10	8
		b. Type T E. Szechwan (28.8.41)			5	5
		ba. Bottom left character repeated at right			3·00	3·00

The Kansu surcharge (Type K), which occurs in six sub-types, was applied unofficially to other values.

肆 暫 分 **4** 作

(76)

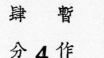

77 Dr. Sun Yat-sen

(Surch by Dah Tung Book Co, Hong Kong)

1940 (23 Oct). *No. 490A surch with T 76, in red.*

582	72	4 c. on 5 c. olive			5	5
		a. Bottom right character repeated at left	..	..	1·25	1·25

(Recess American Bank Note Co, N.Y.)

1941 (21 Feb–21 Apr). *Sun Yat-sen* (*Fourth issue*). *P* 12.

583	**77**	½ c. sepia	..	5	5
584		1 c. orange	..	5	5
585		2 c. ultramarine (21.4)	..	5	5
586		5 c. green	..	5	5
587		8 c. red-orange	..	5	5
588		8 c. turquoise-green (21.4)	..	5	5
589		10 c. emerald-green	..	5	5
590		17 c. olive-green	..	8	10
591		25 c. purple ..	..	5	5
592		30 c. scarlet ..	..	5	5
593		50 c. deep blue	..	5	5
594		$1 black and brown	..	5	5
595		$2 black and blue	..	5	5
		a. Centre inverted	..	£650	
596		$5 black and scarlet	..	8	8
597		$10 black and green (21.4)	..	20	15
598		$20 black and purple (21.4)	..	25	15
583/598		*Set of 16*	..	1·00	90

78 Industry   **(79)**

(Recess Chung Hwa Book Co, Hong Kong)

1941 (21 June). *Thrift Movement. P* 12½.

599	**78**	8 c. green	..	5	5
600		21 c. chocolate	..	5	5
601		28 c. olive-green	..	5	5
602		33 c. scarlet	..	15	10
603		50 c. blue	..	20	20
604		$1 purple	..	25	25
599/604		*Set of 6*	..	70	60
MS605		155×171 mm. Nos. 599/604 in slightly different colours. Typo. Imperf. No gum ..	..	1·25	1·25

A commemorative overprint in Chinese, Russian and French was applied to 5000 miniature sheets by the P.O. for an exhibition of the Russian Philatelic Society in Shanghai, 28 February 1943. These had postal validity.

(Optd by Postal Supply Dept, Shanghai)

1941 (10 Oct). *30th Anniv of Republic. T* **72** and portraits of martyrs as *T* **60**, optd with *T* **79**.

606	**60**	1 c. yellow-orange (508) (B.)	..	5	5
607	**72**	2 c. olive-green (463) (R.)	..	5	5
608	**60**	4 c. lilac (512) (R.)	..	5	5
609	**72**	8 c. sage-green (468) (R.)	..	5	5
610		10 c. green (469) (R.) ..	..	5	5
611		16 c. olive-brown (471) (R.)	..	5	5
612	**60**	21 c. sepia (520) (R.) ..	..	5	5
613		28 c. olive (522) (R.) ..	..	5	5
614	**72**	30 c. scarlet (494) (B.)	..	8	5
615		$1 sepia and red-brown (473) (B.)		12	10
606/615		*Set of 10*	..	50	45

E 3

1941. *EXPRESS LETTER. Litho. No gum. Rouletted.*

E616	**E 3**	(–) Red and yellow ..	..	35	35

1941. *REGISTRATION. As Type* E **3.** *Litho. No gum. Rouletted.*

R617	(–) Blue-green and buff	..	35	35

The above were prepared without indication of value as postal rates were about to be changed. The Express Letter stamp (inscribed "Postage paid for express letter of every 20 grams") was sold at $2 and the Registration stamp (inscribed "Postage paid for registered letter of every 20 grams") was sold at $1.50.

B Chekiang   **D** Fukien

L Kiangsi   **S** Szechwan

1941 (Nov). PROVINCIAL SURCHARGES. 8 c. stamps of *T* **72** surch "7 c." as above, typo.

(a) Chung Hwa. Die III (Nos. 467/8)

618	**B**	On 8 c. sage-green (C) (Chekiang)	..	5	5
619	**S**	a. Type **D** Fukien ..		5	5
619	**S**	On 8 c. sage-green (D) (Szechwan)	..	5	5

(b) Dah Tung. No wmk (Nos. 491/2A)

620	**B**	On 8 c. sage-green (E) (Chekiang)	..	2·00	2·00
621		On 8 c. sage-green (F) (Chekiang)	..	5	5
		a. Type **D** Fukien ..		5	5
		b. Type **L** Kiangsi ..		5	5

D Fukien   **H** Hunan-Kwangtung

L Kiangsi   **N** Kwangsi

(**H** litho; others typo)

1942 (16 May)–**43**. PROVINCIAL SURCHARGES. Various ½ c. stamps surch "1 c." as above, in red.

(a) T **60** *of 1932 (No. 410)*

622	**H**	On ½ c. sep (Hunan-Kwangtung) (8.42)		5	5
		a. Type **N** Kwangsi (7.43) ..		5	5

(b) T **60**, *Hong Kong print. No wmk (No. 507)*

623	**D**	On ½ c. sepia (Fukien) (16.5.42)	..	5	5
		a. Type **H** Hunan-Kwangtung (8.42)		5	5
		b. Type **L** Kiangsi (8.42) ..		5	5
		c. Type **N** Kwangsi (7.43) ..		5	5

(c) T **77.** *Fourth Sun Yat-sen issue (No. 583)*

624	**H**	On ½ c. sep (Hunan-Kwangtung) (8.42)		5	5
		a. Surch double ..		75	

There are 14 sub-types of Type **H** (Hunan-Kwangtung), varying in size, shape of bottom left character, and relative position of figure "1".

H Hunan-Kwangtung   **T** East Szechwan

角40作   **角 40 作**
U West Szechwan   W Yunnan

(H litho; others typo)

1942 (22 Aug–Nov). PROVINCIAL SURCHARGES. *Various 50 c. stamps surch "40 c." as above, in red.*

(a) T 72. Dah Tung. No wmk (No. 495B)

625	T On 50 c. blue (*East Szechwan*) (26.8)		5	5
	a. Type **U** *West Szechwan* (16.11)		15	8
	b. Type **W** *Yunnan* (22.8)		5	5
	ba. Surch inverted		10·00	10·00
	bb. Top left and bottom right characters transposed		10·00	

(b) Martyr type. W 73 (No. 544)

626	H On 50 c. green (*Hunan–Kwangtung*) (Nov)		5	5

(c) T 77, Fourth Sun Yat-sen issue (No. 593)

627	H On 50 c. dp blue (*Hunan-Kwangtung*) (Nov)		5	5

82   *(a)*   *(b)*

The $1, $2, $4 and $5 values of the Paicheng print differ from the same values in the Central Trust print by having a small "c" as shown in (b). In the $3 the "c" is in the corresponding ornament on the right-hand side.

1942–46. Sun Yat-sen (*Fifth issue*). Typo.

(i) Printed by Central Trust, Chungking. No gum. P 10½ to 13½ and compounds (15.9.42–1944)

628	82	10 c. green (1943)		5	5
629		16 c. olive-brown (15.9.42)		70	70
630		20 c. grey-olive (1942)		5	5
631		25 c. purple-brown (1943)		5	5
632		30 c. orange-red (1942)		5	8
633		40 c. red-brown (1942)		5	5
634		50 c. grey-green (1942)		5	5
635		$1 lake (1942)		5	5
636		$1 olive-green (a) (1943)		5	5
637		$1.50 blue (1942)		5	5
638		$2 blue-green (a) (1943)		5	5
639		$3 yellow (a) (1943)		5	5
640		$4 brown (a) (1944)		5	5
641		$5 carmine (a) (1943)		5	5
628/641		Set of 14		1·00	1·00

(ii) Printed by Paicheng Printing Co, Nanping. No gum. P 12 to 13 (1944–46)

642	82	30 c. brown (1946)		5	5
643		$1 olive-green (b) (1945)		10	12
644		$2 blue-green (b)		10	10
		a. Perf 10½		15·00	15·00
645		$2 blue		5	5
646		$2 purple-brown		5	5
		a. Imperf (pair)		30	30
647		$3 yellow (b) (1945)		5	5
648		$4 brown-purple (b) (1945)		5	5
		a. Imperf (pair)		5·00	5·00
649		$5 carmine (b) (1945)		5	5
		a. Perf 10½		15·00	15·00
650		$6 violet-blue (1945)		5	5
651		$10 red-brown (1945)		5	5
		a. Imperf (pair)		6·00	6·00
652		$20 blue (1946)		5	5
653		$50 deep blue-green (1946)		5	5
654		$70 deep lilac (1946)		5	5
655		$100 pale brown (1946)		5	5
642/655		Set of 14		70	75

There are many varieties of shade and paper in both prints and many stamps may be found imperf between, etc.

84 Dr. Sun Yat-sen

(Recess Paicheng Printing Co, Nanping)

1942–45. Sun Yat-sen (*Third issue but redrawn*). *Single colours. No gum.*

(a) Imperf

656	84	$10 red-brown		5	5
657		$20 green		8	5
658		$20 rose-carmine (1944)		35	8
659		$30 purple (1943)		8	8
660		$40 carmine (1943)		5	5
661		$50 blue		5	5
662		$100 brown (1943)		30	12
656/662		Set of 7		85	45

(b) Rouletted 6½

663	84	$5 lilac-grey (1944)		12	10
		a. Rouletted 6½ × perf 12½		2·00	1·50
664		$10 red-brown		12	8
665		$50 blue		12	10

(c) Rough perf 12 to 15½

666	84	$4 blue (1943)		5	5
667		$5 lilac-grey (1943)		5	5
668		$10 red-brown		5	5
669		$20 green (1943)		5	5
670		$20 rose-carmine (1945)		2·00	2·50
671		$30 purple (1943)		5	5
672		$40 carmine (1943)		8	8
673		$50 blue		5	5
674		$100 brown (1945)		2·10	2·25
666/674		Set of 9		4·00	4·50

Beware of forged perforations on Nos. 670 and 674. There are various crude unofficial perforations of the imperforate stamps.

(M 1) Hupeh   **(M 2)** Chungking   **(M 3)** Chungking

(M 4) Chekiang   **(M 5)** Kwangtung   **(M 6)** Hunan

(M 7) Kiangsi   **(M 8)** Kiangsi

1942 (Oct)–**44.** MILITARY FIELD POST. *Sold below current postal rates. Various stamps optd for use on soldiers' correspondence.*

(a) Hupeh issue. Nos. 492 and 588 optd with Type M 1, by the Hupeh Press, Enshih

M675	72	8 c. sage-green (R.) (10.42)		10	12
M676	77	8 c. red-orange (1943?)		3·00	

(b) General issue. Central Trust print of Fifth Sun Yat-sen issue optd by Central Trust, Chungking with Type M 2 (16 c.) or M 3 (rest)

M677	82	16 c. olive-brown (R.) (12.42)		12	15
		a. Black opt		2·40	2·50
M678		50 c. grey-green (R.) (3.43)		10	12
M679		$1 lake (1.8.43)		12	12
M680		$1 olive-green (12.43)		12	12
M681		$2 blue-green (R.) (1.6.44)		12	12

(c) Chekiang issue. Nos. 492 and 471 optd with Type M 4, at Shihshien, Anhwei

M682	72	8 c. sage-green (R.) (12.42)		25	20
M683		16 c. olive-brown (R.) (12.42)		50	35

(d) Kwangtung issue. No. 587 optd with Type M 5, at Chukong

M684	77	8 c. turquoise-grn (R.) (28.12.42)		15	10

(e) Hunan issue. No. 588 optd with Type M 6

M685	77	8 c. turquoise-green (R.) (1942?)		12	12

(f) Kiangsi issue. No. 492 optd with Type M 7, by Dah Tung Book Co, Kanhsien and No. 646 optd with Type M 8

M686	72	8 c. sage-green (R.) (4.43)	15	30
M687	82	$2 purple-brown (1944)	35	30

A Anhwei   **D** Fukien   **F** Honan

G Hunan   **J** Hupeh   **K** Kansu

L Kiangsi   **N** Kwangsi   **P** Kwangtung

Q Kweichow   **R** Shensi   **T** East Szechwan

U West Szechwan   **W** Yunnan

(Surch "Surcharge for Domestic Postage Paid")
(**A** and **G** litho; others typo)

1942 (1 Nov). *PROVINCIAL SURCHARGES. No. 629 surch as above. P 13.*

688	**A** 16 c. olive-brown (*Anhwei*) (R.)	12·00	12·00
	a. Type **D** Fukien (R.)	3·75	3·75
	b. Type **F** Honan	42·00	45·00
	c. Type **G** Hunan	45·00	
	d. Type **J** Hupeh (R.)	55·00	60·00
	da. Perf 10½	40·00	40·00
	e. Type **K** Kansu (R.)	15	30
	f. Type **L** Kiangsi (R.)	40	55
	g. Type **N** Kwangsi	1·75	2·00
	ga. Perf 10½	30·00	
	h. Type **P** Kwangtung (R.)	35·00	40·00
	i. Type **Q** Kweichow (R.)	2·50	3·00
	j. Type **R** Shensi	5·00	6·00
	ja. Surch inverted	7·50	
	k. Type **T** East Szechwan (R.)	60	75
	ka. Perf 10½	40·00	18·00
	l. Type **U** West Szechwan	3·75	3·75
	m. Type **W** Yunnan (R.)	55	55

The above were sold at $1.16 for a few days only except for Anhwei which was on sale until January 1943. Beware of forgeries.

B Chekiang   **C** Chungking G.P.O.   **F** Honan

G Hunan   **N** Kwangsi   **P** Kwangtung

Q Kweichow   **R** Shensi   **T** East Szechwan

U West Szechwan

(**G** litho; others typo)

1943 (Jan–July). *PROVINCIAL SURCHARGES. No. 629 surch "50 c." as above. P 13.*

689	**B** 50 c. on 16 c. olive-brown (*Chekiang*) (R.) (May)	80	
	a. Type **C** Chungking (R.) (Jan)	5	5
	aa. Perf 10½	15	15
	ab. Perf 13×10½	2·00	2·00
	b. Type **F** Honan (Mar)	15	10
	ba. Perf 10½	2·00	2·00
	c. Type **F** Honan (R.) (July)	30	30
	ca. Perf 10½	1·20	1·20
	d. Type **G** Hunan (R.) (Mar)	8	8
	da. Perf 10½	60	
	db. Surch inverted	4·00	
	dc. Surch double		
	e. Type **N** Kwangsi (R.) (June)	8	5
	ea. Perf 10½	35	
	f. Type **P** Kwangtung (R.) (May)	15	12
	fa. Perf 10½	80	80
	fb. Perf 10½×13	4·50	4·50
	g. Type **Q** Kweichow (R.) (Feb)	15	8
	h. Type **R** Shensi (Mar)	8	5
	ha. Perf 10½	1·00	
	hb. Perf 10½×13	4·00	
	hc. Surch double		
	i. Type **T** East Szechwan (R.) (June)	8	5
	ia. Perf 10½	40	
	ib. Perf 13×10½	5·00	
	j. Type **U** West Szechwan (R.) (Feb)	35	20
	ja. Perf 10½	3·00	
	jb. Perf 13×10½	3·00	

Kweichow has two sub-types differing in the overall height of the surcharge and the surcharge for West Szechwan is in two sub-types differing in the size of the "O".

貳 改 貳 改 貳 改
角 20 作   角 20 作   角 20 作
E
Fukien-Chekiang   **F** Honan   **G** Hunan

貳 改 貳 改 貳 改
角 20 作   角 (20) 作   角 20 作
J Hupeh   **K** Kansu   **L** Kiangsi

貳 改 貳 改 貳 改
角 20 作   角 20 作   角 20 作
N Kwangsi   **P** Kwangtung   **Q** Kweichow

貳 改 貳 改 貳 改
角 20 作   角 20 作   角 20 作
R Shensi   **T** East Szechwan   **U** West Szechwan

貳 改
角 20 作
W Yunnan

(**G** litho; others typo)

1943 (Feb–Dec). *PROVINCIAL SURCHARGES. Various stamps surch "20 c." as above.*

(*a*) *Martyr type of 1932 (No. 416)*

690	**G** On 13 c. blue-green (*Hunan*) (R.) (1.9)		65·00	65·00
	a. Type **J** *Hupeh* (R.) (30.12)	..	8	8
	b. Type **K** *Kansu* (10.10)	..	8	8
	c. Type **L** *Kiangsi* (R.) (Aug)	..	8·00	8·00
	d. Type **N** *Kwangsi* (R.) (July)	..	5	5
	e. Type **P** *Kwangtung* (R.) (25.10)	..	1·00	1·00
	f. Type **R** *Shensi* (Dec)	..	5	5
	g. Type **U** *West Szechwan* (May)		8	8

(*b*) *T 72. Chung Hwa. Die III (No. 471)*

691	**F** On 16 c. olive-brown (*Honan*) (Feb)	..	12	12
	a. Type **G** *Hunan* (R.) (1.9)	..	12	10
	b. Type **G** *Hunan* (1.9)	..	5	5
	c. Type **K** *Kansu* (10.10)	..	5	5
	d. Type **L** *Kiangsi* (R.) (Aug)	..	10	10
	e. Type **N** *Kwangsi* (R.) (July)	..	10	10
	f. Type **P** *Kwangtung* (R.) (25.10)	..	1·25	1·25
	g. Type **Q** *Kweichow* (R.) (27.10)	..	8	8
	h. Type **R** *Shensi* (Dec)	..	8	8
	i. Type **U** *West Szechwan* (May)		8	8

(*c*) *Martyr types. No wmk (Nos. 516, 518, 520, 522)*

692	**F** On 13 c. blue-green (*Honan*) (Feb)	..	8	8
	a. Type **G** *Hunan* (R.) (1.9)	..	15	15
	b. Type **J** *Hupeh* (R.) (30.12)	..	5	5
	c. Type **K** *Kansu* (10.10)	..	5	5
	d. Type **L** *Kiangsi* (R.) (Aug)	..	10	10
	e. Type **N** *Kwangsi* (R.) (July)	..	5	5
	f. Type **P** *Kwangtung* (R.) (25.10)	..	5	5
	g. Type **Q** *Kweichow* (R.) (27.10)	..	8	8
	h. Type **R** *Shensi* (Dec)	..	5	5
	i. Type **T** *East Szechwan* (R.) (Oct)	..	5	5
	j. Type **U** *West Szechwan* (May)		60	60
	k. Type **W** *Yunnan* (23.9)		5	5
693	**F** On 17 c. bronze-green (*Honan*) (Feb)	..	1·25	1·00
	a. Type **K** *Kansu* (10.10)	..	12	12
	b. Type **L** *Kiangsi* (R.) (Aug)	..	8	8
	c. Type **P** *Kwangtung* (R.) (25.10)	..	5	5
	d. Type **Q** *Kweichow* (R.) (27.10)	..	8	8
	e. Type **U** *West Szechwan* (May)	..	8	8
694	**E** On 21 c. sepia (*Fukien-Chekiang*) (R.) (5.6)		10	10
	a. Type **F** *Honan* (Feb)	..	8	8
	b. Type **G** *Hunan* (1.9)	..	5	5
	c. Type **J** *Hupeh* (R.) (30.12)	..	5	5
	d. Type **K** *Kansu* (10.10)	..	5	5
	e. Type **L** *Kiangsi* (R.) (Aug)	..	15	15
	f. Type **N** *Kwangsi* (R.) (July)	..	5	5
	g. Type **P** *Kwangtung* (R.) (25.10)	..	5	5
	h. Type **Q** *Kweichow* (R.) (27.10)	..	10	10
	i. Type **T** *East Szechwan* (R.) (Oct)	..	5	5
	j. Type **U** *West Szechwan* (May)	..	8	8
	k. Type **W** *Yunnan* (23.9)	..	20	20
695	**E** On 28 c. olive (*Fukien-Chekiang*) (R.) (5.6)		10	10
	a. Type **F** *Honan* (Feb)	..	85	85
	b. Type **G** *Hunan* (R.) (1.9)	..	5	5
	c. Type **K** *Kansu* (10.10)	..	50	50
	d. Type **L** *Kiangsi* (R.) (Aug)	..	15	15
	e. Type **N** *Kwangsi* (R.) (July)	..	5	5
	f. Type **P** *Kwangtung* (R.) (25.10)	..	5	5
	g. Type **Q** *Kweichow* (R.) (27.10)	..	8	8
	h. Type **U** *West Szechwan* (May)	..	50	40
	i. Type **W** *Yunnan* (23.9)	..	5	5

(*d*) *As last but W 73 (Nos. 535, 537, 539, 541)*

696	**E** On 13 c. blue-green (*Fukien-Chekiang*) (R.) (5.6)		12	12
	a. Type **F** *Honan* (Feb)	..	8·00	7·00
	b. Type **G** *Hunan* (R.) (1.9)	..	10	10
	c. Type **J** *Hupeh* (R.) (30.12)	..	5	5
	d. Type **K** *Kansu* (10.10)	..	15	15
	e. Type **L** *Kiangsi* (R.) (Aug)	..	10	10
	f. Type **N** *Kwangsi* (R.) (July)	..	5	5
	g. Type **P** *Kwangtung* (R.) (25.10)	..	80	80
	h. Type **Q** *Kweichow* (R.) (27.10)	..	5	5
	i. Type **R** *Shensi* (Dec)	..	5	5
	j. Type **T** *East Szechwan* (R.) (Oct)	..	5	5
	k. Type **U** *West Szechwan* (May)	..	8	8
	l. Type **W** *Yunnan* (23.9)	..	50	35
697	**G** On 17 c. bronze-green (*Hunan*) (R.) (1.9)		8	8
	a. Type **N** *Kwangsi* (R.) (July)	..	5	5
	b. Type **P** *Kwangtung* (R.) (25.10)	..	75	75
698	**L** On 21 c. sepia (*Kiangsi*) (R.) (Aug)	..	12	12
699	On 28 c. olive (*Kiangsi*) (R.) (Aug)	..	35·00	30·00

(*e*) *T 77. Fourth Sun Yat-sen issue (No. 590)*

700	**F** On 17 c. olive-green (*Honan*) (Feb)	..	6·00	6·00
	a. Type **G** *Hunan* (R.) (1.9)	..	15	15

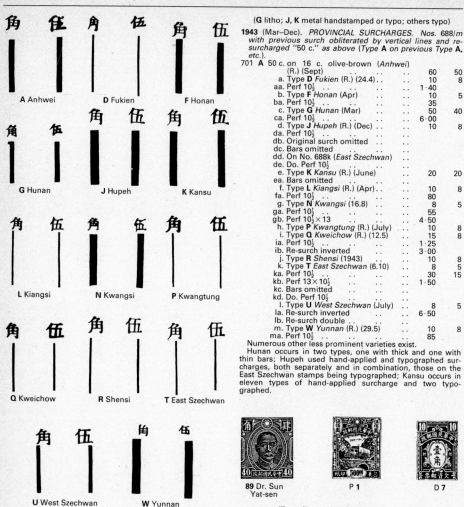

A Anhwei **D** Fukien **F** Honan

G Hunan **J** Hupeh **K** Kansu

L Kiangsi **N** Kwangsi **P** Kwangtung

Q Kweichow **R** Shensi **T** East Szechwan

U West Szechwan **W** Yunnan

(**G** litho; **J, K** metal handstamped or typo; others typo)

1943 (Mar–Dec). *PROVINCIAL SURCHARGES. Nos. 688/m with previous surch obliterated by vertical lines and re-surcharged "50 c." as above (Type A on previous Type A, etc.).*

701	**A**	50 c. on 16 c. olive-brown (*Anhwei*) (R.) (Sept)		60	50
		a. Type **D** *Fukien* (R.) (24.4) ..		10	8
		aa. Perf 10½ ..		1·40	
		b. Type **F** *Honan* (Apr)		10	5
		ba. Perf 10½ ..		35	
		c. Type **G** *Hunan* (Mar)		50	40
		ca. Perf 10½ ..		6·00	
		d. Type **J** *Hupeh* (R.) (Dec) ..		10	8
		da. Perf 10½ ..			
		db. Original surch omitted ..			
		dc. Bars omitted ..			
		dd. On No. 688k (*East Szechwan*)			
		de. Do. Perf 10½ ..			
		e. Type **K** *Kansu* (R.) (June) ..		20	20
		ea. Bars omitted ..			
		f. Type **L** *Kiangsi* (R.) (Apr) ..		10	8
		fa. Perf 10½ ..		80	
		g. Type **N** *Kwangsi* (16.8) ..		8	5
		ga. Perf 10½ ..		55	
		gb. Perf 10½ × 13 ..		4·50	
		h. Type **P** *Kwangtung* (R.) (July) ..		10	8
		i. Type **Q** *Kweichow* (R.) (12.5) ..		15	8
		ia. Perf 10½ ..		1·25	
		ib. Re-surch inverted ..		3·00	
		j. Type **R** *Shensi* (1943) ..		10	8
		k. Type **T** *East Szechwan* (6.10) ..		8	5
		ka. Perf 10½ ..		30	15
		kb. Perf 13 × 10½ ..		1·50	
		kc. Bars omitted ..			
		kd. Do. Perf 10½ ..			
		l. Type **U** *West Szechwan* (July) ..		8	5
		la. Re-surch inverted ..		6·50	
		lb. Re-surch double ..			
		m. Type **W** *Yunnan* (R.) (29.5) ..		10	8
		ma. Perf 10½ ..		85	

Numerous other less prominent varieties exist.

Hunan occurs in two types, one with thick and one with thin bars; Hupeh used hand-applied and typographed surcharges, both separately and in combination, those on the East Szechwan stamps being typographed; Kansu occurs in eleven types of hand-applied surcharge and two typographed.

89 Dr. Sun Yat-sen **P 1** **D 7**

(Typo Chung Hwa Book Co, Chungking)

1944 (June)–46. *Sun Yat-sen (Sixth issue). No gum.* P 12½.

702	**89**	40 c. brown-lake		5	5
703		$2 pale brown (1945) ..		5	5
704		$3 scarlet ..		5	5
		a. Pale orange-red ..		5	5
705		$3 grey-brown (1945) ..		5	5
706		$6 pale purple (1945) ..		5	5
707		$10 claret (1945) ..		5	5
708		$20 rose-red (1945) ..		5	5
		a. Perf 15½ ..		5·00	
709		$50 dull brown (1946) ..		5	5
710		$70 violet (1946) ..		5	5
702/710		Set of 9 ..		35	35

There are numerous shades in this issue.

(Recess Central Trust, Chungking)

1944–45. *PARCELS POST. No gum.* P 13.

P711	**P 1**	$500 green		—	5
P712		$1,000 blue ..		—	5
P713		$3,000 bright carmine ..		—	5
P714		$5,000 brown ..		—	45
P715		$10,000 slate-purple ..		—	75
P716		$20,000 red-orange ..		—	10·00
P711/716		Set of 6 ..		—	10·00

PARCELS POST STAMPS. These were not on sale in unused condition, but were affixed to parcels and cancelled by postal officials. In 1948, permission was given for cancelled stamps to be sold to the public.

Unused Parcels Post stamps now on the market were probably stocks seized by the Communists.

(Litho Central Trust, Chungking)

1944. *POSTAGE DUE. No gum.* P 13.

D717	D **7**	10 c. green	..	5	5
D718		20 c. dull blue	..	5	5
D719		40 c. rose-red	..	5	5
D720		50 c. green	..	5	5
D721		60 c. dull blue	..	5	5
D722		$1 rose-red	..	5	5
D723		$2 brown-purple	..	5	5
D717/723		*Set of 7*	..	25	25

90 War Refugees   91 Savings Bank and Money Box

(Recess American Bank Note Co, N.Y.)

1944 (10 Oct). *War Refugees Relief Fund. As T* **90** *(various frames) surch in black.* P 12.

724	$2+$2 on 50 c.+50 c. ultramarine	..	12	20
725	$4+$4 on 8 c.+8 c. emerald	..	12	20
726	$5+$5 on 21 c.+21 c. red-brown	..	20	25
727	$6+$6 on 28 c.+28 c. olive-green	..	25	30
728	$10+$10 on 33 c.+33 c. scarlet	..	50	50
729	$20+$20 on $1+$1 violet	..	75	1·10
724/729	*Set of 6*	..	1·75	2·25
MS730	190×110 mm. Nos. 724/9	..	2·00	2·00

(Recess Central Trust, Chungking)

1944 (Oct). *Thick paper; Nos. 731/3 also on thin paper. No gum.* P 13.

731	**91**	$40 slate-grey	..	5	5
732		$50 yellow-green	..	5	5
733		$100 yellow-brown	..	5	5
734		$200 deep green	..	5	5
731/734		*Set of 4*	..	15	15

(Recess De La Rue)

1944–46. *As 1931–37. New dollar values in single colours.* P 11½×12½, 12½, 12½×13 or 13½.

735	**58**	$1 violet	..	5	5
736		$2 olive-green	..	5	5
737		$20 apple-green (1946)	..	5	5
738		$30 chocolate (1946)	..	5	5
739		$50 red-orange (1946)	..	5	5
735/739		*Set of 5*	..	20	20

Two dies exist of No. 738.

92 Dr. Sun Yat-sen   M **9** Entrenched Soldiers   93 Dr. Sun Yat-sen

(Litho Central Trust, Chungking)

1944 (25 Dec). *50th Anniv of Kuomintang. No gum.* P 13.

740	**92**	$2 blue-green	..	5	25
741		$5 red-brown	..	5	25
742		$6 purple	..	8	30
743		$10 violet-blue	..	15	40
744		$20 carmine	..	25	80
740/744		*Set of 5*	..	50	1·75

1945 (1 Jan). *MILITARY FIELD POST.* P 12½.

M745	M **9**	(No value) carmine	..	5	15

(Litho Central Trust, Chungking)

1945 (12 Mar). *20th Death Anniv of Dr. Sun Yat-sen. No gum.* P 13.

746	**93**	$2 grey-green	..	5	12
747		$5 red-brown	..	5	12
748		$6 violet-blue	..	5	12
749		$10 light blue	..	8	15
750		$20 rose-carmine	..	10	20
751		$30 orange-brown	..	20	25
746/751		*Set of 6*	..	45	85

D **8**   94

(Litho Central Trust, Chungking)

1945. *POSTAGE DUE. No gum.* P 13.

D752	D **8**	$2 carmine	..	5	5
D753		$6 carmine	..	5	5
D754		$8 carmine	..	5	5
D755		$10 carmine	..	5	5
D756		$20 carmine	..	5	5
D757		$30 carmine	..	5	5
D752/757		*Set of 6*	..	20	20

(Typo Dah Tung Book Co, Chungking)

1945–46. *Sun Yat-sen (Seventh issue). No gum.* P 12½.

758	**94**	$2 green	..	5	5
759		$5 blue-green	..	5	5
760		$10 blue	..	5	5
		a. Imperf (pair)	..	5·00	5·00
761		$20 scarlet (1946)	..	5	5
		a. Imperf (pair)	..	10·00	10·00
		b. Imperf horiz (vert pair)	..	10·00	8·00
758/761		*Set of 4*	..	15	15

95 Gen. Chiang Kai-shek   96 Pres. Lin Sen

(Design recess, flags litho; American Bank Note Co, N.Y.)

1945 (7 July). *Equal Treaties with Great Britain and U.S.A., abolishing Foreign Concessions. Flags in national colours.* P 12.

762	**95**	$1 deep blue	..	5	5
763		$2 green	..	5	5
764		$5 olive-grey	..	5	5
765		$6 brown	..	10	15
766		$10 purple	..	20	25
767		$20 carmine	..	25	30
762/767		*Set of 6*	..	60	75

(Recess American Bank Note Co, N.Y.)

1945 (1 Aug). *In Memory of Pres. Lin Sen.* P 12.

768	**96**	$1 black and ultramarine	..	5	5
769		$2 black and blue-green	..	5	5
770		$5 black and scarlet	..	5	5
771		$6 black and violet	..	8	8
772		$10 black and brown	..	10	15
773		$20 black and olive	..	20	20
768/773		*Set of 6*	..	45	50

COMMUNIST CONQUEST AND POST-WAR INFLATION

Japan surrendered to the Allies on 14 August 1945 and a race ensued between Nationalists and Communists to seize areas which had been occupied by the Japanese. Attempts by the U.S.A. to bring about an understanding between the two parties failed and Communist forces, which had conquered Manchuria by November 1948, finally defeated the Nationalists in the decisive two-month battle of Hwai-Hai in January 1949.

Throughout the period, till the Silver Yuan was introduced in May 1949, inflation of Nationalist currency gained increasing momentum.

Chinese Nationalist Currency
$1 C.N.C.=$200 of Japanese Puppet Govt

(97)   (98)   (99)

(Surch by Union Press, Shanghai)

1945 (Sept). *C.N.C. surcharges. Stamps previously surch in black as T 97 (for the Japanese-controlled puppet government at Nanking and Shanghai, further surch as T 98, in green.*

774	**72**	10 c. on $20 on 3 c. (464) (17.9)	5	5
775	**60**	15 c. on $20 on 2 c. (509) (25.9)	5	5
776	**77**	25 c. on $50 on 1 c. (584) (25.9)	5	5
777	**72**	50 c. on $100 on 3 c. (464) (25.9)	5	5
778	**60**	$1 on $200 on 1 c. (508) (17.9)	5	5
		a. Imperf between (horiz pair)	17·00	
779	**72**	$2 on $400 on 3 c. (464) (17.9)	5	5
780	**77**	$5 on $1,000 on 1 c. (584) (18.9)	5	5
774/780		Set of 7	25	25

The characters at left in surcharge differ in type and number for each value.

(Surch by Honan District Office)

1945 (9 Oct). *Kaifeng provisionals. C.N.C. surcharges. Nos. 166/8 of Japanese Occupation of North China surch as T 99, in green.*

781	**60**	$10 on 20 c. brown-lake	10	25
		a. Bottom left character inverted	2·25	
782		$20 on 40 c. orange	10	25
		a. Surch inverted	2·25	5·00
		b. Surch double	2·50	
		c. Bottom left character inverted		
783		$50 on 30 c. maroon	10	25
		a. Surch inverted	2·00	5·00
		b. Surch double		
		c. Bottom left character inverted		

All values exist with gum on white paper and the $10 and $50 exist without gum on white, yellowish and newsprint papers.

100   101
Pres. Chiang Kai-shek

(Design recess, flag typo; American Bank Note Co, N.Y.)

1945 (10 Oct). *Inauguration of Pres. Chiang Kai-shek. Flag in red and blue. P 12.*

784	**100**	$2 green	8	25
785		$4 blue	8	25
786		$5 grey-olive	8	25
787		$6 yellow-brown	10	40
788		$10 grey	20	50
789		$20 crimson	25	60
784/789		Set of 6	70	2·00

(Litho Chung Hwa Book Co, Chungking)

1945 (10 Oct). *Victory. Flag in red. No gum. P 13.*

790	**101**	$20 green and blue	5	5
		a. Imperf between (horiz pair)	6·00	
791		$50 yellow-brown and blue	8	8
		a. Imperf between (horiz pair)	8·00	
792		$100 blue	5	5
793		$300 carmine and blue	5	5
790/793		Set of 4	15	15

Shades exist of all values.

102 Dr. Sun Yat-sen   (103) Box at top

(Typo Central Trust, Chungking)

1945 (Dec)–**46**. *Sun Yat-sen (Eighth issue). No gum. P 12½ (all values) or 13 ($20, $40, $200).*

794	**102**	$20 carmine	5	5
795		$30 deep blue	5	5
796		$40 orange (1946)	5	10
797		$50 green (1946)	5	5
798		$100 brown (1946)	5	5
799		$200 chocolate (1946)	5	5
794/799		Set of 6	25	30

(Surch by Union Press, Shanghai)

1946 (Jan–Dec). *C.N.C. surcharges. Martyrs issue of 1940–41 (Hong Kong printing), surch as T 103.*

(a) No wmk

800		$3 on 2½ c. claret	10	12
801		$10 on 15 c. maroon	5	5
		a. Imperf between (horiz pair)	2·40	
802		$20 on 8 c. brown-orange	5	5
803		$20 on 20 c. light blue	5	5
		a. Imperf between (horiz pair)	1·75	
804		$30 on ½ c. sepia	5	5
805		$50 on 21 c. sepia	5	5
806		$70 on 13 c. blue-green (No. 416)	1·75	1·75
807		$70 on 13 c. blue-green (No. 516) (Dec)	5	5
808		$100 on 28 c. olive	5	5

(b) W 73

809		$20 on 8 c. brown-orange	5	5
810		$30 on ½ c. sepia	80·00	60·00
811		$50 on 21 c. sepia	5	5
812		$70 on 13 c. blue-green	5	5
813		$100 on 28 c. olive	5	5
800/813		Set of 14	75·00	55·00

P 2   (104)

(Recess De La Rue)

1946. *PARCELS POST. P 12½.*

P814	**P 2**	$3,000 red-orange	—	5
P815		$5,000 indigo	—	5
P816		$10,000 violet	—	5
P817		$20,000 red	—	5
P814/817		Set of 4	—	15

The note after No. P716 also applies here.

(Surch by Central Trust, Chungking)

1946 (2 May). *AIR. C.N.C. surcharges. Surch as T 104.*

(a) On air stamps of 1932–37. P 14

818	**61**	$53 on 15 c. blue-green	8	10
819		$73 on 25 c. orange	50·00	50·00

(b) On air stamps of 1940–41. P 12–13

(i) No wmk

820	**61**	$23 on 30 c. scarlet	5	5
		a. Surch inverted	25·00	
		b. Value omitted	10·00	

821	61	$53 on 15 c. blue-green	..	..	5	5
		a. Imperf between (horiz pair)	..		—	£100
822		$73 on 25 c. orange	..	..	5	5
		a. Surch inverted ..	..	..	85·00	
823		$100 on $2 brown	..	..	5	5
824		$200 on $5 lake	..	..	5	5
		a. Surch inverted ..	..	..	14·00	

(ii) W 73

825	61	$23 on 30 c. scarlet	..	..	5	5
826		$53 on 15 c. blue-green	..	..	45	50
827		$73 on 25 c. orange..	..	..	5	5
828		$100 on $2 brown	..	..	5	5
829		$200 on $5 lake	..	..	5	5
820/829		Set of 10	..	..	80	85

貳 國 念 國
仟 幣 圓 幣
圓 [2000] 圓 [2000]

(105)   (106) Octagonal box,   107 Dr. Sun
Chequered box   Zeros underlined   Yat-sen

(Surch by Union Press, Shanghai)

1946 (May)—**48.** C.N.C. surcharges. Various stamps surch as T 105.

A. Sun Yat-sen issue of 1931–37 (No. 396)

| 830 | 58 | $1,000 on 2 c. olive-green (8.46) | .. | 5 | 5 |

B. Third Sun Yat-sen issue
(a) Chung Hwa. Die III (Nos. 464 etc)

831	72	$20 on 3 c. brown-lake (10.46)	..	5	5
832		$50 on 3 c. brown-lake (12.46)	..	5	5
833		$50 on 5 c. olive-green	..	5	5
834		$100 on 3 c. brown-lake (10.46)	..	5	5
835		$100 on 8 c. sage-green (C) (2.47)	15	5
836		$100 on 8 c. sage-green (D)	..	5	5
837		$200 on 10 c. green (12.47)	..	5	5
838		$300 on 10 c. green (12.47)	..	5	5
839		$500 on 3 c. brown-lake (7.46)	..	5	5

(b) Dah Tung (i) No wmk

840	72	$50 on 5 c. olive (F) (2.47)	..	15	12
841		$100 on 8 c. sage-green (E)	..	15	15
842		$100 on 8 c. sage-green (F)	..	5	5
843		$200 on 10 c. green (2.47)	..	5	5

(ii) W 73

| 844 | 72 | $50 on 5 c. green (F) | .. | 5 | 5 |
| 845 | | $50 on 5 c. olive (F) | .. | 5 | 5 |

C. Martyrs types, Hong Kong printings
(a) No wmk

846	60	$20 on 8 c. brown-orange (10.46)	..	5	5
847		$50 on 5 c. red-orange	..	5	5
848		$100 on 1 c. yellow-orange (508) ..	5	5
		a. Without secret mark (b)	..	8·00	5·00

(b) W 73

| 849 | 60 | $50 on 5 c. red-orange | .. | 5 | 5 |
| 850 | | $100 on 1 c. yellow-orange | .. | 5 | 5 |

D. Fourth Sun Yat-sen issue

851	77	$50 on 5 c. green (5.46)	..	5	5
852		$100 on 8 c. turquoise-green (2.47)	5	5
853		$300 on 10 c. emerald-green (8.46)	5	5

E. Fifth Sun Yat-sen issue

854	82	$50 on $1 olive-green	..	5	5
855		$250 on $1.50 bright blue..	..	5	5
856		$1,000 on $2 blue-green	..	5	5
		a. Imperf (pair)	..	..	5	
857		$1,000 on $2 blue (2.47)	..	8	5
		a. Imperf between (pair)	..		
858		$1,000 on $2 purple-brown (12.47) ..	5	
		a. Imperf (pair)..	..	..	45	80
		b. Imperf between (pair)	..	3·50	
859		$2,000 on $5 carmine	..	5	5

F. Sun Yat-sen issue of 1944–46 (Nos. 735, etc)

860	58	$100 on $1 violet (4.47)	..	5	5
861		$200 on $4 blue* (1.47)	..	5	5
862		$250 on $2 olive-green (5.47)	..	5	5
863		$250 on $5 red* (1.47)	..	5	5
864		$500 on $20 apple-green	..	5	5
865		$800 on $30 chocolate	..	5	5

G. Seventh Sun Yat-sen issue (Nos. 758/9)

| 866 | 94 | $1,000 on $2 green (6.48) | .. | 15 | 8 |
| 867 | | $2,000 on $5 blue-green (R.) (2.48) .. | 5 | 5 |

H. Ninth Sun Yat-sen issue

| 868 | 107 | $100 on $20 carmine (6.47) | .. | 5 | 5 |

*Nos. 861 and 863 were not issued without surcharge.

(Surch by Central Trust, Chungking)

1946 (July)—**47.** C.N.C. surcharges. Various stamps surch as T 106.

A. Third Sun Yat-sen issue
(a) Chung Hwa. Die III

869	72	$20 on 8 c. sage-green (C)	..	5	5
870		$20 on 8 c. sage-green (D)	..	5	5
		a. Surch double	..	..	1·50	
871		$50 on 5 c. green	..	5	5
872		$50 on 5 c. olive-green	..	5	5
		a. Surch inverted	..	..	2·25	
		b. Surch double	..	..	3·00	2·75

(b) Dah Tung (i) No wmk

873	72	$20 on 8 c. sage-green (E)	..	25	30
		a. Surch inverted	..	..	2·25	
874		$20 on 8 c. sage-green (F)	..	5	5
		a. Surch inverted	..	..	1·75	
		b. Surch double	..	..	2·25	
		c. Vert pair, one without surch	..		
		d. Error. On 5 c. green (F)	..	42·00	
875		$50 on 5 c. green (F) (1.10.46)	..	5	5
876		$50 on 5 c. olive (F)	..	5	5

(ii) W 73

| 877 | 72 | $50 on 5 c. green (F) | .. | 5 | 5 |
| 878 | | $50 on 5 c. olive (F) | .. | 5 | 5 |

B. Martyrs types, Hong Kong printings
(a) No wmk

879	60	$20 on 8 c. brown-orange (5.47)	..	5	5
880		$50 on 5 c. red-orange (10.46)	..	5	5
		a. Surch inverted	..	..	3·00	
		b. Surch double	..	..	2·50	

(b) W 73

| 881 | 60 | $20 on 8 c. brown-orange | .. | 6·00 | 6·00 |

C. Fourth Sun Yat-sen issue

882	77	$20 on 8 c. red-orange	..	5	5
883		$20 on 8 c. turquoise-green ..	..	5	5
		a. Surch inverted	..	..	1·25	
		b. Surch double	..	..	1·40	
		c. Surch double, both inverted	..	1·90	
		d. "0" of "20" omitted	..	70	
884		$50 on 5 c. green	..	..	5	5
		a. Surch double, one diagonal	..	2·00	

(Recess Dah Tung Book Co, Shanghai)

1946 (23 July)—**47.** Sun Yat-sen (Ninth issue). No gum. P 14.

885	107	$20 carmine (23.7.46)	..	..	5	5
		a. Imperf vert (horiz pair)	..	3·75	
886		$30 deep blue (1947)	..	..	5	5
887		$50 slate-violet (12.46)	..	..	5	5
		a. Imperf vert (horiz pair)	..	5·00	
888		$70 red-orange (1947)	..	..	8	10
889		$100 crimson (12.46)	..	..	5	5
890		$200 green (1947)..	..	..	5	5
891		$500 blue-green (12.46)	..	..	5	5
892		$700 red-brown (12.46)	..	..	8	10
893		$1,000 claret (12.46)	..	..	5	5
894		$3,000 blue (12.46)	..	..	20	5
895		$5,000 vermilion and green (12.46)	..	30	5
885/895		Set of 11	..	..	90	55

拾 國
圓 [10.00] 幣

(108) Octagonal   109 Aeroplane over
box, Zeros not   Mausoleum of Dr. Sun Yat-sen
underlined

(Surch by Dah Tung Book Co, Chungking)

1946 (Sept–Oct). *C.N.C. surcharges. Surch as T 108, in blue or red (R.).*

A. *Third Sun Yat-sen issue. Chung Hwa. Die III*

896	72	$20 on 2 c. olive-green (B) (R.)			5	5
		a. Surch double			2·50	
		b. Surch double, both inverted			5·00	
897		$20 on 3 c. brown-lake			5	5

B. *Martyrs types, Hong Kong printings*
(a) *No wmk*

898	60	$10 on 1 c. yellow-orange			5	5
		a. Surch inverted			1·25	1·25
		b. Without secret mark (b)			80	80
899		$20 on 3 c. brown			5	5
		a. Surch double			3·00	
900		$30 on 4 c. lilac (R.)			5	5
		a. Surch inverted			2·00	
		b. Surch double			2·25	

(b) *W 73*

901	60	$10 on 1 c. yellow-orange			5	5
		a. Surch inverted			3·25	
902		$20 on 3 c. brown			38·00	23·00

C. *Fourth Sun Yat-sen issue (Oct)*

903	77	$10 on 1 c. orange			5	5
		a. Surch inverted			1·25	
904		$20 on 2 c. ultramarine (R.)			5	5
		a. Surch inverted			1·50	
		b. Surch double			1·40	

(Litho Dah Tung Book Co, Shanghai)

1946 (10 Sept). *AIR. No gum. P 14.*

905	109	$27 blue			5	5

110 Pres. Chiang Kai-shek   **111** National Assembly House, Nanking

1946 (31 Oct). *President's 60th Birthday. Recess.*

A. *P 10½–11½. With or without gum (Dah Yeh Printing Co, Shanghai)*

B. *P 14. No gum (Dah Tung Book Co, Shanghai)*

			A		B	
906	110	$20 carmine	5	5	5	5
		a. Imperf vert (horiz pair)	—	—		†
907		$30 grey-green	5	5	5	5
908		$50 vermilion	5	5	5	5
909		$100 yellow-green	5	5	5	5
		a. Imperf vert (horiz pair)	—	—		†
910		$200 yellow-orange	5	5	5	5
911		$300 claret	8	8	10	8
907/911		*Set of 6*	25	25	30	25

(Litho Dah Tung Book Co, Shanghai)

1946 (15 Nov). *Opening of National Assembly, Nanking. No gum. P 14.*

912	111	$20 green			5	5
913		$30 blue			5	5
914		$50 chocolate			5	5
915		$100 carmine			5	5
912/915		*Set of 4*			12	12

D 9   **P 3**   **112** Entrance to Dr. Sun Yat-sen Mausoleum

(Litho Dah Tung Book Co, Shanghai)

1947 (Jan). *POSTAGE DUE. No gum. P 14.*

D916	D 9	$50 dull purple			5	5
D917		$80 dull purple			5	5
D918		$100 dull purple			5	5
D919		$160 dull purple			5	5
D920		$200 dull purple			5	5
D921		$400 dull purple			5	5
D922		$500 dull purple			5	5
D923		$800 dull purple			5	5
D924		$2,000 dull purple			5	5
D916/924		*Set of 9*			30	30

(Recess Central Trust, Peking)

1947–48. *PARCELS POST. Type P 3 and similar type without inner frame (Nos. P931/8). No gum. P 13½.*

P925		$1,000 yellow			—	5
P926		$3,000 blue-green			—	5
P927		$5,000 orange-red			—	5
P928		$7,000 dull blue			—	5
P929		$10,000 deep carmine			—	5
P930		$30,000 olive-green			—	5
P931		$50,000 blue-black			—	5
P932		$70,000 red-brown			—	5
P933		$100,000 purple			—	5
P934		$200,000 dark green			—	5
P935		$300,000 pink			—	5
P936		$500,000 plum			—	5
P937		$3,000,000 slate-blue (9.48)			—	5
P938		$5,000,000 grey-lilac (9.48)			—	5
P939		$6,000,000 grey (9.48)			—	8
P940		$8,000,000 vermilion (9.48)			—	8
P941		$10,000,000 sage-green (9.48)			—	12
P925/941		*Set of 17*			—	85

Noughts for "cents" are omitted on Nos P935/9.
The note after No. P716 also applies here.

(Recess Central Trust, Peking)

1947 (5 May). *First Anniv of return of Government to Nanking. P 14.*

942	112	$100 green			5	5
943		$200 blue			5	5
944		$250 carmine			5	5
945		$350 yellow-brown			5	5
946		$400 purple			5	5
942/946		*Set of 5*			20	20

113 Dr. Sun Yat-sen   **114** Confucius   **115** Confucius's Lecture School

116 Tomb of Confucius   **117** Confucian Temple

(Recess De La Rue)

1947 (23 May). *Sun Yat-sen (Tenth issue). P 11½ to 13½.*

947	113	$500 olive-green			5	5
948		$1,000 scarlet and green			5	5
949		$2,000 red-brown and blue			5	5
950		$5,000 black and red-orange			5	5
947/950		*Set of 4*			15	15

(T **114** litho, others recess Dah Tung Book Co, Shanghai)

1947 (27 Aug–17 Oct). *Commemorating Confucius. No gum. P 14.*

951	114	$500 carmine			5	5
952	115	$800 brown (17.10)			5	5
953	116	$1,250 green (17.10)			5	5
954	117	$1,800 blue (17.10)			5	5
951/954		*Set of 4*			15	15

118 Dr. Sun Yat-sen and Plum Blossoms

119 Map of Taiwan and Chinese Flag

(120) Box with Diamond Pattern

(Recess Dah Tung Book Co, Shanghai)

1947 (17 Oct)–48. *Sun Yat-sen (Eleventh issue). With two small underlined noughts indicating cents. No gum.* P 14.

955	118	$150 indigo	..	..	5	5
956		$250 slate-violet		..	5	5
957		$500 green	..	..	5	5
958		$1,000 scarlet	..	..	5	5
959		$2,000 red-orange	..	..	5	5
960		$3,000 blue	..	..	5	5
961		$4,000 grey (20.1.48)	..	..	5	5
962		$5,000 brown	..	..	5	5
963		$6,000 bright purple (7.2.48)			5	5
964		$7,000 red-brown (30.3.48)			5	5
965		$10,000 carmine and blue	..		5	5
966		$20,000 green and carmine		..	5	5
967		$50,000 indigo and green ..		..	5	5
968		$100,000 yell-grn & orge (31.3.48)		..	5	5
969		$200,000 blue and purple (31.3.48)			5	5
970		$300,000 orange-brown and sepia (31.3.48)		..	15	10
971		$500,000 sepia and slate-green (31.3.48)	..	..	20	15
955/971		*Set of 17*	..	..	90	80

For similar stamps, but without noughts for cents, see Nos. 1032/43.

(Recess Central Trust, Peking)

1947 (25 Oct). *Second Anniv of Restoration of Taiwan (Formosa).* P 14.

972	119	$500 carmine	..	..	5	5
973		$1,250 green	..	..	5	5

Nos. 972/3 were also issued in Taiwan.

(Surch by Dah Yeh Printing Co, Shanghai)

1947 (25 Oct)–48. *C.N.C. surcharges. Various stamps surch as T* **120.**

A. *Fifth Sun Yat-sen issue*
(a) *Central Trust, Chungking*

974	82	$2,000 on $3 yellow (4.48)	..	..	5	5

(b) *Paicheng Printing Co, Nanping*

975	82	$3,000 on $3 yellow (5.2.48)	..	..	5	5

B. *Sixth Sun Yat-sen issue*

976	89	$2,000 on $3 scarlet (5.11.47)		..	5	5
		a. *Pale orange-red*	..	..	15	12
977		$3,000 on $3 grey-brown (G.)		..	5	5
		a. Surch double	..	..	2·25	

C. *Sun Yat-sen issue of 1946 (No. 737)*

978	58	$500 on $20 apple-green ..		..	5	5
		a. Surch double	..	..	1·50	

D. *Ninth Sun Yat-sen issue*

979	107	$1,250 on $70 red-orange	..		5	5

E. *Eleventh Sun Yat-sen issue*

980	118	$1,800 on $350 yellow-ochre*		..	5	5
974/980		*Set of 7*	..	..	30	30

* No. 980 without surcharge was not issued.

121 Mobile Post Office

122 Postal Kiosk

(Recess Central Trust, Peking)

1947 (5 Nov). *Progress of the Postal Service.* P 14.

981	121	$500 carmine	..	..	5	5
982	122	$1,000 lilac	..	..	5	5
983		$1,250 green	..	..	5	5
984	121	$1,800 blue ..	..	..	5	5
981/984		*Set of 4*	..	..	15	15

123 Air, Sea and Rail Transport

124 Postboy and Motor Van

125 Junk and Aeroplane

126 Book of the Constitution and National Assembly Building

(Recess American Bank Note Co, N.Y.)

1947 (16 Dec). *50th Anniv of Directorate General of Posts.* P 12.

985	123	$100 violet	..	..	5	5
986	124	$200 emerald-green	..	..	5	5
987		$300 lake-brown	..	..	5	5
988	125	$400 scarlet ..	..	..	5	5
989		$500 ultramarine	..	..	5	5
985/989		*Set of 5*	..	..	20	20

(Recess Dah Tung Book Co, Shanghai)

1947 (25 Dec). *Adoption of the Constitution. No gum.* P 14.

990	126	$2,000 vermilion	..	..	5	5
991		$3,000 blue ..	..	..	5	5
992		$5,000 green	..	..	5	5
990/992		*Set of 3*	..	..	10	10

(D 10)

(Stamps recess De La Rue. Surch by Dah Yeh Printing Co, Shanghai)

1948 (8 Mar). POSTAGE DUE. *As Type D* **8,** *but redrawn and surch as Type D* **10.** *P* 13½ × 14.

D993	D 8	$1,000 on $20 purple	..	..	5	5
D994		$2,000 on $30 purple ..		..	5	5
D995		$3,000 on $50 purple ..		..	5	5
D996		$4,000 on $100 purple	..	..	5	5
D997		$5,000 on $200 purple	..	..	5	5
D998		$10,000 on $300 purple		..	5	5
D999		$20,000 on $500 purple		..	5	5
D1000		$30,000 on $1,000 purple		..	5	5
D993/1000		*Set of 8*	..	..	30	30

Nos. D993/1000 were not issued without surcharge.

127 Reproductions of 1947 and 1912 Stamps

128 Sun Yat-sen Memorial Hall

(Litho Dah Yeh Printing Co, Shanghai)

1948. *Philatelic Exhibitions. No gum. P* 14.

    (a) Nanking Philatelic Exhibition (20 March)

| 1001 | **127** | $5,000 claret | .. | .. | .. | 5 | 5 |
| | | a. Imperf | .. | .. | | 5 | 8 |

    (b) Shanghai Philatelic Exhibition (19 May)

| 1002 | **127** | $5,000 blue-green .. | | .. | | 5 | 8 |
| | | a. Imperf | .. | .. | | 8 | 15 |

(Recess Central Trust, Peking)

1948 (28 Apr). *Third Anniv of Restoration of Taiwan (Formosa) to Chinese Rule. P* 14.

| 1003 | **128** | $5,000 lilac | .. | .. | | 5 | 5 |
| 1004 | | $10,000 vermilion .. | | .. | | 5 | 5 |

圓仟伍作改 ☆

圓仟肆作改 ☆
               ☆

5000.00 (129)

400.00 ☆☆ (130)

圓仟伍萬壹作改

圓仟伍萬壹作改

15000 (131)

15000 (132)

1948 (Apr–Oct). *"Re-valuation" surcharges. No gum. Various stamps surcharged.*

A. POSTAGE

(i) *Surch as T* **129** *by Union Press of Chung Hwa Book Co, Shanghai* (Apr–Oct)

1005	**82**	$5,000 on $1 olive-grn (636) (Aug)	5	5
1006		$5,000 on $1 olive-grn (643) (Oct)	25	25
1007		$5,000 on $2 blue-grn (638) (Apr)	5	5
1008	**102**	$10,000 on 20 c. carmine (May) ..	5	5
1009	**82**	$20,000 on 10 c. green (July) ..	5	5
1010		$20,000 on 50 c. grey-green (R.) (Aug)	5	5
1011		$30,000 on 30 c. orange-red (Aug)	5	5
1005/1011		*Set of 7* ..	45	45

(ii) *Surch as T* **130** *by Dah Yeh Printing Co, Shanghai* (May–Aug)

1012	**118**	$4,000 on $100 deep carmine* (Aug)	8	5
1013		$5,000 on $100 deep carmine* ..	8	5
1014		$8,000 on $700 red-brown* (July)	8	5

*Nos. 1012/4 were not issued without surcharge.

(iii) *Surch as T* **131** *by Dah Yeh Printing Co, Shanghai* (Aug–Sept)

1015	**82**	$15,000 on 50 c. grey-green ..	5	5
1016		$40,000 on 20 c. grey-olive (Sept)	5	5
1017		$60,000 on $4 brown (640) (Sept) ..	10	5

(iv) *Surch as T* **132** *by Dah Yeh Printing Co, Shanghai* (Aug–Sept)

1018	**82**	$15,000 on 10 c. green ..	8	5
1019		$15,000 on $4 brown (640) (Sept) ..	8	5
1020		$15,000 on $6 violet-blue (Sept) ..	8	5

改作壹萬圓

10000.00 (134)

B. AIR

Surch by Dah Yeh Printing Co, Shanghai (18 May)

    (i) *As T* **133**

    (a) On 1932–37 issue

| 1021 | **61** | $50,000 on $1 yellow-green (R.) .. | 1·25 | 1·40 |

    (b) On 1940–41 issue

    W **72**

1022	**61**	$10,000 on 30 c. vermilion	..	5	5
1023		$20,000 on 25 c. orange	..	5	5
1024		$30,000 on 90 c. olive (R.) ..		5	5
1025		$50,000 on 60 c. blue (R.)	..	5	5
1026		$50,000 on $1 apple-green (R.)	..	5	5

    No wmk

| 1027 | **61** | $10,000 on 30 c. vermilion | | 5 | 5 |

    (ii) *As T* **134** *on 1946 issue*

| 1028 | **109** | $10,000 on $27 blue | .. | .. | 5 | 5 |
| 1021/1028 | | *Set of 8* .. | .. | | 1·40 | 1·50 |

135 Great Wall of China   **136** Dr. Sun Yat-sen and Plum Blossoms

(Litho Dah Yeh Printing Co, Shanghai)

1948 (5 July). *Tuberculosis Relief Fund. Cross in red. No gum. P* 14.

1029	**135**	$5,000 + $2,000 violet	..	..	5	50
		a. Imperf	..	..	5	50
		b. Imperf between (pair)	..		
1030		$10,000 + $2,000 pale brown		5	50
		a. Imperf	..	..	5	50
		b. Imperf between (horiz pair)		5·00	
1031		$15,000 + $2,000 grey	..	..	5	50
		a. Imperf	..	..	5	50
1029/1031		*Set of 3 (perf or imperf)* ..	∴	12	1·25

(Recess Dah Tung Book Co, Shanghai)

1948 (23 July–Sept). *Sun Yat-sen (Twelfth issue). Without noughts for cents. No gum. P* 14.

1032	**136**	$20,000 rose-carmine	..	..	5	5
1033		$30,000 chocolate	..	..	5	5
1034		$40,000 blue-green	..	..	5	5
1035		$50,000 slate-blue	..	..	5	5
1036		$100,000 sage-green (11.9)	..	5	5
1037		$200,000 purple (11.9)	..	5	5
1038		$300,000 apple-green (11.9)	..	5	5
1039		$500,000 mauve (11.9)	..	5	5
1040		$1,000,000 claret	..	..	10	5
1041		$2,000,000 red-orange	..	8	5
1042		$3,000,000 bistre (11.9)	..	8	5
1043		$5,000,000 ultramarine (11.9)	..	20	10
1032/1043		*Set of 12* ..	..	..	75	60

For similar stamps and with noughts for cents, see Nos. 955/71.

改作壹萬圓

(133)

伍 國
千
圓 5000 幣

137 S.S. *Hai Tien*
and Steamship
of 1872

138 S.S. *Kiang Ya* (138*a*)

(Recess Dah Tung Book Co, Shanghai)

1948 (18 Aug). *75th Anniv of China Merchants' Steam Navigation Company. No gum.* P 14.

1044	**137**	$20,000 blue	..	5	5
1045		$30,000 mauve	..	5	5
1046	**138**	$40,000 yellow-brown	..	5	5
1047		$60,000 vermilion ..	..	5	5
1044/1047		*Set of 4*	..	15	15

1948 (29 Sept). *Kwangsi provisional. C.N.C. surcharge. No. 889 surch at Kweilin with T 138a.*

1048	**107**	$5,000 on $100 crimson	..	30	35

Currency Revaluation
100 Cents = 1 Gold Yuan

On 19 August 1948 the gold yuan replaced legal tender notes at the rate of 1 gold yuan to 3 million dollars and until the following surcharges appeared current stamps were sold on this basis.

金 壹 金
圓 圓 圓

$\frac{1}{2}$分 **3**分 金圓角10圓

(139) (140) (141)

(Surcharged by numerous printers)

1948–49. *Various stamps of 1938–48 variously surch with Gold Yuan values.*

(*a*) As T 139/40

1049	**82**	½ c. on 30 c. orange-red (632) (7.10.48)	..	5	5
1050	**118**	½ c. on $500 green (7.10.48)	..	5	5
		a. Red surch (12.10.48) ..	..	5	
1051	**107**	1 c. on $20 carmine (7.10.48)	..	5	5
		a. Surch double ..	..	1·60	
1052	**82**	2 c. on $1.50, blue (R.) (7.10.48)	..	5	5
1053		3 c. on $5 carm (641) (7.10.48)	..	5	5
1054		4 c. on $1 lake (7.10.48)	..	5	5
1055		5 c. on 50 c. grey-grn (7.10.48)	..	5	5

(*b*) As T 141

1056	**89**	5 c. on $20 rose-red (12.10.48)	..	5	5
1057	**102**	5 c. on $30 dp blue (R.) (7.10.48)	..	5	5
		a. Surch double ..	..	1·50	
1058	**72**	10 c. on 2 c. olive-green (B) (463) (7.10.48)	..	5	5
1059	**60**	10 c. on 2½ c. clar (510) (7.10.48)	..	5	5
		a. Surch inverted ..	..	1·10	
		b. Surch double ..	..	40	
1060		10 c. on 2½ c. clar (529) (7.10.48)		5	5
1061	**82**	10 c. on 25 c. purple-brown (9.10.48)	..	5	5
1062	**89**	10 c. on 40 c. brn-lake (9.10.48)	..	5	5
1063	**82**	10 c. on $1 ol-grn (636) (12.10.48)	..	5	5
		a. Surch double ..	..	25	
1064		10 c. on $1 ol-grn (643) (1948)	..	2·25	2·25
1065	**89**	10 c. on $2 pale brown (9.10.48)	..	5	5
1066	**82**	10 c. on $20 blue (R.) (7.10.48)	..	5	5
1067	**89**	10 c. on $20 rose-red	..	3·75	3·75
1068	**94**	10 c. on $20 scarlet (12.10.48)	..	5	5
		a. Surch inverted ..	..	40	
		b. Surch double ..	..	30	
1069	**107**	10 c. on $20 carmine (12.10.48)	..	5	5

1070	**102**	10 c. on $30 dp blue (R.) (9.10.48) ..		5	5
1071	**89**	10 c. on $70 violet (7.10.48) ..		5	5
		a. Surch double ..	..	1·60	
1072	**118**	10 c. on $7,000 red-brown (7 *mm* wide) (12.48)		5	5
		a. Opt 9 mm wide			
1073	**136**	10 c. on $20,000 rose-carmine (7.12.48)		5	5
		a. Surch double ..	..	40	
1074	**89**	20 c. on $6 pale purple (7.10.48)		5	5
		a. Surch double ..	..	50	
1075	**58**	20 c. on $30 chocolate (7.10.48)	..	5	5
1076	**107**	20 c. on $30 dp blue (R.) (7.10.48) ..		5	5
1077		20 c. on $100 crimson (7.12.48)	..	5	5
		a. Surch inverted ..	..	1·50	
		b. "0" of "20" omitted ..			
1078	**60**	50 c. on ½ c. sepia (410)	..	1·10	1·75
1079		50 c. on ½ c. sepia (507) (12.10.48)		5	5
		a. Surch inverted ..	..	2·50	
		b. Surch double ..	..	75	
1080	**82**	50 c. on ½ c. sepia (526) (12.10.48)		5	5
		a. Surch double ..	..	35	
1081		50 c. on 20 c. grey-ol (12.10.48)		5	5
1082		50 c. on 30 c. orange-red (632) (B.) (9.10.48)		5	5
1083		50 c. on 40 c. red-brn (B.) (9.10.48)		5	5
1084	**89**	50 c. on 40 c. brn-lake (B.) (9.10.48)		5	5
1085	**82**	50 c. on $4 brown-purple (648) (12.10.48)		5	5
		a. Blue surch (9.10.48) ..		5	5
1086		50 c. on $20 blue (R.) (9.10.48)		5	5
1087	**94**	50 c. on $20 scarlet (B.) (9.10.48)		5	5
1088	**107**	50 c. on $20 carmine (12.10.48)		5	5
1089	**82**	50 c. on $70 dp lilac (R.) (12.10.48)		5	5
1090	**118**	50 c. on $6,000 brt purple (12.48)		5	5
		a. Blue surch (12.48) ..		5	5
1091	**82**	$1 on 30 c. brown (642) (12.10.48)		5	5
		a. Surch inverted ..	..	90	
1092		$1 on 40 c. red-brn (9.10.48)	..	5	5
1093	**89**	$1 on $1 lake (12.10.48) ..		5	5
1094		$1 on $5 carmine (649) (12.10.48)		5	5
1095	**89**	$2 on $2 pale brown (R.) (9.10.48)		5	5
1096	**102**	$2 on $20 carmine (12.10.48)	..	5	5
1097	**107**	$2 on $100 crimson (12.10.48)		5	5
1098	**60**	$5 on 17 c. bronze-green (518) (12.10.48)		5	5
1099	**89**	$5 on $2 pale brn (9.10.48)	..	5	5
1100	**118**	$5 on $3,000 blue (R.) (12.10.48)		5	5
		a. Surch double ..	..	90	
1101	**60**	$8 on 20 c. (519) (12.10.48)	..	5	5
1102	**136**	$8 on $30,000 chocolate (R.) (12.10.48)		5	5
1103	**60**	$10 on 40 c. orange (524) (12.10.48)		5	5
1104	**89**	$10 on $2 pale brown (R.) (12.10.48)		5	5
		a. Surch inverted ..	..	1·40	
		b. Green surch (9.10.48) ..		5	5
1105		$20 on $2 pale brown (C.) (9.10.48)		5	5
1106	**107**	$20 on $20 carmine (12.10.48)		5	5
1107	**82**	$50 on 30 c. orange-red (632) (12.10.48)		5	5
1108	**89**	$50 on $2 pale brown (B.) (9.10.48)		5	5
1109	**107**	$80 on $20 carm (12.10.48)		5	5
1110	**82**	$100 on $1 olive-green (643) (12.10.48)		5	5
1111	**89**	$100 on $2 pale brown (R.) (9.10.48)		5	5
1112	**136**	$20,000 on $40,000 blue-green (R.) (30.4.49)		10	12
		a. Error "$10,000" for "$20,000"	..	4·45	
1113		$50,000 on $20,000 rose-carmine (9.10.48)		5	5
1114		$50,000 on $30,000 choc (30.4.49)		12	15
		a. Surch double ..	..	1·00	
1115		$100,000 on $20,000 rose-carmine (30.4.49)		12	12
1116		$100,000 on $30,000 chocolate (B.) (9.10.48)		5	5

1117	**136** $200,000 on $40,000 blue-green (R.)			
	(30.4.49)	.. ..	12	15
	a. Surch double ..		1·25	
1118	$200,000 on $50,000 slate-blue (R.)			
	(30.4.49)	.. ..	12	15
1049/1118	*Set of 70* ..	.. ..	9·00	9·50

No. 1072 was issued in Kiangsu; Nos. 1073 and 1077 at Chengtu and nos. 1112, 1113/4 and 1117/8 at Foochow.

Nos. 830 and 975 further surch 10 c. and 40 c. respectively, in red, were prepared in Kiyang, Hunan, but not officially issued.

金圓貳佰圓 200⁰⁰ 改作郵票

(142)

(Surch by San Yih Printing Press Co, Shanghai)

1948 (17 Dec). *Nos. P814/6 surch as T 142 for use as ordinary stamps.*

1119	**P 2** $200 on $3,000 red-orange	.. ..	5	5
1120	$500 on $5,000 indigo (R.)	.. ..	5	5
1121	$1,000 on $10,000 violet	.. ..	5	5
1119/1121	*Set of 3* ..	.. ..	10	10

143 Ship, Train and Aeroplane

$20

(a)

(b)

$50

(c)   (d)   (e)

$30 $100   & $300

(f)   (g)   (h)   (i)

There are many differences other than those illustrated by (a) to (i) distinguishing the work of each of the printers.

Nos. 1144/6

I Normal   II Retouched Plate

1949 (Jan). *Gold Yuan surcharges. Revenue stamps T 143, from various printers, surch as T 144. No gum. Various perfs 12½ to 14.*

	(i) Litho. Dah Tung Book Co, Shanghai			
1122	50 c. on $20 red-brown (a)	..	5	5
1123	$2 on $50 blue (c) (R.) ..		5	5
1124	$200 on $50 blue	..	5	5
1125	$300 on $50 blue (c) (R.) ..		5	5
1126	$1,500 on $50 blue (B.)	..	5	5
	(ii) Litho. Dah Yeh Printing Co, Shanghai			
1127	$2 on $50 blue (d) (R.) ..		5	5
1128	$3 on $50 blue (d) (R.)	..	5	5
1129	$10 on $50 mauve (f) (B.)	..	5	5
	a. Surch double	..	45	
1130	$80 on $50 blue (P.)	..	5	5
1131	$100 on $50 blue (d)	..	5	5
1132	$300 on $50 blue (Br.)	..	5	8
1133	$300 on $50 blue (d) (R.) ..		5	5
1134	$500 on $30 mauve	..	5	8
1135	$1,000 on $50 blue (R.)	..	12	12
	(iii) Litho. Central Trust, Shanghai			
1136	50 c. on $20 red-brown (b)	..	5	5
1137	$1 on $15 red-orange	..	5	45
1138	$5 on $500 chocolate	..	5	5
1139	$10 on $30 mauve (g) (B.)	..	5	5
1140	$15 on $20 red-brown (B.)	..	5	5
1141	$25 on $20 red-brown (G.)	..	5	5
1142	$200 on $500 chocolate (B.)	..	5	5
1143	$500 on $15 red-orange (B.)	..	5	5
	(iv) Litho. Chung Ming Co			
1144	$3 on $50 dark blue (I) ..	..	5	5
	a. Surch double	..	30	
	b. Type II	..	25	
1145	$50 on $50 dark blue (I) (R.)	..	5	5
	a. Surch double	..	30	
	b. Type II	..	20	
1146	$100 on $50 dark blue (e) (I)	..	5	5
	a. Type II			
	(v) Recess. Dah Tung Book Co, Shanghai			
1147	$50 on $300 green (h) (R.)	..	5	5
1148	$1,000 on $100 olive (h)	..	35	35
	(vi) Recess. Dah Yeh Printing Co, Shanghai			
1149	$50 on $300 green (i) (R.)	..	5	5
	a. Surch double	..	35	
1150	$1,000 on $100 olive (i)	..	25	30
1151	$2,000 on $300 green (i) (B.)	..	8	8
	a. First character in bottom row repeated in 2nd position	..		
1122/1151	*Set of 30* ..	.. ..	1·60	1·90

A $5,000 on $100 olive, recess-ptd by Dah Tung, with red opt, was prepared for use but not issued. (*Price £4.25 un.*)

145 Dr. Sun Yat-sen

1949 (Jan–Apr). *Sun Yat-sen (Thirteenth issue). T 145. No gum.*

	(a) Recess. Dah Tung Book Co, Shanghai. P 14 (6 Jan)			
1152	$1 orange	.. ..	5	5
1153	$10 green	.. ..	5	5
1154	$20 brown-purple	.. ..	5	5
1155	$50 slate-green	.. ..	5	5
1156	$100 chestnut	.. ..	5	5
1157	$200 vermilion	.. ..	5	5
1158	$500 mauve	.. ..	5	5
1159	$800 carmine	.. ..	5	5
1160	$1,000 blue ..	.. ..	5	5
1152/1160	*Set of 9* ..	..	35	35
	(b) Recess. Central Trust, Shanghai. Value re-engraved. Small letter "T" to left of necktie. P 12½ (Jan)			
1161	$10 green	..	8	10
	b. Perf 13	..	15	20
	c. Perf 14	..	25	25
1162	$20 brown-purple	..	5	5
	a. Perf 13	..	5	5
	b. Perf 14	..	25	25

(c) Litho. Dah Tung Book Co, Shanghai. P 12½ (Mar)

1163	$50 slate-green	..	..	8	25
1164	$100 brown	..	..	5	10
1165	$200 red-orange	..	..	5	8
1166	$500 mauve	..	..	5	12
1167	$1,000 blue	..	..	5	5
1168	$2,000 violet	..	..	5	5
1169	$5,000 turquoise-blue	..	..	5	5
1170	$10,000 grey-brown	..	..	5	5
1171	$20,000 apple-green	..	..	5	5
1172	$50,000 pink	..	..	5	5
1173	$80,000 brown-lake	..	..	12	20
1174	$100,000 pale blue-green	..	..	5	5
1163/1174	*Set of 12*	..	..	55	90

(d) Litho. Hwa Nam Printing Co, Chungking. Coarser impression. Shoulder at left ends in a point. P 12½ (Apr)

1175	$50 yellow-green	..	..	8	15
1176	$1,000 deep blue	..	..	8	5
1177	$5,000 carmine	..	..	8	5
1178	$10,000 dull brown	..	..	8	5
1179	$20,000 yellow-orange	..	..	8	8
1180	$50,000 bright blue	..	..	8	8
1181	$200,000 violet-blue	..	..	10	8
1182	$500,000 dull purple	..	..	15	8
1175/1182	*Set of 8*	..	..	65	55

See also Nos. 1343/51.

政郵圓民華中 政郵華民華中

(144a)   (144b)

(Litho Dah Tung Book Co, Shanghai. Surch at Hankow)

1949 (Apr). *Gold Yuan surcharges. Revenue stamps as T 143, surch as T 144 but with key pattern inverted at top and bottom. No gum. P 12½–14.*

1183	$50 on $10 grey-green	..	..	12	10
1184	$100 on $10 grey-green (B.)	..		40	40
1185	$500 on $10 grey-green	..		35	30
	a. Surch double	..		1·50	
1186	$1,000 on $10 grey-green (B.)	..		15	10
	a. Surch double	..		2·00	
1187	$5,000 on $20 red-brown (V.)	..		25	15
1188	$10,000 on $20 red-brown	..		25	15
	a. Error. Incorrect 3rd character (T 144a)				
1189	$50,000 on $20 red-brown (V.)	..		25	15
1190	$100,000 on $20 red-brown	..		35	30
1191	$500,000 on $20 red-brn (V.)	..		5·00	50
	a. Error. Incorrect 3rd character (T 144b)				
1192	$2,000,000 on $20 red-brown (G.)			22·00	11·00
1193	$5,000,000 on $20 red-brown (V.)			35·00	16·00
1183/1193	*Set of 11*	..	..	60·00	28·00

圓拾伍圓金   資欠作改

50   壹   金

圓拾伍圓金   分   圓

              1

(P 4)   (D 11)

1949. PARCELS POST. *Gold Yuan surcharges. Parcels Post stamps of 1947–48 surch as Type P 4.*

P1194	P 3	$10 on $3,000 blue-green	..	—	5
P1195		$20 on $5,000 orange-red	..	—	5
P1196		$90 on $10,000 dp carmine	..	—	5
P1197		$100 on $3,000,000 slate-bl (R.)	..	—	5
P1198		$200 on $5,000 grey-lilac	..	—	5
P1199		$500 on $1,000 yellow	..	—	5
P1200		$1,000 on $7,000 dull blue	..	—	25
P1194/1200		*Set of 7*	..	—	

The note below No. P716 also applies here.

(Surch by Union Press, Shanghai)

1949. POSTAGE DUE. *Gold Yuan surcharges. No. 796 surch as Type D 11. P 12½ or 13.*

D1201	102	1 c. on $40 orange	..	5	5
D1202		2 c. on $40 orange	..	5	5
D1203		5 c. on $40 orange	..	5	5
D1204		10 c. on $40 orange	..	5	5
D1205		20 c. on $40 orange	..	5	5

D1206	102	50 c. on $40 orange	..	5	5
D1207		$1 on $40 orange	..	5	5
D1208		$2 on $40 orange	..	5	5
D1209		$5 on $40 orange	..	5	5
D1210		$10 on $40 orange	..	5	5
D1201/1210		*Set of 10*	..	35	35

"Unit" Stamps

In March and April 1949 inflation of the Gold Yuan currency became so rapid that it was no longer possible to print stamps to keep pace with it. Stamps were therefore produced to be sold at the rate of the day for the service indicated ("Unit" stamps).

Owing to the collapse of the central administration in face of the advance of the Communist armies, stamps were overprinted by the local administrations; temporary labels were also used.

146 "Surface Transport"   **147** "Air Transport"

148 Postman on Motor-cycle   **149** Mountains

1949 (2 May–Sept). *No value indicated. Litho.*

     A. P 12½. Dah Tung Book Co (2 May)
     B. Roul. Ah Chow Ptg Co, Hong Kong (Sept)

				A		B	
1211	146	(–) Brown-orange	..	10	5	30	30
1212	147	(–) Pale blue-green	..	30	20	40	45
1213	148	(–) Magenta	..	15	20	20	40
1214	149	(–) Carmine	..	15	5	15	20
1211/1214		*Set of 4*	..	60	35	95	1·10

This was the most widely used of the "Unit" issues. Nos. 1211/4 were for use as Ordinary postage, Air mail, Express and Registration stamps respectively.

郵資巳   郵   圖
付信甲鳳   資   內
台   巳   平
             付湘   信

(150)   (151)

(1215/6 litho Central Trust, 1217 recess Ying Hua; 1218 recess Dah Tung)

1949. Anhwei Province. *Revenue stamps as T 143 optd as T 150. Issued at Feng Tai. No gum. Various perfs.*

1215	143	$20 red-brown	..	1·25	1·50
1216		$500 chocolate	..	1·25	1·50
1217		$1,000 carmine	..	1·25	1·50
		a. Opt inverted	..	5·00	
1218		$3,000 orange	..	1·25	1·50
1215/1218		*Set of 4*	..	4·50	5·50

Overprint translation: No. 1215, A.R. Fee; 1216, Express Letter Fee; 1217, Domestic Letter Fee; 1218, Registered Letter Fee.

1949. *Hunan Province. Various stamps optd as* T **151.**

1219	**107**	$30 deep blue (R.)	..	..	10	12
		a. Error. On T **102** $30 deep blue (R.)		..	2·00	2·75
1220		$100 crimson	..	..	5	10
		a. Opt inverted	..	..	2·50	
1221	**118**	$7,000 red-brown	..	..	8	30
		a. Opt inverted	..	..	2·00	
1222	**136**	$40,000 blue-green	..	..	20	25
		a. Opt inverted	..	..	3·00	
		b. Error. On T **118** $500 green		12·00	15·00
1219/1222		*Set of 4*	..	..	40	70

Overprint translation: No. 1219, Express Letter Fee; 1220, Domestic Letter Fee; 1221, Registered Letter Fee; 1222, Air Mail Fee.

The arrangement of the overprint varies, but all have the character "sheung" (Hunan) at bottom centre of Type **151**.

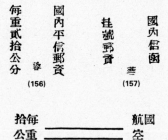

(152) **(153)** **(153a)**

1949 (May). *Kansu, Ninghsia and Chinghai Provinces. Nos.* 1211/2A *handstamped as* T **152.**

1223	**146**	(–) Brown-orange (V.)	..	25·00	45·00
1224	**147**	(–) Pale blue-green (R.)	..	35·00	40·00

Overprint translation: "Limited to use in the Kansu Ninghsia Chinghai area".

1949 (3 May). *Kiangsi Province. Various stamps optd as* T **153.**

1225	**118**	$500 green	..	..	35	40
1226		$3,000 blue	..	..	55	65
1227		$7,000 red-brown (T **153**)	..	1·25	1·50
1228		$7,000 red-brown (T **153a**)	..	1·50	1·75
1229	**136**	$30,000 chocolate	..	..	45	60
1230		$40,000 blue-green	..	..	55	60
1231		$50,000 slate-blue	..	..	1·00	1·25
1225/1231		*Set of 7*	..	..	5·00	6·00

Overprint translation: Nos. 1225, 1227, Registered Letter Fee; 1226, Express Letter Fee; 1228, Air Mail Fee; 1229/31, Domestic Letter Fee.

(154) **(155)**

(1232, 1234 litho Dah Tung; 1233 litho Dah Yeh; 1235/7 recess Dah Tung)

1949 (May). *Kwangtung Province. Revenue stamps as* T **143** *optd as* T **154.** *Issued at Canton. No gum. Various perfs.*

1232	**143**	$10 green (P.)	..	..	55	65
1233		$30 mauve	..	..	1·00	80
1234		$50 blue (R.)	..	..	45	60
1235		$100 olive (B.)	..	..	1·50	1·50
1236		$200 purple	..	..	45	15
1237		$500 grey-green	..	..	45	30
1232/1237		*Set of 6*	..	..	4·00	3·50

Overprint translation: No. 1232, Express Letter Fee; 1233, 1236/7, Domestic Letter Fee; 1234, Registered Letter Fee; 1235, Air Mail Fee.

No. 1237 with a red overprint was prepared for use but not issued (*price $2.50 un*).

1949 (June). *Shensi Province. Various stamps optd with* T **155.**

1238	**102**	$30 deep blue (R.)	..	..	50	60
1239	**107**	$30 deep blue (R.)	..	..	50	60
1240	**118**	$250 slate-violet (R.)	..	90	1·25
1241		$500 green	..	..	30	20
		a. Opt inverted	..	..	3·00	
1242		$3,000 blue	..	..	35	35

1243	**118**	$7,000 red-brown	..	..	1·25	1·50
		a. Opt inverted	..	..	4·00	
		b. Opt double	..	..	5·00	
1238/1243		*Set of 6*	..	..	3·50	4·00

Overprint translation: Nos. 1238/9, Registered Letter Fee; 1240, Express Letter Fee; 1241/2, Domestic Letter Fee; 1243, Air Mail Fee.

(156) **(157)**

(158)

1949. *Szechwan Province. Issued at Chengtu. Various stamps overprinted.*

(a) *As* T **156** (*Domestic Letter Fee*)

1244	**118**	$150 indigo	..	..	4·50	5·00
1245		$250 slate-violet	..	..	4·50	5·00
1246		$500 green	..	..	10	15
1247		$1,000 scarlet	..	..	1·60	2·00
1248		$2,000 red-orange	..	..	8	12
1249		$3,000 blue	..	..	10	15
1250		$4,000 grey	..	..	5	8
1251		$5,000 brown	..	..	5·00	5·00
1252		$6,000 bright purple	..	5	8
1253		$7,000 red-brown	..	..	1·25	1·40
1254		$10,000 carmine and blue	..	12	15
1255	**136**	$20,000 rose-carmine	..	12	15
1256		$30,000 chocolate	..	..	10	12
1257	**118**	$50,000 indigo and green	..	8	10
1258	**136**	$50,000 slate-blue	..	..	5	5
1259	**118**	$100,000 yellow-green & orange		10	8
1260	**136**	$100,000 olive	..	..	10	15
1261	**118**	$200,000 blue and purple	..	12	15
1262	**136**	$200,000 purple	..	..	12	15
		a. Opt inverted	..	..	15	20
1263	**118**	$300,000 orange-brown & sepia		15	20
1264	**136**	$300,000 apple-green	..	20	25
1265	**118**	$500,000 sepia and slate-green		10	12
1266	**136**	$1,000,000 claret	..	..	20	25
1267		$2,000,000 red-orange	..	12	15
1268		$3,000,000 bistre	..	..	12	15
1269		$5,000,000 ultramarine	..	35	40
1244/1269		*Set of 26*	..	..	18·00	20·00

(b) *As* T **157** (*Registered Letter Fee*)

1270	**91**	$100 yellow-brown	..	2·00	2·50
1271	**102**	$100 brown	..	..	4·00	5·00
1272	**91**	$200 deep green	..	..	1·25	1·50
1273	**102**	$200 chocolate	..	..	65	80
1274	**107**	$200 green	..	..	8·00	10·00
1275		$500 blue-green	..	..	8·00	10·00
1276		$700 red-brown	..	..	9·00	12·00
1277		$5,000 vermilion and green	..	6·00	7·50
1270/1277		*Set of 8*	..	..	35·00	45·00

(c) *As* T **158** (*Air Mail Fee*)

1278	**61**	$10,000 on 30 c. verm (1022)	..	20	15
1279	**109**	$10,000 on $27 blue (1028)	..	20	20
		a. T **158** inverted	..	..	23·00	
		b. Error. On $27 (905)	..	4·75	
1280	**61**	$20,000 on 25 c. orange (1023)	..	45	45
1281		$30,000 on 90 c. olive (1024)	..	90	1·25
1282		$50,000 on 60 c. blue (1025)	..	2·75	2·75
1283		$50,000 on $1 apple-grn (1026)	..	1·25	1·25
1278/1283		*Set of 6*	..	..	5·00	5·50

Currency Revaluation
100 Cents=1 Silver Yuan

On 1 May 1949, the Gold Yuan currency, which had collapsed, was replaced by the Silver Yuan currency, based on the silver dollar.

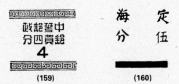

(159)   (160)

(1284/6 recess Dah Tung; 1287, 1292 litho Dah Tung; 1288 recess Central Trust; 1289 litho Central Trust; 1290/1 litho Dah Yeh)

1949 (May). *Silver Yuan surcharges. Revenue stamps as T 143 surch as T 159. No gum. Various perfs.*

1284	143	1 c. on $5,000 olive-brown (G.)	..	8	8
1285		4 c. on $100 olive (B.)	.. ..	5	5
1286		4 c. on $3,000 orange	..	5	5
1287		10 c. on $50 blue (R.)	..	5	5
1288		10 c. on $1,000 carmine	..	5	5
		a. Surch inverted	..	8·00	
1289		20 c. on $1,000 red (B.)	..	5	5
		a. Surch double	..	4·00	
1290		50 c. on $30 mauve (R.)	..	10	10
1291		50 c. on $50 blue (R.)	..	10	10
1292		$1 on $50 blue	.. ..	20	25
1284/1292		*Set of 9*	..	60	65

A 10 c. on $1,000 red stamp, lithographed by Central Trust, with black overprint was prepared for use, but not issued (*Price £4.25 un*).

1949 (June). *Chekiang Province. Silver Yuan surcharges issued on Ting Hai island. Gold Yuan stamps surch as T 160.*

1293	145	1 c. on $100,000 pale blue-green (1174)	..	15·00	15·00
1294		5 c. on $10,000 grey-brown (1170)		12·00	12·00
1295		5 c. on $10,000 grey-brown (1170)		10·00	10·00

On No. 1294 the surcharge is handstamped and on No. 1295 it is machine-printed. The overprint on No. 1293 has four characters in place of the cancelling bar.

(161)   (162)

1949 (May). *Fukien Province. Silver Yuan surcharges. Various stamps surch as T 161, handstamped on No. 1297.*

1296	118	1 c. on $500 green	..	10	25
1297		1 c. on $7,000 red-brown	..	25	15
1298	136	2 c. on $2,000,000 red-orange	..	10	8
		a. Surch double	..	2·25	
		b. Bisected (1 c.) (on cover)	—	5·00	
1299		2½ c. on $50,000 slate-blue	..	60	30
1300	107	4 c. on $100 crimson	..	10	8
1301		10 c. on $200 blue-green	..	15	12
1302	118	10 c. on $3,000 blue	..	10	8
1303		10 c. on $4,000 grey	..	25	25
1304		10 c. on $6,000 bright purple	..	10	10
1305	136	10 c. on $100,000 sage-green	..	12	12
1306		10 c. on $1,000,000 claret	..	10	10
1307		10 c. on $200,000 purple	..	35	35
1296/1307		*Set of 12*	..	2·10	1·60

All the above except No. 1297 may be found with an additional two-character "Foochow" control overprint.

1949. *Hunan Province. Silver Yuan surcharges. Various stamps such as T 162.*

1308	136	1 c. on $2,000,000 red-orange	..	25	25
		a. Surch inverted	..	1·40	
1309		2 c. on $20,000 rose-carmine	..	30	30
		a. Surch inverted	..	1·50	
1310	118	5 c. on $3,000 blue	..	35	35
		a. Surch inverted	..	1·50	
1311		10 c. on $500 green	..	40	40
1308/1311		*Set of 4*	..	1·10	1·10

(Litho Dah Tung. Surch by Fak Ning Press, Hankow)

1949. *Hupeh Province. Silver Yuan surcharges. Revenue stamps as T 143 surch as T 159 but with key pattern inverted at top and bottom. No gum. Various perfs.*

1312	143	1 c. on $20 red-brown (G.)	..	1·00	1·50
1313		10 c. on $20 red-brown	..	1·00	1·50

(163)   (164)

1949 (May). *Kwangsi Province. Silver Yuan surcharges. Various stamps surcharged.*

(a) As T 163

1314	82	5 c. on $20,000 on 10 c. green (C. or Vm.) (1009)	..	75	50
		a. T 163 double	..	1·10	85
1315		5 c. on $40,000 on 20 c. grey-olive (C. or Vm.) (1016)	..	1·10	85

(b) As T 164

1316	136	½ c. on $500,000 mauve	..	85	40
1317		1 c. on $200,000 purple	..	50	20
		a. Surch inverted	..		
1318		2 c. on $300,000 apple-green	..	1·00	1·00
1319	107	5 c. on $3,000 blue	..	45	65
1320	118	5 c. on $3,000 blue	..	30	25
1321	136	5 c. on $40,000 blue-green	..	55	30
1322		13 c. on $50,000 slate-blue	..	45	45
1323		13 c. on $50,000 slate-blue (R.)	..	1·00	80
1324	118	17 c. on $7,000 red-brown	..	35	35
1325	136	21 c. on $100,000 sage-green	..	40	40
1316/1325		*Set of 10*	..	5·00	4·25

(165)   (166)   (167)

1949 (May). *Shantung Province. Silver Yuan surcharges. Issued at Tsingtao. Gold Yuan issues such as T 165 in very fugitive inks.*

1326	145	1 c. on $100 chestnut (B.) (1156)	..	1·50	4·00
1327		4 c. on $5,000 turquoise-blue (V.)	..	1·00	1·25
1328		6 c. on $500 mauve (B.) (1166)	..	1·00	1·25
1329		10 c. on $1,000 blue (R.) (1160)	..	1·00	1·25
1326/1329		*Set of 4*	..	4·00	5·00

1949. *Szechwan Province. Silver Yuan surcharges. Issued at Chengtu.*

(a) Surch with T 166

1330	113	2 c. on $500 olive-green	..	40	60

(b) Handstamped with T 167

1331	145	2½ c. on 4 c. blue-green (V.)	..	50	75

(P 5)   (168)

171 Buddha's Tower, Peking   **172** Bronze Bull

(Recess Dah Tung Book Co, Shanghai)

1949 (20 Aug). *No gum. Rouletted. Values optd in green (15 c.) and carmine (40 c.).*

1358	171	15 c. brown		5	5
1359	172	40 c. grey-green		8	8
		a. Second and third characters of opt transposed		5·00	5·00
		b. Imperf		1·25	2·50
		c. Opt double		20·00	

(173)   (174)

1949 (Aug). *Silver Yuan Surcharges. Issued at Canton. Surch as T 173, by the Nanking Ptg Press, Canton.*

1360	145	1 c. on $100 chestnut (1156)		10	8
		a. Surch inverted		50	
1361		1 c. on $100 brown (1164)		20	20
1362		2½ c. on $500 mauve (1158)		20	10
		a. Surch inverted		65	
1363		2½ c. on $500 mauve (1166)		20	10
1364		15 c. on $10 green (1153)		75	50
		a. Surch inverted		1·50	
		b. Surch double		2·75	
1365		15 c. on $20 brown-purple (1162)		75	50
		a. Surch double		2·00	
1360/1365		*Set of 6*		2·00	

1949. *Silver Yuan surcharges. Issued at Chungking. Surch as T 174, by the Hwa Nan Ptg Press, Chungking.*

1366	145	2½ c. on $50 yellow-green (1175)		5	5
1367		2½ c. on $50,000 bright blue (1180)		5	5
1368		5 c. on $1,000 blue (R.) (1176)		8	5
1369		5 c. on $20,000 yell-orge (1179)		8	5
1370		5 c. on $200,000 vio-bl (R.) (1181)		8	5
1371		5 c. on $500,000 dull purple (1182)		8	5
1372		10 c. on $5,000 carmine (1177)		12	8
1373		10 c. on $10,000 dull brown (1178)		12	12
1374		15 c. on $200 vermilion (1157)		15	25
1375		25 c. on $100 brown (1164)		25	75
1366/1375		*Set of 10*		95	1·40

Chengtu, the last city in Nationalist hands on the Chinese mainland, fell to the Communists on 27 December 1949, a few hours after the last Nationalist Ministers escaped to Formosa, where Taipeh became their new capital. The People's Republic had been proclaimed in Peking on 1 October 1949; in April 1950 it conquered Hainan, the largest island off the Chinese coast.

1949. *PARCELS POST. Szechwan Province. Silver Yuan surcharge. Surch as Type P 5.*

P1332	P 2	1 c. on $20,000 red (P817)		3·00	2·25

Other values were prepared for use but not officially issued.

1949 (May). *Yunnan Province. Silver Yuan surcharges. Issued at Kunming. Various stamps surch as T 168.*

(a) *Values in local currency, not on a par with the rest of China*

1333	136	1 c. on $200,000 purple		20	20
1334		1.2 c. on $40,000 blue-green		60	60
1335	145	6 c. on $200 vermilion (1157)		15	8
1336		10 c. on $20,000 yell-orge (1179)		15	8
1337		12 c. on $50 slate-grn (B.) (1155)		25	8
1338		12 c. on $50 yellow-grn (B.) (1175)		25	8
1339	102	12 c. on $200 chocolate (B.)		25	25
1340	145	30 c. on $20 brown-purple (1154)		40	35
1341	136	$1.20 on $100,000 sage-green		1·10	90

(b) *Values in normal Chinese currency*

1342	145	4 c. on $20 brown-purple (1154)		10·00	10·00
1343	102	12 c. on $200 chocolate (B.)		10·00	10·00
1333/1343		*Set of 11*		21·00	20·00

(Litho Hwa Nam Printing Co, Chungking)

1949 (June). *Sun Yat-sen (Fourteenth issue). Silver Yuan currency. No gum. P 12½, 13 or compound.*

1344	145	1 c. apple-green		5	5
1345		2 c. yellow-orange		5	5
1346		4 c. blue-green		5	5
1347		10 c. deep lilac		5	5
1348		16 c. orange-red		5	5
1349		20 c. pale blue		5	5
1350		50 c. brown		25	25
1351		100 c. blue		8·00	10·00
1352		500 c. scarlet		14·00	16·00
1344/1352		*Set of 9*		17·00	17·00

169 Flying Geese over Globe   **170** Globe and Doves

(Litho Dah Tung Book Co)

1949 (June). *No gum. P 12½.*

1353	169	$1 orange		20	30
1354		$2 blue		45	50
1355		$5 red		90	1·10
1356		$10 blue-green		1·50	1·90
1353/1356		*Set of 4*		2·75	3·50

A 10 c., 16 c. and 50 c. were prepared for use, but not officially issued.

(Recess Dah Tung Book Co, Shanghai)

1949 (1 Aug). *75th Anniv of U.P.U. Value optd in black at Canton. No gum. Imperf.*

1357	170	$1 brown-orange		60	60

COMMUNIST CHINA

I. THE EARLY ISSUES

The Chinese Communist Party was founded in July 1921, and until 1927 was on good terms with the Nationalist Government of the Kuomintang; both were united against the local warlords who ruled north and central China. After Chiang Kai-shek, leader of the right wing of the Kuomintang, had taken Nanking and Shanghai from the warlords, he turned against the communists and on 12 April 1927 killed thousands of them in Shanghai. On 15 July the Communist Party was expelled from the Government and Mao Tse-tung and Chu Teh, their leaders, established themselves with small but growing forces in the Ching Kang Mountains, on the borders of Kiangsi and Hunan provinces, with smaller bases on the borders of Hunan and Hupeh and in West Fukien. Stamps were issued, inscribed "Red Postal Administration".

GUM. The following stamps are without gum.

ISSUES OF THE RED POSTS, 1929–31

RP 1

RP 2

1929–31. *Hunan-Kiangsi Border issue. Litho. Imperf.*
RP1	RP 1	1 c. grey-blue	..	..	75·00	
RP2		2 c. blue-green	..	..		£150
RP3		8 c. blue	..	..		

1929–31. *South-west Kiangsi issue. Litho. Imperf.*
RP4	RP 2	1 c. blue	..	..		
RP5		3 c. red	..	..		
RP6		3 c. sage-green	..	..		
RP7		8 c. blue	..	..	£150	£120

RP 3

RP 4

1929–31. *Hunan-West Hupeh issue. Litho. Imperf.*
RP8	RP 3	4 c. pale red	..	..	50·00
RP9	RP 4	10 c. red/yellow	..	..	

RP 5

1929. *North-east Kiangsi issue. Litho. Imperf.*
RP10	RP 5	1 c. red	..	..	..

RP 6

RP 7

1929–31. *West Fukien issue. Values in copper coins (pien).*
Litho. Imperf.
RP12	RP 6	2 p. light chestnut	..	..
RP13		4 p. light chestnut	..	..
RP14	RP 7	4 p. light chestnut	..	..

In March 1930 the Communist headquarters was moved to Juichin, in south-east Kiangsi. In November 1931 a Chinese Soviet Republic was proclaimed in the area under Communist control, and Mao Tse-tung was elected President on 27 November.

CHINESE SOVIET REPUBLIC, 1931–34

SR 1

SRD 1

1931–34. *Litho. Imperf.*
SR1	SR 1	½ c. brown	..	..		£180
SR2		½ c. blue-violet	..	..		
SR3		1 c. brown	..	..		

1931–34. *POSTAGE DUE. Litho. Imperf.*
SRD4	SRD 1	1 c. brown (23×19 mm)	..	40·00
SRD5		2 c. blue (23×19 mm)	..	£180
SRD6		2 c. blue (27×22 mm)	..	

SR 2

SR 3

1931–34. *Litho. Imperf.*
SR7	SR 2	1 c. red (23×21 mm)	..	..
SR8		1 c. red (25×22 mm)	..	..

No. SR8 also differs in that the value circles are shaded.

1931–34. *Litho. Imperf.*
SR9	SR 3	1 c. green	..	..	..
SR10		2 c. red	..	..	..

SR 4

SR 5

1931. *Litho. Imperf.*
SR11	SR 4	3 c. green	..	..

There are three types of this stamp, differing in the right-hand character in the top central panel.

1931. *Litho. Imperf.*
SR12 SR **5** 3 c. deep red-brown ‥ ‥

SR **6**

SR **7**

1931–34. *Litho. Imperf.*
SR13 SR **6** 5 c. brown ‥ ‥ ‥
SR14   8 c. blue ‥ ‥ ‥
SR15 SR **7** 30 c. deep blue ‥ ‥ ‥

SR **8**

SR **9**

1931–34. *Litho. Imperf.*
SR16 SR **8** 10 c. red ‥ ‥ ‥
SR17 SR **9** 10 c. red ‥ ‥ ‥
SR18   10 c. red ‥ ‥ ‥
No. SR18 differs in that there are no circles with Arabic numerals in bottom corners.

By 1931 the Chinese Soviet forces had a strength of 300,000 men, and from November 1930 to March 1933 they repulsed four Extermination Campaigns launched by Chiang Kai-shek. A fifth campaign in 1933–34, aided by a blockade, was successful, and 120,000 communists began the Long March to North-west China in October 1934. A year later, after fighting and much hardship, 30,000 survivors reached Shensi; in December 1936 they made Yenan their headquarters.

II. ISSUES OF THE BORDER AREAS, 1937–49

On 7 July 1937, the Japanese, who had seized Manchuria in 1931 and the province of Jehol in 1933, launched an invasion of the rest of China. On 22 September, agreement was reached between the Communists and Chiang Kai-shek to co-operate against the Japanese; the communist Yenan troops were re-named the Eighth Route Army. From 1937 until the defeat of Japan in 1945, the Communists fought the Japanese, chiefly in guerrilla warfare from areas under their control; many of these areas were known as Border Areas, as they were situated on the borders of several provinces.

By the spring of 1945, 678 out of 914 country towns in Japanese "occupied" territories were in Communist hands, and the Communists ruled a population of over 95 million. Fighting between Communists and Nationalists was resumed in October 1945, and, except for a short truce early in 1946, did not cease until the Communists had conquered China.

For convenience, the issues of the Border Areas are grouped under the six Government Administrative Areas into which China was divided after the defeat of Japan. In 1949, when the areas came completely under Communist control, these became known as Regions.

GUM. The following stamps are without gum, *unless otherwise stated, and excepting the overprinted Nationalist stamps.*

A. CENTRAL CHINA

The area included under the heading Central China comprises the provinces of Honan, Hupeh, Hunan and Kiangsi.

1. Central Plains Liberated Area, Honan

(CC 1)   CC **2** Mao Tse-tung   (CC 3)

1948 (Mar). *Type NC* **54** *handstamped with new values as Type* CC**1** *at Loyang, Honan. Imperf.*
CC1 NC **54**   c. on $20 rose-red ‥ ‥
CC2 $2 on $100 deep green (R.) ‥
CC3 $5 on $10 emerald (R.) ‥
CC4 $10 on $30 purple ‥ ‥

(Litho at Lushan, Honan)
1948 (1 Apr). A. *Imperf.* B. *P* 10.

		A		B	
CC5 CC **2**	$1 pale red ‥	2·50	2·00	5·00	4·00
CC6	$2 brown ‥	5·00	5·00	7·50	6·00
CC7	$2.50, yellow ‥	2·50	2·50	†	
CC8	$5 red ‥ ‥	2·50	2·00	5·00	4·00
CC9	$10 light green ‥	30·00	25·00	†	
CC10	$20 blue ‥ ‥	20·00	15·00	†	

1948 (11 Nov). *Stamps of Nationalist China optd "Central Plains Liberated Area. Local Currency" and surch new value as Type CC* **3**.

(a) *On Sun Yat-sen Fifth issue*
CC11	**82**	$1 on 50 c. grey-green ‥	‥ 16·00	16·00
CC12		$1 on 50 c. grey-green (R.)	‥ 16·00	16·00

(b) *On Sun Yat-sen Tenth issue*
CC13	**113**	$4 on $2,000 red-brown and blue	15·00	15·00

(c) *On Sun Yat-sen Eleventh and Twelfth issues*
CC14	**118**	$2 on $1,000 scarlet ‥	‥ 12·00	12·00
CC15	**136**	$10 on $20,000 rose-carmine	‥ 12·00	12·00
CC16		$26 on $100,000 sage-green ‥	‥ 14·00	14·00
CC17	**118**	$34 on $5,000 brown ‥	‥ 14·00	14·00
CC18	**136**	$42 on $1,000,000 claret ‥	‥ 14·00	14·00
CC19	**118**	$50 on $7,000 red-brown ‥	‥ 14·00	14·00

CC **4** Mao Tse-tung

(CC **5**)

(CC **6**)

(Litho New China Book Co, Chengchow)
1949 (Jan). A. *P* 9 × 9½. B. *Imperf.*

		A		B	
CC20	CC **4**	$5 bluish violet	20	20	5	5
CC21		$10 brownish red ‥ ‥	5	8	5·00	5·00
		a. Smaller. 17 × 21 mm	80	1·50		†
CC22		$30 apple-green	3·00	2·50	3·00	3·00
CC23		$50 myrtle-green	5	5	1·00	1·00
CC24		$100 ochre ‥	5	8	5	5
CC25		$175 blue ‥	10	10	5	5
CC26		$300 dull verm ‥	60	60	30	30
CC20/26		*Set of 7* ‥	4·00	4·25	8·00	8·00

(Litho Wan Feng Ptg Co, Kaifeng)
1949 (July). *Thick paper.* A. *P* 10½. B. *Imperf.*

		A		B	
CC27	CC **4**	$5 violet ‥		†	20	20
CC28		$50 dull green ‥	20	20	10	10

1949 (July). *No. C22A surch as Type CC* **5**, *by the Chung Chang Ptg Co, Kaifeng.*

			A. P 10½		B. Imp	
CC29	CC **4**	$1 on $30 apple-green	15	15		†
CC30		$25 on $30 apple-green	20	20	4·00	5·00

The surcharge differs on each stamp and appears to have been done by a mimeograph.

1949 (July). *Surch as Type CC* **6**, *by the Chen Ming Chan Ptg Office at Kaifeng, in red.*

(a) On Nos. C22A and C24A

CC31	CC **4**	$90 on $100 ochre	20	25
CC32		$3,000 on $30 apple-green	35	40
CC33		$10,000 on $30 apple-green	60	70

(b) On No. CC28B

CC34	CC **4**	$45 on $50 dull green	10	10
CC31/34	Set of 4		1·10	1·25

2. Honan

The stamps listed under this heading are inscribed in Chinese "Chungchow", an old name for Honan province.

CC **7** Mao Tse-tung   (CC **8**)

(Typo from rubber plates by Hsin Yu Ptg Co, Kaifeng)

1948 (27 Dec). *Imperf.*

CC35	CC **7**	$1 bright orange	5	8
CC36		$4 yellow-olive	5	8
CC37		$10 greyish green	5	8
CC38		$26 blue (*shades*)	5	8
CC39		$34 violet-brown	10	15
CC40		$42 brownish red	30	40
CC35/40	Set of 6		55	80

The $1, $34 and $42 should be mounted in glassine envelopes as they give off colour which penetrates album leaves and affects other stamps.

1949 (May). *Surch as Type CC* **8**, *by the Yung Chong Ptg Co, Kaifeng.*

CC41	CC **7**	$1 on $26 blue	5	10
CC42		$25 on $34 violet-brown	5	10
CC43		$25 on $42 brownish red	5	10

The note after No. CC40 also applies to Nos. CC42/3.

Later issues for Central China are listed under the Regional Issues.

EAST CHINA

The area included under the heading East China comprises the provinces of Shantung, Kiangsu, Anhwei, Chekiang and Fukien.

1. Shantung Wartime Posts

The postal service in the communist areas of Shantung began in February 1942.

EC **1** Map of Shantung

EC **2** Soldier charging

EC **3** Hand with Torch

EC **4** Man pushing Wheel

EC **5** Cavalryman

The extreme right-hand character in the bottom inscription varies as follows:—

A   B

C   D

1942 (Apr)–**43**. *Litho. Imperf.*

EC1	EC **1**	1 c. red (A)			4·00	4·00
EC2		1 c. yellow (A)			25·00	25·00
EC3	EC **2**	2 c. green (A)			6·00	6·00
EC4	EC **3**	2 c. blue (A)			20·00	20·00
		a. Pale blue (B)			6·00	6·00
		b. Light blue (C)			25·00	25·00
		c. Blue (D)			3·00	3·00
EC5	EC **4**	10 c. yellow (A)			38·00	38·00
		a. Type B			38·00	38·00
		b. Type C			38·00	38·00
		c. Type D			10·00	10·00
EC6		10 c. green (B)			40·00	40·00
EC7	EC **5**	50 c. brown (A)			9·00	9·00
		a. Light brown (D)			25·00	25·00
EC8	EC **1**	$1 red (B)			£200	£200

Nos. EC5/7 are inscribed "1" or "5" in the bottom corners (=1 or 5 ten cent pieces).

(EC **6**)   (EC **7**)   (EC **8**)

1942–45. *North-east Shantung. Handstamped with characters "Chiao Tung" (the area E. of Chiao) as Type EC* **6**, *in red, violet, blue or black.*

EC9	EC **1**	1 c. red (R., V., B., Bk.)		5·00	5·00
EC10	EC **2**	2 c. green (R., V., B., Bk.)		4·00	4·00
EC11	EC **3**	5 c. blue (R., V., B., Bk.)		5·00	5·00
EC12	EC **4**	10 c. yellow (R., V., B., Bk.)		22·00	22·00
EC13	EC **5**	50 c. brown (R., Bk.)		25·00	25·00

The handstamp on No. EC11 may be large or small.

1943–45. *North-east Shantung issue. Nos. EC1/3 handstamped "Chiao Tung" and new value as Type EC* **7**, *in red, violet, blue or black.*

EC14	EC **1**	5 c. on 1 c. red (V., B., Bk.)		10·00	10·00
EC15		10 c. on 1 c. red (V., B., Bk.)		15·00	15·00
EC16		10 c. on 1 c. orange (V.)		25·00	25·00
EC17	EC **2**	10 c. on 2 c. green (R., Bk.)		20·00	20·00
EC18		50 c. on 2 c. green (R.)		25·00	25·00
EC19	EC **1**	$1 on 1 c. red (Bk.)			
EC20	EC **3**	$1 on 5 c. blue (R.)			
EC21	EC **2**	$2 on 2 c. green (Bk.)			

1944. *No. EC7 handstamped "War Post General Office" as Type EC* **8**.

EC22	EC **5**	50 c. brown			

EC **9** Mao Tse-tung

EC **15** Chu Teh

EC **16** Mao Tse-tung

EC **17** Chu Teh

1944 (Mar). *Imperf.*

(a) Typo. Fine impression. Thin toned paper

EC23	EC **9**	5 c. deep blue		3·00	3·00
EC24		a. Rouletted		10·00	10·00
		10 c. dull green		9·00	9·00
EC25		50 c. lake-brown		2·00	2·00

(b) Typo. Fine impression. Thick buff paper

EC26	EC **9**	5 c. slate-blue		8·00	8·00
		a. Perf		12·00	12·00
EC27		50 c. red-brown		20·00	20·00

(c) Litho. Coarse impression. Thin toned paper

EC28	EC **9**	10 c. yellow-green		1·50	1·50
		a. Perf		5·00	5·00
EC29		50 c. red-brown		2·75	2·75
		a. Perf		6·00	6·00

EC **10** Ploughing

EC **11** Soldier throwing Grenade

1944–45. *Lu Nan (South Shantung) issue. Litho. Imperf.*

EC30	EC **10**	10 c. green		75·00	40·00
EC31	EC **11**	$1 orange (shades)		55·00	40·00

(EC **12**)

(EC **13**)

(EC **14**)

1945–47. *Handstamped with new values as Type EC* **12.**

EC32	EC **3**	$1 on 5 c. blue	10·00	10·00
EC33		$5 on 5 c. blue (R.) (1947)	5·00	5·00

1945–48. *Surch (a) As Type EC* **13.**

EC34	EC **9**	50 c. on 5 c. blue (R.)	50·00	50·00
EC35		$1 on 5 c. blue (R.)	9·00	9·00
EC36		$1 on 5 c. blue (R.)*	10·00	10·00
EC37		$1 on 5 c. blue (R.)*	4·00	4·00
EC38		$1 on 10 c. green (R.)	2·00	2·00
EC39		$1 on 10 c. green (R.)*	50	50
EC40		$2 on 10 c. green (B.)	2·50	2·50
EC41		$2 on 10 c. green (Bk.)	20·00	20·00
EC42		$5 on 50 c. brown (B.)	5·00	5·00
EC43		$5 on 50 c. brown (Bk.)	5·00	5·00
EC44		$10 on 5 c. blue (R.)	30·00	30·00
EC45		$10 on 10 c. green (R.)	40·00	40·00
EC46		$50 on 50 c. brown (R.)	45·00	45·00

*On Nos. EC36 and EC39 the surcharge consists of two characters only and on No. EC37 the bottom character in the left-hand column is square in shape.

(b) As Type EC **14,** *in red*

EC47	EC **9**	$5 on 10 c. green	3·00	3·00
EC48		$5 on 10 c. green*	5·00	5·00
EC49		$10 on 10 c. green	3·00	3·00

*On No. EC48 the right-hand character of the surcharge is square in shape and on No. EC49 the left-hand character is square in shape.

1945 (1 Aug). *18th Anniv of People's Liberation Army. Litho on newsprint. Imperf.*

EC50	EC **15**	10 c. deep blue (shades)		70·00	25·00

1945 (1 Aug). *7th Congress of the Chinese Communist Party, Yenan. Litho on newsprint. Imperf.*

EC51	EC **16**	5 c. green (shades)		50·00	20·00

1945. *Litho. A. Imperf (Sept). B. P 10–11½ (Dec).*

			A		B
EC52	EC **17**	5 c. light blue	2·00	1·50	†
		a. Deep blue (clearer print)	2·50	2·00	†
EC53		10 c. green (shades)	3·50	3·00	2·00 2·00
EC54		50 c. grey-green	4·00	4·00	30·00 25·00
EC55		50 c. red-brown	†	3·00	3·00
		a. Yell-brn	†	5·00	5·00
EC56		$1 red	30·00	30·00	2·50 2·50
EC57		$1 orange	10·00	10·00	35·00 35·00
EC58		$3 violet	†	3·00	3·00
EC59		$3 dull claret	5·00	5·00	10·00 10·00

(EC **18**)

(EC **19**)

1945–49. *Type EC* **17** *variously surch. (a) As Type EC* **18.**

A. Imperf. B. Perf 10, 11 or compound

		A		B	
EC60	10 c. on 5 c. light blue (R.)	1·60	1·60	†	
EC61	$1 on 5 c. light blue (R.)	3·00	3·00	3·00	3·00
EC62	$1 on 10 c. green (R.)	12·00	12·00	†	
EC63	$3 on 10 c. green (R.)	†		5·00	5·00
EC64	$5 on 5 c. light blue (R.)	1·25	1·25	†	
EC65	$10 on 10 c. green (R.)	1·40	1·40	1·40	1·40
EC66	$20 on 50 c. red-brown	†		2·50	2·50
EC67	$50 on 10 c. green (R.)	†		6·50	6·50
EC68	$3,000 on 10 c. green ('49)	†		1·00	1·00

(b) As Type EC **19.** *Perf 10, 11 or compound*

EC69	50 c. on 10 c. green			5·00	5·00
EC70	50 c. on 10 c. green (R.)			7·00	7·00
EC71	$3 on 10 c. green (R.)			75	75

The surcharge on No. EC60 is handstamped.

2. Shantung Posts

EC 20   EC 21
Mao Tse-tung

1945. *Litho. Value in white. Imperf.*
EC72 EC 20 50 c. lake-brown . . . . 1·25 1·25

1946. *Litho. Value in colour. Imperf.*
EC73 EC 21 50 c. lake-brown . . . . 1·25 1·25
EC74 $2 blue 45 45

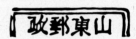

EC 22   EC 23
Chu Teh

1946. *Litho. P 11 (EC75) or imperf (EC76).*
EC75 EC 22 $1 light green . . . . 30·00 30·00
EC76 EC 23 $1 light green . . . . 2·50 2·50
No. EC75 is as Type EC 23 but with a different inscription at top and with double frame as enlarged illustration.

(EC 24)

1947. *Surch with Type EC 24.*
EC77 EC 22 $10 on $1 light green . . . . 20·00 20·00
EC78 EC 23 $10 on $1 light green . . . . 20·00 20·00

3. Pohai Postal Administration, Shantung

This administration operated in the area round the mouths of the Yellow River, south of the Gulf of Pohai.

EC 25 Chu   EC 26 Mao Tse-tung   (EC 27)
Teh

1946–47. *Litho. Imperf.*
EC79 EC 25 $1 green . . . . 25·00 25·00
EC80 $5 green . . . . 8·00 8·00
EC81 $10 blue 75 75
A $10 green was prepared but not issued without surcharge.

1947. *Inscr "East China Liberation Area". Litho. P 10½.*
EC82 EC 26 $5 green 40 40
EC83 $10 orange . . . . 1·60 1·60

1947–49. *Surch as Type EC 27.*

(a) On Type EC 25 (1947–48)
EC84 EC 25 $50 on $1 green (R.) 60 60
EC85 $800 on $10 blue . . . . 8·00 8·00
EC86 $800 on $10 green 50 50
       a. Surch double . . . . 2·00 2·00
       b. Surch double, one inverted 2·00 2·00
EC87 $800 on $50 on $10 green . . 6·00 6·00
The original surcharge on No. EC87 is obliterated with a bar.

(b) On Type EC 26 (1948–49)
EC88 EC 26 $100 on $10 orange . . . . 1·00 1·00
EC89 $200 on $5 green . . . . 1·00 1·00
EC90 $500 on $5 green (R.) 15 15
       a. Surch inverted . . 1·10 1·25
       b. Surch double . . . . 80 1·10
       c. Surch double, one inverted 80 1·10
EC91 $800 on $10 orange . . . . 4·00 4·00

4. Shantung Liberation Area

EC 28 Mao Tse-tung points   EC 29 Heroes'
ahead   Monument

1946. *Victory over Japan. Litho. P 9½–10.*
EC92 EC 28 $1 bright green 20 20
EC93 $5 red-brown 40 40
EC94 $10 lilac . . . . 80 1·00
EC95 $20 dull green, red and blue . . 2·40 2·50
EC92/95 Set of 4 . . . . . . 3·50 3·75

1946 (Dec). *Monument at Ling Shan, near Chefoo, to Heroes of War against Japan. Litho. P 10×9½.*
EC 96 EC 29 $1 bright orange 10 10
       a. Imperf 30 30
EC 97 $2 slate-green 20 20
EC 98 $5 deep brown 45 45
EC 99 $10 dull purple . . . . 1·00 1·00
EC100 $20 violet 60 60
EC96/100 Set of 5 . . . . . . 2·10 2·10

(EC 30)

1947. *Nos. EC66/7 surch with Type EC 30.*

		A		B	
		In black		In blue	
EC101	EC 20	$5 on 50 c. lake-brown . .	3·00	3·00	3·00 3·00
EC102	EC 21	$5 on 50 c. lake-brown . .	5·00	5·00	5·00 5·00

EC 31 Mao   (EC 32)   (EC 33)
Tse-tung

(Litho at Ching Chow (now I Tu))
1947 (Aug)–**48.** *P* 10.

EC103	EC **31**	$5 orange	20	20
EC104		$10 chocolate	20	20
EC105		$10 turquoise-green (10.47) ..	20	20
		a. Imperf	3·00	3·00
EC106		$20 slate-violet	25	25
EC107		$50 red-brown	25	25
EC108		$100 deep blue	4·00	2·40
EC109		$100 yellow-orange (1948) ..	3·00	3·00
		a. Imperf	6·00	5·00
EC103/109		Set of 7	7·00	6·00

For stamps in a similar design, see Nos. EC153/61.

1947–48. *Handstamped with new values as Type EC 32 or with Type EC 33 (No. EC112).*

EC110	EC **29**	$5 on $2 slate-green (R.) ..	10·00	10·00
		a. Surch inverted ..	1·75	1·75
EC111		$10 on $1 bright orange ..	1·90	1·90
EC112		$10 on $1 bright orange ..	50	50
EC113		$20 on $1 bright orange ..	1·00	1·00
EC114		$50 on $1 bright orange ..	1·00	1·00

拾攺 作 暫 東 膠

元作 (EC 34) 圓百壹 (EC 35) 圜百伍 (EC 36)

1947–48. *Surch as Type EC 34.*

EC115	EC **29**	$10 on $1 bright orange ..	30·00	30·00
EC116		$10 on $2 slate-green (R.) ..	30·00	30·00

There are two varieties of the surcharge.

1947–48. *Surch as Type EC 35.*

EC117	EC **31**	$100 on $10 chocolate ..	8·00	8·00
EC118		$200 on $5 orange ..	20	20
		a. Surch inverted ..	2·50	
EC119		$1,000 on $10 chocolate (R.) ..	10·00	10·00

1947–48. *Various stamps surch as Type EC 36.*

EC120	EC **17**	$100 on 10 c. green ..	75·00	75·00
EC121	EC **29**	$200 on $1 bright orange ..	2·50	2·50
		a. Surch inverted ..	3·50	5·00
EC122	EC **31**	$500 on $10 chocolate..	20	20
EC123		$800 on $20 slate-violet (R.) ..	20	20
		a. Surch inverted ..		

貳 佰 圓 (EC 37)

200 (EC 38)

捌 百 圓 (EC 38)

伍 百 圓 (EC 39)

1947–48. *Various stamps surch as Type EC 37.*

EC124	EC **29**	$100 on $1 bright orange ..	10	10
		a. Surch inverted ..	2·50	2·50
		b. Surch double ..	2·50	2·50
		c. Surch double, one invtd ..	2·50	2·50
		d. Imperf (pair) ..	2·50	
EC125	EC **31**	$100 on $20 slate-violet (R.) ..	15	15
		a. Surch double ..	3·50	3·50
EC126		$200 on $5 orange ..	15	15
		a. Surch inverted ..		
		b. Surch double ..		
		c. Surch double, one invtd ..	2·50	2·50

1947–48. *Various stamps surch as Type EC 38, in red.*

EC127	EC **29**	$50 on $2 slate-green ..	8·00	8·00
EC128		$50 on $20 violet ..	20·00	20·00
EC129	EC **31**	$50 on $20 slate-violet ..	75	75
EC130	EC **29**	$100 on $1 bright orange ..	50	50
EC131		$200 on $5 deep brown ..	8·00	8·00
EC132	EC **31**	$200 on $5 orange ..	50	50
EC133		$800 on $10 turquoise-green ..	15	15
		a. Imperf (pair) ..	10·00	10·00

1947–48. *Surch as Type EC 39.*

EC134	EC **31**	$200 on $5 orange ..	15·00	15·00
EC135		$500 on $20 slate-violet ..	6·00	6·00
EC136		$800 on $10 grey-blue ..	6·00	6·00
EC137		$1,000 on $20 slate-violet ..	8·00	8·00
		a. Surch inverted ..	20·00	20·00

叁千元 (EC 40)

貳百圓 (EC 41)

EC **42** Mao Tse-tung

1947–48. *Handstamped diagonally as Type EC 40.*

EC138	EC **29**	$300 on $1 bright orange ..	2·00	2·00
		a. Imperf ..	2·00	2·00
EC139	EC **31**	$500 on $20 slate-violet ..	7·00	7·00
EC140		$500 on $20 slate-violet (R.) ..	5·00	5·00
EC141		$800 on $10 chocolate ..	7·00	7·00
EC142		$800 on $10 turquoise-green ..	7·00	7·00
		a. Imperf ..	5·00	5·00
EC143		$1,000 on $20 slate-violet ..	5·00	5·00
EC144		$1,000 on $20 slate-violet (R.) ..	5·00	5·00
EC145		$1,000 on $50 red-brown ..	1·25	1·25
EC146		$2,000 on $50 red-brown ..	1·50	1·50
EC147		$3,000 on $50 red-brown ..	50	50
EC148		$3,000 on $50 red-brown (R.) ..	3·50	3·50

Nos. EC139/40 and EC147/8 exist with diagonal handstamp in characters differing from Type EC **40.**

1948–49. *Handstamped.*

(a) As Type EC 41 (vertically)

EC149	EC **28**	$100 on $1 bright orange ..	25·00	25·00
EC150		$200 on $5 red-brown ..	30·00	30·00
		a. Smaller handstamp ..	30·00	30·00

(b) As Type EC 40 (diagonally)

EC151	EC **28**	$500 on $10 lilac ..	20·00	20·00
EC152		$800 on $10 lilac ..	4·00	4·00

(Litho at Ching Chow (now I Tu))
1948–49. *P* 9½ *to* 11½ *and compound.*

EC153	EC **42**	$50 yellow..	10	10
		a. Pale orange ..	15	15
EC154		$100 rose	10	10
EC155		$200 blackish lilac ..	12	12
		a. Thin paper. Perf 11 ..	10	10
EC156		$300 green	10	10
EC157		$500 blue	10	10
		a. Thin paper. Perf 11 ..	10	10
EC158		$800 red-orange ..	10	10
EC159		$1,000 deep blue ..	20	20
EC160		$5,000 rose ..	50	50
EC161		$10,000 carmine ..	60	60
EC153/161		Set of 9	1·60	1·60

In the value tablets of Nos. EC159/61 the Arabic numerals are at the left. Nos. EC155a and 157a were printed from the Ching Chow plates by the East China Printing Co, Tsinan.

200°⁰ 山 郵 東 政 貳百圓 (EC 43)

1949 (1 Aug). *Parcels Post stamps of Nationalist China surch as Type EC 43 for use as ordinary postage stamps.*

EC162	P **1**	$200 on $500 green ..		25
EC163	P **3**	$200 on $200,000 deep green ..	2·25	
EC164		$200 on $10,000,000 sage-green ..		25
EC165	P **1**	$500 on $1,000 blue ..		60
EC166	P **3**	$500 on $7,000 dull blue ..	4·25	
EC167		$500 on $50,000 blue-black ..		40
EC168		$1,000 on $10,000 deep carmine ..		40
EC169		$1,000 on $100,000 purple ..		40
EC170		$1,000 on $300,000 pink ..		40

EC171 P 3 $1,000 on $500,000 plum.. .. 2·25
EC172 $1,000 on $8,000,000 vermilion .. 40
EC173 $2,000 on $5,000,000 grey-lilac .. 1·25
    a. Surch double .. .. .. 5·00
EC174 $2,000 on $6,000,000 grey .. 1·25
EC175 $3,000 on $30,000 olive-green .. 1·40
EC176 $3,000 on $70,000 red-brown .. 1·40
EC177 $3,000 on $3,000,000 slate-blue .. 1·40
EC162/177 Set of 16 .. .. .. 16·00

5. Hwai-Nan Area

The Hwai-Nan Area, south of the R. Hwai, was on the borders of Anhwei and Kiangsu Provinces, north of Nanking.

EC 44 Star   (EC 45)

1941. *Printed from wood block. Litho. Imperf.*
EC178 EC 44 20 c. pale sage-green .. .. 15·00 15·00

1941. *Optd with Type EC 45 ("Kao"=despatch) for use by newspaper reporters. Imperf.*
EC179 EC 44 20 c. red .. .. ..

Xuai-Nan
(EC 46)   (EC 47)   (EC 48)

1942. *Unissued Junk type as Type EC 51 (but without surcharge), optd with Type EC 46 ("P'ing"=ordinary post). No value indicated. Litho. Imperf.*
EC180 (—) Blue (R.) .. .. ..
EC181 (—) Red (B.) .. .. ..

1943. *Nos. EC180/1 surch.*
EC182 EC 47 30 c. on (—) red (Br.) .. ..
EC183 EC 48 30 c. on (—) red .. .. ..
EC184   30 c. on (—) blue .. ..

Xuai-Nan
(EC 49)

1943–44. *Unissued Pigeon and Junk types as Types EC 50/51 (but without surcharges), surch as in Type EC 49. Litho. Imperf.*
EC185 30 c. on (—) blue (Pigeon) (R.) ..
EC186 30 c. on (—) blue (Junk) (R.) ..

EC 50 Pigeon   EC 51 Junk

1944. *Unissued surcharged stamps re-surcharged with dollar values, in black. Litho. Imperf.*

(a) *Typographed surcharges as in Types EC 50/51*
EC187 EC 50 $1 on 20 c. (R.) on (—) blue
EC188 EC 51 $1 on 30 c. (R.) on (—) blue ..

(EC 52)

(b) *Airplane type as Type EC 58 (without surcharges), surch as Type EC 52*
EC189 $5 on $2 (B.) on (—) red .. ..

(EC 53)   (EC 54)

(c) *Similar designs with handstamped Dollar surcharges*
EC190 EC 53 $1 on 20 c. (R.) on (—) blue (Pigeon) .. ..
EC191 EC 54 $1 on 30 c. (R.) on (—) blue (Junk) .. ..

EC 55 Warships   EC 56 Airplane

(d) *Handstamped "3" or "5" as in Types EC 55/56*
EC192 EC 55 $3 on $1 (R.) on (—) blue .. — 40·00
EC193 EC 56 $5 on $2 (B.) on (—) red .. — 20·00

(EC 58)   (EC 59)

1944. *No. EC189 handstamped with Type EC 58 (="Provisional for personal correspondence"), in black.*
EC194 $5 on $2 (B.+Bk.) on (—) red (Airplane) .. ..

1944. *No. EC192 handstamped with Type EC 59 (="Changed to ordinary use"), in red.*
EC195 $3 on $1 (R.+Bk.) on (—) blue (Warships) .. ..

6. Yen-Fu Area (North Kiangsu)

Yen-Fu was the name given to the area between the towns of Yencheng and Funing, in the north of Kiangsu province.

(EC 60)   (EC 61)   (EC 62)

1943. *Types of Hwai-Nan area optd "Jan fu ky" and surch as Type EC 60.*
EC196 5 c. on (—) blue (R.) (Pigeon) ..
EC197 10 c. on (—) blue (R.) (Junk) ..
EC198 15 c. on (—) brown (B.) (Warships) ..
EC199 20 c. on (—) brown (B.) (Airplane) ..

1944. *Optd "Jan fu" and surch as Type EC 61, in red.*
EC200 5 c. on (—) pale blue-green (Pigeon .. 25·00 25·00
EC201 5 c. on (—) yellow-green (Pigeon) ..
EC202 10 c. on (—) pale blue-green (Junk) ..

1944. *Optd in black.*

(a) With top two characters of Type EC 62
EC203 5 c. on (–) blue-green (Pigeon)
EC204 10 c. on (–) blue-green (Junk) ..

(b) With Type EC 62
EC205 5 c. on (–) blue-green (Pigeon) ..
EC206 15 c. on (–) brown (Warships) ..
The overprint on Nos. EC203/4 means "New resistance currency" and that on Nos. EC205/6 means "Changed to new resistance currency".

(EC 63)   (EC 64)

1944. *Previous types but with "005" (postal district number) inserted in design, overprinted.*

(a) Junk type optd with Type EC 63
EC207 (–) Red (V.) (Ordinary Mail)
EC208 (–) Violet (R.) (Express Mail).. ..

(b) Type EC 67 optd with Type EC 64
EC209 (–) Orange (Bk.) (Confidential Mail) ..

EC **65** Locomotive

1944. *PARCELS POST. Litho. Imperf. Value surch in red.*
EC210 EC **65** 50 c. blue   .. ..

7. Su-Chung Military District (Central Kiangsu)

Su-Chung is the abbreviation for Central Kiangsu.

EC **66**   EC **67** "Express Mail"   EC **68** "Official
"Confidential   on Hawk   Mail" on Junk
Mail" on Torch

The Chinese characters overprinted on Nos. EC 211/9 are not indications of value, but of the type of mail which the stamp is meant to frank. The colours of the overprints are shown in brackets.

1943. *Litho. P 10½.*

A. 1st issue. Pale colours. B. 2nd issue. Deep colours

		A		B	
EC211	EC **66**	(–) Red (G.) ..	18·00 18·00	8·00	8·00
EC212		(–) Green (R.) ..	18·00 18·00	8·00	8·00
		a. Imperf ..	— —	†	
EC213	EC **67**	(–) Red (G.) ..	18·00 18·00	8·00	8·00
EC214		(–) Green (R.) ..	18·00 18·00	8·00	8·00
EC215	EC **68**	(–) Red (G.) ..	— —	45·00	45·00
EC216		(–) Green (R.) ..	— —	45·00	45·00
		a. Imperf	†	—	

1944. *3rd issue. Colours changed.*

EC217	EC **66**	(–) Brown (R.) ..	..	10·00 10·00
		a. Blue opt ..	..	50·00 50·00
EC218	EC **67**	(–) Red-orange (B.)	..	18·00 18·00
EC219	EC **68**	(–) Blue (R.) ..	..	10·00 10·00

(EC **69**)   (EC **70**)   (EC **71**)

1944. *Stamps as last handstamped with Type EC 69 (="Provisional use for ordinary postage").*

EC220	EC **66**	On No. EC211B (V.) ..	..	
EC221		On No. EC212B (V.) ..	..	
EC222	EC **67**	On No. EC213B (Bk.) ..		
EC223		On No. EC214B (B.) ..	..	
EC224	EC **66**	On No. EC217a (B.) (smaller handstamp) ..	38·00	38·00

On Nos. EC220/1 and EC224 the design differs in that the hand holding the torch is at left.

1945. *Optd "For internal use" with indication of type of mail, as Type EC 70.*

EC225	EC **66**	(–) Reddish brown (R.) (Confidential Mail) ..	1·25	1·25
		a. Opt as on No. EC227 (Bk.) ..	1·25	1·25
EC226	EC **67**	(–) Orange-red (Express Mail)	1·25	1·25
		a. Opt as on No. EC227	16·00	16·00
EC227	EC **68**	(–) Steel-blue (Official Mail) ..	4·00	4·00

On Nos. EC225/a the hand holding torch is at left.

1945. *No. EC225 handstamped with Type EC 71.*
EC228 EC **66** (–) Reddish brown (V.) ..
          a. Smaller handstamp (R.) ..
On No. EC228 the hand holding the torch is at left.

EC **72** Children with   EC **73** Soldier taking Aim
       Buffalo

EC **74** Soldier with Children

EC **75** Soldier   EC **76** Military
                 Theory and Practice

1945. *Types EC 75/6 are surcharged in red. Litho. Imperf.*

EC229	EC **72**	10 c. pale blue-green ..	..	13·00 13·00
EC230	EC **73**	10 c. pale green ..	..	2·50 2·50
EC231	EC **74**	20 c. pale orange-red ..	..	1·00 1·00
		a. Tête-bêche (pair) ..	..	5·00 8·00
EC232	EC **75**	40 c. on 25 c. grey-blue	..	1·00 1·00
		a. Tête-bêche (pair) ..	..	5·00 8·00
EC233	EC **76**	40 c. on 30 c. turquoise-green	..	2·00 2·00
EC229/233		*Set of 5*	..	17·00 17·00

The above are inscribed for use on ordinary mail, printed matter, official mail, confidential mail and express mail, respectively.

(EC 77)

1945–46. *Nos. EC230 and EC232/3 handstamped as Type EC 77 in purple (various types) to alter purpose of stamp. New purpose shown in brackets.*

EC234 EC 73 10 c. pale green (Ordinary Mail)
      a. Red handstamp
      b. Black handstamp .. ..
EC235 EC 75 40 c. on 25 c. grey-blue (Express
      Mail)
EC236 EC 76 40 c. on 30 c. turquoise-green
      (Ordinary Mail) .. ..

There are two varieties of the purple handstamp on No. EC234.

1946. *Colours changed. P 11½.*

EC237	EC 72	10 c. green	20·00	20·00
EC238	EC 74	20 c. green	12·00	12·00
EC239	EC 75	40 c. on 25 c. green (R.)	8·00	8·00
EC240	EC 76	40 c. on 30 c. green (R.)	4·00	4·00
EC237/240		Set of 4	40·00	40·00

The above are for use on ordinary, official, confidential and express mail, respectively.

8. Central Kiangsu: Fifth Sub-Area

The Fifth Sub-Area comprised all Kiangsu Province south of the Yangtze River.

EC **78** Flying Goose   EC **79** Aircraft

1944. *Optd with characters in red for official and confidential mail, respectively. Litho. Imperf.*

EC241	EC 78	(–) Green	75·00	75·00
EC242	EC 79	(–) Red	75·00	75·00

9. Wan-Kiang Area (Central Anhwei)

EC **80** Pigeon with Letter

1945. *Surch with value in red. Litho. Imperf.*
EC243 EC **80** 50 c. on (–) green   ..   30·00   30·00

10. Kiangsu-Anhwei Border Area

The name of this area was abbreviated to Su-Wan Border Area.

郵 簡

角二作改

(EC 82)

EC **81** Mao   (EC **82**)   EC **83** Railway
Tse-tung   Train

1946 (Feb). *As Type EC* **81.** *Litho. Imperf.*

EC244	5 c. dull blue (Ordinary Mail) ..	20	20
	a. Perf 9½ to 11	2·00	2·00
EC245	5 c. dull violet (Printed Matter)	60	60
EC246	10 c. drab (Official Mail) ..	20	20
	a. Perf 9½ to 11	12·00	12·00
EC247	10 c. grey-blue (Official Mail) ..	1·00	1·00
EC248	10 c. grey-blue (Ordinary Mail) ..	1·00	1·00
	a. Tête-bêche (pair)	12·00	12·00
EC249	20 c. dp grey-blue (Confidential Mail)	60	60
	a. Perf 9½ to 11½	4·00	4·00
EC250	20 c. orange-red (Express Letter) ..	40	40
	a. Perf 9½ to 11	16·00	16·00
	b. Pale orange	50	50
EC244/250	Set of 7	3·50	3·50

A different character in a circle appears at the top of each stamp in this issue to denote purpose of use, but there is no character on No. EC248, thus distinguishing it from No. EC247.

1946 (Apr). *Surch as Type EC* **82.** *Imperf.*
EC251 EC **81** 20 c. on 5 c. dull blue ..   15   15
       a. Surch inverted ..   2·50   2·50
EC252   75 c. on 5 c. scarlet ..   15   15
      No. EC252 without surcharge was not issued.

1946. *Type EC* **83.** *Litho.*

A. *Imperf* (Apr).   B. *P* 11 (Sept)

		A		B	
EC253	25 c. pale violet-bl	20	20	30	30
EC254	50 c. light blue ..	20	20	20	20
EC254a	75 c. light red ..	75	75	†	
EC255	$1 greyish red ..	20	20	20	20
EC256	$2 dull blue ..	65	65	†	
	a. Error. $1 dull blue	15·00	20·00	†	
EC257	$5 greyish violet ..	45	45	†	
EC258	$10 purple	8·00	3·00	†	
EC253/258A	Set of 7.. ..	8·50	4·25	†	

No. EC256a resulted from a $1 cliché appearing in the plate of the $2.

11. Hwa-Chung Area

"Hwa Chung" means Central China; but the stamps so inscribed, issued before the creation of the Central China Region, were issued in the provinces comprised in East China.

EC **84** Aircraft

(EC **85**)

1946 (Jan). *Type EC* **84** *and types of Hwai-Nan Area optd "Xuazhung" and surch in red. Imperf.*

EC259	10 c. on (–) blue (Pigeon) ..	6·00	6·00
EC260	10 c. on (–) blue (Junk) ..	6·00	6·00
EC261	20 c. on (–) blue (Warships) ..	20·00	20·00
EC262	40 c. on (–) blue (Type EC **84**) ..	£250	£250

1947–48. *Type EC* **83** *surch as Type EC* **85.**

EC263	$50 on 50 c. light blue (R.) ..	40·00	40·00
EC264	$50 on $5 greyish violet (R.) ..	40·00	40·00
EC265	$50 on $10 purple (R.) ..	45·00	45·00
EC266	$100 on $5 greyish violet ..	55·00	55·00

EC **86**

1949 (1 Jan). *Issue for First Sub-District, Hwa-Chung Area. As Type EC 86. Hectographed. Imperf.*

EC267	$50 black	..	..	.. 22·00 22·00
EC268	$100 black	..	..	.. 35·00 35·00
EC269	$200 black	..	..	.. 23·00 23·00
EC270	$300 black	..	..	.. £100 £100
EC271	$500 black	..	..	.. £150 £150

There are several types of the central characters on these stamps. They were produced in sheets of 35, containing thirteen $50, six $100, twelve $200, two $300 and two $500.

12. North Kiangsu

The North Kiangsu (abbreviated to "Su-peh") Posts and Telegraphs Administration was set up on 1 January 1949.

EC 87 Aircraft   (EC 88)

1949 (1 Jan). *Surch as Type EC 88 at Taichow. Imperf.*

(a) On Type EC 87 (Kiangsu-Anhwei Border Area Money Order stamp)

EC272	$50 on $10 light brown	..	..	5 5
	a. Perf 11			20 20
EC273	$50 on $20 pale red (B.)	..	..	5 5
	a. Error. On $50 pale red (in pair with $20)			10·00
EC274	$50 on $50 red (B.)	..		20 20
EC275	$500 on $1 azure (R.)	..		8 8
	a. Surch inverted			5·00
EC276	$1,000 on $2 light blue (R.)	..		8 8
	a. Surch inverted			5·00
	b. Error. On $1 azure	..		10·00

(b) On Type EC 83

EC277	$100 on 50 c. light blue (R.)	..		5 5
	a. Surch inverted			6·00
	b. Surch double..			6·00
EC278	$100 on 75 c. light red (B.)	..		8 8
EC279	$200 on $1 greyish red (B.)	..		8 8
	a. Surch inverted			5·00
EC272/279	Set of 8	..	..	60 60

13. South Kiangsu

South Kiangsu is the part of the province south of the Yangtze River.

EC 89   (EC 90)

1938. *Issue for Tsingpu Guerrilla District, W. of Shanghai. Type EC 89. Litho. Imperf.*

EC280	1 c. green (Printed Matter)	..
EC281	2 c. red (Local Mail)	..
EC282	5 c. blue (Mail Outside the District)	..
EC283	10 c. violet (Registered Mail)	..

1949. *Surch as Type EC 90.*

EC284	EC 83	$1 on 50 c. light blue (G.)	..	20 20
EC285		$2 on 50 c. light blue	..	12 12
EC286		$4 on 50 c. light blue (O.)	..	20 20
EC287	EC 87	$8 on $1 azure (B.)	..	1·00 1·00
EC288		$8 on $2 light blue (B.)	..	1·50 1·50
EC289		$10 on $1 azure (R.)	..	3·00 3·00
EC284/289	Set of 6	..	..	5·50 5·50

These stamps were issued in the cities of Changchow, Wusih, Soochow and Sungchiang, after their capture in May 1949.

14. Kiang-Hwai Area

Kiang-Hwai was the name given to the parts of Kiangsu and Anhwei provinces between the Yangtze Kiang and the R. Hwai.

EC 91 Map of Kiang-Hwai Area

1949 (Mar). *Litho at Hofei. Imperf.*

EC290	EC 91	$2 vermilion	..	..	.. 20 25
		a. Tête-bêche (pair)	..	..	1·00 1·50

EC 92 Mao Tse-tung   EC 93 Chu Teh   EC 94 "By Air, Sea or Rail"

1949 (May). *Litho at Hofei. Imperf.*

EC291	EC 92	$3 red-brown (*shades*)	..	10 10
		a. Tête-bêche (pair)		50 70
EC292	EC 93	$5 dull blue (*shades*) ..		10 10
		a. Tête-bêche (pair)		50 80
EC293	EC 94	$10 lilac	..	15 15
		a. Tête-bêche (pair)	..	50 80

EC 95 Mao Tse-tung   (EC 96)

(Litho Han Mai Lin Press and Tu Fun Press, Nantung, Kiangsu)

1949 (June). *Imperf.*

EC294	EC 95	$100 brown	..	25 25
EC295		$200 lilac	..	25 25
EC296		$500 red-orange	..	25 25
		a. Printed both sides	..	3·00
EC297		$1,000 orange-yellow (*shades*)		25 25
EC298		$2,000 light green (*shades*)		25 25
		a. Printed both sides	..	1·50 1·50
EC299		$5,000 blue (*shades*)	..	1·50 1·50
		a. Larger Chinese characters to left of portrait	..	2·00 2·00
EC294/299	Set of 6	..	..	2·40 2·40

Though these stamps are inscribed "Central China Liberation Area" in Chinese, they were issued in Kiangsu province.

All values were printed on buff paper; Nos. EC298/9 may also be found on white paper. The column of Chinese characters of value on Nos. EC299/a is 8 mm or 9½ mm high, respectively.

1949 (23 June). *Handstamped in green as Type EC 96, at Anking.*

EC300	EC 91	$50 on $2 vermilion	..	5·00 5·00
EC301		$100 on $2 vermilion	..	5·00 5·00

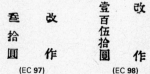

(EC 97)   (EC 98)

1949 (July). (a) *Surch with Type EC 97.*

EC302	EC 91	$30 on $2 vermilion (*Imperf*)		5	5
		a. Tête-bêche (pair)	..	50	50
EC303		$30 on $2 verm (*p 8½×8*)	..	15	15
		a. Tête-bêche (pair)		75	75

(b) Surch as Type EC 98

EC304	EC 92	$90 on $3 red-brown	..	5	5
		a. Tête-bêche (pair)		50	50
EC305	EC 93	$150 on $5 dull blue ..	..	5	5
		a. Tête-bêche (pair)	..	1·25	1·25
EC306	EC 92	$1,000 on $3 blue	..	15	15
		a. Tête-bêche (pair)	..	1·25	1·25
EC302/306		*Set of 5*	..	40	40

Later issues for East China are listed under the Regional Issues.

C. NORTH CHINA

The area included under the heading North China comprises the provinces of Chahar, Hopeh, Shansi and Suiyuan.

1. Shansi-Chahar-Hopeh Border Area

The Shansi-Chahar-Hopeh Command was created on 7 November 1937; it gradually spread over an area of 300,000 square miles, with a population of 25 million. The area was known for short as the Chin-Cha-Chi Area.

NC 1   NC 2

1937 (Dec). *Litho. Imperf.*

NC1	NC 1	1 c. blue	..	..	£200	£125
NC2		5 c. blue	..	..	£200	£175
NC3		5 c. black	..	..		

This issue was made at Wu-Tai-Shan, Shansi, by a Field Post Office of the 115th Regiment, 8th Route Army.

1938 (Feb). *Litho. Imperf.*

A. *1st printing on newsprint.* B. *2nd printing on white paper*

			A	B
NC4	NC 2	1 c. vio (*shades*) ..	20·00 20·00	— —
NC5		5 c. brown	25·00 25·00	— —
NC6		10 c. blue	†	— —

There are differences in design between the first and second printings.

NC 3   NC 4 Soldier

1938 (June). *Tang-Hsien (Hopeh) issue. Litho. Imperf.*

NC7	NC 3	1 c. red ..	..	..	— 90·00

1938 (Sept). *MILITARY POST. Litho. Imperf.*

NC8	NC 4	(–) Scarlet..	..	..	£225

2. Shansi-Chahar-Hopeh Posts

A Shansi-Chahar-Hopeh Postal Administration was set up on 15 October 1945, after the end of the war with Japan.

NC 5 Sun Yat-sen   (NC 6)

暫用

冀察晉

用 暫   冀察晉
(NC 7)   (NC 8)

1945 (20 Oct). *Unissued stamps prepared for Japanese Occupation of Mengkiang variously optd. Litho at Changchun. With gum. P 13½.*

(a) With Type NC 6 (="Temporary use")

NC 9	NC 5	50 c. dull blue (R.)	..	5	5
		a. Opt inverted	..	2·00	1·50
NC10		$1 yellow-brown (R.) ..	..	5	5
		a. Opt inverted	..	2·00	1·50

(b) With Type NC 7 (="Shansi-Chahar-Hopeh temporary use")

NC11	NC 5	50 c. dull blue ..	..	5	5
NC12		$1 yellow-brown	..	5	5
		a. Opt inverted	..	2·25	2·00

(c) With Type NC 8 (="Temporary use Shansi-Chahar-Hopeh")

NC13	NC 5	50 c. dull blue (R.)	..	5	5
NC14		$1 yellow-brown (R.) ..		5	5

NC 9   NC 10
Cavalry Charge

1946 (Mar). *Victory over Japan (1st issue). Litho. P 10.*

(a) No wmk

NC15	NC 9	$1 reddish chestnut	..	60	80
		a. Imperf	..	2·50	3·50

(b) Wmk Wavy Lines

NC16	NC 9	$2 yellow-green	..	60	80
NC17		$4 vermilion	..	30	40
		a. Imperf	..	18·00	24·00
NC18		$5 dull purple	..	30	40
		a. Imperf	..	18·00	24·00
NC19		$8 deep blue	..	30	40
NC20		$10 rose-carmine	..	30	40
NC21		$12 yellow	..	60	70
NC22		$20 dull green	..	70	1·00
		a. Imperf	..	19·00	26·00
NC15/22		*Set of 8* ..	..	3·25	4·50

1946 (May). *Victory over Japan (2nd issue). Litho. P 9.*

(a) No wmk

NC23	NC **10**	$1 dull scarlet			10	15
		a. Imperf	..	..	1·00	1·50
NC24		$2 pale green		..	10	15
		a. Imperf	..	..	2·25	3·25
NC25		$3 pale mauve		..	50	75
NC26		$5 dull violet ..		..	50	75
NC27		$8 deep blue ..		..	50	75
NC28		$10 carmine-rose		..	15	25
		a. Imperf	..	..	2·25	3·25
NC29		$15 deep reddish violet		..	1·00	1·50
NC30		$20 pale green		..	20	30
NC31		$30 turquoise-blue		..	20	30
NC32		$40 mauve		..	20	30
NC33		$50 brown		..	20	30
NC34		$60 slate-green		..	20	30

(b) Wmk Wavy Lines

NC35	NC **10**	$100 orange		..	30	45
NC36		$200 steel-blue ..		..	60	90
NC37		$500 rose-red	..	..	6·00	9·00
NC23/37	*Set of 15*		..	..	9·00	14·00

The four following issues of surcharges were made at Shih Men (or Shihkiachwang) in Central Hopeh, at the junction of the Peking-Hankow and Tsingtao-Lanchow railways.

暂作
100.⁰⁰
(NC 11)

暂作
50.⁰⁰
(NC 12)

1947 (16 Nov). *First Shih Men issue. Handstamped with new values as Type NC 11.*

NC38	NC **9**	$50 on $4 vermilion		..	20·00	20·00
NC39		$100 on $1 reddish chestnut (B.)			1·00	1·00
NC40		$100 on $4 vermilion		..	1·00	1·00
NC41		$100 on $4 vermilion (B.)			1·00	1·00
NC42		$100 on $2 yellow-green (B.)			20·00	18·00
NC43		$100 on $12 yellow (B.)			20·00	18·00

1947 (16 Nov). *Second Shih Men issue. Handstamped with new values as Type NC 12.*

		A		B	
		In black		In blue	
NC44	NC **10**	$50 on $1 dull scarlet	1·00	1·00	1·00	1·00
		a. Imperf	1·25	1·25	1·25	1·25
NC45		$50 on $2 pale green	1·75	1·75	†	
NC46		$50 on $5 dull violet	1·25	1·25	1·00	1·00
NC47		$50 on $10 carm-rose	1·25	1·25	†	
NC48		$50 on $40 mauve	1·25	1·25	1·00	1·00
NC49		$100 on $60 slate-green	1·00	1·00	1·25	1·25

伍佰圓
暂作
(NC 13)

暂作
壹百圓
(NC 14)

1947 (16 Nov). *Third Shih Men issue. Surch by wood blocks with new values in characters as Type NC 13.*

NC50	NC **10**	$300 on $30 turquoise-blue		..	1·00	1·00
		a. Error. Surch in blue			20·00	20·00
NC51		$300 on $30 turquoise-blue (R.)			1·00	1·00
NC52		$500 on $20 pale green			1·00	1·00
NC53		$500 on $20 pale green (B.)			1·00	1·00
NC54		$500 on $20 pale green (R.)			1·00	1·00
NC50/54	*Set of 5*		..	..	4·25	4·25

1947 (16 Nov). *Fourth Shih Men issue. Surch with new values in characters as Type NC 14.*

NC55	NC **10**	$50 on $3 pale mauve		..	15·00	15·00
NC56		$50 on $40 mauve		..	75	75
NC57		$100 on $30 turquoise-blue (R.)			75	75
NC58		$100 on $60 slate-green		..	2·50	2·50
		a. Imperf	..	..	5·00	5·00
NC59		$500 on $20 pale green (R.)			—	30·00

NC 15   NC 16

Mao Tse-tung

1948 (Mar). *Litho at Pingshan, Hopeh.*

A. P 10 to 11. B. Imperf

			A		B	
NC60	NC **15**	$100 slate-blk	5	5	8	8
NC61		$200 bluish red	5	5	8	8
NC62	NC **16**	$500 yell-orge	10	10	15	15
NC63		$1,000 brown ..	10	10	12	12
NC64		$2,000 green ..	20	20	15	15
NC65		$2,500 lake ..	20	20	†	
NC66		$5,000 pale blue	30	30	†	
NC60/66A	*Set of 7*		90	90		
NC60/64B	*Set of 5*			†	50	50

NC 17

1948 (Mar). *Litho at Pingshan, Hopeh. P 9½ to 10½.*

NC64	NC **17**	$500 orange	..	..	50	50

3. East Hopeh

The East Hopeh ("Ki-Tung") Administrative Sub-bureau was set up round Tangshan in January 1946.

冀東區   作 暂

暂售八元 $100.⁰⁰
(NC 18)   (NC 19)

1947 (Jan). *Handstamped as Type NC 18.*

NC68	NC **9**	$4 on $10 rose-carmine ..		..	4·00	4·00
NC69		$8 on $12 yellow		..	4·00	4·00

1947 (Apr). *Handstamped as Type NC 19.*

NC70	NC **9**	$100 on $4 vermilion		..	—	20·00
NC71		$100 on $12 yellow		..	—	25·00

遼熱察冀
作暂
100.⁰⁰
(NC 20)

遼熱察冀
作 暂
100.⁰⁰
(NC 21)

1948 (Aug). *MILITARY POST. (a) Handstamped with Type NC 20.*

| NC72 | NC 9 | $100 on $4 vermilion | .. | .. | 10·00 | 10·00 |
| NC73 | | $100 on $8 deep blue | .. | .. | 25·00 | 25·00 |

(b) Handstamped with Type NC 21

NC74	NC 10	$100 on $1 dull scarlet	..	..	16·00	16·00
NC75		$100 on $2 pale green	..	..	2·00	2·00
NC76		$100 on $3 pale mauve	..	..	2·00	2·00
NC77		$100 on $5 dull violet	..	..	5·00	5·00
NC78		$100 on $8 deep blue	..	..	25·00	25·00
NC79		$100 on $10 carmine-rose	..	..	20·00	20·00
NC80		$100 on $20 pale green	..	..	2·00	2·00
NC81		$100 on $30 turquoise-blue	..	..	12·00	12·00

The first two lines of the Chinese overprint mean "Hopeh, Chahar, Jehol and Liaoning".

The town of Tangshan fell to the Communists on 12 December 1948 and the following seven issues were made there.

(NC 22)

NC 23 Mao Tse-tung

1948 (19 Dec). *First Tangshan issue. Nos. NC75, 77 and 79/81 with handstamp surcharge Type NC 22.*

NC82	$1,000 on $100 on $2 pale green (R.)		5·00	5·00
NC83	$1,000 on $100 on $5 dull violet		5·00	5·00
NC84	$1,000 on $100 on $5 dull violet (R.) ..		18·00	18·00
NC85	$1,000 on $100 on $10 carmine-rose		5·00	5·00
NC86	$1,000 on $100 on $20 pale green (R.)		5·00	5·00
NC87	$1,000 on $100 on $30 turq-blue (R.)		5·00	5·00

1948 (23 Dec). *Second Tangshan issue. Litho. P 11.*

| NC88 | NC 23 | $1,000 dull rose | .. | .. | 75 | 1·00 |

(NC 24)   (NC 25)

1948 (28 Dec). *Third Tangshan issue. Type NC 10 handstamped as Types NC 24/25 (="East Hopeh" and new value).*

NC89	NC 24	$2,000 on $5 dull violet	..	1·50	1·50
NC90	NC 25	$2,000 on $5 dull violet (B.) ..		5·00	5·00
NC91	NC 24	$2,000 on $20 pale green	..	1·50	1·50
NC92	NC 25	$2,000 on $30 turq-blue (V.)			
NC93		$2,000 on $30 turq-blue (R.)		5·00	5·00
NC94		$3,000 on $3 pale mauve		1·50	1·50
NC95		$3,000 on $3 pale mauve (R.)			
NC96		$3,000 on $5 dull violet (R.)		5·00	5·00
NC97		$3,000 on $20 pale green (B.)		1·50	1·50
NC98		$3,000 on $30 turq-blue (V.)		2·50	2·50
		a. Tête-bêche (pair)	..	12·00	14·00
NC99		$4,000 on $3 pale mauve (B.)		1·50	1·50
NC100	NC 24	$4,000 on $5 dull violet	..	5·00	5·00
NC101	NC 25	$4,000 on $30 dull violet	..	5·00	5·00
NC101a		$4,000 on $30 turq-blue (V.)		1·75	1·75

(NC 26)   (NC 27)   (NC 28)

1949 (Jan). *Fourth Tangshan issue. Nos. NC80 and NC88 handstamped "$3,000" with Type NC 26, in violet.*

| NC102 | NC 10 | $3,000 on $100 on $20 pale green | .. | 12·00 | 12·00 |
| NC103 | NC 23 | $3,000 on $1,000 dull rose | .. | 12·00 | 12·00 |

1949 (Jan). *Fifth Tangshan issue. No. 19 of North-Eastern Provinces surch with Types NC 27/28.*

| NC104 | NC 27 | $1,500 on 20 c. apple-green | .. | 1·50 | 1·50 |
| NC105 | NC 28 | $1,500 on 20 c. apple-green | .. | 1·50 | 1·50 |

Both stamps exist with the two characters of the surcharge reversed.

東 冀

伍仟圓

(NC 29)

1949. *Sixth Tangshan issue. Handstamped as Type NC 29 (="East Hopeh" and new value).*

(a) On stamps of Nationalist China

NC106	136	$500 on $300,000 apple-green	5·00	5·00
NC107		$500 on $500,000 mauve	3·00	3·00
NC108	118	$500 on $500,000 sepia & slate-green		
NC109	136	$1,000 on $20,000 rose-carmine		
NC110		$1,000 on $1,000,000 claret	..	

(b) On No. 42 of North-Eastern Provinces

NC111	5	$500 on $500 rose	..	1·00	1·00
NC112		$1,000 on $500 rose	..	1·00	1·00
NC113		$2,000 on $500 rose	..	1·00	1·00
		a. Handstamped in violet	..	15·00	
NC114		$3,000 on $500 rose	..	1·50	1·50
NC115		$4,000 on $500 rose	..	2·00	2·00
NC116		$5,000 on $500 rose	..	1·00	1·00

東 冀   東 冀   東 冀

叁仟圓   肆仟圓   貳仟圓

(NC 30)   (NC 31)   (NC 32)

1949. *Seventh Tangshan issue. Handstamped as Types NC 30/32 (="East Hopeh" and new value).*

(a) On T 89 and 102 of Nationalist China

| NC117 | 102 | $3,000 on $20 carmine (NC 30) .. | 18·00 | 18·00 |
| NC118 | 89 | $4,000 on 40 c. brown-lake (B.) (NC 31) | .. | |

(b) On T 118 and 136 of Nationalist China

NC119	136	$2,000 on $100,000 sage-green (B.) (NC 31)	1·00	1·00
NC120		$3,000 on $100,000 sage-green (NC 32)	1·00	1·00
NC121		$3,000 on $100,000 sage-green (B.) (NC 31)		
NC122		$3,000 on $300,000 apple-green (NC 30)	2·00	2·00
NC123		$3,000 on $300,000 apple-green (NC 31)	4·00	4·00
NC124		$3,000 on $300,000 apple-green (NC 32)	2·00	2·00
NC125	118	$3,000 on $500,000 brn (NC 31) ..	1·00	1·00
NC126	136	$3,000 on $3,000,000 bistre (NC 30)	4·00	4·00
NC127	118	$4,000 on $7,000 red-brown (B.) (NC 31)	—	10·00
NC128	136	$4,000 on $100,000 sage-green (NC 31)	4·00	4·00
NC129		$4,000 on $1,000,000 claret (NC 31)	1·00	1·00
		a. Blue handstamp ..		
NC130		$4,000 on $2,000,000 red-orange (B.) (NC 31)	..	..

(c) On No. 42 of North-Eastern Provinces

NC131	5	$2,000 on $500 rose (NC 31)	1·00	1·00
NC132		$2,000 on $500 rose (NC 32)	1·00	1·00
NC133		$3,000 on $500 rose (NC 30)	1·00	1·00
NC134		$3,000 on $500 rose (NC 31)	4·00	4·00
NC135		$3,000 on $500 rose (NC 32)	1·00	1·00
NC136		$4,000 on $500 rose (NC 31)	1·00	1·00
NC137		$4,000 on $500 rose (NC 32)	1·00	1·00

4. Shansi-Hopeh-Shantung-Honan Border Area

This Border Area, known for short as Chin-Ki-Lu-Yü, was first organised in 1937 in the Taihan Mountains in South Shansi and the area round the Yellow River. A postal service was established in September 1940.

NC 33 Eagle shaded   NC 34 Eagle unshaded

1942 (June). *Inscr "Labels for postage". Litho. Imperf.*

			A NC 33	B NC 34
NC138	2 c. yellow		18·00 20·00	—
NC139	10 c. deep blue		25·00 30·00	—

A 5 c. and 50 c. in Type NC 33 were not issued.

(NC 35)   (NC 36)   (NC 37)

1942 (June). *Surcharged in red.*

		(*a*) As Type NC 35		
NC140	NC 33	2 c. on 10 c. deep blue		
NC141		5 c. on 10 c. deep blue		20·00

		(*b*) As Type NC 36	
NC142	NC 34	2 c. on 10 c. deep blue	
NC143		5 c. on 10 c. deep blue	

		(*c*) With Type NC 37	
NC144	NC 33	10 c. on 2 c. yellow	

NC 38 Eagle on Globe   (NC 40)
Cent Units

1943. *Values in cents. Litho. Imperf.*

NC145	NC 38	2 c. violet (*shades*)	10·00	10·00
NC146		5 c. yellow-orange	10·00	10·00
NC147		10 c. red	10·00	10·00
NC148		20 c. brown	4·00	4·00
		a. Red-brown	5·00	5·00
NC149		50 c. blue	4·00	4·00
NC150		100 c. apple-green	20·00	20·00
NC151		500 c. blue-green	50·00	50·00
NC145/151	Set of 7		£100	£100

See also Nos. NC161/6 and NC172/6.

1943–44. *POSTAGE DUE. Optd with the two large characters from Type NC 40.*

NCD152	NC 38	2 c. violet (R.)	8·00	8·00
NCD153		10 c. red	8·00	8·00
NCD154		20 c. brown	20·00	20·00

1944. *Surch as Type NC 40.*

NC155	NC 38	5 c. on 20 c. brown (R.)	
NC156		5 c. on 20 c. brown	
NC157		10 c. on 5 c. yellow-orange (R.)	
NC158		10 c. on 20 c. brown (R.)	
		a. "10" in centre (Bk.)	
		b. Arabic "10" omitted (Bk.)	
NC159		10 c. on 100 c. apple-green (R.)	

(NCD 41)   NC 42 Eagle on Globe   (NC 43)
10 Cent Units

1944. *POSTAGE DUE. No. NCD104 surch with 5 c. as in Type NCD 41.*

NCD160	NC 38	5 c. on 20 c. brown	

1946 (Mar). *Value in 10 c. units. Litho.*

			A. Imp		B. Roul	
NC161	NC 42	2 (20 c.) brn	2·00	2·00	2·00	2·00
NC162		5 (50 c.) deep blue	2·00	2·00	2·00	2·00
NC163		10 ($1) lt grn	4·00	4·00	3·50	3·50
NC164		20 ($2) greyish red	4·00	4·00	3·50	3·50
NC165		50 ($5) dp vio	24·00	24·00	25·00	25·00
NC166		100 ($10) orge	11·00	11·00	12·00	12·00

1946. *No. NC 162A surch as Type NC 43.*

NC167	NC 42	$1 on 5 (50 c.) deep blue	8·00	8·00
		a. Smaller characters	10·00	10·00
NC168		$2 on 5 (50 c.) deep blue	8·00	8·00
NC169		$4 on 5 (50 c.) deep blue	8·00	8·00

(NC 44)   NC 45 Eagle on Globe   NC 46 Eagle on
Dollar Units   Globe

1946. *Nos. NC161/2A surch with Type NC 44.*

NC170	NC 42	$1 on 2 (20 c.) brown	7·00	7·00
NC171		$1 on 5 (50 c.) deep blue	7·00	7·00
		a. Right-hand characters at left	7·00	7·00

1946. *Values in dollars. Litho. Imperf.*

NC172	NC 45	$1 green	2·50	2·50
NC173		$2 rose-red	7·50	7·50
NC174		$5 violet	2·50	2·50
NC175		$10 orange	10·00	10·00
NC172/175	Set of 4		21·00	21·00

1946. *Bottom panel inscr "Postal Bureau" instead of "Communications Bureau". Litho. Imperf.*

NC176	NC 46	$5 dull blue	5·00	

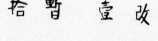

(NC 47)   (NC 48)   (NC 49)

1946. *Imperf. Surch (a) As Type* NC **47.**

NC177	NC **42**	$1 on 2 (20 c.) brown		
NC178		$2 on 2 (20 c.) brown	..	

(b) With Type NC **48**

NC179	NC **42**	$10 on 5 (50 c.) deep blue (R.)		
NC180	NC **45**	$10 on $1 green (B.)	..	

1946–47. *Imperf. Surch as Type* NC **49.**

NC181	NC **42**	$1 on 5 (50 c.) deep blue	..	1·20	1·20
NC182		$2 on 5 (50 c.) deep blue	..	9·00	9·00
NC183		$10 on 5 (50 c.) deep blue	..	2·25	2·25
		a. Characters of surch 1 mm		
		apart	..	12·00	12·00
NC184		$10 on 10 ($1) lt green (R.)	..	7·50	7·50
		a. Characters of surch 1 mm		
		apart	..	15·00	15·00
NC185		$20 on 5 (50 c.) dp blue (R.)	..	7·50	7·50
NC186		$20 on 10 ($1) lt green (R.)	..	5·00	5·00
NC187	NC **46**	$20 on $5 dull blue (R.)	..	9·00	9·00

(NC **50**)

(NC **51**)

(NC **52**)

1946–47. *Imperf. Surch (a) As Type* NC **50.**

NC188	NC **42**	$1 on 2 (20 c.) brown (B.)	..	9·00	9·00
NC189		$2 on 5 (50 c.) deep blue (R.)	12·00	12·00

(b) With Type NC **51**

NC190	NC **42**	$4 on 5 (50 c.) deep blue	..	7·50	7·50

(c) As Type NC **52**

NC191	NC **42**	$20 on 5 (50 c.) deep blue (R.)	12·00	12·00
NC192		$20 on 10 ($1) light green (R.)	5·00	5·00
NC193		$20 on 20 ($2) greyish red	..	6·00	6·00
NC194		$30 on 5 (50 c.) deep blue	12·00	12·00
		a. Surch inverted	..	

NC **53** Chu Teh and Mao Tse-tung

NC **54** Mao Tse-tung

1946 (Sept). *First Anniv of Victory over Japan. Litho. Imperf.*

NC195	NC **53**	$10 light blue ..	..	45·00	45·00

See also No. NC209.

1946 (Dec)**–48.** *Litho. Imperf.*

NC196	NC **54**	$2 deep brown	..	..	6·00	6·00
NC197		$5 orange	..	..	25·00	25·00
NC198		$10 emerald ..		..	80	80
		a. Perf 10	..	..	28·00	28·00
NC199		$20 rose-red ..		..	1·25	1·25
NC200		$30 blue	..	..	2·50	2·50
NC201		$30 purple	..	..	4·00	4·00
NC202		$40 red-brown	..	..	1·60	1·60
NC203		$50 orange	..	..	40·00	40·00
		a. Perf 10	..	..	35·00	32·00
NC204		$60 rose-pink	..	..	1·25	1·25
		a. Perf 10	..	..	28·00	28·00
NC205		$80 lake	..	..	4·00	4·00
		a. On brown paper	..	6·00	6·00
		b. Perf 10	..	..	28·00	28·00
NC206		$100 deep green	..	..	4·00	4·00
NC207		$200 brown	..	..	6·00	6·00
NC208		$500 light blue	..	..	4·00	4·00
		a. Perf 10	..	..	28·00	28·00

There are varieties of paper in this issue.

1947 (Sept). *Second Anniv of Victory over Japan. As No.* NC195 *but with inscription altered. Litho. Imperf.*

NC209	NC **53**	$20 rose-red	..	20·00	18·00
		a. Perf	..	..	30·00	30·00

(NC **55**)

1948. *Surch as Type* NC **55.**

NC210	NC **54**	$50 on $10 emerald ..		
NC211		$200 on $2 deep brown	..	

5. Hopeh-Shantung-Honan Border Area

This area, known as "Chi-Lu-Yu" for short, centred around Hotseh, and comprised territory N.E. of Kaifeng and to the S.E. of the Yellow River. A Communications Bureau was set up in October 1941, but stamps were not issued till 1946.

NC **56** Mao Tse-tung   NC **57**

(litho at Hotseh, S. W. Shantung)

1946 (Apr). *P* 10½.

NC212	NC **56**	50 c. red	..	..	..	—	25·00

(Hectographed at Hotseh, S.W. Shantung)

1946. *Imperf.*

NC213	NC **57**	50 c. blue	..	..	45·00	40·00
NC214		$1 blue	..	..	40·00	35·00
NC215		$2 green	..	..	35·00	30·00

(NC **58**)   (NC **59**)

(NC **60**)

1949. *Optd* "North China People's Postal Administration" *and surch as Types* NC **58/60,** *at Hotseh.*

(a) As Type NC **58.** *P* 10 *to* 11

NC216	NC **16**	$5 on $500 yellow-orange	..	2·00	2·00
NC217		$6 on $500 yell-orange (B.)	..	3·00	3·00
NC218	NC **15**	$12 on $200 bluish red	..	40	40
		a. Imperf	..	..	1·25	1·25

(b) As Type NC **59**

NC219	NC **38**	$3 on 2 (20 c.) brown	..	15·00	15·00
NC220		$3 on 5 (50 c.) deep blue	..	1·50	1·50
NC221		$5 on 2 (20 c.) brown	..	1·50	1·50
NC222		$5 on 5 (50 c.) deep blue	..	27·00	27·00

(c) As Type NC **60**

NC223	NC **54**	$5 on $60 rose-pink	..	2·00	2·00
NC224		$5 on $80 lake	..	1·50	1·50

NC225	NC **54**	$6 on $2 deep brown	5·50	5·50
NC226		$6 on $40 red-brown	1·50	1·50
NC227		$6 on $80 lake	42·00	42·00

6. Shansi-Suiyuan Border Area

A Shansi-Suiyuan base (known for short as "Chin-Sui") was created in October 1937 and in 1946 became one of the main Communist administrative areas.

NC 61   NC 62

1946 (Apr). *No value indicated. Inscr with service for which stamps intended. Litho. Imperf.*

NC228	NC **61**	(–) Green (Ordinary Letter)	
NC229		(–) Blue (Printed Matter: 100 grammes)	
NC230		(–) Violet (Printed Matter; 500 grammes)	
NC231	NC **62**	(–) Salmon (Registered Letter)	
NC232		(–) Red (Double Fee Registered Letter)	

The inscriptions differ on Nos. NC229/30.

NC 63 Mao Tse-tung   (NC 64)

1946 (Dec)–**47**. *Litho. Imperf.*

NC233	NC **63**	$1 pink	12·00	12·00
NC234		$3 blue	90	90
NC235		$10 light brown	90	90
		a. Error. Yellow	—	
NC236		$15 yellow	35·00	30·00
NC237		$20 green	15·00	15·00
NC238		$30 red-brown	50·00	45·00
NC239		$50 lilac	3·00	3·00
NC240		$80 rose-carmine	90	90
NC241		$100 yellow-green	90	90
NC242		$500 deep dull blue (*very coarse print*) (1947)	90	90

1947 (July). *Handstamped surch with Type NC 64.*

NC243	NC **63**	$500 on $1 rose-red	45·00	45·00
NC244		$500 on $3 blue (R.)	3·00	3·00
		a. Rouletted	9·00	9·00

(NC 65)   (NC 66)

1948 (June). *Handstamped surch as Type NC 65.*

NC245	NC **63**	$5,000 on $15 yellow	45·00	45·00
NC246		$10,000 on $3 blue	2·50	2·50
		a. Smaller characters in surch	12·00	12·00

1948 (July). *Handstamped surch as Type NC 66.*

NC247	NC **63**	$500 on $3 blue (R.)	45·00	45·00
NC248		$1,000 on $80 rose-carmine	90	90
NC249		$3,000 on $10 light brown (R.)	9·00	9·00
NC250		$3,000 on $30 ochre	45·00	45·00
NC251		$3,000 on $50 lilac	45·00	45·00
NC252		$4,000 on $20 green (R.)	45·00	45·00

(NC 67)   NC 68 Ploughman

1948 (Sept). *Handstamped surch as Type NC 67.*

NC253	NC **63**	$600 on $1 rose-red	
NC254		$4,000 on $20 green	
NC255		$4,000 on $50 lilac	
NC256		$5,000 on $20 green	
NC257		$5,000 on $50 lilac	

1948. *Litho. Imperf.*

NC258	NC **68**	$1,000 salmon	10	12
NC259		$3,000 claret	10	12
NC260		$5,000 light green	10	12
NC261		$10,000 violet	15	20
NC262		$20,000 rose-red	20	25
NC258/262		Set of 5	55	65

(NC 69)   (NC 70)

1949. *People's Currency. Surch with Type NC 69.*

NC263	NC **63**	$60 on $500 deep dull blue	40	40

1949. *People's Currency. Surch as Type NC 70.*

NC264	NC **68**	50 c. on $5,000 light grn (R.)	30	30
		a. Surch double	2·50	
NC265		$1 on $1,000 salmon	30	30
		a. Surch double	2·50	
NC266		$3 on $3,000 claret	30	30
NC267		$5 on $1,000 salmon	30·00	20·00
NC268		$5 on $5,000 light green	30	30
		a. Surch inverted	—	8·00
NC269		$10 on $10,000 violet	30	30
NC270		$15 on $20,000 rose-red	30	30

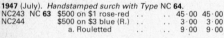

(NC 71)   (NC 72)

1949. *People's Currency. Surch as Type NC 71.*

NC271	NC **68**	50 c. on $5,000 light grn (R.)	50	50
NC272		$20 on $1,000 salmon	50	50
		a. Bottom left character with closed box	1·50	1·50
NC273		$30 on $10,000 violet	50	50
NC274		$90 on $10,000 violet (R.)	50	50
NC275		$100 on $3,000 claret	50	50
NC276		$100 on $20,000 rose-red	50	50
NC271/276		Set of 6	2·50	2·50

1949. *Sho-Hsien (N. Shansi) provisional. Handstamped surch with Type NC 72.*

NC277	NC **63**	$30 on $500 deep dull blue	

7. Suiyuan-Inner Mongolia Border Area

(NC 73)

1949. *Surch as Type NC 73 (No. NC282 handstamped).*

NC278	NC 63	50 c. on $500 dp dull bl (R.)	..	45·00	45·00
NC279	NC 68	$2 on $3,000 claret	..	18·00	18·00
NC280		$5 on $5,000 lt grn (R.)	..	1·00	1·00
NC281		$10 on $10,000 violet (R.)	..	1·50	1·50
NC282		$15 on $20,000 rose-red	..	45·00	45·00

Later issues of North China are listed under the Regional Issues.

NORTH EAST CHINA

For greater convenience these stamps are listed under the heading of Manchuria after the Chinese People's Republic.

D. NORTH WEST CHINA

The area included under the heading North West China comprises the provinces of Kansu, Ninghsia, Shensi, Tsinghai and Sinkiang; for stamps issued in Sinkiang see under that heading.

The main Communist forces reached North Shensi in October 1935, after the Long March from Kiangsi. This area was their headquarters until 1949, with Yenan as chief centre, except from 19 March 1947 to 24 April 1948, when that town was occupied by the Nationalists.

The American writer Edgar Snow, who was at Yenan in 1936, reported that the Communists had issued stamps in Shensi; no examples seem to be known to collectors and the earliest known stamps of this area date from 1946.

1. Shensi-Kansu-Ninghsia Area

NW 1 Yenan Pagoda

1946 (Mar). *Yenan Pagoda (First issue). Litho.*

				A. Imp		B. Roul	
NW1	NW 1	$1 green	..	35	50	6·50	10·00
NW2		$5 blue	..	5·00	6·00	10·00	15·00
NW3		$10 rose-red	..	35	50	6·50	10·00
NW4		$50 grey-purple		70	1·00	†	
NW5		$100 orge-brn	..	1·25	1·60	†	
NW1/5A		*Set of 5*	..	7·00	8·50	†	

(NW 2)   (NW 3)   (NW 4)   (NW 5)

1946 (Nov). *Nos. NW1/2A surch as Types NW 2/5, in red.*

NW6	NW 1	$30 on $1 green (NW 2)		75	75
		a. Square bottom left character in surcharge	..	30·00	30·00
NW7		$30 on $1 green (NW 3)	..	15	15
NW8		$30 on $1 green (NW 4)		20	20
NW9		$60 on $1 green (NW 2 with square bottom left char)	..	50·00	50·00
NW10		$90 on $5 blue (NW 5) ..	..	30	30

NW 6 Yenan Pagoda   NW 7 Yenan Pagoda   (NW 8)   NW 9 Yenan Pagoda

1948 (June). *Yenan Pagoda (Second issue). Litho. Imperf.*

NW11	NW 6	$100 yellow-buff	..	..	20·00	20·00
NW12		$300 rose-red		..	2·00	2·00
NW13		$500 flesh-pink (*shades*)		..	25	25
NW14		$1,000 blue	..	..	10	10
NW15		$2,000 yellow-green		..	2·00	2·00
NW16		$5,000 purple-brown		..	2·00	2·00

1948 (Dec). *Yenan Pagoda (Third issue). Values in People's Currency. Litho. Imperf.*

NW17	NW 7	10c. ochre	..	..	10	15
NW18		20c. yellow	..	..	10	15
NW19		$1 blue	..	..	10	15
NW20		$2 scarlet	..		30	40
NW21		$5 blue-green	..		50	60
NW22		$10 pale violet	..	..	1·50	1·60
NW17/22		*Set of 6*	..	..	2·25	2·50

1949 (Jan). *Nos. NW2A and NW13 surch in People's Currency as Type NW 8.*

NW23	NW 1	$1 on $5 blue (R.)	..	2·00	2·00
NW24	NW 6	$2 on $500 rose-red	..	..	2·00	2·00

1949 (1 May). *Yenan Pagoda (Fourth issue). Values in People's Currency. Litho. Imperf.*

NW25	NW 9	50 c. yellow	..	..	10	15
NW26		$1 indigo	..	..	10	15
NW27		$3 orange-yellow		..	10	15
NW28		$5 blue-green	..	..	10	15
NW29		$10 violet	..	..	20	25
NW30		$20 rose-red ..		..	30	40
NW25/30		*Set of 6*	..	..	75	1·10

No. NW25 is inscribed "5" in the bottom corners (=5 ten cent pieces).

2. Shensi Area

(NW 10)   (NW 11)   (NW 12)

1949 (13 June). *Stamps of Nationalist China optd "People's Posts (Shensi)" as Type NW 10, by the Mao Chi Ptg Co, Sian.*

NW31	146	On (–) brown-orange (1211A)		20	25
NW32	148	On (–) magenta (1213A) ..	..	25	30
NW33	149	On (–) carmine (1214A)	..	25	30

Sian was taken by the Communists on 20 May 1949.

1949 (1 July). *Gold Yuan issues of Nationalist China optd "Shensi People's Posts" as Type NW 11, by Yi Wen Tsai Paper Hong, Sian.*

(a) *On Dah Tung recess-printed issue*

NW34	145	$10 green	..	..	5	5
		a. Opt double	..	..	1·75	
NW35		$20 brown-purple	..		5	5
		a. Opt double	..	..	1·75	
NW36		$50 slate-green (R.)	..		5	5
NW37		$100 chestnut ..		..	5	5
NW38		$500 mauve	..	..	15	15

(b) *On Central Trust issue*

NW39	145	$20 brown-purple	..		5	5
		a. Opt double	..	..	1·75	

(c) *On Dah Tung litho issue*

NW40	145	$2,000 violet (R.)	..	..	40	40

(d) On Hwa Nam issue

NW41	145	$50 yellow-green	..	..	5	5
NW42		$1,000 deep blue (R.)	..	..	40	40
NW43		$5,000 carmine ..		..	80	80
NW44		$10,000 dull purple	..	..	1·75	1·75
NW34/44	Set of 11	..	..	..	3·50	3·50

1949. *North Shensi issue. Surch with Type* NW 12, *at Yenan.*

NW45	NW 9	$50 on $3 orange-yellow (R.)	..	10	10
		a. Surch inverted	..	..	2·00	
		b. Surch double	..	..	1·50	

NW **13** Train

1949 (Dec). *South Shensi issue. Litho. Imperf.*

NW46	NW 13	$50 blue-green	..	..	20·00	20·00
		a. Rouletted ..		..	..	

NW **14**	NW **15**	NW **16**
	Mao Tse-tung	

1949 (Dec). *South Shensi issue. Litho.*

			A. Roul		B. Imp	
NW47	NW 14	$5 yellow	..	40·00	28·00	48·00	32·00
		a. Error.					
		Olive-grn		†		80·00	
NW48		$10 grey	..	20·00	20·00	—	24·00
NW49	NW 15	$20 blue	..	2·00	2·00		†
NW50	NW 16	$50 pale orge	..	1·25	1·25		†
NW51	NW 14	$70 lake	..	8·00	8·00	10·00	10·00
NW52	NW 15	$200 carm-red	..	4·00	4·00	5·00	5·00
NW53	NW 16	$300 dull rose	..	2·00	2·00		†

3. Kansu-Ninghsia-Tsinghai Area

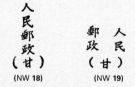

(NW 17)   (NW 18)   (NW 19)

1949 (30 Sept). *Ninghsia Province provisionals. Gold and Silver Yuan issues of Nationalist China surch as Type* NW **17.**

NW54	145	$5 on $20,000 yell-orge (1179)			
NW55		$50 on 4 c. blue-green (1345)	..	—	30·00
NW56		$100 on 1 c. apple-green (1343)	..		
NW57		$200 on 2 c. yellow-orge (1344)	..	—	30·00

1949 (Oct). *Stamps of Nationalist China optd "People's Post (Kansu)" as Type* NW **18**, *at Lanchow.*

NW58	146	On (–) brown-orange (1211B)	..	20	20
		a. Opt double	..	..	1·00	
NW59	148	On (–) magenta (1213A) ..		40	40
		a. Opt double	..	..	1·25	
NW60	149	On (–) carmine (1214A) ..		40	40
		a. Opt double	..	..	1·25	

Lanchow was taken by the Communists on 26 August 1949.

1949 (Oct). *Gold Yuan issues of Nationalist China optd "People's Post (Kansu)" as Type* NW **19**, *at Lanchow.*

(a) On Dah Tung recess-printed issue

NW61	145	$10 green	..	..	5	5
NW62		$20 brown-purple	..	..	5	5
NW63		$50 slate-green	..	..	5	5
NW64		$100 chestnut ..		..	5	5
		a. 4½ mm between vert rows of characters	..	4·50	
NW65		$200 vermilion	..	..	5	5
NW66		$500 mauve	..	..	5	5
NW67		$1,000 blue	..	..	8	10

(b) On Dah Tung litho issue

NW68	145	$100 brown	..	..	15	20
NW69		$1,000 blue	..	..	20	25
NW70		$2,000 violet	..	..	40	50
NW71		$5,000 turquoise-blue	..	80	1·00
NW72		$10,000 grey-brown	..	80	1·00
NW73		$20,000 apple-green	..	..	3·00	3·50
NW61/73	Set of 13	..	..	..	5·00	6·00

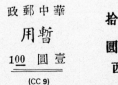

(NW **20**)

1949 (8 Oct). *Tienshui provisionals. Nos.* 1180 *and* 1182 *of Nationalist China handstamped "People's Post (South Kansu)" and surch as Type* NW **20**, *in red.*

NW74	145	$30 on $50,000 bright blue	..	1·00	1·25
NW75		$30 on $500,000 dull purple	..	1·00	1·25

There are three varieties of this surcharge on each value.

Later issues of North West China are listed under the Regional Issues.

III. REGIONAL ISSUES

After their decisive victory in the battle of Hwai-Hai in January 1949, the Communists over-ran China. Liberation Areas of Central China, East China, North China, North West China, South China and South West China were established in 1949 as regional administrative units, each consisting of a group of provinces, and using People's Currency. The regional issues could be used anywhere in China. They were discontinued after the proclamation of the People's Republic and replaced by general issues for all China (see Nos. 1401 onwards).

North East China, where the currency had a lower value, had separate issues of stamps until May 1951, when People's Currency was introduced there (see separate lists under Chinese Provinces (Manchuria).

GUM. All the Regional issues were issued without gum, except for the overprinted Nationalist stamps.

A. CENTRAL CHINA

The Central China Liberation Area consisted of the provinces of Honan, Hupeh, Hunan and Kiangsi.

(CC 9)   (CC 10)

1949 (4 June). *Sun Yat-sen issue of Nationalist China surch as Type CC **9**, at Hankow.*

(a) Thin bars at foot (early printings)

CC44	**145**	$1 on $200 vermilion (1157) ..	5	5
CC45		$6 on $10,000 grey-brn (1170) ..	5	5
CC46		$15 on $1 orange (1152) ..	5	5
CC47		$30 on $100 chestnut (1156)	5	5
CC48		$30 on $100 brown (1164) ..	5	5
CC49		$50 on $20 brown-purple (1162)	5	5
CC50		$80 on $1,000 blue (1167) ..	40	40
CC44/50	*Set of 7*		60	60

(b) Thick bars at foot (later printings)

CC51	**145**	$1 on $200 vermilion (1157) ..	5	5
CC52		$3 on $5,000 turq-blue (1169) ..	5	5
CC53		$10 on $500 mauve (1158) ..	5	5
CC54		$10 on $100 mauve (1166) ..	5	5
CC55		$50 on $20 brown-purple (1154)	5	5
CC56		$50 on $20 brown-purple (1162)	5	5
CC57		$80 on $1,000 blue (1160) ..	5	5
CC58		$80 on $1,000 blue (1167) ..	30	30
CC59		$100 on $50 slate-green (1155) ..	5	5
CC51/59	*Set of 9*		55	55

Hankow was taken by the Communists on 16 May 1949.

1949 (20–30 June). *First issue for Kiangsi. Various stamps of Nationalist China surch as Type CC **10**, by the Jen Sen Ptg Co, Kiukiang.*

*(a) On Sun Yat-sen issues, T **118** and **136***

CC60	**118**	$1 on $250 slate-violet ..	5	5
CC61		$20 on $4,000 grey ..	5	5
CC62	**136**	$30 on $20,000 rose-carmine	5	5
CC63	**118**	$200 on $250 slate-violet ..	20	20

*(b) On Sun Yat-sen issue, T **145***

CC64	**145**	$5 on $1,000 blue (1167) (30.6)	5	5
CC65		$5 on $2,000 violet (1168) (30.6)	5	5
CC66		$5 on $5,000 turquoise-bl (1169)	5	5
CC67		$10 on $1,000 blue (1160) ..	5	5
CC68		$80 on $500 mauve (1166) ..	5	5
CC69		$100 on $1,000 blue (1167) ..	5	5

*(c) On Sun Yat-sen issue, T **107***

CC70	**107**	$30 on $100 crimson (27.6) ..	5	5

*(d) On Revenue stamps, T **143**, Central Trust print*

CC71	**143**	$3 on $30 mauve	5	5
CC72		$15 on $15 red-orange ..	5	5
CC73		$30 on $50 blue (30.6) ..	5	5
CC74		$60 on $50 blue	5	5
CC75		$130 on $15 red-orange ..	20	20
CC60/75	*Set of 16*		90	90

Nanchang was taken by the Communists on 22 May 1949.

(CC 11)

(CC 12)

1949 (2 July). *Second issue for Kiangsi. Various stamps of Nationalist China, surch at Kiukiang.*

*(a) As Type CC **11***

*(i) On Sun Yat-sen issue, T **145***

CC76	**145**	$3 on $5,000 turq-bl (1169) (R.)	5	8
CC77		$30 on $500 mauve (1167) ..	5	8
CC78		$30 on $10,000 grey-brn (1170) ..	5	8

(ii) On Revenue stamps with Gold Yuan surcharges

CC79	**143**	$5 on $2,000 on $300 green (1151) (R.)	5	8
CC80		$10 on $200 on $50 blue (1124) (R.)	5	8
CC81		$10 on $200 on $500 chocolate (1142) (R.)	5	8
CC82		$30 on $50 on $300 green (1149)	5	8
CC83		$50 on $100 on $50 dark blue (1146) (R.)	5	8
CC84		$100 on $25 on $20 red-brn (1141)	5	8

*(b) As Type CC **12***

(i) On "Unit" stamps for Kiangsi (1225/30)

CC85	**118**	$30 on $500 green	5	8
CC86		$30 on $3,000 blue	5	8

CC87	**118**	$30 on $7,000 red-brown (1228)	5	8
CC88	**136**	$30 on $30,000 chocolate ..	5	8
CC89		$30 on $40,000 blue-green ..	5	8

(ii) On Sun Yat-sen issue with Gold Yuan surch

CC90	**136**	$300 on $50,000 on $20,000 rose-carmine (1113)	50	60
CC76/90	*Set of 15*		1·00	1·50

Kiukiang was taken by the Communists on 17 May 1949.

CC **13**
Peasant,
Soldier and
Workman

CC **14** Peasant, Soldier
and Workman

CC **15** Star
enclosing
Map of
Hankow Area

1949 (21 July–Aug.). *P 10 to 12 and compound.*

(a) Litho by Kuo Kwang Ptg Co, Hankow

CC91	CC **13**	$1 yellow-orange ..	5	5
CC92		$3 orange-brown ..	5	5
CC93		$6 apple-green ..	5	5
CC94	CC **14**	$7 yellow-brown (Aug) ..	5	5
CC95	CC **13**	$10 blue-green ..	5	5
CC96	CC **14**	$14 brown (Aug) ..	5	5
CC97	CC **13**	$15 ultramarine ..	5	5
CC98		$30 yellow-green ..	5	5
CC99	CC **14**	$35 slate-grey (Aug) ..	5	5
CC100	CC **13**	$50 purple ..	5	5
CC101	CC **14**	$70 dull green (Aug) ..	5	5
CC102	CC **13**	$80 carmine ..	5	5
CC103	CC **14**	$100 green (Aug) ..	5	5
CC104		$220 rose-red (Aug) ..	8	5

(b) Litho by Dah Ming Ptg Co, Hankow

CC105	CC **13**	$30 yellow-green ..	40	40
CC91/105	*Set of 15*		40	40

No. CC105 differs from No. CC98 in that the top left character has the white upper line unbroken, and there is a white gap in the shadow between the soldier's feet.

$500 I. Thin numerals. II. Thick numerals
$1,000 I. Stop after "1000". II. No stop

(Litho Kuo Kwang Ptg Co, Hankow)

1949 (July). *P 10 to 12 and compound.*

CC106	CC **15**	$110 yellow-brown..	5	8
		a. Imperf ..	40	40
CC107		$130 violet ..	8	5
		a. Imperf ..	40	40
CC108		$200 orange ..	5	5
CC109		$290 brown ..	10	5
CC110		$370 blue ..	15	12
CC111		$500 light blue (I) ..	75	8
CC112		$500 light blue (II) ..	25	5
CC113		$1,000 lake (I) ..	75	10
CC114		$1,000 lake (II) ..	35	5
CC115		$5,000 sepia ..	60	35
CC116		$10,000 carmine-pink ..	90	65
CC106/116	*Set of 11*		3·50	1·50

(CC 16)

(CC 17)

1949 (5 Aug). *Third issue for Kiangsi. Various stamps of Nationalist China surch by Dah Wen Ptg Co, Nanchang.*

*(a) As Type CC **16***

CC117	**82**	$1 on $70 deep lilac (654) ..	5	5
CC118	**107**	$10 on $100 crimson (889) ..	5	5
CC119	**118**	$10 on $500 green (951) ..	5	5
CC120	**72**	$20 on 2 c. olive-green (896) ..	5	5
CC121	**118**	$10,000 on $6,000 brt pur (963) ..	1·25	1·25

On No. CC120 there are two vertical columns of surcharge, with two further bottom characters close together.

(b) As Type CC 17

CC122	60	$10 on 1 c. yellow-orge (508)	20	20
CC123		$10 on 1 c. yellow-orge (527)	5	5
CC124	72	$20 on 3 c. brown-lake (464)	5	5
CC125	107	$1,000 on $100 crimson (889) ..	25	25
CC126	82	$5,000 on $1 ol-grn (1007) (R.) ..	1·00	1·00
CC117/126		Set of 10 ..	2·75	2·75

On No. CC126 there are only two horizontal rows of over-print, with no surcharge of new value

CC 18 Entry of Communist Troops into Hankow

CC 19 River Scene, Hanyang

CC 20 River Wall, Wuchang

(CC 21)

(CC 22)

(Litho Kuo Kwang Ptg Co, Hankow)

1949 (16 Aug). *Liberation of Hankow, Wuchang and Hanyang.*

			A. P 11		B. Imp	
CC127	CC 18	$70 green ..	15	20	15	20
CC128		$220 carmine	15	20	15	20
CC129	CC 19	$290 brown ..	15	20	15	20
CC130		$370 blue ..	15	20	15	20
CC131	CC 20	$500 purple ..	15	20	15	20
CC132		$1,000 scarlet ..	15	20	15	20
CC127/132		Set of 6 ..	80	1·00	80	1·00

1949 (Aug). *Issue for Honan. Surch as Type CC 21, in red.*

CC133	CC 13	$7 on $6 apple-green	5	10
CC134		$14 on $15 ultramarine	5	5
CC135		$70 on $30 yellow-green	5	5

This and the next three issues were made because the currency in Honan Province had a different value from that in the other provinces of Central China.

1949 (Aug). *Issue for Honan. Optd as Type CC 22.*

CC136	CC 13	$3 orange-brown	5	8
CC137	CC 14	$7 yellow-brown..	5	8
CC138	CC 13	$10 blue-green	5	8
CC139	CC 14	$14 brown	5	8
CC140	CC 13	$30 yellow-green ..	5	8
CC141	CC 14	$35 slate-grey	5	8
CC142	CC 13	$50 purple	5	8
CC143		$70 dull green	5	8
CC144	CC 15	$110 yellow-brown..	5	8
CC145		$220 rose-red	8	8
CC146	CC 15	$290 brown	5	8
CC147		$370 blue	5	8
CC148		$500 light blue (I)	8	12
CC149		$1,000 lake (II)	15	25
CC150		$5,000 sepia	60	80
CC151		$10,000 carmine-pink ..	1·50	2·00
CC136/151		Set of 16 ..	2·50	3·50

(CC 23)

(CC 24)

CCP 25

(CC 26)

1949 (Aug). *Issue for Honan. Optd as Type CC 23.*

			A. P 11		B. Imp	
CC152	CC 18	$70 green ..	20	25	20	25
CC153		$220 carmine	20	25	20	25
CC154	CC 19	$290 brown ..	20	25	20	25
CC155		$370 blue ..	20	25	20	25
CC156	CC 20	$500 purple ..	20	25	20	25
CC157		$1,000 scarlet ..	20	25	20	25
CC152/157		Set of 6 ..	1·00	1·25	1·00	1·25

1949 (Sept). *Issue for Honan. No. CC22 surch as Type CC 24, in red.*

CC158	CC 4	$290 on $30 apple-green	20	20
CC159		$370 on $30 apple-green	50	50

(Litho Kuo Kwang Ptg Co, Hankow)

1949 (Nov). *PARCELS POST. P 11 to 11½.*

CCP160	CCP 25	$5,000 brown	75	90
CCP161		$10,000 rose-carmine	1·25	1·50
CCP162		$20,000 deep green	2·75	3·00
CCP163		$50,000 vermilion ..	5·00	6·00
CCP160/163		Set of 4 ..	9·00	10·00

1949 (22 Dec). *Surch as Type CC 26.*

CC164	CC 13	$200 on $1 yellow-orange	5	8
CC165		$200 on $3 orange-brown	5	10
CC166		$200 on $6 apple-green	5	10
CC167	CC 14	$200 on $7 yellow-brown	5	10
CC168		$200 on $14 brown ..	5	8
CC169		$200 on $35 slate-grey	5	10
CC170		$200 on $70 dull green	5	5
CC171	CC 13	$200 on $80 carmine	5	5
CC172	CC 14	$200 on $220 rose-red	5	8
CC173	CC 15	$200 on $370 blue ..	5	5
CC174	CC 14	$300 on $70 dull green	5	5
CC175	CC 13	$300 on $80 carmine	5	5
CC176	CC 14	$300 on $220 rose-red	5	5
CC177	CC 13	$1,200 on $3 orange-brown	10	10
CC178	CC 14	$1,200 on $7 yellow-brown	12	10
CC179		$1,500 on $14 brown ..	15	5
CC180	CC 13	$2,100 on $1 yellow-orange	20	10
CC181		$2,100 on $6 apple-green	30	10
CC182	CC 14	$2,100 on $35 slate-grey	35	10
CC183	CC 15	$5,000 on $370 blue ..	50	8
CC164/183		Set of 20 ..	2·00	1·40

B. EAST CHINA

The East China Liberation Area consisted of the provinces of Shantung, Kiangsu, Anhwei, Chekiang and Fukien.

EC 99 Methods of Transport

(EC 100)

(Litho in Tientsin)

1949 (Apr). *Seventh Anniv of Shantung Communist Postal Administration. A. P 9 to 11. B. Imperf.*

			A		B	
EC307	EC 99	$1 yell-green	5	5	5	5
EC308		$2 blue-green	5	5	5	5
EC309		$3 dp carm ..	5	5	5	5
EC310		$5 dull brown	5	5	5	5
		a. Without optd character	5·00	—	5·00	—

				A		B	
EC311	EC **99**	$10 ultram	..	5	5	5	5
EC312		$13 violet	..	5	5	5	5
EC313		$18 blue	..	5	5	5	5
EC314		$21 vermilion		5	5	5	5
EC315		$30 grey	..	5	5	5	5
EC316		$50 carmine	..	5	5	5	5
EC317		$100 olive	..	5	5	5	5
EC307/317		Set of 11	..	40	40	40	40

The $5 has an overprinted character obliterating a Japanese flag on the tower.

1949 (4 May). *Sun Yat-sen issue of Nationalist China surch as Type EC **100**, at Nanking.*

EC318	**145**	$1 on $10 green (1161) (R.)	..	10	15
EC319		$3 on $20 brown-purple (1162)	..	10	15

Nanking was taken by the Communists on 24 April, 1949.

EC **101** Train and Postal Runner
EC **102** Victorious Troops and Map of Battle
(EC **103**)

(Litho in Tientsin)

1949 (May). *Dated "1949.2.7".*

A. P 8 to 11. B. *Imperf*

				A		B	
EC320	EC **101**	$1 yell-grn		5	5	5	5
EC321		$2 blue-grn		5	5	5	5
EC322		$3 dp carm		5	5	5	5
EC323		$5 brown	..	5	5	5	5
EC324		$10 ultram	..	5	5	5	5
EC325		$13 violet	..	5	5	5	5
EC326		$18 blue	..	5	5	5	5
EC327		$21 vermilion		5	5	5	5
EC328		$30 dp grey		5	5	5	5
EC329		$50 carmine		5	5	5	5
EC330		$100 olive	..	5	5	5	5
EC320/330		Set of 11	..	40	40	40	40

(Litho in Tientsin)

1949 (7 May). *Victory of Hwai-Hai (Hwaiyin and Haichow).* A. P 9½ to 11. B. *Imperf.*

				A		B	
EC331	EC **102**	$1 yell-grn		5	5	5	5
EC332		$2 blue-grn		5	5	5	5
EC333		$3 dull carm		5	5	5	5
EC334		$5 sepia	..	5	5	5	5
EC335		$10 ultram	..	5	5	5	5
EC336		$13 violet	..	5	5	5	5
EC337		$18 blue	..	5	5	5	5
EC338		$21 vermilion		5	5	5	5
EC339		$30 grey	..	5	5	5	5
EC340		$50 carmine		5	5	5	5
EC341		$100 olive	..	5	5	5	5
EC331/341		Set of 11	..	40	40	40	40

1949 (15 May). *Sun Yat-sen issue of Nationalist China surch as Type EC **103**, at Hangchow.*

EC342	**145**	$1 on $1 orange (1152)	..	5	5
EC343		$3 on $20 brown-pur (1162) (R.)	..	5	5
EC344		$5 on $100 chestnut (1156)	..	5	5
EC345		$5 on $100 brown (1164)	..	5	5
EC346		$10 on $50 slate-green (1155) (R.)	..	5	5
EC347		$13 on $10 green (1153)	..	5	5
EC342/347		Set of 6	..	25	25

Hangchow was taken by the Communists on 3 May 1949.

★**200**★
郵 華
政 東
圓百貳作暫 念圓
(EC **104**)

券民人 改
拾圓 作
東華
(EC **105**)

人民
伍
券
(EC **106**)

1949 (May). *Sun Yat-sen issue of Nationalist China surch as Type EC **104**, at Wusih.*

EC348	**145**	$50 on $1,000 blue (1167) (R.)	..	8·00	10·00
EC349		$100 on $5,000 turquoise-blue (1169) (R.)	..	12·00	15·00
EC350		$200 on $20 brown-purple (1162)		16·00	20·00
		a. Error. "500" for "200"	..	32·00	

1949 (May). *Stamps of Nationalist China surch at Wuhu.*

(a) Revenue stamps with Gold Yuan surcharges surch as Type EC **105**

EC351	**143**	$5 on 50 c. on $20 red-brn (1136) (G.)	..	5	5
EC352		$10 on 50 c. on $20 red-brown (1136)	..	5	5
EC353		$20 on 50 c. on $20 red-brn (1122) (R.)	..	5	5
EC354		$50 on 50 c. on $20 red-brn (1136) (R.)	..	5	5
EC351/354		Set of 4	..	15	15

(b) Sun Yat-sen issue surch as Type EC **106**

EC355	**145**	$30 on $1,000 blue (1160)	..	5	5
EC356		$30 on $1,000 blue (1167)	..	5	5
EC357		$50 on $200 red-orange (1165) (B.)	..	5	5
EC358		$100 on $5,000 turquoise-blue (1169) (R.)	..	12	25
EC359		$300 on $10,000 grey-brown (1170) (R.)	..	25	25
EC360		$500 on $200 red-orange (1165) (B.)	..	50	50
EC351/360		Set of 10	..	90	1·00

Wuhu was taken by the Communists on 22 April 1949.

EC **107** Maps of Shanghai and Nanking
EC **108** Train and Postal Runner

1949 (30 May). *Liberation of Nanking and Shanghai. Litho. P 8½ to 11.*

EC361	EC **107**	$1 rose-red	..	5	5
EC362		$2 blue-green	..	5	5
EC363		$3 violet	..	5	5
EC364		$5 purple-brown	..	5	5
		a. Imperf (pair)	..	3·00	
EC365		$10 deep ultramarine	..	5	5
		a. Imperf (pair)	..	3·00	
EC366		$30 deep grey	..	5	5
EC367		$50 carmine	..	5	5
EC368		$100 olive	..	5	5
EC369		$500 orange	..	20	20
EC361/369		Set of 10	..	50	50

Shanghai was taken by the Communists on 27 May 1949.

(Litho San Yih Ptg Co, Shanghai ($10) or Dah Tung Book Co (others))

1949 (July)—**50.** *Dated "1949".*

			A. P 12½		B. P 14	
EC370	EC **108**	$10 ultram	5	5	†	
EC371		$15 verm	5	5	5	5
EC372		$30 grey-black	5	5	5	5
EC373		$50 carm	5	5	†	
EC374		$60 blue-green	†		5	5
EC375		$100 olive	†		5	5
EC376		$1,600 vio-bl (2.50)	30	50	†	
EC377		$2,000 purple (2.50)	60	50	†	
EC370/377		Set of 8	1·00	1·00	†	

EC **109** General Chu Teh, Mao Tse-tung and Troops

(Litho Dah Tung Book Co, Shanghai)

1949 (Aug). *22nd Anniv of Chinese People's Liberation Army. P 12½.*

EC378	EC **109**	$70 brown-orange (1.8)	5	5
EC379		$270 carmine (17.8)	5	5
EC380		$370 emerald-green (17.8)	5	5
EC381		$470 purple (17.8)	5	5
EC382		$570 blue (17.8)	5	5
EC378/382	Set of 5		20	20

For other values in this design and with only three characters in bottom panel, see Nos. SW6/16.

$200	$500	$1,000
$2,000	$5,000	$10,000

(ECP 110)

1949 (7 Sept). *PARCELS POST. No. 1356 of Nationalist China surch as Type ECP* **110.**

ECP383	**169**	$200 on $10 blue-green	6·00	50
ECP384		$500 on $10 blue-green	6·00	50
ECP385		$1,000 on $10 blue-green	6·00	70
ECP386		$2,000 on $10 blue-green	6·00	1·50
ECP387		$5,000 on $10 blue-green	6·00	3·00
ECP388		$10,000 on $10 blue-green	6·00	6·00
ECP383/388	Set of 6		33·00	11·00

EC **111** Mao Tse-tung   (EC **112**)

(Litho San Yih Ptg Co, Shanghai)

1949 (Oct). *P 12½.*

EC389	EC **111**	$10 ultramarine	10	15
EC390		$15 scarlet..	10	15
EC391		$70 brown..	5	5
EC392		$100 deep lilac	5	5
EC393		$150 brown-orange	5	5
EC394		$200 greenish grey	5	5
EC395		$500 bluish grey	5	5
EC396		$1,000 rose	5	5
EC397		$2,000 emerald-green	5	5
EC389/397	Set of 9		30	50

1949 (25 Nov). *Sun Yat-sen issue of Nationalist China surch "Chinese People's Postal Service East China Region" and new value as Type EC* **112.**

EC398	**145**	$400 on $200 orange-red (1165)	5	8
EC399		$1,000 on $50 slate-green (1163) (R.)	5	8
EC400		$1,200 on $100 brown (1164)	5	25
EC401		$1,600 on $20,000 apple-green (1171)	5	10
EC402		$2,000 on $1,000 blue (1167) (R.)	5	10
		a. Perf 14	—	50
EC398/402	Set of 5		15	50

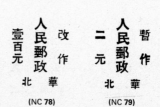

(ECP 113)   (ECP 114)

1950 (28 Jan). *PARCELS POST. Nos. 1353/5 and unissued 10 c. perf 12½ of Nationalist China surch as Type ECP* **113.**

ECP403	**169**	$5,000 on 10 c. blue (R.)	6·00	1·25
ECP404		$10,000 on $1 orange	6·00	1·75
ECP405		$20,000 on $2 blue	6·00	2·00
ECP406		$50,000 on $5 red	18·00	5·00
ECP403/406	Set of 4		34·00	9·00

1950 (28 Jan). *PARCELS POST. Nationalist Chinese Parcels Post stamps of 1944-45 and 1947-48 surch as Type ECP* **114.**

ECP407	P **1**	$5,000 on $500 green (R.)	4·00	1·00
ECP408		$10,000 on $1,000 blue (R.)	4·00	1·00
ECP409	P **3**	$20,000 on $3,000 blue-green	6·00	2·50
ECP410		$50,000 on $5,000 orange-red	10·00	4·00
ECP407/410	Set of 4		22·00	8·00

C. NORTH CHINA

The North China Liberation Area consisted of the provinces of Chahar, Hopeh, Shansi and Suiyuan. Tientsin was taken by the Communists on 15 January 1949 and Peking on 23 January.

NC **74** Infantry   NC **75** Industry

1949 (Jan–June). *Litho. Imperf.*

NC283	NC **74**	50c. purple	15	20
NC284		$1 greyish blue	30	40
NC285		$2 yellow-green (June)	15	20
NC286		$3 violet	15	20
NC287		$5 brown (June)	15	20
NC288	NC **75**	$6 pale claret	15	20
NC289	NC **74**	$10 pale green (June)	15	20
NC290		$12 carmine (June)..	15	20
NC283/290	Set of 8		1·25	1·60

The 50 c. and $6 have the value in Chinese characters only.

NC **76** Pagoda   (NC **77**) (50 c.)   ($1)   ($3)

(Recess Central Trust, Chungking)

1949 (Jan). *Money Order stamps of Nationalist China, Type NC* **76,** *surch "North China Postal Service Provisional Postage Stamps" and new value as Type NC* **77,** *at Tientsin (top central character differs as shown). No gum. P 13.*

NC291	NC **76**	50 c. on $50 grey-brown	10	20
NC292		$1 on $50 grey-brown	20	35
NC293		$3 on $50 grey-brown	20	35
NC294		$6 on $20 brown-purple	25	40
NC291/294	Set of 4		70	1·10

The 50 c. exists with smaller central characters.

(NC **78**)   (NC **79**)   NC **80**

1949 (7 Mar). *Various stamps surch "People's Postal Service North China" and new value as Type* NC **78** *(characters in right-hand column="Changed to")*.

(a) Sun Yat-sen issue of Nationalist China

NC295	**107**	$100 on $100 crimson (B.)* ..	50	10

(b) On stamps of North-Eastern Provinces

NC296	**5**	50 c. on 5 c. lake	5	5
NC297		$1 on 10 c. orange	5	5
NC298		$2 on 20 c. apple-green ..	5	5
		a. Surch inverted ..	5·00	5·00
NC299		$3 on 50 c. red-orange ..	5	5
NC300		$4 on $5 deep green ..	5	5
NC301		$6 on $10 rose-red (32) ..	5	5
NC302		$10 on $300 pale blue-green	8	8
NC303		$12 on $1 blue	8	8
NC304		$18 on $3 brown ..	8	8
NC305		$20 on 50 c. red-orange (B.)*	5	5
NC306		$20 on $20 olive (29) ..	5	8
NC307		$20 on $20 olive (33) ..	20	8
NC308		$30 on $2.50 indigo (R.) ..	25	10
NC309		$40 on 25 c. blkish brown (R.) ..	25	10
NC310		$50 on $109 blue-green (R.) ..	25	10
NC311		$80 on $1 blue (R.)* ..	20	8
NC312		$100 on $65 yellow-green (R.)	20	8
NC295/312		*Set of 18*	1·80	1·00

*On these stamps the bottom character in the left-hand column of the overprint is square in shape.

1949 (Apr). *Various stamps surch "People's Postal Service North China" and new value as Type* NC **79** *(characters in right-hand column="Temporary use")*.

(a) Sun Yat-sen issues of Nationalist China

NC313	**107**	$100 on $100 crimson (G.)* ..	25	10
NC314		$300 on $700 red-brown (B.)* ..	25	10
		a. Surch inverted ..	5·00	
NC315	**118**	$500 on $500 green (R.)* ..	12	8
NC316		$3,000 on $3,000 blue (R.)* ..	70	35

(b) Stamps of North-Eastern Provinces

NC317	**5**	$1 on 25 c. blkish brn (G.)* ..	5	5
		a. Surch in grey ..	5	
NC318		$2 on 20 c. apple-green ..	5	5
NC319		$3 on 50 c. red-orange ..	5	5
NC320		$4 on $5 deep green ..	5	5
NC321		$6 on $10 rose-red (28) ..	5	5
NC322		$6 on $10 rose-red (32) ..	5	5
NC323		$10 on $300 pale bl-grn (R.)*	5	5
NC324		$12 on $1 blue ..	5	5
NC325		$20 on 50 c. red-orange (G.)* ..	5	5
NC326		$20 on $20 olive (29) (R.)* ..	8	8
NC327		$40 on 25 c. blkish brn (R.)* ..	15	15
NC328		$50 on $109 blue-green (R.)* ..	12	12
		a. Surch 15½ mm wide instead of 15½ mm	1·50	75
NC329		$80 on $1 blue (R.)* ..	12	12
NC313/329		*Set of 17*	3·25	2·00

*On these stamps the bottom character in the left-hand column of the overprint is square in shape.

1949 (30 May–June). *Labour Day. Recess.*

			A. P 14		B. Imp	
NC330	NC **80**	$20 scarlet ..	10	10	15	15
NC331		$40 deep blue (13.6) ..	10	10	15	15
NC332		$60 yell-brn (13.6) ..	12	12	15	15
NC333		$80 blue-grn (13.6) ..	15	15	25	25
NC334		$100 violet (13.6) ..	20	20	25	25
NC330/334		*Set of 5* ..	60	60	85	85

Also issued in blocks of four, perforated only on the outside edges (*Price £10 for five blocks un or us*).

政郵民人

元百捌

北　華

(NCP 81)

作圓佰伍暫

電郵北華

作　暫

500

(NCP 82)

1949 (June). *PARCELS POST. Parcels Post stamps of Nationalist China surch as Type* NC **78**, *at Peking*.

NCP335	P **3**	$300 on $6,000,000 grey	—	60
NCP336		$400 on $8,000,000 vermilion	—	60
NCP337		$500 on $10,000,000 sage-grn	—	90
NCP338		$800 on $5,000,000 grey-lilac	—	1·25
NCP339		$1,000 on $3,000,000 slate-blue	—	1·75
NCP335/339		*Set of 5*	—	4·50

1949 (June). *PARCELS POST. Parcels Post stamps of Nationalist China surch as Type* NCP **82**, *at Tientsin*.

NCP340	P **3**	$500 on $3,000,000 slate-blue	—	75
NCP341		$1,000 on $8,000,000 grey-lilac	—	1·50
NCP342		$3,000 on $8,000,000 vermilion	—	2·25
NCP343		$5,000 on $10,000,000 sage-grn	—	3·00
NCP340/343		*Set of 4*	—	6·50

政郵民人　　　北　　華

紙印裏包　　圓拾貳

元　六　　紙印裏包

　　　　　　　圓拾貳

北　華　　　北　　華

(NCP 83)　　(NCP 84)

華

圓拾貳

紙印裏包

圓拾貳

(NCP 85)

1949 (June). *PARCELS POST. Money Order stamps surch as Type* NCP **83**, *at Peking. No gum. P 13*.

NCP344	NC **76**	$6 on $5 red	10	10
NCP345		$20 on $50 grey	20	10
NCP346		$50 on $20 brown-purple	20	10
NCP347		$100 on $10 olive-green	40	10
NCP344/347		*Set of 4*	75	30

1949 (June). *PARCELS POST. Money Order stamps surch as Types* NCP **84** *or* NCP **85** *(No. NCP349), at Tientsin*.

(i) Recess Dah Tung Book Co. P 14

NCP348	NC **76**	$20 on $1 brown-orange ..	20	10
NCP349		$20 on $1 brown-orange ..	40	20
NCP350		$30 on $2 blue-green ..	20	10
NCP351		$30 on $2 blue-green (R.) ..	20	10
NCP352		$30 on $10 green ..	30	10
NCP353		$30 on $10 green (R.) ..	50	20
NCP354		$100 on $10 green (R.) ..	20	10

(ii) Recess Commercial Press. P 12½

NCP355	NC **76**	$20 on $1 brown-orange ..	40	20
NCP356		$100 on $10 yell-grn (R.) ..	40	20

(iii) Litho Central Trust. P 13

NCP357	NC **76**	$50 on $5 red ..	20	10

(iv) Typo Kwang Hwa Printing Co. Roul 9½

NCP358	NC **76**	$30 on $2 blue-green (R.) ..	50	20
NCP348/358		*Set of 11* ..	3·00	1·40

NC 86

NC 87

Mao Tse-tung

1949 (1 July). *28th Anniv of Chinese Communist Party. Recess.*

			A. P 14		B. Imp	
NC359	NC **86**	$10 scarlet ..	5	5	20	30
NC360	NC **87**	$20 blue ..	5	5	25	30
NC361	NC **86**	$50 orange ..	5	5	25	30
NC362	NC **87**	$80 blue-grn ..	5	5	50	60
NC363	NC **86**	$100 violet ..	5	5	50	60
NC364	NC **87**	$120 olive-grn ..	5	5	50	60
NC365	NC **86**	$140 maroon ..	25	25	75	1·00
NC359/365		*Set of 7* ..	40	40	2·75	3·25

Stamps of Type NC **86** have the value in Chinese characters only.

(NC 88)

NCP 89 Railway Train

1949 (Aug). *Various stamps surch "People's Postal Service North China" and new value as Type NC 88.*

(a) Sun Yat-sen issue of Nationalist China

NC366	118	$10 on $7,000 red-brown		35	12

(b) Stamps of North-Eastern Provinces

NC367	5	$10 on $10 rose-red (28) (B.)			25	20
NC368		$10 on $10 rose-red (32) (B.)			20	12
NC369		$30 on 20 c. apple-green (R.)			25	12
NC370		$50 on $44 crimson (B.)			20	8
		a. Surch inverted			5·00	
NC371		$100 on $3 brown (B.)			35	12
NC372		$200 on $4 orge-brn (26) (B.)			6·00	3·00
NC373		$200 on $4 orge-brown (31) (B.)			50	20

1949 (Nov). *PARCELS POST. Recess. P 14.*

NCP374	NCP 89	$500 scarlet		—	60
NCP375		$1,000 deep blue		—	80
NCP376		$2,000 green		—	1·00
NCP377		$5,000 olive		—	2·00
NCP378		$10,000 orange		—	3·00
NCP379		$20,000 brown-red		—	7·00
NCP380		$50,000 deep purple		—	15·00
NCP374/380	*Set of 7*			—	28·00

NC 90 Gate of Heavenly Peace, Peking

NC 91 Field Workers and Factory

(Litho Commercial Press, Shanghai)

1949 (26 Nov). *P 12½.*

NC381	NC 90	$50 brown-orange		5	5
NC382		$100 carmine		5	5
NC383		$200 blue-green		5	5
NC384		$300 purple		5	5
NC385		$400 blue		5	5
NC386		$500 brown		5	5
NC387		$700 violet		15	15
NC381/387	*Set of 7*			35	35

1949 (Dec). *Recess. P 14.*

NC388	NC 91	$1,000 orange		5	5
NC389		$3,000 deep blue		10	10
NC390		$5,000 carmine		25	25
NC391		$10,000 lake-brown		50	50
NC388/391	*Set of 4*			80	80

D. NORTH WEST CHINA

The North West China Liberation Area consisted of the provinces of Kansu, Ninghsia, Shensi, Tsinghai and Sinkiang.

NW 21 Mao Tse-tung

NW 22 Great Wall

(Litho Kwang Hwa Press, Sian)

1949 (15 Oct). *Imperf.*

NW76	NW 21	$50 pink			5	5
NW77	NW 22	$100 blue			5	5
NW78	NW 21	$200 orange			5	5
		a. Error. $200 pink			6·00	6·00
NW79	NW 22	$400 sepia			5	5
NW76/79	*Set of 4*				15	15

E. SOUTH CHINA

The South China Liberation Area consisted of the provinces of Kwangsi and Kwangtung.

SC 1 Ho Nam Bridge, Canton

(SC 2)

(SC 3)

1949 (4 Nov). *Liberation of Canton. Litho. Imperf.*

SC1	SC 1	$10 green		5	5
SC2		$20 brown		5	5
SC3		$30 violet		5	5
SC4		$50 carmine		5	5
SC5		$100 blue		5	5
SC1/5	*Set of 5*			10	20

Canton was taken by the Communists on 15 October 1949.

1949 (9 Nov). *Liberation of Swatow. Silver Yuan surcharges of Nationalist China handstamped "Temporary use: Liberation of Swatow" as Type SC 2, in red.*

SC6	145	2½ c. on $500 mauve (1362)		2·00	2·00
SC7		2½ c. on $500 mauve (1363)		2·00	2·00
SC8		15 c. on $10 green (1364)		2·50	2·50

The handstamp was designed to overprint a block of four stamps at a time. The distance between the top and bottom rows of characters varies from ¾ to 2½ mm; that between the vertical columns of characters is 8½ mm.

1949 (9 Nov). *Liberation of Swatow. Various stamps of Nationalist China optd "Temporary use: Liberation of Swatow" with Type SC 3, in red.*

(a) "Unit" stamps

SC9	146	(—) Brown-orange (1211B)		80	35
SC10	147	(—) Pale blue-green (1212A)		80	1·40
SC11	148	(—) Magenta (1213A)		80	1·40
SC12	149	(—) Carmine (1214A)		80	1·40

(b) Sun Yat-sen (Fourteenth issue)

SC13	145	2 c. yellow-orange (1345)		2·50	1·40
SC14		4 c. blue-green (1346)		4·00	2·25
SC15		10 c. deep lilac (1347)		40	25
SC16		20 c. pale blue (1349)		50	35

(c) Flying Geese issue

SC17	169	$1 orange		1·60	80
SC18		$10 blue-green		20·00	10·00

(d) Silver Yuan surcharges

SC19	145	2½ c. on $500 mauve (1362)		40	30
SC20		2½ c. on $500 mauve (1363)		35	30
SC21		15 c. on $10 green (1364)		40	30

Swatow was taken by the Communists on 17 October 1949.

(SC 4)

1949–50. *Surch as Type SC 4.*

SC22	SC 1	$300 on $30 violet (R.)		5	5
SC23		$500 on $20 brown (R.)		10	5
SC24		$800 on $30 violet (G.)		15	5
SC25		$1,000 on $10 green (R.)		30	5
SC26		$1,000 on $20 brown (R.)		35	5
SC22/26	*Set of 5*			85	20

F. SOUTH WEST CHINA

The South West China Liberation Area consisted of the provinces of Kweichow, Szechwan, Sikang and Yunnan.

(SW 1)

SW 2 Gen. Chu Teh, Mao Tse-tung and Troops

1949 (1 Dec). *Kweichow issue. Silver Yuan issues of Nationalist China optd "Kweichow People's Post" and surch as Type SW 1, by Wen Wei Press, Kweiyang.*

SW1	145	$20 on 2 c. yellow-orange (1345)	5	10
SW2		$50 on 4 c. blue-green (1346) ..	5	5
SW3	169	$100 on $1 orange	5	5
SW4		$400 on $5 red ..	15	20
		a. "4" in "400" omitted	1·00	
SW5		$2,000 on $10 blue-green ..	40	50
SW1/5		*Set of 5*	60	75

Kweiyang was taken by the Communists on 13 November 1949.

(Litho San Yih Ptg Co, Shanghai)

1949 (Dec). P 12½.

SW 6	SW 2	$10 blue	5	8
SW 7		$20 reddish purple ..	5	5
SW 8		$30 red-orange	5	8
SW 9		$50 grey-green	5	8
SW10		$100 carmine	5	5
SW11		$200 light blue ..	5	8
SW12		$300 violet-blue	5	5
SW13		$500 grey-black	15	15
SW14		$1,000 purple ..	25	25
SW15		$2,000 pale green	50	40
SW16		$5,000 yellow-orange	1·00	70
SW6/16		*Set of 11* ..	2·10	1·75

For other values in this design, see Nos. EC378/82.

(SW 3)   (SW 4)

1949–50. *Surch as Type SW 3, at Chungking (number of characters and length as indicated).*

SW17	SW 2	$300 on $100 carmine (SW 3)	10	5
SW18		$500 on $100 carmine (5 characters, 17 mm) ..	10	5
SW19		$1,200 on $100 carm (7 chars.)	50	20
SW20		$1,500 on $200 lt blue (7 chars.)	20	10
SW21		$2,000 on $200 lt blue (5 chars.)	30	10
SW17/21		*Set of 5* ..	1·10	45

Chungking was taken by the Communists on 30 November 1949.

1950 (Jan). *East Szechwan issue. Optd "East Szechwan" in Chinese characters as Type SW 4, at Chungking.*

SW22	SW 2	$100 carmine	15	15
SW23		$200 light blue ..	15	15

(SW 5)   (SW 6)

1950 (Jan). *Handstamped with new value as Type SW 5, at Chungking.*

SW24	SW 2	$1,200 on $100 carmine	60	40
SW25		$1,500 on $200 light blue ..	60	40

No. SW24 exists with eight types of overprint and No. SW25 with four.

1950 (Jan). *West Szechwan issue. Optd "West Szechwan" in Chinese characters as Type SW 6, at Chengtu.*

SW26	SW 2	$100 carmine	15	10
SW27		$200 light blue ..	30	15
SW28		$300 violet-blue ..	45	20

Chengtu was taken by the Communists on 27 December 1949.

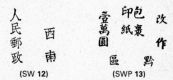

(SW 7) ($800)   (SW 8) ($200)   (SW 9) ($1,000)

1950 (Jan). *West Szechwan issue. Surch as Type SW 7, at Chengtu.*

SW29	SW 2	$500 on $100 carmine ..	15	15
		a. 4½ mm between lines of characters	4·00	4·00
SW30		$800 on $100 carmine (SW 7)	5	5
SW31		$1,000 on $50 grey-green	10	10
SW32		$2,000 on $200 light blue	25	15
SW33		$3,000 on $300 violet-blue	50	50
SW29/33		*Set of 5*	95	85

1950 (Jan). *West Szechwan issue. Sun Yat-sen issue of Nationalist China surch as Types SW 8/9, at Chengtu.*

SW34	145	$100 on 4 c. blue-green (1346) ..	20	15
SW35		$200 on 4 c. blue-green (1346) (SW 8)	30	25
SW36		$800 on 16 c. orange-red (1348)	1·50	1·25
SW37		$1,000 on 16 c. orange-red (1348) (SW 9)	3·00	2·50
SW34/37		*Set of 4* ..	4·50	3·25

(SW 10)

SW 11 Map of China with Flag in S.W.

1950. *Kiunglai (West Szechwan) provisional. Handstamped with new value with Type SW 10.*

SW38	SW 2	$300 on $50 grey-green	4·00	6·50

(Litho at Nanking)

1950 (Jan). *Liberation of the South West. P 9 to 11½.*

SW39	SW 11	$20 deep blue	15	20
SW40		$30 yellow-green ..	15	20
SW41		$50 scarlet	15	20
SW42		$100 brown	15	20
SW39/42		*Set of 4*	50	70

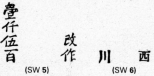

(SW 12)   (SWP 13)

1950 (Feb). *"Unit" stamps of Nationalist China optd as Type SW 12 at Kunming.*

SW43	146	(–) Brown-orange (1211A) ..	12·00	12·00
SW44		(–) Brown-orange (1211B) ..	10·00	10·00
SW45	148	(–) Magenta (1213A) ..	10·00	10·00
SW46	149	(–) Carmine (1214A) ..	10·00	10·00
SW43/46		*Set of 4* ..	38·00	38·00

1950 (Feb). *PARCELS POST. Nos. EC370/2 optd "Parcels Post Stamp. Kweichow" and surch with new value as Type SWP 13, at Kweiyang.*

SWP47	EC 109	$5,000 on $10 ultramarine ..	60	70
SWP48		$10,000 on $15 vermilion ..	75	90
SWP49		$50,000 on $30 grey-black ..	1·75	2·00

(SW **14**) ($3,000)

($5,000)   ($10,000)   ($20,000)   ($50,000)

(Surch characters in left-hand column)

Nos. SW50 and SW52/3 have three characters in left-hand column; Nos. SW51 and SW54 have five.

1950. *Surch as Type* SW **14.**

SW50	SW **11**	$60 on $30 yellow-green ..	20	15
SW51		$150 on $30 yellow-green ..	15	12
SW52		$300 on $20 deep blue (R.) ..	15	8
SW53		$300 on $100 brown	20	12
SW54		$1,500 on $100 brown	20	15
SW55		$3,000 on $50 scarlet	35	20
SW56		$5,000 on $50 scarlet	40	25
SW57		$10,000 on $50 scarlet	1·10	40
SW58		$20,000 on $50 scarlet	3·00	75
SW59		$50,000 on $50 scarlet	6·00	2·50
SW50/59	*Set of 10*		10·00	4·25

(SW **15**)

1950. *Surch as Type* SW **15** (*with bars*).

SW60	SW **2**	$800 on $30 red-orange ..	1·00	1·25
SW61	SW **11**	$1,000 on $50 scarlet	30	10
SW62		$2,000 on $100 brown	30	20
SW63		$4,000 on $20 deep blue ..	70	50
SW64		$5,000 on $30 yellow-green ..	70	50
SW60/64	*Set of 5*		2·75	2·50

IV. CHINESE PEOPLE'S REPUBLIC

(General Issues for China)

The Chinese People's Republic was proclaimed on 1 October 1949.

1949. Yuans
1955. 100 Fen = 1 Yuan

NORTH EAST CHINA ISSUES. From 1949 to 1951 stamps of similar design to some of the following but with additional characters and in different values were issued in North East China (*q.v.*).

GUM or NO GUM. Nos. 1401/1891 were issued *without* gum (except Nos. 1843/5 and 1850/7). From No. 1892 onwards all postage stamps were issued *with* gum, *unless otherwise stated*. From 1965 some issues seem to have no gum, though in fact they bear an adhesive substance.

SERIAL MARKINGS. Issues other than definitive issues are divided into two categories: "commemorative" and "special". Figures below the design of each stamp of such issues indicate: (a) serial number of the issue; (b) number of stamps in the issue; (c) number of the stamp within the issue; and (d) year of issue (from No. 1557 on). Neither chronological order of issue nor sequence of value is always strictly followed. From No. 2343 these serial markings were omitted till they were re-introduced from No. 2433 onwards.

REPRINTS. Collectors should beware of reprints, both unused and cancelled to order, of commemorative and special issues of China and North East China from 1949 to 1952 made in replacement of exhausted stocks by the Chinese Postal Administration for sale to stamp collectors. These reprints were put on sale after the currency revaluation which took place on 1 March 1955, but could be used postally as stamps in the old currency were valid for use until 31 March 1956. However, as this was not their primary function, we do not list them.

Notes with identification details of the reprints are given where reprints are known.

Our prices are for originals.

CANCELLED TO ORDER. Most stamps of the Chinese People's Republic issued from 1961 onwards exist cancelled to order. Where this applies the prices in the used column are for cancelled stamps, postally used copies being worth more.

181 Celebrations at   Original   Reprint
Gate of Heavenly
Peace, Peking

Reprints exist, easily identified by the altered ornament on the lantern and the clearer impression.

(Litho Commercial Press, Shanghai)

1949 (8 Oct). *Celebration of First Session of Chinese People's Political Conference.* P 12½.

1401	**181**	$30 blue ..		..	5	5
1402		$50 carmine	..	..	5	5
1403		$100 emerald-green	..	..	10	5
1404		$200 purple	..	..	12	8
1401/1404	*Set of 4* ..		..	..	30	20

182   Original   Reprint

Reprints exist, easily identified by the heavier shading on the fist.

(Litho Commercial Press, Shanghai)

1949 (16 Nov). *World Federation of Trade Unions, Asiatic and Australasian Congress, Peking.* P 12½.

1405	**182**	$100 carmine	..	.. ..	10	5
1406		$300 deep green		..	12	5
1407		$500 bright blue	..	.. ..	15	8
1405/1407		Set of 3 ..	..	.. ..	35	15

183 Conference Hall

184 Mao Tse-tung

Original Reprint
Reprints exist. T **183**
is completely
re-engraved. The
simplest test is the
smaller "box" in the
first character in the top
scroll.

Original Reprint
T **184** is more lightly
printed and the thin
shading lines on the
rostrum do not reach the
top.

(Recess Dah Tung Book Co, Shanghai)

1950 (1 Feb). *Chinese People's Political Conference.* P 14.

1408	**183**	$50 scarlet		..	5	5
1409		$100 blue ..	..	..	5	5
1410	**184**	$300 brown-purple		..	15	8
1411		$500 green..	..	..	15	8
1408/1411		Set of 4 ..	..	..	35	20

185 Gate of Heavenly Peace, Peking

A Break in top line of
shading

B Top line of shading
unbroken

1950. P 12½.

(a) *Litho at Commercial Press, Shanghai. Top right corner as A* (10 Feb)

1412	**185**	$200 green	..	..	5	5
1413		$300 lake	..	..	5	5
1414		$500 carmine ..		..	5	5
1415		$800 brown-orange		..	12	5
1416		$1,000 lilac	..	..	5	5
1417		$2,000 olive	..	..	12	5
1418		$5,000 pink	..	..	5	5
1419		$8,000 blue	..	..	5	15
1420		$10,000 yellow-brown		..	5	5
1412/1420		Set of 9 ..	..	..	55	50

(b) *Typo at Nanking. Top right corner as B* (9 June)

1420a	**185**	$1,000 lilac	..	..	5	5
1420b		$3,000 lake-brown		..	5	5
1420c		$10,000 yellow-brown		..	5	5

See also Nos. 1459/63, 1481a/7 and 1493/8.

中國人民郵政

壹佰圓

100
(186)

187 Harvesters and Ox

1950. *"Unit" stamps of Nationalist China surch as T **186** (except $200 which has Chinese value at right and tablet at left).*

(a) *Nos. 1211/4A (P 12½)* (March)

1421	**148**	$100 on (–) magenta (B.)		..	5	5
1422	**149**	$200 on (–) carmine		..	5	5
1423	**147**	$300 on (–) blue-green		..	5	5
1424	**146**	$500 on (–) brown-orange (G.)		..	5	5
		a. Perf 14	..	..	1·25	75
1425		$800 on (–) brown-orange (R.)		..	5	5
		a. Perf 14	..	..	1·75	75
1426		$1,000 on (–) brown-orange		..	5	5
		a. Perf 14	..	..	5	5
1421/1426		Set of 6 ..	..	..	25	25

(b) *On Nos. 1211/4B (Rouletted)* (June)

1427	**148**	$100 on (–) magenta (B.)		..	5	5
1428	**149**	$200 on (–) carmine		..	5	5
1429	**147**	$300 on (–) blue-green		..	5	5
1430	**146**	$800 on (–) brown-orange (R.)		..	5	5
1427/1430		Set of 4 ..	..	..	15	15

1950 (May). *Unissued stamp of East China surch as in T **187**.*

1431		$20,000 on $10,000 scarlet	..	2·00	25

188 Mao Tse-tung and
Parade

中國人民郵政

伍拾圓
☆ **50** (189)

中國人民郵政
壹佰圓
★★ **100** (190)

(Litho Dah Tung Book Co, Shanghai)

1950 (1 July). *Foundation of People's Republic on 1 October 1949.* P 14.

1432	**188**	$800 carmine, yellow and green	25	12
1433		$1,000 carmine, yellow and brown	30	12
1434		$2,000 carmine, yellow and purple ..	35	20
1435		$3,000 carmine, yellow and blue ..	60	30
1432/1435		Set of 4	1·40	65

Reprints exist, perf 12½ and with extra dot in collar button.

1950 (July). *Stamps of North-Eastern Provinces surch as T **189**.*

1436	**5**	$50 on 20 c. apple-green (R.)	..	12	20
1437		$50 on 25 c. brown (R.)	..	5	15
1438		$50 on 50 c. orange	..	5	5
1439		$100 on $2.50 indigo (R.)	..	5	5
1440		$100 on $3 brown	..	5	5
1440a		$100 on $4 brown (26) (B.)	..	75	50
1441		$100 on $4 brown (31) (B.)	..	5	10
1442		$100 on $5 green	..	5	5
1443		$100 on $10 rose-red (32) (B.)	..	15	20
1443a		$400 on $20 olive (29) (B.)	..	75	50
1444		$400 on $20 olive (33) (B.)	..	15	20
1445		$400 on $44 crimson (B.)	..	15	8
1446		$400 on $65 yellow-green (R.)	..	10	5
1447		$400 on $100 green (R.)	..	10	5
1448		$400 on $200 red-brown	..	10	5
1449		$400 on $300 blue-green (R.)	..	10	5

1950 (1 Aug). *Nos. 1352/5 of Nationalist China (Flying Geese) and unissued 10 c., 16 c., 50 c. and $20 surch as T* **190.**

1450	**169**	$50 on 10 c. blue (R.)	5	5
1451		$100 on 16 c. olive (B.) ..	5	5
1452		$100 on 50 c. green (B.) ..	5	5
1453		$200 on $1 orange (G.) ..	5	5
1453a		$200 on $2 blue (R.) ..	5	5
1454		$400 on $5 red ..	5	5
1455		$400 on $10 blue-green ..	5	5
1455a		$400 on $20 purple ..	10	10
1450/1455a		*Set of 8*	35	35

Nos. 1451/2 are imperforate.

(Flag litho, rest recess Dah Tung Book Co, Shanghai)

1950 (Oct). *First Anniv of People's Republic. Flag in red, yellow and brown.* P 14.

1464	**193**	$100 violet (31.10) ..	5	5
1465		$400 orange-brown (31.10) ..	5	5
1466		$800 green (1.10) ..	12	5
1467		$1,000 olive (31.10) ..	15	10
1468		$2,000 light blue (31.10) ..	25	12
1464/1468		*Set of 5*	55	40

No. 1466 measures 44×53 *mm* from perf to perf; the remainder, 33½×37½ *mm*.

191 "Peace"   **D 12**   C

(Recess Dah Tung Book Co, Shanghai)

1950 (1 Aug). *Peace Campaign* (1st issue). P 14.

1456	**191**	$400 brown	5	5
1457		$800 green	15	5
1458		$2,000 blue	20	5

Reprints exist. Printing differences are minute but the colours are slightly brighter than those of the originals.

(Typo Nanking Ptg Co)

1950 (1 Sept). *POSTAGE DUE. No gum.* P 12½.

D1459	**D 12**	$100 blue ..	5	5
D1460		$200 blue ..	5	5
D1461		$500 blue ..	5	5
D1462		$800 blue ..	8	5
D1463		$1,000 blue ..	5	5
D1464		$2,000 blue ..	5	5
D1465		$5,000 blue ..	5	5
D1466		$8,000 blue ..	5	5
D1467		$10,000 blue ..	10	12
D1459/1464		*Set of 9* ..	45	45

(Litho People's Ptg Works, Peking)

1950 (6 Oct–Dec). *As T* **185,** *but clouds redrawn as in* C. P 14.

1459	**185**	$100 turquoise	15	8
1459a		$200 emerald-green ..	30	12
1460		$300 lake ..	5	5
1460a		$400 grey-green ..	5	5
1461		$500 carmine (1.12) ..	5	5
1462		$800 orange (*shades*) ..	5	5
1463		$2,000 brown-olive (1.12) ..	5	5
1459/1463		*Set of 7*	60	40

See also Nos. 1481a/7 and 1493/8.

27.24   **194** (47)
"Communications"   **195** Stalin Greets Mao Tse-tung

(Litho Dah Tung Book Co, Shanghai)

1950 (1 Nov). *First All-China Postal Conference.* P 14.

1469	**194**	$400 orange-brown & blue-green	5	5
1470		$800 blue-green and carmine ..	20	8

Reprints exist, perf 12½.

(Recess People's Ptg Works, Peking)

1950 (1 Dec). *Sino-Soviet Treaty.* P 14.

1471	**195**	$400 scarlet	12	10
1472		$800 green	15	10
1473		$2,000 blue	40	15

Reprints exist but the differences are very minute.

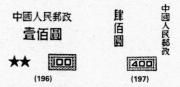

     (196)   (197)

1950 (Dec). *East China Regional stamps surch as T* **196.** P 12½.

1474	**EC 108**	$50 on $10 ultramarine (R.) ..	5	5
1475		$100 on $15 vermilion ..	5	5
		a. Perf 14	5	5
1476		$300 on $50 carmine ..	5	5
1477		$400 on $1,600 violet-blue (Br.) ..	5	5
1478		$400 on $2,000 purple (B.) ..	5	5
1474/1478		*Set of 5*	20	20

1950 (Dec). *East China Regional stamps surch as T* **197.** P 12½.

1479	**EC 111**	$50 on $10 ultramarine (R.) ..	5	5
1480		$400 on $15 scarlet ..	5	5
1481		$400 on $2,000 emerald-green ..	5	5
1479/1481		*Set of 3*	12	12

193 Flag   Original   Reprint

Reprints exist. In the large design the dots forming the shading of the flag are set at a different angle.

In all values the leaves at left below flag are grey-brown instead of reddish brown.

D   **198** Temple of Heaven, and Aeroplane

(Litho East China Revenue Office, Shanghai)

1950 (22 Dec)–**51.** As T **185** but redrawn without small white clouds, as in D. P 12½.

1481a	**185**	$100 turquoise (8.6.51) ..	..	5	5
1482		$200 dull green..	..	5	5
1483		$300 plum ..	..	5	5
1483a		$400 grey-green (8.6.51)	..	5	5
1484		$500 carmine ..	..	5	5
1485		$800 red-orange	..	5	5
1485a		$1,000 violet (8.6.51)	..	5	5
1486		$2,000 olive ..	..	20	5
1486a		$3,000 brown (8.6.51)	..	5	5
1487		$5,000 pink ..	..	5	5
1481a/1487		Set of 10	..	60	40

See also Nos. 1493/8.

(Recess People's Ptg Works, Shanghai)

1951 (1 May). AIR. P 12½.

1488	**198**	$1,000 carmine ..	..	5	5
1489		$3,000 green ..	..	5	5
1490		$5,000 orange ..	..	5	5
1491		$10,000 blue-green and purple	..	12	8
1492		$30,000 brown and blue ..	..	25	15
1488/1492		Set of 5	..	50	35

中國人民郵政

貳拾伍圓

(200)

199 Gate of Heavenly Peace, Peking

(Recess People's Ptg Works, Peking)

1951 (18 Apr). Pink network background. P 14.

1493	**199**	$10,000 brown ..	..	50	20
1494		$20,000 olive ..	..	50	15
1495		$30,000 green ..	..	1·00	65
1496		$50,000 violet ..	..	1·60	40
1497		$100,000 scarlet ..	..	3·75	1·60
1498		$200,000 blue ..	..	7·00	2·50
1493/1498		Set of 6 ..	..	13·00	5·00

1951 (2 May). "Unit" stamps of Nationalist China surch as T **200**.

(a) Nos. 1211/4A (P 12½)

1499	148	$5 on (–) magenta	..	5	5
1500	147	$10 on (–) blue-green	..	5	5
1501	149	$15 on (–) carmine	..	5	5
1502	146	$25 on (–) brown-orange ..	..	5	5
1499/1502		Set of 4	..	12	12

(b) Nos. 1211/4B (Roul)

1503	148	$5 on (–) magenta	..	5	5
1504	147	$10 on (–) blue-green	..	5	5
1505	149	$15 on (–) carmine	..	5	5
1506	146	$25 on (–) brown-orange	..	5	5
1503/1506		Set of 4	..	12	12

These stamps were available in China but were issued for use only in North East China.

201 Mao Tse-tung

203 National Emblem

202 Dove of Peace, after Picasso

(Recess People's Ptg Works, Peking)

1951 (1 July). Thirtieth Anniv of Chinese Communist Party. No gum. P 14.

1507	**201**	$400 brown	..	5·	5
1508		$500 green..	..	10	5
1509		$800 carmine-red ..	..	20	5
1507/1509		Set of 3 ..	..	30	12

Reprints exist on paper which is thin and whiter.

(Recess People's Ptg Works, Shanghai)

1951 (15 Aug). Peace Campaign (2nd issue). P 12½.

1510	**202**	$400 orange-brown	..	15	5
		a. Imperf between (pair)	..		
1511		$800 blue-green ..	..	25	8
		a. Imperf between (pair)	..	10·00	
1512		$1,000 violet ..	..	50	10
		a. Imperf between (pair)	..		
1510/1512		Set of 3 ..	..	80	20

Reprints exist, perf 14 and with small Chinese characters inserted in various parts of the design.

(Recess People's Ptg Works, Peking)

1951 (1 Oct). National Emblem Issue. Yellow network background. P 14.

1513	**203**	$100 deep blue	..	5	5
1514		$200 brown	..	5	5
1515		$400 yellow-orange	..	5	5
1516		$500 green..	..	8	5
1517		$800 carmine	..	12	5
1513/1517		Set of 5 ..	..	30	20

Reprints exist but the differences are very minute.

伍拾圓

★ 50 ★

(204)

205 Lu Hsun

Original   Reprint

T **205.** Reprints exist, easily identified by a small dot in right-hand bottom corner.

1951 (Sept). Money Order stamps as Type NC **76**, surch as T **204**.

(i) Recess, Commercial Press. P 12, 12½, 12½×13, 12½×13½, 13 or 13×12½.

1518	$50 on $2 emerald-green (C.) ..	5	5

(ii) Typo Kwang Hwa Ptg Co. Roul 9½.

1519	$50 on $2 blue-green (C.) ..	5	5
1520	$50 on $5 red-orange (C.) ..	5	5
1521	$50 on $50 grey (C.) ..	5	5
	a. Imperf (pair) ..	4·00	

(iii) Litho. Central Trust. P 13

1522	$50 on $50 brownish grey (C.) ..	5	5

(iv) Litho. Chung Hwa Book Co. P 11½

1523	$50 on $50 black (C.) ..	5	5
	a. Perf 11½×10 ..	5	5

(Litho East China Revenue Office, Shanghai)

1951 (19 Oct). 15th Death Anniv of Lu Hsun (author). P 12½.

1524	**205**	$400 violet..	..	12	5
1525		$800 blue-green ..	..	25	5

206 Rebels at Chintien

Original   Reprint

Reprints exist and are easily identified by a line of shading in top left corner of T **206** and two strokes in bottom right part of coin of unillustrated type.

(Recess Dah Tung Book Co, Shanghai)

1951 (15 Dec). *Centenary of Taiping Rebellion. T* **206** *and similar horiz design inscr "1851–1951". P* 14.

1526	**206**	$400 apple-green	..	..	5	5
1527	–	$800 carmine	..	..	10	5
1528	–	$800 orange	..	..	10	5
1529	–	$1,000 blue	..	..	15	8
1526/1529		*Set of* 4	..	..	35	20

Design:—$800 orange and $1,000, Coin and Documents of Taiping Kingdom.

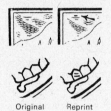

207 Peasants and Tractor

Original   Reprint
Reprints exist and are easily identified by an extra line between legs of ploughman.

(Recess Dah Yeh Co, Shanghai)

1952 (1 Jan). *Agrarian Reform. P* 14.

1530	**207**	$100 carmine	..	..	5	5
1531	–	$200 light blue	..	..	5	5
1532	–	$400 chocolate	..	..	5	5
1533	–	$800 green	..	..	12	5
1530/1533		*Set of* 4	..	..	25	15

208 The Potala, Lhasa

209 "Child Protection"

(Recess People's Ptg Works, Shanghai)

1952 (15 Mar). *Liberation of Tibet. T* **208** *and similar horiz design. P* 12½.

1534	**208**	$400 vermilion	..	..	8	5
1535	–	$800 blue-green	..	..	10	5
1536	**208**	$800 claret	..	..	10	5
1537	–	$1,000 dull violet	..	..	15	5
1534/1537		*Set of* 4	..	..	40	15

Design:—$800 blue-green and $1,000, Tibetan ploughing with yaks.
Reprints exist, perf 14 and with Chinese characters added in bottom left corner of vignette.

(Litho East China Revenue Office, Shanghai)

1952 (12 Apr). *International Child Protection Conference, Vienna. P* 12½.

1538	**209**	$400 green	..	..	5	5
		a. Perf 14 × 12½	..	..	12	10
1539		$800 royal blue	..	..	5	5
		a. Perf 14 × 12½	..	..	12	10

210 Hammer and Sickle

211 Gymnast

(Litho East China Revenue Office, Shanghai)

1952 (1 May). *Labour Day. T* **210** *and similar vert designs inscr "1952". P* 12½.

1540	**210**	$800 scarlet	..	..	5	5
1541	–	$800 turquoise-green	..	..	5	5
1542	–	$800 orange-brown	..	..	5	5
1540/1542		*Set of* 3	..	..	8	8

Designs:—No. 1541, Hand and dove; No. 1542, Hammer and ear of corn.

(Litho East China Revenue Office, Shanghai)

1952 (20 June–23 July). *Gymnastics by Radio. T* **211** *and similar vert designs. P* 12½.

1543		$400 scarlet (14–17) (20.6)	..	..	5	5
1544		$400 deep blue (18–21) (7.7)	..	..	5	5
1545		$400 brown-purple (22–25) (7.7)	..	..	5	5
1546		$400 green (26–29) (7.7)	..	..	5	5
1547		$400 vermilion (30–33) (23.7)	..	..	5	5
1548		$400 blue (34–37) (23.7)	..	..	5	5
1549		$400 orange (38–41) (23.7)	..	..	5	5
1550		$400 reddish violet (42–45) (23.7)	..	..	5	5
1551		$400 yellow-brown (46–49) (23.7)	..	..	5	5
1552		$400 pale blue (50–53) (23.7)	..	..	5	5
1543/1552		*Set of* 10	..	..	35	25
1543/1552		*Set of* 10 *blocks of* 4	..	2·00	2·00	

The stamps in each colour are arranged in blocks of four throughout the sheet, each block showing four stages of the exercise depicted. Where two stages are the same, the stamps differ only in the serial number in brackets, in the right-hand corner of the bottom margin of the stamp. These serial numbers are shown above after the colours of the stamps.
Prices are for single stamps.
Reprints exist, on smoother and slightly thicker paper. In some instances shades differ considerably.

212 "A Winter Hunt" (A.D. 386–580)

213 Marco Polo Bridge, Lukouchiao

(Recess People's Ptg Works, Shanghai)

1952 (1 July). *"Glorious Mother Country"* (1st issue). *T* **212** *and similar horiz designs showing Tun Huang mural paintings. P* 12½.

1553	212	$800 brown-black ..	..	5	5
1554	–	$800 red-brown	..	5	5
1555	–	$800 slate-black	..	5	5
1556	–	$800 slate-purple	..	5	5
1553/1556		*Set of 4*	..	10	10

Paintings:—No. 1554, "Benefactor" (A.D. 581–617): 1555, "Celestial Flight" (A.D. 618–906); 1556, "Dragon" (A.D. 618–906).

(Litho People's Ptg Works, Peking)

1952 (7 July). *15th Anniv of War with Japan. T* **213** *and similar horiz designs inscr.* "1937–1952". *P* 14.

1557	213	$800 blue ..	..	5	5
1558	–	$800 blue-green	..	5	5
1559	–	$800 plum ..	..	5	5
1560	–	$800 carmine-red ..	..	5	5
1557/1560		*Set of 4*	..	10	10

Designs:—No. 1558, Victory at Pinghsingkwan; 1559, Departure of New Fourth Army from Central China; 1560, Mao Tse-tung and Chu Teh.

214 Airman, Sailor and Soldier

215 Soldier, Tanks and Guns

(Recess People's Ptg Works, Shanghai)

1952 (1 Aug). *25th Anniv of People's Liberation Army. T* **214/5** *and similar designs inscr* "1927–1952". *P* 12½.

1561	214	$800 carmine-red ..	..	5	5
1562	215	$800 deep green ..	..	5	5
1563	–	$800 reddish violet	..	5	5
		a. Imperf between (horiz pair) ..			
1564	–	$800 chestnut	..	5	5
1561/1564		*Set of 4*	..	10	10

Designs:—As *T* **215**—No. 1563, Sailor and warships; 1564, Pilot and aeroplanes.

216 Dove of Peace over Pacific Ocean

217 Huai River Barrage

(Recess Dah Yeh Ptg Co, Shanghai)

1952 (2 Oct). *Asia and Pacific Ocean Peace Conference. T* **216** *and similar design inscr* "1952". *P* 14.

1565	216	$400 deep claret ..	..	5	5
1566	–	$800 yellow-orange	..	5	5
1567	216	$800 carmine-red	..	5	5
1568	–	$2,500 deep green ..	..	5	5
1565/1568		*Set of 4*	..	12	10

Design: *Horiz*—Nos. 1566 and 1568, Doves and globe.

(Recess Dah Yeh Ptg Co, Shanghai)

1952 (1 Oct). *"Glorious Mother Country"* (2nd issue). *T* **217** *and similar horiz designs. P* 14.

1569	217	$800 violet ..	..	5	5
		a. Imperf between (vert pair) ..			
1570	–	$800 scarlet	..	5	5
1571	–	$800 maroon	..	5	5
1572	–	$800 deep blue-green	..	5	5
1569/1572		*Set of 4*	..	10	10

Designs:—No. 1570, Chungking-Chengtu railway viaduct; 1571, Oil refinery; 1572, Tractor, disc harrows and combine drill.

218 Peasants collecting Food for the Front   **220** Textile Worker

(Recess Dah Yeh Ptg Co, Shanghai)

1952 (25 Oct). *Second Anniv of Chinese Volunteer Force in Korea. T* **218** *and similar horiz designs inscr* "1950–1952". *P* 14.

1573	–	$800 turquoise	..	5	5
1574	218	$800 vermilion	..	5	5
1575	–	$800 violet ..	..	5	5
1576	–	$800 lake-brown	..	5	5
1573/1576		*Set of 4* ..	..	10	10

Designs:—No. 1573, Marching troops; 1575, Infantry attack; 1576, Meeting of Chinese and North Korean soldiers.

(Recess Dah Yeh Ptg Co, Shanghai)

1953 (10 Mar). *International Women's Day. T* **220** *and similar horiz design. P* 14.

1578	220	$800 scarlet	..	5	5
1579	–	$800 emerald (Woman harvesting grain)	..	5	5

221 Shepherdess   **222** Karl Marx   **223** Workers and Flags

1953 (25 Mar–May). *T* **221** *and similar vert designs. Litho. P* 14.

1580		$50 reddish purple ..	..	5	5
1581		$200 emerald	..	5	5
1582		$250 ultramarine	..	5	5
1583		$800 turquoise-green	..	5	5
1584		$1,600 grey	..	5	5
1585		$2,000 red-orange (23.5)	..	5	5
1580/1585		*Set of 6* ..	..	20	20

Designs:—$50, Mill girl; $250, Carved lion; $800, Lathe-operator; $1,600, Miners; $2,000, Old Palace, Peking.

1953 (20 May). *135th Birth Anniv of Karl Marx. Recess. P* 14.

1586	222	$400 chocolate	..	5	5
1587		$800 bronze-green	..	5	5

PRINTERS. From here onwards all stamps were printed at the People's Printing Works, Peking, *unless otherwise stated.*

1953 (25 June). *7th National Labour Union Conference. Recess. P* 14.

1588	223	$400 blue ..	..	5	5
1589		$800 carmine	..	5	5

224 Dove of Peace

M **8**

1953 (25 July). *Peace Campaign* (3rd issue). *Recess.* P 14.
1590	**224**	$250 bluish green ..	..	5	5
1591	–	$400 orange-brown	..	5	5
1592	–	$800 violet ..	..	5	5
1590/1592		*Set of 3* ..	..	8	8

1953 (1 Aug)–**57**. *MILITARY POST. Litho. Without gum.* P 14.
M1593	M **8**	$800 yellow and red ..	25	65
M1594		$800 red, yellow-orange and reddish purple (1957)	1·40	
M1595		$800 red, orange-yellow and blue (1957)	30·00	

Nos. M1593/5 were issued for the use of the Army, Air Force and Navy, respectively.

A later printing of No. M1593 is on whiter paper and the yellow colour is brighter.

225 Horseman and Steed (A.D. 386–580)

226 Mao Tse-tung and Stalin at Kremlin

1953 (1 Sept). *"Glorious Mother Country"* (3rd issue) T **225** *and similar horiz designs showing Tun Huang mural paintings. Recess.* P 14.
1593	**225**	$800 bluish green ..	..	5	5
1594	–	$800 red-orange ..	..	5	5
1595	–	$800 blue ..	..	5	5
1596	–	$800 carmine-red ..	..	5	5
1593/1596		*Set of 4* ..	..	10	10

Paintings:—No. 1594, Court Players (A.D. 386–580); 1595, Battle scene (A.D. 581–617); 1596, Ox-drawn palanquin (A.D. 618–906).

1953 (5 Oct). *35th Anniv of Russian Revolution.* T **226** *and similar designs inscr.* "1917–1952". *Recess.* P 14.
1597	**226**	$800 bluish green ..	..	5	5
1598	–	$800 carmine-red ..	..	5	5
1599	–	$800 blue ..	..	5	5
1600	–	$800 orange-brown	..	5	5
1597/1600		*Set of 4* ..	..	10	10

Designs: *Horiz*—No. 1598, Lenin addressing revolutionaries. *Vert*—1599, Statue of Stalin; 1600, Stalin making speech.

Four stamps similar to Nos. 1597/1600 but in different colours and with two additional characters meaning "SOVIET-UNION" in the single-line Chinese inscription had been issued earlier but withdrawn. However, they appear to have done normal postal duty for about a month from early February 1953 at post offices in Western Hunan (*Price* £100 *un*, £40 *us*).

227 Compass (300 B.C.)

228 Rabelais (writer)

1953 (1 Dec). *"Glorious Mother Country"* (4th issue). T **227** *and similar horiz designs showing scientific instruments. Recess.* P 14.
1601	**227**	$800 blue-black	..	..	5	5
1602	–	$800 deep green	..	..	5	5
1603	–	$800 slate-blue	..	..	5	5
1604	–	$800 chocolate	..	..	5	5
1601/1604		*Set of 4*	..	..	10	10

Designs:—No. 1602, Seismoscope (A.D. 132); 1603, Drum cart for measuring distances (A.D. 300); 1604, Armillary sphere (A.D. 1437).

1953 (30 Dec). *Famous Men.* T **228** *and similar vert portraits. Recess.* P 14.
1605		$250 blackish green ..		5	5
1606		$400 slate-purple ..		5	5
1607		$800 indigo ..	..	5	5
1608		$2,200 chocolate ..	..	5	5
1605/1608		*Set of 4* ..	..	10	10

Portraits:—$400, J. Marti (revolutionary); $800, Chü Yüan (poet); $2,200, Copernicus (astronomer).

229 Flax Mill, Harbin

230 Gate of Heavenly Peace, Peking

1954 (1 May). *Industrial Development.* T **229** *and similar vert designs. Recess.* P 14.
1609		$100 olive-brown ..		5	5
1610		$200 deep bluish green		5	5
1611		$250 violet ..	..	5	5
1612		$400 brown-black ..		5	5
1613		$800 deep reddish purple		5	5
1614		$800 indigo ..	..	5	5
1615		$2,000 scarlet ..	..	5	5
1616		$3,200 deep brown ..		5	5
1609/1616		*Set of 8* ..	..	30	30

Designs:—$200, Tangku harbour; $250, Tienshui-Lanchow railway; $400, Heavy machine works; $800 (1613), Blast furnace; $800 (1614), Open-cast mines, Fuhsin; $2,000. North-East electric power station; $3,200, Geological survey team.

1954 (1 May–Sept). *Litho.* P 14.
1617	**230**	$50 claret (1.7)	..	5	5
1618		$100 light blue ..	..	5	5
1619		$200 green (15.9)	..	5	5
1620		$250 ultramarine (1.7)	..	5	5
1621		$400 grey-green ..	..	5	5
1622		$800 orange ..	..	5	5
1623		$1,600 grey (15.9) ..	..	5	5
1624		$2,000 olive (1.7) ..	..	5	5
1617/1624		*Set of 8* ..	..	25	25

231 Statue of Lenin and Stalin at Gorki

232 Lenin Speaking

1954 (30 June). *30th Anniv of Lenin's Death.* T **231/2** *and similar vert design inscr* "1870–1924". *Recess.* P 14.
1625	**231**	$400 deep turquoise-green	..	5	5
1626	–	$800 blackish brown	..	5	5
1627	**232**	$2,000 carmine-lake	..	5	5
1625/1627		*Set of 3* ..	..	12	10

Design: (25×37 *mm*).—$800, Lenin (full-face portrait).

D 13

233 Painted Pottery
(c. 2000 B.C.)

1954 (18 Aug). *POSTAGE DUE. Litho. No gum. P* 14.
D1628	**D 13**	$100 carmine-red	..	..	5	5
D1629		$200 carmine-red	..	..	5	5
D1630		$500 carmine-red	..	..	5	5
D1631		$800 carmine-red	..	..	5	5
D1632		$1,600 carmine-red	..	..	5	5
D1628/1632		*Set of 5* ..	..	..	15	15

1954 (25 Aug). *"Glorious Mother Country" (5th issue). T* **233**
and similar horiz designs. Recess. P 14.
1628	**233**	$800 chocolate	..	..	5	5
1629	–	$800 black ..	..	..	5	5
1630	–	$800 deep turquoise-blue	..		5	5
1631	–	$800 lake	..	..	5	5
1628/1632		*Set of 4* ..	..	..	15	15

Designs:—No. 1629, Musical stone (1200 B.C.); 1630, Bronze basin (816 B.C.); 1631, Lacquered wine cup and cosmetic tray (403–221 B.C.).

234 Heavy Rolling Mill   **235** Statue of Stalin

1954 (1 Oct). *Anshan Steel Works. T* **234** *and similar vert design. Recess. P* 14.
1632	$400 deep turquoise-blue	..	..	5	5
1633	$800 maroon ..	..	..	5	5

Design:—$400, Seamless steel-tubing mill.

1954 (16 Oct). *First Anniv of Stalin's Death. T* **235** *and other designs inscr "1953–1954". Recess. P* 14.
1634	$400 black ..	..	..	5	5
1635	$800 sepia ..	..	..	5	5
1636	$2,000 deep rose-red ..	..	..	10	10
1634/1636	*Set of 3* ..	..	..	15	15

Designs: *Vert* (26×37 *mm*)—$800, Full-face portrait of Stalin. *Horiz* (42½×25 *mm*)—$2,000, Stalin and hydro-electric station.

236 Exhibition Building

1954 (7 Nov). *Russian Economic and Cultural Exhibition, Peking. Recess. P* 14.
1637	**236**	$800 red-brown/*yellow*	25	12

This stamp may be found in various sizes, due to paper shrinkage during printing.

237 Instructor and Apprentices   **238** Woman Worker

239 Rejoicing Crowds

1954 (15 Dec). *Technical Development. T* **237** *and similar horiz design. Recess. P* 14.
1638	**237**	$400 bronze-green	..	..	5	5
1639	–	$800 vermilion (Workers and machinery)	..	..	8	8
1638/1639		*Set of 2* ..	...	..	10	10

1954 (30 Dec). *First Session of National Congress. Recess. P* 14.
1640	**238**	$400 brown-purple	..	..	5	5
1641	**239**	$800 vermilion	..	..	8	8
1640/1641		*Set of 2* ..	..	..	10	10

240 "New Constitution"   **241** Pylons

1954 (30 Dec). *Constitution Commemoratives. Recess. P* 14.
1642	**240**	$400 sepia/*buff*	..	..	5	5
1643	–	$800 vermilion/*yellow*	..	..	5	5
1642/1643		*Set of 2* ..	..	..	8	8

1955 (26 Feb). *Development of Overhead Transmission of Electricity. Recess. P* 14.
1644	**241**	$800 deep blue	..	..	5	5

Currency Revaluation
100 Fen=1 Yuan (=10,000 old Yuan)

242 Nurse and Red Cross Worker

1955 (25 June). *50th Anniv of Chinese Red Cross. Recess; cross typo in red. P* 14.
1645	**242**	8 f. deep green	..	..	10	8

243 Miner

244 Gate of Heavenly Peace, Peking

1955 (16 July)–56. *P* 14.

(a) Litho **T 243** *and similar designs*

1646	½ f. yellow-brown (3.11.55)	..	5	5
1647	1 f. purple	..	5	5
1648	2 f. bluish green (3.11.55)	..	5	5
1648a	2½ f. blue (28.12.56)	..	5	5
1649	4 f. brown-olive	..	5	5
1650	8 f. orange-red	..	5	5
	a. Perf 12½. Shanghai ptg	..	35	12
1650b	10 f. crimson (28.12.56)	..	8	5
1651	20 f. blue	..	12	5
1652	50 f. grey (3.11.55)	..	25	5

(b) Recess. **T 244** (20.9.55)

1653	$1 brownish lake	..	40	10
1654	$2 sepia	..	80	10
1655	$5 deep slate	..	2·00	20
1656	$10 orange-red	..	4·00	80
1657	$20 slate-violet	..	8·00	1·25
1646/1657	*Set of 14*	..	14·00	2·50

Designs:—1 f. Lathe operator; 2 f. Airman; 2½ f. Nurse; 4 f. Soldier; 8 f. Foundry worker; 10 f. Chemist; 20 f. Farm girl; 50 f. Sailor.

245 Stalin and Mao Tse-tung

246 Workmen and Industrial Plant

1955 (25 July). *Fifth Anniv of Sino-Russian Treaty. Recess. P* 14.

1658	**245**	8 f. red-brown	..	5	5
1659	**246**	20 f. blackish olive	..	12	5
1658/1659		*Set of 2*	..	12	8

247 Chang-Heng (A.D. 78–139, astronomer)

248 Foundry

(Des Sun Chuan-che (after Chiang Choa-ho). Eng Tang Lin-kun)

1955 (25 Aug). *Scientists of Ancient China. Various vert portraits as* **T 247**. *Recess. P* 14.

1660	8 f. deep olive-brown/*buff*	..	10	5
1661	8 f. greenish blue/*buff*	..	10	5
1662	8 f. black/*buff*	..	10	5
1663	8 f. brown-purple/*buff*	..	10	5
1660/1663	*Set of 4*	..	35	15

MS1663a Four sheets each 63×90 mm. Nos. 1660/3 but printed on white paper.

Imperf	..	..	75	40

Portraits No. 1661, Tsu Chung-chi (429–500, mathematician); 1662, Chang Sui (683–727, astronomer); 1663, Li Shih-chen (1518–1593, pharmacologist).

1955 (1 Oct)–56. *Five Year Plan.* **T 248** *and similar horiz designs. Litho. P* 12½.

1664	8 f. red, orange and black	..	8	5
1665	8 f. brown, yellow and black	..	8	5
1666	8 f. greenish yellow, black & blue-black		8	5
1667	8 f. reddish violet, blue and blue-black		8	5
1668	8 f. yellow, red-brown and black	..	8	5
1669	8 f. yellow, carmine and blue-black	..	8	5
1670	8 f. grey, deep blue and blue-black	..	8	5
1671	8 f. orange, black and grey-black	..	8	5
1672	8 f. yellow, brown and blue-black	..	8	5
1673	8 f. red, orange & grey-black (15.12.55)		8	5
1674	8 f. yellow, green & grey-blk (15.12.55)		8	5
1675	8 f. red, yellow and blue-black (24.2.56)		8	5
1676	8 f. yellow, grey & blue-black (15.12.55)		8	5
1677	8 f. yellow, blue & grey-black (15.12.55)		8	5
1678	8 f. orange, blue & grey-blk (15.12.55)		8	5
1679	8 f. yellow, brown & blue-blk (15.12.55)		8	5
1680	8 f. red, brown & grey-black (15.12.55)		8	5
1681	8 f. yellow, brown & grey-blk (24.2.56)		8	5
1664/1681	*Set of 18*	..	1·25	50

Designs:—No. 1665 Electricity pylons; 1666, Mining machinery; 1667, Oil tankers and derricks; 1668, Heavy machinery workshop; 1669, Factory guard and industrial plant; 1670, Textile machinery; 1671, Factory workers; 1672, Combine harvester; 1673, Dairy herd and farm girl; 1674, Dam; 1675, Artists decorating pottery; 1676, Lorry; 1677, Ship and wharf; 1678, Surveyors; 1679, Students; 1680, Man, woman and child; 1681, Workers' rest home.

249 Lenin

250 Engels

1955 (15 Dec). *85th Birth Anniv of Lenin. Recess. P* 14.

1682	**249**	8 f. deep turquoise-blue	..	10	5
1683		20 f. carmine-lake	..	15	5
1682/1683		*Set of 2*	..	20	8

1955 (15 Dec). *60th Death Anniv of Engels. Recess. P* 14.

1684	**250**	8 f. orange-red	..	10	5
1685		20 f. sepia	..	15	5
1684/1685		*Set of 2*	..	20	8

251 Capture of Lu Ting Bridge

1955 (30 Dec). *Twentieth Anniv of Long March by Communist Army.* **T 251** *and vert design inscr "1934.10 1935. 10". Recess. P* 14.

1686	**251**	8 f. brown-lake	..	20	5
1687		8 f. deep greenish blue	..	20	5
1686/1687		*Set of 2*	..	35	8

Design: (28×46 mm)—No. 1687, Crossing the Ta Hsueh Mountains.

252 Convoy of Lorries **253** Tatu River Suspension Bridge

1956 (30 Mar). *Opening of Sikang-Tibet and Tsinghai-Tibet Highways. T 252/3 and similar design. Recess. P 14.*

1688	252	4 f. blue	..	5	5
1689	253	8 f. deep olive-brown	..	8	5
1690	–	8 f. carmine-red	..	8	5
1688/1690		Set of 3	..	15	10

Design: *As T 252*—No. 1690, Opening ceremony, Lhasa.

254 Summer Palace **255** Salt Production

1956 (15 June)–57. *Views of Peking. T 254 and similar horiz designs. Recess. P 14.*

1691		4 f. carmine	..	5	5
1692		4 f. deep turquoise-green	..	5	5
1693		8 f. orange-red (2.57)	..	10	5
1694		8 f. greenish blue	..	10	5
1695		8 f. bistre-brown	..	10	5
1691/1695		Set of 5	..	35	15

Views:—No. 1692, Peihai Park; 1693, Gate of Heavenly Peace; 1694, Temple of Heaven; 1695, Tai Ho Palace.

A stamp similar to No. 1693 (with background rays of sunlight) was not officially issued, although copies are known cancelled from post offices in Kiangsi Province between 10 and 15 June 1956.

1956 (1 Oct). *Archaeological Discoveries at Chengtu. T 255 and similar horiz designs showing brick carvings of the Tung Han Dynasty (A.D. 25–200). Recess. P 14.*

1696		4 f. bronze-green	..	5	5
1697		4 f. grey-black	..	5	5
1698		8 f. brownish black	..	12	5
1699		8 f. sepia	..	12	5
1696/1699		Set of 4	..	30	10

Designs:—No. 1697, House; 1698, Hunting and farming; 1699, Carriage crossing a bridge.

256 **257** Gate of Heavenly Peace, Peking

1956 (1 Oct). *National Savings. Recess. P 14.*

1700	256	4 f. ochre	..	5	5
1701		8 f. vermilion	..	12	5
1700/1701		Set of 2	..	15	5

1956 (10 Nov). *Eighth National Communist Party Congress. Recess. P 14.*

1702	257	4 f. deep green	..	5	5
1703		8 f. vermilion	..	12	5
1704		16 f. deep carmine-red	..	20	5
1702/1704		Set of 3	..	30	10

258 Dr. Sun Yat-sen **259** Putting the Shot

1956 (12 Nov). *90th Birth Anniv of Dr. Sun Yat-sen. Recess. P 14.*

1705	258	4 f. brown	..	5	5
1706		8 f. blue	..	15	8
1705/1706		Set of 2	..	15	10

1957 (20 Mar). *First Chinese Workers' Athletic Meeting, 1955. T 259 and similar sports designs, each with red flower. Litho. P 12½.*

1707		4 f. deep carmine-lake and brown	..	5	5
1708		4 f. deep purple and brown	..	5	5
1709		8 f. deep bluish green and brown	..	12	5
1710		8 f. deep blue and brown	..	12	5
1711		8 f. deep yellow-brown and brown	..	12	5
1707/1711		Set of 5	..	40	20

Designs:—No. 1708, Weightlifting; 1709, Sprinting; 1710, Football; 1711, Cycling.

260 Assembly Line

1957 (1 May). *Lorry Production. T 260 and similar horiz design. Recess. P 14.*

1712		4 f. yellow-brown (Changchun motor plant)	..	15	5
1713		8 f. slate-blue	..	5	5
1712/1713		Set of 2	..	15	5

261 Nanchang Revolutionaries **262** Congress Emblem

1957 (10 Aug–30 Dec). *30th Anniv of People's Liberation Army. T 261 and similar horiz designs. Recess. P 14.*

1714		4 f. blackish violet	..	5	5
1715		4 f. deep bluish green (30.12)	..	5	5
1716		8 f. red-brown	..	12	5
1717		8 f. deep blue (30.12)	..	12	5
1714/1717		Set of 4	..	30	15

Designs:—No. 1715, Meeting of Red Armies at Chinkangshan; 1716, Liberation Army crossing the Yellow River; 1717, Liberation of Nanking.

1957 (30 Sept). *Fourth World Trade Unions Congress, Leipzig. Recess. P 14.*

1718	262	8 f. red-brown	..	12	5
1719		22 f. indigo	..	25	10
1718/1719		Set of 2	..	35	10

263 Yangtse River Bridge   **264** Fireworks over Kremlin

1957 (1 Oct). *Opening of Yangtse River Bridge. T **263** and similar horiz design. Recess. P 14.*
1720	8 f. carmine-red	..	..	12	5
1721	20 f. slate-blue	..	..	25	10
1720/1721	*Set of 2*	..	..	35	10
Design:—20 f. Aerial view of Yangtse River Bridge.

1957 (7 Nov). *40th Anniv of Russian Revolution. T **264** and similar vert designs dated "1917 1957". Recess. P 14.*
1722	4 f. deep red	..	..	5	5
1723	8 f. deep brown	..	..	8	5
1724	20 f. deep emerald	..	..	20	5
1725	22 f. lake-brown	..	..	20	5
1726	32 f. deep blue	..	..	35	12
1722/1726	*Set of 5*	..	..	80	25
Designs:—8 f. Soviet emblem, globe and broken chains; 20 f. Dove of Peace and plant; 22 f. Hands supporting book bearing portraits of Marx and Lenin; 32 f. Electricity power pylon.

265 Airport Scene   **266** Yellow River Dam and Power Station

1957 (7 Nov)–**58**. *AIR. T **265** and similar vert designs. Recess. P 14.*
1727	16 f. blackish blue	..	..	10	5
1728	28 f. deep olive	..	..	20	10
1729	35 f. slate-black	..	..	25	12
1730	52 f. greenish blue (1958)	..	35	15
1727/1730	*Set of 4*	..	..	80	35
Designs: 'Plane over—28 f. mountain highway; 35 f. railway tracks; 52 f. collier at coaling station.

1957 (30 Dec). *Harnessing of the Yellow River. Various horiz designs as T **266**. Recess. P 14.*
1731	4 f. red-orange	..	..	5	5
1732	4 f. deep blue	..	..	5	5
1733	8 f. carmine-lake	..	..	12	5
1734	8 f. deep bluish green	..	..	12	5
1731/1734	*Set of 4*	..	..	30	15
Designs:—No. 1731, Map of Yellow River; 1733, Motorship; 1734, Aerial view of irrigation on Yellow River.

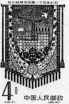

267 Ploughing   **268** "Peaceful Construction"   **269** High Peak Pagoda, Tenfeng

1957 (30 Dec). *Co-operative Agriculture. T **267** and similar vert designs. Multicoloured. Litho. P 14.*
1735	8 f. Farmer enrolling for co-operative farm	..	..	8	5
1736	8 f. Type **267**	..	..	8	5
1737	8 f. Tree-planting	..	..	8	5
1738	8 f. Harvesting	..	..	8	5
1735/1738	*Set of 4*	..	..	25	15

1958 (30 Jan). *Completion of First Five Year Plan. T **268** and similar vert designs. Designs recess; backgrounds litho. P 14.*
1739	4 f. emerald and cream	..	..	5	5
1740	8 f. red and cream	..	..	12	5
1741	16 f. ultramarine and cream	..	..	25	5
1739/1741	*Set of 3*	..	..	35	10
Designs:—8 f. "Industry and Agriculture" (grapple and wheat-sheaves); 16 f. "Communications and Transport" (train on viaduct and ship).

1958 (15 Mar). *Ancient Chinese Pagodas. Various vert designs as T **269**. Recess. P 14.*
1742	8 f. deep olive-brown	..	..	15	5
1743	8 f. slate-blue	..	..	15	5
1744	8 f. purple-brown	..	..	15	5
1745	8 f. deep green	..	..	15	5
1742/1745	*Set of 4*	..	..	50	15
Designs:—No. 1742, T **269**; 1743, One Thousand League Pagoda, Tali; 1744, Buddha Pagoda, Yinghsien; 1745, Flying Rainbow Pagoda, Hungchao.

270 Trilobite of Hao Li Shan   **271**

1958 (15 Apr). *Chinese Fossils T **270** and similar vert designs. Recess. P 14.*
1746	4 f. indigo	..	..	8	5
1747	8 f. sepia	..	..	15	5
1748	16 f. slate-green	..	..	30	5
1746/1748	*Set of 3*	..	..	45	12
Designs:—8 f. Dinosaur of Lufeng; 16 f. Sinomegaceros pachyospeus (deer).

1958 (1 May). *Unveiling of People's Heroes Monument, Peking. P 14.*
1749	**271** 8 f. carmine	..	..	15	5
MS1749a	137×87 mm. No. 1749. Imperf	50	50

272 Karl Marx (after Zhukov)   **273** Cogwheels of Industry

1958 (5 May). *140th Birth Anniv of Karl Marx. T **272** and similar vert design. P 14.*
1750	8 f. chocolate	..	..	8	5
1751	22 f. deep green	..	..	25	10
1750/1751	*Set of 2*	..	..	30	12
Design:—22 f. Karl Marx addressing audience at the German Workers' Educational Association, London.

1958 (25 May). *Eighth All-China Trade Union Congress, Peking. Recess. P 14.*
1752	**273** 4 f. turquoise-blue	..	..	5	5
1753	8 f. bright purple	..	..	10	5
1752/1753	*Set of 2*	..	..	12	8

274 Federation Emblem   **275** Mother and Child   **276** Kuan Han-ching

1958 (1 June). *4th International Democratic Women's Federation Congress, Vienna. Recess.* P 14.

1754	**274**	8 f. ultramarine	..		10	5
1755		20 f. turquoise-green	..	..	20	8
1754/1755		*Set of 2*	..	..	25	10

1958 (1 June). *Chinese Children. Various vert designs as T 275. Multicoloured. Litho.* P 14.

1756	8 f. Type 275	..	12	5
1757	8 f. Children watering sunflowers	..	12	5
1758	8 f. "Hide and seek"	..	12	5
1759	8 f. Children sailing boat	..	12	5
1756/1759	*Set of 4*	..	45	15

1958 (20 June). *700th Anniv of Works of Kuan Han-ching (playwright). Various vert designs as T 276. Recess.* P 14.

1760	4 f. black-green/cream	..	8	8
1761	8 f. deep maroon/cream	..	15	10
1762	20 f. black/cream	..	35	15
1760/1762	*Set of 3*	..	50	25
MS1762a	100×128 mm. Nos. 1760/2 but printed on white paper. Imperf ..		1·25	60

Designs: Scenes from Kuan comedies;—4 f. "The Butterfly Dream"; 20 f. "The Riverside Pavilion".

277 Peking Planetarium   **278** Marx and Engels

1958 (25 June). *Peking Planetarium. T 277 and similar horiz design. Recess.* P 14.

1763	8 f. deep grey-green	..	..	15	10
1764	20 f. indigo (Planetarium in operation)		35	15
1763/1764	*Set of 2*	..	..	45	20

1958 (1 July). *110th Anniv of "Communist Manifesto". T 278 and similar vert designs inscr. "1848 1958". Recess.* P 14.

1765	4 f. reddish purple	..	15	5
1766	8 f. deep greenish blue	..	40	10
1765/1766	*Set of 2*	..	50	12

Design:—8 f. Front cover of first German *Communist Manifesto*.

279 Wild Goose and Radio Pylon   **280** Peony and Doves   **281** Chang Heng's Weather-cock

---

1958 (10 July). *Communist Postal Conference, Moscow. Recess.* P 14.

1767	**279**	4 f. ultramarine	..	..	15	5
1768		8 f. deep emerald	..		40	10
1767/1768		*Set of 2*	..		50	12

1958 (20 July). *International Disarmament Conference, Stockholm. T 280 and similar vert designs. Recess.* P 14.

1769	4 f. red	..	..	30	10
1770	8 f. emerald	..		30	10
1771	22 f. red-brown..	..		60	25
1769/1771	*Set of 3*	..	..	1·00	40

Designs:—8 f. Olive branch; 22 f. Atomic symbol and factory plant.

1958 (25 Aug). *Chinese Meteorology. T 281 and similar vert designs. Recess.* P 14.

1772	8 f. black/olive-yellow ..	..	12	5
1773	8 f. black/blue	..	12	5
1774	8 f. black/blue-green	..	12	5
1772/1774	*Set of 3*	..	30	10

Designs:—No. 1773, Meteorological balloon; 1774, Typhoon signal-tower.

282 Union Emblem within figure "5"   **283** Chrysanthemum   **284** Telegraph Building, Peking

1958 (4 Sept). *Fifth International Students' Union Congress, Peking. Recess.* P 14.

1775	**282**	8 f. bright purple ..	..	10	5
1776		22 f. deep bluish green	..	25	8
1775/1776		*Set of 2*	..	30	10

Stamps with a slightly different series of characters below the date "1958" meaning "5th Congress of World Students' Representatives" instead of "International Students' Union, 5th Congress" were withdrawn before issue, but it is understood that No. 1775 with wrong inscription were on sale in Liaoning Province in North East China for one day.

1958 (25 Sept). *Various flowers as T 283. Recess.* P 14.

1777	–	1½ f. mauve (Peony)	..	5	5
1778	–	3 f. blue-green (Hibiscus) ..		5	5
1779	**283**	5 f. orange-red	..	5	5
1777/1779		*Set of 3*	..	10	8

1958 (29 Sept). *Opening of Peking Telegraph Building. Recess.* P 14.

1780	**284**	4 f. deep olive-green	5	5
1781		8 f. rose-carmine ..	12	5
1780/1781		*Set of 2*	12	5

285 Exhibition Emblem and Symbols   **286** Labourer on Reservoir Site

1958 (1 Oct). *National Exhibition of Industry and Communications. Various designs as T 285. Recess.* P 14.

1782	8 f. blackish green	..	..	10	5
1783	8 f. rose-carmine	..		10	5
1784	8 f. red-brown ..	..		10	5
1782/1784	*Set of 3*	..	..	25	10

Designs:—No. 1783, Chinese dragon riding the waves; 1784, Horses in the sky.

1958 (25 Oct). *Inauguration of Ming Tombs Reservoir. T 286 and similar horiz design. Recess.* P 14.

1785	4 f. deep red-brown	..	5	5
1786	8 f. deep greenish blue	..	15	5
1785/1786	*Set of 2*	..	15	8

Design:—8 f. Ming Tombs Reservoir.

287 Sputnik and ancient Theodolite

288 Chinese and North Korean Soldiers

1958 (30 Oct). *Russian Sputnik Commemoration. Various horiz designs as T* **287**. *Recess. P* 14.
1787	4 f. rose-red	..	..	12	8
1788	8 f. bluish violet	..	..	25	10
1789	10 f. deep bluish green	..	..	30	12
1787/1789	Set of 3	..	..	60	25

Designs:—8 f. Third Russian sputnik encircling globe; 10 f. Three Russian sputniks encircling globe.

1958 (20 Nov). *Return of Chinese People's Volunteers from Korea. T* **288** *and similar horiz designs. Recess. P* 14.
1790	8 f. purple	..	..	12	5
1791	8 f. chestnut	..	..	12	5
1792	8 f. carmine	..	..	12	5
1790/1792	Set of 3	..	..	30	10

Designs:—No. 1791, Chinese soldier embracing Korean woman; 1792, Girl presenting bouquet to Chinese soldier.

289 Forest Landscape

290 Atomic Reactor

1958 (15 Dec). *Afforestation Campaign. Various designs as T* **289**. *Recess. P* 14.
1793	8 f. bluish green	..	..	12	5
1794	8 f. slate-blue	..	..	12	5
1795	8 f. reddish violet	..	..	12	5
1796	8 f. deep blue	..	..	12	5
1793/1796	Set of 4	..	..	40	12

Designs: *Vert*—No. 1794, Forest patrol. *Horiz*—No. 1795, Tree-felling by power-saw; 1796, Tree-planting.

1958 (30 Dec). *Inauguration of China's First Atomic Reactor. T* **290** *and similar horiz design. Recess. P* 14.
1797	8 f. deep blue	..	..	10	5
1798	20 f. deep brown (Cyclotron in action)	..	25	8
1797/1798	Set of 2	..	..	30	10

291 Children with model Aircraft

292 Rooster

293 Mao Tse-tung and Steel Workers

1958 (30 Dec). *Aviation Sports. Various vert designs as T* **291**. *Recess. P* 14.
1799	4 f. carmine	..	..	8	5
1800	8 f. deep olive (Gliders in flight)	..	10	5
1801	10 f. sepia (Parachutists)	..	..	12	5
1802	20 f. slate-blue (Light planes in flight)	..	20	5
1799/1802	Set of 4	..	..	45	15

1959 (1 Jan). *Chinese Folk Paper-cuts. Various vert designs as T* **292**. *Recess; background photo. P* 14.
1803	8 f. black/*violet* (Camel)	..	..	12	5
1804	8 f. black/*blue-green* (Pomegranate)	..	12	5
1805	8 f. black/*vermilion* (T **292**)	..	..	12	5
1806	8 f. black/*blue* (Actress on stage)	..	12	5
1803/1806	Set of 4	..	..	40	12

1959 (15 Feb–25 May). *Steel Production Progress. T* **293** *and similar vert designs inscr "1958". Recess. P* 14.
1807	4 f. scarlet	..	..	8	5
1808	8 f. deep magenta	..	..	12	5
1809	10 f. scarlet (25.5)	..	..	15	5
1807/1809	Set of 3	..	..	30	12

Designs:—8 f. Battery of steel furnaces; 10 f. Steel "blowers" and workers.

294 Chinese Women

295 Natural History Museum, Peking

1959 (8 Mar). *International Women's Day. T* **294** *and similar vert design. Recess. P* 14.
1810	8 f. emerald/*cream*	..	..	12	5
1811	22 f. magenta/*cream*	..	..	25	8
1810/1811	Set of 2	..	..	30	10

Design:—22 f. Russian and Chinese women.

1959 (1 Apr). *Opening of Natural History Museum, Peking. Recess. P* 14.
1812	**295** 4 f. turquoise-blue	..		5	5
1813	8 f. olive-brown	..	..	12	5
1812/1813	Set of 2	..	..	12	5

296 Barley

297 Workers with Marx-Lenin Banner

1959 (25 Apr). *Successful Harvest, 1958. T* **296** *and similar horiz designs inscr "1958" Recess. P* 14.
1814	8 f. red (Type **296**)	..	..	12	5
1815	8 f. red (Rice)	..	..	12	5
1816	8 f. red (Cotton)	..	..	12	5
1817	8 f. red (Soya beans, groundnuts and rape)	..		12	5
1814/1817	Set of 4	..	..	45	15

The four stamps were issued together in sheets of 120.

1959 (1 May). *Labour Day. T* **297** *and similar vert design "1889–1959". Recess. P* 14.
1818	4 f. ultramarine	..	..	5	5
1819	8 f. light red	..	..	12	5
1820	22 f. emerald	..	..	25	5
1818/1820	Set of 3	..	..	35	12

Designs:—8 f. Hands clasping Red Flag; 22 f. "5.1" and workers.

298 Airport Building

299 Students with Banners

1959 (20 June). *Inauguration of Peking Airport. T* **298** *and similar horiz design. Recess; background litho. P* 14.
1821	8 f. black/*lilac*	..	..	12	5
1822	10 f. black/*light grey-green*	..	15	5
1821/1822	Set of 2	..	..	25	5

Design:—10 f. Chinese airliner at airport.

1959 (1 July). *40th Anniv of "May 4th" Students' Rising.* **T 299** *and similar horiz design inscr "1919–1959".* *Photo.* P 11 × 11½.

1823	4 f. red, chocolate and pale olive			8	5
1824	8 f. red, chocolate and yellow-bistre			15	5
1823/1824	Set of 2			20	8

Design:—8 f. Workers with banners.

300 F. Joliot-Curie

301 Stamp Printing Works, Peking

1959 (25 July). *Tenth Anniv of World Peace Council.* **T 300** *and similar vert design inscr "1949–1959".* *Recess.* P 11½.

1825	8 f. dull purple			15	5
1826	22 f. violet			30	10
1825/1826	Set of 2			40	10

Design:—Silhouette of European, Chinese and Negro.

1959 (15 Aug). *Sino-Czech Co-operation in Postage Stamp Production.* *Recess.* P 11 × 11½.

1827	**301**	8 f. deep bluish green		12	5

302

303 Moon Rocket

1959 (30 Aug). *World Table-Tennis Championships, Dortmund.* *Litho.* P 14.

1828	**302**	4 f. blue and black			8	5
1829		8 f. red and black			12	5
1828/1829	Set of 2				15	8

1959 (10 Sept). *Launching of First Cosmic Rocket.* *Photo.* P 11½.

1830	**303**	8 f. scarlet, blue and black			50	10

304 "Prologue"

305 Mao Tse-tung and Gate of Heavenly Peace, Peking

1959 (25 Sept). *First Anniv of People's Communes.* *Vert designs as* **T 304**. *Recess.* P 11½.

1831	8 f. rose-red				8	5
1832	8 f. dull purple				8	5
1833	8 f. orange-red				8	5
1834	8 f. bronze-green				8	5
1835	8 f. blue				8	5
1836	8 f. olive				8	5
1837	8 f. indigo				8	5
1838	8 f. magenta				8	5
1839	8 f. black				8	5
1840	8 f. emerald				8	5
1841	8 f. violet				8	5
1842	8 f. red				8	5
1831/1842	Set of 12				80	50

Designs:—No. 1832, Steel worker ("Rural Industries");1833, Farm girl ("Agriculture"); 1834, Salesgirl ("Trade"); 1835, Peasant ("Study"); 1836, Militiaman ("Militia"); 1837, Cook with tray of food ("Community Meals");

1838, Child watering flowers ("Nursery"); 1839, Old man with pipe ("Old People's Homes"); 1840, Health worker ("Public Health"); 1841, Young flautist ("Recreation and Entertainment"); 1842, Star-shaped flower ("Epilogue").

1959 (28 Sept). *Tenth Anniv of People's Republic* (1st issue). **T 305** *and similar vert designs inscr "1949–1959".* *Photo.* With gum. P 11½ × 11.

1843	8 f. red and yellow-brown			10	5
1844	8 f. red and grey-blue			10	5
1845	22 f. red and blue-green			30	10
1843/1845	Set of 3			45	15

Designs:—No. 1844, Marx and Lenin, and Kremlin; 1845, Dove of peace, and globe.

306 Republican Emblem

307 Steel Plant

1959 (1 Oct). *Tenth Anniv of People's Republic* (2nd issue). *Litho.* P 14.

1846	**306**	4 f. red, yellow and turquoise		8	5
1847		8 f. red, yellow and lilac		12	5
1848		10 f. red, yellow and blue		15	5
1849		20 f. red, yellow and buff		25	8
1846/1849	Set of 4			55	20

1959 (1 Oct). *Tenth Anniv of People's Republic* (3rd issue). *Various vert designs as* **T 307** *inscr "1949–1959".* *Centres photo; frames recess.* With gum. P 11½ × 11.

1850	8 f. rose-red and maroon			15	5
1851	8 f. grey and maroon			15	5
1852	8 f. yellow-brown and maroon			15	5
1853	8 f. grey-blue and maroon			15	5
1854	8 f. orange and maroon			15	5
1855	8 f. olive-green and maroon			15	5
1856	8 f. blue-green and maroon			15	5
1857	8 f. blackish violet and maroon			15	5
1850/1854	Set of 8			1·00	30

Designs:—No. 1851, Coal-mine; 1852, Steel-mill; 1853, Double-decked bridge; 1854, Combine-harvester; 1855, Dam construction; 1856, Textile mill; 1857, Chemical works.

308 Rejoicing Populace

1959 (1 Oct). *Tenth Anniv of People's Republic* (4th issue). **T 308** *and similar designs inscr "1949–1959".* *Litho.* P 14.

1858	8 f. multicoloured/*cream*			15	5
1859	10 f. multicoloured/*cream*			20	5
1860	20 f. multicoloured/*cream*			30	8
1858/1860	Set of 3			60	15

Designs: *Vert*—People rejoicing and: 10 f. Industrial plant; 20 f. Banners and tree.

309 Mao Tse-tung proclaiming Republic

310 Boy Bugler ("Summer Camps")

1959 (1 Oct). *Tenth Anniv of People's Republic (5th issue). Recess.* P 14.

1861	**309**	20 f. carmine-lake	..	..	40	25

1959 (10 Nov). *Tenth Anniv of Chinese Youth Pioneers. Various vert designs as T 310. Photo. Black inscr recess. (No. 1862). P 11½.*

1862	4 f. yellow, vermilion and black	..	5	5
1863	4 f. red and Prussian blue	..	5	5
1864	8 f. red and brown	..	8	5
1865	8 f. red and blue	..	8	5
1866	8 f. red and green	..	8	5
1867	8 f. red and deep reddish purple	..	8	5
1862/1867	*Set of 6*	..	40	25

Designs:—No. 1862, Pioneers' emblem; 1863, T 310; 1864, Schoolgirl with flowers and satchel ("Study"); 1865, Girl with rain gauge ("Science"); 1866, Boy with sapling ("Forestry"); 1867, Girl skater ("Athletic Sports").

311 Exhibition Emblem and Symbols of Communication

312 Cultural Palace of the Nationalities

1959 (1 Dec). *National Exhibition of Industry and Communications, Peking. T 311 and similar vert design inscr "1949–1959". Recess.* P 11½.

1868	4 f. deep blue	..	..	5	5
1869	8 f. red	..	..	10	5
1868/1869	*Set of 2*	..	..	12	5

Design:—8 f. Exhibition emblem and symbols of industry.

1959 (10 Dec). *Inauguration of Cultural Palace of the Nationalities, Peking. Recess; frame litho.* P 14.

1870	**312**	4 f. black and vermilion	..	5	5
1871		8 f. black and blue-green	..	10	5
1870/1871	*Set of 2*	..	..	12	5

313 "Statue of Sport"

314 Wheat (Main Pavilion)

1959 (28 Dec). *First National Sports Meeting, Peking. Various sports designs as T 313. Multicoloured.* P 14.

1872	8 f. Type **313**	..	..	8	5
1873	8 f. Parachuting	..	..	8	5
1874	8 f. Pistol-shooting	..	..	8	5
1875	8 f. Diving	..	..	8	5
1876	8 f. Table tennis	..	..	8	5
1877	8 f. Weight-lifting	..	..	8	5
1878	8 f. High jumping	..	..	8	5
1879	8 f. Rowing	..	..	8	5
1880	8 f. Running	..	..	8	5
1881	8 f. Basketball	..	..	8	5
1882	8 f. Fencing	..	..	8	5
1883	8 f. Motor-cycling	..	..	8	5
1884	8 f. Gymnastics	..	..	8	5
1885	8 f. Cycling	..	..	8	5
1886	8 f. Horse-racing	..	..	8	5
1887	8 f. Football	..	..	8	5
1872/1887	*Set of 16*	..	..	1·10	60

1960 (20 Jan). *Opening of National Agricultural Exhibition Hall, Peking. T 314 and similar horiz designs. Recess; background litho.* P 14.

1888	4 f. black, red and red-orange	..	5	5
1889	8 f. black, blue and light blue..	..	8	5
1890	10 f. black, brown and brown-orange ..		8	5
1891	20 f. black, violet and greenish blue	..	15	8
1888/1891	*Set of 4*	..	..	30	20

Designs:—8 f. Meteorological symbols (Meteorological Pavilion); 10 f. Cattle (Animal Husbandry Pavilion); 20 f. Fishes (Aquatic Products Pavilion).

315 Crossing the Chinsha River

316 Clara Zetkin (founder)

1960 (25 Jan). *25th Anniv of Conference during the Long March, Tsunyi, Kweichow. T 315 and similar horiz designs inscr "1935–1960". Recess (4 f., 10 f.) or photo (8 f.). P 11 × 11½.*

1892	4 f. deep ultramarine ..	..	5	5
1893	8 f. sepia, lt turquoise, yellow & red ..		8	5
1894	10 f. deep green	..	10	8
1892/1894	*Set of 3*	..	..	20	15

Designs:—4 f. Conference Hall, Tsunyi; 8 f. Mao Tse-tung and flags.

1960 (8 Mar). *50th Anniv of International Women's Day. Vert designs as T 316. Photo. Frame and inscriptions black; centre colours below.* P 11½ × 11.

1895	4 f. blue, black and flesh	..	5	5
1896	8 f. multicoloured	..	8	5
1897	10 f. multicoloured	..	10	8
1898	22 f. multicoloured	..	25	10
1895/1898	*Set of 4*	..	..	45	25

Designs:—8 f. Mother, child and dove; 10 f. Woman tractor-driver; 22 f. Women of three races.

317 Chinese and Soviet Workers

318 Flags of Hungary and China

1960 (10 Mar). *Tenth Anniv of Sino-Soviet Treaty. T 317 and similar vert designs inscr "1950–1960". Photo. (4 f., 10 f.) or recess; background litho (8 f.). P 11½ × 11.*

1899	4 f. deep brown	..	15	8
1900	8 f. black, yellow and red	..	12	8
1901	10 f. blue	..	..	20	12
1899/1901	*Set of 3*	..	..	40	25

Designs:—8 f. Flowers and Sino-Soviet emblems; 10 f. Chinese and Soviet soldiers.

1960 (4 Apr). *15th Anniv of Hungarian Liberation. T* **318** *and similar horiz design inscr "1945–1960". Photo. P* 11 × 11½.

1902	8 f. red, green, black and yellow		..	15	8
1903	8 f. red, black and blue..	..	..	15	8
1902/1903	*Set of 2*	..	..	25	12

Designs:—No. 1902, T **318**; 1903, Parliament Buildings, Budapest.

319 Lenin Speaking   **320** Lunik 2

1960 (22 Apr). *90th Birth Anniv of Lenin. T* **319** *and vert designs inscr "1870–1960". Recess; background photo* (8 f.). *P* 11½ × 11.

1904	4 f. deep lilac ..	..	..	5	5
1905	8 f. black and vermilion	..	..	10	8
1906	20 f. deep chocolate ..	..	..	20	10
1904/1906	*Set of 3*	..	..	30	20

Designs:—8 f. Portrait of Lenin; 20 f. Lenin talking with Red Guards (after Vasilyev).

1960 (30 Apr). *Cosmic Rocket Flights. T* **320** *and similar vert design. Recess. P* 11½.

1907	8 f. scarlet	..	..	20	10
1908	10 f. bluish green (Lunik 3)	..	..	25	12
1907/1908	*Set of 2* ..	..	..	40	20

321 View of Prague   **322** "Out-folded Operculum and Nostril Bouquet"

1960 (9 May). *15th Anniv of Liberation of Czechoslovakia. T* **321** *and similar design inscr "1945–1960". Photo. P* 11½ × 11 (*No.* 1909) *or* 11 × 11½ (*No.* 1910).

1909	8 f. red, blue, sepia & greenish yellow	15	10
1910	8 f. deep myrtle-green ..	..		15	10
1909/1910	*Set of 2*	..	..	25	15

Design: *Vert*—No. 1909, Child pioneers and flags of China and Czechoslovakia.

1960 (1 June). *Chinese Goldfish. Horiz designs as T* **322**. *Multicoloured. P* 11 × 11½.

1911	4 f. (1) Type **322**	..	..	15	10
1912	4 f. (2) "Black-back Dragon-eye"	..	15	10
1913	4 f. (3) "Bubble-eye"	..	..	15	10
1914	4 f. (4) "Red Tigerhead"	..	..	15	10
1915	8 f. (5) "Pearl-scale" ..	..	..	20	10
1916	8 f. (6) "Blue Dragon-eye"	..	..	20	10
1917	8 f. (7) "Skyward-eye" ..	..	..	20	10
1918	8 f. (8) "Red-cap"	..	..	20	10
1919	8 f. (9) "Purple-cap"	..	..	20	10
1920	8 f. (10) "Red-head"	..	..	20	10
1921	8 f. (11) "Red and White Dragon-eye"		20	10
1922	8 f. (12) "Red Dragon-eye"	..	..	20	10
1911/1922	*Set of 12*	..	..	2·00	1·00

SERIAL NUMBERS. In the above and most later multicoloured sets containing several stamps of the same denomination, the serial number is quoted in brackets to assist identification. This is the last figure in the bottom left corner of the stamp.

323 Sow with Litter   **324** "Serving the Workers"

1960 (15 June). *Pig-breeding. Horiz designs as T* **323**. *Photo. P* 11 × 11½.

1923	8 f. black and vermilion	..	..	12	5
1924	8 f. black and green	..	..	12	5
1925	8 f. black and magenta..	..	..	12	5
1926	8 f. black and yellow-olive	..	..	12	5
1927	8 f. black and orange ..	..	..	12	5
1923/1927	*Set of 5*	..	..	55	20

Designs:—No. 1923, T **323**; 1924 Pig being inoculated; 1925, Group of pigs; 1926, Pig and feeding pens; 1927, Pig and crop-bales.

1960 (30 July). *Third National Literary and Art Workers' Congress, Peking. T* **324** *and similar vert design inscr "1960". Photo* (4 f.) *or recess; background photo* (8 f.). *P* 11½ × 11.

1928	4 f. red, sepia and dull green	..	10	5
1929	8 f. red, bistre and pale turquoise	..	15	5
1928/1929	*Set of 2*	..	..	20	8

Design:—8 f. Inscribed stone seal.

325 N. Korean and Chinese Flags, and Flowers   **326** Peking Railway Station

1960 (15 Aug). *15th Anniv of Liberation of Korea. T* **325** *and similar vert design inscr "1945–1960". Photo. P* 11½ × 11.

1930	8 f. red, blue, yellow and green	..	15	10
1931	8 f. red, indigo and bright blue	..	15	10
1930/1931	*Set of 2*	..	..	25	15

Design:—No. 1931, "Flying Horse" of Korea.

1960 (30 Aug). *Opening of New Peking Railway Station. T* **326** *and similar horiz design. Photo. P* 11½.

1932	8 f. brown, cream, black and blue	..	20	8
1933	10 f. indigo, cream and turquoise	..	20	8
1932/1933	*Set of 2*	..	..	35	12

Design:—10 f. Train arriving in station.

327 Chinese and N. Vietnamese Flags, and Children   **328** Worker and Spray Fan

1960 (2 Sept). *15th Anniv of North Vietnam Republic. T* **327** *and similar vert design inscr "1945–1960". Photo. P* 11 × 11½ (*No.* 1934) *or* 11½ × 11 (*No.* 1935).

1934	8 f. red, yellow, and black	..	..	10	5
1935	8 f. red, grey-green, green and black	..	10	5
1934/1935	*Set of 2*	..	..	15	5

Design: *Vert*—No. 1935, "Lake of the Returning Sword", Hanoi.

1960 (10 Sept). *Public Health Campaign. Various vert designs as T* **328**. *Photo.* P 11½.

1936	8 f. black and orange	12	5
1937	8 f. blackish green and grey-blue ..	12	5
1938	8 f. deep brown and light blue..	12	5
1939	8 f. lake and light orange-brown ..	12	5
1940	8 f. deep ultramarine and turq-green ..	12	5
1936/1940	*Set of 5*	55	20

Designs:—No. 1936, T **328**; 1937, Spraying insecticide; 1938, Cleaning windows; 1939, Medical examination of child; 1940, "Tai Chi Chuan" (Chinese physical drill).

329 Façade of Great Hall   **330** Dr. N. Bethune operating on Soldier

1960 (1 Oct). *Completion of "Great Hall of the People". T* **329** *and similar horiz design. Multicoloured. Photo.* P 11½.

1941	8 f. Type **329**	12	5
1942	10 f. Interior of Great Hall	15	12
1941/1942	*Set of 2*	25	15

1960 (20 Nov). *Dr. Norman Bethune (Canadian surgeon with 8th Route Army) Commemoration. T* **330** *and similar vert design. Photo.* (*No.* 1943) *or recess* (*No.* 1944). P 11½×11.

1943	8 f. grey, black & verm (Dr. N. Bethune)	15	5
1944	8 f. sepia (Type **330**)	25	8
1943/1944	*Set of 2*	25	8

331 F. Engels   **332** Big "Ju-I"   **333** Freighter

1960 (28 Nov). *140th Birth Anniv of Friedrich Engels. T* **331** *and similar vert design. Recess* (8 *f.*) *or photo* (10 *f.*). P 11½×11.

1945	8 f. chocolate	10	5
1946	10 f. red-orange and grey-blue ..	15	5
1945/1946	*Set of 2*	20	8

Design:—8 f. Engels addressing congress at The Hague.

1960 (10 Dec)—**61**. *Chrysanthemums. Vert designs as T* **332**. *Flowers in natural colours; background colours below. Photo.* P 11½×11.

1947	4 f. violet-blue (24.2.61)	5	5
1948	4 f. pink (24.2.61)	5	5
1949	8 f. grey (24.2.61)	8	5
1950	8 f. blue (18.1.61)	8	5
1951	8 f. green (18.1.61)	8	5
1952	8 f. bright violet (18.1.61)	8	5
1953	8 f. olive	8	5
1954	8 f. greenish blue	8	5
1955	10 f. greenish grey	10	8
1956	10 f. chocolate-brown (24.2.61) ..	10	8
1957	20 f. bright blue (24.2.61)	12	10
1958	20 f. vermilion (24.2.61)	12	10
1959	22 f. yellow-bistre (18.1.61)	15	12
1960	22 f. carmine (18.1.61)	15	12
1961	30 f. light grey-green (18.1.61) ..	25	20
1962	30 f. magenta	25	20
1963	35 f. bluish green	30	25
1964	52 f. bright purple	45	30
1947/1964	*Set of 18*	2·25	1·60

Chrysanthemums:—No. 1947, "Hwang Shih Pa"; 1948, "Green Peony"; 1949 "Er Chiao"; 1950, T **332**; 1951 "Ju-I"

with Golden Hooks; 1952, "Golden Peony"; 1953, "Generalissimo's Banner"; 1954, "Willow Thread"; 1955, "Cassia on Salver of Hibiscus"; 1956, "Pearls on Jade Salver"; 1957, "Red Gold Lion"; 1958, "Milky White Jade"; 1959, "Purple Jade with Fragrant Beads"; 1960, "Cassia on Ice Salver"; 1961, "Inky Black Lotus"; 1962, "Jade Bamboo Shoot of Superior Class"; 1963, "Smiling Face"; 1964, "Swan Ballet".

1960 (15 Dec). *Launching of First Chinese-built Freighter. Photo. No gum.* P 11½.

1965	**333** 8 f. blue	15	5

334 Pantheon, Paris   **335** Table-Tennis Match –

1961 (18 Mar). *90th Anniv of Paris Commune. T* **334** *and similar vert design. Recess, flags photo.* P 11½×11.

1966	8 f. black and red	10	5
1967	8 f. sepia and red	10	5
1966/1967	*Set of 2*	15	8

Design:—No. 1967, Proclamation of Commune.

1961 (5 Apr). *26th World Table-Tennis Championships, Peking. T* **335** *and similar horiz designs. Multicoloured. Photo.* P 11.

1968	8 f. Championship emblem and jasmine	8	5
1969	10 f. Table-tennis bat and ball, and Temple of Heaven	10	5
1970	20 f. Type **335**	12	5
1971	22 f. Peking Workers' Gymnasium ..	15	5
1968/1971	*Set of 4*	40	15
MS1971a	150×100 mm. Nos. 1968/71. No gum. Imperf	2·75	2·75

1961 (20 June). *Birth Centenary of Chan Tien-yu (railway construction engineer). T* **336** *and similar vert design inscr "1861–1961". Photo.* P 11½×11.

1972	8 f. black and sage-green	15	5
1973	10 f. orange-brown and sepia	20	5
1972/1973	*Set of 2*	30	5

Design:—10 f. Train on Peking-Changchow Railway.

1961 (1 July). *40th Anniv of Chinese Communist Party. T* **337** *and similar horiz designs inscr "1921–1961". Flags red, frames gold, centre colours below. Photo.* P 11½.

1974	4 f. reddish purple	5	5
1975	8 f. blue-green	8	5
1976	10 f. orange-brown	10	5
1977	20 f. ultramarine	20	5
1978	30 f. orange-red	25	5
1974/1978	*Set of 5*	60	20

Designs:—8 f. "August 1" Building, Nanchang; 10 f. Provisional Central Govt. Building, Juichin; 20 f. Pagoda Hill, Yenan; 30 f. Gate of Heavenly Peace, Peking.

336 Chan Tien-yu   **337** Congress Building, Shanghai

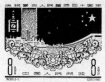

338 "August 1"
Building, Nanchang

339 Flags of China and
Mongolia

1961 (20 July)–**62**. *T* **338** *and similar horiz designs* (24×16½ mm). *Recess. No gum.* P 11.

1979	**338**	1 f. ultramarine (20.7.62) ..	..	5	5
1980		1½ f. lake (20.7.62) ..	..	5	5
1981		2 f. deep slate-blue ..	..	5	5
1982	–	3 f. violet ..	..	5	5
1983	–	4 f. emerald ..	..	5	5
1984	–	5 f. blackish green (20.7.62) ..		5	5
1985	–	8 f. sepia ..	..	5	5
1986	–	10 f. bright purple ..	..	8	5
1987	–	20 f. deep turquoise-blue ..		10	5
1988	–	22 f. chocolate ..	..	10	5
1989	–	30 f. blue ..	..	20	10
1990	–	50 f. scarlet..	..	30	15
1979/1990		*Set of 12* ..	..	90	50

Designs:—3 f., 4 f., 5 f. Tree and Sha Chow Pa Building, Juichin; 8 f. 10 f., 20 f. Yenan Pagoda; 22 f., 30 f., 50 f. Gate of Heavenly Peace, Peking.
Some of the above exist also on vertically laid paper.
See also Nos. 2010/21.

1961 (11 July). *40th Anniv of Mongolian People's Revolution. T* **339** *and similar horiz design inscr* "1921–1961". *Photo.* P 11×11½.

1991	8 f. red, ultramarine and yellow	..	15	10
1992	10 f. orange, yellow and deep olive	..	20	15
1991/1992	*Set of 2* ..	..	30	20

Design:—10 f. Mongolian Government Building.

340 Military Museum

1961 (1 Aug). *People's Revolutionary Military Museum. Centre recess; background photo.* P 11½.

1993	**340**	8 f. chocolate, green & grey-blue		10	8
1994		10 f. black, green and grey-brown ..		15	8
1993/1994		*Set of 2* ..	..	20	10

341 Uprising at Wuhan   **342** Donkey

1961 (10 Oct). *50th Anniv of 1911 Revolution. T* **341** *and similar design inscr* "1911–1961". *Photo.* P 11×11½ (8 f.) *or* 11½×11 (10 f.).

1995	8 f. black and grey ..	..	10	5
1996	10 f. black and yellow-brown ..		15	5
1995/1996	*Set of 2* ..	..	20	5

Design: Vert—10 f. Dr. Sun Yat-sen.

1961 (10 Nov). *Tang Dynasty Pottery* (618–907 A.D.). *T* **342** *and similar vert designs. Centres multicoloured; background colours below. Photo.* P 11½×11.

1997	4 f. grey-blue ..	..	..	5	5
1998	8 f. grey-green	..	..	5	5
1999	8 f. purple	..	..	5	5
2000	10 f. slate-blue ..	..	..	10	8
2001	20 f. yellow-olive	..	..	20	10
2002	22 f. bluish green	..	..	20	10
2003	30 f. brown-red..	..	..	30	15
2004	50 f. slate	..	..	50	20
1997/2004	*Set of 8* ..	..	1·25	65

Designs:—No. 1998, Donkey; Nos. 1999/2002, Various horses; Nos. 2003/4, Various camels.

343 Tibetans Rejoicing   **344** Lu Hsun (after Hsieh Chia-seng)

1961 (25 Nov). *"Rebirth of the Tibetan People". Photo.* P 11½×11. *and similar vert designs.*

2005	4 f. chocolate and buff	..	..	5	5
2006	8 f. chocolate and turquoise-green		8	5
2007	10 f. chocolate and yellow	..	10	5
2008	20 f. chocolate and pink	..	15	5
2009	30 f. chocolate and pale slate-blue	..	20	10
2005/2009	*Set of 5* ..	..	..	50	25

Designs:—8 f. Sower; 10 f. Tibetans celebrating "bumper crop"; 20 f. "Responsible citizens"; 30 f. Tibetan children.

1962 (Jan)–**71**. *Designs similar to Nos.* 1979/90 *but smaller* (20½×16½ *mm*). *Litho. No gum.* P 12½.

2010	1 f. ultramarine	..	..	5	5
2011	2 f. grey-green	..	..	5	5
	a. Perf 11	..	..		
	b. Roul×perf 13	..	..		
2012	2 f. slate-green (p 11) (1.7.70)..		5	5
2013	3 f. slate-violet	..	..	5	5
2014	3 f. agate (p 11) (1.7.70)	..	5	5
2015	4 f. emerald	..	..	5	5
	a. Perf 13	..	..		
	b. Perf 14	..	..		
2016	4 f. bright rose (p 11) (1.7.70) ..		5	5
2017	8 f. sepia	..	..	8	5
	a. Perf 14	..	..		
	b. Perf 11×11½	..	..		
2018	10 f. bright purple	..	..	8	5
	a. Perf 11 (1.7.70)	..	..	5	5
2019	20 f. deep turquoise-blue	..	15	5
	a. Perf 11 (1.7.70)	..	..	8	5
2020	30 f. blue	..	..	25	12
2021	52 f. orange-red (p 11) (10.2.71)		30	20
2010/2021	*Set of 12* ..	..	1·00	60

Designs:—Nos. 2010/2, 2014, "August 1" Building, Nanchang; Nos. 2013, 2015, Tree and Sha Chow Pa Building, Juichin; Nos. 2016, 2020/1, Gate of Heavenly Peace, Peking; Nos. 2017/9, Yenan Pagoda.
The 2 f. grey-green, 4 f. emerald and 8 f. exist on thin and thick paper.

1962 (26 Feb). *80th Birth Anniv of Lu Hsun* (writer). *Photo.* P 11½×11.

2022	**344**	8 f. black and lake ..	..	10	5

PUZZLED?

Then you need
PHILATELIC TERMS ILLUSTRATED
to tell you all you need to know about printing
methods, papers, errors, varieties, watermarks,
perforations, etc. 192 pages, almost half in full
colour, soft cover. £1 post paid.

345 Anchi Bridge, Chaohsien

346 Tu Fu

1962 (15 May). *Ancient Chinese Bridges.* T 345 *and similar horiz designs. Photo.* P 11.

2023	4 f. deep bluish violet and lavender	..	5	5
2024	8 f. slate-green and green	..	8	5
2025	10 f. sepia and light bistre-brown		10	5
2026	20 f. ultramarine and turquoise	..	15	5
2023/2026	*Set of 4*	..	35	15

Bridges:—8 f. Paotai, Soochow; 10 f. Chupu, Kuanhsien; 20 f. Chenyang, Sankiang.

1962 (25 May). *1,250th Birth Anniv of Tu Fu (poet).* T 346 *and similar vert design. Photo.* P 11½×11.

2027	4 f. black and yellow-bistre	..	8	5
2028	8 f. black and turquoise-blue	..	12	5
2027/2028	*Set of 2*	..	15	5

Design:—4 f. Tu Fu's Memorial, Chengtu.

347 Two Cranes and Trees

348 Cuban Soldier

1962 (10 June). *"The Sacred Crane".* T 347 *and similar vert designs. Photo.* P 11½×11.

2029	8 f. black, red, turquoise-green & drab	12	5
2030	10 f. black, red, buff and blue	..	15	5
2031	20 f. black, red, blue and buff	..	25	10
2029/2031	*Set of 3*	..	45	15

Designs:—10 f. Two cranes in flight; 20 f. Crane on rock. (All from paintings by Chen Chi-fo.)

1962 (10 July). *"Support for Cuba".* T 348 *and similar horiz designs. Photo.* P 11×11½.

2032	8 f. black and lake	..	12	10
2033	10 f. black and yellow-green	..	15	12
2034	22 f. black and violet-blue	..	30	15
2032/2034	*Set of 3*	..	50	30

Designs:—10 f. Sugar-cane planter; 22 f. Militiaman and woman.

349 Torch and Map

350 Mei Lan-fang (actor)

1962 (10 July). *"Support for Algeria".* T 349 *and similar vert design. Photo.* P 11½×11.

2035	8 f. orange-red and deep brown	..	10	5
2036	22 f. choc & ochre (Algerian patriots)	..	15	10
2035/2036	*Set of 2*	..	20	12

1962 (8 Aug–15 Sept). *"Stage Art of Mei Lan-fang".* T 350 *and similar vert designs. Photo.* P 11½×11 or 11½ (**MS**2044a).

2037	4 f. multicoloured	..	..	..	8	5
2038	8 f. multicoloured	..	..	..	10	5
2039	8 f. multicoloured	..	..	..	10	5
2040	10 f. multicoloured	..	..	..	15	8
2041	20 f. multicoloured (1.9)	..	..	20	12
2042	22 f. multicoloured (1.9)	..	..	25	12
2043	30 f. multicoloured (1.9)	..	..	40	20
2044	50 f. multicoloured (1.9)	..	..	55	30
2037/2044	*Set of 8*	..	..	1·60	90
MS2044a	108×147 mm. 3 f. multicoloured (15.9)		2·75	2·75

Designs: *Vert*—Mei Lan-fang in stage costume with: No. 2038, Drum; 2039, Fan; 2040, Swords; 2041, Bag. *Larger:* (48×58 mm)—3 f. With partner in "Drunken Beauty" opera. *Horiz*—No. 2042, Ribbons; 2043, Loom; 2044, Long sleeves. Nos. 2037/44 exist imperforate (*Price £8 un or used*).

351 Han "Flower Drum" Dance

352 Soldiers storming the Winter Palace, Petrograd

1962 (15 Oct). *Chinese Folk Dances* (1st issue). T 351 *and similar vert designs, inscr "246" to "251" at bottom right. Multicoloured. Litho. No gum.* P 12½.

2045	4 f. Type 351	..	..	5	5
2046	8 f. Mongolian "Ordos"	..	5	5
2047	10 f. Chuang "Catching shrimp"	..	10	5
2048	20 f. Tibetan "Fiddle"	..	15	5
2049	30 f. Yi "Friend"	..	..	25	8
2050	50 f. Uighur "Tambourine"	..	40	12
2045/2050	*Set of 6*	..	..	90	30

See also Nos. 2104/15.

1962 (7 Nov). *45th Anniv of the Russian Revolution.* T 352 *and similar design. Photo.* P 11½.

2051	8 f. black-brown and red	..	10	5
2052	20 f. deep bronze-green and red	..	20	8
2051/2052	*Set of 2*	..	25	10

Design: *Vert*—8 f. Lenin leading soldiers.

353 Revolutionary Statue and Map

354 Tsai Lun (A.D.?–121, inventor of papermaking process)

1962 (28 Nov). *50th Anniv of Albanian Independence.* T 353 *and similar vert design. Photo.* P 11½×11.

2053	8 f. sepia and slate-blue	..	10	5
2054	10 f. black, red, yellow and grey-blue	..	15	5
2053/4	*Set of 2*	..	20	8

Design:—10 f. Albanian flag and girl pioneer.

1962 (1 Dec). *Scientists of Ancient China.* T 354 *and similar vert designs. Multicoloured. Photo.* P 11½×11.

2055	4 f. Type 354	..	..	5	5
2056	4 f. Paper-making	..	..	5	5
2057	8 f. Sun Szu-miao (581–682, physician)	..	8	5
2058	8 f. Preparing medical treatise	..	8	5
2059	10 f. Shen Ko (1031–1095, geologist)	..	10	5
2060	10 f. Making field notes	..	..	10	5

1964 (1 May). *Labour Day.* T **369** *and similar horiz design. Recess and photo.* P 11½
2166	8 f. black, red and gold..	..	..	10	5
2167	8 f. black, red and gold..	..	..	10	5
2166/2167	Set of 2	..	..	15	8

Design:—No. 2167, Workers and banners.

370 Date Orchard, Yenan   **371** Map of Vietnam and Flag

1964 (1 July). *"Yenan—Shrine of the Chinese Revolution".* T **370** *and similar horiz designs showing Yenan Buildings. Multicoloured. Photo.* P 11 × 11½.
2168	8 f. (1) Type **370**			8	5
2169	8 f. (2) Central Auditorium, Yang Chia Ling			8	5
2170	8 f. (3) Mao Tse-tung's Office and Residence, Date Orchard, Yenan			8	5
2171	8 f. (4) Auditorium, Wang Chia Ping	..		8	5
2172	8 f. (5) Border Region Assembly Hall			8	5
2173	52 f. (6) Pagoda Hill	..	..	30	12
2168/2173	Set of 6	..	..	60	30

1964 (20 July). *South Vietnam Victory Campaign. Photo.* P 11½.
2174	**371** 8 f. olive-grey, blue, red and yellow		12	5

372 "The Alchemist's Glowing Crucible" (peony)   **373** "Church" (wine cup)

1964 (5 Aug). *Chinese Peonies. Vert designs as* T **372**. *Multicoloured. Photo.* P 11½ × 11 or 11½ (MS2189a).
2175	4 f. (1) Type **372**	..	..	5	5
2176	4 f. (2) Night-shining Jade	..	..	5	5
2177	8 f. (3) Purple Kuo's Cap	..		5	5
2178	8 f. (4) Chao Pinks		..	5	5
2179	8 f. (5) Yao Yellows	..		5	5
2180	8 f. (6) Twin Beauties ..			5	5
2181	8 f. (7) Ice-veiled Rubies	..		5	5
2182	10 f. (8) Gold-sprinkled Chinese Ink	..		8	5
2183	10 f. (9) Cinnabar Jar	..	..	8	5
2184	10 f. (10) Lantien Jade	..	..	8	5
2185	10 f. (11) Imperial Robe Yellow		..	8	5
2186	10 f. (12) Hu Reds	..	..	8	5
2187	20 f. (13) Pea Green	..	..	15	8
2188	43 f. (14) Wei Purples	..	..	35	15
2189	52 f. (15) Intoxicated Celestial Peach	..	45	20
2175/2189	Set of 15	..	..	1·50	90
MS189a	77 × 136 mm. 2 y. Glorious Crimson and Great Gold Pink (*Larger,* 48 × 59 mm) ..	..	..	3·50	3·50

1964 (25 Aug).ˑ *Bronze Vessels of the Yin Dynasty* (*Before* 1050 B.C.). *Vert designs as* T **373**. *Centres in various shades of green, olive or blue; values, inscr and frames in black. Recess and photo.* P 11½ × 11.
2190	4 f. (1) Type **373**	.:	..	5	5
2191	4 f. (2) "Ku" (beaker) ..		..	5	5
2192	8 f. (3) "Kuang" (wine urn)	..		5	5
2193	8 f. (4) "Chia" (wine cup)		.ˑ	5	5
2194	10 f. (5) "Tsun" (wine vessel)	..		10	5
2195	10 f. (6) "Yu" (wine urn)	..		10	5
2196	20 f. (7) "Tsun" (wine vessel)	..		15	5
2197	20 f. (8) "Ting" (ceremonial cauldron)		15	5
2190/2197	Set of 8	..	..	60	30

374 "Harvesting"   **375** Marx, Engels and Trafalgar Square, London (vicinity of old St. Martin's Hall)

1964 (26 Sept). *Agricultural Students. Vert designs as* T **374**. *Multicoloured. Photo.* P 11½ × 11.
2198	ˑ8 f. (1) Type **374**	..	..	12	5
2199	8 f. (2) "Sapling planting"	..		12	5
2200	8 f. (3) "Study" ..	..	..	12	5
2201	8 f. (4) "Scientific experiment"	..		12	5
2198/2201	Set of 4	..	..	40	15

1964 (28 Sept). *Centenary of "First International". Photo.* P 11½.
2202	**375** 8 f. red, orange-brown and gold	..	25	12

376 Rejoicing People   **377** Oil Derrick

1964 (1 Oct). *15th Anniv of People's Republic. Vert designs as* T **376**. *Multicoloured. Photo.* P 11½.
2203	8 f. (1) Type **376**	..	..	12	5
2204	8 f. (2) Chinese flag	..	..	12	5
2205	8 f. (3) As T **376** in reverse	..		12	5
2203/2205	Set of 3	..	..	30	10
MS2205a	150 × 114 mm. Nos. 2203/5 forming a composite design without dividing perfs ..	..	..	30	20

Nos. 2203/5 were issued in the form of a triptych, in sheets.

1964 (1 Oct). *Petroleum Industry.* T **377** *and similar designs. Multicoloured. Photo.* P 11½.
2206	4 f. Geological surveyors and van (*horiz*)			5	5
2207	8 f. Type **377**	..	..	8	5
2208	8 f. Oil-extraction equipment ..			8	5
2209	10 f. Refinery	..	..	10	5
2210	20 f. Railway petroleum trucks (*horiz*) ..		15	5
2206/2210	Set of 5	..	..	40	20

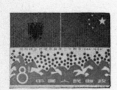

378 Albanian and Chinese Flags and Plants

379 Dam under Construction

1964 (29 Nov). *20th Anniv of Liberation of Albania. T 378 and similar horiz design. Photo. P 11×11½.*
2211	8 f. red, black, green and yellow	..	10	5
2212	10 f. black, red and yellow	.. ..	12	5
2211/2212	Set of 2	.. ..	20	8

Design:—10 f. Enver Hoxha and Albanian arms.

1964 (15 Dec). *Hsinankiang Hydro-Electric Power Station. T 379 and similar vert designs. Multicoloured. Photo. P 11½.*
2213	4 f. Type **379** ..		5	5
2214	8 f. Installation of turbo-generator rotor	.. .. ..	8	5
2215	8 f. Main dam ..	.. ..	8	5
2216	20 f. Pylon	.. .. ..	12	5
2213/2216	Set of 4	.. .. ..	30	15

380 Fertilisers

1964 (30 Dec). *Chemical Industry. Horiz designs as T 380. Main design and inscr in black; background colours given below. Recess and photo. P 11½.*
2217	8 f. (1) vermilion (Type **380**)	..	8	5
2218	8 f. (2) yellow-green (Plastics) ..		8	5
2219	8 f. (3) brown-orge (Medicinal drugs) ..		8	5
2220	8 f. (4) magenta (Rubber)	..	8	5
2221	8 f. (5) bright blue (Insecticides)	..	8	5
2222	8 f. (6) orange (Acids)	..	8	5
2223	8 f. (7) bright lilac (Alkalis)	..	8	5
2224	8 f. (8) brt blue-green (Synthetic fibres)		8	5
2217/2224	Set of 8	.. .. ..	55	30

381 Mao Tse-tung standing in Room   **382** Conference Hall

1965 (31 Jan). *30th Anniv of Tsunyi Conference. T 381 and similar designs. Multicoloured. Photo. P 11½×11 (No. 2226) or 11 (others).*
2225	8 f. Type **381** ..	.. ..	15	8
2226	8 f. Mao Tse-tung (26½×36 mm)	..	15	8
2227	8 f. "Victory at Loushan Pass" ..		15	8
2225/2227	Set of 3	.. .. ..	40	20

1965 (18 Apr). *Tenth Anniv of Bandung Conference. T 382 and similar vert design inscr "1955–1965". Multicoloured. Photo. P 11½×11.*
2228	8 f. Type **382** ..	.. ..	10	5
2229	8 f. Rejoicing Africans and Asians	..	10	5
2228/2229	Set of 2 ..	.. .. ..	15	5

383 Lenin   **384** Table-tennis Player   **385** Government Building

1965 (22 Apr). *95th Anniv of Lenin's Birth. Photo. P 11½×11.*
2230	**383** 8 f. multicoloured ..	..	8	5

1965 (25 Apr). *World Table-tennis Championships, Peking. T 384 and similar horiz designs showing different views of table-tennis players, each red, gold, black and green. Photo. P 11½.*
2231	**384** 8 f. (1)	.. ..	10	5
2232	— 8 f. (2)	.. ..	10	5
2233	— 8 f. (3)	.. ..	10	5
2234	— 8 f. (4)	.. ..	10	5
2231/2234	Set of 4	.. ..	35	15

Nos. 2231/4 were issued together in blocks of 4 within the sheets.

1965–66. *T 385 and similar vert designs. Litho. No gum. P 11½×11.*
2235	**385**	1 f. brown	..	..	5	5
2236	A	1½ f. bright purple..		..	5	5
2237	B	2 f. grey-green	..	..	5	5
2238	C	3 f. turquoise-green		..	5	5
2239	**385**	4 f. new blue	..	..	5	5
2239a	A	5 f. plum (1966)	..	..	8	5
2240	B	8 f. rose-red	..	..	5	5
2241	C	10 f. drab ..	..	..	5	5
2242	**385**	20 f. violet..	..	..	10	5
2243	A	22 f. yellow-orange	..	..	10	5
2244	B	30 f. yellow-green..		..	20	5
2244a	C	50 f. ultramarine (1966)		..	35	10
2235/2244a	Set of 12 ..		..	..	1·00	50

Designs:—A, Gate of Heavenly Peace; B, People's Hall; C, Military Museum.

386 All-China T.U. Federation Team scaling Mt. Minya Konka   **387** Marx and Lenin

1965 (25 May). *Chinese Mountaineering Achievements. T 386 and similar vert designs each black, pale yellow and blue. Recess and photo. P 11½.*
2245	8 f. (1) Type **386**	.. .. ..	8	5
2246	8 f. (2) Men and women's mixed team on slopes of Muztagh Ata	..	8	5
2247	8 f. (3) Climbers on Mt. Jolmo Lungma		8	5
2248	8 f. (4) Women's team camping on Kongur Tiubie Tagh	..	8	5
2249	8 f. (5) Climbers on Shishma Pangma	..	8	5
2245/2249	Set of 5 ..	.. .. ..	35	20

1965 (21 June). *Postal Ministers' Congress, Peking. Photo.*
P 11½ × 11.

2250 **387** 8 f. multicoloured 20 8

388 Tseping

1965 (1 July). *"Chingkang Mountains—Cradle of the Chinese Revolution". T* **388** *and similar horiz designs. Multicoloured. Photo. P* 11 × 11½.

2251	4 f. (1) Type **388**		5	5
2252	8 f. (2) Sanwantsun	.. ..	8	5
2253	8 f. (3) Octagonal Building, Maoping	8	5
2254	8 f. (4) River and bridge at Lungshih	..	8	5
2255	8 f. (5) Tachingtsun	..	8	5
2256	10 f. (6) Bridge at Lungyuankou	..	8	5
2257	10 f. (7) Hwangyangchieh	..	8	5
2258	52 f. (8) Chingkang peaks	.. ..	30	12
2251/2258	*Set of 8*	.. .. ..	75	30

389 Soldiers with Texts

1965 (1 Aug). *People's Liberation Army. T* **389** *and similar multicoloured designs. Photo. P* 11½.

2259	8 f. (1) Type **389**	.. ..	8	5
2260	8 f. (2) Soldiers reading book	..	8	5
2261	8 f. (3) Soldier with grenade-thrower	..	8	5
2262	8 f. (4) Giving tuition in firing rifle	..	8	5
2263	8 f. (5) Soldiers at rest (*vert*)	..	8	5
2264	8 f. (6) Bayonet charge (*vert*)	..	8	5
2265	8 f. (7) Soldier with banners (*vert*)	..	8	5
2266	8 f. (8) Military band (*vert*)	..	8	5
2259/2266	*Set of 8*	.. .. ..	55	30

390 "Welcome to Peking"

391 Soldier firing Weapon

1965 (25 Aug). *Chinese–Japanese Youth Meeting, Peking. T* **390** *and similar vert designs. Multicoloured. Photo. P* 11½ × 11.

2267	4 f. (1) Type **390**	..	5	5
2268	8 f. (2) Chinese and Japanese youths with linked arms	.. ..	8	5
2269	8 f. (3) Chinese and Japanese girls	..	8	5
2270	10 f. (4) Musical entertainment	..	8	5
2271	22 f. (5) Emblem of Meeting	..	12	8
2267/2271	*Set of 5*	.. .. ..	35	20

1965 (2 Sept). *"Vietnamese People's Struggle". T* **391** *and similar designs. Photo. P* 11½ (*No.* 2275) *or* 11½ × 11 (*others*).

2272	8 f. (1) chestnut and red	.. ..	10	5
2273	8 f. (2) blackish olive and red	..	10	5
2274	8 f. (3) maroon and red	.. ..	10	5
2275	8 f. (4) black and vermilion	..	10	5
2272/2275	*Set of 4*	.. ..	35	15

Designs: *Vert*—(1) *T* **391**; (2) Soldier with captured weapons; (3) Soldier giving victory salute. *Horiz* (48½ × 26 *mm*)—(4) "Peoples of the world".

392 "Victory"

393 Football

1965 (3 Sept). *20th Anniv of Victory over Japanese. T* **392** *and similar designs. Photo. P* 11 (*No.* 2276), 11½ × 11 (*No.* 2278) *or* 11 × 11½ (*others*).

2276	8 f. (1) multicoloured	..	10	5
2277	8 f. (2) slate-green and red	..	10	5
2278	8 f. (3) sepia and red	..	10	5
2279	8 f. (4) slate-green and red	..	10	5
2276/2279	*Set of 4*	..	35	15

Designs: *Horiz* (50½ × 36 *mm*)—(1) Mao Tse-tung writing. As *T* **392**: *Horiz*—(2) Soldiers crossing Yellow River; (4) Recruits in cart.

1965 (28 Sept). *National Games. T* **393** *and similar multicoloured designs. Photo. P* 11½ × 11.

2280	4 f. (1) Type **393**	.. ..	5	5
2281	4 f. (2) Archery	.. ..	5	5
2282	8 f. (3) Throwing the javelin	..	8	5
2283	8 f. (4) Gymnastics	.. ..	8	5
2284	8 f. (5) Volleyball	.. ..	8	5
2285	10 f. (6) Opening ceremony (56 × 35½ *mm*)	..	10	5
2286	10 f. (7) Cycling	.. ..	10	5
2287	20 f. (8) Diving	.. ..	12	5
2288	22 f. (9) Hurdling	.. ..	15	8
2289	30 f. (10) Weightlifting	..	20	12
2290	43 f. (11) Basketball	..	25	15
2280/2290	*Set of 11*	.. ..	1·10	55

394 Textile Workers

1965 (30 Nov). *Women in Industry. T* **394** *and similar vert designs. Multicoloured. Photo. P* 11½ × 11.

2291	8 f. (1) Type **394**	..	10	5
2292	8 f. (2) Machine building	..	10	5
2293	8 f. (3) Building construction	..	10	5
2294	8 f. (4) Studying	.. ..	10	5
2295	8 f. (5) Militia guard	.. ..	10	5
2291/2295	*Set of 5*	.. ..	45	20

395 Children playing with Ball

1966 (25 Feb). *Children's Games. T* **395** *and similar horiz designs. Multicoloured. Photo. P* 11.

2296	4 f. (1) Type **395**	..	5	5
2297	4 f. (2) Racing	..	5	5
2298	8 f. (3) Tobogganing	..	5	5
2299	8 f. (4) Exercising	..	5	5
2300	8 f. (5) Swimming	..	5	5
2301	8 f. (6) Shooting	..	5	5
2302	10 f. (7) Jumping with rope	..	8	8
2303	52 f. (8) Playing table-tennis	..	35	15
2296/2303	*Set of* 8	..	65	40

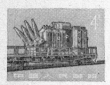

396 Mobile Transformer

397 Women of Military and other Services

1966 (30 Mar). *New Industrial Machines. T* **396** *and similar designs. Recess and photo. P* 11×11½ *(horiz) or* 11½×11 *(vert).*

2304	4 f. (1) black and light yellow	..	5	5
2305	8 f. (2) black and violet-blue	..	8	5
2306	8 f. (3) black and pink	..	8	5
2307	8 f. (4) black and yellow-olive	..	8	5
2308	8 f. (5) black and bright purple	..	8	5
2309	10 f. (6) black and light greenish grey	..	10	5
2310	10 f. (7) black and turquoise	..	10	5
2311	22 f. (8) black and lilac	..	20	8
2304/2311	*Set of* 8	..	70	30

Designs: *Vert*—(2) Electron microscope; (4), Vertical boring and turning machine; (6), Hydraulic press; (8), Electron accelerator, *Horiz*—(3), Lathe; (5), Gear-grinding machine; (7), Milling machine.

1966 (10 May). *Women in Public Service. T* **397** *and similar horiz designs. Multicoloured. Photo. P* 11×11½.

2312	8 f. (1) Type **397**	..	8	5
2313	8 f. (2) Train conductress	..	8	5
2314	8 f. (3) Red Cross worker	..	8	5
2315	8 f. (4) Kindergarten teacher	..	8	5
2316	8 f. (5) Roadsweeper	..	8	5
2317	8 f. (6) Hairdresser	..	8	5
2318	8 f. (7) Bus conductress	..	8	5
2319	8 f. (8) Travelling sales-woman	..	8	5
2320	8 f. (9) Canteen worker	..	8	5
2321	8 f. (10) Rural postwoman	..	8	5
2312/2321	*Set of* 10	..	70	35

398 "Thunderstorm" (sculpture)

399 Dr. Sun Yat-sen

1966 (27 June). *Afro-Asian Writers' Meeting. T* **398** *and similar horiz design. Photo. P* 11×11½.

2322	8 f. black and red	..	10	5
2323	22 f. gold, yellow and red (Meeting emblem)	..	20	8
2322/2323	*Set of* 2	..	25	10

1966 (12 Nov). *Birth Centenary of Dr. Sun Yat-sen. Photo. P* 11½×11.

2324	**399** 8 f. sepia and light buff	..	10	5

400 Athletes with Mao Tse-tung's Portrait

401 Mao's Appreciation of Lu Hsun (patriot and writer)

1966 (31 Dec). *"Cultural Revolution" Games. T* **400** *and similar multicoloured designs. Photo. P* 11 *(Nos. 2325/6) or* 11×11½ *(others).*

2325	8 f. (1) Type **400**		15	5
2326	8 f. (2) Athletes with linked arms holding Mao texts		15	5
2327	8 f. (3) Two women athletes with Mao texts		15	5
2328	8 f. (4) Athletes reading Mao texts		15	5
2325/2328	*Set of* 4		50	15

Sizes:—No. 2326, As T **400**, but vert; Nos. 2327/8, 36½×25 mm.

1966 (31 Dec). *Lu Hsun Commemoration. T* **401** *and similar vert designs. Photo. (No. 2330) or recess and photo (others). P* 11½.

2329	8 f. (1) black and red-orange	..	15	5
2330	8 f. (2) black, flesh and red		15	5
2331	8 f. (3) black and red-orange		15	12
2329/2331	*Set of* 3		40	12

Designs.—(1) Type **401**; (3) Lu Hsun's manuscript.

402 "Be Resolute . . ." (Mao Tse-tung)

403 Liu Ying-chun (military hero)

1967 (10 Mar). *Heroic Oilwell Firefighters. T* **402** *and similar designs. Photo. P* 11½ *(No. 2333) or* 11½×11 *(others)*

2332	8 f. (1) gold, scarlet and black	..	15	5
2333	8 f. (2) black and light vermilion		15	5
2334	8 f. (3) black and light vermilion		15	5
2332/2334	*Set of* 3		40	12

Designs: *Vert*—(1) Type **402**; (3) Smothering flames with tarpaulins. *Horiz* (48×27 *mm*)—(2) Drilling Team No. 32111 fighting flames.

1967 (25 Mar). *Liu Ying-chun Commemoration. T* **403** *and similar vert designs. Multicoloured. Photo. P* 11½×11

2335	8 f. (1) Type **403**		10	5
2336	8 f. (2) Liu Ying-chun holding book of Mao texts	..	10	5
2337	8 f. (3) Liu Ying-chun holding horse's bridle	..	10	5
2338	8 f. (4) Liu Ying-chun looking at film slide		10	5
2339	8 f. (5) Liu Ying-chun lecturing	..	10	5
2340	8 f. (6) Liu Ying-chun making fatal attempt to stop bolting horse	..	10	5
2335/2340	*Set of* 6	..	55	25

404 Soldier, Nurse, Workers and Banners

1967 (15 Apr). *Third Five-Year Plan.* T **404** *and similar horiz design. Multicoloured. Photo.* P 11.

2341	8 f. Type **404**	..	..	15	5
2342	8 f. Armed woman, peasants and banners	..	..	15	5
2341/2342	*Set of 2*	..	..	25	8

405 Mao Tse-tung

406 Mao Text (39 characters)

1967 (20 Apr). *"Thoughts of Mao Tse-tung"* (1st issue). T **406** *and similar vert designs showing Mao texts, each gold and red, and* T **405**. *To assist identification of Nos. 2344/53 the total numbers of Chinese characters within the frames are given. Photo.* P 11½.

(a) Type **405**

2343	8 f. multicoloured	..	..	..	20	10

(b) As Type **406**. *Red outer frames*

2344	8 f. Type **406**	..	..	..	12	8
2345	8 f. (50 characters)	..	..	..	12	8
2346	8 f. (39—in six lines)	..	..	..	12	8
2347	8 f. (53) ..	..	..	..	12	8
2348	8 f. (46) ..	..	..	..	12	8

(c) As Type **406**. *Gold outer frames*

2349	8 f. (41) ..	..	..	..	12	8
2350	8 f. (49) ..	..	..	..	12	8
2351	8 f. (35) ..	..	..	..	12	5
2352	8 f. (22) ..	..	..	..	12	5
2353	8 f. (29) ..	..	..	..	12	5
2343/2353	*Set of 11*	..	..	..	1·25	80

Nos. 2344/8 and 2349/53 were respectively issued together *se-tenant* in strips of five within the sheet.

See also No. 2404.

407 Mao Text

1967 (1 May). *Labour Day.* T **407** *and similar vert designs. Multicoloured. Recess and photo* (4 f.) *or photo* (others). P 11 (No. 2358) *or* 11 × 11½ (*others*).

2354	4 f. Type **407**	..	..	10	8
2355	8 f. Mao Tse-tung and poem	..	12	10
2356	8 f. Mao Tse-tung and multi-racial crowd with texts	..	12	10
2357	8 f. Mao Tse-tung with Red Guards	..	12	10
2358	8 f. Mao Tse-tung with hand raised in greeting (*smaller* 36 × 50½ *mm*)	..	12	10
2354/2358	*Set of 5*	..	..	50	40

For stamps similar to No. 2358 see Nos. 2367/9.

408 Mao Text

1967 (23 May). *25th Anniv of Mao Tse-tung's "Talks on Literature and Art".* T **408** *and similar horiz designs. Photo,* P 11 (No. 2361) *or recess and photo,* P 11½ (*others*).

2359	8 f. black, and yellow	..	..	15	10
2360	8 f. black, red and yellow	..	15	10
2361	8 f. multicoloured	..	..	15	10
2359/2361	*Set of 3*	..	..	40	25

Designs:—No. 2359, Type **408**; No. 2360. As Type **408** but different text. *Larger* (50 × 36½ *mm*)—No. 2361, Mao supporters in procession.

409 Mao Tse-tung

410 Mao Tse-tung and Lin Piao

1967 (1 July–Sept). *46th Anniv of Chinese Communist Party. Recess.* P 11.

2362	**409**	4 f. Venetian red	..	..	8	5
2363		8 f. carmine-red (Sept)	..	10	5
2364		35 f. purple-brown (Sept)	..	25	10
2365		43 f. orange-red (Sept)	..	30	15
2366		52 f. cerise (Sept)	..	35	20
2362/2366	*Set of 5*	..	..	1·00	50

1967 (20 Sept). *"Our Great Teacher"*. *T* 410 *and similar multicoloured designs. Photo. P* 11.

2367	8 f.	Type **410**	..	..	15	15
2368	8 f.	Mao Tse-tung (*horiz*)			15	15
2369	10 f.	Mao Tse-tung conferring with Lin Piao (*horiz*)			40	40
2367/2369	Set of 3	..	..	..	65	65

For 8 f. stamp showing Mao with hand raised in greeting see No. 2358.

411 Mao Tse-tung as "Sun"

1967 (1 Oct). 18*th Anniv of People's Republic. T* 411 *and similar horiz design. Multicoloured. Photo. P* 11½ × 11.

2370	8 f.	Type **411**		..	15	8
2371	8 f.	Mao Tse-tung with representatives of Communist countries	..	..	15	8
2370/2371	Set of 2	..	..	..	25	12

412 (*Reduced size illustration. Actual size* 62 × 26 *mm*)

413 (*Reduced size illustration. Actual size* 62 × 26 *mm*)

414 Mao writing Poems at Desk

1967 (1 Oct). *"Poems of Mao Tse-tung"* (1*st issue*).

(*a*) *Recess and photo. P* 11½

2372	**412**	8 f. black, yellow and red	..	..	12	5
2373	**413**	8 f. black, yellow and red	..		12	5

(*b*) *Photo. P* 11

2374	**414**	10 f. multicoloured	..	..	20	10
2372/2374	Set of 3	..	..	..	40	15

See also Nos. 2385/7 and 2389/96.

415 Epigram on Chairman Mao by Lin Piao

1967 (26 Dec). *Fleet Expansionists' Congress. Photo. P* 11 × 11½.

2375	**415**	8 f. gold and red	..	..	12	5

416 Mao Tse-tung and Procession

1968 (30 Jan). *"Revolutionary Literature and Art"* (1*st issue*). *T* 416 *and similar multicoloured designs showing scenes from People's Operas. Photo. P* 11 (*vert*) *or* 11½ × 11 (*horiz*).

2376	8 f.	Type **416**			15	5
2377	8 f.	"Raid on the White Tiger Regiment"			15	5
2378	8 f.	"Taking Tiger Mountain"	..		15	5
2379	8 f.	"On the Docks"	..		15	5
2380	8 f.	"Shachiapang"	..		15	5
2381	8 f.	"The Red Lantern" (*vert*)			15	5
2376/2381	Set of 6	..	..		80	25

417 "Red Detachment of Women" (ballet)

1968 (1 May). *"Revolutionary Literature and Art"* (2*nd issue*). *T* 417 *and similar horiz designs. Photo. P* 11 (*No.* 2384) *or* 11½ (*others*).

2382	**417**	8 f. multicoloured	..		15	5
2383	—	8 f. multicoloured	..		15	5
2384	—	8 f. multicoloured	..		15	5
2382/2384	Set of 3	..			40	12

Designs: As *T* 417—No. 2383, "The White-haired Girl" (ballet). *Larger* (50 × 36 *mm*)—No. 2384, Mao Tse-tung, Symphony Orchestra and Chorus.

418   **419**

420

1968 (1 May). *"Poems of Mao Tse-tung" (2nd issue). Recess and photo. P 11 (No. 2387) or 11½ (others).*

2385	**418**	8 f. black, yellow and red	12	5
2386	**419**	8 f. black, yellow and red	12	5
2387	**420**	10 f. black, yellow and red	15	5
2385/2387		*Set of 3*	35	12

421 Mao Tse-tung ("Unite still more closely . . .")

1968 (31 May). *Mao's Anti-American Declaration. Photo. P 11.*

2388	**421**	8 f. red-brown, gold and red ..	25	10

422 (*Reduced size illustration. Actual size 81×20 mm*)

423 (*Actual size 81×20 mm*)

424 (*Actual size 62×26 mm*)

425 (*Actual size 62×26 mm*)

426 (*Actual size 54×40 mm*)

427 (*Actual size 31×52 mm*)

428 (*Actual size 31×52 mm*)   429 (*Actual size 54×40 mm*)

1968 (July). *"Poems of Mao Tse-tung" (3rd issue). Recess and photo. P 11 (Nos. 2389/90, 2393 and 2396) or 11½ (others).*

2389	**422**	4 f. black, yellow and red	10	5
2390	**423**	4 f. black, yellow and red	10	5
2391	**424**	8 f. black, yellow and red	12	5
2392	**425**	8 f. black, yellow and red	12	5
2393	**426**	8 f. black, yellow and red	12	5
2394	**427**	8 f. black, yellow and red	12	5
2395	**428**	8 f. black, yellow and red	12	5
2396	**429**	10 f. black, yellow and red	15	10
2389/2396		*Set of 8*	85	40

430   431

HAVE YOU READ THE NOTES AT THE BEGINNING OF THIS CATALOGUE?

These often provide answers to the enquiries we receive.

432

433

434

435 Inscription by Lin Piao, 26 July 1965

1968 (20 July). *"Directives of Mao Tse-tung".* Photo. P 11½.

2397	430	8 f. brown, red and pale yellow	..	12	5
2398	431	8 f. brown, red and pale yellow	..	12	5
2399	432	8 f. brown, red and pale yellow	..	12	5
2400	433	8 f. brown, red and pale yellow	..	12	5
2401	434	8 f. brown, red and pale yellow	..	12	5
2397/2401		Set of 5	.. .. ..	55	20

Nos. 2397/2401 were issued together *se-tenant* in strips of five within the sheet.

1968 (1 Aug). *41st Anniv of the People's Liberation Army.* Recess and photo. P 11½.

2402	435	8 f. black, gold and red	..	15	10

436 "Chairman Mao goes to Anyuan" (Chiang Ching)

1968 (1 Aug). *Mao's Youth.* Photo. P 11×11½.

2403	436	8 f. multicoloured	..	60	75
		a. 2nd ptg. Red omitted right of Mao	..	60	75

An 8 f. value entitled "The Whole Country is Red", depicting workers and map of China in a vertical format, was issued on 24 November, 1968. Apparently this stamp was on sale for two days only in Canton, before being withdrawn, possibly because Taiwan had been left white.

438 Mao Tse-tung and Text

1968 (30 Nov). *"Thoughts of Mao Tse-tung"* (2nd issue). Photo. P 11½.

2405	438	8 f. blackish brown and bright red	12	12

439 Displaying "Words of Mao Tse-tung"

1968 (26 Dec). *"The Words of Mao Tse-tung".* Photo. No gum. P 11×11½.

2406	439	8 f. multicoloured	..	..	..	25	25

440 Yangtse Bridge

1968 (29 Dec). *Completion of Yangtse Bridge.* T 440 and similar horiz designs. Multicoloured. Litho (4 f., 10 f.) or photo (others). No gum. P 11½×11 (4 f., 10 f.) or 11½ (others).

2407		4 f. Type 440	..	..	..	25	25
2408		8 f. Buses crossing bridge	..	..	25	25
2409		8 f. Bridge portal	..	..	..	25	25
2410		10 f. Aerial view of bridge	..	..	20	20
2407/2410		Set of 4	..	..	..	85	85

The two 8 f. values are larger, 49×27 mm.

441 Li Yu-ho singing "I am filled with Courage and Strength"   442 Communist Party Building, Shanghai

1969 (Aug). *Songs from "The Red Lantern" Opera.* T 441 and similar horiz design. Multicoloured. Photo. No gum. P 11×11½.

2411		8 f. Type 441	..	..	..	12	12
2412		8 f. Li Li-mei singing "Hatred in my Heart"	..	..	12	12
2411/2412		Set of 2	..	..	..	20	20

PERFORATIONS. Some of the following issues up to early in 1971 exist with both rough and clear-cut perforations. The rough perforations were done in Shanghai and the clean-cut in Peking.

1969 (Oct)–**70.** *T* **442** *and similar horiz designs. Litho (Nos. 2413, 2416/17) or photo (others). No gum. P* 10 *(Nos. 2413, 2416/17) or* 11½ *(others).*

2413	1½ f. verm, pur-brn & slate-lilac (6.70) ..	10	5
2414	8 f. brown, grey-green and cream ..	10	5
2415	8 f. scarlet and plum	10	5
2416	8 f. yellow-brown and new blue (7.70)	15	8
	a. Perf 11½	20	20
2417	20 f. blue, purple and carmine (1.70) ..	20	12
	a. Perf 11½	25	25
2418	50 f. buff and blackish green (7.70) ..	50	35
2413/2418	*Set of 6*	1·00	60

Designs "Historic Sites of the Revolution": *Size* 27 × 22 *mm*—No. 2414, Pagoda Hill, Yenan; No. 2415, Gate of Heavenly Peace, Peking; No. 2418, Mao Tse-tung's house, Yenan. *Size as T* **442**—No. 2416, Heroes' Monument, Peking; No. 2417, Conference Hall, Tsunyi.

Stamps of this issue exist with clean-cut or with rough perforations.

See also Nos. 2455/65.

443 Rice Harvesters   **444** Snow Patrol

1969 (Oct). *Agricultural Workers. T* **443** *and similar horiz designs. Multicoloured. Photo. No gum.* P 11 × 11½.

2419	4 f. Type **443**	25	12
2420	8 f. Grain harvest	25	12
2421	8 f. Study group with "Thoughts of Mao"	25	12
2422	10 f. Red Cross worker with mother and child	25	12
2419/2422	*Set of 4*	90	45

1969 (Oct). *Defence of Chen Pao Tao in the Ussuri River. T* **444** *and similar multicoloured designs. Photo. No gum.* P 11½.

2423	8 f. Type **444**	15	15
2424	8 f. Guards by river	15	15
2425	8 f. Servicemen and Militia ..	15	15
2426	35 f. As No. 2424	45	45
2427	43 f. Type **444**	50	50
2423/2427	*Set of 5*	1·25	1·25

445 Farm Worker   **446** Chin Hsün-hua in Water

1969 (Oct). *"The Chinese People" (woodcuts). T* **445** *and similar horiz designs. Litho. No gum.* A. P 10. B. P 11½.

		A		B	
2428	4 f. maroon and red-orange ..	10	10	10	10
2429	8 f. deep dull purple & red-orange ..	10	10	10	10
2430	10 f. deep bronze-grn & red-orange ..	10	10	10	10

Designs:—8 f. Foundryman; 10 f. Soldier.

Stamps of this issue exist with clean-cut or with rough perforations.

1970 (Jan). *Heroic Death of Chin Hsün-hua in Kirin Border Floods. Photo. No gum.* P 11½.

2431	**446** 8 f. black and vermilion *(shades)* ..	20	20

447 Cavalry Patrol   **448** "Yang Tse-jung, Army Scout"

1970 (1 Aug). *43rd Anniversary of People's Liberation Army. Photo. No gum.* P 11½.

2432	**447** 8 f. multicoloured *(shades)* ...	25	25

SERIAL NUMBERS. These were reintroduced for commemorative stamps from No. 2433 onwards. The numbers are given in brackets after the face value to help the identification of designs, where this is necessary.

1970 (1 Aug)–**71.** *"Taking Tiger Mountain" (Revolutionary opera). T* **448** *and similar multicoloured designs. Photo. No gum.* P 11½ *(Nos. 2436/7),* 11½ × 11 *(Nos. 2433, 2435) or* 11 × 11½ *(Nos. 2434, 2438).*

2433	8 f. (1) Type **448**	20	20
2434	8 f. (2) "The patrol sets out" *(horiz)* (9.70)	20	20
2435	8 f. (3) "Leaping through the forest" ..	20	20
2436	8 f. (4) "Li Yung-chi's farewell" (9.70) ..	20	20
2437	8 f. (5) "Yang Tse-jung in disguise" (9.70)	20	20
2438	8 f. (6) "Congratulating Yang Tse-jung" *(horiz)* (12.71)	10	10
2433/2438	*Set of 6*	1·00	1·00

Nos. 2436/7 are larger, 27 × 48 mm.

449 Tractor-driver   **450** Soldiers in Snow

1970. *T* **449** *and similar design. Litho. No gum.* P 10.

2439	5 f. black, red and salmon (10.70) ..	8	8
	a. Perf 11½	15	15
2440	1 y. black and red (8.70)	60	30
	a. Perf 11	60	30
	b. Perf 11½	60	30

Design: *Horiz*—1 y. Foundryman.

These stamps exist with clean-cut or with rough perforations.

1971 (Jan). *2nd Anniversary of Defence of Chen Pao Tao. Litho. No gum. P* 10.

2441	**450**	4 f. multicoloured	..	..	5 5
		a. Perf 11½	..	..	5 5

This stamp exists with clean-cut or with rough perforations.

451 Communard Standard

453 Workers and People's Hall, Peking

452 Communist Party Building, Shanghai

1971 (18 Mar). *Centenary of the Paris Commune. T* **451** *and similar designs. Photo* (4, 22 f.) *or recess and litho* (8, 10 f.). *No gum. P* 11½×11 (*vert*) *or* 11×11½ (*horiz*).

2442		4 f. multicoloured	..	..	8 8
2443		8 f. blackish brown, pale pink & rosine		12 12
2444		10 f. vermilion, blksh brn & pale pink	..	12 12
2445		22 f. purple-brown, verm & brown-rose		25 25
2442/2445		*Set of* 4	..	..	50 50

Designs: *Horiz*—8 f. Fighting in Paris, March 1871; 22 f. Communards in Place Vendôme. *Vert*—10 f. Commune proclaimed at the Hôtel de Ville.

1971 (1 July). *50th Anniversary of Chinese Communist Party. Photo. No gum. P* 11½.

(a) Horiz views as T **452**. *Multicoloured*

2446		4 f. (12) Type **452**	..	..	5 5
2447		4 f. (13) National Peasant Movement Institute, Canton	..	5 5
2448		8 f. (14) Chingkang Mountains	..	8 8
2449		8 f. (15) Conference Building, Tsunyi		8 8
2450		8 f. (16) Pagoda Hill, Yenan	..	..	8 8
2451		22 f. (17) Gate of Heavenly Peace, Peking	..	..	20 20

(b) Vert designs as T **453**. *Multicoloured*

2452		8 f. (18) Workers and Industry	..	8 8
2453		8 f. (19) Type **453**	..	..	8 8
2454		8 f. (20) Workers and Agriculture	..	8 8
		a. Horiz strip of 3. Nos. 2452/4	..	25 25
2446/2454		*Set of* 9	..	..	70 70

Nos. 2452/4 were issued in *se-tenant* strips within the sheet, forming a continuous design.

PUZZLED?

Then you need
PHILATELIC TERMS ILLUSTRATED
to tell you all you need to know about printing methods, papers, errors, varieties, watermarks, perforations, etc. 192 pages, almost half in full colour, soft cover. £1 post paid.

454 National Peasant Movement Institute, Canton

455 Welcoming Bouquets

1971 (20 Sept)–72. *T* **454** *and similar multicoloured designs, showing "Revolutionary Sites". Photo. No gum. P* 11½.

2455		1 f. Communist Party Building, Shanghai (*vert*) (20.12.71)	..	5 5
2456		2 f. Type **454**	..	..	5 5
2457		3 f. Site of 1929 Congress, Kutien		5 5
2458		4 f. Mao Tse-tung's house, Yenan (25.3.72)	..	..	5 5
2459		8 f. Gate of Heavenly Peace, Peking (25.3.72)	..	..	8 5
2460		10 f. Monument, Chingkang Mountains		8 5
2461		20 f. River bridge, Yenan (20.12.71)	..	15 8
2462		22 f. Mao's birthplace, Shaoshan	..	15 8
2463		35 f. Conference Building, Tsunyi	..	20 10
2464		43 f. Start of the Long March, Chingkang Mountains	..	..	25 15
2465		52 f. People's Palace, Peking	..	..	30 20
2455/2465		*Set of* 11	..	..	1·25 75

1971 (3 Nov). *"Afro-Asian Friendship" Table-tennis Tournament, Peking. T* **455** *and similar vert designs. Multicoloured. Photo. No gum. P* 11½.

2466		8 f. (22) Type **455**	..	..	8 8
2467		8 f. (23) Group of players	..	..	8 8
2468		8 f. (24) Asian and African players	..	8 8
2469		43 f. (21) Tournament badge	..	..	40 40
2466/2569		*Set of* 4	..	..	55 55

456 Enver Hoxha making Speech

457 Conference Hall, Yenan

1971 (8 Nov). *30th Anniversary of Albanian Workers' Party. T* **456** *and similar multicoloured designs. Photo. No gum. P* 11×11½ (52 f.) *or* 11½×11 (*others*).

2470		8 f. (25) Type **456**	..	..	8 8
2471		8 f. (26) Party Headquarters	..	..	8 8
2472		8 f. (27) Albanian flag, rifle and pick	..	8 8
2473		52 f. (28) Soldier and Workers' Militia (*horiz*)	..	..	50 50
2470/2473		*Set of* 4	..	..	65 65

1972 (23 May). *30th Anniversary of Publication of "Yenan Forum's Discussions on Literature and Art". T* **457** *and similar vert designs. Multicoloured. Photo. No gum. P* 11.

2474		8 f. (33) Type **457**	..	..	5 5
2475		8 f. (34) Army choir	..	..	5 5
2476		8 f. (35) "Brother and Sister"	..	5 5
2477		8 f. (36) "Open-air Theatre"	..	5 5
2478		8 f. (37) "The Red Lantern" (opera)	..	5 5
2479		8 f. (38) "Red Detachment of Women" (ballet)	..	..	5 5
2474/2479		*Set of* 6	..	..	25 25

458 Ball Games

459 Gymnastics

461 Championship Badge

460 Freighter *Fenglei*

462 Wang Chin-hsi, the "Iron Man"

463 Cliff-edge Construction

1972 (25 Dec). *Wang Chin-hsi (workers' hero) Commemoration. Recess and photo. No gum. P* 11½×11.

2493	**462**	8 f. multicoloured	..	..	5	5

1972 (30 Dec). *Construction of Red Flag Canal. T 463 and similar vert designs. Recess and photo. Multicoloured. P* 11.

2494	8 f. (49) Type **463**	..	..	5	5
2495	8 f. (50) "Youth" tunnel	..	..	5	5
2496	8 f. (51) Taoyuan bridge	..	..	5	5
2497	8 f. (52) Cliff-edge canal	..	..	5	5
2494/2497	*Set of 4*	..	..	20	20

464 Panda eating Bamboo Shoots

465 "New Power in the Mines" (Yang Shi-guang)

1972 (10 June). *10th Anniversary of Mao Tse-tung's Edict on Physical Culture. T 458, and vert designs as T 459. Multicoloured. Photo. No gum. P* 11 *(No.* 2480) *or* 11½×11 *(others).*

2480	8 f. (39) Type **458**	..	..	..	5	5
2481	8 f. (40) Type **459**	..	..	..	5	5
2482	8 f. (41) Tug-of-war	..	..	..	5	5
2483	8 f. (42) Rock-climbing	..	..	..	5	5
2484	8 f. (43) High-diving	..	..	..	5	5
2480/2484	*Set of 5*	..	..	..	20	20

1972 (10 July). *Chinese Merchant Shipping. T 460 and similar horiz designs. Multicoloured. Photo. No gum. P* 11½.

2485	8 f. (29) Type **460**	..	..	5	5
2486	8 f. (30) Tanker *Taching No.* 30	..	..	5	5
2487	8 f. (31) Cargo-liner *Chang-seng*	..	..	5	5
2488	8 f. (32) Dredger *Xian-feng*	..	..	5	5
2485/2488	*Set of 4*	..	..	..	20	20

1972 (2 Sept). *1st Asian Table-tennis Championships, Peking. T 461 and similar multicoloured designs. Photo. No gum. P* 11½×11 *(vert) or* 11×11½ *(horiz).*

2489	8 f. (45) Type **461**	..	..	5	5
2490	8 f. (46) Welcoming crowd *(horiz)*	..	5	5
2491	8 f. (47) Game in progress *(horiz)*	..	5	5
2492	22 f. (48) Players from three countries	12	12
2489/2492	*Set of 4*	..	..	..	25	25

1973 (15 Jan). *China's Giant Pandas. T 464 and similar designs, showing brush and ink drawings of pandas. Photo. P* 11.

2498	4 f. (63) Type **465**	..	..	5	5
2499	8 f. (59) multicoloured *(horiz)*	..	5	5
2500	8 f. (60) multicoloured *(horiz)*	..	5	5
2501	10 f. (58) multicoloured	..	..	8	5
2502	20 f. (57) multicoloured	..	..	15	8
2503	43 f. (62) multicoloured	..	..	25	15
2498/2503	*Set of 6*	..	..	..	55	40

1973 (8 Mar). *International Working Women's Day. T 465 and similar vert designs, showing paintings. Multicoloured. Photo. P* 11.

2504	8 f. (63) Type **465**	..	..	..	5	5
2505	8 f. (64) "Woman Committee Member" (Tang Xiao-ming)	..	5	5
2506	8 f. (65) "I am a Sea-gull" (Army telegraph line-women) (Pan Jia-jun)	5	5

CHINESE PROVINCES, ETC

FORMOSA

This is included with the issues for Taiwan after the list of Chinese Provinces.

MANCHURIA

A. KIRIN AND HEILUNGKIANG

Stamps were overprinted for use in these North Eastern Provinces because the currency there had lost about 70% of its value. They were used in Liaoning, the third province of Manchuria, as well as in Kirin and Heilungkiang.

貼   吉

用貼黑吉限   用   黑

    (1)   (2)

1927. *Stamps of China, Nos. 309 etc, optd with T* **1.**

1	43	½ c. sepia	.. ..	5	5
2		1 c. bright yellow-orange	..	5	5
3		1½ c. violet	.. ..	5	5
4		2 c. yellow-green	.. ..	8	5
5		3 c. blue-green	.. ..	5	5
6		4 c. olive-green	.. ..	8	5
7		5 c. rosy mauve	.. ..	8	5
8		6 c. bright scarlet	.. ..	8	5
9		7 c. violet	.. ..	8	5
10		8 c. orange	.. ..	8	5
11		10 c. deep blue	.. ..	8	5
12	44	13 c. yellow-brown	.. ..	25	10
13		15 c. deep blue	.. ..	10	8
14		16 c. olive-green	.. ..	10	8
15		20 c. red-brown	.. ..	20	8
16		30 c. purple	.. ..	20	8
17		50 c. green	.. ..	50	25
18	45	$1 sepia and brown-orange	..	70	35
19		$2 red-brown and deep blue	..	1·10	75
20		$5 grey-green and scarlet	..	3·50	3·50
1/20		Set of 20	..	7·00	5·00

1928. *Chang Tso-lin issue of China optd with T* **2.**

21	55	1 c. orange (R.)	.. ..	8	8
22		4 c. olive-green (R.)	.. ..	8	8
23		10 c. blue (R.)	.. ..	25	20
24		$1 scarlet (B.)	.. ..	2·50	2·25
21/24		Set of 4	..	2·50	2·25

1929. *Unification issue of China optd as T* **2** *but spaced* 11 *mm horizontally between characters in carmine.*

25	56	1 c. orange	.. ..	10	8
26		4 c. olive-green	.. ..	20	12
27		10 c. blue	.. ..	55	25
28		$1 scarlet	.. ..	3·25	3·00
25/28		Set of 4	..	3·50	3·00

1929. *Sun Yat-sen Memorial issue of China optd as T* **2** *but spaced* 16 *mm horizontally between characters.*

29	57	1 c. orange	.. ..	10	5
30		4 c. olive-green	.. ..	20	8
31		10 c. blue	.. ..	50	20
32		$1 scarlet	.. ..	4·75	2·40
29/32		Set of 4	..	5·00	2·50

B. MANCHUKUO

100 Fen=1 Yuan

In 1905, after the Russo-Japanese War, Japan took over from Russia the lease of Port Arthur and Dairen in Kwantung and obtained the right to station troops in Manchuria to guard the South Manchurian Railway, also leased to Japan. On 18 September 1931 these troops began the complete seizure of Manchuria, the independence of which, as the state of Manchukuo, was declared by Japan on 18 February 1932. Pu Yi, who as a child had been the last Emperor of China, was made Chief Executive, and in March 1934 was enthroned as Emperor Kang-teh. In January 1933 the Chinese province of Jehol was annexed to Manchukuo.

State of Manchukuo
1 March 1932–28 February 1934

1 White Pagoda, Liaoyang   2 Pu Yi, later Emperor Kang-teh

A.   B.

C.   D.

A and C (5 characters)="Manchu State Postal Administration"

B and D (6 characters)="Manchu Empire Postal Administration"

(Des Y. Yoshida. Litho Japanese Govt Ptg Bureau)

1932 *(26 July). Top panels as A or C. P* 13×13½.

1	1	½ f. bistre-brown	..	5	5
2		1 f. brown-red	..	5	5
3		1½ f. dull purple	..	25	10
4		2 f. slate	..	25	5
5		3 f. chestnut	..	30	15
6		4 f. yellow-olive	..	8	5
7		5 f. emerald	..	8	5
8		6 f. vermilion	..	30	5
9		7 f. deep grey	..	12	5
10		8 f. yellow-brown	..	50	15
11		10 f. red-orange	..	30	5
12	2	13 f. red-brown	..	35	15
13		15 f. rosine	..	60	8
14		16 f. turquoise-blue	..	65	15
15		20 f. bistre-brown	..	30	5
16		30 f. orange	..	30	8
17		50 f. yellow-olive	..	60	10
18		1 y. violet	..	1·25	35
1/18		Set of 18	..	5·50	1·50

Nos. 1/18 were overprinted in black or vermilion with four Chinese characters meaning "Chinese Postal Administration" during a rebellion by General Su Ping-wen in late 1932. The stamps were of local validity.
See also Nos. 23/31 and 40/56.

3 Map and Flags   4 Council Hall, Hsinking   5

(Des Y. Yoshida. Litho Japanese Govt Ptg Bureau)

1933 (1 Mar). *1st Anniv of Republic. P* 12½.

19	3	1 f. orange	.. ..	35	35
20	4	2 f. yellow-green	.. ..	75	50
21	3	4 f. rosine	.. ..	35	35
22	4	10 f. blue	.. ..	1·10	70
19/22		Set of 4	..	2·25	1·75

(Des Y. Yoshida. Recess Japanese Govt Ptg Bureau)

1934 (Jan–Aug). *Top panels as A or C. Granite paper. W* **5.**
P 13×13½.

23	1	½ f. sepia (Aug)	..	8	5
24		1 f. lake-brown	..	8	5
25		1½ f. violet (April)	..	10	5
26		2 f. indigo	..	12	5
27		3 f. red-brown (Feb)	..	15	5
28		4 f. olive-brown (March)	..	90	8
29		10 f. red-orange (April)	..	25	5
30	2	15 f. rosine (March)	..	25·00	10·00
31		1 y. deep violet (April)	..	90	30
23/31		Set of 9	..	25·00	10·00

Empire
Emperor Kang-teh, 1 March 1934–14 August 1945

6 Emperor's Palace   **7** Phœnixes

(Des T. Oona. Recess Japanese Govt Ptg Bureau)
1934 (1 Mar). *Enthronement of Emperor. W* **5**. *P* 12½.

32	**6**	1½ f. chestnut	..	..	20	10
33	**7**	3 f. scarlet	..	..	30	10
34	**6**	6 f. green	..	..	65	30
35	**7**	10 f. steel-blue	..	..	90	30
32/35		*Set of 4*	..	..	1·75	70

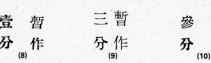

(8)   (9)   (10)

(*Trans. T* **8** "Temporarily made 1 fen". *T* **9**, **10** "... 3 fen")

(Surcharges typo Chikazawa Yoko Co, Harbin)

1934–35. *Various stamps surch as T* **8/10**.

36	**8**	1 f. on 4 f. yellow-olive (6) (1.6.34)	..	8	5
		a. Surch in brown		1·50	1·10
37	**9**	3 f. on 4 f. yellow-olive (6) (3.35)	..	1·75	1·50
38		3 f. on 4 f. olive-brown (28) (3.35)	..	8	5
39	**10**	3 f. on 16 f. turq-blue (14) (13.2.35)	..	75	50
36/39		*Set of 4*	..	3·75	2·75

Specialists recognise four types of T **8**, three of T **9** and four of T **10**.

11 Repeated pattern of six characters meaning "Manchu Empire Postal Administration", each row covering about seven stamps

(Des Y. Yoshida. Recess Japanese Govt Ptg Bureau)
1934 (1 Nov)–**36**. *Top panels as* B *or* D. *Granite paper. P* 13×13½.

(a) *W* **5**

40	**1**	½ f. sepia	..	..	..	5	5
41		1 f. lake-brown	..	..	..	5	5
42		1½ f. violet	..	..	..	5	5
43		3 f. red-brown	..	..	..	5	5
44		5 f. blue (1935)	..	..	..	35	5
45		5 f. slate-blue (4.36)	..	..	12	5
46		6 f. rosine	..	..	..	12	5
47		7 f. deep grey	..	..	..	12	5
48		9 f. orange-red	..	..	..	8	5
49	**2**	15 f. rosine	..	..	..	8	5
50		18 f. turquoise-green	..	..	80	12
51		20 f. sepia	..	..	..	12	8
52		30 f. orange-brown	..	..	20	5
53		50 f. bronze-green	..	..	25	5
54		1 y. deep violet	..	..	60	20

(b) *W* **11** (July 1935)

55	**1**	10 f. deep blue	..	..	15	5
56	**2**	13 f. orange-brown	..	..	15	10
40/56		*Set of 18*	..	..	3·00	85

The 4 f. and 8 f. in Type **1** were prepared but not issued.

12 Orchid Crest of Manchukuo   **13** Changpai Mountain and Sacred Lake   **14**

I   II   III   IV

(Des H. Oya)

1935–37. *China Mail. Granite paper. P* 13×13½.

(a) *Litho by Manchukuo Central Bank. Crests as* I *and* III
(i) *W* **14** (1.1.35)

57	**12**	2 f. yellow-green	..	35	15
58	**13**	4 f. yellow-olive	..	12	8
59	**12**	8 f. yellow	..	30	15
60	**13**	12 f. orange-red	..	55	45

(ii) *W* **11** (1.3.35)

61	**12**	2 f. yellow-green	..	15	12
62		8 f. yellow	..	15	12
63	**13**	12 f. chestnut	..	30	15

(b) *Recess by Manchukuo Govt Supplies Division. Crest as* II *and* IV. *W* **11** (1936–37)

64	**12**	2 f. yellow-green (1.1.36)	..	5	5
65		2½ f. reddish violet (4.37)	..	5	5
66	**13**	4 f. yellow-olive (4.12.36)	..	10	5
67		5 f. indigo (22.4.37)	..	5	5
68	**12**	8 f. ochre (3.36)	..	5	5
69	**13**	12 f. red-orange (3.36)	..	95	50
70		13 f. chocolate (28.4.37)	..	8	5
57/70		*Set of 14*	..	3·00	1·75

Although produced for use on mail to China, Nos. 57/70 were valid for any postal service. Nos. 57/60 imperforate are official samples for publicity purposes. The 5 f. in red-brown is a fake.

See also No. 149.

15 Mt. Fuji   **16** Phœnixes

(Des H. Oya. Recess Manchukuo Central Bank)

1935 (2 Apr). *Visit of Emperor Kang-teh to Japan. Granite paper. W* **11**. *P* 11.

71	**15**	1½ f. deep bluish green	..	12	8
72	**16**	3 f. orange	..	12	8
73	**15**	6 f. carmine-red	..	20	10
		a. Imperf between (horiz pair)	28·00	
		b. Perf compound of 11 and 12½	4·00	4·00
74	**16**	10 f. steel-blue	..	30	15
		a. Perf compound of 12½ and 11	2·75	2·75
71/74		*Set of 4*	..	65	35

17 Symbolic of Accord

18 Department of Communications

(Des H. Oya. Recess Manchukuo Central Bank)

1936 (26 Jan). *Japan–Manchukuo Postal Agreement. Granite paper.* W **11**. *P* 12×12½ (1½, 6 f.) *or* 12½×12 (3, 10 f.).

75	**17**	1½ f. blackish brown	..	..	8	5
76	**18**	3 f. reddish purple	..	..	8	5
77	**17**	6 f. carmine-red	..	..	30	15
78	**18**	10 f. greenish blue	..	..	40	25
75/78		*Set of 4*	..	..	75	45

19 State Council Building, Hsinking

20 Chengte Palace, Jehol

(Des H. Oya. Recess Manchukuo Govt Supplies Division)

1936 (5 Dec)–**37**. *T* **19/20** *and similar designs. Granite paper.* W **11**. *P* 13×13½.

79	**19**	½ f. brown	..	..	5	5
80	—	1 f. brown-lake	..	..	5	5
81	—	1½ f. slate-lilac	..	..	12	5
82	—	2 f. yellow-green (1.4.37)	..	5	5
83	**19**	3 f. chocolate	..	..	5	5
84	—	4 f. yellow-olive (1.4.37)	..	5	5
85	**19**	5 f. slate	..	..	40	15
86	—	6 f. rosine	..	..	5	5
87	—	7 f. grey-black	..	..	5	5
88	—	9 f. orange-red	..	..	8	5
89	**20**	10 f. blue	..	..	5	5
90	—	12 f. orange (4.37)	..	..	5	5
91	—	13 f. chocolate	..	..	65	30
92	—	15 f. rose-red	..	..	8	5
93	—	18 f. blue-green	..	..	40	25
94	—	19 f. blue-green (4.37)	..	25	15
95	—	20 f. brown	..	..	10	5
96	**20**	30 f. orange-brown	..	..	10	8
97	—	38 f. blue	..	..	40	20
98	—	39 f. blue (14.9.37)	..	..	20	5
99	—	50 f. yellow-orange	..	..	10	10
100	**20**	1 y. violet	..	..	˙35	25
79/100		*Set of 22*	..	..	3˙25	1˙75

Designs:—2, 6, 20, 50 f. Carting soya beans; 4, 7, 9, 12, 13, 15 f. Peiling Mausoleum; 18, 19 f. 'Plane and grazing sheep (domestic and China air mail); 38, 39 f. 'Plane over Sungari River bridge (air mail to Japan).

Imperforate and diagonally perforated sheets of the ½, 1, 2 and 4 f. are from stocks stolen from the printing works. A 20 f. in bronze-green is a fake.

See also Nos. 150/4.

21 Sun rising over Fields

22 Shadowgraph of old and new Hsinking

(Des H. Oya. Litho Manchukuo Govt Supplies Division)

1937 (1 Mar). *5th Anniv of Founding of State. P* 12½.

101	**21**	1½ f. carmine	..	..	15	15
102	**22**	3 f. myrtle-green	..	..	12	12

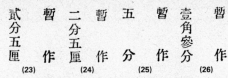

(23)   **(24)**   **(25)**   **(26)**

(*Trans. T* **23/4** ''Temporarily made 2½ fen''. **T 25** ''... 5 fen''. **T 26** ''... 13 fen'')

(Surch by Manchukuo Govt Supplies Division)

1937 (Apr). *China Mail provisionals. Surch with T* **23/6**.

(a) *Vert columns of characters spaced 6½ mm apart* (1 April)

103	**23**	2½ f. on 2 f. yellow-green (61)	..	15	10
104	**23**	2½ f. on 2 f. yellow-green (64)	..	15	8
105	**25**	5 f. on 4 f. yellow-olive (66)	..	15	10
106	**26**	13 f. on 12 f. chestnut (63)	..	7˙00	6˙00
107		13 f. on 12 f. red-orange (69)	..	35	35

(b) *Spaced 4½ mm* (12 April?)

108	**24**	2½ f. on 2 f. yellow-green (64)	..	12	8
		a. Surch inverted	..	10˙00	10˙00
109	**25**	5 f. on 4 f. yellow-olive (58)	..	12	10
110		5 f. on 4 f. yellow-olive (66)	..	12	10
111	**26**	13 f. on 12 f. chestnut (63)	..	35	30

27 Pouter Pigeon and Hsinking

28 Flag over Imperial Palace

(Des K. Ishikawa. Recess Manchukuo Government Supplies Division)

1937 (16 Sept). *Completion of Five-year Reconstruction Plan for Hsinking. P* 12×12½.

112	**27**	2 f. purple	..	..	5	5
113	**28**	4 f. scarlet	..	..	5	5
114	**27**	10 f. grey-green	..	..	15	15
115	**28**	20 f. blue	..	..	30	25
112/115		*Set of 4*	..	..	50	45

29 Manchukuo

30 Japanese Residents' Association Bldg

31 Ministry of Justice

32 ''Twofold Happiness''

33 Red Cross on Map and Globe

(Des H. Oya. Litho Manchukuo Govt Supplies Division)

1937 (1 Dec). *Japan's Relinquishment of Extra-territorial Rights.* T **29/31** *and similar design.*

116	**29**	2 f. carmine-red (p 12×12½)		5	5
117	**30**	4 f. blue-green (p 13×13½)		5	5
		a. Perf 13		8	8
		b. Perf 12½×13		5	5
118		8 f. red-orange (p 13×13½)		15	12
		a. Perf 13		15	12
119		10 f. blue (p 13×13½)		15	12
		a. Perf 13		15	12
		b. Perf 13½×13		15	12
120	**31**	12 f. violet (p 13½×13)		15	15
		a. Perf 13		15	15
		b. Perf 13×13½		15	15
121		20 f. red-brown (p 13×13½)		25	20
		a. Perf 13		25	25
116/121		*Set of 6*		70	60

Design: As T **30**—10 f., 20 f. Department of Communications Building.

(Des H. Oya. Frame recess, centre typo Manchukuo Govt Supplies Division)

1937 (15 Dec). *New Year's Greetings.* P 12×12½.

122	**32**	2 f. vermilion and blue		12	8

(Des T. Yamashita. Litho Manchukuo Govt Supplies Division)

1938 (15 Oct). *Inauguration of Manchukuo Red Cross Society. Cross in red. Granite paper.* W **11**. P 13.

123	**33**	2 f. lake		8	8
124		4 f. grey-green		8	8
123/124		*Set of 2*		12	12

PERFORATION. Worn machinery led to further variations of perforation in the 1939–40 issues.

34 Map of Railway Lines

35 "Asia" Express

36 Cranes over Shipmast

(Des J. Sasaki, R. H. Akagi and T. Yamashita. Litho Manchukuo Govt Supplies Division)

1939 (21 Oct). *Completion of 10,000 Km of Railways. Granite paper.* W **11**. P 13.

125	**34**	2 f. blue and orange		5	5
126	**35**	4 f. indigo and greenish blue		8	8
125/126		*Set of 2*		10	10

(Des Y. Ota. Photo Japanese Govt Ptg Bureau)

1940 (26 June). *2nd Visit of Emperor Kang-teh to Japan.* P 13.

127	**36**	2 f. bright purple		5	5
128		4 f. emerald		8	8
127/128		*Set of 2*		10	10

37 Census Official and Manchukuo

38 Census Slogans in Chinese and Mongolian

(Des Y. Ota. Litho Manchukuo Govt Ptg Bureau)

1940 (10 Sept). *National Census. Granite paper.* W **11**. P 13 or 13×13½.

129	**37**	2 f. chocolate and yellow		5	5
130	**38**	4 f. blackish green and green		5	5
129/130		*Set of 2*		8	8

39 Message of Congratulation

40 Dragon Dance

(Des Y. Ota (2 f.) and Li Ping-ho (4 f.). Eng Japanese Govt Ptg Bureau and recess Manchukuo Govt Ptg Bureau)

1940 (19 Sept). *2600th Anniv of Founding of Japanese Empire. Granite paper.* W **11**. P 13×13½ (2 f.) or 13½×13 (4 f.).

131	**39**	2 f. rose-red		5	5
132	**40**	4 f. steel-blue		5	5
		a. Imperf (pair)		19·00	
131/132		*Set of 2*		8	8

41 Recruit

(42)

(Des Y. Ota. Photo Japanese Govt Ptg Bureau)

1941 (25 May). *Enactment of Conscription Law.* P 13×13½.

133	**41**	2 f. carmine		5	5
134		4 f. blue		5	5
133/134		*Set of 2*		8	8

(Opt typo Manchukuo Govt Ptg Bureau)

1942 (16 Feb). *Fall of Singapore. Nos. 82 and 84 optd with T* **42**.

135		2 f. yellow-green (R.)		5	5
136		4 f. yellow-olive (B.)		5	5
135/136		*Set of 2*		8	8

43 Kengoka Shrine

44 Achievement of Fine Crops

45 Women of Five Races Dancing

46 Map of Manchukuo

(Des H. Oya (2 f., 4 f.); Li Ping-ho (3 f.); Y. Ota (others). Eng Japanese Govt Ptg Bureau, recess Manchukuo Govt Ptg Bureau)

1942 (1 Mar–15 Sept). *10th Anniv of Founding of State. Granite paper.* W **11**. P 12×12½ or 12½×12 (horiz designs).

137	**43**	2 f. carmine		5	5
138	**44**	3 f. yellow-orange (15.9)		5	5
139	**43**	4 f. reddish lilac		5	5
140	**45**	6 f. green (15.9)		5	5
141	**46**	10 f. red/*lemon*		5	5
142		20 f. indigo/*lemon*		5	5
137/142		*Set of 6*		20	20

Design: *Horiz*—20 f. Flag of Manchukuo.

(47)   (48)   49 Nurse and Stretcher   50 Furnace at Anshan Plant

(Opt des H. Oya. Litho Manchukuo Govt Ptg Bureau)

1942 (1 Dec). *1st Anniv of "Greater East Asia War". Nos. 83 and 86 optd with T 47.*
143	3 f. chocolate (G.)	..	..	..	5	5
144	6 f. rosine (B.)	..	..	..	5	5
143/144	Set of 2				8	8

(Opt des H. Oya. Litho Manchukuo Govt Ptg Bureau)

1943 (1 May). *Proclamation of Labour Service Law. Nos. 83 and 86 optd with T 48.*
145	3 f. chocolate (R.)	..	..	..	5	5
146	6 f. rosine (B.)	..	..	..	5	5
145/146	Set of 2				8	8

(Des Y. Ota. Photo Japanese Govt Ptg Bureau)

1943 (1 Oct). *5th Anniv of Manchukuo Red Cross Society. Perf in Hsinking 13 × 13½.*
147	49	6 f. emerald	..	..	5	5

(Des B. Tachibana. Photo Japanese Govt Ptg Bureau)

1943 (8 Dec). *2nd Anniv of "Greater East Asia War". Perf in Hsinking 13 × 13½.*
148	50	6 f. brown-red	..	..	5	5

(Des H. Oya. Litho Manchukuo Govt Ptg Bureau)

1944–45. *Previous types with change of printing process. W 11. P 13 × 13½.*
149	13	5 f. black (as 67) (11.6.44)	..		5	5
150	—	6 f. red (as 86) (26.6.44)	..		5	5
151	20	10 f. light blue (10.6.44)	..		5	5
152	—	20 f. brown (as 95) (18.6.44)	..		5	5
153	20	30 f. orange-brown (15.2.45)	..		5	5
154	—	1 y. dull purple (as 100) (7.11.44)	..		25	12
149/154		Set of 6			40	30

A 3 f. brown and 5 f. black, both imperf, are known but are of doubtful status.

51 Chinese Characters   52 Japanese Characters   53 "One Heart, One Soul"

(Des H. Oya. Litho Manchukuo Govt Ptg Bureau)

1944 (1–9 Oct). *Friendship with Japan. W 11. P 13 × 13½.*

(a) Chinese characters
155	51	10 f. rose			5	5
156		40 f. bronze-green (9.10)			12	12
		a. Frame with rounded corners (as 10 f.)			10·00	10·00

(b) Japanese characters
157	52	10 f. rose			5	5
158		40 f. bronze-green (9.10)			12	12
155/158		Set of 4			30	30

Horizontal rows of both values alternate in Chinese and Japanese inscription (which reads "Japan's prosperity is Manchukuo's prosperity").

No. 156a occurs on some sheets at position 45, probably resulting from using a 10 f. transfer to repair top and centre portions of a damaged 40 f.

Imperforate stamps are of doubtful status.

(Des Y. Ota. Litho Manchukuo Govt Ptg Bureau)

1945 (2 May). *10th Anniv of Emperor's Edict. W 11. P 13 × 13½.*
159	53	10 f. orange-red	..	..	5	5

This is known imperforate but status is doubtful.

The Soviet Union declared war on Japan on 8 August 1945 and her troops rapidly over-ran Manchukuo and brought the puppet Empire to an end. Sovereignty over Manchuria reverted to China.

C. NORTH-EASTERN PROVINCES

Under this heading are listed the issues made in Manchuria by the Chinese Nationalists. After the surrender of Japan, Nationalist troops were moved to Manchuria, from which Soviet troops had, however, arrived there first, and occupied the rural areas and, in April 1946, the cities of Harbin, Kirin and Tsitsihar as soon as the Russians left them. The Nationalists took Mukden on 13 March 1946 and Changchun on 23 May, and held territory along the railways between them and down to Dairen and Antung.

1 Dr. Sun Yat-sen   (2)   (3)

1946. *Surch with new values in Chinese characters as T 2. Litho. P 14.*
1	1	50 c. on $5 red	..	..	5	5
2		50 c. on $10 green	..	..	5	5
3		$1 on $10 green	..	..	5	5
4		$2 on $20 purple	..	..	5	5
5		$4 on $50 brown	..	..	5	5
1/5		Set of 5			15	15

There are many shades and several varieties of paper in this issue.

1946. *Stamps of China, optd with T 3 (="Limited for use in North East").*
6	60	1 c. yellow-orange (508)			5	5
7		3 c. brown (511)			5	5
8		5 c. red-orange (513)			5	5
9	72	10 c. green (469)			5	5
10		10 c. green (493A)			5	5
11	60	20 c. light blue (519)			5	5
6/11		Set of 6			20	20

1946–48. *MILITARY POST. No. M745 of China optd as T 3 (a) 18 mm long or (b) 15½ mm long.*
M12	M 9	(—) Carmine (a) (4.46)			20	60
M13		(—) Carmine (b) (21.2.48)			10	30

(4)

1946 (Aug). *Stamps of China surch as T 4, but larger (19 mm long), in red.*
14	60	$5 on $50 on 21 c. sepia (805)	..	2·00	2·50
15		$10 on $100 on 28 c. olive (808)	..	2·00	2·50
16	91	$20 on $200 deep green (734)	..	2·00	2·50
14/16		Set of 3		5·50	6·50

5 Dr. Sun Yat-sen   A   B

(Recess Central Trust, Peking)

1946–48. *No gum.* P 14.

(a) *Character to left of sun emblem as* A.

17	5	5 c. lake	..	..	5	5
18		10 c. orange	..	..	5	5
19		20 c. apple-green	..	..	5	5
20		25 c. blackish brown	..	..	5	5
21		50 c. red-orange	..	..	5	5
22		$1 blue	..	..	5	5
23		$2 deep purple	..	..	5	5
24		$2.50, indigo	..	..	5	5
25		$3 brown	..	..	5	5
26		$4 orange-brown	..	..	5	5
27		$5 deep green	..	..	5	5
28		$10 rose-red	..	..	5	5
29		$20 olive	..	..	5	5
30		$50 violet-blue	..	..	5	5
17/30		*Set of 14*	..	..	50	50

(b) *Re-engraved character as* B (1947–48)

31	5	$4 orange-brown	..	..	5	5
32		$10 rose-red	..	..	5	5
33		$20 olive	..	..	5	5
34		$22 black (5.11.47)	..	..	1·00	1·40
35		$44 crimson (1948)	..	..	12	12
36		$50 violet	..	..	5	5
37		$65 yellow-green (5.11.47)	..	1·40	1·50
38		$100 green	..	..	5	5
39		$109 blue-green (5.11.47)	..	1·75	1·90
40		$200 red-brown	..	..	5	5
41		$300 pale blue-green	..	..	5	5
42		$500 rose	..	..	5	5
43		$1,000 brown-orange	..	..	5	5
31/43		*Set of 13*	..	..	4·00	4·75

10⁰⁰

(6)

限東北貼用

圓拾

D 1

7 Pres. Chiang Kai-shek

1946. *Opening of National Assembly, Nanking. Nos. 912/5 of China surch as T 6, by Chung Hwa Book Co, Shanghai.*

44	111	$2 on $20 green	..	..	5	5
45		$3 on $30 blue	..	..	5	5
46		$5 on $50 chocolate	..	..	5	5
47		$10 on $100 carmine	..	..	5	5
44/47		*Set of 4*	..	..	12	15

(Recess Central Trust, Peking)

1947 (Jan). *POSTAGE DUE. No gum.* P 14.

D48	D 1	10 c. deep blue	..	..	5	5
D49		20 c. deep blue	..	..	5	5
D50		50 c. deep blue	..	..	5	5
D51		$1 deep blue	..	..	5	5
D52		$2 deep blue	..	..	5	5
D53		$5 deep blue	..	..	5	5
D48/53		*Set of 6*	..	..	20	20

(Recess Dah Yeh Printing Co, Shanghai)

1947 (5 Mar). *President's 60th Birthday.* P 10½–11½.

54	7	$2 carmine	..	..	5	5
55		$3 grey-green	..	..	5	5
56		$5 vermilion	..	..	5	5
57		$10 yellow-green	..	..	5	5
58		$20 yellow-orange	..	..	5	5
59		$30 claret	..	..	5	5
54/59		*Set of 6*	..	..	20	25

用貼北東限

壹佰圓 改 100⁰⁰ 作

(8)

9 Entrance to Dr. Sun Yat-sen Mausoleum

1947 (31 Mar)–**48.** *Stamps of China surch as T 8, by Chung Hwa Book Co, Shanghai.*

60	107	$100 on $1,000 claret (893)	..	..	5	5
61		$300 on $3,000 blue (894)	..	..	5	5
62	58	$500 on $30 chocolate (738)	..	..	5	5
63	107	$500 on $5,000 vermilion and green (895) (1948)	..	5	5
60/63		*Set of 4*	..	..	15	15

(Recess Central Trust, Peking)

1947 (5 May). *First Anniv of Return of Government to Nanking.* P 14.

64	9	$2 green	..	..	5	5
65		$4 blue	..	..	5	5
66		$6 carmine	..	..	5	5
67		$10 yellow-brown	..	..	5	5
68		$20 purple	..	..	5	5
64/68		*Set of 5*	..	..	20	20

軍郵
暫作
肆拾肆圓

(M 1)

改
仟捌
圓 8000 作

(10)

1947 (Sept). *MILITARY POST. No. 21 surch with Type M 1, by Central Trust, Peking.*

M69	5	$44 on 50 c. red-orange	..	..	20	45

1948 (Sept). *Surch as T 10, by Central Trust, Peking.*

70	5	$1,500 on 20 c. apple-green (19)	..	5	10
71		$3,000 on $1 blue (22)	..	..	5	5
72		$4,000 on 25 c. blackish brn (20) (R.)		5	5
73		$8,000 on 50 c. red-orange (21)	..	5	5
74		$10,000 on 10 c. orange (18)	..	5	5
75		$50,000 on $109 blue-green (39) (R.)	..	8	10
76		$100,000 on $65 yellow-green (37)	..	5	5
77		$500,000 on $22 black (34) (R.)	..	8	10
70/77		*Set of 8*	..	..	35	45

用貼北東限
伍拾萬圓 改 10000 作

P 1

拾圓 改 作

(D 2)

(Recess Central Trust, Peking)

1948. *PARCELS POST. No gum.* P 13½.

P78	P 1	$500 orange-red	..	..	—	50
P79		$1,000 crimson	..	..	—	50
P80		$3,000 olive-green	..	..	—	50
P81		$5,000 dark blue	..	..	—	75
P82		$10,000 pale green	..	..	—	75
P83		$20,000 pale blue	..	..	—	1·50
P78/83		*Set of 6*	..	..	—	4·00

1948 (Oct). *PARCELS POST. No. P938 of China surch with Type P 2.*

P84		$500,000 on $5,000 grey-lilac	..	—	4·50

These Parcels Post stamps were not officially issued in unused condition.

1948. *POSTAGE DUE. Surch as Type D 2 (three characters at left on $20 and $50), in red.*

D85	D 1	$10 on 10 c. deep blue	..	..	5	5
D86		$20 on 20 c. deep blue	..	..	5	5
D87		$50 on 50 c. deep blue	..	..	5	5
D85/87		*Set of 3*	..	..	8	8

On 5 January 1948 the Communist commander, Lin Piao, began his eighth offensive and isolated Changchun and Mukden; in a final offensive Changchun fell on 20 October and Mukden ten days later; by 5 November 1948 the Nationalists had lost the North-East.

D. NORTH EAST CHINA

Under this heading are listed the issues made in Manchuria by the Communists, who had to use local resources to produce stamps in the smaller towns under their control.

In addition to the stamps listed below and under the heading North-Eastern Provinces, stamps of Manchukuo were handstamped by Communists or Nationalists in many places, usually with characters for "Chinese Republic" or "Chinese Postal Service" and "Temporary use". Altogether over 3,300 different handstamped Manchukuo stamps are known; they are outside the scope of this catalogue.

GUM. All the following were issued without gum.

NE 1   NE 2

Mao Tse-tung

1946 (Feb). *Litho.*

			A. P 11		B. Imp	
NE1	NE **1**	$1 pale violet	15	20	1·50	2·00
NE2	NE **2**	$2 rose-red	8	15	40	60
NE3		$5 orange	8	15	80	1·20
NE4		$10 blue	8	20	45	65
NE1/4		*Set of 4*	35	65	2·75	4·00

NE 3 Torch·   NE 4

1946 (July). *Pamiencheng issue. Litho. P 11.*

NE5	NE **3**	50 c. yellow-ochre	45	1·25
NE6	NE **4**	$1 apple-green	40	1·25

NE 5 Map of China   "(NE 6)"   NE 7 Dove of Peace

1946 (Aug). *Tsitsihar issue. Litho. Roul 12½.*

NE7	NE **5**	50 c. light blue	35	70
NE8		$1 vermilion	35	70

1946 (Aug). *Tsitsihar issue. First Anniv of Victory. Optd with Type NE 6.*

NE 9	NE **5**	50 c. light blue (R.)	35	70
NE10		$1 vermilion (G.)	35	70

1946. *Chao-Yuan issue. Litho. Rough perf about 10 × 12.*

NE11	NE **7**	50 c. violet-blue	5·00	8·00

NE 8 Mao Tse-tung   (NE 9)

1946. *Tung-Hwa issue. Litho. Imperf.*

NE12	NE **8**	$2 deep violet	£100	£150
		a. *Black*	80·00	£100
NE13		$5 scarlet	35·00	38·00
NE14		$10 turquoise-blue	40·00	45·00

1946 (Sept). *Harbin issue. Victory Commemoration. Nos. 1 and 3/5 of North-Eastern Provinces optd with Type NE* **9.**

NE15	**1**	50 c. on $5 red (G.)	12	20
NE16		$1 on $10 green (R.)	15	20
NE17		$2 on $20 purple (G.)	25	30
NE18		$4 on $50 brown (R.)	35	50
NE15/18		*Set of 4*	80	1·10

Harbin was taken by the Communists on 25 April 1946.

NE **10** Mao Tse-tung   NE **11** Chu Teh

NE **12** Chu Teh and Mao Tse-tung

1946 (Sept). *First Antung issue. Litho. White wove paper. Roul.*

NE19	NE **10**	$1 dull blue	30	45
NE20	NE **11**	$1 dull blue	2·25	3·00
NE21	NE **10**	$2 violet	60	90
NE22	NE **11**	$2 violet	60	90
NE23	NE **12**	$5 turquoise-green	1·75	2·50
NE24		$10 carmine-vermilion	1·50	2·25
NE25		$15 orange-vermilion	1·00	1·40
NE19/25		*Set of 7*	7·00	10·00

Antung was taken by the Nationalists on 27 October 1946.
See also Nos. NE73/4.

(NE **13**)   NE **14** Map of China with Communist Lion, Japanese Wolf and Chiang Kai-shek   (NE **15**)

1946 (10 Oct). *35th Anniv of Chinese Revolution. Nos. 1 and 3/5 of North-Eastern Provinces optd with Type NE* **13.**

NE26	**1**	50 c. on $5 red (G.)	12	20
NE27		$1 on $10 green (R.)	15	20
NE28		$2 on $20 purple (G.)	25	30
NE29		$4 on $50 brown (G.)	35	50
NE26/29		*Set of 4*	80	1·10

1946 (12 Dec). *10th Anniv of Seizure of Chiang Kai-shek at Sian. Litho. P 11.*

NE30	NE **14**	$1 violet	30	45
NE31		$2 brown-orange	30	45
NE32		$5 brown	40	60
NE33		$10 yellow-green	55	80
		a. Imperf (pair)		
NE30/33		*Set of 4*	1·40	2·10

1947. *Shwangcheng issue. Victory Commemoration. Nos. 1 and 3/5 of North-Eastern Provinces optd with Type NE* **15.**

NE34	**1**	50 c. on $5 red (G.)	12	20
NE35		$1 on $10 green (R.)	15	20
NE36		$2 on $20 purple (G.)	25	30
NE37		$4 on $50 brown (R.)	35	50
NE34/37		*Set of 4*	80	1·10

NE 16 Railwaymen   NE 17 Women   (NE 18)
Cheering

1947 (7 Feb). *24th Anniv of Massacre of Strikers at Cheng-chow Station. Litho.* P 10½.

NE38	NE 16	$1 carmine-pink	..	15	20
NE39		$2 dull green ..	..	25	30
NE40		$5 carmine-pink	..	40	55
NE41		$10 dull green ..	..	60	80
NE38/41		Set of 4	..	1·25	1·60

1947 (8 Mar). *International Women's Day. Litho. Wmk characters in sheet.* P 10½×11.

NE42	NE 17	$5 vermilion ..	..	15	20
NE43		$10 brown ..	..	20	25

1947 (18 Mar). *Optd with Type* NE 18 (="North East Postal Service"), *in green.*

NE44	NE 17	$5 vermilion ..	..	20	25
NE45		$10 brown ..	..	25	30

NE 19 Children's   (NE 20)   (NE 21)
Troop-comforts Unit

1947 (4 Apr). *Children's Day. Litho. Granite paper wmkd with characters in sheet.* P 11×10½.

NE46	NE 19	$5 rose-carmine	..	20	25
NE47		$10 yellow-green	..	30	45
NE48		$30 orange	..	40	55

1947. *Hailar issue. No.* NE7 *handstamped with new values as Type* NE 20.

NE49	NE 5	$30 on 50 c. light blue	..	10·00	15·00
NE50		$50 on 50 c. light blue (R.)	..	10·00	15·00

1947 (Apr). *Nos.* NE1/2A *surch as Type* NE 21.

NE51	NE 1	$50 on $1 pale violet (R.)	..	60	90
NE52		$50 on $1 pale violet (Br.)	..	60	90
NE53	NE 2	$50 on $2 rose-red	..	60	90
NE54		$50 on $2 rose-red (Br.)	..	60	90
NE55	NE 1	$100 on $1 pale violet	..	70	1·00
		a. Surch inverted	..	5·00	6·50
NE56		$100 on $1 pale violet (G.)	..	70	1·00
		a. Imperf (No. NE1B)	..	8·00	
NE57	NE 2	$100 on $2 rose-red (B.)	..	80	1·10
NE58		$100 on $2 rose-red (G.)	..	80	1·10
		a. Imperf (No. NE2B)	..	4·00	5·50
NE51/58		Set of 8	..	5·00	7·00

NE 22 Peasant and   NE 23 "Freedom"
Workman

1947 (1 May). *Labour Day. Litho. Wmk characters in sheet.* P 11×10½.

NE59	NE 22	$10 rose-red ..	..	12	20
NE60		$30 ultramarine	..	15	20
NE61		$50 grey-green ..	..	20	30

1947 (4 May). *28th Anniv of Students' Rebellion, Peking University. Litho. Wmk characters in sheet.* P 10½×11.

NE62	NE 23	$10 emerald-green	..	20	30
NE63		$30 grey-brown	..	25	35
NE64		$50 violet	..	30	45

NE 24 Youths with Banner   NE 25 Mao Tse-tung

1947 (30 May). *22nd Anniv of Nanking Road Incident, Shanghai. Litho.* P 11×10½.

NE65	NE 24	$2 red and mauve ..	..	20	30
NE66		$5 red and bright green	..	20	30
NE67		$10 red and yellow	..	20	30
NE68		$20 red and violet ..	..	25	35
NE69		$30 red and red-brown	..	30	45
NE70		$50 red and blue	..	30	45
NE71		$100 red and brown	..	50	75
NE65/71		Set of 7 ..	..	1·75	2·50
MS NE72		218×160 mm. Nos. NE65/71. Imperf		15·00	

1947 (? June). *Second Antung issue. Imperf.*

NE73	NE 12	$10 dull scarlet ..	..	1·00	2·00
NE74		$10 dull vermilion	..	1·00	2·00

No. NE73 is on grey paper and No. NE74 is on surfaced paper with coloured illustrations on the back.

Antung was recaptured by the Communists on 10 June 1947.

1947 (1 July). *26th Anniv of Chinese Communist Party. Litho. Wmk characters in sheet.* P 11×10½.

NE75	NE 25	$10 rose-red ..	..	25	35
NE76		$30 pale mauve ..	..	30	45
NE77		$50 purple ..	..	50	75
NE78		$100 scarlet ..	..	75	1·10
NE75/78		Set of 4 ..	..	1·60	2·40

NE 26 Hand grasping   NE 27 Mountains and
Rifle   River

1947 (7 July). *10th Anniv of Outbreak of War with Japan. Litho. Wmk characters in sheet.* P 10½.

NE79	NE 26	$10 orange ..	..	25	35
NE80		$30 green ..	..	35	50
NE81		$50 grey-blue ..	..	45	65
NE82		$100 brown ..	..	90	1·40
NE79/82		Set of 4 ..	..	1·75	2·50
MS NE83		150×110 mm. Nos. NE79/82. Imperf		12·00	

1947 (15 Aug). *2nd Anniv of Japanese Surrender. Litho.* P 11.

NE84	NE 27	$10 pale brown ..	..	20	30
NE85		$30 pale olive ..	..	25	35
NE86		$50 green ..	..	45	65
NE87		$100 sepia ..	..	90	1·40
NE84/87		Set of 4 ..	..	1·60	2·40

(NE 28)   (NE 29)   (NE 30)

1947 (29 Aug). *Nos.* NE1/2A *surch as Type* NE **28**.

NE88	NE 1	$5 on $1 pale violet (R.)	..	50	65
NE89		$5 on $1 pale violet (G.)	..	50	65
		a. Surch inverted	..	2·10	2·75
NE90		$5 on $1 pale violet	..	50	65
		a. Surch inverted	..	2·50	3·25
NE91	NE 2	$10 on $2 rose-red (B.)	..	60	80
		a. Surch inverted on imperf (No. NE1B)	..	2·10	2·75
NE92		$10 on $2 rose-red (G.)	..	60	80
NE93		$10 on $2 rose-red	..	60	80
NE88/93	*Set of 6*	..	..	3·00	4·00

1947–48. Tung-Hwa issue.

(a) Nos. NE1/2A *surch as Type* NE **29**

NE 94	NE 2	$20 on $2 rose-red	..	45·00	60·00
NE 95	NE 1	$40 on $1 pale violet (R.)	..	45·00	60·00
NE 96		$50 on $1 pale violet (R.)	..	50·00	65·00

(b) Nos. NE12/14 *surch as Type* NE **30**

NE 97	NE 8	$20 on $5 scarlet	..	60·00	75·00
NE 98		$40 on $2 deep violet (R.)	..	90·00	£110
NE 99		$50 on $5 scarlet	..	60·00	75·00
NE100		$100 on $3 deep violet (R.)	..	90·00	£110
NE101		$100 on $10 turquoise-blue (R.)	..	80·00	£100

NE 31 Map of Manchuria   NE 32 Offices of N.E. Political Council   NE 33 Mao Tse-tung

1947 (18 Sept). *16th Anniv of Japanese attack on Manchuria. Litho.* P 11.

NE102	NE 31	$10 grey-green	..	40	60
NE103		$20 mauve	..	45	65
NE104		$30 grey-brown	..	60	90
NE105		$50 carmine	..	75	1·10
NE102/105	*Set of 4*	..	..	2·00	3·00

1947 (10 Oct). *35th Anniv of Chinese Republic. Litho.* P 10½.

NE106	NE 32	$10 yellow	..	1·10	1·50
NE107		$20 carmine	..	1·25	1·90
NE108		$100 brown	..	5·00	7·50

1947 (Oct). *Litho.* P 11.

NE109	NE 33	$1 purple	..	5	10
NE110		$5 grey-green	..	5	10
NE111		$10 bright green	..	5	15
NE112		$15 violet	..	5	20
NE113		$20 carmine-pink	..	5	15
NE114		$30 green	..	5	20
NE115		$50 sepia	..	15	25
NE116		$90 pale blue	..	15	25
NE117		$100 scarlet	..	15	20
NE118		$500 orange	..	50	65
NE109/118	*Set of 10*	..	..	1·10	2·00

1947 (? Nov). *Type* NE **33** *redrawn (with larger panel below portrait). Litho.* P 10½×11.

(a) No wmk

NE119	NE 33	$50 pale green	..	12	15
NE120		$150 pale red	..	15	20
NE121		$250 lilac	..	30	40

(b) Wmk characters

NE122	NE 33	$250 lilac	..	40	55

1947 (? Dec). *Type* NE **33** *redrawn (with larger panel below portrait and no digits "Fco" for cents in value). Litho.* P 11.

NE123	NE 33	$300 blue-green	..	60	90
NE124		$1,000 yellow	..	40	55

There are several varieties of paper in this issue. See also T 43.

NE 34   NE 35 Tomb of Gen. Li Chao-lin

1947 (12 Dec). *11th Anniv of Seizure of Chiang Kai-shek at Sian. Litho.* P 11.

NE125	NE 34	$30 carmine	..	30	40
NE126		$90 blue	..	60	90
NE127		$150 green	..	90	1·25

1948 (9 Mar). *2nd Death Anniv of Gen. Li Chao-lin. Litho.* P 10½.

A. Thin paper without watermark
B. Granite paper with watermark

			A		B	
NE128	NE 35	$30 grey-grn	50	70	50	70
NE129		$150 grey-lilac	1·25	1·75	1·25	1·75

(NE 36)   (NE 37)

1948. *Antung surcharges. Handstamped with new values as Types* NE **36/37**.

(a) Nos. NE23/4 *as Type* NE **36**

NE130	NE 12	$60 on $5 turquoise-green	..	
NE131		$60 on $10 carmine-vermilion		

(b) No. NE82 *as Type* NE **37**

NE132	NE 12	$30 on $10 dull scarlet (B.)	..	1·10	1·60
NE133		$90 on $10 dull scarlet	..	1·10	1·60
NE134		$150 on $10 dull scarlet	..	1·50	2·25

(c) No. NE83 *as Type* NE **36**. *Imperf*

NE135	NE 12	$50 on $10 dull vermilion	..	15·00	25·00
NE136		$90 on $10 dull vermilion	..	4·00	6·50
NE137		$100 on $10 dull vermilion	..	5·00	8·00
NE138		$100 on $10 dull vermilion (B.)	..	5·00	8·00
NE139		$150 on $10 dull vermilion	..	3·00	5·50

(d) No. NE83 *but perf, as Type* NE **37**

NE140	NE 12	$30 on $10 dull vermilion	..	25·00	35·00
NE141		$30 on $10 dull vermilion (V.)	..	25·00	35·00
NE142		$50 on $10 dull vermilion	..	20·00	30·00
NE143		$100 on $10 dull vermilion	..	7·00	10·00

NE 38 Flag and Globe   NE 39 Youth with Torch

1948 (1 May). *Labour Day. Litho. Wmk large characters in sheet.* P 11×10½.

NE143	NE 38	$50 rose-red	..	3·50	5·00
NE144		$150 green	..	6·00	9·00
NE145		$250 violet	..	12·00	18·00

1948 (4 May). *Youth Day. Litho.* P 10½×11.

NE146	NE 39	$50 green	..	50	75
NE147		$150 brown-purple	..	75	1·00
NE148		$250 lake	..	1·00	1·50

NE **40** Crane Operator   (NE **41**)   NE **42** Workman, Soldier and Peasant   NE **46** Workers' Procession   NE **47** North East Heroes' Monument   NE **48** Celebrations at Gate of Heavenly Peace, Peking

1948 (May). *All-China Labour Conference. Harbin. Litho. Wmk characters in sheet.* P 11.

NE149	NE **40**	$100 rose and pink ..	20	30
NE150		$300 brown and yellow	50	70
NE151		$500 blue and green ..	65	1·00

1948 (July). *Surch as Type NE* **41**.

NE152	NE **33**	$100 on $1 purple ..	1·25	1·60
NE153		$100 on $1 purple (B.)	1·00	1·25
NE154		$100 on $15 violet ..	1·00	1·25
NE155		$100 on $15 violet (B.)	1·00	1·25
NE156		$300 on $5 grey-green (R.)	1·00	1·25
NE157		$300 on $30 green (R.)	1·00	1·25
NE158		$300 on $90 pale blue (R.)	1·00	1·25
NE159		$500 on $50 pale green (R.)	25	40
NE160		$1,500 on $150 pale red (G.)	40	50
NE161		$2,500 on $300 blue-green	60	80
		a. Surch inverted..	2·50	
NE152/161		Set of 10 ..	7·50	10·00

1948 (? Nov). *Nos. NE2/4A, surch as Type NE* **41**.

NE162	NE **2**	$500 on $2 rose-red ..	25	35
NE163		$1,500 on $5 orange (R.)	35	45
NE164		$2,500 on $10 blue (C.)..	55	70

1948 (3 Dec). *Liberation of the North East. Litho.* P 11 or 11 × 10½.

NE165	NE **42**	$500 rose-red	25	40
NE166		$1,500 green ..	35	50
NE167		$2,500 brown ..	55	75

NE **43** Mao Tse-tung. ("YUAN" at top right)   NE **44** Workers and Banners   NE **45** "Production in Field and Industry"

1949 (Feb). *Litho.* P 11.

NE168	NE **43**	$300 olive ..	5	10
NE169		$500 orange ..	5	10
NE170		$1,500 blue-green ..	5	10
NE171		$4,500 purple-brown ..	12	15
NE172		$6,500 blue ..	15	20
NE168/172		Set of 5 ..	35	60

1949 (1 May). *Labour Day. Litho.* P 11½ × 11.

NE173	NE **44**	$1,000 red and blue ..	12	20
NE174		$1,500 red and turquoise	15	20
NE175		$4,500 rose and bistre	20	30
NE176		$6,500 orange-brown & green	25	35
NE177		$10,000 maroon & ultramarine	30	40
NE173/177		Set of 5 ..	90	1·25

1949. *Litho.* P 10–11.

NE178	NE **45**	$5,000 pale blue ..	10	15
NE179		$10,000 brown-orange ..	20	35
NE180		$50,000 green ..	65	1·00
NE181		$100,000 violet ..	1·40	1·00
NE178/181		Set of 4 ..	2·10	2·25

1949 (1 July). *28th Anniv of Chinese Communist Party. Litho.* P 11.

NE182	NE **46**	$1,500 rose, violet and blue ..	12	20
NE183		$4,500 red, chocolate and blue	15	25
NE184		$6,500 carmine, pink and blue	20	30

1949 (15 Aug). *4th Anniv of Japanese Surrender. Litho.* P 11½ × 11.

NE185	NE **47**	$1,500 pale red ..	12	20
NE186		$4,500 yellow-green ..	15	25
NE187		$6,500 pale blue ..	20	30

(Litho Commercial Press, Shanghai)

1949 (12 Sept). *First Session of Chinese People's Political Conference.* P 12½.

NE188	NE **48**	$1,000 blue ..	15	20
NE189		$1,500 carmine ..	15	20
NE190		$3,000 emerald-green..	15	20
NE191		$4,500 purple ..	20	30
NE188/191		Set of 4 ..	60	80

Reprints exist, with same differences as noted under Nos. 1401/4 of China.

NE **49** Factory   (NE **50**)   NE **51**

1949 (Oct). *Litho.* P 11 × 10½.

NE192	NE **49**	$1,500 orange-red ..	12	15

1949 (Nov). *Various stamps surch as Type NE* **50**.

NE193	NE **43**	$2,000 on $300 olive ..	10	10
NE194		$2,000 on $4,500 pur-brn (G.)	35	35
NE195		$2,500 on $1,500 blue-green	45	45
NE196		$2,500 on $6,500 blue	20	20
NE197	NE **49**	$5,000 on $1,500 orange-red	30	30
		a. Surch inverted	2·25	2·25
		b. Surch double ..	4·50	4·50
NE198	NE **43**	$20,000 on $4,500 purple-brn	25	25
NE199		$35,000 on $300 olive ..	35	35
NE193/199		Set of 7 ..	1·75	1·75

(Litho Commercial Press, Shanghai)

1949 (16 Nov). *World Federation of Trade Unions, Asiatic and Australasian Conference, Peking.* P 12½.

NE200	NE **51**	$5,000 carmine ..	1·25	1·25
NE201		$20,000 green ..	1·75	1·75
NE202		$35,000 blue ..	2·75	2·75

Reprints exist, with same differences as noted under Nos. 1405/7 of China.

NE **52** Conference
Hall

NE **53** Mao Tse-tung

(Recess Dah Tung Book Co, Shanghai)

1950 (1 Feb). *Chinese People's Political Conference. P* 14.
NE203	NE **52**	$1,000 scarlet	..	12	12
NE204		$1,500 blue	..	15	15
NE205	NE **53**	$5,000 brown-purple	..	25	25
NE206		$20,000 green ..	..	40	40
NE203/206		*Set of* 4 ..	..	80	80

Reprints exist, with same differences as noted under Nos. 1408/11 of China.

NE **54** Gate of
Heavenly
Peace, Peking

(NE **55**)

NE **56** Gate of
Heavenly Peace,
Peking

NEP **1**

1950 (Mar–Nov). *Litho. P* 10½.
NE207	NE **54**	$500 olive ..	..	5	5
NE208		$1,000 orange	..	5	5
NE209		$1,000 magenta (Nov)	..	5	5
NE210		$2,000 deep green	..	5	5
NE211		$2,500 yellow	..	5	5
NE212		$5,000 red-orange	..	5	5
NE213		$10,000 orange-brown	..	10	10
NE214		$10,000 red-brown (Nov)	..	10	10
NE215		$20,000 purple-brown	..	20	20
NE216		$35,000 blue ..	..	30	30
NE217		$50,000 bright green ..	..	35	35
NE207/217		*Set of* 11 ..	..	1·10	1·10

(Litho Dah Tung Book Co)

1950 (1 July). *Foundation of People's Republic on* 1 *Oct,* 1949. *As T* **188** *of China, but with additional characters, Type* NE **55** *at left. P* 14.
NE218	$5,000 carmine, yellow and green ..		30	40
NE219	$10,000 carmine, yellow and brown		40	50
NE220	$20,000 carmine, yellow and purple		45	60
NE221	$30,000 carmine, yellow and blue ..		60	90
NE218/221	*Set of* 4 ..	..	1·60	2·10

Reprints exist, perf 12½ and with extra dot in collar button.

1950 (1 Aug). *Peace Campaign. As T* **191** *of China, but with four additional characters below olive branch. P* 14.
NE222	$2,500 brown	..	10	12
NE223	$5,000 green	..	15	20
NE224	$20,000 blue ..	..	40	60

Reprints exist. See note under No. 1458 of China.

(Flag litho, remainder recess Dah Tung Book Co)

1950 (1–31 Oct). *First Anniv of People's Republic. As T* **193** *of China, but with four additional characters, Type* NE **55** *at left. Flag in red, yellow and brown. P* 14.
NE225	$1,000 violet (31.10)	..	8	12
NE226	$2,500 orange-brown (31.10)	..	10	15
NE227	$5,000 green	..	20	30
NE228	$10,000 olive (31.10)..	..	25	35
NE229	$20,000 light blue (31.10)	..	50	75
NE225/229	*Set of* 5 ..	..	1·00	1·50

No. NE227 measures 44×53 *mm* from perf to perf; the remainder, 32½×37½ *mm.*
Reprints exist with the same differences as noted under Nos. 1464/8 of China.

(Litho Dah Tung Book Co)

1950 (1 Nov). *First All-China Postal Conference. As T* **194** *of China, but with four additional characters, Type* NE **55** *at left. P* 14.
NE230	$2,500 orange-brown and blue-green		10	10
NE231	$5,000 blue-green and carmine	..	15	15

Reprints exist, perf 12½.

(Litho People's Ptg Wks, Peking)

1950 (Nov)**–51**. *As Type* NE **54** *but with lines of shading wider apart. P* 10½.

(a) No wmk
NE232	NE **56**	$5,000 red-orange	..	10	10
NE233		$30,000 carmine	..	75	75
NE234		$100,000 violet	..	1·25	1·25

(b) W **14** *of Manchukuo (sideways)*
NE235	NE **56**	$250 brown	..	5	5
NE236		$500 olive ..	..	5	5
NE237		$1,000 magenta	..	5	5
NE238		$2,000 green ('51)	..	5	5
NE239		$2,500 yellow	..	5	5
NE240		$5,000 red-orange	..	5	5
NE241		$10,000 orange-brown ('51) ..		15	15
NE242		$12,500 purple	..	20	20
NE243		$20,000 purple-brown ('51) ..		40	40
NE232/243		*Set of* 12 ..	..	2·75	2·75

A $50,000 bright green with watermark exists, but is not known to have been issued.

(Recess People's Printing Works, Peking)

1950 (1 Dec). *Sino-Soviet Treaty. As T* **195** *of China, but with four additional characters, Type* NE **55** *in top right-hand corner. P* 14.
NE244	$2,500 scarlet	..	12	15
NE245	$5,000 green	..	15	25
NE246	$20,000 blue ..	..	35	50

Reprints exist but the differences are very minute.

1951. *PARCELS POST. Litho. P* 10½ (*No.* NEP247) *or imperf (others)*.
NEP247	NEP **1**	$100,000 bluish violet	..	6·00	7·50
NEP248		$300,000 pale claret	..	12·00	
NEP249		$500,000 pale turq-blue	..	18·00	
NEP250		$1,000,000 red	..	35·00	

With the introduction of People's Currency in North East China in May 1951, there was no further need for special stamps, and the stamps of China came into use.

E. PORT ARTHUR AND DAIREN

By the Sino-Soviet Treaty of August 1945, Port Arthur was to be used jointly as a naval base by China and the Soviet Union, and Dairen was to be a free port, with all the installations leased to the Soviet Union. China was to have the civil administration of both places.

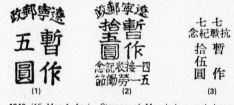

(1)   (2)   (3)

1946 (15 Mar–1 Apr). *Stamps of Manchukuo and Japan handstamped "Liaoning Posts" and new value as T* **1**.

(a) Stamps of Manchukuo (15 March)
1	20	c. on 30 f. orange-brown (153) (V.)	..	15	20
2		$1 on 12 f. orange (90) (V.)	..	15	20

(b) Stamps of Japan (sideways on Nos. 5/6) (1 April)
3	20	c. on 3 f. green (319) (V.)	..	20	25
4		$1 on 17 s. grey-violet (402) (C.)	..	30	35
		a. Violet opt	..	3·00	
5		$5 on 6 s. carmine (242)	..	60	70
6		$5 on 6 s. carmine (301)	..	60	70
7		$5 on 6 s. orange (322)	..	45	50
8		$15 on 40 s. purple (406)	..	1·00	1·10
1/8		*Set of* 8 ..	..	3·00	3·50

1946 (1 May). *Transfer of Administration on 1 April and Labour Day. Stamps of Manchukuo, 1936–37, handstamped as T 2.*

9	$1 on 1 f. brown-lake (80) (G.) ..	..	60	90
10	$5 on 4 f. yellow-olive (84) (C.) ..	..	80	1·10
11	$15 on 30 f. orange-brown (96)	..	1·00	1·40

1946 (June). *Nos. 319 and 322 of Japan, surch as T 1, but with smaller characters and two horiz bars instead of top line of characters.*

12	$1 on 3 s. green ..	..	3·00	3·50
13	$5 on 6 s. orange	..	1·10	1·40

1946 (7 July). *9th Anniv of Outbreak of War with Japan. Stamps of Manchukuo surch as T 3.*

14	$1 on 6 f. red (150) (G.) ..	..	35	50
15	$5 on 2 f. yellow-green (82) (R.)	..	45	65
16	$15 on 12 f. orange (90)	..	60	90

(4)   **(5)**   **(6)**

1946 (15 Aug). *1st Anniv of Japanese Surrender. Stamps of Manchukuo surch as T 4.*

17	$1 on 12 f. orange (90) ..	..	35	50
18	$5 on 1 f. brown-lake (80) (G.) ..	..	45	65
19	$15 on 5 f. black (149) (R.)	..	90	1·40

1946 (10 Oct). *35th Anniv of Chinese Revolution. Stamps of Manchukuo surch as T 5.*

20	$1 on 6 f. red (150) (G.) ..	..	35	50
21	$5 on 12 f. orange (90)	..	45	65
22	$15 on 2 f. yellow-green (82) (R.)	..	90	1·40

1946 (19 Oct). *10th Death Anniv of Lu Hsun (author). Stamps of Manchukuo surch as T 6.*

23	$1 on 1 f. brown-lake (80)	..	1·75	2·50
24	$5 on 6 f. red (150) (G.) ..	..	2·25	3·25
25	$15 on 12 f. orange (90) (B.) ..	..	4·50	6·50

(7)   **(8)**   **(9)**

1947 (20 Feb). *29th Anniv of Red Army. Stamps of Manchukuo surch as T 7.*

26	$1 on 2 f. yellow-green (82) (R.)	..	1·50	2·25
27	$5 on 6 f. red (150) (G.) ..	..	3·00	4·50
28	$15 on 13 f. chocolate (70)	..	5·50	7·50

1947 (1 May). *Labour Day. Stamps of Manchukuo surch as T 8.*

29	$1 on 2 f. yellow-green (82) (R.)	..	70	1·00
30	$5 on 6 f. red (150) (G.) ..	..	1·40	2·10
31	$15 on 30 f. orange-brown (153)..	..	1·75	2·50

1947 (15 Sept). *Stamps of Manchukuo surch "Kwantung Postal Service, China" and new value as T 9.*

32	$5 on 2 f. yellow-green (82) ..	..	2·50	2·75
33	$15 on 4 f. yellow-olive (84)	..	3·00	3·25
34	$20 on 30 f. orange-brown (96) ..	..	4·25	4·75
35	$20 on 30 f. orange-brown (153)..	..	5·00	5·50
32/35	Set of 4	..	13·00	15·00

10   **(11)**

1948 (20 Feb). *30th Anniv of Red Army. Stamps of Manchukuo and Label surch as in T 10.*

(a) Stamps of Manchukuo

36	$10 on 2 f. yellow-green (82) (R.)	..	6·50	10·00
37	$20 on 6 f. red (150) (G.)	..	10·00	13·00

(b) Label commemorating 2600th Anniv of Japanese Empire, T 10

38	$100 on (–) blue and red-brown ..	..	18·00	25·00

1948 (1 July). *Stamps of Manchukuo surch "Kwantung Postal Administration" and new value as T 11.*

39	$20 on 2 f. yellow-green (82) (R.)	..	8·00	9·00
40	$50 on 4 f. yellow-olive (84)	..	10·00	11·00
41	$100 on 20 f. brown (152) (G.)	..	12·00	13·00

(12)   **(13)**   **(14)**

1948 (1 Nov). *31st Anniv of Russian October Revolution. Stamps of Manchukuo surch as T 12.*

42	$10 on 1 f. brown-lake (80) (B.) ..	..	15·00	20·00
43	$50 on 2 f. yellow-green (82) (R.)	..	25·00	32·00
44	$100 on 4 f. yellow-olive (84)	..	45·00	55·00

1948 (15 Nov). *Kwantung Agricultural and Industrial Exhibition. Stamps of Manchukuo surch as T 13.*

45	$10 on 2 f. yellow-green (82) (R.)	..	16·00	22·00
46	$50 on 20 f. brown (152) (G.)	..	65·00	95·00

1948 (Dec)–**49**. *Stamps of Japan and Manchukuo surch "Chinese Postal Administration: Kwantung Posts and Telegraphs" and new value as T 14.*

(a) No. 319 of Japan surch with T 14

47	$5 on 3 s. green (R.) ..	..	3·00	3·00

(b) Stamps of Manchukuo surch as T 14

48	$10 on 1 f. brown-lake (80) (B.) ..	..	20·00	22·00
49	$50 on 2 f. yellow-green (82)	..	25·00	28·00
50	$100 on 4 f. yellow-olive (84)	..	38·00	40·00

(c) Stamps of Manchukuo surch as T 14 but with smaller characters in bottom line (3.49)

51	$10 on 2 f. yellow-green (82)	..	14·00	15·00
52	$50 on 1 f. brown-lake (80)	..	18·00	20·00

15 Peasant and Artisan   **16** "Transport"   **17** Dock

1949 (1 Apr). *Bottom panel inscr "Kwantung Postal and Telegraphic General Administration". Litho. P 11 or 11½.*

53	**15**	$5 pale green	..	60	90
54	**16**	$10 yellow-orange	..	90	1·40
55	**17**	$50 rose-red	..	1·00	1·50

(18)   **(19)**   **(20)**

1949 (Apr)–**50.** *Nos. 53/5 surch as T* **18/20.**

56	**18**	$7 on $5 pale green (R.)	1·00	1·00
57		$7 on $5 pale green (1950) ..	1·00	1·00
58	**19**	$50 on $5 pale green (R.) (1950)	2·50	2·50
59		$100 on $10 yellow-orange (1950)	4·50	4·50
60	**20**	$500 on $5 pale green (R.) (1950)	40·00	
61		$500 on $10 yellow-orange (R.) (1950)	28·00	25·00

The surcharge on No. 57 measures 16×19 mm.

21 "Labour"	22 Mao Tse-tung

1949 (1 May). *Labour Day. Litho. No gum.* P 11.

62	**21**	$10 rose ..	50	70
63		$10 vermilion ..	1·25	1·50

No. 63 is a later printing from a worn plate.

1949 (1 July). *28th Anniv of the Chinese Communist Party. Litho. No gum.* P 11½.

64	**22**	$50 vermilion ..	1·40	1·50

23 Dock	24 Heroes' Monument, Dairen

1949 (7 July). *Bottom panel inscr "Port Arthur and Dairen Postal and Telegraphic Administration". Litho. No gum.* P 11.

65	**23**	$50 red ..	1·40	1·50

1949 (3 Sept). *4th Anniv of Victory over Japan and Opening of Dairen Industrial Fair. Litho.* P 11, 11½ or compound.

66	**24**	$10 red, blue and light blue ..	2·00	2·25
67		$10 red, blue and grey-green ..	1·00	1·10

25 Acclamation of Mao Tse-tung	26 Stalin and Lenin

1949 (1 Nov). *Founding of the Chinese People's Republic. Litho. No gum.* P 11×11½.

68	**25**	$35 red, yellow and blue ..	1·50	1·75

1949 (5 Nov). *32nd Anniv of the Russian October Revolution. Litho. No gum.* P 11×11½.

69	**26**	$10 grey-green ..	50	70

27 Josef Stalin	28 Gate of Heavenly Peace, Peking

1949 (20 Dec). *Stalin's 70th Birthday. Litho. No gum.* P 11½.

70	**27**	$20 purple ..	1·50	1·75
71		$35 rose-red ..	1·50	1·75

1950 (10 Mar). *Typo. No gum.* P 10½.

72	**28**	$10 blue ..	70	70
73		$20 dull green ..	1·00	1·10
74		$35 red ..	1·25	1·40
75		$50 indigo ..	2·25	2·40
76		$100 bright purple ..	5·00	5·50
72/76		Set of 5 ..	9·00	10·00

All Soviet forces were withdrawn by 26 May 1955 and the stamps of the Chinese People's Republic are now in use.

SINKIANG

(Chinese Turkestan)

Stamps were overprinted for special use in Sinkiang because of the debasement of the silver coinage in that province to about a quarter of the value of the silver coinage of China.

Stamps of China overprinted or surcharged

限新省貼用 (1)   限新省貼用 (2)

1915. T **43/5** (*first Peking printings*), optd at Shanghai, with T **1** (*first character not in alignment*).

1	**43**	½ c. sepia	8	8
2		1 c. bright yellow-orange ..	5	5
3		2 c. yellow-green ..	8	8
4		3 c. blue-green ..	8	8
5		4 c. bright scarlet ..	10	10
6		5 c. rosy mauve ..	10	10
7		6 c. grey ..	10	10
8		7 c. violet ..	15	15
9		8 c. brown-orange ..	12	12
10		10 c. deep blue ..	15	15
11	**44**	15 c. brown ..	15	15
12		16 c. olive ..	25	25
13		20 c. brown-lake ..	30	30
14		30 c. deep brownish purple ..	40	30
15		50 c. deep green ..	80	55
16	**45**	$1 black and orange-yellow (R.) ..	3·00	1·75
		a. 2nd and 3rd characters of opt transposed .	£375	
1/16		Set of 16 ..	5·50	4·00

1916–19. T **43/5** (*first Peking printings*) optd with T **2** (*first character in alignment*).

17	**43**	½ c. sepia ..	5	5
18		1 c. bright yellow-orange ..	8	8
19		1½ c. violet (1919) ..	8	8
20		2 c. yellow-green ..	5	5
21		3 c. blue-green ..	8	5
22		4 c. bright scarlet ..	8	8
23		5 c. rosy mauve ..	12	8
24		6 c. grey ..	12	8
25		7 c. violet ..	20	20
26		8 c. brown-orange ..	8	8
27		10 c. deep blue ..	5	5
28	**44**	13 c. brown (1919) ..	20	10
29		15 c. brown ..	20	12
30		16 c. olive ..	12	10
31		20 c. brown-lake ..	10	10
32		30 c. deep brownish purple ..	20	12
33		50 c. deep green ..	20	10
34	**45**	$1 black and orange-yellow (R.) ..	70	25
35		$2 black and blue (R.) ..	90	40
36		$5 black and scarlet (R.) ..	3·25	1·00
37		$10 black and green (R.) ..	9·00	7·00
38		$20 black and yellow (R.) (1919) ..	23·00	19·00
17/38		Set of 22 ..	35·00	26·00

貼　　　新
　　　　　疆
用貼省新限　月　　省
(3)　　　　　(4)

1921. *25th Anniv of Chinese National Postal Service. Optd with T 3.*
39	48	1 c. orange	..	..	..	15	15
40		3 c. blue-green			..	15	15
41		6 c. grey		..	..	40	40
42		10 c. blue			..	3·25	3·25
39/42		*Set of 4*			..	3·50	3·50

1923 (Nov). *Adoption of the Constitution. Optd with T 4.*
43	53	1 c. orange			..	5	5
44		3 c. blue-green			..	10	10
45		4 c. scarlet			..	15	15
46		10 c. blue			..	30	15
43/46		*Set of 4*			..	55	40

1924–36. *Redrawn types of 1923–33 optd as T 2.*
47	43	½ c. sepia			..	5	5
48		1 c. bright yellow-orange			..	5	5
49		1½ c. violet	..		..	5	5
50		2 c. yellow-green			..	5	5
51		3 c. blue-green			..	5	5
52		4 c. slate-grey			..	15	15
53		4 c. olive (1926)			..	5	5
54		5 c. rosy mauve			..	5	5
55		6 c. bright scarlet	..		..	5	5
56		6 c. yellow-brown (1936)			..	1·75	1·40
57		7 c. violet			..	5	5
58		8 c. brown-orange			..	5	5
59		10 c. deep blue			..	5	5
60	44	13 c. brown	..		..	8	8
61		15 c. deep blue			..	8	8
62		16 c. olive			..	10	8
63		20 c. red-brown			..	10	8
64		30 c. purple			..	12	8
65		50 c. green			..	15	10
66	45	$1 sepia and brown-orange (R.)			..	35	10
67		$2 brown and deep blue (R.)			..	65	20
68		$5 grey-green and scarlet (R.)			..	2·50	50
69		$10 rosy mauve and green (R.)			..	7·00	7·00
70		$20 blue and plum (R.)			..	14·00	12·00
47/70		*Set of 24*			..	24·00	20·00

Stamps optd with T 1 and T 2, and certain later issues, were perforated with Chinese characters for use on official correspondence.

貼　　　新
用　　　疆
(5)　　　(6)　空航

1928 (21 May). *Assumption of Title of Marshal of the Army and Navy by Chang Tso-lin. Optd with T 5.*
71	55	1 c. orange (R.)			..	5	5
72		4 c. olive-green (R.)	..		..	8	8
73		10 c. blue (R.)	..		..	12	12
74		$1 scarlet (B.)			..	1·40	1·40
71/74		*Set of 4*			..	1·50	1·50

1929 (21 May). *Unification of China. Optd as T 5, but spaced 10½ mm horiz between characters.*
75	56	1 c. orange (C.)			..	5	5
76		4 c. olive-green (C.)	..		..	8	8
77		10 c. blue (C.)			..	12	12
78		$1 scarlet (C.)			..	1·50	1·50
75/78		*Set of 4*			..	1·60	1·60

1929 (15 July). *State Burial of Dr. Sun Yat-sen. Optd as T 5, but spaced 15½ mm horiz between characters.*
79	57	1 c. orange			..	5	5
80		4 c. olive-green			..	8	8
81		10 c. blue			..	12	12
82		$1 scarlet			..	1·50	1·50
79/82		*Set of 4*		..	..	1·60	1·60

1932 (25 Nov)–**33.** *AIR. Stamps of Sinkiang handstamped as T 6 but larger (="By Air Mail"), in red.*
83	43	5 c. rosy mauve (54) (8.6.33)	..	..	20·00	15·00
84		10 c. deep blue (59) (8.6.33)	..	..	20·00	14·00
85	44	15 c. deep blue (61)	..	..	£150	45·00
86		30 c. deep brownish purple (32)	..	70·00	50·00
83/86		*Set of 4*		..	£225	£110

These stamps were authorised for payment of air mail postage on correspondence carried by a service from Tihwa, owing to shortage of the regular air stamps. The 15 c. and 30 c. paid the original rate to Lanchow and Eastern China respectively, while the 5 c. and 10 c. were used, with other stamps, to make up the later rates of 50 c. and $1 to the same destinations.
Beware of forged overprints.

1932–41. *Dr. Sun Yat-sen issue optd as T 3.*
I. Emblem with double circles
(a) London optd (11½ mm long) (1932)
87	58	1 c. red-orange		..	5	5
88		2 c. olive-green		..	8	8
89		4 c. green	..	..	5	5
90		20 c. ultramarine		..	5	8
91		$1 sepia and red-brown		..	25	25
92		$2 red-brown and blue		..	35	40
93		$5 black and scarlet		..	80	90

(b) Shanghai opt (12 mm long) (1941)
94	58	2 c. olive-green		..	5	5
87/94		*Set of 8*		..	1·50	1·60

II. Emblem with thick circle
(a) London opt (11½ mm long) (1932)
95	58	2 c. olive-green		..	8	10
96		4 c. green		..	50	25
97		15 c. blue-green		..	15	15
98		25 c. ultramarine		..	15	15
99		$1 sepia and red-brown		..	35	35
100		$2 red-brown and blue		..	40	45
101		$5 deep green and scarlet	..	80	90
95/101		*Set of 7*		..	2·10	2·10

(b) Peking opt (12½ mm long) (1933)
102	58	2 c. olive-green		..	5	5
103		4 c. green		..	5	5
104		5 c. yellow-green		..	8	10
105		15 c. blue-green		..	5	5
106		15 c. scarlet		..	5	5
107		25 c. ultramarine		..	5	5
108		$1 sepia and red-brown		..	20	25
109		$2 red-brown and blue		..	35	40
110		$5 deep green and scarlet..	..	80	90
102/110		*Set of 9*		..	1·50	1·75

(c) Shanghai opt (12 mm long) (1941)
111	58	2 c. olive-green		..	8	8
112		4 c. green		..	5	5
113		5 c. yellow-green		..	5	5
114		15 c. scarlet		..	5	5
115		20 c. ultramarine		..	5	5
116		25 c. ultramarine		..	5	8
111/116		*Set of 6*		..	25	30

As in China there are two types of the 4 c. and four types of the 5 c. with Peking overprint.

1933 (1 Feb). *Tan Yen-kai Memorial. Optd with T 5.*
117	62	2 c. olive-green		..	5	5
118		5 c. green		..	15	15
119		25 c. blue		..	30	30
120		$1 scarlet		..	2·40	2·40
117/120		*Set of 4*		..	2·50	2·50

1933–41. *Martyrs issue as T 60, optd as T 3. P 14.*
(a) Peking opt (12½ mm long) (1933–34)
121		½ c. sepia		..	5	5
122		1 c. yellow-orange		..	5	5
123		2½ c. claret		..	5	5
124		3 c. brown		..	5	5
125		8 c. orange-red ..		..	5	5
126		10 c. purple		..	5	5
127		13 c. green		..	5	5
128		17 c. bronze-green		..	5	5
129		20 c. brown-lake..		..	5	5
130		30 c. maroon		..	5	5
131		40 c. orange		..	5	5
132		50 c. green		..	5	5
121/132		*Set of 12*		..	50	50

(b) Shanghai opt (12 mm long) (1941)
133		1 c. yellow-orange		..	5	5
134		2½ c. claret		..	25	12

135	3 c. brown	..	..	..	..	6·00	4·00
136	13 c. green		..	..	5	5
137	20 c. brown-lake..		..		5	5
138	40 c. orange			..	40	40
133/138	Set of 6	..		..	6·00	4·00

1940 (3 Dec)–**43**. *Third Sun Yat-sen issue, T* **72**, *optd as T* **3**, *at Shanghai.*

(a) P 12½

139	2 c. olive-green (A) (462)			5	5
140	3 c. brown-lake (464) (11.5.42)	..		5	5
141	5 c. green (465)			5	5
142	5 c. olive-green (466) (21.4.41)	..		5	5
143	8 c. sage-green (C) (467) (11.5.42)	..		5	5
144	10 c. green (469) (1.5.42)	..		5	5
145	15 c. scarlet (470)			5	5
146	16 c. olive-brown (471) (11.5.42)	..		5	5
147	25 c. violet-blue (472)	..		5	5
148	$1 sepia & red-brown (460) (18.1.43)		30	20
149	$2 red-brown & blue (458) (18.1.43)		30	25
150	$2 dp green & scarlet (475) (18.1.43)		85	80
139/150	Set of 12	..		1·60	1·40

(b) P 14

151	5 c. olive (F) (490B)	..		5	5
152	8 c. sage-green (E) (491A) (3.2.41)	..		5	5
153	8 c. sage-green (F) (492A) (11.5.42)	..		35	35
154	10 c. green (493B)			5	5
155	10 c. green (493A) (1941)	..		10	10
156	30 c. scarlet (494B)			5	5
157	30 c. scarlet (494A) (18.1.43)	..		5	5
158	50 c. blue (495B)			5	5
159	50 c. blue (495A) (18.1.43)	..		5	10
160	$1 sepia and red-brown (496A)	..		5	5
161	$2 red-brown and blue (497A)	..		5	5
162	$5 deep green and scarlet (498A)	..		8	8
163	$10 violet and green (499A)	..		12	12
164	$20 ultramarine and purple (500A)	..		25	25
151/164	Set of 14	..		1·10	1·10

1941–45. *Martyrs issue as T* **60**, *optd as T* **3**, *at Shanghai. P 12, 12½, 13 or compound.*

(a) No wmk

165	½ c. sepia			5	5
166	1 c. yellow-orange	..	..	5	5
167	2 c. blue			5	5
168	3 c. brown			5	5
169	4 c. lilac			5	5
170	8 c. brown-orange			5	5
171	13 c. blue-green ..			5	5
172	15 c. maroon			5	5
173	17 c. bronze-green			5	5
174	20 c. light blue			5	5
175	21 c. sepia			5	5
176	28 c. olive			5	5
177	40 c. orange			12	12
178	50 c. green			5	5
165/178	Set of 14			50	50

(b) W **73**

179	1 c. yellow-orange			5	5
180	2½ c. claret			5	5
181	8 c. brown-orange			5	5
182	10 c. dull purple ..			5	5
183	13 c. blue-green ..			5	5
184	17 c. bronze-green			5	5
185	25 c. purple			5	5
186	40 c. orange			5	5
179/186	Set of 8			30	30

用貼省新限 (7)　用貼省新限 (8)

1942 (30 Nov)–**44**. *AIR. Air stamps handstamped in Sinkiang.*

I. *With T* **7**, *in red* (30.11.42)

(a) P 14

187	**61**	15 c. blue-green			25	25
188		25 c. orange		..	40·00	40·00
189		30 c. scarlet			25	30
190		45 c. purple			25	25
191		50 c. chocolate			1·50	1·50
192		60 c. blue			20	25
193		90 c. bronze-green			2·10	2·10
194		$1 yellow-green			25	25
187/194		Set of 8			40·00	40·00

(b) P 12, 12½, 13 or compound

(i) *W* **73**

195	**61**	15 c. blue-green			25	30
196		25 c. orange			25	30

(ii) *No wmk*

197	**61**	25 c. orange			15	15
198		30 c. scarlet			15	15
199		50 c. chocolate			15	15
200		$2 brown			1·40	1·40
201		$5 lake			1·40	1·40
195/201		Set of 7			3·50	3·50

II. *With T* **8**, *in black* (25.5.44)

(a) P 14

202	**61**	15 c. blue-green			20	
203		25 c. orange			50	
204		45 c. purple			15	
205		60 c. blue			15	
206		$1 yellow-green			15	
202/206		Set of 5			1·00	

(b) P 12, 12½, 13 or compound

(i) *W* **73**

207	**61**	25 c. orange			15	

(ii) *No wmk*

208	**61**	15 c. blue-green			12·00	
209		25 c. orange			10	
210		30 c. scarlet			20	
211		50 c. chocolate			35	
212		$2 brown			40	
213		$5 lake			55	
207/213		Set of 7			12·00	

1942 (30 Nov)–**44**. *Thrift Movement. Handstamped as T* **8**, *in Sinkiang.*

(a) In red (30.11.42)

214	**78**	8 c. green			20·00	20·00
215		21 c. chocolate			15	15
216		28 c. olive-green			15	15
217		33 c. scarlet			10·00	10·00
218		50 c. blue			35	35
219		$1 purple			1·75	1·75
MS220		155×171 mm. China No. MS605			5·00	5·00

(b) In black (1944)

221	**78**	8 c. green			15	15
222		21 c. chocolate			15	15
223		33 c. scarlet			15	15
224		50 c. blue			8·00	5·00
225		$1 purple			30	30
MS226		155×171 mm. China No. MS605			10·00	

1943. *Fifth Sun Yat-sen (Central Trust, Chungking printing), optd in Sinkiang or Chungking as T* **3**, *but slightly larger* (14 mm)

227	**82**	10 c. green (R.)			5	5
228		20 c. grey-olive (R.)			5	5
229		25 c. purple-brown			5	5
230		30 c. orange-red			5	5
231		40 c. red-brown			5	5
232		50 c. grey-green			5	5
233		$1 lake			5	5
234		$1 olive-green			5	5
235		$1.50 blue (R.)			5	5
236		$2 blue-green (R.)			5	5
237		$3 yellow			5	5
238		$5 carmine..			5	5
227/238		Set of 12			45	45

Specialists recognise three types of the overprint.

角 改
貳 作
分 壹

用貼省新限 (9)　(10)

1943. *Various stamps optd with T* **9**, *in Chengtu.*

239	**72**	10 c. green (469)			20	25
240	**60**	20 c. light blue (519)		..	20	25
241	**72**	50 c. blue (495B)			20	25

1944. *Sun Yat-sen (Third issue but redrawn), optd as T 3, in Chungking.*

(a) *Imperf (Nos. 656, etc)*

242	$10 red-brown..	..	..	2·50	2·50
243	$20 rose-carmine	..	..	5	5
244	$30 purple	..	..	8	10
245	$40 carmine	..	..	10	12
246	$50 blue	..	..	30·00	30·00
247	$100 brown	..	..	15	15

(b) *Rough perf 12½ to 15 (Nos. 666/74)*

248	$4 blue	..	..	5	5
249	$5 lilac-grey	..	..	5	5
250	$10 red-brown..	..	..	5	5
251	$20 green	..	..	10	10
252	$20 rose-carmine	..	..	4·00	4·00
253	$30 purple	..	..	15	15
254	$40 carmine	..	..	20	20
255	$50 blue	..	..	20	25
256	$100 brown	..	..	4·50	4·50
248/256	*Set of 9*	..	..	8·50	8·50

1944 (1 Aug). *Nos. 227 and 229 of Sinkiang surch as T 10.*

257	82	12 c. on 10 c. green	..	..	5	10
		a. Surch inverted	..		2·50	
258		24 c. on 25 c. purple-brown	..		5	10
		a. Surch inverted	..		2·50	

1945. *Fifth Sun Yat-sen issue optd as T 3, in Chungking.*

259	89	40 c. brown-lake	..	..	5	5
260		$3 scarlet	..	..	5	5

(11)   (12)

1949 (May). *Silver Yuan surcharges. Sun Yat-sen issues surch as T 11.*

261	107	1 c. on $100 crimson	..	..	30	30
262		3 c. on $200 green (R.)	..	..	40	40
263		5 c. on $500 blue-green (R.)	..		50	50
264	136	10 c. on $20,000 rose-carmine	..		50	50
265	118	50 c. on $4,000 grey (R.)	..		80	80
266		$1 on $6,000 bright purple	..		2·00	2·00
261/266	*Set of 6*	..	..	..	3·25	3·25

After the Communists took over Sinkiang, they handstamped the above issue, and also China Nos. 1356/8, in October 1949, with violet characters meaning "People's Postal Service". Three types of handstamp were used, and many forgeries exist. No. 1292 was similarly handstamped with two types of red overprint. Owing to the difficulty of distinguishing genuine handstamps, we do not list these stamps.

1949 (Oct). *Various stamps optd "People's Postal Service, Sinkiang" and surch with new value as T 12, at Tihwa.*

267	136	10 c. on $50,000 slate-blue (R.)	..		30	30
268	146	$1 on (–) brown-orange (1211A)..			2·25	2·25
		a. No brackets round central character	..		5·00	
269	136	$1.50 on $100,000 sage-green (R.)			60	60
270	149	$3 on (–) carmine (1214A)	..		2·25	2·25
267/270	*Set of 4*	..	..	..	5·00	5·00

Tihwa was taken by the Communists on 20 October 1949, after Sinkiang had gone over to them on 25 September. The stamps of the People's Republic have been in use since then.

THE ILI REPUBLIC

In 1945 the Uighur inhabitants of the Ili valley, in N.W. Sinkiang on the border with Kazakhstan, declared their independence of China and issued stamps.

(13)

1945 (Aug). *Tah-Cheng issue. Handstamped with T 13, in red.*

(a) *Nos. 182, etc of Sinkiang*

271	82	20 c. grey-olive	..	..	20·00	
272		25 c. purple-brown	..	..	8·00	
273		40 c. red-brown	..	..	12·00	
274		$1 olive-green	..	..	6·00	
275		$1.50 blue	..	..	8·00	
276		$2 blue-green	..	..	£100	
277		$3 yellow	..	..	16·00	
278		$4 blue	..	..	15·00	
279		$5 carmine	..	..	25·00	

(b) *No. D573 of China*

280	D 5	50 c. orange..	..	..	11·00

14   15

16   17

1949 (Feb). *Printed from woodblocks. No gum. Imperf.*

281	14	$50 blue	..	..	2·00	8·00
		a. Tête-bêche (pair)	..		15·00	
282	15	$100 blue	..	..	2·00	5·00
		a. Tête-bêche (pair)	..		15·00	
283	16	$200 blue	..	..	2·00	5·00
		a. Tête-bêche (pair)	..		15·00	
284	17	$500 blue	..	..	40·00	60·00
		a. Tête-bêche (pair)	..		£110	
281/284	*Set of 4*	..	..	..	42·00	70·00

The Ili Republic joined the Chinese People's Republic at the end of 1949.

SZECHWAN PROVINCE

Stamps were overprinted for special use in Szechwan because of the devaluation of the local currency.

Stamps of China overprinted

用貼川四限

(1)

1933. *Redrawn types of 1923–33, optd with T 1, at Peking.*

1	43	1 c. bright yellow-orange	..	..	10	5
2		5 c. rosy mauve	..	..	10	5
3	44	50 c. green	..	..	40	8

1933–34. *Dr. Sun Yat-sen issue with thick circle, optd with T 1, at Peking.*

4	58	2 c. olive-green	..	..	5	5
5		5 c. yellow-green	..	..	5	5
6		15 c. blue-green	..	..	12	5
7		15 c. scarlet	..	..	15	12
8		25 c. ultramarine	..	..	15	5
9		$1 sepia and red-brown	..	..	70	8
10		$2 red-brown and blue	..	..	1·60	15
11		$5 deep green and scarlet	..	..	4·75	85
4/11	*Set of 8*	..	..	..	7·00	1·25

There are three types of the 5 c. with the overprint.

1933–34. *Martyrs issue as T 60, optd with T 3, at Peking.*
P 14.

12	½ c. sepia				5	5
13	1 c. yellow-orange				5	5
14	2½ c. claret				5	5
15	3 c. brown				8	5
16	8 c. orange-red				8	5
17	10 c. purple				15	5
18	13 c. green				15	5
19	17 c. bronze-green				20	12
20	20 c. brown-lake				20	5
21	30 c. maroon				20	5
22	40 c. orange				80	5
23	50 c. green				1·25	8
12/23	*Set of* 12				3·00	50

Special issues for Szechwan were withdrawn on 31 October 1936, with the introduction of the Chinese National Currency.

YUNNAN PROVINCE

Stamps were overprinted for special use in Yunnan because of the devaluation of the local currency.

Stamps of China overprinted

貼　滇

用貼省滇限　用　省　用貼省滇限

(1)　　　(2)　　(3)

1926 (15 Aug). *Redrawn types of* 1923–33, *optd as T* 1, *at Peking.*

1	43	½ c. sepia				5	5
2		1 c. bright yellow-orange				5	5
3		1½ c. violet				5	5
4		2 c. yellow-green				5	5
5		3 c. blue-green				5	5
6		4 c. olive				5	5
7		5 c. rosy mauve				5	5
8		6 c. bright scarlet				5	5
9		7 c. violet				8	8
10		8 c. brown-orange				8	8
11		10 c. deep blue				8	8
12	44	13 c. yellow-brown				10	8
13		15 c. deep blue				8	8
14		16 c. olive				10	8
15		20 c. red-brown				15	5
16		30 c. purple				30	8
17		50 c. green				40	10
18	45	$1 sepia and brown-orange				80	20
19		$2 red-brown and deep blue			1·25	55
20		$5 grey-green and scarlet			5·00	4·25
1/20	*Set of* 20				8·00	5·50

1929 (28 Apr). *Unification of China. Optd with T* 2.

21	56	1 c. orange (C.)				8	8
22		4 c. olive-green (C.)				8	8
23		10 c. blue (C.)				20	20
24		$1 scarlet (C.)				1·75	1·75
21/24	*Set of* 4				1·90	1·90

1929. *State Burial of Dr. Sun Yat-sen. Optd as T* 2, *but spaced* 15½ *mm horiz between characters.*

25	57	1 c. orange				8	8
26		4 c. olive-green				8	8
27		10 c. blue				15	15
28		$1 scarlet				1·25	1·25
25/28	*Set of* 4				1·40	1·40

1932–34. *Dr. Sun Yat-sen issue optd as T* 3.

I. Emblem with double circles, optd in London

29	58	1 c. red-orange				5	5
30		2 c. olive-green				5	5
31		4 c. green				8	8
32		20 c. ultramarine				15	15
33		$1 sepia and red-brown			1·50	1·50
34		$2 red-brown and blue			3·00	3·00
35		$5 deep green and scarlet			8·00	8·00
29/35	*Set of* 7				11·00	11·00

II. Emblem with thick circle
(a) London opt (11 *mm long*) (1932)

36	58	2 c. olive-green				8	8
37		4 c. green				8	8
38		15 c. blue-green				5·00	5·00
39		25 c. ultramarine				60	60
40		$1 sepia and red-brown			30·00	30·00
41		$2 red-brown and blue			25·00	25·00
42		$5 deep green and scarlet			28·00	28·00
36/42	*Set of* 7				80·00	80·00

(b) Peking opt (12 *mm long*) (1933–34)

43	58	2 c. olive-green				5	5
44		4 c. green				8	5
45		5 c. yellow-green				5	5
46		15 c. blue-green				25	25
47		15 c. scarlet				15	15
48		25 c. ultramarine				15	15
49		$1 sepia and red-brown			1·50	1·50
50		$2 red-brown and blue			3·00	3·00
51		$5 deep green and scarlet			6·50	6·50
43/51	*Set of* 9				10·00	10·00

As in China there are two types of the 4 c. and three of the 5 c. with Peking overprint.

1933. *Tan Yen-kai Memorial. Optd as T* 2, *but spaced* 13 *mm horiz between characters.*

52	62	2 c. olive-green				8	8
53		5 c. green				8	8
54		25 c. blue				20	20
55		$1 scarlet				2·00	1·75
52/55	*Set of* 4				2·10	1·90

1933–34. *Martyrs issue as T* 60, *optd as T* 3, *at Peking. P* 14.

56		½ c. sepia				5	5
57		1 c. yellow-orange				5	5
58		2½ c. claret				5	5
59		3 c. brown				10	10
60		8 c. orange-red				15	15
61		10 c. purple				10	10
62		13 c. green				12	8
63		17 c. bronze-green				25	12
64		20 c. brown-lake				15	12
65		30 c. maroon				20	20
66		40 c. orange				1·25	1·00
67		50 c. green				1·75	1·10
56/67	*Set of* 12				3·75	2·75

Special issues for Yunnan were withdrawn on 31 July 1935, with the introduction of the Chinese National Currency.

TIBET

In 1720 the Chinese Emperor K'ang Hsi sent an expedition to Lhasa, restored the Dalai Lama, and established Chinese influence there. Two resident Chinese officials, the *ambans*, were first appointed in 1726. During the 18th century, there was a series of Chinese military expeditions to Tibet as crises arose in Lhasa, each followed by waning interest until the next crisis. After 1792 Tibet closed its doors to foreigners and during the 19th century Chinese influence was dormant.

In 1903, British attempts, prompted by suspicion of Russia, to persuade Tibet to negotiate an agreement on trade and boundaries, were ignored. A British force under Colonel Francis Younghusband was sent to Lhasa, which it reached, after fighting, on 3 August 1904. Conventions between Britain and Tibet were signed in 1904, between Britain and China in 1906 and between Britain and Russia in 1907. The Chinese interpreted the convention of 1906 as recognition of their sovereignty over Tibet.

A. CHINESE OFFICES

12 Pies=1 Anna. 16 Annas=1 Indian Rupee

In 1910 a Chinese force under General Chung Ying was sent to Lhasa, and Chinese post offices were opened in Tibet. With Chinese support the Panchen Lama, rival of the Dalai Lama, was installed in Lhasa.

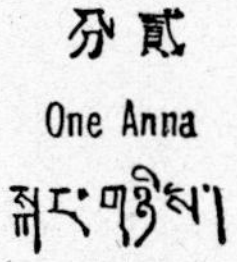

(C 1)

1911 (Mar). *Nos.* 122 *and* 151, *etc, of China, surch as Type* C **1**.

C 1	**32**	3 p. on 1 c. brownish orange	75	1·25
C 2		$\frac{1}{2}$ a. on 2 c. deep green	1·00	1·50
C 3		1 a. on 4 c. scarlet	1·00	1·50
C 4		2 a. on 7 c. crimson-lake	1·00	1·50
C 5		$2\frac{1}{2}$ a. on 10 c. dull blue	1·00	1·50
C 6	**33**	3 a. on 16 c. olive-green	1·50	2·00
		a. Large inverted "S" in "Annas"	£100	£130
C 7		4 a. on 20 c. maroon	2·00	3·00
C 8		6 a. on 30 c. vermilion	2·50	3·50
C 9		12 a. on 50 c. green	4·00	5·50
C10	**34**	1 r. on $1 red and flesh	10·00	15·00
C11		2 r. on $2 claret and bright yellow	50·00	65·00
C1/11		*Set of* 11	65·00	85·00

After the Chinese Revolution of 1911, a revolt broke out in Tibet and the Chinese troops there, cut off from supplies, had to be shipped home by way of India in 1912. The Dalai Lama was restored.

B. INDEPENDENT STATE

$6\frac{2}{3}$ Tranka=1 Sang

PRINTING. All Tibetan stamps were typographed at Lhasa on locally made paper, of varying thickness and texture, without gum.

COLOURS. Owing to the primitive method of production, numerous shades exist of most values. Our colour descriptions have therefore been simplified, and where we have felt that we must list more than one colour for any one value, our namings are intended to cover groups of shades which, for the purpose of this catalogue, fall within the one description.

1 ($\frac{1}{6}$ t.)

$\frac{1}{3}$ t. $\frac{1}{2}$ t. $\frac{2}{3}$ t. 1 t. 1 s.

1912–50. *Imperf.*

A. *Dull ink.* B. *Shiny enamel paint*

			A		B	
1	**1**	$\frac{1}{6}$ t green	1·00	1·00	†	
		a. Perf	—	40·00	†	
		b. *Dull yell-green* ('20)	1·50	1·25	†	
		ba. Do Perf	28·00	—	†	
		c. *Olive-green* (1922)	†		3·50	2·00
2		$\frac{1}{3}$ t. blue	1·75	2·50	†	
		a. *Ultramarine*	2·50	3·50	†	
		b. *Grey-blue* (1932)	2·50	3·50	22·00	8·00
3		$\frac{1}{2}$ t. violet	1·50	2·50	†	
		a. Perf	—	65·00	†	
		b. *Lilac* (1914)	3·00	3·50	8·00	4·50
		c. *Purple* (1930)	3·00	4·00	12·00	6·00
4		$\frac{2}{3}$ t. carmine	2·50	3·00	5·00	3·50
		a. "POTSAGE" for "POSTAGE"	6·00	7·50	10·00	12·00
		b. *Brown-red*	4·00	5·00	†	
		c. *Lake* (1923)	3·00	4·00	6·00	4·00
5		1 t. vermilion	3·00	5·00	†	
		a. *Brown-red* (1925)	5·00	6·00	†	
		b. *Carmine* (1930)	†		12·00	10·00
6		1 s. grey-green (1950)	15·00	15·00	†	
		a. *Blue-green* (1950)	9·00	9·00	†	

No. 4a occurs on all shades and the prices quoted are for the cheapest shade.

2

1914–? *Imperf.*

A. *Dull ink.* B. *Shiny enamel paint*

			A		B	
7	**2**	4 t. deep blue	50·00	40·00	60·00	50·00
		a. *Indigo*	†		80·00	60·00
		b. *Dull grey-blue*	40·00	40·00	†	
8		8 t. vermilion	50·00	45·00	†	
		a. *Carmine*	†		65·00	50·00
		b. *Pink*	25·00	25·00	†	

3 (1 t.)

$\frac{1}{2}$ t. $\frac{2}{3}$ t. 2 t. 4 t.

Normal

3*a*

1933 (May)–**60.** A. *Pin-perf.* B. *Imperf.*

			A		B	
9	**3**	$\frac{1}{2}$ t. orange	3·50	4·00	1·50	1·75
		a. *Yellow* (1935)	†		1·25	1·50
		b. *Bistre* (1940)	†		8·50	—
10		$\frac{1}{6}$ t. deep blue	3·00	4·50	1·50	2·00
		a. *Grey-blue* (1942)	†		1·50	2·00
		b. *Indigo* (1950)	†		1·25	1·50
		c. *Violet-blue* (1960)	†		1·50	2·00
11		1 t. carmine	3·00	4·50	2·00	2·25
		a. *Scarlet* (1938)	†		1·00	1·50
		b. *Orange* (1947)	†		1·00	1·50
		c. *Cinnamon* (1954)	†		6·50	4·00

12	**3**	2 t. scarlet	3·00	4·50	2·50	2·00
	aa.	Bisected (1 t.) (on cover)		†	—	20·00
	a.	*Rose-carmine* (1946)		†	1·25	1·50
	b.	*Cinnamon* (1950)		†	2·50	3·00
	c.	*Orange* (1951)		†	1·25	1·50
	ca.	Bisected (1 t.) (on cover)		†	—	20·00
13		4 t. emerald-green	3·00	4·00	1·25	1·25
	a.	*Olive-green* (1938)		†	6·00	7·50
	b.	*Apple-green* (1947)		†	2·00	2·00
	c.	*Myrtle-green* (1950)		†	3·00	3·00
	ca.	Quartered (1 t.) (on cover)		†	—	50·00
	d.	*Dull green* (1951)		†	1·25	1·25
	da.	Quartered (1 t.) (on cover)		†	—	50·00
	e.	Type **3**a (shades)		†	2·50	3·50

The original perforations were pin-perf 6½ to 12½. In 1952 stamps appeared with a clean-cut hand punched perf 10 but these are believed to be unofficial.

The bisected and quartered stamps were in use in 1953/54 owing to a shortage of the 1 t. value.

Stamps of Type **3** were printed in sheets of 12 from loose blocks, individually engraved and therefore each identifiable. In the various printings these blocks appear in differing sheet positions.

One block of the 4 t. value was lost, and sheets are found with only 11 stamps. Later a new block was made. This is slightly larger (25 mm instead of 24 mm) the difference being most noticeable in the centre and in the word "TIBET". This is separately listed as No. 13e.

The Chinese occupied Eastern Tibet in 1950 and started setting up Chinese post offices in 1951. Chinese rule was gradually established over the whole country although a Tibetan Government continued to exist until dissolved on 28 March 1959 following an abortive revolt against Chinese rule. Tibet became an autonomous region of China on 9 September 1965 and Chinese stamps are now used.

TAIWAN

(FORMOSA)

In 1590 the Portuguese made unsuccessful attempts to make settlements in Taiwan, called by the Europeans Formosa (Beautiful). The Dutch made a trading settlement at Anping in 1624 and the Spaniards another at Chilung in 1626, and till 1642, when the Dutch drove out the Spaniards, these traders divided the island between them. In 1662 the last Dutch stronghold fell to Cheng Ch'eng-kung (Koxinga), who had fought for the Chinese Ming dynasty against the Manchus, and founded his own dynasty in Taiwan. In 1683 his grandson had to surrender the island, which was made a dependency of the Chinese province of Fukien. In 1886 Taiwan became a province of China. The Governor, Liu Mingchuan, organised a postal service, for which stamps were issued.

A. CHINESE PROVINCE

16 Cash=1 Candarin

Essay overprints, of "FORMOSA" diagonally, or of four characters for "Taiwan Postage Stamp", were made on the 3 c. and 5 c. of Type **2** of China in 1886, also on unwatermarked imperforate proofs in the issued colours.

Nos. C1/4 were completed in manuscript by the Postmaster with the amount received, the destination, date and weight. The right-hand portion was normally detached and used on the mail. Prices in the used column are for this half only.

C **1** Clear impression

C **1** Worn impression

The used portions of Nos. C1 and C2 can easily be distinguished from one another by the character indicated by the arrows in Types C **1** and C **2**. In Type C **1** the tail of this character curves to the right and in Type C **2** it curves to the left.

Nos. C1/4 are all handstamped, believed from woodblocks, with control character handstamped separately in red.

1886 (Aug)–**95**. *OFFICIAL. Wove paper. Imperf.*

A. *Clear impression*
B. *Worn impression with blurred and defective characters*

			A	B
C1	C **1**	(–) Black	11·00 16·00	7·50 22·00
	a.	Laid paper	11·00 16·00	7·50 22·00

There are nine dies varying in size from 58½ × 40 mm to 60 × 44½ mm.

C 2

1888–95. *Laid paper. Imperf.*
C2 C **2** (–) Black .. .. — 25·00
   a. Wove paper .. .. .. † —
  This is inscribed "Postage Stamp for Public" in top right panel.
  Only one or two entire copies are known of No. C2 and no entire unused copy of No. C2a has been recorded.

C 4

1894–95. *OFFICIAL. Laid paper. Imperf.*
C4 C **4** (–) Black .. .. .. 9·00 30·00

  The above were used in the north of Taiwan until the issue of the "Horse and Dragon" stamps of 1888, and sometimes even later. They continued to be used in the south of the island until the Black Flag Republic stamps were issued in August 1895.

C 3

1893. *"Commercial Postal Matter Receipt" stamp. Laid paper. Imperf.*
C3 C **3** (–) Black/*deep buff* .. .. .. † £225
  The exact purpose of this stamp is questionable. It may have been a stamp used for registered post or else a post office receipt for an item of mail. Only some six used portions have been recorded.

C 5

  We illustrate Type C **5** as it is often taken for a postage stamp but in fact it is believed to be a telegram receipt. Provision is given for insertion of the destination and the number of words in the message. The left half was kept in the despatch office and the right half was given to the sender as a receipt. This is not known used. (*Price £6 un.*)

C **6** Horse and Dragon

(Recess Bradbury, Wilkinson & Co)

1888 (Apr). *P 14* (*outer edges imperf*).
C5 C **6** 20 c. green .. .. .. 25·00 30·00
C6   20 c. carmine .. .. .. 25·00 30·00
  These stamps were used in the north of Taiwan only, until late in 1892.

HAVE YOU READ THE NOTES AT THE BEGINNING OF THIS CATALOGUE?

These often provide answers to the enquiries we receive.

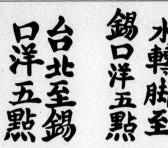

(C 7) (= "Taipeh to Hsi Kou Foreign 5 cents")

(C 8) (= "Shui Chuan Chiao to Hsi Kou Foreign 5 cents")

(C 13) (= "Taipeh to Sui Chuan Chiao Foreign 10 cents")

(C 14) (= "Hsi Kou 5 cents")

(C 15) (= "Shui Fan Chiao 10 cents")

1888. Carriage of Letters on Stages of Taipeh-Keelung Railway. Nos. C5/6 handstamped with Types C **7/13**. Surcharged in silver cents.

C7	C **7**	5 c. on 20 c. green	..	..	
C8		5 c. on 20 c. carmine	..	..	
C9	C **8**	5 c. on 20 c. green	..	..	
C10		5 c. on 20 c. green (R.)	..	..	35·00
C11		5 c. on 20 c. carmine	..	..	35·00
C12	C **9**	10 c. on 20 c. green (R.)	..	..	35·00
C13		10 c. on 20 c. carmine (R.)	..	..	35·00
C14	C **10**	10 c. on 20 c. green (R.)	..	..	35·00
C15	C **11**	10 c. on 20 c. green (R.)	..	..	35·00
C16	C **12**	10 c. on 20 c. carmine	..	..	35·00
C17	C **13**	10 c. on 20 c. green	..	..	
C18		10 c. on 20 c. carmine	..	..	

Nos. C7/8 additionally handstamped with Type C **14**, in red

C19	C **7**	5 c. on 5 c. on 20 c. green	..	
C20		5 c. on 5 c. on 20 c. carmine		

Nos. C17/8 additionally handstamped with Type C **15**, in red

C21	C **13**	10 c. on 10 c. on 20 c. green	..	
C22		10 c. on 10 c. on 20 c. carmine		

These surcharges indicate the rates for carriage of letters on different stretches, as shown, of the railway from Taipeh to Keelung. Handstamps of Types C **9/11** with the Chinese characters "Hsi" (West) or "Tung" (East) are believed to indicate use on up or down trains. Some of the carmine stamps are said to have been used as railway tickets on this line for about a month after they were withdrawn from postal use.

The above listing may not be complete but represents all that have been recorded.

There are also numerous surcharges made by brush and ink.

(C 9)

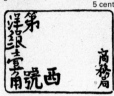

(C 10)
(= "Foreign Silver 10 cents. Number ... West. Commercial Office")

(C 11) (= "Foreign Silver 10 cents. Number ... East. Commercial Office")

(C 12) (= "Shui Chuan Chiao to Taipeh Foreign 10 cents")

B. REPUBLIC

24 May to 21 October 1895

16 Cash=1 Candarin

At the end of the Sino-Japanese War, 1894–95, China ceded Formosa to Japan by the Treaty of Shimonoseki, 18 April 1895. The Governor of the Province, Tan Ching-sun, refused to acknowledge the treaty and on 24 May 1895 a Republic was set up, known as the Black Flag Republic, with Tang as President. Japanese troops landed and occupied Taipeh and most Chinese officials, including the Governor, obeyed an order to return to the mainland. The Republic remained in being in the south, based on Tainan, with Liu Yung-fu as President. Stamps were printed, for obligatory use on all mail. With the capture of Anping and Tainan by the Japanese on 21 October, the Republic came to an end.

R 1 Die I   R 2 Die II

R 3 Die III   R 4 Die IIIA

"Tiger" Emblem of Black Flag Republic

To help with identification Types R 1/4 are shown in actual size. The differences between Die II and Die III lie in the curve of the tiger's tail. Die IIIA can be distinguished from Die III by the rounded corners, due to wear.

Value Types (enlarged)

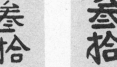

A 8½ mm   B 7 mm   C 7 mm

30 Cash

A 8½ mm   C 7 mm

50 Cash

A 8½ mm   B 7½ mm   C 7 mm

100 Cash

In the following issues the values are struck separately by hand. These differ as shown in the enlarged illustrations and the actual vertical measurements are given for each. On Die II of the 50 cash the characters appear to be indistinguishable from Type A. The value tablets were sometimes applied to the wrong dies and these are listed as errors.

1895 (Aug–Sept). *Die I. Value tablets Type* A. *Very thin transparent silky native paper. Imperf.*

R1	**R 1**	30 c. yellow-green	3·00	4·50
		a. Blue-green	4·00	4·00
		b. Value omitted	25·00	
R2		50 c. vermilion to red	4·50	4·00
		a. Value omitted	25·00	
		b. Tête-bêche (pair)	65·00	
R3		100 c. purple	3·50	3·00
		a. Value omitted	30·00	
		b. Tête-bêche (pair)	75·00	

Wide, medium and narrow settings of the sheet exist, with make-up of 10×10, 16×11 and 12×12 or more, respectively. No. R1 is printed in fugitive ink.

1895 (Oct). *Die II. Value tablets Type* A (50 c.) *or* B (others). *Wove paper.* P 12.

R4	**R 2**	30 c. blue	4·50	6·50
		a. Se-tenant with Die III	70·00	
		b. Value Type C	25·00	
R5		50 c. vermilion	14·00	11·00
		a. Value Type C		
R6		100 c. violet	11·00	10·00
		a. Value Type A		
		b. Value omitted		
		c. Bronze-violet	14·00	13·00

1895 (Oct). *Die III. Value tablets Type* C. *Wove paper.*

			A. P 11½		B. P 12	
R 7	**R 3**	30 c. blue	1·50	20·00	1·75	2·00
		a. Value omitted	18·00		—	
		b. Value Type B			5·00	5·00
		c. Blue-black	2·50	2·00	†	
R 8		30 c. blue-green		†	13·00	13·00
R 9		50 c. vermilion	2·00	3·00	1·50	1·25
		a. Value omitted	—		—	
		b. Deep red	2·50	2·50	†	
R10		100 c. pur/yellowish		†	1·00	1·50
		a. Vio (aniline)	75	75	†	
		b. Value omitted	—		—	
R11		100 c. blue-black	1·50	1·50	†	

1895. *Die IIIA (worn). Value tablets Type* C. *Wove paper.* P 12.

R12	**R 4**	30 c. emerald-green		3·50
R13		50 c. red		1·50
R14		100 c. violet		60
R15		100 c. sky-blue		7·50

Nos. R12/15 have not been found in used condition. Most copies of No. R12 are badly washed and these are worth considerably less than the price quoted.

The value handstamps are sometimes found in a different ink from that of the stamps; they are also found inverted, sideways or completely double. Double impressions of the stamps also occur.

Stamps from Die III and Die IIIA are on paper with paper-maker's watermark: either "DORLING & CO. LONDON" in two lines covering six stamps, once on a sheet; or "1011" covering two stamps on each half of the sheet or sometimes on each quarter. Prices are for stamps without watermark but stamps bearing portions of watermark are worth about double.

No. R7 exists with a 10 c. surcharge in Chinese characters applied by brush and ink.

C. JAPANESE ISLAND

100 Sen = 1 Yen

From 1895 to 1945 Taiwan was part of the Japanese Empire and stamps of Japan were used there. From March 1945 operations of the U.S. Navy round Okinawa cut Taiwan off from Japan. Stamps were printed in Taipeh when supplies ran short.

J 1 Numeral and Chrysanthemum

(Des M. Hioki. Litho Taiwan Photographic Ptg Co, Taipeh)

1945 (Oct). *Imperf.*

J1	J **1**	3 s. carmine (21.10)	..	..	1·50	1·90
J2		5 s. blue-green (21.10)		..	85	1·00
J3		10 s. pale blue (31.10)	..	..	2·50	3·00

30 s., 40 s., 50 s. and 1 y. values were prepared for use but not issued without overprint.

D. CHINESE PROVINCE

1945. 100 Sen=1 Yen

1947. 100 Cents=1 Yuan (C.N.C.)

After the surrender of Japan in August 1945, Taiwan was returned to Chinese rule on 25 October 1945, under the Cairo Agreement of 1943.

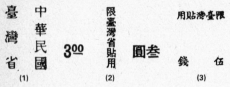

臺灣省	中華民國	3⁰⁰	限臺灣省貼用	用貼灣臺限
(1)	(2)	圓叁 (3)	錢 伍	

1945 (4 Nov). *Optd with T* **1** (="Taiwan Province, Chinese Republic"), *by Chao Hsiang Ptg Works, Taipeh.*

(a) On Nos. J1/3 and other unissued values

1	J **1**	3 s. carmine	..	..	5	5
2		5 s. blue-green	..	..	5	5
3		10 s. pale blue	..	..	5	5
		a. Opt inverted		..	6·50	
		b. Opt double		..	7·00	
4		30 s. blue	..	..	8	5
5		40 s. violet	..	..	8	5
6		50 s. brownish grey	..	..	8	5
7		1 y. olive-green	..	..	8	8

(b) On stamps similar to Nos. 424/5 of Japan

8	87	5 y. grey-green	..	..	15	12
9		10 y. purple	..	..	20	15
		a. Opt inverted		..	5·00	
1/9		*Set of 9*		..	65	55

There are many shades in this issue and most values exist on white, grey and buff paper. There are two varieties of overprint on Nos. 2 and 3.

1946 (Nov). *Opening of National Assembly, Nanking. Nos. 912/5 of China surch as T* **2**, *by Chung Hwa Book Co, Shanghai.*

10	**111**	70 s. on $20 green	..	..	5	5
		a. Surch inverted	..	..	25·00	
11		$1 on $30 blue	..	..	5	5
12		$2 on $50 chocolate		..	5	5
13		$3 on $100 carmine		..	5	5
10/13		*Set of 4*		..	12	12

1946 (June–Dec). *Stamps of China surch as T* **3**, *with two to four characters in lower line denoting value, by Chung Hwa Book Co, Shanghai.*

(a) Martyrs issue as T **60**, *Hong Kong printings*

14	2 s. on 2 c. blue (509) (Sept)		..	5	5
15	5 s. on 5 c. red-orange (513)		..	5	5
16	10 s. on 4 c. lilac (512)	..	..	5	5
17	30 s. on 15 c. maroon (517)	..	..	5	5
18	30 s. on 15 c. maroon (536)	..	..	1·00	1·00
19	$1 on 20 c. light blue (519)		..	5	5

(b) Sun Yat-sen issue of 1944–46 (Aug)

20	**58**	65 s. on $20 apple-green (737)	..	5	5
		a. 7 mm instead of 10 mm between lines of surch ..		8	8
21		$1 on $30 chocolate (738) ..		5	5
		a. 7 mm instead of 10 mm between lines of surch ..		40	40
22		$2 on $50 chocolate (738) ..		5	5
		a. 7 mm instead of 10 mm between lines of surch ..		10	10

(c) Ninth Sun Yat-sen issue

23	**107**	50 s. on $20 carmine (Aug)	..	5	5
24		$3 on $100 crimson (Dec)	..	5	5
25		$5 on $200 green (Sept)	..	5	5

26	**107**	$10 on $500 blue-green (Dec)	..	5	5
27		$20 on $700 red-brown (Dec)	..	5	5
28		$50 on $1,000 claret (Dec)	..	12	12
29		$100 on $3,000 blue (Dec) ..	..	15	15

See also Nos. 65/85.

4 Pres. Chiang Kai-shek	**5** Entrance to Dr. Sun Yat-sen Mausoleum
	6 Sun Yat-sen and Palms

(Recess Dah Yeh Printing Co, Shanghai)

1947 (5 Mar). *President's 60th Birthday. P* 10½–11½.

30	**4**	70 s. carmine	..	..	5	5
31		$1 grey-green	..	..	5	5
32		$2 vermilion	..	..	5	5
33		$3 yellow-green	..	..	5	5
34		$7 yellow-orange	..	..	5	5
35		$10 claret	..	..	5	5
30/35		*Set of 6*		..	20	20

(Recess Central Trust, Peking)

1947 (5 May). *Chinese National Currency. First Anniv of Return of Government to Nanking. P* 14.

36	**5**	50 s. green	..	..	5	5
37		$3 blue	..	..	5	5
38		$7.50, carmine	..	..	5	5
39		$10 yellow-brown	..	..	5	5
40		$20 purple	..	..	5	5
36/40		*Set of 5*		..	15	15

(Recess Dah Tung Book Co, Shanghai)

1947 (1 Oct–5 Nov). *T* **6** (*with small underlined noughts for cents*). *No gum. P* 14.

41	**6**	$1 olive-brown	..	..	5	5
42		$2 orange-brown (5.11)	..	..	5	5
43		$3 green (5.11)	..	..	5	5
44		$5 red-orange	..	..	5	5
45		$9 blue (5.11)..	..	..	5	5
46		$10 carmine	..	..	5	5
47		$20 blue-green	..	..	5	5
48		$50 purple	..	..	5	5
49		$100 blue	..	..	5	5
50		$200 lake-brown	..	..	5	5
41/50		*Set of 10*		..	35	35

USE OF STAMPS OF CHINA. Nos. 972/3 of China, issued to commemorate the second anniversary of the return of Taiwan, were also issued in Taiwan on 25 October 1947. The $500 was sold at $7 local currency and the $1250 at $18.

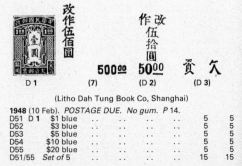

D **1**	(7)	(D **2**)	(D **3**)
	500⁰⁰	50⁰⁰	貢 欠

(Litho Dah Tung Book Co, Shanghai)

1948 (10 Feb). *POSTAGE DUE. No gum. P* 14.

D51	D **1**	$1 blue	..	..	5	5
D52		$3 blue	..	..	5	5
D53		$5 blue	..	..	5	5
D54		$10 blue	..	..	5	5
D55		$20 blue	..	..	5	5
D51/55		*Set of 5*		..	15	15

1948 (May)–**49.** *"Re-valuation" surcharges. Surch as T 7.*

51	6	$25 on $100 blue (7.48)	.. ..	5	5
		a. Top character same as second			
		character	.. ..	3·50	2·00
52		$300 on $3 green (2.49)	.. ..	5	8
53		$500 on $7.50, orange	.. ..	10	8
54		$1,000 on 30 c. grey	.. ..	20	15
55		$1,000 on $3 green (R.) (3.49)	..	10	5
56		$2,000 on $3 green (V.) (3.49)	..	5	5
57		$3,000 on $3 green (C.) (2.49)	..	20	12
58		$3,000 on $7.50, orange (2.49)	..	1·00	50

Nos. 53/4 and 58 were not issued without surcharge.

(Recess Dah Tung Book Co, Shanghai)

1948 (Oct)–**49.** *As T 6, but without noughts for cents in figures of value. No gum. P 14.*

59	6	$25 green	.. ..	5	5
60		$5,000 yellow-orange (1949)	..	10	5
61		$10,000 yellow-green (1949)	..	5	5
62		$20,000 bistre-brown (1949)	..	5	5
63		$30,000 indigo (1949)	..	8	5
64		$40,000 brown-purple (1949)	..	15	5
59/64		Set of 6	.. ..	40	20

1948 (4 Dec). *POSTAGE DUE. "Re-valuation" surcharges. Surch as Type D 2, in carmine.*

D65	D 1	$50 on $1 blue	.. ..	15	15
D66		$100 on $3 blue	.. ..	15	15
D67		$300 on $5 blue	.. ..	15	15
D68		$500 on $10 blue	.. ..	25	25
D65/68		Set of 4	.. ..	60	60

1948. *PARCELS POST. As Parcels Post stamps of China of 1947–48, with six characters in the sky above the lorry. No gum. P 13½.*

P65	P 3	$100 blue-green	.. ..	—	5
P66		$300 carmine	.. ..	—	5
P67		$500 olive-green	.. ..	—	5
P68		$1,000 blue-black	.. ..	—	5
P69		$3,000 red-purple	.. ..	—	5
P65/69		Set of 5	.. ..	—	20

These stamps were not on sale in unused condition, but were affixed to parcels and cancelled by postal officials. Cancelled stamps were sold to the public at the Shanghai post office.

1948–49. *Various stamps of China surch as T 3, with two to four characters in lower line denoting value.*

(a) *Martyrs issue of 1932–34*

65	60	$2 on 2½ c. claret (510)	..	5	5

(b) *Third Sun Yat-sen issue of 1938–41*

66	72	$20 on 2 c. olive-green (B) (463)		5	5

(c) *Fifth Sun Yat-sen issue, Central Trust, of 1942–43*

67	82	$10 on $3 yellow (639) (1949)	..	5	5
68		$50 on 50 c. grey-green	..	15	5
69		$800 on $4 brown (640) (1949)	..	30	10

(d) *Third Sun Yat-sen issue redrawn of 1942–44*

70	72	$500 on $30 purple (671) (1949)		15	8

(e) *Sixth Sun Yat-sen issue of 1944–46*

71	89	$20 on $3 scarlet (1949)	..	12	5
72		$100 on $20 rose-red	..	5	5

(f) *Seventh Sun Yat-sen issue of 1945–46*

73	94	$100 on $20 scarlet (1949)	..	5·00	4·50
74		$200 on $10 blue (R.) (1949)	..	10	5
75		$5,000 on $10 blue	..	20	5
76		$10,000 on $20 scarlet	..	50	30

(g) *Eighth Sun Yat-sen issue of 1945–46*

77	102	$5 on $40 orange (1949)	..	5	5

(h) *Ninth Sun Yat-sen issue of 1946–47*

78	107	$5 on $50 slate-violet (R.)	..	5	5
79		$5 on $70 red-orange	..	5	5
80		$5 on $100 crimson	..	5	5
81		$600 on $100 crimson (1949)	..	50	20

(i) *Eleventh Sun Yat-sen issue of 1947–48*

82	118	$10 on $150 indigo (R.)	..	5	8
83		$20 on $250 slate-violet (R.)	..	5	5
84		$200,000 on $3,000 blue (R.) (1949)	..	5·00	3·75

(j) *Twelfth Sun Yat-sen issue of 1948*

85	136	$1,000 on $20,000 rose-carm (1949)		30	10

1949 (5 Aug). *POSTAGE DUE. Nos. 55, 57 and 60 hand-stamped with Type D 3 (="Postage Due"), in violet.*

D86	6	$1,000 on $3 green	.. ..	45	45
D87		$3,000 on $3 green	.. ..	60	60
D88		$5,000 yellow-orange	.. ..	90	90

Two slightly different handstamps were used.

1949 (16 Oct). *Nos. 1211/4B of China optd with five Chinese characters, similar to T 3.*

86	146	(–) Brown-orange	.. ..	12	5
87	147	(–) Pale blue-green	.. ..	15	15
88	148	(–) Magenta	.. ..	12	15
89	149	(–) Carmine	.. ..	12	15
86/89		Set of 4	.. ..	45	45

Sold at the rate for the day for Ordinary Postage, Air Mail, Express Delivery and Registration, respectively.

In November 1949, Chiang Kai-shek moved his Government to Taiwan just before his complete loss of the mainland of China.

E. CHINESE NATIONALIST REPUBLIC
(Republic of China)

100 Cents=1 Silver Yuan

After Chiang Kai-shek and his government retired to Taiwan, with Taipeh as their capital, they continued to claim that they were the legitimate government of all China, and Taiwan was styled the Republic of China. They kept the seats allotted to China in the Assembly and on the Security Council of the United Nations until 25 October 1971.

Silver Yuan Surcharges

10	**10**	**20**	★★★	**20**
(8) Small figures	**(9)** Large figures		**(10)**	

1949 (1 Dec). *Stamps of Taiwan Province surch.*

(a) *No. 48 surch with T 8, by Central Eng and Ptg Works, Taipeh*

90	6	10 c. on $50 purple	.. ..	50	40

(b) *Nos. 63/4 surch as T 9 (figures at right), by Dah Tung Ptg Co, Taiwan*

91	6	2 c. on $30,000 indigo (V.)	..	50	40
92		10 c. on $40,000 purple	..	75	50

1949 (12 Dec)–**50.** *No. 35 of North-Eastern Provinces, surch as T 10, by Central Eng and Ptg Works.*

93	5	2 c. on $44 crimson (G.)	..	15	15
94		5 c. on $44 crimson (V.)	..	25	20
95		5 c. on $44 crimson (P.) (23.1.50)		15	15
96		10 c. on $44 crimson (V.) (23.1.50)		30	12
97		20 c. on $44 crimson (Bk.) (1.1.50)		55	20
98		30 c. on $44 crimson (B.) (1.1.50)		80	40
99		50 c. on $44 crimson (B.) (1.1.50)		2·50	1·00
93/99		Set of 7	.. ..	4·00	1·90

1 00	**20**
(11)	**(D 4)**

1950 (1 Jan). *Flying Geese type of China, without indication of value, surch as T* **11** *by Central Engraving and Printing Works.*

100	**169**	$1 on (–) blue-green (Bk.) ..	.. 1·40	25
101		$2 on (–) blue-green (R.) ..	.. 2·50	80
102		$5 on (–) blue-green (V.) ..	.. 10·00	2·75
103		$10 on (–) blue-green (Br.) ..	.. 27·00	6·50
104		$20 on (–) blue-green (B.) ..	.. 50·00	25·00
100/104		*Set of 5*	.. 80·00	32·00

The $1 exists in two settings, 10 mm or 12 mm across Chinese characters.

On 1 September 1950, a further printing of No. 101 was issued, overprinted by Dah Tung Printing Co. In the original printing the top left (value) character has a dot above the first horizontal stroke whilst in the Dah Tung printing the dot appears to the left, forming a straight line. Also the bottom left character in the original printing has the upper right-hand corner rounded, whereas this is sharp and square in the Dah Tung printing.

1950 (26 Jan). *POSTAGE DUE. No. 49 surch "Postage Due" in Chinese characters and new value as Type D* **4**, *by Central Eng and Ptg Works.*

D105	**6**	4 c. on $100 blue (Br.) ..	.. 50	50
D106		10 c. on $100 blue (C.) ..	.. 25	25
D107		20 c. on $100 blue (Bk.) ..	.. 40	40
D108		40 c. on $100 blue (R.) ..	.. 1·10	1·40
D109		$1 on $100 blue (B.) ..	.. 1·50	1·60
D105/109		*Set of 5*	.. 3·25	3·75

1950 (25 Mar). *Stamps of China surch.*

(a) *As T* **8** *("5" at left), by Central Eng and Ptg Works*

105	**136**	5 c. on $200,000 purple ..	.. 30	12
		a. Surch double ..	.. 1·25	

(b) *As T* **9** *(figures at left), by Dah Tung Ptg Co*

106	**136**	3 c. on $30,000 chocolate..	.. 20	15
107		3 c. on $40,000 blue-green (R.) ..	.. 20	15
108		3 c. on $50,000 slate-blue (R.) ..	.. 25	15
108a	**118**	10 c. on $4,000 grey ..	.. 65	25
109		10 c. on $6,000 bright purple ..	.. 40	20
110	**136**	10 c. on $20,000 rose-carmine ..	.. 65	20
110a		10 c. on $2,000,000 red-orange ..	.. 1·00	30
110b		20 c. on $500,000 mauve ..	.. 1·10	30
110c		20 c. on $1,000,000 claret ..	.. 1·25	50
110d		30 c. on $3,000,000 bistre ..	.. 60	35
110e		50 c. on $5,000,000 ultramarine (R.) ..	.. 1·60	70
105/110e		*Set of 12*	.. 7·00	3·00

GUM. All the following postage stamps to No. 616 were issued without gum *except where otherwise stated.*

12 Koxinga	**13** Peasant and Ballot Box		**(14)**

(Litho Dah Tung Printing Co)

1950. *Roul* 8. (a) *POSTAGE.*

111	**12**	3 c. grey-green (26.9) ..	.. 20	10
112		10 c. yellow-brown (26.9) ..	.. 5	5
113		15 c. orange-yellow (26.9) ..	.. 55	30
114		20 c. apple-green (15.6) ..	.. 5	5
115		30 c. claret (26.9) ..	.. 2·00	1·00
116		40 c. red-orange (26.9) ..	.. 8	5
117		50 c. purple-brown (15.6) ..	.. 12	5
118		80 c. carmine (26.9) ..	.. 40	20
119		$1 violet-blue (26.9)	.. 30	5
120		$1.50 green (26.9) ..	.. 80	25
121		$1.60 light blue (26.9) ..	.. 80	5
122		$2 magenta (26.9) ..	.. 1·00	10
123		$5 turquoise (26.9) ..	.. 4·75	50

(b) *AIR. Additional character each side of head*

124	**12**	60 c. blue (26.9) ..	.. 1·25	50
111/124		*Set of 14*	.. 10·00	2·75

(Des Liao Wei-lin. Recess Central Eng and Ptg Works)

1951 (20 Mar). *Division of Country into Self-governing Districts.* A. *P* 12½ *or* 13. B. *Imperf.*

			A		B	
125	**13**	40 c. carmine ..	20	5	50	50
126		$1 blue ..	1·00	20	1·00	1·00
127		$1.60 purple ..	1·25	20	1·25	1·25
128		$2 yellow-brown ..	1·40	50	1·25	1·25
125/128		*Set of 4*	3·50	85	3·50	3·50
MS128a		102×71 mm. **13** $2				
		blue-green. Imperf ..	..	†	4·00	4·00

1951 (19 July). *Silver Yuan surcharges. Flying Geese type of China, but without indication of value, surch as T* **14**, *by Central Eng and Ptg Works.*

129	**169**	$5 on (–) blue-green (Br.) ..	.. 3·00	85
130		$10 on (–) blue-green (Bk.) ..	.. 15·00	65
131		$20 on (–) blue-green (R.) ..	.. 20·00	3·00
132		$50 on (–) blue-green (V.) ..	.. 35·00	4·50
129/132		*Set of 4*	.. 65·00	8·00

(D 5)		**15**

1951 (13 Aug). *POSTAGE DUE. No. 524 of China surch as Type D* **5**, *by Central Eng and Ptg Works.*

D133	**60**	40 c. on 40 c. orange (G.) ..	.. 25	15
D134		80 c. on 40 c. orange ..	.. 30	20

(Des Shen Sho. Eng Pao Liang-yu. Recess Bank of Taiwan First Printing Plant)

1952 (1 Jan). *Land Tax Reduction.*

			A. P 14		B. Imp	
133	**15**	20 c. orange ..	25	10	50	50
134		40 c. blackish green ..	25	15	70	70
135		$1 brown ..	1·25	70	95	95
136		$1.40, blue ..	90	45	1·00	1·00
137		$2 grey ..	4·00	3·50	1·60	1·60
138		$5 carmine-red ..	4·50	1·10	2·50	2·50
133/138		*Set of 6* ..	10·00	5·50	6·50	6·50

16 President and Rejoicing Crowds		**(17)**

(Des Liao Wei-lin. Eng Pao Liang-yu. Recess: flag typo. Bank of Taiwan First Printing Plant)

1952 (1 Mar). *Second Anniv of Re-election of President Chiang Kai-shek. Flag in red and blue.*

			A. P 14		B. Imp	
139	**16**	40 c. carmine-red ..	5	5	50	30
140		$1 deep green ..	50	10	70	50
141		$1.60, orange-brn ..	1·25	15	1·00	80
142		$2 blue ..	1·70	1·00	1·50	1·50
143		$5 purple-brown ..	1·50	45	2·25	1·50
139/143		*Set of 5* ..	4·50	1·50	5·00	4·00

1952 (1 Aug). *Stamps of China, Nos. 1345/6 and 1348/9 surch with T* **17**, *by Central Eng and Ptg Works.*

144	**145**	3 c. on 4 c. dull green ..	.. 20	10
145		3 c. on 10 c. deep lilac ..	.. 20	10
146		3 c. on 20 c. pale blue ..	.. 20	10
147		3 c. on 50 c. brown ..	.. 20	10
144/147		*Set of 4*	.. 70	35

(18)

(D 6)

(19)

1952 (8 Dec). *Flying Geese type of China, but without value, surch as T* **18**, *by Central Eng and Ptg Works.*

148	**169**	$10 on (–) blue-green (B.)	..	..	4·00	1·00
149		$20 on (–) blue-green (R.)	..		8·00	2·25
†50		$50 on (–) blue-green (Bk.)	..	..	40·00	40·00

(Litho (Nos. D151, D153) or recess (D152, D154) Dah Tung. Litho (D155) Dah Yeh)

1953 (1 Feb). *POSTAGE DUE. Revenue stamps as T* **143** *of China, surch as Type D* **6**, *by Central Eng and Ptg Wks.*

D151	10 c. on $50 blue (R.)	..	15	5
D152	20 c. on $100 olive (Br.)	..	15	5
D153	40 c. on $20 red-brown (Bk.)	..	15	5
D154	80 c. on $500 grey-brown (B.)		40	5
D155	100 c. on $30 mauve (G.)	..	30	12
D151/155	*Set of 5*	..	1·00	25

PRINTERS. All the following issues were printed by Central Engraving and Printing Works, Taipeh, *unless otherwise stated.*

(Recess: flag typo)

1953 (1 Mar). *Third Anniv of Re-election of President Chiang Kai-shek. As T* **16** *but re-engraved, with eleven characters in scroll at foot. Flag in red and blue.*

				A. P 12½		B. Imp	
151	**16**	10 c. orange-red	..	15	5	60	35
152		20 c. green	..	20	5	60	35
153		40 c. carmine	..	15	5	80	45
154		$1.40, blue	..	65	12	1·25	70
155		$2 sepia	..	1·10	20	2·00	90
156		$5 deep purple	..	3·00	70	3·00	2·25
151/156	*Set of 6*	..	4·75	70	7·50	4·50

1953–54. *Surch as T* **19** *(different ornament at foot for each value).*

157	**12**	3 c. on $1 violet-blue (R.) (25.5.53)	..	10	5
158		10 c. on 15 c. orange-yell (G.) (1.2.54)	15	5
159		10 c. on 30 c. claret (B.) (16.7.53)	..	15	5
160		20 c. on $1.60 light blue (13.6.53)	..	15	5
157/160	*Set of 4*	..	..	50	15

20 Doctor, Nurses and Patients

21 President Chiang Kai-shek

1953 (1 July). *Establishment of Anti-Tuberculosis Association. Litho. On paper with network in colours shown in italics. P* 12½.

161	**20**	40 c. red and brown/*stone*	..	..	60	8
162		$1.60, red & pale blue/*turquoise*	..	2·25	12
163		$2 red and emerald/*yellow*	..	1·00	15
164		$5 red and red-orange/*flesh*		3·50	50
161/164	*Set of 4*	..	..	..	6·50	75

1953 (31 Oct). *Recess. P* 12½.

165	**21**	10 c. sepia	..	5	5
166		20 c. deep reddish purple	..	5	5
167		40 c. green	..	5	5
168		50 c. bright reddish purple	..	5	5
169		80 c. yellow-brown	..	25	10
170		$1 olive-green	..	8	5
171		$1.40, blue	..	15	5
172		$1.60, carmine	..	50	5

173	**21**	$1.70, bright green	..	15	10
174		$2 brown	..	20	5
175		$3 deep blue	..	.:	2·00	25
176		$4 turquoise	..	60	12
177		$5 orange-red	..	65	12
178		$10 deep bluish green	..	1·50	25
179		$20 brown-purple	..	2·75	50
165/179	*Set of 15*	..	8·00	1·50

Imperforate stamps of this issue are from souvenir booklets.

22 Silo Bridge over R. Cho-Shui-Chi

23 Sapling, Tree and Plantation

24 Runner

(Eng Pao Liang-yu. Recess)

1954 (28 Jan). *Completion of Silo Bridge. T* **22** *and similar horiz design. Various frames. P* 12½.

180	**22**	40 c. orange-red	..	..	30	8
181		— $1.60, deep ultramarine	..	1·75	15
182	**22**	$3.60, brownish black	..	1·75	25
183		— $5 deep magenta	..	..	2·50	50
180/183	*Set of 4*	..	..	5·50	90

Design:—$1.60, $5, Silo Bridge.
The note below No. 179 also applies to Nos. 180/3.

(Eng Pao Liang-yu. Recess)

1954 (12 Mar)–**55.** *Afforestation Campaign. T* **23** *and similar vert design. P* 12½.

184		40 c. deep blue-green	..	1·00	5
185		$10 reddish violet	..	2·50	40
186		$20 scarlet (1.4.55)	..	1·25	20
187		$50 blue (1.4.55)	..	3·00	65
184/187	*Set of 4*	..	..	7·00	1·10

Designs:—$10, Tree plantation and houses; $20, Planting seeding; $50, Map of Taiwan and tree.

(Eng Pao Liang-yu. Recess)

1954 (29 Mar). *Youth Day. P* 12½.

188	**24**	40 c. deep blue	..	1·60	45
189		$5 carmine	..	..	4·50	1·00

25 'Plane over City Gate, Taipeh

26 Refugees crossing Pontoon Bridge

27 Junk and Bridge

(Des Chin Yu-chang. Recess)

1954. *AIR. 15th Anniv of Air Force Day. T* **25** *and similar horiz designs. P* 12.

190		$1 brown (1.9)	..	30	8
191		$1.60, brown-black (14.8)	..	20	5
192		$5 turquoise-blue (1.9)	..	40	8

Designs:—$1.60, Three jet fighters over Chung Shang Bridge, Taipeh; $5, Doves over Chi Kan Lu (Fort Zeelandia) in Tainan City.

(Des Y. S. Lin. Eng Pao Liang-yu. Recess)

1954 (1 Oct). *Relief Fund for Chinese Refugees from North Vietnam. P* 12.

193	**26**	40 c. + 10 c. deep blue	..	70	15
194		$1.60 + 40 c. purple	..	2·25	40
195		$5 + $1 scarlet	..	7·00	3·50

1954 (21 Oct). *Second Anniv of Overseas Chinese League. Recess. P* 12.

196	**27**	40 c. red-orange	..	25	5
197		$5 deep blue	..	..	85	25

28 "Chainbreaker" (29)

1955 (23 Jan). *Freedom Day. T **28** and similar vert designs. Recess. P 12.*
198 40 c. blue-green 10 5
199 $1 blackish olive .. .. 1·00 30
200 $1.60, carmine-red 80 25
Designs:—$1 Soldier holding torch and flag; $1.60 Hand holding torch and figures "1.23".

1955 (18 Feb). *Surch as T **29**.*
201 **12** 3 c. on $1 violet-blue (Br.) 5 5
202 20 c. on 40 c. red-orange (G.).. .. 5 5

31 Pres. Chiang Kai-shek and (32)
Sun Yat-sen Memorial
Building

(Des Chin-Yu-ch'ang. Eng Li Ping-chien and Chen Lien-huei. Recess)

1955 (20 May). *First Anniv of President Chiang Kai-shek's Second Re-election. P 12.*
203 **31** 20 c. brown-olive 8 5
204 40 c. deep blue-green 15 5
205 $2 carmine.. .. .. 20 5
206 $7 deep ultramarine 50 15
203/206 *Set of 4* 85 25
MS206a 147 × 104 mm. Nos. 203/6. Imperf .. 1·00 1·00
This miniature sheet also exists with the outer frame inverted. This can be distinguished by the two arrows in the filigree work which are at centre top in the normal stamp and at bottom in the variety.

1955 (1 Aug). *Surch with T **32**, in blue.*
207 **12** 10 c. on 80 c. carmine 10 5
208 10 c. on $1.50 green 8 5

33 Air Force Badge (34)

(Des Liao Wei-lin and Hsi Teh-chin. Eng Li Ping-chien. Recess)

1955 (3 Sept). *Armed Forces Day. P 12.*
209 **33** 40 c. deep blue 10 5
210 $2 red 65 15
211 $7 deep blue-green 65 15
MS211a 148 × 105 mm. Nos. 209/11. Imperf 2·25 1·90

1955 (16 Sept). *Surch with T **34**, in purple.*
212 **12** 20 c. on 40 c. red-orange 10 5
213 20 c. on 50 c. purple-brown 10 5
214 20 c. on 60 c. blue 15 5

35 Flags of U.N. and Taiwan 36 President Chiang
Kai-shek

(Des Liao Wei-lin. Eng Pao Liang-yu. Recess)

1955 (24 Oct). *Tenth Anniv of United Nations. P 12.*
215 **35** 40 c. deep blue 15 5
216 $2 carmine-red 60 12
217 $7 slate-green 60 20

(Photo Govt Ptg Works, Tokyo)

1955 (31 Oct). *69th Birthday of President. With gum. P 13½.*
218 **36** 40 c. bistre-brown, dp bl & rose-red 5 5
219 $2 dp bl, dp grey-grn & rose-red .. 20 10
220 $7 dull green, sepia and rose-red .. 45 15
MS220a 148 × 105 mm. Nos. 218/20. Imperf.
No gum 80 80

37 Sun Yat-sen's (38) 39 Old and
Birthplace Modern Postal
Transport

(Des Chin Yu-ch'ang. Eng Li Ping-chien. Recess)

1955 (12 Nov). *Ninetieth Birth Anniv (1956) of Dr. Sun Yat-sen. P 12.*
221 **37** 40 c. blue 5 5
222 $2 red-brown 25 10
223 $7 carmine 35 15

1956 (10 Feb). *No. 1211B of China surch with T **38**.*
224 **146** 20 c. on (–) brown-orange (G.) .. 5 5

(Des Liao Wei-lin. Eng Pao Liang-yu. Recess)

1956 (20 Mar). *60th Anniv of Postal Service. Wmk Wavy Lines. P 12.*
225 **39** 40 c. carmine-red 5 5
226 $1 blue-black 10 5
227 $1.60, deep brown 12 5
228 $2 deep myrtle-green 15 5
225/228 *Set of 4* 35 15
MS228a Two sheets each 149 × 103 mm. No.
228 in red and in crimson. Imperf. Pair 2·00 1·50

40 Children at Play (41)

(Des P'i Ta-ch'un. Eng Li Ping-chien. Recess)

1956 (4 Apr). *Children's Day. P 12.*
229 **40** 40 c. bright emerald 5 5
230 $1.60, blue 12 5
231 $2 carmine-red 15 5

1956 (25 Apr). *Nos. 1214A/B of China surch with T **41**.*
A. P 12½ B. Roul
232 **148** 3 c. on (–) magenta .. 5 5 5 5

42 Earliest and Latest Locomotives   **D 7**   **43** President Chiang Kai-shek

(Des Liao Wei-lin. Eng Pao Liang-yu. Recess)

1956 (9 June). *75th Anniv of Chinese Railways. Wmk Wavy Lines. P 12.*
233	**42**	40	c. carmine-red	..	5	5
234			$2 deep blue	..	12	5
235			$8 myrtle-green	..	45	15

(Des Tso Teh-wu. Litho)

1956 (1 Sept). *POSTAGE DUE. P 12½.*
D236	D **7**	20	c. magenta and light blue	5	5
D237		40	c. myrtle-green and buff	5	5
D238		80	c. bistre-brown and grey	5	5
D239		$1	blue and pale mauve	5	5
D236/239		*Set of 4*	..	15	15

(Des P'i Ta-ch'un and Tso Te-wa. Photo Harrison)

1956 (31 Oct). *70th Birthday of President Chiang Kai-shek. T 43 and similar portraits. With gum. P 14½×13½ (20 c., 40 c.), 14½ ($1, $1.60) or 13½×14½ ($2, $8).*
236	20	c. orange-red	..	5	5
237	40	c. carmine	..	5	5
238	$1	ultramarine	..	5	5
239	$1.60,	bright purple	..	10	5
240	$2	red-brown	..	15	5
241	$8	deep turquoise-blue	..	45	15
236/241	*Set of 6*		..	75	35

Portraits: As *T 43*—40 c.; (26½×26½ *mm*)—$1, $1.60; (30×21½ *mm*)—$2, $8.

(44)   **(45)**   **46** Telecommunications Symbols

1956 (11 Nov). *No. 1212B of China surch with T 44.*
242	147	3 c. on (–) pale blue-green (R.)	..	5	5

1956 (25 Dec). *No. 1214B of China surch with T 45.*
243	149	10 c. on (–) carmine	..	..	5	5

(Des Liao Wei-lin. Eng Pao Liang-yu. Recess)

1956 (28 Dec). *75th Anniv of Chinese Telegraph Service. Wmk Wavy Lines. P 12.*
244	**46**	40 c. deep violet-blue	..	5	5
245		$1.40, brown-red	..	5	5
246		$1.60, deep bluish green	..	12	5
247		$2 sepia	..	50	8
244/247		*Set of 4*	..	65	20

47 Map of China   **48** Mencius with his Mother

(Des Liao Wei-lin. Eng Chen.Lien-hui. Litho)

1957 (1–20 Mar). *No wmk (Nos. 252/3). Wmk Wavy Lines (others). P 12½.*
248	**47**	3 c. blue (20.3)	..	5	5
249		10 c. violet (20.3)	..	5	5
250		20 c. red-orange	..	5	5
251		40 c. carmine-red	..	5	5
252		$1 brown	..	5	5
253		$1.60, green (20.3)	..	5	5
248/253		*Set of 6*	..	25	25

See also Nos. 268/73.

(Des Liao Wei-lin. Eng Li Ping-chien (40 c.) and Chen Lien-hui ($3). Recess)

1957 (12 May). *Mother's Teaching. T 48 and similar design. P 12.*
254	40	c. deep green	..	5	5
255		$3 reddish brown	..	15	5

Design:—$3, Marshal Yueh Fei with his mother.

49 Chinese Scout Badges and Rosettes   **50** Globe, Radio Mast and Microphone

(Des Chiang Nai-yu. Eng Pao Liang-yu. Recess)

1957 (11 Aug). *50th Anniv of Boy Scout Movement and Birth Centenary of Lord Baden-Powell. P 12.*
256	**49**	40 c. reddish violet	..	5	5
257		$1 myrtle-green	..	8	5
258		$1.60, deep blue	..	15	5

(Des Ch'en Chao-erh. Eng Pao Liang-yu. Recess)

1957 (16 Sept). *30th Anniv of Chinese Broadcasting Service. P 12.*
259	**50**	40 c. orange-red	..	5	5
260		50 c. bright purple	..	5	5
261		$3.50, deep blue	..	12	10

51 Highway Map of Taiwan   **52** Motor-ship *Hai Min* and River-vessel *Kiang Foo*

1957 (25 Oct). *First Anniv of Taiwan Cross-Island Highway Project. Recess. P 12.*
262	**51**	40 c. bluish green	..	5	5
263		$1.40, ultramarine	..	5	5
264		$2 olive-brown	..	8	5

(Des Wen Hsueh-ju. Eng Pao Liang-yu. Recess)

1957 (16 Dec). *85th Anniv of China Merchants' Steam Navigation Co. P 12.*
265	**52**	40 c. deep blue	..	5	5
266		80 c. brown-purple	..	8	5
267		$2.80, orange-red	..	15	8

1957 (25 Dec). *As Nos. 248/53 but typo in two colours. Frames grey-blue, centres given below. No wmk.*
268	**47**	3 c. blue	..	5	5
269		10 c. violet	..	5	5
270		20 c. red-orange	..	5	5
271		40 c. carmine-red	..	5	5
272		$1 orange-brown	..	8	5
273		$1.60, green	..	8	5
268/273		*Set of 6*	..	30	20

53 *Batocera lineolata*
(beetle)

54 *Phalaenopsis amabilis*
(orchid)

(Des Wen Hsueh-ju. Photo Govt Printing Works, Tokyo)

1958 (20 Mar). *Formosan Insects. Vert designs as T* **53**. *Multicoloured. With gum.* P 13 × 13½.

274	10 c. Type **53**	..	5	5
275	40 c. *Agehana maraho* (butterfly)	..	5	5
276	$1 *Attacus atlas* (moth)	..	5	5
277	$1.40, *Erasmia pulchella chinensis* (moth)	..	8	5
278	$1.60, *Propomacrus macleayi* (beetle)		10	5
279	$2 *Papilio memnon agenor* (butterfly)		15	8
274/279	Set of 6	..	40	25

(Des Wen Hsueh-ju. Photo Govt Printing Bureau, Tokyo)

1958 (20 Mar). *Formosan Orchids. Various designs as T* **54**. *With gum.* P 13.

280	20 c. multicoloured	..	5	5
281	40 c. multicoloured	..	5	5
282	$1.40, multicoloured	..	15	5
283	$3 multicoloured	..	20	12
280/283	Set of 4	..	40	20

Orchids: *Vert*—40 c. *Laelia-cattleya;* $1.40, *Cycnoches chlorochilon klotzsch. Horiz*—$3, *Dendrobium phalaenopsis*.

55 W.H.O. Emblem

(Des Wen Hsueh-ju. Eng Pao Liang-yu. Recess)

1958 (28 May). *Tenth Anniv of World Health Organization.* P 12.

284	**55** 40 c. deep blue	..	5	5
285	$1.60, orange-red	..	5	5
286	$2 bright purple	..	5	5

56 Presidental
Mansion, Taipeh

57 Chinese Seal
Character "Yu".

WATERMARKS. From 1961 the impressions of W **57** are so arranged as to give stamps with upright and sideways watermarks in the same sheet.

(Des Wen Hsueh-ju. Eng Yang Lien. Recess)

1958 (20 Sept)–*62. Ordinary or granite paper.* W **57**. P 12.

286a	**56** $5 grey-green (20.7.62)	..	15	5
286b	$5.60, reddish violet (20.7.62)	..	20	5
286c	$6 red-orange (20.7.62)	..	20	5
287	$10 blue-green	..	40	5
288	$20 carmine-red	..	80	5
289	$50 red-brown	..	2·50	25
290	$100 deep blue	..	5·50	55
286a/290	Set of 7	..	8·50	90

58 Ploughman

59 Pres. Chiang Kai-shek
reviewing Troops

(Des Cheng Yueh-po. Eng Pao Liang-yu. Recess)

1958 (1 Oct). *Tenth Anniv of Joint Commission on Chinese Rural Reconstruction.* P 12.

291	**58** 20 c. emerald-green	..	5	5
292	40 c. black	..	5	5
293	$1.40, bright purple	..	5	5
294	$3 bright blue	..	10	5
291/294	Set of 4	..	20	12

(Des Wen Hsueh-ju. Photo Govt Ptg Works, Tokyo)

1958 (31 Oct). *72nd Birthday of Pres. Chiang Kai-shek and National Day Review. With gum.* P 13½.

295	**59** 40 c. multicoloured	..	5	5

60 U.N.E.S.C.O. Headquarters,
Paris

61 Flame of
Freedom encircling
Globe

(Des Wen Hsueh-ju. Eng Pao Liang-yu. Recess)

1958 (3 Nov). *Inauguration of U.N.E.S.C.O. Headquarters Building, Paris.* P 12.

296	**60** 20 c. deep blue	..	5	5
297	40 c. blue-green	..	5	5
298	$1.40, orange-red	..	5	5
299	$3 bright purple	..	12	8
296/299	Set of 4	..	20	15

(Des Wen Hsueh-ju. Eng Pao Liang-yu. Recess)

1958 (10 Dec). *Tenth Anniv of Declaration of Human Rights.* P 11½ × 12.

300	**61** 40 c. deep green	..	5	5
301	60 c. sepia	..	5	5
302	$1 carmine-red	..	5	5
303	$3 ultramarine	..	12	5
300/303	Set of 4	..	20	15

0.20

角貳

(62)

350

(63)

1958 (11 Dec). *No. 1211B of China surch with T* **62**, *and No. 192 of Taiwan surch with T* **63**. (a) POSTAGE.

304	**146** 20 c. on (–) brown-orange (G.)	..	5	5

(b) AIR

305	$3.50 on $5 turquoise-blue (R.)	..	15	8

64 The Constitution	65 Chü Kwang Tower, Quemoy

(Des Wen Hsueh-ju. Eng Pao Liang-yu. Recess)

1958 (25 Dec). *Tenth Anniv of Constitution. P* 12.
306 **64** 40 c. deep green 5 5
307 50 c. deep purple 5 5
308 $1.40, carmine 8 5
309 $3.50, deep blue 15 10
306/309 *Set of 4* 30 20

PRINTERS. The Central Engraving and Printing Works, Taipeh, was renamed China Engraving and Printing Works in 1959. All the following issues were printed there, *unless otherwise stated.*

(Des Wen Hsueh-ju. Litho)

1959 (26 Feb)–**60.** W **57.** P 12.
310 **65** 3 c. orange (27.4.59) 5 5
311 5 c. yellow-olive (1.8.60) 5 5
312 10 c. reddish lilac (27.4.59) 5 5
313 20 c. deep ultramarine 5 5
314 40 c. brown (27.4.59).. .. .. 5 5
315 50 c. blue-green (5.11.59) 5 5
316 $1 rose-red 5 5
317 $1.40, light green 8 5
318 $2 bronze-green 12 5
319 $2.80, rose-magenta (5.11.59) .. 15 5
320 $3 deep slate (27.4.59) 15 5
310/320 *Set of 11* 75 30
See also Nos. 367/82g.

66 Seagull	67 I.L.O. Emblem and Headquarters, Geneva

(Des Wen Hsueh-ju. Photo Govt Ptg Works, Tokyo)

1959 (20 Mar). *AIR. With gum. P* 13½.
321 **66** $8 black, blue and green 20 8

(Des Wen Hsueh-ju. Eng Pao Liang-yu. Recess)

1959 (15 June). *40th Anniv of the International Labour Organization.* W **57.** P 12.
322 **67** 40 c. blue 5 5
323 $1.60, sepia 5 5
324 $3 blue-green 10 5
325 $5 vermilion 15 8
322/325 *Set of 4* 30 20

68 Scout Bugler	69 Inscribed Rock, Mt. Tai-wu, Quemoy

(Des Wen Hsueh-ju. Eng Pao Liang-yu. Recess)

1959 (8 July). *Tenth World Scout Jamboree, Manila. P* 12.
326 **68** 40 c. carmine-red 5 5
327 50 c. deep blue 5 5
328 $5 deep green 20 8

(Des Wen Hsueh-ju (T **69**), Tsai Cheng-lun (others). Eng Pao Liang-yu. Recess)

1959 (3 Sept). *Defence of Quemoy* (*Kinmen*) *and Matsu Islands,* 1958. T **69** *and similar design. P* 12.
329 **69** 40 c. brown 5 5
330 – $1.40, ultramarine 5 5
331 – $2 bluish green 8 5
332 **69** $3 deep blue 10 5
329/332 *Set of 4* 25 15
Design: 41×23½ mm.—$1.40, $2, Map of Taiwan, Quemoy and Matsu Islands.

70	71 National Science Hall

(Des Wen Hsueh-ju. Eng Pao Liang-yu. Recess)

1959 (4 Oct). *International Correspondence Week. P* 12.
333 **70** 40 c. deep ultramarine 5 5
334 $1 crimson 5 5
335 $2 blackish brown 5 5
336 $3.50, orange-red 12 8
333/336 *Set of 4* 25 15

(Des Liu Pao-chin. Photo Govt Ptg Works, Tokyo)

1959 (12 Nov). *Inauguration of Taiwan National Science Hall.* T **71** *and similar vert design. With gum. P* 13½.
337 40 c. multicoloured 5 5
338 $3 multicoloured 12 5
Design:—$3 Different view of Science Hall.

72 Confederation Emblem

(Des Lin Shen-yung. Eng Pao Liang-yu. Recess)

1959 (7 Dec). *Tenth Anniv of International Confederation of Free Trade Unions* (*ICFTU*). *P* 12.
339 **72** 40 c. multicoloured 5 5
340 $1.60, purple 5 5
341 $3 orange 12 5

73 Sun Yat-sen and Abraham Lincoln	74 "Bomb Burst" by "Thunder Tiger" Aerobatic Squadron

(Des Wen Hsueh-ju. Photo Govt Ptg Works, Tokyo)

1959 (25 Dec). *150th Birth Anniv of Lincoln. With gum.* P 12 or 13½.

342	**73**	40 c. multicoloured	..	..	..	5	5
343		$3 multicoloured	..	..	..	12	5

(Des Wen Hsueh-ju. Photo Govt Ptg Works, Tokyo)

1960 (29 Feb). *AIR. Chinese Air Force Commemoration. T* **74** *and similar designs. With gum.* P 13.

344	$1 black, red, ultramarine and light blue	12	5
345	$2 multicoloured	..	..	10	5
346	$5 multicoloured	..	..	30	10

Designs: *Horiz*—(Various aerobatics) $2 Loop; $5 Diamond formation flying over jet fighter.

75 Night Delivery

76 "Uprooted Tree"

(Des Yang Kia-chen. Eng Pao Liang-yu ($1.40). Des Wen Hsueh-ju. Eng Chen Lien-hui ($1.60). Recess)

1960 (20 Mar). *Introduction of "Prompt Delivery" and "Postal Launch" Services. T* **75** *and similar horiz design.* P 12.

347	$1.40, deep maroon	..	..	..	5	5
348	$1.60, bright blue (Postal launch)	..	8	5

(Des Wen Hsueh-ju. Photo Govt Ptg Works, Tokyo)

1960 (7 Apr). *World Refugee Year. With gum.* P 12½×13.

349	**76**	40 c. lt green, lt red-brown and black	5	5
350		$3 dp bluish green, red-orge & blk	12	5

77 Cross-Island Highway

WELCOME
U.S. PRESIDENT
DWIGHT D. EISENHOWER
1960
(78)

(Des Wen Hsueh-ju. Eng Pao Liang-yu. Recess)

1960 (9 May). *Inauguration of Taiwan Cross-Island Highway. T* **77** *and similar design.* P 12.

351	**77**	40 c. blue-green	..	..	..	5	5
352		$1 deep blue	..	..	..	8	5
353		$2 maroon	..	..	..	8	5
354	**77**	$3 bistre-brown	..	..	12	5
351/354		Set of 4	..	..	30	15

MS354*a* 144×103 mm. Nos. 352 and 354.
W **57**. Imperf. .. .. 1·60 1·60
Design: *Vert*—$1, $2 Tunnels on Highway.

1960 (18 June). *President Eisenhower's Visit to Taiwan. Nos.* 331/2 *optd as T* **78**, *in red.*

355	–	$2 bluish green	..	..	..	8	5
356	**69**	$3 deep blue	..	..	..	15	8

79 Winged Tape-reel   **80** "Flowers and Birds" (after Hsiao Yung)

(Des Wen Hsueh-ju. Eng Li Ping-ch'en. Recess)

1960 (27 June). *Phonopost (tape-recordings) Service.* P 12.

357	**79**	$2 orange-red	..	..	..	8	5

(Photo Govt Ptg Wks, Tokyo)

1960 (4 Aug). *Ancient Chinese Paintings from Palace Museum Collection (1st series). T* **80** *and similar designs. With gum.* P 13½.

358	$1 multicoloured	..	..	..	15	5
359	$1.40, multicoloured	..	..	15	5
360	$1.60, multicoloured	..	..	20	5
361	$2 multicoloured	..	..	30	10
358/361	Set of 4	..	..	60	20

Paintings: *Horiz*—$1 "Two Riders" (after Wei Yen); $1.40, "Two Horses and Groom" (after Han Kan); $2, "A Pair of Mandarin Ducks in a Rivulet" (after Monk Hui Ch'ung).
See also Nos. 451/4, 577/80 and 716/19.

81 Youth Corps Flag and Summer Activities   **82** "Forest Cultivation"   **83** Chü Kwang Tower, Quemoy

(Des Kin Yu-ch'ang. Eng Pao Liang-yu. Recess)

1960 (20 Aug). *Youth Summer Activities. T* **81** *and similar design.* P 12.

362	50 c. blackish green	..	..	..	5	5
363	$3 chestnut	..	..	..	12	8

Design: *Horiz*—$3 Youth Corps Flag and other summer activities.

(Des Yen Ki-shih. Photo Govt Ptg Wks, Tokyo)

1960 (29 Aug). *Fifth World Forestry Congress, Seattle. T* **82** *and similar vert designs. Multicoloured. With gum.* P 13½×13.

364	$1 Type **82**	..	..	5	5
365	$2 "Forest Protection" (trees)	..	..	15	5
366	$3 "Lumber Production" (cable-railway)	15	5

MS366*a* 100×145 mm. Nos. 364/6 forming a composite design. Imperf. No gum 30 30

1960 (5 Oct)–**64**. *Litho.* W **57**. P 12½.

(a) Plain wove paper (1960–62)

367	**83**	3 c. red-brown (15.11.60) ..	..	5	5
368		40 c. violet ..	..	..	5	5
369		50 c. brown-orange (28.1.61)	..	5	5
370		60 c. red-purple	..	..	5	5
371		80 c. dull green	..	..	5	5
372		$1 grey-green (28.1.61)	..	..	8	5
373		$1.20, yellow-olive (24.12.60)	..	5	5

374	83	$1.50, dull ultramarine (24.12.60)		5	5
375		$2 cerise (28.1.61)	.. ..	8	5
376		$2.50, pale blue	..	8	5
377		$3 blue-green (24.12.60) ..		8	5
378		$3.20, purple-brown	..	20	5
379		$3.60, ultramarine (28.1.61)	..	15	5
380		$4.50, vermilion (15.11.60)	..	25	5

(b) Granite paper (1962–64)

381	83	3 c. red-brown (20.2.62)	..	5	5
382	10	c. light emerald (15.12.63)	..	10	5
382a	40	c. violet (20.2.62)	..	5	5
382b	80	c. dull green (20.3.62)	..	5	5
382c		$1 grey-green (23.1.63) ..	..	20	5
382d		$2 cerise (1.12.62)	..	20	5
382e		$3.20, purple-brown (25.1.64)	..	30	5
382f		$4 turquoise-green (30.6.62)	..	35	5
382g		$4.50, vermilion (1.12.62)	..	20	5
367/382g		Set of 16	..	1·50	60

84 Diving

85 Bronze Wine Vase (Shang Dynasty)

(Des Wen Hsueh-ju. Photo Govt Ptg Wks, Tokyo)

1960 (25 Oct). *Sports. Vert designs as T **84**. With gum.* P 12½ × 13.

383	50 c. orange-red, yellow & ultramarine	5	5
384	80 c. deep violet, yell and reddish pur ..	5	5
385	$2 black, pale grn, orge-red and yell	8	5
386	$2.50, black and orange	8	5
387	$3 black, red, brown and buff	10	5
388	$3.20, black, yellow-orge, yell & red	12	8
383/388	Set of 6	45	25

Designs:—80 c. Discus throwing; $2 Basketball; $2.50, Football; $3 Hurdling; $3.20, Sprinting.

(Photo Govt Ptg Wks, Tokyo)

1961 (1 Feb–1 May). *Ancient Chinese Art Treasures (1st series).* T **85** *and similar vert designs. With gum.* P 12½ × 13.

389	80 c. purple, indigo, black & yell-olive ..	5	5
390	$1 indigo, ultram & salmon-red (1.5)	5	5
391	$1.20, dp blue, black sepia & yellow	10	5
392	$1.50, sepia, dp blue & mauve (1.5)	10	5
393	$2 red-brown, violet & yell-ol (1.5)	12	5
394	$2.50, brown-black, dp lilac & turq-bl	15	8
389/394	Set of 6	50	25

Designs:—$1, Bronze cauldron (Chou); $1.20, Porcelain vase (Sung); $1.50, Jade perforated tube (Chou); $2, Porcelain jug (Ming); $2.50, Jade flower vase (Ming).
See also Nos. 408/3, 429/34.

86 Farmer and Mechanical Plough

87 Mme. Chiang Kai-shek

(Des Yen Ki-shih. Eng Pao Liang-yu. Recess)

1961 (4 Feb). *Agricultural Census.* P 12.

395	86	80 c. purple	5	5
396		$2 green	8	5
397		$3.20, orange-red	10	5

(Des Yang Kia-chen. Photo Govt Ptg Wks, Tokyo)

1961 (8 Mar). *Tenth Anniv of Chinese Women's Anti-Aggression League. With gum.* P 13.

398	87	80 c. black, red and green ..	5	5
399		$1 black, red and yellow-green	8	5
400		$2 black, red and orange-brown	10	5
401		$3.20, black, red and purple ..	12	10
398/401		Set of 4	30	20

88 Taiwan Lobster

89 Jeme Tien-yao and Locomotive

(Des Chen Hung-wei. Eng Pao Liang-yu. Recess)

1961 (20 Mar). *Mail Order Service.* P 12.

402	88	$3 blackish green	15	5

(Des Liu Chih-yen. Eng Chen Lien-hui and Li Ping-chien. Recess)

1961 (26 Apr). *Birth Centenary of Jeme Tien-yao (railway engineer).* T **89** *and similar design.* P 12.

403	80 c. reddish violet	5	5
404	$2 black	10	5

Design: *Vert*—80 c. As T **89** but locomotive heading right.

90 Pres. Chiang Kai-shek

91 Convair 880-M Jetliner ("The Mandarin Jet"), Biplane and Flag

(Des Wen Hsueh-ju. Photo Govt Ptg Wks, Tokyo)

1961 (20 May). *1st Anniv of Chiang Kai-shek's Third Term Inauguration.* T **90** *and similar design. With gum.* P 13½.

405	80 c. multicoloured	5	5
406	$2 multicoloured	12	5
MS406a	139 × 100 mm. Nos. 405/6. Imperf.		
	No gum	20	20

Design: *Horiz*—80 c. Map of China.

(Des Lin Yuan-shen. Photo Govt Ptg Wks, Tokyo)

1961 (1 July). *40th Anniv of Chinese Civil Air Service. With gum.* P 13.

407	91	$10 multicoloured	40	12

1961 (15 Aug–15 Sept). *Ancient Chinese Art Treasures (2nd series). Various designs as T **85**. With gum.* P 13.

408	80 c. blue, yellow, black and carmine ..	5	5
409	$1 indigo, brown and bistre ..	12	5
410	$1.50, deep blue and salmon ..	15	8
411	$2 red, black, and pale blue (15.9)	15	5
412	$4 blue, sepia and rose-red (15.9)	40	5
413	$4.50, chestnut, deep brown & light blue (15.9) ..	35	15
408/413	Set of 6	1·10	35

Designs: *Vert*—80 c. Palace perfumer (Ching); $1, Corn vase (Warring States); $2, Jade tankard (Sung). *Horiz*—$1.50, Bronze bowl (Chou); $4, Porcelain bowl (Southern Sung); $4.50, Jade chimera (Han).

92 Sun Yat-sen and Chiang Kai-shek

93 Lotus Lake

(D 8)

97 Postal Segregating, Facing and Cancelling Machine

(Des Wen Hsueh-ju and Liu Chih-yen. Photo Govt Ptg Wks, Tokyo)

1961 (10 Oct). *Fiftieth National Day. T 92 and similar design. With gum.* P 13.
414	80 c. brown, blue and grey	..	8	5
415	$5 blue, red, brown and grey	..	25	10
MS415a	135×100 mm. Nos. 414/5. Imperf.			
	No gum	.. ..	30	30
	Design: *Horiz*—$5, Map and flag.			

(Des Wu T'ing-piao and Yen Ki-shih. Photo Harrison)

1961 (31 Oct). *Taiwan Scenery. T 93 and similar designs. Multicoloured. With gum.* P 13½ × 14½ (vert) or 14½ × 13½ (horiz).
416	80 c. Pitan (Green Lake) (vert)	..	5	5
417	$1 Type 93	.. ..	5	5
418	$2 Sun-Moon Lake	.. ..	8	5
419	$3.20, Wulai Waterfall (vert)	..	20	10
416/419	Set of 4	.. ..	35	20

94 Steel Furnace

95 Atomic Reactor, National Tsing Hwa University

96 Telegraph Wires and Micro-wave Reflector Pylons

(Photo Courvoisier)

1961 (14 Nov). *Taiwan Industries. T 94 and similar designs. With gum.* P 11½.
420	80 c. indigo, brown and blue	..	5	5
421	$1.50, multicoloured	..	10	8
422	$2.50, multicoloured	..	12	8
423	$3.20, indigo, ochre and blue	..	15	10
420/423	Set of 4	..	35	20
	Designs: *Vert*—80 c. Oil Refinery; $2.50, Aluminium manufacture. *Horiz*—$3.20, Fertilizer plant.			

(Des Wen Hsueh-ju. Photo Govt Ptg Wks, Tokyo)

1961 (2 Dec)–**62**. *Inauguration of First Taiwan Atomic Reactor. T 95 and similar designs. With gum.* P 13.
424	95 80 c. multicoloured	..	10	5
425	– $2 multicoloured (20.3.62)	..	30	10
426	– $3.20, multicoloured (20.3.62)	..	35	8
	Designs: *Vert*—$2, Interior of reactor. *Horiz*—$3.20, Reactor building.			

(Des Wen Hsueh-ju. Photo Govt Ptg Wks, Tokyo)

1961 (28 Dec). *80th Anniv of Chinese Telecommunications. T 96 and similar design inscr "1881–1961". With gum.* P 13.
427	80 c. multicoloured	.. ..	8	5
428	$3.20, multicoloured	..	20	8
	Design: *Horiz*—$3.20, Micro-wave parabolic antenna.			

1961 (28 Dec). *POSTAGE DUE. No. 288 surch with Type D 8, in deep blue.*
D429	56 $5 on $20 carmine-red	.. ..	15	5

1962 (15 Jan–15 Feb). *Ancient Chinese Art Treasures (3rd series). Various designs as T 85. With gum.* P 13.
429	80 c. yellow-brown, deep violet and carmine-red (15.2)		5	5
430	$1 deep purple black-brown & lt bl	..	10	5
431	$2.40, grey-blue, sepia & brown-red		15	8
432	$3 bronze-green, pink, black and light blue (15.2)	..	35	15
433	$3.20, rose-red, emerald & blue (15.2)		45	5
434	$3.60, red-brn, dp blue, sepia & yell		50	10
429/434	Set of 6	.. ..	1·40	40
	Designs: *Vert*—80 c. Jade topaz twin wine vessel (Ching); $1, Bronze pouring vase (Warring States); $2.40, Porcelain vase (Ming); $3, Tsun bronze wine vase (Shang); $3.20, Porcelain jar (Ching); $3.60, Jade perforated disc (Han).			

(Des Wen Hsueh-ju. Eng Pao Liang-yu. Recess)

1962 (20 Mar). *Postal Mechanisation. W 57.* P 12.
435	97 80 c. deep maroon	.. ..	5	5

98 Mt. Yu Weather Station

99 Distribution of Milk, and U.N. Emblem

(Des Yen Ki-shih, Wen Hsueh-ju, Tsai Cheng-lun. Eng Chen Lien-hui, Pao Liang-yu, Li Ping-chien. Recess)

1962 (23 Mar–7 May). *World Meteorological Day. T 98 and similar vert design.* P 12.
436	80 c. deep brown	.. ..	5	5
437	$1 deep blue (7.5)	..	15	5
438	$2 deep green	..	20	10
	Design: *$1*, Route-map of typhoon Pamela; $2, Weather balloon passing globe.			

(Des Wen Hsueh-ju. Eng Pao Liang-yu. Recess)

1962 (4 Apr). *15th Anniv of U.N.I.C.E.F.* P 12.
439	99 80 c. carmine-red	..	5	5
440	$3.20, deep green	..	12	8
MS440a	135×100 mm. Nos. 439/40. Imperf	20	20

ALBUM LISTS

Write for our latest lists of albums and accessories.

These will be sent free on request.

100 Campaign Emblem

101 Yü Yu-jen (journalist)

102 Koxinga

(Des Wen Hsueh-ju. Photo Govt Ptg Wks, Tokyo)

1962 (7 Apr). *Malaria Eradication. With gum.* P 13.
441	**100**	80 c. red, light green & deep blue	5	5
442		$3.60, pale brn, turq-grn & dp brn	15	8

(Des Tso Te-wu. Photo Govt Ptg Wks, Tokyo)

1962 (24 Apr). *"Elder Reporter" Yü Yu-jen Commemoration. With gum.* P 13½ × 13.
443	**101**	80 c. deep sepia and pink	5	5

(Des Wen Hsueh-ju. Photo Govt Ptg Wks, Tokyo)

1962 (29 Apr). *300th Anniv of Koxinga's Recovery of Taiwan. With gum.* P 13.
444	**102**	80 c. brown-purple	5	5
445		$2 slate-green	10	5

103 Co-operative Emblem

104 U.N.E.S.C.O. Symbols

(Des Tsai Cheng-lun, Wu T'ing-piao. Eng Pao Liang-yu. Recess)

1962 (7 July). *40th International Co-operative Day.* T **103** *and similar vert design.* W **57**. P 12.
446		80 c. brown	5	5
447		$2 deep lilac (Global handclasp)	15	5

(Des Wen Hsueh-ju. Eng Pao Liang-yu. Recess)

1962 (28 Aug). *U.N.E.S.C.O. Activities Commemoration.* T **104** *and similar designs.* W **57**. P 12.
448		80 c. magenta	5	5
449		$2 lake	12	8
450		$3.20, yellow-green	20	8
Designs: *Horiz*—$2, U.N.E.S.C.O. emblem on open book; $3.20, Emblem linking hemispheres.

105 Emperor T'ai Tsu (Ming Dynasty)

106 "Lions" Emblem and Activities

(Photo Courvoisier)

1962 (20 Sept). *Ancient Chinese Paintings from Palace Museum Collection (2nd series).* T **105** *and similar vert designs showing Emperors. Multicoloured. With gum.* P 11½.
451	80 c. T'ai Tsung (Tang)			10	5
452	$2 T'ai Tsu (Sung)			40	15
453	$3.20, Genghis Khan (Yuan)			60	12
454	$4 Type **105**			50	20
451/454	*Set of 4*			1·40	45

(Des Wen Hsueh-ju. Photo Govt Ptg Wks, Tokyo)

1962 (8 Oct). *45th Anniv of "Lions International". With gum.* P 13½.
455	**106**	80 c. multicoloured	5	5
456		$3.60, multicoloured	20	8
MS456a	100 × 75 mm. Nos. 455/6. Imperf. No gum			25	25

107 Pole-vaulting

108 Young Farmers

109 Liner

(Des Liao Wei-lin. Photo Govt Ptg Wks, Tokyo)

1962 (25 Oct). *Sports.* T **107** *and similar design but horiz. With gum.* P 12½ × 13 (80 c.) or 13 × 12½ ($3.20).
457	80 c. brown, black and blue		5	5
458	$3.20, multicoloured (Rifle-shooting)		12	5

(Des Liang Nai-yu, Yen Ki-shih. Eng Li Ping-chien, Chen Lien-hui. Recess)

1962 (7 Dec). *Tenth Anniv of Chinese 4-H Clubs.* T **108** *and similar vert design.* W **57**. P 12.
459	80 c. carmine-red		5	5
460	$3.20, dp green (4-H Clubs emblem)		12	5
MS460a	135 × 100 mm. Nos. 459/60. Imperf		15	15

(Des Wen Hsueh-ju. Photo Govt Ptg Wks, Tokyo)

1962 (16 Dec). *90th Anniv of China Merchants' Steam Navigation Co.* T **109** *and similar multicoloured design. With gum.* P 13½.
461	80 c. Type **109**		5	5
462	$3.60, Freighter and Pacific route-map (*horiz*)		25	10

110 Harvesting

111 Youth, Girl, Torch, and Martyrs' Monument, Huang Hua Kang

(Des Yen Ki-shih. Photo Govt Ptg Wks, Tokyo)

1963 (21 Mar). *Freedom from Hunger. With gum.* P 13.
463	**110**	$10 multicoloured	45	10

(Des Liao Wei-lin. Eng Chen Lien-hui. Recess)

1963 (29 Mar). *20th Youth Day.* W **57**. P 12.
464	**111**	80 c. reddish violet	5	5
465		$3.20, emerald-green	12	5

112 Swallows and Pagoda   **113** Refugee in Tears   **114** Jetliner over Tropic of Cancer Monument, Kiai

(Des Lin Yuan-shen. Photo Govt Ptg Wks, Tokyo)

1963 (1 Apr). *First Anniv of Asian-Oceanic Postal Union. T 112 and similar designs. With gum. P 13½.*
466   80 c. multicoloured   20   5
467   $2 multicoloured   20   5
468   $6 multicoloured   50   20
Designs: *Horiz*—$2, Seagulls. *Vert*—$6, Crane and pine tree.

(Des Yen Ki-shih. Eng Pao Liang-yu, Li Ping-chien. Recess)

1963 (27 June). *Refugees' Flight from Mainland. T 113 and similar design. W 57. P 12.*
469   80 c. black   10   5
470   $3.20, brown-lake   ..   15   5
Design: *Horiz*—$3.20, Refugees on march.

(Des Lin Yuan-shen. Photo Govt Ptg Wks, Tokyo)

1963 (14 Aug). *AIR. T 114 and similar designs. Multicoloured. With gum. P 13½.*
471   $2.50, Suspension Bridge, Pitan (*horiz*)   8   5
472   $6 Type **114**   15   5
473   $10 Lion-head Mountain, Sinchu   ..   30   10

115 Red Cross Nurse and Emblem   **116** Basketball

(Des Liang Nai-yu, Liu Chih-yen. Photo Govt Ptg Wks, Tokyo)

1963 (1 Sept). *Red Cross Centenary. T 115 and similar horiz design. With gum. P 13×12½.*
474   80 c. red and black   10   5
475   $10 red, grey-green and grey-blue   ..   55   20
Design:—$10, Globe and scroll.

(Des Wu T'ing-piao, Kin Wen-hung. Eng Li Ping-chien, Pao Liang-yu. Recess)

1963 (20 Nov). *Second Asian Basketball Championships, Taipeh. T 116 and similar vert design. W 57. P 12.*
476   80 c. magenta   5   5
477   $2 bluish violet   12   5
Design:—$2, Hands reaching for inscribed ball.

117 Freedom Torch   **118** Country Scene

(Des Wen Hsueh-ju. Eng Pao Liang-yu, Chen Lien-hui. Recess)

1963 (10 Dec). *15th Anniv of Declaration of Human Rights. T 117 and similar design. Recess. W 57. P 12.*
478   80 c. emerald   5   5
479   $3.20, brown-lake   10   5
Design: *Horiz*—$3.20, Human figures and scales of justice.

(Des Liao Wei-lin. Photo Govt Ptg Wks, Tokyo)

1963 (17 Dec). *"Good People, Good Deeds" Campaign. T 118 and similar vert design. Multicoloured. With gum. P 13½×13.*
480   40 c. Type **118**   5   5
481   $4.50, Lighting candle   ..   30   8

119 Dr. Sun Yat-sen and his Book *Three Principles of the People*   **120** Torch of Liberty

(Des Yen Ki-shih. Photo Govt Ptg Wks, Tokyo)

1963 (25 Dec). *Tenth Anniv of Land-to-Tillers Programme. With gum. P 13×13½.*
482   **119** $5 multicoloured   20   8

(Des Wen Hsueh-ju. Eng Pao Liang-yu. Recess)

1964 (23 Jan). *Tenth Anniv of Liberty Day. T 120 and similar design. W 57. P 12.*
483   80 c. red-orange   5   5
484   $3.20, indigo   10   5
Design: *Vert*—$3.20, Hands with broken manacles.

121 Broadleaf Cactus   **122** Wu Chih-hwei   **123** Chü Kwang Tower, Quemoy

(Des Wen Hsueh-ju. Photo Govt Ptg Wks, Tokyo)

1964 (27 Feb). *Formosan Cacti. T 121 and similar vert designs. Multicoloured. With gum. P 13.*
485   80 c. Type **121**   5   5
486   $1 Crab cactus   10   5
487   $3.20, Nopalxochia   15   5
488   $5 Grizzly-Bear cactus   ..   20   5
485/488   *Set of 4*   45   12

(Des Tso Te-wu. Eng Pao Liang-yu. Recess)

1964 (25 Mar). *99th Birth Anniv of Wu Chih-hwei (politician). W 57. P 11½.*
489   **122** 80 c. deep purple-brown   ..   5   5

1964 (29 Mar)–65. *POSTAGE DUE. Nos. 371, 379/80 surch as Type D 8.*
D490   **83** 10 c. on 80 c. dull green   ..   5   5
D491   20 c. on $3.60, ultram (C.) (15.12.65)   5   5
D492   40 c. On $4.50, verm (B.) (15.12.65)   5   5
D490/492   *Set of 3*   8   8

(Des Chen Lien-hui. Litho)

1964 (28 Apr)–**66.** *Granite paper.* W **57.** P 13½×12½.
490	**123**	3	c. slate-purple (1.12.64)	..	5	5
491		5	c. yellow-green (26.6.65)		5	5
492		10	c. yellow-olive (1.12.64) ..		5	5
493		20	c. deep bluish green (26.6.65)	..	5	5
494		40	c. carmine-red	..	5	5
495		50	c. claret (1.12.64)	..	5	5
496		80	c. orange (23.1.65)	..	5	5
497		$1	violet (23.1.65)	..	5	5
498		$1.50,	purple (25.4.66)	..	5	5
499		$2	bright purple	..	5	5
500		$2.50,	bright blue (10.12.65)	..	8	5
501		$3	deep grey	..	8	5
502		$3.20,	light blue	..	8	5
504		$4	green ..	..	8	5
490/504			Set of 14	..	60	35

124 Nurse and Florence Nightingale

125 Weir

(Des Yen Ki-shih, Wu T'ing-piao. Eng Chen Lien-hui, Li Ping-chien. Recess)

1964 (12 May). *Nurses Day.* T **124** *and similar design.* W **57.** P 11½.
506	80 c. bluish violet	.. ..	5	5
507	$4 red	.. ..	20	5

Design: *Horiz*—80 c. Nurses holding candlelight ceremony.

(Des Lin Yuan-shen. Photo Govt Ptg Wks, Tokyo)

1964 (14 June). *Inauguration of Shihmen Reservoir.* T **125** *and similar horiz designs. Multicoloured. With gum.* P **13.**
508	80 c. Type **125**	..	5	5
509	$1 Irrigation channel ..	..	5	5
510	$3.20, Dam and powerhouse	..	12	5
511	$5 Main spillway	..	20	10
508/511	*Set of 4*	..	35	20

126 Ancient Treasure Ship and Modern Freighter

127 Bananas

(Des Wen Hsueh-ju. Eng Pao Liang-yu. Recess)

1964 (11 July). *Navigation Day.* W **57.** P 11½.
512	**126** $2 orange-red	..	5	5
513	$3.60, blue-green	..	12	5

(Des Wen Hsueh-ju. Photo Harrison)

1964 (25 July). *Formosan Fruits.* T **127** *and similar horiz designs. Multicoloured. With gum.* P 14½.
514	80 c. Type **127** ..		5	5
515	$1 Oranges	..	15	10
516	$3.20, Pineapples	..	20	5
517	$4 Water-melons	..	30	15
514/517	*Set of 4*	..	60	30

128 Aircraft, Warships and Artillery

129 Globe and Flags of Taiwan and U.S.A.

(Des Kin Wen-hung. Eng Chen Lien-hui. Recess)

1964 (3 Sept). *Armed Forces Day.* W **57.** P 11½.
518	**128** 80 c. grey-blue	.. ..	5	5
519	$6 brown-purple ..		20	5

(Des Huang Chih-yang. Photo Courvoisier)

1964 (10 Sept). *New York World's Fair* (1st *issue*). T **129** *and similar design. With gum.* P 11½.
520	80 c. multicoloured	.. ..	5	5
521	$5 multicoloured	.. ..	20	8

Design: *Horiz*—$5, Taiwan Pavilion at Fair.
See also Nos. 550/1.

130 Cowman holding Calf

131 Cycling

(Des Kin Wen-hung. Eng Pao Liang-yu. Recess)

1964 (24 Sept). *Animal Protection.* W **57.** P 11½.
522	**130** $2 brown-purple	..	5	5
523	$4 ultramarine	..	15	5

(Des Lin Yuan-shen, Kin Wen-hung. Eng Pao Liang-yu, Chen Lien-hui, Li Ping-chien. Recess)

1964 (10 Oct). *Olympic Games, Tokyo.* T **131** *and similar vert designs.* W **57.** P 12.
524	80 c. ultramarine	.. ..	5	5
525	$1 red	.. ..	5	5
526	$3.20, deep bluish green	..	20	5
527	$10 reddish violet	..	45	25
524/527	*Set of 4*	.. ..	65	30

Designs:—$1, Runner breasting tape; $3.20, Gymnastics; $10, High-jumping.

132 Hsu Kuang-chi (statesman)

133 Factory-bench ("Pharmaceutics")

134 Dr. Sun Yat-sen (founder)

(Des Liu Chih-yen. Eng Pao Liang-yu. Recess)

1964 (8 Nov). *Famous Chinese.* W **57.** P 12.
528	**132** 80 c. deep blue	.. ..	5	5

See also Nos. 558/9, 586/7, 599, 606/9, 610 and 738/40.

(Photo Courvoisier)

1964 (11 Nov). *Taiwan Industries.* T **133** *and similar designs. Multicoloured. With gum.* P 11½.
529	40 c. Type **133**			5	5
530	$1.50, Loom ("Textiles") (*horiz*)		..	15	8
531	$2 Refinery ("Chemicals")		..	10	5
532	$3.60, Cement-mixer ("Cement") (*horiz*)			20	5
529/532	*Set of 4*	..	..	45	20

(Des Yen Ki-shih. Eng Pao Liang-yu. Recess)

1964 (24 Nov). *70th Anniv of Kuomintang.* W **57**. P 12.
533	**134**	80 c. deep green	..	..	5	5
534		$3.60, purple			12	5

135 Mrs. Eleanor Roosevelt and "Human Rights" Emblem

136 Law Code and Scales of Justice

137 Rotary Emblem and Mainspring

(Des Kin Wen-hung. Photo Govt Ptg Wks, Tokyo)

1964 (10 Dec). *16th Anniv of Declaration of Human Rights. With gum.* P 12½×13.
535	**135**	$10 orange-brown and violet	..	25	8

(Des Kin Wen-hung. Eng Liu Yueh-ch'iao. Recess)

1965 (11 Jan). *20th Judicial Day.* W **57**. P 12.
536	**136**	80 c. carmine	..	..	5	5
537		$3.20, olive-green	..	..	10	5

(Des Wen Hsueh-ju. Eng Pao Liang-yu. Recess)

1965 (23 Feb). *60th Anniv of Rotary International.* W **57**. P 12.
538	**137**	$1.50, red	..	..	5	5
539		$2 emerald	..	..	8	5
540		$2.50, blue	..	..	10	5

138 "Double Carp"

139 Mme. Chiang Kai-shek

(Des Liao Wei-lin. Eng Pao Liang-yu. Recess)

1965 (29 Mar). *Granite paper.* W **57**. P 12.
541	**138**	$5 reddish violet	..	..	35	5
542		$5.60, blue	..	..	15	5
543		$6 brown	..	..	15	5
544		$10 magenta	..	..	15	5
545		$20 carmine	..	..	40	5
546		$50 green	..	..	90	25
547		$100 vermilion	..	..	2·00	65
541/547		*Set of 7*	..	..	3·75	1·00

For T **138** redrawn, see Nos. 695/8.

(Des Wu T'ing-piao. Photo Courvoisier)

1965 (17 Apr). *15th Anniv of Chinese Women's Anti-Aggression League. With gum.* P 11½.
548	**139**	$2 multicoloured	..	5	5
549		$6 multicoloured	..	25	10

140 Unisphere and Taiwan Pavilion, N.Y. Fair

(Des Huang Chih-yung. Photo Courvoisier)

1965 (8 May). *New York World's Fair* (2nd issue). T **140** *and similar horiz design. Multicoloured. With gum.* P 11½.
550	$2 Type **140**		..	12	5
551	$10 Peacock and various birds ("100 birds paying tribute to Queen Phoenix")		..	40	10

141 I.T.U. Emblem and Symbols

142 Red Bream

(Des Wen Hsueh-ju. Photo Govt Ptg Wks, Tokyo)

1965 (17 May). *I.T.U. Centenary.* T **141** *and similar multicoloured design. With gum.* P 13½×13 (80 c.) or 13×13½ ($5).
552	80 c. Type **141**		..	5	5
553	$5 I.T.U. emblem and symbols (*vert*)			20	8

(Des Wen Hsueh-ju. Photo Govt Ptg Wks, Tokyo)

1965 (1 July). *Taiwan Fishes.* T **142** *and similar multicoloured designs. With gum.* P 13½×13 ($2) or 13×13½ (others).
554	40 c. Type **142**		..	5	5
555	80 c. White pomfret	..	..	8	5
556	$2 Skipjack (*vert*)	..	..	10	5
557	$4 Moonfish	..	..	15	5
554/557	*Set of 4*	..	..	35	15

(Eng Pao Liang-yu. Recess)

1965 (28 Sept). *Famous Chinese Portraits as* T **132**. W **57**. P 12.
558	$1 carmine (Confucius)	..	..	5	5
559	$3.60, royal blue (Mencius)	..		15	5

143 I.C.Y. Emblem

144 Road Crossing

145 Dr. Sun Yat-sen

(Des Wen Hsueh-ju. Photo Govt Ptg Wks, Tokyo)

1965 (24 Oct). *International Co-operation Year.* T **143** *and similar multicoloured design. With gum.* P 13×13½ ($2) or 13½×13 ($6).
560	$2 Type **143**		..	5	5
561	$6 I.C.Y. emblem (*horiz*)		..	25	12

(Des Lin Yuan-shen. Eng Pao Liang-yu. Recess)

1965 (1 Nov). *Road Safety.* W **57**. P 12.
562	**144**	$1 maroon	..	..	5	5
563		$4 red	..	..	15	5

(Des Yen Ki-shih. Photo Govt Ptg Wks, Tokyo)

1965 (12 Nov). *Birth Centenary of Dr. Sun Yat-sen.* T **145** *and similar multicoloured designs. With gum.* P 13½.
564	$1 Type **145**	5	5
565	$4 As T **145** but with portrait, etc on right	12	5
566	$5 Dr. Sun Yat-sen and flags (*horiz*) ..	25	15

146 Children with Firework   **147** Lien Po, *Marshal and Prime Minister Reconciled*   **148** Pigeon holding Postal Emblem

(Des Wen Hsueh-ju. Photo Govt Ptg Wks, Tokyo)

1965 (1 Dec). *Chinese Folklore* (1*st series*). T **146** *and similar vert design. Multicoloured. With gum.* P 13.
567	$1 Type **146**	15	5
568	$4.50, Dragon dance	15	8

See also Nos. 581/3 and 617.

(Des P'i Ta-ch'un. Photo Courvoisier)

1966 (15 Feb). *Painted Faces of Chinese Opera.* T **147** *and similar vert designs. With gum.* P 11½.
569	$1 multicoloured	25	5
570	$3 multicoloured	12	5
571	$4 multicoloured	20	5
572	$6 multicoloured	25	15
569/572	Set of 4	75	25

Faces (role and opera):—$3, Kuan Yu, *Reunion at Ku City*; $4, Chang Fei, *Long Board Slope*; $6, Buddha, *The Flower-scattering Angel*.

(Des Kin Wen-hung, Yen Ki-shih, Wen Hsueh-ju. Photo Govt Ptg Wks, Tokyo)

1966 (20 Mar). *70th Anniv of Chinese Postal Services.* T **148** *and similar multicoloured designs. With gum.* P 13.
573	$1 Type **148**	8	5
574	$2 Postman by Chu memorial stone (*horiz*)	8	5
575	$3 Postal Museum (*horiz*) ..	10	5
576	$4 "Postman climbing"	15	8
573/576	Set of 4	35	20

149 "Fishing on a Snowy Day" (after artist of the "Five Dynasties")   **150** Flags of Argentine and Chinese Republics

(Photo Govt Ptg Wks, Tokyo)

1966 (20 May). *Ancient Chinese Paintings from Palace Museum Collection* (3*rd series*). T **149** *and similar vert designs. Multicoloured. With gum.* P 13½.
577	$2.50, Type **149**	15	5
578	$3.50, "Calves on the Plain" ..	10	5
579	$4.50, "Snowscape"	10	5
580	$5 "Magpies" (after Lin Ch'un)..	30	8
577/580	Set of 4	55	20

Nos. 578/9 both after Sung artists.

(Des Wen Hsueh-ju. Photo Govt Ptg Wks, Tokyo)

1966. *Chinese Folklore* (2*nd series*). *Designs as* T **146.** *Multicoloured. With gum.* P 13.
581	$2.50, Dragon-boat racing (*horiz*) (23.6)	20	5
582	$4 "Lady Chang O Flying to the Moon" (*horiz*) (29.9) ..	15	5
583	$6 Lion Dance (*vert*) (26.11)	15	5

(Des Kin Wen-hung. Photo Govt Ptg Wks, Tokyo)

1966 (9 July). *150th Anniv of Argentine Republic's Independence. With gum.* P 13½.
584	**150**	$10 multicoloured	25	8

151 Lin Sen   D **9**   **153** Flying Geese

(Des Kin Wen-hung. Eng Pao Liang-yu. Recess)

1966 (1 Aug). *Birth Centenary of Lin Sen* (*statesman*). W **57.** P 12.
585	**151**	$1 sepia	5	5

(Des Wu T'ing-piao. Eng Pao Liang-yu. Recess)

1966 (3 Sept). *Famous Chinese. Portraits as* T **132.** W **57.** P 12.
586	$2.50, blackish brown	5	5
587	$3.50, carmine-red	12	5

Portraits:—$2.50, General Yueh Fei; $3.50, Wen Tien-hsiang (statesman).

(Des Kin Wen-hung. Litho)

1966 (1 Oct)–**73.** *POSTAGE DUE. Granite paper.* W **57.** P 12½.
D588	D **9**	10 c. chocolate and pale lilac ..	5	5
D589		20 c. greenish blue and pale greenish yellow	5	5
D590		50 c. ultramarine & light blue (*with gum*) (4.5.70)	5	5
D591		$1 violet and pale flesh ..	5	5
		a. With gum (11.7.68) ..	5	
D592		$2 deep green and pale blue ..	5	5
		a. With gum (10.1.73) ..	5	
D593		$5 carmine-red and pale buff ..	10	5
D588/593		Set of 6	30	20

(Des Yen Ki-shih. Eng Chen Lien-huei. Recess)

1966 (10 Oct)–**72.** *Granite paper.* W **57.** P 11½.
588	**153**	$3.50, brown		5
		a. With gum (6.6.72) ..		5
589		$4 red (10.12.66)	8	5
		a. With gum (31.8.70) ..	5	
590		$4.50, emerald (10.12.66) ..	8	5
		a. With gum (18.8.71) ..	8	
591		$5 bright purple (10.12.66) ..	10	5
		a. With gum (20.6.70) ..	8	
592		$5.50, yellow-green (15.2.67) ..	10	5
593		$6 new blue (10.12.66)	20	10
		a. With gum (18.8.71) ..	15	
594		$6.50, violet..	12	5
595		$7 black	15	5
		a. With gum (25.6.71) ..	12	
596		$8 cerise (15.2.67)	15	5
		a. With gum (25.6.71) ..	12	
588/596		Set of 9	85	35

HAVE YOU READ THE NOTES AT THE BEGINNING OF THIS CATALOGUE?

These often provide answers to the enquiries we receive.

154 Pres. Chiang
Kai-shek

155 Various Means of
Transport

(Des Yen Ki-shih. Photo Govt Ptg Wks, Tokyo)

1966 (31 Oct). *President Chiang Kai-shek's Re-election for Fourth Term.* T **154** *and similar vert design. Multicoloured. With gum.* P 13.
597	$1 Type **154**	5	5
598	$5 President in uniform	20	8

(Des Yen Ki-shih. Eng Pao Liang-yu. Recess)

1967 (11 Jan). *Famous Chinese. Portrait as* T **132**. *Granite paper.* W **57**. P 12.
599	$1 ultramarine (Tsai Yuan-pei (scholar))	5	5

(Des Yen Ki-shih. Photo Govt Ptg Wks, Tokyo)

1967 (15 Mar). *Development of Taiwan Communications.* T **155** *and similar multicoloured design. With gum.* P 13.
600	$1 Mobile postman and microwave station (*vert*)	5	5
601	$5 Type **155**	12	5

156 Boeing "727"
over Chilin
Pavilion, Grand
Hotel, Taipeh

157 Pres. Chiang
Kai-shek

158 "God of
Happiness"
(woodcarving)

(Des Lin Yuan-shen. Photo Govt Ptg Wks, Tokyo)

1967 (1 Apr). *AIR.* T **156** *and similar vert design. Multicoloured. With gum.* P 13.
602	$5 Type **156**	12	5
603	$8 Boeing "727" over Palace Museum, Taipeh	12	5

(Des Yen Ki-shih. Photo Govt Ptg Wks, Tokyo)

1967 (20 May). *Chiang Kai-shek's Fourth Presidential Term. With gum.* P 13.
604	**157** $1 multicoloured	5	5
605	$4 multicoloured	12	5

(Eng Li Ping-chien, Chen Lien-huei. Recess)

1967 (12 June). *Chinese Poets. Portrait designs as* T **132**. *Granite paper.* W **57**. P 12.
606	$1 black (Chu Yuan)	5	5
607	$2 brown (Li Po)	8	5
608	$2.50, agate (Tu Fu)	8	5
609	$3 blackish olive (Po Chu-i)	10	5
606/609	*Set of 4*	25	15

(Des Yen Ki-shih. Eng Pao Liang-yu. Recess)

1967 (15 July). *Famous Chinese. Portrait as* T **132**. W **57**. P 12.
610	$1 black (Chiu Ching, female revolutionary)	5	5

(Photo Courvoisier)

1967 (12 Aug). *Chinese Handicrafts.* T **158** *and similar vert designs. Multicoloured. With gum.* P 11½.
611	$1 Type **158**	5	5
612	$2.50, Vase and dish	5	5
613	$3 Chinese dolls	8	5
614	$5 Palace lanterns	15	8
611/614	*Set of 4*	30	15

159 "W A C L" on World
Map

160 Formosan Barbet

(Des Yen Ki-shih. Eng Pao Liang-yu. Recess)

1967 (25 Sept). *First World Anti-Communist League Conference, Taipeh. Granite paper.* W **57**. P 12.
615	**159**	$1 vermilion	5	5
616		$5 new blue..	8	5

GUM. All issues from No. 617 are with gum, *unless otherwise stated.*

(Des Wen Hsueh-ju. Photo Govt Ptg Wks, Tokyo)

1967 (10 Oct). *Chinese Folklore* (3rd series). *Stilts Pastime. Design as* T **146**. P 13.
617	$4.50, multicoloured	8	5

Design:—$4.50, "The Fisherman and the Woodcutter" (Chinese play on stilts).

(Des Wen Hsueh-ju. Photo Courvoisier)

1967 (25 Nov). *Taiwan Birds.* T **160** *and similar multicoloured designs.* P 11½.
618	$1 Type **160**	5	5
619	$2 Maroon oriole (*horiz*)	5	5
620	$2.50, Formosan green pigeon (*horiz*) ..	5	5
621	$3 Blue magpie (*horiz*)	8	5
622	$5 Crested serpent-eagle	15	5
623	$8 Mikado long-tailed pheasant (*horiz*) ..	20	10
618/623	*Set of 6*	50	30

161 Chung Hsing
Pagoda

162 Flags and China Park,
Manila

(Photo Govt Ptg Wks, Tokyo)

1967 (10 Dec). *International Tourist Year.* T **161** *and similar multicoloured designs.* P 13.
624	$1 Type **161**	5	5
625	$2.50, Yeh Liu National Park (coastal scene) (*horiz*)..	10	5
626	$4 Statue of Buddha (*horiz*)	12	5
627	$5 National Palace Museum, Taipeh (*horiz*)	15	8
624/627	*Set of 4*	35	20

(Des Yen Ki-shih. Photo Govt Ptg Wks, Tokyo)

1967 (30 Dec). *China–Philippines Friendship Year.* P 13½.
628	**162** $1 multicoloured	5	5
629	$5 multicoloured	12	5

163 Sun
Yat-sen
Building,
Yangmingshan

164 Taroko Gorge

165 Harvesting
Sugar-cane

(Des Wen Hsueh-ju. Litho)

1968 (23 Jan–11 July). *Granite paper.* W **57**. P 13½ × 12½.
630	**163**	5 c. yellow-brown (11.7)		5	5
631		10 c. slate-green (11.7)		5	5
632		50 c. bright purple		5	5
633		$1 red		5	5
634		$1.50, emerald (11.7)		5	5
635		$2 reddish purple (11.7)		5	5
636		$2.50, blue		5	5
637		$3 turquoise-blue (11.7)		8	5
630/637		*Set of 8*		35	35

For T **163** redrawn, see Nos. 791/8.

(Photo Govt Ptg Wks, Tokyo)

1968 (12 Feb). *17th Pacific Area Travel Association Conference, Taipeh.* T **164** and similar horiz design. Multicoloured. P 13.
638	$5 Type **164**		10	5
639	$8 Sun Yat-sen Building, Yangmingshan		15	8

(Des Huang Chih-yung. Photo Govt Ptg Wks, Tokyo)

1968 (1 Mar). *Sugar-cane Technologists Congress, Taiwan.* P 13½ × 13.
640	**165**	$1 multicoloured		5	5
641		$4 multicoloured		12	5

166 Vice-Pres.
Cheng

167 Flying Geese

168 Jade Cabbage
(Ching dynasty)

(Des Yen Ki-shih. Photo Govt Ptg Wks, Tokyo)

1968 (5 Mar). *Third Death Anniv of Vice-President Chen Cheng.* P 13½ × 13.
642	**166**	$1 multicoloured		5	5

(Des Yen Ki-shih. Litho)

1968 (20 Mar). *90th Anniv of Chinese Postage Stamps.* Granite paper. W **57**. P 12.
643	**167**	$1 rose-red		5	5
MS644		75 × 100 mm. **167** $3 turq-grn. Imperf	10	10

(Photo Govt Ptg Wks, Tokyo)

1968 (29 Mar). *Chinese Art Treasures, National Palace Museum (First series).* T **168** and similar designs. Multicoloured. P 13.
645	$1 Type **168**		5	5
646	$1.50, Jade battle-axe (Warring States period)		5	5
647	$2 Lung-ch'uan porcelain flower bowl (Sung dynasty) (*horiz*)		8	5
648	$2.50, Yung Cheng enamelled vase (Ching dynasty)		10	5

649	$4 Agate "fingered" flowerholder (Ching dynasty) (*horiz*)		10	5
650	$5 Sacrificial vessel (Western Chou)		12	5
645/650	*Set of 6*		45	20

See also Nos. 682/7 and 732/7.

169 W.H.O. Emblem
on "20"

170 Sun, Planets, and
"Rainfall"

(Des Wen Hsueh-ju. Eng Li Ping-chien, Pao Liang-yu. Recess)

1968 (7 Apr). *20th Anniv of World Health Organization.* Granite paper. W **57**. P 12.
651	**169**	$1 blue-green		5	5
652		$5 red		8	5

(Des Wen Hsueh-ju. Litho)

1968 (6 June). *International Hydrological Decade.* Granite paper. W **57**. P 12.
653	**170**	$1 deep green and red-orange		5	5
654		$4 new blue and red-orange		8	5

171 "A City of Cathay" (section of hand-scroll painting)

(Photo Govt Ptg Wks, Tokyo)

1968 (18 June). *"A City of Cathay" (Scroll, Palace Museum) (1st series).* T **171** and similar horiz designs. P 13½ (Nos. 655/9) or 13 × 13½ (others).
655	$1 (1) multicoloured		5	5
656	$1 (2) multicoloured		5	5
657	$1 (3) multicoloured		5	5
658	$1 (4) multicoloured		5	5
659	$1 (5) multicoloured		5	5
660	$5 multicoloured		20	10
661	$8 multicoloured		25	15
655/661	*Set of 7*		60	45

Designs: As T **171**—Nos. 655/9 together show panorama of the city ending with the palace. *Larger* (61 × 32 mm)—$5, City wall and gate; $8, Great bridge.

The five $1 stamps were issued together *se-tenant* in horizontal strips, representing the last 11 feet of the 37 foot scroll, which is viewed from right to left as it is unrolled. The stamps may be identified by the numbers given in brackets which correspond to the numbers in the bottom right-hand corners of the stamps.

See also Nos. 699/703.

172 Map and Radio
"Waves"

173 Human Rights
Emblem

(Des Yen Ki-shih, Lin Chao-tung. Litho)

1968 (1 Aug). *40th Anniv of Chinese Broadcasting Service.*
T **172** *and similar design. Granite paper.* W **57**. P 12½.
662　$1 pale grey, ultramarine & greenish bl ... 5　5
663　$4 red and ultramarine ... 8　5
Design: *Vert*—$4, Stereo broadcast "waves".

(Des Wen Hsueh-ju. Litho)

1968 (3 Sept). *Human Rights Year. Granite paper.* W **57**. P 12½.
664　**173**　$1 multicoloured ... 5　5
665　$5 multicoloured ... 10　5

174 Harvesting Rice　　175 Throwing the Javelin

(Des Yen Ki-shih. Litho)

1968 (30 Sept). *Rural Reconstruction. Granite paper.* W **57**. P 12½.
666　**174**　$1 deep brown, yellow-ochre and light greenish yellow ... 5　5
667　$5 deep green, bright grn & lemon ... 10　5

(Des Yen Ki-shih. Photo Govt Ptg Wks, Tokyo)

1968 (12 Oct). *Olympic Games, Mexico. T* **175** *and similar designs. Multicoloured.* P 13.
668　$1 Type **175** ... 5　5
669　$2.50, Weightlifting ... 5　5
670　$5 Pole-vaulting (*horiz*) ... 10　5
671　$8 Hurdling (*horiz*) ... 12　5
668/671　*Set of 4* ... 25　15

176 President Chiang Kai-shek and Main Gate, Whampoa Military Academy

(Des Wen Hsueh-ju, Yen Ki-shih. Photo Courvoisier)

1968 (31 Oct). *"President Chiang Kai-shek's Meritorious Services". T* **176** *and similar horiz designs. Multicoloured.* P 11½.
672　$1 Type **176** ... 5　5
673　$2 Reviewing Northern Expedition Forces ... 5　5
674　$2.50, Suppression of bandits ... 5　5
675　$3.50, Marco Polo Bridge, and Victory Parade, Nanking, 1945 ... 8　5
676　$4 Chinese Constitution ... 8　5
677　$5 National flag ... 12　5
672/677　*Set of 6* ... 40　25
Each stamp bears the portrait of President Chiang Kai-shek as in Type **176**.

177 Cockerel　　178 National Flag

(Des Wen Hsueh-ju. Litho)

1968 (12 Nov). *New Year Greetings. Granite paper.* W **57**. P 12½.
678　**177**　$1 multicoloured ... 10　5
679　$4.50, multicoloured ... 30　8

(Des Huang Chih-yung. Litho)

1968 (25 Dec). *20th Anniv of Chinese Constitution. Granite paper.* W **57**. P 12½.
680　**178**　$1 multicoloured ... 5　5
681　$5 multicoloured ... 10　5

(Photo Govt Ptg Wks, Tokyo)

1969 (15 Jan). *Chinese Art Treasures, National Palace Museum (Second series). Multicoloured designs as T* **168**. P 13.
682　$1 Jade buckle (Ching dynasty) (*horiz*) ... 5　5
683　$1.50, Jade vase (Sung dynasty) (*vert*) ... 5　5
684　$2 Cloisonné enamel teapot (Ching dynasty) (*horiz*) ... 5　5
685　$2.50, Bronze sacrificial vessel (Kuei) (*horiz*) ... 8　5
686　$4 Hsuan-te "heavenly ball" vase (Ming dynasty) (*vert*) ... 10　5
687　$5 "Gourd" vase (Ching dynasty) (*vert*) ... 12　8
682/687　*Set of 6* ... 40　25

GRANITE PAPER. All issues from No. 688 which were produced by the China Engraving and Printing Works are on granite paper, *unless otherwise stated.*

179 Servicemen and Savings Emblem　　180 Ti (flute)

(Des Yen Ki-shih. Eng Pao Liang-yu. Recess)

1969 (1 Feb). *Tenth Anniv of Forces' Savings Services.* W **57**. P 12.
688　**179**　$1 purple-brown ... 5　5
689　$4 blue ... 8　5

(Des Yen Ki-shih. Photo Govt Ptg Wks, Tokyo)

1969 (16 Mar). *Chinese Musical Instruments. T* **180** *and similar horiz designs. Multicoloured.* P 13.
690　$1 Type **180** ... 5　5
691　$2.50, Sheng (pipes) ... 5　5
692　$4 P'i-p'a (lute) ... 10　5
693　$5 Cheng (zither) ... 10　5
690/693　*Set of 4* ... 25　15

181 Chung Shan Building, Mt. Yangmin　　182 "Double Carp"

(Des Yen Ki-shih. Litho)

1969 (29 Mar). *Tenth Kuomintang Congress. Ordinary paper.* P 13½×14.
694　**181**　$1 multicoloured ... 5　5

(Des Huang Chih-yung. Eng Pao Liang-yu. Recess)

1969 (21 Apr). *T* **138** *redrawn as T* **182**. W **57**. P 12.
695　**182**　$10 blue ... 20　5
696　$20 chocolate ... 30　5
697　$50 emerald ... 1·10　25
698　$100 vermilion ... 2·10　60
695/698　*Set of 4* ... 3·25　85

183 "Emigrants with Ox-cart"

(Photo Govt Ptg Wks, Tokyo)

1969 (20 May). *"A City of Cathay" (scroll) (2nd series).* T **183** *and similar horiz designs, showing details from the scroll. Multicoloured.* P 13.

699	$1 "Musicians"	..	..	5	5
700	$1 "Bridal chair"	..	..	5	5
701	$2.50, Type **183**	..	..	8	5
702	$5 "Scroll gallery"	..	..	12	10
703	$8 "Roadside cafe"	..	..	15	10
699/703	*Set of 5*	..	..	40	30

Nos. 699/700 form a composite picture of a bridal procession and were issued *se-tenant* within the sheet.

184 I.L.O. Emblem   185 "Food and Clothing"

(Des Wen Hsueh-ju. Eng Li Ping-chien. Recess)

1969 (15 June). *50th Anniversary of International Labour Organization.* W **57**. P 12.

704	**184**	$1 deep blue	..	5	5
705		$8 carmine-red	..	15	8

(Des Yen Ki-shih. Eng Pao Liang-yu. Recess)

1969 (15 July). *"Model Citizen's Life" Movement.* T **185** *and similar horiz designs. Ordinary paper.* W **57**. P 12.

706	$1 vermilion	..	..	5	5
707	$2.50, blue	..	..	5	5
708	$4 green	..	..	8	5

Designs:—$2.50, "Housekeeping and Road Safety"; $4, "Schooling and Recreation".

**186 Wild Geese over   187 Children and Symbols of
Mountains   Learning**

(Des Yen Ki-shih. Photo Govt Ptg Wks, Tokyo)

1969 (14 Aug). *AIR.* T **186** *and similar multicoloured designs.* P 13.

709	$2.50, Type **186**	..	..	5	5
710	$5 Geese over sea	..	..	10	5
711	$8 Geese over river (*horiz*)	..	15	8

(Des Yen Ki-shih. Eng Pao Liang-yu. Recess)

1969 (1 Sept). *1st Anniv of Nine Year Free Education System.* T **187** *and similar design.* W **57**. P 12.

712	**187**	$1 red	..	5	5
713	–	$2.50, emerald	..	5	5
714	–	$4 deep blue	..	8	5
715	**187**	$5 chocolate	..	10	5
712/715		*Set of 4*	..	25	12

Design: Vert—$2.50, $4, Children and school.

**188 "Flowers and   189 "Charles Mallerin"
Pheasants" (Lu Chih, Ming   Rose
dynasty)**

(Photo Govt Ptg Wks, Tokyo)

1969 (9 Oct). *Ancient Chinese Paintings from Palace Museum Collection (4th series). "Birds and Flowers".* T **188** *and similar vert designs. Multicoloured.* P 13½.

716	$1 Type **188**	..	..	5	5
717	$2.50, "Bamboos and Birds" (Sung dynasty)			5	5
718	$5 "Flowers and Birds" (Sung dynasty)		10	5
719	$8 "Twin Cranes and Flowers" (G. Castiglione, Ching dynasty)		15	10
716/719	*Set of 4*	..	..	30	20

(Des Wen Hsueh-ju. Litho De La Rue)

1969 (31 Oct). *Taiwan Roses.* T **189** *and similar vert designs. Multicoloured.* P 14.

720	$1 Type **189**	..	..	5	5
721	$2.50, "Golden Sceptre"	..	..	5	5
722	$5 "Peace"	..	..	10	5
723	$8 "Josephine Bruce"	..	..	15	10
720/723	*Set of 4*	..	..	30	20

**190 Launching   191 A.P.U. Emblem
Missile**

(Des Yen Ki-shih. Eng Pao Liang-yu. Recess)

1969 (21 Nov). *30th Air Defence Day. Ordinary paper.* W **57**. P 12.

724	**190**	$1 claret	..	5	5

(Des Wen Hsueh-ju. Eng Pao Liang-yu. Recess)

1969 (25 Nov). *5th General Assembly of Asian Parliamentarians' Union, Taipeh. Ordinary paper.* W **57**. P 12.

725	**191**	$1 deep claret	..	5	5
726		$5 green	..	10	5

192 Pekinese Dogs   193 Satellite and Earth Station

(Des Yen Ki-shih. Litho)

1969 (1 Dec). *New Year Greetings. "Year of the Dog".* W **57**. P 12.

727	**192**	50 c. multicoloured	..	5	5
728		$4.50, multicoloured	..	15	5

(Des Wen Hsueh-ju. Photo Govt Ptg Wks, Tokyo)

1969 (28 Dec). *Inauguration of Satellite Earth Station, Yangmingshan. P* 13.

729	**193**	$1 multicoloured	.. .. ..	5	5
730		$5 multicoloured	.. .. ..	10	5
731		$8 multicoloured	.. .. ..	15	8

(Photo Govt Ptg Wks, Tokyo)

1970 (23 Jan). *Chinese Art Treasures, National Palace Museum* (3rd series). *Multicoloured designs as T* **168.** *P* 13.

732	$1 Lacquer vase (Ching dynasty) ..	5	5
733	$1.50, Agate grinding-stone (Ching Dynasty) (*horiz*)	5	5
734	$2 Jade carving (Ching dynasty) (*horiz*)	5	5
735	$2.50, "Shepherd and Ram" jade carving (Han dynasty) (*horiz*) ..	5	5
736	$4 Porcelain jar (Ching dynasty) ..	8	5
737	$5 "Bull" porcelain urn (Northern Sung dynasty)	10	5
732/737	*Set of* 6	35	25

(Des Wu T'ing-piao ($1, $4), Yen Ki-shih ($2.50). Eng Pao Liang-yu. Recess)

1970. *Famous Chinese. Portraits as T* **132.** *W* **57.** *P* 12.

738	$1 carmine (20.2)	5	5
739	$2.50, deep bluish green (17.3).. ..	5	5
740	$4 steel blue (20.2)	8	5

Portraits:—$1, Hsuan Chuang (traveller); $2.50, Hua To (physician); $4, Chu Hsi (philosopher).

194 Taiwan Pavilion and EXPO Emblem   **195** Sun Yat-sen Building, Yangmingshan

(Des Lin Yuan-shen, Liao Wei-lin. Photo Govt Ptg Wks, Tokyo)

1970 (13 Mar). *World Fair "EXPO 70", Osaka, Japan. T* **194** *and similar horiz design. Multicoloured. P* 13.

741	$5 Type **194**	10	5
742	$8 Pavilion encircled by national flags ..	15	8

(Des Wen Hsueh-ju. Photo Govt Ptg Wks, Tokyo)

1970 (20 Mar). *Coil Stamp. P* 13 × *imperf.*

743	**195** $1 carmine-red	5	5

196 Rain-cloud, Palm and Recording Apparatus   **197** Martyrs' Shrine

(Des Yen Ki-shih. Litho)

1970 (23 Mar). *World Meteorological Day. T* **196** *and similar multicoloured design. W* **57.** *P* 13½.

744	$1 Type **196**	5	5
745	$8 "Nimbus 3" satellite (*horiz*) ..	15	8

(Photo Govt Ptg Wks, Tokyo)

1970 (29 Mar). *Revolutionary Martyrs' Shrine. T* **197** *and similar horiz design. Multicoloured. P* 13.

746	$1 Type **197**	5	5
747	$8 Shrine gateway	15	8

198 General Yueh Fei ("Loyalty")   **200** Old Lai-tsu dropping Buckets

199 "Three Horses at Play"

(Photo Govt Ptg Wks, Tokyo)

1970 (4 May). *Chinese Opera. "The Virtues". T* **198** *and similar vert designs, showing opera characters. P* 13½.

748	$1 Type **198**	5	5
749	$2.50, Emperor Shun tortured by stepmother ("Filial Piety") ..	5	5
750	$5 Chin Liang-yu, "The Lady General" ("Chastity")	10	5
751	$8 Kuan Yu and groom ("Fidelity") ..	15	8
748/751	*Set of* 4	30	20

(Photo Govt Ptg Wks, Tokyo)

1970 (18 June). *"One Hundred Horses" (hand-scroll painting by Lang Shih-ning (G. Castiglione)). T* **199** *and similar horiz designs. Multicoloured. P* 13.

752	$1 (1)	5	5
753	$1 (2)	5	5
754	$1 (3)	5	5
755	$1 (4)	5	5
756	$1 (5)	5	5
757	$5 Type **199**	12	5
758	$8 "Groom roping Horses"	15	10
752/758	*Set of* 7	45	30

Nos. 752/6 form a continuous picture of the scroll and were issued in *se-tenant* horiz strips within the sheet.

SE-TENANT STRIPS. The different designs of Nos. 752/6 and later strips can be determined by the Chinese numbers given in brackets at the bottom right-hand corners of the stamps. For key to Chinese numerals see table at the beginning of CHINA.

(Des Liao Wei-lin. Litho)

1970 (10 July). *Chinese Folk-tales* (1st series). *T* **200** *and similar vert designs. Multicoloured. W* **57.** *P* 13½.

759	10 c. Type **200**	5	5
760	10 c. Yien-tsu disguised as a deer ..	5	5
761	10 c. Hwang Hsiang with fan ..	5	5
762	10 c. Wang Shiang fishing	5	5
763	10 c. Chu Hsiu-chang reunited with mother	5	5
764	50 c. Emperor Wen tasting mother's medicine	5	5
765	$1 Lu Chi dropping oranges ..	5	5
766	$1 Yang Hsiang fighting tiger ..	5	5
759/766	*Set of* 8	25	25

See also Nos. 817/24.

201 Chiang Kai-shek's
Moon Message

202 Productivity Symbol

(Des Wen Hsueh-ju. Photo Govt Ptg Wks, Tokyo)

1970 (21 July). *First Man on the Moon. T 201 and similar
multicoloured designs. P 13½.*
767	$1 Type **201**	..	..	5	5
768	$5 "Apollo 11" astronauts (*horiz*)	..	10	5
769	$8 "First step on the Moon"	..	..	15	8

(Des Wen Hsueh-ju. Litho)

1970 (18 Aug). *Asian Productivity Year. W 57. P 13½.*
770	**202**	$1 multicoloured	..	..	5	5
771		$5 multicoloured	..	..	10	5

203 Flags of Taiwan
and United Nations

204 Postal Zone Map

(Des Wen Hsueh-ju. Litho)

1970 (19 Sept). *25th Anniversary of United Nations. W 57.
P 12½.*
772	**203**	$5 multicoloured	..	..	10	5

(Des Liao Wei-lin. Litho)

1970 (8 Oct). *Postal Zone Numbers Campaign. T 204 and
similar multicoloured design. W 57. P 12½.*
773	$1 Type **204**	..	..	5	5
774	$2.50, Postal Zone emblem (*horiz*)	..	5	5

205 "Cultural Activities"
(10th month)

206 "Planned Family"

(Photo Govt Ptg Wks, Tokyo)

1970–71. *"Occupations of the Twelve Months" Hanging
Scrolls. T 205 and similar vert designs. Multicoloured.
P 13.*

(a) "Winter" (21.10.70)
775	$1 Type **205**	..	5	5
776	$2.50, "School Buildings" (11th month)	5	5
777	$5 "Games in the Snow" (12th month)	10	5

(b) "Spring" (14.1.71)
778	$1 "Lantern Festival" (1st month)	..	5	5
779	$2.50, "Apricots in Blossom (2nd month)	..	5	5
780	$5 "Purification Ceremony" (3rd month)	10	5

(c) "Summer" (26.4.71)
781	$1 "Summer Shower" (4th month)	..	5	5
782	$2.50, "Dragon-boat Festival" (5th month)	..	5	5
783	$5 "Lotus Pond" (6th month)	..	10	5

(d) "Autumn" (27.8.71)
784	$1 "Weaver Festival" (7th month)	5	5
785	$2.50, "Moon Festival" (8th month)	5	5
786	$5 "Chrysanthemum Blossom" (9th month)	..	10	5
775/786	*Set of 12*	..	70	40

The month numbers are given by the Chinese characters in
brackets, which follow the face value on the stamps.

(Des Yen Ki-shih. Litho)

1970 (11 Nov). *Family Planning. T 206 and similar multicoloured design. W 57. P 13½.*
787	$1 Type **206**	..	..	5	5
788	$4 "Family excursion" (*vert*)	..	8	5

207 Toy Pig

208 Sun Yat-sen
Building,
Yangmingshan

(Des Yen Ki-shih. Litho)

1970 (1 Dec). *New Year Greetings. "Year of the Boar".
W 57. P 12½.*
789	**207**	50 c. multicoloured	..	..	5	5
790		$4.50, multicoloured	..	8	5

(Des Wen Hsueh-ju. Litho)

1971. *T 163 redrawn as T 208. W 57. P 13½ × 12½.*
791	**208**	5 c. brown (22.2)	..		5	5
792		10 c. slate-green (10.6)	..	5	5
793		50 c. magenta (10.6)	..	5	5
794		$1 vermilion (1.3)	..	5	5
795		$1.50, blue (1.5)	..	5	5
796		$2 reddish purple (1.5)	..	5	5
797		$2.50, bright emerald (10.6)	..	5	5
798		$3 turquoise-blue (1.5)	..	5	5
791/798	*Set of 8*	..	..	25	25

Nos. 791/8 were issued for use with automatic facing and
cancelling equipment, the thick frame being needed to oper-
ate an electronic eye.

209 *Tibia fusus*

210 Savings Book and
Certificate

(Photo De La Rue)

1971 (25 Feb). *Taiwan Shells. T 209 and similar horiz designs. Multicoloured. P 13.*

799	$1 Type **209**	..	..	..	..	5	5
800	$2.50, *Harpeola kurodai*		..	..	5	5
801	$5 *Conus stupa kuroda* ..		..	..	12	5
802	$8 *Entemnotrochus rumphii*		..	..	20	15
799/802	*Set of 4*	..	..	..	..	35	25

(Des Yen Ki-shih. Litho)

1971 (20 Mar). *National Savings Campaign. T 210 and similar horiz design. Multicoloured. W 57. P 13½.*

803	$1 Type **210**	..	..	..	5	5
804	$4 Hand dropping coin into savings bank ..	..	..	..	10	5

211 Chinese greeting
African Farmer

212 White-faced Flying
Squirrel

(Des Yen Ki-shih. Photo Govt Ptg Wks, Tokyo)

1971 (20 May). *10th Anniversary of Sino-African Technical Co-operation Committee. T 211 and similar multicoloured design. P 13.*

805	$1 Type **211**	..	..	..	5	5
806	$8 Rice-growing (*horiz*)..	..	..	20	15

(Des Wen Hsueh-ju. Photo Courvoisier)

1971 (25 June). *Taiwan Animals. T 212 and similar multicoloured designs. P 11½.*

807	$1 Taiwan rock-monkey (*vert*) ..	..	5	5
808	$2 Type **212**	..	..	5	5
809	$3 Chinese pangolin	..	..	8	5
810	$5 Taiwan sika deer	..	..	10	5
807/810	*Set of 4*	..	..	..	25	12

213 Pitcher delivering
Ball

(214)

(Des Wen Hsueh-ju. Photo Govt Ptg Wks, Tokyo)

1971 (29 July). *World Little League Baseball Championships (Pacific Area), Taiwan. T 213 and similar multicoloured designs. P 13.*

811	$1 Type **213**	..	..	..	5	5
812	$2.50, Players at base (*horiz*)	..	..	5	5
813	$4 Striker and catcher	..	..	10	5

1971 (9 Sept). *Victory of "Tainan Giants" in World Little League Baseball Championships, Williamsport (U.S.A.). Nos. 633 and 636/7 optd with T 214.*

814	**163**	$1 red (V.)	..	..	..	5	5
815		$2.50, blue (R.)	..	..	..	5	5
816		$3 turquoise-blue (R.)	..	..	8	5

1971 (22 Sept). *Chinese Folk-tales (2nd series). Vert designs as T 200. Multicoloured. P 13½.*

817	10 c. Yu Hsun and elephant	..	..	5	5
818	10 c. Tsai Hsun with mulberries	..	5	5
819	10 c. Tseng Sun with firewood ..	..	5	5
820	10 c. Kiang Keh and bandits	..	5	5
821	10 c. Tsu Lu with sack of rice	..	5	5
822	50 c. Meng Chung gathering bamboo shoots	..	..	..	5	5
823	$1 Tung Yung and wife	..	..	5	5
824	$1 Tzu Chien shivering with cold	..	5	5
817/824	*Set of 8*	..	..	..	25	25

215 60th Anniversary
Emblem and Flag

216 A.O.P.U. Emblem

(Des Yen Ki-shih. Photo Govt Ptg Wks, Tokyo)

1971 (10 Oct). *60th National Day. T 215 and similar horiz designs. Multicoloured. P 13.*

825	$1 Type **215**	..	..	..	5	5
826	$2.50, National anthem, map and flag ..		5	5
827	$5 Pres. Chiang Kai-shek, constitution and flag	..	..	..	12	5
828	$8 Dr. Sun Yat-sen, "Three Principles" and flag	..	..	..	20	15
825/828	*Set of 4*	..	..	..	35	25

F. NATIONALIST RÉGIME

On 25 October 1971 the Assembly of the United Nations voted to admit the Chinese People's Republic to membership with a permanent seat on the Security Council. Taiwan was expelled from the United Nations.

(Des Wen Hsueh-ju. Litho)

1971 (8 Nov). *Asian-Oceanic Postal Union Executive Committee Session, Taipeh. W 57. P 13½.*

829	**216**	$2.50, multicoloured	..	..	5	5
830		$5 multicoloured	..	..	12	5

217 "White Frost Hawk"

222 Flags of Taiwan and
Jordan

218/221 Squirrels

(Litho De La Rue)

1971 (16 Nov)–**72**. *"Ten Prized Dogs" (paintings on silk by Lang Shih-ning (G. Castiglione). T 217 and similar vert designs. Multicoloured. P 13.*

831	$1 Type 217	5	5
832	$1 "Black Dog with Snow-white Claws" (12.1.72)	5	5
833	$2 "Star-glancing Wolf"	5	5
834	$2 "Yellow Leopard" (12.1.72)	5	5
835	$2.50, "Golden-winged Face"	5	5
836	$2.50, "Flying Magpie" (12.1.72)	5	5
837	$5 "Young Black Dragon"	12	5
838	$5 "Heavenly Lion" (12.1.72)	12	5
839	$8 "Young Grey Dragon"	20	15
840	$8 "Mottle-coated Tiger" (12.1.72)	20	15
831/840	Set of 10	80	50

(Des Wen Hsueh-ju. Litho)

1971 (1 Dec). *New Year Greetings. "Year of the Rat". W 57. P 13 × 12½.*

841	**218** 50 c. multicoloured	5	5
842	**219** 50 c. multicoloured	5	5
843	**220** 50 c. multicoloured	5	5
844	**221** 50 c. multicoloured	5	5
	a. *Se-tenant* block of 4. Nos. 841/4		
845	**218** $4.50, multicoloured	12	5
846	**219** $4.50, multicoloured	12	5
847	**220** $4.50, multicoloured	12	5
848	**221** $4.50, multicoloured	12	5
	a. *Se-tenant* block of 4. Nos. 845/8		
841/848	Set of 8	60	30

Types *218/221* were issued in *se-tenant* blocks of four within the sheet, forming a composite design.

(Des Wen Hsueh-ju. Litho)

1971 (16 Dec). *50th Anniversary of Hashemite Kingdom of Jordan. W 57. P 13½.*

849	**222** $5 multicoloured	12	5

223 Freighter *Hai King*   **224** Downhill Skiing

(Des Wang Kai. Litho)

1971 (16 Dec). *Centenary of China Merchants Steam Navigation Company. T 223 and similar design. W 57. P 12½.*

850	$4 chalky blue, vermilion and emerald	10	5
851	$7 multicoloured	15	8

Design: Vert—$7, Liner on Pacific.

1972 (3 Feb). *Winter Olympic Games, Sapporo, Japan. T 224 and similar horiz designs. Litho. W 57. P 13½.*

852	$1 black, orange-yellow and light blue	5	5
853	$5 black, orange and light green	12	5
854	$8 black, vermilion and pale grey	20	15

Designs:—$5, Cross-country skiing; $8, Giant slalom.

225 Yung Cheng Vase   **226** Doves

1972 (20 Mar). *Chinese Porcelain (1st series). Ching Dynasty. T 225 and similar vert designs. Multicoloured. Photo. P 11½.*

855	$1 Type 225	5	5
856	$2 Kang Hsi jar	5	5
857	$2.50, Yung Cheng jug	5	5
858	$5 Chien Lung vase	12	5
859	$8 Chien Lung jar	20	15
855/859	Set of 5	40	25

See also Nos. 914/18 and 927/31.

1972 (1 Apr). *10th Anniversary of Asian-Oceanic Postal Union. Litho. W 57. P 13½.*

860	**226** $1 black and light blue	5	5
861	$5 black and lavender	12	5

227 "Dignity with Self-Reliance" (Pres. Chiang Kai-shek)   **228** "Mounted Messengers"

1972. *Litho. W 57. P 13 × 12½.*

862	**227** 5 c. red-brown and lemon (24.10)	5	5
863	10 c. new blue and orange (24.10)	5	5
864	50 c. pale lilac and bright purple	5	5
865	$1 red and light blue (20.5)	5	5
866	$1.50, yellow and blue (20.5)	5	5
867	$2 reddish violet, bright purple and orange (20.5)	5	5
868	$2.50, emerald & rosine (24.10)	5	5
869	$5 red & turquoise-green (20.5)	8	5
862/869	Set of 8	40	30

See also No. **MS**901.

1972. *"The Emperor's Procession" (Ming dynasty hand-scrolls). T 228 and similar horiz designs. Multicoloured. Photo. P 13.*

(a) *"The Departure from the Palace"* (14 June)

870	$1 (1)	5	5
871	$1 (2)	5	5
872	$1 (3)	5	5
873	$1 (4)	5	5
874	$1 (5)	5	5
875	$2.50, Type 228	5	5
876	$5 "Guards with Fans"	12	5
877	$8 "Imperial Sedan-chair"	20	15

(b) *"The Return to the Palace"* (12 July)

878	$1 (1)	5	5
879	$1 (2)	5	5
880	$1 (3)	5	5
881	$1 (4)	5	5
882	$1 (5)	5	5

883	$2.50, "City Guard"	..	..	5	5
884	$5 "Mounted Orchestra"	..	..	12	5
885	$8 "Barge Procession" ..	..	..	20	15
870/885	*Set of* 16	..	..	1·10	80

Nos. 870/74 and 878/82 were each issued in *se-tenant* strips within the sheet, forming composite designs depicting "Emperor leaving the Palace" and "Procession by the River", respectively.

229 First Day Covers

(230)

1972 (9 Aug). *Philately Day. T* **229** *and similar designs. Recess. W* **57**. *P* 12.

886	$1 blue ..	..	..	5	5
887	$2.50, emerald ..	..	..	5	5
888	$8 scarlet	..	..	20	15

Designs: *Vert*—$2.50, Magnifying glass and stamps. *Horiz*—$8, Magnifying glass, perforation-gauge and tweezers.

1972 (9 Sept). *Victories by Taiwan in Senior and Little World Baseball Leagues. Nos. 865/7 and 869 optd with T* **230**.

889	**227**	$1 red and light blue (Blk.) ..		5	5
890		$1.50, yellow and blue (R.) ..		5	5
891		$2 reddish vio, brt pur & orge (R.) ..		5	5
892		$3 red and turquoise-green (B.) ..		8	5
889/892		*Set of* 4	..	20	15

231 Emperor Yao

232 Mountaineering

1972 (20 Sept)–73. *Chinese Cultural Heroes. T* **231** *and similar vert portraits. Recess. W* **57**. *P* 12.

893	$3.50, deep blue	..	..	8	5
894	$4 rose-red	..	..	10	5
895	$4.50, reddish violet	..	..	10	5
896	$5 emerald	..	..	12	5
897	$5.50, brown-purple (2.4.73)	..	12	5
898	$6 orange-red (2.4.73)	..	15	8
899	$7 olive-brown (2.4.73) ..	..	15	10
900	$8 indigo (2.4.73)	..	..	20	15
893/900	*Set of* 8	..	..	90	45

Designs:—$4, Emperor Shun; $4.50, Yu the Great; $5, King T'ang; $5.50, King Weng; $6, King Wu; $7, Chou Kung; $8, Confucius.

1972 (24 Oct). *"ROCPEX" Stamp Exhibition, Taipeh. Nos. 867 and 869 in miniature sheet* 71×100 *mm. Litho. W* **57**. *Without gum. Imperf.*

MS901	**227**	$2 reddish vio, brt pur & orge;		
		$3 red and tyrquoise-green	12	12

1972 (31 Oct). *20th Anniversary of China Youth Corps. T* **232** *and similar vert designs. Multicoloured. Photo. P* 11½.

902	$1 Type **232**	..	..	5	5
903	$2.50, Winter sports	..	..	5	5
904	$4 Diving	..	..	10	5
905	$8 Parachuting ..	..	..	20	15
902/905	*Set of* 4	..	..	35	25

233 Microwave Systems and Electronic Sorting Machine

234 "Eyes" and J.C.I. Emblem

1972 (12 Nov). *Improvement of Communications. T* **233** *and similar designs. Recess. W* **57**. *P* 12.

906	$1 vermilion	..	..	5	5
907	$2.50, new blue..	..	..	5	5
908	$5 brown-purple	..	..	12	5

Designs: *Horiz*—$2.50, Jet airliner and container-ship; $5, Modern train and motorway.

1972 (12 Nov). *27th World Congress of Junior Chamber International, Taipeh. Litho. W* **57**. *P* 12½.

909	**234**	$1 multicoloured	..	5	5
910		$5 multicoloured	..	12	5
911		$8 multicoloured ..	..	20	15

235 Cow and Calf

236 "Kicking the Shuttlecock"

1972 (1 Dec). *New Year Greetings. "Year of the Ox". Litho. W* **57**. *P* 12½.

912	**235**	50 c. black and red ..	..	5	5
913		$4.50, brown, red and yellow	..	10	5

(Photo Courvoisier)

1973 (10 Jan). *Chinese Porcelain (2nd series). Ming Dynasty. Vert designs as T* **225**. *Multicoloured P* 11½.

914	$1 Fu vase	..	..	5	5
915	$2 Floral vase	..	..	5	5
916	$2.50, Ku vase	..	..	5	5
917	$5 Hu flask	..	..	12	5
918	$8 Garlic-head vase	..	..	20	15
914/918	*Set of* 5	..	..	40	25

(Photo Courvoisier)

1973 (7 Feb). *Chinese Folklore. T* **236** *and similar multicoloured designs. P* 11½.

919	$1 Type **236**	..	..	5	5
920	$4 "The Fisherman and the Oyster-fairy" (*horiz*)	..	..	10	5
921	$5 "Lady in a Boat" (*horiz*)	..	12	5
922	$8 "The Old Man and the Lady"	..	20	15
919/922	*Set of* 4	..	..	45	25

237 Bamboo Sampan

238 Contractors' Equipment

1973 (9 Mar). *Taiwan Handicrafts. T 237 and similar multi-coloured designs. Photo. P 13 × 14 (horiz) or 14 × 13 (vert).*

923	$1 Type **237**	..	..	5	5
924	$2.50, Marble vase (vert)	..	..	5	5
925	$5 Glass plate	..	..	12	5
926	$8 Aborigine doll (vert) ..	..	..	20	15
923/926	Set of 4	..	..	35	25

(Photo Courvoisier)

1973 (24 Mar). *Chinese Porcelain (3rd series). Ming Dynasty. Multicoloured designs as T 225, but all horiz. P 11½.*

927	$1 Dragon stem-bowl	..	..	5	5
928	$2 Dragon pot	..	..	5	5
929	$2.50, Covered jar with lotus decor	..	5	5
930	$5 Covered jar showing horses	..	12	5
931	$8 "Immortals" bowl	..	..	20	15
927/931	Set of 5	..	..	40	25

1973 (2 Apr). *12th Convention of International Federation of Asian and Western Pacific Contractors Association. T 238 and similar design. Litho. W 57. P 12.*

932	$1 multicoloured	..	5	5
933	$5 new blue & black (Bulldozer) (horiz)	12	5

FOREIGN POST OFFICES IN CHINA

PROPOSED BELGIAN POST OFFICE

In 1908 stamps were prepared for a Belgian consular post office in China, but as the Chinese P.M.G., a Frenchman, had had no application for the establishment of another non-Chinese office, he took diplomatic steps to ensure that it was not opened. The stamps, which were not issued, were Belgium Nos. 99, 101, 103/5 and 106/8, overprinted "CHINE" in black; and also with surcharges in "cents" in two sorts of lettering. Nearly all the existing copies are handstamped "Specimen". All are very rare.

FRENCH POST OFFICES

1894. 100 Centimes=1 Franc
1907. 100 Cents=1 Piastre

A French Post Office was opened by the consular authorities in Shanghai in November 1862 and another at Tientsin on 16 March 1889. Unoverprinted stamps of France were used until 1894. French Post Offices were opened at Chefoo in November 1898; at Peking in December 1900; at Amoy in January 1902; and at Foochow and Ningpo in 1902. A Postal Agency was opened at Hankow in November 1898 and this became a Post Office in October 1902.

All overprints are on stamps of France, the "Tablet", Type X inscribed "INDO-CHINE" or the Type of Indo-China illustrated below.

X "Tablet" Type

6 "Grasset" Type

Chine	25	16 Cents	5
(1)	(2)	(3)	(4)

1894–1903. *Peace and Commerce type optd with T* 1. *All Type (b) except where otherwise stated.*

1 **10**	5 c. deep green/*green* (*b*) (Vm.)	..	15	12
	a. Carmine opt		20	20
2	5 c. yellow-green (*a*) (C.) (1900)		15	12
3	5 c. yellow-green (*b*) (C.) (1900)	..	2·25	1·00
4	10 c. black/*lilac* (*a*) (C.) (1900)	..	1·10	70
5	10 c. black/*lilac* (*b*) (C.) ..		35	25
	a. Vermilion opt		45	20
6	15 c. blue (C.)		30	20
	a. Vermilion opt	..	35	20
7	15 c. blue/*bluish* (C.) (1903)	..	17·00	11·00
8	20 c. red/*green* ..	..	30	20
9	25 c. black/*rose* (C.)	..	30	15
	a. Vermilion opt	..	80	25
10	30 c. cinnamon ..	..	30	20
11	40 c. red/*yellow* (1900) ..		40	30
12	50 c. carmine (*b*)	..	90	45
	a. Pale carmine	..	80	40
13	50 c. carmine (*a*) (1900)	..	1·25	95
14	75 c. brown/*orange* (Vm.)	..	4·50	3·00
	a. Carmine opt		5·50	3·50
15	1 f. olive-green ..	..	70	20
	a. Opt double	..	20·00	
	b. Grey-green	..	70	20
16	2 f. brown/*pale blue* (*a*) (1900)	..	1·75	1·50
17	5 f. lilac/*pale lilac*	..	10·00	4·00
	a. Mauve/*pale lilac* ..	..	6·00	4·00

No. 7 was issued at Tientsin.
The 50 c. (*b*) and 5 f. with carmine overprint exist but were not issued.

1900 (25 Oct). *Provisional for Shanghai. No.* 15 *surch with T* 2.

18 **10**	25 on 1 f. olive-green ..	..	5·50	3·75

1901 (20 Apr). *Provisionals for Peking. No.* 9 *surch as T* 3.

19 **10**	2 c. on 25 c. black/*rose* (R.)	..	80·00	26·00
20	4 c. on 25 c. black/*rose* (R.)	..	75·00	26·00
21	6 c. on 25 c. black/*rose* (R.)	..	90·00	30·00
22	16 c. on 25 c. black/*rose* (R.)	..	24·00	14·00
	a. Surch in black ..	..	—	£500

1901–7. POSTAGE DUE. *Postage Due stamps of France optd with T* 1.

D23 **D 3**	5 c. pale blue (C.) ..	..	20	20
D24	10 c. pale brown (C.)	..	45	35
D25	15 c. pale green (C.) ..		60	30
D26	20 c. olive-green (1907)	..	35	30
D27	30 c. carmine	..	70	50
D28	50 c. dull claret	..	60	45
D23/28	*Set of 6*	..	2·50	1·90

1902 (Oct)–6. *"Blanc"* (11), *"Mouchon"* (14) *and "Merson"* (13) *types of France, inscr* "CHINE". *P* 14×13½.

23 **11**	5 c. yellow-green	..	5	5
	a. Blue-green (1906)	..	5	5
24 **14**	10 c. carmine (3.03)	..	5	5
25	15 c. pale red (3.03)	..	8	5
26	20 c. purple-brown (2.03)	..	30	25
27	25 c. blue (3.03)	..	12	8
28	30 c. mauve (5.03)	..	25	15
29 **13**	40 c. red and pale blue..	..	50	40
30	50 c. brown and lavender	..	50	40
31	1 f. lake and yellow-green	..	90	65
32	2 f. deep lilac and buff	..	2·50	2·40
33	5 f. deep blue and buff	..	6·00	4·25
23/33	*Set of 12*	..	10·00	8·00

All the above are inscribed "POSTE FRANCAISE".

1903 (4 July). *Provisional for Shanghai. No.* 25 *surch with T* 4.

34 **14**	5 on 15 c. pale red (B.) ..	..	1·25	70
	a. Surch inverted ..	..	6·00	5·00

CHINE	CHINE
仙六十	仙六十
(5)	(6)

(Surch at Hanoi)

1902 (Sept). *Type X inscr* "INDO-CHINE" *surch* "CHINE" *and value in Chinese only as in T* 5.

35 **X**	1 c. black/*azure*	..	15	10
36	2 c. brown/*buff*	..	20	15
37	4 c. purple-brown/*grey*	..	20	15
38	5 c. pale green ..	..	25	20
39	10 c. rose-red	..	20	15
40	15 c. grey	..	35	25
41	20 c. red/*green*	..	65	50
42	25 c. black/*rose* ..	..	1·00	70
43	30 c. cinnamon/*drab*	..	1·25	1·10
44	40 c. red/*yellow* ..	..	3·50	2·00
45	50 c. carmine/*rose*	..	3·25	2·25
46	75 c. brown/*orange*	..	3·25	2·25
47	1 f. olive-green/*toned* ..	..	3·25	2·25
48	5 f. mauve/*pale lilac*	..	6·50	5·50
35/48	*Set of 14*	..	22·00	16·00

This issue was in use for a short time at post offices in Canton, Chungking, Hoihow, Mengtsz and Pakhoi. It was replaced by individual sets for each of these places (see Indo-Chinese Post Offices) and in 1904 this issue was put on sale again with revised surcharge as Type 6. (*See* Nos. 49/62.)

A PERCEVOIR	A PERCEVOIR
(D 1)	(D 2)

1903 (Sept). *POSTAGE DUE. Provisional issue handstamped at Peking as Type* D **1**.

(*a*) *Stamps of* 1894–1903

			A. In red		B. In violet	
D49	**10**	5 c. deep green/*green* (No. 1) ..	£500	—		†
D50		5 c. brt yell-grn (*a*) ..	£250	70·00	£250	£110
D51		10 c. black/*lilac* (*a*) ..	£500	£300	£500	£300
D52		15 c. blue ..	£250	55·00	£250	55·00
D53		30 c. cinnamon ..	£140	6·00	£140	6·00

(*b*) *Stamps of* 1902–06

D54	**11**	5 c. yellow-green ..	£110	55·00	£110	55·00
D55	**14**	10 c. carmine ..	60·00	10·00	60·00	10·00
D56		15 c. pale red ..	65·00	12·00	65·00	12·00

The above were for use in Peking and Tientsin.

Two types of handstamp exist. One with the "A" above the space between "C" and "E" and the other with "A" above the second "E".

1903 (13 Oct). *POSTAGE DUE. Handstamped as Type* D **2**.

(*a*) *Stamps of* 1894–1903

			A. In red		B. In violet	
D57	**10**	5 c. deep green/*green* (No. 1) ..	£500	—		†
D58		5 c. brt yell-grn (*a*) ..	£130	24·00	£130	26·00
D59		10 c. black/*lilac* (*a*) ..	£500	£300	£500	£300
D60		15 c. blue	£100	8·00	£100	8·00
D61		30 c. cinnamon ..	35·00	8·00	35·00	8·00

(*b*) *Stamps of* 1902–06

D62	**11**	5 c. yellow-green ..	90·00	25·00	90·00	25·00
D63	**14**	10 c. carmine ..	25·00	3·50	25·00	3·50
D64		15 c. pale red ..	55·00	3·50	55·00	3·50

There are two types of handstamp. The first a rubber stamp with an open "C" and the second a leather stamp with an almost closed "C".

(Surch at Hanoi)

1904. *Type* X *inscr* "INDO-CHINE" *surch* "CHINE" *and value in Chinese only as in T* **6**.

49	X	1 c. black/*azure*	12	10
50		2 c. brown/*buff*	55	25
51		4 c. purple-brown/*grey*	12	12
52		5 c. pale green	15	12
53		10 c. rose-red	55	35
54		20 c. red/*green*	50	45
55		25 c. black/*rose*	65	55
56		25 c. blue	30	25
57		30 c. cinnamon/*drab*	30	25
58		40 c. red/*yellow*	1·90	1·60
59		50 c. brown/*azure*	50	50
60		75 c. brown/*orange*	2·10	1·75
61		1 f. olive-green/*toned*	2·40	1·90
62		5 f. mauve/*pale lilac*	8·00	7·00
49/62		*Set of* 14	16·00	14·00

A variety exists on all the values in which the letter "C" of "CHINE" is slightly larger than the normal type.

Stamps with inverted surcharges or with surcharge incomplete in this and the following issue are of clandestine origin.

Two types of 15 c.: (I) as Type **6**; (II) with Chinese characters above "CHINE". Type II are from a different printing and occur on the same sheet with Type I.

1904–05. *T* **6** *of Indo-China surch as in T* **6**.

63	**6**	1 c. olive-green	5	5
64		2 c. claret/*yellow*	8	8
65		4 c. purple-brown/*grey*	£110	75·00
66		5 c. deep green	10	10
67		10 c. rose	15	15
68		15 c. brown/*azure* (I)	10	10
69		15 c. brown/*azure* (II)	15	15
70		20 c. red/*green*	75	75
71		25 c. blue	20	20
72		40 c. black/*greyish*	20	20
73		1 f. pale olive-green	25·00	20·00
74		2 f. brown/*yellow*	1·50	1·50
75		10 f. red/*green*	15·00	15·00
63/75		*Set of* 13	£130	£100

The variety mentioned after No. 62 may be found on all values.

(7)

(8)

1907. *Stamps of* 1902–06 *surch as T* **7**.

76	**11**	2 c. on 5 c. yellow-green	5	5
		a. *Blue-green*	5	5
77	**14**	4 c. on 10 c. carmine	5	5
78		6 c. on 15 c. pale red	8	8
79		8 c. on 20 c. purple-brown	15	15
		a. "8" inverted	1·90	1·90
80		10 c. on 25 c. blue	5	5
81	**13**	20 c. on 50 c. brown and lavender ..	15	10
		a. Surch treble	22·00	22·00
82		40 c. on 1 f. lake and yellow-green ..	1·25	1·00
83		2 pi. on 5 f. deep blue and buff ..	1·40	1·10
		a. Surch double	£110	75·00
76/83		*Set of* 9	3·00	2·40

1911–21. *As last but surch as T* **8**.

84	**11**	2 c. on 5 c. blue-green	5	5
85	**14**	4 c. on 10 c. carmine	8	5
86		6 c. on 15 c. orange (1915)	12	8
87		8 c. on 20 c. purple-brown	8	5
88		10 c. on 25 c. blue (1921)	8	8
89		20 c. on 50 c. blue (1921)	3·00	2·75
90	**13**	40 c. on 1 f. lake and yellow	15	12
91		$2 on 5 f. deep blue and buff (1921)	15·00	13·00
84/91		*Set of* 8	17·00	15·00

1911. *POSTAGE DUE. Postage Due stamps of France surch as T* **8**.

D92	D **3**	2 c. on 5 c. pale blue	15	10
		a. Surch double	7·00	
D93		4 c. on 10 c. brown	15	10
		a. Surch double	7·00	
D94		8 c. on 20 c. olive-green	20	15
		a. Surch double	7·00	
D95		20 c. on 50 c. dull claret	20	15
D92/95		*Set of* 4	60	45

1922 (Dec). *Types of* 1902–06 *in new colours surch with new values as T* **8**. *P* $14\times13\frac{1}{2}$.

92	**11**	1 c. on 5 c. orange	20	15
93	**14**	2 c. on 10 c. green	50	35
94		3 c. on 15 c. orange	70	55
95		4 c. on 20 c. purple-brown	1·10	70
96		5 c. on 25 c. purple	30	25
97		6 c. on 30 c. red	1·00	80
98		10 c. on 50 c. blue	1·25	90
99	**13**	20 c. on 1 f. lake and yellow-green ..	2·50	1·90
100		40 c. on 2 f. red and blue-green ..	2·50	1·90
101		1 pi. on 5 f. blue and buff	13·00	13·00
92/101		*Set of* 10	21·00	19·00

1922. *POSTAGE DUE. As Nos.* D92/5 *but surch different values as T* **8**.

D102	D **3**	1 c. on 5 c. pale blue	4·50	4·00
D103		2 c. on 10 c. brown	7·50	5·50
D104		4 c. on 20 c. olive-green	7·50	5·50
D105		10 c. on 50 c. dull claret	7·50	5·50

The French post offices in China were closed down on 31 December 1922.

GERMAN POST OFFICES

1898. 100 Pfennige=1 Mark
1905. 100 Cents=1 Dollar

An Imperial German Postal Agency was opened in the Consulate at Shanghai on 16 August 1886. Branch offices were opened at Tientsin and Chefoo in October 1889 and on 1 June 1892 respectively. Tientsin became a Postal Agency (with its own canceller) on 1 April 1893 and both Tientsin and Chefoo became full Post Offices on 1 January 1900. German Post Offices were opened later at Amoy, Canton, Foochow, Hankow, Ichang, Nanking, Peking, Swatow and Chinkiang. Stamps of Germany were used till 1898.

ERRORS. Errors such as double and inverted overprints or surcharges were never issued but come from waste sheets which later leaked out of the printers.

(1)

(2)

1898. *Stamps of Germany, 1889–90, optd "China".*

(a) Overprint sloping as T 1 (48°) (Mar–June)

1	8	3 pf. grey-brown	..	..	18·00	£900
		a. Bistre-brown (June)		..	35·00	
2		5 pf. green	..	..	1·50	1·50
3	9	10 pf. carmine	..	..	2·00	1·00
4		20 pf. ultramarine	..	..	1·75	90
5		25 pf. orange (May)	..	..	6·50	10·00
6		50 pf. chocolate ..	..	..	3·00	1·25

(b) Overprint sloping as T 2 (56°) (Dec)

7	8	3 pf. grey-brown	..	..	35	50
		a. Bistre-brown	..	..	75	1·00
		b. Red-brown	..	..	5·00	6·00
8		5 pf. green	..	..	30	30
9	9	10 pf. carmine	..	..	70	70
10		20 pf. ultramarine	..	..	2·00	2·75
11		25 pf. orange	..	..	3·00	4·00
12		50 pf. chocolate ..	..	..	1·50	1·00
7/12		Set of 6 ..	..	..	7·00	8·50

5 pf (3)   **China** (4)

1900. *Foochow provisional. Handstamped with T 3.*

13	9	5 pf. on 10 pf. carmine (No. 3)	..		70·00	80·00
14		5 pf. on 10 pf. carmine (No. 9)	..		70·00	80·00

The first printing of 8 July comprised 100 of No. 13 and 1400 of No. 14 and there was a second printing on 7 November consisting of 2500 of No. 13. It follows therefore that copies of No. 13 showing dated postmarks prior to November 1900 are very rare.

1900 (24 Nov)**–1901** (Jan). *Tientsin provisionals. Stamps of Germany (inscr "REICHSPOST") handstamped as T 2.*

15	10	3 pf. brown	..	..	65·00	65·00
16		5 pf. green	..	..	32·00	35·00
17		10 pf. carmine	..	..	75·00	65·00
18		20 pf. blue	..	..	95·00	90·00
19	11	30 pf. black and orange/buff	..		£500	£500
20		50 pf. black and purple/buff (24.11.00)		£1800	£1400
21		80 pf. black and carmine/rose	..		£475	£450

The 25 and 40 pf. and 2 and 3 marks are known with this surcharge, but were not issued.

1901 (Jan)**–04.** *Stamps of Germany (inscr "REICHSPOST") optd with T 4, horizontally, (on 3 m. vertically at sides).*

22	10	3 pf. brown	..	..	20	25
23		5 pf. green	..	..	20	15
24		10 pf. carmine	..	..	30	15
25		20 pf. ultramarine	..	..	45	20
26	11	25 pf. black and red/yellow	..		1·50	2·00
27		30 pf. black and orange/buff	..		1·50	1·60
28		40 pf. black and carmine	..		1·50	1·00
29		50 pf. black and purple/buff	..		1·50	1·00
30		80 pf. black and carmine/rose	..		1·75	1·75
31	12	1 m. carmine	..	..	4·00	4·00
32	13	2 m. blue	..	..	3·50	3·25
33	14	3 m. violet-black (R.)	..		5·50	7·50
35	15	5 m. lake and black (I)	..		40·00	55·00
		a. Type II (4.04)	..	..	23·00	50·00

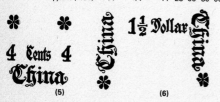

(5)   (6)

1905 (1 Oct). *Chinese currency. Stamps of Germany (inscr "DEUTSCHES REICH") surch as T 5 (cent values) and 6 (dollar values). No wmk.*

36	17	1 c. on 3 pf. brown	..		50	45
37		2 c. on 5 pf. green	..		50	12
38		4 c. on 10 pf. carmine	..		1·10	15
39		10 c. on 20 pf. ultramarine	..		50	30
40		20 c. on 40 pf. black and carmine		2·00	50
41		40 c. on 80 pf. black and carmine/rose		5·50	1·50
42	18	½ d. on 1 m. carmine	..		3·50	3·75
43	20	1 d. on 2 m. blue	..		4·25	4·00
44	21	1½ d. on 3 m. violet-black (R.)	..		2·50	3·75

45	22	2½ d. on 5 m. lake and black	..		17·00	30·00
36/45		Set of 10	..	..	35·00	40·00

1905–13. *As last, but wmk Lozenges.*

46	17	1 c. on 3 pf. brown		10	20
47		2 c. on 5 pf. green (1911)		10	12
48		4 c. on 10 pf. carmine (1911)	..	10	12
49		10 c. on 20 pf. ultramarine (1913)		25	1·50
50		20 c. on 40 pf. black & carmine (1908)	30	40
51		40 c. on 80 pf. black and carmine/rose	25	4·50
52	18	½ d. on 1 m. carmine (1906)	..	65	1·75
53	20	1 d. on 2 m. blue (1907)	..	1·10	5·00
54	21	1½ d. on 3 m. violet-black (1912)		1·50	14·00
55	22	2½ d. on 5 m. lake and black (1906)	..	3·25	11·00
46/55		Set of 10	..	..	6·00	35·00

German Post Offices in China were closed down on 17 March 1917.

INDO-CHINESE POST OFFICES

1901. 100 Centimes=1 Franc

1918. 100 Cents=1 Piastre

The following are surcharged or overprinted on the "Tablet" Type X inscribed "INDO-CHINE" (see under French Post Offices in China) or on other stamps of Indo-China.

A. CANTON

An Indo-Chinese Post Office was opened at Canton, the chief city of Kwangtung province, on 15 June 1901.

CANTON
州廣 (1)   **CANTON**
仙四 (2)   **CANTON**
花銀八厘 (3)

1901 (15 June). *Type X ("Tablet") inscr "INDO-CHINE" optd with T 1 (="CANTON" in French and Chinese), in carmine, at Hanoi.*

1	X	1 c. black/azure	..		10	8
2		2 c. brown/buff	..		10	8
3		4 c. purple-brown/grey	..		15	15
4		5 c. bright yellow-green	..		12	12
5		5 c. green/green	..		40·00	35·00
6		10 c. black/lilac	..		40	35
7		15 c. blue/quadrillé	..		20	20
8		15 c. grey	..		20	20
9		20 c. red/green	..		65	60
10		25 c. black/rose	..		65	60
11		30 c. cinnamon/drab	..		2·00	1·90
12		40 c. red/yellow ..	..		2·00	1·90
13		50 c. carmine/rose	..		3·00	2·50
14		75 c. brown/orange	..		2·00	1·90
15		1 f. olive-green/toned ..		2·50	2·25
16		5 f. mauve/pale lilac	..		24·00	24·00
1/16		Set of 16	..	..	70·00	65·00

1903–04. *As last, but surch as T 2 (Chinese characters represent value), in black, at Hanoi.*

17	X	1 c. black/azure		15	15
18		2 c. brown/buff		20	20
19		4 c. purple-brown/grey	..	20	20
20		5 c. bright yellow-green		15	15
21		10 c. rose-red	..		15	15
22		15 c. grey	..		15	15
23		20 c. red/green	..		1·10	1·10
24		25 c. blue	..		40	30
25		25 c. black/rose	..		45	45
26		30 c. cinnamon/drab	..		1·00	1·00
27		40 c. red/yellow ..	..		3·00	2·40
28		50 c. carmine/rose	..		32·00	26·00
29		50 c. brown/azure (1904)		6·50	6·50
30		75 c. brown/orange	..		7·00	7·00
		a. "INDO-CHINE" in label inverted	..	£5000	
31		1 f. olive-green/toned ..		7·00	7·00
32		5 f. mauve/pale lilac	..		7·00	7·00
17/32		Set of 16	..	..	60·00	55·00

Only two copies are known of No. 30a.

1906 (Oct). *As last and T 6 but surch as T 3, at Hanoi.*

33	**6**	1 c. olive-green (R.)	..	..	8	8
34		2 c. claret/*yellow*	..	..	8	8
35		4 c. magenta/*azure* (R.)	..	..	10	10
36		5 c. deep green (R.)	..	..	10	10
37		10 c. rose	..	..	15	15
38		15 c. brown/*azure*	..	..	15	15
39		20 c. red/*green*	..	..	10	10
40		25 c. blue	..	..	15	15
41		30 c. brown/*cream*	..	..	30	30
42		35 c. black/*yellow* (R.)	..	..	8	8
43		40 c. black/*greyish* (R.)	..	..	35	35
44		50 c. brown/*toned*	..	..	30	25
45	X	75 c. brown/*orange* (R.)..	..	..	4·00	4·00
46	**6**	1 f. pale olive-green	..	..	1·10	85
47		2 f. brown/*yellow* (R.)	..	..	2·25	1·75
48	X	5 f. mauve/*pale lilac*	..	..	8·00	8·00
49	**6**	10 f. red/*green* ..	..	..	8·00	8·00
33/49		*Set of 17*	..	..	22·00	22·00

In the first printing the surcharge was applied at a separate operation; the ink is bright and clear. There were two printings in 1908 in which the overprint and surcharge were applied together and the ink is dull and paler.

CANTON

(4) (5)

1908. *Stamps of Indo-China, 1907, surch as T 4 (1 c. to 50 c.) or 5 (others), in Paris. Centre and value in black.*

50	**7**	1 c. sepia (R.)	..	..	8	8
51		2 c. brown (R.) ..	..	..	8	8
52		4 c. blue (R.)	..	..	12	8
53		5 c. pale green (R.)	..	..	15	8
54		10 c. scarlet (R.)	..	..	15	12
		a. With surch of 5 c. ..	..	..	2·00	2·00
55		15 c. violet (R.) ..	..	..	20	15
56	**8**	20 c. violet (R.) ..	..	..	20	15
57		25 c. blue (R.) ..	..	..	30	15
58		30 c. chocolate (R.)	..	..	55	45
59		35 c. olive-green (R.)	..	..	55	45
60		40 c. brown (R.)	..	..	55	40
61		50 c. carmine (B.)	..	..	45	30
62	**9**	75 c. orange (B.)..	..	..	65	50
63		1 f. lake (B.)	..	..	1·10	1·10
64		2 f. green (R.) ..	..	..	3·25	3·00
65		5 f. blue (R.) ..	..	..	3·50	3·25
66		10 f. violet (R.) ..	..	..	9·00	9·00
50/66		*Set of 17*	..	..	19·00	18·00

No. 54a was surcharged in complete sheets.

(6) (a) Normal (b) Error

1919 (Jan). *As last, further surch in new currency as T 6, in Paris.*

67	**7**	½ c. on 1 c. sepia	..	..	5	5
68		½ c. on 2 c. brown	..	..	5	5
69		1½ c. on 4 c. blue (R.)	..	..	10	10
70		2 c. on 5 c. pale green ..	..	..	10	10
71		4 c. on 10 c. scarlet (B.) (*a*)	..	..	5	5
		a. "4" with closed top	..	..	1·25	1·25
		b. Chinese "2" for "4" (*b*)	..	..	1·50	1·50
72		6 c. on 15 c. violet	..	..	10	8
73	**8**	8 c. on 20 c. violet	..	..	15	12
74		10 c. on 25 c. blue	..	..	15	10
75		12 c. on 30 c. chocolate ..	..	..	12	10
		a. "12 CENTS" double	..	..	9·00	9·00
76		14 c. on 35 c. olive-green	..	..	5	5
		a. "4" with closed top	..	..	50	50
77		16 c. on 40 c. brown	..	..	12	8
78		20 c. on 50 c. carmine (B.)	..	..	12	8

79	**9**	30 c. on 75 c. orange (B.)	..	..	12	8
		a. "30 CENTS" double	..	..	40·00	40·00
80		40 c. on 1 f. lake (B.)	..	..	85	30
81		80 c. on 2 f. green (R.) ..	..	..	60	35
82		2 pi. on 5 f. blue (R.) ..	..	..	80	80
83		4 pi. on 10 f. violet (R.)..	..	..	85	85
67/83		*Set of 17*	..	..	4·00	3·50

This office was closed down on 31 December 1922.

B. CHUNGKING

An Indo-Chinese Post Office was opened at Chungking, the chief city of Szechwan province, on 7 February 1902.

Stamps of Indo-China, 1892–1902, overprinted "TCHONG-KING" only, in small capitals, in red or black, were sold at Chungking and used for franking letters. They were not, however, officially authorised.

Tch'ong K'ing

TCHONGKING

四之五仙   花銀八厘

(1) (2)

1903–04. *Type X ("Tablet") inscr "INDO-CHINE" surch as T 1, at Hanoi.*

1	X	1 c. black/*azure*	..	..	20	20
2		2 c. brown/*buff*	..	..	15	15
3		4 c. purple-brown/*grey*	..	..	15	15
4		5 c. pale green ..	..	..	15	15
5		10 c. rose-red	..	..	15	15
6		15 c. grey	..	..	12	12
7		20 c. red/*green* ..	..	..	15	15
8		25 c. blue	..	..	3·50	3·50
9		25 c. black/*rose* ..	..	..	15	15
10		30 c. cinnamon/*drab*	..	..	15	15
11		40 c. red/*yellow*..	..	..	3·00	3·00
12		50 c. carmine/*rose*	..	..	22·00	22·00
13		50 c. brown/*azure* (1904)	..	..	14·00	14·00
14		75 c. brown/*orange*	..	..	3·00	3·00
15		1 f. olive-green/*toned* ..	..	..	3·00	3·00
16		5 f. mauve/*pale lilac*	..	..	7·00	7·00
1/16		*Set of 16*	..	..	50·00	50·00

1906 (Oct). *Stamps of Indo-China surch as T 2, at Hanoi.*

17	**6**	1 c. olive-green (R.)	..	..	15	15
18		2 c. claret/*yellow*	..	..	15	15
19		4 c. magenta/*azure* (R.)	..	..	15	15
20		5 c. deep green (R.)	..	..	15	15
21		10 c. rose	..	..	15	15
22		15 c. brown/*azure*	..	..	30	20
23		20 c. red/*green* ..	..	..	15	15
24		25 c. blue	..	..	20	20
25		30 c. brown/*cream*	..	..	20	20
26		35 c. black/*yellow* (R.)	..	..	20	20
27		40 c. black/*greyish* (R.)	..	..	30	30
28		50 c. brown/*toned*	..	..	40	40
29	X	75 c. brown/*orange* (R.)..	..	..	1·40	1·40
30	**6**	1 f. pale olive-green	..	..	1·75	1·75
31		2 f. brown/*yellow* (R.) ..	..	..	1·75	1·75
32	X	5 f. mauve/*pale lilac*	..	..	10·00	10·00
33	**6**	10 f. red/*green* ..	..	..	13·00	13·00
17/33		*Set of 17*	..	..	27·00	27·00

The note about printings under No. 49 of Canton also applies here.

貳 圓

TCHONGKING

壹 苑   **TCHONGKING**

(3) (4)

1908. Stamps of Indo-China, 1907, surch as *T 3* (1 *c.* to 50 *c.*) or *4* (others), in Paris. Centre and value in black.

34	7	1 c. sepia (R.)			5	5
35		2 c. brown (R.)			5	5
36		4 c. blue (R.)			5	5
37		5 c. pale green (R.)			12	12
38		10 c. scarlet (B.)			15	15
39		15 c. violet (R.)			15	15
40	8	20 c. violet (R.)			15	15
41		25 c. blue (R.)			15	15
42		30 c. chocolate (R.)			15	15
43		35 c. olive-green (R.)			40	40
44		40 c. brown (R.)			90	90
45		50 c. carmine (B.)			70	70
46	9	75 c. orange (B.)			40	40
47		1 f. lake (B.)			70	70
48		2 f. green (R.)			6·50	6·50
49		5 f. blue (R.)			2·50	2·50
50		10 f. violet (R.)			28·00	28·00
34/50		*Set of 17*			38·00	38·00

1919 (Jan). As last, further surch in new currency as *T 6* of Canton, in Paris.

51	7	¾ c. on 1 c. sepia			5	5
52		½ c. on 2 c. brown			5	5
53		1½ c. on 4 c. blue (R.)			10	10
54		2 c. on 5 c. pale green			8	8
55		4 c. on 10 c. scarlet (B.)			8	8
56		6 c. on 15 c. violet			5	5
57	8	8 c. on 20 c. violet			5	5
58		10 c. on 25 c. blue			12	5
59		12 c. on 30 c. chocolate			12	8
60		14 c. on 35 c. olive-green			12	8
		a. "4" with closed top			1·10	
61		16 c. on 40 c. brown			12	12
		a. T 4 double			7·00	
62		20 c. on 50 c. carmine (B.)			90	70
63	9	30 c. on 75 c. orange (R.)			15	15
64		40 c. on 1 f. lake (R.)			30	30
65		80 c. on 2 f. green (R.)			30	30
66		2 pi. on 5 f. blue (R.)			60	60
67		4 pi. on 10 f. violet (R.)			60	60
51/67		*Set of 17*			3·50	3·50

This office was closed down on 31 December 1922.

C. HOIHOW

An Indo-Chinese Post Office was opened at Hoihow, the chief town of the island of Hainan, on 15 May 1900.

HOI HAO   HOI HAO   **HOI-HAO**

州 瓊   仙 六   花銀八厘

(1)   (2)   (3)

1901. Type X ("Tablet") inscr "INDO-CHINE" optd with *T 1* (="HOI HAO" in French and Chinese), in carmine, at Hanoi.

1	X	1 c. black/azure			20	20
2		2 c. brown/buff			20	20
3		4 c. purple-brown/grey			20	20
4		5 c. pale green			20	20
5		10 c. black/lilac			20	20
6		15 c. blue/quadrillé			£130	£60
7		15 c. grey			15	15
8		20 c. red/green			1·25	1·25
9		25 c. black/rose			55	30
10		30 c. cinnamon/drab			1·75	1·40
11		40 c. red/yellow			2·50	2·00
12		50 c. carmine/rose			3·25	2·50
13		75 c. brown/orange			16·00	16·00
14		1 f. olive-green/toned			55·00	50·00
15		5 f. mauve/pale lilac			50·00	48·00

1903-04. As last but surch as *T 2* (Chinese characters represent value), in black, at Hanoi.

16	1 c. black/azure			8	8
17	2 c. brown/buff			10	10
18	4 c. purple-brown/grey			15	15
19	5 c. pale green			15	15
20	10 c. rose-red			15	15
21	15 c. grey			15	15
22	20 c. red/green			30	30
23	25 c. blue			20	20
24	25 c. black/rose			20	20
25	30 c. cinnamon/drab			30	30
26	40 c. red/yellow			2·10	2·10
27	50 c. carmine/rose			2·50	2·50
28	50 c. brown/azure (1904)			10·00	10·00
29	75 c. brown/orange			3·50	3·50
	a. "INDO-CHINE" inverted			£2000	
30	1 f. olive-green/toned			4·00	4·00
31	5 f. mauve/pale lilac			14·00	14·00
16/31	*Set of 16*			34·00	34·00

1906 (Oct). As last and *T 6* but surch as *T 3*, at Hanoi.

32	6	1 c. olive-green (R.)			12	12
33		2 c. claret/yellow			15	15
34		4 c. magenta/azure (R.)			15	15
35		5 c. deep green (R.)			25	25
36		10 c. rose			25	25
37		15 c. brown/azure			25	25
38		20 c. red/green			40	40
39		25 c. blue			40	40
40		30 c. brown/cream			50	50
41		35 c. black/yellow (R.)			55	55
42		40 c. black/greyish (R.)			55	55
43		50 c. brown/toned			1·10	1·10
44	X	75 c. brown/orange (R.)			3·00	3·00
45	6	1 f. pale olive-green			2·25	2·25
46		2 f. brown/yellow (R.)			3·25	3·25
47	X	5 f. mauve/pale lilac			12·00	12·00
48	6	10 f. red/green			13·00	13·00
32/48		*Set of 17*			34·00	34·00

The note about printings under No. 49 of Canton also applies here.

貳圓

HOI HAO

寶祭   HOI-HAO

(4)   (5)

1908. Stamps of Indo-China, 1907, surch as *T 4* (1 *c.* to 50 *c.*) or *5* (others), in Paris. Centre and value in black.

49	7	1 c. sepia (R.)			5	5
50		2 c. brown (R.)			5	5
51		4 c. blue (R.)			8	8
52		5 c. pale green (R.)			15	15
53		10 c. scarlet (B.)			20	20
54		15 c. violet (R.)			40	40
55	8	20 c. violet (R.)			50	50
56		25 c. blue (R.)			50	50
57		30 c. chocolate (R.)			50	50
58		35 c. olive-green (R.)			50	50
59		40 c. brown (R.)			45	45
60		50 c. carmine (R.)			70	70
61	9	75 c. orange (B.)			50	50
62		1 f. lake (B.)			1·50	1·50
63		2 f. green (R.)			3·25	3·25
64		5 f. blue (R.)			8·00	8·00
65		10 f. violet (R.)			9·50	9·50
49/65		*Set of 17*			24·00	24·00

1919 (Jan). As last, further surch in new currency as *T 6* of Canton, in Paris.

66	7	¾ c. on 1 c. sepia			5	5
67		½ c. on 2 c. brown			8	8
68		1½ c. on 4 c. blue (R.)			8	8
69		2 c. on 5 c. pale green			5	5
70		4 c. on 10 c. scarlet (B.) (a)			5	5
		a. Chinese "2" for "4" (b)			6·00	6·00
71		6 c. on 15 c. violet			8	8
72	8	8 c. on 20 c. violet			5	5
		a. "CENT" for "CENTS"			8·00	8·00
73		10 c. on 25 c. blue			35	35
74		12 c. on 30 c. chocolate			8	8
75		14 c. on 35 c. olive-green			10	10
		a. "4" with closed top			90	90
76		16 c. on 40 c. brown			5	5

77 **8** 20 c. on 50 c. carmine (B.) 12 12
78 **9** 30 c. on 75 c. orange (B.) 20 20
79 40 c. on 1 f. lake (B.) 45 45
80 80 c. on 2 f. green (R.) .. .. .. 1·25 1·25
81 2 pi. on 5 f. blue (R.) .. .. .. 4·00 4·00
a. "2 PIASTRES" treble .. .. 30·00
82 4 pi. on 10 f. violet (R.) .. .. .. 18·00 18·00
66/82 *Set of* 17 .. .. .. 22·00 22·00

This office was closed down on 31 December 1922.

D. KWANGCHOW

(French Leased Territory)

The territory of Kwangchow, with an area of 328 square miles, was leased for 99 years by France from China, as a coaling station and naval base, in April 1898. In January 1900 it was placed under the authority of the Governor-General of Indo-China.

Although not having the same status as the Indo-Chinese Post Offices, these stamps are listed here for convenience.

贰圓

KOUANG-TCHÉOU

Kouang
Tchéou-Wan

花銀八厘 (1) 壹角 (2) KOUANG-TCHEOU (3)

1906 (Oct). *Stamps of Indo-China, surch as T* **1**, *at Hanoi.*
1 **6** 1 c. olive-green (R.) 20 20
2 2 c. claret/*yellow* 20 20
3 4 c. magenta/*azure* (R.) 20 20
4 5 c. deep green (R.) 20 20
5 10 c. rose 20 20
6 15 c. brown/*azure* 20 20
7 20 c. red/*green* 20 20
8 25 c. blue 20 20
9 30 c. brown/*cream* 20 20
10 35 c. black/*yellow* (R.) 20 20
11 40 c. black/*greyish* (R.) 20 20
12 50 c. brown/*toned* .. .. .. 1·10 1·10
13 **X** 75 c. brown/*orange* (R.) .. .. .. 1·10 1·10
14 **6** 1 f. pale olive-green .. .. .. 1·40 1·40
15 2 f. brown/*yellow* (R.) .. .. .. 1·50 1·50
16 **X** 5 f. mauve/*pale lilac* .. .. .. 14·00 14·00
17 **6** 10 f. red/*green* .. .. 18·00 18·00
1/17 *Set of* 17 .. .. 35·00 35·00

The note about printings under No. 49 of Canton also applies here.

1908. *Stamps of Indo-China,* 1907, *surch as T* **2** (1 *c. to* 50 *c.*) *or* **3** (*others*), *in Paris. Centre and value in black.*
18 **7** 1 c. sepia (R.) 5 5
19 2 c. brown (R.) 5 5
20 4 c. blue (R.) 5 5
21 5 c. pale green (R.) 5 5
22 10 c. scarlet (B.) 5 5
23 15 c. violet (R.) 15 15
24 **8** 20 c. violet (R.) 30 30
25 25 c. blue (R.) 30 30
26 30 c. chocolate (R.) 40 40
27 35 c. olive-green (R.) 65 65
28 40 c. brown (R.) 65 65
29 50 c. carmine (B.) 65 65
30 **9** 75 c. orange (B.) 60 60
31 1 f. lake (B.) 90 90
32 2 f. green (R.) .. .. 3·25 3·25
33 5 f. blue (R.) .. .. 6·50 6·50
34 10 f. violet (R.) .. .. 9·00 8·00
a. Surch double .. .. .. 40·00
b. Surch treble .. .. .. 40·00
18/34 *Set of* 17 .. .. 22·00 21·00

1919 (Jan). *As last, further surch in new currency as T* **6** *of Canton, in Paris.*
35 **7** $\frac{2}{5}$ c. on 1 c. sepia 5 5
36 $\frac{4}{5}$ c. on 2 c. brown 5 5
37 1$\frac{3}{5}$ c. on 4 c. blue (R.) 5 5
38 2 c. on 5 c. pale green 8 5
a. "2 CENTS" inverted .. .. 6·00
39 4 c. on 10 c. scarlet (B.) 15 8
40 6 c. on 15 c. violet 5 5
41 **8** 8 c. on 20 c. violet 40 25
42 10 c. on 25 c. blue 90 75
43 12 c. on 30 c. chocolate 8 8
44 14 c. on 35 c. olive-green 15 15
a. "4" with closed top .. .. 2·25 2·25
45 16 c. on 40 c. brown 8 8
46 20 c. on 50 c. carmine (B.) 8 8
47 **9** 30 c. on 75 c. orange (B.) 30 25
48 40 c. on 1 f. lake (B.) 55 35
a. "40 CENTS" inverted .. ..
49 80 c. on 2 f. green (R.) 40 30
50 2 pi. on 5 f. blue (R.) .. .. .. 15·00 15·00
51 4 pi. on 10 f. violet (R.) .. .. .. 1·50 1·50
35/51 *Set of* 17 .. .. 18·00 17·00

OVERPRINTS. The following were all overprinted in Paris on stamps of Indo-China.

KOUANG-TCHÉOU (4) KOUANG-TCHÉOU (5)

1923 (July). *Stamps of* 1922–23 *optd with T* **4**. *Values and centres in black* (*except* $\frac{1}{10}$ *c.*).
52 **7** $\frac{1}{10}$ c. red and grey (B.) 5 5
53 $\frac{1}{5}$ c. blue (R.) 5 5
a. Surch in black .. .. ..
54 $\frac{2}{5}$ c. sepia (R.) 5 5
55 $\frac{4}{5}$ c. rosine 5 5
56 1 c. brown (B.) 5 5
57 2 c. green (R.) 5 5
58 3 c. violet (R.) 5 5
59 4 c. orange 5 5
60 5 c. carmine 5 5
61 **8** 6 c. red 8 8
62 7 c. olive-green 5 5
63 8 c. black/*lilac* (R.) 10 10
64 9 c. yellow/*greenish* 10 10
65 10 c. blue 10 10
66 11 c. violet 10 10
67 12 c. chocolate 12 12
68 15 c. yellow-orange 15 15
69 20 c. blue/*buff* (R.) 15 15
70 40 c. scarlet (B.) 25 25
71 1 pi. blue-green/*greenish* 50 50
72 2 pi. purple/*rose* (B.) .. .. .. 1·10 1·10
52/72 *Set of* 21 .. .. 3·00 3·00

1927 (26 Sept). *Pictorial stamps of* 1927 *optd with T* **5**.
73 **21** $\frac{1}{10}$ c. olive-green (R.) 5 5
74 $\frac{1}{5}$ c. yellow 5 5
75 $\frac{2}{5}$ c. pale blue (R.) 5 5
76 $\frac{4}{5}$ c. brown 5 5
77 1 c. orange 5 5
78 2 c. green (R.) 5 5
79 3 c. indigo (R.) 5 5
80 4 c. pink 8 8
81 5 c. violet 5 5
82 **22** 6 c. scarlet 8 8
83 7 c. bistre-brown 5 5
84 8 c. olive-green (R.) 8 8
85 9 c. purple 8 8
86 10 c. pale blue (R.) 8 8
87 11 c. orange 8 8
88 12 c. slate (R.) 8 8
89 **23** 15 c. brown and carmine 20 20
90 20 c. slate and bright violet (R.) .. 15 15
91 **24** 25 c. magenta and red-brown 15 15
92 30 c. olive and blue (R.) 15 15
93 **25** 40 c. pale blue and vermilion 10 10
94 50 c. slate and yellow-green (R.) .. 15 15
95 **26** 1 pi. black, yellow and blue (R.) .. 45 45
96 2 pi. blue, orange and red (R.) .. 20 20
73/96 *Set of* 24 .. .. 2·25 2·25

1937 (15 Apr). *International Exhibition, Paris. As No.* **MS**246*a of Indo-China, colour changed, optd* "KOUANG-TCHEOU" *in black. Imperf.*
MS97 30 c. green 30 35
a. Inscription inverted £200

KOUANG-TCHÉOU
(6)

1937 (19 May). *Pictorial stamps of 1931–41 optd with T* **6**.
98	30	½ c. greenish blue	..	5	5
99		1 c. deep lake-blue	..	5	5
100		2 c. brown-orange	..	5	5
101		2 c. red-brown	..	5	5
102		2 c. violet	..	5	5
103		1 c. sepia	..	5	5
104		2 c. green	..	5	5
105	31	3 c. green	..	5	5
106		4 c. deep blue (R.)	..	5	5
107		5 c. purple	..	5	5
108		5 c. vermilion	..	5	5
109	32	10 c. blue (R.) ..	..	10	10
110		15 c. deep blue (R.)	..	5	5
111		20 c. carmine	..	5	5
112		21 c. deep green	..	5	5
113		25 c. purple	..	25	25
114		30 c. chestnut..	..	5	5
115	33	50 c. sepia	..	5	5
116		60 c. purple	..	5	5
117		1 pi. bright green	..	12	12
118		2 pi. scarlet ..	..	5	5
98/118		*Set of 21*	..	1·10	1·10

1939 (10 May). *New York World's Fair. As T* **20** *of Cameroun.*
119		13 c. lake	..	5	5
120		23 c. bright ultramarine	..	5	5

1939 (5 July). *150th Anniv of French Revolution. As T* **25** *of Cameroun.*
121		6 c. + 2 c. green	..	55	55
122		7 c. + 3 c. brown	..	55	55
123		9 c. + 4 c. red-orange	..	55	55
124		13 c. + 10 c. carmine	..	55	55
125		23 c. + 20 c. blue..	..	55	55
121/125		*Set of 5*	..	2·50	2·50

1941–42. *Pictorial stamps of 1931–41 optd with T* **6**.
126	31	3 c. brown	..	5	5
127		4 c. blue-green	..	5	5
128		4 c. yellow	..	15	15
129		5 c. green	..	5	5
130		7 c. grey-black (R.)	..	5	5
131		8 c. deep lake	..	5	5
132		9 c. black/yellow (R.)	..	5	5
		a. Opt in black	..	65	65
133	32	10 c. blue/pink (R.)	..	5	5
134		18 c. bright blue (R.)	..	5	5
135		22 c. blue-green	..	5	5
136		25 c. deep blue (R.)	..	5	5
137		70 c. light blue (R.)	..	5	5
126/137		*Set of 13*	..	1·00	1·00

During 1941/44 other stamps of Indo-China were overprinted and issued in Paris but were not in use in Kwangchow.

The territory was returned by France to China in February 1943 and was promptly occupied by Japanese troops. It was eventually returned to China, after the defeat of Japan, by a Convention signed at Chungking on 18 August 1945.

E. MENGTSZ

An Indo-Chinese Post Office was opened at Mongtze (now Mengtsz), a town in the south of Yunnan province, on 25 January 1900.

MONGTZE

Mong-Tseu

仙 二
(1)

花銀八厘
(2)

1903–06. *Type* X *("Tablet") inscr "INDO-CHINE" surch as* T **1**, *at Hanoi.*
1	X	1 c. black/azure	..	..	55	55
2		2 c. brown/buff		..	50	50
3		4 c. purple-brown/grey		..	50	50
4		5 c. pale green..	..	..	40	40
5		10 c. rose-red	..	..	50	50
6		15 c. grey	..	..	50	50
7		20 c. red/green	..	..	60	60
8		25 c. blue	..	..	60	60
9		25 c. black/rose (1906)	..	48·00	48·00
10		30 c. cinnamon/drab		..	60	60
11		40 c. red/yellow..	..	..	5·00	5·00
12		50 c. carmine/rose	..	28·00	28·00
13		50 c. brown/azure (1906)	..	8·00	8·00
14		75 c. brown/orange	..	..	6·00	6·00
		a. "INDO-CHINE" in label inverted		£3500	
15		1 f. olive-green/toned..	..	6·00	6·00
16		5 f. mauve/pale lilac	..	7·00	7·00
1/16		*Set of 16*	..	..	£100	£100

Only one copy is known of No. 14a.

1906 (Oct)–**08.** *Stamps of Indo-China surch as* T **2**, *at Hanoi.*
17	6	1 c. olive-green (R.)	..	..	8	8
18		2 c. claret/yellow		..	8	8
19		4 c. magenta/azure (R.)	..	8	8
20		5 c. deep green (R.)	..	..	15	15
21		10 c. rose	..	..	12	12
22		15 c. brown/azure	..	..	20	20
23		20 c. red/green	..	..	30	30
24		25 c. blue	..	..	45	45
25		30 c. brown/cream	..	..	40	40
26		35 c. black/yellow (R.)	..	..	35	35
27		40 c. black/greyish (R.)	..	..	35	35
28		50 c. brown/toned	..	..	1·00	1·00
29	X	75 c. brown/orange (R.)..	..	2·10	2·10
		a. "INDO-CHINE" in label inverted		£4000	
30	6	1 f. pale olive-green	..	..	1·25	1·25
31		2 f. brown/yellow (R.)..	..	3·25	3·25
32	X	5 f. mauve/pale lilac	..	..	5·50	5·50
33	6	10 f. red/green (opt inverted)	..	£150	£150
34		10 f. red/green (1908)	..	..	10·00	10·00

Only one copy is known of No. 29a.
The note about printings under No. 49 of Canton also applies here. All the first printing of the 10 f. (150) had the overprint inverted (No. 33).

捌 角

MONGTSEU

(3)

MONGTSEU
(4)

1908. *Stamps of Indo-China, 1907, surch as* T **3** (*1 c. to 50 c.*) *or* **4** (*others*), *in Paris. Centre and value in black.*
35	7	1 c. sepia (R.)	..	..	5	5
36		2 c. brown (R.)	..	..	5	5
37		4 c. blue (R.)	..	..	5	5
38		5 c. pale green (R.)	..	..	5	5
39		10 c. scarlet (B.)	..	..	8	8
40		15 c. violet (R.)	..	..	12	12
41	8	20 c. violet (R.)	..	..	20	20
42		25 c. blue (R.)	..	..	20	20
43		30 c. chocolate (R.)	..	..	15	15
44		35 c. olive-green (R.)	..	..	30	30
45		40 c. brown (R.)	..	..	15	15
46		50 c. carmine (B.)	..	..	20	20
47	9	75 c. orange (B.)	..	..	70	70
48		1 f. carmine (B.)	..	..	65	65
49		2 f. green (R.)	..	..	65	65
50		5 f. blue (R.)	..	..	10·00	10·00
51		10 f. violet (R.)	..	..	10·00	10·00
35/51		*Set of 17*	..	..	21·00	21·00

1919 (Jan). *As last, further surch in new currency as* T **6** *of Canton, in Paris.*
52	7	²⁄₅ c. on 1 c. sepia	..	..	5	5
53		⁴⁄₅ c. on 2 c. brown	..	..	5	5

54	7	1¾ c. on 4 c. blue (R.)	.. .. ..	12	12
55		2 c. on 5 c. green	.. .. ..	5	5
56		4 c. on 10 c. scarlet (B.)	.. .. ..	12	12
57		6 c. on 15 c. violet	.. .. ..	12	12
58	8	8 c. on 20 c. violet	.. .. ..	25	25
59		10 c. on 25 c. blue	.. .. ..	20	20
60		12 c. on 30 c. chocolate	.. .. ..	20	20
61		14 c. on 35 c. olive-green	.. .. ..	20	20
		a. "4" with closed top		70	70
62		16 c. on 40 c. brown	.. .. ..	30	30
63		20 c. on 50 c. carmine (B.)	.. .. ..	25	25
64	9	30 c. on 75 c. orange (B.)	.. .. ..	15	15
65		40 c. on 1 f. carmine (B.)	.. .. ..	55	55
66		80 c. on 2 f. green (R.)	.. .. ..	20	20
		a. Surch treble, one inverted	.. ..	20·00	20·00
67		2 pi. on 5 f. blue (R.)	.. ..	14·00	14·00
		a. Surch double	.. ..	20·00	20·00
		b. Surch treble, one inverted	..	20·00	20·00
68		4 pi. on 10 f. violet (R.)	.. ..	1·50	1·50
52/68		*Set of 17*	.. .. ..	16·00	16·00

This office was closed down on 31 December 1922.

F. PAKHOI

An Indo-Chinese Post Office was opened at Pakhoi, a sea-port in Kwangtung province, on 1 February 1902.

PAK·HOI

PACKHOI

仙二
(1)

花銀八厘
(2)

1903 (Apr)–**04.** *Type X ("Tablet") inscr "INDO-CHINE" surch as T 1, at Hanoi.*

1	X	1 c. black/*azure*	.. .. ..	55	55
2		2 c. brown/*buff*	.. .. ..	30	30
3		4 c. purple-brown/*grey*	.. ..	20	20
4		5 c. pale green	.. .. ..	20	20
5		10 c. rose-red	.. .. ..	20	20
6		15 c. grey	.. .. ..	20	20
7		20 c. red/*green*	.. .. ..	45	45
8		25 c. blue	.. .. ..	45	45
9		25 c. black/*rose*	.. .. ..	20	20
10		30 c. cinnamon/*drab*	.. ..	50	50
11		40 c. red/*yellow*	.. .. ..	4·25	4·25
12		50 c. carmine/*rose*	.. ..	30·00	30·00
13		50 c. brown/*azure* (1904)	..	6·00	6·00
14		75 c. brown/*orange*	.. ..	5·50	5·50
		a. "INDO-CHINE" in label inverted	..	£2000	
15		1 f. olive-green/*toned*	..	6·00	6·00
16		5 f. mauve/*pale lilac*	.. ..	10·00	10·00
1/16		*Set of 16*	.. .. ..	60·00	60·00

Only three copies of No. 14a are known.

1906 (Oct). *Stamps of Indo-China surch as T 2, at Hanoi.*

17	6	1 c. olive-green (R.)	.. ..	15	15
18		2 c. claret/*yellow*	.. ..	15	15
19		4 c. magenta/*azure* (R.)	..	15	15
20		5 c. deep green (R.)	.. ..	15	15
21		10 c. rose	.. .. ..	15	15
22		15 c. brown/*azure*	.. ..	50	40
23		20 c. red/*green*	.. ..	30	30
24		25 c. blue	.. .. ..	30	30
25		30 c. brown/*cream*	.. ..	30	30
26		35 c. black/*yellow* (R.)	..	30	30
27		40 c. black/*greyish* (R.)	..	30	30
28		50 c. brown/*toned*	.. ..	60	55
29	X	75 c. brown/*orange* (R.)	..	3·00	2·40
30	6	1 f. pale olive-green	..	2·50	2·25
31		2 f. brown/*yellow* (R.)	..	3·75	3·00
32	X	5 f. mauve/*pale lilac*	..	11·00	10·00
33	6	10 f. red/*green*	.. ..	11·00	10·00
17/33		*Set of 17*	.. ..	32·00	28·00

The note about printings under No. 49 of Canton also applies here.

PAKHOI

骂骂 **PAKHOI**
(3) | **(4)**

1908. *Stamps of Indo-China, 1907, surch as T 3 (1 c. to 50 c.) or 4 (others), in Paris. Centre and value in black.*

34	7	1 c. sepia (R.)	.. .. ..	5	5
35		2 c. brown (R.)	.. .. ..	5	5
36		4 c. blue (R.)	.. .. ..	5	5
37		5 c. pale green (R.)	.. ..	10	10
38		10 c. scarlet (R.)	.. ..	10	10
39		15 c. violet (R.)	.. ..	15	15
40	8	20 c. violet (R.)	.. ..	15	15
41		25 c. blue (R.)	.. ..	15	15
42		30 c. chocolate (R.)	.. ..	20	20
43		35 c. olive-green (R.)	..	20	20
44		40 c. brown (R.)	.. ..	20	20
45		50 c. carmine (R.)	.. ..	20	20
46	9	75 c. orange (B.)	.. ..	50	50
47		1 f. lake (B.)	.. .. ..	50	50
48		2 f. green (R.)	.. ..	1·40	1·40
49		5 f. blue (R.)	.. ..	6·00	6·00
50		10 f. violet (R.)	.. ..	16·00	16·00
34/50		*Set of 17*	.. ..	23·00	23·00

1919 (Jan). *As last, further surch in new currency as T 6 of Canton, in Paris.*

51	7	½ c. on 1 c. sepia	.. ..	5	5
		a. "PAKHOI" double	..	10·00	
52		¼ c. on 2 c. brown	.. ..	5	5
53		1¾ c. on 4 c. blue (R.)	..	5	5
54		2 c. on 5 c. green	.. ..	5	5
55		4 c. on 10 c. scarlet (B.)	..	20	20
56		6 c. on 15 c. violet	.. ..	5	5
57	8	8 c. on 20 c. violet	.. ..	15	15
58		10 c. on 25 c. blue	.. ..	30	30
59		12 c. on 30 c. chocolate	..	12	12
		a. "12 CENTS" double	..	8·00	
60		14 c. on 35 c. olive-green	..	5	5
		a. "4" with closed top	..	50	50
61		16 c. on 40 c. brown	..	12	12
62		20 c. on 50 c. carmine (B.)	..	12	12
63	9	30 c. on 75 c. orange (B.)	..	12	12
64		40 c. on 1 f. lake (B.)	..	1·00	1·00
65		80 c. on 2 f. green (R.)	..	20	20
66		2 pi. on 5 f. blue (R.)	..	80	80
67		4 pi. on 10 f. violet (R.)	..	1·50	1·50
51/67		*Set of 17*	.. ..	4·50	4·50

This office was closed down on 31 December 1922.

G. YUNNANFU (now KUNMING)

An Indo-Chinese Post Office was opened at Yunnan-Sen, chief city of Yunnan province, on 15 February 1900.

"Sen" and "Fu" both mean "town" in Chinese, the latter indicating a place of greater importance than the former. In 1906 Yunnansen was raised in rank, and was then known as Yunnanfu.

Yunnan·Fou

YUNNANSEN

仙四
(1)

花銀八厘
(2)

1903–04. *Type X ("Tablet") inscr "INDO-CHINE" surch as T 1, at Hanoi.*

1	X	1 c. black/azure	.. .. ..	45 *	45
2		2 c. brown/buff	.. ..	35	35
3		4 c. purple-brown/grey	.. ..	45	35
4		5 c. pale green ..	.. ..	45	35
5		10 c. rose	.. ..	45	35
6		15 c. grey	.. ..	50	35
7		20 c. red/green ..	.. ..	50	40
8		25 c. blue	.. ..	50	40
9		30 c. cinnamon/drab	.. ..	50	40
10		40 c. red/yellow ..	.. ..	5·00	4·00
11		50 c. carmine/rose	.. ..	32·00	32·00
12		50 c. brown/azure (1904)	..	16·00	16·00
13		75 c. brown/orange	.. ..	4·25	3·25
		a. "INDO-CHINE" in label inverted		£2500	
14		1 f. olive-green/toned ..	..	4·25	3·25
15		5 f. mauve/pale lilac	.. ..	9·00	9·00
1/15		*Set of 15*	.. ..	65·00	65·00

Only three copies of No. 14a are known.

1906 (Oct). *Stamps of Indo-China surch as T 2, at Hanoi.*

16	6	1 c. olive-green (R.)	.. ..	15	15
17		2 c. claret/yellow	.. ..	12	12
18		4 c. magenta/azure (R.)	..	20	20
19		5 c. deep green (R.)	.. ..	20	20
20		10 c. rose	.. ..	20	20
21		15 c. brown/azure	.. ..	25	25
22		20 c. red/green	.. ..	25	25
23		25 c. blue	.. ..	25	25
24		30 c. brown/cream	.. ..	30	30
25		35 c. black/yellow (R.) ..	..	40	40
26		40 c. black/greyish (R.) ..		40	40
27		50 c. brown/toned	.. ..	40	40
28	X	75 c. brown/orange (R.)..	..	3·50	3·50
29	6	1 f. pale olive-green	..	1·60	1·60
30		2 f. brown/yellow (R.) ..		2·10	2·10
31	X	5 f. mauve/pale lilac	..	6·50	6·50
32	6	10 f. red/green ..	..	7·00	7·00
16/32		*Set of 17*	.. ..	21·00	21·00

The note about printings under No. 49 of Canton also applies here.

貳 圓

VUNNANFOU

壹 角　　　**YUNNANFOU**

(3)　　　　(4)

1908. *Stamps of Indo-China, 1907, surch as T 3 (1 c. to 50 c.) or 4 (others), in Paris. Centre and value in black.*

33	7	1 c. sepia (R.)	.. ..	5	5
34		2 c. brown (R.) ..	..	5	5
35		4 c. blue (R.)	.. ..	5	5
36		5 c. pale green (R.)	..	12	12
37		10 c. scarlet (B.) ..	..	5	5
38		15 c. violet (R.)	.. ..	25	15
39	8	20 c. violet (R.) ..	..	30	20
40		25 c. blue (R.)	.. ..	40	30
41		30 c. chocolate (R.)	..	40	30
42		35 c. olive-green (R.)	..	40	30
43		40 c. brown (R.) ..	..	60	50
44		50 c. carmine (B.)	..	60	50
45	9	75 c. orange (B.)..	..	60	50
46		1 f. lake (B.)	.. ..	1·00	80
47		2 f. green (R.)	.. ..	1·75	1·25
		a. Error. "YUNNANFOU"	..	£180	
48		5 f. blue (R.)	.. ..	3·50	3·25
		a. Error. "YUNNANFOU"	..	£180	
49		10 f. violet (R.)	.. ..	9·00	9·00
		a. Error. "YUNANNFOU"	..	£180	
33/49		*Set of 17*	.. ..	17·00	16·00

1919 (Jan). *As last, further surch in new currency as T 6 of Canton, in Paris.*

50	7	⅜ c. on 1 c. sepia	.. ..	5	5
		a. "⅜ CENT" double ..	..	7·00	

51	7	¼ c. on 2 c. brown	.. ..	5	5
52		1½ c. on 4 c. blue (R.)	..	12	12
53		2 c. on 5 c. green	.. ..	10	10
		a. "2 CENTS" treble ..	..	9·00	
54		4 c. on 10 c. scarlet (B.)	..	5	5
55		6 c. on 15 c. violet	.. ..	8	8
56	8	8 c. on 20 c. violet	.. ..	15	12
57		10 c. on 25 c. blue	.. ..	20	15
58		12 c. on 30 c. chocolate ..		12	12
59		14 c. on 35 c. olive-green	..	25	25
		a. "4" with closed top	..	8·00	
60		16 c. on 40 c. brown	..	30	30
61		20 c. on 50 c. carmine	..	12	12
62	9	30 c. on 75 c. orange (B.)	..	40	40
63		40 c. on 1 f. lake (B.)	..	40	40
64		80 c. on 2 f. green (R.)	..	70	70
		a. "80 CENTS" double	..	45·00	
		b. "80 CENTS" treble, one inverted	..	16·00	
65		1 pi. on 5 f. blue (R.)	..	3·25	3·25
66		4 pi. on 10 f. violet (R.) ..		1·25	1·25
50/66		*Set of 17*	.. ..	6·50	6·50

This office was closed down on 31 December 1922.

ITALIAN POST OFFICES

100 Cents=1 Chinese Dollar

Italian troops were stationed in China from July 1900 and a concession was granted for their use of unoverprinted Italian stamps on 21 January 1901. In September 1917 Italian Post Offices were opened in Peking and Tientsin for which the following stamps were issued. Their use was limited to legation and consular staff and Italian troops.

Stamps of Italy overprinted or surcharged

A. PEKING

PECHINO 2 CENTS	Pechino
(1)	(2)

1917 (Sept–Nov). *Stamps of 1901–16, surch locally by hand as T 1.*

1	37	2 c. on 5 c. green	.. ..	3·75	2·50
		a. Surch inverted	.. ..	5·00	5·00
		b. Surch double, one inverted		12·00	10·00
		c. Error. 4 c. on 5 c.	..	£200	
2	33	4 c. on 10 c. lake	.. ..	£325	£325
		a. Surch inverted	.. ..	£550	£550
3	38	4 c. on 10 c. rose	.. ..	10·00	6·00
		a. Surch inverted	.. ..	12·00	10·00
		b. Surch double, one inverted		25·00	17·00
4	36	6 c. on 15 c. slate	.. ..	20·00	11·00
		a. Surch inverted	.. ..	22·00	14·00
		b. Error. 8 c. on 15 c. ..		£100	60·00
5	49	8 c. on 20 c. on 15 c. slate (No. 100)		65·00	38·00
		a. Surch inverted	.. ..	80·00	45·00
6	41	8 c. on 20 c. orange (No. 101) ..		£110	60·00
		a. Surch inverted	.. ..	£130	75·00
7	33	20 c. on 50 c. violet (No. 70a)	..	£450	£225
		a. Surch inverted	.. ..	£450	£225
		b. Error. 40 c. on 50 c.	..	£150	80·00
8	34	40 c. on 1 l. brown and green	..	£1800	£800

1917 (1 Dec)–**18.** *Stamps of 1901–16 optd with T 2. Typo at Turin.*

9	30	1 c. brown	.. ..	20	25
15	31	2 c. red-brown	.. ..	20	25
11	37	5 c. green	.. ..	5	5
12	38	10 c. rose	.. ..	5	5
13	41	20 c. orange (No. 101) ..		35	35
14	39	25 c. blue	.. ..	5	5
15	40	50 c. violet	.. ..	5	5
16	34	1 l. brown and green ..		12	15
17		5 l. blue and rose	.. ..	12	25
18	44	10 l. sage-green and rose	..	1·00	1·40
9/18		*Set of 10*	.. ..	2·00	2·50

1917 (1 Dec). *EXPRESS LETTER. No.* E80 *optd with T 2.*

E19	E 2	30 c. blue and rose	.. ..	20	25

1917 (1 Dec). *POSTAGE DUE. Optd with T* **2**.

D19	D 3	10 c. magenta and orange	..	..	5	5
D20		20 c. magenta and orange	..	..	5	5
D21		30 c. magenta and orange	..	..	5	5
D22		40 c. magenta and orange	..	..	15	20
D19/22		*Set of 4*	..	..	25	30

10 CENTS

Pechino

(3)

2 dollari

Pechino

(4)

1918/19. *Stamps of 1901–16 surch as T* **3** *or* **4** *(No. 27). Typo at Turin.*

19	30	½ c. on 1 c. brown	..	..	1·40	1·40
		a. "1 CENTS"	..	..	5·00	5·00
20	31	1 c. on 2 c. red-brown	..	..	5	5
		a. "1 CENTS"	..	..	2·50	2·50
21	37	2 c. on 5 c. green	..	..	5	5
22	38	4 c. on 10 c. rose	..	..	5	5
23	41	8 c. on 20 c. orange (No. 101)	..	..	5	10
24	39	10 c. on 25 c. blue	..	..	5	10
25	40	20 c. on 50 c. violet	..	..	10	15
26	34	40 c. on 1 l. brown and green	..	..	1·25	1·75
27		2 d. on 5 l. blue and rose	..	..	13·00	15·00
19/27		*Set of 9*	..	..	14·00	17·00

1918 (June). *EXPRESS LETTER. No. E80 surch as T* **3**.

E28	E 2	12 c. on 30 c. blue and rose	..		1·50	1·75

1918 (July). *POSTAGE DUE. Surch as T* **3**.

D28	D 3	4 c. on 10 c. magenta and orange	..	£2000	£1600
D29		8 c. on 20 c. magenta and orange	..	5	8
D30		12 c. on 30 c. magenta and orange	..	1·75	1·75
D31		16 c. on 40 c. magenta and orange	..	4·50	4·50

2 dollari

2 DOLLARI

10 CENTS
Pechino

(5)

Pechino

(6)

Pechino

(7)

1918–19. *Stamps of 1901–08 surch locally by hand with T* **5**/**7**.

28	39	10 c. on 25 c. blue	..	..	10	15
29	34	2 d. on 5 l. blue and rose (T **6**)	..	£325	£250
30		2 d. on 5 l. blue and rose (T **7**)	..	£2250	£1600·

B. TIENTSIN

1917 (Sept–Oct). *Stamps of 1901–16 surch locally by hand "TIENTSIN" and new value, as T* **1**.

31	37	2 c. on 5 c. green	..	..	7·50	5·00
		a. Surch inverted	..		10·00	7·50
		b. Surch double, one inverted	..	11·00	8·50
		c. Error. 4 c. on 5 c.	..		£450	
32	38	4 c. on 10 c. rose	..		17·00	12·00
		a. Surch inverted	..		20·00	13·00
		b. Surch double, one inverted	..	20·00	13·00
33	36	6 c. on 15 c. slate	..		30·00	20·00
		a. Error. 4 c. on 15 c.	..		75·00	60·00
		b. Surch inverted	..	..	35·00	22·00

1917 (1 Dec)–**18**. *Stamps of 1901–16 optd "Tientsin" as T* **2**. *Typo at Turin.*

34	30	1 c. brown	..	..	..	15	25
35	31	2 c. red-brown	..	..		15	25
36	37	5 c. green	..	..	..	5	5
37	38	10 c. rose	..	..	..	5	5
38	41	20 c. orange (No. 101)	..	..	30	35
39	39	25 c. blue	..	..	..	5	5
40	40	50 c. violet	..	..		5	10
41	34	1 l. brown and green	..	..	12	15
42		5 l. blue and rose	..	..		12	25
43	44	10 l. sage-green and rose	..	..	1·00	1·40
34/43		*Set of 10*	..	..		1·75	2·50

1917 (1 Dec). *EXPRESS LETTER. No. E80 optd "Tientsin" as T* **2**.

E44	E 2	30 c. blue and rose	..	..	..	20	25

1917 (1 Dec). *POSTAGE DUE. Optd "Tientsin" as T* **2**.

D44	D 3	10 c. magenta and orange	..	..	5	5
D45		20 c. magenta and orange	..	..	5	5
D46		30 c. magenta and orange	..	..	5	5
D47		40 c. magenta and orange	..	..	15	20
D44/47		*Set of 4*	..	..	20	25

2 Dollari

Tientsin

(8)

1918–19. *Stamps of 1901–16 surch "Tientsin" and new value as T* **3** *or* **8** *(No. 52). Typo at Turin.*

44	30	½ c. on 1 c. brown	..	..	65	75
		a. "1 CENTS"	..	..	4·00	4·00
45	31	1 c. on 2 c. red-brown	..	..	5	5
		a. "1 CENTS"	..	..	3·25	3·25
46	37	2 c. on 5 c. green	..	..	5	5
47	38	4 c. on 10 c. rose	..	..	5	5
48	41	8 c. on 20 c. orange (No. 101)	..	5	10
49	39	10 c. on 25 c. blue	..	..	5	10
50	40	20 c. on 50 c. violet	..	..	10	15
51	34	40 c. on 1 l. brown and green	..	90	1·25
52		2 d. on 5 l. blue and rose	..	12·00	13·00
44/52		*Set of 9*	..	..	13·00	14·00

1918 (June). *EXPRESS LETTER. No. E80 surch "Tientsin" and new value as T* **3**.

E53	E 2	12 c. on 30 c. blue and rose	..	1·50	1·75

1918 (July). *POSTAGE DUE. Surch "Tientsin" and new value as T* **3**.

D53	D 3	4 c. on 10 c. magenta and orange	..	£130	£140
D54		8 c. on 20 c. magenta and orange	..	5	8
D55		12 c. on 30 c. magenta and orange	..	1·25	1·50
D56		16 c. on 40 c. magenta and orange	..	3·75	4·25

1919–21. *Stamps of 1901 surch locally by hand.*
(a) As T **8** *but with small "d"*

53	34	2 d. on 5 l. blue and rose (1919)	..	£325	£250

(b) In thin sans-serif letters and with capital "D"

54	34	2 d. on 5 l. blue and rose (1921)	..	£325	£250

The Italian offices were closed down on 31 December 1922.

JAPANESE POST OFFICES

100 Sen=1 Yen

An Imperial Japanese Post Office was opened in Shanghai on 15 April 1876 and Agencies were set up at Chefoo, Chinkiang, Foochow, Hankow, Kiukiang, Newchwang (now Yingkow), Ningpo and Tientsin. In 1896, following the war with China, further offices were opened at Hanghow, Shasi and Soochow. Unoverprinted stamps of Japan were in use until 1 January 1900.

邶 圣
(1)

Stamps of Japan overprinted with T 1

1900 (1 Jan)–08. *Stamps of 1899–1908. Opt characters are 6 mm apart in 5 y. and 10 y.*

				A. P 11½–12 line		B. P 12½ line		C. P 12×12½ comb		D. P 13×13½ comb	
1	28	5 r. slate (R.)	..	70	40	70	45	†		†	
2		½ s. slate (R.) (27.3.01)		35	12	35	15	†		†	
3		1 s. pale brown (R.)		35	10	35	10	†		35	15
4		1½ s. pale ultramarine (1.10.00)		1·10	65	1·25	70	†		40	12
5		1½ s. violet (15.5.06)		55	15	60	20	—		†	
6		2 s. yellow-green (R.)		60	10	65	12	†		65	20
		a. Black opt								70	15
7		3 s. dull maroon	..	75	15	75	15	—	—		
8		3 s. rosine (15.5.06)		40	8	45	10	—	—	50	10
9		4 s. rosine	..	50	15	50	15	—	—	60	20
10		5 s. orange-yellow (R.)		1·75	20	2·00	25	†		†	
11	29	6 s. maroon (20.8.07)		2·25	1·75	2·50	2·00	†		†	
12		8 s. olive (R.)		2·50	2·00	2·50	2·00	—	—		
13		10 s. deep blue	..	1·25	10	1·25	12	†		1·50	20
14		15 s. purple	..	2·75	20	2·75	25	—	—		
15		20 s. orange	..	2·50	10	2·50	10	—	—	†	
16	30	25 s. pale blue-green (R.)		5·50	50	5·50	50	†		†	
17		50 s. brown	..	6·00	40	6·00	40	†		—	
18	31	1 y. carmine	..	10·00	35	10·00	35	†		†	
19	32	5 y. green (20.2.08)		70·00	6·00	†		†		†	
20		10 y. violet (20.2.08)		£120	15·00	†		†		†	

As in Japan there are a number of shades in this issue.

1900 (28 Apr). *Wedding of Prince Imperial.*

21	33	3 s. carmine (*perf 11½–12*)	..	..	3·25	1·50
		a. Perf 12½	..	..	6·00	3·00

1913. *Stamps of 1913. White paper. No wmk. P 12×12½.*

22	36	½ s. brown (31.10)		..	1·60	1·25
		a. Perf 13×13½		..	1·40	1·25
23		1 s. orange (31.10)		..	1·75	1·25
24		1½ s. pale blue (31.8)		..	5·00	1·75
		a. Perf 13×13½		..	4·50	1·60
25		2 s. green (31.10)		..	6·00	3·00
26		3 s. carmine (31.8)		..	3·00	80
		a. Perf 13×13½		..	2·75	80
27	37	4 s. scarlet (31.10)		..	8·00	6·50
28		5 s. violet (31.10)		..	8·50	5·00
29		10 s. deep blue (31.10)	..	..	8·00	1·25
30		20 s. claret (31.10)		..	32·00	12·00
31		25 s. olive (31.10)		..	13·00	1·50
32	38	1 y. pale green & choc (*perf 11½–12*)	..	95·00	60·00

1914 (20 May)–19. *Stamps of 1914–25. Granite paper. W 39.* (a) *Perf 13×13½.*

33	36	½ s. brown	..	..	20	12
		a. Perf 12×12½	..	..	30	12
34		1 s. orange	..	..	30	12
		a. Perf 12×12½	..	..	30	12
35		1½ s. pale blue	..	..	35	12
		a. Perf 12×12½	..	..	35	12
		b. Perf 11½–12				
36		2 s. green	..	..	40	15
		a. Perf 12×12½	..	..	—	15
		b. Perf 11½–12				
37		3 s. carmine	..	..	25	12
		a. Perf 12×12½	..	..	25	12
		b. Perf 11½–12				
38	37	4 s. scarlet	..	..	1·00	50
39		5 s. violet	..	..	1·50	30
		a. Perf 12×12½	..	..	2·00	30
40		6 s. brown (16.8.19)	..	..	3·75	2·00
		a. Perf 12×12½				
41		8 s. grey (16.8.19)	..	..	4·50	3·25
42		10 s. deep blue	..	..	1·75	30
		a. Perf 12×12½	..	..	1·75	20
		b. Perf 11½–12				
43		20 s. claret	..	..	5·00	50
		a. Perf 12×12½	..	..	—	45
		b. Perf 11½–12				

44		25 s. olive	..	..	6·50	60
		a. Perf 12×12½	..	..	—	85
45	38	30 s. chestnut (16.8.19)	..	12·00	3·50
		a. Perf 11½–12				
46		50 s. chocolate (16.8.19)	..	35·00	3·50

(b) Perf 11½–12

47	38	1 y. pale green and chocolate	..	13·00	4·50
48	32	5 y. green	..	..	£140	65·00
49		10 y. violet	..	..	£225	£100

The use of overprinted Japanese stamps was discontinued by Japanese military post offices on 21 February 1905, in post offices of the Kwangtung leased territory on 20 March 1908, and in Japanese post offices in the Chinese Eastern Railway Zone on 1 June 1918; the remaining offices were closed down on 31 December 1922.

RUSSIAN POST OFFICES

1899. 100 Kopecks=1 Rouble
1917. 100 Cents=1 Dollar

Imperial Russian Post Offices were opened in Peking, Kalgan, Tientsin and Urga (now Ulan-Bator, capital of Mongolia), in 1870 and in Shanghai and Chefoo by 1897. Hankow had a Russian Postal Agency by 1897 and an Imperial Post Office by 1904. There were also Russian Post Offices at Port Arthur and Dalny in the Russian Leased Territory of Liaotung and many Russian Field Post Offices and civilian Post Offices in Manchuria during the Russian military occupation, 1900–07. Stamps of Russia were used till 1899, and later than that in Manchuria and on the Chinese Eastern Railway.

Stamps of Russia overprinted or surcharged

(1)

1899–1908. *Arms types (with thunderbolts), optd with T* **1.**

(a) Horizontally laid paper (1899–1904)

1	9	1 k. orange (B.)	.. ..	5	5
2		2 k. green (R.) ..	.. ..	5	5
3		3 k. carmine (B.)	.. ..	5	5
4		5 k. purple (B.)	.. ..	5	5
5		7 k. deep blue (R.)	.. ..	5	5
		a. Opt inverted	.. ..		
6	14	10 k. blue (R.) ..	.. ..	10	10
7		50 k. green and purple (B.) (1904)	..	35	35
8	15	1 r. orge & brown/*pale brn* (B.) (1904)		2·00	2·00
1/8		*Set of 8*	.. ..	2·40	2·40

(b) Vertically laid paper (1904–8)

9	14	4 k. red (B.) (1907)	.. ..	5	5
10	9	7 k. deep blue (R.) (1907)	..	2·75	2·25
11	14	10 k. deep blue (R.)	.. ..	40·00	40·00
12	10	14 k. rose and blue (R.) (1907) ..		20	20
13		15 k. pale blue and plum (B.) (1908)		65	65
14	14	20 k. carmine and blue (B.)	..	8	8
15	10	25 k. mauve and dull green (R.) (1908)		70	70
16		35 k. green and deep lilac (R.) (1907)	..	30	30
17	14	50 k. green and purple (B.) (1908)	..	8·00	8·00
18	10	70 k. orange and brown (B.) (1907)	..	65	65
19	15	1 r. orge & brown/*pale brn* (B.) (1907)		1·50	1·25
20	11	3 r. 50, grey and black (R.) (1907)	..	45	35
21	20	5 r. pale and deep blue/*grn* (R.) (1907)		1·00	1·00
		a. Opt inverted			
22	11	7 r. yellow and black (B.) (1907)	..	70	45
23	21	10 r. pale grey and scar/*yell* (B.) (1907)	..	6·00	6·00
9/23		*Set of 15*	..	55·00	55·00

1910–16. *Arms types of 1909–15, optd with T* **1.** *Wove paper with varnish lines on face. Perf.*

24	22	1 k. yellow-orange (B.)	.. ..	5	5
		a. Opt inverted			
		b. Opt double			
		c. Blue-black opt		1·10	1·10
25		2 k. deep green ..	.. ..	5	5
		a. Opt inverted			
		b. Blue opt		1·10	1·10
		c. Opt double (Bk. + B.) ..			
26		3 k. rose-red (B.) ..	..	5	5
		a. Black opt		2·25	2·25
27	23	4 k. rose-carmine (B.)..	..	5	5
		b. Black opt		2·00	2·00
28	22	7 k. blue	..	5	5
29	23	10 k. deep blue..	.. ..	5	5
		a. Opt double			
30	10	14 k. rose-red and blue	..	12	12
		a. Opt inverted			
31		15 k. blue and purple-brown	..	8	8
32	14	20 k. scarlet and blue (1916)	..	8	8
		a. Opt inverted			
33	10	25 k. pale violet and light green	..	5	5
		a. Blue opt		40	40
34		35 k. green and purple..	..	5	5
		a. Opt inverted			
		b. Blue opt			
35	14	50 k. green and purple (B.)	..	5	5
		a. Black opt		2·50	2·50
36	10	70 k. orange and cinnamon (B.)	..	5	5
37	15	1 r. pale orange & brn/*pale brn* (B.)..		10	10
38	20	5 r. pale & deep blue/*green* (R.) (1916)		1·40	1·00
		a. Opt inverted			
24/38		*Set of 15*	..	2·00	1·75

(2)　　(3)　　(4)　　(5)

1917. *Arms types surch as T* **3** *(on 10, 14 and 20 k.),* **2** *(other kopeck values) or* **4** *(on rouble values). Perf.*

(a) Vertically laid paper

39	11	3 d. 50 on 3 r. 50, grey and black	..	80	1·00
		a. Surch inverted			
40	20	5 d. on 5 r. pale blue & dp blue/*green*		80	1·00
		a. Surch inverted ..	..	13·00	13·00
41	11	7 d. on 7 r. yellow and black ..		55	65

(b) Wove paper with varnish lines on face

42	22	1 c. on 1 k. orange ..	..	5	5
43		2 c. on 2 k. green (*shades*) ..	..	5	5
44		3 c. on 3 k. carmine-red ..	..	5	5
		a. Surch inverted ..	..	10·00	10·00
45	23	4 c. on 4 k. red ..	..	5	5
46	22	5 c. on 5 k. brown-lilac ..	..	5	5
47	23	10 c. on 10 k. deep blue ..	..	5	5
		a. Surch inverted ..	..	12·00	
		b. Surch double			
48	10	14 c. on 14 k. deep carmine and blue ..		10	10
		a. Imperf		1·10	60
49		15 c. on 15 k. blue and purple-brown ..		5	8
50	14	20 c. on 20 k. scarlet and blue ..	..	5	8
		a. Surch inverted			
51	10	25 c. on 25 k. violet and deep green ..		5	8
52		35 c. on 35 k. deep green & brown-pur	..	8	10
		a. Surch inverted		6·00	6·00
53	14	50 c. on 50 k. green and dull purple ..		8	10
		a. Surch inverted			
54	10	70 c. on 70 k. vermilion and brown ..		8	10
55	15	1 d. on 1 r. orange-vermilion and deep brown/*pale brown* ..		12	12
56	20	5 d. on 5 r. pale blue & deep blue/*grn*		1·90	1·50
		a. Surch inverted			
57	21	10 d. on 10 r. pearl-grey and red/*yellow*		3·25	4·00
39/57		*Set of 19*	..	7·50	8·50

Beware of dangerous forgeries of these surcharges.

1920. *Arms types of 1912–18, surch as T* **5,** *at Harbin.*

(a) Perf $14 \times 14\frac{1}{2}$

58	22	1 c. on 1 k. orange ..	..	1·90	1·90
59		2 c. on 2 k. green (*shades*) (R.)	..	30	30
60		3 c. on 3 k. carmine-red ..	..	30	30
61	23	4 c. on 4 k. red ..	..	55	55
62	22	5 c. on 5 k. brown-lilac ..	..	1·00	1·00
63	23	10 c. on 10 k. deep blue (R.) ..	..	5·00	5·00
64	22	10 c. on 10 k. on 7 k. deep blue (R.) ..		3·75	3·75

(b) Imperf

65	22	1 c. on 1 k. orange ..	..	65	65
66		5 c. on 5 k. brown-lilac ..	..	1·90	1·90
		a. Surch inverted			
		b. Surch double			
58/66		*Set of 9*	..	14·00	14·00

Minor varieties occur twice on each sheet: thick "t", broken "f" for "t", italic "C", and wide "C".

These surcharged stamps were for use on the Chinese Eastern Railway. Dangerous forgeries exist.

UNITED STATES POSTAL AGENCY IN SHANGHAI

100 Cents=1 Dollar (Chinese)

These stamps were valid for use on mail despatched from the U.S. Postal Agency in Shanghai to addresses in the United States.

The numbering of shades and varieties in this list follows the style of the United States list. See note at the beginning of Canal Zone.

(1)　　(2)

FOR WELL CENTRED COPIES ADD 50%

1919 (1 July). *U.S. stamps of 1917–19 (Nos. 505 etc), surch as T **1**. No wmk. Flat plate printings.* P 11.

1	**128**	2 c. on 1 c. blue-green	..	80	80
2		4 c. on 2 c. carmine-rose (I)		80	80
3		6 c. on 3 c. violet (II)	..	80	80
4		8 c. on 4 c. yellow-brown ..		1·10	1·10
5		10 c. on 5 c. Prussian blue ..		1·60	1·60
6		12 c. on 6 c. red-orange	..	1·75	1·75
7		14 c. on 7 c. jet-black (R.)	..	1·60	1·60
8	**137**	16 c. on 8 c. deep yellow-olive		1·60	1·60
8A		16 c. on 8 c. olive-yellow	..	1·40	1·40
9		18 c. on 9 c. salmon	..	1·40	1·40
10		20 c. on 10 c. chrome-yellow	..	1·25	1·25
11		24 c. on 12 c. claret-brown ..		3·00	3·00
11A		24 c. on 12 c. brown-carmine		1·60	1·60
12		30 c. on 15 c. grey	..	1·90	1·90
13		40 c. on 20 c. ultramarine	..	1·90	1·90
14		60 c. on 30 c. vermilion	..	2·00	2·00
15		$1 on 50 c. lilac ..		11·00	11·00
16		$2 on $1 purple-black (R.)	..	6·50	6·50
		va. Surch double ..	..	70·00	45·00
1/16		*Set of 16*	..	38·00	38·00

FOR WELL CENTRED COPIES ADD 100%

1922 (3 July). *As last, but surch as T **2**.*

17	**128**	2 c. on 1 c. blue-green	..	2·75	2·75
18		4 c. on 2 c. carmine	..	3·50	3·50

This agency was closed on 31 December 1922.

KIAOCHOW

(German Leased Territory)

1900. 100 Pfennige=1 Mark

1905. 100 Cents=1 Dollar

On 14 November 1897 the port of Tsingtao was occupied by German naval forces after the murder of two German missionaries in China. By a treaty of 6 March 1898 the Kiaochow (now Kiaohsien) territory of 117 square miles, including Tsingtao, was leased by China to Germany for 99 years.

ERRORS. Errors such as double and inverted overprints or surcharges were never issued but come from waste sheets which later leaked out of the printers.

5 Pfg. (1)   5 Pfg. (2)   5 Pfg. (3)

5 Pfg. (4)   5 Pfg. (5)   5 Pfg (6)

1900 (9 May). *Issued at Tsingtao. Stamps of German P.O's in China, surch with T **1** to **6**.*

(a) On No. 3 ("China" sloping 48°)

1	**1**	5 Pfg. on 10 pf. carmine ..	..	23·00	23·00
2	**2**	5 Pfg. on 10 pf. carmine ..	..	28·00	28·00

(b) On No. 9 ("China" sloping 56°)

3	**1**	5 Pfg. on 10 pf. carmine ..		6·50	6·00
4	**2**	5 Pfg. on 10 pf. carmine ..		6·50	6·00
5	**3**	5 Pfg. on 10 pf. carmine ..		6·50	6·00
6	**4**	5 Pfg. on 10 pf. carmine ..		7·50	6·50
7	**5**	5 Pfg. on 10 pf. carmine ..		7·50	6·50
8	**6**	5 Pfg. on 10 pf. carmine ..			

1900 (19 July). *Issued at Tsingtao. No. 3 of German P.O's in China, surch as T **1**, but "5 Pf." instead of "5 Pfg.".*

8a	5 Pf. on 10 pf. carmine ..		£225	£250

With additional handstamp "5"

9	5 on 5 Pf. on 10 pf. carmine ..		£1500	£2000

With additional handstamp "5 Pf."

10	5 Pf. on 5 Pf. on 10 pf. carmine ..		£500	£700

For illustrations and notes about German Colonial Types A and B, see under Cameroun.

1901 (Jan). *No wmk.*

11	A	3 pf. brown	..	..	15	12
12		5 pf. green	..	..	12	12
13		10 pf. carmine	..	..	25	20
14		20 pf. ultramarine		..	80	85
15		25 pf. black and red/*yellow*		1·60	2·00
16		30 pf. black and orange/*buff*	..	1·60	2·00
17		40 pf. black and carmine	..	2·00	2·25
18		50 pf. black and purple/*buff*	..	2·00	3·25
19		80 pf. black and carmine/*rose* ..		3·25	7·50
20	B	1 m. carmine (*a*)	..	..	5·50	7·50
21		2 m. blue (*a*)	..	..	9·00	11·00
22		3 m. violet-black (*a*)	..		9·00	25·00
23		5 m. carmine and black (Frame II, centre I) (*a*) ..		18·00	65·00
11/23		*Set of 13*	..	..	48·00	£110

1905 (1 Oct). *Chinese currency. No wmk.*

24	A	1 c. brown	..	..	15	15
25		2 c. green	..	..	25	12
26		4 c. carmine	..	..	45	12
27		10 c. ultramarine	..	..	1·10	60
28		20 c. black and carmine	..	3·00	2·75
29		40 c. black and carmine/*rose*	..	9·00	10·00
30	B	½ d. carmine (*c*)	..	..	7·00	7·00
31		1 d. blue (*a*)	..	..	22·00	13·00
		a. 25×16 holes	..	..	14·00	13·00
32		1½ d. violet-black (*a*)	..	75·00	£130
33		2½ d. carmine and black (II) (*a*) ..		£150	£300
		a. 25×16 holes	..	..	£250	£325

1906–18. *Wmk Lozenges.*

34	A	1 c. brown (1906)	..	..	5	10
35		2 c. green (1908)	..	..	5	10
36		4 c. carmine (1909)	..	..	5	10
37		10 c. ultramarine (1908)	..	..	12	40
38		20 c. black and carmine (1908) ..		25	3·00
39		40 c. black and carmine/*rose*	..	40	7·50
40	B	½ d. carmine (*a*) (1907)..		70	8·00
		a. 25×17 holes (1918)	..		60	
41		1 d. blue (*a*) (1907)	..	..	1·00	6·00
		a. 25×17 holes (1918)	..		90	
42		1½ d. violet-black (*a*) (1907)	..	2·00	25·00
		a. 25×17 holes (1918)	..		1·50	
43		2½ d. carmine and black (II) (*a*) (1906) ..		5·00	60·00
		a. 25×17 holes (1918)	..	..	4·00	

In the First World War, Tsingtao surrendered to Japanese forces after a 3 months siege on 7 November 1914. The Japanese later occupied much of Shantung province, which was not returned to China until 4 February 1922, after the Washington Disarmament Conference of 1921–22.

JAPANESE OCCUPATION OF CHINA

100 Cents=1 Dollar

A. KWANGTUNG

Japanese troops occupied Canton on 21 October 1938 and by August 1945 had occupied most of Kwangtung Province. Unoverprinted stamps of China were used in the occupied area until smuggling of stamps from unoccupied China, to take advantage of discrepancies in currency values, caused the Japanese to overprint stamps for Kwangtung in 1942.

貼 粵

用 省

(1) (="Special for Kwangtung")   (2)

1942 (13 June). *Stamps of China optd with T* **1**.

1	60	1 c. yellow-orange (508)	5	5
2	77	1 c. orange ..	5	5
3	58	2 c. olive-green (396)	5	5
4	72	3 c. brown-lake (464)	5	5
5	77	5 c. green	5	5
7	72	8 c. sage-green (F) (492A) ..	5	5
8	77	8 c. turquoise-green	5	5
9	72	10 c. green (469) (R.) ..	5	5
10		10 c. green (493A) (R.)	5	5
11	77	10 c. emerald-green ..	5	5
12	72	16 c. olive-brown (471)	5	5
13	77	17 c. olive-green	8	8
14	60	20 c. light blue (519) ..	5	5
15	72	30 c. scarlet (494A)	5	5
16	77	30 c. scarlet	8	8
17	72	50 c. blue (495A) (R.) ..	5	5
18	77	50 c. deep blue	8	8
19	72	$1 sepia and red-brown (H) (496A)	8	8
20		$2 red-brown and blue (H) (497A)	8	8
21		$5 deep green & scar (H) (498A) ..	12	12
22		$10 violet and green (H) (499A)	20	20
23		$20 ultramarine & purple (H) (500A)	12	12
1/23		Set of 22	1·25	1·25

1942 (20 Nov). *Stamps of China optd with T* **2**.

(a) Third Sun Yat-sen issue, 1938–41

24	72	2 c. olive-green (B) (463)	5	5
25		3 c. brown-lake (464)	5	5
26		5 c. olive-green (466)	5	5
27		8 c. sage-green (C) (467) ..	7·00	7·00
28		8 c. sage-green (D) (468)	5	5
29		10 c. green (469)	5	5
30		16 c. olive-brown (471)	5	5
31		25 c. violet-blue (472)	5	5
32		30 c. scarlet (494A)	5	5
33		50 c. blue (495A)	5	5
34		$1 sepia and red-brown (H) (496A)	8	8
35		$1 sepia and red-brown (H) (496B)	20	20
36		$2 red-brown and blue (H) (497A)	8	8
37		$2 red-brown and blue (H) (497B)	20	20
38		$5 deep green & scarlet (H) (498A)	12	12
39		$5 deep green & scarlet (H) (498B)	25	25
40		$10 violet and green (H) (499A) ..	20	20
41		$10 violet and green (H) (499B)	25	25
42		$20 ultram and purple (H) (500A)	20	20
43		$20 ultram and purple (H) (500B)	35	35
24/43		Set of 20	8·50	8·50

(b) Fourth Sun Yat-sen issue, 1941

44	77	2 c. ultramarine ..	5	5
45		5 c. green ..	5	5
46		8 c. red-orange	5	5
47		8 c. turquoise-green	5	5
48		10 c. emerald-green ..	5	8
49		17 c. olive-green	8	8
50		25 c. purple ..	8	8
51		30 c. scarlet ..	8	8
52		50 c. deep blue	8	8
53		$1 black and brown	10	10
54		$2 black and blue ..	10	10
55		$5 black and scarlet	12	12
56		$10 black and green	12	12
57		$20 black and purple	20	20
44/57		Set of 14	1·00	1·00

(D 1) (3) (4)

1945. *POSTAGE DUE. No. D575 of China surch with Type* **D 1**.

D58	D 5	$100 on $2 orange ..	.. ..	25·00 25·00

1945 (July). *Canton provisionals. Nos. 29 and 28 surch as* **T 3**.

58	72	$200 on 10 c. green	..	2·50 1·60
59		$400 on 8 c. sage-green	..	3·50 1·90

1945 (22 Aug). *Swatow provisional. No. 508 of China surch with T* **4**

60	72	$400 on 1 c. yellow-orange	..	.. 40·00 32·00

Japanese forces in China capitulated on 9 September 1945.

B. MENGKIANG

(Inner Mongolia)

Japanese troops captured Kalgan on 27 August 1937 and Kweisui (re-named Huhehot) on 13 October. The Inner Mongolian leaders, Prince Yun and Prince Teh, were encouraged to federate the autonomous governments of South Chahar, North Shansi and the Mongol League which the Japanese had established. A Federated Committee for Mengkiang ("The Mongolian Borderlands") was set up at Kalgan on 22 November 1937, and on 1 September 1939 a Federated Autonomous Government of Mengkiang was formed at Huhehot, with Prince Teh as Chief Executive.

(1) Small   (2) Large

See notes under "Six Districts" overprints in Japanese Occupation of North China.

(Optd by Chinese Bureau of Engraving and Printing, Peking)

1941. *Stamps of China overprinted "Mengkiang".*

A. With T **1** (1 July).   B. With T **2** (15 July).
(a) On T **58**, *1931–37 De La Rue single circle issue*

				A		B	
1		2 c. ..	(396)	5	5	5	5
2		4 c. ..	(397)	65	65	50	50
3		15 c. scarlet ..	(400)	5	5	10	8
4		20 c. ..	(401)	8	8	15	8
5		25 c. ..	(402)	1·00	1·00	15	8

(b) On T **72**, *1938–41, Chung Hwa. P 12½. No wmk*

6		2 c. (B)	(463)	†		5	5
7		3 c. ..	(464)	5	5	5	5
8		5 c. olive-green	(466)	5	5	5	5
9		8 c. (C)	(467)	5	5	5	5
10		8 c. (D)	(468)	†		12	10
11		10 c. ..	(469)	†		5	5
12		16 c. ..	(471)	†		8	8
13		$1 Die II	(460)	1·90	2·00	†	
14		$1 Die III	(473)	20·00	20·00	20	20
15		$5 ..	(475)	†		1·25	1·25

(c) On T **72**. *1939–41, Dah Tung. P 14. No wmk*

16		5 c. olive (F)..	(490A)			5	5
17		8 c. (E)	(491A)	—	—	5	5
18		8 c. (F)	(492A)	5	5	†	
19		10 c. ..	(493A)	5	5	5	5
20		30 c. ..	(494A)	8	8	8	8
21		50 c. ..	(495A)	10	8	8	8
22		$1 (H)	(496A)	35	20	45	40
23		$2 (H)	(497A)	35	25	90	55
24		$5 (H)	(498A)	1·40	1·40	2·10	2·10
25		$10 (H)	(499A)	2·50	2·50	2·10	2·10
26		$20 (H)	(500A)	3·50	3·50	3·00	3·00

(d) As last but W **73**

27		5 c. green (F)	(489B)			†	
28		5 c. olive (F)..	(490B)	†		1·40	—
29		10 c. ..	(493B)			10	10
30		30 c. ..	(494B)	3·00	3·00	15	15
31		50 c. ..	(495B)			15	15

(e) On T **60**, *1932–34, Martyrs, Peking. P 14*

32		½ c. ..	(410)	5	5	55	55
33		2½ c. ..	(412)	5	5	5	5
34		13 c. ..	(416)	3·75	3·75	5	5
35		30 c. ..	(419)	†		2·10	2·10

(f) On T **60**, *1939–41, Hong Kong print. P 12, 12½, 13 or compound. No wmk*

36		½ c. ..	(507)	5	5	5	5
37		1 c. ..	(508)	5	5	5	5
38		1 c. (b)	(508b)	—	—	1·40	—
39		2 c. ..	(509)	5	5	†	
40		3 c. ..	(511)	5	5	5	5

41	4 c.	..	..	(512)	†	5	5
42	8 c.	..	..	(514)	5·00 5·00	20	20
43	10 c.	..	..	(515)	50 35	1·25	1·25
44	13 c.	..	..	(516)	10 8	15	15
45	15 c.	..	..	(517)	†	5	5
46	17 c.	..	..	(518)	5 5	5	5
47	20 c.	..	..	(519)	5 5	5	5
48	21 c.	..	..	(520)	†	5	5
49	25 c.	..	..	(521)	5 5	†	
50	28 c.	..	..	(522)	†	8	8
51	50 c.	..	..	(525)	25 15	12	12

(g) As last but W 73

52	½ c.	..	..	(526)	1·25 —	20	15
53	1 c.	..	..	(527)	5 5	5	5
54	2 c.	..	..	(528)	†	35	—
55	2½ c.	..	..	(529)	2·00 —	2·00	—
56	3 c.	..	..	(530)	†	5	5
57	8 c.	..	..	(533)	†	1·60	1·25
58	10 c.	..	..	(534)	20 10	35	—
59	13 c.	..	..	(535)	†	50	—
60	17 c.	..	..	(537)	3·00 —	1·25	—
61	20 c.	..	..	(538)	†	5·50	—
62	25 c.	..	..	(540)	†	15	5
63	30 c.	..	..	(542)	2·40 2·40	1·50	1·25
64	40 c.	..	..	(543)	10 10	5	5
65	50 c.	..	..	(544)	25 15	1·25	1·25

疆 蒙

半 分

(3)

(Surch by Chinese Bureau of Engraving and Printing, Peking)

1942 (1 June). *Stamps of China and unissued "New Peking" printings, optd "Mengkiang" (top two characters) and surch half original value as T 3 (four characters at foot in 15 c. and 25 c.).*

(a) On 1931–37 De La Rue single circle issue

66	**58**	1 c. on 2 c. olive-green	(396)	10	10
67		2 c. on 4 c. green	(397)	8	8
68		10 c. on 20 c. ultramarine	(401)	50	50

(b) On Third Sun Yat-sen issue, 1938–41

69	**72**	1 c. on 2 c. olive-green (B)	(463)	5	5
70		4 c. on 8 c. sage-green (C)	(467)	25	20
71		4 c. on 8 c. sage-green (D)	(468)	8	8
72		4 c. on 8 c. sage-green (F)	(492A)	5	5
73		5 c. on 10 c. green	(469)	5	5
74		8 c. on 16 c. olive-brown	(471)	8	5
75		15 c. on 30 c. scarlet	(494A)	5	5
76		15 c. on 30 c. scarlet	(494B)	2·25	2·25
77		25 c. on 50 c. blue	(495A)	12	10
78		50 c. on $1 sepia & red-brown	(460)	2·50	2·50
79		50 c. on $1 sepia & red-brown	(473)	25	20
80		50 c. on $1 sepia & red-brn	(496A)	15	12
81		$1 on $2 red-brown & blue	(474)	1·00	90
82		$1 on $2 red-brn & blue	(497A)	25	20
83		$5 on $10 violet & green	(499A)	1·00	1·00
84		$10 on $20 ultram & pur	(500A)	5·00	4·75

(c) On Martyrs types

85	**60**	½ c. on 1 c. yellow-orange	(411)	1·50	40
86		½ c. on 1 c. yellow-orange	(508)	5	5
87		2 c. on 4 c. lilac	(512)	5	5
88		10 c. on 20 c. light blue	(519)	5	5
89		15 c. on 30 c. maroon	(542)	1·00	1·00
90		20 c. on 40 c. orange	(524)	20	20
91		20 c. on 40 c. orange	(543)	25	20
92		25 c. on 50 c. green	(525)	40	35

(d) On Sun Yat-sen "New Peking" printings

93	**58**	1 c. on 2 c. olive-green	..	5	5
94		2 c. on 4 c. yellow-green	..	5	5
95	**72**	8 c. on 16 c. olive-brown	..	5	5
96		50 c. on $1 sepia & orange-brown	..	20	15
97		$1 on $2 brown and blue	..	40	35
98		$5 on $10 violet and green	..	1·50	1·40

(e) On Martyrs "New Peking" printings

99	**60**	5 c. on 10 c. purple	..	5	5
100		10 c. on 20 c. brown-lake	..	5	5
101		15 c. on 30 c. maroon	..	5	5
102		20 c. on 40 c. orange	..	8	8
103		25 c. on 50 c. green	..	10	10

See note below No. 138 of Japanese Occupation of North China.

4 Dragon Pillar, Peking   **5** Miners

(Recess Imperial Printing Bureau, Tokyo)

1943 (16 Apr). *Fifth Anniv of Establishment of Mengkiang Post and Telegraph Service. Granite paper. Wmk Characters in circle in sheet (none on some stamps). P 11½×11 or 12×11.*

104	**4**	4 c. red-orange	..	..	..	5	5
105		8 c. deep blue	..	..	..	5	8

(Photo Imperial Printing Bureau, Tokyo)

1943 (8 Dec). *Second Anniv of War in East Asia. P 12.*

106	**5**	4 c. blue-green	..	..	..	5	5
107		8 c. lake	..	..	..	8	8

6 Stylised Horse   **7** Prince Yun   **8** Blast Furnace

(Photo Imperial Printing Bureau, Tokyo)

1944 (1 Sept). *Fifth Anniv of Federation of Autonomous Governments of Mongolian Provinces. P 12½×12 (4 c.) or 12×12½ (8 c.).*

108	**6**	4 c. rose	..	..	..	5	5
109	**7**	8 c. deep blue	..	..	..	8	8

(Photo Imperial Printing Bureau, Tokyo)

1944 (8 Dec). *Productivity Campaign. P 12×12½.*

110	**8**	8 c. brown	..	..	..	5	5

1945 (June). *Unissued "New Peking" printings optd as top characters of T 3. No gum.*

(a) On Sun Yat-sen types

111	**58**	2 c. olive-green	..	..	5	5
112		4 c. yellow-green	..	..	12	12
113		5 c. green	..	..	5	5
114	**72**	$1 sepia and orange-brown	..	8	8
115		$2 brown and blue	..	40	40
116		$5 green and rose-red	..	1·00	1·00

(b) On Martyrs types

117	**60**	1 c. yellow-orange	..	..	5	5
118		8 c. brown-orange	..	..	5	5
119		10 c. purple	..	..	5	5
120		20 c. brown-lake	..	..	5	5
121		30 c. maroon	..	..	5	5
122		40 c. orange	..	..	5	5
123		50 c. green	..	..	8	8
111/123		Set of 13	..	..	1·75	1·75

角 壹   角 伍   圓 壹

(9)   (10)   (11)

1945 (July). *Surch with new values in Chinese characters as T 9* (10 c.), **10** (50 c.) *or* **11** ($1).

(a) On Chinese stamps previously optd "Mengkiang"
A. With T **1** (*small*).   B. With T **2** (*large*)

				A		B	
124	60	10 c. on ½ c. (36) (R.)	..	5	5	5	5
125		10 c. on ½ c. (52) (R.)	..	†		10	10
126		10 c. on 1 c. (37) (R.)	..	10	10	5	5
127		10 c. on 1 c. (38) (R.)	..	†		70	70
128		10 c. on 1 c. (53) (R.)	..	8	8	8	8
129	58	50 c. on 2 c. (1)	..	25	25	10	10
130	72	50 c. on 2 c. (6)	..	†		5	5
131	60	50 c. on 4 c. (41) (R.)	..	†		5	5
132	72	50 c. on 5 c. (8) (R.)	..	5	5	5	5
133		50 c. on 5 c. (16) (R.)	..	†		5	5

(b) On "New Peking" printings optd as top characters of T **3**

134	60	10 c. on 1 c. yellow-orange (R.)	..	5	5
135	58	50 c. on 4 c. yellow-green	..	5	5
136		50 c. on 4 c. yellow-green (R.)	..	20	20
137		50 c. on 5 c. green (R.)	..	5	5
138	60	$1 c. on 8 c. brown-orange (R.)	..	5	5

After the Japanese surrender in 1945, Inner Mongolia was occupied by the Chinese Communists, who later created an Inner Mongolian Autonomous Region within the People's Republic.

C. NORTH CHINA

After the "Marco Polo Bridge incident" at Lukouchiao, near Peking, on 7 July 1937, the Japanese army began to try to conquer China. On 8 August it entered Peking, and on 14 December founded there a puppet Provisional Government of China. On 30 March 1940, this was combined with the Reformed Government of the Republic of China, established by the Japanese at Nanking on 27 March 1938, to form the Reorganised National Government of the Republic of China, with Wang Ching-wei as Chairman and Nanking as capital. Civil affairs in North China were conducted by the North China Political Council at Peking. The areas occupied by the Japanese army consisted mostly of large towns and lines of communication between them.

"NEW PEKING PRINTINGS". In 1941 the Chinese Bureau of Engraving and Printing was ordered to print stamps for the Japanese-controlled areas of North China in the designs current in areas under the Government of Chiang Kai-shek. The 8 c. Martyrs type (No. 1) was the only value officially issued without some sort of overprint.

Stamps of this issue overprinted in 1942–45 comprise the 2 c., 4 c. and 5 c. in the 1931–37 Sun Yat-sen type (second issue); the 9 c., 16 c. and 18 c. and $1, $2, $5, $10 and $20 in the 1939–41 Dah Tung Book Co type; and the 1 c., 8 c., 10 c., 20 c., 30 c., 40 c. and 50 c. in the 1932–34 Martyrs type. There are minute differences of design between the "New Peking" and earlier printings, but the "New Peking" printings may be distinguished easily by the fact that the execution is less finished, and the paper used is of poor quality, resembling newsprint. The stamps were first issued with a dull yellowish gum and later without gum. The "New Peking" Martyr stamps are also usually ½ mm to ¾ mm wider than the Martyr issue of 1932–34.

"SIX DISTRICTS" OVERPRINTS. The characters below respectively represent the names of the Provinces of Honan, Hopeh, Shansi and Shantung and the District of Supeh, (Northern Kiangsu); the corresponding overprint for the sixth district, i.e. the autonomous District of Mengkiang (Inner Mongolia), will be found listed uner Mengkiang, Nos. 1 to 65, together with the other issues for that district.

Each overprint exists in two types, known as "small" and "large", differing slightly in size but more particularly in shape.

Overprinting was carried out to combat speculation. The currency in the south having depreciated, stamps could be smuggled to the Japanese-occupied north for re-sale at a profit. The overprints acted as controls, use being restricted to the province or district named on the stamp. Their sale was discontinued on 31 May 1942.

Some values were philatelically manipulated by postal officials but contradictory information and the absence of authoritative records makes it difficult to be sure which. Our list is of values known to exist.

1941 (5 June). *"New Peking" printing. As No. 414 of China but re-engraved by the Chinese Bureau of Engraving and Printing, Peking. Recess. P* **14**.

1	**60**	8 c. red-orange	..	..	..	..	20	40

南	河	南	河	北	河	北	河	西	山	西	山

(A) Small Honan   (B) Large Honan   (C) Small Hopeh   (D) Large Hopeh   (E) Small Shansi   (F) Large Shansi

東	山		東	山		北	蘇		北	蘇

(G) Small Shantung   (H) Large Shantung   (I) Small Supeh   (J) Large Supeh

1941. *Stamps of China overprinted with Types A to J.*

Small types (1 July). Large types (15 July)
(a) On T **58**, 1931–37 De La Rue single circle issue

					Honan			Hopeh				Shansi		
					A		B		C		D		E		F
2	2 c.	..	..	(396)	10	5	5	5	5	5	5	5	8	5	5
3	4 c.	..	..	(397)	6·00	3·50	50	45	5	5	25	25	20	5	3·00 3·00
4	15 c. scarlet	..	..	(400)	5	5	5	5	10	10	1·50	1·50	5	5	5 5
5	20 c.	..	..	(401)	15	5	†		7·00	6·50	5	5	†		5
6	25 c.	..	..	(402)	—	—	45	40	4·00	4·00	15	15	1·75	1·75	8 5

					Shantung				Supeh			
					G		H		I		J	
2	2 c.	..	..	(396)	..	..	..	..	5	5	8	8	20	20
3	4 c.	..	..	(397)	..	..	..	..	8	5	5	5	3·50	—
4	15 c. scarlet	..	..	(400)	..	..	..	..	5	5	4·00	2·50	3·50	—
5	20 c.	..	..	(401)	..	..	..	..	5	5	†		5	5
6	25 c.	..	..	(402)	..	..	..	..	6·00	6·00	8	8	2·00	—	†

(b) On T 72, 1938–41, Chung Hwa. P 12½. No wmk

No.	Value	Cat.	Honan A		Honan B		Hopeh C		Hopeh D		Shansi E		Shansi F	
7	2 c. (A)	(462)	†		†		†		5	5	†		†	
8	2 c. (B)	(463)	†		15	15	†		12	12	†		5	5
9	3 c.	(464)	5	5	5	5	5	5	5	5	20	8	5	5
10	5 c. green	(465)	†		†		†		5	5	†		†	
11	5 c. olive-green	(466)	5	5	5	5	5	5	5	5	8	5	5	5
12	8 c. (C)	(467)	5	5	5	5	5	5	5	5	8	5	5	5
13	8 c. (D)	(468)	†		15	15	†		15	5	†		1·00	20
14	10 c.	(469)	†		5	5	†		5	5	†		5	5
15	15 c.	(470)	†		†		†		2·10	—	†		†	
16	16 c.	(471)	†		8	8	†		5	5	†		5	5
17	$1 (II)	(460)	3·00	3·00	†		2·00	1·60			—	—	†	
18	$1 (III)	(473)	12·00	12·00	50	25			20	20	†		35	20
19	$2	(474)	†		†		1·75	1·50	30	30	†		1·00	70
20	$5	(475)	†		3·00	2·50	1·50	1·50	1·40	1·40	†		2·10	2·10
21	$10	(476)	†		†		†		6·00	6·00	†		†	
22	$20	(477)	†		—		†		20·00	20·00	†		†	

No.	Value	Cat.	Shantung G		Shantung H		Supeh I		Supeh J	
7	2 c. (A)	(462)			5	5	†		†	
8	2 c. (B)	(463)			5	5	†		5	5
9	3 c.	(464)	5	5	5	5	5	5	5	5
11	5 c. olive-green	(466)	5	5	5	5	5	5	5	5
12	8 c. (C)	(467)	5	5	5	5	5	5	8	5
13	8 c. (D)	(468)	†		5	5	†		1·50	1·25
14	10 c.	(469)	†		5	5	†		5	5
16	16 c.	(471)	†		8	8	†		5	5
17	$1 (II)	(460)	3·50	3·25	†		10·00	9·00	†	
18	$1 (III)	(473)	20·00	25·00	20	15	†		30	20
19	$2	(474)	†		†		†		†	
20	$5	(475)	†		1·50	1·50	†		10·00	—

(c) On T 72, 1939–41, Dah Tung. P 14. No wmk

No.	Value	Cat.	Honan A		Honan B		Hopeh C		Hopeh D		Shansi E		Shansi F	
23	5 c. green	(489A)	†		†		—		†		†		†	
24	5 c. olive	(490A)	†		5	5	5	5	5	5	†		5	5
25	8 c. (F)	(492A)	†		5	5	1·75	1·50	5	5	·†		5	5
26	10 c.	(493A)	†		5	5	5	5	5	5	5	5	5	5
27	30 c.	(494A)	5	5	5	5	†		5	5	5	5	5	5
28	50 c.	(495A)	5	5	5	5	8	8	5	5	8	8	8	8
29	$1	(496A)	20	15	3·50	3·50	20	15	20	15	40	20	1·00	20
30	$2	(497A)	35	25	50	25	35	25	35	25	50	20	50	20
31	$5	(498A)	50	50	50	50	1·60	1·25	1·25	1·25	5·00	4·75	1·25	1·25
32	$10	(499A)	7·00	7·00	2·50	2·50	2·10	2·10	2·00	2·00	2·75	2·25	2·00	2·00
33	$20	(500A)	3·25	3·25	4·00	4·00	3·00	3·00	3·00	3·00	3·00	3·00	3·00	3·00

No.	Value	Cat.	Shantung G		Shantung H		Supeh I		Supeh J	
23	5 c. green	(489A)	†		†		†		5	5
24	5 c. olive	(490A)	†		5	5	†		5	5
25	8 c. (F)	(492A)	5	5	5	5	†		5	5
26	10 c.	(493A)	†		5	5	5	5	8	5
27	30 c.	(494A)	10	5	5	5	5	5	8	5
28	50 c.	(495A)	10	5	5	5	5	5	8	5
29	$1	(496A)	20	15	20	15	20	15	1·25	1·25
30	$2	(497A)	35	20	35	20	35	20	60	60
31	$5	(498A)	1·60	1·25	1·25	1·25	1·25	1·25	3·00	—
32	$10	(499A)	2·00	2·00	2·00	2·00	3·00	3·00	2·50	2·00
33	$20	(500A)	3·00	3·00	3·00	3·00	4·00	4·00	3·25	3·00

(d) As last but W 73

No.	Value	Cat.	Honan A		Honan B		Hopeh C		Hopeh D		Shansi E		Shansi F	
34	5 c. green	(489B)	†		50	10	†		5	5	†		5	5
35	5 c. olive	(490B)	†		20	5	†		5	5	†		5	5
36	10 c.	(493B)	†		10·00	—	†		5	5	†		5	5
37	30 c.	(494B)	70	40	40	12	40	40	5	5	3·00	2·50	3·00	3·00
38	50 c.	(495B)	†		75	60	†		8	5	15	10	†	

No.	Value	Cat.	Shantung G		Shantung H		Supeh I		Supeh J	
34	5 c. green	(489B)	†		5	5	†		†	
35	5 c. olive	(490B)	†		5	5	†		†	
36	10 c.	(493B)	†		20	12	†		5	5
37	30 c.	(494B)	1·00	40	15	10	40	20	†	
38	50 c.	(495B)	30	15	10	8	50	20	†	

(e) On T 60, 1932–34 Martyrs, Peking. P 14

No.	Value	Cat.	Honan A		Honan B		Hopeh C		Hopeh D		Shansi E		Shansi F	
39	½ c.	(410)	5	5	35	35	5	5	5	5	5	5	5	5
40	2½ c.	(412)	5	5	5	5	5	5	5	5	5	5	5	5
41	13 c.	(416)	1·75	85	8	5	8	8	5	5	7·00	6·00	5	5
42	30 c.	(419)	†		30	10	†		8	5	†		10	5
43	40 c.	(420)	†		2·10	50	†		3·00	—	—		†	

			Shantung		Supeh	
			G	H	I	J
39	½ c.	(410)	5 5	5 5	5 5	60 —
40	2½ c.	(412)	5 5	5 5	5 5	5 5
41	13 c.	(416)	50 35	5 5	8 8	5 5
42	30 c.	(419)	†	3·00 —	†	†

(f) On T **60**, 1939–41, Hong Kong print. P 12, 12½, 13 or compound. No wmk.

			Honan		Hopeh		Shansi	
			A	B	C	D	E	F
44	½ c.	(507)	5 5	5 5	5 5	5 5	5 5	5 5
45	1 c.	(508)	5 5	5 5	5 5	5 5	5 5	5 5
46	1 c. *(b)*	(508b)	†	— —	†	†		
47	2 c.	(509)	10 5	†	5 5	5 5	†	5 5
48	3 c.	(511)	5 5	5 5	5 5	5 5	15 5	45 —
49	4 c.	(512)	†	5 5	†	5 5	†	5 5
50	8 c.	(514)	60 —	5 5	5 5	5 5	20 5	20 5
51	10 c.	(515)	1·00 25	†	— —	5 5	75 40	2·00 2·00
52	13 c.	(516)	30 10	5 5	5 5	5 5	40 8	40 25
53	15 c.	(517)	†	5 5	†	5 5	†	5 5
54	17 c.	(518)	25 10	5 5	5 5	5 5	5 5	5 5
55	20 c.	(519)	1·00 25	5 5	5 5	5 5	5 5	5 5
56	21 c.	(520)	†	5 5	†	5 5	†	5 5
57	25 c.	(521)	8 5	†	5 5	5 5	5 5	3·00
58	28 c.	(522)	†	8 8	†	5 5	†	5 —
60	50 c.	(525)	†	3·00 2·10	†	3·50 —	†	15 8

			Shantung		Supeh	
			G	H	I	J
44	½ c.	(507)	5 5	5 5	5 5	5 5
45	1 c.	(508)	5 5	5 5	3·75 —	5 5
46	1 c. *(b)*	(508b)	†	1·90 1·90	15 12	†
47	2 c.	(509)	†	5 5	15 12	†
48	3 c.	(511)	5 5	5 5	5 5	40 —
49	4 c.	(512)	†	5 5	†	5 5
50	8 c.	(514)	30 15	5 5	2·50 —	40 —
51	10 c.	(515)	10 8	†	1·25 70	†
52	13 c.	(516)	5 5	5 5	5 5	40 —
53	15 c.	(517)	†	5 5	†	5 5
54	17 c.	(518)	5 5	5 5	5 5	5 5
55	20 c.	(519)	5 5	5 5	5 5	5 5
56	21 c.	(520)	†	5 5	†	5 5
57	25 c.	(521)	5 5	†	5 5	20 12
58	28 c.	(522)	†	5 5	†	5 5
59	30 c.	(523)	†	— —	†	†
60	50 c.	(525)	†	20 20	†	3·00 —

(g) As last but W **73**

			Honan		Hopeh		Shansi	
			A	B	C	D	E	F
61	½ c.	(526)	†	5 5	†	5 5	†	5 5
62	1 c.	(527)	5 5	5 5	5 5	5 5	5 5	5 5
63	2 c.	(528)	†	25 —	†	5 5	†	5 5
64	2½ c.	(529)	†	50 25	†	5 5	8 8	†
65	3 c.	(530)	†	†	†	5 5	†	†
66	8 c.	(533)	†	†	†	3·50	†	4·00 —
67	10 c.	(534)	5 5	25 20	5 5	5 5	10 5	45 —
68	13 c.	(535)	†	8 5	†	5 5	†	5 5
69	17 c.	(537)	25 8	8 5	5 5	5 5	1·10 50	†
70	20 c.	(538)	†	†	†	2·50 —	†	†
71	25 c.	(540)	†	10 5	†	5 5	†	5 5
72	30 c.	(542)	†	†	55 55	5 5	3·50 3·00	3·50 3·50
73	40 c.	(543)	30 5	12 5	8 5	5 5	1·00 30	5 5
74	50 c.	(544)	†	†	†	2·75 —	1·25 35	5 5

			Shantung			
61	½ c.	(526)	†	5 5	— —	5 5
62	1 c.	(527)	5 5	5 5	5 5	5 5
63	2 c.	(528)	†	50 —	†	5 5
64	2½ c.	(529)	8 8	5 5	50 45	5 5
65	3 c.	(530)	†	†	†	1·75 —
66	8 c.	(533)	†	†	†	3·50 —
67	10 c.	(534)	5 5	50 —	25 12	60
68	13 c.	(535)	†	5 5	†	5 5
69	17 c.	(537)	10 8	5 5	2·75 2·25	5 5
71	25 c.	(540)	†	5 5	†	5 5
72	30 c.	(542)	60 50	5 †	25 12	3·00
73	40 c.	(543)	45 20	5 5	10 10	5 5
74	50 c.	(544)	— —	5 5	3·50 3·50	†

坡　嘉　新
念　紀　落　陷

(1)

國　建　國　洲　滿
念　紀　年　週　十

(2)

1942 (19 Feb–1 Aug). *Fall of Singapore. Stamps of preceding issues with Large character overprints, further optd with* **T 1**, *in red.*

				Honan B		Hopeh D		Shansi F		Shantung H		Supeh J	
75	**58**	4 c.	(3)	†		†		†		†		2·50	2·50
76	**60**	4 c.	(49)	5	5	5	5	5	5	5	5	10	10
77	**72**	8 c. (C)	(12)	50	45	8	8	·10	10	15	15	15	15
78		8 c. (D)	(13)	15	15	12	12	65	65	70	70	50	50
79		8 c. (F)	(25)	15	15	15	15	15	15	15	15	†	

Dates of issue: 1 June, Nos. 78B, 78D, 78F, 78J and 79F; 1 Aug, Nos. 75J and 77H; 19 Feb, remainder.

1942 (1 Mar). *Tenth Anniv of Manchukuo. Stamps of preceding issues with Large character overprints, further optd with* **T 2**, *in red.*

				Honan B		Hopeh D		Shansi F		Shantung H		Supeh J	
80	**72**	2 c. (B)	(8)	15	15	15	15	10	10	10	10	12	12
81	**60**	4 c.	(49)	25	25	8	8	8	8	8	8	10	10
82	**72**	8 c. (C)	(12)	1·10	1·10	1·60	1·60	90	90	45	45	2·25	2·25
83		8 c. (D)	(13)	90	90	†		1·25	1·25	75	75	1·25	1·25
84		8 c. (F)	(25)	†		12	12	90	90	8	8	†	

The 2 c. Type **58**, De La Rue (No. 2) was similarly overprinted for Honan, Shansi, Shantung and Supeh but the stamps were not officially issued.

(3)

(Surch by Chinese Bureau of Engraving and Printing, Peking)

1942 (1 June). *Stamps of China and unissued "New Peking printings, optd "Hwa Pei" (two top characters, meaning "North China") and surch half original value as* **T 3**.

(a) On 1931–37 De La Rue single circle issue

85	**58**	1 c. on 2 c. olive-green (396)		5	5
86		2 c. on 4 c. green (397)		5	5

(b) On Third Sun Yat-sen issue, 1938–41

87	**72**	1 c. on 2 c. olive-green (A) (462)		10	10
88		1 c. on 2 c. olive-green (B) (463)		5	5
89		4 c. on 8 c. sage-green (C) (467)		5	5
90		4 c. on 8 c. sage-green (D) (468)		5	5
91		4 c. on 8 c. sage-green (F) (492A)		5	5
92		5 c. on 10 c. green (469)		5	5
93		5 c. on 10 c. green (493A)		5	5
94		5 c. on 10 c. green (493B)		5	5
95		8 c. on olive-brown (471)		5	5
96		15 c. on 30 c. scarlet (494A)		5	5
97		15 c. on 30 c. scarlet (494B)		5	5
98		25 c. on 50 c. blue (495A)		5	5
99		25 c. on 50 c. blue (495B)		5	5
100		50 c. on $1 sepia & red-brn (457)		20·00	20·00
101		50 c. on $1 sepia & red-brn (460)		2·00	2·00
102		50 c. on $1 sepia & red-brn (473)		10	
103		50 c. on $1 sepia & red-brown (496A)		8	5
104		$1 on $2 red-brown & blue (458)		50	50
105		$1 on $2 red-brown & blue (461)		5·00	5·00
106		$1 on $2 red-brown & blue (474)		20	20
107		$1 on $2 red-brown & blue (497A)		15	15
108		$5 on $10 violet & green (499A)		75	75
109		$10 on $20 ultram & pur (500A)		1·00	1·00

(c) On Martyrs types

110	**60**	½ c. on 1 c. yellow-orange (411)		5	5
111		½ c. on 1 c. yellow-orange (508)		5	5
112		½ c. on 1 c. yellow-orange (508b)		20	20
113		½ c. on 1 c. yellow-orange (527)		5	5
114		1 c. on 2 c. blue (509)		5	5
115		1 c. on 2 c. blue (528)		5	5
116		2 c. on 4 c. lilac (512)		5	5
117		4 c. on 8 c. orange-red (414)		1·60	1·25
118		4 c. on 8 c. brown-orange (514)		5	5
119		4 c. on 8 c. brown-orange (533)		15	12
120		5 c. on 10 c. dull purple (515)		5	5
121		5 c. on 10 c. dull purple (534)		5	5
122		10 c. on 20 c. light blue (519)		5	5
123		15 c. on 30 c. maroon (536)		8	5
124		20 c. on 40 c. orange (519)		5	5
125		20 c. on 40 c. orange (543)		5	5
126		25 c. on 50 c. green (525)		5	5
127		25 c. on 50 c. green (544)		5	5

(d) On Sun Yat-sen "New Peking" printings

128	**58**	1 c. on 2 c. olive-green		5	5
129		2 c. on 4 c. yellow-green		5	5

130	**72**	8 c. on 16 c. olive-brown		5	5
131		50 c. on $1 sep. and orange-brown		5	5
132		$1 on $2 brown and blue		10	8
133		$5 on $10 violet and green		50	50

(e) On Martyrs "New Peking" printings

134	**60**	4 c. on 8 c. brown-orange		5	5
135		10 c. on 20 c. brown-lake		5	5
136		15 c. on 30 c. maroon		5	5
137		20 c. on 40 c. orange		5	5
138		25 c. on 50 c. green		5	5

Postal rates in the occupied areas to the south were doubled in April 1942 because of currency depreciation, but those in the north were unchanged. These half-value surcharges thus indicated the actual purchase price in North China (and Mengkiang).

邦友
界租　還交　局總　政郵
立成
念紀　念紀年週五

(4)　　(5)

1943 (30 Mar). *Return to China of Foreign Concessions. Stamps of preceding issues further optd with* **T 4**, *in red.*

139	**58**	2 c. on 4 c. yellow-green	(129)	5	5
140	**72**	4 c. on 8 c. sage-green	(91)	5	5
141		8 c. on 16 c. olive-brown	(130)	5	5
139/141		Set of 3		10	10

1943 (15 Aug). *Fifth Anniv of Directorate General of Posts for North China. Stamps of preceding issues further optd with* **T 5**, *in red.*

142	**58**	2 c. on 4 c. yellow-green	(129)	5	5
143	**72**	4 c. on 8 c. sage-green	(90)	5	5
144		8 c. on 16 c. olive-brown	(130)	5	5
142/144		Set of 3		10	10

1943 (1 Nov). *Stamps of China and unissued "New Peking" printings, optd "Hwa Pei" (= North China) as top characters of* **T 3**.

(a) On Third Sun Yat-sen issue, 1938–41

145	**72**	10 c. green (469)		5	5
146		$2 red-brown and blue	(497A)	60	60
147		$5 deep green and scarlet	(475)	30	30
148		$5 deep green & scarlet	(498A)	20	20
149		$10 violet and green	(499A)	80	80
150		$20 ultramarine & purple	(500A)	2·50	2·50

(b) On Martyrs issue

151	**60**	1 c. yellow-orange	(411)	5	5
152		1 c. yellow-orange	(508)	5	5

(c) On Sun Yat-sen "New Peking" printings

153	**58**	2 c. olive-green		5	5
154		4 c. yellow-green		5	5
155		5 c. green		5	5
156	**72**	9 c. sage-green		5	5
157		16 c. olive-brown		5	5
158		18 c. olive-brown		5	5
159		$1 sepia and orange-brown		10	8
160		$2 brown and rose-red		15	12
161		$5 green and rose-red		20	15

162	$10 violet and green	25	25
163	$20 ultramarine and purple	55	55

The 16 c. was issued only with gum and the $20 only without gum; the remaining values were issued both with and without gum.

(d) On Martyrs "New Peking" printings

164 **60**	1 c. yellow-orange..	5	5
165	10 c. purple ..	5	5
166	20 c. brown-lake	5	5
167	30 c. maroon	5	5
168	40 c. orange	5	5
169	50 c. green ..	5	5

The 1 c. was issued only with gum; the other values were issued both with and without gum.

戰　參
念紀年週一
(6)

會員委務政
念紀年週四
(7)

華
北
玖
分
(8)

1944 (9 Jan). *First Anniv of Declaration of War on Allies by Japanese-controlled Nanking Govt. Optd with T* **6**.

170 **58**	4 c. yellow-green (154)	5	5
171 **72**	10 c. green (145)	5	5

1944 (30 Mar). *Fourth Anniv of Establishment of North China Political Council. Optd with T* **7**, *in red*.

172 **72**	9 c. sage-green (156)	5	5
173	19 c. olive-brown (158)	5	5
174 **60**	50 c. green (169)	10	10
175 **72**	$1 sepia and orange-brown (159) ..	15	15
172/175	Set of 4	30	30

1944 (July). *Nos. 114/7 of Japanese Occupation of Nanking and Shanghai surch "Hwa Pei" and new values in Chinese characters variously as T* **8**.

176 **5**	5 c. on 50 c. orange	5	5
177	18 c. on $1 green (R.)	5	5
178 **6**	36 c. on $2 violet-blue (R.)	5	5
179	90 c. on $5 carmine	8	8
176/179	Set of 4	20	20

No. 176 is overprinted with Type **8**; No. 177 with six characters vertically; No. 178 with six characters in two columns; No. 179 with a group of four characters.

立成局總政郵
念紀年週六
(9)

席　主　汪
念　紀　典　葬
(10)

年週二戰　參
念　紀
(11)

1944 (15 Aug). *Sixth Anniv of Directorate General of Posts for North China. Optd with T* **9**.

180 **72**	9 c. sage-green (156) (R.)	5	5
181	18 c. olive-green (158) (R.)	5	5
182 **60**	50 c. green (169) (R.)..	5	5
183 **72**	$1 sepia and orange-brown (159)..	12	12
180/183	Set of 4	20	20

1944 (5 Dec). *Death of Wang Ching-wei. Optd with T* **10**.

184 **60**	20 c. brown-lake (166) (B.)	5	5
185	50 c. green (169) (B.) ..	5	5
186 **72**	$1 sepia and orge-brown (159) (B.)	5	5
187	$2 brown and blue (160)	5	5
184/187	Set of 4	15	15

1945 (9 Jan). *Second Anniv of Declaration of War on Allies by Nanking Govt. Optd with T* **11**.

188 **60**	20 c. brown-lake (166)	5	5
189	50 c. green (169) (R.) ..	8	8
190 **72**	$1 sepia and orange-brown (159)..	8	8
191	$2 brown and blue (160)	12	12
188/191	Set of 4	30	30

華
北
壹
圓
(12)

13 Dragon Pillar

14 Long Bridge

15 Imperial City Tower

16 Marble Boat, Summer Palace

17

1945 (7 Feb). *Nos. 118/9 of Japanese Occupation of Nanking and Shanghai, surch with new values as T* **12**, *in red, for use in North China*.

192 **7**	50 c. on $3 yellow-orange	5	5
193	$1 on $6 blue	5	5

(Litho Hsin Min Press, Peking)

1945 (30 Mar). *Fifth Anniv of Establishment of North China Political Council. Views of Peking. No gum. P* 14.

194 **13**	$1 yellow	5	5
195 **14**	$2 blue	5	5
196 **15**	$5 scarlet	5	5
197 **16**	$10 green	5	5
194/197	Set of 4	15	15

(Litho Hsin Min Press, Peking)

1945 (5 May). *Optd "Hwa Pei" as top characters in T* **3**. *No gum. P* 14.

198 **17**	$1 red-brown	5	5
199	$2 blue	5	5
200	$5 red	8	5
201	$10 green	10	8
202	$20 purple	12	8
203	$50 brown	45	40
198/203	Set of 6	75	60

These stamps exist in many shades and several varieties of paper. They were not issued without overprint.

Imperforate copies of the $50 in unissued colours and without overprint are proofs.

18 Wutai Mountain, Shansi

19 Kaifeng Iron Pagoda, Honan

20 International Bridge, Tientsin

21 Taishan Mountain, Shantung

22 G.P.O., Peking

(Litho Hsin Min Press, Peking)

1945 (15 Aug). *Seventh Anniv of Directorate General of Posts for North China. No gum. P* 14.

204 **18**	$5 green	5	5
205 **19**	$10 grey-brown	5	5
206 **20**	$20 purple	5	5
207 **21**	$30 slate-grey	5	5
208 **22**	$50 carmine ..	5	5
204/208	Set of 5	20	20

D. NANKING AND SHANGHAI

The Japanese army captured Shanghai on 9 November 1937, Nanking on 13 December 1937 and Hankow on 25 October 1938. On 27 March 1938 Nanking was made the seat of government of a Japanese-controlled Chinese government for areas in the Yangtse basin, and on 30 March 1940 it was made the capital of Wang Ching-wei's government for all Japanese-occupied China. The stamps listed below were used in parts of Anhwei, Southern Kiangsu, Chekiang, Hupeh, Kiangsi, Hunan and Fukien.

念紀界租回收

20   八月一日   三十二年

付巳貸空航之函信內國   角 伍

(1)   (2)

1941 (23 Dec)–**42.** AIR. Air stamps of China, 1940–41, surch in Japanese currency as T **1**.

1	61	10 s. on 50 c. chocolate (549)	5	5
2		18 s. on 90 c. olive (551)	5	5
3		20 s. on $1 apple-green (552)	5	5
4		20 s. on $1 apple-green (562)	70	80
5		25 s. on 90 c. olive (551) (1.5.42)	5	5
6		35 s. on $2 brown (553)	5	5

No. 6 further surch in red (1.5.42)

7	61	60 s. on 35 s. on $2 brown	5	5
1/7		Set of 7	90	1·00

A second printing of No. 1 has the "10" directly above the first Chinese character instead of to the left of it.

1943 (1 Aug). *Return of Shanghai Foreign Concessions. Stamps of China surch as T* **2**.

8	72	25 c. on 5 c. green (465) (R.)	5	5
9	77	50 c. on 8 c. red-orange (B.)	5	5
10	72	$1 on 16 c. olive-brown (471) (R.)	5	5
11	77	$2 on 50 c. deep blue (R.)	5	5
8/11		Set of 4	15	15

The Post Office put these on sale at above face value, *i.e.* at $4 per set.

(Recess Chung Hwa Book Co, Hong Kong)

1943 (22 Nov). T **72** *of China without overprint. P* 12½.

12	72	15 c. brown	30	40

A small quantity of this stamp was issued at Shanghai; the bulk of the printing was surcharged as below.

壹 暫   壹 暫

角 **10** 售   圓柒角 **170** 售

(3)   (4)

1943 (22 Nov)–**45.** *Stamps of China and No.* 12 *above, surch in Chinese currency as T* **3** (*cent values*) *or* **4** (*dollar values*).

(a) On Type **58**, *1931–37 issue*

13		$6 on 5 c. yellow-green (398) (30.3.45)	5	5
14		$20 on 15 c. scarlet (400) (30.3.45)	5	5
15		$500 on 15 c. bl-grn (399) (3.9.45)	5	5
16		$1,000 on 20 c. ultram (392) (7.7.45)	30·00	
17		$1,000 on 20 c. ultram (401) (7.7.45)	5	5
18		$1,000 on 25 c. ultram (402) (7.7.45)	5	5

(b) On Type **72**

(i) Chung Hwa printings, 1938–41. No wmk

19		25 c. on 5 c. olive-green (466)	5	5
20		30 c. on 2 c. ol-grn (B) (463) (1.5.44)	5	5
21		50 c. on 3 c. brn-lake (464) (1.9.44)	5	5
22		50 c. on 5 c. ol-grn (466) (1.3.44)	5	5
23		50 c. on 8 c. sage-green (C) (467)	5	5
24		$1 on 8 c. sage-green (C) (467)	5	5
25		$1 on 8 c. sage-green (D) (468)	8	8
26		$1 on 15 c. brown	5	5
27		$1.30 on 16 c. olive-brown (471)	5	5

28		$1.50 on 3 c. brown-lake (464) (1.9.44)	5	5
29		$2 on 5 c. ol-grn (466) (1.9.44)	5	5
30		$2 on 10 c. green (469) (1.3.44)	5	5
31		$3 on 15 c. brown (1.3.44)	5	5
32		$4 on 16 c. ol-brn (471) (1.3.44)	5	5
33		$5 on 15 c. brown (1.3.44)	5	5
34		$6 on 5 c. green (465) (30.3.45)	5	5
35		$6 on 5 c. ol-grn (466) (27.11.44)	5	5
		a. Perf 14*	1·75	1·75
36		$6 on 8 c. sage-green (C) (467) (30.3.45)	5	5
37		$6 on 8 c. sage-green (D) (468) (30.3.45)	50·00	40·00
38		$6 on 10 c. green (469) (1.9.44)	5	5
39		$10 on 10 c. green (469) (27.11.44)	5	5
40		$10 on 16 c. ol-brn (471) (1.3.44)	5	5
41		$20 on 3 c. brown-lake (464) (30.3.45)	5	5
42		$20 on 15 c. scarlet (470) (30.3.45)	5	5
43		$20 on 15 c. brown (27.11.44)	5	5
44		$20 on $2 red-brown and blue (474) (1.9.44)	8	8
45		$100 on 3 c. brown-lake (464) (7.7.45)	5	5
46		$500 on 8 c. sage-green (C) (467) (3.9.45)	5	5
47		$500 on 10 c. green (469) (3.9.45)	5	5
48		$500 on 15 c. scarlet (470) (3.9.45)	5	5
49		$500 on 15 c. brown (3.9.45)	5	5
50		$500 on 16 c. ol-brn (471) (3.9.45)	5	5
51		$1,000 on 25 c. vio-bl (472) (3.9.45)	5	5
52		$2,000 on $5 deep green and scarlet (475) (3.9.45)	5	5

(ii) Dah Tung printings, 1939–41. No wmk

53		$1 on 8 c. sage-green (F) (492A) (1.3.44)	5	5
54		$1.70 on 30 c. scarlet (494A)	5	5
		a. Perf 12½*	5	5
55		$2 on 5 c. olive-green (F) (490A) (30.3.45)	5	5
56		$2 on $1 sep & red-brn (496A)	5	5
57		$3 on 8 c. sage-green (F) (492A) (1.9.44) (flat top 3)	5	5
		a. Perf 12½*	5	5
58		$3 on 8 c. sage-green (E) (491A) (1.9.44) (round top 3)	12	12
59		$3 on 8 c. sage-green (F) (492A) (1.9.44) (round top 3)	5	5
60		$6 on 5 c. olive-green (F) (490A) (27.11.44)	5	5
61		$6 on 5 c. green (E) (489A) (30.3.45)	5	5
62		$6 on 8 c. sage-green (F) (492A) (30.3.45)	5	5
		a. Perf 12½*	5	5
63		$10 on 10 c. green (493A) (30.3.45)	5	5
		a. Perf 12½*	5	5
64		$20 on $2 red-brown and blue (497A) (1.5.44)	5	5
65		$50 on 30 c. scarlet (494A) (30.3.45)	5	5
66		$50 on 50 c. blue (495A) (30.3.45)	5	5
67		$50 on $5 deep green and scarlet (498A) (1.9.44)	5	5
68		$50 on $20 ultram & purple (500A)	12	10
69		$100 on $10 violet and green (499A) (30.3.45)	5	5
70		$200 on $20 ultramarine and purple (500A) (30.3.45)	5	5
71		$500 on 8 c. sage-green (E) (491A) (3.9.45)	8	8
72		$500 on 8 c. sage-green (F) (492A) (3.9.45)	5	5
73		$500 on 10 c. green (493A) (3.9.45)	5	5
74		$1,000 on 30 c. scar (494A) (3.9.45)	5	5
75		$1,000 on 50 c. blue (495A) (3.9.45)	5	5
76		$1,000 on $2 red-brown and blue (497A) (7.7.45)	15	15
77		$2,000 on $5 deep green and scarlet (498A) (3.9.45)	12	12

(iii) Dah Tung printings, 1940–41. W **73**

78		$2 on $1 sep & red-brn (p. 12½)*	5	5
79		$6 on 5 c. green (F) (489B) (30.3.45)	5	5
80		$6 on 5 c. olive-green (F) (490B) (30.3.45)	5	5
81		$50 on 30 c. scarlet (494B) (1.3.44)	6·50	6·50

82	$50 on $5 deep green and scarlet (498B) (27.11.44)	5	5
	a. Violet and black surch ..	5	5
83	$100 on $10 violet and green (496B) (1.5.44)	5	5
84	$200 on $20 ultramarine and purple (500B) (1.5.44) ..	5	5
85	$500 on 10 c. green (493B) (3.9.45)	5	5
86	$1,000 on 30 c. scarlet (494B) (3.9.45)	5	5
87	$5,000 on $10 violet and green (499B) (3.9.45)	3·00	3·00
	a. Perf 12½*	40	40

*Not officially issued without surcharge.
No. 82a has the value tablet in violet and the Chinese characters in black.

(c) On Martyrs issue as T 60, 1939–41 (3.9.45)

88	$7.50 on ½ c. sepia (507) ..	5	5
89	$15 on 1 c. yellow-orange (508) ..	5	5
90	$15 on 1 c. yellow-orange (508b) ..	5·00	5·00
91	$30 on 2 c. blue (509) ..	5	5
92	$30 on 2 c. blue (528) ..	3·25	3·25
93	$200 on 1 c. yellow-orange (508) ..	5	5
94	$200 on 8 c. brown-orange (514) ..	5	5

(d) On Type 77, 1941 New York issue

95	5 c. on ½ c. sepia (1.5.44) ..	5	5
96	10 c. on 1 c. orange (1.3.44) ..	5	5
97	20 c. on 1 c. orange (1.5.44) ..	5	5
98	40 c. on 5 c. green (1.5.44) ..	5	5
99	$5 on 5 c. green (30.3.45)	5	5
100	$10 on 10 c. emer-grn (30.3.45)	5	5
101	$50 on ½ c. sepia (7.7.45) ..	5	5
102	$50 on 1 c. orange (7.7.45)	5	5
103	$50 on 17 c. olive-green (30.3.45)	5	5
104	$200 on 5 c. green (7.7.45) ..	5	5
105	$200 on 8 c. turq-green (3.9.45)	5	5
106	$200 on 8 c. red-orange (3.9.45)	5	5
107	$500 on $5 blk & scarlet (30.3.45)	5	5
108	$1,000 on 1 c. orange (3.9.45)	5	5
109	$1,000 on 25 c. purple (3.9.45)	5	5
110	$1,000 on 30 c. scarlet (3.9.45)	5	5
111	$1,000 on $2 black and blue (7.7.45)	8	8
112	$1,000 on $10 black & green (30.3.45) ..	5	5
113	$2,000 on $5 black and scarlet (7.7.45)	8	8

5 Wheat and Cotton Flower

6 Purple Mountain, Nanking

1944 (30 Mar). Fourth Anniv of Establishment of Chinese Puppet Government at Nanking. Recess. P 12½×12 (T 5) or 12×12½ (T 6).

114	5	50 c. orange ..	..	..	5	5
115		$1 green ..	..	..	5	5
116	6	$2 violet-blue ..	..	..	5	5
117		$5 carmine ..	..	..	5	5
114/117		Set of 4 ..	..	..	15	15

7 Map of Shanghai and Foreign Concessions   (D 1)

1944 (1 Aug). First Anniv of Return to China of Shanghai Foreign Concessions. Recess. P 12×12½.

118	7	$3 yellow-orange	..	5	5
119		$6 blue	..	5	5

1944 (27 Nov). POSTAGE DUE. Postage Due stamps of China, 1932, surch as Type D 1.

D120	D 5	$1 on 2 c. orange..	..	5	5
D121		$2 on 5 c. orange	..	5	5
D122		$5 on 10 c. orange	..	5	5
D123		$10 on 20 c. orange	..	5	5
D120/123		Set of 4 ..	..	15	15

1945 (30 Mar). Fifth Anniv of Establishment of Chinese Puppet Government at Nanking. Surch with new values as T 4.

124	5	$15 on 50 c. orange ..	..	5	5
125		$30 on $1 green	..	5	5
126	6	$60 on $2 violet-blue..	..	5	5
127		$200 on $5 carmine	..	5	5
124/127		Set of 4 ..	..	15	15

(8)

(Surch by Union Printing Co, Shanghai)

1945 (9 Aug). Air Raid Precaution Propaganda Issue. Air stamps of China, 1940–41, no wmk, surch as T 8.

128	61	$150 on 15 c. blue-green (Vm.) ..	5	5
129		$250 on 25 c. orange (G.) ..	5	5
130		$600 on 60 c. blue (Vm.) ..	5	8
131		$1,000 on $1 apple-green (C.) ..	5	10
128/131		Set of 4	15	20

These stamps were for use on all kinds of mail.

CHUNGKING ((Tchongking). See under China (Indo-Chinese Post Offices).

Cilicia

40 Paras = 1 Piastre

(A)   (B)   (C)   (D)   (E)

CILICIE   CILICIE   Cilicie
(1)   (2)   (3)

FRENCH OCCUPATION

By the Armistice Agreement of 30 October 1918 with the Allies, Turkey withdrew troops from Cilicia, the area of Turkey-in-Asia between the Taurus Mts. and the Gulf of Alexandretta, consisting mostly of the pre-1918 Turkish vilayet of Adana. Cilicia was occupied by French troops from the end of 1918 until, after warfare between these troops and those of Kemal Atatürk, the occupation was ended by the Angora Agreement of 20 October 1921 between France and the Turkish Nationalists.

Stamps of Turkey variously overprinted

NOTE. Being handstamped, Types **1** to **4** may be found double or inverted on most of the stamps listed, and occasionally double, one inverted.

1919 (4 Mar). *Handstamped with T* **1**, *in black. Turkish Crescent opts in black or red* (R.).

(a) 1897 Printed Matter stamp, No. N161. P 13½

N1	**15**	5 pa. on 10 pa. green (E) (R.)	..	12	10

(b) 1901 type. P 12 or 13½

2	**21**	1 pi. blue (B) (R.) ..	..	..	12	12
3		1 pi. blue (D) (R.) ..	..	..	25	25

(c) 1909 type. P 12

4	**28**	20 pa. rose-carmine (B)	..	..	10	10
5		20 pa. rose-carmine (C)	..	..	7·00	5·50
6		20 pa. rose-carmine (D)	..	..	12	10
7		1 pi. ultramarine (A+C) (R.)	..	£150	50·00
		a. Type A omitted	..	..	£180	£140
8		1 pi. ultramarine (D) (R.)	..	..	60	50

(d) 1913 type. P 12

9	**30**	20 pa. rose (B)	..	..	20	20

(e) 1914 pictorial issue. P 12

10	**32**	2 pa. claret ..	..	..	20	15
11	**33**	4 pa. sepia ..	..	..	5	5
12	**35**	6 pa. deep blue	..	..	90	45
13	**40**	1¾ pi. red-brown and grey ..	..	30	30

(f) 1916 Postal Anniversary issue. P 12½ *or* 13½

14	**60**	5 pa. green ..	..	..	16·00	7·00
15		20 pa. blue ..	..	..	10	10
16		1 pi. black and violet	..	..	15	15
17		5 pi. black and brown	..	..	12	12

(g) Pictorial issues of 1916–18. P 11½ *or* 12½

18	**73**	10 pa. green ..	..	..	12	12
19	**76**	50 pa. blue ..	..	..	60	20
20	**69**	5 pi. on 2 pa. greenish blue	..	50	30
21	**63**	25 pi. carmine/buff ..	..	..	12	12

22	**64**	50 pi. carmine	..	..	..	12	12
23		50 pi. indigo	..	..	..	1·40	1·40

(h) Armistice issue of 1919 with opt Turkey T **81**. *P* 11½ *or* 12½

24	**76**	50 pa. blue (R.)	..	..	..	60	35
25	**77**	2 pi. indigo and chestnut ..	..	20	15
26	**78**	5 pi. black and blue-green (R.)	..	60	20

(i) Postage Due stamps of 1914. P 12

D27	D **6**	5 pa. purple	..	..	..	12	12
D28	D **7**	20 pa. carmine	..	..	..	10	10
D29	D **8**	1 pi. deep blue	..	..	..	30	30
D30	D **9**	2 pi. grey ..	..	..	..	25	25

1919 (14 Mar). *As previous issues but handstamped with T* **2**.

(a) 1897 Printed Matter stamp, No. N161. P 13½

N31	**15**	5 pa. on 10 pa. green (E) (R.)	..	10	10

(b) 1901 type. P 12 or 13½

32	**21**	1 pi. blue (B) (R.)	..	..	12	12
33		1 pi. blue (D) (R.)	..	..	20	20

(c) 1909 type. P 12

34	**28**	20 pa. rose-carmine (C)	..	10·00	8·00
35		20 pa. rose-carmine (D)	..	..	5	5

(d) 1913 type. P 12

36	**30**	20 pa. rose (B)	..	..	8	8

(e) 1914 pictorial issue. P 12

37	**32**	2 pa. claret ..	..	..	5	5
38	**33**	4 pa. sepia ..	..	..	15	15

(f) 1916 Postal Anniversary issue. P 12½ *or* 13½

39	**60**	20 pa. blue ..	..	..	12	12
40		1 pi. black and violet	..	..	10	8

(g) Pictorial issue of 1918. P 11½ *or* 12½

41	**69**	5 pi. on 2 pa. greenish blue	..	10	10

(h) Postage Due stamps of 1914. P 12

D42	D **6**	5 pa. purple	..	..	..	12	12
D43	D **7**	20 pa. carmine	..	..	..	10	10
D44	D **8**	1 pi. deep blue	..	..	..	30	25
D45	D **9**	2 pi. grey ..	..	..	..	30	20

1919 (1 Apr). *As previous issues but handstamped with T* **3**.

(a) 1897 Printed Matter stamp, No. N161. P 13½

N46	**15**	5 pa. on 10 pa. green (E) (R.)	..	10	10

(b) 1901 type. P 12 or 13½

47	**21**	1 pi. blue (B) (R.)	..	..	5	5
48		1 pi. blue (D) (R.)	..	..	10	10
49		1 pi. blue (E) (R.)	..	..	5·00	2·75

(c) 1908 type. P 12, 13½ *or* 12×13½

50	**25**	20 pa. rose-carmine (A (B.)+D)	..	35	35

(d) 1909 type. P 12

51	**28**	20 pa. rose-carmine (B)	..	50·00	24·00
52		20 pa. rose-carmine (A (B.)+D)	..	12	12
		a. Type A omitted	..	..	7·00	3·25

(e) 1913 type. P 12

53	**30**	5 pa. bistre (B) (R.) ..	..	..	20	20
54		20 pa. rose (B)	..	..	..	12	12

(f) 1914 pictorial issue. P 12

55	**32**	2 pa. claret ..	..	..	8	8
56	**33**	4 pa. sepia ..	..	..	8	8

(g) 1916 Postal Anniversary issue. P 12½ *or* 13½

57	**60**	20 pa. blue ..	..	..	10	10
58		1 pi. black and violet	..	..	8	8
59		5 pi. black and brown	..	..	8	8

(h) Pictorial issues of 1917–18. P 11½ *or* 12½

60	**72**	5 pa. orange	..	..	..	20	20
61	**75**	1 pi. violet-blue	..	..	..	12	12
62	**69**	5 pi. on 2 pa. greenish blue	..	..	30	30
63	**64**	50 pi. green/yellow ..	..	..	1·90	1·25

		(i) Postage Due stamps of 1914. P 12				
D64	D 6	5 pa. purple	..	..	10	10
D65	D 7	20 pa. carmine	..	..	10	10
D66	D 8	1 pi. deep blue	..	..	30	30
D67	D 9	2 pi. grey ..	..	..	25	20

T.E.O.   T. E. O.

Cilicie   Cilicie

(4)   **(5)**

("T.E.O." = Territoires Ennemis Occupés)

1919 (1 May). *Stamp of 1917–18 handstamped with T 4. P 11½ or 12½.*

68	73	10 pa. green	..	..	5	5

1919 (23 May). *Optd with T 5.*

(a) 1897 Printed Matter stamp, No. N161. P 13½

N69	15	5 pa. on 10 pa. green (E) (R.)	..		5	5

(b) Type of 1892 surch with T 56 of Turkey, No. 630. P 13½

70	15	10 pa. on 20 pa. claret (D)	..	..	5	5

(c) 1909 type. P 12

71	28	20 pa. rose-carmine (B)	..	..	12	8
72		20 pa. rose-carmine (D)	..	..	8	8

(d) Type of 1909 optd with Turkey T 82, in red and surch with T 83, in blue, No. 938

73	28	5 pa. on 2 pa. olive-green	..	..	5	5
		a. Opt T 82 double	..	..		
		b. Surch T 83 double	..	..		

(e) 1914 pictorial stamp. P 12

74	38	1 pi. bright blue (R.)	..	..	5	5

(f) 1916 Postal Anniversary issue. P 12½ or 13½

75	60	5 pa. green ..	..	..	22·00	8·00
76		20 pa. blue	..	..	5	5
77		1 pi. black and violet	..	..	5	5

(g) As last but with opt Type D, in blue. P 12½ or 13½

78	60	10 pa. carmine	..	..	5	5

(h) Pictorial issues of 1916–18. P 11½ or 12½

79	72	5 pa. orange (B.)	..	..	5	5
80	73	10 pa. green ..	..	..	5	5
81	74	20 pa. carmine (B.)	..	..	5	5
		a. Black opt	..	..	5	5
82	77	2 pi. indigo and chestnut	..	..	5	5
83	78	5 pi. sepia and greenish blue (R.)	..	..	5	5
84	69	5 pi. on 2 pa. greenish blue	..	..	30	20
85	63	25 pi. carmine/*buff*	..	..	30	15
86	64	50 pi. green/*yellow*	..	..	5·00	4·50

(i) War Charity stamp of 1917. P 12½

87	65	10 pa. purple ..	..	..	5	5

Type **5** is known inverted, double and double, one inverted on most of the above. There are numerous minor varieties such as stop after "O" of "T.E.O." on the line instead of being raised. Also "Cilicie" occurs spelt "Cilcte", "Ciltcte", "Cilicle", etc. and accents are known instead of dots over one of the "i's".

T E O
20
PARAS

(6)   20   *20*   *20*   20

     I   II   III

I. Thick figures.
II. Thin figures. Wide "O"
III. Thin figures. Narrow "O"

1920. *No. 14 of French Post Offices in the Turkish Empire (Mouchon type of France inscr "LEVANT") surch as T 6.*

88		20 pa. on 10 c. carmine (I)	..	..	5	5
		a. "PARAS" omitted ..	..	..	1·50	1·50
		b. "P ARS" for "PARAS"	..	..	2·25	2·25
		c. "S" inverted	..	..	20	20
		d. Type II	..	..	15	15
		e. Type III	..	..	12	12

MILITAIRE

PARAS

OCCUPATION   70   Française

CILICIE

7   **(8)**

1920. *Fiscal stamp of Turkey, surch as T 8, in blue. P 11½.*

89	7	70 pa. on 5 pa. red	..	..	5	5
90		3½ pi. on 5 pa. red	..	..	5	5

The above exist with surcharge inverted, double and double, one inverted and with numerous errors such as "OCCCPATION", "OCCUPTTION", "MLITAIRE", "PIATSRES", etc. (*price £1 each*).

Stamps of France surcharged

O M F   O. M. F.   O. M. F.
Cilicie   Cilicia   Cilicie
     1   SAND. EST
5 PARAS   PIASTRE   5 PARAS

(9)   **(10)**   **(11)**

("O.M.F." = Occupation Militaire Française)

1920. *Surch as T 9 or in four lines (5 pi. to 100 pi.).*

91	11	5 pa. on 2 c. claret ..		..	5	5
92	18	10 pa. on 5 c. green ..		..	5	5
93		20 pa. on 10 c. red	..	..	10	10
		a. Thin figure "2"	..	..	6·00	
94		1 pi. on 25 c. blue ..		..	10	10
95	15	2 pi. on 15 c. slate-green	..	..	30	30
96	13	5 pi. on 40 c. red and pale blue	..	..	40	40
		a. Small "O" in "O.M.F."	..	..	2·00	
97		10 pi. on 50 c. cinnamon & lavender	..	..	50	50
		a. Small "O" in "O.M.F."	..	..	2·75	
98		50 pi. on 1 f. lake and yellow	..	..	12·00	12·00
		a. Small "O" in "O.M.F."	..	..	30·00	
99		100 pi. on 5 f. deep blue and buff	..	..	80·00	80·00

1920. *Surch as T 10 (thicker letters).*

100	11	5 pa. on 2 c. claret ..		..	5	5
		a. "Cililie"	..	..	1·25	1·25
		b. "Syrie" for "Cilicie" ..		..	3·00	3·00
		c. "PIASTRES" for "PARAS"	..		1·60	1·60
		d. "PARAS" for "Cilicie"	..		2·50	2·50
		e. "Cilicie" omitted	..	..	2·50	2·50
		f. Surch inverted	..	..	80	80
		g. Surch double ..	..	..	1·75	1·75
101	18	10 pa. on 5 c. green	..	..	5	5
		a. "Syrie" for "Cilicie" ..		..	3·00	3·00
		b. "PARAS" for "Cilicie"	..		2·50	2·50
		c. "5 PARAS" for "10 PARAS"	..		1·00	1·00
		d. Do. and surch inverted	..		3·00	3·00
		e. Normal surch inverted	..		1·00	1·00
		f. Surch double ..	..	..		
102		20 pa. on 10 c. red	..	..	5	5
		a. "10 PARAS" for "20 PARAS"	..		1·10	1·10
		b. Do. and surch inverted	..		3·00	3·00
		c. Normal surch inverted	..		90	90
		d. Surch double ..	..	..	2·25	2·25
		e. Surch double, one inverted	..		3·25	3·25
103		1 pi. on 25 c. blue ..		..	5	5
		a. Thin figure "1"	..	..	1·25	1·25
		b. Surch inverted	..	..	1·00	1·00
104	15	2 pi. on 15 c. slate-green ..		..	5	5
		a. "S" omitted ..	..	..	3·00	
		b. Surch inverted	..	..	80	80
		c. Surch double ..	..	..	2·50	2·50
		d. Surch double, one inverted	..		5·00	
105	13	5 pi. on 40 c. red and pale blue	..		5	5
		a. Thin figure "5"	..	..	6·50	6·50
		b. "PIASRTES" ..	..	..	2·50	2·50
		c. Surch inverted	..	..	2·25	2·25
		d. Surch double ..	..	..	3·25	

106	**13**	10 pi. on 50 c. cinnamon & lavender		5	5
		a. "PIASRTES"	..	2·75	2·75
		b. Surch inverted	..	3·00	3·00
		c. Surch double..	..	5·00	5·00
107		50 pi. on 1 f. lake and yellow	..	10	10
		a. Thin figure "5" ..	..	6·50	
		b. "50" omitted ..	..	10·00	
		c. "PIASRTES"	..	3·00	3·00
		d. Surch inverted	..	4·00	4·00
108		100 pi. on 5 f. deep blue and buff	..	1·00	1·00
		a. "PIASTRES"	..	8·00	8·00
		b. Surch inverted	..	10·00	10·00
100/108		*Set of 9*	..	1·25	1·25

All values also exist with 1 or 2 mm spacing between value and "Cilicie" and with the "e" of "Cilicie" open or closed, appearing inverted.

("SAND. EST" = Sandjak de l'Est)

1920. *Surch as T* **11.**

109	**11**	5 pa. on 2 c. claret ..	..	..	40
110	**18**	10 pa. on 5 c. green ..	..	..	40
		a. Surch double ..	..	..	5·00
111		20 pa. on 10 c. red ..	..	..	10
		a. Surch inverted..	..	..	3·00
112		1 pi. on 25 c. blue ..	..	..	12
113	**15**	2 pi. on 15 c. slate-green ..	..	..	65
114	**13**	5 pi. on 40 c. red and pale blue	..	7·00	
		a. "N" inverted	..	12·00	
		b. Small "O" in "O.M.F."	..	12·00	
115		20 pi. on 1 f. lake and yellow	..	8·00	
		a. "N" inverted	..	16·00	
		b. Small "O" in "O.M.F."	..	16·00	
		c. "O.M.F. Cilicie" omitted	..	27·00	
		d. Surch double	..	30·00	
109/115		*Set of 7*	..	15·00	

The words "SAND. EST" read vertically at side on the 5 and 20 pi. These stamps were intended for use in the Eastern Sandjak of Cilicia.

(12)   **13**

1921. *AIR. Nos.* 104 *and* 105 *optd with T* **12.**

116	**15**	2 pi. on 15 c. slate-green	..	£500	£400
		a. Optd on No. 95 ..	..	£500	
117	**13**	5 pi. on 40 c. red and pale blue	..	£500	£450
		a. Optd on No. 96 ..	..	£500	

Beware of forgeries of these stamps.
It is believed that genuine copies of the 10 pi. on 50 c. and 50 pi. on 1 f. do not exist.

1921. *POSTAGE DUE. Postage Due stamps of France surch as T* **10.**

D118	D **3**	1 pi. on 10 c. pale brown ..	..	35	45
		a. Thin figure "1"	..	2·00	2·00
		b. No stop after "M"	..	1·50	1·50
D119		2 pi. on 20 c. olive-green	..	30	35
		a. No stop after "M"	..	1·50	1·50
D120		3 pi. on 30 c. carmine	..	45	45
		a. No stop after "M"	..	1·50	1·50
D121		4 pi. on 50 c. dull claret	..	45	45
D118/121		*Set of 4*	..	1·40	1·50

1921. *Cilis provisional. Thin paper. P* 9.

122	**13**	1 pi. violet	..	2·00	2·00

COCHIN-CHINA. See under Indo-China.

Colombia

100 Centavos = 1 Peso

The Spanish conquest of what is now Colombia began in 1525 and lasted till 1550. From 1740 Colombia, together with Venezuela and Ecuador, formed the Spanish Viceroyalty of New Granada. A rising in Bogotá on 20 July 1810 ejected Spanish officials and, after Bolivar's victory over the Spaniards at Boyacá, the Republic of Colombia, including Ecuador and Venezuela, was founded on 17 December 1819. Ecuador and Venezuela broke away in 1830 and from 1831 to 1858 Colombia was known as the Republic of New Granada. A new constitution of 22 May 1858 created a Confederation of nine states, the Granadine Confederation.

For GREAT BRITAIN stamps used in Colombia with obliterations "C56" (or "C65"), "C62", "E88" or "F69" see Great Britain Stamps Used Abroad in the *British Commonwealth Catalogue*.

PRICES. The stamps of the early issues were mostly cancelled in pen and ink, as cancelling handstamps were furnished in very few places. As these stamps are not known to have been used for fiscal purposes, pen-cancellation denotes postal use. The prices quoted in the used column are for postmarked copies, pen-cancelled stamps being worth very much less.

REPRINTS. Most issues from 1859 to 1889 have been reprinted or forged and these are generally on different coloured papers or have other distinguishing characteristics.

A. GRANADINE CONFEDERATION

1   2

(Litho C. and J. Martinez)

1859 (Aug). *Imperf.*
1	1	2½ c. deep green ..	..	..	6·50	5·50
		a. Olive-green ..	..	..	6·50	5·50
2		5 c. bright blue ..	..	..	7·50	7·50
		a. Tête-bêche (pair)	..	..	£750	£750
3		5 c. violet	..	..	12·00	6·50
		a. Lilac..	..	..	10·00	6·50
		b. Slate	..	..	9·00	6·50
		c. Tête-bêche (pair)	..	..	£750	£750
		d. Error. "50" for "5" ..	..	..	—	£900
4		10 c. bistre-brown	..	..	6·00	5·00
		a. Buff ..	..	..	7·00	6·00
5		20 c. blue ..	..	..	3·00	3·00
		a. Tête-bêche (pair)	..	..	£2500	£3000
		b. Error. In pair with 5 c.	..		£3750	£3500
6		1 p. carmine	..	..	3·50	3·50
7		1 p. rose/bluish ..	..	..	50·00	

No. 7 is not known used. The 10 c. in green is believed to be a proof.

(Litho D. Ayala and I. Medrano)

1860 (June?). *Wove paper. Imperf.*
8	2	5 c. rosy lilac ..	..	..	6·50	6·50
		a. Laid paper ..	..	..	50·00	35·00
		b. Grey-lilac ..	..	..	6·50	6·50
9		10 c. yellow	..	..	6·50	5·00
		a. Tête-bêche (pair)	..	..	£700	£600
10		20 c. blue	..	..	25·00	20·00

A rising against the "Conservative" (Catholic) Government began in 1859 and in July 1861 anti-clerical "Democrats"

captured Bogotá, where they issued stamps inscribed for the United States of New Granada. Later in 1861 a congress at Bogotá adopted a new federal constitution and established the United States of Colombia.

B. UNITED STATES OF NEW GRANADA

3

(Litho, Bogotá)

1861. *Imperf.*
11	3	2½ c. black	..	..	£200	80·00
12		5 c. orange-buff	..	..	35·00	10·00
		a. Pale yellow	..	..	35·00	10·00
13		10 c. blue	..	..	50·00	20·00
14		20 c. red ..	..	..	80·00	25·00
15		1 p. rose	..	..	90·00	50·00

There are no varieties of the lower values, but there is a variety of the 20 c. red, showing traces of the "1" of the fraction "½" from the original die, viz. that of the 2½ c., from which the 20 c. was made, and there are as many varieties of the 1 peso as there are stamps on the sheet (? 54).

C. UNITED STATES OF COLOMBIA

4   5   6

(T **4/6** litho D. Ayala and I. Medrano)

1862. *Imperf.*
16	4	10 c. blue	..	..	20·00	10·00
17		20 c. red ..	..	..	£300	80·00
18		50 c. blue-green..	..	..	45·00	12·00
		a. Pale green ..	..	..	45·00	12·00
19		1 p. lilac	..	..	60·00	25·00
20		1 p. lilac/bluish..	..	..	£700	£400

1862–63. *Imperf. (a) White paper.*
21	5	5 c. orange	..	..	6·00	3·50
		a. Star after "CENT" ..	..			
22		10 c. blue (1862. July?)	..	..	7·00	2·00
23		20 c. red ..	..	..	7·50	6·50
		a. Star after "CENT" ..	..		15·00	10·00
		b. 50 c. on sheet of 20 c.	..		£2500	£1000

(*b*) *Bluish paper*
24	5	10 c. blue	..	..	9·00	2·00
25		50 c. green	..	..	12·00	8·00
		a. Star after "CENT" ..	..		13·00	10·00

There are ten varieties of each value.

1863. *Imperf.*
26	6	5 c. orange	..	..	6·00	2·00
		a. Yellow	..	..	6·00	2·00
		b. Tête-bêche (pair)	..	..	70·00	60·00
27		10 c. blue	..	..	3·50	1·50
28		20 c. red ..	..	..	7·00	2·50
29		50 c. green	..	..	7·00	2·50
30		1 p. mauve	..	..	30·00	15·00

There are two varieties of each value.

7   8   9

(A)   (B)

(Litho D. Ayala and I. Medrano)

1865. *Imperf.*

31	7	1 c. rose	..	..	..	1·00	1·00
		a. Bluish pelure paper		..	..	2·00	2·00
32	8	2½ c. black/*lilac* ..	..	..	..	1·50	1·50
33	9	5 c. orange	..	..	..	1·50	1·00
		a. *Lemon*	..	..	..	1·50	1·00
34		10 c. violet	..	..	..	1·50	75
		a. *Lilac*	..	..	..	2·00	75
35		20 c. blue	..	..	..	2·00	1·25
36		50 c. green (A)	..	..	..	6·00	2·50
37		50 c. green (B)	..	..	..	6·00	2·50
38		1 p. vermilion	..	..	..	6·00	1·00
		a. *Rose*	..	..	..	6·00	1·00

10   11

(Litho D. Ayala and I. Medrano)

1865. *T* 10/11 *and similar type inscr* "SOBREPORTE".
Imperf.

39	10	25 c. black/*blue*	..	..	..	6·00	6·00
40	11	50 c. black/*yellow*	..	..	..	7·00	6·50
41	–	1 p. black/*rose*	..	..	..	9·00	8·00

These stamps prepaid an additional charge to certain overseas countries with which Colombia had no postal conventions.

R 1   R 2

(Litho D. Ayala and I. Medrano)

1865. *REGISTRATION. Imperf.*

R42	R 1	5 c. black	..	..	..	6·00	6·00
R43	R 2	5 c. black	..	..	..	6·00	6·00

12   13   14

15   16   17   18

(Litho D. Ayala and I. Medrano)

1866 (Aug?). *Imperf.*

44	12	5 c. orange	..	..	..	3·00	1·50
45	13	10 c. lilac	..	..	..	75	50
46	14	20 c. blue	..	..	..	5·00	2·50
47	15	50 c. blue-green	..	..	..	2·00	1·50
		a. *Yellow-green*	..	..	..	2·00	1·50
48	16	1 p. vermilion	..	..	..	3·50	1·50
		a. *Carmine*	..	..	..	3·50	1·50
49	17	5 p. black/*green*	..	..	..	40·00	25·00
50	18	10 p. black/*vermilion*	..	..	30·00	18·00

There are some varieties of the "UN PESO" having the letters "U", "N", "S" or "O" contracted, all of which occur on the same sheet as the normal. The 20 c., 50 c. and 1 peso are found perf. 11 unofficially. The two highest values are on surface-coloured paper.

19   20   21

22   23   24

Two types of 10 c.
A. "B" of "COLOMBIA" over "V" of "CENTAVOS".
B. "B" over "VO".

Three types of 1 p.
C. Long thin spearheads; diagonal lines in lower part of shield.
D. Short thick spearheads; horiz and some diagonal lines in lower part of shield.
E. Short thick spearheads; crossed lines in shield; ornaments at each side of circle broken (No. 92).

(Litho D. Ayala and D. Paredes)

1868–70. *Imperf.*

51	19	5 c. dull orange-yellow	..	..	8·00	6·00
52	20	10 c. violet (A) ..	..	..	1·00	25
		a. *Lilac*	..	..	..	1·00	25
53		10 c. violet (B) ..	..	..	1·00	25
		a. *Lilac*	..	..	..	1·00	25
54	21	20 c. blue	..	..	..	90	50
55	22	50 c. yellow-green	..	..	1·50	60
56	23	1 p. rose-red (C)	..	..	40·00	4·00
		a. Type D	..	..	..		
57		1 p. vermilion (D)	..	..	1·10	75
		a. Tête-bêche (pair) ..	..	..	70·00	60·00

The 1 p. is found perf 11 unofficially.
See also Nos. 82/3 and 91/2.

(Litho D. Ayala and D. Paredes)

1869–70. *Wove paper. Imperf.*

58	24	2½ c. black/*violet*	..	..	2·50	2·50
		a. Laid paper (1870) ..	..	..	35·00	35·00
		b. Laid bâtonné paper (1870)	..	25·00	25·00

There are two varieties of these stamps. They were used as carrier stamps.

PRINTERS. On 27 November 1869 a contract was made with D. Paredes to be the sole printer of Colombian stamps until this was invalidated on 4 July 1892. These stamps were all lithographed.

25   26   27

| 28 | 29 | 32 | 33 | 34 |

Two types of 10 c.
A. "OS" of "CORREOS" same size.
B. "S" is larger than "O".

1870–74. *Wove paper. Imperf.*

59	25	1 c. green (1872)	..	..	..	45	40
		a. Olive-green				40	30
60		1 c. carmine (1873)	..	..		25	25
		a. Rose	..	..	..	25	25
61	26	2 c. brown	..	..	..	25	30
		a. Cinnamon	..	..		40	40
62	27	5 c. orange	..	..	..	25	25
		a. Yellow	..	..	..	40	40
63	28	10 c. violet (*laid paper*) (A) (1872)	..	12·00	9·00
64		10 c. violet (*laid paper*) (B) (1872)	..	12·00	9·00
65		10 c. violet (A) (1874)	..	..	60	20
		a. Mauve	..	..	..	40	20
66		10 c. violet (B) (1874)	..	..	60	20
		b. Mauve	..	..	..	40	20
67	29	25 c. black/*blue*	..	..	3·25	3·00

No. 67 served for the same purpose as Nos. 39/41 although
not inscribed "SOBREPORTE". It also exists on pink and on
yellow but these are believed to be proofs.
See also No. 87.

| 30 | 31 |

Two Dies of 5 p.
I. Ornament on the left side of "C" of "CINCO" impinges on
it; stars above arms indistinct.
II. Ornament only touches the "C"; stars more distinct.

Three Dies of 10 p.
I. Middle band of shield has some lines of shading; stars
have extra rays between the points.
II. Shading removed; stars are distinctly five-pointed.
III. Similar to Die II but a line across the top left corner cuts
through the corner of the design.

1870–77. *Surface-coloured paper. Imperf.*

68	30	5 p. black/*green* (I)	..	..	7·00	2·00
69		5 p. black/*green* (II) (1877)	..	7·00	2·00
70	31	10 p. black/*vermilion* (I)	..	7·00	1·90
		a. Black/*rose*	..	..	10·00	4·00
71		10 p. black/*rose* (II) (1877)	..	7·00	1·50
72		10 p. black/*rose* (III) (Date?)	..	7·00	1·50

See also Nos. 118/9a.

| R 3 | R 4 |

1870–77. *REGISTRATION. Imperf.*

(a) Vertical lines in centre

| R73 | R 3 | 5 c. black | .. | .. | .. | 1·00 | 1·00 |
| R74 | R 4 | 5 c. black | .. | .. | .. | 1·00 | 1·00 |

(b) Horizontal lines in centre (1877)

R75	R 3	5 c. black	..	..	2·00	2·00
R76		5 c. black/*bluish*	..	..	2·00	2·00
R77	R 4	5 c. black	..	..	2·00	2·00
R78		5 c. black/*bluish*	..	..	2·00	2·00

1876–80. *Imperf.*

(a) White laid paper (July 1876–79)

79	32	5 c. pale lilac	..	..	1·50	1·50
		a. Mauve	..	..	..	1·50	1·50
80	33	10 c. brown	..	..	..	4·50	1·70
81	34	20 c. greenish blue	..	..	6·00	4·00
		a. Deep blue	..	..	..	6·00	3·00
82	22	50 c. green (1879)	..	..	8·50	3·50
83	23	1 p. pale red (1879)	..	..	12·00	1·00

(b) White wove paper (1877–79)

84	32	5 c. lilac	..	..	..	40	15
		a. Mauve	..	..	..	40	10
		b. Violet	..	..	..	45	15
85	33	10 c. bistre-brown	..	..	30	10
		a. Cinnamon	..	..	..	35	20
		b. Purple-brown	..	..	50	15
86	34	20 c. greenish blue	..	..	35	20
		a. Blue	..	..	..	40	30
		b. Violet-blue	..	..	2·50	1·25
87	29	25 c. blue-green (1879)	..	..	3·50	3·50

(c) Bluish wove paper (1880)

88	32	5 c. mauve	..	..	..	3·50	1·00
		a. Violet	..	..	..	3·50	1·00
89	33	10 c. brown	..	..	..	1·25	75
90	34	20 c. pale blue	..	..	2·00	1·00
91	22	50 c. emerald	..	..	..	3·00	2·00
92	23	1 p. vermilion (E)	..	..	5·00	3·50

Stamps of the above issue are found perforated unofficially.

| 35 | 36 | 37 | 38 |

Original issue	Redrawn issue
1 c. Stop before "UNION" is round; rays between stars and condors.	Stop is square. Rays are partially or completely erased.
2 c. "2's" and "C's" in corners are upright.	"2's" and "C's" arranged diagonally.
5 c. Five pearls around figure "5" in upper left corners shaded.	Pearls are unshaded.
10 c. Lettering is thin; there are rays between stars and condors.	Lettering is thicker, also the white lines of design; rays have been removed.

1881 (1 July)**–83.** *Imperf.*

93	35	1 c. blue-green	..	..	..	30	25
94	36	2 c. vermilion	..	..	25	25
		a. Rose	..	..	..	25	25
95	35	5 c. blue	..	..	..	40	20
		a. Printed both sides	..	35·00	10·00
96		10 c. purple	..	..	..	50	30
97	37	20 c. black	..	..	..	75	50

Redrawn (Jan 1883)

98	35	1 c. green	..	..	..	40	30
99	38	2 c. bright rose	..	..	20	20
100	35	5 c. blue	..	..	..	20	15
		a. Ultramarine	..	..	40	20
		b. Printed both sides	..	12·00	10·00
101		10 c. purple	..	..	..	40	25

The above issues are found perf 11 unofficially.

39   R 5

42   43 General Sucre   44 Bolivar

1881 (1 July). *On coloured paper. Imperf.*
102	**39**	1 c. black/*green*	.. .. ..	30	30
103		2 c. black/*rose*	.. .. ..	30	30
104		5 c. black/*lilac* ..	.. .. ..	50	35

The above are found perf 11 unofficially.

1881. REGISTRATION. *Imperf.*
R **5** 10 c. lilac 2.25 .. .. .. 2·25 2·25

45 President   46 General Narino   L 1
Nunez   (inscr "REPULICA")

1886–88. *Tinted papers. P* 13½ (*T* **43, 45/6**) *or* 10½ (*others*).
120	**42**	1 c. yellow-green/*bluish*	.. ..	10	10
		a. Blue-green/*bluish*	.. ..	10	10
		b. Imperf (pair)	.. ..	1·00	1·50
121	**43**	2 c. red/*rose* (1887) ..	.. ..	20	20
		a. Imperf (pair)	.. ..	1·25	1·60
122		2 c. red/*yellow* (1887)	.. ..	1·40	1·40
123		2 c. red/*white* (1887)	.. ..	2·50	2·50
124	**44**	5 c. blue/*blue*	.. ..	12	5
		a. Imperf (pair)	.. ..	1·75	1·75
		b. Perf 13½ ..	.. ..		
		c. Ultramarine/*blue*	.. ..	15	5
125	**45**	10 c. orange	.. ..	20	10
		a. Imperf (pair)	.. ..	1·25	1·25
		b. Pelure paper	.. ..	50	20
126	**46**	20 c. violet/*lilac* (1877)	.. ..	40	25
		a. Imperf (pair)	.. ..	2·75	2·10
127		20 c. violet/*white* (1877)	.. ..	3·00	3·00
		a. Imperf (pair)	.. ..	9·00	9·00
128		20 c. purple/*mauve* (1877)	.. ..	50	30
		a. Imperf (pair)	.. ..	3·75	
129		20 c. violet/*green* (1877)	.. ..	2·00	
		a. Imperf (pair)	.. ..	5·50	
130	**42**	50 c. brown/*buff* (1888)	.. ..	12	12
		a. Imperf (pair)	.. ..	1·40	1·40
131		1 p. rosy mauve/*bluish* (1888)	.. ..	60	35
132		1 p. rosy mauve/*white* (1888)	.. ..	20	12
		a. Imperf between (pair)			
133		5 p. brown/*white* (1888)	.. ..	1·40	1·40
134		5 p. black/*white* (1888)	.. ..	80	80
135		10 p. black/*rose* (1888)	.. ..	1·40	70

See also Nos. 162/4a.

40   41   R 6

1883–86. *Tinted papers. P* 10½ (*T* **40**) *or* 13½ (*T* **41**).
106	**40**	1 c. yellow-green/*green*	..	12	10
		a. Blue-green/*green*	..	12	10
		b. Blue-green/*bluish green*		12	10
107	**41**	2 c. red/*rose* ..	..	12	10
		a. Perf 12 ..	..	6·50	
108		2 c. red/*buff* ..	..	2·75	2·75
		a. Perf 12 ..	..		
109	**40**	5 c. blue/*blue*	..	30	8
110		5 c. dull blue/*white*	..	1·10	50
111	**41**	10 c. orange/*yellow* ..	..	35	25
		a. Perf 12 ..	..	6·50	
		b. "DE LOS" as 20 c.*	..	3·25	1·40
		c. As b. Perf 12	..		
112		20 c. mauve/*lilac*	..	35	25
		a. Perf 12 ..	..	1·60	
113	**40**	50 c. brown/*buff*	..	35	30
		a. Perf 12 ..	..	80	
114		1 p. lake/*bluish*	..	70	40
		a. Perf comp of 10½ and 12	..	6·50	
115		5 p. yellow-brown/*yellow* (1886)	..	2·10	1·25
		a. Perf 12 ..	..	11·00	
116		10 p. black/*rose* (1886)	..	2·00	1·40
		a. Perf 12 ..	..	7·50	

*In the 20 c. the words "DE LOS" are rather larger than in the 2 c. and 10 c.
All values exist imperforate. There are numerous shades in this issue.

1883. REGISTRATION. *P* 13½.
R117 R **6** 10 c. red/*orange* 60 40

1886. *As 1870–77 but colours changed and P* 10½.
118	**30**	5 p. orange-brown (II)	.. ..	2·10	1·10
119	**31**	10 p. black/*lilac* (III) ..	.. ..	2·10	1·10
		a. Perf 12 ..	.. ..	—	6·50

Both values exist imperforate.

D. REPUBLIC OF COLOMBIA

By a new constitution of 5 August 1886 the country was re-named the Republic of Colombia. The sovereignty of the states was abolished and they became departments.

1888. LATE FEE. *P* 10½.
L136 L **1** 2½ c. black/*lilac* 5 5

47   R 7

1889. "REPULICA" *corrected to* "REPULICA". *Tinted papers. P* 13½.
137	**47**	20 c. violet/*lilac*	.. ..	10	10
		a. Imperf (pair)	.. ..	1·50	
138		20 c. violet/*white*	.. ..	3·00	3·00
		a. Imperf (pair)	.. ..	9·00	
139		20 c. purple/*mauve*	.. ..	20	20
140		20 c. violet/*green*	.. ..	4·00	4·00
		a. Imperf (pair)	.. ..	8·00	

1889. REGISTRATION. *Tinted papers. P* 13½.
R141	R **7**	10 c. red/*greyish* ..	.. ..	20	20
R142		10 c. red/*yellowish* ..	.. ..	55	55

See also Nos. R165/6b.

48   49   50

51   52

1890–91. *Tinted papers.* P 10½ (*T* **49**) *or* 13½ (*others*).

143	48	1 c. green/*pale green*	..	15	10
144	49	2 c. rose-red/*rose*	..	15	10
145	50	5 c. blue/*greenish blue*	..	8	5
		a. Imperf (pair)	..	90	90
146		5 c. deep blue/*blue*	..	12	5
		a. Imperf (pair)	..	1·40	1·40
		b. Perf 13½ × 10½	..		
147	51	10 c. brown/*yellow*	..	8	5
148	52	20 c. violet/*white* (*pelure*)	..	20	12

See also Nos. 149, etc.

53   54   55

56   58   L 2

57

T **57** is T **56** redrawn. In the redrawn type all the lettering is larger and thicker; the numerals are smaller; the flag of the figure "5" is much thinner; all the exterior ornaments are altered and the lower spear-head at left is absent.

1892–99. *Old designs in new colours and new types. Tinted papers.* P 13½.

149	48	1 c. red/*yellow*	..	5	5
		a. Perf 12	..	5	5
		b. Perf comp of 13½ and 12	..	5	5
		c. Imperf (pair)	..	2·00	2·00
150	53	2 c. red/*rose*	..	50	45
151		2 c. blue-green/*white*	..	5	5
		a. Perf 12	..	5	5
		b. Perf comp of 13½ and 12	..	5	5
		c. Imperf (pair)	..		
152	50	5 c. black/*buff*	..	5·00	75
		a. Perf 10½	..	5	5
		b. Perf 12	..	5	5
		c. Perf comp of 13½ and 12	..	2·50	15
		d. Perf comp of 10½ and 12	..	—	15
		e. Perf 14 to 15½	..	—	1·25
		f. Imperf (pair)	..		

153	54	5 c. brown/*buff* (1895)	..	5	5
		a. Perf 12	..	5	5
		b. Perf comp of 13½ and 12	..	12	5
		c. Imperf (pair)	..	1·75	1·75
154		5 c. red-brown/*pale brown* (1897)	..	5	5
		a. Perf 12	..	15	5
		b. Perf comp of 13½ and 12	..	5	5
		c. Imperf (pair)	..	2·00	2·00
155	51	10 c. brown/*rose*	..	5	5
		a. Perf 12	..	8	5
		b. Perf comp of 13½ and 12	..	5	5
		c. Perf comp of 10½ and 12	..		
		d. Imperf (pair)	..	2·00	2·00
156	55	20 c. brown/*blue*	..	5	5
		a. Perf 10½	..	5	5
		b. Perf 12	..	5	5
		c. Perf comp of 13½ and 12	..	5	5
		d. Perf 14 to 15½	..	—	2·75
157		20 c. yellow-brown/*greenish blue* (p comp of 13½ and 12) (1897)	..	25	25
		a. Perf 14 to 15½	..		
158		20 c. brown/*buff* (1897)	..	2·25	
		a. Perf 10½	..	3·50	2·50
		b. Perf comp of 13½ and 12	..	2·25	
		c. Perf 14 to 15½	..		
159	56	50 c. violet/*lilac* (p 12)	..	8	8
160	57	50 c. dull violet/*lilac* (p 12) (1899)	..	75	75
		a. Perf comp of 13½ and 12	..	40	20
161	58	1 p. blue/*green*	..	10	10
		b. Perf comp of 13½ and 12	..		
		c. Imperf (pair)	..	2·00	2·00
162	42	5 p. red/*lilac-rose* (p 10½)	..	15	15
163		5 p. red/*buff* (p 10½)	..	35	
164		10 p. blue/*white*	..	30	30
		a. Perf 10½	..	30	20

1892. *REGISTRATION. Colour changed. Tinted papers.* P 13½.

R165	R **7**	10 c. brown/*red-brown*	..	20	12
		a. Perf 12	..	20	20
R166		10 c. yellow-brown/*buff*	..	12	12
		a. Perf 12	..	20	20
		b. Imperf between (pair)	..	2·50	

1892. *TOO LATE. Tinted paper. Litho.* P 13½.

L167	L **2**	2½ c. blue/*rose*	..	5	5
		a. Perf 12	..	5	5

AR **1** 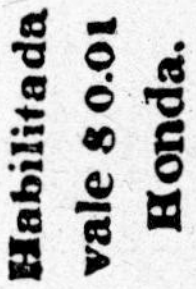   (59)

1894. *ACKNOWLEDGMENT OF RECEIPT. Litho.* P 13½.

AR168	AR **1**	5 c. vermilion/*bluish*	..	40	30
AR169		5 c. vermilion/*white* (p 12)	..	15	15

1896. *Honda provisional.* No. 151a surch with T **59**.

170	53	1 c. on 2 c. blue-green	..	7·00	6·00

Forgeries exist in smaller type, struck diagonally.

61    62

1898–1901. *Litho.* P 13½.

171	61	1 c. red/*yellow*	..	8	5
172		5 c. brown/*pale brown*	..	8	5
		a. Imperf	..	—	35
		b. Imperf between (pair)	..	40	80
173	62	10 c. brown/*rose*	..	20	8
174		50 c. blue/*lilac*	..	15	10

E. CIVIL WAR PROVISIONAL ISSUES

On 17 October 1899 the "Liberals" (Anti-clericals) rose against the "Conservative" (Catholic) Government and a devastating civil war began which ended on 21 November 1902 with victory for the Government.
As supplies were cut off from Bogotá, provisional issues were made in various parts of the country.

Cartagena Issues

PRINTERS. Types **63** and **74** were lithographed by E. E. Delgado, Cartagena.

    63   **64**   **65**

1899 (8 Nov). *T 63 and similar type. Optd with control mark in blue or violet.* (a) *Imperf.*

175	63	5 c. red/*buff*	..	..	70	70
176	–	10 c. blue/*buff*	..	..	70	70

(b) *Pin-perf by sewing machine, about 12*

177	63	5 c. red/*buff* ..	..	..	2·25	2·25
178	–	10 c. blue/*buff*	..	..	2·25	2·25

1899 (8 Dec). *Colours changed and optd with 7 parallel lines, in mauve. Pin-perf about 6½.*

179	63	5 c. maroon/*green*	..	..	75	75
		a. Tête-bêche (pair)	..	38·00	38·00	
180	–	10 c. red/*rose* ..	..	..	80	80

The 1 c. and 2 c. were formed from the 5 c. and 10 c. of Type **63** by erasing the labels at top and bottom, and replacing them with type-set inscriptions and a type-set frame round the stamp. There are ten types of each value, nine formed from the 5 c. and one from the 10 c.
Types **64/5** are made from the 5 c. as can clearly be seen from the presence of the top flag of the "5". This is lacking from Nos. 181a and 182a and there are other differences.

1899 (18 Dec). *T 64/5 optd with 7 parallel lines, in mauve. Pin-perf 8 to 9.*

181	64	1 c. brown/*buff*	..	..	20	20
		a. Altered from 10 c.	..	..	40	40
182		2 c. black/*buff*..	..	..	20	20
		a. Altered from 10 c.	..	..	55	55

    66   **67**   **68**

1900 (16 Jan). *Optd with 7 parallel wavy lines, in mauve.*

				A. Imp		B. P12	
183	66	5 c. vermilion	..	20	20	70	70

1901. *Optd with letters "S" (repeated) in frame, in violet. Pin-perf.*

184	67	1 c. black	..	..	5	5
		a. Imperf (pair)	..	..	30	30
184b	68	2 c. black/*red*	..	..	5	5
		c. Imperf (pair)	..	..	40	40

    69   **70**

1902. *Optd with chain pattern, in red. Pin-perf.*

185	69	1 c. pale blue ..	..	..	5	5
		a. Imperf (pair)	..	..	60	60
186	70	2 c. brown	..	..	5	5
		a. Imperf (pair)	..	..	60	60

    71   **72**

1902. *Optd with five-pointed star, in magenta. Pin-perf.*

187	71	5 c. violet	..	..	25	20
		a. No star ..	..	..	40	40
		b. With two stars	..	..	45	45
		c. Perf 12 ..	..	..	25	20
		d. Imperf (pair)	..	..		
188	72	10 c. brown	..	..	8	8
		a. No star ..	..	..	40	40
		b. With two stars	..	..	40	40
		c. Perf 12 ..	..	..	5	5
		ca. Perf 12. No star ..	..	..	40	40
		cb. Perf 12. Two stars	..	..	60	60
		cc. Perf 12. Star is carmine-red	..	15	15	

    73   **74**

1902. *Optd with 7 parallel wavy lines, in magenta or mauve. Pin-perf.*

189	73	5 c. bistre-brown	..	..	15	15
190		10 c. black	..	..	20	25
191	74	20 c. maroon ..	..	..	25	25

The above stamps are found with the overprint vertical, and also with a vertical and horizontal overprint on the same stamp.

Cucuta Issues

The city of Cúcuta was captured by the rebels early in the war and they issued the following stamps.

Goblerno Provisional
CORREOS.

5 ctvos.
74a

1900. *Black on coloured paper. Litho. P 12 vert. Values expressed as indicated, in roman letters.*

(a) "Gobierno Provisorio" at top

191a	74a	1 ctvo. *blue-green*	..	..	1·50	85
191b		1 cvo. *blue-green*	..	..	3·50	1·90
191c		2 cvos. *white*	..	..	1·00	70
191d		5 cvos. *deep pink*	..	..	1·00	70
191e		10 cvos. *deep pink*	..	..	1·00	70
191f		20 cvos. *yellow*	..	..	1·60	80

(b) *Optd "Andrez B. Fernandez" at side reading up, in addition*

191g	74a	5 cvos. *deep pink* (V.)	..	2·00	1·50	
191h		10 cvos. *deep pink*	..	2·00	1·50	
191i		20 cvos. *yellow* (G.)	..	2·50	2·40	

(c) *"Gobierno Provisional" at top and optd "Andrez B. Fernandez" at side reading up. Values in italics*

191j	74a	1 centavo, *blue-green* (G.)	..	6·00	5·00	
191k		1 ctvo. *blue-green*	..	..	70	40

191*l*	**74a**	2 *ctvos. blue-green* (G.) ..	..	45	45
191*m*		5 *ctvos. white* (G.)	..	40	35
		ma. *"ctvos."* smaller..	..	1·75	1·75
191*n*		10 *ctvos. deep pink*	..	50	35
191*o*		20 *ctvos. yellow* (G.)	..	1·10	45
		oa. *"Provisorio"*	..		

Beware of forgeries of the above.

The above were formerly listed under the Colombian States but are more correctly classed under the Civil War Provisional issues, as they are inscribed "GOBIERNO PROVISIONAL".

Tumaco Issue

In 1902 Tumaco was under rebel control and the following were issued.

74b

1902. *Type-set. Imperf.*

191*p*	**74b**	5 c. grey-blue/*toned*	..	45·00	30·00
191*q*		10 c. red/*toned*	..	35·00	25·00

The design of the 10 c. value differs slightly.
The footnote at the end of Cúcuta also applies here.

Bogotá Issues

75

76

77

78

79

80

81

82

83

84

1902–05. *Litho.* A. *Imperf.* B. *Pin-perf.*

				A		B	
192	**75**	2 c. black/*rose*	..	5	5	12	12
		a. Perf 12	..	†		20	20
193	**76**	4 c. red/*green*	..	5	5	12	12
		a. Perf 12	..	†		—	
194		4 c. blue/*green* ('03)		5	5	8	8
		a. Perf 12	..	†		—	
195	**77**	5 c. green/*green*	..	5	5	5	5
196		5 c. blue/*blue* ('03)		5	5	12	12
		a. Perf 12	..	†		20	20
197	**78**	10 c. black/*pink*		5	5	12	12
		a. Perf 12	..	†		12	12
		b. Black/*rose*		5	5	15	—
198	**79**	20 c. bistre/*buff*		5	5	12	12
		a. Perf 12	..	†		35	35
199		20 c. blue/*buff* ('03)		5	5	35	35
		a. Perf 12	..	†		40	40
		b. Blue/*yellowish*		5	5	50	50
200	**80**	50 c. green/*rose*		8	8	20	20
		a. Perf 12	..	†		—	
201		50 c. blue/*rose* ('03)		10	10	30	30
		a. Perf 12	..	†		80	80
202	**81**	1 p. purple/*buff*		8	8	40	40
		a. Perf 12	..	†		40	40
203	**82**	5 p. blue-green/*blue*		55	35	80	70
		a. Perf 12	..	†		1·10	1·10
204	**83**	10 p. green/*pale grn*		55	40	1·10	70
		a. Perf 12	..	†		1·75	1·75
205	**84**	50 p. orange/*pale rose* (1905)	..	17·00	17·00	†	
206	–	100 p. blue/*deep rose* (1905)	..	14·00	14·00	†	

The design of the 100 p. is similar to the 50 p.
See also Nos. 261/3a.

R 8

1902–03. *REGISTRATION. Litho.* A. *Imperf.* B. *Pin-perf*

				A		B	
R207	**R 8**	20 c. red-brown/*bl* ..		30	15	55	55
		a. Perf 12	..	†		55	55
R208		20 c. blue/*blue* ('03)		15	15	55	55
		a. Perf 12	..	†		55	55

See also No. R264.

L 3

AR 2

1902. *LATE FEE. Litho.* A. *Imperf.* B. *Pin-perf.*

				A		B	
L209	**L 3**	5 c. purple/*rose*	..	5	5	45	55
		a. Perf 12 ..	..	†		70	70

1902. *ACKNOWLEDGMENT OF RECEIPT. Litho. A. Imperf. B. Pin-perf.*

			A		B	
AR210	AR **2**	10 c. blue/*blue* ..	10	10	30	30
AR211		10 c. deep blue/				
		greenish ..	10	10	30	30

See also No. AR265.

Barranquilla Issues

PRINTER. These issues were lithographed by Francisco Valiente F., Barranquilla.

85 River Magdalena   86 Iron Quay, Savanilla

87 Hill of La Popa

1902–03. A. *Imperf.* B. *Pin-perf.*

			A		B	
212	**85**	2 c. blue-green ..	10	10	70	70
		a. Printed both sides ..	30	30	†	
213		2 c. blue ..	10	12	50	60
		a. Perf 12 ..	†		70	70
214		2 c. rose ..	40	40	†	
		a. Perf 12 ..	†		1·00	1·00
215	**86**	10 c. scarlet ..	8	8	15	20
		a. Perf 12 ..	†		45	45
216		10 c. rose ..	8	8	8	8
217		10 c. magenta ..	8	8	10	10
218		10 c. maroon ..	8	8	12	12
219		10 c. orange ..	50	50	50	50
220	**87**	20 c. violet (*shades*) ..	1·60	1·60	8	8
		a. Printed both sides ..			35	25
		b. Perf 12 ..	†		8	8
221		20 c. dull blue ..	70	70	35	35
222		20 c. dull blue/*pink* ..	3·00	3·00	†	
223		20 c. purple/*crimson* ..	†		4·25	4·25
224		20 c. carmine-rose ..	1·00	1·00	2·50	2·50
		a. Perf 12 ..	†		—	—

See also Nos. 242/7.

88 Cruiser *Cartagena*   89 Bolivar

90 General Pinzon   91   92

1903–04. A. *Imperf.* B. *P* 12.

			A		B	
225	**88**	5 c. blue	5	5	50	50
226		5 c. bistre	8	8	50	50
		a. Printed both sides	—	—	†	
227	**89**	50 c. green	8	8	†	
		a. Pin-perf.. ..	†		50	50
228		50 c. brown	8	8	†	
		a. Pin-perf.. ..	†		65	65
229		50 c. yellow	5	5	†	
230		50 c. orange	5	5	†	
		a. Pin-perf.. ..	†		50	50
231		50 c. vermilion ..	12	12	†	
		a. Pin-perf.. ..	†		1·00	1·00
232		50 c. rosine	15	15	50	50
233	**90**	1 p. brown	8	8	1·00	1·00
		a. Printed both sides	—	—	†	
		b. Pin-perf.. ..	†		50	50
234		1 p. rosine	8	8	1·00	1·00
		a. Pin-perf.. ..	†		50	50
235		1 p. blue	10	10	50	50
		a. Pin-perf.. ..	†		50	50
236		1 p. deep purple ..	3·50	3·50	1·75	1·75
237	**91**	5 p. brown ..	10	10	1·25	1·25
238		5 p. purple	12	12	1·40	1·40
239		5 p. blue-green ..	20	20	1·25	1·25
240	**92**	10 p. green	12	12	1·40	1·40
241		10 p. claret	12	12	1·40	1·40

Nos. 235/6 are smaller than Nos. 233/4a.

1903–4. *On coloured laid paper.* A. *Imperf.* B. *P* 12.

			A		B	
242	**86**	10 c. blue/*brown* ..	10	10	1·25	1·25
243		10 c. blue/*pale green* ..	25	25	2·40	2·40
244		10 c. blue/*salmon* ..	10	10	1·75	1·75
245		10 c. blue/*pale lilac* ..	12	12	1·40	1·40
246		10 c. blue/*pale grey* ..	20	20	75	60
247		10 c. blue/*rose* ..	10	10	1·25	1·25

Medellin Issues

93   R 9

(Litho J. L. Arango, Medellin)

1902. *P* 12.

248	**93**	1 c. green/*pale yellow*		5	5
		a. Imperf (pair) ..			
249		2 c. red/*pale salmon*		5	5
		a. Imperf (pair) ..			
250		5 c. blue/*bluish*		5	5
		a. Imperf (pair) ..			
251		10 c. brown/*pale yellow* ..		5	5
252		20 c. mauve/*pale salmon* ..		5	5
		a. Imperf (pair) ..			
253		50 c. red/*greenish*		8	8
254		1 p. black/*bright yellow* ..		15	15
		a. Imperf (pair) ..		2·25	
255		5 p. deep blue/*azure*.. ..		1·00	1·00
		a. Imperf (pair) ..		—	2·25
256		10 p. brown/*pale salmon* ..		75	75
		a. Imperf (pair)		2·25	1·60

(Litho J. L. Arango, Medellin)

1902. *REGISTRATION. Laid paper. P* 12.

R257	R **9**	10 c. slate-purple		40	40

(AR 3)

1903. *ACKNOWLEDGMENT OF RECEIPT. No. 197A optd with Type* AR **3.**

AR258	**78**	10 c. black/*pink* (V.)	.. ..	7·00

F. NATIONAL ISSUES
Gold Currency

AR

94	95	(AR 4)

1904. *Types of 1902–05 and T* **94/5.** *Thin paper. Imperf.*

259	**94**	½ c. pale brown	.. .. ..	15	15
		a. Perf 13 ..	..	45	45
260	**95**	1 c. yellow-green	.. ..	12	8
		a. Perf 13 ..	..	35	35
		b. *Blue-green*	..	15	10
261	**75**	2 c. blue	.. ..	10	10
		a. Perf 13 ..	..	30	30
262	**77**	5 c. rose	.. ..	15	12
		a. Perf 12 ..	..	40	40
263	**78**	10 c. mauve	.. ..	20	12
		a. Perf 12 ..	..	50	50

1904. *REGISTRATION. Thin paper. Imperf.*

R264	R **8**	10 c. purple..	.. ..	40	40
		a. Perf 12	.. ..	50	50

1904. *ACKNOWLEDGMENT OF RECEIPT. Thin paper. Imperf.*

AR265	AR **2**	5 c. pale blue	..	30	30
		a. Perf 12	.. ..	70	70

1904. *ACKNOWLEDGMENT OF RECEIPT. No. 262 optd with Type* AR **4.**

AR266	**77**	5 c. rose	..	2·40	2·40
AR267		5 c. rose (G.)	..	2·40	2·40

96	97	98 Pres. Marroquin

Type 96

(a)   (b)

Types of ½ c. and 1 c.

Type I.   Left-hand hook turned out as A; printer's imprint spaced from foot of stamp; top line of value label overlapped by foliate sprays (*a*).

Type II.   As I, but left-hand hook turned in as B.

Type III.   As II, but three white lines between "REPUBLICA" and rows of pearls above it, instead of two lines.

Type IV.   Imprint close to foot of stamp; value label overlapped as I.

Type V.   Imprint as IV; value label overlapped (*b*).

Types of 2 c. and 5 c.

Type I.   Left-hand hook turned out as A; label overlapped by foliate sprays (*a*); imprint low; two lines in front curl of foot of "2" in 2 c.

Type II.   Left-hand hook turned in as B; label overlapped by foliate spray (*a*); imprint close; two lines in front curl of foot of "2" in 2 c.

Type III.   Left-hand hook as B; label not overlapped as (*b*); imprint close; one line in front curl of foot of "2" in 2 c.

Type IV.   As II, but label not overlapped.

Types of 20 c.

Type I.   Imprint spaced from foot of stamp.

Type II.   Imprint close to foot of stamp.

(Litho J. L. Arango, Medellin)

1904. *Wove paper. P* 12.

268	**96**	½ c. yellow (II)	..	..	10	8
269		½ c. yellow (IV)	..	..	20	15
270		½ c. deep yellow (V) ..		..	8	5
		a. Imperf (pair)	..	..		
271		1 c. green (I) ..	..	..		
272		1 c. green (II)	..	..	10	5
273		1 c. green (III)	..	..	8	5
274		1 c. yellow-green (IV)		..	5	5
		a. Imperf (pair)	..	..		
275		1 c. yellow-green (V)		..	5	5
276		2 c. carmine (I)	..	..	15	5
		a. Imperf (pair)	..	..	85	
277		2 c. carmine (II)	..	..	—	5
278		2 c. carmine (III)	..	..	12	5
279		2 c. carmine (IV)	..	..		5
280		5 c. blue (I) ..	..	..	20	5
		a. Imperf (pair)	..	..		
281		5 c. blue (II) ..	..	..	15	5
		a. Imperf (pair)	..	..	2·25	
282		5 c. blue (III) ..	..	..	15	5
283		10 c. violet	..	..	12	5
		a. Imperf (pair)	..	..		
		b. Imperf between (vert pair)		..		
284		20 c. grey-black (I)	..	..	20	5
		a. Imperf between (pair)		..	—	2·25
285		20 c. grey-black (II)	..	..	35	5
286	**97**	1 p. brown	..	..	70	12
		a. Imperf (pair)	..	..		
287	**98**	5 p. black and red/*yellowish*		..	1·75	1·75
288		10 p. black and blue/*bluish*	..		2·40	2·25

Type **96** overprinted "OFICIAL" is believed to be a "specimen".

R 10	AR 5

(Litho J. L. Arango, Medellin)

1904. *REGISTRATION. P* 12.

R289	R **10**	10 c. purple	..	..	..	15	10

(Litho J. L. Arango, Medellin)

1904. *ACKNOWLEDGMENT OF RECEIPT. P* 12.

AR290	AR **5**	5 c. blue ..	..	..	..	20	10

101

Two dies of the 2 c.

Die I. Diagonal line joining "D" of "DOS" to top of "O". (This is sometimes faint or broken, but traces may always be seen at top of "O".)

Die II. No line between "D" and "O". Line running from "L" of "NACIONAL" diagonally to top of "A" and thence to bottom frameline of design.

Two dies of the 5 c.

Die I. The arches above the "5" are clear of any mark.

Die II. There is an extra line in the second arch, counting from the right-hand point of the top of the "5". A small mark, like an L, below the final letter of "NACIONAL" in the imprint denotes a third state of the die.

(Litho National Ptg Works, Bogotá)

1908–16. *Imprint,* "LIT NACIONAL" *at left* (2 c.), *at right* (1 c., 10 c., 20 c.) *or at left and right* (½ c., 5 c.).

(a) P 13½

291	**101**	½ c. orange (1909) ..	.. ..	8	5
		a. Imperf (pair) ..	..		
		b. Yellow (shades)	..	15	5
292		1 c. green (no imprint) (1910)	..	15	5
293		1 c. green (with imprint) (1911)	..	15	5
		a. Imperf (pair) ..	..		
294		2 c. red (Die I)	..	5	5
		a. Imperf (pair) ..	..		
295		2 c. red (Die II) (1913)	..	5	5
		a. Imperf (pair) ..	..	75	75
		b. Imprint at right..	..		
296		5 c. blue (Die I)	..	12	5
297		5 c. blue (Die II) (1914)	..	12	5
		a. Imperf (pair) ..	..	3·00	
298		10 c. violet (1912) ..	..	1·00	20
299		20 c. grey-black (1916)	..	1·25	25

(b) P 10

300	**101**	½ c. orange (1909) ..	..	35	5
		a. Perf comp of 10 and 13½	..	1·25	1·25
		b. Yellow (shades)	..	35	5
301		1 c. green (no imprint) (1910)	..	25	20
		a. Perf comp of 10 and 13½	..	20	5
302		1 c. green (with imprint) (1911)	..	20	5
		a. Perf comp of 10 and 13½	..		
303		2 c. red (Die I)	..	25	5
		a. Perf comp of 10 and 13½	..	1·00	5
		b. Do. Imperf between (pair)	..	2·75	
304		2 c. red (Die II) (1913)	..	25	5
		a. Perf comp of 10 and 13½	..	1·00	5
305		5 c. blue (Die I)	..	40	8
		a. Perf comp of 10 and 13½	..	2·25	1·75
306		5 c. blue (Die II) (1914)	..	50	8
307		10 c. violet (perf comp of 10 and 13½) (1912) ..	.. ..		

(Litho National Ptg Works, Bogotá)

1909. REGISTRATION. *With imprint* "LIT NACIONAL".

R308	**R 10**	10 c. violet	..	45	12
		a. Imperf between (vert pair)	..		
		b. Perf comp of 10 and 13½	..	50	16

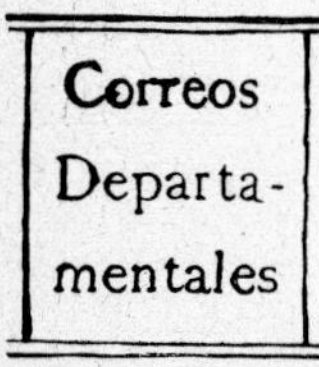

(D 1)

(D 2)

The following stamps were supplied to Government Departments (or Ministries) at half face value as a contribution to their postage costs.

1909. DEPARTMENTAL. *Various stamps handstamped with Types* D **1** *or* D **2**.

(a) No. 256, with Type D **1**

D309	93	10 p. brown/pale salmon ..	..	9·00	9·00
		a. In green	..		
		b. In violet	..		

(b) No. 66 of Tolima, with Type D **1**

D310	–	1 p. brown	..	1·25	1·25
		a. In green	..	1·25	1·25
		b. In violet	..		

(c) T **96/7**
(i) With Type D **1**

D311	96	½ c. deep yellow (V) (270)	..		
		a. In green	..	20	20
		b. In violet	..		
D312		1 c. yellow-green (V) (275)	..	20	20
		a. In violet	..	35	35
D313		2 c. carmine (III) (278)	..	35	35
D314		5 c. blue (I) (280)	..	35	35
D315		5 c. blue (II) (281)	..		
D316		10 c. violet..	..	55	55
D317		20 c. grey-black	..	1·60	1·60
D318	97	1 p. brown	..	2·25	2·25

(ii) With Type D **2**

D319	96	½ c. deep yellow (V) (270)	..		
		a. In green	..	20	20
D320		1 c. yellow-green (V) (275)	..		
		a. In violet	..		
D321		2 c. carmine (III) (278)	..		
D322		5 c. blue (I) (280) ..	..		
D323		10 c. violet..	..	55	55
D324		20 c. grey-black	..	1·60	1·60

(d) T **101**
(i) With Type D **1**. P 13½

D325	**101**	½ c. orange	..	20	20
		a. Imperf (pair) ..	..	2·00	2·00
		b. In green	..	20	20
		c. In violet	..		
D326		2 c. red	..	55	55
D327		5 c. blue	..		
D328		10 c. violet..	..	65	65

P 10

D329	**101**	½ c. orange	..	55	55
D330		1 c. green (p comp of 10 and 13½) (V.)	..	20	20
D331		2 c. red	..		
		a. Perf comp of 10 and 13½	..		
D332		5 c. blue ..	..	55	55

(ii) With Type D **2**. P 13½

D333	**101**	½ c. orange	..	20	20
		a. In green	..	20	20
D334		2 c. red ..	..	55	55
D335		5 c. blue ..	..	55	55

P 10

D336	**101**	½ c. orange	..		
D337		2 c. red	..		
		a. Imperf (pair) ..	..	2·00	2·00
D338		5 c. blue ..	..		

(d) Registration stamps, Type R **10**

D339	D **1**	10 c. purple (R289)	..	1·25	1·00
D340	D **2**	10 c. purple (R289)	..	1·25	1·25
D341	D **1**	10 c. violet (R308) ..	..	70	75
D342	D **2**	10 c. violet (R308)	..	1·00	1·00

(e) Acknowledgment of Receipt stamp, Type AR **5**

D343	D **1**	5 c. blue	..	65	65
D344	D **2**	5 c. blue	..	65	65

Being handstamped, these overprints also occur inverted.

HAVE YOU READ THE NOTES AT THE BEGINNING OF THIS CATALOGUE?

These often provide answers to the enquiries we receive.

102 Camilo Torres

103 Policarpa Salavarrieta

104 Narino demanding Liberation of Slaves

(Eng and recess American Bank Note Co)

1910 (20 July). *Centenary of Independence. T 102/4 and portraits as T 103, inscr "1810 1910". P 12.*

345	102	½ c. black and dull purple	..	20	12
		a. Centre inverted	..	28·00	28·00
346	103	1 c. green	..	20	12
347	–	2 c. scarlet (Narino)	..	20	10
348	–	5 c. blue (Bolivar)	..	20	10
349	–	10 c. plum (Caldas)	..	60	30
350	–	20 c. grey-brown (Santander)	..	1·75	70
351	104	1 p. purple	..	3·75	1·90
352	–	10 p. lake (Narino in group)	..	30·00	20·00
345/352		*Set of 8*	..	33·00	21·00

R 11 Execution of 24 Feb, 1816   AR 6 A. Gomez

(Eng and recess American Bank Note Co)

1910 (Aug). *Centenary of Independence. P 12.*

(a) REGISTRATION

R353	R 11	10 c. black and red	..	5·00	5·00

(b) ACKNOWLEDGMENT OF RECEIPT

AR354	AR 6	5 c. green and orange	..	1·00	1·00

L 4

110 C. Torres

111 Boyacá Monument

112 Cartagena

113 Arms

(Litho National Ptg Works, Bogotá)

1914. *LATE FEE. A. P 13½. B. P 10.*

				A		B	
L335	L 4	2 c. chocolate	..	25	25	45	45
L356		5 c. blue-green	..	25	25	55	55

(Eng and recess Perkins, Bacon & Co)

1917. *T 110/3 and portraits as T 110. P 13½.*

357	–	½ c. bistre (Caldas)	..	..	5	5
358	110	1 c. green	..	..	5	5
359	–	2 c. carmine (Narino)	..	..	5	5
360	–	4 c. purple (Santander)	..	..	5	5
361	–	5 c. dull blue (Bolivar)	..	..	5	5
362	–	10 c. grey (Cordoba)	..	..	12	5
363	111	20 c. red	..	..	25	5
364	112	50 c. carmine	..	..	55	5
365	–	1 p. sky-blue (Sucre)	..	..	1·00	15
		a. Steel-blue	..	..	80	15
366	–	2 p. orange (Cuervo)	..	..	1·60	20
367	–	5 p. grey (Ricaurte)	..	..	4·25	80
368	113	10 p. deep brown	..	..	10·00	5·00
357/368		*Set of 12*	..	..	17·00	6·00

The 1 c., 5 c., 10 c., 50 c., 2 p., 5 p. and 10 p. also exist perf 11½ and perf compound of 13½ and 11½.

Stamps of this issue overprinted "OFICIO" are believed to be "specimens".

See also Nos. 380 and 393/402.

R 12 Port of Colombia

R 13 Tequendama Falls

(Eng and recess Perkins, Bacon & Co)

1917. *REGISTRATION. P 11, 11½, 13½, 14 and compound.*

R369	R 12	4 c. blue and green	..	..	50	50
		a. Centre inverted	..	..	£130	£130
R370	R 13	10 c. deep blue	..	..	20	5

AR 7 Sabana Station

AR 8 Map of Colombia

E 1 Express Messenger

(Eng and recess Perkins, Bacon & Co)

1917. *ACKNOWLEDGMENT OF RECEIPT. P 13½.*

AR371	AR 7	4 c. bistre-brown	..	..	45	45
AR372	AR 8	5 c. chestnut-brown	..	..	60	60

(Recess Perkins, Bacon & Co)

1917. *SPECIAL DELIVERY. P 13½.*

E373	E 1	5 c. green	..	..	45	50

(114)   (115)   (116)

1918. *Surch as T 114 reading up or down, in red.*

374	96	0.00½ on 20 c. grey-black	..	70	20
375	101	0.00½ on 20 c. grey-black	..	1·25	60
376	96	0.03 on 10 c. violet	..	1·00	55
377	101	0.03 on 10 c. violet	..	1·90	70

Nos. 374/77 exist with "s" of "Especie" omitted and with small zero before the decimal point.

1918. *Provisional issue for Bogotá. Litho. P 13½.*
378 **115** 3 c. lake 20 5
   a. Imperf between (pair) .. .. 3·00

1919. *AIR. No. 359 optd with T* **116**, *at Barranquilla.*
379 2 c. carmine £350 £170
   a. Figures "1" of "18" and "19" with
   serifs £1000 £350
Used for the first flight, Barranquilla to Puerto Colombia on
18 June 1919. This overprint did not have the prior authority
of the Ministry of Posts and Telegraphs. Beware of forgeries.

1920. *New value. P 13½.*
380 **113** 3 c. red/yellow 20 5

  117   118   119

(Litho National Ptg Works, Bogotá)
1920–22. A. *P 13½.* B. *P 10 or compound.*

		A		B	
381 **117**	½ c. yellow ..	..	25	12	
382	1 c. green ..	..	10	5	75	30
383	2 c. red ..	..	5	5	75	30
384 **118**	3 c. bright green	..	5	5	15	8
	a. Sage-green ..		5	5	15	8
385 **117**	5 c. blue ..	..	10	5	40	25
386	10 c. violet ..	..	20	10	40	20
387	10 c. dp blue (1922)	..	80	60	†	
388	20 c. green ..	..	1·50	30	2·00	1·10
389 **119**	50 c. red ..	..	1·75	90	2·00	1·10
381/389A	Set of 9	..	4·25	2·00		

The tablet with "PROVISIONAL" was added separately to
each design on the lithographic stones and its position varies
on different stamps in the sheet. In the ½ c., 1 c. and 5 c. the
angle of inclination also varies.
There are numerous shades in this issue.

PROVICIONAL   **PROVISIONAL**   **PROVISIONAL**
$003   **$0.03**   **$003**
  (120)   (121)   (122)

1921–24. *No. 360 surch, in red.*
390 **120** $003 on 4 c. purple.. .. .. 15 5
   a. Surch double .. .. .. 5·00
391 **121** $0.03 on 4 c. purple (1922) 60 30
392 **122** $003 on 4 c. purple (1924) 75 20
   a. Surch double .. .. .. 6·00
   b. Surch double, one inverted .. 6·00

LATE FEE STAMPS. Stamps overprinted "RETARDO" or
"Retardo 1921" were unauthorised.

  123 Sabana Station   **124**

(Recess Perkins, Bacon & Co)
1923–29. *As 1917. New values, colours changed and new
design (T* **123***). Portraits are as T* **110***. P 13½.*
393 **113** 1½ c. chocolate 10 8
394 3 c. blue 8 5
395 – 4 c. blue (Santander) (1926) .. 8 5
396 – 5 c. claret (Bolivar) (1924) .. 8 5
397 **113** 8 c. blue (1926) 10 5
398 – 10 c. blue (Cordoba) 40 5
399 – 30 c. bistre (Caldas) (1926) .. 45 5
400 **123** 40 c. brown (1926) 45 5
401 – 5 p. violet (Ricaurte) (1926) .. 4·50 30
   a. Perf 11 (1929) .. .. 5·00 2·00
402 **113** 10 p. green (1926) .. .. 9·00 2·00
   a. Perf 11 (1929) .. .. 10·00 5·00
393/402 Set of 10 .. .. .. 14·00 2·50

The 4 c., 8 c. and 30 c. differ from previous stamps in the
same general designs in many details, notably in the fact that
the vertical frameline between "CORREOS" and the central
background is unshaded.

(Litho Villaveces, Bogotá)
1924 (17 Nov)–**25.** *P 10 × 13½* (3 c. *also P 10*).
403 **124** 1 c. scarlet 5 5
404 3 c. blue (1925) 15 5

CENTAVO   **PROVISIONAL**
  (125)   (126)

1925. *Large fiscal stamps surch with T* **125** *or optd with
T* **126**.
 (a) *With imprint of Waterlow & Sons. P* 14, 15
405 1 c. on 3 c. brown 5 5
406 4 c. purple (R.) 8 5
   a. Opt inverted .. .. .. 4·00 4·00
 (b) *With imprint of American Bank Note Co. P* 12
407 1 c. on 3 c. brown 45 40
   a. Surch inverted .. .. .. 6·50 6·00
408 4 c. violet (G.) 35 20
   a. Opt inverted .. ..
Beware of forgeries of the errors.

          R **14**

1925. *REGISTRATION. Inscr* "PROVISIONAL". *Litho.
P* 10 × 13½.
R409 R **14** (10 c.) light blue .. .. .. 1·00 1·00

  127   128

(Litho National Ptg Works, Bogotá)
1926. *Coarse greyish paper. W* **128**. *P 13½ × 10.*
410 **127** 1 c. green 5 5
   a. Figure "1" crosses "PROVI-
   SIONAL" 75 75
   b. Perf 10 .. .. 30 8
   c. Perf 10 × 13½ .. .. ..
411 4 c. deep blue 5 5
   a. "CUATRC" 25 40
   b. Perf 10 × 13½ 12 5
   c. Perf 10 .. .. 5 5
   d. Imperf between (horiz pair) .. 1·00 1·50
The 4 c. without watermark comes from an unauthorised
printing made by an employee of the printing works.

  129 Death of Bolivar

(Recess Waterlow & Sons)

1930 (17 Dec). *Death Centenary of Bolivar. P 12½.*
412 **129** 4 c. black and blue 15 10

130

131

CORREO AEREO
(132)

CORREO AEREO
(133)

(Stamps typo Govt Printing Works, Berlin. Overprinted at Bogotá)

1932 (12 Jan). *AIR. T* **130** *and* **131** *optd with T* **132** *and* **133** *respectively. W* **46** *of Germany. P* 14.

413	130	5 c. yellow ..	..	..	..	3·25	3·00
414		10 c. maroon	..	..	..	55	12
415		15 c. green ..	..	..	..	50	25
416		20 c. rose	..	..	..	25	5
417		30 c. grey-blue	..	..	..	30	5
418		40 c. lilac	..	..	..	35	25
419		50 c. olive ..	..	..	..	45	40
420		60 c. red-brown	..	..	..	40	40
421		80 c. yellow-green ..	..	..	3·75	3·75
422	131	1 p. blue	..	..	..	3·50	75
423		2 p. red	..	..	..	8·00	4·00
424		3 p. mauve ..	..	..	..	14·00	14·00
425		5 p. olive-green	..	..	..	22·00	22·00
413/425		*Set of 13*	..	..	..	50·00	45·00

R
(R 15)

20
CENTAVOS
(134)

1932 (12 Jan). *REGISTRATION AIR. No.* 416 *optd with Type* R **15**.
R426 **130** 20 c. rose .. .. .. 3·00 2·50

PRIVATE AIR COMPANIES. Prior to the issue of the stamps listed above, which resulted from the Colombian Government taking over the control of the air services, stamps of the SOCIEDAD COLOMBO-ALEMANA DE TRANSPORTES AEREOS (S.C.A.D.T.A.) in various types were used. While officially authorised by the Government for prepayment of charges on letters carried by Colombian air-routes, the stamps were issued by a private company holding the concession for this service.

They are at present outside the scope of this catalogue, although the stamps of other private air companies with government concessions for carrying mail are listed at the end of Colombia.

1932 (20 Jan). *Nos.* 395 *and* 399 *surch as T* **134**.
427 1 c. on 4 c. blue (R.) 5 5
    a. Surch inverted .. .. .. 3·50 3·50
428 20 c. on 30 c. bistre (B.) 35 10

135

136 Emerald Mine

137 Oil Wells

138 Coffee Plantation

139 Platinum Mine

140 Gold Mining

141 Columbus

(Recess Waterlow & Sons)

1932 (June). "WATERLOW & SONS LTD. LONDRES" *imprint at foot. W* **135**. *P* 12½.

429	136	1 c. deep green	..	..	..	5	5
430	137	2 c. scarlet ..	..	..	..	5	5
431	138	5 c. brown ..	..	..	..	12	5
432	139	8 c. blue	..	..	..	30	12
433	140	10 c. yellow ..	..	..	..	25	5
434	141	20 c. blue ..	..	..	..	25	5
429/434		*Set of 6*	..	..	..	90	30

For litho issue, see Nos. 479/86a.

142 Coffee

143 Gold

R
(R 16)

(Des Fräulein D. Suffrian. Photo Govt Printing Works, Berlin)

1932 (1 Aug)–**39**. *AIR. T* **142**/3 *and similar designs. W* **46** *of Germany. P* 14.

435	142	5 c. chocolate and orange ..	..	10	5
436	–	10 c. black and lake ..	..	..	5	5
437	–	15 c. violet and deep green ..	..	10	5
438	–	15 c. violet and scarlet (28.7.39)	..	30	5
439	–	20 c. bronze-green and carmine	..	15	5
440	–	20 c. ol-green & emerald (28.7.39) ..	50	10
441	142	30 c. chocolate and blue	..	..	20	5
442	–	40 c. olive-bistre and violet ..	..	25	5
443	–	50 c. chocolate & blackish green	..	25	5
444	–	60 c. violet and chocolate ..	..	35	5
445	142	80 c. sepia and green	..	..	75	20
446	143	1 p. olive-bistre and blue ..	..	1·60	8
447	–	2 p. olive-bistre and brown-lake ..	2·75	25
448	–	3 p. emerald and violet ..	..	4·00	80
449	–	5 p. emerald and olive-green ..	6·00	1·75
435/449		*Set of 15*	..	..	..	16·00	3·25

Designs: As T **142**—10 c., 50 c. Cattle; 15 c., 60 c. Oil wells; 20 c., 40 c. Bananas. As T **143**—3 p., 5 p. Emeralds.

1932 (1 Aug). *REGISTRATION AIR. No.* 439 *optd as Type* R **16**.
R450 20 c. bronze-green and carmine .. .. 2·50 70

144 Pedro de Heredia

(Litho National Ptg Works, Bogotá)

1933 (30 Dec). *400th Anniv of Cartagena. P* 11½.
451	144	1 c. grey-green	..	..	40	20
452		5 c. brown	..	..	20	10
453		8 c. blue	..	..	30	15

(145) (146)

1934 (2 Jan). *AIR. 400th Anniv of Cartagena. Nos. 443 and 445 surch as T* **145** *and Nos. 446/7 surch as T* **146**.
454	–	10 c. on 50 c. chocolate & green	..	1·00	1·00
455	142	15 c. on 80 c. sepia and green		1·00	1·00
456	143	20 c. on 1 p. bistre and blue..		1·25	1·25
457		30 c. on 2 p. bistre and lake ..		1·60	1·60
454/457		Set of 4	..	4·25	4·25

Nos. 454/7 were sold at Cartagena from 30 December 1933 to 6 January 1934 for use on air mail but from 2 January they were on sale at all air mail offices in Colombia.

147 Oil Wells **148** Coffee Plantation **149** Gold Mining

(Recess American Bank Note Co)

1934 (Dec)–**35**. *"AMERICAN BANK NOTE CO" at foot. No wmk. P* 12.
458	147	2 c. carmine (3.35) ..	..	5	5
459	148	5 c. brown	..	5	5
460	149	10 c. orange (1935) ..	..	15	5

For 2 c. and 10 c. with watermark, see Nos. 534 and 537; for 2 c. recess by Columbia Bank Note Co, see No. 589; and for 2 c. litho by National Printing Works, see No. 604.

150 Discus Thrower **151** Runners

(Litho National Ptg Works, Bogotá)

1935 (26 Jan). *Third National Olympiad. T* **150**/1 *and similar designs inscr* "III OLIMPIADA BARRANQUILLA 1935". *P* 11½.
461		2 c. orange and blue-green	..	80	50
462		4 c. deep green	..	80	50
463		5 c. yellow and brown ..	..	80	50
		a. Imperf between (horiz pair)		75·00	
464		7 c. carmine	..	1·25	80
465		8 c. violet and black	..	1·25	80
466		10 c. light blue and chocolate	..	1·25	80
467		12 c. deep blue ..	..	1·60	1·25
468		15 c. lake and blue	..	2·50	1·50
469		18 c. yellow and purple ..	..	3·00	1·90
470		20 c. green and violet ..	..	3·50	2·40
471		24 c. ultramarine and green	..	4·00	3·00
472		50 c. orange and ultramarine	..	5·00	5·00
473		1 p. light blue and olive	..	10·00	7·00
474		2 p. light blue and deep green ..		35·00	30·00
475		5 p. light blue and deep violet ..		65·00	60·00
476		10 p. light blue and black	..	£140	£130
461/476		Set of 16	..	£250	£225

Designs: *Vert*—2 c. Footballers; 1 p. G.P.O.; 2 p. "Flag of the Race" Monument; 5 p. Arms; 10 p. Condor. *Horiz*—5 c. Allegory of 1935 Olympiad; 7 c. Runners; 8 c. Tennis player; 10 c. Hurdler; 12 c. Puerto Pier; 15 c. Athlete; 18 c. Baseball; 20 c. Seashore; 24 c. Swimmer; 50 c. Aerial view of Barranquilla.

152 Nurse and Sick (153)

(Litho National Ptg Works, Bogotá)

1935 (27 May). *OBLIGATORY TAX. Red Cross Fund. P* 11½.
477	152	5 c. scarlet and olive-green	..	35	15

1935. *No. 365 surch with T* **153**.
478		12 c. on 1 p. sky-blue	..	30	20

(Litho National Ptg Works, Bogotá)

1935–44. *Waterlow types of 1932 printed litho in Bogotá.* "LIT. NACIONAL BOGOTA" *at foot. No wmk. Various perfs.*
479	136	1 c. emerald-green (p 11½) (10.35)		5	5
		a. Imperf (pair) ..	..	1·75	1·25
		b. Imperf between (horiz pair)	..	1·25	
		c. Perf 11 (10.36) ..		5	5
480	137	2 c. rose-red (p 10½) (5.12.38)		5	5
481	138	5 c. brown (p 11 × 11½) (27.4.36)		5	5
482		5 c. light brown (p 10½) (14.8.36)		5	5
483		5 c. chocolate (p 10½) (1938)		5	5
484		5 c. orange-brown (p 12½) (1944)		5	5
485	140	10 c. orange (p 10½) (5.12.38)	..	20	5
		a. Perf 12½ (1944)	..	12	5
486	141	20 c. blue (p 10½) (5.12.38)	..	40	5
		a. Perf 12½ (1944)	..	1·25	5

154 Simon Bolivar **155** Tequendama Falls

(Recess Waterlow)

1937–48. *W* **135**. *P* 12½.
487	154	1 c. green ..	..	5	5
		a. Perf 14 ..	..		
488	155	10 c. scarlet (12.48) ..	..	8	5
489		12 c. blue	..	25	15

156 Footballer **157** Discus Thrower **158** Runner

(Photo Waterlow)

1937 (4 Jan). *Fourth National Olympiad. P* 12½.
490	156	3 c. emerald-green..		75	20
491	157	10 c. carmine	..	2·50	50
492	158	1 p. black ..	..	10·00	3·00

159 Exhibition Palace

160 "Flag of the Race" Monument

164 Entrance to Church of the Rosary

165 Gonzálo Jiménez de Quesada

166 "Bochica" (Indian God)

(Photo Waterlow)

1937 (4 Jan). *Barranquilla Industrial Exhibition. T* **159/60** *and similar horiz design. P* 12½.

493	159	5 c. maroon	..	15	8
494	–	15 c. light blue (Stadium)	..	1·00	15
495	160	50 c. red-brown	..	1·40	50

OFICIAL
(O 1)

OFICIAL
(O 2)

1937 (Febr). *OFFICIAL. Various stamps optd with Type* O **1** (1 c. to 12 c.) *or Type* O **2** (others).

O496	136	1 c. emerald-green (479c)		5	5
O497	137	2 c. scarlet (430)	..	5	5
O498	138	5 c. brown (431)	..	5	5
		a. Opt double	..	2·50	2·50
O499	149	10 c. orange (460)	..	20	5
O500	156	12 c. blue (489) (R.)	..	8	8
O501	141	20 c. blue (434) (R.)	..	12	5
O502	–	30 c. bistre (399)	..	20	5
O503	123	40 c. brown (400)	..	30	5
O504	112	50 c. carmine (364)		40	8
O505	–	1 p. sky-blue (365)	..	60	20
O506	–	2 p. orange (366)	..	1·25	60
O507	–	5 p. grey (367)	..	4·00	1·40
O508	113	10 p. deep brown (368)	..	7·50	2·25
O496/508		Set of 13	..	13·00	4·50

The overprint is horizontal on the 5, 40 and 50 c. and vertical on the others. Beware of forgeries.

The 5 p. and 10 p. usually had "ANULADO" punched through them before use, but the above prices are for unpunched stamps.

161 Mother and Child

5 CENTAVOS (162)

2 CENTAVOS (163)

(Litho National Ptg Works, Bogotá)

1937 (24 May). *OBLIGATORY TAX. Red Cross Fund. P* 10½.

509	161	5 c. rose (shades)	..	12	5

1937–38. 2 c. surch with T **163**, others as T **162**.

510	156	1 c. on 3 c. emerald-green (3.11.37)	30	10
		a. Surch inverted ..	..		
511	155	2 c. on 12 c. blue (3.11.37) ..		5	5
512	139	5 c. on 8 c. blue (432) (26.10.37)		5	5
513	113	5 c. on 8 c. blue (397) (5.11.37)		5	5
514	155	10 c. on 12 c. blue (1938) ..		12	5

Inverted surcharges of No. 514 are clandestine productions from the genuine type.

PUZZLED?

Then you need
PHILATELIC TERMS ILLUSTRATED
to tell you all you need to know about printing methods, papers, errors, varieties, watermarks, perforations, etc. 192 pages, almost half in full colour, soft cover. £1 post paid.

167 First Mass on Site of Bogotá

168 Proposed P.O., Bogotá

(Photo Waterlow)

1938 (27 July). *400th Anniv of Bogotá. As T* **164/7** (*inscr* "1538 1938 IV CENTENARIO BOGOTA"). *P* 12½.

515	1 c. green	..	..	5	5
516	2 c. scarlet	..	..	10	8
517	5 c. black	..	..	10	8
518	10 c. sepia	..	..	15	8
519	15 c. light blue	..	..	20	15
520	20 c. magenta	..	..	35	35
521	1 p. red-brown	..	..	2·00	1·60
515/521	Set of 7	..	..	2·75	2·10

Designs: *Vert*—1 c. "Calle del Arco" ("Street of the Arch"), Old Bogotá; 5 c. Arms of Bogotá; 20 c. Convent of Santo Domingo.

(Litho National Ptg Works, Bogotá)

1939 (15 Jan). *OBLIGATORY TAX. P.O. Rebuilding Fund. P* 10½.

522	168	½ c. blue	..	..	5	5
523		½ c. carmine	..	..	5	5
524		1 c. violet	..	..	5	5
525		2 c. green	..	..	5	5
526		20 c. brown	..	..	20	12
522/526		Set of 5	..	..	30	25

A 25 c. orange was issued for compulsory use on receipts for renewal of rents for P.O. boxes.

See also Nos. 564/7a.

5 cts

15

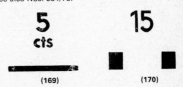

(169)   (170)

1939–40. *AIR. Air stamps of 1932 surch with T* **169/70** *or as T* **169** *but larger* (Nos. 530/1).

527	5 c. on 20 c. bronze-green and carmine (11.5.39)	10	5
528	5 c. on 40 c. olive-bistre and violet (R.) (1.3.39)	10	5
529	15 c. on 20 c. bronze-green and carmine (15.1.39)	..	15	5
	a. Surch inverted	..	6·00	
	b. Surch double	..	5·00	
530	15 c. on 30 c. chocolate and blue (20.10.40)	..	35	5
	a. Surch inverted	..	5·00	
531	15 c. on 40 c. olive-bistre and violet (R.) (20.10.40)	..	35	5
	a. Surch double	..	5·00	
527/531	Set of 5	..	95	20

1939 (1 Mar). *REGISTRATION AIR. No. R450 surch with T* **169**.

R532	5 c. on 20 c. bronze-green and carmine	60	40

171 Bolivar

172 Coffee Plantation

173 Arms of Colombia

174 Columbus

175 Caldas

176 Sabana Station

177

178 Proposed new P.O., Bogotá

(Recess American Bank Note Co)

1939 (3 Mar)–49. W **177**. P 12.

533	171	1 c. blue-green	..	5	5
534	147	2 c. carmine	..	5	5
535	172	5 c. reddish brown (9.3.39) ..	..	5	5
536		5 c. light blue (4.8.49)	..	5	5
537	149	10 c. orange ..	..	10	5
538	173	15 c. blue (9.3.39)	..	15	5
539	174	20 c. slate-black (9.3.39)	..	25	5
540	175	30 c. olive-green	..	30	5
541	176	40 c. olive-brown	..	50	15
533/541		Set of 9	..	1·40	40

For stamps recess by Columbia Bank Note Co, see Nos. 588/91 and for stamps litho by National Printing Works, see Nos. 603/5.

(Recess De La Rue)

1940 (20 Jan). *OBLIGATORY TAX. P.O. Rebuilding Fund.* W **135**. P 12½×13 (*Nos.* 542/6) *or* 13½–14 (542, 544) *or* 13½ (543).

542	178	¼ c. ultramarine	..	5	5
543		½ c. scarlet ..	..	5	5
544		1 c. bright violet	..	5	5
545		2 c. green ..	..	5	5
546		20 c. brown ..	..	15	8
542/546		Set of 5	..	25	20

A 25 c. grey-black was issued for fiscal use. For ¼ c. litho, see No. 608.

(Recess De La Rue)

1940 (6 May). *Death Centenary of Gen. Santander. As* T **179/80** *designs dated* "1840 1940"). W **135**. P 13×13½ (1 *c. to* 15 *c.*) *or* 13½×13 (*others*).

547		1 c. sage-green	..	..	..	15	12
548		2 c. carmine	..	..	..	15	12
549		5 c. chocolate ..	..	..	..	20	10
550		8 c. carmine	..	..	..	25	15
551		10 c. yellow-orange	..	..	..	35	25
552		15 c. blue	..	..	..	40	20
553		20 c. emerald-green	..	..	..	65	40
554		50 c. violet	..	..	..	80	80
555		1 p. carmine	..	..	..	2·25	1·90
556		2 p. orange	..	..	..	8·50	6·00
547/556		Set of 10	..	..	..	12·00	9·00

Designs: As T **179**. *Vert*—1 c. Gen. Santander; 5 c. Medallion of Santander by David; 8 c. Statue of Santander, Cucuta; 15 c. Church at Rosario. *Horiz*—10 c. Santander's birthplace, Rosario. As T **180**. *Horiz*—20 c. Battlefield at Paya; 1 p. Death of Santander; 2 p. Victorious Army at Zamora.

181 Tobacco Plant

182 Santander

183 Garcia Rovira

184 Gen. Sucre

185 "Protection"

(Recess American Bank Note Co)

1940–47. T **181/4** *and another portrait type.* W **177**. P 12.

557	181	8 c. green and carmine	..	60	30
558	182	15 c. blue (1943)	..	12	5
559	183	20 c. slate-grey (1941)	..	20	5
560	–	40 c. bistre-brown (Galan) (1941)	..	40	5
561	184	1 p. black	..	1·25	10
562		1 p. violet (1947)	..	60	5
557/562		Set of 6	..	2·75	55

For 20 c. without watermark, see No. 591.

(Recess American Bank Note Co)

1940 (Aug). *OBLIGATORY TAX. Red Cross Fund.* W **177**. P 12.

563	185	5 c. carmine ..	..	5	5

For lithographed stamp, see No. 607.

1940–44. *OBLIGATORY TAX. P.O. Rebuilding Fund. As Nos.* 522/4 *but colours changed.* P 12½.

564	168	¼ c. maroon (1944)	..	5	5
565		½ c. rose-red ..	..	5	5
566		1 c. dark violet	..	5	5
567		1 c. yellow-orange (1944)	..	5	5
		a. Reddish orange ..	..	5	5
564/567		Set of 4	..	15	15

179 "Arms and the Law"

180 Bridge at Boyacá

186 Pre-Colombian Monument

187 Proclamation of Independence

(Recess American Bank Note Co)

1941 (28 Jan). *AIR. Various designs as T* **186/7**. *P* 12.

568	186	5 c. grey	.. ..	5	5
569	–	10 c. yellow-orange	.. ..	5	5
570	–	15 c. carmine	.. .. ..	5	5
571	–	20 c. green	.. .. ..	5	5
572	186	30 c. blue	.. .. ..	12	5
573	–	40 c. maroon	.. .. ..	20	5
574	–	50 c. blue-green	.. ..	25	5
575	–	60 c. brown-purple	.. ..	25	5
576	186	80 c. grey-olive	.. ..	40	5
577	187	1 p. black and blue	.. ..	70	5
578	–	2 p. black and red	.. ..	1·60	20
579	187	3 p. black and violet	..	2·50	35
580	–	5 p. black and green	..	4·50	90
568/580		*Set of 13*	.. ..	10·00	1·75

Designs: As T **186**—10 c., 40 c. "El Dorado" Monument; 15 c., 50 c. Spanish Fort, Cartagena; 20 c., 60 c. Street in Old Bogotá. As T **187**—2 p., 5 p. National Library, Bogotá.

For same designs in different colours, see Nos. 691/703 and 749/58. No. 570 was reissued in 1952.

188 Arms of Palmira

189 Home of Jorge Isaacs (author)

(Litho Colombia Printing Works, Bogotá)

1942 (4 July). *Eighth National Agricultural Exhibition, Palmira. P* 11.

581	188	30 c. claret	..	45	20

(Litho Colombia Printing Works, Bogotá)

1942 (4 July). *Honouring J. Isaacs. P* 11.

582	189	50 c. green	.. .. ..	55	20

190 Peace Conference Delegates

(191) MEDIO CENTAVO $ 0,0½

(Litho Colombia Printing Works, Bogotá)

1942. *40th Anniv of Wisconsin Peace Treaty ending Civil War. P* 11.

583	190	10 c. orange	.. .. ..	25	10

1943. *OBLIGATORY TAX. P.O. Rebuilding Fund. Surch with T* **191**.

584	168	½ c. on 1 c. violet	.. ..	5	5
585		½ c. on 2 c. green	.. ..	5	5
586		½ c. on 20 c. brown	.. ..	5	5
584/586		*Set of 3*	.. ..	10	10

(192) 5 Centavos

193 National Shrine

194 San Pedro Alejandrino

1944. *No.* 537 *surch with T* **192**.

587	149	5 c. on 10 c. orange	.. ..	5	5

(Recess Columbian Bank Note Co)

1944. *With imprint* "COLUMBIAN BANK NOTE CO" *at foot. No wmk. P* 11.

588	171	1 c. blue-green	.. ..	5	5
589	147	2 c. carmine	.. ..	5	5
590	172	5 c. reddish brown	..	5	5
591	183	20 c. slate-grey	.. ..	20	8
592	193	30 c. slate-green	.. ..	30	10
593	194	50 c. carmine	.. ..	45	12
588/593		*Set of 6*	.. ..	1·00	40

See also Nos. 603/4.

1944 (Oct). *No.* 590 *surch as T* **163**.

594	172	1 c. on 5 c. reddish brown		5	5
595		2 c. on 5 c. reddish brown	..	5	5

Inverted and double surcharges on these stamps were not authorised.

195 Banner　　　　　**196** Virrey Solis

(Litho Colombia Printing Works, Bogotá)

1944 (10 Oct). *75th Anniv of General Benevolent Institution of Cundinamarca. As T* **195/6** (*inscr* "1869 AGOSTO 15 1944"). *P* 11–11½.

596		2 c. blue and yellow	.. ..	10	5
597		5 c. blue and yellow	.. ..	10	8
598		20 c. black and green	..	35	20
599		40 c. black and scarlet	..	50	45
600		1 p. black and scarlet	..	1·60	1·50
596/600		*Set of 5*	.. ..	2·40	2·00
MS601		100×87 mm. Nos. 596/600. Stamps imperf but sheet perf 11–11½		3·00	3·00

Designs: As T **195**—5 c. Arms of the Institution; 20 c. Murillo Toro. As T **196**:—40 c. St. Juan de Dios Maternity Hospital.

199 Murillo Toro

200 San Pedro Alejandrino

201 Proposed New P.O., Bogotá

(Litho National Ptg Works, Bogotá)

1944. *P* 11.

602	199	5 c. brown-olive	.. ..	10	5

(Litho National Ptg Works, Bogotá)

1944 (Oct). *With imprint* "LITOGRAFIA NACIONAL BOGOTA" *at foot. No wmk. P* 12½.

603	171	1 c. blue-green	.. ..	5	5
		a. Grey-olive	.. ..	5	5
		b. Imperf (pair)			
604	147	2 c. carmine	.. ..	5	5
605	175	30 c. olive-green	.. ..	45	5
606	200	50 c. carmine	.. ..	90	15
603/606		*Set of 4*	.. ..	1·25	25

(Litho Colombia Printing Works, Bogotá)

1944. *OBLIGATORY TAX. Red Cross Fund. As No.* 563, *but inscr* "LITOGRAFIA COLOMBIA, BOGOTA" *at foot. No wmk. P* 11.

607	185	5 c. carmine	.. ..	10	5

1944. *OBLIGATORY TAX. P.O. Rebuilding Fund. With imprint* "LITO-COLOMBIA BOGOTA-COLOMBIA" *at foot. As No.* 542, *but litho. No wmk. P* 11.

608	178	¼ c. ultramarine	.. ..	20	5

(Recess American Bank Note Co)

1945–48. *OBLIGATORY TAX. P.O. Rebuilding Fund.* *W* **177.** *P* 12

609	**201**	¼ c. ultramarine	5	5
610		¼ c. sepia (1946)	5	5
611		½ c. carmine	5	5
612		½ c. magenta (1946)	5	5
613		1 c. violet (1946)	5	5
614		1 c. red-orange (1946)	5	5
615		1 c. olive-green (1947)	5	5
616		2 c. green (1946)	5	5
617		20 c. brown (1946)	12	5
		a. Red-brown (1948)	12	5

For 25 c. deep grey, see No. 757.

(202) Stalin, Roosevelt and Churchill

203 Clock Tower, Cartagena

1945 (19 July). *No.* 535 *optd with T* **202.**

618	**172**	5 c. reddish brown (R.)	20	5
619		5 c. reddish brown (G.)	20	5
620		5 c. reddish brown (B.)	20	5

(Recess American Bank Note Co)

1945. *W* **177.** *P* 12.

621	**203**	50 c. blackish olive	45	15

204 Control Tower

205 National Capitol, Bogotá

(Litho Colombia Printing Works, Bogotá)

1945 (Nov). *AIR. As T* **204/5** (*inscr* "SOBREPORTE AEREO"). *P* 11.

622	**204**	5 c. blue-grey (15 Nov)	5	5
623	–	10 c. yellow-orange	5	5
624	–	15 c. carmine (3 Nov)	5	5
625	**204**	20 c. yellow-green	12	5
626	–	30 c. blue (15 Nov)	15	5
627	–	40 c. claret	20	5
628	**204**	50 c. blue-green	25	5
629	–	60 c. brown-purple	25	5
630	–	80 c. greenish grey	75	5
631	**205**	1 p. blue	75	5
632		2 p. red-orange	2·25	20
622/632		*Set of* 11	4·50	60

Designs: As T **204**—10 c., 30 c., 60 c. Tequendama Falls; 15 c., 40 c., 80 c. Santa Marta Bay.

207 Sierra Nevada of Santa Maria

1
UN CENTAVO

(208)

(Litho Colombia Printing Works, Bogotá)

1945 (14 Dec). *25th Anniv of First Air Mail Service in America. T* **207** *and similar horiz designs. P* 11.

633	20 c. emerald-green	30	12
634	30 c. blue	40	15
635	50 c. carmine	70	15

Designs:—30 c. Seaplane *Tolima*; 50 c. San Sebastian Fortress, Cartagena.

1946. *Nos.* 481 *and* 484 *surch with T* **208.**

636	**138**	1 c. on 5 c. brown (*p* 11×11½)	5	5
637		1 c. on 5 c. orange-brown (*p* 12½)	5	5

209 Gen. Sucre

(210)

211 Map of South America

(Recess American Bank Note Co)

1946 (16 Apr). *W* **177.** *P* 12.

(*a*) 19¼×26½ *mm*

638	**209**	1 c. greenish blue and bistre-brown	5	5
639		2 c. carmine and violet	5	5

(*b*) 23×31¼ *mm*

640	**209**	5 c. blue and olive-brown	5	5
641		9 c. scarlet and blue-green	40	40
642		10 c. orange and ultramarine	15	8
643		20 c. orange and black	15	5
644		30 c. emerald and lake	20	8
645		40 c. claret and grey-green	25	12
646		50 c. violet and purple	35	20
638/646		*Set of* 9	1·50	95

1946 (25 May). *OBLIGATORY TAX. Red Cross Fund. No.* 535 *optd with T* **210,** *in red.*

647	**172**	5 c. reddish brown	5	5

(Litho Colombia Printing Works, Bogotá)

1946 (7 June). *P* 11.

648	**211**	15 c. blue	12	5

212 Bogotá Observatory

213 Andres Bello

214 Joaquin de Cayzedo y Cuero

(Litho Colombia Printing Works, Bogotá)

1946 (Aug)–**48.** *P* 11.

649	**212**	5 c. purple-brown	8	5
650		5 c. blue (1948)	5	5

(Recess American Bank Note Co)

1946 (3 Sept). *80th Death Anniv of Andres Bello* (*poet and teacher*). *W* **177.** *P* 12.

(*a*) *POSTAGE*

651	**213**	3 c. purple-brown	5	5
652		10 c. orange	8	5
653		15 c. black	15	8

(*b*) *AIR. Inscr* "SERVICIO AEREO"

654	**213**	5 c. blue	5	5
651/654		*Set of* 4	30	20

(Recess Waterlow)

1946 (20 Sept)–**48.** *J. de Cayzedo y Cuero* (*Hero of Independence*). *P* 12½. (*a*) *W* **135.**

655	**214**	2 p. blue-green	1·90	30

(*b*) *No wmk* (1948)

656	**214**	2 p. grey-green	65	15

215 Proposed New P.O., Bogotá

V JUEGOS C.
A. Y DEL C.
1946

(216)

(Litho Colombia Printing Works, Bogotá)

1946. *OBLIGATORY TAX. P.O. Rebuilding Fund.* P 11.
657 **215** 3 c. blue 5 5

1946 (6 Dec). *Fifth Olympic Games, Barranquilla. As No.* 621 *(colour changed), optd with T* **216.** A. *In black.* B. *In green.*
  A   B
658 **203** 50 c. red .. .. 2·25 1·10 2·25 1·10

217 Coffee Plant   **218** *Masdevallia Nicterina*

(Frame recess, centre litho Waterlow)

1947 (10 Jan). *W* **135.** *P* 12½.
659 **217** 5 c. red, green, yellow and brown .. 35 5

(Frame recess, centres litho A.B.N. Co)

1947 (7 Feb). *Colombian Orchids. T* **218** *and similar vert designs. Multicoloured. W* **177.** *P* 12.
660 1 c. Type **218** 30 10
661 2 c. *Miltonia Vexillaria* 30 8
662 5 c. *Cattleya Dowiana Aurea* 45 8
663 5 c. *Cattleya Chocoensis* 35 5
664 5 c. *Odontoglossum Crispum* 40 8
665 10 c. *Cattleya Labiata Trianae* 70 12
660/665 *Set of* 6 .. .. 2·25 . 45

SOBRETASA
(219)   **220** Antonio Narino   **221** M. del Socorro Rodriguez

1947. *OBLIGATORY TAX. No.* 591 *optd with T* **219.**
666 **183** 20 c. slate-grey (R.) 35 5

(Litho Waterlow)

1947 (9 May). *Fourth Pan-American Press Conference, Bogotá. As T* **220/1** *(portraits in various frames). P* 12½. *(a) POSTAGE.*
667 **220** 5 c. blue/*azure* 5 5
668 **221** 10 c. brown/*azure* 12 5

(b) AIR. Inscr "SERVICIO AEREO"
669 – 5 c. blue/*azure* 8 5
670 – 10 c. orange-red/*azure* 12 10
667/670 *Set of* 4 .. .. 30 20
Portraits:—No. 669, Alberto Urdaneta y Urdaneta; No. 670, Francisco José de Caldas.

222 Arms of Colombia and Cross   **223** J. C. Mutis and J. J. Triana

(Recess Waterlow)

1947 (Sept). *OBLIGATORY TAX. Red Cross Fund. P* 12½.
671 **222** 5 c. lake *(shades)* 5 5
For similar stamp, litho, see No. 705.

(Recess Waterlow)

1947 (8 Nov)–**48.** *P* 12½. *(a) No wmk*
672 **223** 25 c. dull green 15 5

(b) W **135**
673 **223** 25 c. sage-green (1948) .. .. 20 ·5

224 M. A. Caro and R. J. Cuervo   **225** Bogotá Cathedral

(Recess Waterlow)

1947 (Dec)–**48.** *P* 12½. *(a) W* **135.**
674 **224** 3 p. slate-purple .. .. .. 1·60 40

(b) No wmk (1948)
675 **224** 3 p. purple 90 30

1947. *OBLIGATORY TAX. No.* 486e *optd with T* **219.**
676 **141** 20 c. blue (R.) .. .. .. 1·75 1·75

(Recess Waterlow)

1948 (2 Apr). *Ninth Pan-American Congress, Bogotá. As T* **225** *(horiz designs inscr* "IX CONFERENCIA INTERNA-CIONAL AMERICANA"). *W* **135.** *P* 12½. *(a) POSTAGE.*
677 5 c. sepia 5 5
678 10 c. orange 20 12
679 15 c. grey-blue 25 15
MS679a 91×91 mm. 50 c. slate. Imperf .. 35 35
Designs:—10 c. National Capitol; 15 c. Foreign Office; 50 c. Map of N. America and Arms of Bogotá.

(b) AIR. Inscr "SERVICIO AEREO"
680 5 c. brown 5 5
681 15 c. blue 80 70
MS681a 91×91 mm. 50 c. yellow-brown. Imperf .. .. 1·00 1·00
677/681 *Set of* 5 .. .. .. 1·25 90
Designs:—5 c. Chancellery; 15 c. Raphael Court, Capitol; 50 c. Map of S. America and Arms of Colombia.

COLOMBIA
SOBRETASA
1
CENTAVO
(229)   **C**   **CORREOS**
230   **(231)**
("C" = "CORREOS")

(Litho Colombia Printing Works, Bogotá)

1948 (May). *OBLIGATORY TAX. Savings Bank Stamps surch, with T* **229.** *Various designs.* P 11 (5 c., 25 c.) *or* 11½ (10 c., 50 c.).
682 1 c. on 5 c. brown 5 5
683 1 c. on 10 c. lilac 5 5
684 1 c. on 25 c. scarlet 5 5
685 1 c. on 50 c. blue 5 5
682/685 *Set of* 4 .. .. .. 20 20

1948. *No.* 567 *optd with T* **230.** *No gum.*
686 **168** 1 c. yellow-orange 5 5

1948. *Nos.* 615/6 *and* 617a *optd with T* **231.**
687 **201** 1 c. olive-green (18.11) 5 5
688 2 c. green 5 5
689 20 c. red-brown 15 5

COLOMBIA
CORREOS

1783   1830

15 CENTAVOS 15

232 Simon Bolivar

233 Proposed New P.O., Bogotá

COLOMBIA
1847
1903

40 CVS CARLOS MARTINEZ SILVA 40 CVS

234 C. M. Silva

(Recess American Bank Note Co)

1948. W **177.** P 12.
690 **232** 15 c. green 10 5

1948 (21 July). AIR. As Nos. 568/80, but colours changed.
691 **186** 5 c. yellow 5 5
692 – 10 c. vermilion 5 5
693 – 15 c. blue 5 5
694 – 20 c. violet 5 5
695 **186** 30 c. green 12 5
696 – 40 c. grey 15 5
697 – 50 c. claret 20 5
698 – 50 c. grey-olive 25 5
699 **186** 80 c. brown 35 5
700 **187** 1 p. slate-purple and sage-green .. 40 5
701 – 2 p. blue and blue-green .. 80 12
702 **187** 3 p. black and rose-carmine .. 1·75 50
703 – 5 p. turquoise and sepia .. 2·50 75
691/703 Set of 13 .. .. 6·00 1·60
For Nos 691/703 and also the same stamps but with colours changed again and overprinted "L" or "A", see under "Private Air Companies" at the end of the postage issues.

1948. OBLIGATORY TAX. Red Cross Fund. As No. 671, but inscr "LITO-COLOMBIA BOGOTA" at foot. P 11.
704 **222** 5 c. pale vermilion 5 5

(Recess American Bank Note Co)

1948–50. OBLIGATORY TAX. P.O. Rebuilding Fund. W **177.** P 12.
705 **233** 1 c. carmine (1949) 5 5
706 ,, 2 c. green (7.50) 5 5
707 ,, 3 c. blue 5 5
708 ,, 5 c. grey 5 5
709 ,, 10 c. violet 5 5
705/709 Set of 5 .. .. 20 15
See also Nos. 756 and 758.

(Litho De La Rue)

1948 (21 Dec). P 13½.
710 **234** 40 c. carmine 25 5

COLOMBIA
CORREOS

4 JULIO GARAVITO ARMERO 4
CENTAVOS

235 J. G. Armero (mathematician)

COLOMBIA
CORREOS

75 ANIVERSARIO DE LA SOCIEDAD DE AGRICULTORES DE COLOMBIA 1871–1946

5 CENTAVOS

DR JUAN DE DIOS CARRASQUILLA 1833–1908

236 Dr. Juan de Dios Carrasquilla

(Recess Waterlow)

1949 (24 Apr). W **177.** P 12.
711 **235** 4 c. green 5 5

(Litho Waterlow)

1949 (20 May). 75th Anniv of National Society of Agriculture. W **177.** P 12½.
712 **236** 5 c. olive-bistre 5 5

15 CTAVOS 15

237 Arms of Colombia

LOOK A LA ... Y A LAS LEYES 5 C's

238 Allegory of Justice

COLOMBIA
CONGRESO FORESTAL 13-X-1945
5 CENTAVOS 5

239 Tree and Shield

(Recess Institut de Gravure, Paris)

1949 (7 Oct). New Constitution. T **237/8** and similar type. P 13. (a) POSTAGE.
713 **237** 15 c. blue 10 5

(b) AIR
714 **238** 5 c. blue-green 5 5
715 – 10 c. orange (Allegory of Constitution) 5 5

(Recess Waterlow)

1949 (13 Oct). First Forestry Congress, Bogotá. W **176.** P 12½.
716 **239** 5 c. olive-green 5 5

CORREOS DE COLOMBIA

FRANCISCO JAVIER CISNEROS 28-XII-1836 7-VII-1898
50 CVS

240 F. X. Cisneros

1950
5 CENTAVOS

241 Mother and Child

(Photo Waterlow)

1949 (15 Dec). 50th Death Anniv of Francisco Xavier Cisneros (engineer). P 12½.
717 **240** 50 c. ligth blue and brown 25 5
718 ,, 50 c. violet and green 25 5
719 ,, 50 c. bright yellow & bright purple .. 25 5
717/719 Set of 3 .. .. 65 12

1950 (25 May). OBLIGATORY TAX. Red Cross Fund. Surch with new value and date as in T **241.** Litho. P 11.
720 **241** 5 on 2 c. grey, blk, yell & red (B.) .. 40 20
Outside edges of sheet of 44 imperf.

SOBRETASA
(242)

1950 (26 May). OBLIGATORY TAX. No. 536 optd with T **242.**
721 **172** 5 c. light blue 5 5

COLOMBIA 1874 U.P.U. 1949

1 CENTAVO 1 MASDEVALLIA CHIMAERA

243 Masdevallia Chimaera

COLOMBIA 1874 U.P.U. 1949

CORREO COLONIAL S/F DOMINGO

244 Santo Domingo Palace

244a Globe

(Photo Waterlow)

1950. *T 247 and similar arms type.* W **177.** *P* 12.
733		5 p. green	.. ..	1·90	40
734		10 p. red-orange (Arms of Colombia)	..	3·50	80

1951 (30 Jan). *60th Anniv of Colombian Society of Engineers. Photo.* P 12½.
735	**248**	20 c. red, yellow and blue	..	..	15	5

249 Arms of Colombia and Cross

250 Fray Bartolomé de Las Casas

251 D. G. Valencia

(Ptd by Waterlow)

1951 (May)–53. *OBLIGATORY TAX. Red Cross Fund.* P 12½.

(a) Recess
736	**249**	5 c. scarlet	..	..	5	5
737	**250**	5 c. carmine	..	..	5	5

(b) Design recess; cross litho
738	**250**	5 c. green and carmine-red (1953)	..	5	5

(Recess Waterlow)

1951 (20 Oct). P 13.
739	**251**	25 c. black	..	..	15	5

1950 (22 Aug). *75th Anniv of Universal Postal Union.*

(a) POSTAGE. T 243 and similar orchid designs inscr "1874 U.P.U. 1949", and T 244. P 13
722	**243**	1 c. yellow-brown	..	..	..	12	5
723	–	2 c. violet	..			12	5
724	–	3 c. magenta	..	..	..	15	5
725	–	4 c. emerald-green	..	..	..	20	5
726	–	5 c. red-orange	..	..	..	25	5
727	–	11 c. scarlet	..	..	..	45	12
728	**244**	18 c. light blue	..	..	..	55	20
722/728		Set of 7	..	..	..	1·60	50

Orchids:—2 c. *Odontoglossum Crispum;* 3 c. *Cattleya Labiata Trianae;* 4 c. *Masdevallia Nycterina;* 5 c. *Cattleya Dowiana Aurea;* 11 c. *Miltonia Vexillaria.*

(b) POSTAGE. T 244a. Imperf
MS728a	90×90 mm. 50 c. yellow	..	..	20	20

(c) AIR. T 244a. Inscr "AEREO". Imperf
MS728b	90×90 mm. 50 c. slate	..	60	60

REVERSION
CONCESION MARES

 centavo

(252)

25 Agosto 1951

(253)

1951. *No. 707 surch with T* **252.**
740	**233**	1 c. on 3 c. blue	..	..	5	5

1951 (11 Dec). *Nationalization of Barranca Oil Fields. No. 534 optd with T* **253.**
741	**147**	2 c. carmine	..	..	..	5	5

1952 (10 May). *AIR. As Nos. 568/72 but colours changed.*

(a) Internal air mail
742	**186**	5 c. ultramarine	..	..	5	5
743	–	10 c. ultramarine	..	..	5	5
744	–	15 c. ultramarine	..	..	5	5
745	–	20 c. ultramarine	..	..	15	5
746	**186**	30 c. ultramarine	..	..	20	5

(b) External air mail
747	**186**	5 c. carmine	..	..	5	5
748	–	10 c. carmine	..	..	5	5
749	–	20 c. carmine	..	..	15	5
750	**186**	30 c. carmine	..	..	20	5
742/750		Set of 9	..	..	..	80	30

245 Antonio Baraya (patriot)

246 Farm

(Recess De La Rue)

1950 (27 Nov). P 12½.
729	**245**	2 c. scarlet	..	..	..	5	5

(Photo Courvoisier)

1950 (28 Dec). P 11½.
730	**246**	5 c. carmine-lake and buff	..	8	5
731		5 c. blue-green and turquoise	..	8	5
732		5 c. blue and light blue	..	..	8	5
730/732		Set of 3	..	..	20	10

247 Arms of Bogotá

248 Map and Badge

254 Dr. J. M. Lombana

255 Proposed New P.O., Bogotá

255a

(Recess Waterlow)

1952 (6 Aug). *Colombian Doctors. T 254 and similar horiz portraits. No wmk. P 11½.*

751	1 c. blue (N. Osorio)	..	..	5	5
752	1 c. blue (P. Martinez)	..	..	5	5
753	1 c. blue (E. Uriocoechea)	..	..	5	5
754	1 c. blue (J. M. Lombana)	..	..	5	5
751/754	Set of 4	..	..	15	10

These four stamps were printed together in sheets of 100 stamps, with each design in a separate pane of 25, divided by double rows of ornamental labels.

(Recess American Bank Note Co)

1952. *P 12. (a) No wmk.*

755	255	5 c. bright blue (10.9)	..	5	5

(b) W 177

756	233	20 c. red-brown	..	5	5
757	201	25 c. deep grey	..	4·75	1·75
758	233	25 c. bluish green	..	60	8
759	255a	50 c. orange	..	1·10	12
760		1 p. carmine	..	1·90	20
761		2 p. reddish purple	..	3·00	35
762		2 p. violet	..	2·75	30
755/762		Set of 8	..	13·00	2·50

No. 758 had been issued earlier as a compulsory tax stamp but only for use on telegrams. In 1952 it was made valid as a postage stamp. The price in the used column is for postally used copies.

Owing to a shortage of postage stamps the above in obligatory tax types were issued for ordinary postal use.

1952. *OBLIGATORY TAX. No. 759 surch as T 252.*

763	255a	8 c. on 50 c. orange	..	5	5

256 Manizales Cathedral

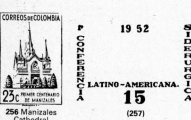

(257)

(Photo Courvoisier)

1952 (10 Oct). *Centenary of Manizales. P 11¼.*

764	256	23 c. black and pale blue	..	..	20	5

1952 (30 Oct). *First Latin-American Siderurgical Conference.*

(a) POSTAGE. No. 672 surch with T 257, in blue

765	233	15 c. on 25 c. dull green	..	..	20	5

(b) AIR. Unissued stamp as No. 699, colour changed, surch as T 257, but smaller, in blue.

766	186	70 c. on 80 c. carmine	..	..	40	25

258 Queen Isabella and Columbus Monument

(259)

AEREO (260)

(Recess Wright Bank Note Co, Philadelphia)

1953 (10 Mar). *Fifth Birth Centenary of Isabella the Catholic. P 12½.*

767	258	23 c. black and pale blue	..	..	20	5

1953. *AIR. Nos. 756, 758 and unissued stamp (8 c.), in similar design.*

(a) Surch as T 259

768	233	5 c. on 8 c. blue	..	..	5	5
769		15 c. on 20 c. red-brown	..	5	5
		a. Pair, one without surch		9·00	
770		15 c. on 25 c. bluish green (Oct)	..	5	5

(b) Optd "CORREO AEREO" only, as in T 259

771	233	25 c. bluish green (Aug)	..	10	5
		a. Opt double	..	..	

No. 768 exists without surcharge.

1953 (Aug). *AIR. No. 488 optd with T 260.*

772	155	10 c. scarlet (B.)	..	..	5	5
		a. Opt inverted	..	..	2·25	

"EXTRA RAPIDO". Stamps bearing this overprint or inscription were used to prepay the additional cost on air carriage of inland mail handled by the National Postal Service from 1953 to 1964. Subsequently remaining stocks of these stamps were used for other classes of correspondence. Since the 1920's regular air service for inland and foreign mail has been provided by the Air Postal Service, a separate undertaking, which is administered by the Avianca airline and for which the regular air stamps are used. (See note above No. 968.)

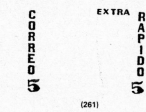

(261)

1953. *AIR. No. 727 surch with T 261.*

773		5 c. on 11 c. scarlet (B.)	..	..	30	15

262   263

1953. *AIR. Fiscal stamps optd "CORREO EXTRA-RAPIDO" as in T 262, surch also (1 c.).*

774	262	1 c. on 2 c. green	..	..	5	5
775		50 c. orange-red	..	..	25	15

1953. *AIR. Real Estate Tax stamps optd "CORREO EXTRA-RAPIDO" as in T 263.*

776	263	5 c. red-orange	..	..	5	5
777		20 c. brown (R.)	..	..	12	8

40

(264)

CTVOS. (264)   **50** CENTAVOS (265)

1953 (19 Oct). *Nos. 760 and 656 surch with T 264/5, in blue.*

778	255a	40 c. on 1 p. carmine	..	..	20	10
779	214	50 c. on 2 p. grey-green	..	..	20	10

266 Don. M. Ancizar   267

(Recess Waterlow)

1953 (12 Nov). *Centenary of Colombian Chorographical Commission. T 266 and similar vert portraits inscr "1850 1950". P 13 × 13½.*

780	14 c. rose-red and black..	..	..	5	5
781	23 c. ultramarine and black	..	..	12	5
782	30 c. sepia and black	..	..	15	8
783	1 p. emerald and black..	..	..	45	25
780/783	*Set of 4*	..	..	70	40

Portraits:—23 c. J. J. Triana; 30 c. M. Ponce de Leon; 1 p. A. Codazzi.

1953 (12 Dec). *Second National Philatelic Exhibition, Bogotá. Real Estate Tax stamps surch as in T 267. Recess. W 177. P 12. (a) POSTAGE.*

784	267	5 c. on 5 p. yellow, magenta, brown and deep blue ..	..	10	5

(b) AIR

785	–	15 c. on 10 p. green, magenta, lilac and brown	..	30	20

Design:—15 c. Map of Colombia.

CORREO
2

EXTRA-RAPIDO
(268)

1953–56. *AIR. Unissued stamp surch with T 268, and No. 709 similarly optd but without figure "2".*

786	233	2 c. on 8 c. blue (1956)	..	5	5
787		10 c. violet ..	..	10	5

269 Fountain, Tunja   270 Pastelillo Fort, Cartagena

271 Map of Colombia   272

(Recess De La Rue)

1954 (15 Jan)–**58.** *AIR. T 269/71 and similar designs. P 13.*

788	5 c. purple	..	..	..	..	5	5
789	10 c. black	..	..	..	..	5	5
790	15 c. carmine	..	..	..	..	5	5
791	15 c. vermilion	..	..	..	..	5	5
792	20 c. bistre-brown	..	..	..	..	8	5
793	25 c. blue (20.6.58)	..	..	..	5	5
794	25 c. deep purple (20.6.58)	..	..	5	5
795	30 c. chestnut	..	..	..	..	8	5
796	40 c. blue	..	..	..	..	10	5
797	50 c. blackish purple	..	..	..	15	5
798	60 c. sepia	..	..	..	..	20	5
799	80 c. brown-lake	..	..	..	..	30	5
800	1 p. black and blue	..	..	..	35	5
801	2 p. black and green	..	..	..	60	8
802	3 p. blackish violet and carmine	..	90	50
803	5 p. slate-green and brown	..	..	1·50	45
804	10 p. olive-green and orange-red	..	3·25	80
788/804	*Set of 17*	..	..	..	7·00	2·25

Designs: *Vert (27×32 mm)*—5 c., 30 c. Galeras Volcano, Pasto; 15 c. (No. 790), 50 c. Bolivar Monument, Boyacá; 15 c. (No. 791), 25 c. Sanctuary of the Rocks, Nariño; 20 c., 80 c., Nevado del Ruiz Mts., Manizales; 40 c. J. Isaacs Monument, Cali; 60 c. *T 269.* (*32×38½ mm*)—10 p. *T 271. Horiz (32×27 mm)*—10 c. San Diego Monastery, Bogotá. (*37½×27 mm*)—1 p. Giradot Stadium, Medellin; 2 p. *T 270*; 3 p. Santo Domingo Gateway and University, Popayán. (*38½×32 mm*)—5 p. Sanctuary of the Rocks, Nariño.

1954. *Nos. 780 and 764 surch.*

805	266	5 c. on 14 c. rose-red and black	..	8	5
806	256	5 c. on 23 c. black and pale blue (R.)	8	5

(Litho Talleres Banco de la Republica)

1954 (23 Apr). *AIR. P 12½.*

807	272	5 c. reddish purple	..	..	8	5

273   (274)

(Photo Courvoisier)

1954 (23 Apr). *400th Anniv of Franciscan Community in Colombia. P 11½.*

808	273	5 c. chocolate, green and sepia	..	8	5

1954. *AIR. OBLIGATORY TAX. Red Cross Fund. No. 807 optd with T 274.*

809	272	5 c. reddish purple (R.)	..	..	5	5

275 Soldier, Flag and Arms of Republic   276

(Recess De La Rue)

1954 (13 June). *National Army Commemoration. P 13. (a) POSTAGE.*

810	275	5 c. Prussian blue ..	..	..	5	5

(b) AIR. Inscr "AEREO"

811	275	15 c. carmine-red	..	..	8	5

For Nos. 810/1 in different colours, in miniature sheets, see Nos. **MS845** and **MS848**.

(Recess De La Rue)

1954 (18 July). *Seventh National Athletic Games, Cali. T 276 and similar design inscr "VII JUEGOS ATHLETICOS" etc. P 13. (a) POSTAGE.*
812	–	5 c. deep blue	..	..	..	10	5
813	276	10 c. red	..	..	..	15	5

(b) AIR. Inscr "AEREO"
814	–	15 c. deep brown	..	..	..	15	5
815	276	20 c. emerald	..	..	..	20	5
812/815		Set of 4	..	..	..	50	15

Design: *Vert*—5 c., 15 c. Badge of the games.

CORREOS DE COLOMBIA

281 Virgin of Chiquinquirá   **282** Tapestry Presented by Queen Margaret of Austria

277

278 Saint's Convent and Cell

(Recess Waterlow)

1954 (24 July). *50th Anniv of Colombian Academy of History. P 13.*
816	277	5 c. bluish green and bright blue	..	5	5

(Recess De La Rue)

1954 (9 Sept). *Third Centenary of San Pedro Claver. T 278 and similar vert design inscr "1654–1954". P 13. (a) POSTAGE.*
817	278	5 c. deep myrtle-green	..	..	5	5
MS818		121×130 mm. No. 817 but printed in green	..	..	..	30	30

(b) Inscr "AEREO"
819	–	15 c. brown	..	..	8	5
MS820		121×130 mm. No. 819 but printed in red-brown	..	..	..	20	20

Design:—15 c. San Pedro Claver Church, Cartagena.

(Centre litho, frame recess De La Rue)

1954 (4 Dec)—**57**. *AIR. P 13.*
825	281	5 c. blue, yellow, red & orange-brn	..	10	5
826		5 c. blue, yellow, red and reddish violet (23.5.57)	..	..	5	5

(Recess De La Rue)

1954 (6 Dec). *Tercentenary of Senior College of Our Lady of the Rosary, Bogotá. T 282 and other designs inscr "1653 1953". P 11½×13 (horiz) or 13×11½ (vert). (a) POSTAGE.*
827		5 c. black and brown-orange	..	..	5	5
828		10 c. Prussian blue	..	..	..	10	5
829		15 c. purple-brown	..	..	..	12	5
830		20 c. reddish brown and black	..	..	20	8
MS831		125×131 mm. Nos. 827/30 in new colours	..	..	..	70	70

(b) AIR. Inscr "AEREO"
832		15 c. black and orange-red	..	..	10	5
833		20 c. ultramarine	..	..	..	15	5
834		25 c. sepia	..	..	..	20	8
835		50 c. carmine and black	..	..	35	15
MS836		125×131 mm. Nos. 832/5 in new colours	..	..	..	1·00	1·00
827/835		Set of 8	..	..	..	1·10	50

Designs: *Vert*—5 c., 15 c. (No. 832), T **282**; 10 c., 20 c. (No. 833), Friar Cristobal de Torres (founder). *Horiz*—15 c. (No. 829), 25 c. Cloisters and statue; 20 c. (No. 830), 50 c. Chapel and coat-of-arms.

279 Mercury

280 Archbishop Mosquera

283 Paz del Rio Steel Plant

284 J. Marti

(Recess De La Rue)

1954 (29 Oct). *First International Fair, Bogotá. P 13.*

(a) POSTAGE
821	279	5 c. orange	..	..	..	5	5

(b) AIR. (i) Inscr "CORREO AEREO"
822	279	15 c. blue	..	..	..	10	5

(ii) Inscr "CORREO EXTRA RAPIDO"
823	279	50 c. red	..	..	..	40	25

(Recess De La Rue)

1954 (17 Nov). *AIR. Death Cent. of Archbishop Mosquera. P 13.*
824	280	2 c. yellow-green	..	..	5	5

(Recess De La Rue)

1954 (12 Dec). *Inauguration of Paz del Rio Steel Plant. P 13.*

(a) POSTAGE
837	283	5 c. black and ultramarine	..	..	5	5

(b) AIR
838	283	20 c. black and green	..	..	12	5

(Recess De La Rue)

1955 (28 Jan). *Birth Cent of Marti (Cuban revolutionary). P 13. (a) POSTAGE.*
839	284	5 c. carmine-red	..	..	5	5

(b) AIR. Inscr "AEREO"
840	284	15 c. deep green	..	..	10	5

285 Badge, Flags and Korean Landscape

286 Ship's Wheel and Map

(Recess De La Rue)

1955 (23 Mar). *Colombian Forces in Korea.* P 12½. (a) POSTAGE.
841 285 10 c. maroon 15 5

(b) AIR. Inscr "AEREO AEREO"
842 285 20 c. deep bluish green 20 8
For Nos. 841/2 in different colours, in miniature sheets, see Nos. MS845 and MS848.

(Recess De La Rue)

1955 (12 Apr). *Greater Colombia Merchant Marine Commemoration.* T **286** *and horiz design inscr "FLOTA MERCANTE GRANCOLOMBIANA".* P 13. (a) POSTAGE.
843 286 15 c. deep green 5 5
844 – 20 c. violet 12 5
MS845 125×131 mm. Nos. 810, 841, 843/4 in new colours. P 12½ 70 70

(b) AIR. Inscr "AEREO"
846 286 25 c. black 12 8
847 – 50 c. deep myrtle-green 35 10
MS848 125×131 mm. Nos. 811, 842, 846/7 in new colours. P 12½ .. .. .. 1·10 1·10
843/847 *Set of 4* 55 25
Design: *Horiz*—20 c., 50 c. M.S. *City of Manizales* and skyscrapers.

287 M. Fidel Suarez

288 San Pedro Claver Feeding Slaves

(Recess De La Rue)

1955 (23 Apr). *AIR. Birth Cent. of President Suarez.* P 13.
849 287 10 c. deep blue 5 5

(Recess; cross typo De La Rue)

1955. *OBLIGATORY TAX. Red Cross Fund and Third Birth Centenary of San Pedro Claver.* P 13.
850 288 5 c. light maroon and vermilion .. 5 5

289 Hotel Tequendama and San Diego Church

290 Bolivar's Country House

(Photo Courvoisier)

1955 (16 May). P 11½. (a) *POSTAGE.*
851 289 5 c. blue and pale blue 5 5

(b) AIR. Inscr "AEREO"
852 289 15 c. brown-lake and pink 10 5

(Recess De La Rue)

1955 (28 Sept). *50th Anniv of Rotary International.* P 12½. (a) POSTAGE.
853 290 5 c. deep blue 5 5

(b) AIR. Inscr "AEREO"
854 290 15 c. carmine 10 5

291 Belalcazar, De Quesada and Balboa

292 J. E. Caro

(Des Mosdossy. Design recess, background litho (No. 863); centres photo, frames recess (others) De La Rue)

1955 (12 Oct). *Seventh Postal Union Congress of the Americas and Spain.* T **291** *and similar horiz designs inscr "VII CONGRESO DE LA UNION POSTAL" etc.* P 13. (a) POSTAGE.
855 2 c. sepia and yellow-green 5 5
856 5 c. deep brown and greenish blue .. 5 5
857 23 c. black and blue 15 10
MS858 120×130 mm. Nos. 855/7 in slightly different colours. (Sold at 50 c.) .. 30 30

(b) AIR. (i) Inscr "AEREO"
859 15 c. black and carmine.. .. 8 5
860 20 c. black and dull brown .. 10 5
MS861 120×130 mm. Nos. 859/60 in slightly different colours. (Sold at 50 c.) .. 35 35

(ii) Inscr "CORREO EXTRA RAPIDO"
862 2 c. black and brown 5 5
863 5 c. deep brown and yellow .. 5 5
864 1 p. deep brown & deep brown-olive .. 40 35
865 2 p. black and pale violet 80 60
855/865 *Set of 9* .. .. .. 1·50 1·25
Designs:—2 c. (No. 855), T **291**; 2 c. (No. 862), Atahualpa, Tisquesuza and Moctezuma; 5 c. (No. 856), San Martin, Bolivar and Washington; 5 c. (No. 863), King Ferdinand, Queen Isabella and coat-of-arms; 15 c. O'Higgins, Santander and Sucre; 20 c. Marti, Hidalgo and Petion; 23 c. Columbus, *Santa Maria, Pinta* and *Nina*; 1 p. Artigas, Lopez and Murillo; 2 p. Calderon, Baron de Rio Branco and De La Mar.

(Recess De La Rue)

1955 (29 Nov). *Death Centenary of Caro.* P 13.

(a) POSTAGE
866 292 5 c. reddish brown 5 5

(b) AIR. Inscr "AEREO"
867 292 15 c. bronze-green 8 5

293 Salamanca University

294 Gold Mining, Nariño

(Recess De La Rue)

1955 (29 Nov). *AIR. Seventh Centenary of Salamanca University.* P 13.
868 293 20 c. brown 10 8

(Recess De La Rue)

1956–58. *T 294 and similar designs inscr "PROVIDENCIA" (No. 874), "INTENDENCIA" (Nos. 891/3), "COMISARIA" (No. 894) or "DEPARTMENTO" (others). P 13.*

869	2 c. myrtle-green and carmine-red (24.7.56)		5	5
870	3 c. black and dull purple (11.9.56)	..	5	5
871	3 c. brown and blue (1958)	..	5	5
872	3 c. deep reddish violet and bronze-green (1958)	..	5	5
873	4 c. black and deep emerald (1956)	..	5	5
874	5 c. black and pale blue (5.4.56)	..	5	5
875	5 c. slate-blue & carmine-red (5.4.56)	..	5	5
876	5 c. bronze-green & red-brn (31.7.56)	..	5	5
877	5 c. chocolate & brown-olive (31.7.56)		5	5
878	5 c. cobalt and sepia (1956)	..	5	5
879	10 c. black & yellow-orange (24.7.56)	..	10	5
880	10 c. brown and olive-green (1958)	..	5	5
881	10 c. brown and deep blue (1958)	..	5	5
882	15 c. black and bright blue (1956)	..	5	5
883	20 c. grey-blue & deep brown (24.7.56)		8	5
884	23 c. orange-red & ultramarine (1956)	..	8	5
885	25 c. black and bronze-green (23.4.56)	..	10	5
886	30 c. brown and deep blue (5.3.56)	..	10	5
887	40 c. reddish brn & slate-pur (24.7.56)	..	15	8
888	50 c. black and deep green (1956)	..	12	8
889	60 c. myrtle-green and sepia (24.7.56)	..	15	10
890	1 p. slate-blue & reddish purple (1956)		25	12
891	2 p. brown and green (31.7.56)	..	50	30
892	3 p. black and carmine-red (1956)	..	90	55
893	5 p. blue and brown (24.7.56)	..	1·40	80
894	10 p. bluish green & yellow-brn (1956)	..	2·75	1·50
869/894	Set of 26	..	6·50	3·75

Designs as T 294: *Horiz*—2 c. Barranquilla naval workshops, Atlantico; 2 c. Fishing, Cartagena Port, Bolivar; 5 c. (No. 875) View of Port, San Andrés; 5 c. (876) Cocoa, Cauca; 5 c. (877) Prize cattle, Córdoba; 23 c. Rice harvesting, Huila; 25 c. Bananas, Magdalena; 40 c. Tobacco, Santander; 50 c. Oil wells of Catatumbo, Norte de Santander; 60 c. Cotton harvesting, Tolima. *Vert*—3 c. Allegory of Industry, Antioquia; 5 c. (874) Map of San Andrés Archipelago; 5 c. (878) Steel plant, Boyacá; 10 c. Coffee, Caldas; 15 c. Cathedral of Sal Salinas de Zipaquira, Cundinamarca; 20 c. Platinum and map, Chocó. (37½×27 *mm*)—1 p. Sugar factory, Valle del Cauca; 2 p. Cattle fording river, Meta; 3 p. Statue and R. Amazon, Leticia, Amazon; 5 p. Landscape, La Guajira. (27×37½ *mm*)—10 p. Rubber-tapping, Vaupés.

295 Henri Dunant and S. Samper Brush

(Des Mosdossy. Photo De La Rue)

1956 (1 June). *OBLIGATORY TAX. Red Cross Fund. Cross, and "CRUZ ROJA" recess, in red. P 13.*

895	**295**	5 c. bistre-brown	..	5	5

EXTRA-RAPIDO
(296) **297** Columbus and Lighthouse

1956. *AIR. No. 783 optd with T 296.*

896		1 p. emerald and black	..	40	25

(Des Mosdossy, Photo State Ptg Wks, Vienna)

1956 (12 Oct)–**58.** *Columbus Memorial Lighthouse. P 12. (a) POSTAGE.*

897	**297**	3 c. black	..	5	5

(b) AIR. (i) Inscr "AEREO"

898	**297**	15 c. deep greenish blue	..	5	5

(ii) Inscr "EXTRA RAPIDO"

899	**297**	3 c. deep green (9.1.58)	..	5	5

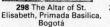

298 The Altar of St. Elisabeth, Primada Basilica, Bogotá

299 St. Ignatius of Loyola

(Des Mosdossy. Photo State Ptg Wks, Vienna)

1956 (19 Nov). *Seventh Centenary of St. Elisabeth of Hungary. P 12. (a) POSTAGE.*

900	**298**	5 c. bright reddish purple	..	5	5

(b) AIR. Inscr "AEREO"

901	**298**	15 c. red-brown	..	8	5

(Des Mosdossy. Recess De La Rue)

1956 (26 Nov). *Fourth Death Centenary of St. Ignatius of Loyola. P 13. (a) POSTAGE.*

902	**299**	5 c. deep blue	..	5	5

(b) AIR. Inscr "AEREO"

903	**299**	5 c. sepia	..	5	5

300 Javier Pereira (1789–1956)

EXTRA-RAPIDO
(301)

(Recess American Bank Note Co)

1956 (28 Dec). *Pereira Commemoration. P 12. (a) POSTAGE.*

904	**300**	5 c. deep blue	..	5	5

(b) AIR. Inscr "AEREO"

905	**300**	20 c. carmine	..	10	5

1957. *AIR. No. 874 optd with T 301.*

906	5 c. black and pale blue (R.)	..	5	5

1957. *AIR. As No. 580 but in new colours, optd with T 301.*

907	5 p. black and yellow (R.)	..	1·10	75

302 Dairy Farm

303 Racing Cyclist

(Des Mosdossy. Photo De La Rue)

1957. 25th Anniv of Agricultural Credit Bank. T 302 and similar designs. P 14×13½.

(a) POSTAGE (5 Mar)

908	302	1 c. olive-green	..	..	5	5
909	–	2 c. light brown	..	..	5	5
910	–	5 c. pale blue	..	..	5	5

(b) AIR. (i) Inscr "AEREO" (23 May)

911	302	5 c. yellow-orange ..	..	..	5	5
912	–	10 c. green ..	..	..	5	5
913	–	15 c. black ..	..	..	8	5
914	–	20 c. carmine-red ..	..	..	12	5

(ii) Inscr "EXTRA RAPIDO" (5 Mar)

915	–	5 c. deep brown	..	5	5
908/915	Set of 8	..	..	40	25

Designs:—2 c., 10 c. Farm tractor; 5 c. (No. 910), 15 c. Emblem of agricultural prosperity; 5 c. (No. 915), 20 c. Livestock.

(Des Mosdossy. Photo State Ptg Wks, Vienna)

1957 (6 July). AIR. Seventh Round-Colombia Cycle Race. P 12.

916	303	2 c. brown ..	..	..	5	5
917		5 c. bright blue	..	..	5	5

304 Arms and General Reyes (founder)

305 Father J. M. Delgado

(Des Mosdossy. Recess De La Rue)

1957 (20 July). 50th Anniv of Military Cadet School. T 304 and similar horiz design inscr "CINCUENTENARIO DE LA ESCUELA MILITAR DE CADETES". P 13. (a) POSTAGE.

918	304	5 c. slate-blue	..	..	5	5
919	–	10 c. yellow-orange ..	..	..	5	5
MS920		130×120 mm. Nos. 918/9 in slightly different colours	..	..	30	30

(b) AIR. Inscr "AEREO"

921	304	15 c. carmine	..	..	8	5
922	–	20 c. bistre-brown	..	..	10	5
918/922	Set of 4	..	..	..	25	15

Design:—10 c., 20 c. Arms and Military Cadet School.

(Des Mosdossy. Photo State Ptg Wks, Vienna)

1957 (16 Sept). Father Delgado Commemoration. P 12. (a) POSTAGE.

923	305	2 c. brown-lake	..	5	5

(b) AIR. Inscr "AEREO"

924	305	10 c. slate-blue	..	5	5

306 St. Vincent de Paul with Children

307 Signatories to Bogotá Postal Convention of 1838, and U.P.U. Monument, Berne

(Des Mosdossy. Photo State Ptg Wks, Vienna)

1957 (18 Oct). Centenary of Foundation of Colombian Order of St. Vincent de Paul. P 12. (a) POSTAGE.

925	306	1 c. deep bronze-green	..	5	5

(b) AIR. Inscr "AEREO"

926	306	5 c. deep brown-red ..	..	5	5

(Des Mosdossy. Photo State Ptg Wks, Vienna)

1957 (20 Oct). 14th U.P.U. Congress, Ottawa, and International Correspondence Week. P 12. (a) POSTAGE.

927	307	5 c. green ..	..	..	5	5
928		10 c. deep olive-grey	..	..	5	5

(b) AIR. Inscr "AEREO"

929	307	15 c. deep brown	..	..	5	5
930		25 c. blue ..	..	..	8	5
927/930	Set of 4	..	..	..	20	15

308 Fencer

309 Discovery of Hypsometry by F. J. de Caldas

(Des Mosdossy. Photo State Ptg Wks, Vienna)

1957 (22 Nov). Third South American Fencing Championships. P 12½. (a) POSTAGE.

931	308	4 c. purple ..	..	5	5

(b) AIR. Inscr "AEREO"

932	308	20 c. purple-brown ..	..	10	5

(Des Mosdossy. Photo State Ptg Wks, Vienna)

1958 (12 May). International Geophysical Year. P 12. (a) POSTAGE.

933	309	10 c. black ..	..	5	5

(b) AIR. (i) Inscr "AEREO"

934	309	25 c. deep green	..	10	5

(ii) Inscr "EXTRA RAPIDO"

935	309	1 p. deep lilac	..	25	20

E 2

310 Nurses with Patient, and Ambulance

(Des Mosdossy. Photo State Printing Works, Vienna)

1958 (19 May). EXPRESS AIR. P 12.

E936	E 2	25 c. scarlet and blue	..	5	5

(Des Mosdossy. Photo State Ptg Wks, Vienna)

1958 (2 June). OBLIGATORY TAX. Red Cross Fund. P 12.

936	310	5 c. red and grey-black	..	5	5

5¢

(311)

AEREO

(312)

1958 (30 Sept)–59. Nos. 882 and 884 surch as T 311.

937		5 c. on 15 c. black and bright blue (B.) ..		5	5
938		5 c. on 23 c. orange-red and ultramarine (G.) (1959) ..	..	5	5

1958 (16 Oct). AIR. No. 888 optd with T 312.

939		50 c. black and deep green (R.) ..	..	10	5

313 Father R. Almanza and **(314)**
San Diego Church, Bogotá

(Des Mosdossy. Photo Enschedé, Haarlem)

1958 (23 Oct). *Father Almanza Commemoration. P* 14×12½.

(*a*) POSTAGE
940 **313** 10 c. deep lilac 5 5

(*b*) AIR. (i) *Inscr* "AEREO"
941 **313** 25 c. grey-black 8 5

(ii) *Inscr* "EXTRA RAPIDO"
942 **313** 10 c. bronze-green 5 5

1958–59. *Nos.* 780/2 *vert surch* "CINCO" (5 *c.*) *or* "VEINTE"
(20 *c.*) *as T* 314.
943 5 c. on 14 c. rose-red and black (B.)
(18.2.59) 5 5
944 5 c. on 30 c. sepia and black (1958) .. 5 5
945 20 c. on 23 c. ultramarine and black
(23.10.58) 8 5

315 Mons. Carrasquilla and Rosario College, Bogotá

(Des Mosdossy. Photo Enschedé)

1959 (22 Jan). *Birth Centenary of Mons. R. M. Carrasquilla.
P* 14×13. (*a*) POSTAGE.
946 **315** 10 c. brown 5 5

(*b*) AIR. *Inscr* "AEREO"
947 **315** 25 c. carmine-red 5 5
948 1 p. grey-blue 20 10

2

318 Luz Marina **(319)**
Zuluaga ("Miss
Universe 1959")

(Des Mosdossy. Photo Courvoisier)

1959 (26 June). *"Miss Universe* 1959" *Commemoration.
P* 11½. (*a*) POSTAGE.
952 **318** 10 c. brown, blue, carmine & grn 8 5

(*b*) AIR. (i) *Inscr* "AEREO"
953 **318** 1 p. 20, brown, blue, carm & green 25 20

(ii) *Inscr* "EXTRA RAPIDO"
954 **318** 5 p. brown, lt blue, carmine & grn 6·50 5·50

1959 (3 July). *No.* 873 *surch with T* 319.
955 2 c. on 4 c. black and deep emerald (B.) 5 5

10¢

320 G. E. Gaitan **(321)**
(political leader)

(Recess Waterlow)

1959 (28 July). *Gaitan Commemoration.* (*a*) POSTAGE. *No.*
956 *is surch with T* 321. *P* 12½×13½.
956 **320** 10 c. on 3 c. grey (B.) 5 5
957 30 c. purple 10 5

(*b*) AIR. *T* 320 *surch as T* 321 *and with* "EXTRA-RAPIDO" *in
addition.*
958 **320** 2 p. on 1 p. black 30 25
959 2 p. on 1 p. black (B.) 30 25
956/959 *Set of* 4 .. .. 70 50

50¢

(322)

1959 (24 Aug). *AIR. No.* 798 *surch with T* 322.
960 **269** 50 c. on 60 c. sepia (B.) 12 8

10¢

20¢

(316) **(317)**

1959 (11 Mar). *No.* 767 *surch with T* 316.
949 **258** 20 c. on 23 c. black and pale blue .. 8 5

1959 (20 Mar). *No.* 826 *with* "CORREO EXTRA RAPIDO"
obliterated by solid rectangle, in blue.
950 **281** 5 c. blue, yellow, red & reddish vio .. 5 5

1959 (9 Apr). *No.* 794 *surch with T* 317.
951 10 c. on 25 c. deep purple (B.) 5 5

323 Capitol, Bogotá **324** Santander

(Des Mosdossy. Litho State Ptg Wks, Bogotá)

1959 (12 Nov)–60. *T* **323, 324** *and similar portrait. P* 12½.

(a) POSTAGE

961	323	2 c. red-brown and blue	5	5
962		3 c. reddish violet & blk (26.11.59)	5	5
963	324	5 c. slate-purple and yellow ..	5	5
964	–	5 c. dp blue & lt blue (26.11.59) ..	5	5
965	–	10 c. black and red	5	5
966	324	10 c. black & bluish grn (26.11.59) ..	5	5

(b) AIR. Inscr "AEREO"

967	–	35 c. black and grey (23.11.60) ..	10	5
961/967		*Set of 7*	35	25

Portrait. As T **324**: Nos. 964/5, 967, Bolivar.

"UNIFICADO"=Unified. Combining the air mail rate with the ordinary surface rate. Hitherto the air fee had to be added by means of another stamp (see note above No. 773).

(325)

1959–60. *AIR. Unification of Airmail Rates. Various issues optd with T* **325** *(vert on Nos.* 970, 984 *and* 988).

968	299	5 c. sepia (R.)	15	5
969	302	5 c. yellow-orange (1.12.59) ..	12	5
970	306	5 c. dp brown-red (Bk. & Sil.) (860)	20	5
971	155	10 c. scarlet (772)(1.12.59) ..	15	5
972	–	10 c. black (889)	12	5
973	304	15 c. carmine	20	5
974	–	20 c. bistre-brown (792) ..	15	5
975	–	20 c. bistre-brown (922) ..	15	5
976	308	20 c. purple-brown (1960) ..	20	5
977	–	25 c. blue (793)	20	5
978	–	25 c. deep purple (794) (1960) ..	20	5
979	313	25 c. grey-black (1.12.59) ..	20	5
980	315	25 c. carmine-red (1.12.59) ..	25	5
981	–	30 c. chestnut (795) ..	25	5
982	269	50 c. on 60 c. sepia (960) ..	25	5
983	315	1 p. grey-blue	30	12
984	318	1 p. 20, brown, light blue, carmine and green	55	20
985	–	2 p. black and green (801) ..	50	20
986	–	3 p. blackish violet & carmine (802)	80	35
987	–	3 p. slate-green and brown (803) ..	1·00	65
988	–	10 p. olive-green & orange-red (804)	2·25	1·25
968/988		*Set of 21*	7·50	3·25

1959. *EXPRESS AIR. Unification of Airmail Rates. No.* E936 *optd with T* **325,** *vert downwards.*

E989	E 2	25 c. scarlet and blue (R.)	10	5

326 Colombian 2½ c. stamp of 1859 and Postmen with Mule

327 "Tête-bêche" 5 c. stamps of 1859.

(Des Mosdossy. Litho National Ptg Wks, Bogotá (**MS**997). Photo State Ptg Wks, Vienna (others))

1959 (1 Dec). *Centenary of First Colombian Postage Stamps. Designs as T* **326** *inscr "1859 1959". P* 12. *(a) POSTAGE.*

989	5 c. green and yellow-orange	5	5
990	10 c. blue and lake	5	5
991	15 c. green and carmine	5	5
992	25 c. red-brown and blue	8	5

(b) AIR. (i) Inscr "AEREO"

993	25 c. red and deep brown	5	5
994	50 c. bright blue and red	12	8
995	1 p. 20, brown-red and yellow-brown ..	30	20

(ii) Inscr "EXTRA RAPIDO"

996	10 c. lilac and bistre	5	5
989/996	*Set of 8*	70	50

(iii) *Miniature sheet. Inscr "EXTRA RAPIDO" W* **330.** *Imperf*
MS997 74×70 mm. **327** 5 c. blue/pink (sold
at 5 p.) .. .. 1·25 1·25
Designs: *Vert*—10 c. (No. 990), Colombian 5 c. stamp of 1859, and river steamer; 10 c. (996), Colombian 5 c. stamp of 1859, and map of Colombia; 15 c. T **326**; 25 c. (992) Colombian 10 c. stamp of 1859, and railway train; 25 c. (993) Postal decree of 1859, and Pres. M. Ospina. *Horiz*—50 c. Colombian 20 c. stamp of 1859 and seaplane; 1 p. 20, Colombian 1 p. stamp of 1859, and "Super Constellation" airliner flying over valley.

328 Colombian 2 c. air stamp of 1918, Seaplane and "Super Constellation" Airliner

(Des Mosdossy. Photo State Ptg Wks, Vienna)

1959 (5 Dec). *AIR. 40th Anniv of Colombian AVIANCA Air Mail Services. T* **328** *and a similar horiz design inscr "1919 AVIANCA 1959". P* 12.

998	35 c. scarlet, black and cobalt	12	8
999	60 c. black and yellow-green	15	10
MS1000	90×50 mm. Two 1 p. stamps in designs of Nos. 998/9 but in different colours	65	65
MS1001	Sheet as last but containing two 1 p. 50 stamps in different colours and inscr "EXTRA RAPIDO"	75	75

Design:—60 c. Similar to T **328** but without Colombian 2 c. stamp.

329 Eldorado Airport, Bogotá

330

(Des Mosdossy. Litho)

1959 (10 Dec)–60. *AIR. W* **330.** *P* 12½. (i) *Inscr "AEREO".*

1002	329	35 c. yellow-orange and black ..	8	5
1003		60 c. red and grey (29.7.60) ..	12	8

(ii) *Inscr "EXTRA RAPIDO"*

1004	329	1 p. deep blue and grey (29.7.60) ..	20	12

331 A. von Humboldt

332 *Anthurium andreanum*

(Des Mosdossy. Photo State Ptg Wks, Vienna)

1960 (12 Feb). *Death Centenary of Von Humboldt (naturalist).* T 331 *and various animal designs.* P 12, *also* 11 × 12 (20 c.). (a) POSTAGE.

1005	5 c. bistre-brown and turquoise	5	5
1006	10 c. sepia and scarlet ..	5	5
1007	20 c. slate-purple and olive-yellow ..	8	5

(b) AIR. *Inscr* "AEREO"

1008	35 c. deep brown	8	5
1009	1 p. 30, brown and rose ..	35	12
1010	1 p. 45, lemon and greenish blue ..	35	15
1005/1010	Set of 6	85	40

Designs: *Vert*—5 c. Sloth; 20 c. Monkey. *Horiz*—35 c. Anteater; 1 p. 30, Armadillo; 1 p. 45, Parrot fish.

(Des Mosdossy. Photo State Ptg Wks, Vienna)

1960 (10 May)–**62.** *Colombian Flowers.* T 332 *and similar vert designs.* P 12. (a) POSTAGE.

1011	332	5 c. yell, rose-red, green & sep ..	5	5
1012	A	20 c. yellow, yellow-green & sep ..	8	5

(b) AIR. (i) *Inscr* "CORREO AEREO"

1013	B	5 c. magenta, yell, grn & dp bl ..	5	5
1014	B	5 c. magenta, yellow, green and deep grey (30.1.62)	5	5
1015	A	10 c. yellow, yellow-green and grey-blue (30.1.62)	5	5
1016	C	20 c. yellow, brown-red, green and reddish purple (30.1.62) ..	5	5
1017	D	25 c. yellow, brown-red, grey and yellow-olive (30.1.62) ..	5	5
1018	C	35 c. yellow, green and lake ..	8	5
1019	B	60 c. magenta, yellow, green and deep slate-blue	10	8
1020	332	60 c. yellow, rose-red, green and bistre-brown (30.1.62) ..	10	8
1021		1 p. 45, yellow, rose-red, green and sepia	25	15

(ii) *Inscr* "EXTRA RAPIDO"

1022	C	5 c. red-brown, yell, grn & mar ..	5	5
1023	D	10 c. yellow, brown-red, grey-green and sepia	5	5
1024	332	1 p. yellow, bright rose-red, green and sepia	30	15
1025	A	1 p. yellow, yellow-grn and sepia	30	15
1026	B	1 p. magenta, yell, grn & dp bl ..	30	15
1027	C	1 p. red-brown, yell, grn & mar ..	30	15
1028	D	1 p. yellow, brown-red, grey-green and sepia	30	15
1029	C	2 p. yellow, brown-red, green and orange-red (30.1.62)	30	20
1011/1029		Set of 19	2·50	1·60

Flowers:—A, *Espeletia grandiflora;* B, *Passiflora mollissima;* C, *Odontoglossuom luteo purpureum;* D, *Stanhopea tigrina.*

(Des Mosdossy. Litho Editorial Retina)

1960 (10 June). *150th Birth Anniv of Abraham Lincoln.* P 11.

(a) POSTAGE

1032	334	20 c. black and mauve	5	5

(b) AIR. *Inscr* "AEREO"

1033	334	40 c. black and chocolate	12	8
1034		60 c. black and carmine-red ..	15	10

335 "House of the Flower Vase"

336 St. Luisa de Marillac and Sanctuary

(Des Mosdossy. Photo State Ptg Wks, Vienna)

1960 (19 July). *150th Anniv of Independence.* T 335 *and similar designs inscr* "INDEPENDENCIA NACIONAL 1810–1960". P 12. (a) POSTAGE.

1035		5 c. orange-brown and deep green ..	5	5
1036		20 c. purple and bistre-brown ..	5	5
1037		20 c. yellow, deep blue and magenta ..	5	5

(b) AIR. (i) *Inscr* "AEREO"

1038	5 c. multicoloured	5	5
1039	5 c. sepia and bright reddish violet ..	5	5
1040	35 c. yellow, red, blue and grey ..	5	5
1041	60 c. deep green and Venetian red ..	10	8
1042	1 p. bronze-green and rose-red ..	20	12
1043	1 p. 20, indigo and blue	25	12
1044	1 p. 30, black and red-orange.. ..	25	15
1045	1 p. 45, yell, red, bl & dp grey-grn ..	30	20
1046	1 p. 65, brown and deep green ..	30	20
1035/1046	Set of 12	1·50	1·00

(ii) *Miniature sheet. Inscr* "EXTRA RAPIDO"

MS1047 90 × 75 mm. As designs of postage and air stamps but in new colours .. ..

50 c. (As No. 1037)..		
50 c. (As No. 1038)..	} 75	75
1 p. (As No. 1040)..		
1 p. (As No. 1035)..		

Designs: *Vert*—No. 1035, Cartagena coins of 1811–13; 1038, Arms of Cartagena; 1037, Arms of Mompós; No. 1043, Statue of A. Galan. *Horiz*—1036, T 335; 1039, J. Camacho, J. T. Lozano and J. M. Pey; 1040, 1045, Colombian Flag; 1041, A. Rosillo, A. Villavicencio and J. Caicedo; 1042, B. Alvarez and J. Gutierrez; No. 1044, Front page of *La Bagatela* (newspaper); 1046, Antonia Santos, J. A. Gomez and L. Meija.

(Des J. Sarmiento. Litho Editorial Retina)

1960 (1 Sept). *OBLIGATORY TAX. Red Cross Fund.* T 336 *and similar horiz design.* P 11.

1048	5 c. red and brown	5	5
1049	5 c. red and deep violet-blue ..	5	5

Design:—No. 1049, H. Dunant and battle scene.

333 Refugee Family

334 Lincoln Statue, Washington

(Litho Colombia Printing Works, Bogotá)

1960 (12 May). AIR. *World Refugee Year.* P 11.

1030	333	60 c. olive-grey and blue-green ..	20	8
		a. Perf 10	12	8
		ab. Imperf between (vert pair) ..	50·00	

1960 (28 May). AIR. *Eighth Pan-American Highway Congress.* Sheet 46 × 56 mm. W 330. Imperf.

MS1031 339 2 p. 50, brown & turquoise-blue 70 70

337 St. Isidro Labrador

338 U.N. Headquarters, New York

Colombia 1961

(Des Mosdossy. Photo State Ptg Wks, Vienna)

1960 (26 Sept). *St. Isidro Labrador Commemoration* (1*st issue*). *T* 337 *and similar vert design.* P 12½×12.

(a) POSTAGE
1050	337	10 c. multicoloured	.. ..	5	5
1051	–	20 c. multicoloured	.. ..	5	5

(b) AIR. (i) *Inscr "AEREO"*
1052	337	35 c. multicoloured	.. ..	10	5

(ii) *Miniature sheet. Inscr "EXTRA RAPIDO"*
MS1053 90×60 mm. As designs of postage stamps but in slightly different colours ..
1 p. 50 (As T 337) .. .. } 65 65
1 p. (As No. 1051).. .. .. ..
Design:—20 c. "The Nativity" (after Vasquez).
See also No. 1126/8.

(Des Retina. Litho National Ptg Wks, Bogotá)

1960 (24 Oct). *United Nations Day.* W 330. P 11.
1054	338	20 c. rose and black	.. ..	8	5
MS1055	338	55×49 mm. 50 c. pale blue-green and chocolate. Imperf	.. ..	25	25

339 Highway Map, Northern Colombia **340** Alfonso Lopez (statesman)

(Des Mosdossy. Litho Litografia Colombia)

1961 (7 Mar). *Eighth Pan-American Highway Congress.* P 11. *(a) POSTAGE.*
1056	339	20 c. brown and light blue ..	..	8	5

(b) AIR. (i) *Inscr "AEREO"*
1057	339	10 c. bright purple and emerald	..	5	5
1058		20 c. scarlet and light blue ..	..	5	5
1059		30 c. black and emerald	..	10	5

(ii) *Inscr "EXTRA RAPIDO"*
1060	339	10 c. ultramarine and emerald	..	5	5
1056/1060		*Set of 5*	..	30	20

For miniature sheet, see No. **MS**1031.

(Photo De La Rue)

1961 (22 Mar). P 13. *(a) POSTAGE.*
1061	340	10 c. brown and bright carmine	..	5	5
1062		20 c. brown and violet	..	5	5

(b) AIR. (i) *Inscr "AEREO"*
1063	340	35 c. brown and blue	..	8	5

(ii) *Inscr "EXTRA RAPIDO"*
1064	340	10 c. brown and bluish green	..	5	5
MS1065		74×60 mm. **340** 1 p. yellow-brown and reddish violet	.. ..	25	25

341 **342** Arms and View of Cúcuta

(Des Mosdossy. Photo State Ptg Wks, Tokyo)

1961 (17 Aug)–**62**. *50th Anniv of Valle del Cauca. T 341 and similar designs inscr "VALLE DEL CAUCA".* P 13½×13 (*vert*) *or* 13×13½ (*horiz*). *(a) POSTAGE.*
1066		10 c. red-brown, blue, green and red (26.4.62)	..	5	5
1067		20 c. brown and black ..	..	5	5

(b) AIR. (i) *Inscr "AEREO"*
1068		35 c. chocolate and olive-brown	..	8	5
1069		35 c. bistre-brown and emerald	..	8	5
1070		1 p. 30, sepia and brown-purple	..	20	15
1071		1 p. 45, bronze-green & orge-brown ..		20	15

(ii) *Inscr "EXTRA RAPIDO"*
1072		10 c. chocolate and yellow-olive	..	5	5
1066/1072		*Set of 7*	..	60	50

Designs: *Horiz*—10 c. (No. 1066), La Ermita Church, bridge and arms of Cali; 35 c. (1068), St. Francis' Church, Cali; 1 p 30, Conservatoire; 1 p. 45, Agricultural College, Palmira. *Vert*—10 c. (No. 1072), Aerial view of Cali; 35 c. (1069), University emblem.

(Des Mosdossy. Photo State Ptg Wks, Tokyo)

1961 (29 Aug). *50th Anniv of North Santander. T 342 and similar designs inscr "1910—NORTE DE SANTANDER—1960".* P 13×13½ (*horiz*) *or* 13½×13 (*vert*). *(a) POSTAGE.*
1073		20 c. red, blue, sepia and yellow-brown		5	5
1074		20 c. red, yellow, blue and indigo	..	5	5

(b) AIR. (i) *Inscr "AEREO"*
1075		35 c. bluish green, bistre & bistre-brn ..		8	5

(ii) *Inscr "EXTRA RAPIDO"*
1076		10 c. dull purple and green	.. ..	5	5
1073/1076		*Set of 4*	..	20	15

Design: *Horiz*—No. 1073, Arms of Ocana and Pamplona; 1074, T 342; 1075, Panoramic view of Cúcuta. *Vert*—No. 1076, Villa del Rosario, Cúcuta.

(343) **(344)** **345** Arms of Barranquilla

1961 (30 Sept). *AIR. Optd with T 343* (*No.* 1077) *or T 344* (*others*) *or surch also.*
1077	332	5 c. yellow, rose-red, green and sepia	..	5	5
1078	–	5 c. bistre-brown & turq (1005) ..		5	5
1079	–	10 c. on 20 c. slate-purple and olive-yellow (1007) ..	..	5	5
1077/1079		*Set of 3*	..	10	10

(Des Mosdossy. Photo J. Enschedé)

1961 (10 Oct). *Atlántico Tourist Issue. T 345 and similar designs.* P 12½×13 (*vert*) *or* 13×12½ (*horiz*). *(a) POSTAGE.*
1080		10 c. yellow, blue, red and silver	..	5	5
1081		20 c. red, blue and yellow	..	5	5
1082		20 c. yellow, blue, red and gold	..	5	5

(b) AIR. (i) *Inscr "AEREO"*
1083		35 c. sepia and carmine	..	10	5
1084		35 c. red, yellow and green	..	10	5
1085		35 c. blue and gold	..	10	5
1086		1 p. 45, brown and yellow-green	..	20	15
1080/1088		*Set of 8*	..	60	45

MS1087 90×76 mm. As designs of postage and air stamps, but in new colours: 35 c. (As T 345); 40 c. (As 1080): 1 p. (As 1084); 1 p. (As 1088) 50 50

THE WORLD CENTRE FOR
FINE STAMPS IS 391 STRAND

(ii) *Inscr* "EXTRA RAPIDO"
1088	10 c. yellow and brown	..	..	5	5
MS1089	90×76 mm. As designs of postage and air stamps but in new colours: 50 c. (As 1085); 50 c. (As 1083); 50 c. (As 1082); 50 c. (As 1088)		..	50	50

Designs: *Vert*—No. 1080, Arms of Ponayán; 1081, T **345**; 1082, Arms of Bucaramanga; 1083, Courtyard of Tourist Hotel, Popayán; 1088, Holy Week procession, Popayán; *Horiz*—No. 1084, View of San Gil; 1085, Barranquilla Port; 1086, View of Velez.

346 Nurse M. de la Cruz   **347** Boxing

(Recess Govt Ptg Wks, Madrid)

1961 (2 Nov). *OBLIGATORY TAX. Red Cross Fund. Crosses in red.* P 13.
1090	**246**	5 c. chocolate	..	5	5
1091		5 c. reddish violet	..	5	5

DE LA RUE PRINTINGS. All De La Rue issues up to this point were printed in London; later printings were made at their subsidiary in Bogotá.

(Litho De La Rue, Bogotá)

1961 (16 Dec). *Fourth Bolivar Games.* T **347** *and similar vert designs inscr* "IV JUEGOS DEPORTIVOS BOLIVARIANOS" *etc.* P 13½×14. (*a*) *POSTAGE.*
1092	20 c. dp green, yellow, flesh & dp blue		5	5
1093	20 c. sepia, flesh, yellow and green	..	5	5
1094	20 c. sepia, flesh, yellow and chestnut		5	5
1095	25 c. deep green, yellow, flesh and bistre-brown	..	8	5

(*b*) *AIR* (i) *Inscr* "AEREO"
1096	35 c. yellow, flesh, brown & bright blue		8	5
1097	35 c. sepia, flesh, yellow & rose-carmine	..	8	5
1098	1 p. 45, sepia, flesh, yellow and dp greenish blue	..	20	15

(ii) *Inscr* "EXTRA RAPIDO"
1099	10 c. multicoloured		5	5
1100	10 c. deep sepia, flesh, yellow and crimson	..	5	5
1092/1100	*Set of 9*	..	60	50
MS1001	74×106 mm. Multicoloured. 50 c. Statue and flags; 50 c. Baseball; 1 p. Football; 1 p. Basketball ..	..	60	60

Designs:—No. 1092, T **347**; 1093, Basketball; 1094, Running; 1095, Football; 1096, Diving; 1097, Tennis; 1098, Baseball; 1099, Statue and flags; 1100, Runner with Olympic torch.

348 "S.E.M." Emblem and Mosquito   **349** Society Emblem

(Photo State Ptg Wks, Vienna)

1962 (12 Apr). *Malaria Eradication.* T **348** *and similar vert design.* P 11½×12. (*a*) *POSTAGE.*
1102	**348**	20 c. red and ochre	..	5	5
1103	–	50 c. ultramarine and ochre	..	12	8

(*b*) *AIR.* (i) *Inscr* "AEREO"
1104	**348**	40 c. red and yellow	..	10	5
1105	–	1 p. 45, ultramarine and grey	..	20	15

(ii) *Inscr* "EXTRA RAPIDO"
1106	–	1 p. ultramarine and green	..	20	12
1102/1106	*Set of 5*	..	..	60	40

Design:—50 c., 1 p., 1 p. 45, Campaign emblem and mosquito.

(Des Mosdossy. Photo State Ptg Wks, Vienna)

1962 (12 June). *Sixth National Engineer's Congress, 1961, and 75th Anniv of Colombian Society of Engineers.* T **349** *and similar vert designs.* P 12. (*a*) *POSTAGE.*
1107	**349**	10 c. black, yellow, red and blue	..	5	5

(*b*) *AIR* (i) *Inscr* "AEREO"
1108	–	5 c. carmine and blue	..	5	5
1109	–	10 c. brown and green	..	5	5
1110	–	15 c. brown and purple	..	5	5

(ii) *Inscr* "EXTRA RAPIDO"
1111	**349**	2 p. black, yellow, red and blue	..	30	25
1107/1111	*Set of 5*	..	45	35

Designs:—No. 1108, A. Ramos and Engineering Faculty, Cauca University, Popayán; 1109, M. Triana, A. Arroyo and Monserrate cable and funicular railways; 1110, D. Sanchez and first Society H. Q., Bogotá.

350 O.E.A. Emblem   **351** Mother Voting and Statue of Policarpa Salavarrieta

352 Parallel Curved Lines   **353** Scouts in Camp

(Des Mosdossy. Photo De La Rue, Bogotá)

1962 (28 June). *70th Anniv of O.E.A. (Organization of American States). Flags multicoloured; background colours below.* P 13. (*a*) *POSTAGE.*
1112	**350**	25 c. orange-red and black..	..	5	5
MS1113	41×45 mm. **350** 2 p. 50, yellow and black..	..	..	35	35

(*b*) *AIR. Inscr* "AEREO"
1114	**350**	35 c. blue and black	..	5	5

(Des Mosdossy. Litho De La Rue, Bogotá)

1962 (20 July)–**64.** *Women's Franchise. Black and grey. Background colour given below.* W **352.** P 12×12½. (*a*) *POSTAGE.*
1115	**351**	5 c. orange-brown (11.7.63)	..	5	5
1116		10 c. light blue	..	5	5

(*b*) *AIR. Inscr* "CORREO AEREO"
1117	**351**	5 c. pink (14.3.64) ..	..	5	5
1118		35 c. yellow-orange	..	8	5

1119	351	45 c. green (25.5.63)	..	..	8	5
1120		45 c. mauve (25.5.63)	..	..	8	5
1115/1120		Set of 6	..	..	30	25

(Des Mosdossy. Photo State Ptg Wks, Vienna)

1962 (26 July). *30th Anniv of Colombian Boy Scouts and 25th Anniv of Colombian Girl Scouts Movements. T* **353** *and similar vert design. P 11½ × 12 or 12.*

(a) POSTAGE. Inscr "CORREOS"

| 1121 | 353 | 10 c. brown and turquoise.. | .. | 5 | 5 |

(b) AIR. (i) Inscr "AEREO"

1122	353	15 c. brown and red	..	..	5	5
1123	–	40 c. brown-purple and carmine	..	8	5
1124	–	1 p. blue and salmon	..	..	12	8

(ii) Inscr "EXTRA RAPIDO"

| 1125 | 353 | 1 p. violet and yellow | .. | .. | 15 | 12 |
| 1121/1125 | | Set of 5 | .. | .. | .. | 40 | 30 |

Design:—40 c., 1 p. Girl Scouts.

354 St. Isidro   **355** Railway Map   **356** Posthorn
Labrador

(Des Mosdossy. Photo State Ptg Wks, Vienna)

1962 (28 Aug). *St. Isidro Labrador Commemoration (2nd issue). T* **354** *and similar vert design. P 12½ × 12.*

(a) POSTAGE

| 1126 | 354 | 10 c. multicoloured | .. | .. | 5 | 5 |

(b) AIR. Inscr "EXTRA RAPIDO"

| 1127 | – | 10 c. multicoloured | .. | .. | 5 | 5 |
| 1128 | 354 | 2 p. multicoloured | .. | .. | 30 | 20 |

Design: *Vert*—10 c. (No. 1127), "The Nativity" (after G. Vasquez).

(Recess (Nos. 1132/3); photo (others) Govt Ptg Wks, Madrid)

1962 (28 Sept). *Completion of Colombia Atlantic Railway. T* **355** *and similar designs. P 13 × 12½ (vert), or 12½ × 13 (horiz). (a) POSTAGE.*

| 1129 | 355 | 10 c. carmine, blue-green and blackish olive.. | .. | .. | 5 | 5 |

(b) AIR. (i) Inscr "AEREO"

1130	–	5 c. blackish green and sepia	..	5	5
1131	355	10 c. carmine, greenish blue & bistre-brown ..	..	5	5
1132	–	1 p. chocolate and purple..	..	12	8

(ii) Inscr "EXTRA RAPIDO"

| 1133 | – | 5 p. brown, ultram & dp grey-grn | 65 | 45 |
| 1129/1133 | | Set of 5 | .. | .. | .. | 80 | 60 |

Designs: *Horiz*—5 c. 1854 and 1961 locomotives; 1 p., 5 p. Pres. A. Parra and R. Magdalena railway bridge.

(Des Mosdossy. Litho De La Rue, Bogotá)

1962 (18 Oct). *50th Anniv of U.P.A.E. Postal Union of the Americas and Spain. T* **356** *and similar vert design. W* **352**. *P 13½ × 14. (a) POSTAGE.*

| 1134 | 356 | 20 c. gold and indigo | .. | .. | 5 | 5 |

(b) AIR. Inscr "AEREO"

| 1135 | – | 50 c. gold and deep grey-green | .. | 5 | 5 |
| 1136 | 356 | 60 c. gold and purple | .. | .. | 8 | 5 |

Design:—50 c. Posthorn, dove and map.

357 Virgin of the   **358** Centenary Emblem
Mountain, Bogotá

(Des Mosdossy. Litho De La Rue, Bogotá)

1963 (11 Mar). *Ecumenical Council, Vatican City. T* **357** *and similar vert design. W* **352**. *P 13½ × 14. (a) POSTAGE.*

| 1137 | 357 | 60 c. multicoloured | .. | .. | 8 | 5 |

(b) AIR Inscr "AEREO"

| 1138 | – | 60 c. brown-red, yellow and gold | .. | 10 | 8 |

Design:—No. 1138, Pope John XXIII.

(Des Mosdossy. Litho De La Rue, Bogotá)

1963 (1 May). *OBLIGATORY TAX. Red Cross Centenary. W* **352**. *P 12 × 12½.*

| 1139 | 358 | 5 c. red and bistre .. | .. | .. | 5 | 5 |

359 Hurdling and Flags

(Des Mosdossy. Litho De La Rue, Bogotá)

1963 (12 Aug). *AIR. South American Athletic Championships, Cali. W* **352**. *P 13½ × 14.*

| 1140 | 359 | 20 c. multicoloured | .. | .. | 5 | 5 |
| 1141 | | 80 c. multicoloured | .. | .. | 12 | 8 |

360. Bolivar Monument.

(Des Mosdossy. Litho De La Rue, Bogotá)

1963 (30 Aug). *AIR. Centenary of Pereira. P 14 × 13½.*

| 1142 | 360 | 1 p. 90, bistre-brown and light blue | 20 | 15 |

E **3** Jetliner on back of "Express" Letter

361 Tennis-player

(Des Mosdossy. Litho De La Rue, Bogotá)

1963 (4 Oct). *EXPRESS AIR. P* 14.
E1143 E **3** 50 c. black and red 5 5

(Des Mosdossy. Litho De La Rue, Bogotá)

1963 (11 Oct). *AIR. 30th South American Tennis Championships, Medellin. P* 13½×14.
1143 **361** 55 c. flesh, brown, yellow-green & bluish green 8 5

362 Pres. Kennedy and Alliance Emblem

363 Veracruz Church

(Des Mosdossy. Litho De La Rue, Bogotá)

1963 (17 Dec). *AIR. "Alliance for Progress". P* 14×13½.
1144 **362** 10 c. sepia, green, blue and grey .. 5 5

(Des J. Pardo and T. Nel Molina. Photo De La Rue, Bogotá)

1964 (10 Mar). *AIR. National Pantheon, Veracruz Church. T 363 and similar vert design. Multicoloured. P* 13½×14.
1145 1 p. Type **363** 10 8
1146 2 p. "The Crucifixion" 20 12

364 Cartagena

365 Eleanor Roosevelt

(Des Mosdossy. Litho De La Rue, Bogotá)

1964 (18 Mar). *AIR. Cartagena Commemoration. P* 14×13½.
1147 **364** 3 p. multicoloured 35 20

(Des T. N. Molina. Photo State Ptg Wks, Vienna)

1964 (10 Nov). *AIR. 15th Anniv of Declaration of Human Rights. P* 12.
1148 **365** 20 c. brown-red & lt yellow-green .. 5 5

366 A. Castilla (composer and founder) and Music

367 Manuel Mejia and Coffee Growers' Flag Emblem

(Des J. Pardo. Photo State Ptg Wks, Vienna)

1964 (10 Nov). *AIR. Tolima Conservatoire Commemoration. P* 12.
1149 **366** 30 c. deep bluish green and bistre 5 5

(Recess Govt Ptg Wks, Madrid)

1965 (10 Feb). *Manuel Mejia Commemoration T **367** and similar horiz designs, each including portrait of Mejia, director of the National Coffee Growers' Association. P* 12½×13. (*a*) *POSTAGE.*
1150 25 c. sepia and rose 5 5

(*b*) *AIR. Inscr "CORREO AEREO"*
1151 45 c. sepia and brown 5 5
1152 5 p. black and grey-green 35 25
1153 10 p. black and ultramarine 75 55
1150/1153 *Set of* 4 .. .. 1·10 80
Designs: 45 c. Gathering coffee-beans; 5 p. Mule transport; 10 p. Freighter *Manuel Mejia* at Buenaventura port.

368 Nurse with Patient

369 I.T.U. Emblem and "Waves"

(Des T. Molina. Photo State Ptg Wks, Vienna)

1965 (30 Apr). *OBLIGATORY TAX. Red Cross Fund. P* 12.
1154 **368** 5 c. indigo and red 5 5

(Des T. Molina. Photo State Ptg Wks, Vienna)

1965 (25 Oct). *AIR. I.T.U. Centenary. P* 12.
1155 **369** 80 c. deep Prussian blue, red and light blue 8 5

370 Orchid (*Cattleya trianae*)

371 Satellites, Telegraph Pole and Map

(Des T. Molina. Litho De La Rue, Bogotá)

1965 (31 Oct). *AIR. Fifth Philatelic Exhibition, Bogotá. P* 13½×14.
1156 **370** 20 c. multicoloured 5 5

(Des T. Molina. Litho De La Rue, Bogotá)

1965 (1 Nov). *AIR. Centenary of Colombian Telegraphs. T **371** and similar multicoloured design. P* 14×13½ (1157) or 13½×14 (1158).
1157 60 c. Type **371** 10 5
1158 60 c. Statue of President Murrilo-Toro, Bogotá (*vert*) 5 5

372 Junkers "F-13" Seaplane (1920)

373 Badge, and Car on Mountain Road

(Des Mosdossy. Photo De La Rue, Bogotá)

1965–66. *AIR. "History of Colombian Aviation".* **T 372** *and similar horiz designs. Multicoloured.* P 14×13½. (a) AIR.

1159	5 c. Type **372** (13.12.65)	5	5
1160	10 c. Dornier "Wal" (1924) (15.7.66)	5	5
1161	20 c. Dornier "Mercury" seaplane (1926) (14.12.66)	5	5
1162	50 c. Ford "Trimotor" (1932) (14.12.66)	5	5
1163	60 c. De Havilland "Moth" (1930) (13.12.65)	5	5
1164	1 p. Douglas "DC-4" (1947) (15.7.66)	8	5
1165	1 p. 40, Douglas "DC-3" (1944) (15.7.66)	10	8
1166	2 p. 80, Super Constellation (1951) (14.12.66)	20	15
1167	3 p. Boeing "720 B" jetliner (1961) (13.12.65)	25	20

(b) EXPRESS AIR. Inscr "EXPRESO"

E1168	80 c. Boeing "727" jetliner (1966) (14.12.66)	8	5
1159/E1168	Set of 10	90	70

(Des T. N. Molina. Litho De La Rue, Bogotá)

1966 (16 Feb). *25th Anniv of Colombian Automobile Club (1956).* P 14×13½.

1168	**373**	20 c. multicoloured	5	5

374 J. Arboleda (writer)

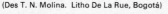

375 Red Cross and Children as Nurse and Patient

(Des T. N. Molina. Litho De La Rue, Bogotá)

1966 (9 Mar). *Julio Arboleda Commemoration.* P 14×13½.

1169	**374**	5 c. multicoloured	5	5

(Des J. Vargas. Litho De La Rue, Bogotá)

1966 (26 Apr). *OBLIGATORY TAX. Red Cross Fund.* P 13½×14.

1170	**375**	5 c.+5 c. multicoloured	5	5

376 16th-century Galleon   377 Hogfish

(Photo De La Rue, Bogotá)

1966 (16 June). *History of Maritime Mail.* **T 376** *and similar horiz designs. Multicoloured.* P 14×13½.

1171	5 c. Type **376**	5	5
1172	15 c. Riohacha brigantine (1850)	5	5
1173	20 c. Uraba schooner	5	5
1174	40 c. Magdalena steamboat and barge (1900)	5	5
1175	50 c. Modern motor-ship	5	5
1171/1175	Set of 5	20	15

(Photo Govt Ptg Wks, Madrid)

1966 (25 Aug). *Fishes.* **T 377** *and similar horiz designs. Multicoloured.* P 12½×13. (a) POSTAGE.

1176	80 c. Type **377**	8	8
1177	10 p. Flying Fish	70	50

(b) AIR. Inscr "AEREO"

1178	2 p. Angel Fish	12	10
1179	2 p. 80, Electric Ray	20	15
1180	20 p. Spanish Mackerel	1·25	1·00
1176/1180	Set of 5	2·10	1·60

378 Arms of Colombia, Venezuela and Chile   379 C. Torres (patriot)

(Des C. Alonso. Litho De La Rue, Bogotá)

1966 (11 Oct). *Visits of Chilean and Venezuelan Presidents.* P 14×13½. (a) POSTAGE.

1181	**378**	40 c. multicoloured	5	5

(b) AIR. Inscr "AEREO"

1182	**378**	1 p. multicoloured	8	8
1183		1 p. 40, multicoloured	10	8

(Des T. N. Molina, Litho De La Rue, Bogotá)

1967 (18 Jan). *Famous Colombians.* **T 379** *and similar vert portraits.* P 13½×14. (a) POSTAGE.

1184	25 c. violet and olive-yellow	5	5
1185	60 c. brown-purple and olive-yellow	5	5
1186	1 p. dull green and olive-yellow	8	5

(b) AIR. Inscr "AEREO"

1187	80 c. deep grey-blue and olive-yellow	8	5
1188	1 p. 70, black and olive-yellow	12	10
1184/1188	Set of 5	35	25

Portraits:—60 c. J. T. Lozano (naturalist); 80 c. Father F. R. Mejia (scholar); 1 p. F. A. Zea (writer); 1 p. 70, J. J. Casas (diplomat).

380 Map of Signatory Countries

(Des T. N. Molina. Litho De La Rue, Bogotá)

1967 (2 Feb). *"Declaration of Bogotá"* (16.8.66). P 14×13½.

(a) POSTAGE

1189	**380**	40 c. multicoloured	5	5
1190		60 c. multicoloured	5	5

(b) AIR. Inscr "AEREO"

1191	**380**	3 p. multicoloured	20	15

381 *Monochaetum* and Bee

(Litho De La Rue, Bogotá)

1967 (7 Apr–23 May). *National Orchid Congress and Tropical Flora and Fauna Exhibition, Medellin.* T **381** and similar multicoloured designs. P 14. (*a*) POSTAGE.

1192	25 c. Type **381** (23.5)	..	5	5
1193	2 p. *Passiflora vitifolia* and butterfly (*horiz*) (23.5)	.. .. ..	15	10

(*b*) AIR. *Inscr* "AEREO"

1194	1 p. *Cattleya dowiana* (*vert*) (23.5)	..	8	5
1195	1 p. 20, *Masdevallia coccinea* (*vert*)	..	10	8
1196	5 p. *Catasetum macrocarpum* and bee (*horiz*) (23.5)	.. .. ..	35	25
1192/1196	*Set of 5*	.. .. ..	65	45
MS1197	100×150 mm. Nos. 1194/6	..	60	60

382 Nurse's Cap

383 Lions Emblem

(Des C. Alonso. Litho De La Rue, Bogotá)

1967 (1 June). *OBLIGATORY TAX. Red Cross Fund.* P 12½×12.

1198	**382** 5 c. red and light greenish blue	..	5	5

(Des T. N. Molina. Litho De La Rue, Bogotá)

1967 (12 July). *50th Anniv of Lions International.* P 13½×14.

(*a*) POSTAGE

1199	**383** 10 p. multicoloured	.. ..	60	45

(*b*) AIR. *Inscr* "AEREO"

1200	**383** 25 c. multicoloured	.. ..	5	5

384 "Caesarian Operation 1844" (from painting by Grau)

385 S.E.N.A. Emblem

(Litho De La Rue, Bogotá)

1967 (7 Sept). *AIR. Sixth Colombian Surgeons Congress, Bogotá, and Centenary of National University.* P 14×13½.

1201	**384** 80 c. multicoloured	.. ..	8	5

(Des C. Alonso. Litho (centre embossed). De La Rue, Bogotá)

1967 (20 Sept). *Tenth Anniv of National Apprenticeship Service.* P 13½×14. (*a*) POSTAGE.

1202	**385** 5 p. black, gold and emerald	..	30	20

(*b*) AIR. *Inscr* "AEREO"

1203	**385** 2 p. black, gold and red	..	12	10

386 Calima Diadem

387 Radio Antennae

(Des C. Alonso. Photo De La Rue, Bogotá)

1967 (13 Oct). *Administrative Council of U.P.U. Consultative Commission of Postal Studies.* T **386** and similar designs. Main design and lower inscr in brown and gold. P 13½×14 or 14×13½ (3 p.). (*a*) POSTAGE.

1204	1 p. 60, bright purple	..	..	10	8
1205	3 p. deep blue	..	..	20	15

(*b*) AIR. *Inscr* "AEREO"

1206	30 c. vermilion	..	..	5	5
1207	5 p. red	..	..	30	20
1208	20 p. violet	..	..	1·25	1·00
1204/1208	*Set of 5*	..	..	1·75	1·25
MS1209	92×92 mm. Nos. 1206/7 but in new colours. Imperf	..		75	75

Designs (Colombian archaeological treasures): *Vert*—30 c. Chief's head-dress; 1 p. 60, T **386**; 5 p. Cauca breastplate; 20 p. Quimbaya jug. *Horiz*—3 p. Tolima anthropomorphic figure and postal "pigeon on globe" emblem. The miniature sheet is inscr "VI EXPOSICION FILATELICA NACIONAL BOGOTA OCTUBRE 1967".

(Litho De La Rue, Bogotá)

1968 (14 May). *"21 Years of National Telecommunications Services"* (*inscr* "1947–1968"). T **387** and similar vert designs. P 13½×14. (*a*) POSTAGE.

1210	50 c. black, red, brown & bright green		5	5
1211	1 p. red, green, blue and light grey	..	8	5

(*b*) AIR. *Inscr* "AEREO"

1212	50 c. red, green, yellow and black	..	5	5
1213	1 p. yellow, grey and blue	..	8	5
1210/1213	*Set of 4*	..	20	15

Designs:—No. 1210, Type **387**; 1211, Communications network; 1212, Diagram; 1213, Satellite.

388 The Eucharist

389 "St. Augustine" (Vasquez)

(Des C. Alonso. Litho De La Rue, Bogotá)

1968 (6 June). *39th International Eucharistic Congress, Bogotá* (1st *issue*). P 13½×14. (*a*) POSTAGE.

1214	**388** 60 c. multicoloured	..	5	5

(*b*) AIR. *Inscr* "AEREO"

1215	**388** 80 c. multicoloured	..	8	5
1216	3 p. multicoloured	..	20	15

(Photo Japanese Govt Ptg Wks, Tokyo)

1968 (13 Aug). *39th International Eucharistic Congress, Bogotá* (2nd *issue*). T **389** and similar multicoloured designs showing paintings. P 13. (*a*) POSTAGE.

1217	25 c. Type **389**	..	5	5
1218	60 c. "Gathering Manna" (Vasquez)	..	5	5
1219	1 p. "Betrothal of the Virgin and St. Joseph" (B. de Figueroa)	..	8	5
1220	5 p. "La Lechuga" (Jesuit statuette)	..	35	20
1221	10 p. "Pope Paul VI" (painting by Franciscan Missionary Mothers)	..	65	50

(b) AIR. Inscr "AEREO"
1222 80 c. "The Last Supper" (Vasquez)
(horiz) 5 5
1223 1 p. "St. Francis Xavier's Sermon"
(Vasquez).. .. .. .. 8 5
1224 2 p. "Elias's Dream" (Vasquez) .. 12 10
1225 3 p. As No. 1220 .. .. .. 20 12
1226 20 p. As No. 1221 .. .. .. 1·25 85
1217/1226 Set of 10 .. .. .. 2·50 1·75
MS1227 91×90 mm. Nos. 1220/1. Imperf 80 80

PRINTERS. From No. 1228 all issues were printed in lithography by De La Rue, Bogotá, *unless otherwise stated.*

390 Pope Paul VI

391 University Arms

1968 (22 Aug). *Pope Paul's Visit to Colombia. T 390 and similar multicoloured designs. P 14×13½ (80 c.) or 13½×14 (others). (a) POSTAGE.*
1228 25 c. Type **390** 5 5

(b) AIR. Inscr "AEREO"
1229 80 c. Reception podium (horiz) .. 5 5
1230 1 p. 20, Pope Paul giving Blessing .. 10 8
1231 1 p. 80, Cathedral, Bogotá 15 8
1228/1231 Set of 4 .. .. .. 30 20

1968 (29 Oct). *Centenary of National University. T 391 and similar vert design. P 13½×14. (a) POSTAGE.*
1232 80 c. multicoloured 5 5

(b) AIR. Inscr "AEREO"
1233 20 c. carmine, emer & lt ochre-yellow 5 5
Design:—20 c. Computer symbols.

392 Antioquia 2½ c.
Stamp of 1868

393 Institute Emblem and
Split Leaf

1968 (20 Nov). *Centenary of First Antioquia Stamps. P 12×12½.*
1234 **392** 30 c. blue and emerald .. 5 5
MS1235 59×79 mm. **392** 5 p. blue and bistre 30 30

1969 (5 Mar). *25th Anniv (1967) of Inter-American Agricultural Sciences Institute. P 13½×14. (a) POSTAGE.*
1236 **393** 20 c. black, yellow, green & lt blue 5 5

(b) AIR. Inscr "AEREO"
1237 **393** 1 p. black, yellow, green & lt grey 8 5

394 Pen and Microscope

(Des C. A. Corbo)

1969 (24 Mar). *AIR. 20th Anniv of the University of the Andes. P 14.*
1238 **394** 5 p. black, red, violet and yellow .. 30 15

395 Von Humboldt and
Andes (Quindio Region)

396 Junkers "F-13" Seaplane
and Map

(Des T. N. Molina)

1969 (3 June). *AIR. Birth Bicent of Alexander von Humboldt (naturalist). P 14×13½.*
1239 **395** 1 p. green and chocolate 5 5

(Des I. Mosdossy)

1969 (18 June). *AIR. 50th Anniv of First Colombian Airmail Flight. T 396 and similar horiz design. Multicoloured. P 14×13½.*
1240 1 p. Type **396** 5 5
1241 1 p. 50, Boeing "720-B" and Globe .. 8 5
MS1242 93×92 mm. Two 5 p. designs as
Nos. 1240/1 but colours changed. Imperf .. 55 55
MS1242 was issued in connection with "EXFILBA 69"
National Philatelic Exhibition, Barranquilla.
For similar designs see Nos. 1249/50.

397 Red Cross

398 "Battle of Boyacá" (J. M.
Espinosa)

1969 (1 July). *OBLIGATORY TAX. Colombian Red Cross. P 12×12½.*
1243 **397** 5 c. red and bluish violet 5 5

1969 (24 July). *150th Anniversary of Independence. T 398 and similar horiz designs, showing paintings. Multicoloured. P 13½×14. (a) POSTAGE.*
1244 20 c. Type **398** 5 5
1245 30 c. "Death on the Pisba" (F. A. Caro) 5 5

(b) AIR. Inscr "AEREO"
1246 2 p. 30, "Entry into Santa Fé" (I.
Castillo-Cervantes) 10 8

399 "Human Being"

400 Cranial Diagram

(Des T. N. Molina)

1969 (29 Oct). *AIR. 20th Anniversary of Colombian Social Security Institute. P 13½×14.*
1247 **399** 20 c. bright green and black .. 5 5

(Des T. N. Molina)

1969 (29 Oct). *AIR. 13th Latin-American Neurological Congress, Bogotá. P 13½ × 14.*
1248 **400** 70 c. multicoloured 5 5

401 Junkers "F-13" Seaplane and Puerto Colombia

402 Child posting Christmas Card

(Des I. Mosdossy)

1969 (28 Nov). *AIR. 50th Anniversary of "AVIANCA" Airline. T 401 and similar horiz design. Multicoloured. P 14 × 13½.*
1249   2 p. Type **401** 10 8
1250   3 p. 50, Boeing "720-B" and Globe .. 15 10
MS1251   93 × 91 mm. As Nos. 1249/50, but face values changed to 3 p. 50 and 5 p. Imperf 40 40
MS1251 was issued in connection with "EXFILBO 69" Interamerican Philatelic Exhibition, Bogotá.

(Des M. C. Castro)

1969 (16 Dec). *AIR. Christmas. T 402 and similar vert design. Multicoloured. P 13½ × 14.*
1252   60 c. Type **402** 5 5
1253   1 p. Type **402** 5 5
1254   1 p. 50, Child with Christmas presents 8 5
1252/1254   Set of 3 .. .. 15 12

403 "Poverty"

404 Dish Aerial and Ancient Head

1970 (1 Mar). *Colombian Social Welfare Institute, and 10th Anniv of Children's Rights Law. P 14.*
1255 **403** 30 c. multicoloured 5 5

(Des C. Alonso)

1970 (25 Mar). *AIR. Opening of Satellite Earth Station, Chocontá. P 14 × 13½.*
1256 **404** 1 p. black, salmon-red & dp green 5 5

STAMP MONTHLY

—finest and most informative magazine for all collectors. Obtainable from your newsagent or by postal subscription—details on request.

405 National Sports Institute Emblem

406 "A B C" of Art

1970 (6 Apr). *AIR. 9th National Games, Ibagué (1st issue). T 405 and similar vert design. P 13½ × 14.*
1257   1 p. 50, black, yellow and bronze-green 8 5
1258   2 p. 30, multicoloured 12 10
Design:—2 p. 30, Dove and rings (Games emblem).

(Des E. R. Villamizar)

1970 (30 Apr). *AIR. 2nd Fine Arts Biennial, Medellin. P 13½ × 14.*
1259 **406** 30 c. multicoloured 5 5

407 Dr. E. Santos (founder) and Buildings

408 U.N. Emblem, Scales and Dove

(Des I. Mosdossy)

1970 (18 June). *AIR. 30th Anniv (1969) of Territorial Credit Institute (housing organization). P 14 × 13½.*
1260 **407** 1 p. black, greenish yellow & bl-grn 5 5

(Des I. Mosdossy)

1970 (26 June). *AIR. 25th Anniversary of United Nations. P 13½ × 14.*
1261 **408** 1 p. 50, greenish yellow, light blue and deep ultramarine 8 5

409 Hands protecting Child

410 Theatrical Mask

(Des I. Mosdossy)

1970 (1 Aug). *OBLIGATORY TAX. Colombian Red Cross. P 12½ × 12.*
1262 **409** 5 c. red and light blue 5 5

(Des I. Mosdossy)

1970 (12 Sept). *Latin-American University Theatre Festival, Manizáles. P 14 × 13½.*
1263 **410** 30 c. brown-ochre, red-orge & black 5 5

411 Postal Emblem, Letter and Stamps

412 Discus-thrower and Ibagué Arms

(Des T. N. Molina)

1970 (24 Sept). *Philatelic Week.* P 14×13½.
1264 **411** 2 p. multicoloured 10 8

(Des I. Mosdossy)

1970 (13 Oct). *9th National Games, Ibagué (2nd issue).* P 14×13½.
1265 **412** 80 c. sepia, emerald & pale yellow 5 5

413 "St. Teresa" (B. de Figueroa)

414 Int Philatelic Federation Emblem

1970 (26 Oct)–**72**. *Elevation of St. Teresa of Avila to Doctor of the Universal Church.* P 13½×14. (a) POSTAGE.
1266 **413** 2 p. multicoloured 10 8

(b) AIR. Optd "AEREO" (15.2.72)
1267 **413** 2 p. multicoloured 10 8

(Des C. Alonso)

1970 (12 Nov). *AIR. "EXFILCA 70" Int Stamp Exhib, Caracas, Venezuela.* P 13½×14.
1268 **414** 10 p. black, gold and new blue .. 50 40

415 Chicha Maya Dance

416 Stylised Athlete

(Des I. Mosdossy (60 c. to 1 p. 30))

1970–71. *Folklore Dances and Costumes. T 415 and similar vert designs, showing costumes from various regions.* Multicoloured. P 13½×14. (a) POSTAGE.
1269 1 p. Type **415** (20.12.71) .. 5 5
1270 1 p. 10, Currulao dance (5.8.71) .. 8 5

(b) AIR. Inscr "AEREO"
1271 60 c. Napanga costume (18.11.70) .. 5 5
1272 1 p. Joropo dance (4.12.70) .. 5 5
1273 1 p. 30, Guabina dance (15.12.70) 8 5
1274 1 p. 30, Bambuco dance (9.3.71) .. 8 5
1275 1 p. 30, Cumbia dance (22.4.71) .. 8 5
1269/1275 Set of 7 .. .. .. 45 30
MS1276 Two sheets, each 80×110 mm. Face values and colours changed. Imperf. (a) 2 p. 50, As No. 1271; 2 p. 50, As No. 1272; 5 p. As No. 1273. (b) 4 p. As No. 1270; 4 p. As No. 1274; 4 p. As No. 1275 (10.8.71).
 Pair 1·00 1·00
In **MS**1276 "AEREO" is omitted from the designs.

(Des C. Alonso)

1971 (11 Mar). *AIR. 6th Pan-American Games, Cali (1st issue). T 416 and similar vert design.* P 13½×14.
1277 1 p. 50, multicoloured 8 8
1278 2 p. red-orange, emerald and black .. 10 8
Design:—2 p. Games emblem.

417 G. Alzate Avendaño

418 Priest's House, Guacari

(Des I. Mosdossy)

1971 (29 Apr). *AIR. 10th Death Anniv of Gilberto Alzate Avendaño (politician).* P 14×13½.
1279 **417** 1 p. multicoloured 5 5

(Des I. Mosdossy)

1971 (20 May). *400th Anniversary of Guacari (town).* P 14×13½.
1280 **418** 1 p. 10, multicoloured 8 5

419 Commemorative Medal

(Des T. N. Molina. Litho and embossed)

1971 (21 June). *AIR. Centenary of Bank of Bogotá.* P 14×13½.
1281 **419** 1 p. gold, light brn & dp bluish grn 5 5

420 Sports Centre

421 Weightlifting

(Des C. Alonso)

1971 (16 July). *AIR. 6th Pan-American Games (2nd issue) and "EXFICALI 71" Stamp Exhibition, Cali. T 420/1 and similar vert designs.* Multicoloured. P 13½×14.
1282 1 p. 30, Type **420** (yellow emblem) .. 8 5
1283 1 p. 30, Football 8 5
1284 1 p. 30, Wrestling 8 5
1285 1 p. 30, Cycling 8 5
1286 1 p. 30, Volleyball 8 5
1287 1 p. 30, Diving 8 5
1288 1 p. 30, Fencing 8 5
1289 1 p. 30, Type **420** (green emblem) .. 8 5
1290 1 p. 30, Sailing 8 5
1291 1 p. 30, Show-jumping 8 5
1292 1 p. 30, Athletics 8 5
1293 1 p. 30, Rowing 8 5
1294 1 p. 30, Cali emblem 8 5
1295 1 p. 30, Netball 8 5
1296 1 p. 30, Type **420** (blue emblem) .. 8 5
1297 1 p. 30, Stadium 8 5
1298 1 p. 30, Baseball 8 5
1299 1 p. 30, Hockey 8 5
1300 1 p. 30, Type **421** 8 5
1301 1 p. 30, Medals 8 5

1302	1 p. 30, Boxing ..	..	..	..	8	5
1303	1 p. 30, Gymnastics	..	..	..	8	5
1304	1 p. 30, Rifle-shooting ..	..	..		8	5
1305	1 p. 30, Type **420** (red emblem)	..			8	5
1282/1305	Set of 24 ..	..	..		1·60	1·00

Nos. 1282/1305 were issued *se-tenant* in sheets of 25 containing two stamps as No. 1296 and one example of each of the other stamps. (*Price for complete sheet* £1.75 *un.*)

422 "Bolivar at Congress"
(S. Martinez-Delgado)

424 C.I.M.E. Emblem

423 "Battle of Carabobo" (M. Tovar y Tovar)

1971 (6 Oct). *150th Anniversary of Greater Colombia Constituent Assembly, Rosario del Cúcuta.* P 14.
1306 **422** 80 c. multicoloured 5 5

1971 (25 Nov). *AIR. 150th Anniversary of Battle of Carabobo.* P 13½ × 14.
1307 **423** 1 p. 50, multicoloured 8 5

(Des C. Rojas)

1972 (24 Feb). *20th Anniversary of Inter-Governmental Committee on European Migration (C.I.M.E.).* P 13½ × 14.
1308 **424** 60 c. black and light grey 5 5

425 ICETEX Symbol

426 Rev. Mother
Francisca del Castillo

(Des I. Mosdossy)

1972 (15 Mar). *20th Anniversary of Institute of Educational Credit and Technical Training Abroad (ICETEX).* P 14 × 13½.
1309 **425** 1 p. 10, brown and myrtle-green .. 5 5

1972 (6 Apr). *300th Birth Anniv of Rev. Mother Francisca Josefa del Castillo.* P 13½ × 14.
1310 **426** 1 p. 20, multicoloured 8 5

427 Soldier and Frigate
Almirante Padilla

428 Hat and Ceramics

(Des I. Mosdossy)

1972 (7 Apr). *20th Anniversary of Colombian Troops' Participation in Korean War.* P 14 × 13½.
1311 **427** 1 p. 20, multicoloured 8 5

(Des I. Mosdossy)

1972 (11 Apr). *Colombian Crafts and Products.* T **428** *and similar vert designs. Multicoloured.* P 13½ × 14.

(a) POSTAGE
1312 1 p. 10, Type **428** 5 5

(b) AIR. Inscr "AEREO"
1313	50 c. Woman in shawl ..	..		5	5
1314	1 p. Male doll ..	..	..	5	5
1315	3 p. Female doll	..	..	12	10
1312/1315	Set of 4 ..	..	..	25	20

429 Maxillaria triloris
(orchid)

430 Uncut Emeralds and
Pendant

(Des I. Mosdossy)

1972 (20 Apr). *10th National Stamp Exhibition and 7th World Orchid-growers Congress, Medellin.* T **429** *and similar multicoloured design.* P 13½ × 14 (20 p.) or 14 × 13½ (1 p. 30). (a) POSTAGE.
1316 20 p. Type **429** 85 60

(b) AIR. Inscr "AEREO"
1317 1 p. 30, Mormodes rolfeanum (horiz) 8 5

(Des I. Mosdossy)

1972 (16 June). *Colombian Emeralds.* P 13½ × 14.
1318 **430** 1 p. 10, multicoloured 5 5

431 Gen. Narino's House

432 Congo Dance

(Des I. Mosdossy)

1972 (17 June). *400th Anniversary of Leyva (town).* P 14 × 13½.
1319 **431** 1 p. 10, multicoloured 5 5

1972 (21 June). *AIR. Barranquilla International Carnival.*
P 13½×14.
1320 **432** 1 p. 30, multicoloured 8 5

$ 1.30 ▬

433 Island Scene (**434**)

(Des I. Mosdossy)

1972 (24 June). *150th Anniversary of Annexation of San Andrés and Providencia Islands. P 13½×14.*
1321 **433** 60 c. multicoloured .. 5 5

1972 (5 Oct). *AIR. No. 1142 surch with T 434, in bistre-brown.*
1322 **360** 1 p. 30 on 1 p. 90, bistre-brn & lt bl 8 5

435 "Pres. Laureano Gomez" (R. Cubillos)   **436** Postal Administration Emblem

1972 (17 Oct). *AIR. President Laureano Gomez Commemoration. P 13½×14.*
1323 **435** 1 p. 30, multicoloured 8 5

(Des C. Alonso)

1972 (15 Nov). *National Postal Administration. P 12½×12.*
1324 **436** 1 p. 10, emerald 5 5

437 Colombian Family   **438** Pres. Guillermo Valencia

(Des C. Alonso)

1972 (23 Nov). *"Social Front for the People" Campaign.*
P 12½×12.
1325 **437** 60 c. yellow-orange 5 5

1972 (28 Nov). *AIR. President Guillermo Valencia Commemoration. P 13½×14.*
1326 **438** 1 p. 30, multicoloured 8 5

439 Benito Juárez   **440** "La Rebeca" Statue

1972 (12 Dec). *AIR. Death Centenary of Benito Juárez (Mexican statesman). P 13½×14.*
1327 **439** 1 p. 50, multicoloured 8 5

(Des C. Alonso)

1972 (19 Dec). *AIR. "La Rebeca" Monument, Centenary Park, Bogotá. P 13½×14.*
1328 **440** 80 c. multicoloured 5 5
1329   1 p. multicoloured 5 5

441 "350" and Arms of Bucaramanga

(Des "Consuegra 72")

1972 (22 Dec). *AIR. 350th Anniversary of Bucaramanga (city). P 14×13½.*
1330 **441** 5 p. multicoloured 20 15

442 University Buildings   **443** League Emblem

(Des I. Mosdossy)

1973 (8 May). *AIR. 350th Anniv of Javeriana University.*
P 14×13½.
1331 **442** 1 p. 30, bistre-brown & lt emerald .. 8 5
1332   1 p. 50, bistre-brown and light blue 8 5

(Des I. Mosdossy)

1973 (10 May). *40th Anniv of Colombian Radio Amateurs League. P 12×12½.*
1333 **443** 60 c. red, new blue and pale blue .. 5 5

PRIVATE AIR COMPANIES

At various times Private Air Companies which carried air mail under Government contracts maintained their own post offices and issued stamps. Until 1932 when the first Government air stamps were issued (apart from the 1919 Barranquilla-Cartagena first flight stamp), these were the only legal franking for air mail correspondence, both internal and international. The stamps only paid the air fee and Government stamps had to be used in addition for the ordinary postage fee.

A. Compania Colombiana de Navegacion Aérea

This Company was under contract only during 1920.

1 Mother and Child

2 Pilot in Flight signalling Biplane

(Litho Curtis Co)

1920 (27 Feb). *Private advertising labels surch "COMPANIA COLOMBIANA DE NAVEGACION AEREA Porte Aéreo: $0,10" as in T* **1**. *Various designs. Multicoloured. No gum. Imperf.*

1	10 c. Type **1**				£300	£200
2	10 c. 'Plane over two clouds				£300	£200
3	10 c. Left wings of biplane..				£300	£200
4	10 c. Pilot in flight signalling biplane (As T **2**)				£300	£200
5	10 c. Lighthouse				£300	£200
6	10 c. Fuselage, tail and right wings of biplane				£400	£250
7	10 c. Condor on cliff				£300	£300
8	10 c. 'Plane on airfield and pilots				£300	£300
9	10 c. Ocean liner				£300	£300

The above were valid for use on one flight between Barranquilla and Cartagena.

(Litho C. Valiente M., Barranquilla)

1920 (20 Mar). *No gum. Imperf.*

10	**2**	10 c. green			25·00 35·00

3 Sea and Mountains

4 Cliffs and Lighthouse

(Litho C. Valiente M., Barranquilla)

1920 (20 Mar). *No gum. Imperf.*

11	**3**	10 c. green						15·00
12	**4**	10 c. green						15·00
13	**3**	10 c. brick-red						25·00
		a. Brown-red ..						15·00
14	**4**	10 c. brick-red						25·00
		a. Brown-red ..						15·00

It is believed that Nos. 11/14a were not used.

Nos. 11/14 were printed in sheets of 72 comprising twelve rows of six, each design being in alternate rows, thus producing vertical *se-tenant* pairs.

Nos. 13a and 14a were from a later printing in sheets of 68 comprising ten rows of six (with designs alternating as before) and in the 11th row there were four of each design arranged alternately and placed sideways to the rest, thus producing *tête-bêche* combinations.

B. SCADTA
(Sociedad Colombo-Alemana de Transportes Aéreos)

This international Company operated under Government contracts from 1920 to January 1941. It had its own stamps until 1932 when regular Government air mail stamps were issued. It issued stamps for Colombia and also for Ecuador as well as a general issue. Consideration will be given to listing these in a future edition.

C. LANSA
(Lineas Aereas Nacionales, S.A.)

This Company had a contract for the carriage of air mail on internal services and issued the following stamps.

1 Wing   **(2)**   **(3)**

(Litho A. Garcia-Bergen, Barranquilla)

1950 (22 June). *AIR. P* 12.

1	**1**	5 c. yellow					12	10
2		10 c. red					15	10
3		15 c. new blue					20	10
4		20 c. green					35	35
5		30 c. dull purple					35	35
6		60 c. brown					1·10	1·10

With background network in colours in brackets

7	**1**	1 p. grey (*buff*)					2·25	2·00
8		2 p. Prussian blue (*green*)					4·50	4·00
9		5 p. dull claret (*dull claret*)					12·00	11·00
1/9		*Set of* 9					20·00	17·00

The 1 p. was also issued without the network.

1950 (18 July–Sept). *Nos. 691, etc, optd with T* **2**, *by Garcia Muñoz, Bogotá.*

10		5 c. yellow					5	5
11		10 c. vermilion					8	5
12		15 c. blue ..					10	5
13		20 c. violet					12	5
14		30 c. green					15	5
15		40 c. grey ..					20	5
16		50 c. claret (Aug)					25	5
17		1 p. slate-purple and sage-green (Sept)					80	25
18		2 p. blue and blue-green					1·25	25
19		3 p. black and rose-carmine					3·50	2·75
20		5 p. turquoise and sepia					5·00	2·75
10/20		*Set of* 11					10·00	6·00

1951 (15 Sept). *As Nos. 696, etc but colours changed, optd with T* **3**, *at bottom right.*

21		40 c. yellow-orange					20	5
22		50 c. ultramarine ..					25	8
23		60 c. grey ..					30	5
24		80 c. carmine-rose					40	8
25		1 p. brown-red and orange-red ..					75	30
26		2 p. blue and carmine					1·50	35
27		3 p. emerald and chocolate					2·50	1·25
28		5 p. grey and orange-yellow					7·00	6·00
21/28		*Set of* 8					12·00	7·00

D. AVIANCA

(Aerovias Nacionales de Colombia, S.A.)

This Company, an affiliate of Pan American Airways, took over the contract held by SCADTA in January 1941, and issued its own stamps in 1950–53.

(1)

(2)

1950 (12 July). *Nos. 691/703 optd with T* **1**, *by Garcia Muñoz, Bogotá.*

1	5 c. yellow	5	5
2	10 c. vermilion	8	5
3	15 c. blue	10	5
4	20 c. violet	12	5
5	30 c. green	15	5
6	40 c. grey	20	5
7	50 c. claret	25	5
8	60 c. grey-olive	30	5
9	80 c. brown	40	8
10	1 p. slate-purple and sage-green	80	5
11	2 p. blue and blue-green	1·10	12
12	3 p. black and rose-carmine	2·00	65
13	5 p. turquoise and sepia	3·75	1·50
1/13	*Set of* 13	8·50	2·50

1951 (1 Oct)–**53.** *As Nos. 696, etc but colours changed, optd with T* **2**, *at bottom right.*

14	40 c. yellow-orange	20	5
15	50 c. ultramarine	30	5
16	60 c. grey	35	5
	a. Opt in centre	25	5
17	80 c. carmine-rose	50	8
18	1 p. brown-red and orange-red	1·00	8
19	1 p. violet-brown and olive-green (1953)	70	15
20	2 p. blue and carmine	1·50	20
21	3 p. emerald and chocolate	2·50	55
22	5 p. grey and orange-yellow	5·00	70
14/22	*Set of* 9	11·00	1·75

All values except the 2 p. and 3 p. exist without the overprint.

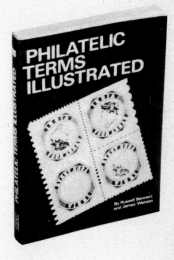

COLOMBIAN STATES

(From 1886, constituted as Departments)
100 Centavos=1 Peso

The 1832 constitution of the Republic of New Granada divided the country into eighteen provinces, each with control of its local affairs. Until communications improved, this was inevitable in a land divided by mountains and jungle. In 1858 the provinces were reorganised as the nine states of Antioquia, Bolivar, Boyacá, Cauca, Cundinamarca, Magdalena, Panama, Santander and Tolima.

With the encouragement of the federal government many of them set up their own postal services and, from 1865 onwards, issued their own stamps. In 1886 the power of the states was much reduced and they became departments of the newly constituted Republic of Colombia. By 1900 the departmental posts had been largely taken over by the national government, and the stamps were ordered to be withdrawn by decrees, the last of these being dated 28 July 1906.

7

8

9

10   11   12

ANTIOQUIA

1

2

3

4

1868. *Litho. Imperf.*

1	1	2½ c. blue			£150	£100
2	2	5 c. green			£130	80·00
3	3	10 c. lilac			£400	£150
4	4	1 p. red			£100	65·00

Used prices are for fine copies with pen cancellation.

The 2½ c., 10 c., and 1 peso were reprinted in 1879 upon white to bluish paper, and at the same time a bogus variety of the 5 c. was made by altering the value on the die of the 2½ c. to 5 c. The reprints (except the 10 c.) usually show diagonal lines or cuts across the design, the result of the cancellation of the dies from which the plates were made.

13   14

1873. *Litho. Imperf.*

11	7	1 c. yellow-green			1·00	80
		a. Green			1·00	80
12	8	5 c. green			1·40	1·10
13	9	10 c. mauve			6·00	4·50
14	10	20 c. yellow-brown			1·40	1·40
		a. Deep brown			1·40	1·40
15	11	50 c. blue			45	45
16	12	1 p. red			50	50
17	13	2 p. black/*yellow*			1·10	1·10
18	14	5 p. black/*rose*			9·00	7·00

5

6

A

B

In Type B the figures "5" in corners are shaded instead of solid and the stars above the Eagle are smaller.

(Litho Ayala, Bogotá)

1869–71. *T 5 (and similar types) and T 6 (1 p.). Imperf.*

5		2½ c. blue			80	55
6		5 c. deep green (A)			1·00	1·00
7		5 c. blue-green (B)			1·10	1·10
8		10 c. lilac			1·40	60
9		20 c. brown			1·10	60
10		1 p. carmine			2·40	2·25
		a. Vermilion			4·50	4·25

Reprints of Nos. 7, 8 and 10 were made in 1879 on *bluish* paper, the 1 p. being in dull rose and in carmine-rose. The 2½ c., 10 c. and 1 p. were reprinted in 1887 (?) on *white* paper, the 1 p. being in bright vermilion.

The 10 c. exists in blue from a new plate made from a defaced die, but this is believed to be a reprint.

17 White figures   18 Coloured figures   19 J. Berrfo

1875–77. *Litho. Imperf.*

(a) Wove paper

19	15	1 c. black/*emerald (glazed paper)*			60	55
20		1 c. black/*green* (1876)			30	30
21		1 c. black (1877)			30	30
22	16	2½ c. deep blue			60	60
23	17	5 c. green			4·50	3·00
24	18	5 c. green			4·50	3·00
25	19	10 c. mauve			6·00	3·00

(b) Laid paper

26	15	1 c. black			35·00	25·00
27	17	5 c. green			25·00	10·00
28	18	5 c. green			25·00	12·00
29	19	10 c. mauve			35·00	30·00

See also Nos. 43/4 and 52.

20 Condor	**21** Liberty	**22** Arms

28

1879. *Thin (pelure) wove paper. Litho. Imperf.*

30	20	2½ c. blue	..	..	55	55
31	21	5 c. green	..	..	6·00	3·00
32	22	10 c. violet	..	..	£125	90·00

23	**24**
	Liberty

1882–83. *Colours changed and new designs. Litho. Imperf.*

(a) Laid paper (1882–83)

33	20	2½ c. green (1883)	..	..	15·00	10·00
34	21	5 c. green	..	..	6·00	80
35		5 c. purple	..	..	85·00	60·00
36	23	10 c. violet	..	..	35·00	6·00
37	24	20 c. brown	..	..	50	50

(b) Wove paper (1883)

38	20	2½ c. grey-green	..	..	55	50
39	21	5 c. deep green	..	..	40	40
		a. Yellow-green	..	..	80	45
40		5 c. violet	..	..	80	50
		a. Bluish violet	..	..	1·25	1·25
41	23	10 c. vermilion	..	..	50	50
		a. Tête-bêche (pair)	..	..	12·00	12·00
42	24	20 c. brown	..	..	50	45

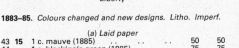

25	**26**	**27**
	Liberty	

1883–85. *Colours changed and new designs. Litho. Imperf.*

(a) Laid paper

43	15	1 c. mauve (1885)	..	..	50	50
44		1 c. black/pale green (1885)	..	..	75	75
45	20	2½ c. black/buff (1885)	..	..	1·25	1·25
46	25	5 c. brown	..	..	35·00	18·00
47		5 c. yellow (1885)	..	..	65	65
48		5 c. green (1885)	..	..	15·00	10·00
49	26	10 c. blue-green	..	..	60	55
50		10 c. mauve (1885)	..	..	1·25	1·25
51	27	20 c. blue (1885)	..	..	55	55

(b) Wove paper

52	15	1 c. blue-green (1885)	..	..	50	50
53	25	5 c. brown	..	..	85	55
54		5 c. green (1885)	..	..	15·00	9·00
55	26	10 c. blue/azure (1885)	..	..	75	70
56		10 c. mauve (1885)	..	..	15·00	9·00

1886. *Wove paper. Litho. Imperf.*

57	28	1 c. green/flesh	..	..	15	15
58		2½ c. black/orange	..	..	12	12
		a. Centre erased (block of 9)	..	12·00	
59		5 c. blue/buff	..	..	45	25
		a. Ultramarine/buff	..	..	70	30
60		10 c. rose-carmine/buff	..	..	30	20
		a. 50 c. rose-carm (in sheet of 10 c.)	20·00	20·00
		b. Centre erased (block of 9)	..	18·00	
61		20 c. purple/buff	..	..	35	20
62		50 c. ochre/buff	..	..	55	55
63		1 p. yellow/bluish green	..	..	60	60
64		2 p. green/deep lilac	..	..	60	60

1888. *Colours changed. Litho. Imperf.*

65	28	1 c. red/deep lilac	..	..	8	8
66		2½ c. mauve/flesh	..	..	15	12
67		5 c. red/green	..	..	60	50
68		5 c. lake/buff	..	..	20	20
69		10 c. deep brown/green	..	..	20	20

29	**30**

31	**32**

1888–89. *Medellin issue. Type-set. Imperf.*

70	29	2½ c. black/yellow	..	..	5·00	4·50
71	30	2½ c. red (1889)	..	..	1·25	1·25
72	31	5 c. black/yellow	..	..	80	80
73	32	5 c. red/orange	..	..	55	55

There are two types of No. 70 and six of No. 72 which are printed in the same sheet, the two types of No. 70 forming the last row. There are ten types each of Nos. 71 and 73.

33	**34**	**35**

1889–90. *Inscr "REPUBLICA DE COLOMBIA." T 33 (1 c. to 5 c.), 34 and similar types. Litho. P 13½.*

74		1 c. black/rose	..	..	5	5
75		2½ c. black/pale blue	..	..	5	5
76		5 c. black/yellow	..	..	10	8
77		10 c. black/green	..	..	15	20
78		20 c. blue (1890)	..	..	35	30
79		50 c. brown-violet (1890)	..	..	85	95
		a. 20 c. brown-violet (in sheet of 50 c.)	25·00	
80		50 c. green (1890)	..	..	55	55
81		1 p. vermilion (1890)	..	..	45	45

82	2 p. black/*magenta* (1890)		..	..	4·00	3·00
83	5 p. black/*vermilion* (1890)			..	5·00	4·50

The 1 c. to 10 c. exist printed on different coloured papers but these are believed to be proofs. The 1 c. to 10 c., 2 p. and 5 p. exist imperforate in the issued colours but it is not known if these were issued.

See also No. 95.

1890. T **85** *and similar types. Type-set. Perf irregularly about* 14.

84	2½ c. black/*buff*	..	..	..	20	20
85	5 c. black/*yellow*..			..	20	20
86	10 c. black/*buff*	..	..	..	1·25	1·25
87	10 c. black/*rose*		..	..	1·00	1·00
88	20 c. black/*yellow*..		..	..	1·00	1·00

There are ten types of each of the above. There are two settings of the 5 c.

36

37

1892–93. *Litho.* P 13½.

89	**36**	1 c. cinnamon/*buff*	..	..	15	10
90		1 c. blue (1893)	..	..	5	5
91		2½ c. violet/*lilac*	..	..	12	8
92		2½ c. green (1893)	..	..	12	8
93		5 c. black	..	..	25	15
		a. 2½ c. black (in sheet of 5 c.)		..	50·00	
94		5 c. red (1893)..	..	..	5	5
95	**34**	10 c. grey-brown (1893)	..	..	5	5

(Litho American Bank Note Co, N.Y.)

1896. *Values in the middle.* P 14.

96	**37**	2 c. grey	..	..	10	10
		a. Error. Lilac	..	..	30·00	
97		2½ c. Venetian red	..	..	10	10
98		3 c. red	..	..	12	12
99		5 c. green	..	..	5	5
100		10 c. lilac	..	..	20	20
101		20 c. yellow-brown	..	..	25	25
102		50 c. sepia	..	..	35	35
103		1 p. black and ultramarine	..	..	4·00	4·00
104		2 p. black and orange	..	..	10·00	10·00
105		5 p. black and mauve	..	..	12·00	12·00

R 1

(Litho American Bank Note Co)

1896. *REGISTRATION.* P 14.

R106	R **1**	2½ c. pink	..	..	20	20

1896. *Colours changed.*

107	**37**	2 c. claret	..	..	8	10
108		2½ c. blue	..	..	8	10
109		3 c. olive-green	..	..	8	10
110		5 c. dull yellow	..	..	5	8
111		10 c. purple-brown	..	..	20	20
112		20 c. bright blue	..	..	35	35
113		50 c. rose	..	..	50	50
114		1 p. black and rose	..	..	4·00	4·00
115		2 p. black and myrtle-green	..	..	10·00	10·00
116		5 p. black and violet	..	..	12·00	12·00

Nos. 105 and 116 are known with centres omitted but these are considered to be proofs.

1896. *REGISTRATION. Colour changed.*

R117	R **1**	2½ c. blue	..	..	20	20

39   L 1

General Cordova

1899. *Litho.* P 11.

118	**39**	½ c. slate-blue		..	5	5
		a. Imperf between (pair)	..	..	20	
119		1 c. slate-blue		..	5	5
		a. Imperf between (pair)	..	..	60	
120		2 c. grey-black	..	..	5	5
121		3 c. red	..	..	5	8
122		4 c. sepia	..	..	5	5
123		5 c. green	..	..	5	5
124		10 c. red	..	..	5	5
125		20 c. slate-purple	..	..	5	5
126		50 c. ochre	..	..	5	5
127		1 p. greenish black	..	..	5	8
128		2 p. bronze-green	..	..	5	12
118/128		*Set of* 11	..	..	45	60

Many reprints of this issue are in circulation.

1899. *LATE FEE. Litho.* P 11.

L129	L **1**	2½ c. bluish green	..		5	5

R 2 General Cordova

1899. *REGISTRATION. Litho.* P 11.

R130	R **2**	2½ c. slate-blue	..	..	5	5
R131	R **3**	10 c. dull purple	..	..	5	5

40   41   L 2

1901. *Type-set in blocks of four varieties.* P 12.

132	**40**	1 c. carmine	..	..	8	12
133	**41**	1 c. stone	..	..	20	20
134		1 c. blue	..	..	20	20
135	–	1 c. red	..	..	35	35
136	–	1 c. blue	..	..	3·00	2·00

Nos. 135/6 are as Type **41**, but have the word "CENTAVO" inside the inner rectangle before the figure "1".

1901–02. *LATE FEE. Type-set in blocks of four varieties. Laid paper.* P 12.

L137	L **2**	2½ c. purple ..	..	..	45	50
		a. Wove paper (1.02)	..	..	20	20

Four new types were used in the setting for No. L137a.

42   43   44 Girardot

45 Girardot.
(Head
smaller)

46 Dr. J. Felix de
Restrepo

L 3

(Litho J. L. Arango, Medellin)

1902–03. *P* 12.

(a) Wove paper

138	42	1 c. rose	..	..	5	5
		a. Imperf (pair)	..	..	1·00	
139		1 c. blue (1903)	..	..	5	5
140		2 c. blue	..	..	5	5
		a. 3 c. blue (in sheet of 2 c.)	..	1·50	1·50	
141		2 c. dull violet (1903)	..	..	5	5
142		3 c. green	..	..	5	5
		a. Imperf (pair)	..	..	1·00	
143		4 c. slate-purple	..	..	5	5
144	43	5 c. rose-red	..	..	5	5
		a. Thin bluish paper	..	..	5	5
145	44	10 c. mauve	..	..	5	5
146	45	10 c. mauve	..	..	1·50	1·50
147	44	20 c. green	..	..	8	10
148		30 c. rose	..	..	8	5
149		40 c. blue	..	..	8	5
150		50 c. brown/*yellow*	..	..	10	10

(b) Laid paper

151	42	1 c. rose	..	..	25	30
152	46	1 p. black and violet	..	..	25	30
153		2 p. black and rose	..	..	25	30
154		5 p. black and grey-blue	..	..	30	35

(Litho J. L. Arango, Medellin)

1902. *LATE FEE. P* 12.

L155	L 3	2½ c. lilac	..	..	5	5

R 4

AR 1

(Litho J. L. Arango, Medellin)

1902. *REGISTRATION. P* 12.

R156	R 4	10 c. violet/*greenish*	..	..	8	8

(Litho J. L. Arango, Medellin)

1902–03. *ACKNOWLEDGMENT OF RECEIPT. P* 12.

AR157	AR 1	5 c. black/*rose*	..	..	25	15
AR158		5 c. slate-green (1903)	..	..	8	8

47

48

49 Zea

(Litho J. L. Arango, Medellin)

1903–04. *T* **47/9** *and portraits as T* **49.** *P* 12.

159	47	4 c. pale brown	..	..	..	5	5
160		5 c. blue	..	..	..	5	5
161	48	10 c. yellow	..	..	..	5	5
162		20 c. lilac	..	..	..	5	8
163		30 c. brown	..	..	..	20	25
164		40 c. green	..	..	..	20	25
165		50 c. rose	..	..	..	8	10
166	49	1 p. olive-grey	..	..	..	20	12
167	–	2 p. bright mauve (G. Rovira)	..	20	12		
168	–	3 p. deep blue (La Pola)	..	25	25		
169	–	4 p. dull red (J. M. Restrepo)	..	40	25		
170	–	5 p. purple-brown (F. Madrid)	..	40	30		
171	–	10 p. carmine (J. del Corral)	..	1·50	1·50		
159/171		*Set of 13*	..	..	..	3·25	3·00

Local Issues

Stamps in this design were issued without authority for a private post in Manizales in 1909.

Stamps in the above types were issued in Medellin between 1903 and 1913 but without authority.

BOLIVAR

1

2

3

4

5

1863–66. *Seal of Colombia.* 10 *c. have* 6 *stars below the arms. Litho. Imperf.*

1	1	10 c. green	..	..	..	£200	£150
		a. 5 stars under arms	..				
2		10 c. rose (1866)	..	..	..	9·00	9·00
		a. 5 stars under arms	..				
3		1 p. red	..	..	..	3·00	3·00

There are fourteen varieties of each.
These are generally considered to be the smallest stamps issued.

1872. *Litho. Imperf.*

4	2	5 c. blue..	..	..	75	90
5	3	10 c. mauve	..	..	1·00	1·00
6	4	20 c. green	..	..	6·50	6·50
7	5	80 c. vermilion	..	..	17·00	15·00

6	7	8

1874–78. *Litho. Imperf.*

8	6	5 c. blue	..	..	5·00	1·50
9	7	5 c. blue (1878)..	..	..	2·50	1·50
10	8	10 c. mauve (1877)	..	..	35	35

9	10	11
	Simon Bolivar	

IMPERF. Many of the stamps of 1879–82 exist imperforate and also in pairs, imperforate between.

1879. *T 9 (portraits in various frames, dated "1879"). Litho. P 12½. (a) Wove paper.*

11	5 c. blue ..	..	..	10	10
12	10 c. mauve	..	..	10	10
13	20 c. red	..	..	12	10
	a. Error of colour. Green	..	5·00	5·00	

(b) Blue laid paper

14	5 c. blue ..	..	..	8	8
15	10 c. mauve	..	..	65	65
16	20 c. red	..	..	10	10

The 80 c. and 1 p. on wove paper and the 1 p. on blue laid paper were prepared but not issued.

1879. *REGISTRATION. As T 9 but additionally inscr "CERTIFICADA" and dated "1879". Litho. P 12½. (a) Wove paper.*

R17	40 c. brown	..	..	30	30

(b) Blue laid paper

R18	40 c. brown	..	..	25	25

1880. *As 1879 issue but dated "1880". (a) Wove paper.*

19	5 c. blue ..	..	..	10	10
20	10 c. mauve	..	..	12	12
21	20 c. red	..	..	12	12
	a. Error of colour. Green	..	5·00	5·00	
22	80 c. green	..	..	60	60
23	1 p. orange	..	..	75	75

(b) Blue laid paper

24	5 c. blue ..	..	..	10	10
25	10 c. mauve	..	..	75	75
26	20 c. red	..	..	12	15
27	1 p. orange	..	..	£150	

1880. *REGISTRATION. As 1879 issue but dated "1880". (a) Wove paper.*

R28	40 c. brown	..	..	15	20

(b) Blue laid paper

R29	40 c. brown	..	..	25	25

1882. *Recess. P 12.*

30	10	5 p. carmine and blue	..	50	50
		a. Perf 16	..	2·10	1·40
		b. Perf 14	..	3·50	
31		10 p. blue and maroon..	..	50	50
		a. Perf 16	..	1·75	1·00
		b. Rouletted..	..		

(Litho Manhattan Bank Note Co, N.Y.)

1882–85. *T 11 (portraits in various frames).*

A. P 12.   B. P 16×12
(a) Dated "1882" (1882)

					A		B	
32	5 c. ultramarine..	..	1·00	1·10	8	10
33	10 c. mauve	..	10	10	10	10
34	20 c. carmine	..	15	20	12	15
35	80 c. green	..	25	25	30	35
36	1 p. orange	..	30	35	30	35

(b) Dated "1883" (1883)

37	5 c. ultramarine..	..	1·25	55	10	10
38	10 c. mauve	..	15	20	10	12
39	20 c. carmine	..	25	25	10	12
40	80 c. green	..	25	35	20	25
41	1 p. orange	..	25	35	1·00	1·00

(c) Dated "1884" (1884)

42	5 c. ultramarine..	..	4·00	—	20	20
43	10 c. mauve	..	10	12	8	8
44	20 c. carmine	..	2·00	1·75	8	8
45	80 c. green	..	1·10	1·60	10	12
46	1 p. orange	..	30	35	20	25

(d) Dated "1885" (1885)

47	5 c. ultramarine..	..	15	15	5	5
48	10 c. mauve	..	10	10	5	5
49	20 c. carmine	..	15	20	5	5
50	80 c. green	..	25	25	10	12
51	1 p. orange	..	25	25	15	20

1882–85. *REGISTRATION. As T 11 but additionally inscr "CERTIFICADA". Dated as shown.*

A. P 12   B. P 16×12

R52	40 c. brown ("1882")	..	9·00	—	12	15
R53	40 c. brown ("1883")	..	—	5·00	15	15
R54	40 c. brown ("1884")	..	—	4·50	8	8
R55	40 c. brown ("1885")	..	—	—	12	15

12

(Litho Manhattan Bank Note Co, N.Y.)

1891. *Litho. P 14.*

56	12	1 c. black	..	..	8	8
		a. On buff	..	..	8	8
57		5 c. orange	..	..	15	10
58		10 c. red	..	..	20	20
59		20 c. blue	..	..	25	25
60		50 c. green	..	..	35	35
61		1 p. violet	..	..	35	35
56/61		Set of 6	..	..	1·25	1·25

1901. *Cartagena provisional. No. 56 optd with parallel wavy lines, in mauve.*

62	12	1 c. black	..	..	20·00	20·00

13 Bolivar	14 Fernandez Madrid	15 Rodriguez Torices

16 Garcia de
Toledo

R 1

17 J. M. del
Castillo

18 Manuel Anguiano

19 Pantaleon G.
Ribon

(Litho F. Francisco Valiente F., Barranquilla)

1903. *Laid paper.* A. *Imperf.* B. *P* 12.

				A	B		
63	13	50 c. green/*rose*	..	30	30	60	60
64		50 c. blue/*rose*	..	20	20	60	60
		a. Printed both sides		1·10	1·25	†	
		b. On *bluish*	..	20	20	30	30
		ba. Printed both sides		1·25	1·25	†	
65		50 c. violet/*green*	..	60	70	50	50
66		50 c. purple	..	60	70	70	70
67	14	1 p. verm/*pale red*	..	35	35	50	50
		a. Orange/*greenish*		4·25	4·25	6·00	6·00
68		1 p. green/*lavender*	..	50	55	75	75
		a. On *yellow*	..	2·25	2·25	1·50	1·50
69	15	5 p. carmine/*lavender*		25	25	75	75
		a. On *brown*		25	30	75	75
		b. On *yellow*		35	35	65	65
		c. On *greenish*	..	1·25	1·25	†	
		d. On *crimson*	..	3·25	3·25	†	
70	16	10 p. blue	..	40	40	†	
		a. On *lavender*	..	3·75	3·75	†	
		b. On *pale blue*	..	30	35	†	
		c. On *salmon*	..	2·00	2·00	†	
		d. On *greenish*	..	40	40	1·40	1·40
		e. On *yellow*	..		†	3·25	3·25
71		10 p. violet/*greenish*	..	2·00	2·00	1·75	1·75
		a. On *rose*	..	2·00	2·00	†	
		b. On *brown*	..	2·00	2·00	†	
		c. On *bluish*	..	2·00	2·00	2·50	2·50
		d. On *yellow*	..		†	3·75	3·75
		e. On *crimson*	..		†	2·75	2·75

Stamps of the above issue, as also of the Registration, Late Fee and Acknowledgment of Receipts stamps were put on the market in many other colours in 1907, but they are of doubtful origin.

The sheets of the above issue were made up very irregularly, with stamps sideways, etc. and sometimes with the printer's name "VALIENTE" between two stamps.

(Litho F. Francisco Valiente F., Barranquilla)

1903. *REGISTRATION. Laid paper.* A. *Imperf.* B. *P* 12.

				A	B		
R72	R 1	20 c. orange/*rose*	.	25	25	†	
		a. On *salmon*	..	30	30	†	
		b. On *greenish blue*	..	1·50	1·50	1·25	1·25

L 1

AR 1

(Litho F. Francisco Valiente F., Barranquilla)

1903. *LATE FEE. Laid paper.* A. *Imperf.* B. *P* 12.

				A	B		
L73	L 1	20 c. carm-rose/*bluish*		20	20	20	20
L74		20 c. violet/*bluish*		20	20	25	25
		a. On *rose*	..	55	55	55	55
		b. On *brown*	..	55	55	†	

(Litho F. Francisco Valiente F., Barranquilla)

1903. *ACKNOWLEDGMENT OF RECEIPT. Laid paper.*
A. *Imperf.* B. *P* 12

				A	B		
AR75	AR 1	20 c. orange/*yell*		45	45	2·75	2·75
		a. On *greenish*		1·40	1·40	2·25	2·25
		b. On *rose*	..	60	60	†	
AR76		20 c. blue/*yellow*		35	35	2·25	2·25

1904. *Litho.* A. *Pin-perf.* B. *Imperf.*

					A		B	
77	17	5 c. black	..	..	8	8	35	40
78	18	10 c. brown	..	..	8	8	20	20
79	19	20 c. scarlet	..	..	12	12	40	40
80		20 c. red-brown	..	..	25	25	†	

20

21

22

R 2

1904. *Gold value currency. Litho. Imperf.*

81	20	½ c. black	..	..	..	20	15
		a. Tête-bêche (pair)	..	..	1·10	1·10
82	21	1 c. blue	..	..	..	35	30
83	22	2 c. violet	..	..	..	50	45

1904. *REGISTRATION. Litho. Imperf.*

R84	R 2	5 c. black	..	..	..	1·25	1·25

AR 2

1904. *ACKNOWLEDGMENT OF RECEIPT. Litho. Imperf.*

AR85	AR 2	2 c. vermilion	..	..	..	25	25

BOYACÁ

1 Mendoza Perez

1899–1902. *Litho.* *P* 13½. (*a*) *White wove paper.*

1	1	5 c. blue-green	.. .. ..	..	30	30
		a. Imperf (pair)	..	..	5·00	5·00
		b. Laid paper	..	..	30·00	30·00

(*b*) *Bluish paper* (1902)

2	1	5 c. blue-green/*bluish*	..	..	30·00	30·00

2	3	4 General Pinzon

5	6 Battle of Boyacá Monument	7 President Marroquin

(Des J. E. Lenher. Litho R. Ronderos, Bogotá)

1903. A. *Imperf.* B. *P* 12.

				A		B	
3	2	10 c. grey-black..	..	8	8	10	10
		a. Bluish grey	..	30	25	20	20
4		10 c. blue	..	†	40	40
5	3	20 c. brown	..	12	12	20	20
		a. Maroon	..	15	15	20	25
6	4	50 c. green	..	†	12	12
7		50 c. dull blue	..	†	60	65
8	5	1 p. vermilion	..	1·10	75	15	12
9		1 p. claret	..	1·25	1·25	1·00	1·00
10	6	5 p. black/*rose*..	..	30	20	30	20
		a. Error. On *buff*	5·00	5·00	†
		b. "5" omitted	..	†	1·50	1·50
11	7	10 p. black/*buff* ..	..	30	30	30	25
		a. Tête-bêche (pair)	4·50	4·50	3·25	3·50
		b. Error. On *rose*	6·00	6·00	†
		ba. Tête-bêche (pair) ..	15·00	15·00	†

8

1904. *Litho.* (*a*) *P* 12.

12	8	10 c. yellow-orange	..	..	..	12	10

(*b*) *Imperf*

13	8	10 c. yellow-orange	..	..	50	50

CAUCA

1	2	3

1879. *Issue for Chocó. Handstamped. Imperf.*

1	1	(5 c.) Black	..	..	..	£500

1902. *Type-set. Imperf.*

2	2	10 c. black/*red*	..	..	..	40	45
		a. Pin-perf	..	..	..	45	45
3		20 c. black/*orange*	..	..	30	35
		a. Pin-perf	..	..	..	35	35

Various stamps as Type **3** and another 5 c. stamp inscribed "PROVISIONAL P. de A." were not authorised by the national government.

Barbacaos, Cali and Tumaco

We do not list the various postmasters' provisionals as they were not authorised by the national government.

The Tumaco stamps inscribed "GOBIERNO PROVISIONAL" issued in 1902 are listed under the Civil War Provisional issues as Nos. 191*p/q* of Colombia.

CUNDINAMARCA

PRICES. The prices in the used column for all issues up to 1885 inclusive are for pen-cancelled copies.

1	2

1870. *Litho. Imperf.*

1	1	5 c. pale blue	..	..	..	1·00	1·00
2	2	10 c. scarlet	..	..	..	5·00	5·00

These stamps have been reprinted. The reprints show traces of the diagonal lines or cuts made across the die at the time it was cancelled. The lines may be traced crossing the figure in the right upper corner, and across the "C" of "CINCO," etc.

3	4	5

1877–82. *Imperf.*

(*a*) *Laid paper* (1877)

3	3	10 c. salmon	..	..	..	1·00	1·00
		a. Thick paper. *Rose*	..	..	3·75
4	4	20 c. green	..	..	..	3·50	3·50

(*b*) *Wove paper* (1882)

5	3	10 c. red	..	..	..	70	70
6	4	20 c. green	..	..	..	1·75	1·75
7	5	50 c. mauve	..	..	..	2·25	2·25
8	–	1 p. deep brown..	..	..	3·50	3·50
		a. Chestnut	..	..	..	3·00	3·00

The 1 p. is similar to the 50 c.

6	7

Colombia CUNDINAMARCA

8   **9**

1883. *Type-set. Imperf.*
9	6	10 c. black/*yellow*	..	..	5·00	5·00
10	7	50 c. black/*magenta*	..	..	4·00	4·00
		a. Black/*rose* ..	..	..	4·00	4·00
11	8	1 p. black/*brown*	..	..	12·00	12·00
12	9	2 r. black/*green*	..	..	£450	

There are four types of the 10 c., and two each of the 50 c. and 1 p. The 10 c. and 2 reales are signed by the postmaster, but it is doubtful if the 2 r. was ever issued, the value not being expressed in the proper currency of the country. A stamp exists similar to T **9**, but without value or signature, "(2 r.), black on *green* wmk flowers" but it is probably a proof.

R 1

1883. *REGISTRATION. Litho. Imperf.*
R13	R **1**	(No value) black/*orange*	..	.. 4·50	4·50

The stamps were signed in *MS.* in the lower left division by a postal official, and a serial number was inserted in the lower right division when the stamps were used.

10   (*a*)   (*b*)

There are two types of this stamp, one (*a*) with a larger ball to the figures "5" than in the other (*b*). In (*a*) there is also a stop after "COLOMBIA" which does not exist in (*b*).

1883–84. *Litho. Imperf.*
14	**10**	5 c. blue (*a*)	..	..	30	40
		a. Tête-bêche (pair)	..	..	10·00	
15		5 c. blue (*b*) (1884)	..	..	60	60
		a. Tête-bêche (pair)	..	..	15·00	

(11)

12

1884. *No. 2 surch with T* **11.**
16	**2**	1 p. on 10 c. scarlet	..	..	— 50·00

1885. *T* **12** (5 *c. and* 50 *c.*) *and similar type. Litho. Imperf.*
17	5 c. blue ..	..	..	..	25	25
18	10 c. vermilion	..	..	..	1·00	1·00
19	10 c. vermilion/*lilac*	..	..	65	65
20	20 c. green	..	..	,1·00	1·00
	a. Yellow-green	..	..	1·10	1·10
21	50 c. mauve	..	..	1·10	1·10
22	1 p. chestnut	..	..	1·40	1·40

The above have all been reprinted. The colours are aniline and differ and the impressions are coarse and blurred.

13   **14**   **15**

(Des J. E. Lenher. Litho R. Ronderos, Bogotá)

1904. *Types in various frames as* **13** (*large numerals:* 1 *c.,* 2 *c.*), (*large numerals and arms:* 3 *c.,* 5 *c.*), *as* **14** (*arms:* 10 *c. to* 50 *c.*) *and* **15.** (*a*) *P* 12.
23	1 c. orange	..	..	12	12
24	2 c. blue ..	..	..	12	12
25	3 c. rose ..	..	..	15	15
26	5 c. grey-green ..	..	..	15	15
27	10 c. pale brown ..	..	..	15	15
28	15 c. pink ..	..	..	20	20
29	20 c. blue/*green* ..	..	..	15	15
30	50 c. rosy mauve ..	..	..	20	20
31	1 p. grey-green ..	..	..	20	20

(*b*) *P* 10½
32	20 c. blue ..	..	..	30	30
	a. Perf comp of 10½ and 11½			30	30
33	40 c. blue ..	..	..	30	30
	a. Perf comp of 10½ and 11½		1·75	1·75

(*c*) *Imperf*
34	1 c. orange	..	..	30	30
35	2 c. blue ..	..	..	30	30
	a. Slate-grey	..	..	1·50	1·50
36	3 c. rose ..	..	..	45	45
37	5 c. grey-green ..	..	..	50	50
38	10 c. pale brown ..	..	..	60	60
39	15 c. pink ..	..	..	20	20
40	20 c. blue ..	..	..	50	50
41	20 c. blue/*green* ..	..	..	75	75
42	40 c. blue ..	..	..	30	30
43	40 c. blue/*buff* ..	..	..	5·50	5·50
44	50 c. rosy mauve ..	..	..	25	25
45	1 p. grey-green ..	..	..	25	25

R 2

1904. *REGISTRATION. Litho.*
R46	R **2**	10 c. brown (*perf* 12)	..	..	35	35
R47		10 c. brown (*imperf*)..	..	..	1·25	1·25

MAGDALENA

Stamps in the above and a similar design were issued by the Postmaster of Rio Hacha but without the authority of the national government.

PANAMA

The list of stamps issued by the Colombian state and Department of Panama will be found, for convenience, before the issues of the Republic of Panama in Vol. 3.

SANTANDER

1   **2**

1884. *Inscr* "ESTADOS UNIDOS DE COLOMBIA." *Litho. Imperf.*

1	**1**	1 c. blue ..	..	..	..	10	10
		a. Ultramarine ..	..	..	..	60	60
2		5 c. vermilion	..	..	..	20	20
3		10 c. violet	..	..	..	40	40
		a. Bright mauve	..	..	..	40	40
		b. Tête-bêche (pair)	..	..			

The 5 c. exists perf 14 but this was unofficial.

1886. *T* **2** *and similar types. Litho. Imperf.*

4		1 c. blue ..	..	..	..	25	25
		a. Ultramarine ..	..	..	10·00	10·00
5		5 c. red ..	..	..	..	8	8
		a. Turned sideways (block of 3)	..	2·00	
6		10 c. indigo-lilac	..	..	..	15	15
		a. Turned sideways (block of 3)	..	2·00	
		b. "CINCO" for "DIEZ" ..	..	6·00	6·00

In the 1 c. there are numerals also in the upper corners and the 10 c. has numerals only in the upper corners.
The 10 c. exists perf 12 but this was unofficial.

1887. *As T* **1** *but inscr* "REPUBLICA DE COLOMBIA". *Litho. Imperf.*

7		1 c. blue ..	..	..	..	8	8
		a. Ultramarine ..	..	..	..	40	40
8		5 c. vermilion	..	..	..	35	35
9		10 c. violet ..	..	..	..	1·00	1·00

3   **4**   **5**

1889. *Litho. Thin paper. (a) P* 13½.

10	**3**	1 c. blue	..	..	..	8	8
		a. Imperf between (horiz pair)	..	50	
11	**4**	5 c. vermilion ..	..	..	40	40
12	**5**	10 c. violet ..	..	..	..	20	20
		a. Imperf (pair)	..	..			

(b) P 11½

13	**3**	1 c. grey-blue ..	..	..	2·10	2·10

6   **7**

1892. *Litho. P* 13½.

14	**6**	5 c. red/buff	..	..	..	20	15

1895–96. *Litho. P* 13½.

15	**7**	5 c. chocolate ..	..	..	25	25
16		5 c. yellow-green (1896)..	..	25	25
		a. Perf 12	..	..	..	2·75	1·50

8   **9**   **10**

1899. *Litho. P* 10 (1 c., 5 c.) *or* 13½ (10 c.).

17	**8**	1 c. black/green	..	..	..	15	15
18	**9**	5 c. black/rose	..	..	..	15	15
19	**10**	10 c. blue	..	..	..	25	25
		a. Perf 12	..					

Provisional.

Correos de Santander.

F 1   **(11)**

1903. *POSTAL FISCAL. Litho. Imperf.*

F20	**F 1**	50 c. red	..	..	..	10	10
		a. Rose	..	..	..	12	12

1903. *Optd with T* **11**.

21	**F 1**	50 c. red	..	..	..	10	10
		a. Rose	..	..	..	12	12
		b. Tête-bêche (pair)	..	..	1·25	1·25
		c. Error "Corceos" ..	..	65	65
		d. Error "Corrcos" ..	..	65	65
		e. Error "Santender"	..	65	65

Stamps as above and other designs in the values of 5, 10, 20 and 50 c. and 1, 5 and 10 p. and also surcharged ½, 1 or 2 c. do not appear to have been authorised by the national government.

Cúcuta

The stamps formerly listed here and inscribed "Gobierno Provisional" are now listed under the Civil War Provisional issues as Nos. 101a/o of Colombia.

Stamps as above and other designs in the values of 1, 2, 5, 10, 20 and 50 c. and 1 p. (each in two colours) and also surcharged ½, 1 or 2 c. do not appear to have been authorised by the national government.

TOLIMA

1

1870. T 1. *Type-set. Ten varieties arranged in 5 horizontal rows of 2. Black impression. Imperf.*

Plate I. Blue paper

1	5 c. horizontally laid	..	..	..	35·00	30·00
2	5 c. vertically laid	..	..	..	20·00	10·00
3	5 c. vertically laid ruled in blue	..	..		
4	5 c. wove				
5	5 c. quadrillé	..	..	..	30·00	25·00

It was formerly thought that Nos. 4, 8 and 10 on the plate were altered to form a reset plate but it is now believed that the alterations are due to the method of printing.

Plate II. Blue paper

6	5 c. wove	..	..	..	15·00	10·00
7	5 c. laid	..	..	..	£150	
8	5 c. quadrillé	..	..	..	30·00	20·00
9	5 c. laid ruled in blue				

All the types on this plate, except No. 7, differ from those on Plate I.

Plate II. Reset
(i) Buff paper

10	5 c. wove	..	..	..	25·00	12·00
11	5 c. laid	..	..			

(ii) White wove paper

12	5 c. plain..	..	..	..	15·00	9·00
13	10 c. plain..	..	..	..	15·00	9·00

The last two rows of Plate II were altered by changing the figure "5" to "10". There are therefore six types of the 5 c. and four of the 10 c.

So-called reprints of these stamps were made in 1886 upon blue and upon white papers, but as the original setting of the types had long before been broken up, these impressions are only official imitations.

2   3

4   5

1871. *Yellowish white wove paper. Litho. Imperf.*

14	2	5 c. deep brown	..	..	..	35	35
		a. Red-brown	..	..	..	35	35
		b. "CINGO" for "CINCO"	..	..	7·00	7·00
15	3	10 c. blue	..	..	..	1·10	1·10
		a. Printed both sides..	..	..		
		b. Laid paper..	..	..	..	—	8·00
16	4	50 c. deep green	..	..	15·00	15·00
17	5	1 p. rose-red	..	..	..	1·75	1·75
						3·25	3·25

The unused 10 c., 50 c. and 1 p. usually found are printed from new plates, made from the original dies after they had been defaced. These stamps can be recognised by the fine lines across the stamp, which are, of course, always *identical*.

Reprints of the 5 c. were also made at the same time, but the die of this value had been so effectually cancelled that it had to be entirely reengraved. These reprints have a much larger star ornament at the top of the stamp.

6   7

8   9   10

1879–80. *Litho. Imperf. White paper.*

18	6	5 c. brown	..	..	..	15	15
		a. On greyish..	..	..	12	12
		b. Purple-brown	..	..	15	15
19	7	10 c. blue	..	..	..	15	15
		a. On greyish..	..	..	15	15
20	8	50 c. green (1880)	..	..	40	40
		a. On greyish..	..	..	15	20
21	9	1 p. vermilion (1880)	..	..	90	90
		a. On greyish..	..	..	50	55
		b. Carmine	..	..		

1883. *Colours changed and new value. Litho. Imperf.*

22	6	5 c. orange	..	..	..	15	15
23	7	10 c. scarlet	..	..	..	20	20
24	10	20 c. violet	..	..	..	30	30

The 5 p. value in yellow or orange-red is believed to be bogus.

11   12   13

14   15
Condor with long wings touching flagstaffs

1884. *Litho. Imperf.*

25	11	1 c. grey	..	..	..	5	5
26		2 c. dull rose	..	..	..	5	5
		a. Error. Slate-blue	..	..	1·50	
27		2½ c. dull orange	..	..	5	5
28		5 c. brown	..	..	..	5	5
		a. Purple-brown	..	..	15	15
29		10 c. blue	..	..	..	25	25
		a. Slate-blue	..	..	10	12
30		20 c. olive-yellow	..	..	15	15
		a. Laid paper	..	..		
31		25 c. black	..	..	..	10	10
32		50 c. blue-green	..	..	15	15
		a. Deep green	..	..	15	15
33		1 p. vermilion	..	..	15	15
34		2 p. violet	..	..	..	30	20
		a. Value omitted	..	..	6·00	
35		5 p. orange	..	..	..	20	20
36		10 p. lilac-rose	..	..	35	35
		a. Laid paper	..	..		
		b. Slate	..	..	..	50·00	

1886. *Litho. P 10½, 11.*

(a) White paper, clear impressions (Jan)

37	12	5 c. brown	..	..	..	30	30
		a. Yellow-brown	..	..	35	35
		b. Imperf (pair)	..	..	3·00	
38	13	10 c. blue	..	..	..	1·25	1·25
		a. Imperf (pair)	..	..	5·00	
39	14	50 c. green	..	..	..	40	40
		a. Imperf (pair)	..	..	5·00	5·00
40	15	1 p. vermilion..	..	..	80	80
		a. Imperf (pair)	..	..	6·00	

(b) Mauve tinted paper, blurred impressions (Apr)

41	12	5 c. red-brown	..	4·00	4·00
42	13	10 c. indigo	..	4·00	4·00
43	14	50 c. green	..	2·50	2·50
44	15	1 p. vermilion..	..	2·00	2·00

The 50 c. has been reprinted in pale grey-green on white paper, perf 10½ and the 1 p. in bright vermilion on white paper, perf 11½. The impressions show signs of wear.

16   **17**
Condor with short wings

1886 (Apr). *Value labels of 10 c. and 1 p. now octagonal. Litho. P 12.*

45	12	1 c. grey	..	2·00	2·00
46		2 c. dull claret	..	2·50	2·50
47	14	2½ c. flesh	..	6·00	8·00
48	12	5 c. brown	..	3·00	3·00
		a. Imperf (pair)	..	9·00	
49	16	10 c. bright blue	..	4·00	4·00
		a. Imperf (pair)	..	9·00	
50		20 c. olive-yellow	..	2·50	2·50
		a. Tête-bêche (pair) ..	..	35·00	
51		25 c. black	..	2·00	2·00
52	14	50 c. green	..	1·00	1·00
		a. Imperf between (horiz pair)	..	4·00	
53	17	1 p. vermilion ..	..	1·60	1·60
		a. Imperf (pair)	..	9·00	
54		2 p. violet	..	3·00	3·00
		a. Tête-bêche (pair) ..	..	35·00	
		b. Imperf (pair)	..	7·00	
		c. Imperf between (horiz pair)	..	9·00	
55		5 p. orange	..	6·00	6·00
		a. Imperf (pair)	..	18·00	
56		10 p. rose	..	2·50	2·50
		a. Imperf (pair)	..	6·00	

The other values probably exist imperforate.

18   **19**
Condor with long wings. Upper Flagstaffs omitted

1888. *Litho on white paper. (a) Imperf.*

57	12	1 c. black	..	50·00

(b) P 12, 12½

58	16	2½ c. dull orange	..	20·00	
		a. Imperf (pair)	..	50·00	
59	18	5 c. brown	..	2·50	2·50
		a. Imperf (pair)	..	6·00	
		b. Error. 10 c. in sheet of 5 c. Imperf		10·00	
60	13	10 c. ultramarine	..	3·50	3·50
		a. Imperf (pair)	..	8·00	
61	19	2 p. red-violet ..	..	3·50	3·50
		a. Imperf (pair)	..	7·00	
		b. Corner numerals omitted. Imperf		10·00	
62		5 p. orange	..	6·00	
		a. Imperf (pair)	..	15·00	

The 1 c., 2½c. and 10 c. are similar to T **12, 16** and **13** but without upper flagstaffs.

20   **21**   **22**

1888. *Litho. P 10½, 11.*

63	20	5 c. vermilion ..	..	..	..	8	8
64		10 c. green	..	..	..	20	20
65		50 c. blue	..	..	..	35	35
66		1 p. brown	..	..	..	60	60

1895–1902. *Litho. (a) P 12.*

67	20	1 c. blue/*rose* ..	..	..		12	12
68		2 c. green/*pale green* ..	..			12	12
69		5 c. vermilion ..	..	..		5	5
70		10 c. green	..	..		15	20
71		20 c. blue/*yellow*	..	..		25	25
72		1 p. brown	..	..		40	40

(b) P 13½

73	20	1 c. blue/*rose* ..	..	..		15	20
74		2 c. green/*pale green* ..	..			15	20
75		5 c. vermilion ..	..	..		8	8
76		20 c. blue/*yellow*	..	..		35	40

(Des J. E. Lenher. Litho R. Ronderos, Bogotá)

1903–04. *T 21, 22 and similar types in various frames.*

(a) Imperf

77		4 c. black/*green* ..	..	..		10	10
78		10 c. dull blue	..	..		8	8
79		20 c. orange	..	..		30	30
80		50 c. black/*rose*	..	..		55	55
		a. On *flesh*	..	..		20	30
81		1 p. brown	..	..		5	5
82		2 p. slate-grey	..	..		5	5
83		5 p. scarlet	..	..		8	8
		a. Tête-bêche (pair)	..		1·50		
84		10 p. black/*pale blue*	..	..	1·25	1·25
		a. Tête-bêche (pair)	..				
		b. On *pale green*	..	..	1·25	1·25
		c. On *green* (glazed paper)	..		4·50	4·50

(b) P 12

85		4 c. black/*green* ..	..	..		8	8
		a. Imperf between (pair)	..	..		25	
86		10 c. dull blue	..	..		8	8
87		20 c. orange	..	..		8	8
88		50 c. black/*rose*	..	..		10	10
		a. On *flesh*	..	..		10	10
89		1 p. brown	..	..		5	5
90		2 p. slate-grey	..	..		5	5
91		5 p. scarlet	..	..		5	5
		a. Tête-bêche (pair)	..		1·50		
92		10 p. black/*pale blue*	..	..		8	8
		a. On *pale green*	..	..		8	8
		b. On *green* (glazed paper)	..		1·40	1·40

```
┌┼┼┼─┼┼─┼┼┼┐
  R DE C
 GARZON 1894
┤NO HAY, Estampillas├
┤ PAGÓ $0.01. ┤
└┼┼┼─┼┼─┼┼┼┘
```

Stamps in the above and similar types were issued by the Postmaster of Garzon but without the authority of the national government.

For stamp surcharged "Habilitada vale $0.01 Honda" see No. 170 of Colombia.

Comoro Islands

100 Centimes = 1 Franc

The Comoro Archipelago consists of the islands of Anjouan, Great Comoro, Mayotte and Mohéli, lying between Madagascar and Mozambique. France took possession of Mayotte as a colony in 1843 and the Sultans of Anjouan, Great Comoro and Mohéli placed themselves under French protection in 1886. In 1891 the protected islands became French colonies, and from 1898 to 1912 they were French dependencies. On 25 July 1912 the islands were again given the status of French colonies, until 23 February 1914 when the whole archipelago was subordinated to the Governor-General of Madagascar. From 1914 to 1950 the stamps of Madagascar were used in the islands.

PRINTERS. All stamps were printed at the Government Printing Works, Paris, *unless otherwise stated.*

IMPERFORATE STAMPS. Stamps exist imperforate in their issued colours but they were not valid for postage. Imperforate stamps in other colours are colour trials.

ANJOUAN

X. "Tablet" Type

1892 (Nov). *Type X inscr "SULTANAT D'ANJOUAN" in red (1, 5, 15, 25, 75 c. and 1 f.) or blue (others). P 14 × 13½.*

1	1 c. black/azure	..	12	12
2	2 c. brown/buff	..	12	12
3	4 c. purple-brown/grey	..	15	15
4	5 c. green/pale green	..	30	25
5	10 c. black/lilac	..	30	25
6	15 c. blue	..	55	30
7	20 c. red/green	..	80	55
8	25 c. black/rose	..	80	55
9	30 c. cinnamon/drab	..	1·75	1·25
10	40 c. red/yellow	..	2·75	1·25
11	50 c. carmine/rose	..	1·75	1·25
12	75 c. brown/orange	..	1·75	1·75
13	1 f. olive-green/toned	..	5·00	4·50
1/13	*Set of 13*	..	14·00	11·00

1900 (Dec)–07. *Type X. Colours changed and new values. Inscr in blue (10 c.) or red (others). P 14 × 13½.*

14	10 c. rose-red	..	1·50	1·25
15	15 c. grey	..	1·00	70
16	25 c. blue	..	1·10	90
17	35 c. black/yellow (7.06)	..	75	50
18	45 c. black/green (10.07)	..	12·00	10·00
19	50 c. brown/azure	..	1·75	1·25
14/19	*Set of 6*	..	16·00	13·00

05 10

(2) (3)

In Type A the space between "0" and "5" is 1½ mm and between "1" and "0" 2½ mm. In Type B the spacing is 2 mm and 3 mm respectively.

1912 (Nov). *Type X surch with T 2 or 3.*

A. *Narrow spacing.* B. *Wide spacing*

			A		B	
20	05 on 2 c. brown/buff	..	5	5	65	65
21	05 on 4 c. purple-brown/grey (R.)	..	5	5	45	45
	a. Pair , one without surch	..	—	—	†	
22	05 on 15 c. blue (R.)	..	5	5	40	40
	a. Pair, one without surch	..	—	—	†	
23	05 on 20 c. red/green	..	5	5	50	50
	a. Pair, one without surch	..	—	—	†	
24	05 on 25 c. black/rose (R.)	..	5	5	65	65
25	05 on 30 c. cinna/drab (R.)	..	5	5	65	65
26	10 on 40 c. red/yellow	..	5	5	4·00	4·00
27	10 on 45 c. black/grn (R.)	..	5	5	4·00	4·00
28	10 on 50 c. carmine	..	20	20	9·00	9·00
29	10 on 75 c. brown/orange	..	12	12	4·00	4·00
30	10 on 1 f. olive-grn/toned	..	12	12	9·00	9·00
	a. Pair, one without surch	..	—	—	†	
20/30	*Set of 11*	..	70	70	30·00	30·00

GREAT COMORO

1897 (Nov). *Type X inscr "GRANDE COMORE", in red (1, 5, 15, 25, 75 c., 1 f.) or blue (others). P 14 × 13½.*

1	1 c. black/azure	..	..	..	5	5
2	2 c. brown/buff	..	..	..	5	5
3	4 c. purple-brown/grey	..	..	..	12	12
4	5 c. green/pale green	..	..	..	12	12
5	10 c. black/lilac	..	..	..	45	30
6	15 c. blue	..	..	..	1·00	40
7	20 c. red/green	..	..	..	1·00	90
8	25 c. black/rose	..	..	..	1·25	80
9	30 c. cinnamon/drab	..	..	..	1·25	90
10	40 c. red/yellow	..	..	..	1·40	1·10
11	50 c. carmine/rose	..	..	..	2·10	1·40
12	75 c. brown/orange	..	..	..	3·25	2·25
13	1 f. olive-green/toned	..	..	..	2·10	1·60
1/13	*Set of 13*	..	..	..	11·00	9·00

1900 (Dec)–07. *Type X. Colours changed. Inscr in blue (10 c) or red (others). P 14 × 13½.*

14	10 c. rose-red	..	..	..	1·10	1·10
15	15 c. grey	..	..	..	40	40
16	25 c. blue	..	..	..	1·00	1·00
17	35 c. black/yellow (7.06)	..	..	..	1·40	1·25
18	45 c. black/green (11.07)	..	..	..	8·00	7·00
19	50 c. brown/azure	..	..	..	3·00	2·50
14/19	*Set of 6*	..	..	..	13·00	11·00

1912 (Nov). *Type X surch as T 2 and 3 of Anjouan.*

A. *Narrow spacing.* B. *Wide spacing*

			A		B	
20	05 on 2 c. brown/buff	..	5	5	30	30
21	05 on 4 c. purple-brown/grey (R.)	..	5	5	30	30
22	05 on 15 c. blue (R.)	..	5	5	40	40
23	05 on 20 c. red/green	..	5	5	85	85
24	05 on 25 c. black/rose (R.)	..	8	8	45	45
25	05 on 30 c. cinna/drab (R.)	..	8	8	45	45
26	10 on 40 c. red/yellow	..	8	8	5·00	5·00
27	10 on 45 c. black/grn (R.)	..	10	10	4·00	4·00
28	10 on 50 c. carmine/rose	..	12	12	4·00	4·00
29	10 on 75 c. brown/orange	..	10	10	9·00	9·00
20/29	*Set of 10*	..	60	60	22·00	22·00

For note *re* spacing see Anjouan.

MAYOTTE

1892 (Nov)**–99.** *Type X inscr "MAYOTTE". Name in red (1, 5, 15, 25, 75 c. and 1 f.) or blue (others). P 14×13½.*
1	1 c. black/*azure* ..	..	..	5	5
2	2 c. brown/*buff* ..	..	..	5	5
	a. Name double	..	..	14·00	14·00
3	4 c. purple-brown/*grey* ..	..	8	8
4	5 c. green/*pale green*	..	..	15	12
5	10 c. black/*lilac* ..	..	..	20	15
6	15 c. blue ..	..	..	90	75
7	20 c. red/*green*	..	..	80	60
8	25 c. black/*rose* ..	..	..	55	45
9	30 c. cinnamon/*drab*	..	..	80	75
10	40 c. red/*yellow* ..	..	..	95	75
11	50 c. carmine/*rose*	..	..	1·00	1·00
12	75 c. brown/*orange*	..	..	1·40	1·00
13	1 f. olive-green/*toned* ..	..	1·00	85
14	5 f. mauve/*pale lilac* (1899)	..	..	9·00	7·00
1/14	*Set of 14*	..	..	15·00	12·00

1900 (Dec)**–07.** *Type X. Colours changed and new values. Name in blue (10 c.) or red (others). P 14×13½.*
15	10 c. rose-red	..	..	3·25	2·50
16	15 c. grey ..	..	..	9·00	8·00
17	25 c. blue ..	..	..	60	40
18	35 c. black/*yellow* (7.06)	..	..	50	30
19	45 c. black/*green* (10.07) ..	..	65	55
20	50 c. brown/*azure*	..	..	1·10	1·00
15/20	*Set of 6*	..	..	13·00	11·00

1912 (Nov). *Type X surch as T 2 and 3 of Anjouan.*
A. *Narrow spacing.* B. *Wide spacing*
		A		B	
21	05 on 2 c. brown/*buff* ..	8	8	80	80
	a. Pair, one without surch	—	—	†	
22	05 on 4 c. purple-brown/*grey* (R.) ..	8	8	55	55
23	05 on 15 c. blue (R.) ..	8	8	55	55
24	05 on 20 c. red/*green* ..	8	8	55	55
25	05 on 25 c. black/*rose* (R.)	10	10	55	55
	a. Surch double ..	10·00	—	£100	
26	05 on 30 c. cinna/*drab* (R.)	10	10	55	55
27	10 on 40 c. red/*yellow* ..	8	8	4·00	4·00
	a. Surch double ..	12·00	—	£120	
28	10 on 45 c. black/*grn* (R.)	5	5	2·40	2·40
	a. Surch double ..	10·00	—	£120	
29	10 on 50 c. carmine	15	15	6·00	6·00
30	10 on 75 c. brown/*orange*	15	15	6·00	6·00
31	10 on 1 f. olive-grn/*toned*	15	15	8·00	8·00
21/31	*Set of 11* ..	90	90	27·00	27·00

For note *re* spacing see Anjouan.

MOHELI

1906–07. *Type X inscr "MOHÉLI" in blue (2, 4, 10, 20, 30, 40 c. and 5 f.) or red (others). P 14×13½.*
1	1 c. black/*azure* ..	..	..	12	10
2	2 c. brown/*buff* ..	..	..	10	8
3	4 c. purple-brown/*grey* ..	..	10	10
4	5 c. yellow-green	..	..	20	15
5	10 c. rose-red	..	..	20	20
6	20 c. red/*green* ..	..	..	60	40
7	25 c. blue ..	..	..	60	30
8	30 c. cinnamon/*drab*	..	..	1·00	75
9	35 c. black/*yellow*..	..	..	35	20
10	40 c. red ..	..	..	1·00	75
11	45 c. black/*green* (1907) ..	..	4·25	3·50
12	50 c. brown/*azure*	..	..	1·00	60
13	75 c. brown/*orange*	..	..	1·50	1·10
14	1 f. olive-green/*toned* ..	..	1·10	85
15	2 f. violet/*rose* ..	..	..	2·75	2·10
16	5 f. mauve/*pale lilac* ..	..	14·00	13·00
1/16	*Set of 16* ..	..	..	26·00	21·00

1912 (Nov). *Type X surch as T 2 and 3 of Anjouan.*
A. *Narrow spacing.* B. *Wide spacing*
		A		B	
17	05 on 4 c. purple-brown/*grey* (R.) ..	..	8	8	85	85
18	05 on 20 c. red/*green* ..	30	30	3·50	3·50
19	05 on 30 c. cinna/*drab* (R.)	12	12	3·00	3·00
20	10 on 40 c. red/*yellow* ..	12	12	8·50	8·50
21	10 on 45 c. black/*grn* (R.)	12	12	4·25	4·25
	a. Name double ..	15·00	—	†	
22	10 on 50 c. brn/*azure* (R.)	15	15	9·00	9·00
17/22	*Set of 6* ..	80	80	26·00	26·00

For note *re* spacing, see Anjouan.

COMORO ISLANDS

(General Issues)

On 9 May 1946 the Comoro Archipelago was given administrative autonomy within the French Republic.

1 Anjouan Bay　　2 Native woman

3 Mosque at Moroni

4 Ouani Mosque, Anjouan (22½×36 *mm*)
5 Coelacanth (36×22½ *mm*)

6 Mutsamudu Village　　D 1 Mosque in Anjouan

7 Natives and Mosque de Vendredi (48×27 *mm*)
8 Ouani Mosque, Anjouan (48×27 *mm*)

(Postage. Des Barlangue (T 1, 4), Mahias (T 2/3). Eng Barlangue (T 1, 4), Dufresne (T 2) and Munier (T 3). Air. Des and eng Gandon (T 5), Pheulpin (T 6) and Serres (T 7/8). Recess)

1950 (15 May)**–54.** *P 13.* (a) *POSTAGE.*
1	1	10 c. blue ..	..	..	5	5
2		50 c. yellowish green	..	..	5	5
3		1 f. brown ..	..	..	5	5
4	2	2 f. emerald-green	..	..	5	5
5		5 f. bright violet	..	..	5	5
6		6 f. plum ..	..	..	5	5
7	3	7 f. scarlet	..	..	5	5
8		10 f. green ..	..	..	5	5
9		11 f. blue ..	..	..	8	8
10	4	15 f. purple-brown (1.12.52)	..	..	8	5
11		20 f. lake-brown (1.12.52)	..	..	12	5
12	5	40 f. indigo & turquoise-blue (20.9.54)	..	35	25

(b) *AIR*
13	6	50 f. lake and green	..	..	35	12
14	7	100 f. chocolate and scarlet	..	..	70	20

15 **8** 200 f. lake-brown, deep blue-green and
    reddish violet (15.1.53) .. .. 1·25   65
1/15 *Set of 15* .. .. 3·00   1·50

(Des Giat. Eng E. Feltesse. Recess)

1950 (15 May). *POSTAGE DUE. P 14×13.*
D16 **D 1** 50 c. bright green 5   5
D17   1 f. brownish black 5   5

1952 (1 Dec). *Centenary of Médaille Militaire. As T **48** of Cameroun.*
16   15 f. blue, yellow and green .. .. 2·25   2·25

1954 (6 June). *AIR. Tenth Anniv of Liberation. As T **50** of Cameroun.*
17   15 f. brown-red and deep brown .. .. 1·75   1·75

D **2** Coelacanth

9 Village Pump

(Des and eng P. Camors. Recess)

1954 (13 Aug). *POSTAGE DUE. P 13.*
D18 **D 2**   5 f. sepia and deep green 5   5
D19   10 f. violet-grey and red-brown .. 5   5
D20   20 f. indigo and light blue 8   5

(Des and eng H. Cheffer. Recess)

1956 (25 Apr). *Economic and Social Development Fund. P 13.*
18 **9** 9 f. bluish violet 10   5

10 "Human Rights"

11 Radio Station, Dzaoudzi

(Des and eng R. Cami. Recess)

1958 (10 Dec). *Tenth Anniv of Declaration of Human Rights. P 13.*
19 **10** 20 f. bronze-green and blue 60   60

1959 (5 Jan). *Tropical Flora. As T **58** of Cameroun.*
20   10 f. red, yellow, green and violet-blue .. 20   15
    Design:—10 f. Colvillea.

(Des P. Chapelet. Eng Combet. Recess)

1960 (23 Dec). *Inauguration of Comoro Broadcasting Service. T **11** and similar design. P 13.*
21   20 f. green, bluish violet & brown-pur .. 15   12
22   25 f. emerald, red-brown & ultramarine .. 20   12
    Design:—25 f. Radio mast and map.

12 Bull Mouth Helmet

13 Marine Plants

(Des R. Chapelet. Photo Hélio-Comoy)

1962 (13 Jan–27 Oct). *Multicoloured.*

    (*a*) *POSTAGE. Seashells as T **12**. P 13.*
23   50 c. Type **12** 5   5
24   1 f. Conoidal harp 5   5
25   2 f. White murex 5   5
26   5 f. Green turban (27.10) 5   5
27   20 f. Scorpion conch (27.10) 12   12
28   25 f. Pacific triton 15   15

    (*b*) *AIR. Marine plants as T **13**. P 12½×13½*
29   100 f. Type **13** (27.10) 45   30
30   500 f. Stoney-coral .. .. .. 2·25   1·25
23/30 *Set of 8* .. .. 2·75   1·75

1962 (7 Apr). *Malaria Eradication. As T **11** of Central African Republic.*
31   25 f. + 5 f. rose-carmine 35   35

13a "Telstar" Satellite and part of Globe

(Des C. Durrens. Eng P. Béquet. Recess)

1962 (5 Dec). *AIR. First Trans-Atlantic Television Satellite Link. P 13.*
32 **13**a 25 f. bright purple, purple and violet   35   20

14 Emblem in Hands, and Globe

14a Centenary Emblem

(Des and eng J. Derrey. Recess)

1963 (21 Mar). *Freedom from Hunger. P 13.*
33 **14** 20 f. deep bluish green & chocolate .. 30   20

(Des and eng J. Combet. Recess)

1963 (2 Sept). *Red Cross Centenary. P 13.*
34 **14**a 50 f. red, grey and bright emerald .. 40   40

15 Globe and Scales of Justice

16 Tobacco Pouch

(Des and eng A. Decaris. Recess)

1963 (10 Dec). *15th Anniv of Declaration of Human Rights. P 13.*
35 **15** 15 f. green and carmine-red 25   25

(Des and eng J. Combet. Recess)

1963 (27 Dec). *Handicrafts.* **T 16** *and similar vert designs.*
P 13. (*a*) *POSTAGE.*

36	3 f. ochre, carmine-red and emerald ..	5	5
37	4 f. deep grey-green, brown-pur & orge	5	5
38	10 f. chocolate, green and chestnut ..	5	5

(*b*) *AIR. Inscr "POSTE AERIENNE". Size* 27×48 *mm*

39	65 f. carmine-red, yellow-brn and green	35	20
40	200 f. claret, red and turquoise	90	60
36/40	*Set of 5*	1·10	80

Designs:—4 f. Perfume-burner; 10 f. Lamp-bracket; 65 f.
Baskets; 200 f. Filigree pendant.

16*a* "Philately"

17 Pirogue

(Des and eng P. Gandon. Recess)

1964 (31 Mar). *"PHILATEC 1964" International Stamp Exhibi-tion, Paris. P* 13.

41	**16***a* 50 f. red, green and deep blue ..	25	25

(Des R. Chapelet. Photo So.Ge.Im.)

1964 (7 Aug). *Native Craft.* **T 17** *and similar vert designs.*
Multicoloured. (*a*) *POSTAGE. Size as* 22×37 *mm.*
P 13×12½.

42	15 f. Type **17**	10	5
43	30 f. Boutre felucca	15	10

(*b*) *AIR. Inscr "POSTE AERIENNE". Size* 27×48½ *mm. P* 13.

44	50 f. Mayotte pirogue	25	15
45	85 f. Schooner	40	20
42/45	*Set of 4*	80.	45

18 Boxing (ancient
bronze plaque)

19 Medal

(Des and eng C. Haley. Recess)

1964 (10 Oct). *AIR. Olympic Games, Tokyo. P* 13.

46	**18** 100 f. bronze-green, chestnut & choc ..	50	35

(Des P. Lambert. Photo So.Ge.Im.)

1964 (10 Dec). *AIR. Star of Great Comoro. P* 13.

47	**19** 500 f. multicoloured	1·75	1·25

20 "Syncom"
Communications
Satellite, Telegraph
Poles and Morse Key

21 Hammer-head Shark

(Des and eng J. Combet. Recess)

1965 (17 May). *AIR. I.T.U. Centenary. P* 13.

48	**20** 50 f. turquoise-blue, yellow-ol & slate	65	65

(Des and eng J. Combet. Recess)

1965 (2 Dec). *Marine Life.* **T 21** *and similar designs. P* 13.

49	1 f. myrtle-green, orange & reddish vio	5	5
50	12 f. black, indigo and carmine	5	5
51	20 f. brown-red and bluish green ..	10	8
52	25 f. purple-brown, verm & bluish grn ..	12	8
49/52	*Set of 4*	25	20

Designs: *Vert*—1 f. Spiny lobster; 25 f. Grouper.
Horiz—20 f. Scaly turtle.

21*a* Rocket "Diamant"

(Des and eng C. Durrens. Recess)

1966 (17 Jan). *AIR. Launching of 1st French Satellite.* **T 21***a*
and similar horiz design. P 13.

53	25 f. plum, reddish violet and ultramarine	15	15
54	30 f. plum, reddish violet and ultramarine	20	15

Design:—30 f. Satellite "A1".
Nos. 53/4 were printed together in sheets of 16, giving 8
horiz strips containing one of each value separated by a half
stamp-size inscr label. (*Price per strip un or us* 35*p.*)

21*b* Satellite "D1"

(Des and eng C. Durrens. Recess)

1966 (16 May). *AIR. Launching of Satellite "D1". P* 13.

55	**21***b* 30 f. maroon, myrtle-green & orange	12	10

22 Lake Salé

23 Comoro Sunbird

(Des R. Chapelet. Photo So.Ge.lm.)

1966 (19 Dec). *Comoro Views. T 22 and similar multicoloured designs. (a) POSTAGE. P 12½ × 13.*
56	15 f. Type **22**	..	..	5	5
57	25 f. Itsandra Hotel, Moroni	..	..	10	8

(b) AIR. Inscr "POSTE AERIENNE". P 13
58	50 f. The Battery, Dzaoudzi	..	..	15	12
59	200 f. Ksar Fort, Mutsamudu	..	..	60	40
56/59	Set of 4	..	..	80	60

Sizes:—25 f. As T **22**; 50 f. 48 × 27 mm; 200 f. 27 × 48 mm.

(Des P. Lambert. Photo So.Ge.lm.)

1967 (20 June). *Birds. T 23 and similar designs. Multicoloured. P 12½ × 13 (horiz) or 13 (vert). (a) POSTAGE.*
60	2 f. Type **23**	..	..	5	5
61	10 f. Kingfisher	..	..	5	5
62	15 f. Fody	..	..	5	5
63	30 f. Cuckoo-roller	..	..	12	8

(b) AIR. Inscr "POSTE AERIENNE"
64	75 f. Flycatcher	..	..	30	12
65	100 f. Blue-cheeked bee-eater	..	..	40	15
60/65	Set of 6	..	..	85	40

Designs: *Horiz (as T 23)*—10 f., 15 f., 30 f. *Vert (Larger, 27 × 48 mm)*—75 f., 100 f.

28 Human Rights Emblem

29 Swimming

(Des and eng A. Decaris. Recess)

1968 (10 Aug). *Human Rights Year. P 13.*
73	**28** 60 f. blue-green, chocolate & orange ..		20	15

(Des G. Bétemps. Photo Delrieu)

1968 (28 Dec). *AIR. Olympic Games, Mexico (1968). P 12½.*
74	**29** 65 f. multicoloured	..	..	20	12

24 Nurse tending Child

25 Slalom Skiing

(Des and eng P. Forget. Recess)

1967 (3 July). *Comoro Red Cross. P 13.*
66	**24** 25 f. + 5 f. purple-brown, red & bl-grn ..		12	12

(Des and eng P. Forget. Recess)

1968 (29 Apr). *AIR. Winter Olympic Games, Grenoble. P 13.*
67	**25** 70 f. purple-brn, greenish bl & bl-grn ..		25	12

26 Bouquet, Sun and W.H.O. Emblem

27 Powder Blue Surgeon

(Des and eng A. Decaris. Recess)

1968 (4 May). *20th Anniv of World Health Organization. P 13.*
68	**26** 40 f. crimson, violet and blue-green ..		15	8

(Des and eng J. Derrey. Recess)

1968 (1 Aug). *Fishes. T 27 and similar horiz designs. P 13.*

(a) POSTAGE. Size 36 × 21½ mm
69	20 f. violet-blue, yellow and brown-red ..		8	5
70	25 f. ultramarine, orange & turq-blue	..	8	5

(b) AIR. Inscr "POSTE AERIENNE". Size 48 × 27 mm
71	50 f. yellow-ochre, indigo and purple ..		15	10
72	90 f. yellow-ochre, grey-green and emer	..	25	20

Designs: 25 f. Imperial angelfish; 50 f. Moorish idol; 90 f. Yellow-banded sweetlips.

30 Prayer Mat and Worshipper

31 Vanilla Flower

(Des and eng C. Guillame. Recess)

1969 (27 Feb). *Msoila Prayer Mats. T 30 and similar horiz designs. P 13.*
75	20 f. carmine, blue-green and violet	..	5	5
76	30 f. blue-green, violet and carmine	..	10	5
77	45 f. violet, carmine and blue-green	..	15	10

Designs:—As T **30**, but worshipper stooping (30 f.) or kneeling upright (45 f.).

(Des P. Lambert. Photo So.Ge.lm.)

1969 (5 Mar). *Flowers. Multicoloured designs as T 31.*

(a) POSTAGE. Horiz designs size 36½ × 23 mm. P 12½ × 13
78	10 f. Type **31**	..	..	5	5
79	15 f. Ylang-ylang blossom	..	..	5	5

(b) AIR. Inscr "POSTE AERIENNE". Vert designs size 27 × 49 mm. P 13
80	50 f. Heliconia	..	..	15	10
81	85 f. Tuberose	..	..	30	20
82	200 f. Orchid	..	..	70	45
78/82	Set of 5	..	..	1·10	75

32 "Concorde" in Flight

33 I.L.O. Building, Geneva

(Des and eng C. Durrens. Recess)

1969 (17 Apr). *AIR. First Flight of "Concorde". P 13.*
83	**32** 100 f. plum and orange-brown	..	35	25

(Des and eng J. Derrey. Recess)

1969 (24 Nov). *50th Anniversary of International Labour Organization. P 13.*
84	**33** 5 f. grey, emerald and salmon ..		5	5

(Des C. Guillame. Photo)

1971 (12 Mar). *Birds. T 38 and similar vert designs. Multicoloured. P 12½ × 13.*

94	5 f. Type **38**	..	..	5	5
95	10 f. Comoro pigeon	..	..	5	5
96	15 f. Green-backed heron	..	..	5	5
97	25 f. Sganzin's wart pigeon	..	..	8	5
98	35 f. *Humblotia flavirostris*	..	..	10	8
99	40 f. Allen's gallinule	..	..	12	10
94/99	*Set of 6*	..	..	35	30

34 Poinsettia **35** "EXPO" Panorama

(Des P. Lambert. Photo Delrieu)

1970 (5 Mar). *Flowers. P 12½ × 12.*

85	**34** 25 f. multicoloured	..	..	10	5

1970 (20 May). *New U.P.U. Headquarters Building, Berne. Design as T 156 of Cameroun.*

86	65 f. lake-brown, blue-green and violet ..	15	8

(Des P. Lambert. Photo)

1970 (13 Sept). *AIR. World Fair "EXPO 70", Osaka, Japan. T 35 and similar vert design. Multicoloured. P 13.*

87	60 f. Type **35**	..	..	15	10
88	90 f. Geisha and map of Japan	..	..	25	20

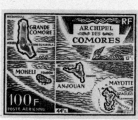

39 Sunset, Moutsamoudou (Anjouan)

40 Map of Comoro Archipelago

(Des P. Lambert. Photo (15 f. to 85 f.). Des and eng P. Béquet. Recess (100 f.))

1971 (3 May). *AIR. Comoro Landscapes. P 13.* (a) *T 39 and similar horiz designs. Multicoloured.*

100	15 f. Type **39** ..	..	..	5	5
101	20 f. Sada village (Mayotte)	..	..	5	5
102	65 f. Ruined palace, Iconi (Great Comoro)	..	..	20	12
103	85 f. Off-shore islands, Moumatchoua, (Mohéli)	..	..	25	15

(b) *T 40*

104	100 f. brown-red, blue-green and ultram	30	20
100/104	*Set of 5*	75	50

See also Nos. 124/8.

36 Chiromani Costume, Anjouan **37** Friday Mosque, Moroni

(Des P. Lambert. Photo)

1970 (30 Oct). *Comoro Costumes. T 36 and similar vert design. Multicoloured. P 12½ × 13.*

89	20 f. Type **36** ..	..	..	8	5
90	25 f. Bouiboui, Great Comoro	..	..	8	5

(Des P. Lambert. Eng E. Lacaque. Recess)

1970 (18 Dec). *P 12½ × 13.*

91	**37** 5 f. turquoise-blue, blue-grn & cerise	5	5
92	10 f. reddish violet, blue-grn & purple	5	5
93	40 f. red-brown, blue-green and red ..	10	8

41 *Pyrostegia venusta* **42** *Conus lithoglyphus*

(Des S. Gauthier. Photo)

1971 (12 July). *Tropical Plants. T 41 and similar multicoloured designs. P 13.* (a) *POSTAGE. Size as T 41.*

105	1 f. Type **41**	..	5	5
106	3 f. *Allamanda cathartica* (horiz)	..	5	5
107	20 f. *Plumeria rubra*	..	5	5

(b) *AIR. Inscr "POSTE AERIENNE". Size 27 × 48 mm*

108	60 f. *Hibiscus schizopetalus*	..	20	12
109	85 f. *Acalypha sanderii* ..	..	25	15
105/109	*Set of 5* ..	..	55	35

38 White Egret

(Des P. Lambert. Photo)

1971 (4 Oct). *Seashells. T 42 and similar horiz designs. Multi-coloured. P* 13.

110	5 f. Type **42**	..	..	..	5	5
111	10 f. *Conus litteratus*	..	..	..	5	5
112	20 f. *Conus aulicus*	..	..	..	5	5
113	35 f. *Nerita polita*	..	..	..	10	8
114	60 f. *Cypraea caputserpentis*	..	..	15	12
110/114	*Set of 5*	..	..	..	35	30

43 De Gaulle in Uniform (June 1940)

44 Mural, Airport Lounge

(Des G. Bétemps. Eng J. Miermont (20 f.), G. Bétemps (35 f.). Recess)

1971 (9 Nov). *1st Death Anniv of Gen. Charles de Gaulle. T* **43** *and similar vert portrait. P* 13.

115	20 f. black and bright purple	..	5	5
116	35 f. black and bright purple	..	10	8

Design:—35 f. De Gaulle as President of France (1970).

(Des and eng N. Hanniquet. Recess (100 f.). Photo (others))

1972 (31 Mar). *AIR. Inauguration of New Airport, Moroni. T* **44** *and similar horiz designs. P* 13.

117	65 f. multicoloured	..	20	12
118	85 f. multicoloured	..	25	15
119	100 f. myrtle-grn, light brn & new blue ..		30	20

Designs:—85 f. Mural similar to T **44**; 100 f. Airport buildings.

45 Eiffel Tower, Paris, and Telecommunications Centre, Moroni

(Des and eng N. Hanniquet. Recess)

1972 (24 Apr). *AIR. Inauguration of Paris–Moroni Radio-Telephone Link. T* **45** *and similar horiz design. P* 13.

120	35 f. red, slate-purple and light blue	..	10	8
121	75 f. lake, violet and new blue	..	20	15

Design:—75 f. Telephone conversation.

46 Underwater Spear-fishing

(Des and eng J. Combet. Recess)

1972 (5 July). *AIR. Aquatic Sports. P* 13.

122	**46** 70 f. lake, blue-green and deep blue ..		20	15

47 Pasteur, Crucibles and Microscope

48 Pres. Said Mohamed Cheikh

(Des and eng R. Quillivic. Recess)

1972 (2 Aug). *150th Birth Anniv of Louis Pasteur. P* 13×12½.

123	**47** 65 f. slate-blue, olive-brn & red-orge		20	12

(Des P. Lambert. Photo (20 f. to 60 f.). Des P. Béquet. Eng E. Lacaque. Recess (100 f.))

1972 (15 Nov). *AIR. Anjouan Landscapes. P* 13. *(a) Horiz views similar to T* **39**. *Multicoloured.*

124	20 f. Fortress wall, Cape Sima ..		..	5	5
125	35 f. Bambao Palace	..	..	10	8
126	40 f. Palace, Domoni	..	..	12	10
127	60 f. Gomajou Island	..	..	20	12

(b) Horiz map design as T **40**

128	100 f. myrtle-grn, new blue & brn-lake ..		30	20
124/128	*Set of 5*	..	..	70	50

Design:—100 f. Map of Anjouan.

(Photo Delrieu)

1973 (16 Mar). *AIR. Said Mohamed Cheikh, President of Comoro Council, Commemoration. P* 13.

129	**48** 20 f. multicoloured	..	5	5
130	35 f. multicoloured	..	..	10	8

CONFEDERATE STATES. See after United States.

CONGO (KINSHASA). See Zaire Republic.

CONGO (PORTUGUESE). See after Angola.

Congo

100 Centimes = 1 Franc

PRINTERS. All stamps were printed at the Government Printing Works, Paris, *unless otherwise stated.*

IMPERFORATE STAMPS. Stamps exist imperforate in their issued colours but they were not valid for postage. Imperforate stamps in other colours are colour trials.

A. FRENCH CONGO

The explorer Savorgnan de Brazza made a treaty with the King of the Bateke, who ceded his rights to France, in 1880, and Brazzaville was founded. De Brazza secured Pointe Noire and Loango, on the coast, for France by 1882 and in 1888 Paul Crampel opened up the region between the French Congo and Lake Chad. The French Congo, to which Gabon was joined, and which included the Chad and Ubangi-Shari territories, was created a Colony on 11 December 1888. The colony, at first Gabon-Congo, was given the title of "Congo Français" on 20 April 1891.

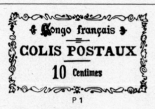

P 1

1891. *PARCEL POST. Type-set. Imperf.*

P13	P **1**	10 c. black/*blue*	.. 12·00	6·00
		a. Tête-bêche (pair)	.. 35·00	30·00

Congo français (1) **COngo Français** (2)

5c. (1)   **5 c.** (2)

(3)   (P 2)   **Valeur 15** (5)

1891–92. *Type J of French Colonies (General Issues) surch.* P 14 × 13½.

(a) As T 1

1	5 c. on 1 c. black/*azure* (R.) (2.9.91)	.. £450	£350
2	5 c. on 1 c. black/*azure* (2.9.91)	.. 12·00	7·00
	a. Surch double (Bk.)	.. 16·00	15·00
	b. Surch double (Bk.+R.)	.. £650	£600
3	5 c. on 15 c. blue (24.3.91)	.. 18·00	7·50
	a. Surch double	.. 20·00	18·00
	b. Surch vert		
4	5 c. on 25 c. black/*rose* (4.12.91)	:. 7·00	2·00
	a. Surch inverted	.. 12·00	5·00
	b. Surch vert		

(b) As T 2

5	5 c. on 20 c. red/*green* (13.5.92)	.. 95·00	45·00
	a. Surch double	.. —	90·00
6	5 c. on 25 c. black/*rose* (9.7.92)	.. 6·00	2·00
	a. Surch vert	.. 6·00	2·00
	b. Vert surch double		
7	10 c. on 25 c. black/*rose* (9.7.92)	.. 12·00	3·50
	a. Surch double	.. 16·00	6·50
	b. Surch inverted	.. 12·00	4·50
	c. Surch vert	.. 12·00	3·50
8	10 c. on 40 c. red/*yellow* (13.5.92)	.. £160	30·00
	a. Surch double	.. —	£100
9	15 c. on 25 c. black/*rose* (5.8.92)	.. 9·00	2·25
	a. Surch double	.. 12·00	6·00
	b. Surch inverted	.. 10·00	4·00
	c. Surch vert	.. 9·00	2·40

(c) As T 1 but vert and no stop after "c" (20.9.92)

10	5 c. on 25 c. black/*rose*	.. 6·00	5·00
11	10 c. on 25 c. black/*rose*	.. 10·00	3·50
12	15 c. on 25 c. black/*rose*	.. 10·00	3·50

The 5 c. on 1 c. were first surcharged in red as Type **1**, but the type was reset for the black surcharge. The "5" and "c" are 4 mm apart in the red surcharge and 1 mm in the black.

There were two printings of No. 3, but they are practically indistinguishable.

The vertical surcharges exist reading up or down, the value being about the same for each.

1892. *Type U of French Colonies (General issues), hand-stamped locally as T 3. Imperf.*

13	5 c. on 5 c. black (R.) (9.11)	.. 10·00	9·00
14	5 c. on 20 c. black (R.) (9.11)	.. 10·00	8·00
15	5 c. on 30 c. black (R.) (9.11)	.. 12·00	9·00
16	10 c. on 1 f. brown (8.9)	.. 12·00	7·00
	a. Surch horiz	.. 75·00	75·00

Nos. 13/16 exist with surcharge reading up or down and the prices are the same for each. In the 10 c. the word "Timbres" is in the plural.

1892 (Nov)–**1900.** *Type X of Anjouan inscr "CONGO FRANCAIS". Name in red (1, 5, 15, 25, 50 (No. 31), 75 c. and 1 f.) or blue (others). P 14 × 13½.*

17	1 c. black/*azure*	.. 8	8
	a. Name double		
18	2 c. brown/*buff*	.. 10	10
	a. Name in red and black	.. 8·00	8·00
19	4 c. purple-brown/*grey*	.. 12	12
	a. Name in black and blue	.. 10·00	10·00
20	5 c. green/*pale green*	.. 30	30
21	10 c. black/*lilac*	.. 1·10	80
	a. Name double	.. 28·00	28·00
22	10 c. rose-red (12.00)	.. 15	10
23	15 c. blue	.. 3·00	1·10
24	15 c. grey (12.00)	.. 55	50
25	20 c. red/*green*	.. 1·75	1·25
26	25 c. black/*rose*	.. 1·50	85
27	25 c. blue (12.00)	.. 85	70
28	30 c. cinnamon/*drab*	.. 1·60	85
29	40 c. red/*yellow*	.. 3·00	2·00
30	50 c. carmine/*rose*	.. 3·00	2·00
31	50 c. brown/*azure* (12.00)	.. 80	70
	a. Name double	.. 30·00	30·00
32	75 c. brown/*orange*	.. 2·50	2·00
33	1 f. olive-green/*toned*	.. 3·25	1·90
17/33	*Set of 17*	.. 21·00	13·00

1893. *PARCEL POST. Receipt stamp of France handstamped with Type P 2.*

P34	10 c. grey	.. 5·00	4·00

1900 (8 July). *Brazzaville Provisionals. Type X of Anjouan surch as T* **5.** *P* 14×13½.

34	5 on 20 c. red/*green*	..	—	£750
35	15 on 30 c. cinnamon/*drab*	..	—	£300
	a. Surch double	..	—	£700

Nos. 34/5 were authorised by the Lieutenant-Governor by decree of 9 July. They were withdrawn on 12 July.

6 Leopard in Ambush   **7** Branch of Thistle

8 Bakalois Woman   **10** Coconut Palms, Libreville

9 Rose Branch   **11** Branch of Olive

(Des Paul Merwart. Eng B. Damman. Typo by M. Chassepot)

1900 (May)–**4.** *P* 11. (*a*) *T* **6.** *W* **7.**

36	1 c. deep purple and sepia	..	..	5	5
	a. Background and value inverted	..	2·75	2·75
	b. Value tablet double ..	..		
	c. Red-brown and grey (5.04) ..	..	5	5
37	2 c. brown and yellow	..	..	5	5
	a. Imperf (pair)..	..	..	2·75	2·75
	b. Error. Red and pale red	..	10·00	12·00
38	4 c. vermilion and grey ..	..	5	5
	a. Background and value inverted	..	3·50	3·50
	b. Error. Red and pale red	..	70·00	
39	5 c. green and grey-green	..	12	5
	a. Imperf (pair)..	..	..	3·00	3·00
40	10 c. red and pale red	..	35	20
	a. Imperf (pair)..	..	..	6·00	6·00
41	15 c. dull violet and olive-green ..		12	5
	a. Imperf (pair)..	..	..	3·50	3·50

(*b*) *T* **8.** *W* **9**

42	20 c. green and pale red ..		..	8	5
43	25 c. blue and pale blue	..		12	12
	a. Blue and greenish blue	..	..	12	12
44	30 c. carmine and yellow..		..	15	10
45	40 c. chestnut and green ..		..	20	15
	a. Imperf (pair)..	..	..	3·50	3·50
	b. Background and value inverted	..	10·00	10·00

46	50 c. deep violet and lilac	..	..	35	25
47	75 c. claret and orange	..		55	35
	a. Imperf (pair)..	..	..	4·75	4·75
	b. Red and orange	..	..	85	85

(*c*) *T* **10.** *W* **11**

48	1 f. drab and slate-green	..	..	1·25	1·10
	a. Imperf (pair)..	..	..		
	b. Background and value inverted	..	18·00	18·00
	c. Value misplaced and inverted	..	9·00	9·00
49	2 f. carmine and grey-brown	..	..	1·75	1·50
	a. Imperf (pair)..	..	..	8·00	8·00
	b. Pink and grey-brown	..	..	1·75	1·50
50	5 f. orange and black	..	..	5·50	5·50
	a. Imperf (pair)..	..	..	25·00	25·00
	b. Error. Wmk T **9**	..		26·00	
	c. Background and value inverted	..	32·00	32·00
	d. Value misplaced and inverted	..	22·00	22·00
	e. Value tablet double ..	..	25·00	25·00
	f. Ochre and black	..	..	40·00	
36/50	Set of 15	..	..	..	9·50	8·50

(12)   (13)

1903 (13 July). *Stamps of 1900–4 surch with T* **12** *or* **13.**

51	5 c. on 30 c. carmine and yellow	..	30·00	14·00
	a. Surch inverted	..	..	£140	
52	0,10 on 2 f. carmine and grey-brown	..	35·00	15·00
	a. Surch inverted	..	..	£150	
	b. Surch double	..	..		

B. MIDDLE CONGO

By decree of 29 December 1903, the French Congo Colony was divided, as from 1 July 1904, into Middle Congo (Moyen Congo), Gabon, Ubangi-Shari and Chad. Middle Congo was the area which now forms the Congo Republic.

1 Leopard in Ambush

2 Bakalois Woman   **3** Coconut Palms, Libreville

(Designs adapted from those of French Congo. Eng J. Puy-
plat. Typo)

1907–17. *Frames in first colour.* P 14×13½ (T 1) or 13½×14
(*others*).

1	**1**	1 c. olive and brown	..	..	5	5
2		2 c. violet and brown	..	..	5	5
3		4 c. blue and brown	..	..	5	5
4		5 c. green and blue	..	..	5	5
5		10 c. carmine and blue	..	..	5	5
6		15 c. dull purple and pink (1917)	..	12	5
7		20 c. pale brown and blue	..	20	12
8	**2**	25 c. blue and grey-green	..	5	5
9		30 c. salmon-pink and green	..	12	10
10		35 c. chocolate and blue	..	8	8
11		40 c. dull green and pale brown	..	10	5
12		45 c. violet and salmon	..	40	25
13		50 c. green and salmon	..	12	12
14		75 c. brown and blue	..	60	55
15	**3**	1 f. deep green and pale violet	..	75	75
16		2 f. violet and grey-green	..	45	45
17		5 f. blue and pink	..	..	1·75	1·75
1/17		*Set of* 17	..	..	4·50	4·00

All values, *except* the 15, 35 and 45 c., exist on chalk-
surfaced paper.
See also Nos. 21/5.
For stamps in different colours see "Opt omitted" errors of
Cameroun, Central African Republic and Chad.

(4)   (5)

1916. *Surch locally with* T **4.** (*a*) *In centre of stamp.*

18	**1**	10 c.+5 c. carmine and blue	..	..	10	8
		a. Surch inverted	..	..	6·00	5·50
		b. Surch double	..	..	6·00	5·50
		c. Surch double, one inverted	..	7·00	6·00
		d. Pair. one without surch	..	2·00	2·00

(*b*) *In left lower corner*

19	**1**	10 c.+5 c. carmine and blue	..	..	8	8
		a. Surch double	..	..		

No. 19 was surcharged at Bangui for use there.

1916. *Surch with* T **5** *in red. Chalk-surfaced paper.*

20	**1**	10 c.+5 c. carmine and blue	..	..	5	5

1922 (1 Jan). *New colours.* P 14×13½ (T **1**) or 13½×14 (T **2**).

21	**1**	5 c. yellow and blue	..	..	5	5
22		10 c. green and blue-green	..	..	20	20
23	**2**	25 c. green and grey	..	..	5	5
24		30 c. carmine	..	..	5	5
25		50 c. blue and green	..	..	5	5
21/25		*Set of* 5	..	..	30	30

AFRIQUE ÉQUATORIALE
FRANÇAISE
(6)

AFRIQUE
EQUATORIALE
FRANÇAISE
(7)

1ᶠ25

25ᶜ   65   90   90
(8)   (9)   (10)   (11)

1924 (June)–**27.** *Stamps as* T **2/3**, *some with colours
changed, optd with* T **7** *in blue (Nos. 28/9) or black (others),
and further surch.*

(*a*) *With* T **8** *and obliterating bars. Chalk-surfaced paper
(No. 26)* (6.24)

26	**3**	25 c. on 2 f. violet and grey-green	..	5	5
27		25 c. on 5 f. blue and pink (B.)	..	5	5

(*b*) *As* T **9** (1.2.25)

28	**3**	65 on 1 f. red and brown	..	..	5	5
		a. Opt T **7** omitted	..	..	14·00	
29		85 on 1 f. red and brown	..	..	5	5
		a. Opt T **7** double	..	..	6·00	

(*c*) *With* T **10** (11.4.27)

30	**2**	90 on 75 c. scarlet and rose-red...		8	8

(*d*) *As* T **11** (1926–27)

31	**3**	1 f. 25 on 1 f. blue & ultramarine (R.) (14.6.26)	..	5	5
		a. Surch T **11** omitted	..	5·00	
32		1 f. 50 on 1 f. ultram & blue (11.4.27)	..	12	12
		a. Surch T **11** omitted	..	8·50	
33		3 f. on 5 f. chestnut & rose (19.12.27)	..	20	20
		a. Surch T **11** omitted	..	15·00	
34		10 f. on 5 f. rose-red and green (11.4.27)	85	75
35		20 f. on 5 f. brown and purple (11.4.27)	85	75
26/35		*Set of* 10	..	..	2·00	1·90

1924 (Nov)–**30.** *Stamps as* T **1/3**, *some with colours
changed, optd with* T **6** (1 *c. to* 20 *c.*) *or* **7.**

36	**1**	1 c. olive and brown	..	..	5	5
		a. Opt double	..	..	7·00	5·00
37		2 c. violet and brown	..	..	5	5
38		4 c. blue and brown	..	..	5	5
39		5 c. yellow and blue	..	..	5	5
40		10 c. green and blue-green (R.)	..	5	5
41		10 c. carmine and grey (1.12.25)	..	5	5
42		15 c. purple and pink (B.)	..	5	5
		a. Opt double	..	..	6·00	6·00
43		20 c. brown and blue	..	..	5	5
44		20 c. green and pale green (1.3.26)	..	5	5
45		20 c. brown and magenta (6.27)	..	5	5
46	**2**	25 c. green and grey	..	..	5	5
47		30 c. carmine (B.)	..	..	5	5
48		30 c. grey and mauve (R.) (1.12.25)	..	5	5
49		30 c. olive-green and green (14.11.27)	..	12	10
50		35 c. chocolate and blue (B.)	..	5	5
51		40 c. sage-green and brown	..	5	5
		a. Opt double	..	..	12·00	10·00
52		45 c. violet and salmon (B.)	..	5	5
		a. Opt inverted	..	..	6·50	5·00
53		50 c. blue and green (R.)	..	5	5
54		50 c. yellow and black (1.12.25)	..	5	5
		a. Opt omitted	..	..	13·00	
55		65 c. brown-red and blue (19.12.27)	..	25	20
56		75 c. brown and blue	..	..	5	5
		a. Opt double (Blk.+R.)	..	14·00	
		b. Opt quadruple (2 Blk.+2 R.)	..	16·00	
57		90 c. scarlet and bright rose (22.3.30)	..	20	20
58	**3**	1 f. green and violet	..	..	8	8
		a. Opt double	..	..	18·00	18·00
59		1 f. 10, mauve and chocolate (25.9.28)	..	25	25
60		1 f. 50, ultramarine and blue (22.3.30)	..	50	40
61		2 f. violet and grey-green	..	..	8	8
62		3 f. magenta/*rose* (22.3.30)	..	80	45
63		5 f. blue and pink	..	..	20	20
36/63		*Set of* 28	..	..	3·00	3·00

Of the 1924 values the 2, 4, 20, 40, 75 c., 1, 2 and 5 f. exist
on chalk-surfaced paper, the 40, 75 c. and 1 f. do not exist on
ordinary paper.
For similar stamps in other colours see "Opt omitted" errors of Central African Republic and Chad.

MOYEN-CONGO

A. E. F.
(D 1)

1928 (2 Apr). *POSTAGE DUE. Type* D **3** *of France optd with
Type* D **1.** P 14×13½.

D64		5 c. light blue	..	..	5	5
D65		10 c. brown	..	..	5	5
D66		20 c. olive-green	..	..	8	8
D67		25 c. rosine	..	..	8	8
D68		30 c. rose	..	..	8	8
D69		45 c. green	..	..	12	12
D70		50 c. claret	..	..	15	15
D71		60 c. yellow-brown/*cream*	..	15	15
D72		1 f. maroon/*cream*	..	..	15	15
D73		2 f. rose-red	..	..	15	15

D74	3 f. bright violet	..	..	..	30	30
D64/74	Set of 11	..	..	..	1·10	1·10

D 2 Village   **D 3** Steamer on the R. Congo

(Des J. Piel. Typo)

1930 (17 Feb). *POSTAGE DUE. P* 14 × 13½.

D75	D 2	5 c. drab and deep blue	..	..	5	5
D76		10 c. chocolate and scarlet	..		8	8
D77		20 c. chocolate and green	..	..	35	35
D78		25 c. chocolate and light blue			35	35
D79		30 c. blue-green and yellow-brown			35	35
D80		45 c. drab and blue-green	..		40	40
D81		50 c. chocolate and magenta			40	40
D82		60 c. black and lilac	..		60	60
D83	D 3	1 f. slate-black and yellow-brown	..		60	60
D84		2 f. chocolate and magenta			60	60
D85		3 f. chocolate and scarlet	..		60	60
D75/85	Set of 11	..	..	..	3·75	3·75

1931 (13 Apr). *International Colonial Exhibition, Paris. As T* 9/12 *of Cameroun.*

65	40 c. green	..	..	..	40	30
66	50 c. mauve	..	..	..	20	20
67	90 c. vermilion	..	..	..	20	20
68	1 f. 50, blue	..	..	..	35	25
65/68	Set of 4	..	..	..	1·00	85

12 Mindouli Viaduct   **13** Pasteur Institute, Brazzaville

(Des Herviault. Photo Vaugirard, Paris)

1933 (1 May–25 Sept). *T* 12/13 *and similar horiz design. P* 13½.

69	12	1 c. chocolate ..	..	..	..	5	5
70		2 c. greenish blue	..	..	..	5	5
71		4 c. bronze-green	..	..	..	5	5
72		5 c. claret	..	..	..	5	5
73		10 c. deep blue-green	..	..	..	5	5
74		15 c. purple	..	..	..	5	5
75		20 c. red/rose	..	..	..	65	50
76		25 c. orange	..	..	..	5	5
77		30 c. green	..	..	..	25	20
78	13	40 c. red-brown	..	..	..	15	12
79		45 c. black/green	..	..	..	15	15
80		50 c. slate-purple	..	..	..	8	5
81		65 c. red/green ..	..	..	..	12	10
82		75 c. black/rose	..	..	..	65	50
83		90 c. rosine	..	..	..	8	8
84		1 f. vermilion ..	..	..	..	10	5
85		1 f. 25, green (25.9)	..	..	..	15	15
86		1 f. 50, blue	..	..	..	60	55
87	–	1 f. 75, violet (25.9)	..	..	..	15	15
88	–	2 f. myrtle-green	..	..	..	12	10
89	–	3 f. black/red ..	..	..	..	20	15
90	–	5 f. blackish blue	..	..	..	1·10	1·00
91	–	10 f. black	..	..	..	1·90	1·40
92	–	20 f. brown	..	..	..	1·50	90
69/92	Set of 24	..	..	..	7·50	6·00

Design: 1 f. 75 to 20 f. Govt Building, Brazzaville.
The above issue overprinted "AFRIQUE ÉQUATORIALE FRANÇAISE" and with "MOYEN CONGO" obliterated by bars, will be found listed under French Equatorial Africa.

D 4 "Le Djoué"

(Des Herviault. Photo Vaugirard, Paris)

1933 (1 May). *POSTAGE DUE. P* 13½.

D 93	D 4	5 c. yellow-green ..	..	..	5	5
D 94		10 c. blue/blue	..	..	..	5	5
D 95		20 c. red/yellow	..	..	..	5	5
D 96		25 c. red-brown	..	..	..	8	8
D 97		30 c. vermilion	..	..	..	5	5
D 98		45 c. purple	..	..	..	5	5
D 99		50 c. blackish green	..	..	8	8
D100		60 c. black/red	..	..	..	25	25
D101		1 f. carmine	..	..	..	30	30
D102		2 f. orange	..	..	..	35	35
D103		3 f. Prussian blue ..	..	..	35	35
D93/103	Set of 11	..	..	..	1·50	1·50

On 15 January 1910 Middle Congo became part of the federation of French Equatorial Africa, but continued to have its own stamps until 16 March 1937, after which the stamps of French Equatorial Africa were used there until 1959.

C. CONGO REPUBLIC

Middle Congo became the Congo Republic on 28 November 1958, and an independent republic, within the French Community, on 15 August 1960.

1 "Birth of the Republic"   **2** President Youlou

(Des and eng R. Cami.)

1959 (28 Nov). *First Anniv of Republic. P* 13.
1	1	25 f. brown-purple, yell, brn & bronze-grn	15	5

1960 (21 May). *Tenth Anniv of African Technical Co-operation Commission. As No.* 3 *of Central African Republic.*
2	50 f. lake and deep bluish green	..	..	30	30

1960 (15 Dec). *AIR. Olympic Games. No.* 192 *of French Equatorial Africa surch as T* 5 *of Central African Republic in red, but opt includes* "REPUBLIQUE DU CONGO".
3	250 f. on 500 f. deep blue, blk & dp bl-grn	2·25	2·25

(Des and eng P. Munier. Recess)

1960 (15 Dec). *P* 13.
4	2	15 f. deep grey-green, carmine & bl-grn ..	12	5
5		85 f. deep grey-blue and carmine	..	45	20

3 U.N. Emblem,   **4** *Thesium tencio*
Map and Flag

(Des J. Combet. Eng J. Pheulpin. Recess)

1961 (11 Mar). *Admission of Congo Republic into U.N.O. P* 13.
6	3	5 f. multicoloured	..	..	..	5	5
7		20 f. multicoloured	..	..	..	12	8
8		100 f. multicoloured	..	..	..	65	50

(Des P. Lambert. Eng P. Munier (100 f.), J. Pheulpin (200 f.),
C. Mazelin (500 f.). Recess)

1961 (28 Sept). *AIR. T 4 and similar horiz floral designs.
P* 13.

9	100 f. bright purple, yellow and green	..		50	30
10	200 f. yellow, blue-green and brown	..	1·10		45
11	500 f. yellow, blackish green and chestnut	2·40	1·10		

Designs:—100 f. *Helicrysum mechowiam*; 200 f. *Cogniauxia podolaena.*

5 Airliners and Congolese

(Des and eng A. Decaris. Recess)

1961 (25 Nov). *AIR. Foundation of "Air Afrique" Airline.
P* 13.

12	**5**	50 f. bright purple, slate-grn and green	25	20

6 *Elagatis bipinnulatus*   **7** Brazzaville Market

(Des Cottet (50 c., 2 f. (No. 15a), 3 f., 10 f., 15 f.), Samson (1 f.,
2 f. (No. 15), 5 f.). Eng Cottet. Recess)

1961 (28 Nov)**–64.** *Tropical Fish as* **T 6.** *P* 13.

13	**6**	50 c. yellow-green, orange & dp grn	..	5	5
14	–	1 f. bistre-brown and blue-green		5	5
15	–	2 f. bistre-brown and blue	..	5	5
15a	–	2 f. verm, brown & grn (20.10.64)	..	5	5
16	**6**	3 f. yellow-green, orange and ultram		5	5
17	–	5 f. sepia, chestnut and emerald	..	5	5
18	–	10 f. red-brown and turquoise-blue	..	5	5
18a	–	15 f. mar, yell-grn & dp vio (20.10.64)		5	5
13/18a		*Set of 8*	..	30	30

Fishes:—1 f., 2 f. (No. 15), *Chauliodus sloanei*; 2 f. (No.
15a), *Lycoteuthis diadema*; 5 f. *Argyropelecus gigas*; 10 f.
Caulolepis longidens; 15 f. *Melanocetus johnsoni.*

D 1 Letter-carrier

(Des Serres. Eng Forget (Nos. D19/20, D29/30), Béquet
(D21/2, D27/8), Aufschneider (D23/6). Recess)

1961 (4 Dec). *POSTAGE DUE. Various designs showing old
and new forms of mail transport as Type* D **1.** *P.* 11.

D19	50 c. bistre, red and blue		5	5
D20	50 c. bistre, purple and blue	..	5	5
D21	1 f. yellow-brown, red & yellow-green		5	5
D22	1 f. yellow-green, red and lake	..	5	5
D23	2 f. red-brown, green and blue		5	5
D24	2 f. red-brown and blue		5	5
D25	5 f. deep sepia and violet		5	5
D26	5 f. deep sepia and violet	..	5	5
D27	10 f. chocolate, blue and green		5	5
D28	10 f. chocolate and green	..	5	5
D29	25 f. chocolate, blue and deep turquoise	12	12
D30	25 f. black and blue	..	12	12
D19/30	*Set of 12*	..	55	55

Designs:—Nos. D19, Type D **1**; D20, "Broussard" monoplane; D21, Hammock-bearers; D22, "Land-Rover" car; D23,
Pirogue; D24, River steamer; D25, Cyclist; D26, Motor lorry;
D27, Steam locomotive of 1932; D28 Diesel locomotive; D29
Seaplane of 1935; D30 "Boeing 707" jet airliner.
The two designs in each value are arranged in *tête-bêche*
pairs throughout the sheet.

(Des Moutala and Combet. Eng Barre. Typo)

1962 (23 Mar). *P* 13½×14.

19	**7**	20 f. red, emerald-green and black	..	10	5

1962 (7 Apr). *Malaria Eradication. As T* **11** *of Central African
Republic.*

20	25 f. + 5 f. yellow-brown ..	..	..	15	15

8 Export of Timber, Pointé Noire

(Des R. Chapelet. Photo Delrieu)

1962 (8 June). *AIR. International Fair, Pointe Noire.
P* 13×12.

21	**8**	50 f. multicoloured	.. ..	25	15

(Des Ringard. Photo Delrieu)

1962 (21 July). *Sports. Designs as T* **12** *of Central African
Republic. Inscr* "JEUX SPORTIFS". *P* 12×13 (100 f.) or
12½×12.

(a) POSTAGE

22	20 f. brown, red, magenta and black	..	12	10
23	50 f. brown, red, magenta and black	..	30	15

(b) AIR. Inscr "POSTE AERIENNE"

24	100 f. brown, red, magenta and black	..	55	40

Designs: *Horiz*—20 f. Boxing; 50 f. Running. *Vert* (26×47
mm)—100 f. Basketball.

1962 (8 Sept). *First Anniv of Union of African and Malagasy
States. As T* **14** *of Central African Republic.*

25	30 f. blue-green, red, gold and violet	..	15	15

1963 (21 Mar). *Freedom from Hunger. As T* **16** *of Central
African Republic.*

26	25 f. + 5 f. turq-blue, red-brn & ultram	..	15	15

9 Town Hall, Brazzaville, and Pres.   **9a** *Costus spectabilis*
Youlou   (K. Schum)

(Photo Delrieu)

1963 (31 July). *AIR. P* 13×12.

27	**9**	100 f. multicoloured	.. ..	15·00	15·00

(Des P. Lambert. Photo So.Ge.Im.)

1963. *AIR. Flowers as T* **9a.** *Multicoloured. P* 13.

28	100 f. Type **9a** (9 Aug)		50	25
29	250 f. *Acanthus montanus T. anders* (4 Nov)		90	60

1963 (8 Sept). *AIR. African and Malagasian Posts and Telecommunications Union. As T* **18** *of Central African Republic.*

30	85 f. red, buff and violet ..	.. ..	45	30

1963 (19 Sept). *Space Telecommunications. As Nos. 37/8 of Central African Republic.*
31   25 f. blue, orange and green   15   12
32   100 f. reddish violet, light brown & blue ..   60   50

10 King Makoko's   **11** Airline Emblem
     Gold Chain

(Des and eng C. Mazelin. Recess)

1963 (21 Oct). *Folklore and Tourism. T **10** and similar vert design. P* 13.
33   10 f. bistre and black   5   5
34   15 f. brown-purple, red, yellow and blue   5   5
Design:—15 f. Kébékébé mask.

(Des E. Baudry. Photo Delrieu)

1963 (19 Nov). *AIR. First Anniv of "Air Afrique", and Inauguration of "DC-8" Service. P* 13 × 12.
35   **11** 50 f. black, green, light brown and blue   25   20

12 Liberty Square, Brazzaville   **13** Statue of Hathor, Abu Simbel

(Des P. Béquet. Photo Delrieu)

1963 (28 Nov). *AIR. P* 13 × 12.
36   **12** 25 f. multicoloured   12   10

1963 (30 Nov). *AIR. European-African Economic Convention. As T **24** of Central African Republic.*
37   50 f. deep brown, yellow, ochre & ol-grey   30   20

1963 (10 Dec). *15th Anniv of Declaration of Human Rights. As T **26** of Central African Republic.*
38   25 f. deep blue, blue-green and brown   ..   12   10

(Des and eng G. Bétemps. Recess)

1964 (9 Mar). *AIR. Nubian Monuments Preservation. P* 13.
39   **13** 10 f. + 5 f. violet and brown   ..   12   10
40   25 f. + 5 f. orge-brn & dp bluish grn   20   15
41   50 f. + 5 f. deep bluish green & red-brn   35   35

14 Barograph   **15** Machinist

(Des and eng C. Haley. Recess)

1964 (23 Mar). *World Meteorological Day. P* 13.
42   **14** 50 f. red-brown, ultramarine & bl-grn ..   25   20

(Des and eng C. Haley. Recess)

1964 (8 Apr). *"Technical Instruction". P* 13.
43   **15** 20 f. chocolate, magenta & turq-bl   ..   12   5

16 Emblem and Implements   **17** Diaboua Ballet
     of Manual Labour

(Des J. Combet. Eng A. Frères. Recess)

1964 (24 Apr). *Manual Labour Rehabilitation. P* 13.
44   **16** 80 f. green, brown-red and sepia   ..   35   20

(Des and eng P. Gandon. Recess)

1964 (8 May). *Folklore and Tourism. T **17** and similar vert design. Multicoloured. P* 13.
45   30 f. Type **17**   15   8
46   60 f. Kébékébé dance   30   15

18 Tree-felling   **19** Wood Carving

(Des and eng J. Derrey. Recess)

1964 (12 May). *AIR. P* 13.
47   **18** 100 f. sepia, brown-red & yellow-green   45   20

(Des and eng J. Combet. Recess)

1964 (22 May). *Congo Sculpture. P* 13.
48   **19** 50 f. sepia and brown-red   20   15

20 Students in Classroom   **21** Sun, Ears of Wheat and Globe within Cogwheel

(Des P. Gandon. Eng R. Cami. Recess)

1964 (26 May). *Development of Education. P* 13.
49   **20** 25 f. vermilion, brown-purple and blue   12   8

1964 (23 June). *AIR. 5th Anniv of Equatorial African Heads of State Conference. As T **31** of Central African Republic.*
50   100 f. multicoloured   25   15

(Des J. Combet. Photo Delrieu)

1964 (20 July). *AIR. First Anniv of European-African Convention. P* 12 × 13.
51   **21** 50 f. yellow, greenish bl & brn-red   ..   25   15

22 Stadium, Olympic Flame and Throwing the Hammer

(Des and eng C. Haley. Recess)

1964 (30 July). *AIR. Olympic Games, Tokyo. T 22 and similar designs. P 13.*

52	25 f. orange, ultramarine & red-brown ..		15	8
53	50 f. orange, bright purple & olive-green		25	20
54	100 f. orange, deep bluish grn & red-brn		55	45
55	200 f. orange, deep olive-green & red ..		1·00	75
52/55	*Set of 4*		1·75	1·25
MS55a	191×100 mm. Nos. 52/5 ..		1·90	1·90

Designs: Stadium, Olympic Flame and: *Vert*—50 f. Weight-lifting; 100 f. Volley-ball. *Horiz*—200 f. High-jumping.

1964 (15 Aug). *First Anniv of Revolution, and National Festival. As T 12 but inscr "1er ANNIVERSAIRE DE LA REVOLUTION FETE NATIONALE 15 AOÛT 1964" in red. P 13×12.*

56	20 f. multicoloured	.. .. ..	10	5

23 Posthorns, Envelope and Radio Mast   24 Dove, Envelope and Radio Mast

(Des J. Combet. Litho So.Ge.lm.)

1964 (2 Nov). *AIR. Pan-African and Malagasy Posts and Telecommunications Congress, Cairo. P 12½×13.*

57	**23** 25 f. sepia and Venetian red ..	..	12	10

1964 (7 Nov). *French, African and Malagasy Co-operation. As T 547 of France.*

58	25 f. chocolate, emerald and red ..	..	12	8

(Des J. Combet. Litho So.Ge.lm.)

1965 (1 Jan). *Establishment of Posts and Telecommunications Office, Brazzaville. P 12½×13.*

59	**24** 25 f. Venetian red, yell-ol, grey & blk ..		12	10

25 Town Hall, Brazzaville and Arms

(Des J. Combet. Photo Delrieu)

1965 (30 Jan). *AIR. P 12½.*

60	**25** 100 f. multicoloured	.. ..	45	25

26 "Europafrique"

(Des H. Biais. Photo Delrieu)

1965 (27 Feb). *AIR. "Europafrique." P 13×12.*

61	**26** 50 f. multicoloured	.. .. ..	25	15

27 Elephant   29 Pres. Massamba-Debat

28 Cadran de Breguet's Telegraph and "Telstar"

(Des and eng J. Pheulpin. Recess)

1965 (15 Mar). *Folklore and Tourism. T 27 and similar designs. P 13.*

62	15 f. brown-purple, deep bluish grn & bl		8	5
63	20 f. black, blue and deep bluish green ..		12	5
64	85 f. multicoloured	.. ..	40	25

Designs: *Vert*—15 f. Antelope; 85 f. Dancer on stilts.

(Des and eng P. Béquet. Recess)

1965 (17 May). *AIR. I.T.U. Centenary. P 13.*

65	**28** 100 f. brown, yell-brn & deep ultram ..		55	35

(Photo Delrieu)

1965 (1 June)—**66**. *P 12×12½.*

66	**29** 20 f. multicoloured	.. ..	10	5
66a	25 f. multicoloured (14.2.66) ..	..	12	5
66b	30 f. multicoloured (14.2.66) ..	..	15	5

30 Sir Winston Churchill   31 Pope John XXIII

(Photo Delrieu)

1965. *AIR. Famous Men. T* **30** *and similar vert designs.*
P 12½.

67	25 f. on 50 f. sepia and red (25.6)		12	12
	a. Surch omitted	..	7·00	7·00
68	50 f. sepia and yellow-green (26.6)	..	25	25
69	80 f. sepia and turquoise-blue (25.6)	..	30	30
70	100 f. sepia and yellow (26.6)	..	50	40
67/70	*Set of 4*	..	1·00	95
MS70a	106×145 mm. Nos 67/70 (26.6)	..	1·25	1·25
	b. Surch omitted	..	10·00	10·00

Portraits:—25 f. Lumumba; 80 f. Pres. Boganda; 100 f. Pres. Kennedy.

(Des P. Lambert. Photo So.Ge.Im.)

1965 (26 June). *AIR. Pope John Commemoration.*
P 12½×13.

71	**31**	100 f. multicoloured	..	..	..	45	40

RÉPUBLIQUE DU CONGO
POSTE AÉRIENNE
50F

32 Athletes and Map of Africa   **33** Natives hauling Log

(Des C. Haley. Photo Delrieu)

1965 (17 July). *First African Games, Brazzaville. T* **32** *and similar designs inscr "PREMIERS JEUX AFRICAINS". Multicoloured. P* 12½.

72	25 f. Type **32**	..	..	..	..	12	10
73	40 f. Football	..	..	..	..	20	15
74	50 f. Handball	..	..	..	..	25	20
75	85 f. Running	..	..	..	..	40	30
76	100 f. Cycling	..	..	..	..	45	40
72/76	*Set of 5*	..	..	..	..	1·25	1·00
MS76a	137×169 mm. No. 72/6		..	..	1·25	1·25

Nos. 73/6 are larger (34½×34½ mm).

(Des L. Fylla. Eng C. Haley. Recess)

1965 (14 Aug). *AIR. National Unity. P* 13.

77	**33**	50 f. purple-brown, blue-green and greenish black	..	20	15

34 "World Co-operation"   **35** Arms of Congo

(Des and eng J. Gauthier. Recess)

1965 (18 Oct). *AIR. International Co-operation Year. P* 13.

78	**34**	50 f. multicoloured	..	..	25	15

(Des S. Gauthier, after L. Mühlemann. Litho So.Ge.Im.)

1965 (15 Nov). *P* 13.

79	**35**	20 f. multicoloured	..	..	10	5

36 Lincoln

(Des P. Lambert. Photo So.Ge.Im.)

1965 (15 Dec). *AIR. Death Centenary of Abraham Lincoln. P* 13.

80	**36**	90 f. multicoloured	..	..	45	25

37 Trench-digging   **39** Weaving

38 De Gaulle and Flaming Torch

(Des J. Combet. Photo So.Ge.Im.)

1966 (18 Feb). *Village Co-operative. P* 12½×13.

81	**37**	25 f. multicoloured	..	..	12	5

(Des J. Combet. Photo So.Ge.Im.)

1966 (18 Feb). *National Youth Day. Horiz design similar to T* **37** *but showing Youth Display. P* 12½×13.

82	30 f. multicoloured	..	..	15	12

(Des and eng P. Gandon. Recess)

1966 (28 Feb). *AIR. 22nd Anniv of Brazzaville Conference. P* 13.

83	**38**	500 f. purple-brown, red & myrtle-grn	3·50	2·25

(Des G. Fylla (30 f.), J. Combet (others). Photo So.Ge.Im.)

1966 (9 Apr). *World Festival of Negro Arts, Dakar. T* **39** *and similar designs. Multicoloured. P* 12½×13 (85 f.) *or* 13×12½ (others).

84	30 f. Type **39**	..	..	..	12	10
85	85 f. Musical instrument (*horiz*)	..	..	35	20
86	90 f. Mask..	..	..	..	40	25

40 People and Clocks   **41** W.H.O. Building

(Des P. Béquet. Photo Delrieu)

1966 (15 Apr). *Establishment of Shorter Working Day. P* 12½×12.

87	**40**	70 f. multicoloured	..	..	..	30	15

(Des H. Biais. Photo So.Ge.lm.)

1966 (3 May). *Inauguration of W.H.O. Headquarters, Geneva.* P 12½×13.
88 41 50 f. violet, yellow and light blue . . 25 12

42 Satellite "D1" and Brazzaville Tracking Station

43 St. Pierre Claver Church

(Des and eng J. Combet. Recess)

1966 (15 May). *AIR. Launching of Satellite "D1".* P 13.
89 42 150 f. black, brown-red & turquoise-grn 70 40

(Des J. Combet. Photo So.Ge.lm.)

1966 (25 June). P 13×12½.
90 43 70 f. multicoloured 30 12

44 Volleyball

45 Jules Rimet Cup and Globe

(Des Forget. Eng Monvoisin (1 f.), Fenneteaux (2 f.), Gandon (3 f.), Mazelin (5 f.), Forget (10 f., 15 f.). Recess)

1966 (15 July). *Sports.* T **44** *and similar designs.* P 13.
91 1 f. purple-brown, bistre and bright blue 5 5
92 2 f. purple-brown, green and new blue . . 5 5
93 3 f. purple-brown, crimson & dp grn . . 5 5
94 5 f. purple-brown, grey-blue and emer . . 5 5
95 10 f. violet, turquoise-blue & blackish grn 5 5
96 15 f. purple-brown, bluish violet and lake 5 5
91/96 Set of 6 . . . . . . 25 25
  Designs: *Vert*—2 f. Basketball; 5 f. Sportsmen; 10 f. Athlete; 15 f. Football. *Horiz*—3 f. Handball.

(Des Monvoisin. Photo Delrieu)

1966 (15 July). *World Cup Football Championships.* P 12½×12.
97 **45** 30 f. gold, black, lt bl & brt orge-red . . 15 5

46 Corn, Atomic Emblem and Map

47 Pres. Massamba-Debat and Presidential Palace, Brazzaville

(Des C. Haley. Photo Delrieu)

1966 (20 July). *AIR. "Europafrique".* P 12×13.
98 **46** 50 f. gold, yellow-green, vio & light bl 20 12

(Des Monvoisin. Photo Delrieu)

1966 (15 Aug). *AIR. Third Anniv of Congolese Revolution.* T **47** *and similar horiz designs. Multicoloured.* P 12½.
99 25 f. Type **47** 12 5
100 30 f. Robespierre and Bastille, Paris . . 12 5
101 50 f. Lenin and Winter Palace, St. Petersburg 20 12
MS102 132×160 mm. Nos. 99/101 . . . . 50 50

1966 (31 Aug). *AIR. Inauguration of "DC-8" Air Services. As* T **54** *of Central African Republic.*
103 30 f. olive-yellow, black and light violet 12 5

48 Dr. Albert Schweitzer

(Des J. Gauthier. Photo Delrieu)

1966 (4 Sept). *AIR. Schweitzer Commemoration.* P 12½.
104 **48** 100 f. multicoloured 45 25

49 Savorgnan de Brazza High School

50 Pointe-Noire Railway Station

(Des G. Aufschneider. Photo Delrieu)

1966 (15 Sept). *Inauguration of Savorgnan de Brazza High School.* P 12½×12.
105 **49** 30 f. multicoloured 12 5

(Des and eng Monvoisin. Recess)

1966 (15 Oct). P 13.
106 **50** 60 f. carmine-red, brown and green . . 25 12

51 Silhouette of Congolese, and U.N.E.S.C.O. Emblem

52 Balumbu Mask

(Des Hanniquet. Eng C. Hertenberger. Recess)

1966 (28 Nov). *20th Anniv of U.N.E.S.C.O.* P 13.
107 **51** 90 f. indigo, brown and blue-green . . 40 25

(Des P. Gandon. Eng P. Gandon (5 f., 15 f.), C. Haley (10 f., 20 f.). Recess)

1966 (12 Dec). *Congolese Masks.* T **52** *and similar vert designs.* P 13.
108 5 f. sepia and carmine-red 5 5
109 10 f. brown and greenish blue 5 5
110 15 f. blue, sepia and orange-brown . . 8 5
111 20 f. brown-red, blue, yellow and green 10 5
108/111 Set of 4 . . . . 25 15
  Masks:—10 f. Kuyu; 15 f. Bakwéle; 20 f. Batéké.

53 Cancer "The Crab",
Microscope and Pagoda

54 Social Weaver

(Des G. Aufschneider. Photo So.Ge.Im.)

1966 (26 Dec). *AIR. Ninth International Cancer Congress,
Tokyo. P* 13.
112 **53** 100 f. multicoloured 45 25

(Des P. Lambert. Photo So.Ge.Im.)

1967. *AIR. Birds. T* **54** *and similar vert designs inscr
"1967". Multicoloured. P* 13.
113 50 f. Type **54** (13.2) 20 12
114 75 f. Bee-eater (13.2) 30 20
115 100 f. Lilac-breasted roller (13.2) .. 40 25
116 150 f. Regal sunbird (20.6) 60 30
117 200 f. Crowned crane (20.6) 90 45
118 250 f. Secretary bird (20.6) .. .. 1·10 65
119 300 f. Knysna lourie (20.6) .. .. 1·25 75
113/119 *Set of* 7 .. .. 4·25 2·40

55 Medal, Ribbon
and Map

56 Learning the Alphabet
(Educational Campaign)

(Des P. Lambert. Photo Delrieu)

1967 (15 Mar). *"Companion of the Revolution" Order.
P* 12 × 12½.
120 **55** 20 f. multicoloured 10 5

(Des Guillame, after J. Balou. Photo Delrieu)

1967 (15 Mar). *Education and Sugar Production Campaigns.
T* **56** *and similar horiz design. Multicoloured. P* 12½ × 12.
121 25 f. Type **56** 12 5
122 45 f. Cutting sugar-cane 20 8

57 Mahatma Gandhi

58 Prisoner's Hands in Chains

(Des A. Spitz. Eng Mazelin. Recess)

1967 (21 Apr). *Gandhi Commemoration. P* 13.
123 **57** 90 f. black and blue 40 15

(Des P. Lambert. Photo So.Ge.Im.)

1967 (24 May). *AIR. African Liberation Day. P* 12½ × 13.
124 **58** 500 f. multicoloured .. .. .. 2·00 1·00

59 Ndumba, Lady of
Fashion

60 Congo Scenery

(Des P. Lambert. Photo So.Ge.Im)

1967 (5 June). *Congolese Dolls. T* **59** *and similar vert
designs. Multicoloured. P* 13 × 12½.
125 5 f. Type **59** 5 5
126 10 f. Fruit vendor 5 5
127 25 f. Girl pounding saka-saka 12 5
128 30 f. Mother and child 12 8
125/128 *Set of* 4 .. .. 30 15

(Des and eng J. Combet. Recess)

1967 (5 July). *International Tourist Year. P* 13.
129 **60** 60 f. claret, yellow-orange & ol-grn .. 25 15

61 "Europafrique"

62 "Sputnik I" and "Explorer 6"

(Des J. Gauthier. Photo Delrieu)

1967 (20 July). *Europafrique. P* 12 × 12½.
130 **61** 50 f. multicoloured 20 10

(Des and eng C. Haley. Recess)

1967 (1 Aug). *AIR. Space Exploration. T* **62** *and similar horiz
designs. P* 13.
131 50 f. greenish blue, reddish vio & chest 20 10
132 75 f. lake and slate 30 15
133 100 f. blue, brown-red and greenish blue 45 35
134 200 f. vermilion, new blue and lake .. 90 65
131/134 *Set of* 4 .. .. 1·60 1·10
Designs:—75 f. "Ranger 6" and "Lunik 2"; 100 f. "Mars 1"
and "Mariner 4"; 200 f. "Gemini" and "Vostok".

63 Brazzaville Arms

64 Jamboree Emblem, Scouts and
Tents

(Des S. Gauthier, after P. Lods. Photo So.Ge.Im.)

1967 (15 Aug). *Fourth Anniv of Congo Revolution. P* 13.
135 **63** 30 f. multicoloured 12 5

1967 (9 Sept). *AIR. Fifth Anniv of U.A.M.P.T. Horiz design as* T **66** *of Central African Republic.*
136   100 f. light emerald, red and olive-brown   45   30

    (Des and eng Monvoisin. Recess)

1967 (29 Sept). *AIR. World Scout Jamboree, Idaho.* T **64** *and similar horiz design.* P 13.
137   50 f. light blue, red-brown & orge-brn ..   20   12
138   70 f. brown-red, blackish green and greenish blue   30   15
Design:—70 f. Saluting hand, Jamboree camp and emblem.

65 Sikorsky "S-43" Flying-boat and Map

66 Dove, Human Figures and U.N. Emblem

68 Albert Luthuli (winner of Nobel Peace Prize), and Dove

70 Arms of Pointe Noire

    (Des J. Combet. Photo So.Ge.Im.)

1967 (2 Oct). *AIR. 30th Anniv of Aeromaritime Airmail Link.* P 13.
139   **65**   30 f. multicoloured   15   8

    (Des P. Béquet. Photo)

1967 (24 Oct). *U.N. Day and Campaign in Support of U.N.* P 13×12.
140   **66**   90 f. multicoloured   40   20

69 Global Dance

    (Des and eng J. Combet. Recess)

1968 (29 Jan). *Luthuli Commemoration.* P 13.
142   **68**   30 f. bistre-brown and bluish green ..   12   5

    (Des and eng P. Béquet (after Balou). Recess)

1968 (8 Feb). *AIR. "Friendship of the Peoples".* P 13.
143   **69**   70 f. chocolate, emerald & ultram   ..   30   15

    (Des S. Gauthier (after Paci). Litho So.Ge.Im.)

1968 (20 Feb). P 13.
144   **70**   10 f. multicoloured   5   5

67 Young Congolese

O **1** Arms

    (Des Béquet. Eng Monvoisin. Recess)

1967 (11 Dec). *21st Anniv of U.N.I.C.E.F.* P 13.
141   **67**   90 f. black, bright blue and lake-brown   40   20

(Des and die eng G. Aufschneider, after Muhlemann. Typo)
1968 (1 Jan)–**70**. *OFFICIAL.* P 14×13.
O142   O **1**   1 f. multicoloured (1.1.70)   ..   5   5
O143   2 f. multicoloured (1.1.70)   ..   5   5
O144   5 f. multicoloured (1.1.70)   ..   5   5
O145   10 f. multicoloured (1.1.70)   ..   5   5
O146   25 f. multicoloured (1.1.70)   ..   8   5
O147   30 f. multicoloured   8   5
O148   50 f. multicoloured (1.1.70)   ..   12   8
O149   85 f. multicoloured (1.1.70)   ..   15   15
O150   100 f. multicoloured (1.1.70)   ..   20   20
O151   200 f. multicoloured (1.1.70)   ..   35   35
O142/151   *Set of 10* ..   ..   ..   1·00   95

71 "Old Man and His Grandson" (Ghirlandaio)

72 "Mother and Child"

    (Photo and litho Delrieu)

1968 (20 Mar). *AIR. Paintings.* T **71** *and similar designs. Multicoloured.* P 12½.
145   30 f. Type **71**   15   8
146   100 f. "The Horatian Oath" (J.-L. David) (*horiz*)   40   25
147   200 f. "The Negress with Peonies" (F. Bazille) (*horiz*)   80   45
See also Nos. 209/13.

    (Des P. Lambert, after Soumbou. Eng C. Guillame. Recess)

1968 (25 May). *Mothers' Festival.* P 13.
148   **72**   15 f. black, new blue and brown-lake   5   5

73 Train crossing
Mayombé Viaduct

74 Beribboned Rope

(Des Mariscalchi. Eng Miermont. Recess)

1968 (24 June). *P* 13.
149 **73** 45 f. brown-lake, greenish blue and
     myrtle-green   20   10

(Des Dessirier. Photo So.Ge.Im.)

1968 (20 July). *AIR. Fifth Anniv of "Europafrique". P* 13.
150 **74** 50 f. red, yellow, green and sepia .. 20   12

75 Daimler, 1889

76 Dr. Martin Luther
King

(Des P. Lambert. Photo So.Ge.Im.)

1968 (29 July). *Veteran Motor Cars. T* **75** *and similar horiz
designs. Multicoloured. P* 13×12½.

(a) POSTAGE

151	5 f. Type **75** ..	5	5
152	20 f. Berliet, 1897	10	5
153	60 f. Peugeot, 1898	20	10
154	80 f. Renault, 1900	30	12
155	85 f. Fiat, 1902 ..	35	15

(b) AIR. Inscr "POSTE AERIENNE"

156	150 f. Ford, 1915..	60	30
157	200 f. Citroën, 1922	80	40
151/157	*Set of 7*	2·10	1·00

1968 (30 July). *Inauguration of Petroleum Refinery, Port
Gentil, Gabon. Design as T* **80** *of Central African Republic.*
158   30 f. new blue, red, green & chestnut .. 12   5

(Photo Delrieu)

1968 (5 Aug). *AIR. Martin Luther King Commemoration.
P* 12½.
159 **76** 50 f. black, dp bluish grn & pale emer   20   10

77 "The Barricade" (Delacroix)

78 Robert Kennedy

(Photo Delrieu)

1968 (15 Aug). *AIR. Fifth Anniv of the Revolution. Paintings. T* **77** *and similar horiz design. Multicoloured. P* 12½.
160   25 f. Type **77**   12   5
161   30 f. "Destruction of the Bastille" (H.
        Robert) ..   .· ..   15   10

(Photo Delrieu)

1968 (30 Sept). *AIR. Robert Kennedy Commemoration.
P* 12½.
162 **78** 50 f. black, light apple-grn & carm-red   20   10

79 "Tree of Life"
and W.H.O.
Emblem

80 Start of Race

(Des and eng J. Combet. Recess)

1968 (28 Nov). *20th Anniv of World Health Organization.
P* 13.
163 **79** 25 f. scarlet, purple and myrtle-green   10   5

(Des and eng J. Combet. Recess)

1968 (27 Dec). *AIR. Olympic Games, Mexico. T* **80** *and
similar designs. P* 13.

164	5 f. chocolate, new blue and emerald ..	5	5
165	20 f. myrtle-green, light brown and blue	8	5
166	60 f. chocolate, blue-green and crimson	20	12
167	85 f. chocolate, cerise and slate.. ..	35	20
164/167	*Set of 4*	60	35

Designs: *Vert*—20 f. Football; 60 f. Boxing. *Horiz*—85 f.
High-jumping.

(Photo Delrieu)

1968 (30 Dec). *AIR. "Philexafrique" Stamp Exhibition, Abidjan, Ivory Coast* (1969) (1st *issue). Vert design as T* **86** *of
Central African Republic. P* 12½.
168   100 f. multicoloured   55   50
Design:—100 f. "G. de Gueidan writing" (N. de Largilliere).
No. 168 was issued in sheets with *se-tenant* "PHILEX-
AFRIQUE" *stamp-size label.*

(Des and eng C. Durrens. Recess)

1969 (14 Feb). *AIR. "Philexafrique" Stamp Exhibition, Abidjan, Ivory Coast* (2nd *issue). Horiz design similar to T* **87** *of
Central African Republic. P* 13.
169   50 f. myrtle-green, orange-brown & mag 25   20
Design:—50 f. Pointe-Noire harbour, lumbering and Middle
Congo stamp of 1933.

(Photo Delrieu)

1969 (20 May). *AIR. Birth Bicentenary of Napoleon Bonaparte. Horiz designs as T* **144** *of Cameroun. Multicoloured. P* 12×12½.

170	25 f. "Battle of Rivoli" (Vernet) ..	12	5
171	50 f. "Battle of Marengo" (Pajou) ..	20	10
172	75 f. "Battle of Friedland" (Vernet) ..	30	12
173	100 f. "Battle of Jena" (Thévenin) ..	45	20
170/173	*Set of 4*	95	40

81 "Che" Guevara **82 Doll and Toys**

(Photo Delrieu)

1969 (10 June). *AIR. Ernesto "Che" Guevara (Latin-American revolutionary) Commemoration. P 12½.*
174 **81** 90 f. blackish brn, red-orge & lake-brn .. 30 15

(Des and eng C. Guillame. Recess)

1969 (20 June). *AIR. International Toy Fair, Nuremberg. P 13.*
175 **82** 100 f. slate, magenta and orange .. 35 20

83 Beribboned Bar **84 Astronauts**

(Des Dessirier. Photo Delrieu)

1969 (5 Aug). *AIR. "Europafrique". P 13×12.*
176 **83** 50 f. reddish violet, black & turquoise 20 12

1969 (10 Sept). *5th Anniversary of African Development Bank. As T 146 of Cameroun.*
177 25 f. orge-brown, emerald & carm-red .. 10 5
178 30 f. orge-brown, emerald & new blue .. 12 5

(Des Martimor. Embossed on gold foil Societé Pierre Mariotte)

1969 (15 Sept). *AIR. First Man on the Moon. Sheet 65×51 mm containing T 84 and similar vert design. Imperf.*
MS179 1000 f. Type **84**; 1000 f. Lunar module .. .. 6·00

(Des and eng J. Combet. Recess)

1969 (6 Oct). *Cycles and Motor-cycles. T 85 and similar horiz designs. P 13.*
180 50 f. bright purple, orange & olive-brn 20 8
181 75 f. black, lake and orange 25 10
182 80 f. dp bluish grn, new blue & purple 30 12
183 85 f. blue-green, slate and bistre-brown 35 12
184 100 f. maroon, carmine, violet-bl & black 40 15
185 150 f. bistre-brown, brown-red & black 50 30
186 200 f. bright purple, deep grn & blue-grn 65 35
187 300 f. emerald, bright purple & black .. 90 60
180/187 *Set of 8* .. .. 3·25 1·60
Design:—75 f. "Hirondelle" cycle; 80 f. Folding cycle; 85 f. "Peugeot" cycle; 100 f. "Excelsior Manxman" motor-cycle; 150 f. "Norton" motor-cycle; 200 f. "Brough Superior" motor-cycle; 300 f. "Matchless and N.L.G.-J.A.P.S." motor-cycle.

(Des J. Combet. Photo So.Ge.Im.)

1969 (20 Oct). *African Tourist Year. T 86 and similar multi-coloured design. P 13×12½ (40 f.) or 12½×13 (60 f.).*
188 40 f. Type **86** 15 5
189 60 f. Train crossing the Mayombe (*horiz*) 20 8

87 Mortar Tanks **88 Harvesting Pineapples**

(Des and eng C. Haley. Recess)

1969 (10 Dec). *Loutété Cement Works. T 87 and similar designs. P 13.*
190 10 f. slate, bistre-brown and lake .. 5 5
191 15 f. reddish violet, turq-blue & lake-brn 5 5
192 25 f. greenish blue, light brown & rose .. 10 5
193 30 f. indigo, reddish vio & ultramarine .. 12 5
190/193 *Set of 4* 25 15
MS194 170×101 mm. Nos. 190/3 .. .. 25 25
Designs: *Vert*—15 f. Mixing tower; 25 f. Cableway. *Horiz*—30 f. General view of works.

1969 (12 Dec). *10th Anniversary of ASECNA. As T 150 of Cameroun.*
195 100 f. bistre-brown 35 20

(Des and eng M. Monvoisin. Recess)

1969 (20 Dec). *50th Anniversary of International Labour Organization. T 88 and similar horiz design. P 13.*
196 25 f. chestnut, yellow-grn & new blue .. 10 5
197 30 f. slate, dull purple and red 12 5
Design:—30 f. Operating lathe.

PEOPLE'S REPUBLIC OF THE CONGO

By a new constitution, based on Marxist-Leninist principles, promulgated on 3 January 1970, the Congo Republic became the People's Republic of the Congo. This change was first reflected in the inscriptions on Nos. 214/5.

85 Modern Bicycle **86 Train entering Mbamba Tunnel**

89 Textile Plant **90 Linzolo Church**

(Des and eng G. Bétemps. Recess)

1970 (20 Jan). *"SOTEXCO" Textile Plant, Kinsoundi. T 89 and similar horiz designs. P 13.*
198	15 f. black, reddish violet and emerald ..	5	5
199	20 f. myrtle-green, carmine and purple	8	5
200	25 f. light brown, slate-blue & new blue	10	5
201	30 f. chocolate, cerise and slate.. ..	12	5
198/201	Set of 4	30	15

Designs:—20 f. Spinning machines; 25 f. Printing textiles; 30 f. Checking finished cloth.

(Des and eng G. Bétemps (25 f.), M. Monvoisin (90 f.). Recess)

1970. *Buildings. T 90 and similar design. P 13.*
202	25 f. bright green, choc & indigo (10.2) ..	10	5
203	90 f. choc, myrtle-green & new bl (20.1)	30	15

Design: *Horiz*—90 f. Cosmos Hotel, Brazzaville.

91 Artist at Work   **92** Diosso Gorges

(Des P. Béquet. Eng C. Guillame (100 f.), M. Monvoisin (others). Recess)

1970 (20 Feb). *AIR. "Art and Culture". T 91 and similar vert designs. P 13.*
204	100 f. chestnut, plum and blue-green ..	40	20
205	150 f. deep plum, brn-lake & myrtle-grn	55	25
206	200 f. lake-brown, choc & yellow-ochre	75	40

Designs:—150 f. Lesson in wood-carving; 200 f. Potter at wheel.

(Des and eng J. Gauthier. Recess)

1970 (25 Feb). *Tourism. T 92 and similar horiz design. P 13.*
207	70 f. bright purple, choc & myrtle-green	20	10
208	90 f. bright purple, deep grn & ol-brn ..	30	12

Design:—90 f. Foulakari Falls.

(Photo Delrieu)

1970 (10 Mar). *AIR. Paintings. Vert designs as T 71. Multicoloured. P 12½×12.*
209	150 f. "Child with Cherries" (J. Russell)	55	20
210	200 f. "Erasmus" (Holbein the younger)	75	30
211	250 f. "Silence" (B. Luini)	90	40
212	300 f. "Scio Massacre" (Delacroix)	1·10	60
213	500 f. "Capture of Constantinople" (Delacroix)	1·75	1·10
209/213	Set of 5	4·50	2·40

93 Aurichalcite   **94** *Volvaria esculenta*

(Des P. Lambert. Photo Delrieu)

1970 (20 Mar). *AIR. Minerals. T 93 and similar horiz design. Multicoloured. P 12½.*
214	100 f. Type **93** ..	35	20
215	150 f. Dioptase .. ..:	50	25

(Des P. Lambert, after N. Hallé (50 f.) or R. Heim (others). Photo)

1970 (31 Mar). *Mushrooms. T 94 and similar vert designs. Multicoloured. P 13.*
216	5 f. Type **94**	5	5
217	10 f. *Termitomyces entolomoides* ..	5	5
218	15 f. *Termitomyces microcarpus* ..	5	5
219	25 f. *Termitomyces aurantiacus* ..	10	5
220	30 f. *Termitomyces mammiformis* ..	12	5
221	50 f. *Tremella fuciformis*	20	10
216/221	Set of 6	50	30

95 Laying Cable   **96** Mother feeding Child

(Des and eng G. Bétemps. Recess)

1970 (30 Apr). *Laying of Coaxial Cable Brazzaville–Pointe Noire. T 95 and similar horiz design. P 13.*
222	25 f. chocolate, light brown & deep blue	10	5
223	30 f. purple-brown and grey-green ..	12	5

Design:—30 f. Diesel locomotive and cable-laying gang.

1970 (20 May). *New U.P.U. Headquarters Building, Berne. As T 156 of Cameroun.*
224	30 f. reddish purple, deep slate & plum	12	5

(Des P. Lambert. Photo)

1970 (30 May). *Mothers' Day. T 96 and similar vert design. Multicoloured. P 13.*
225	85 f. Type **96**	30	15
226	90 f. Mother suckling baby	30	15

97 U.N. Emblem and Trygve Lie   **98** Lenin in Cap

(Des and eng M. Monvoisin. Recess)

1970 (20 June). *25th Anniversary of United Nations. T 97 and similar designs, each showing U.N. emblem. P 13.*
227	100 f. bright blue, indigo and lake ..	35	30
228	100 f. slate-lilac, rose-carmine and lake	35	30
229	100 f. yellow-green, blue-green & lake ..	35	30
MS230	130×100 mm. Nos. 227/9	95	80

Designs: *Horiz*—No. 227, T **97**; No. 229, U Thant. *Vert*—No. 228, Dag Hammarskjöld.

(Photo Delrieu)

1970 (25 June). *AIR. Birth Centenary of Lenin. T 98 and similar vert design. P 12½.*
231	45 f. orge-brn, orge-yell and deep green	15	8
232	75 f. plum, claret and ultramarine ..	25	12

Design:—75 f. Lenin seated (after Vassiliev).

99 *Brillantaisia vogeliana*   **100** Karl Marx

(Des P. Lambert (1 f. to 5 f. after N. Hallé). Photo So.Ge.lm. (10, 15 f.) or Delrieu (others))

1970 (30 June). *Flora and Fauna. Multicoloured designs as T* **99**, *showing flowers (horiz designs) or insects (vert designs). P* 13 × 12½ (10, 15 f.), 12 × 12½ (20 f.) or 12½ × 12 *(others)*.

233	1 f. Type **99**	5	5
234	2 f. *Plectranthus decurrens*	5	5
235	3 f. *Myrianthemum mirabile*	5	5
236	5 f. *Connarus griffonianus*	5	5
237	10 f. *Sternotomis variabilis (vert)*	5	5
238	15 f. *Chelorrhina polyphemus (vert)*	5	5
239	20 f. *Metopodontus savagei (vert)*	5	5
233/239	*Set of 7*	25	25

(Des and eng M. Monvoisin. Recess)

1970 (10 July). *AIR. Founders of Communism. T* **100** *and similar vert design. P* 13.

240	50 f. chocolate, bright green and lake	15	8
241	50 f. chocolate, bright blue and lake	15	8

Designs:—No. 240, T **100**; No. 241, Friedrich Engels.

101 Kentrosaurus   **102** "Mikado 141" Steam Engine (1932)

(Des C. Guillame. Photo Delrieu)

1970 (20 July). *Prehistoric Creatures. T* **101** *and similar multicoloured designs. P* 12½ × 12 (horiz) or 12 × 12½ (vert).

242	15 f. Type **101**	5	5
243	20 f. *Dinotherium (vert)*	5	5
244	60 f. *Brachiosaurus (vert)*	20	10
245	80 f. *Arsinoitherium*	25	15
242/245	*Set of 4*	50	30

(Des J. Pheulpin. Eng J. Pheulpin (40 f.), G. Aufschneider (60 f.), A. Frères (75 f.), J. Miermont (85 f.). Recess)

1970 (20 Aug). *Locomotives of Congo Railways. T* **102** *and similar horiz designs. P* 13.

246	40 f. black, turq-green & bright purple	12	5
247	60 f. black, emerald and new blue	15	10
248	75 f. black, red and new blue	20	12
249	85 f. carmine, myrtle-green & yell-orge	25	15
246/249	*Set of 4*	65	35

Designs:—60 f. Type 130 + 032 steam loco (1947); 75 f. Alsthom "BB 1100" engine (1962); 85 f. C.E.M. C.A.F.L. "BB BB 232" diesel (1969).

103 Lilienthal's Glider, 1891

(Des C. Guillame. Eng M. Monvoisin (90 f.), C. Guillame (others). Recess)

1970 (5 Sept). *AIR. History of Flight and Space Travel. T* **103** *and similar horiz designs. P* 13.

250	45 f. bistre-brown, new blue & crimson	15	8
251	50 f. myrtle-green, lt brn & bright grn	15	8
252	70 f. bistre-brown, brown-lake & new bl	20	12
253	90 f. brown, blackish olive & new blue	25	15
250/253	*Set of 4*	70	40

Designs:—50 f. Lindbergh's "Spirit of St. Louis", 1927; 70 f. "Sputnik 1", 1957; 90 f. First man on the Moon, 1969.

104 "Wise Man"   **105** *Cogniauxia padolaena*

(Des P. Lambert. Photo Delrieu)

1970 (10 Dec). *AIR. Christmas. Stained-glass from Brazzaville Cathedral. T* **104** *and similar vert designs. Multicoloured. P* 12½.

254	100 f. Type **104**	30	15
255	150 f. "Shepherd"	45	20
256	250 f. "Angels"	75	40
MS257	152 × 116 mm. Nos 254/6	1·50	1·50

(Des "Lacroix" (H. Ouin). Photo Delrieu)

1971. *Tropical Flowers. Vert designs as T* **105**. *Multicoloured. P* 12 × 12½. (a) POSTAGE (10 Feb).

258	1 f. Type **105**	5	5
259	2 f. *Celosia cristata*	5	5
260	5 f. *Plumeria acutifolia*	5	5
261	10 f. *Bauhinia variegata*	5	5
262	15 f. *Euphorbia pulcherrima*	5	5
263	20 f. *Thunbergia grandiflora*	5	5
258/263	*Set of 6*	25	25

(b) POSTAGE DUE. Inscr "TIMBRE-TAXE" (25 Mar).

D264	1 f. Stylised bouquet	5	5
D265	2 f. *Phaeomeria magnifica*	5	5
D266	5 f. *Millettia laurentii*	5	5
D267	10 f. *Polianthes tuberosa*	5	5
D268	15 f. *Pyrostegia venusta*	5	5
D269	20 f. *Hibiscus rosa sinensis*	5	5
D264/269	*Set of 6*	25	25

HAVE YOU READ THE NOTES AT THE BEGINNING OF THIS CATALOGUE?

These often provide answers to the enquiries we receive.

106 Marilyn Monroe

108 Telecommunications Map

107 "Carrying the Cross" (Veronese)

(Des and eng C. Haley. Recess)

1971 (16 Mar). *AIR. Great Names of the Cinema.* T **106** *and similar vert portraits.* P 13.

270	100 f. lake-brown, ultram & emerald	..	30	15
271	150 f. bright purple, ultram & purple	..	45	20
272	200 f. purple-brown and ultramarine	..	60	30
273	250 f. plum, ultramarine and emerald	..	75	40
270/273	*Set of 4*		1·90	95

Designs:—150 f. Martine Carol; 200 f. Eric von Stroheim; 250 f. Sergei Eisenstein (wrongly inscr "Serghei").

(Photo Delrieu)

1971 (26 Apr). *AIR. Easter. Religious paintings as* T **107**. *Multicoloured.* P 13.

274	100 f. Type **107** ..	..	35	15
275	150 f. "Christ on the Cross" (Burgundian School c 1500) (*vert*)	..	50	20
276	200 f. "Descent from the Cross" (Van der Weyden)	..	70	30
277	250 f. "The Entombment" (Flemish School c 1500) (*vert*)	..	80	40
278	500 f. "The Resurrection" (Memling) (*vert*)	..	1·60	80
274/278	*Set of 5*	..	3·50	1·60

(Photo Delrieu)

1971 (18 June). *AIR. Pan-African Telecommunications Network.* P 12½.

279	**108** 70 f. chocolate, light blue and grey ..	25	12
280	85 f. chocolate, cobalt & pale mauve	30	15
281	90 f. choc, turq-green & olive-yell ...	30	20

(Photo Delrieu)

1971 (19 June). *AIR. World Telecommunications Day* (17 May). P 12½.

282	**109** 65 f. multicoloured ..	..	..	20	12

(Des M. Monvoisin. Photo Delrieu)

1971 (26 June). *Reptiles.* T **110** *and similar multicoloured designs.* P 12 × 12½ (*vert*) or 12½ × 12 (*horiz*).

283	5 f. Type **110**	..	5	5
284	10 f. African egg-eating snake (*horiz*)	..	5	5
285	15 f. Flap-necked chameleon	..	..	5	5
286	20 f. Nile crocodile (*horiz*)	..	..	8	5
287	25 f. Rock python (*horiz*)	..	..	10	5
288	30 f. Gabon viper	..	..	10	5
289	40 f. Brown house snake (*horiz*)	..	15	8
290	45 f. Jameson's mamba..	..	..	15	10
283/290	*Set of 8*	..	..	65	40

111 Afro-Japanese Allegory

112 *Pseudimbrasia deyrollei*

(Des and eng J. Combet. Recess)

1971 (28 June). *AIR. "PHILATOKYO '71" Stamp Exhibition, Tokyo.* T **111** *and similar vert design.* P 13.

291	75 f. black, magenta & reddish violet ..	25	15
292	150 f. pur-brn, brown-red & bright pur ..	50	30

Design:—150 f. "Tree of Life", Japanese geisha and masked African.

(Des Baillais. Photo)

1971 (3 July). *Caterpillars.* T **112** *and similar multicoloured designs.* P 13.

293	10 f. Type **114** ..	..	..	5	5
294	15 f. *Bunaea alcinoe* (*vert*)	..	5	5
295	20 f. *Epiphora vacuna ploetzi*	..	8	5
296	25 f. *Imbrasia eblis*	..	..	10	5
297	30 f. *Imbrasia dione* (*vert*)	..	10	5
298	40 f. *Holocera angulata* ..	..	15	8
293/298	*Set of 6* ..	..	..	45	25

109 Global Emblem

110 Green Night Adder

113 Japanese Scout

114 Olympic Torch

(Embossed on foil Boccard)

1971 (14 July). *World Scout Jamboree, Asagiri, Japan (1st issue)*. *P* 10½. *(a) POSTAGE. Vert designs as T* **113**.

299	90 f. silver (Type 113)..	..	..	30	
300	90 f. silver (French scout)	..	..	30	
301	90 f. silver (Congolese scout)..	..	30	
302	90 f. silver (Lord Baden-Powell)	..	30	

(b) AIR. Design 47×36 *mm inscr* "Poste Aérienne"

| 303 | 1000 f. gold (Scouts and Lord Baden-Powell) | .. | .. | .. | 3·25 | |
| 299/303 | *Set of* 5 | .. | .. | .. | 4·00 | |

Nos. 299/302 were issued in *se-tenant* blocks of four within the sheet.

(Des and eng M. Monvoisin. Recess)

1971 (20 July). *AIR. Olympic Games, Munich* (1972). *T* **114** *and similar design. P* 13.

| 304 | 150 f. verm, slate-green & bright purple | 50 | 30 |
| 305 | 350 f. reddish violet, emerald & yell-brn | 1·20 | 75 |

Design: *Horiz*—350 f. Sporting cameos within Olympic rings.

115 Scout Badge, Dragon and Congolese Wood-carving

(Des and eng J. Combet. Recess)

1971 (25 Aug). *AIR. World Scout Jamboree, Asagiri, Japan (2nd issue)*. *T* **115** *and similar designs. P* 13.

306	85 f. bright purple, brown & turq-blue	30	15
307	90 f. red-brown, reddish violet & lake ..	30	15
308	100 f. turquoise-grn, lake and olive-brn	35	20
309	250 f. chocolate, carmine-red & bl-grn ..	80	45
306/309	*Set of* 4	..	..	..	1·60	85

Designs: *Vert*—90 f. African and Japanese mask; 100 f. Japanese woman and African. *Horiz*—250 f. Congolese mask, geisha and Scout badge.

116 Running

(Des and eng A. Decaris. Recess)

1971 (30 Sept). *AIR. 75th Anniversary of Modern Olympic Games. T* **116** *and similar horiz designs. P* 13.

310	75 f. red-brown, new blue & brn-lake ..	25	12
311	85 f. purple-brn, slate-blue & rose-red	30	15
312	90 f. brown and bluish violet ..	..	30	15
313	100 f. brown and slate-blue ..	..	35	20
314	150 f. purple-brown, red and blue-grn ..	50	30
310/314	*Set of* 5	..	..	..	1·50	80

Designs:—85 f. Hurdling; 90 f. Various events; 100 f. Wrestling; 150 f. Boxing.

117 *Cymothae sangaris*

118 African and European Workers

(Des Baillais. Photo Delrieu)

1971 (15 Oct). *Butterflies. T* **117** *and similar multicoloured designs. P* 12½×12 *(horiz) or* 12×12½ *(vert)*.

315	30 f. Type 117 ..	..	..	..	10	5
316	40 f. *Papilio dardanus* (vert)	..	..	15	5
317	75 f. *Iolaus timon*	..	..	..	25	12
318	90 f. *Papilio phorcas* (vert)	..	..	30	20
319	100 f. *Euchloron megaera*	..	..	35	20
315/319	*Set of* 5	..	..	..	1·00	55

(Des Baillais. Photo Delrieu)

1971 (30 Oct). *Racial Equality Year. P* 13.

| 320 | **118** 50 f. multicoloured .. | .. | .. | 15 | 10 |

119 De Gaulle and Congo 1966 Brazzaville Conference Stamp

(Des and eng J. Combet. Recess (500 f.). Des Martimor. Litho and embossed on gold foil Societé Pierre Mariotte (1000 f.))

1971 (9 Nov). *AIR. 1st Death Anniv of General De Gaulle. T* **119** *and similar designs. P* 13 (500 f.) *or* 12½ (1000 f.).

321	500 f. brown, slate-green and scarlet ..	1·75	1·25
322	1000 f. scarlet and emerald/*gold*	..	3·75	
323	1000 f. scarlet and emerald/*gold*	..	3·75	

Designs: *Vert* (29×38 *mm*)—No. 322, Tribute by Pres. Ngouabi; No. 323, De Gaulle and Cross of Lorraine.

1971 (13 Nov). *AIR. 10th Anniversary of African and Malagasy Posts and Telecommunications Union. Design similar to T* **184** *of Cameroun*.

| 324 | 100 f. Headquarters and Congolese woman .. | .. | .. | .. | 35 | 20 |

REPUBLIQUE POPULAIRE
DU CONGO
30F

INAUGURATION
DE LA LIAISON COAXIALE
18-11-71

(120)

1971 (18 Nov). *Inauguration of Brazzaville–Pointe Noire Cable Link. Nos.* 222/3 *surch with T* **120** *and similar type*.

| 325 | **95** 30 f. on 25 f. choc, light brn & dp blue | 10 | 5 |
| 326 | – 40 f. on 30 f. purple-brown & grey-grn | 12 | 8 |

121 Congo Republic Flag and Allegory of Revolution

(Des J. Chesnot. Photo)

1971 (30 Nov). *AIR. 8th Anniversary of Revolution. P* 13.

| 327 | **121** 100 f. multicoloured .. | .. | .. | 35 | 20 |

122 Congolese with Flag

(Des J. Chesnot. Photo)

1971 (31 Dec). *AIR. 2nd Anniv of Congolese Workers' Party (30 f.) and Adoption of New National Flag (40 f.). T* **122** *and similar horiz design. Multicoloured. P* 13.
| 328 | 30 f. Type **122** | .. | .. | .. | 10 | 5 |
| 329 | 40 f. National flag | .. | .. | .. | 12 | 8 |

123 Map and Emblems

124 Lion

(Des Baillais. Photo)

1971 (31 Dec). *"Work–Democracy–Peace". P* 12½ × 13.
330	**123**	30 f. multicoloured..	..	..	10	5
331		40 f. multicoloured..	..	..	12	8
332		100 f. multicoloured..	..	..	35	20

(Des M. Monvoisin. Eng C. Guillame (2 f.), M. Monvoisin (others). Recess)

1972 (31 Jan). *Wild Animals. T* **124** *and similar designs. P* 13.
333	1 f. brown, blue and emerald	..	..	5	5
334	2 f. bistre-brown, myrtle-green and red		5	5
335	3 f. bistre-brn, orge-red & brn-lake	..	5	5
336	4 f. chocolate, turq and reddish violet ..	5	5
337	5 f. bistre-brown, blue-green & brn-red		5	5
338	20 f. bistre-brown, turq & red-orange	..	5	5
339	30 f. slate-green, emerald & yell-brown	8	5
340	40 f. black, emerald and greenish blue ..	10	8
333/340	*Set of 8*			35	25

Designs: *Horiz*—2 f. Elephants; 3 f. Leopard; 4 f. Hippopotamus; 20 f. Potto; 30 f. De Brazza's monkey. *Vert*—5 f. Gorilla; 40 f. Chimpanzee.

125 Book Year Emblem

126 Team Captain with Cup

(Litho Delrieu)

1972 (3 June). *AIR. International Book Year. P* 12½.
| 341 | **125** | 50 f. yellow-green, yellow and red .. | 15 | 10 |

(Des B. Le Sourd. Photo Delrieu)

1973 (22 Feb). *AIR. Congolese Victory in Africa Cup Football Championship, 1972. T* **126** *and similar multicoloured design. P* 13½ × 13 (*No. 342*) *or* 13 × 13½ (*No. 343*).
| 342 | 100 f. Type **126** | .. | .. | .. | 35 | 20 |
| 343 | 100 f. Congolese team (*horiz*) | .. | .. | 35 | • 20 |

127 Girl with Bird   **128** Miles Davis

(Des and eng P. Forget. Recess)

1973 (5 Mar). *AIR. U.N. Environmental Conservation Conference, Stockholm* (1972). *P* 13.
| 344 | **127** | 85 f. myrtle-grn, new blue & orge | .. | 30 | 15 |

(Des B. Le Sourd. Photo Delrieu)

1973 (5 Mar). *AIR. Famous Negro Musicians. T* **128** *and similar horiz designs. P* 13.
345	125 f. magenta, turq-blue & ultram	..	40	25
346	140 f. brt purple, dp mauve & vermilion	45	30
347	160 f. orange-yellow, brt emer & ol-yell	55	35
348	175 f. red-orge, ultram & reddish vio	..	60	40
345/348	*Set of 4*		1·90	1·25

Designs:—140 f. Ella Fitzgerald; 160 f. Count Basie; 175 f. John Coltrane.

129 Hurdling

(Des Dessirier. Eng Larrivière (250 f.), Jumelet (others). Recess)

1973 (15 Mar). *AIR. Olympic Games, Munich* (1972). *T* **129** *and similar designs. P* 13.
349	100 f. violet and magenta	..	..	35	20
350	150 f. reddish violet and emerald	..	50	30
351	250 f. crimson and new blue	..	85	50

Designs: *Vert*—150 f. Pole-vaulting. *Horiz*—250 f. Wrestling.

130 Oil Tank Farm, Djéno

(Des and eng A. Decaris. Recess)

1973 (20 Mar). *AIR. Oil Installations, Pointe Noire.* *T* **130** *and similar designs.* *P* 13.

352	180 f. indigo, brown-red & new blue	..		60	40
353	230 f. black, brown-red & new blue	..		75	45
354	240 f. maroon, indigo and brown-red	..		80	50
355	260 f. black, brown-red & new blue	..		85	55
352/355	*Set of 4*	..	.. ..	2·75	1·75

Designs: *Vert*—230 f. Oil-well head; 240 f. Drill in operation. *Horiz*—260 f. Off-shore oil-well.

131 Lunar Module and Astronaut on Moon

(Des and eng P. Béquet. Recess)

1973 (31 Mar). *AIR. Moon Flight of "Apollo 17".* *P* 13.

356	**131**	250 f. multicoloured ..	..	..	85	50

CORDOBA. See Argentine Republic.

CORRIENTES. See Argentine Republic.

Costa Rica

1862. 8 Reales = 1 Peso
1866. 100 Centavos = 1 Peso
1900. 100 Centimos = 1 Colon

Costa Rica was discovered by Columbus in 1502 and was made a Spanish province in 1540. On 15 September 1821 it became an independent republic.

1

(Eng and recess A.B.N. Co, N.Y.)

1863 (Apr)–75. *P* 12.

1	1	½ r. deep blue	..	..	..	..	12	20
2		½ r. light blue (7.75)	..	..	..	12	35
		a. Imperf between (pair)		..	..	28·00	
3		2 r. red /..	..	..	..	25	50
4		4 r. green (3.64) ..	..	..	..	1·00	1·25
5		1 p. orange (1.64)..	..	..	..	4·00	4·50

No. 2 was printed from a different plate and shows little or no sky over the mountains.

cto.	cto.	cts.	Cts.
(2)	(3)	(4)	(5)

1881–82. *No. 1 surch as T 2/5, in red.*

6	2	1 c. on ½ r. blue (1882)	..		..	60	1·25
7	3	1 c. on ½ r. blue (10.82)	..		..	2·50	5·00
8	4	2 c. on ½ r. blue (1.81)	..		..	45	85
		a. Error. Surch T 5	..		..	35·00	
9		5 c. on ½ r. blue (11.82)	..		..	1·25	1·75

A block of six of No. 8a has been found in one pane. The error was quickly corrected.

10 cts. U.P.U.	20 CTS U.P.U.	
(6)	(7)	

8 General P. Fernandez

1882 (Dec). *Surch as T 6 or 7 (20 c.). P* 12.

10	1	5 c. on ½ r. blue (R.)	..	17·00	20·00
11		10 c. on 2 r. red	..	9·00	10·00
12		20 c. on 4 r. green (R.)	..	20·00	20·00

Surcharges of other values or types on stamps of Type 1 are bogus productions made by the dealer who bought the remainder stocks of the first issue.

Dangerous forgeries of Nos. 10/12 exist.

(Eng and recess A.B.N. Co, N.Y.)

1883 (1 Jan). *Tablets containing numerals vary for each value. Date on stamp that of first issue under U.P.U. P* 12.

13	8	1 c. green	..	..	..	25	20
14		2 c. carmine	..	..	..	30	25
15		5 c. violet	..	..	..	45	20
16		10 c. orange	..	..	..	2·50	80
17		40 c. blue	..	..	..	30	25

USED OFFICIAL STAMPS. As it was not the practice to cancel the stamps on official mail, postmarked copies are extremely rare. Some have foreign postmarks applied on arrival. Our prices in the used column for Official stamps of 1883 to 1902 (No. O58) are for unused stamps without gum and prices in the unused column are for mint stamps. Later issues were postmarked.

Oficial	OFICIAL	OFICIAL
(O 1) 13½ mm	(O 2) 13 mm	(O 3) 15½ mm

Oficial	OFICIAL.
(O 4) 12 mm	(O 5) 15 mm

There are two types of Type O 5, in Antique or Roman capitals.

1883–87. OFFICIAL. **T 8** optd.

(a) With Type O **1** (Apr 1883–85)

O18	1 c. green (R.) ..		..	..	25	25
O19	1 c. green		..	..	30	30
O20	2 c. carmine (B.)		..	..	40	40
O21	2 c. carmine		..	..	30	30
O22	5 c. violet (R.) ..		..	..	1·10	1·10
O23	10 c. orange (G.)		..	..	1·25	1·25

(b) With Type O **2** (Aug 1886)

O24	1 c. green		..	..	35	35
O25	2 c. carmine		..	..	50	50
O26	5 c. violet (R.)		..	..	3·50	3·50
O27	10 c. orange		..	..	3·50	3·50

(c) With Type O **3** (Aug 1886)

O28	1 c. green		..	..	30	30
O29	2 c. carmine		..	..	50	50
O30	5 c. violet (R.)		..	..	3·00	3·00
O31	10 c. orange		..	..	3·00	3·00

(d) With Type O **4** (1886)

O32	5 c. violet		..	..	8·00	8·00
O33	10 c. orange		..	..	20·00	16·00

(e) With Type O **5** (1887)

O34	1 c. green		..	..	20	20
	a. "OFICAL" ..		..	..	1·40	1·40
	a. Stop omitted		..	..	30	30
O35	2 c. carmine		..	..	25	25
	a. "OFICAL" ..		..	..	2·25	2·00
	b. Stop omitted		..	..	35	* 35
O36	10 c. orange		..	..	1·10	1·10
	a. "OFICAL" ..		..	..	2·00	2·00
	b. Stop omitted		..	..	1·40	1·40
	c. Opt double		..	..		
O37	40 c. blue		..	..	25	30
	a. "OFICAL" ..		..	..	1·50	1·50
	b. Stop omitted		..	..	40	40

OFICIAL

F **1** General P.
Fernandez

F **2** President B. Soto

9 President B.
Soto

19   **20**   (O **7**)

(Eng and recess A.B.N. Co, N.Y.)

(Eng and recess Waterlow)

1884–88. *POSTAL FISCAL. P* 12.

F18	F **1**	1 c. carmine			5	5
F19		2 c. blue			25	20
F20	F **2**	5 c. brown-red (1888)			65	50
F21		10 c. blue (1888)			8	15

(Eng and recess A.B.N. Co, N.Y.)

1887 (Jan). *Numeral tablets vary. P* 12.

18	**9**	5 c. violet			80	20
19		10 c. orange			40	30

1887. *OFFICIAL. T* **9** *optd with Type O* **5**.

O38	5 c. violet			85	85
	a. "OFICAL"			1·75	1·75
	b. Stop omitted			90	90
O39	10 c. orange			25	25
	a. "OFICAL"			1·10	1·10
	b. Stop omitted			50	50
	c. Opt double			3·25	

CORREOS
(10)

1889 (July). *Provisionals. Fiscal stamps optd horiz with T* **10**.

20	F **1**	1 c. dull carmine			45	45
		a. Opt inverted			3·00	
21	F **2**	5 c. brown-red			35	35

It is understood that the 1 c. with overprint vertical is a fake.

OFICIAL

11 Pres. Soto   **12** Pres. Soto   (O **6**)

(Eng and recess Waterlow, London)

1889 (20 Sept–9 Oct). *T* **11/12** *and portrait of Pres. Soto in various frames. P* 14, 15.

22	1 c. sepia				10	10
	a. Imperf (pair)				7·50	
	b. Imperf vert (horiz pair)				1·25	
	c. Imperf between (pair)				6·00	
23	2 c. green				10	10
	a. Imperf (pair)				1·50	
	b. Imperf horiz (vert pair)				1·50	
	c. Imperf between (pair)				1·50	
24	5 c. deep orange				15	10
	a. Imperf (pair)					
25	10 c. brown-lake				10	10
	a. Imperf between (vert pair)				1·00	
26	20 c. green				10	10
	a. Imperf between (horiz pair)				1·50	
	b. Imperf horiz (vert pair)				1·50	
27	50 c. rose-carmine				20	20
28	1 p. blue				40	40
	a. Greenish blue				60	60
29	2 p. violet				1·25	1·10
30	5 p. olive-green				7·00	6·00
31	10 p. black (9 Oct)				12·00	10·00

1889. *OFFICIAL. Nos.* **22/27** *optd with Type O* **6**.

O40	1 c. sepia			8	10
O41	2 c. greenish blue			8	10
O42	5 c. deep orange			8	10
O43	10 c. brown-lake			8	10
	a. Imperf between (horiz pair)				
O44	20 c. green			8	10
O45	50 c. rose-carmine			40	50

1892 (Mar). *T* **19**, **20** *and similar arms types in various frames. P* 14, 15.

32	1 c. greenish blue			10	10
	a. Imperf between (horiz pair)				
33	2 c. orange			10	10
34	5 c. violet			1·25	10
	a. Reddish lilac			10	10
	b. Imperf between (pair)				
35	10 c. green			12	10
	a. Reddish lilac			10	10
	b. Imperf between (pair)				
36	20 c. scarlet			1·25	10
	a. Imperf between (horiz pair)			3·75	
37	50 c. ultramarine			1·25	1·25
38	1 p. bronze-green/*straw*			40	30
39	2 p. red/*grey*			40	30
40	5 p. blue/*buff*			40	40
41	10 p. brown/*buff*			1·75	1·00
	a. Brown/*yellow*			1·50	1·00

1892. *OFFICIAL. Nos.* **32/37** *optd with Type O* **7**.

O46	1 c. greenish blue			10	10
O47	2 c. orange			10	10
O48	5 c. violet			10	10
O49	10 c. green			40	40
O50	20 c. scarlet			8	8
O51	50 c. ultramarine			20	25
O46/51	*Set of 6*			90	90

BARRED CANCELLATIONS. Our prices in the used column for the following issues are for postally used specimens. Stamps cancelled with five black bars can be supplied at the prices indicated in brackets, where these are given, if in stock.

There is another cancellation consisting of four concentric circles which was used for both postal and telegraph purposes and these cannot be distinguished. However, on values from 50 c. upwards, they were invariably telegraphically used.

29 Juan
Santamaria

30 Juan Mora F.

31 Port Limon

32 Braulio Carrillo
(wrongly inscr
"BRANLIO")

33 National Theatre

34 José M. Castro

35 Birris Bridge

36 Juan Rafael Mora

D 1

(42)

(Eng and recess Waterlow)

1903 (Sept). *POSTAGE DUE. Numerals in centre in black.*
P 14.

D55	D 1	5 c. slate-blue	..	..	1·75	45
D56		10 c. orange-brown	..	..	1·75	45
D57		15 c. green	..	..	65	45
D58		20 c. carmine	..	..	85	45
D59		25 c. ultramarine	..	..	85	95
D60		30 c. deep brown	..	..	1·75	95
D61		40 c. olive-bistre	..	..	1·75	95
D62		50 c. magenta	..	..	1·75	70
D55/62		*Set of 8*	..	..	10·00	4·75

37 Jesus Jimenez

38 Arms

PROVISORIO

OFICIAL

(O 8)

(Eng and recess Waterlow)

1901 (Jan). *New Currency. P* 13½ *to* 16.

42	29	1 c. black and green	..	..	10	15
43	30	2 c. black and vermilion (B. 5p.)	..	20	15
		a. Centre inverted	..	..		
44	31	5 c. black and pale blue	..	..	10	5
		a. Imperf (pair)	..	..	10·00	9·00
45	32	10 c. black and yellow-brown (B. 8p.)	..	25	5
46	33	20 c. black and lake (B. 10p.)	..	65	8
47	34	50 c. blue and dull claret (B. 10p.)	..	65	25
48	35	1 col. black and olive (B. 10p.)	..	2·75	60
49	36	2 col. greenish blk & car (B. 12p.)	..	1·75	40
50	37	5 col. black and brown (B. 35 p)	..	3·25	40
51	38	10 col. brown-red & pale grn (B. 20p.)	..	4·00	60
42/51		*Set of 10*	..	..	12·00	2·40

1901–02. *OFFICIAL. Nos.* 42/48 *optd with Type* O **7.**

O52	29	1 c. black and green	..	..	15	15
O53	30	2 c. black and vermilion	..	..	15	15
O54	31	5 c. black and pale blue (B. 5p.)	..	15	15
O55	32	10 c. black and yellow-brown	..	20	20
O56	33	20 c. black and lake	..	..	40	40
O57	34	50 c. blue and dull claret	..	..	75	75
O58	35	1 col. black and olive	..	..	1·50	1·50
O52/58		*Set of 7*	..	..	3·00	3·00

1903 (Jan). *OFFICIAL. No.* 43 *optd with Type* O **8.**

O59	30	2 c. black and vermilion (G.)	..	1·00	1·00
		a. Opt inverted	..	..	1·50	1·50
		b. "PROVISIORO"	..	..	1·75	1·75
		c. "PROVISIORO" inverted	..	5·00	5·00

39 José M. Cañas

40 Julian Volio

41 Eusebio Figueroa

(Eng and recess Waterlow)

1903 (8 Sept). *P* 13½–14.

52	39	4 c. black and purple	..	..	50	25
53	40	6 c. black and olive (B. 10p.)	..	1·40	50
54	41	25 c. brown and pale lilac	..	1·00	5

1903. *OFFICIAL. Nos.* 52/4 *optd with Type* O **7.**

O60	39	4 c. black and purple	..	..	40	40
O61	40	6 c. black and olive	..	..	50	50
O62	41	25 c. brown and pale lilac	..	1·25	1·00

1905–06. *No.* 46 *surch with T* 42.

(*a*) *Surch horizontal* (Aug 1905)

55	33	1 c. on 20 c. black and lake	..	..	15	15
		a. Surch inverted	..	..	50	50
		b. Surch double	..	..		

(*b*) *Surch diagonal* (Feb 1906)

56	33	1 c. on 20 c. black and lake	..	..	15	15

Stamps are also known surcharged with Type 42 in *red,*
green, yellow or *gold,* but these are colour trials.

43 Juan Santamaria

44 Juan Mora

45 José M. Cañas

46 Mauro Fernandez

47 Braulio Carrillo

48 Julian Volio

49 Eusebio Figueroa

50 José M. Castro

51 Jesus Jimenez

52 Juan Rafael Mora

OFICIAL

(O 9)

(Eng and recess Waterlow)

1907 (1 Oct). *No wmk or papermaker's wmk "JAS WRIGLEY & SON LD 219" in two lines.* (*a*) *P* 14.

57	43	1 c. indigo and chestnut-brown	..	10	5
58	44	2 c. black and yellow-green	..	25	8
59	45	4 c. indigo and carmine-red/toned	..	35·00	4·00
60	46	5 c. indigo and orange-buff	..	20	8
		a. Centre inverted	..	26·00	
61	47	10 c. black and blue	..	20	10
62	48	20 c. slate and olive	..	85	50
63	49	25 c. myrtle and lavender (**B.** 50p.)	..	60	25
64	50	50 c. indigo-blue and dull claret	..	8·00	2·50
65	51	1 col. black and sienna (**B.** 50p.)	..	3·00	2·00
66	52	2 col. myrtle and claret (**B.** 75p.)	..	10·00	7·00

(*b*) *P* 11½ × 14

67	43	1 c. indigo and chestnut-brown	..	12	5
68	44	2 c. black and yellow-green	..	30	10
69	45	4 c. indigo and carmine-red/toned	..	1·40	65
70	46	5 c. indigo and orange-buff	..	75	15
71	47	10 c. black and blue	..	15	10
72	48	20 c. slate and olive (**B.** 10p.)	..	75	25
73	49	25 c. myrtle and lavender (**B.** 1.50		1·50	70
74	50	50 c. indigo-bl & dull claret (**B.** 20p.)	..	6·50	1·75
75	51	1 col. black and sienna (**B.** 20p.)	..	2·50	1·50
76	52	2 col. myrtle and claret (**B.** £1)	..	8·00	5·00

All values of the 1907 issue are known imperforate but these are clandestine.

1908 (Jan). *OFFICIAL. Stamps of* 1907 *optd with Type* O **9**. *P* 14.

O77	43	1 c. indigo and chestnut-brown	..	5	5
O78	44	2 c. black and yellow-green..	..	5	5
O79	45	4 c. indigo and carmine-red/toned	..	5	5
O80	46	5 c. indigo and orange-buff..		8	8
O81	47	10 c. black and blue	..	15	8
O82	49	25 c. myrtle and lavender	..	15	·10
O83	50	50 c. indigo-blue and dull claret	..	15	15
O84	51	1 col. black and sienna	..	40	30
O77/84		Set of 8	..	95	75

53   **54**

(Eng and recess A.B.N. Co, N.Y.)

1910 (6 Apr). *T* **53, 54** *and similar portraits, all inscr* "U.P.U. 1909". *P* 12.

77	1 c. brown (J. Santamaria)	..	5	5
78	2 c. deep green (J. Mora)	..	5	5
79	4 c. scarlet (J. M. Cañas)	..	5	5
80	5 c. orange (M. Fernandez)	..	5	5
81	10 c. deep blue (B. Carrillo)	..	5	5
82	20 c. olive (J. Volio)	..	12	10
83	25 c. purple (E. Figueroa)..	..	85	20
84	1 col. grey-brown (J. Jimenez)	..	40	20
77/84	Set of 8	.. ..	1·50	65

✶₁₉₁₁✶   **.✶ 1911 .✶**
(62)   **(63)**

1910–11. *Optd with T* **62** (i) *or* **63** (ii).

(*a*) *P* 14, 15 (*No.* 85) *or* 14

85	29	1 c. black and green (i) (R.) (4.11)	..	20	15
		a. Stars arranged thus ✶₊1911₊✶	..	75	60
		b. Surch in black	.. ..	5·00	4·00
86	43	1 c. indigo & chestnut-brown (i) (4.11)		20	10
		a. Opt inverted	..	1·40	1·40
		b. Stars arranged thus ✶₊1911₊✶	..	20	20
87	44	2 c. black and yellow-green (ii) (R.) (12.10)		35	30
		a. Opt inverted	..	1·10	1·10
		b. With opt (i) and (ii)	..	1·25	1·25
		c. With stars level	..	70	70
88		2 c. black and yellow-green (i) (**B.** 5p.)		20	10
		a. Stars arranged thus ✶₊1911₊✶	..	45	35

(*b*) *P* 11½ × 14

89	44	2 c. black and yellow-green (i)..		35	10
		a. Stars arranged thus ✶₊1911₊✶	..		

Hab·litado   **Habilitado**

ɪ₉ɪɪ   **1911**
(64)   **(65)**

1911–12. (i) *Optd with T* **64**. (*a*) *P* 14.

90	46	5 c. indigo & orange-buff (B.) (7.6.11)		10	8
		a. Opt double	..	1·10	1·10
		b. "Habilitada"	..	85	75
		c. Dated "2911"	..	2·00	1·10
91	47	10 c. black and blue (**B.** 5p.) (1.12)		40	25
		a. Surch in red	..	12·00	5·00

(*b*) *P* 11½ × 14.

92	47	10 c. black and blue (**B.** 5p.) (1.12)		40	25
		a. Surch in red	..	1·25	1·25

(ii) *Optd with T* **65**. *P* 14, 15

93	39	4 c. black and purple (**B.** 10p.) (1.12)	..	25	20

The variety "Habilitada" is to be found on the sheets with double impression. The date is found with either figure "1" in Roman type (Type **64** only).

Correos   **Correos**
           5
Un centimo   **5 centimos**
66   **(67)**   **(68)**

(Eng and recess A.B.N. Co, N.Y.)

1911 (19 Nov–Dec). *Telegraph stamps, T* **66** *surch as T* **67/8**. *P* 12. *Space between lines of surch* 8 *mm.*

94		1 c. on 10 c. blue (R.) (**B.** 5p.)	..	10	8
		a. Error. "COEREOS"	..	2·00	2·00
		b. Space between lines 9¼ mm	..	30	20
		ba. Do Surch inverted	..	1·25	
95		1 c. on 10 c. blue	..	12·00	12·00
96		1 c. on 25 c. violet (**B.** 5p.)	..	8	8
		a. Error "COEREOS"	..	2·00	2·00
97		1 c. on 50 c. red-brown (B.)	..	12	10
98		1 c. on 1 col. brown (R.) ..	..	12	12
99		1 c. on 5 col. red (B.)	..	25	20
100		1 c. on 10 col. brown (R.)	..	25	20
101		5 c. on 5 col. orange (B.) (**B.** 5p.) (Dec)		12	10
		a. Surch double	..	1·50	1·25
		b. Surch inverted	..	1·50	1·25
		c. Pair, one without surch			

Correos
Dos centimos
           2
69   **(70)**

(Eng and recess Waterlow)

1911 (Dec). *Telegraph stamps, T* **69**, *surch as T* **70**.

(*a*) *P* 14

102		2 c. on 5 c. yellow-brown	..	80	80
		a. Surch inverted	..	1·40	1·40
		b. "Correos" inverted	..	2·50	2·00
		c. Surch double	..	1·50	1·50
103		2 c. on 10 c. blue (R.)	..	12·00	9·00
		a. "Correos" inverted ..	..	42·00	42·00
104		2 c. on 50 c. claret	..	15	15
105		2 c. on 1 col. brown (**B.** 5p.)	..	30	25
106		2 c. on 2 col. rose-red	..	2·75	2·40
107		2 c. on 5 col. green	..	30	25
		a. Surch inverted			
108		2 c. on 10 col. maroon	..	30	30

(*b*) *P* 14 × 11½

109		2 c. on 10 c. blue (R.)	..	6·00	5·00
		a. "Correos" inverted ..	..	28·00	28·00
110		2 c. on 50 c. claret (**B.** 5p.)	..	15	12
		a. Surch inverted	..	80	80
		b. Surch double	..	3·75	4·00

111	2 c. on 1 col. brown (**B.** 5*p.*)	..	..	35	30
	a. Surch inverted	..	..	3·50	3·50
	b. Surch double	..	..	4·25	4·25
112	2 c. on 2 col. rose-red (**B.** 5*p.*)	..	..	35	30
	a. Surch inverted	..	..	1·60	1·60
	b. "Correos" inverted ..	..	..	2·25	2·00
113	2 c. on 5 col. green (**B.** 5*p.*)	..	..	35	30
	a. Surch inverted	..	..	2·25	2·25
	b. "Correos" inverted ..	..	..	2·25	2·00
114	2 c. on 10 col. maroon (**B.** 5*p.*)	..	..	35	30
	a. "Correos" inverted ..	..	..		

Beware of forgeries of the 1910–11 surcharges.

OFICIAL

15 - VI - 1917

D 2   (O 10)

OFICIAL

✳ **15** ✳

CENTIMOS

(O 11)

(Litho A.B.N. Co, N.Y.)

1915. *POSTAGE DUE.* P 12.

D115	D 2	2 c. orange	..	..	5	5
D116		4 c. blue ..	..	..	5	5
D117		8 c. green ..	..	..	20	20
D118		10 c. violet ..	..	..	8	8
D119		20 c. brown	..	..	12	12
D115/119		*Set of 5*	..	..	45	45

1917 (June). *OFFICIAL. Nos. 80/81 optd with Type* O **10.**

O115	5 c. orange	..	..	12	12
	a. Opt inverted	..	..	1·10	1·10
O116	10 c. deep blue	..	..	10	10
	a. Opt inverted	..	..	5·00	5·00

Overprints in red were not authorised.

1920. *OFFICIAL. No.* 82 *surch with Type* O **11.**

O117	15 c. on 20 c. olive (R.)	..	..	25	25

71   **72** Bolivar

(Litho Litografia Nacional)

1921 (17 June). *Centenary of Coffee Cultivation.* P 11½.

115	**71** 5 c. black and blue	..	..	50	50
	a. Tête-bêche (pair) ..	..	..	1·25	1·00
	b. Imperf (pair)	..	..	3·50	

(Eng and recess A.B.N. Co, N.Y.)

1921 (24 July). P 12.

116	**72** 15 c. violet	..	..	12	8

73   **74** Juan Mora and Julio Acosta

(Des G. Prudhomme. Recess in France)

1921 (15 Sept). *Independence Centenary.* P 11.

117	**73** 5 c. violet	..	..	30	15
	a. Imperf (pair)	..	..	12·00	

(Litho Litografia Nacional)

1921 (15 Sept). *Independence Centenary.* P 11½.

118	**74** 2 c. black and orange	..	..	25	20
119	3 c. black and green ..	..	..	20	20
120	6 c. black and scarlet	..	..	35	30
121	15 c. black and deep blue	..	..	1·50	1·25
122	30 c. black and brown	..	..	2·00	1·75
118/122	*Set of 5*	..	..	4·00	3·25

Stamps imperforate or with inverted centres are of clandestine manufacture. Though the decree authorising this issue only called for 2000 of the 30 c. and 5000 of the remainder, we believe that a very much larger number was printed surreptitiously.

1921 – 22

20 CTS.   **10 CTS.**

(O 12)   (O 13)   (75)

1921. *OFFICIAL. Official stamps of* 1908 *surch with Type* O **12,** *or optd with date only.*

O123	**45** 4 c. indigo and carmine-red	..	20	15
	a. "1291" for "1921"	..	..	1·50	1·50
O124	**43** 6 c. on 1 c. ind & chestnut-brn	..	20	20
	a. No stop after "CTS"	..	..	2·25	2·25
O125	**49** 20 c. on 25 c. black and lavender	..	20	20
	a. No stop after "CTS"	..	..	1·50	
O126	**50** 50 c. indigo and pink	..	..	1·10	1·10
	a. Hyphen omitted	..	..	2·50	2·50
O127	**51** 1 col. black and sienna	..	..	1·60	1·60
	a. Hyphen omitted	..	..	5·50	5·50

1921 (Dec). *OFFICIAL. No.* O115 *surch with Type* O **13.**

O128	10 c. on 5 c. orange	..	..	20	20
	a. Surch inverted	..	..	5·00	5·00

1922 (11 Jan). *Coffee Publicity. Nos.* 77/81 *and* 116 *optd with* T **75.**

123	1 c. brown (B.) ..	..	..	8	5
124	2 c. deep green (R.)	..	..	10	5
125	4 c. scarlet	..	..	12	8
126	5 c. orange	..	..	12	10
127	10 c. deep blue (R.)	..	..	20	12
128	15 c. violet (Gold)	..	..	70	50
123/128	*Set of 6*	..	..	1·25	80

All values exist with inverted overprint.
This overprint has been extensively forged.

CORREOS

1922   ✚ **5ᶜ**

(76)   (77)   (78)

1922 (Mar). *No.* 117 *optd with* T **76.**

129	**73** 5 c. violet	..	..	20	8
	a. Opt inverted	..	..	1·00	
	b. Opt double	..	..	2·00	

1922 (Oct). *Red Cross Fund. No.* 80 *surch with* T **77.**

130	5 c. + 5 c. orange (R.)	..	..	45	15

This stamp was re-issued for ordinary postal use as a 5 c. denomination in 1928.

1923 (Jan). *No.* 80 *optd with* T **78.**

131	5 c. orange	..	..	20	12
	a. "VD" for "UD"	..	..	2·00	1·60
	b. Large stop between "CAFE" and "COMPRE"	..	..	75	60
	c. "CCMPRE" for "COMPRE" ..		2·00	1·60

OFICIAL
(O 14)

79

(Litho National Printing Works)

1923 (18 June). *Birth Centenary of J. Jiménez. P 11½.*
132	**79**	2 c. brown	..	..	8	5
133		4 c. green	..	..	10	8
134		5 c. dull blue	..	..	12	8
135		20 c. carmine	..	..	10	10
136		1 col. violet-blue	..	..	20	15
132/136		*Set of 5*	..	..	55	40

All values exist imperforate but these were not regularly issued.

1923. OFICIAL. *Optd with Type O 14.*
O137	**79**	2 c. brown	..	..	15	15
O138		4 c. green	..	..	8	8
O139		5 c. dull blue	..	..	15	15
O140		20 c. carmine	..	..	10	10
O141		1 col. violet-blue	..	..	20	20
O137/141		*Set of 5*	..	..	60	60

All values exist imperforate but these were not regularly issued.

80 National Monument   **81** Coffee-growing

82 Columbus and Isabella I   **83** Columbus

84 Manuel M. Gutierez   **85** Don R. A. Maldonado y Velasco

(Eng and recess A.B.N. Co, N.Y.)

1923 (Sept)–26. *First Pan-American Postal Congress. T 80/4 and various designs inscr "UPU 1923". P 12.*
137	**80**	1 c. purple	..	..	5	5
138	**81**	2 c. chrome-yellow	..	..	15	5
139	–	4 c. green	..	..	20	15
140	–	5 c. light blue	..	..	25	5
141	–	5 c. green (6.3.26)	..	..	8	5
142	**82**	10 c. brown	..	..	50	10
143	–	10 c. carmine (6.3.26)	..	..	10	5
144	**83**	12 c. carmine	..	..	90	75
145	–	20 c. blue	..	..	1·40	65
146	–	40 c. orange	..	..	2·50	1·10
147	**84**	1 col. olive-green	..	..	70	30
137/147		*Set of 11*	..	..	6·00	3·00

Designs: As T **80**—5 c. G.P.O., San José; 20 c. Columbus at Cariari; 40 c. Map of Costa Rica. As T **81**—4 c. Banana-growing.
See also Nos. 174 and 176.

(Des T. S. Guell. Eng and recess Waterlow)

1924 (4 May). *Without printer's imprint. P 14.*
148	**85**	2 c. green	..	..	8	5
		a. Perf 12½	..	..	5	5

See also Nos. 211 and 308/12.

86 Map of Guanacaste   **87** Church at Nicoya

(Litho American Bank Note Co)

1924 (25 July). *Centenary of Incorporation of Nicoya (Guanacaste). P 12.*
149	**86**	1 c. carmine	..	..	25	15
150		2 c. purple	..	..	25	15
151		5 c. green	..	..	25	10
152		10 c. orange	..	..	70	30
153	**87**	15 c. blue	..	..	45	30
154		20 c. grey-black	..	..	60	55
155		25 c. pale red-brown	..	..	1·25	70
149/155		*Set of 7*	..	..	3·25	2·00

All values exist imperforate.

88 Discus Thrower   **89** Trophy

90 Parthenon   **(91)**

(Litho National Printing Office)

1924 (Dec). *Central American Olympic Games.*

			A. Imp		B. P 12	
156	**88**	5 c. (+ 10 c.) green	2·40	2·00	2·40	2·00
157	**89**	10 c. (+ 10 c.) carmine	2·40	2·00	2·40	2·00
158	**90**	20 c. (+ 10 c.) indigo	4·50	3·50	4·50	3·50
		a. Tête-bêche (pair)	11·00	10·00	10·00	9·00

1925 (28 Nov). *Surch with T 91 and similar types.*
159	–	3 c. on 5 c. light blue (140)	..		12	12
160	**82**	6 c. on 10 c. brown	..		15	15
161	–	30 c. on 40 c. orange (146)	..		25	20
162	**84**	45 c. on 1 col. olive-green	..		30	25
159/162		*Set of 4*	..		75	65

$$=10 \qquad 10=$$

(92)

1926 (Apr). *Surch with T 92.*
163	**83**	10 on 12 c. carmine	..	..	60	10

93   94 Heredia Normal School

(Recess A.B.N. Co, N.Y.)

1926 (4 June). P 12½.
164   93   20 c. ultramarine   85   20
Although inscribed "Correo Aereo", no air mail service existed until 1930.

(Eng and recess Waterlow)

1926 (8 Sept). T **94** and similar types, all inscr "1926–1926". P 12½.
165   3 c. ultramarine   12   10
166   6 c. brown   20   12
167   30 c. orange   25   15
168   45 c. slate-violet   35   20
165/168   Set of 4   80   50
Designs:—3 c. St. Louis College, Cartago; 6 c. Chapui Asylum, San José; 45 c. Ruins of Ujarras.

O 15   (95)

(Eng and recess Waterlow)

1926 (20 Oct). OFFICIAL. Coat of arms and value in black. P 12½.
O169   O **15**   2 c. ultramarine   5   5
O170   3 c. carmine   5   5
O171   4 c. light blue   5   5
O172   5 c. green   5   5
O173   6 c. bistre   5   5
O174   10 c. scarlet   5   5
O175   20 c. olive-green   5   5
O176   30 c. orange   8   8
O177   45 c. brown   10   10
O178   1 col. deep lilac   15   15
O169/178   Set of 10   50   50
See also Nos. O231/43.

1928 (7 Jan). Lindbergh "Good Will Tour" of Central America. Surch with T **95**.
169   **83**   10 c. on 12 c. carmine   ..   2·75   2·25
Beware of forgeries.

CORREOS

5

(96)

5   5   CENTIMOS

(96)   (97)

5   5   5   5   5

(A)   (B)   (C)   (D)   (E)

1928 (28 Apr). Surch with T **96**.
170   **73**   5 c. on 5 c. violet   15   5
     a. Surch inverted   ..   ..

1929. Telegraph stamp as T **69**, surch as T **97**. P 12½.
     (a) Surch typo
171   5 c. on 2 col. rose-red (A to D) (19.1)   ..   5   5
     a. Type E   40   40
     (b) Surch litho
172   5 c. on 2 col. rose-red (E) (26.1)   ..   5   5
173   13 c. on 40 c. green (2.11)   8   5
The lithographed surcharge has thicker letters and shinier ink than the typographed surcharge.

98 Post Office   (99)

(Recess Waterlow)

1930. Types of 1923–26 redrawn (26×21½ mm). Dated "1929", as T **98**. P 12½.
174   **80**   1 c. purple   5   5
175   **98**   5 c. green   5   5
176   **84**   10 c. carmine   20   5

1930 (11 Mar). AIR. Type O **15** surch as T **99**, in red.
177   O **15**   8 c. on 1 col. deep lilac   ..   35   30
178   20 c. on 1 col. deep lilac   ..   40   35
179   40 c. on 1 col. deep lilac   ..   85   70
180   1 col. on 1 col. deep lilac   90   75
177/180   Set of 4   ..   ..   ..   2·25   1·90

CORREO AEREO

(100)

Correo Aereo

20   Correo
CENTIMOS   Aereo
(101)   (102)

1930 (14 Mar)–**32.** AIR.
     (a) No. 143 optd with T **100**
181   **82**   10 c. carmine   30   8
     (b) Telegraph stamps as T **69** (P 12½) surch as T **101**
182   **69**   5 c. on 10 c. brown (7.3.32)   ..   10   8
     a. Surch inverted   ..   ..   1·75
     b. Surch double, one inverted   ..   1·75
183   20 c. on 50 c. ultramarine (19.3.30)   12   10
184   40 c. on 50 c. ultramarine (19.3.30)   15   10
     (c) Stamp as last optd with T **102**
185   **69**   1 col. orange (19.3.30)   55   15
The surcharge on No. 182 is in slightly different type and the first "é" of "Aereo" has an accent.
Errors other than those listed are considered to be clandestine.

Habilitado
1931
Correo Aéreo
¢ 2.00

103 Juan Rafael Mora   (104)

(Recess Waterlow)

1931 (29 Jan). P 12½.
186   **103**   13 c. carmine   15   10

1931–32. *AIR. Fiscal stamps inscr "TIMBRE 1929" (or "1930", 3 col.) surch as T* **104.** *P* 12.

(a) 19.12.31. *First printing. Toned paper. Brownish vermilion surcharge.*

187	2 col. on 2 col. grey-green	..	..	5·00	5·00
188	3 col. on 5 col maroon	..	..	5·00	5·00
189	5 col. on 10 col. black	..	..	6·00	6·00

(b) 20.6.32. *Second printing. White paper. Scarlet surcharge*

190	2 col. on 2 col. grey-green	..	..	4·00	4·00
191	3 col. on 5 col. maroon	..	..	4·00	4·00
192	5 col. on 10 col. black	..	..	4·00	4·00

(105)   106

1932 (8 Mar). *AIR. Telegraph stamp as T* **69** *(P* 12½*), optd with T* **105.**

193	40 c. green	..	..	..	90	15
	a. Opt inverted	..	..	5·00	4·00	

(Recess A.B.N. Co)

1932 (12 Oct). *National Philatelic Exhibition. P* 12.

194	**106**	3 c. orange ..	..	..	10	10
195		5 c. deep green	..	..	15	15
196		10 c. carmine	..	..	20	20
197		20 c. blue	..	..	25	25
194/197		*Set of 4*	..	..	60	60

See also Nos. 231/4.

107 Landing Ground, San José   **108** Allegory of the Air Mail

(Recess A.B.N. Co)

1934 (14 Mar). *AIR. P* 12.

198	**107**	5 c. green	..	..	10	5
199		10 c. carmine	..	..	10	5
200		15 c. chocolate	..	..	25	10
201		20 c. blue	..	..	25	5
202		25 c. orange ..	..	..	35	10
203		40 c. grey-brown	..	..	35	5
204		50 c. black	..	..	40	8
205		60 c. orange-yellow ..	..	..	75	10
206		75 c. violet	..	..	1·25	30
207	**108**	1 col. carmine	..	..	85	5
208		2 col. light blue	..	..	1·50	20
209		5 col. black ..	..	..	2·00	1·50
210		10 col. red-brown	..	..	3·00	2·25
198/210		*Set of 13*	..	..	10·00	4·50

For other colours and new value in T **107,** see Nos. 507/12.

OFICIAL

(O 16)   **109** Nurse at Altar

1934 (14 Apr). *OFFICIAL AIR. Optd with Type O* **16,** *in red.*

O211	**107**	5 c. green ..	..	..	15	15
O212		10 c. carmine	..	..	15	15
O213		15 c. chocolate	..	..	25	25
O214		20 c. blue	..	..	35	35
O215		25 c. orange	..	..	35	35
O216		40 c. grey-brown	..	..	40	35
O217		50 c. black ..	..	..	40	40
O218		60 c. orange-yellow	..	..	50	50
O219		75 c. violet ..	..	..	50	50
O220	**108**	1 col. carmine	..	..	75	50
O221		2 col. light blue	..	..	2·50	2·50
O222		5 col. black	..	..	4·00	4·00
O223		10 col. red-brown ..	..	..	5·00	5·00
O211/223		*Set of 13*	..	..	14·00	14·00

(Eng and recess Waterlow)

1934 (11 Aug). *With Waterlow's imprint. P* 12½.

211	**85**	3 c. myrtle-green	..	..	5	5

See also Nos. 308/12.

(Recess A.B.N. Co)

1935 (31 May). *Costa Rican Red Cross Jubilee. P* 12.

212	**109**	10 c. carmine	..	..	20	10

110 Aerial View of Cartago   **111** Our Lady of the Angels

(Recess Waterlow)

1935 (1 Aug). *Tercentenary of Apparition of Our Lady of the Angels. T* **110/1** *and another design dated "1635 1935". P* 12½.

213	**110**	5 c. green ..	..	..	20	10
214	**111**	10 c. carmine	..	..	30	12
215	**110**	30 c. orange ..	..	..	60	20
216	—	45 c. violet	..	..	1·40	30
217	**111**	50 c. blue-black	..	..	2·00	70
213/217		*Set of 5*	..	..	4·00	1·25

Design:—45 c. Allegory of the Apparition (as T **110**).

112 Cocos Island   **113** Cocos Is. and Fleet of Columbus

(Recess Perkins, Bacon & Co)

1936 (29 Jan). *P* 14 *or* 11½ *(*25 *c.).*

218	**112**	4 c. yellow-brown ..	..	..	15	10
219		8 c. violet	..	..	20	12
220		25 c. orange ..	..	..	25	15
221		35 c. red-brown	..	..	30	15
222		40 c. brown	..	..	35	20
223		50 c. yellow	..	..	40	25
224		2 col. yellow-green ..	..	..	1·50	1·00
225		5 col. blue-green ..	..	..	5·00	2·50
218/225		*Set of 8*	..	..	7·00	4·00

All values exist imperforate.

(Recess A.B.N. Co)

1936 (5 Dec). *P* 12.

226	**113**	5 c. green	..	..	8	5
227		10 c. carmine	..	..	8	5

1936 (5 Dec). *OFFICIAL. Optd with Type O* **16.**

O228	**113**	5 c. green ..	..	..	5	5
O229		10 c. carmine	..	..	5	5

114 Aeroplane over Mt. Poás

(Recess A.B.N. Co)

1937 (10 Feb). *AIR. First Annual Fair. P* 12.

228	**114**	1 c. black	..	8	8
229		2 c. red-brown	.. ..	8	8
230		3 c. violet	.. .. ..	8	8
228/230		*Set of 3*	.. ..	20	20

(Recess A.B.N. Co)

1937 (24 July). *OFFICIAL. New values and colours changed. Arms and values in black. P* 12½.

O231	O **15**	2 c. lilac ..	.. ..	5	5
O232		3 c. bistre-brown	.. ..	5	5
O233		4 c. carmine	.. ..	5	5
O234		5 c. olive-green ..	.. ..	5	
O235		8 c. sepia	.. ..	5	
O236		10 c. carmine	.. ..	5	
O237		20 c. indigo	.. ..	5	5
O238		40 c. vermilion	.. ..	8	10
O239		55 c. lilac ..	.. ..	12	
O240		1 col. red-brown..	.. ..	15	15
O241		2 col. grey-blue ..	.. ..	30	35
O242		5 col. orange	.. ..	75	85
O243		10 col. blue and black	.. ..	2·50	2·50
O231/243		*Set of 13*	.. ..	3·75	†
		Set of 9	.. .. ..	†	3·75

The values which have used prices in the above issue were issued to officials for postal purposes with perforated star. Unpunched copies were sold to collectors but had no franking value. Prices for unused are for unpunched stamps.

1937 (15 Dec). *2nd National Philatelic Exhibition. As T* **106** *but inscr* "DICIEMBRE 1937". *P* 12.

231	**106**	2 c. slate-purple	.. ..	8	8
232		3 c. black ..	.. ..	8	8
233		5 c. green ..	.. ..	10	10
234		10 c. orange-red	.. ..	12	10
231/234		*Set of 4*	.. ..	35	30
MS234a		164 × 101 mm. Nos. 231/4. Imperf	..	30	30

115 Tunny

116 Native and Donkey   **117** Puntarenas
carrying Bananas

(Recess American Bank Note Co)

1937 (15 Dec). *National Exhibition, San José* (1st issue). *P* 12. (*a*) *POSTAGE.*

235	**115**	2 c. olive-grey	.. ..	25	12
236	**116**	5 c. blue-green	.. ..	30	12
237	–	10 c. carmine (Coffee gathering)	..	40	25

(*b*) *AIR*

238	**117**	2 c. black ..	.. ..	5	5
239		5 c. green ..	.. ..	10	8
240		20 c. blue ..	.. ..	25	20
241		1 col. 40, sepia	.. ..	1·75	1·50
235/241		*Set of 7*	.. ..	2·75	2·10

118 Orchid (*Guaria Morada*)

119 National Bank

(Recess Waterlow)

1938 (11 Jan). *National Exhibition, San José* (2nd issue). *W* **135** *of Colombia* (*Wavy Lines*). *P* 12½. (*a*) *POSTAGE. T* **118** *and similar design.*

242	**118**	1 c. violet and green	..	20	20
243	–	3 c. chocolate (Cocoa-bean)	..	25	15

(*b*) *AIR*

244	**119**	1 c. violet	.. ..	5	5
245		3 c. vermilion	.. ..	5	5
246		10 c. carmine	.. ..	10	10
247		75 c. brown ..	.. ..	1·25	1·25
242/247		*Set of 6*	.. ..	1·60	1·60

1938

(**120**)   **121** La Sabana Airport

1938 (23 Sept). *No.* 145 *optd with T* **120**.

248		20 c. blue	.. ..	15	12

(Recess A.B.N. Co)

1940 (2 May). *AIR. Opening of La Sabana Airport, San José, P* 12.

249	**121**	5 c. green ..	.. ..	5	5
250		10 c. carmine	.. ..	8	8
251		25 c. blue ..	.. ..	12	10
252		35 c. red-brown	.. ..	20	20
253		60 c. red-orange	.. ..	40	30
254		85 c. violet ..	.. ..	90	75
255		2 col. 35, blue-green	..	4·75	4·50
249/255		*Set of 7*	.. ..	6·00	5·50

(**122**)   (**123**)   (**124**)

(**125**)   (**126**)

1940. *No.* 168 *surch litho with* T **122/5,** *in scarlet.*
256	122	15 c. on 45 c. slate-violet (8.9)	..	15	12
257	123	15 c. on 45 c. slate-violet (9.9)	..	15	12
258	124	15 c. on 45 c. slate-violet (18.9)	..	15	12
259	125	15 c. on 45 c. slate-violet (1.10)	..	15	12

1940 (13 Nov). *No.* 168 *with type-set surch, in scarlet.*
| 260 | 126 | 15 c. on 45 c. slate-violet | .. | .. | 12 | 8 |
| | | a. Surch inverted .. | .. | .. | | |

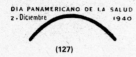

DIA PANAMERICANO DE LA SALUD
2 - Diciembre   1940

(127)

DIA PANAMERICANO DE LA SALUD
2 - DICIEMBRE   1940

(128)

(Stamps recess A.B.N. Co)

1940 (2 Dec). *Pan-American Health Day. Various unissued stamps, prepared for the 8th Pan-American Child Welfare Congress (inscr "VIII CONGRESO PANAMERICANO DEL NIÑO OCTOBRE 1939"). P* 12.

(a) POSTAGE *(Allegorical). Optd with* T **127**
261	5 c. green	..	..	..	..	10	8
262	10 c. carmine	..	..	..	..	15	8
263	20 c. blue	..	..	...	..	20	10
264	40 c. brown	..	..	..	..	30	20
265	55 c. orange-yellow	..	..	..	90	45

(b) AIR *(View of Duran Sanatorium). Optd with* T **128**
266	10 c. scarlet	..	..	..	8	5
267	15 c. violet	..	..	..	10	8
268	25 c. blue	..	..	..	20	12
269	35 c. sepia	..	..	..	25	20
270	60 c. turquoise-blue	..	..	40	35
271	75 c. olive-green..	..	..	80	70
272	1 col. 35, red-orange	..	2·75	2·25
273	5 col. chocolate	..	..	9·00	9·00
274	10 col. magenta ..	..	20·00	20·00
261/274	Set of 14	..	..	32·00	30·00

These are known without overprint.

AEREO

Aviación Panamericana

Dic. 17   1940

15 CENTIMOS 15
(129)

1940 (17 Dec). *AIR. Pan-American Aviation Day. Surch as* T **129.**
275	112	15 c. on 50 c. yellow..	..	..	30	30
		a. Error. On 25 c. orange ..	..	15·00	15·00
276		30 c. on 50 c. yellow (B.)	..	..	30	30

15
CENTIMOS
15
(130)

1941 (14 Feb). *Surch with* T **130.**
277	112	15 c. on 25 c. orange	..	..	15	12
278		15 c. on 35 c. red-brown	..	..	15	12
279		15 c. on 40 c. brown..	..	..	15	12
280		15 c. on 2 col. yellow-green ..	..	15	12
281		15 c. on 5 col. blue-green	..	..	15	12
277/281	Set of 5	..	..	..	70	50

All values exist with surcharge inverted.

131 Stadium and Flag

132 Football Match

1941 (8 May). *Central American and Caribbean Football Championship.*

(a) POSTAGE. *Recess Flags typo in national colours. Columbian Bank Note Co. P* 12½
282	131	5 c. yellow-green	..	..	..	75	15
		a. Flags omitted	..	..	..	7·50	
283		10 c. orange	..	..	..	55	15
284		15 c. carmine	..	..	..	90	20
285		25 c. blue	..	..	..	1·50	30
286		40 c. brown ..	..	..	..	2·75	1·00
287		50 c. violet	..	..	..	4·25	1·00
288		75 c. red-orange	..	..	..	7·50	2·00
289		1 col. carmine	..	..	..	13·00	3·50

(b) AIR. *Recess American Bank Note Co. P* 12
290	132	15 c. rose	..	..	..	50	12
291		30 c. ultramarine	..	..	..	65	15
292		40 c. brown ..	..	..	..	65	20
293		50 c. violet	..	..	..	80	50
294		60 c. green	..	..	..	1·00	50
295		75 c. yellow	..	..	..	1·75	75
296		1 col. mauve	..	..	..	3·25	2·00
297		1 col. 40, carmine	..	..	6·00	4·00
298		2 col. blue-green	..	..	12·00	8·00
299		5 col. black	..	..	..	26·00	20·00
282/299	Set of 18	..	..	..	75·00	40·00

See also Nos. 410/2.

Mayo   1941

Tratado Limítrofe
Costa Rica - Panamá

CINCO CENTIMOS

(133)

1941 (2 June). *AIR. Costa Rica–Panama Boundary Treaty. Variously optd as* T **133** *or surch also.*
300	107	5 c. on 20 c. blue	..	..	..	8	5
301		15 c. on 20 c. blue	..	..	..	10	5
302		40 c. on 75 c. violet ..	..	..	15	10
303	108	65 c. on 1 col. carmine	..	..	30	25
304		1 col. 40 on 2 col. light blue	..	1·50	1·25
305		5 col. black ..	..	..	..	6·00	5·00
306		10 col. red-brown	..	..	..	7·00	7·00
300/306	Set of 7	..	..	..	14·00	12·00

5 Céntimos 5

(134)

135 C. Gonzalaz Viquez

1941 (26 July). *No.* 186 *surch with* T **134.**
| 307 | 103 | 5 c. on 13 c. carmine | .. | .. | 8 | 5 |

(Eng and recess Waterlow)

1941 (25 Aug)–**48**. *T* **135** *and similar portrait types with Waterlow's imprint. P* 12½.

308	135	3 c. red-orange	..	5	5
309		3 c. maroon (19.1.43)	..	5	5
310		3 c. carmine (27.12.45)	..	5	5
310a	–	3 c. ultramarine (21.8.48)	..	5	5
311	–	5 c. violet	..	5	5
312	–	5 c. black (19.1.43)	..	5	5
308/312		*Set of 6*	..	25	20

Portraits:—3 c. ultram. Bishop Bernardo Augusto Thiel; 5 c. (2) Jose Joaquin Rodriguez.
For 3 c. myrtle-green, see No. 211.

136 New Decree and Restored University

(Recess A.B.N. Co)

1941 (26 Aug). *Restoration of National University. T* **136** *and similar design. P* 12. (a) *POSTAGE.*

313	–	5 c. green	..	15	8
314	136	10 c. yellow-orange	..	15	8
315	–	15 c. carmine	..	25	5
316	136	25 c. blue	..	35	12
317	–	50 c. brown	..	1·25	60

(b) *AIR. Inscr "CORREO AEREO"*

318	136	15 c. rose-red	..	10	5
319	–	30 c. blue	..	15	5
320	136	40 c. red-orange	..	20	12
321	–	60 c. turquoise	..	30	20
322	136	1 col. violet	..	85	70
323	–	2 col. black	..	2·10	1·75
324	136	5 col. brown-purple	..	6·50	5·50
313/324		*Set of 12*	..	11·00	8·50

Design: Others—The original Decree and University.

15 CENTIMOS 15

(138)

1942. *Nos.* 166 *and* 248 *surch as T* **138**.

325		5 c. on 6 c. brown (28.4)	..	10	5
		a. Surch inverted	..		
326		15 c. on 20 c. blue (R.) (19.4)	..	12	8
		a. Surch inverted	..		
		b. Surch double	..		

139 "V", Torch and Flags   **140** Francisco Morazan

(Recess A.B.N. Co)

1942 (25 Sept). *War Effort. P* 12.

327	139	5 c. carmine	..	10	8
328		5 c. red-orange	..	10	8
329		5 c. green	..	10	8
330		5 c. blue	..	10	8
331		5 c. violet	..	10	8
327/331		*Set of 5*	..	45	35

(Recess A.B.N. Co)

1943–48. *As T* **140** (*various portraits and dates). P* 12.

(a) *POSTAGE*

332		1 c. reddish purple	..	5	5
333		2 c. grey-black	..	5	5
334		3 c. blue	..	5	5
335		5 c. deep blue-green	..	5	5
336		5 c. emerald-green (1947)	..	5	5
337		15 c. vermilion	..	5	5
338		25 c. ultramarine	..	15	8
339		50 c. violet	..	20	12
340		1 col. sepia	..	55	25
341		2 col. red-orange	..	85	55

(b) *AIR. Inscr "CORREO AEREO"*

341a		5 c. sepia (1.6.48)	..	5	5
342		10 c. carmine	..	5	5
342a		10 c. olive-black (1.6.48)	..	5	5
342b		15 c. violet (1.6.48)	..	5	5
343		25 c. bright blue (13.5.46)	..	8	5
344		30 c. red-brown (13.5.46)	..	8	8
345		40 c. light blue	..	10	5
346		40 c. carmine (10.7.45)	..	10	8
347		45 c. claret	..	20	12
348		45 c. black (10.7.45)	..	10	8
349		50 c. blue-green	..	60	10
350		50 c. red-orange (10.7.45)	..	15	12
351		55 c. claret (13.5.46)	..	15	10
352		60 c. ultramarine	..	30	10
353		60 c. emerald-green (10.7.45)	..	12	10
354		65 c. vermilion	..	40	12
355		65 c. ultramarine (10.7.45)	..	12	10
356		75 c. blue-green (13.5.46)	..	20	15
357		85 c. red-orange	..	45	15
358		85 c. slate-violet (10.7.45)	..	50	20
359		1 col. grey-black	..	55	25
360		1 col. vermilion (10.7.45)	..	20	10
361		1 col. 05, bistre-brown (10.7.45)	..	30	15
362		1 col. 15, lake-brown	..	85	75
363		1 col. 15, green (10.7.45)	..	1·25	60
364		1 col. 40, violet	..	1·40	90
365		1 col. 40, yellow-orange (10.7.45)	..	80	70
366		2 col. black	..	2·25	40
367		2 col. olive-green (10.7.45)	..	60	20
322/367		*Set of 39*	..	13·00	6·00

Portraits:—J. Mora Fernandez, 1 c., 10 c.; B. Carranza, 2 c., 1 col. 40; T. Guardia, 3 c., 2 col.; M. Aguilar, 5 c., 40 c.; Salvador Lara, 5 c. (No. 341a); F. Morazan, 15 c. (337), 45 c. (347); Carlos Durán, 15 c. (342b); J. M. Alfaro, 25 c. (338), 50 c. (349/50); Aniceto Esquivel, 25 c. (343); V. Herrera, 30 c.; J. R. de Gallegos, 45 c. (348); F. M. Oreamuno, 50 c. (339), 60 c.; Próspero Fernández, 55 c.; J. M. Castro, 65 c., 1 col. (340); B. Soto, 75 c.; J. R. Mora, 85 c., 2 col. (341); J. M. Montealegre, 1 col. (359/60); B. Carrillo, 1 col. 05; J. Jiménez, 1 col. 15.

Legislación Social
15 Setiembre 1943
(141)

1943 (16 Sept). *Nos.* 209/10 *optd with T* **141**.

368	108	5 col. black (R.)	..	1·50	75
369		10 col. red-brown (B.)	..	2·25	2·00

142 San Ramon   **143** Allegory of Flight

(Recess A.B.N. Co)

1944 (19 Jan). *Centenary of Foundation of San Ramon. P* 12. (a) *POSTAGE.*

370	142	5 c. blue-green	..	5	5
371		10 c. orange	..	8	5
372		15 c. carmine	..	12	5
373		40 c. grey	..	30	15
374		50 c. blue	..	45	30

(b) *AIR*

375	143	10 c. orange	..	8	5
376		15 c. carmine-lake	..	10	5

377	**143**	40 c. ultramarine	..	..	..	20	12
378		45 c. rose-lilac	..	..	..	25	15
379		60 c. emerald-green	..	..	..	30	25
380		1 col. brown	..	..	..	60	50
381		1 col. 40, grey	..	..	..	3·25	2·75
382		5 col. violet..	..	..	..	7·50	7·50
383		10 col. black ..	..	..	..	17·00	16·00
370/383		Set of 14	..	..	..	27·00	25·00

La entrevista
de los
Presidentes
De la Guardia
y Picado
contribuirá a
afianzar la
unidad
Continental.
18 setiembre
1944
(144)

1944
(145)

1944 (18 Sept). *Ratification of Costa Rica and Panama Boundary Treaty. Nos. 328/331 optd with T* **144**.

384	**139**	5 c. red-orange	..	..	5	5
385		5 c. green	..	..	5	5
386		5 c. blue (R.) ..	..	..	5	5
387		5 c. violet (R.)	..	..	5	5
384/387		Set of 4	..	..	15	12

1944 (22 Nov). *AIR. No. O220 optd with T* **145**.

388	**108**	1 col. carmine	..	..	35	15
		a. Blue opt	..	..	10·00	

1945
(146)

**CORREO AEREO
1945**
(147)

1945 (12 Jan). *AIR. Nos. O211/23 optd with T* **146**.

389	**107**	5 c. green (R.)	..	..	20	20
		a. Black opt				
390		10 c. carmine	..	..	25	25
391		15 c. chocolate (R.)	..	..	25	25
392		20 c. blue (R.)	..	..	15	15
393		25 c. orange ..	..	..	25	25
394		40 c. grey-brown (R.)	..	..	20	15
395		50 c. black (R.)	..	..	30	30
396		60 c. orange-yellow ..	..	..	40	20
397		75 c. violet (R.)	..	..	40	35
398	**108**	1 col. carmine	..	..	30	20
399		2 col. light blue (R.)	..	..	2·25	1·75
400		5 col. black (R.)	..	..	3·00	3·00
401		10 col. red-brown	..	..	5·00	5·00
389/401		Set of 13	..	..	12·00	11·00

1945 (28 Feb). *AIR. Telegraph stamps as T* **69** *optd with T* **147** *Recess. P* 12½.

402		40 c. green (R.)	..	..	10	5
403		50 c. ultramarine (R.)	..	..	10	5
404		1 col. orange	..	..	25	12

148 Mauro Fernández

149 Coffee Gathering

(Recess Chilean Mint, Santiago)

1945 (21 July). *Birth Centenary of Fernández. P* 14.

405	**148**	20 c. green	..	..	8	5

(Recess A.B.N. Co)

1945 (9 Oct). *P* 12.

406	**149**	5 c. black and green	..	..	5	5
407		10 c. black and orange	..	..	10	5
408		20 c. black and carmine	..	..	12	8

150 Florence Nightingale and
Edith Cavell

15   **15**

(151)

(Recess Waterlow)

1945 (27 Dec). *AIR. 60th Anniv of National Red Cross Society. Cross in red. P* 12½.

409	**150**	1 col. black	..	..	25	12

(Recess A.B.N. Co)

1946 (13 May). *AIR. Central American and Caribbean Football Championship. As T* **132** *but inscr* "FEBRERO 1946". *P* 12.

410	**132**	25 c. green	..	..	60	50
411		30 c. orange ..	..	..	60	50
412		55 c. blue	..	..	70	50

1946 (18 May). *No. 405 surch with T* **151**.

413	**148**	15 c. on 20 c. green (R.)	..	8	5
		a. Surch inverted ..	..	6·00	

152 San Juan de Dios
Hospital

153 Ascensión
Esquivel

(Recess Hamilton Bank Note Co)

1946 (23 June). *AIR. Centenary of San Juan de Dios Hospital. P* 12½.

414	**152**	5 c. black and green	..	..	5	5
415		10 c. black and chocolate	..	..	5	5
416		15 c. black and carmine	..	..	5	5
417		25 c. black and blue ..	..	..	8	5
418		30 c. black and orange	..	..	15	10
419		40 c. black and olive-green	..	..	8	5
420		50 c. black and violet	..	..	15	10
421		60 c. black and grey-green	..	..	15	10
422		75 c. black and brown	..	..	25	15
423		1 col. black and light blue ..	..	30	15
424		2 col. black and orange-brown	..	50	35
425		3 col. black and brown-purple	..	1·10	90
426		5 col. black and yellow	..	..	1·50	1·50
414/426		Set of 13	..	..	4·00	3·25

(Recess Chilean Mint, Santiago)

1947 (20 Jan). *AIR. Former Presidents. As T* **153** *(portraits). W* 68 *of Chile (Mult Shields). P* 14.

427		2 col. black and blue	..	..	40	25
428		3 col. black and rose	..	..	60	50
429		5 col. black and green ..	..	..	80	50
430		10 col. black and orange	..	..	1·90	1·40
427/430		Set of 4	..	..	3·25	2·40

Portraits:—2 col. Rafael Iglesias; 5 col. Cleto Gonzalez Viquez; 10 col. Ricardo Jiménez.

**CORREOS
1947**
(154)

1947 (19 Mar). *No. O 228 optd with T* **154**

431	**113**	5 c. green (R.)	..	..	5	5

Habilitado para

₡ 0.15

Decreto Nº 16 de
28 de abril de 1947
(155)

156 Columbus at Cariari

1947 (5 May). *AIR. Nos. 410/2 surch with T* **155.**

432	**132**	15 c. on 25 c. green	..	..	55	45
		a. Surch inverted ..				
		b. Surch double, one inverted	..			
433		15 c. on 30 c. orange	..	..	55	45
		a. Surch inverted ..		..		
434		15 c. on 55 c. blue	..	..	55	45
		a. Surch inverted ..		..		

(Recess Waterlow)

1947 (19 May). *AIR. P* 12½.

435	**156**	25 c. black and green	..	..	12	8
436		30 c. black and ultramarine ..		..	12	8
437		40 c. black and orange	..	..	20	10
438		45 c. black and violet	..	..	25	12
439		50 c. black and carmine	..	..	30	12
440		65 c. black and orange-brown		..	45	30

₡0.15
(157)

158 Franklin D. Roosevelt

1947 (4 June). *AIR. Nos. 350, 353, 356 and 360/1 surch with T* **157.**

441		15 c. on 50 c. red-orange	..	..	10	8
442		15 c. on 60 c. emerald-green (R.)	..	..	10	8
443		15 c. on 75 c. blue-green (R.)	..	..	10	8
444		15 c. on 1 col. scarlet	..	..	10	8
445		15 c. on 1 col. 05, sepia	..	..	10	8
441/445		*Set of 5*	..	..	45	35

(Recess A.B.N. Co)

1947 (26 Aug). *P* 12. (a) *POSTAGE.*

446	**158**	5 c. emerald-green ..		..	5	5
447		10 c. carmine	..	..	5	5
448		15 c. ultramarine	..	..	5	5
449		25 c. red-orange	..	..	12	10
450		50 c. claret	..	..	20	15

(b) *AIR. Inscr* "CORREO AEREO"

451	**158**	15 c. yellow-green	..	..	5	5
452		30 c. carmine	..	..	8	8
453		45 c. red-brown	..	..	15	15
454		65 c. orange ..		..	15	15
455		75 c. light blue	..	..	15	15
456		1 col. olive-green	..	..	30	25
457		2 col. black ..		..	85	75
458		5 col. vermilion	..	..	1·50	1·25
446/458		*Set of 13*	..	..	3·25	3·00

159 Cervantes

160 Steam Locomotive

(Recess Chilean Mint, Santiago)

1947 (10 Nov). *400th Birth Anniv of Cervantes. W* **68** *of Chile (Mult Shields). P* 14.

459	**159**	30 c. blue	..	..	10	5
460		55 c. claret ..	..	..	20	12

(Recess Wright Bank Note Co, Philadelphia)

1947 (10 Nov). *AIR. Fiftieth Anniv of Electrification of Pacific Railway. P* 12½.

461	**160**	35 c. black and green	..	..	45	15

161 National Theatre   162 Rafael Iglesias

(Recess Waterlow)

1948 (26 Jan). *AIR. Fiftieth Anniv of Opening of National Theatre. P* 12½.

462	**161**	15 c. black and ultramarine ..		..	5	5
463		20 c. black and scarlet	..	..	8	5
464	**162**	35 c. black and blue-green	..	..	10	10
465	**161**	45 c. black and violet	..	..	10	8
466		50 c. black and carmine	..	..	10	10
467		75 c. black and bright purple	..	..	30	20
468		1 col. black and olive-green	..	..	40	25
469		2 col. black and brown-lake	..	..	65	50
470	**162**	5 col. black and orange-yellow	..	1·40	1·10
471		10 col. black and blue	..	..	2·40	2·00
462/471		*Set of 10*	..	..	5·00	4·00

1824-1949

HABILITADO PARA	125 Aniversario de la Anexión Guanacaste
₡ 0.35	**₡ 0.55**
(163)	(164)

1948 (21 Apr). *AIR. Surch with T* **163.**

472	**156**	35 c. on 40 c. black and orange (R.) ..		15	12

1949 (28 Aug). *AIR. 125th Anniv of Annexation of Guanacaste. Various stamps surch as T* **164** (*larger opt on No.* 474).

473		35 c. on 1 col. 05, sepia (361) (R.)	..	8	5
474		50 c. on 1 col. black and red (409) (R.)	..	15	12
		a. 2nd and 3rd lines both read "125 Aniversario"	..	..	3·00	3·00
475		55 c. on 1 col. 15, green (363) (R.)	..	25	20
476		55 c. on 1 col. 40, yellow-orange (365)	..	25	20

165 Globe and Dove

(Photo Courvoisier, La Chaux-de-Fonds)

1950 (11 Jan). *AIR. 75th Anniv of U.P.U. P* 11½.

477	**165**	15 c. carmine-pink ..		..	8	5
478		25 c. blue	..	..	10	8
479		1 col. grey-green	..	..	20	10

166 Battle of El Tejar, Cartago   **167** Capture of Limon

(Centres photo, frames recess Waterlow)

1950 (20 July). *AIR. As T* **166/7** *(battle scenes and portraits inscr* "GUERRA DE LIBERACION NACIONAL 1948"). *P* 12½.

480	15 c. black and carmine ..	..	..	5	5
481	20 c. black and green	..	..	10	5
482	25 c. black and grey-blue	..	..	12	8
483	35 c. black and brown ..	..	..	15	8
484	55 c. black and violet	..	..	25	10
485	75 c. black and vermilion	..	..	40	12
486	80 c. black and grey	..	..	50	15
487	1 col. black and orange	..	..	60	25
480/487	*Set of 8*	..	..	2·00	80

Designs: *Horiz*—25 c. La Lucha Ranch; 35 c. Trench of San Isidro Battalion; 55 c., 75 c. Observation post. *Vert*—80 c., 1 col. Dr. C. L. Valverde.

169 Bull   **170** Queen Isabella and Caravels

(Centres photo, frames recess Waterlow)

1950 (27 July). *AIR. National Agricultural, Cattle and Industries Fair. Inscr* "FERIA NACIONAL AGRICOLA" *etc., as T* **169**. *P* 12½.

488	1 c. black and yellow-green	..	..	10	10
489	2 c. black and light blue	..	..	10	10
490	3 c. black and brown ..	..	..	10	10
491	5 c. black and ultramarine	..	..	10	10
492	10 c. black and blue-green	..	..	20	10
493	30 c. black and violet ..	..	..	15	10
494	45 c. black and vermilion	..	..	20	10
495	50 c. black and grey	..	..	25	10
496	65 c. black and deep blue	..	..	30	15
497	80 c. black and carmine ..	..	..	50	25
498	2 col. black and yellow-orange	..	..	1·50	75
499	3 col. black and light blue	..	..	1·60	1·25
500	5 col. black and scarlet..	..	..	3·00	2·50
501	10 col. black and claret ..	..	..	3·75	3·00
488/501	*Set of 14*	..	..	11·00	8·00

Designs: *Vert*—1 c., 10 c., 2 col. T **169**; 2 c., 30 c., 3 col. Fishing; 3 c., 65 c. Pineapple; 5 c., 50 c., 5 col. Bananas; 45 c., 80 c., 10 col. Coffee.

(Recess De La Rue)

1952 (4 Mar). *AIR. Fifth Birth Centenary of Isabella the Catholic. P* 13 × 12½.

502	**170** 15 c. carmine-red	..	..	5	5
503	20 c. orange ..	..	..	5	5
504	25 c. bright blue	..	..	10	5
505	55 c. deep green	..	..	20	12
506	2 col. deep violet	..	..	50	25
502/506	*Set of 5*	..	..	80	45

1952 (23 Apr)–**53**. *AIR. As Nos.* 198/200, *but colours changed and new value. P* 12.

507	**107** 5 c. blue	..	..	..	5	5
508	5 c. pale blue (17.8.53)	..	..	5	5
509	10 c. green	..	..	..	5	5
510	10 c. bluish green (17.8.53)	..	5	5
511	15 c. carmine (17.8.53)	..	..	8	5
512	35 c. violet (5.52)	..	..	15	8
507/512	*Set of 6*	..	..	..	35	25

HABILITADO PARA CINCO CENTIMOS 1953

(171)   (172)

1953 (11 Apr). *AIR. Nós.* 452/4 *surch with T* **171**.

513	**158** 15 c. on 30 c. carmine	..	..	10	8
514	15 c. on 45 c. red-brown	..	..	10	8
515	15 c. on 65 c. orange	..	..	10	8

1953 (24 Apr). *AIR. Surch with T* **172**, *in red.*

515a	**155** 5 c. on 30 c. black and ultramarine	70	50
516	5 c. on 40 c. black and orange	..	8	8
517	5 c. on 45 c. black and violet	..	8	8
518	5 c. on 65 c. black & orange-brown	15	12

173   **174** "Vegetable Oil"

1953 (25 June). *Fiscal stamp inscr* "TIMBRE DE ARCHIVO" *surch as in T* **173**.

519	5 c. on 10 c. green	..	..	10	5

(Centres photo, frames recess State Ptg Wks, Vienna (Nos. 520a, 521a, 522a, 533a); De La Rue, London (others))

1954 (1 Sept)–**59**. *AIR. National Industries. T* **174** *and similar horiz designs. P* 13 × 12½.

520	5 c. black and scarlet ..	..	..	5	5
520a	5 c. black and bright blue (17.2.56)	..	8	5
521	10 c. black and indigo ..	..	..	8	5
521a	10 c. black & dp violet-blue (17.2.56)	..	10	5
522	15 c. black and green ..	..	..	8	5
522a	15 c. black & yellow-orange (17.2.56)	..	10	5
523	20 c. black and violet	..	..	8	5
524	25 c. black and crimson	..	..	8	5
525	30 c. black and deep lilac (10.54)	..	25	8
526	35 c. black and bright purple (10.54)	..	12	5
527	40 c. black ..	..	..	20	10
528	45 c. black and deep myrtle-green	..	35	12
529	50 c. black and maroon	..	..	25	8
530	55 c. black and yellow ..	..	..	15	8
531	60 c. black and sepia (10.54)	..	..	35	15
532	65 c. black and carmine-red (10.54)	..	45	20
533	75 c. black and bluish violet (10.54)	..	65	15
533a	75 c. black and orange-red (17.2.56)	..	12	10
533b	80 c. black and violet (2.10.59) ..	..	25	12
534	1 col. black and turquoise-blue	..	20	10
	a. Imperf (pair)	..	..	8·00	
535	2 col. black and magenta (10.54)	..	45	25
536	3 col. black & deep yellow-grn (10.54)	65	50
537	5 col. black ..	..	..	1·25	60
538	10 col. black and lemon	..	..	3·75	2·50
520/538	*Set of 24*	..	..	9·00	5·00

Designs:—5 c. T **174**; 10 c. Pottery; 15 c. Sugar; 20 c. Soap; 25 c. Timber; 30 c. Matches; 35 c. Textiles; 40 c. Leather; 45 c. Tobacco; 50 c. Confectionery; 55 c. Canned foods; 60 c. General industries; 65 c. Metals; 75 c., 80 c. Pharmaceutics; 1 col. Paper and cardboard; 2 col. Rubber; 3 col. Aircraft reconstruction; 5 col. Marble; 10 col. Beer.

175　　　**176** Rotary Emblem over Central America

1955–56. *Fiscal stamps optd for postal use as in T* **175.** *Recess.* P 12.

539	**175**	5 c. on 2 c. emerald (R.) (14.10.55)	5	5
540		15 c. on 2 c. emerald (B.) (19.10.55)	8	5
541		15 c. on 2 c. emerald (R.) (1956) ..	8	5

See also Nos. 750/2.

(Recess Austrian State Ptg Wks, Vienna)

1956 (7 Feb). AIR. *50th Anniv of Rotary International.* T **176** *and similar vert designs inscr "1905 1955".* P 12.

542	10 c. blue-green ..	..	..	..	5	5
543	25 c. deep blue	..	..	..	10	5
544	40 c. sepia	..	..	..	12	8
545	45 c. vermilion	..	..	..	15	10
546	60 c. maroon	..	..	..	15	10
547	2 col. brown-orange	..	..	..	30	20
542/547	*Set of 6*	..	..	..	80	50

Designs:—25 c. Emblem, hand and boy; 40 c., 2 col. Emblem and hospital; 45 c. Emblem, leaves and Central America; 60 c. Emblem and lighthouse.

SELLO DE NAVIDAD

PRO - CIUDAD
DE LOS NIÑOS
5　　**5**

177 Map of Costa Rica　　　**(178)**

(Recess Waterlow)

1957 (21 June). AIR. *Centenary of War of 1856–57.* T **177** *and similar vert designs inscr "CENTENARIO DE LA GUERRA 1856–57".* P 14×13½.

548	5 c. blue	..	..	..	5	5
549	10 c. green	..	..	..	5	5
550	15 c. orange	..	..	..	5	5
551	20 c. yellow-brown	..	..	..	5	5
552	25 c. deep ultramarine	..	..	..	8	8
553	30 c. violet	..	..	..	10	8
554	35 c. carmine	..	..	..	12	8
555	40 c. grey-black ..	..	..	..	12	10
556	45 c. scarlet	..	..	..	12	10
557	50 c. bright blue ..	..	..	..	15	10
558	55 c. yellow-ochre	..	..	..	15	10
559	60 c. rose-carmine	..	..	..	20	12
560	65 c. carmine-red	..	..	..	20	12
561	70 c. yellow	..	..	..	25	15
562	75 c. emerald-green	..	..	..	20	15
563	80 c. deep brown	..	..	..	30	20
564	1 col. black	..	..	..	40	25
548/564	*Set of 17* ..	..	..	..	2·25	1·60

Designs:—10 c. Map of Guanacaste Province; 15 c. War-time inn; 20 c. Santa Rosa house; 25 c. General D. J. M. Quirós; 30 c. Old Presidential Palace; 35 c. Minister D. J. B. Calvo; 40 c. Minister L. Molina; 45 c. General D. J. J. Mora; 50 c. General D. J. M. Cañas; 55 c. Juan Santamaria Monument; 60 c. National Monument; 65 c. A. Vallerriestra; 70 c. Pres. R. Castilla y Marquesado of Peru; 75 c. San Carlos Fort; 80 c. Vice-President D. F. M. Oreamuno of Costa Rica; 1 col. President D. J. R. Mora of Costa Rica.

1958. OBLIGATORY TAX. *Juvenile Delinquents' Fund.* No. 489 *surch with T* **178,** *and No.* 521a *with similar surch.*

565	5 c. on 2 c. black & lt blue (R.) (1.12.58)	8	5
566	5 c. on 10 c. black & deep violet-blue (G.)	8	5
	a. Surch inverted	..	..	..

179 Pres. Gonzalez Viquez　　　**180** Pres. R. J. Oreamuno and Electric Train

(Recess Waterlow)

1959 (23 Nov). AIR. *Birth Centenaries of Gonzalez Viquez* (1958) *and Oreamuno* (1959). *Designs as T* **179/80.** P 13½ (5 c., 10 c.) *or* 13½×13 (*others*).

567	5 c. ultramarine and carmine-red	..	5	5
568	10 c. slate and brown-red	..	5	5
569	15 c. black and slate-blue	..	5	5
570	20 c. red-brown and carmine	..	8	8
571	35 c. blue and purple	..	..	10	10
572	55 c. violet and olive-brown	..	12	10
573	80 c. ultramarine	..	..	20	12
574	1 col. lake and red-orange	..	25	12
575	2 col. lake and black	..	..	45	30
567/575	*Set of 9* ..	..	..	1·25	85

Designs: *Vert* (as T **179**): 10 c. Pres. Oreamuno. *Horiz* (as T **180**): Pres. Gonzalez Viquez and: 15 c. Highway bridge; 55 c. Water pipe-line; 80 c. National Library. Pres. Oreamuno and: 20 c. Puntarenas quay; 35 c. Post Office, San José. 2 col. Presidents Gonzalez Viquez and Oreamuno, and open book inscr "PROBIDAD" ("Honesty").

181 Father Flanagan　　　**182** Goal Attack

(Photo State Ptg Wks, Vienna)

1959 (25 Nov). OBLIGATORY TAX. *Christmas. As T* **181** *inscr "SELLO DE NAVIDAD".* P 14.

576	5 c. green	..	..	..	10	8
577	5 c. magenta	..	..	..	10	8
578	5 c. olive-brown ..	..	..	10	8
579	5 c. grey-black	..	..	..	10	8
576/579	*Set of 4* ..	..	..	35	20

Designs: Famous paintings—No. 577, "Girl with braids" (after Modigliani); 578, "Boy with a club-foot" (after Ribera); 579 "The boy blowing on charcoal" (after El Greco).

(Photo State Ptg Wks, Vienna)

1960 (7 Mar). AIR. *Third Pan-American Football Games. Horiz designs as T* **182.** P 14.

580	10 c. indigo	..	..	8	5
581	25 c. ultramarine	..	..	10	8
582	35 c. orange-red ..	..	..	15	10
583	50 c. lake-brown ..	..	..	20	12
584	85 c. deep bluish green ..	..	30	20
585	1 col. brown-purple	..	..	1·50	1·25
580/585	*Set of 6* ..	..	..	2·10	1·60
MS585a	139×80 mm. 2 col. blue (as 35 c.).		
	Imperf	..	..	..	75	75

Designs:—25 c. Player heading ball; 35 c. Defender tackling forward; 50 c. Referee bouncing ball; 85 c. Goalkeeper seizing ball; 5 col. Player kicking high ball.

183 "Uprooted Tree"   **184** Prof. J. A. Facio

(Photo Courvoisier)

1960 (7 Apr). *AIR. World Refugee Year. P* 11½.
586 **183** 35 c. bright violet-blue and yellow .. 15 10
587   85 c. black and rose-carmine .. 25 15

(Photo State Ptg Wks, Vienna)

1960 (20 Apr). *Birth Centenary of Facio. P* 14.
588 **184** 10 c. lake-red 5 5

185

1960 (15 Aug). *AIR. 6th and 7th Chancellors' Reunion Conferences, Organization of American States, San José. T* **185** *and similar designs. Litho. P* 10.
589 25 c. multicoloured 10 8
  a. Flags sideways .. .. .. 10·00
590 35 c. multicoloured 15 10
  a. Imperf between (pair) .. .. 20·00
591 55 c. multicoloured 25 20
592 5 col. multicoloured .. .. 1·90 1·40
593 10 col. multicoloured .. .. 2·50 1·90
589/593 *Set of* 5 .. .. .. 4·50 3·25
MS593a 124×76 mm. 2 col. multicoloured.
  Imperf 70 70
Designs:—35 c. "OEA" within oval of chains; 55 c. Clasped hands and chains; 2 col. "OEA" and map of Americas; 5 col. Flags in form of flying bird; 10 col. "OEA" on map of Costa Rica, and flags.

186 St. Louise de Marillac, Sister of Charity, and Children   **187** Father Peralta

(Recess J. Enschedé & Sons, Haarlem)

1960 (26 Oct). *AIR. 300th Death Anniv of St. Vincent de Paul. T* **186** *and similar designs. P* 13×14 (5 *col.*) *or* 14×13 (*others*).
594 10 c. deep green.. .. .. 5 5
595 25 c. carmine-lake 8 5
596 50 c. deep blue 12 10
597 1 col. yellow-brown 30 20
598 5 col. sepia .. .. 1·25 90
594/598 *Set of* 5 .. .. 1·60 1·10
Designs: *Horiz*—St. Vincent de Paul and: 25 c. Two-storey building; 1 col. Modern building; 50 c. As T **186** but scene shows sister at bedside. *Vert*—5 col. Stained-glass window picturing St. Vincent de Paul with children.

Nos. 594/8 exist imperforate but these were not regularly issued.

(Photo State Ptg Wks, Vienna)

1960 (1 Dec). *OBLIGATORY TAX. Christmas. As T* **187** *inscr* "SELLO DE NAVIDAD" *etc. P* 14.
599 5 c. chocolate 20 5
600 5 c. orange 20 5
601 5 c. deep claret 20 5
602 5 c. grey-blue 20 5
599/602 *Set of* 4 .. .. .. 70 15
Designs:—No. 600, "Girl" (after Renoir); 601, "The Drinkers" (after Velazquez); 602, "Children Singing" (sculpture, after Zuniga).

188 Running

(Photo Enschedé)

1960 (14 Dec). *AIR. Olympic Games. T* **188** *and similar designs. P* 14×13.
603 1 c. black and greenish yellow.. .. 5 5
604 2 c. black and cobalt 5 5
605 3 c. black and rose-red.. .. 5 5
606 4 c. black and orange-yellow .. 5 5
607 5 c. black and yellow-green .. 5 5
608 10 c. black and vermilion 5 5
609 25 c. black and bluish green .. 10 8
610 85 c. black and light reddish violet .. 45 35
611 1 col. black and grey 60 40
612 10 col. black and lavender .. .. 3·25 2·75
603/612 *Set of* 10 .. .. .. 4·25 3·50
MS612a 100×65 mm. 5 col. multicoloured .. 2·00 2·00
Designs: As T **188**—2 c. Diving; 3 c. Cycling; 4 c. Weightlifting; 5 c. Tennis; 10 c. Boxing; 25 c. Football; 85 c. Basketball; 1 col. Baseball; 10 col. Pistol-shooting. *Square* (27×27 *mm*)—5 col. Romulus and Remus statue.
Nos. 603/12 exist imperforate but these were not regularly issued.

XV Campeonato Mundial de Beisbol de Aficionados
(189)

190 M. Aguilar   **191** Prof. M. Obregon

1961 (21 Apr). *AIR. 15th World Amateur Baseball Championships. No. 533a optd with T* **189**, *or additionally surch* (25 *c.*), *in blue.*
613 25 c. on 75 c. black and orange-red .. 5 5
614 75 c. black and orange-red 20 12

(Photo State Ptg Wks, Vienna)

1961 (14 June). *AIR. First Continental Lawyers' Conference. T* **190** *and portrait designs of lawyers. P* 12.
615 10 c. Prussian blue 5 5
616 10 c. brown-purple (A. Brenes) .. 5 5
617 25 c. violet (A. Gutierrez) .. 8 5
618 25 c. deep sepia (V. Herrera) .. 8 5
615/618 *Set of* 4 .. .. .. 20 15
See also Nos. 628/31.

(Litho State Ptg Wks, Vienna)

1961 (19 July). *AIR. Birth Centenary of Obregon. P* 14.
619 **191** 10 c. deep turquoise-green 5 5

SELLO DE NAVIDAD

PRO - CIUDAD
DE LOS NIÑOS

5   **5**

192 Granary (F.A.O.)   (193)

(Recess Bradbury, Wilkinson)

1961 (24 Oct). *AIR. United Nations Commemoration. T 192 and similar square designs. P 11½.*

620	10 c. emerald	..	5	5
621	20 c. orange	..	5	5
622	25 c. slate	..	8	8
623	30 c. deep blue	..	12	8
624	35 c. carmine	..	50	10
625	45 c. deep violet . .	..	20	12
626	85 c. light blue	..	30	20
627	10 col. black	..	2·75	2·10
620/627	*Set of 8*	..	3·50	2·50
MS627a	100×65 mm. 5 col. blue. Imperf	..	1·75	1·75

Designs:—20 c. "Medical Care" (W.H.O.); 25 c. Globe and workers (I.L.O.); 30 c. Globe and communications satellite "Correo 1B" (I.T.U.); 35 c. Compass and rocket (W.M.O.); 45 c. "The Thinker" (statue) and open book (U.N.E.S.C.O.); 85 c. Airliner and globe (I.C.A.O.); 5 col. "United Nations covering the world"; 10 col. "Spiderman" on girder (International Bank).

(Photo Govt Ptg Bureau, Tokyo)

1961 (29 Nov). *AIR. Ninth Central American Medical Congress. Portrait designs of doctors as T 190 but inscr "NOVENO CONGRESO MEDICO" etc. P 13½.*

628	10 c. violet (E. Rojas Roman)	..	5	5
629	10 c. turquoise-blue (J. M. Soto Alfaro)	..	5	5
630	25 c. sepia (A. Saenz Llorente)	..	8	5
631	25 c. maroon (J. J. Ulloa Giralt)	..	8	5
628/631	*Set of 4*	..	20	15

1961 (1 Dec). *AIR. Children's City Christmas Issue. No. 522 surch with T 193.*

632	5 c. on 15 c. black and green	..	10	5

II CONVENCION FILATELICA

CENTROAMERICANA

10   SETIEMBRE 1962

(194)   (195)

1962 (30 May). *AIR. Various stamps surch as T 194.*

633	10 c. on 15 c. black and green.(522)	..	5	5
634	25 c. on 15 c. black and green (522)	..	10	8
635	35 c. on 50 c. black & maroon (529) (R.)	..	12	8
	a. Surch double	..		
636	85 c. on 80 c. ultramarine (573) (R.)	..	20	15
633/636	*Set of 4*	..	40	30

1962 (12 Sept). *AIR. 2nd Central American Philatelic Convention. Nos. 575 and 623 optd with T 195, in red.*

637	30 c. deep blue	..	25	20
638	2 col. lake and black	..	50	40

₡ 0.10

(196)

197

1962 (Nov). *AIR. (a) No. 522 surch with T 196, in red.*

639	10 c. on 15 c. black and green	..	5	5

(b) As T 197. *Fiscal stamps surch in red*

640	25 c. on 2 c. emerald	..	5	5
641	35 c. on 2 c. emerald	..	8	8
642	45 c. on 2 c. emerald	..	10	10
643	85 c. on 2 c. emerald	..	20	15
639/643	*Set of 5*	..	40	35

198 "Virgin and   199 Jaguar
Child" (after
Bellini)

(Photo State Ptg Wks, Vienna)

1962 (1 Dec). *OBLIGATORY TAX. Christmas. Designs as T 198 inscr "SELLO DE NAVIDAD", etc., "1962". P 14.*

644	5 c. sepia	..	20	5
645	5 c. deep bluish green	..	20	5
646	5 c. blue . .	..	20	5
647	5 c. claret	..	20	5
644/647	*Set of 4*	..	70	15

Designs:—No. 645, "Angel with Violin" (after Mellozo); 646, Mgr. Ruben Odio; 647, "Child's Head" (after Rubens). See also Nos. 674/7.

(Photo Govt Ptg Bureau, Tokyo)

1963 (23 Jan–June). *AIR. T 199 and similar designs. P 13½.*

648	5 c. brown and yellow-olive (3.6)	..	5	5
649	10 c. grey-blue and orange (6.4)	..	5	5
650	25 c. yellow and blue	..	8	5
651	30 c. brown and yellow-green (6.4)	..	8	8
652	35 c. orange-brown and bistre	..	10	8
653	40 c. light blue and light green (3.6)	..	15	10
654	85 c. black and green (3.6)	..	25	15
655	5 col. chocolate and olive-green (6.4)	..	1·00	75
648/655	*Set of 8*	..	1·60	1·10

Animals:—5 c. Paca; 10 c. Tapir; 30 c. Ocelot; 35 c. Deer; 40 c. Manatee; 85 c. Cebus monkey; 5 col. Peccary.

1963

10

CENTIMOS

200 Arms and Campaign   (201)
Emblem

(Photo Courvoisier)

1963 (14 Feb). *AIR. Malaria Eradication. P 11½.*

656	200	25 c. carmine	..	10	5
657		35 c. orange-brown	..	12	8
658		45 c. ultramarine	..	15	10
659		85 c. emerald	..	20	15
660		1 col. deep blue	..	25	20
656/660		*Set of 5*	..	70	50

1963 (Feb). *OBLIGATORY TAX. Fund for Children's Village. Nos. 644/7 surch with T 201, in red.*

661	10 c. on 5 c. sepia	..	5	5
662	10 c. on 5 c. deep bluish green	..	5	5
663	10 c. on 5 c. blue	..	5	5
664	10 c. on 5 c. claret	..	5	5
661/664	*Set of 4*	..	15	12

202 Anglo-Costa Rican Bank

203 ½ real Stamp of 1863 and Packet-ship *William le Lacheur*

(Photo Govt Ptg Bureau, Tokyo)

1963 (25 June). *Centenary of Anglo-Costa Rican Bank.* P 13½.
665 **202** 10 c. indigo 5 5

(Litho Govt Ptg Bureau, Tokyo)

1963 (26 June). *Stamp Centenary.* T **203** *and similar horiz designs.* P 13½. (a) POSTAGE.

666	25 c. blue and reddish purple ..	8	5
667	2 col. orange-brown and grey ..	40	30
668	3 col. green and light ochre ..	55	45
669	10 col. yellow-brown and grey-green	1·75	1·40
666/669	*Set of 4*	2·50	2·00

(b) AIR. Miniature sheet
MS669a 60×100 mm. 5 col. blue, orange-brown, green and yellow-brown .. .. 1·50 1·50
Designs:—2 col. 2 reales stamp of 1863 and Postmaster-General R. B. Carrillo; 3 col. 4 reales stamp of 1863 and mounted postman and pack-mule of 1839; 5 col. ½ real, 2 reales, 4 reales and 1 peso stamps of 1863 (as in Nos. 666/9); 10 col. 1 peso stamp of 1863 and burro-drawn mail-car.

₡ 0.10
(204)

1963 (14 Sept). *AIR. Unissued triangular stamps as T* **199** *surch as T* **204**, *in red.*

670	10 c. on 1 c. orange-brown and bl-green	5	5
671	25 c. on 2 c. sepia and brown-orange ..	8	5
672	35 c. on 3 c. light brown & myrtle-green	10	8
673	85 c. on 4 c. brown and lake ..	20	10
670/673	*Set of 4*	35	25

Animals:—1 c. Little ant-eater; 2 c. Grey fox; 3 c. Armadillo; 4 c. Great ant-eater.

(Photo State Ptg Wks, Vienna)

1963 (2 Dec). *OBLIGATORY TAX. Christmas.* As T **198** *but inscr "SELLO DE NAVIDAD" etc., "1963" and colours changed.* P 14.

674	5 c. blue (As 644)	12	5
675	5 c. claret (As 645)	12	5
676	5 c. black (As 646)	12	5
677	5 c. sepia (As 647)	12	5
674/677	*Set of 4*	40	15

205 Pres. Orlich (Costa Rica)

206 Puma (clay statuette)

(Photo Heraclio Fournier, Vitoria (Spain))

1963 (7 Dec). *AIR. Presidential Reunion, San José. Portrait designs as T* **205**. *Portraits in black-brown.* P 14½.

678	25 c. dull purple	8	5
679	30 c. magenta	10	8
680	35 c. yellow-ochre	10	10
681	85 c. light grey-blue	15	12
682	1 col. chestnut	30	15
683	3 col. light olive-green ..	70	50
684	5 col. slate	2·00	1·40
678/684	*Set of 7*	3·00	2·10

Presidents:—30 c. Rivera (El Salvador); 35 c. Ydigoras (Guatemala); 85 c. Villeda (Honduras); 1 col. Somoza (Nicaragua); 3 col. Chiari (Panama); 5 col. Kennedy (U.S.A.).

(Photo State Ptg Wks, Vienna)

1963 (26 Dec)–**64**. *AIR. Archaeological Discoveries.* T **206** *and similar designs.* P 12.

685	5 c. turquoise and light apple-green ..	5	5
686	10 c. deep bluish green & light yellow ..	5	5
687	25 c. sepia and rose-red	5	5
688	30 c. blue-green and buff (29.2.64) ..	8	5
689	35 c. bronze-green and light salmon ..	8	8
690	45 c. brown and light blue	8	8
691	50 c. bistre-brown and pale blue ..	10	8
692	55 c. bistre-brown and light yell-green ..	10	8
693	75 c. chocolate and yellow-buff ..	12	8
694	85 c. red-brown and greenish yellow ..	20	12
695	90 c. brown and yellow (29.2.64)	20	15
696	1 col. brown and light blue (29.2.64)	15	12
697	2 col. bluish green & lt yellow (29.2.64)	25	15
698	3 col. brown and light green (29.2.64) ..	50	25
699	5 col. lt olive-brn & apple-yell (29.2.64)	1·10	75
700	10 col. bronze-green & mauve (29.2.64)	1·50	1·00
685/700	*Set of 16*	4·00	2·75

Designs: *Horiz*—10 c. Ceremonial stool; 1 col. Twin beakers; 2 col. Alligator. *Vert*—25 c. Man (statuette); 30 c. Dancer; 35 c. Vase; 45 c. Deity; 50 c. Simian effigy; 55 c. "Eagle" bell; 75 c. Multi-limbed deity; 85 c. Kneeling figure; 90 c. "Bird" jug; 3 col. Twin-tailed lizard; 5 col. Child; 10 col. Stone effigy of woman.

207 Flags

₡ 0.15
(208)

(Photo Heraclio Fournier, Vitoria (Spain))

1964 (11 Mar). *AIR. "Centro America".* P 14½×14.
701 **207** 30 c. black, grey, red and blue .. 25 10

1964 (Oct). *AIR. Various stamps surch as T* **208**.

702	5 c. on 30 c. (No. 688) (15.10) ..	5	5
703	15 c. on 30 c. (No. 701) (15.10) ..	5	5
704	15 c. on 85 c. (No. 694) (9.10) ..	5	5
702/704	*Set of 3*	10	10

See also Nos. 745/9.

₡ 0.15

**CONFERENCIA POSTAL
DE PARIS - 1864**
(209)

210 Mgr. R. Odio and Children

1964 (22 Nov). *Paris Postal Conference.* No. 695 *surch with* T **209**.
705 15 c. on 90 c. brown and yellow .. 5 5

(Litho Fotolitografia Universal, San José)

1964 (10 Dec). *OBLIGATORY TAX. Christmas.* T **210** *and similar designs inscr "SELLO DE NAVIDAD", etc., "1964".* P 12½.

706	5 c. brown	8	5
707	5 c. blue (Teacher and child) ..	8	5
708	5 c. bright purple (Children at play)	8	5
709	5 c. blue-green (Children in class) ..	8	5
706/709	*Set of 4*	25	12

75 ANIVERSARIO
ASILO CHAPUI
1890—1965
211 A. Gonzalez F.   (212)

(Photo State Ptg Wks, Vienna)

1965 (June). *AIR. 50th Anniv of National Bank. P* 12.
710 211 35 c. deep bluish green 8 5

1965 (14 Aug). *AIR. 75th Anniv of Chapui Hospital. No.* 697 *optd with T* 212.
711 2 col. bluish green and light yellow .. 35 25

213 Handfuls of Grain

214 National Children's Hospital

(Litho Litografia Nacional, Oporto, Portugal)

1965 (25 Oct). *AIR. Freedom from Hunger. T* 213 *and similar designs. P* 14.
712 15 c. black, grey and yellow-brown .. 5 5
713 35 c. black and buff 8 5
714 50 c. deep bluish green and blue .. 10 8
715 1 col. silver, black and blue-green .. 20 12
712/715 *Set of 4* 35 25
Designs: *Horiz*—15 c. Map and grain silo; 1 col. Jetliner over map. *Vert*—50 c. Children and population graph.

(Litho Fotolit Ltda, San José)

1965 (10 Dec). *OBLIGATORY TAX. Christmas. T* 214 *and similar designs inscr "SELLO DE NAVIDAD", etc. P* 10.
716 5 c. deep emerald 8 5
717 5 c. red-brown (Father Casiano) .. 8 5
718 5 c. scarlet (Poinsettia) 8 5
719 5 c. ultramarine (Father Christmas with children) 8 5
716/719 *Set of 4* 25 12
No. 719 is diamond-shaped.

215 L. Briceño B.

216 Running

(Litho De La Rue, Bogotá)

1965 (20 Dec). *AIR. Incorporation of Nicoya District. T* 215 *and similar vert designs. P* 13½×14.
720 5 c. deep slate, black and chestnut .. 5 5
721 10 c. deep slate and light blue .. 5 5
722 15 c. deep slate and bistre .. 5 5
723 35 c. deep slate and light blue .. 5 5
724 50 c. violet-blue and greenish grey .. 8 5
725 1 col. deep slate and ochre .. 12 10
720/725 *Set of 6* 35 30
Designs:—10 c. Nicoya Church; 15 c. Incorporation scroll; 35 c. Map of Guanacaste Province; 50 c. Provincial dance; 1 col. Guanacaste map and produce.

(Des C. Alonso. Litho De La Rue, Bogotá)

1965 (23 Dec). *AIR. Olympic Games* (1964). *T* 216 *and similar vert designs. Multicoloured. P* 13×13½.
726 5 c. Type 216 .. .. 5 5
727 10 c. Cycling 5 5
728 40 c. Judo 10 10
729 65 c. Handball 15 15
730 80 c. Football 20 20
731 1 col. Olympic torches 25 25
726/731 *Set of 6* 70 70
MS731a 68×95 mm. No. 731 (×2) in different colours 60 60

217 Pres. Kennedy, and Capsule encircling Globe   218 Fire Engine

(Des C. Alonso. Litho De La Rue, Bogotá)

1965 (23 Dec). *AIR. 2nd Anniv of President Kennedy's Death. T* 217 *and similar multicoloured designs. P* 13½×13 (45 *c.) or* 13×13½ (*others*).
732 45 c. Type 217 .. .. 10 10
733 55 c. Pres. Kennedy making speech .. 15 15
734 85 c. Pres. Kennedy with son 20 20
735 1 col. Façade of White House, Washington 25 25
732/735 *Set of 4* 60 60
MS735a 68×94 mm. No. 735 (×2) in different colours 50 50
Nos. 733/5 are vertical.

(Litho British-American Bank Note Co, Ottawa)

1966 (12 Mar). *AIR. Centenary of Fire Brigade. T* 218 *and similar designs. P* 11.
736 5 c. rose-red and black 5 5
737 10 c. rose-red and olive-yellow .. 5 5
738 15 c. black and rose-red 5 5
739 35 c. lemon and black 5 5
740 50 c. red and blue 8 5
736/740 *Set of 5* 20 15
Designs: *Vert*—10 c. Fire engine of 1866; 15 c. Firemen with hoses; 35 c. Brigade badge; 50 c. Emblem of Central American Fire Brigades Confederation.

219 Angel   (220)

(Litho Fotolit Ltda, San José)

1966 (1 Dec). *OBLIGATORY TAX. Christmas. T* 219 *and similar designs inscr "SELLO DE NAVIDAD", etc. P* 11.
741 5 c. blue 5 5
742 5 c. red (Trinkets) 5 5
743 5 c. emerald (Church) 5 5
744 5 c. bistre-brown (Reindeer) 5 5
741/744 *Set of 4* 15 12

1966 (Dec). *AIR. Various stamps surch as T* 208.
745 15 c. on 30 c. (688) 5 5
746 15 c. on 45 c. (690) 5 5
747 35 c. on 75 c. (693) 5 5
748 35 c. on 55 c. (733) 5 5
749 50 c. on 85 c. (734) 5 5
745/749 *Set of 5* 25 20
The surcharges differ from *T* 208 as follows:—Nos. 745/7 have a more rounded "C" and figures; No. 784 has tall, narrow "C" and rounded figures; No. 749 has tall, narrow "C" and figures.

1967 (Jan). *AIR. Revenue stamps (as T **175**) surch as T **220**. P* 12.

750	15 c. on 5 c. blue	..	..	5	5
751	35 c. on 10 c. claret	..	..	5	5
752	50 c. on 20 c. vermilion	..	..	8	5

220a Post Office, San José   221 Central Bank, San José

(Litho Fotolit Ltda, San José)

1967 (Mar). *OBLIGATORY TAX. Social Plan for Postal Workers. P* 11.

753	**220**a 10 c. bright greenish blue	..	..	5	5

On 15 December 1972 instructions were given for the above to be re-issued for ordinary postal use.

(Litho Fotolit Ltda, San José)

1967 (1 Mar). *AIR. 50th Anniv of Central Bank. P* 11.

754	**221** 5 c. light blue-green	..	..	5	5
755	15 c. yellow-brown	..	..	5	5
756	35 c. rosine	..	..	5	5
754/756	*Set of 3*	..	..	12	10

222 Telecommunications Building, San Pedro   223 *Chondrorhyncha aromatica*

(Litho Fotolit Ltda, San José)

1967 (24 Apr). *AIR. Costa Rican Electrical Industry. T **222** and similar designs. P* 11.

757	5 c. black	..	..	5	5
758	10 c. magenta	..	..	5	5
759	15 c. brown-orange	..	..	5	5
760	25 c. ultramarine	..	..	5	5
761	35 c. emerald	..	..	5	5
762	50 c. lake-brown	..	..	8	5
757/762	*Set of 6*	..	..	25	20

Designs: *Vert*—5 c. Electricity pylons; 15 c. Central Telephone Exchange, San José. *Horiz*—25 c. La Garita dam; 35 c. Rio Macho reservoir; 50 c. Cachi dam.

(Recess and litho De La Rue, Bogotá)

1967 (15 June). *AIR. University Library. Orchids. T **223** and similar vert designs. Multicoloured. P* $13 \times 13\frac{1}{2}$.

763	5 c. Type **223**	..	..	5	5
764	10 c. *Miltonia endresii*	..	..	5	5
765	15 c. *Stanhopea cirrhata*	..	..	5	5
766	25 c. *Trichopilia suavis*	..	..	5	5
767	35 c. *Odontoglossum schlieperianum*	..	8	5
768	50 c. *Cattleya skinneri*	..	..	10	8
769	1 col. *Cattleya dowiana*	..	..	20	12
770	2 col. *Odontoglossum chiriquense*	..	40	25
763/770	*Set of 8*	..	..	90	60

224 O.E.A. Emblem and Split Leaf   225 Madonna and Child   226 L.A.C.S.A. Emblem

(Recess and litho Courvoisier)

1967 (6 Oct). *AIR. 25th Anniv of Inter-American Institute of Agricultural Science. P* $13 \times 13\frac{1}{2}$.

771	**224** 50 c. ultramarine and new blue	..	8	5

(Litho Fotolit Ltda, San José)

1967 (1st Dec). *OBLIGATORY TAX. Christmas. P* 11.

772	**225** 5 c. olive-green	..	..	5	5
773	5 c. magenta	..	..	5	5
774	5 c. new blue	..	..	5	5
775	5 c. turquoise-blue	..	..	5	5
772/775	*Set of 4*	..	..	15	12

1967 (12 Dec). *AIR. 20th Anniv of Lineas Aereas Costaricenses (L.A.C.S.A.—Costa Rican Airlines)* (1966). *T **226** and similar designs. Multicoloured. Embossed and litho. P* $13 \times 13\frac{1}{2}$ *(vert) or* $13\frac{1}{2} \times 13$ *(horiz)*.

776	40 c. Type **226**	..	..	5	5
777	45 c. L.A.C.S.A. emblem and jetliner (horiz)	..	..	5	5
778	50 c. Wheel and emblem	..	..	8	5

227 Church of Solitude   228 Scouts in Camps

(Recess U.S. Banknote Corp)

1967 (15 Dec). *AIR. Churches and Cathedrals. T **227** and similar vert designs. P* $12\frac{1}{2}$.

779	5 c. green	..	..	5	5
780	10 c. blue	..	..	5	5
781	15 c. purple	..	..	5	5
782	25 c. ochre	..	..	5	5
783	30 c. chestnut	..	..	5	5
784	35 c. light blue	..	..	5	5
785	40 c. red-orange	..	..	8	5
786	45 c. bluish green	..	..	10	5
787	50 c. yellow-olive	..	..	10	5
788	55 c. brown	..	..	10	5
789	65 c. magenta	..	..	10	5
790	75 c. sepia	..	..	12	8
791	80 c. yellow	..	..	12	8
792	85 c. slate-purple	..	..	12	8
793	90 c. yellow-green	..	..	12	8
794	1 col. slate	..	..	15	10
795	2 col. turquoise-green	..	..	30	15
796	3 col. yellow-orange	..	..	45	30
797	5 col. violet-blue	..	..	75	45
798	10 col. carmine	..	..	1·40	1·00
779/798	*Set of 20*	..	..	3·75	2·50

Designs:—10 c. Santo Domingo Basilica, Heredia; 15 c. Tilaran Cathedral; 25 c. Alajuela Cathedral; 30 c. Church of Mercy; 35 c. Our Lady of the Angels Basilica; 40 c. San Rafael Church, Heredia; 45 c. Ruins, Ujarras; 50 c. Ruins of Parish Church, Cartago; 55 c. San José Cathedral; 65 c. Parish Church, Puntarenas; 75 c. Orosi Church; 80 c. Cathedral of San Isidro the General; 85 c. San Ramon Church; 90 c. Church of the Forsaken; 1 col. Coronado Church; 2 col. Church of St. Teresita; 3 col. Parish Church, Heredia; 5 col. Carmelite Church; 10 col. Limon Cathedral.

ALBUM LISTS

Write for our latest lists of albums and accessories.

These will be sent free on request.

(Recess and litho Courvoisier)

1968 (15 Mar). *AIR. Golden Jubilee of Scout Movement in Costa Rica* (1966). *T* **228** *and similar designs. Multicoloured. P* 13×13½ (*vert*) *or* 13½×13 (*horiz*).

799	15 c. Scout on traffic control	..	5	5
800	25 c. Scouts tending camp-fire	..	5	5
801	35 c. Scout badge and flags	..	8	5
802	50 c. Type **228**	..	8	5
803	65 c. First scout troop on parade, 1916	..	8	5
799/803	*Set of 5*		30	20

The 15 c., 25 c. and 35 c. are vertical designs.

1968 (1 Aug). *AIR. Third National Philatelic Exhibition, San José. Sheet No.* **MS**669a *optd* "III EXPOSICION FILATELICA NACIONAL 2–4 AGOSTO 1968 COSTA RICA 68" *in three lines.*

MS804 60×100 mm. 5 col. blue, orange-brown, green and yellow-brown 90 90

229 "Madonna and Child"

230 Running

231 Exhibition Emblem

(Litho Fotolitografia Universal, San José)

1968 (Dec). *OBLIGATORY TAX. Christmas. P* 12½.

805	**229**	5 c. grey-black	..	5	5
806		5 c. maroon	..	5	5
807		5 c. orange-brown	..	5	5
808		5 c. light red	..	5	5
805/808		*Set of 4*		15	10

(Litho Fotolit Ltda, San José)

1969 (Jan). *AIR. Olympic Games, Mexico. T* **230** *and similar vert designs. Multicoloured. P* 10×11.

809	30 c. Type **230**	..	5	5
810	40 c. Woman breasting tape	..	8	5
811	55 c. Boxing	..	10	5
812	65 c. Cycling	..	10	5
	a. "IMPIADA" for "OLIMPIADA"	..		
813	75 c. Weightlifting	..	12	8
814	1 col. High-diving	..	15	10
815	3 col. Rifle-shooting	..	45	35
809/815	*Set of 7*	..	95	60

(Litho Fotolit Ltda, San José)

1969 (5 June). *AIR. "Costa Rica 69" Philatelic Exhibition, San José. P* 11×10.

816	**231** 35 c. multicoloured	..	5	5
817	40 c. multicoloured	..	5	5
818	50 c. multicoloured	..	8	5
819	2 col. multicoloured	..	25	15
816/819	*Set of 4*	..	40	25

232 Arms of San José

233 I.L.O. Emblem

(Litho Litografia Nacional, Oporto, Portugal)

1969 (14 Sept). *Provincial Coats-of-Arms. T* **232** *and similar vert designs. Multicoloured. P* 14×13½.

820	15 c. Type **232**	..	5	5
821	35 c. Cartago	..	5	5
822	50 c. Heredia	..	8	8
823	55 c. Alajuela	..	8	8
824	65 c. Guanacaste	..	10	8
825	1 col. Puntarenas	..	15	10
826	2 col. Limón	..	30	20
820/826	*Set of 7*	..	75	60

(Litho Fotolit Ltda, San José)

1969 (29 Oct). *AIR. 50th Anniversary of International Labour Organization. P* 10.

827	**233** 35 c. turquoise and black	..	5	5
828	50 c. carmine-red and black	..	8	5

234 Map on Football

235 Madonna and Child

(Litho Fotolit Ltda, San José)

1969 (23 Nov). *AIR. 4th North and Central American Football Championship* (*CONCACAF*). *T* **234** *and similar vert designs. Multicoloured. P* 11×10.

829	65 c. Type **234**	..	..	8	8
830	75 c. Goal-mouth mêlée	..	..	8	8
831	85 c. Player with ball	..	..	10	8
832	1 col. Two players with ball	..	12	10
829/832	*Set of 4*	..	..	35	30

(Litho Fotolitografia Universal, San José)

1969 (1 Dec). *OBLIGATORY TAX. Christmas. P* 12½.

833	**235** 5 c. deep bluish green	..	5	5
834	5 c. brown-lake	..	5	5
835	5 c. deep blue	..	5	5
836	5 c. orange	..	5	5
833/836	*Set of 4*	..	12	8

236 Stylised Crab

E 237 New U.P.U. Building, and Monument, Berne

(Des A. Calder. Litho Fotolitografia Universal, San José)

1970 (14 May). *AIR. 10th Inter-American Cancer Congress, San José. P* 12½.

837	**236** 10 c. black and light magenta	..	5	5
838	15 c. black and greenish yellow	..	5	5
839	50 c. black and orange	..	8	5
840	1 col. 10, black and bright green	..	12	10
837/840	*Set of 4*	..	25	20

(Litho Fotolit Ltda, San José)

1970 (20 May). *AIR SPECIAL DELIVERY. Opening of New U.P.U. Headquarters Building, Berne. P* 10×11.

E841	E **237** 35 c. multicoloured	..	5	5
E842	60 c. multicoloured	..	8	5

Nos. E841/2 were issued with *se-tenant* tab at foot. For No. E841 this tab is inscribed as shown in Type E **237**; the tab for No. E842 is inscribed "EXPRES". Prices are for stamps with tab attached.

Without these tabs the two stamps could be used for ordinary airmail postage.

238 Costa Rican Stamps and Magnifier

239 Japanese Vase and Flowers

(Des R. Coto. Litho Fotolit Ltda, San José)

1970 (14 Sept). *AIR. "Costa Rica 70" Philatelic Exhibition, San José. T 238 and similar vert design. P 11.*

843	1 col. carmine-red, sepia and bright blue		12	8
844	2 col. black, pale mauve and bright blue		25	15

Design:—2 col. Father and son with stamps.

(Des and litho Kyoto Ptg Co, Tokyo)

1970 (22 Oct). *AIR. "EXPO 70" World Fair, Osaka, Japan. T 239 and similar multicoloured designs. P 13 × 13½ (vert) or 13½ × 13 (horiz).*

845	10 c. Type **239**	..	5	5
846	15 c. Costa Rican ornamental cart (*horiz*)		5	5
847	35 c. Sun Tower, Osaka (*horiz*)	..	5	5
848	40 c. Japanese tea ceremony (*horiz*)		5	5
849	45 c. Coffee-picking	..	5	5
850	55 c. View of Earth from the Moon		8	5
845/850	*Set of 6*	..	25	20

240 "Irazu" (R. A. Garcia)

241 "Holy Child"

(Litho Moller & Rothe, Gothenburg, Sweden)

1970 (4 Nov). *AIR. Costa Rican Paintings. T 240 and similar multicoloured designs. P 12½.*

851	25 c. Type **240**	..	5	5
852	45 c. "Escazu Valley" (M. Bertheau) (*horiz*)		5	5
853	80 c. "Estuary Landscape" (T. Quiros) (*horiz*)		10	8
854	1 col. "The Other Face" (C. Valverde) (*horiz*)		12	8
855	2 col. 50, "Madonna" (L. Daell)		25	20
851/855	*Set of 5*	..	50	35

(Des Sister Maria de la Salette. Litho Casa Grafica Ltda, San José)

1970 (Dec). *OBLIGATORY TAX. Christmas. P 12½.*

856	**241** 5 c. magenta..	..	5	5
857	5 c. yellow-brown	..	5	5
858	5 c. olive	..	5	5
859	5 c. light reddish violet	..	5	5
856/859	*Set of 4*	..	12	10

242 Costa Rican Arms, 21 Oct 1964

243 National Theatre, San José

(Litho Litografia Nacional, Oporto, Portugal)

1971 (10 Feb). *AIR. Development of the Costa Rican National Coat-of-Arms. Vert designs as T 242, showing arms from different periods. Multicoloured. P 14 × 13½.*

860	5 c. Type **242**	..	5	5
861	10 c. Arms, 27 Nov 1906		5	5
862	15 c. Arms, 29 Sept 1848		5	5
863	25 c. Arms, 21 April 1840		5	5
864	35 c. Arms, 22 Nov 1824		5	5
865	50 c. Arms, 2 Nov 1824	..	8	5
866	1 col. Arms, 6 March 1824		12	8
867	2 col. Arms, 10 May 1823		25	15
860/867	*Set of 8*	..	65	45

(Litho Fotolit Ltda, San José)

1971 (14 Apr). *AIR. Meeting of Organization of American States (O.E.A.), San José. P 11.*

868	**243** 2 col. purple	..	25	15

244 J. M. Delgado and M. J. Arce (El Salvador)

245 Cradle on "PAX"

(Litho Moller & Rothe, Gothenburg, Sweden)

1971. *AIR. 150th Anniversary of Central American Independence from Spain. T 244 and similar multicoloured designs. P 13.*

869	5 c. Type **244** (1.11)	..	5	5
870	10 c. M. Larreinaga and M. A. de la Cerda (Nicaragua) (1.11)		5	5
871	15 c. J. C. del Valle and D. de Herrera (Honduras) (1.11)		5	5
872	35 c. P. Alvarado and F. del Castillo (Costa Rica) (1.11)		5	5
873	50 c. A. Larrazabal and P. Molina (Guatemala) (1.11)		8	5
874	1 col. United States of Central America flag (*vert*) (14.9)		15	10
875	2 col. United States of Central America arms (*vert*) (14.9)		25	15
869/875	*Set of 7*	..	60	45

(Des Sister Maria de la Salette. Litho Casa Grafica Ltda, San José)

1971 (29 Nov). *OBLIGATORY TAX. Christmas. P 12½.*

876	**245** 10 c. red-orange	..	5	5
877	10 c. lake-brown	..	5	5
878	10 c. green	..	5	5
879	10 c. blue	..	5	5
876/879	*Set of 4*	..	10	8

HAVE YOU READ THE NOTES AT THE BEGINNING OF THIS CATALOGUE?

These often provide answers to the enquiries we receive.

246 Federation Emblem

247 "Children of the World"

(Litho Fotolitografia Universal, San José)

1971 (6 Dec). *AIR. 50th Anniversary of Costa Rican Football Federation. P 12½.*
880 **246** 50 c. multicoloured 8 5
881 60 c. multicoloured 8 5

(Litho Fotolitografia Universal, San José)

1972 (11 Jan). *AIR. 25th Anniversary of U.N.I.C.E.F. P 12½.*
882 **247** 50 c. multicoloured 8 5
883 1 col. 10, multicoloured 12 10

248 Guanacaste Tree

E **249** Winged Letter

(Litho Fotolit Ltda, San José)

1972 (28 Feb). *AIR. Bicentenary of Liberia City. T 248 and similar designs. P 11.*
884 20 c. sage-green, yellow-brn & emerald 5 5
   a. Imperf between (vert pair).. ..
885 40 c. brown and sage-green 5 5
886 55 c. brown and black 8 5
887 60 c. scarlet, black and pale buff .. 8 5
   a. Imperf horiz (vert pair) .. ..
884/887 *Set of 4* 20 15
Designs: *Horiz*—40 c. Hermitage, Liberia; 55 c. Mayan petroglyphs. *Vert*—60 c. Painted head sculpture.

(Litho Fotolit Ltda, San José)

1972 (20 Mar–19 Dec). *SPECIAL DELIVERY. P 11×12 (No. E889) or 11 (others).*
E888 E **249** 75 c. bistre-brown and red .. 8 5
E889 75 c. green (19.12) 8 5
E890 1 col. 50, new blue and red .. 15 8
The 75 c. stamps were for domestic use and for mail to member countries of the Spanish-American Postal Union. The 1 col. 50 was for other foreign mail.

250 Farmer's Family and Farm

251 Inter-American Stamp Exhibitions

(Litho Fotolitografia Universal, San José)

1972 (30 June). *AIR. 30th Anniversary of Inter-American Institute of Agricultural Sciences. T 250 and similar designs. P 12½.*
891 20 c. multicoloured 5 5
892 45 c. multicoloured 5 5
893 50 c. yellow-bistre, emerald and black .. 8 5
894 10 col. multicoloured .. .. .. 1·25 75
891/894 *Set of 4* .. .. .. 1·25 80
Designs: *Horiz*—45 c. Meat production. *Vert*—50 c. Treeplanting; 10 col. Agricultural worker and map.

(Litho Casa Grafica, Ltda, San José)

1972 (26 Aug). *AIR. "EXFILBRA 72" Philatelic Exhibition, Rio de Janeiro. P 13.*
895 **251** 50 c. purple-brown and orange .. 8 5
896 2 col. violet and light blue 25 15

252 Madonna and Child

253 First Book printed in Costa Rica

(Des Sister Maria de la Salette. Litho Fotolit Ltda, San José)

1972 (30 Nov). *OBLIGATORY TAX. Christmas. P 11½.*
897 **252** 10 c. rosine 5 5
898 10 c. bright mauve 5 5
899 10 c. blue 5 5
900 10 c. green 5 5
897/900 *Set of 4* 10 8

(Litho Fotolitografia Universal, San José)

1972 (7 Dec). *AIR. International Book Year. T 253 and similar multicoloured design. P 12½.*
901 20 c. Type **253** 5 5
902 50 c. National Library, San José (horiz) 8 5
903 75 c. Type **253** 10 8
904 5 col. As 50 c. 60 40
901/904 *Set of 4* 75 50

254 View near Irazú

(Litho Fotolit Ltda, San José)

1972 (26 Dec)–73. *AIR. American tourist Year. T 254 and similar multicoloured designs. P 11×12 (horiz) or 12×11 (vert).*
905 5 c. Type **254** (21.3.73) 5 5
906 15 c. Entrance to Culebra Bay (21.3.73) .. 5 5
907 20 c. Type **254** 5 5
908 25 c. As 15 c. 5 5
909 40 c. Manuel Antonio Beach (21.3.73) .. 5 5
910 45 c. Costarican Tourist Institute emblem (21.3.73) 5 5
911 50 c. Lindora Lake (21.3.73) 8 5
912 60 c. Post Office Building, San José (vert) (21.3.73) 8 5
913 80 c. As 40 c. 10 8
914 90 c. As 45 c. 12 8
915 1 col. As 50 c. 12 8
916 2 col. As 60 c. 25 15
905/916 *Set of 12* 85 50

GUANACASTE

In the 1880's the Costa Rican central postal authorities allowed a discount on purchases of $25 worth of stamps or more by local post offices. As the province of Guanacaste was then three days' journey from San José, twice the rate of discount was allowed to post offices there. To prevent speculation, stamps sold in Guanacaste were overprinted from 1886 to 1889 with the name of the province.

(Types G 1/10 optd by National Printing Office, San José)

1885. *Stamps of 1883, T 8. P 12.*

Overprinted

Guanacaste   **Guanacaste**   **Guanacaste**
(G 1) 15¾ mm   (G 2) 17½ mm   (G 3) 18½ mm

(a) With Type G 1 horizontally
A. *In black.* B. *In red*

			A		B	
G1	1 c. green	..	1·00	1·00	80	80
	a. "Gnanacaste"	..	12·00	—	8·00	—
	b. Opt double (Bk.+R.)	..	16·00	—		
G2	2 c. carmine	..	70	80	†	
	a. "Gnanacaste"	..	8·50	—	†	
G3	5 c. violet	..	†		3·75	80
	a. "Gnanacaste"	..	†		14·00	
G4	10 c. orange	..	2·50	2·50	†	
	a. "Gnanacaste"	..	14·00		†	
G5	40 c. blue	..	†		5·00	5·00
	a. "Gnanacaste"	..			—	—

(b) With Type G 2 horizontally
A. *In black.* B. *In red*

			A		B	
G 6	1 c. green	..	2·25	2·00	†	
G 7	2 c. carmine	..	2·00	2·00	†	
G 8	5 c. violet	..	4·50	1·00	8·00	2·10
G 9	10 c. orange	..	4·25	2·60	†	
G10	40 c. blue	..	10·00	7·00	£100	—

(c) With Type G 3
(i) Horizontally

G11	1 c. green (R.)	..	1·75	1·50
	a. Opt double (R.+Bk.)	..	25·00	
G12	2 c. carmine	..	1·90	1·50
G13	5 c. violet (R.)	..	8·00	1·25
G14	10 c. orange	..	8·00	6·00
G15	40 c. blue (R.)	..	8·00	8·00

(ii) Vertically

G16	1 c. green	..	75·00	75·00
G17	2 c. carmine	..	75·00	75·00
G18	5 c. violet	..	20·00	20·00
G19	10 c. orange	..	12·00	12·00

Guanacaste   **GUANACASTE**   **GUANACASTE**   **GUANACASTE**
(G 4)   (G 5)   (G 6)   (G 7)
20 mm

(d) With Type G 4 vertically (reading up or down)

G20	1 c. green	..	..	..	22·00	22·00
G21	2 c. carmine	..	..	..	22·00	22·00
G22	5 c. violet	..	..	..	13·00	11·00
G23	10 c. orange	..	..	..	13·00	13·00

(e) With Type G 5 vertically

G24	1 c. green	..	..	..	24·00	24·00
G25	2 c. carmine	..	..	..	24·00	24·00
G26	5 c. violet	..	..	..	16·00	13·00
G27	10 c. orange	..	..	..	13·00	13·00

(f) With Type G 6 vertically

G28	1 c. green	..	..	..	26·00	26·00
G29	2 c. carmine	..	..	..	16·00	16·00
G30	5 c. violet	..	..	..	16·00	16·00
G31	10 c. orange	..	..	..	8·00	8·00

(g) With Type G 7 vertically

G32	1 c. green	..	..	..	85·00	85·00
G33	2 c. carmine	..	..	..	85·00	85·00
G34	5 c. violet	..	..	..	50·00	35·00
G35	10 c. orange	..	..	..	40·00	35·00

Types G 3 (vertically) and G 4/7 all occur on the same sheet.

Guanacaste
(G 8)

(h) With Type G 8 horizontally

G36	2 c. carmine	..	..	..	55	55

Guanacaste   **Guanacaste**
(G 9)   (G 10)

1887. *Stamps of 1887, T 9, optd horizontally. P 12.*

G37	G 9	5 c. violet	..	..	..	4·50	90
G38	G 10	5 c. violet	..	..	..	5·50	90
G39	G 9	10 c. orange	..	..	..	55	55

Types G 9 and G 10 are in a setting of 50, repeated twice on the sheet. The two top rows and first five stamps of third row are Type G 10, the rest of third row and the two bottom rows are Type G 9.

Fiscal stamps as Type F 1 optd with T 10 and Type G 2, both horizontally

G40	1 c. dull carmine	..	..	..		
G41	2 c. blue	..	..	..	7·00	7·00

Fiscal stamps as Type F 1 optd horizontally with T 10 and with Types G 3/7 vertically

G42	G 3	1 c. carmine					
G43	G 4	1 c. carmine					
G44	G 5	1 c. carmine	..	..		35·00	35·00
G45	G 6	1 c. carmine					
G46	G 7	1 c. carmine					
G47	G 3	2 c. blue	..	..		35·00	35·00
G48	G 4	2 c. blue	..	..		16·00	11·00
G49	G 5	2 c. blue	..	..		25·00	
G50	G 6	2 c. blue	..	..		22·00	22·00
G51	G 7	2 c. blue	..	..		50·00	50·00

GUANACASTE   **GUANACASTE**
(G 11)   (G 12)

(Types G 11/12 optd by Waterlow)

1889. *Contemporary stamps, as T 11/12, optd horizontally with Type G 11. P 14, 15.*

G52	1 c. sepia	..	..	..	1·40	60
G53	2 c. greenish blue	..	..	..	1·40	60
G54	5 c. deep orange	..	..	..	2·25	40
G55	10 c. brown-lake	..	..	..	2·75	60
G56	20 c. green	..	..	..	30	30
G57	50 c. rose-carmine	..	..	..	80	80
	a. "GUAGACASTE"	..	..	..	18·00	
G58	1 p. pale blue	..	..	..	1·40	1·40
	a. "GUAGACASTE"	..	..	..	18·00	13·00
G59	1 p. blue	..	..	..	1·40	1·40
G60	2 p. violet	..	..	..	1·50	1·50
	a. "GUAGACASTE"	..	..	..	18·00	18·00
G61	5 p. olive-green	..	..	..	8·00	7·00
	a. "GUAGACASTE"	..	..	..	22·00	22·00

Costa Rica

1889. *POSTAL FISCAL. Nos. F18/19 optd (a) Horizontally.*

GF66	G **2**	2 c. blue	..	..	..	..	1·10	1·40

(b) Vertically

GF67	G **3**	1 c. carmine	..	..	..	5·50	8·00
GF68	G **4**	1 c. carmine	..	..	..	3·25	3·50
GF69	G **5**	1 c. carmine	..	..	..	10·00	10·00
GF70	G **6**	1 c. carmine	..	..	..	10·00	
GF71	G **7**	1 c. carmine	..	..	..	10·00	11·00
GF72	G **3**	2 c. blue	..	..	..	5·00	4·75
GF73	G **4**	2 c. blue	..	..	..	3·00	3·75
GF74	G **5**	2 c. blue	..	..	..	10·00	
GF75	G **6**	2 c. blue	..	..	..	3·25	3·25
GF76	G **7**	2 c. blue	..	..	..	10·00	11·00

Most of the issues of Guanacaste have been forged.

Cuba

1855. 8 Reales Plata Fuerte (strong silver reales) = 1 Peso
1866. 100 Centesimos = 1 Escudo
1871. 100 Centesimos = 1 Peseta
1881. 1000 Milesimas = 100 Centavos = 1 Peso
1898. 100 Cents = 1 Dollar
1899. 100 Centavos = 1 Peso

I. SPANISH COLONY

Cuba was discovered by Columbus on 27 October 1492, and was conquered for Spain by Diego Velasquez with about 300 man during 1511–13. From 1855 until 1873 joint issues were made for Cuba and Puerto Rico. During the period 1869 to 1879 some stamps of Cuba and Puerto Rico and separate issues for Cuba were also used in Fernando Poo.

For GREAT BRITAIN stamps used in Cuba with obliterations "C58" or "C88" see Great Britain Stamps Used Abroad in the British Commonwealth Catalogue.

A. CUBA AND PUERTO RICO

Queen Isabella of Spain, 1833–68

$Y\frac{1}{4}$ $Y\frac{1}{4}$ $Y\frac{1}{4}$

1 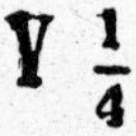   (2) 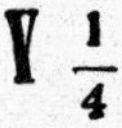   (3)    (4)

(Dies eng J. P. Varela. Typo)
1855. Bluish paper. Wmk Loops. Imperf.

1	1	½ r. blue-green	..	1·25	20
2		1 r. yellow-green ..	..	1·25	20
		a. Green..	..	1·25	15
3		2 r. deep carmine..	..	5·50	65
		a. Dull red	..	11·00	80

1855 (19 Nov). Surch in Havana.

4	2	Y¼ on 2 r. deep carmine	..	22·00	4·00
		a. Dull red	..	45·00	11·00
5	3	Y¼ on 2 r. deep carmine	..	22·00	4·00
		a. Dull red	..	45·00	11·00

Nos. 4, 5 and 12 were only used in Cuba.

1856. Yellowish paper. Wmk Crossed Lozenges. Imperf.

6	1	½ r. blue-green	..	15	10
7		1 r. bright green	..	20·00	1·10
		a. Yellow-green ..	..	16·00	75
8		2 r. red	..	10·00	75

1857. White paper. No wmk. Imperf.

9	1	½ r. greenish blue	..	15	5
		a. Pale blue	..	30	5
		b. Left upper corner white			
		c. Repaired corner	..		
10		1 r. bright green ..	..	12	5
		a. Deep green ..	..	12	8
		b. Yellow-green	..	25	10
11		2 r. rose-red	..	35	15
		a. Orange-red ..	..	50	20

1860. Surch in Havana.

12	4	Y¼ on 2 r. rose-red	..	6·50	4·50

Varieties exist (i) with the figure "1" of "¼" inverted, and (ii) with the fraction bar (which is not an ordinary bar, but a letter "I") reversed.

5    6   **66** (7)

(T **5/6** dies eng J. P. Varela. Typo)
1862. Imperf.

13	5	¼ r. black ..	..	..	1·25	75

1864. Imperf.

14	6	¼ r. black/buff	..	..	1·25	65
15		½ r. green	..	..	12	5
16		½ r. green/rose ..	..	..	85	8
17		1 r. dull blue/pale brown	..	..	12	5
		a. Bright blue/salmon ..	..	..	12	5
18		2 r. red/rose	..	..	1·60	65
		a. Red/buff	..	..	1·40	70

1866. No. 14 optd with T **7.**

19	6	¼ r. black/buff	..	..	6·00	3·00

Nos. 13, 14 and 19 were for local use in Havana and were not used in Puerto Rico.

8    9

(T **8/9** dies eng J. P. Varela. Typo)
1866. New Currency. Dated 1866. Imperf.

20	8	5 c. dull mauve..	..	..	2·00	1·00
21		10 c. blue	..	..	20	8
22		20 c. green	..	..	12	8
23		40 c. rose	..	..	60	45

1867. Dated 1867. P 14.

24	8	5 c. dull mauve..	..	..	1·25	80
25		10 c. blue	..	..	40	8
26		20 c. green	..	..	40	8
27		40 c. rose	..	..	60	45

The 10 c. and 20 c. are known imperf.
The currency change of 1866 did not take effect in Puerto Rico until 1868 so Nos. 20/27 were not used there.

1868. Dated 1868. P 14.

28	9	5 c. dull lilac	..	..	1·25	65
29		10 c. blue	..	..	20	8
		a. Deep blue ..	..	..	20	8
30		20 c. green	..	..	60	20
		a. Deep green	..	..	60	20
31		40 c. rose	..	..	60	30

1869. Dated 1869. P 14.

32	9	5 c. rose	..	..	1·75	1·00
33		10 c. brown	..	..	20	12
34		20 c. orange	..	..	35	15
35		40 c. dull rose	..	..	2·10	65

No. 32 was used locally in Havana and is not known used in Puerto Rico.

Provisional Government of Spain 1868–70

HABILITADO
POR LA
NACION.
(10)

This overprint is generally diagonal, but exists in various positions.

1868–69. Optd with T **10**. (a) Dated 1868.

36	9	5 c. dull lilac	..	..	..	3·25	2·00
37		10 c. blue	..	..	..	3·25	2·00
38		20 c. green	..	..	..	3·25	2·00
39		40 c. rose	..	..	..	3·25	2·00

(b) Dated 1869

40	9	5 c. rose	..	..	..	4·75	3·00
41		10 c. brown	..	..	..	4·00	2·75
42		20 c. orange	..	..	..	4·00	2·75
43		40 c. dull lilac	..	..	..	4·75	3·00

11   **12**

(T **11/12** dies eng E. Julia. Typo)

1870. P 14.

44	11	5 c. blue	..	..	..	7·50	3·00
45		10 c. green	..	..	..	8	8
		a. Deep green	..	..	..	8	8
46		20 c. brown	..	..	..	8	8
		a. Pale brown	..	..	..	8	8
47		40 c. rose	..	..	..	8·50	2·50

The 5 c. was not used in Puerto Rico.

King Amadeo of Spain, 1870–73

1871. New Currency. Dated 1871. P 14.

48	12	12 c. pale mauve	..	..	..	1·00	40
		a. Grey-lilac . .	..	..	..	1·40	40
49		25 c. pale ultramarine ..	..	..	10	5
		a. Deep ultramarine	..	..	10	5
50		50 c. green	..	..	..	10	5
		a. Deep green	..	..	..	10	5
51		1 p. pale brown	..	..	..	1·50	50
		a. Brown	..	..	..	1·50	50

All the values of this set are known imperf.
The 12 c. was not used in Puerto Rico.

B. SEPARATE ISSUES FOR CUBA

From 1873 Cuba had its own stamps. Until 1877 these were overprinted with a monogram for use in Puerto Rico. Both these monogram overprints and further issues of Puerto Rico will be found listed under that territory.

13   **14**   **15**

(Dies eng E. Julia. Typo)

1873. P 14.

52	13	12½ c. green	..	..	..	2·00	1·00
53		25 c. pearl-grey	..	..	..	10	5
		a. Pale lilac ..	..	..	..	10	5
54		50 c. brown	..	..	..	8	5
55		1 p. chestnut ..	..	..	..	12·00	5·50

The 25 c. and 50 c. are known imperf.

Spanish Republic, 1873–75

1874. Dated 1874. P 14.

56	12	12½ c. brown	..	..	..	70	40
57		25 c. pale ultramarine	..	..	8	5
		a. Deep ultramarine	..	..	8	5
58		50 c. indigo-lilac	..	..	8	5
		a. Grey	..	..	..	8	5
59		1 p. carmine	..	..	..	5·00	1·50
		a. Pale carmine	..	..	5·00	1·50

The 1 p. is known imperf.

(Dies eng L. Plañol. Typo)

1875. P 14.

60	14	12½ c. mauve	..	..	..	8	5
		a. Lilac	..	..	..	25	30
61		25 c. ultramarine	..	..	5	5
62		50 c. green	..	..	..	5	5
63		1 p. brown	..	..	..	35	30
		a. Deep brown	..	..	40	35

The 12½, 25 and 50 c. are known imperf.

King Alfonso XII of Spain, 1875–86

(Dies eng J. G. Morago. Typo)

1876. P 14.

64	15	12½ c. green	..	..	..	8	5
		a. Deep green	..	..	10	12
65		25 c. mauve	..	..	..	12	5
		a. Grey-lilac	..	..	..	5	5
		b. Pearl-grey	..	..	..	5	5
66		50 c. ultramarine	..	..	5	5
67		1 p. black	..	..	..	40	35

The 50 c. and 1 p. are known imperf.

16   **17**   **18**

(T **16/18** dies eng E. Julia. Typo)

1877. Dated 1877. P 14.

68	16	10 c. yellow-green	..	..	2·40	1·50
		a. Emerald-green	..	..	2·40	1·50
69		12½ c. grey-lilac	..	..	25	12
		a. Lilac	..	..	..	25	12
70		25 c. blue-green	..	..	8	5
71		50 c. black	..	..	..	8	5
72		1 p. brown	..	..	..	1·50	75
		a. Deep brown	..	..	1·50	75

The 12½, 25 and 50 c. are known imperf.

1878. Dated 1878. P 14.

73	16	5 c. blue	..	..	..	5	5
		a. Deep blue	..	..	..	5	5
74		10 c. black	..	..	..	3·25	2·50
75		12½ c. grey-bistre	..	..	5	5
		a. Bistre-buff	..	..	5	5
76		25 c. yellow-green	..	..	5	5
		a. Bluish green	..	..	5	5
77		50 c. blue-green	..	..	5	5
		a. Deep blue-green	..	..	5	5
78		1 p. carmine	..	..	..	55	40

1879. Dated 1879. P 14.

79	16	5 c. olive-black	..	..	5	5
80		10 c. ochre-red	..	..	7·00	3·50
81		12½ c. aniline rose	..	..	8	5
82		25 c. ultramarine	..	..	5	5
		a. Deep ultramarine	..	..	5	5
83		50 c. grey	..	..	..	5	5
84		1 p. olive-bistre	..	..	1·10	55

Many stamps of T **16** may be found imperf but they are merely proofs or from trial sheets.

1880. Dated 1880. P 14.

85	17	5 c. green	..	..	..	5	5
86		10 c. carmine	..	..	..	4·00	2·00
87		12½ c. grey-lilac	..	..	5	5
88		25 c. dull lavender	..	..	5	5
		a. Grey-blue	..	..	..	5	5
89		50 c. sepia	..	..	..	5	5
90		1 p. chestnut ..	..	..	30	20

1881. *New Currency. Dated 1881.* P 14.

91	**17**	1 c. grey-green	..	5	5
92		2 c. lake-rose ..	..	2·00	1·40
93		2½ c. grey-bistre	..	8	5
		a. Olive-bistre	..	8	5
94		5 c. dull lavender	..	5	5
95		10 c. brown ..	..	5	5
		a. Deep brown	..	5	5
96		20 c. sepia ..	..	25	20

1882. P 14.

97	**18**	1 c. green ..	..	5	5
98		2 c. carmine-rose	..	8	8
99		2½ c. grey-brown	..	8	8
100		5 c. dull lavender	..	8	5
		a. Slate-violet	..	20	15
101		10 c. olive-bistre	..	5	5
102		20 c. brown ..	..	4·50	2·40

(19) (20) (21)

1883. *Stamps of the preceding issue optd or surch.*

(a) With T **19**

103	**18**	5 c. (R.)	..	15	10
104		10 c. (B.)	..	20	15
105		20 c. ..	..	3·50	2·00

(b) As T **20**

106	**18**	5 on 5 c. (R.)	..	10	10
107		10 on 10 c. (B.)	..	12	12
108		20 on 20 c. ..	..	1·00	1·00

(c) As T **21**

109	**18**	5 on 5 c. (R.)	..	10	10
110		10 on 10 c. (B.)	..	12	12
111		20 on 20 c. ..	..	50	45

(22) (23)

(d) As T **22**

112	**18**	5 on 5 c. (R.) ..	..	8	8
113		10 on 10 c. (B.)	..	10	10
114		20 on 20 c. ..	..	1·10	1·10
		a. Error. 10 on 20 c. (Bk.) ..	..	8·00	7·50

(e) As T **23**

115	**18**	5 on 5 c. (R.) ..	..	8	8
116		10 on 10 c. (B.)	..	8	8
117		20 on 20 c. ..	..	2·10	1·60

Most of the above surcharges may be found *inverted* and *double*.

The various surcharges have been reprinted on the 20 c., but are handstamped instead of machine-printed.

1883–88. P 14.

118	**18**	2½ c. bistre	..	5	5
119		2½ c. mauve (1884)	..	5	5
		a. Bright mauve (1885)	..	5	5
120		2½ c. chestnut (1887) ..	..	8	8
		a. Pale brown (1888)	..	8	8
121		20 c. olive-bistre	..	60	35
122		20 c. brown-lilac (1887)	..	40	25

A B C D

The plate for T **18**, which was used for Philippine Islands, Puerto Rico, and Fernando Poo, as well as Cuba, was retouched three times. The second retouch is only known in Philippine stamps, but for convenience of reference we illustrate all the differences here.

A. *Original state*—The medallion is surrounded by a heavy line of colour, of nearly even thickness, touching the horizontal line below the inscription in the upper label; the opening in the hair above the temple is narrow and pointed. All the preceding stamps of T **18** are as A.

B. *First retouch*—The line above the medallion is thin, except at the upper right, and does not touch the horizontal line above it; the opening in the hair is slightly wider and a trifle rounded; the lock of hair above the forehead is shaped like a broad "V", and ends in a point; there is a faint white line below it, which is not found in the original state.

C. *Second retouch*—The opening is still wider and more rounded; the lock of hair does not extend as far down on the forehead, is very slightly rounded, instead of being pointed, and the white line below it is thicker.

D. *Third retouch*—The opening in the hair forms a semicircle; the lock above the forehead has only a slight wave, and the white line is broader than before.

T **18** retouched. P 14.
First retouch (B)

123	**18**	5 c. grey	..	20	8
124		5 c. dull lavender	..	12	5
125		10 c. deep brown	..	20	8
		a. Pale chestnut	..	10	8
126		10 c. blue	..	8	8

Third retouch (D)

127	**18**	1 c. grey-green	..	10	8
128		5 c. dull lavender	..	40	25

P 1   24   P 2

(T **24** and P **1/2**. Dies eng. E. Julia. Typo)

1888. *PRINTED MATTER.* P 14.

P129	P **1**	½ m. black ..	..	5	5
P130		1 m. black ..	..	5	5
P131		2 m. black ..	..	5	5
P132		3 m. black ..	..	8	8
P133		4 m. black ..	..	12	12
P134		8 m. black ..	..	30	30
P129/134		*Set of 6*	..	45	45

King Alfonso XIII of Spain, 1886–1931

1890. P 14.

135	**24**	1 c. brown	..	40	20
136		2 c. indigo ..	..	12	8
137		2½ c. blue-green	..	30	10
138		5 c. slate	..	8	5
139		10 c. purple-brown	..	20	8
140		20 c. dull purple	..	10	8
135/140		*Set of 6*	..	1·00	50

1890. *PRINTED MATTER.* P 14.

P141	P **2**	½ m. red-brown	..	5	5
P142		1 m. red-brown	..	5	5
P143		2 m. red-brown	..	8	5
P144		3 m. red-brown	..	8	5
P145		4 m. red-brown	..	15	10
P146		8 m. red-brown	..	30	20
P141/146		*Set of 6* ..	..	60	45

1891. P 14.

147	**24**	1 c. olive-grey	..	12	5
148		2 c. purple-brown	..	8	5
149		2½ c. salmon ..	..	1·25	30
150		5 c. blue-green	..	5	5
151		10 c. dull rose..	..	10	5
152		20 c. blue	..	40	20
147/152		*Set of 6*	..	1·75	50

1892. *PRINTED MATTER. P 14.*

P153	P 2	½ m. dull lilac	5	5
P154		1 m. dull lilac	5	5
P155		2 m. dull lilac	5	5
P156		3 m. dull lilac	8	5
P157		4 m. dull lilac	12	10
P158		8 m. dull lilac	30	25
P153/158		Set of 6	55	45

1894. *P 14.*

159	24	1 c. blue	10	5
160		2 c. aniline pink	70	20
161		2½ c. lilac	10	5
		a. Bright mauve	60	60
162		20 c. brown	35	20

1894. *PRINTED MATTER. P 14.*

P163	P 2	½ m. aniline pink	5	5
P164		1 m. aniline pink	5	5
P165		2 m. aniline pink	5	5
P166		3 m. aniline pink	10	5
P167		4 m. aniline pink	10	8
P168		8 m. aniline pink	25	15
P163/168		Set of 6	50	30

1896–97. *P 14.*

169	24	1 c. dull purple	5	5
170		2 c. lake	15	5
171		2½ c. aniline pink	5	5
172		.5 c. indigo	5	5
173		10 c. blue-green	8	5
174		20 c. lilac	40	15
175		40 c. chestnut	2·00	1·50
176		80 c. chocolate	3·00	2·00
169/176		Set of 8	5·00	3·50

Note after No. 84 also applies to stamps of T **24**.

1896. *PRINTED MATTER. P 14.*

P177	P 2	½ m. blue-green	5	5
P178		1 m. blue-green	5	5
P179		2 m. blue-green	5	5
P180		3 m. blue-green	10	5
P181		4 m. blue-green	15	8
P182		8 m. blue-green	20	10
P177/182		Set of 6	50	25

25

(Dies eng B. Maura. Typo)

1898. *P 14.*

183	25	1 m. chestnut	5	5
184		2 m. chestnut	5	5
185		3 m. chestnut	5	5
186		4 m. chestnut	25	15
187		5 m. chestnut	5	5
188		1 c. plum	5	5
189		2 c. blue-green	5	5
190		3 c. deep brown	5	5
191		4 c. orange	50	25
192		5 c. aniline rose	5	5
193		6 c. blue	5	5
194		8 c. grey-brown	12	10
195		10 c. vermilion	12	10
196		15 c. olive-slate	20	12
197		20 c. maroon	8	5
198		40 c. mauve	20	8
199		60 c. black	20	8
200		80 c. chocolate	75	55
201		1 p. yellow-green	1·00	80
202		2 p. indigo	1·75	1·00
183/202		Set of 20	4·50	2·75

Risings against Spanish rule led to wars of independence from 1868 to 1878 and 1895 to 1898. Following the unexplained sinking of the U.S. battleship *Maine* on 15 February 1898, a Spanish-American war began on 24 April. The Spanish-American War ended with the Treaty of Paris, 10 December 1898, by which Spain relinquished Cuba to the United States, in trust for the island's inhabitants.

II. UNITED STATES MILITARY RULE

1 January 1899–19 May 1902

FOR WELL CENTRED COPIES ADD 50%

HABILITADO   HABILITADO

1   **1**

cent.   **cents.**

(26)   (27)

2   **2**   **3**   **3**   **5**   **5**

A   B   C   D   E   F

1899. *Stamps of Spanish Cuba, of 1896 and 1898, surcharged with new values. Issued under the authority of the U.S. Post Office in Puerto Principe.*

*Surch as T **26** or **27** (taller)*

(a) On postage stamps of 1898

203	26	1 cent on 1 m. chestnut	5·50	3·50
204	27	1 cents on 1 m. chestnut	2·40	1·75
		a. Surch inverted	—	15·00
		b. Surch double		
205	26	2 c. on 2 m. chestnut (A)	1·10	75
		a. Surch inverted	35·00	6·00
206		2 c. on 2 m. chestnut (B)	2·40	1·75
		a. Surch inverted	55·00	12·00
207	27	3 c. on 1 m. chestnut (C)	30·00	11·00
		a. Surch double		
208		3 c. on 1 m. chestnut (D)	£150	50·00
		a. Surch double		
209	26	3 c. on 2 m. chestnut (C)	—	£150
210		3 c. on 2 m. chestnut (D)	£325	£150
211		3 c. on 3 m. chestnut (C)	2·40	1·25
		a. Surch inverted	—	7·00
212		3 c. on 3 m. chestnut (D)	4·75	3·50
		a. Surch inverted	—	38·00
213	27	3 c. on 1 c. plum (C) (R.)	3·50	1·75
		a. Surch inverted	—	12·00
214		3 c. on 1 c. plum (D) (R.)	9·50	7·00
		a. Surch inverted	—	23·00
215	26	5 c. on 1 m. chestnut (E)	38·00	9·50
		a. Surch inverted	—	60·00
216		5 c. on 1 m. chestnut (F)	90·00	25·00
		a. Surch inverted	—	70·00
217		5 c. on 2 m. chestnut (E)	80·00	17·00
218		5 c. on 2 m. chestnut (F)	£160	48·00
219		5 c. on 3 m. chestnut (E)	—	12·00
		a. Surch inverted	—	60·00
220		5 c. on 3 m. chestnut (F)	—	35·00
		a. Surch inverted	—	70·00
221		5 c. on 5 m. chestnut (E)	4·00	4·00
		a. Surch inverted	50·00	12·00
		b. Surch double		
222		5 c. on 5 m. chestnut (F)	29·00	18·00
		a. Surch inverted	—	38·00
223	27	5 c. on 1 c. plum (E) (R.)	1·10	1·10
		a. Surch inverted	—	9·50
		b. Surch double	48·00	48·00
224		5 c. on 1 c. plum (F) (R.)	2·75	2·00
		a. Surch inverted	—	18·00
		b. Surch double	60·00	
225		10 c. on 1 c. plum (R.)	2·00	2·00

(b) On printed matter stamps of 1896

226	27	3 c. on 1 m. blue-green (C)	17·00	12·00
		a. Surch inverted	—	29·00
		b. "eents."	60·00	29·00
		c. Surch inverted and "eents."	—	£100
227		3 c. on 1 m. blue-green (D)	48·00	35·00
		a. Surch inverted	—	60·00

228	27	3 c. on 2 m. blue-green (C) ..	.. 70·00	14·00
		a. Surch inverted ..	.. —	£110
		b. "eents."	.. 95·00	29·00
		c. Surch inverted and "eents."	.. —	£160
229		3 c. on 2 m. blue-green (D) ..	.. £150	48·00
		a. Surch inverted ..	.. —	£100
230		3 c. on 3 m. blue-green (C) ..	.. 80·00	14·00
		a. Surch inverted ..	.. —	35·00
		b. "eents."	.. £120	29·00
		c. Surch inverted and "eents."	.. —	£100
231		3 c. on 3 m. blue-green (D) ..	.. £130	29·00
		a. Surch inverted ..	.. —	95·00
232	26	5 c. on ½ m. blue-green (E) ..	.. 14·00	3·50
		a. Surch inverted ..	.. 35·00	9·50
233		5 c. on ½ m. blue-green (F) ..	.. 17·00	5·50
		a. Surch inverted ..	.. —	35·00
234	27	5 c. on ½ m. blue-green (E) ..	.. 70·00	12·00
235		5 c. on ½ m. blue-green (F) ..	.. 60·00	14·00
236		5 c. on 1 m. blue-green (E) ..	.. —	£150
		a. "eents."		
237		5 c. on 1 m. blue-green (F) ..	.. —	£250
238		5 c. on 2 m. blue-green (E) ..	.. —	35·00
		a. "eents."		
239		5 c. on 2 m. blue-green (F) ..	.. —	23·00
240		5 c. on 3 m. blue-green (E) ..	.. —	29·00
		a. "eents."	.. —	60·00
241		5 c. on 3 m. blue-green (F) ..	.. —	£120
242		5 c. on 4 m. blue-green (E) ..	.. £225	48·00
		a. Surch inverted ..	.. —	£120
		b. "eents."	.. —	£120
		c. Surch inverted an "eents."	.. —	£170
243		5 c. on 4 m. blue-green (F) ..	.. —	£170
		a. Surch inverted ..	.. —	£225
244		5 c. on 8 m. blue-green (E) ..	.. £225	£110
		a. Surch inverted ..	.. —	£120
		b. "eents."	.. —	£120
		c. Surch inverted and ""eents."	.. —	£150
245		5 c. on 8 m. blue-green (F) ..	.. —	£225
		a. Surch inverted ..	.. —	£300

CUBA

1 c.
de PESO.

(28)

1899 (20 Jan). *Stamps of United States surch as T 28.*

246	1 c. on 1 c. yellow-green (No. 283A) ..	25	10
	a. Surch double ..	15·00	
247	2 c. on 2 c. carmine (III) (No. 270) ..	25	10
	a. "CUPA" for "CUBA" ..	6·50	
	b. Surch inverted ..	£120	85·00
	c. On 2 c. rose-pink (III) (No. 270A) ..	65	12
248	2½ c. on 2 c. red (III) (No. 284) ..	15	12
	a. On 2 c. rose-carmine (III) (No. 284A)	65	55
249	3 c. on 3 c. violet (No. 271) ..	40	20
250	5 c. on 5 c. deep blue (No. 286) ..	50	15
	a. "CUPA" for "CUBA" ..	1·60	1·10
	b. "CUBA" at bottom.. ..		
251	10 c. on 10 c. brown (I) (No. 288) ..	1·60	1·10
	a. "CUBA" omitted	£200	
	b. "CUBA" at bottom.. ..	17·00	

The 2½ c. value was not needed and was sold to the public for 2 c.

The 10 c. on 10 c. brown Type II exists from a Special Printing made in 1899.

1899 (1 Oct). *SPECIAL DELIVERY. No E5 of United States surch as T 28, but with stop after "CUBA".*

E252	10 c. on 10 c. indigo (R.) ..	6·00	6·00
	a. No stop after "CUBA" ..	15·00	15·00

1899 (15 Nov). *POSTAGE DUE. Nos. D38/9 and D41/2 of United States surch as T 28.*

D253	1 c. on 1 c. lake	1·25	70
D254	2 c. on 2 c. lake	1·25	55
	a. Surch inverted ..	—	£110
D255	5 c. on 5 c. lake	50	40
	a. "CUPA" for "CUBA" ..		
D256	10 c. on 10 c. lake	25	20

29 Statue of Columbus   **30** Palms   **31** Statue of "La India"

32 Liner ("Commerce")   **33** Sugar Cultivation

A 1 c.   B 1 c.   A 2 c.   B 2 c.

A 5 c.   B 5 c.   A 10 c.   B 10 c.

The following differences distinguish B from A:—

1 c. Corners of label containing "CENTAVO" scalloped.
2 c. Foliate ornaments at side of value ovals removed.
5 c. Central prong of trident extended to top line and two small coloured right angles added to label containing "CUBA".
10 c. Small white ball added to projection of label containing "CUBA".

(Eng and recess Bureau of Engraving and Printing, Washington)

1899 (1 Sept). *Designs as A illustrations. Wmk U.S.—C. P 12.*

301	29	1 c. green ..	..	..	30	5
302	30	2 c. carmine-red	..	..	40	5
303	31	3 c. purple ..	..	..	20	5
304	32	5 c. deep blue ..	..	..	40	5
305	33	10 c. brown ..	..	..	1·40	12
301/305		Set of 5 ..	..	..	2·40	25

See also Nos. 307/10.

E 34

(Eng and recess Bureau of Engraving and Printing, Washington)

1900 (15 Dec). *SPECIAL DELIVERY. Inscr "immediata". Wmk US—C. P 12.*

E306	E 34	10 c. orange ..	.. 1·00	75

See also No. E307.

III. INDEPENDENT REPUBLIC

Cuba became an independent republic on 20 May 1902 but this was subject to the "Platt Amendment" under which the United States reserved the right to intervene by sending troops if Cuba entered into treaty relationships with a foreign power. Troops were in fact sent in 1906, 1913, 1917 and 1933 but the right was abrogated in 1934.

HABILITADO

(35)

36 Major-General
Antonio Maceo

1902 (30 Sept). *No.* 303 *surch with T* **35**, *in red.*
306 **31** 1 c. on 3 c. purple 25 25
     a. Surch inverted .. .. 6·00 6·00
     b. Surch double .. .. 7·50 7·50

(Eng and recess Bureau of Engraving and Printing,
Washington)

1902 (21 Nov). *SPECIAL DELIVERY. As Type E* **34**, *but with
inscr corrected to "inmediata".*
E307 10 c. orange 10 10

(Eng and recess American Bank Note Co, N.Y.)

1905 (Jan). *Designs as* B *illustrations. No wmk. P* 12.
307 **29** 1 c. green 25 5
308 **30** 2 c. carmine 20 5
309 **32** 5 c. deep blue .. .. 2·10 15
310 **33** 10 c. brown 45 12
307/310 *Set of 4* .. .. .. 2·75 30

(Eng and recess A.B.N. Co, N.Y.)

1907 (19 Feb). *P* 12.
311 **36** 50 c. black and slate 25 12

37 B. Maso   38 Carlos Roloff   E 39 J. B. Zayas

(Eng and recess A.B.N. Co, N.Y.)

1910 (1 Feb). *As T* **37/8** (*various portraits*) *and* **36** (50 c.).
P 12.
312 1 c. violet and green 10 5
     a. Centre inverted .. .. 5·00 5·00
313 2 c. green and carmine (M. Gomez) .. 30 5
     a. Centre inverted .. .. 50·00 50·00
314 3 c. blue and violet (J. Sanguily) .. 15 5
315 5 c. green and blue (I. Agramonte) .. 1·75 12
316 8 c. violet and olive (C. Garcia) .. 15 5
317 10 c. blue and sepia (Mayia) .. 65 5
     a. Centre inverted .. .. 75·00 75·00
318 50 c. black and violet 25 15
319 1 p. black and slate .. .. 1·25 75
312/319 *Set of 8* .. .. .. 4·00 1·10

(Eng and recess A.B.N. Co, N.Y.)

1910 (1 Feb). *SPECIAL DELIVERY. No wmk. P* 12.
E320 E **39** 10 c. blue and orange .. 45 25
     a. Centre inverted .. 55·00

1911 (15 July)–**13**. *As* 1910 *issue, colours changed.*
320 1 c. green 12 5
321 2 c. carmine-rose 12 5
322 5 c. blue 30 5
323 8 c. black and olive 20 10
324 1 p. black (10.7.13) .. .. 1·00 30
320/324 *Set of 5* .. .. .. 1·50 50

40 Map   E 41 Aeroplane near Morro
Castle

(Eng A.B.N. Co. Recess J. L. Rodriguez, Havana)

1914 (24 Feb)–**15**. *P* 12.
325 **40** 1 c. green 8 5
326 2 c. carmine 8 5
     a. Rose 15 5
327 2 c. red (1915) 8 5
328 3 c. violet 50 10
329 5 c. blue 25 8
330 8 c. olive 75 15
331 10 c. brown 75 12
332 10 c. olive (1915) 80 12
333 50 c. orange .. .. 4·00 2·10
334 1 p. slate .. .. 5·50 2·40
325/334 *Set of 10* .. .. 11·00 4·75

(Eng A.B.N. Co, N.Y. Recess J. L. Rodriguez, Havana)

1914 (24 Feb). *SPECIAL DELIVERY. P* 12.
E335 E **41** 10 c. deep blue 70 8
See also No. E352.

Nos. 325/6, 328 and E335 were overprinted "4 Fbro. 1917
Gob. Constitucional Camaguey" in black (2 c.) or red during
the revolt of General Gomez. These are not known used.

D 42   43 Gertrudis Gomez de
Avellaneda

(Eng and recess J. L. Rodriguez, Havana)

1914 (1 July)–**27**. *POSTAGE DUE. P* 12.
D335 D **42** 1 c. carmine 15 10
D336 1 c. rosine (1927) 20 15
D337 2 c. carmine 20 12
D338 2 c. rosine (1927) 40 20
D339 5 c. carmine 45 20
D340 5 c. rosine (1927) 40 20
D335/340 *Set of 6* .. .. 1·60 85

(Recess J. L. Rodriguez)

1914 (1 Oct). *Birth Centenary of Gertrudis de Avellaneda*
(*poetess*). *P* 12.
335 **43** 5 c. deep blue .. .. .. 1·50 65

44 José Marti   45 Antonio Maceo   46 C. M. de
Cespedes

1917–18. *T* **44** (*various portraits*), **45** *and* **46**. *Recess. No
wmk. P* 12.
336 1 c. green (*shades*) (10.6.17) .. 5 5
337 2 c. rose-red (Gomez) (1.4.17) 5 5
     a. Brown-red (1918) 5 5
338 3 c. purple (*shades*) (La Luz) (10.5.17) .. 12 5
     a. Imperf (pair)
339 5 c. blue (Garcia) (10.5.17) .. 20 5
340 8 c. red-brown (Agramonte) (10.5.17) 40 5
341 10 c. bistre-brown (Palma) (10.6.17) .. 40 5
342 20 c. olive-green (Saco) (10.6.17) 75 12
343 50 c. brown-carmine (10.6.17) .. .. 1·00 15
344 1 p. black (10.6.17) .. .. 1·25 10
336/344 *Set of 9* .. .. 3·75 50

1925–45. *T* **44** *(various portraits as before) but wmk Star.*
P 12.

345	1 c. green (shades)	..	..	20	5
	a. Imperf (1926)	..	..	20	8
	b. Perf 10 (1930)	..	..	15	5
	c. Perf 10. Rotary press			8	5
346	2 c. rose-carmine (shades)	..	..	20	5
	a. Imperf (1926)	..	..	20	8
	b. Perf 10 (1930)	..	..	12·00	8·00
	c. Perf 10. Rotary press			8	5
347	3 c. purple (p 10) (1942)	..	..	25	8
	a. Rotary press (1941)	..	..	12	5
348	5 c. blue	..	..	40	5
	a. Imperf (1926)	..	..	35	15
	b. Perf 10 (1930)	..	..	45	5
349	8 c. red-brown (1928)	..	..	60	10
	a. Perf 10 (1945)	..	..	35	5
350	10 c. bistre-brown (1927)	..	..	75	5
	a. Perf 10 (1935)	..	..	60	5
351	20 c. olive-green	..	..	80	10
	a. Perf 10 (1941)	..	..	40	5

The perf 10 flat plate printings are size 18½ × 21½ mm and
the rotary press printings measure 19 × 22 mm.

1927–35. *SPECIAL DELIVERY. Wmk Star. P* 12.

E352	E **41**	10 c. deep blue	..	50	12
		a. Perf 10 (1935)	..	50	8

47

48 Seaplane over Havana
Harbour

(Recess Canadian Bank Note Co, Ottawa)

1927 (20 May). *25th Anniv of Republic. P* 12.

352	**47**	25 c. deep violet	..	1·50	50

(Des O. Fontes y Acosta. Eng Security Bank Note Co, Philadelphia. Recess Cia Nacional de Artes Gráficos de Cuba)

1927 (1 Nov). *AIR. Wmk Star. P* 12.

353	**48**	5 c. deep blue	..	40	5

49 T. Estrada Palma

LINDBERGH
FEBRERO 1928
(50)

(Recess Cia Nacional de Artes Gráficos)

1928 (2 Jan). *6th Pan-American Conference. Horiz portraits
and views as T* **49**. *Wmk Star. P* 12.

354	1 c. green	..	..	15	10
355	2 c. deep carmine	..	..	15	10
356	5 c. deep blue	..	..	20	15
357	8 c. red-brown	..	..	40	40
358	10 c. brown	..	..	35	12
359	13 c. orange	..	..	40	30
360	20 c. olive-green	..	..	45	40
361	30 c. deep violet	..	..	85	35
362	50 c. carmine	..	..	1·50	70
363	1 p. black	..	..	2·75	1·40
354/363	*Set of 10*	..	..	6·50	3·50

Designs:—2 c. General G. Machado; 5 c. El Morro, Havana;
8 c. Railway Station, Havana; 10 c. President's Palace; 13 c.
Tobacco plantation; 20 c. Treasury Secretariat; 30 c. Sugar
Mill; 50 c. Havana Cathedral; 1 p. Galician Immigrants Centre, Havana.

1928 (8 Feb). *AIR. Lindbergh's Goodwill Flight over Central
America. As No.* 353 *but new colour, optd with T* **50.**

364	**48**	5 c. deep carmine	..	60	30

Forged double overprints are known.

51 The Capitol, Havana   52 Hurdler

(Recess Cia Impresora de Cuba)

1929 (18 May). *Inauguration of the Capitol. Wmk Star. P* 12.

365	**51**	1 c. green	..	12	8
366		2 c. carmine	..	15	8
367		5 c. blue	..	15	8
368		10 c. brown	..	35	15
369		20 c. purple	..	80	50
365/369		*Set of 5*	..	1·40	80

(Recess Cia Impresora de Cuba)

1930 (15 Mar). *Second Central American Games, Havana.
Wmk Star. P* 12.

370	**52**	1 c. green	..	35	15
371		2 c. carmine	..	35	15
372		5 c. blue	..	50	15
373		10 c. brown	..	70	35
374		20 c. purple	..	1·75	80
370/374		*Set of 5*	..	3·25	1·40

CORREO AEREO NACIONAL

10¢   10¢
(53)

1930 (27 Oct). *AIR. Surch with T* 53.

375	**47**	10 c. on 25 c. deep violet (R.)	..	50	25

54   55

(*T* **54**/5. Des O. Fonts. Recess Cia. Impresora de Cuba)

1931 (26 Feb)–**48.** *AIR. For Foreign Mail. Wmk Star. P* 10.

376	**54**	5 c. green	..	10	5
377		8 c. brown-red (15.6.48)	..	20	5
378		10 c. blue	..	15	5
379		15 c. deep carmine	..	30	15
380		20 c. brown	..	30	5
381		30 c. purple	..	45	5
382		40 c. orange	..	55	10
383		50 c. olive-green	..	1·00	5
384		1 p. grey-black	..	1·50	10
376/384		*Set of 9*	..	4·00	50

1931 (15 Aug)–**56.** *AIR. Internal Mail. Wmk Star. P* 10.

385	**55**	5 c. purple (5.4.32)	..	5	5
386		10 c. black	..	15	5
387		20 c. carmine	..	80	12
388		20 c. pink (1946)	..	40	10
389		50 c. blue	..	85	20
390		50 c. greenish blue (1956)	..	65	20
385/390		*Set of 6*	..	2·50	60

56 Mangos of   57 Battle of Mal Tiempo
Baragua

(Photo Waterlow & Sons, Ltd)

1933 (20 May). *35th Anniv of War of Independence. Various designs as T* **56/7**. *Wmk Wavy lines.* P 12½.

391	3 c. chocolate	..	..	..	20	8
	a. Two palm trees only between mangos..	..	..	..	5·00	3·00
392	5 c. ultramarine	..	..	..	35	15
393	10 c. emerald	..	..	..	45	10
394	13 c. scarlet	..	..	..	60	15
395	20 c. black	..	..	..	1·25	45
391/395	*Set of 5*	..	..	..	2·50	80

Designs: As T **57**—10 c. Battle of Coliseo; 13 c. Maceo, Gomez and Zayas. As T **56**—20 c. Campaign Monument.

No. 391a occurs once in every sheet of the 3 c. value. On the remaining stamps in the sheet there are four palm trees between the trunks of the mangos.

(58) 59 Dr. Carlos J. Finlay

1933 (23 Dec). *Establishment of Revolutionary Govt. Nos. 345b and 347* (shades), *optd or surch as T* **58**. A. *Reading up.* B. *Reading down.*

			A		B	
396	1 c. yellow-green (R.)	..	8	5	8	5
397	2 on 3 c. dull purple	..	8	5	8	5

1934 (3 Dec). *101st Birth Anniv of Finlay ("yellow fever" researcher). Recess. Wmk Star.* P 10.

398	**59**	2 c. carmine-red	..	..	20	8
399		5 c. blue	..	..	40	8

PRIMER TREN AEREO
INTERNACIONAL. 1935

O'Meara y du Pont **+10 cts.**

(60)

1935 (1 May). *AIR. Havana–Miami "Air Train". New colour. Surch with T* **60**. *Wmk Star.*

			A. Imp		B. P 10	
400	**54**	10 c. + 10 c. scarlet	..	6·50 6·50	1·25 1·25

A set of stamps commemorating Columbus, released in 1935, was a private issue and had no franking value.

61 Matanzas Bay and Free Zone E 62 Mercury

(Photo Waterlow)

1936 (5 May). *Free Port of Matanzas. As T* **61** (*inscr* "ZONA FRANCA DEL PUERTO DE MATANZAS"). *Wmk Wavy Lines.* P 12½ *or imperf* (same prices).

(a) POSTAGE (inscr "CORREOS")

401	1 c. blue-green	..	..	..	10	8
402	2 c. scarlet	..	..	..	15	8
403	4 c. maroon	..	..	..	20	8
404	5 c. bright blue	..	..	..	25	10
405	8 c. brown	..	..	..	45	25
406	10 c. bright green	..	..	..	65	25
407	20 c. red-brown	..	..	..	85	35
408	50 c. slate	..	..	..	1·60	1·10

(b) SPECIAL DELIVERY

E409	E **62**	10 c. maroon	..	..	50	35

Designs:—1 c. Map of Caribbean; 4 c. S.S. *Rex* in Matanzas Bay; 5 c. Ships in the Free Zone; 8 c. Bellamar Caves; 10 c. Yumuri Valley; 20 c. Yumuri River; 50 c. Sailing vessel and steamboat.

(c) AIR (inscr "CORREO AEREO")

409	5 c. bright violet	..	..	..	15	8
410	10 c. orange	..	..	..	40	20
411	20 c. deep green	..	..	..	85	60
412	50 c. greenish black	..	..	..	1·90	1·10

(d) AIR EXPRESS (inscr "CORREOS ENTREGA AEREA ESPECIAL")

E413	15 c. light blue	..	..	..	75	40
401/E413	*Set of 14*	..	..	..	8·00	4·50

Designs:—5 c. Aerial panorama; 10 c. Airship *Macon* over Puente de la Concordia; 15 c. Maya Lighthouse; 20 c. Aeroplane *Cuatro Vientos* over Matanzas; 50 c. San Severino Fortress.

63 Pres. J. M. Gómez 64 Gen. J. M. Gómez Monument

(Recess P. Fernandez, Havana)

1936 (19 May). *Inauguration of Gómez Monument. Wmk Star.* P 10.

413	**63**	1 c. green	..	..	20	15
414	**64**	2 c. carmine	..	..	30	12

65 "Peace and Labour" 66 Maximo Gómez Monument

E 67 "Triumph of the Revolution" 68 Caravel and Sugar Cane

(Photo Waterlow)

1936 (18 Nov). *Birth Centenary of Máximo Gómez. As T* **65/6** (*inscr* "18 NOV 1935"). *Wmk Wavy Lines.* P 12½.

(a) POSTAGE. Inscr "CORREOS"

415	1 c. emerald-green	..	..	..	10	5
416	2 c. scarlet	..	..	..	12	5
417	4 c. plum	..	..	..	20	8
418	5 c. bright blue	..	..	..	50	15
419	8 c. olive-green	..	..	..	80	45

(b) AIR. Inscr "CORREO AEREO"

420	5 c. bright violet	..	..	..	65	25
421	10 c. red-brown	..	..	..	75	20

(c) SPECIAL DELIVERY

E422	E **67**	10 c. orange	..	..	50	25
415/E422	*Set of 8*	..	..	..	3·25	1·25

Designs: *Vert*—4 c. Flaming torch; 8 c. Dove of Peace. *Horiz*—5 c. (No. 418), Army of Liberation; 5 c. (No. 420), Lightning; 10 c. "Flying wing".

(Recess P. Fernandez, Havana)

1937 (2 Oct). *400th Anniv of Cane Sugar Industry. As T 68 (inscr "IV CENTENARIO AZUCAR CANA"). Wmk Star. P 10.*

422	1 c. emerald-green	..	..	15	8
423	2 c. scarlet	..	..	12	5
424	5 c. pale blue	..	..	30	12

Designs: *Horiz*—2 c. Caravel and early sugar mill; 5 c. Caravel and modern sugar mill.

69 Mountain View (Bolivia)

70 Camilo Henriquez (Chile)

E **71** Temple of Quetzalcoatl (Mexico)

(Recess P. Fernandez, Havana)

1937 (13 Oct). *Association of American Writers and Artists. T 69/70 and similar designs showing scenes or portraits. Wmk Star. P 10. (a) POSTAGE.*

424a	1 c. green	..	..	..	12	12
424b	1 c. bright green	..	..	..	15	15
424c	2 c. carmine-red	..	..	..	12	12
424d	2 c. carmine-red	..	..	..	15	15
424e	3 c. bluish violet	..	..	..	30	30
424f	3 c. bluish violet	..	..	..	30	30
424g	4 c. bistre-brown	..	..	..	30	30
424h	4 c. bistre-brown	..	..	..	30	30
424i	5 c. dull blue	..	..	..	30	30
424j	5 c. dull blue	..	..	..	30	30
424k	8 c. yellow-olive	..	..	..	75	75
424l	8 c. yellow-olive	..	..	..	50	50
424m	10 c. brown-lake	..	..	..	60	60
424n	10 c. brown-lake	..	..	..	60	60
424o	25 c. lilac	..	..	..	4·00	4·00

Designs: *Vert*—No. 424a, Arms of the Republic (Argentina); 424c, Arms (Brazil); Type **70**; 424f, Gen. F. de Paula Santander (Colombia); 424g, Autograph of José Marti (Cuba); 424j, Juan Montalvo (Ecuador); 424k, Abraham Lincoln (U.S.A.); 424l, Quetzal and scroll (Guatemala); 424m, Arms (Haiti); 424n, Francisco Morazán (Honduras). *Horiz*—No. 424b, Type **69**; 424d, River scene (Canada); 424h, National Monument (Costa Rica); 424i, Columbus Lighthouse (Dominican Republic); 424o, Ships of Columbus.

(b) AIR. Inscr "AEREO"

424p	5 c. scarlet	..	..	..	1·10	90
424q	5 c. scarlet	..	..	..	1·10	90
424r	10 c. greenish blue	..	..	..	1·10	90
424s	10 c. greenish blue	..	..	..	1·10	90
424t	20 c. myrtle-green	..	..	..	1·40	1·25
424u	20 c. myrtle-green	..	..	..	1·40	1·25

Designs: *Horiz*—No. 424p, Arch (Panama); 424q, Carlos Lopez (Paraguay). *Vert*—No. 424r, Inca gate, Cuzco (Peru); 424s, Atlacatl (Indian warrior) (El Salvador); 424t, Simon Bolivar (Venezuela); 424u, José Rodó (Uruguay).

(c) SPECIAL DELIVERY. Type E **71** and similar design, inscr "ENTREGA INMEDIATA"

E424v	10 c. orange (Type E **71**)	..		60	60
E424w	10 c. orange (Ruben Dario, Nicaragua)	..	..	60	60
424a/E424w	Set of 23	..	..	16·00	15·00

Nos. 424a/E424w were on sale from the Cuban Post Office for three days only. During this period no other stamps were available. All profits, above 30,000 pesos, were paid by the Cuban authorities to the Association. Unsold remainders were later overprinted "S V P" = without postal value.

1837   1937

PRIMER CENTENARIO
FERROCARRIL EN CUBA

10¢   10¢

(72)

1937 (18 Nov). *Railway Centenary. No. 352 surch with T **72**.*

425	**47**	10 c. on 25 c. deep violet (G.)..	..	1·00	25

1913   1938

ROSILLO

Key West-Habana

(73)

1938 (15 May). *AIR. 25th Anniv of D. Rosillo's Overseas Flight from Key West to Havana. T **48** in new colour, optd with T **73**. Wmk Star. P 10.*

426	**48**	5 c. red-orange	..	60	30

74 Pierre and Marie Curie   **75** Allegory of Child Care

1938 (23 Nov). *International Anti-Cancer Fund. 40th Anniv of Discovery of Radium. Recess. Wmk Star. P 10.*

427	**74**	2 c. + 1 c. scarlet	..	50	20
428		5 c. + 1 c. bright blue ..	..	1·00	45

1938 (1 Dec). *OBLIGATORY TAX. Anti-Tuberculosis Fund. Recess. Wmk Star. P 10.*

429	**75**	1 c. emerald-green	..	5	5

76 Native and Cigar   **77** Cigar, Globe and Wreath of Leaves   **78** Tobacco Plant and Cigars

(Des E. A. Cabrera. Recess)

1939 (28 Aug). *Havana Tobacco Industry. Wmk Star. P 10.*

430	**76**	1 c. green	..	..	5	5
431	**77**	2 c. scarlet	..	..	10	5
432	**78**	5 c. bright blue	..	..	25	5

EXPERIMENTO DEL
COHETE Postal
AÑO DE 1939

(79)

1939 (15 Oct). *AIR. Experimental Rocket Post. Optd with T **79**. Wmk Star. P 10.*

433	**55**	10 c. emerald-green	..	..	12·00	1·75

80 Calixto Garcia   **81** Garcia on Horseback   **82** Nurse and Child

1939 (6 Nov). *Birth Centenary of Gen. Calixto Garcia. Recess. Wmk Star.*

		A. Imp		B. P 10	
434	**80**	2 c. scarlet	12	8	10	5
435	**81**	5 c. bright blue	25	15	20	12

1939 (1 Dec). *OBLIGATORY TAX. Anti-Tuberculosis Fund. Recess. Wmk Star. P 10.*

436 **82** 1 c. scarlet   5   5

83 Gonzalo de Quesada and Union Flags   **84** Rotarian Symbol, Flag and Tobacco Plant   **85** Lions Emblem, Flag and Palms

1940 (30 Apr). *50th Anniv of Pan-American Union. Recess. Wmk Star. P 10.*

437 **83** 2 c. scarlet   15   12

1940 (18 May). *Rotary International Convention, Havana. Recess. Wmk Star. P 10.*

438 **84** 2 c. carmine   50   20

1940 (23 July). *Lions International Convention, Havana. Recess. Wmk Star. P 10.*

439 **85** 2 c. scarlet   30   20

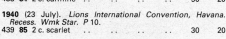

86 Dr. Gutierrez

1940 (28 Oct). *Centenary of Publication of First Cuban Medical Review. Recess. Wmk Star. P 10.*

440	**86**	2 c. scarlet	12	5
441		5 c. bright blue	25	8

MS442 127×177 mm. Two each of Nos. 440/1. No wmk. Imperf (sold at 25 c.) .. 60   60
See also Nos. MS560/1.

87 Sir Rowland Hill, G.B. 1d. of 1840 and Cuba Issues of 1855 and 1899   **88** "Health" Protecting Children

(Recess P. Fernandez, Havana)

1940 (28 Nov). *AIR. Centenary of First Adhesive Postage Stamps. Wmk Star. P 10.*

443 **87** 10 c. brown   ..   ..   ..   1·25   25
MS444 128×178 mm. No. 443 in block of four. No wmk. Imperf (sold at 60 c.) .. 2·25   2·00

1940 (1 Dec). *OBLIGATORY TAX. Anti-Tuberculosis Fund. Recess. Wmk Star. P 10.*

445 **88** 1 c. deep blue   5   5

89 Heredia and Niagara Falls

(Recess P. Fernandez, Havana)

1940 (30 Dec). *AIR. Death Centenary of J. M. Heredia y Campuzana (poet). T 89 and similar type. Wmk Star. P 10.*

446   5 c. emerald-green (Heredia and palms)   40   15
447   10 c. bluish grey   60   30

90 General Moncada and Sword   **91** Moncada riding into Battle

1941 (25 June). *Birth Centenary of Moncada. Recess. Wmk Star. P 10.*

448	**90**	3 c. brown	..	..	20	8
449	**91**	5 c. blue	..	..	25	15

92 Mother and Child

1941 (1 Dec). *OBLIGATORY TAX. Anti-Tuberculosis Fund. Recess. Wmk Star. P 10.*

450 **92** 1 c. yellow-brown   5   5

93 Western Hemisphere   **95** "Labour, Wealth of America"

97 Statue of Liberty

102 "Unmask Fifth Columnists"

103 "Be Careful! The Fifth Column is Spying on You"

96 Tree of Fraternity, Havana

94 Maceo, Bolivar, Juarez and Lincoln and Coat of Arms

(Des Cabrera and Cuesta. Recess)

1942 (23 Feb)–**43.** *American Democracy. Wmk Star. P* 10 *or imperf, without gum* (23.2.43). *Same prices.*

451	93	1 c. emerald-green	..	..	10	8
452	94	3 c. chestnut	..	..	15	10
453	95	5 c. blue	..	..	25	12
454	96	10 c. magenta	..	..	50	20
455	97	13 c. carmine-rose	..	..	70	25
451/455		Set of 5	..	..	1·50	70

104 "Don't be Afraid of the Fifth Column. Attack it"

1943 (5 July). *"Fight the Fifth Column". T* 102/4 *and similar designs. Recess. Wmk Star. P* 10.

461		1 c. green	..	..	10	5
462		3 c. vermilion	..	..	12	5
463		5 c. blue	..	..	20	12
464		10 c. brown	..	..	45	20
465		13 c. purple	..	..	75	45
461/465		Set of 5	..	..	1·50	75

Designs: *Horiz* (45×25 *mm*)—5 c. Woman in snake's coils ("The Fifth Column is like the Serpent—destroy it"); 10 c. Men demolishing column with battering-ram ("Fulfil your patriotic duty by destroying the Fifth Column").

98 Gen. Ignacio Agramonte Loynaz

99 Rescue of Sanguily

1942 (10 Apr). *Birth Centenary of Gen. Ignacio Agramonte Loynaz (patriot). Recess. Wmk Star. P* 10.

456	98	3 c. sepia	..	..	15	5
457	99	5 c. blue	..	..	30	20

105 Eloy Alfaro, Flags of Ecuador and Cuba and Scroll of Independence

106 "The Long Road to Retirement"

1943 (20 Sept). *Birth Centenary of Eloy Alfaro (former President of Ecuador). Recess. Wmk Star. P* 10.

466	105	3 c. green	..	..	20	10

1943 (8 Nov)–**44.** *Postal Employees' Retirement Fund. Recess. Wmk Star. P* 10.

467	106	1 c. blue-green	..	..	5	5
468		1 c. yellow-green (18.3.44)	..	..	8	5
469		3 c. red	..	..	12	5
470		3 c. rose-red (18.3.44)	..	..	8	5
471		5 c. blue	..	..	20	12
472		5 c. bright blue (18.3.44)	..	..	20	12
467/472		Set of 6	..	..	60	40

100 "Victory"

1942 (101)

1942 (1 July)–**44.** *OBLIGATORY TAX. Red Cross Fund. Recess. Wmk Star. P* 10.

458	100	½ c. orange	..	..	5	5
459		½ c. grey (3.10.44)	..	..	5	5

(Design recess. Opt typo)

1942 (1 Dec). *OBLIGATORY TAX. Anti-Tuberculosis Fund. As No.* 450, *but colour changed and optd with T* 101. *Wmk Star. P* 10.

460	92	1 c. vermilion	..	..	5	5
		a. Opt inverted	..	..		

107 "Health" Protecting Children

108 Columbus

109 Discovery of Tobacco

1943 (1 Dec). *OBLIGATORY TAX. Anti-Tuberculosis Fund. Recess. Wmk Star. P* 10.
473 **107** 1 c. brown 5 5

(Recess P. Fernandez, Havana)

1944 (19 May). *450th Anniv of Discovery of America. As T* **108/9** (*inscr "1492 1942"). Wmk Star. P* 10.

(a) POSTAGE. Inscr "CORREOS"
474 1 c. green 10 5
475 3 c. brown 12 5
476 5 c. blue 20 10
477 10 c. violet 40 25
478 13 c. carmine 80 40

(b) AIR. Inscr "CORREO AEREO"
479 5 c. olive 25 15
480 10 c. grey 50 30
474/480 *Set of 7* .. .. .. 2·10 1·10
Designs: *Vert*—3 c. Bartolomé de las Casas; 5 c. (No. 476), Statue of Columbus. *Horiz*—5 c. (No. 479), Mountains of Gibara; 10 c. (480), Columbus lighthouse; 13 c. Columbus at Pinar del Rio.

110 Carlos Roloff

111 American Continents and Brazilian "Bull's Eyes" Stamps

1944 (21 Aug). *Birth Centenary of Maj.-Gen. Carlos Roloff. Recess. Wmk Star. P* 10.
481 **110** 3 c. violet 15 5

1944 (20 Dec). *Centenary of First American Postage Stamps. Recess. Wmk Star. P* 10.
482 **111** 3 c. orange-brown 30 8

112 Society Seal

113 Governor Las Casas and Bishop Peñalver

1945 (5 Oct). *150th Anniv of Economic Society of Friends of Havana. Recess. Wmk Star. P* 10.
483 **112** 1 c. emerald-green 5 5
484 **113** 2 c. red 10 5

E **114** Symbols of Express Delivery   **115** Old Age Pensioners

1945 (30 Oct). *SPECIAL DELIVERY. Recess. P* 10.
E485 E **114** 10 c. brown 30 5

1945 (27 Dec)—**46.** *Postal Employees' Retirement Fund. Recess. Wmk Star. P* 10.
485 **115** 1 c. green 5 5
486 1 c. yellow-green (26.3.46) .. 5 5
487 2 c. scarlet 10 5
488 2 c. rose (26.3.46) 10 5
489 5 c. greenish blue 15 8
490 5 c. light blue (26.3.46) .. 15 8
485/490 *Set of 6* 50 30

116 "Placido"   **117** Manuel Marquez Sterling

1946 (5 Feb). *Death Centenary of Gabriel de la Concepción Valdés* (*poet). Recess. Wmk Star. P* 10.
491 **116** 2 c. scarlet 10 5

1946 (30 Apr). *Founding of "Manuel Marquez Sterling" Professional School of Journalism. Recess. Wmk Star. P* 10.
492 **117** 2 c. scarlet 8 5

118 Red Cross and Globe   **119** Prize Cattle and Dairymaid

1946 (4 July). *80th Anniv of Int Red Cross. Recess. Wmk Star. P* 10.
493 **118** 2 c. scarlet 15 5

1947 (20 Feb). *National Cattle Show. Recess. Wmk Star. P* 10.
494 **119** 2 c. scarlet 15 5

120 Franklin D. Roosevelt

121 Antonio Oms and Pensioners

1947 (12 Apr). *Second Death Anniv of Franklin D. Roosevelt. Recess. Wmk Star.* P 10.
495 **120** 2 c. scarlet 15 5

1947 (20 Oct). *Postal Employees' Retirement Fund. Recess. Wmk Star.* P 10.
496 **121** 1 c. green 5 5
497 2 c. scarlet 8 5
498 5 c. blue 15 8

122 Marta Abreu

123 Armauer Hansen and Isle of Pines

1947 (29 Nov). *Birth Centenary of Marta Abreu (philanthropist). As T* **122** *(inscr "MARTA ABREU/1845–1945"). Recess. Wmk Star.* P 10.
499 1 c. green 12 5
500 2 c. scarlet 12 5
501 5 c. blue 15 8
502 10 c. violet 30 15
499/502 *Set of 4* 60 25
Designs: *Vert*—2 c. Allegory of Charity; 5 c. Marta Abreu Monument; 10 c. Allegory of Patriotism.

1948 (9 Apr). *International Leprosy Relief Congress, Havana. Recess. Wmk Star.* P 10.
503 **123** 2 c. scarlet 10 5

124 Council of War

125 Woman and Child

(Recess Waterlow)

1948 (21 May). *AIR. Fiftieth Anniv of War of Independence. Wmk Wavy Lines.* P 12½.
504 **124** 8 c. black and orange-yellow .. 25 12

1948 (21 May). *AIR. American Air Mail Society Convention, Havana. Sheet* **MS**444 *optd "CONVENCION MAYO 21–22–23 1948 AMERICAN AIR MAIL SOCIETY" in blue, across the block of four.*
MS505 128×178 mm. No. 443 in block of four. No wmk. Imperf (sold at 60 c.) .. 2·00 2·00

1948 (15 Oct). *Postal Employees' Retirement Fund. Recess. Wmk Star.* P 10.
506 **125** 1 c. green 8 5
507 2 c. scarlet 10 5
508 5 c. blue 15 8

126 Death of Marti

127 Gathering Tobacco

128 Girl and Flag

1948 (10 Nov). *50th Anniv of Death of José Marti. T* **126** *and similar type. Recess.* P 10.
509 **126** 2 c. scarlet 10 5
510 – 5 c. blue 15 8
Design:—5 c. Marti disembarking at Playitas.

1948 (6 Dec). *Havana Tobacco Industry. T* **127/8** *and similar type. Recess. Wmk Star.* P 10.
511 **127** 1 c. green 5 5
512 **128** 2 c. scarlet 5 5
513 – 5 c. blue (Cigar and Shield) 8 5
For stamps redrawn smaller, see Nos. 537/9.

129 Antonio Maceo

130 Gen. Maceo and Raised Swords

(Recess Waterlow)

1948 (15 Dec). *Birth Centenary of General Maceo. Designs as T* **129/30**. *Wmk Wavy Lines.* P 12½.
514 1 c. blue-green 5 5
515 2 c. scarlet 8 5
516 5 c. blue 10 5
517 8 c. brown and black 15 10
518 10 c. green and brown 20 8
519 20 c. red and blue 50 25
520 50 c. ultramarine and red .. 1·10 60
521 1 p. violet and black .. .. 2·25 90
514/521 *Set of 8* .. .. .. 4·00 1·75
Designs: *Vert*—1 c. Equestrian statue of Maceo; 5 c. Mausoleum at El Cacahual. *Horiz*—10 c. Maceo leading charge; 20 c. Maceo at Peralejo; 50 c. Declaration at Baragua; 1 p. Death of Maceo at San Pedro.

131 Symbol of Medicine

132 Morro Castle and Lighthouse

1948 (28 Dec). *First Pan-American Pharmaceutical Congress, Havana. Recess. Wmk Star.* P 10.
522 **131** 2 c. rose-carmine 8 5

(Recess Waterlow)

1949 (17 Jan). *Centenary of El Morro Lighthouse. Wmk Wavy Lines.* P 12½.
523 **132** 2 c. carmine 5 5

133 Jagua Castle   **134** M. Sanguily

1949 (27 Jan). *Centenary of Newspaper "Hoja Economica" and Bicentenary of Jagua Fortress. Recess. Wmk Star. P 10.*
524 **133** 1 c. yellow-green 8 5
525   2 c. scarlet 10 5

1949 (31 Mar). *Birth Centenary of Manuel Sanguily y Garritte (poet). Recess. Wmk Star. P 10.*
526 **134** 2 c. scarlet 8 5
527   5 c. bright blue 15 8

135 Isle of Pines   **136** Ismael Cespedes   **137** Woman and Child

1949 (26 Apr). *20th Anniv of Return of Isle of Pines to Cuba. Recess. Wmk Star. P 10.*
528 **135** 5 c. bright blue 15 8

1949 (28 Sept). *Postal Employees' Retirement Fund. Recess. Wmk Star. P 10.*
529 **136** 1 c. green 8 5
530   2 c. scarlet 10 5
531   5 c. blue 20 10

1949 (9 Dec). *OBLIGATORY TAX. Anti-Tuberculosis Fund. Recess. Wmk Star. P 10.*
532 **137** 1 c. light blue 8 5
See also No. 547.

138 Enrique Collazo   **139** E. J. Varona

1950 (28 Feb). *Birth Centenary of General Collazo. Recess. Wmk Star. P 10.*
533 **138** 2 c. scarlet 8 5
534   5 c. blue 20 10

1950 (28 Feb). *Birth Centenary of Enrique José Varona (writer). Recess. Wmk Star. P 10.*
535 **139** 2 c. scarlet 8 5
536   5 c. blue 20 10

1950 (Apr). *Havana Tobacco Industry. As Nos. 511/3 but redrawn and design 21 × 25 mm instead of 22½ × 26 mm.*
537 **127** 1 c. green 8 5
538 **128** 2 c. scarlet 10 5
539   – 5 c. blue 15 5

1950 (27 Apr). *Opening of National Bank of Cuba. No. 538 optd with T 140.*
540 **128** 2 c. scarlet 20 10

U.P.U.
1874
1949
(141)   **142** Balanzategui, Pausa and Railway Crash   **143** F. Figueredo

1950 (19 May). *75th Anniv of U.P.U. As Nos. 537/9, but colours changed. Optd with T 141, in red.*
541 **127** 1 c. apple-green 10 5
542 **128** 2 c. pink 12 5
543   – 5 c. pale blue 15 8

1950 (21 Sept). *Postal Employees' Retirement Fund. Recess. Wmk Star. P 10.*
544 **142** 1 c. green 10 5
545   2 c. scarlet 10 5
546   5 c. blue 20 10

1950 (1 Dec). *OBLIGATORY TAX. Anti-Tuberculosis Fund. As No. 532, but colour changed.*
547 **137** 1 c. rose-carmine 5 5

1951 (17 Mar). *Postal Employees' Retirement Fund. Recess. Wmk Star. P 10.*
548 **143** 1 c. green 10 5
549   2 c. scarlet 10 5
550   5 c. blue 20 10

144 Foundation Stone   **145** Narciso López   E **146** Government House, Cárdenas

1951 (5 June). *OBLIGATORY TAX. P.O. Rebuilding Fund. Recess. Wmk Star. P 10.*
551 **144** 1 c. violet 5 5

(Recess Waterlow)

1951 (3 July). *Centenary of Cuban Flag. T 145/E 146, and similar types inscr "CENTENARIO DE LA BANDERA CUBANA". Wmk Wavy Lines. P 13.*

(a) *POSTAGE. Inscr "CORREOS"*
552   1 c. scarlet, ultram and green .. 8 5
553   2 c. black and scarlet 10 5
554   5 c. scarlet and ultramarine .. 25 10
555   10 c. carm, greenish bl & violet .. 35 15

(b) *AIR. Inscr "SERVICIO AEREO"*
556   5 c. scarlet, ultramarine & olive 30 12
557   8 c. scar, greenish bl & red-brn 40 12
558   25 c. scar, greenish bl & black .. 80 35

(c) *SPECIAL DELIVERY*
E559 E **146** 10 c. scarlet, ultram & brn-orge .. 40 10
552/E559 *Set of 8* .. .. 2·40 90
Designs: *Horiz*—5 c. (No. 556) López landing at Cárdenas. *Vert*—1 c. Miguel Teurbe Tolón; 5 c. (No. 554) Emilia Teurbe Tolón; 8 c. Raising the flag; 10 c. Flag; 25 c. Flag and El Morro lighthouse.

147 Clara Maass, Newark Memorial and Las Animas, Havana, Hospitals

V

1951 (24 Aug). 50th Death Anniv of Clara Maass (nurse). Recess. Wmk Star. P 10.
559 147 2 c. scarlet 12 8

1951 (24 Aug). 50th Anniv of Discovery of Cause of Yellow-fever by Dr. Carlos J. Finlay, and to honour Martyrs of Science. Sheet MS442 optd "50 ANIVERSARIO DESCUBRI-MIENTO AGENTE TRANSMISOR", etc., across the block of four.

(a) POSTAGE. Optd in black
MS560 127×177 mm. Two each of Nos.
440/1. No wmk. Imperf (sold at 25 c.) .. 1·50 1·50

(b) AIR. Optd in green, as last but with aeroplane motif and "CORREO AEREO" in addition.
MS561 127×177 mm. Two each of Nos.
440/1. No wmk. Imperf (sold at 25 c.) .. 1·50 1·50

148 J. R. Capablanca   149 Chess-board

E 150 Capablanca Club, Havana

(Photo Waterlow)

1951 (1 Nov). 30th Anniv of World Chess Championship won by Capablanca. T 148/E 150 and similar designs. Wmk Wavy Lines. P 13. (a) POSTAGE. Inscr "CORREOS".
562 148 1 c. orange and emerald .. 25 10
563 – 2 c. chocolate and rose 40 15
564 – 5 c. ultramarine and black .. 80 25

(b) AIR. Inscr "CORREO AEREO"
565 149 5 c. yellow and green 50 12
566 – 8 c. reddish purple and ultram .. 80 20
567 148 25 c. sepia and brown .. .. 1·50 50

(c) SPECIAL DELIVERY
E568 E 150 10 c. brown-purple and green .. 50 15
562/E568 Set of 7 .. .. 4·25 1·25
Designs: Horiz—5 c. (No. 564) Capablanca Club, Havana. Vert—2 c., 8 c. Capablanca playing chess.

151 Dr. A. Guiteras Holmes   152 Morillo Fortress

1951 (22 Nov). 16th Death Anniv of Dr. Guiteras in skirmish at Morillo. T 151/2 and similar type. Recess. Wmk Star. P 10.

(a) POSTAGE. Inscr "CORREOS"
568 151 1 c. yellow-green 10 5
569 – 2 c. rose 15 5
570 152 5 c. bright blue 20 12

(b) AIR. Inscr "CORREO-AEREO"
571 151 5 c. mauve 20 8
572 – 8 c. deep green 25 12
573 152 25 c. blackish brown 70 35
568/573 Set of 6 .. .. 1·40 70

MS574 Two sheets 125×133 mm each containing Nos. 568/73 (a) stamps in green. Imperf. (b) stamps in blackish brown. P 12½.
Each sold at 60 c. .. .. 15·00 15·00
Design: Horiz—2 c., 8 c. Guiteras framing social laws.

153 Mother and Child   154 Christmas Emblems   155 José Maceo

1951 (1 Dec). OBLIGATORY TAX. Anti-Tuberculosis Fund. Recess. Wmk Star. P 10.
575 153 1 c. yellow-brown 5 5
576 1 c. claret 5 5
577 1 c. green 5 5
578 1 c. violet-blue 5 5
575/578 Set of 4 .. .. 15 10

1951 (1 Dec). Christmas Greetings. Frame recess; centre typo. Wmk Star. P 10.
579 154 1 c. carmine and green 35 15
580 2 c. green and scarlet 50 20

1952 (8 Feb). Birth Centenary of Gen. José Maceo. Recess. Wmk Star. P 10.
581 155 2 c. yellow-brown 12 5
582 5 c. indigo 25 10

156 General Post Office   157 Isabella the Catholic   (158)   AEREO 5¢

1952 (8 Feb)–57. OBLIGATORY TAX. P.O. Rebuilding Fund. Recess. Wmk Star. P 10.
583 156 1 c. indigo 5 5
584 1 c. rose-red (18.1.57) 5 5
For similar stamp see No. 860.

1952 (22 Feb). Fifth Centenary of Birth of Isabella the Catholic. Recess. No wmk. P 10.

(a) POSTAGE
585 157 2 c. orange-red 15 5

(b) AIR. Inscr "AEREO"
586 157 25 c. dull purple 65 25
MS587 Two sheets each 108×108 mm containing Nos. 585/6. (a) 2 c. indigo and 25 c. carmine. Imperf. (b) 2 c. carmine and 25 c. indigo. Perf 10. Both Wmk Star .. .. 4·00 4·00
Stamps in T 157 vertically optd "GOBIERNO REVOLUCIONARIO 10 MARZO 1952", are fraudulent.

1952 (18 Mar). As No. 549, but colour changed.

(a) POSTAGE. Surch with new value
588 143 10 c. on 2 c. yellow-brown (G.) .. 25 10

(b) AIR. Surch as T 158
589 143 5 c. on 2 c. yellow-brown (Bk.) .. 20 8
590 8 c. on 2 c. yellow-brown (R.) .. 30 10
591 10 c. on 2 c. yellow-brown (B.) .. 35 12
592 25 c. on 2 c. yellow-brown (V.) .. 40 20
593 50 c. on 2 c. yellow-brown (R.) .. 1·10 50
594 1 p. on 2 c. yellow-brown (B.) .. 1·90 1·25

(c) SPECIAL DELIVERY. Surch similar to T 158, but "E. ESPECIAL" instead of "AEREO"
E595 143 10 c. on 2 c. yellow-brown (P.) .. 45 12
588/E595 Set of 8 .. .. 4·50 2·10

159 Proclamation of Republic

160 Statue, Havana University

E 161 National Anthem and Arms

(Recess P. Fernandez, Havana)

1952 (27 May). *50th Anniv of Republic of Cuba. As* **T 159**/**E 161** (*inscr "1902 1952"*). *P* 12½. (*a*) *POSTAGE.*

595	1 c. black and green	..	8	5
596	2 c. black and brown-red		10	5
597	5 c. black and blue	..	15	8
598	8 c. black and lake-brown	..	20	8
599	20 c. black and bronze-green	..	40	20
600	50 c. black and orange	..	65	30

(*b*) *AIR. Inscr "AEREO"*

601	5 c. green and deep violet	..	20	10
602	8 c. grey-green and scarlet	..	25	12
603	10 c. emerald and blue	..	30	15
604	25 c. emerald and purple	..	65	30

(*c*) *SPECIAL DELIVERY*

E605 **E 161**	10 c. blue and orange	..	45	12
595/E605	*Set of 11* ..	..	3·00	1·40

Designs: *Horiz*—2 c. Estrada Palma and Estevez Romero; 5 c. (No. 597) Barnet, Finlay, Guiteras and Nuñez; 5 c. (No. 601) Rural school; 8 c. (No. 598) The Capitol; 10 c. Presidential Palace; 20 c. Map showing central highway; 25 c. Peso banknote; 50 c. Sugar factory.

162 Route of Flight

163 A. Parlá and Biplane

(Recess P. Fernandez, Havana)

1952 (22 July). *AIR. 39th Anniv of Florida–Cuba Flight by Agustin Parlá. Wmk Star. P* 10.

605 **162**	8 c. black	..	20	8
606 **163**	25 c. violet-blue	..	50	25
MS607	Four sheets each 111×92 mm. Nos. 605/6 each in deep blue and in green. P 11		4·00	4·00

164 Coffee Beans

165 Col. C. Hernandez

(Recess Waterlow & Sons)

1952 (22 Aug). *200th Anniv of Coffee Cultivation. T* **164** *and similar horiz designs inscr "1748–1948". Wmk Wavy Lines. P* 13½.

608	1 c. green	..	..	8	5
609	2 c. carmine-red ..		..	12	8
610	5 c. slate-green and deep ultramarine	..	25	12

Designs:—2 c. Plantation worker and map of Cuba; 5 c. Coffee plantation.

(Recess P. Fernandez, Havana)

1952 (7 Oct). *Postal Employees' Retirement Fund. Wmk Star. P* 10. (*a*) *POSTAGE.*

611 **165**	1 c. green ..	..	..	..	5	5
612	2 c. red ..	..	..	..	8	5
613	5 c. blue ..	..	..	..	12	5
614	8 c. black ..	..	..	..	20	10
615	10 c. Venetian red ..	..	..	30	10
616	20 c. brown	..	..	..	75	30

(*b*) *AIR. Inscr "AEREO"*

617 **165**	5 c. yellow-orange	..	..	12	5
618	8 c. bright green ..	..	..	20	10
619	10 c. olive-brown ..	..	..	25	12
620	15 c. blackish green	..	..	30	15
621	20 c. turquoise	..	..	..	40	25
622	25 c. scarlet	..	..	..	45	30
623	30 c. violet ..	..	..	1·00	50
624	45 c. bright mauve ..	..	..	1·10	70
625	50 c. deep blue	..	..	..	80	50
626	1 p. yellow-ochre ..	..	..	1·75	80

(*c*) *SPECIAL DELIVERY. Inscr "ENTREGA ESPECIAL"*

E627 **165**	10 c. pale olive-green	..	30	10
611/E627	*Set of 17* ..	..	..	7·00	3·75

166 A. A. de La Campa

167 Statue, Havana University

168 Dominquez, Estébanez and Capdevila (defence lawyers)

169 Child's Face

1952 (27 Nov). *Martyrs of 1871 Revolution. Frames recess; centres typo. Wmk Star. P* 10. (*a*) *POSTAGE. T* **166** *and similar portraits.*

627	1 c. black and deep green ..	..	5	5
628	2 c. black and carmine-red ..	..	8	5
629	3 c. black and deep violet ..	..	10	5
630	5 c. black and blue ..	..	..	12	8
631	8 c. black and sepia ..	..	..	15	10
632	10 c. black and red-brown ..	..	20	10
633	13 c. black and bright purple ..	..	30	15
634	20 c. black and bronze-green	..	50	25

(*b*) *AIR*

635 **167**	5 c. blue and indigo	..	..	15	8
636 **168**	25 c. green and orange	..	..	70	35
627/636	*Set of 10* ..	..	..	2·10	1·10

Portraits:—2 c. C. A. de la Torre; 3 c. A. Bermúdez; 5 c. E. G. Toledo; 8 c. A. Laborde; 10 c. J. de M. Medina; 13 c. P. Rodriguez; 20 c. C. Verdugo.

1952 (1 Dec). *OBLIGATORY TAX. Anti-Tuberculosis Fund. Recess. Wmk Star. P* 10.

637 **169**	1 c. yellow-orange	..	..	8	5
638	1 c. rose-red ..	..	..	..	8	5
639	1 c. bright green ..	..	..	8	5
640	1 c. blue ..	..	..	..	8	5
637/640	*Set of 4* ..	..	..	..	25	10

170 Christmas Tree **171** Marti's Birthplace

1952 (30 Dec). *Christmas Greetings. Frame recess; centre typo. Wmk Star. P·*10.
641 170 1 c. scarlet and bright green .. 70 30
642 3 c. emerald and bluish violet .. 70 30

1953 (Jan–Dec). *Birth Centenary of A. J. Marti. Various designs inscr "CENTENARIO DE MARTI 1853 1953", as T* 171. *Recess. Wmk Star. P* 10. (a) *POSTAGE.*
643 1 c. red-brown and deep green (28.1) .. 5 5
644 1 c. red-brown and deep green (25.8) .. 5 5
645 3 c. sepia and violet (25.8) 8 5
646 3 c. sepia and deep violet (*vert*) (25.8) 8 5
647 5 c. sepia and deep blue (25.8) .. 12 8
648 5 c. brown and blue (*vert*) (17.11) .. 15 8
649 10 c. black and red-brown (*vert*) (25.8) .. 25 12
650 ·10 c. black and red-brown (*vert*) (17.11) 25 12
651 13 c. bistre-brown and bronze-green (*vert*) (17.11) 35 15
652 13 c. bistre-brown & bronze-grn (17.11) 35 15

(b) *AIR. Inscr* "CORREO(S) AEREO"
653 5 c. black and carmine-red (17.11) 12 5
654 5 c. black and carmine-red (*vert*) (17.11) 12 5
655 8 c. black and deep green (*vert*) (25.8) 15 8
656 8 c. black and deep green (17.11) .. 15 8
657 10 c. carmine-red & indigo (*vert*) (23.12) 20 10
658 10 c. indigo and carmine-red (23.12) .. 20 10
659 15 c. black and bluish violet (*vert*) (23.12) 25 12
660 15 c. black and bluish violet (*vert*) (23.12) 25 12
661 25 c. scarlet and sepia (*vert*) (23.12) .. 40 20
662 25 c. scarlet and sepia (*vert*) (23.12) .. 40 20
663 50 c. blue and yellow (23.12) 70 30
643/663 *Set of* 21 .. .. .. 4·00 2·00
Designs: Nos. 643, T 171; 644, Marti before Council of War; 645, Prison wall; 646, Marti in prison; 647, "El Abra" ranch; 648, Allegory of Marti's poems; 649, Marti and Bolivar statue, Caracas; 650, Marti writing; 651, Revolutionaries' meeting place; 652, First edition of "Patria"; 653, Marti in Kingston, Jamaica; 654, Marti in Ibor City; 655, Montecristi manifesto; 656, House of Maximo Gómez, Montecristi; 657, Marti's portrait; 658, Marti as an orator; 659, Marti's first tomb; 660, Obelisk at Dos Rios; 661, Monument in Havana; 662, Marti's present tomb; 663, "Fragua Martiana" (modern building).

172 Rafael Montoro **173** Dr. F. Carrera Justiz

1953 (5 Mar). *Birth Centenary of Montoro (statesman). Recess. Wmk Star. P* 10.
664 172 3 c. slate-purple 10 5

1953 (10 Mar). *Recess. Wmk Star. P* 10.
665 173 3 c. scarlet 10 5

174 **E 175**

(Recess (8, 15 c.). Centre recess, background typo (others) P. Fernandez, Havana)

1953 (22 May)–**55**. *AIR. T* 174 *and similar horiz aeroplane design. Wmk Star.* (a) *P* 10.
666 174 8 c. deep orange-brown 15 5
667 15 c. scarlet 35 25
668 – 2 p. bistre-brown and green .. 3·50 1·50
669 – 5 p. chocolate and pale blue .. 7·50 3·00

(b) *P* 12½ (21.9.55)
670 – 2 p. bronze-green and blue .. 2·25 1·25
671 – 5 p. bronze-green and rose .. 6·00 3·00
666/671 *Set of* 6 .. .. .. 18·00 8·00
Design:—Nos. 668/71, Four-engined 'plane facing right.

1953 (16 June). *No.* 538 *surch with new value.*
672 128 3 c. on 2 c. scarlet 8 5

1953 (28 July). *SPECIAL DELIVERY. Recess. P.*10.
E673 E 175 10 c. blue.. .. .. .. 30 12

176 Congress Building **177**

(Recess P. Fernandez, Havana)

1953 (3 Nov). *First International Accountancy Congress, Havana. T* 176 *and similar horiz designs inscr* "TRIBUNALES DE CUENTAS" *etc. P* 10. (a) *POSTAGE.*
673 176 3 c. ultramarine 10 5

(b) *AIR. Inscr* "CORREO-AEREO"
674 – 8 c. carmine 20 8
675 – 25 c. deep green 40 15
Designs:—8 c. Congress building and "Cuba"; 25 c. Aerial view of building and aeroplane.

1953 (1 Dec). *OBLIGATORY TAX. Anti-Tuberculosis Fund. Recess. P* 10.
676 177 1 c. carmine-rose 5 5

178 M. Coyula Llaguno **179** Postal Employees. Retirement Association Flag **180** José Marti

(Recess P. Fernandez, Havana)

1954 (26 Jan–23 Feb). *Postal Employees' Retirement Fund. T* 178 *and similar portraits inscr* "1953" *and T* 179. *P* 10. (a) *POSTAGE.*
677 1 c. green 5 5
678 3 c. scarlet 5 5
679 5 c. pale blue (23.2) 12 5
680 8 c. brown-lake (23.2) 20 10
681 10 c. bistre-brown 30 5

(b) *AIR. Inscr* "CORREO AEREO"
682 5 c. indigo 12 5
683 8 c. bright purple 15 8
684 10 c. orange (23.2) 30 10
685 1 p. black (23.2) .. .. .. 1·60 90

(c) *SPECIAL DELIVERY. Inscr* "ENTREGA ESPECIAL"
E686 10 c. olive-green (23.2) 20 8
677/E686 *Set of* 10 .. .. 2·75 1·25
·ortraits: *Vert*—3 c., 8 c. (No. 680), E. L. Calleja Hensell; 8 c. (683), 10 c. A. Ginard Rojas; 10 c. (684, E686) G. Hernández Saez. *Horiz*—5 c. (No. 679) as T 179; 5 c. (682), M. Coyula Llaguno.

1954 (6 Apr)–**56**. *T* **180** *and similar portraits. Recess. P* 10.

686	1 c. green	5	5
687	2 c. carmine (Gómez) ..	5	5
688	3 c. violet (J. de la Luz)	5	5
689	4 c. bright purple (M. Aldama) (17.1.56)	5	5
690	5 c. deep slate-blue (Garcia) ..	8	5
691	8 c. brownish lake (Agramonte) (13.7.54)	10	5
692	10 c. sepia (Estrada Palma) (13.7.54) ..	12	5
693	13 c. orange-red (Finlay) (13.7.54)	20	5
694	14 c. grey (S. Sánchez) (14.2.56)	15	5
695	20 c. yellow-olive (Saco) (13.7.54)	30	15
696	50 c. yellow-ochre (A. Maceo) (13.7.54)	50	15
697	1 p. orange (Cespedes) (13.7.54)	1·10	15
686/697	*Set of 12*	2·40	50

See also Nos. 990/1, 1180a/b and 1680/2.

181 Hauling Sugar | **182** José M. Rodriguez

(Recess P. Fernandez, Havana)

1954 (27 Apr)–**56**. *AIR. Sugar Industry. T* **181** *and similar designs. P* 10.

698	5 c. bright green	5	5
699	8 c. bistre-brown	12	5
700	10 c. deep green	20	5
701	15 c. Venetian red	25	10
702	20 c. pale blue	25	10
703	25 c. rose-red	30	10
704	30 c. bright purple	1·10	30
	a. Deep mauve (1956) ..	50	15
705	40 c. deep blue	60	30
706	45 c. violet	50	30
707	50 c. blue	1·00	30
708	1 p. indigo	1·90	45
698/708	*Set of 11*	5·00	1·60

Designs: *Vert*—5 c. Sugar cane; 1 p. A. Reinoso. *Horiz*—8 c. Sugar harvesting; 15 c. Train-load of sugar cane; 20 c. Modern sugar factory; 25 c. Evaporators; 30 c. Stacking sacks of sugar; 40 c. Loading sugar on ship; 45 c. Oxen hauling cane; 50 c. Primitive sugar factory.

1954 (8 June). *Birth Centenary of Maj.-Gen. Rodriguez. T* **182** *and similar vert design Inscr "1851 1951". Recess. Wmk Star. P* 12½.

709	2 c. sepia and brown-red	5	5
710	5 c. sepia and blue	12	8

Design:—5 c. Rodriguez on horseback.

183 Sanatorium | **184**

(Recess P. Fernandez, Havana)

1954 (21 Sept). *General Batista Sanatorium. P* 10.

(a) POSTAGE

711	**183** 9 c. deep grey-blue	8	5

(b) AIR. Inscr "CORREO AEREO"

712	**183** 9 c. deep green	15	8

1954 (1 Nov). *OBLIGATORY TAX. Anti-Tuberculosis Fund. Recess. P* 10.

713	**184** 1 c. scarlet ..	5	5
714	1 c. bright green ..	5	5
715	1 c. blue	5	5
716	1 c. bright violet	5	5
713/716	*Set of 4*	15	10

185 Father Christmas | **186** Maria Luisa Dolz

1954 (15 Dec). *Christmas Greetings. Recess. P* 10.

717	**185** 2 c. deep dull grn & carm-lake	50	8
718	4 c. carmine-lake and emerald ..	50	8

(Recess P. Fernandez, Havana)

1954 (23 Dec). *Birth Centenary of Maria Luisa Dolz (educationist). P* 10. *(a) POSTAGE.*

719	**186** 4 c. chalky blue	10	5

(b) AIR. Inscr "CORREO AEREO"

720	**186** 12 c. cerise	20	5

187 Boy Scouts and Cuban Flag | **188** P. P. Harris and Rotary Emblem

(Des E. Caravia. Recess)

1954 (27 Dec). *3rd National Scouts Camp. P* 12½.

721	**187** 4 c. deep dull green	10	5

(Des Galigarcia. Recess P. Fernandez, Havana)

1955 (23 Feb). *50th Anniv of Rotary International. P* 12½. *(a) POSTAGE. Inscr "CORREOS".*

722	**188** 4 c. blue	8	5

(b) AIR

723	**188** 12 c. carmine	20	8

189 Major-Gen. F. Carrillo | **190** 1855 Stamp and "La Volanta"

1955 (8 Mar). *Birth Centenary of Carrillo. T* **189** *and similar vert portrait. Recess. P* 10.

724	2 c. deep greenish blue and scarlet ..	5	5
725	5 c. sepia and blue	8	5

Design:—5 c. Half-length portrait of Carrillo.

(Des B. Cruz Planas. Recess P. Fernandez, Havana)

1955 (24 Apr). *Centenary of First Cuban Postage Stamps and 50th Anniv of First Republican Stamps. T* **190** *and similar horiz designs. Wmk Star. P* 12½. *(a) POSTAGE.*

726	2 c. Prussian blue and bright purple ..	8	5
727	4 c. deep dull green and brown-orange	10	5
728	10 c. scarlet and ultramarine	25	20
729	14 c. red-orange and bluish green ..	40	15

(b) AIR. Inscr "CORREO AEREO"

730	8 c. deep dull green & dp greenish blue	20	10
731	12 c. red and bronze-green ..	20	10
732	24 c. deep violet-blue and scarlet	45	20
733	30 c. reddish brown and red-orange ..	85	25
726/733	*Set of 8* ..	2·25	1·00

Designs:—*(a)* 1855 stamp and: 2 c. Old Square and Convent of St. Francis; 10 c. Havana in 19th century; 14 c. Captain-General's residence and Plaza de Armas. *(b)* 1855 and 1905 stamps and: 8 c. Palace of Fine Arts; 12 c. Plaza de la Fraternidad; 24 c. Aerial view of Havana; 30 c. Plaza de la Republica.

191 Major-Gen. Menocal

192 Mariel Bay

1955 (22 June). *Postal Employees' Retirement Fund. Recess. Wmk Star.* P 12½. (a) POSTAGE. T **191** and similar portraits.

734	2 c. green	..	..	..	5	5
735	4 c. bright purple	..	..	5	5
736	10 c. blue	..	..	..	15	8
737	14 c. grey-violet	..	..	20	8

Portraits: *Horiz*—4 c. Gen. Nuñez; 14 c. Dr. A. de Bustamante. *Vert*—10 c. J. G. Gómez.

(b) AIR. T **192** and similar horiz designs

738	8 c. deep green and carmine-red	..	15	8
739	12 c. bright blue and yellow-brown		20	8
740	1 p. ochre and deep green	..	1·25	90

Designs:—12 c. Varadero Beach; 1 p. Viñales Valley.

(c) SPECIAL DELIVERY. *Vert portrait as* T **191**, *but inscr* "ENTREGA ESPECIAL"

E741	10 c. lake (Felix Varela)	..	15	8
734/E741	*Set of 8*	..	..	1·90	1·25

193 Cuban Academy

194 Route of 1914 Flight

(Recess P. Fernandez, Havana)

1955 (1 July). *AIR. Centenary of Tampa, Florida. Wmk Star.* P 12½.

741	**193**	12 c. deep bistre-brown and scarlet	20	10

(Recess P. Fernandez, Havana)

1955 (4 July). *AIR. 35th Death Anniv of Crocier (aviator).* T **194** and another horiz design inscr "JAIME GONZALEZ CROCIER". *Wmk Star.* P 10.

742	12 c. green and scarlet	..	20	5
743	30 c. bright purple and deep grey-green	55	20

Design:—30 c. Crocier in aircraft cockpit.

195

196 Wright Brothers' Biplane

197 Turkey

1955 (1 Nov). *OBLIGATORY TAX. Anti-Tuberculosis Fund. Recess. No wmk.* P 10.

744	**155**	1 c. red-orange	..	..	10	5
745		1 c. yellow-ochre	..	..	10	5
746		1 c. blue	..	..	..	10	5
747		1 c. bright mauve	..	..	10	5
744/747	*Set of 4*	..	..	35	10

(Des B. Cruz Planas. Recess, background photo, P. Fernandez, Havana)

1955 (12 Nov). *AIR. International Philatelic Exhibition, Havana.* T **196** and similar horiz designs. *Wmk Star.* P 12½.

748	8 c. black, rose-red and blue	..	25	10
749	12 c. black, emerald and carmine-red	..	30	12
750	24 c. black, bluish violet & carm-red	60	20
751	30 c. black, blue and red-orange	..	70	40
752	50 c. black, olive-green and red-orange	1·25	50
748/752	*Set of 5*	..	..	2·75	1·00

MS753 175×140 mm. Nos. 748/52 in new colours. No gum. Imperf (13 Nov) .. 3·00 3·00
Designs:—12 c. *Spirit of St. Louis;* 24 c. *Graf Zeppelin;* 30 c. "Super-Constellation" aircraft; 50 c. "Convair" delta-wing 'plane.

1955 (15 Dec). *Christmas Greetings. Recess. Wmk Star.* P 12½.

754	**197**	2 c. deep green and red	50	8
755		4 c. carmine-red and green	..	50	8

198 Expedition Disembarking

199 Bishop de St. Cruz

(Recess P. Fernandez, Havana)

1955 (27 Dec). *Birth Centenary of Gen. Nuñez.* T **198** and other designs. *Wmk Star.* P 12½. (a) POSTAGE. *Inscr* "CORREOS".

756	4 c. lake	..	..	8	5

(b) AIR

757	8 c. bright blue and carmine-red	..	15	8
758	12 c. deep green and brown	..	20	8

Designs: *Vert* (22½×32½ mm)—4 c. Portrait of Nuñez. *Horiz* (38½×24 mm)—8 c. *Three Friends* (ship).

(Recess P. Fernandez, Havana)

1956 (27 Mar). *200th Anniv of Cuban Postal Service.* T **199** and similar vert portrait. *No wmk.* P 12½. (a) POSTAGE. Inscr "CORREOS".

759	4 c. deep turquoise-blue & dp brown	..	8	5

(b) AIR

760	12 c. deep green and deep brown	..	20	8

Portrait:—4 c. F. C. de la Vega.

200 J. del Casal

201 Victor Muñoz

202 Mother and Baby

(Recess P. Fernandez, Havana)

1956 (2 May). *Postal Employees' Retirement Fund.* T **200** and similar vert portraits inscr "RETIRO DE COMUNICACIONES 1955". *No wmk.* P 12½. (a) POSTAGE.

761	2 c. black and green	..	5	5
762	4 c. black and mauve ..	..	8	5
763	10 c. black and blue	..	15	5
764	14 c. black and violet	..	20	5

(b) AIR. *Inscr* "AEREO"

765	8 c. black and bistre-brown	..	10	5
766	12 c. black and ochre	..	20	5
767	30 c. black and indigo	..	45	30

(c) SPECIAL DELIVERY. *Inscr* "ENTREGA ESPECIAL"

E768	10 c. black and carmine	..	15	5
761/E768	*Set of 8*	..	1·25	45

Portraits:—4 c. Luisa Pérez de Zambrana; 8 c. Gen. J. Sanguily; 10 c. (No. 763), J. Clemente Zenea: 10 c. (No. E768), J. Jacinto Milanés;12 c. Gen. J. M. Aguirre; 14 c. J. J. Palma; 30 c. Col. E. Fonts Sterling.

(Recess P. Fernandez, Havana)

1956 (13 May). *Muñoz Commemoration. No wmk.* P 12½.

768	**201**	4 c. deep brown and emerald	..	8	5

(Recess P. Fernandez, Havana)

1956 (13 May). *AIR. Mothers' Day. No wmk.* P 12½.

769	**202**	12 c. bright blue and scarlet..	25	8

203 Aerial View of Temple   **204**   **205** H. de Blanck

(Des E. R. Almeyda. Recess P. Fernandez, Havana)

1956 (5 June). *Masonic Grand Lodge of Cuba Temple, Havana. T 203 and similar vert design. No wmk. P 12½.*
(a) POSTAGE.

770	4 c. pale blue	8	5

(b) AIR. Inscr "AEREO"

771	12 c. deep yellow-green . .	20	8

Design:—4 c. Ground level view of Temple.

(Recess P. Fernandez, Havana)

1956 (26 June). *AIR. Various bird designs as T 204. P 12½.*

(a) Wmk Star

772	8 c. blue (29.8.56)		10	8
773	12 c. blue-grey . .		1·00	20
774	14 c. blackish olive		25	8
775	19 c. brown		25	10
776	24 c. rose-magenta		30	12
777	29 c. green		35	12
778	30 c. light bistre-brown (29.8.56)		50	12
779	50 c. grey-black (29.8.56)		75	20
780	1 p. carmine-red (29.8.56)		1·40	50
781	2 p. purple (29.8.56)		2·75	90
782	5 p. scarlet (29.8.56)		5·50	2·00
772/782	Set of 11		12·00	4·00

(b) Wmk 234

783	12 c. bluish green (12.2.60)		10	5
784	1 p. blue (20.7.62)		80	20
785	2 p. scarlet (20.7.62)		1·50	50
786	5 p. purple (20.7.62)		4·00	1·60
783/786	Set of 4		5·50	2·00

Designs: *Horiz*—8 c. Wild duck; 12 c. Pigeon; 29 c. Wild geese; 30 c. Quails; 2 p. Sand pipers. *Vert*—19 c. Seagulls; 24 c. Pelicans; 50 c. Herons; 1 p. Black vulture; 5 p. Woodpeckers.

(Recess P. Fernandez, Havana)

1956 (6 July). *AIR. Birth Centenary of De Blanck (composer). Wmk Star. P 12½.*

787	**205** 12 c. bright blue		15	5

(206)   **207** Church of Our Lady of Charity

1956 (13 July). *AIR. Inauguration of Philatelic Club of Cuba Building. As No. 776 but colour changed. Surch with T 206.*

788	8 c. on 24 c. orange		15	5

(Recess P. Fernandez, Havana)

1956 (8 Sept). *Our Lady of Charity, Cobre. T 207 and similar vert design inscr "NTRA. SRA. DE LA CARIDAD" etc. Wmk Star. P 12½.* (a) POSTAGE.

789	4 c. greenish blue and lemon . .	8	5

(b) AIR

790	12 c. deep green and carmine-red	25	8
MS791	76×77 mm Nos. 789/90. Imperf	60	60

Design:—4 c. Our Lady of Charity over landscape.

208   **209**

(T **208**/9 recess P. Fernandez, Havana)

1956 (5 Oct). *AIR. 260th Birth Anniv of Benjamin Franklin. Wmk Star. P 12½.*

792	**208** 12 c. deep red-brown	25	8

1956 (10 Oct). *"Grito de Yara" (War of Independence) Commemoration. Wmk Star. P 12½.*

793	**209** 4 c. sepia and deep dull green	8	5

(210)   **211**

1956 (26 Oct). *12th Inter-American Press Association Meeting, Havana. As No. 781 but colour changed and surch with T 210, in blue.*

794	12 c. on 2 p. deep grey . .	25	15

1956 (1 Nov). *OBLIGATORY TAX. Anti-Tuberculosis Fund. Recess. No wmk. P 10.*

795	**211** 1 c. rose-red . .		5	5
796	1 c. green		5	5
797	1 c. blue		5	5
798	1 c. brown		5	5
795/798	Set of 4		15	10

212   **213** Prof. R. G. Menocal

(Nos. 799/804. Recess P. Fernandez, Havana)

1956 (1 Dec). *Christmas Greetings. Wmk Star. P 12½.*

799	**212** 2 c. red and deep green		50	5
800	4 c. deep green and red		50	5

1956 (3 Dec). *Birth Centenary of Prof. R. G. Menocal. Wmk Star. P 12½.*

801	**213** 4 c. purple-brown		8	5

214 Martin M. Delgado

215 Scouts around Camp Fire

1957 (30 Jan). *Birth Centenary of Delgado (patriot). Wmk Star. P 12½.*
802 **214** 4 c. deep green 10 5

1957 (22 Feb). *Birth Centenary of Lord Baden-Powell. T 215 and another design. Wmk Star. P 12½. (a) POSTAGE.*
803 4 c. deep green and red 10 5

(b) AIR. Inscr "AEREO"
804 12 c. deep greenish slate 25 10
Design: *Vert—12 c. Lord Baden-Powell.*

216 "The Art Critics" (Melero)

217 Hanabanilla Falls

(Des V. Acosta. Recess)

1957 (29 Mar). *Postal Employees' Retirement Fund. T 216/17 and similar horiz designs inscr "RETIRO DE COMUNICACIONES". Wmk Star. P 12½. (a) POSTAGE. As T 216.*
805 2 c. deep olive-green and sepia .. 5 5
806 4 c. orange-red and sepia .. 8 5
807 10 c. bronze-green and sepia 15 8
808 14 c. ultramarine and brown 25 10
Designs: (Paintings)—2 c. "The Blind" (Vega); 10 c. "Carriage in the Storm" (Menocal); 14 c. "The Convalescent" (Romanach).

(b) AIR. As T 217
809 8 c. blue and scarlet 12 5
810 12 c. green and scarlet 20 8
811 30 c. deep olive-grn & blackish violet .. 35 15
Designs:—12 c. Sierra de Cubitas; 30 c. Puerto Boniato.

(c) SPECIAL DELIVERY. As T 216, but inscr "ENTREGA ESPECIAL"
E812 10 c. turquoise-blue and brown .. 25 8
Design:—10 c. "Ayer" (Cabrera).
805/E812 *Set of 8* .. .. .. 1·25 55

218 Posthorn Emblem of Cuban Philatelic Society

219 Juan F. Steegers

(Recess, centre and frame litho P. Fernandez, Havana)

1957 (24 Apr). *Stamp Day. Cuban Philatelic Exhibition. T 218 and similar vert design. Wmk Star. P 12½.*

(a) POSTAGE
812 4 c. blue, yellow-brown and red .. 8 5

(b) AIR. Inscr "AEREO"
813 12 c. brown, orange-yellow and green .. 20 8
Design:—12 c. Philatelic Society Building, Havana.

1957 (30 Apr). *Birth Centenary of Steegers (fingerprint pioneer). T 219 and similar vert design. Recess. Wmk Star. P 12½. (a) POSTAGE.*
814 4 c. blue 8 5

(b) AIR. Inscr "AEREO"
815 12 c. chocolate (Thumbprint) 20 8

220 Baseball Player

221 Nurse Victoria Brú Sanchez

222 J. de Aguero leading Patriots

1957 (17 May). *AIR. Youth Recreation. Designs as T 220. Recess, background litho. Wmk Star. P 12½.*
816 8 c. red-brown, pale grn & dull green .. 15 5
817 12 c. red-brn, pale lilac & pale violet .. 25 10
818 24 c. red-brown, pale blue and blue .. 50 20
819 30 c. red-brown, flesh and orange .. 55 25
816/819 *Set of 4* .. .. .. 1·25 50
Designs:—12 c. Ballet dancer; 24 c. Diver; 30 c. Boxers.

1957 (3 June). *Nurse Sanchez Commemoration. Recess. Wmk Star. P 12½.*
820 **221** 4 c. indigo 8 5

PRINTERS. Nos. 821 to E859 were recessprinted by P. Fernandez, Havana.

1957 (4 July). *Joaquin de Aguero Commemoration. T 222 and similar vert design. Wmk Star. P 12½. (a) POSTAGE.*
821 4 c. grey-green 5 5

(b) AIR. Inscr "AEREO"
822 12 c. indigo 25 10
Design:—12 c. Joaquin de Aguero (patriot).

223 Youth with Dogs and Cat

224 Colonel R. Manduley del Rio (patriot)

225 J. M. Heredia Girard (poet)

1957 (17 July). *50th Anniv of Young Helpers' League. T 223 and another vert design. Wmk Star. P 12½. (a) POSTAGE.*
823 4 c. deep blue-green 8 5

(b) AIR. Inscr "AEREO"
824 12 c. red-brown 25 10
Design:—12 c. Jeannette Ryder (founder).

1957 (31 July). *Colonel Manduley del Rio Commemoration. Wmk Star. P 12½.*
825 **224** 4 c. slate-green 8 5

1957 (16 Aug). *AIR. Heredia Girard Commemoration. Wmk Star. P 12½.*
826 **225** 8 c. deep violet 12 8

226 Palace of Justice, Havana

1957 (2 Sept). *Inauguration of Palace of Justice. Wmk Star.*
P 12½. (a) POSTAGE.
827 226   4 c. greenish slate 8 5
       (b) AIR. Inscr "AEREO"
828 226   12 c. green 20 10

227 Army Leaders of 1856

228 J. R. Gregg
(shorthand pioneer)

1957 (26 Sept). *Centenary of Cuban Army of Liberation.
Wmk Star. P 12½.*
829 227   4 c. chestnut and grey-green .. 8 5
830   4 c. red-brown and Prussian blue .. 8 5
831   4 c. brown and rose-pink .. 8 5
832   4 c. deep brown and orange-yellow 8 5
833   4 c. sepia and light violet .. 8 5
829/833   Set of 5 .. .. 35 15

1957 (1 Oct). *AIR. Gregg Commemoration. Wmk Star.
P 12½.*
834 228   12 c. deep green 20 10

229 Cuba's First
Publication, 1723

230 José Marti National
Library

1957 (18 Oct). *José Marti National Library. Designs inscr
"BIBLIOTECA NACIONAL". Wmk Star. P 12½.*
       (a) POSTAGE
835 229   4 c. deep slate 8 5
       (b) AIR. Inscr "AEREO"
836 –   8 c. ultramarine 12 5
837 230   12 c. deep green 20 8
Design: (22½ × 32 mm)—8 c. D. Figarola Caneda, first director of National Library.

231 U.N. Emblem and Map
of Cuba

232 Aeroplane and Map

1957 (24 Oct). *AIR. United Nations Day. Recess, map litho.
Wmk Star. P 12½.*
838 231   8 c. red-brown and bronze-green .. 20 10
839   12 c. green and carmine 30 12
840   30 c. magenta and deep blue .. 60 30

1957 (28 Oct). *AIR. 30th Anniv of Inauguration of Air Mail
Service between Havana and Key West, Florida. Plane and
map, litho, frame recess. Wmk Star. P 12½.*
841 232   12 c. blue and brown-lake 25 12

233

234 "R de C" Italics

1957 (1 Nov). *OBLIGATORY TAX. Tuberculosis Relief Fund.
W 234. P 10.*
842 233   1 c. brown-red 5 5
843   1 c. light emerald 5 5
844   1 c. light blue 5 5
845   1 c. olive-grey 5 5
842/845   Set of 4 .. .. 15 10

235 Courtyard

236 Street Scene, Trinidad

1957 (19 Nov). *Centenary of First Cuban Normal School.
T 235 and similar designs inscr "CENTENARIO DE LA
PRIMERA ESCUELA NORMAL DE CUBA". Wmk Star.
P 12½. (a) POSTAGE.*
846 194   4 c. red-brown and deep green .. 8 5
       (b) AIR. Inscr "AEREO"
847 –   12 c. yellow-brown and indigo .. 25 8
848 –   30 c. deep sepia and carmine .. 35 15
Designs: *Vert*—12 c. School façade. *Horiz*—General view of
school.

1957 (17 Dec). *Postal Employees' Retirement Fund. T 236
and similar pictorial designs inscr "RETIRO DE COMUNI-
CACIONES 1957". Wmk Star. P 12½. (a) POSTAGE.*
849   2 c. brown and indigo 5 5
850   4 c. grey-green and brown .. 8 5
851   10 c. deep sepia and red .. 15 5
852   14 c. myrtle-green and red .. 20 8
       (b) AIR. Inscr "AEREO"
853   8 c. grey-black and red .. 15 8
854   12 c. grey-black and red-brown .. 20 8
855   30 c. orange-brown and grey .. 35 15
       (c) SPECIAL DELIVERY. Inscr "ENTREGA ESPECIAL"
E856   10 c. deep violet and brown .. 20 8
849/E856   Set of 8 .. .. .. 1·25 55
Designs: *Vert*—4 c. Sentry-box on old wall of Havana; 10 c.
(No. 851), Calle Padre Pico (street), Santiago de Cuba; 12 c.
Sancti Spiritus Church; 14 c. Church and street scene,
Camaguey. *Horiz*—8 c. "El Viso" Fort, El Caney; 10 c. (No.
E856), Statue of General A. Maceo, Independence Park, Pinar
del Rio; 30 c. Concordia Bridge, Matanzas.

237 Christmas Crib

E **238** Motor-cyclist in Havana

1957 (20 Dec). *Christmas. Recess, centres typo. Multicoloured centres, frame colours given. Wmk Star. P 12½.*
856 237   2 c. sepia 20 5
857   4 c. black 20 5

1958 (17 Jan). *SPECIAL DELIVERY. No wmk. P 12½.*
E858 E **238** 10 c. blue..   15   8
E859   20 c. green   30   8
   For 10 c. wmk **234** see Nos. E954/5.

239 Dayton Hedges and   **240** Dr. F. D. Roldán
   Textile Factories   (physiotherapy
                    pioneer)

1958 (30 Jan). *Dayton Hedges (founder of Cuban Textile Industry) Commemoration. Recess. Wmk Star. P 12½. (a) POSTAGE.*
858 **239** 4 c. grey-blue   8   5

            (b) AIR. Inscr "AEREO"
859 **239** 8 c. green   15   8

1958 (Feb). *OBLIGATORY TAX. P.O. Rebuilding Fund. As No. 584 but W **234**.*
860 **156** 1 c. rose-red   5   5

1958 (21 Feb). *Roldán Commemoration. Recess. Wmk Star. P 12½.*
861 **240** 4 c. deep green   8   5

241 "Diario de la   **242** Map of Cuba showing Postal
   Marina" Building   Routes of 1756

1958 (1 Apr). *125th Anniv of "Diario de la Marina" Newspaper. T **241** and vert portrait. Recess. Wmk Star. P 12½. (a) POSTAGE.*
862 –   4 c. deep yellow-olive   8   5

              (b) AIR
863 **241** 29 c. black   50   25
   Portrait:—4 c. J. I. Rivero y Alonso (journalist).

1958 (24 Apr). *Stamp Day and National Philatelic Exhibition, Havana. T **242** and similar horiz design. Recess, map and background typo. Wmk Star. P 12½. (a) POSTAGE.*
864 **242** 4 c. blackish grn, buff & light bl ..   12   8

             (b) AIR. Inscr "AEREO"
865 –   29 c. deep blue, buff and light blue ..   40   20
   Design:—29 c. Ocean map showing sea-post routes of 1765.

243 General J. M.   **244** Dr. T. Romay
    Gómez   Chacon

1958 (6 June). *Birth Centenary of Gómez. T **243** and similar vert design. Recess. Wmk Star. P 12½. (a) POSTAGE.*
866 **243** 4 c. blue-black   8   5

             (b) AIR. Inscr "AEREO"
867 –   12 c. greenish black   20   8
   Design:—12 c. Gómez at Arroyo Blanco.

1958 (27 June). *Famous Cubans. Various portraits as T **244**. Recess. Wmk Star. P 12½. (a) Doctors. With emblem of medicine.*
868   2 c. brown and deep green   5   5
869   4 c. black and green   8   5
870   10 c. carmine and deep green   15   5
871   14 c. deep blue and green   20   8

       (b) Lawyers. With emblem of law
872   2 c. sepia and red   5   5
873   4 c. black and red   8   5
874   10 c. bronze-green and red   15   8
875   14 c. slate-blue and red   20   8

      (c) Composers. With lyre emblem of music
876   2 c. deep brown and indigo .·. ..   5   5
877   4 c. grey-purple and indigo   8   5
878   10 c. bronze-green and indigo   15   5
879   14 c. red and indigo   20   8
868/879   *Set of 12* .. ..   1·25   60
   Portraits:—Doctors—4 c. Dr. A. A. Aballi; 10 c. Dr. F. G. del Valle; 14 c. Dr. V. A. de Castro. Lawyers—2 c. J. M. G. Montes; 4 c. J. A. González Lanuza; 10 c. J. B. Hernández Barreiro; 14 c. P. González Llorente. Composers—2 c. N. R. Espadero; 4 c. I. Cervantes; 10 c. J. White; 14 c. B. de Salas.

PRINTERS. Nos. 880 to 902 were recessprinted by P. Fernandez, Havana.

245 Dr. C. de la Torre   **246** Polymita picta

1958 (29 Aug). *Birth Centenary of De la Torre (naturalist). T **245** and horiz designs as T **246**. Recess; centre typo. (8 c.). W **234** (sideways on 4 c.). P 12½. (a) POSTAGE.*
880 **245**   4 c. deep ultramarine   8   5

             (b) AIR. Inscr "AEREO"
881 **246**   8 c. scarlet, yellow and black ..   30   15
882   –   12 c. sepia/yellow-green   70   30
883   –   30 c. green/pink .. .. ..   1·00   45
880/883   *Set of 4* .. ..   1·75   80
   Fossils:—12 c. Megalocnus rodens; 30 c. Ammonite.

247 Felipe Poey   **248** Papilio   **249** Theodore
   (naturalist)   caiguanabus   Roosevelt
                 (butterfly)

1958 (26 Sept). *Poey Commemoration. Various designs as T **247/8** inscr "1799—FELIPE POEY—1891." Recess (2 c., 4 c.); centres typo (others). Wmk Star. P 12½.*

           (a) POSTAGE
884   2 c. black and lavender   10   5
885   4 c. brown-black   12   5

          (b) AIR. Inscr "AEREO"
886   8 c. sepia, yellow, black & vermilion ..   35   10
887   12 c. orange, black and green   55   10
888   14 c. yellow, black, orange and purple   75   15
889   19 c. yellow, sepia, black and blue ..   1·25   30
890   24 c. rose, yellow, slate-blue and black   1·40   35
891   29 c. blue, brown and black .. ..   1·40   40
892   30 c. purple-brown, green and black ..   1·50   50

    (c) SPECIAL DELIVERY. Inscr "ENTREGA ESPECIAL"
E893   10 c. rose, yellow, blue and black ..   50   30
E894   20 c. carmine, ultramarine and black ..   1·25   60
884/E894   *Set of 11* .. .. ..   8·00   2·50

Designs: *Vert*—2 c. Cover of Poey's book; 4 c. T **247**; 8 c. T **248**; 12 c. *Teria gundlachia*; 14 c. *Teria ebriola*; 19 c. *Nathalis felicia* (all butterflies). *Horiz*—10 c. Rabiche; 20 c. Guajacon; 24 c. Jacome; 29 c. Anil; 30 c. Diana (all fishes).

1958 (27 Oct). *Birth Centenary of Theodore Roosevelt.* T **249** and horiz design inscr "LOS ROUGH RIDERS" etc. Wmk Star. P 12½. (a) POSTAGE.
893   4 c. grey-green   8   5

(b) AIR. Inscr "AEREO"
894   12 c. sepia   20   10
Design:—12 c. Roosevelt leading Rough Riders at San Juan, 1898.

250 National
Tuberculosis
Hospital

251 U.N.E.S.C.O.
Headquarters, Paris

1958 (1 Nov). OBLIGATORY TAX. *Tuberculosis Relief Fund.* W **234**. P 10.
895 **250** 1 c. red-brown   5   5
896   1 c. light emerald   5   5
897   1 c. rose-red   5   5
898   1 c. grey   5   5
895/898 Set of 4   15   10

1958 (28 Nov). AIR. *Inauguration of U.N.E.S.C.O. Headquarters Building, Paris.* T **251** and similar horiz design. Wmk Star. P 12½.
899   12 c. deep bronze-green   ..   30   12
900   30 c. ultramarine   60   30
Design:—30 c. Façade composed of letters "UNESCO" and map of Cuba.

252 *Cattleyopsis lindenii* (orchid)

253 "The Revolutionary"

1958 (1 Dec). *Christmas.* T **252** and similar vert design inscr "1958–NAVIDADES–1959". Centre photo; frame recess. Wmk Star. P 12½.
901   2 c. yellow, purple, dp bluish grn & blk   35   5
902   4 c. yellow, red, deep violet-blue & blk ..   35   5
Orchid:—4 c. *Oncidium guibertianum.*

SOCIALIST STATE

Following a revolution Dr. Fidel Castro established a Socialist State on 1 January 1959.

(Des V. Acosta. Typo)

1959 (28 Jan). *Liberation Day.* W **234** (sideways). P 12½.
903 **253** 2 c. black and carmine-red   ..   8   5

254 Gen. A. F. Crombet

255 Postal Notice of 1765

(Recess P. Fernandez, Havana)

1959 (18 Mar). *Crombet Commemoration.* Wmk Star. P 12½.
904 **254** 4 c. blackish green   10   5

1959 (24 Apr). AIR. *Stamp Day and National Philatelic Exhibition, Havana.* T **255** and similar vert design. Recess. W **234** (sideways). P 12½.
905   12 c. sepia and blue   25   8
906   30 c. blue and sepia   45   20
Design:—30 c. Administrative postal book of St. Cristobal, Havana, 1765.

256 Hand supporting Sugar Factory

1959 (7 May). *Agricultural Reform.* T **256** and similar horiz design inscr "PRO REFORMA AGRARIA". Centre typo, frame recess. W **234** (sideways). P 12½. (a) POSTAGE.
907 **256** 2 c.+1 c. ultramarine & carm-red ..   8   5

(b) AIR. Inscr "CORREO AEREO"
908   –   12 c.+3 c. yellow-grn & carm-red ..   25   15
Design: (42×30 mm)—12 c. Farm workers and factory plant.

257 Red Cross Nurse

258 Pres. C. M. de Cespedes

(Photo Waterlow)

1959 (22 Sept). *"For Charity".* Wmk Wavy Lines. P 12½.
909 **257** 2 c.+1 c. bright red   8   5
         a. Imperf   8   5

(Recess P. Fernandez, Havana)

1959 (10 Oct). *Cuban Presidents. Portraits as T* **258**. Wmk Star. P 12½.
910   2 c. slate-blue   5   5
911   2 c. deep green (S. C. Betancourt)   ..   5   5
912   2 c. deep bluish violet (M. de Jesus Calvar)   5   5
913   2 c. chestnut (B. Maso)   5   5
914   4 c. carmine-red (J. B. Spotorno)   ..   10   5
915   4 c. chocolate (T. Estrada Palma)   ..   10   5
916   4 c. black (F. J. de Cespedes)   ..   10   5
917   4 c. deep violet (V. Garcia)   ..   10   5
910/917 Set of 8   50   25

(259)

260 Teresa G. Montes (founder)

1959 (17 Oct). AIR. *American Society of Travel Agents Convention, Havana.* No. 780 with colour changed and surch with T **259**, in blue.
918   12 c. on 1 p. light emerald   20   10

(Recess P. Fernandez, Havana)

1959 (11 Nov). *Musical Arts Society Festival, Havana.* T **260** *and similar design inscr "SOCIEDAD PRO-ARTE MUSICAL" etc. Wmk Star.* P 12½. (*a*) POSTAGE.

919 **260** 4 c. brown 8 5

(*b*) AIR. Inscr "AEREO"

920 – 12 c. bronze-green 20 8
Design: *Horiz*—12 c. Society Headquarters, Havana.

261 Rebel Attack at Cuartel Moncada

262

(Des E. Hermández (1 c.), P. F. Morales (2, 29 c.), A. M. Penalver (10 c.), A. B. Jiménez (8 c., 12 c. (No. 924)), A. S. Soler (12 c. (No. 926)). Recess Giesecke & Devrient, Leipzig)

1960 (28 Jan). *First Anniv of Cuban Revolution. Horiz designs as* T **261**. W **262**. P 12½. (*a*) POSTAGE.

921 1 c. bronze-green, vermilion & grey-bl 5 5
922 2 c. bronze-green, sepia and blue .. 5 5
923 10 c. bronze-green, red and grey-blue .. 20 10
924 12 c. bronze-green, deep maroon & bl .. 25 12

(*b*) AIR. Inscr "AEREO"

925 8 c. bronze-green, vermilion & grey-bl 12 5
926 12 c. bronze-green dp mar & yell-brn .. 20 12
927 29 c. red, black and deep bronze-green 40 20
921/927 *Set of 7* .. .. 1·10 60
Designs:—2 c. Rebels disembarking from the *Granma*; 8 c. Battle of Santa Clara; 10 c. Battle of the Uvero; 12 c. (No. 924), "The Invasion (Rebel and map of Cuba); 12 c. (No. 926), Rebel army entering Havana; 29 c. Banknote changing hands ("Clandestine activities in the cities").

HABILITADO PARA

2 ¢

(**263**)

264 Pres. T. Estrada Palma Monument

(**265**)

1960 (3 Feb–20 Sept). *Various stamps surch as* T **263** (*No. 932 with "HABILITADO" and value only*).

(*a*) POSTAGE

928 2 c. on 2 c.+1 c. (907) (R.) 5 5
929 2 c. on 4 c. (689) (B.) (16.7) 5 5
930 2 c. on 5 c. (690) (R.) (16.7) 5 5
931 2 c. on 13 c. (693) (16.7) 5 5
932 10 c. on 20 c. (351a) (20.9) 15 8

(*b*) AIR

933 12 c. on 12 c.+3 c. (908) (R.) 20 10
928/933 *Set of 6* 45 30

1960 (3 Feb). *Various stamps surch as* T **263**, *but with value only.* (*a*) POSTAGE.

934 1 c. on 4 c. (869) (R.) 5 5
935 1 c. on 4 c. (873) (R.) 5 5
936 1 c. on 4 c. (877) (R.) 5 5
937 1 c. on 4 c. (880) (R.) 5 5
938 1 c. on 4 c. (902) (Silver) 5 5
939 1 c. on 4 c. (904) (R.) 5 5
940 1 c. on 4 c. (919) (R.) 5 5
941 2 c. on 14 c. (694) (R.) 5 5

(*b*) AIR. Inscr "CORREO AEREO"

942 12 c. on 40 c. (382) (R.) 20 10
943 12 c. on 45 c. (706) (R.) 20 10
934/943 *Set of 10* 65 40

(Recess P. Fernandez, Havana)

1960 (28 Mar). *Postal Employees' Retirement Fund.* T **264** *and similar designs of monuments inscr "RETIRO DE COMMUNICACIONES 1958". W 234.* P 12½. (*a*) POSTAGE.

944 1 c. brown and deep blue 5 5
945 2 c. deep green and red 5 5
946 10 c. sepia and red 15 10
947 12 c. olive-green and violet 20 12

(*b*) AIR. Inscr "AEREO"

948 8 c. grey and carmine 12 8
949 12 c. carmine-red and grey-blue .. 15 8
950 30 c. violet and red-brown 40 20
944/950 *Set of 7* .. .. 1·00 60
Monuments: *Vert*—2 c. "Mambi Victorioso"; 8 c. Marti; 10 c. Marta Abreu; 12 c. (No. 947), Agramonte; 12 c. (No. 949), Heroes of Cacarajicara. *Horiz*—30 c. Dr. C. de la Torriente.

1960 (24 Apr). AIR. *Stamp Day and National Philatelic Exhibition, Havana.* (*a*) *As Nos. 772/3, but colours changed, optd with* T **265** *in deep blue.*

951 8 c. yellow 15 8
952 12 c. rose-carmine 20 10

(*b*) *Miniature sheet. No.* MS**444** *optd with* T **265** *on each stamp, in deep blue.*

MS953 128×178 mm. No. 443 in block of four. No wmk. Imperf (sold at 60 c.) .. 1·75 1·75
No. MS953 also commemorates the centenary of the Spanish Cuba and Puerto Rico ¼ r. on 2 r. stamps.

(Recess P. Fernandez, Havana)

1960 (30 June)**—61**. *SPECIAL DELIVERY. W 234.* P 12½.

E954 E **238** 10 c. bright violet 20 10
E955 10 c. orange (28.6.61) 20 10

266 Pistol-shooting

267 C. Cienfuegos and View of Escolar

(Des L. M. Pedro. Eng E. A. Wright. Recess P. Fernandez, Havana)

1960 (22 Sept). *Olympic Games.* T **266** *and similar designs.* W **234**. P 12½. (*a*) POSTAGE.

954 1 c. violet (Sailing) 5 5
955 2 c. yellow-orange 5 5

(*b*) AIR. Inscr "AEREO"

956 8 c. bright blue (Boxing) 15 8
957 12 c. carmine (Running) 20 10
954/957 *Set of 4* 40 25
MS958 79×91 mm. Nos. 954/5 each in deep blue. Imperf 80 80

(Des C. A. Parada. Litho)

1960 (27 Oct). *First Death Anniv of Cienfuegos (revolutionary leader). Centre multicoloured; frame colour below.* P 12½.

959 **267** 2 c. sepia 5 5

268 Air Stamp of 1930, Plane and Sputnik

1930 CUBA-AEREO 1960

HABILITADO

ENTREGA ESPECIAL

10 ¢

(E **269**)

(Des C. A. Parada. Litho)

1960 (30 Oct). *AIR. 30th Anniv of National Airmail Service. Centre multicoloured; inscriptions colour below.* P 12½.

960	**268**	8 c. deep violet	.. .. ..	75	30

1960 (18 Nov). *SPECIAL DELIVERY. Nos. 388 and 390 surch with Type E 269.*

E961	**55**	10 c. on 20 c. pink	.. .. ..	20	10
E962		10 c. on 50 c. greenish blue (R.)	..	20	10

270 Aguinaldo

271 Tobacco

1960 (1 Dec). *Christmas. Inscr "NAVIDAD 1960–61". Litho.* P 12½. (a) T **270**.

961	1 c. multicoloured	.. .. ..	10	5
962	2 c. multicoloured	.. .. ..	12	5
963	10 c. multicoloured	.. .. ..	35	10

(b) *Horiz designs as* T **271**

964	1 c. multicoloured	.. .. ..	10	5
965	2 c. multicoloured	.. .. ..	12	5
966	10 c. multicoloured	.. .. ..	35	10

Nos. 961 and 964, 962 and 965, 963 and 966 were printed together in three sheets of 25, each comprising nine stamps of T **270** forming a centre cross and four blocks of four different stamps as T **271** in each corner. The four-stamp design incorporates various floral subjects with an oval border of music (the "Christmas Hymn"). (*Price for three sheets un* £4.50.)

272

273 J. Menéndez

1961 (10 Jan). *Conference of Sub-Industrialized Countries.* T **272** *and similar designs. Photo.* P 11½. (a) *POSTAGE.*

967	1 c. black, yellow and red	.. ..	5	5
968	2 c. red, grey, black and blue	..	5	5
969	6 c. red, black and cream	.. ..	20	8

(b) *AIR. Inscr "AEREO"*

970	8 c. black, green, yellow, red and yellow-brown	.. ..	12	5
971	12 c. light blue, buff, black & bright blue	15	8
972	30 c. red and grey-black	..	35	20
973	50 c. red, pale blue, blue and black	..	55	30
967/973	*Set of 7*	.. ..	1·40	70

Designs: *Horiz*—2 c. Graph and symbols; 6 c. Cogwheels; ·12 c. Workers holding lever; 30 c. Maps. *Vert*—8 c. Hand holding machete; 50 c. Upraised hand.

1961 (22 Jan). *Jesus Menéndez Commemoration. Litho.* P 12½.

974	**273**	2 c. sepia and deep green	.. ..	8	5

274 "Declaration of Havana"

1961 (28 Jan). *AIR. Declaration of Havana. Litho.* P 12½.

975	**274**	8 c. orange-red, black and pale greenish yellow	12	10
976		12 c. violet, black and buff	25	15
977		30 c. red-brown, black and pale blue	45	30
MS978		103×80 mm. Nos. 975/7. No gum.		
		Imperf	80	80

Nos. 975/7. Background text in English, French or Spanish. Price same for each language (*price for set of 9 £2 un* £1.40 *us*).

No. **MS**978. Background texts are as follows:—8 c. Spanish, 12 c. English and 30 c. French.

275 U.N. Emblem within Dove of Peace

(Des A. Evora. Litho)

1961 (12 Apr). *15th Anniv of U.N.* P 12½. (a) *POSTAGE.*

979	**275**	2 c. red-brown and apple-green ..	8	5
980		10 c. green and purple	15	8
MS981		102×64 mm. Nos. 979/80. No gum.		
		Imperf	40	40

(b) *AIR. Inscr "AEREO"*

982	**275**	8 c. cerise and yellow	12	5
983		12 c. blue and orange	15	10
MS984		102×64 mm. Nos. 982/3. No gum.		
		Imperf	50	50

276 10 c. Revolutionary label of 1874 and CUBA MAMBISA "postmark"

(277)

1961 (24 Apr). *Stamp Day.* T **276** *and similar horiz designs inscr "24 DE ABRIL. DIA DEL SELLO".* P 12½.

985	1 c. dull red, green and black	5	5
986	2 c. orange, slate and black	5	5
987	10 c. light turquoise-grn, carmine & blk	15	8

Designs:—2 c. 1907 50 c. stamp and CUBA REPUBLICANA "postmark"; 10 c. 1959 2 c. stamp and CUBA REVOLUCIONARIA "postmark".

1961 (1 May). *Labour Day. No. 974 optd with* T **277**.

988	**273**	2 c. sepia and deep green (R.)	..	5	5

278

1961 (26 July). *"For Peace and Socialism". Litho. P* 12½.
989 **278** 2 c. red, black, yellow and grey .. 5 5
No. 989 is lightly printed on the back with an overall pattern of wavy lines and the multiple inscription "CORREOS CUBA" in buff.

1961 (1 Aug). *As Nos. 686/7 but colours changed and 2 c. redrawn. P* 12½.
990 **180** 1 c. red-brown 5 5
991 – 2 c. bronze-green 5 5
The date of birth (1833) originally shown on the 2 c. has been replaced by a question mark.
For 2 c. in different shade see No. 1681.

HABILITADO
PARA
8 cts.
(279)

primera
exposicion
filatélica
oficial
oct. 7-17. 1961
(280)

1961 (Oct). *AIR. Surch with T* **279**.
992 **174** 8 c. on 15 c. scarlet (667) 15 8
993 **54** 8 c. on 20 c. brown (380) 15 8

1961 (7 Oct). *First Official Philatelic Exhibition. No. 987 optd with T* **280**, *in red*.
994 **276** 10 c. light turq-grn, carm & blk .. 15 10

281 Book and Lamp

1961 (22 Nov). *Education Year. T* **281** *and similar horiz designs. Litho. P* 12½.
995 1 c. red, black and blue-green 5 5
996 2 c. red, black and blue 5 5
997 10 c. red, black and violet 12 8
998 12 c. red, black and yellow-orange .. 15 8
995/998 *Set of 4* 30 20
Designs:—As T **281** but showing letters: 2 c. "U"; 10 c. "B"; 12 c. "A"; forming word "CUBA".

282 *Polymita S. Flammulata T.* (snail)

283 *Polymita P. Fulminata T.* (snail)

1961 (1 Dec). *Christmas. Inscr* "NAVIDAD 1961–62". *Multicoloured. Litho. P* 12½.

(a) Various designs as T **282**
999 1 c. Type **282** .. 5 5
1000 2 c. Bird (*vert*).. 5 5
1001 10 c. Butterfly (*horiz*) 15 10

(b) Various designs as T **283**
1002 1 c. Snails (*horiz*) 5 5
1003 2 c. Birds (*vert*) 5 5
1004 10 c. Butterflies (*horiz*) 15 10
Nos. 999 and 1002, 1000 and 1003, 1001 and 1004 were printed together in three sheets of 25, each comprising four stamps as T **282** plus five *se-tenant* stamp-size labels showing pealing bells, and a star forming a centre cross and four blocks of four different stamps as T **283** in each corner. The four-stamp design incorporates different subjects, which together form a composite picture. (*Price for three sheets un* £4.)

284 Castro Emblem   **285** Hand with Machete

1962 (3 Jan). *Third Anniv of Cuban Revolution. Emblem yellow, red, grey and blue; colours of background and inscriptions below. Litho. P* 12½. (*a*) *POSTAGE*.
1005 **284** 1 c. deep green and pink 5 5
1006 2 c. black and yellow-orange .. 5 5

(*b*) *AIR. Inscr* "AEREO"
1007 **284** 8 c. brown and light blue 10 5
1008 12 c. yellow-ochre and pale green 20 10
1009 30 c. violet and pale yellow .. 45 20
1005/1009 *Set of 5* 75 40

1962 (16 Jan). *AIR. First Anniv of "Socialist People's First Sugar Harvest". Litho. P* 12½.
1010 **285** 8 c. sepia and rose-red 10 5
1011 12 c. black and lilac 15 5

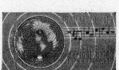

286 Armed Peasant and Tractor

1962 (26 Feb). *National Militia. T* **286** *and similar horiz designs. Litho. P* 12½.
1012 1 c. black and green 5 5
1013 2 c. black and blue 5 5
1014 10 c. black and orange 15 8
Designs:—2 c. Armed worker and welder; 10 c. Armed woman and sewing-machinist.

287 Globe and Music Emblem   **288** Soldiers, Aircraft and Burning Ship

1962 (26 Mar). *AIR. International Radio Service. Inscriptions and aerial yellow; musical notation black; lines on globe brown; background colours below. Litho.* W **234**. P 12½.

1015	**287**	8 c. grey	..	..	10	5
1016		12 c. light blue	..	..	12	8
1017		30 c. light green	..	..	25	15
1018		1 p. lilac	..	..	1·00	55
1015/1018		Set of 4	..	..	1·25	75

1962 (17 Apr). *First Anniv of "Playa Giron" (Invasion attempt by Cuban exiles). Litho.* W **234**. P 12½.

1019	**288**	2 c. multicoloured	..	..	5	5
1020		3 c. multicoloured	..	..	8	5
1021		10 c. multicoloured	..	..	12	5

289 Arrival of First Mail from the Indies

1962. (24 Apr). *Stamp Day. T* **289** *and similar horiz design. Litho.* W **234**. P 12½. *(a) POSTAGE.*

1022	**289**	10 c. black and carmine-red/cream	15	8

(b) SPECIAL DELIVERY. Inscr "ENTREGA ESPECIAL"

E1023	—	10 c. light brown and blue/cream	25	10

Design:—No. E1023, 18th-century sailing packet.

290 Cubans raising Fists

291 Wrestling

1962 (1 May). *Labour Day. Litho.* W **234**. P 12½.

1023	**290**	2 c. black/buff	..	..	5	5
1024		3 c. black/vermilion	..	..	8	5
1025		10 c. black/light blue	..	..	12	5

1962 (25 July). *National Sports Institute (I.N.D.E.R.) Commemoration. Sports designs as T* **291**. *Litho.* W **234**. P 12½.

1026		1 c. brown and vermilion/cream	..		5	5
1027		2 c. lake and green/cream	..		5	5
1028		3 c. ultramarine and lake/cream	..		8	5
1029		9 c. maroon and deep blue/cream	..		12	5
1030		10 c. red-orange and purple/cream	..		12	5
1031		13 c. black and carmine/cream	..		15	5

The above were each printed in five different sports designs repeated five times in the sheet of twenty-five stamps.

Price per set of 30 £2.50 un, £1.25 us.

292 A. Santamaria and Soldiers

293 Dove and Festival Emblem

1962 (26 July). *Ninth Anniv of "Rebel Day". T* **292** *and similar horiz design inscr "26 DE JULIO 1962". Litho.* W **234**. P 12½.

1032		2 c. lake and ultramarine	..	5	5
1033		3 c. ultramarine and lake	..	8	5

Design:—3 c. A. Santamaria and children.

1962 (28 July). *World Youth Festival, Helsinki. T* **293** *and similar design. Litho.* W **234**. P 12½.

1034		2 c. multicoloured	..	5	5
1035		3 c. multicoloured	..	8	5
MS1036		91×52 mm. Nos. 1034/5. Imperf	25	25

Design:—3 c. As T **293** but with "clasped wrists" in place of dove.

294 Czech 5 k. "Praga 1962" stamp of 1961

1962 (18 Aug). *AIR. International Stamp Exhibition, Prague. Litho.* W **234**. P 12½.

1037	**294**	31 c. multicoloured	..	35	15
MS1038		150×123 mm. No. 1037. Imperf	..	1·00	1·00

295 Rings and Boxing Gloves

296 "Cuban Women"

1962 (27 Aug). *Ninth Central American and Caribbean Games, Jamaica. T* **295** *and similar horiz designs. Litho.* W **234**. P 12½.

1039		1 c. ochre and rose-red	..	..	5	5
1040		2 c. ochre and blue	..	..	5	5
1041		3 c. ochre and purple	..		5	5
1042		13 c. ochre and emerald	..	..	15	8
1039/1042		Set of 4	..	..	25	15

Designs:—Rings and: 2 c. Tennis rackets: 3 c. Baseball bats; 13 c. Rapiers and mask.

1962 (1 Oct). *First Cuban Women's Federation National Congress. T* **296** *and similar design inscr "1962". Litho.* W **234**. P 12½.

1043		9 c. carmine, green and black	..	10	5
1044		13 c. black, blue and green	..	12	8

Design: Vert—13 c. Mother and child, and Globe.

297 Running

1962 (13 Oct). *First Latin-American University Games. T* **297** *and similar horiz designs inscr "JUEGOS UNIVERSITARIOS" etc., "1962". Multicoloured. Litho.* Wmk Star. P 12½.

1045		1 c. Type **297**	..	..	5	5
1046		2 c. Baseball	..	..	5	5
1047		3 c. Netball	..	..	8	5
1048		13 c. Globe	..	..	15	8
1045/1048		Set of 4	..	..	30	15

298 Microscope and Parasites

(Des L. Contreras. Litho)

1962 (14 Dec). *Malaria Eradication.* T **298** *and similar horiz designs. Multicoloured. Wmk Star. P* 12½.
1049   1 c. Type **298** 5   5
1050   2 c. Mosquito and pool 5   5
1051   3 c. Cinchona plant and formulae .. 5   5
1049/1051 Set of 3 12   8

299 *Epicrates angulifer* B.   **300** *Cricolepis typica* (lizard)
(snake)

1962 (21 Dec). *Christmas. Inscr "NAVIDAD 1962–63". Multicoloured. Litho. P* 12½.

(a) *Designs as* T **299**
1052   2 c. Type **299** 5   5
1053   3 c. Beetle (*vert*) 8   5
1054   10 c. Bat (*horiz*) 15   10

(b) *Designs as* T **300**
1055   2 c. Reptiles (*horiz*) 5   5
1056   3 c. Insects (*vert*) 8   5
1057   10 c. Mammals (*horiz*) 15   10
Nos. 1052 and 1055, 1053 and 1056, 1054 and 1057 were printed together in three sheets of 25, each comprising four stamps as T **299** plus five *se-tenant* stamp-size labels showing pealing bells, and a star forming a centre cross and four blocks of four different stamps as T **300** in each corner. The four-stamp design incorporates different subjects, which together form a composite picture. (*Price for three sheets un* £3.)

301 Titov and "Vostok 2"

(Des J. D. Batista. Litho)

1963 (26 Feb). *Cosmic Flights* (1st issue). T **301** *and similar horiz designs. W* **234**. *P* 12½.
1058   1 c. yellow, brown-red and ultramarine   5   5
1059   2 c. yellow, brown-purple and green ..   8   5
1060   3 c. yellow, red and reddish violet ..   10   5
Designs:—1 c. Gagarin and "Vostok 1"; 3 c. Nikolaev, Popovich and "Vostok 3 and 4".
See also Nos. 1133/4.

302 Attackers   **303** Baseball

(Des L. Contreras. Litho)

1963 (13 Mar). *Sixth Anniv of Attack on Presidential Palace.* T **302** *and similar horiz designs. W* **234**. *P* 12½.
1061   9 c. black and red 10   5
1062   13 c. maroon and light blue .. 15   8
1063   30 c. green and orange-red .. 30   15
Designs:—13 c. Rodriguez, C. Servia, Machado and Westbrook; 30 c. J. Echeverria and M. Mora.

1963 (20 Apr). *Fourth Pan-American Games, São Paulo.* T **303** *and similar horiz design. Litho. W* **234**. *P* 12½.
1064   1 c. bluish green 10   5
1065   13 c. red (Boxing) 25   10

304 "Mask" Letter-box   **305** Revolutionaries
and Statue

1963 (25 Apr). *Stamp Day.* T **304** *and similar horiz design. Litho. W* **234**. *P* 12½.
1066   3 c. black and orange-brown ..   8   5
1067   10 c. black and deep violet .. 12   8
Design:—10 c. 19th-century Post Office, Cathedral Place, Havana.

1963 (1 May). *Labour Day.* T **305** *and similar design. Multicoloured. Litho. W* **234**. *P* 12½.
1068   3 c. Type **305** 8   5
1069   13 c. Workers celebrating Labour Day   12   10

306 Cuban Child   **307** Ritual Effigy

1963 (1 June). *Children's Week. Litho. W* **234**. *P* 12½.
1070   **306**   3 c. light brown and deep blue ..   5   5
1071   30 c. carmine-red and deep blue ..   25   12

1963 (29 June). *60th Anniv of Montane Anthropological Museum.* T **307** *and similar designs. Litho. W* **234**. *P* 12½.
1072   2 c. chocolate and red-orange ..   5   5
1073   3 c. brown-purple and ultramarine   8   5
1074   9 c. grey and claret 15   8
Designs: *Horiz*—3 c. Carved chair. *Vert*—9 c. Statuette.

308 "Breaking Chains of   **309** Caimito (plum)
Old Regime"

1963 (26 July). *Tenth Anniv of "Rebel Day". Horiz designs as* T **308**. *Litho. W* **234**. *P* 12½.
1075   1 c. black and pink 5   5
1076   2 c. brown-purple and pale blue ..   5   5
1077   3 c. sepia and reddish lilac ..   8   5
1078   7 c. reddish purple and light emerald   8   5
1079   9 c. purple and olive-yellow ..   10   5
1080   10 c. green and ochre 12   8
1081   13 c. blue and buff 15   10
1075/1081 Set of 7 55   30
Designs:—2 c. Palace attack; 3 c. "The Insurrection"; 7 c. "Strike of April 9th" (defence of radio station); 9 c. "Triumph of the Revolution" (upraised flag and weapons); 10 c. "Agrarian Reform and Nationalization" (artisan and peasant); 13 c. "Victory of Giron" (soldiers in battle).

1963 (19 Aug). *Cuban Fruits. Vert designs as* T **309**. *Fruits in natural colours; inscr in black; frame colours given. Litho.* W **234**. P 12½.

1082	1 c. light blue	..	..	5	5
1083	2 c. orange (Chirimoya)	..	..	5	5
1084	3 c. olive (Marañon)	..	..	5	5
1085	10 c. reddish purple ("Anon")	..	..	12	5
1086	13 c. purple (Mango)	..	..	15	8
1082/1086	Set of 5	..	..	35	20

314 Fish in Net

316 Symbolic "1"

310 "Roof and Window"

311 Hemingway and Scene from "The Old Man and the Sea"

315 V. M. Pera (1st Director of Military Posts, 1868–71)

1963 (29 Sept). *Seventh International Architects Union Congress, Havana.* T **310** *and similar designs. Litho.* P 12½.

1087	3 c. orange-red, carmine, deep blue and bistre		5	5
1088	3 c. orge-red, blk, pur, vio, red & grn		5	5
1089	3 c. black, blue and bistre	..	5	5
1090	3 c. bistre, purple, blue and black	..	5	5
1091	13 c. blue, purple, orange-red, grey, black and bistre	..	15	8
1092	13 c. black, light blue, purple and red	..	15	8
1093	13 c. red, yellow-olive and black	..	15	8
1094	13 c. black, blue, pur, red & orge-red	..	15	8
1087/1094	Set of 8	..	70	40

Designs: *Vert*—No. 1087, T **310**; Nos. 1088, 1091 and 1092, Symbols of building construction as T **310**. *Horiz*—Nos. 1089/90 and 1093, Sketches of urban buildings; No. 1094. As T **310** (girders and outline of house).

1963 (5 Dec). *Ernest Hemingway Commemoration.* T **311** *and similar horiz designs. Litho.* W **234**. P 12½.

1095	3 c. brown and pale blue	..	8	5
1096	9 c. deep bluish green & pale mauve	12	8
1097	13 c. black and pale yellow-green	..	15	10

Designs:—Hemingway and: 9 c. Scene from "For Whom the Bell Tolls"; 13 c. Residence at San Francisco de Paula, near Havana.

1964 (17 Apr). *Third Anniv of Girón Victory.* T **314** *and similar designs. Litho.* P 12½.

1106	3 c. orange, lt brown, black & turq-grn		5	5
1107	10 c. black, grey and bistre	..	10	5
1108	13 c. slate-blue, black and orange-red		15	8

Designs: *Horiz*—10 c. Victory Monument. *Vert*—13 c. Fallen eagle.

1964 (24 Apr). *Stamp Day.* T **315** *and similar horiz design. Litho.* P 12½.

1109	3 c. grey-blue and light orange-brown		5	5
1110	13 c. grey-green and lilac	..	..	12	8

Design:—13 c. Cuba's first (10 c.) military stamp.

1964 (1 May). *Labour Day.* T **316** *and similar vert design. Litho.* P 12½.

1111	3 c. multicoloured	..	..	5	5
1112	13 c. multicoloured	..	..	12	8

Designs:—13 c. As T **316** but different symbols within "1".

317 Chinese Monument, Havana

318 Globe

1964 (15 May). *Cuban-Chinese Friendship.* T **317** *and similar designs. Litho.* P 12½.

1113	1 c. grey, black, green and red..		5	5
1114	2 c. brown-red, olive-yellow and black		5	5
1115	3 c. multicoloured	..	..	8	5

Designs: *Horiz*—2 c. Cuban and Chinese. *Vert*—3 c. Flags of Cuba and China.

312 "Zapateo" (dance), after V. P. de Landaluze

313 B. J. Borrell (revolutionary)

1964 (19 Mar). *50th Anniv of National Museum.* T **312** *and similar designs. Litho.* P 12½.

1098	2 c. multicoloured	..	..	5	5
1099	3 c. multicoloured	..	..	8	5
1100	9 c. orange, brown-buff and black	..	10	8
1101	13 c. black and violet	..	..	15	10
1098/1101	Set of 4	..	..	35	20

Designs: *Vert* (32×42½ *mm*)—3 c. "The Rape of the Mulattos" (after C. Enriquez); 9 c. Greek amphora; 13 c. "Dilecta Mea" (bust, after J. A. Houdon).

1964 (9 Apr). *Fifth Anniv of Revolution.* T **313** *and similar vert portrait designs. Litho.* P 12½.

1102	2 c. black, orange and green	..	5	5
1103	3 c. black, orange and red	..	5	5
1104	10 c. black, orange and reddish purple		10	5
1105	13 c. black, orange and blue	..	15	8
1102/1105	Set of 4	..	..	30	15

Portraits:—3 c. M. Salado; 10 c. O. Lucero; 13 c. S. González (revolutionaries).

1964 (29 May). *U.P.U. Congress, Vienna.* T **318** *and similar horiz designs. Litho.* P 12½.

1116	13 c. orange-brown, bluish green & red	12	5
1117	30 c. black, bistre and red	..	..	20	12
1118	50 c. black, blue and red	..	..	40	20

Designs:—30 c. H. von Stephan (founder of U.P.U.); 50 c. U.P.U. Monument, Berne.

319 Fish   **321** Vietnamese Fighter

323 Start of Race

320 Rio Jibacoa

324 "R de C" Roman

1964 (10 Oct). *Olympic Games, Tokyo. T* **323** *and similar designs. Litho. W* **324**. P 10.

1135	1 c. yellow-orange, blue & reddish pur		5	5
1136	2 c. multicoloured		5	5
1137	3 c. yellow-brown, black and red	..	8	5
1138	7 c. reddish violet, turq-blue & orge	..	10	5
1139	10 c. yellow, purple and blue	..	12	5
1140	13 c. multicoloured		15	8
1135/1140	*Set of 6*	.. .. ..	50	25

Designs: *Vert*—1 c. Gymnastics; 2 c. Rowing; 3 c. Boxing. *Horiz*—10 c. Fencing; 13 c. Games symbols.

1964 (16 June). *Popular Savings Movement. T* **319** *and similar horiz designs. Multicoloured. Litho. P* 12½.

1119	1 c. Type **319**	..	5	5
1120	2 c. Cow		5	5
1121	13 c. Poultry	..	12	8

1964 (30 June). *Cuban Merchant Fleet. T* **320** *and similar horiz designs. Multicoloured. Litho. P* 12½.

1122	1 c. Type **320**		5	5
1123	2 c. Camilo Cienfuegos		5	5
1124	3 c. Sierra Maestra	..	5	5
1125	9 c. Bahia de Siguanea		10	8
1126	10 c. Oriente		12	8
1122/1126	*Set of 5*	..	30	20

1964 (20 July). *"Unification of Vietnam" Campaign. T* **321** *and similar vert designs. Multicoloured. Litho. P* 12½.

1127	1 c. Type **321**	..	5	5
1128	3 c. Vietnamese shaking hands across map	..	5	5
1129	10 c. Hand and mechanical ploughing		10	8
1130	13 c. Vietnamese, Cuban and flags	..	15	10
1127/1130	*Set of 4*	.. .. ..	30	20

322 Raul Gómez Garcia and Poem

1964 (25 July). *11th Anniv of "Rebel Day". T* **322** *and another design (inscr "LA HISTORIA ME ABSOLVERA"). Litho. P* 12½.

1131	3 c. black, red and yellow-ochre	..	5	5
1132	13 c. yellow-ochre, red, black & lt blue	15	8

Design:—13 c. Castro's book "La Historia Me Absolvera".

1964 (15 Aug). *Cosmic Flights* (2nd issue). *Horiz designs as T* **301**. *Litho. P* 12½.

1133	9 c. yellow, reddish violet and red	..	10	5
1134	13 c. yellow, claret and dp bluish grn	..	15	5

Designs:—9 c. "Vostok 5" and Bykovsky; 13 c. "Vostok 6" and Tereshkova.

325 Satellite and Globe

326 Rocket and part of Globe

1964 (15 Oct). *25th Anniv of Cuban Postal Rocket Experiment. Litho. W* **324** *(sideways). P* 10. (a) *Horiz designs as T* **325**.

1141	1 c. multicoloured	..	5	5
1142	2 c. multicoloured	..	5	5
1143	3 c. multicoloured	..	5	5
1144	9 c. multicoloured	..	10	8
1145	13 c. multicoloured	..	15	10

(b) Horiz designs as T **326**

1146	1 c. multicoloured	..	5	5
1147	2 c. multicoloured	..	5	5
1148	3 c. multicoloured	..	5	5
1149	9 c. multicoloured	..	10	8
1150	13 c. multicoloured	..	15	10

(c) Larger 44 × 28 mm

1151	50 c. green and black		50	30
MS1152	110 × 74 mm. As No. 1151 but recess-printed and W **234**	..	1·00	1·00

Designs:—50 c. Cuban Rocket Post 10 c. stamp of 1939. Others, various rockets and satellites.

Nos. 1141 and 1146, 1142 and 1147, 1143 and 1148, 1144 and 1149, 1145 and 1150 were printed together in five sheets of 25, each comprising four stamps as T **325** plus five se-tenant stamp-size labels inscribed overall "1939–COHETE POSTAL CUBANO–1964" forming a centre cross and four blocks of four different stamps as T **326** in each corner. The four-stamp design incorporates different subjects, which together form a composite design around globe. (*Price for five sheets un £4.50.*)

PRIMERA TRIPULACION DEL ESPACIO

(327)

1964 (17 Oct). *First Three-Manned Space Flight. As No.* 1151 *but colours changed, optd with T* **327**, *in silver*
1153   50 c. yellow-green and brown   55   30

328 Lenin addressing   **329** Leopard
     Meeting

1964 (7 Nov). *40th Anniv of Lenin's Death. T* **328** *and similar designs.* W **324** *(sideways on* 13 *c.).* P 10.
1154   3 c. black and red-orange   5   5
1155   13 c. rose and violet   12   5
1156   30 c. black and pale blue   20   10
   Designs: *Horiz*—13 c. Lenin mausoleum. *Vert*—30 c. Lenin and hammer and sickle emblem.

1964 (25 Nov). *Havana Zoo Animals. T* **329** *and similar designs. Multicoloured.* W **324** *(sideways on horiz designs).* Litho. P 10.
1157   1 c. Type **284**   5   5
1158   2 c. Elephant (*vert*)   5   5
1159   3 c. Fallow deer (*vert*)   5   5
1160   4 c. Kangaroo   5   5
1161   5 c. Lions   5   5
1162   6 c. Eland   5   5
1163   7 c. Zebra   5   5
1164   8 c. Hyena   8   5
1165   9 c. Tiger   8   5
1166   10 c. Guanaco   8   5
1167   13 c. Chimpanzees   10   5
1168   20 c. Peccary   15   8
1169   30 c. Raccoon (*vert*)   20   10
1170   40 c. Hippopotamus   30   12
1171   50 c. Tapir   40   20
1172   60 c. Dromedary (*vert*). .   . .   60   30
1173   70 c. Bison   70   35
1174   80 c. Bear (*vert*)   75   40
1175   90 c. Water buffalo   80   45
1176   1 p. Deer at Zoo Entrance   . .   90   50
1157/1176   *Set of* 20 . .   . .   . .   4·75   2·40

330 José Marti

1964 (7 Dec). *"Liberators of Independence". T* **330** *and similar horiz designs showing portraits and campaigning scenes. Multicoloured.* W **324** *(sideways).* Litho. P 10.
1177   1 c. Type **330**   5   5
1178   2 c. A. Maceo   5   5
1179   3 c. M. Gómez   5   5
1180   13 c. C. Garcia   12   8
1177/1180   *Set of* 4   20   15

1964 (7 Dec). *As Nos.* 688 *and* 693, *but colours changed.* *Roul.*
1180a   3 c. red-orange   5   5
1180b   13 c. orange-brown   12   5

331

332

1964 (18 Dec). *Christmas. Inscr* "NAVIDAD 1964–65". *Horiz designs showing marine life.* Litho. W **324**. P 10.

(a) *As T* **331**
1181   2 c. multicoloured (T **331**)   . .   5   5
1182   3 c. multicoloured   8   5
1183   10 c. multicoloured   12   8

(b) *As T* **332**
1184   2 c. multicoloured   5   5
1185   3 c. multicoloured   8   5
1186   10 c. multicoloured   12   8
   Nos. 1181 and 1184, 1182 and 1185, 1183 and 1186 were printed together in three sheets of 25, each comprising four stamps as T **331** plus five *se-tenant* stamp-size labels showing pealing bells, and a star forming a centre cross and four blocks of four different stamps as T **332** in each corner. The four-stamp design incorporates different subjects, which together form a composite marine picture. (*Price for three sheets un* £4.)

333 Dr. Tomas Romay   **334** Map of Latin America
                             and Part of Declaration

1964 (21 Dec). *Birth Bicentenary of Dr. Tomas Romay (scientist). T* **333** *and similar designs inscr* "TOMAS ROMAY". Litho. W **324** *(sideways on* 3 *c. and* 10 *c.).* P 10.
1187   1 c. black and bistre   5   5
1188   2 c. blackish sepia and orange-brown   5   5
1189   3 c. red-brown and pale bistre   . .   5   5
1190   10 c. black and bistre   12   5
1187/1190   *Set of* 4   25   12
   Designs: *Vert*—2 c. First vaccination against smallpox. *Horiz*—3 c. Dr. Romay and extract from his treatise on the vaccine; 10 c. Dr. Romay's statue.

1964 (23 Dec). *2nd Declaration of Havana. T **334** and similar design. Multicoloured. Litho. W **324**. P 10.*
1191   3 c. Type **334** 5   5
1192   13 c. Map of Cuba with native receiving
           revolutionary message 15   10
   The two stamps have the declaration superimposed in tiny print across each horizontal row of five stamps, thus requiring strips of five to show the complete declaration.

335 "Maritime Post" (diorama)

1965 (4 Jan). *Inauguration of Cuban Postal Museum. T **335** and similar horiz design. Multicoloured. Litho. W **324** (sideways). P 10.*
1193   13 c. Type **335** 20   10
1194   30 c. "Insurgent Post" (diorama) .. 35   15
MS1195   127×76 mm. As Nos. 1193/4 but
       with blue instead of yellow frames. Imperf   75   75

336 Schooner, *Goleta*

1965 (1 Mar). *Cuban Fishing Fleet. T **336** and similar horiz designs showing fishing craft. Multicoloured. Litho. W **324** (sideways). P 10.*
1196   1 c. Type **336** 5   5
1197   2 c. Omicron 5   5
1198   3 c. Victoria 5   5
1199   9 c. Cardenas 8   5
1200   10 c. Sigma 10   5
1201   13 c. Lambda 20   10
1196/1201   Set of 6 45   25

337 Lydia Doce

338 José Antonio Echeverria
University City

1965 (8 Mar). *International Women's Day. T **337** and similar vert design. Multicoloured. Litho. W **324**. P 11×10.*
1202   3 c. Type **337** 5   5
1203   13 c. Clara Zetkin 15   10

1965 (31 Mar). *"Technical Revolution". T **338** and similar horiz design inscr "REVOLUCION TECNICA". Litho. W **324** (sideways). P 10.*
1204   3 c. black, brown and Venetian red .. 5   5
1205   13 c. black, yellow, violet and blue .. 12   8
Design:—13 c. Scientific symbols.

339 Leonov

340 "Figure" (after E. Rodriguez)

1965 (2 Apr). *Space Flight of "Voskhod 2". T **339** and similar horiz design. Litho. W **324** (sideways). P 10.*
1206   30 c. brown and blue 25   12
1207   50 c. deep blue and magenta 40   20
   Design:—50 c. Beliaiev, Leonov and "Voskhod 2".

1965 (12 Apr). *National Museum Treasures. T **340** and similar multicoloured deisgns. Litho. W **324** (sideways). P 10.*
1208   2 c. Type **340** (27×42 mm) .. 5   5
1209   3 c. "Landscape with sunflowers" (V.
           Manuel) (31×42 mm) 8   5
1210   10 c. "Abstract" (W. Lam) (42×31 mm) 12   5
1211   13 c. "Children" (E. Ponce) (39×33½
           mm) 15   8
1208/1211   Set of 4 35   15

341 Lincoln Statue,
Washington

342 Sailing Packet and Old
Postmarks (Bicentenary of
Maritime Mail)

1965 (15 Apr). *Death Centenary of Abraham Lincoln. T **341** and similar designs. Litho. W **324**. P 10.*
1212   1 c. deep brown, red-brn, grey & yell   5   5
1213   2 c. ultramarine, blue and light blue ..   5   5
1214   3 c. black, red and blue 5   5
1215   13 c. black, orange and blue 15   8
1212/1215   Set of 4 25   15
Designs: *Horiz*—1 c. Cabin at Hodgenville, Kentucky (Lincoln's birthplace); 2 c. Lincoln Monument, Washington. *Vert*—13 c. Abraham Lincoln.

1965 (24 Apr). *Stamp Day. T **342** and similar horiz design. Litho. W **324** (sideways). P 10.*
1216   3 c. bistre-brown and orange-red .. 5   5
1217   13 c. red, black and light blue .. 15   8
Design:—13 c. Cuban 10 c. "Air Train" stamp of 1935 and glider train over Capitol, Havana.

343 Sun and Earth's Magnetic Pole

(Des G. Menendez. Litho)

1965 (10 May). *International Quiet Sun Year.* T **343** *and similar multicoloured designs.* W **324** (*sideways on horiz stamps*). P 10.

1218	1 c. Type **343** ..	..	5	5
1219	2 c. I.Q.S.Y. emblem (*vert*)	..	5	5
1220	3 c. Earth's magnetic fields	..	8	5
1221	6 c. Solar rays..	..	10	5
1222	30 c. Effect of solar rays on various atmospheric layers (*vert*)..		30	15
1223	50 c. Effect of solar rays on satellite orbits	..	50	25
1218/1223	*Set of 6*	..	95	50
MS1224	94×70 mm. No. 1223. Imperf	..	70	70

Nos. 1221/3 are larger, 47×20 mm or 20×47 mm (30 c.).
For miniature sheet containing stamp similar to No. 1223 but inscr "EXHIBICION FILATELICA 'CONQUISTA DEL ESPACIO" at top, see No. **MS**1272.

344 Telecommunications Station

(Des G. Menendez. Litho)

1965 (17 May). *I.T.U. Centenary.* T **344** *and similar multicoloured designs.* W **324** (*sideways on horiz stamps*). P 10.

1225	1 c. Type **344**	..	5	5
1226	2 c. Satellite (*vert*)	..	5	5
1227	3 c. "Telstar" ..	..	8	5
1228	10 c. "Telstar" and receiving station (*vert*)	..	10	5
1229	30 c. I.T.U. emblem	..	30	15
1225/1229	*Set of 5* ..	..	50	30

345 Festival Emblem and Flags

(Des J. R. Radillo. Litho)

1965 (10 June). *World Youth and Students Festival.* T **345** *and similar horiz design inscr with "IX" symbol. Multicoloured.* W **324** (*sideways*). P 10.

1230	13 c. Type **345**	..	12	8
1231	30 c. Soldiers of three races and flags	30	15

346 M. Perez (pioneer balloonist), Balloon and Satellite

347 Rose (Europe)

(Des J. R. Radillo. Litho)

1965 (25 June). *Matias Perez Commemoration.* T **346** *and similar horiz design.* W **324**. P 10.

1232	3 c. black and rose	..	8	5
1233	13 c. black and ultramarine	..	15	8

Design:—13 c. As T **346**, but with rocket in place of satellite.

(Des R. Cordero. Litho)

1965 (20 July). *Flowers of the World.* T **347** *and similar vert designs. Multicoloured.* W **324**. P 10.

1234	1 c. Type **347** ..		5	5
1235	2 c. Chrysanthemum (Asia)	..	5	5
1236	3 c. Strelitzia (Africa) ..	..	5	5
1237	4 c. Dahlia (N. America)	..	8	5
1238	5 c. Orchid (S. America)	..	8	5
1239	13 c. *Grevillea banksii* (Oceania)	..	15	8
1240	30 c. *Brunfelsia nitida* (Cuba)	..	30	15
1234/1240	*Set of 7* ..	..	70	40

348 Swimming

(Des L. Contreras. Litho)

1965 (25 July). *First National Games.* T **348** *and similar horiz designs.* W **324**. P 10.

1241	1 c. orange, light blue, black and deep grey	..	5	5
1242	2 c. black, red, yellow-orange and deep grey..	..	5	5
1243	3 c. black, red and grey	..	8	5
1244	30 c. black, red and deep grey ..	..	30	20
1241/1244	*Set of 4* ..	..	40	30

Sports:—2 c. Basketball; 3 c. Gymnastics; 30 c. Hurdling.

349 Anti-tank Gun **350** C. J. Finlay

(Des J. R. Radillo. Litho)

1965 (26 July). *Museum of the Revolution.* T **349** *and similar horiz designs. Multicoloured.* W **324**. P 10.

1245	1 c. Type **349** ..	..	5	5
1246	2 c. Tank ..	..	5	5
1247	3 c. Bazooka ..	..	8	5
1248	10 c. Rebel uniform	..	12	5
1249	13 c. Launch *Granma* and compass	..	15	8
1245/1249	*Set of 5* ..	..	40	20

(Des M. Rivadulla. Litho)

1965 (20 Aug). *50th Death Anniv of Carlos J. Finlay* (*malaria researcher*). T **350** *and similar designs.* W **324**. P 10.

1250	1 c. black, blue-green and light blue ..		5	5
1251	2 c. brown, yellow-ochre and black ..		5	5
1252	3 c. chestnut and black	..	5	5
1253	7 c. black and slate-lilac	..	10	5
1254	9 c. bronze-green and black	..	12	5
1255	10 c. black and new blue	..	10	8
1256	13 c. multicoloured	..	15	8
1250/1256	*Set of 7* ..	..	55	35

Designs: *Horiz*—1 c. Finlay's signature. *Vert*—2 c. Mosquito; 7 c. Finlay's microscope; 9 c. Dr. C. Delgado; 10 c. Finlay's monument; 13 c. Finlay demonstrating his theories, after painting by Valderrama.

351 *Anetia numidia* (butterfly)

(Des J. Delgado. Litho)

1965 (22 Sept). *Cuban Butterflies. T* **351** *and similar horiz designs. Multicoloured.* P 10.

1257	2 c. Type **351**	..	..	5	5
1258	2 c. Carathis gortynoides	..	..	5	5
1259	2 c. Hymenitis cubana	..	..	5	5
1260	2 c. Eubaphe heros	..	..	5	5
1261	2 c. Dismorphia cubana	..	..	5	5
1262	3 c. Siderone nemesis	..	..	5	5
1263	3 c. Syntomidopsis variegata	..	..	5	5
1264	3 c. Ctenuchidia virgo	..	..	5	5
1265	3 c. Lycorea ceres	..	..	5	5
1266	3 c. Eubaphe disparilis	..	..	5	5
1267	13 c. Anetia cubana	..	..	15	8
1268	13 c. Prepona antimache	..	..	15	8
1269	13 c. Sylepta reginalis	..	..	15	8
1270	13 c. Chlosyne perezi	..	..	15	8
1271	13 c. Anaea clytemnestra	..	..	15	8
1257/1271	Set of 15	..	..	1·00	75

The five designs in each value were issued in sheets of 25 (5×5) arranged *se-tenant* horizontally and vertically.

1965 (10 Oct). *"Conquest of Space" Philatelic Exhibition, Havana. Sheet containing stamp as No. 1223 but inscr "EXHIBICION FILATELICA 'CONQUISTA DEL ESPACIO'".* W **324** (sideways). *No gum. Imperf.*
MS1272   94×65 mm. 50 c. multicoloured   ..   1·00   1·00

CUBA CORREOS

352 20 c. Coin of 1962   **353** Oranges

(Des G. Menendez. Litho)

1965 (13 Oct). *50th Anniv of Cuban Coinage. T* **352** *and similar horiz designs. Multicoloured.* P 10.

1273	1 c. Type **352**	..	..	5	5
1274	2 c. 1 p. coin of 1934	..	..	5	5
1275	3 c. 40 c. coin of 1962	..	..	5	5
1276	8 c. 1 p. coin of 1915	..	..	10	5
1277	10 c. 1 p. coin of 1953	..	..	10	8
1278	13 c. 20 p. coin of 1915	..	..	15	8
1273/1278	Set of 6	..	..	45	30

(Des J. Delgado. Litho)

1965 (15 Nov). *Tropical Fruits. T* **353** *and similar vert designs. Multicoloured.* P 12½.

1279	1 c. Type **353**	..	..	5	5
1280	2 c. Custard apples	..	..	5	5
1281	3 c. Papayas	..	..	5	5
1282	4 c. Bananas	..	..	5	5
1283	10 c. Avocado pears	..	..	10	5
1284	13 c. Pineapples	..	..	15	8
1285	20 c. Guavas	..	..	20	12
1286	50 c. Mameys	..	..	50	20
1279/1286	Set of 8	..	..	1·00	55

354   **355**

(Des J. Delgado. Litho)

1965 (1 Dec). *Christmas. Inscr "NAVIDAD 1965–66". Vert designs showing bird life.* P 12½. (*a*) As *T* **354.**

1287	3 c. multicoloured (T **354**)	..	..	5	5
1288	5 c. multicoloured	..	..	8	5
1289	13 c. multicoloured	..	..	15	8

(*b*) As *T* **355**

1290	3 c. multicoloured	..	..	5	5
1291	5 c. multicoloured	..	..	8	5
1292	13 c. multicoloured	..	..	15	8

Nos. 1287 and 1290, 1288 and 1291, 1289 and 1292 were printed together in three sheets of 25, each comprising four stamps as T **354** plus five *se-tenant* stamp-size labels showing pealing bells, and a star forming a centre cross and four blocks of four different stamps as T **355** in each corner. The four-stamp design incorporates different subjects, which together form a composite picture. (*Price for three sheets un* £4.25.)

356 Hurdling

(Des J. R. Radillo. Litho)

1965 (11 Dec). *Seventh Anniv of International Athletics, Havana. T* **356** *and similar multicoloured designs.* W **324**. P 10.

1293	1 c. Type **356**	..	..	5	5
1294	2 c. Throwing the discus	..	..	5	5
1295	3 c. Putting the shot	..	..	5	5
1296	7 c. Throwing the javelin	..	..	8	5
1297	9 c. High-jumping	..	..	10	5
1298	10 c. Throwing the hammer	..	..	10	5
1299	13 c. Running	..	..	15	8
1293/1299	Set of 7	..	..	50	30

CUBA CORREOS

357 Shark-sucker

(Des J. Delgado. Litho)

1965 (15 Dec). *National Aquarium. T* **357** *and similar horiz designs. Multicoloured.* P 12½.

1300	1 c. Type **357**	..	..	5	5
1301	2 c. Bonito	..	..	5	5
1302	3 c. Sergeant Major	..	..	5	5
1303	4 c. Sailfish	..	..	5	5
1304	5 c. Nassau grouper	..	..	8	5
1305	10 c. Muttonfish	..	..	10	5
1306	13 c. Yellowtail snapper	..	..	15	8
1307	30 c. Atlantic squirrelfish	..	..	30	15
1300/1307	Set of 8	..	..	75	45

358 A. Voisin, Cuban and French Flags

(Des J. R. Radillo. Litho)

1965 (21 Dec). *First Death Anniv of Professor Andre Voisin (scientist). T* **358** *and similar horiz design. W* **324**. *P* 12½.
1308　3 c. multicoloured　..　..　..　5　5
1309　13 c. multicoloured　..　..　..　15　8
　Design:—13 c. Similar to T **358** but with microscope and plant in place of cattle.

362 Guardalabarca Beach

1966 (10 Feb). *Tourism. T* **362** *and similar multicoloured designs. Litho. W* **324**. *P* 12½.
1326　1 c. Type **362**　..　..　..　5　5
1327　2 c. La Gran Piedra (mountain resort)　5　5
1328　3 c. Guama, Las Villas (country scene)　5　5
1329　13 c. Waterfall, Soroa (*vert*)　..　..　15　8
1326/1329　*Set of 4*　..　..　..　25　12

359 "Skoda" Omnibus　　360 Infantry Column

363 Congress Emblem and "Treating Patient" (old engraving)　　364 Afro-Cuban Doll

(Des J. R. Radillo. Litho)

1965 (30 Dec). *Cuban Transport. T* **359** *and similar horiz designs. Multicoloured. W* **324**. *P* 12½.
1310　1 c. Type **359**　..　..　..　5　5
1311　2 c. "Ikarus" omnibus　..　..　5　5
1312　3 c. "Leyland" omnibus　..　..　5　5
1313　4 c. "Tem-4" diesel locomotive　..　5　5
1314　7 c. "BB.69,000" diesel locomotive　..　8　5
1315　10 c. Tugboat *Remolcador*　..　..　10　5
1316　13 c. Freighter *15 de Marzo*　..　..　15　8
1317　20 c. Ilyushin "Il-18" airliner　..　..　25　15
1310/1317　*Set of 8*　..　..　..　70　40

(Des R. M. Pazos. Litho)

1966 (2 Jan). *7th Anniv of Revolution. T* **360** *and similar multicoloured designs inscr* "1966 VII ANIVERSARIO". *W* **324** (*sideways on* 10 *c.,* 13 *c.*). *P* 12½.
1318　1 c. Type **360**　..　..　..　5　5
1319　2 c. Soldier and tank　..　..　5　5
1320　3 c. Sailor and torpedo-boat　..　..　5　5
1321　10 c. MiG-21 jet fighter..　..　..　10　5
1322　13 c. Rocket missile　..　..　..　15　8
1318/1322　*Set of 5*　..　..　..　35　20
　Sizes: As T **360**—2 c., 3 c. *Horiz* (38½ × 23½ *mm*)—10 c., 13 c.

(Des R. Cordero. Litho)

1966 (23 Feb). *Medical and Stomachal Congresses, Havana. T* **363** *and similar horiz design. Multicoloured. W* **324**. *P* 12½.
1330　3 c. Type **363**　..　..　..　5　5
1331　13 c. Congress emblem and children
　　receiving treatment　..　..　15　8

(Des R. Cordero. Litho)

1966 (28 Feb). *Cuban Handicrafts. T* **364** *and similar multicoloured designs. W* **324**. *P* 12½.
1332　1 c. Type **364**　..　..　..　5　5
1333　2 c. Sombreros　..　..　..　5　5
1334　3 c. Vase　..　..　..　5　5
1335　7 c. Gourd lampshades　..　..　8　5
1336　9 c. Rare-wood lampshade　..　..　10　5
1337　10 c. "Horn" shark (*horiz*)　..　..　12　5
1338　13 c. Snail-shell necklace and ear-rings
　　(*horiz*)　..　..　..　15　8
1332/1338　*Set of 7*　..　..　..　50　30

365 "Chelsea College" (after Canaletto)　　366 Cosmonauts in Training

361 Conference Emblem

(Des R. Suarez and F. Valdes. Litho)

1966 (3 Jan). *Tricontinental Conference, Havana. T* **361** *and similar horiz designs. W* **324** (*sideways*). *P* 12½.
1323　2 c. multicoloured　..　..　..　5　5
1324　3 c. multicoloured　..　..　..　5　5
1325　13 c. multicoloured　..　..　..　15　8
　Designs:—3 c., 13 c. As T **361**, but rearranged.

1966 (31 Mar). *National Museum Exhibits. T* **365** *and similar multicoloured designs inscr* "1966". *Litho. W* **324**. *P* 12½.
1339　1 c. Ming Dynasty vase (*vert*)..　..　5　5
1340　2 c. Type **365**　..　..　..　5　5
1341　3 c. "Portrait of a Young Girl" (after
　　Goya) (*vert*)　..　..　..　8　5
1342　13 c. Portrait of Fayum (*vert*)　..　..　20　10
1339/1342　*Set of 4*　..　..　..　35　20

(Des E. C. Formoza. Litho)

1966 (12 Apr). *Fifth Anniv of First Manned Space Flight. T* **366** *and similar multicoloured designs inscr "5e aniversario", etc. W* **324** *(sideways on horiz designs). P* 12½.

1343	1 c. Tsiolkovsky and diagram (*horiz*) ..	5	5
1344	2 c. Type **366**	5	5
1345	3 c. Gagarin, rocket and Globe (*horiz*)	5	5
1346	7 c. Nikolaev and Popovich ..	8	5
1347	9 c. Tereshkova and Bykovsky (*horiz*)	10	5
1348	10 c. Komarov, Feoktistov and Yegorov (*horiz*)	12	5
1349	13 c. Leonov in space (*horiz*)	15	8
1343/1349	*Set of 7*	55	30

367 Tank in Battle

(Des G. Menendez. Litho)

1966 (17 Apr). *Fifth Anniv of Giron Victory. T* **367** *and similar horiz designs inscr "1966/V ANIVERSARIO". etc. W* **324** *(sideways). P* 12½.

1350	2 c. black, green and bistre ..	5	5
1351	3 c. black, grey-blue and light red ..	5	5
1352	9 c. black, light brown and grey ..	10	5
1353	10 c. black, grey-blue & light yell-grn ..	12	5
1354	13 c. black, light brown and blue ..	15	8
1350/1354	*Set of 5*	40	20

Designs:—3 c. Sinking ship; 9 c. Disabled tank and poster hoarding; 10 c. Young soldier; 13 c. Operations map.

368 Interior of Postal Museum (1st anniv)

369 Bouquet and Anvil

(Des C. A. Parada. Litho)

1966 (24 Apr). *Stamp Day. T* **368** *and similar horiz design inscr "DIA DEL SELLO 1966". W* **324** *(sideways). P* 12½.

1355	3 c. grey-green and red	5	5
1356	13 c. brown, black and red	15	8

Design:—13 c. Stamp collector and Cuban 2 c. stamp of 1959.

(Des G. Menendez. Litho)

1966 (1 May). *Labour Day. T* **369** *and similar vert designs inscr "1° DE MAYO 1966". Multicoloured. W* **324**. *P* 12½.

1357	2 c. Type **322**	5	5
1358	3 c. Bouquet and machete	5	5
1359	10 c. Bouquet and hammer	12	5
1360	13 c. Bouquet and parts of globe and cogwheel	15	8
1357/1360	*Set of 4*	30	15

ALBUM LISTS

Write for our latest lists of albums and accessories. These will be sent free on request.

370 W.H.O. Building

371 Athletics

(Des R. Cordero. Litho)

1966 (3 May). *Inauguration of W.H.O. Headquarters, Geneva. T* **370** *and similar horiz designs. W* **324** *(sideways). P* 12½.

1361	2 c. black, grey-green & orge-yellow ..	5	5
1362	3 c. black, light blue and yellow ..	5	5
1363	13 c. black, yellow and light blue ..	15	8

Designs:—W.H.O. building on: 3 c. U.N. flag; 13 c. W.H.O. emblem.

(Des G. Menendez. Litho)

1966 (11 June). *Tenth Central American and Caribbean Games. T* **371** *and similar designs. W* **324**. *P* 12½.

1364	1 c. sepia and yellow-green	5	5
1365	2 c. sepia and orange	5	5
1366	3 c. brown and greenish yellow ..	5	5
1367	7 c. deep blue and magenta	8	5
1368	9 c. black and greenish blue	10	5
1369	10 c. black and light brown	12	5
1370	13 c. deep blue and orange-red ..	15	8
1364/1370	*Set of 7*	55	30

Designs:—*Horiz*—2 c. Rifle-shooting. *Vert*—3 c. Baseball; 7 c. Volleyball; 9 c. Football; 10 c. Boxing; 13 c. Basketball.

372 Makarenko Pedagogical Institute

373 "Agrarian Reform"

(Des J. R. Peña. Litho)

1966 (15 June). *Educational Development. T* **372** *and similar horiz designs. W* **324**. *P* 12½.

1371	1 c. black, green and light green ..	5	5
1372	2 c. black, ochre and light yellow ..	5	5
1373	3 c. black, new blue and pale blue ..	5	5
1374	10 c. black, brown, yellow-brown and light green	12	5
1375	13 c. black, rose-red, new blue and pur	15	8
1371/1375	*Set of 5*	35	20

Designs:—2 c. Alphabetisation Museum; 3 c. Lamp (Fifth anniv of National Alphabetisation Campaign); 10 c. Open-air class; 13 c. "Farmers' and Workers' Education".

(Des G. Menendez. Litho)

1966 (26 July). *AIR. "Conquests of the Revolution". T* **373** *and similar horiz designs. Multicoloured. W* **324**. *P* 12½.

1376	1 c. Type **373**	5	5
1377	2 c. "Industrialisation"	5	5
1378	3 c. "Urban Reform"	5	5
1379	7 c. "Eradication of Unemployment"	8	5
1380	9 c. "Education"	10	5
1381	10 c. "Public Health"	12	5
1382	13 c. Paragraph from Castro's book, *History Will Absolve Me*	15	8
1376/1382	*Set of 7*	55	30

374 Workers with Flag

1966 (12 Aug). *Third Revolutionary Workers' Union Congress, Havana. Litho. W* **324** *(sideways). P* 12½.
1383 **374** 3 c. multicoloured 5 5

375 *Liguus flammellus*   **376** Pigeon and Breeding Pen

1966 (25 Aug). *Cuban Shells. T* **375** *and similar vert designs. Multicoloured. Litho. P* 12½.
1384	1 c. Type **375** ..	..	..	5	5
1385	2 c. *Cypraea zebra*	..	..	5	5
1386	3 c. *Strombus pugilis* ..		..	5	5
1387	7 c. *Aequipecten muscosu*		..	8	5
1388	9 c. *Liguus fasciatus crenatus*		..	10	5
1389	10 c. *Charonia variegata*		..	12	5
1390	13 c. *Liguus fasciatus archeri*	..		15	8
1384/1390	*Set of 7* ..	..	..	55	30

1966 (18 Sept). *Pigeon-breeding. T* **376** *and similar horiz designs. Multicoloured. Litho. W* **324**. *P* 12½.
1391	1 c. Type **376** ..	..	..	5	5
1392	2 c. Pigeon and time-clock	..	..	5	5
1393	3 c. Pigeon and pigeon-loft	..	..	5	5
1394	7 c. Pigeon and breeder tending pigeon-loft		..	8	5
1395	9 c. Pigeon and pigeon-yard ..		..	10	5
1396	10 c. Pigeon and breeder placing message in capsule ..		..	12	5
1397	13 c. Pigeons in flight over map of Cuba (*larger* 44½×28 *mm*)		..	15	8
1391/1397	*Set of 7* ..	..	..	55	30

377 Arms of Pinar del Rio   **378** "Queen" and Mass Games

379 Emblem and Chessboard (Capablanca–Lasker game, 1914)

1966 (10 Oct). *National and Provincial Arms. T* **377** *and similar vert designs. Multicoloured. Litho. W* **324**. *P* 12½.
1398	1 c. Type **377** ..	..	..	5	5
1399	2 c. Arms of Havana ..	..	..	5	5
1400	3 c. Arms of Matanzas	..	..	5	5
1401	4 c. Arms of Las Villas	..	..	5	5
1402	5 c. Arms of Camaguey	..	..	8	5
1403	9 c. Arms of Oriente ..	..	..	10	5
1404	13 c. National Arms (*larger,* 26×44 *mm*)		..	15	8
1398/1404	*Set of 7* ..	..	..	45	30

1966 (18 Oct). *World Chess Olympiad, Havana. T* **378/9** *and similar designs. Litho. W* **324**. *P* 12½ *or imperf (No.* **MS**1411).
1405	1 c. black and blue-green	..	..	5	5
1406	2 c. black and grey-blue	..	..	5	5
1407	3 c. black and orange-red	..	..	5	5
1408	9 c. black and ochre ..	..	..	8	5
1409	10 c. black and magenta	..	..	10	5
1410	13 c. black, new blue & turq-blue	..	..	15	8
1405/1410	*Set of 6* ..	..	..	40	25

MS1411 77×61 mm 30 c. black, blue and yellow 40 40
Designs: *Vert*—1 c. "Pawn"; 2 c. "Rook"; 3 c. "Knight"; 9 c. "Bishop". *Horiz*—10 c. T **378**; 13 c. Olympiad emblem and "King"; 30 c. T **379**.

380 Lenin Hospital

1966 (7 Nov). *Cuban-Soviet Friendship. T* **380** *and similar horiz designs. Multicoloured. Litho. W* **324**. *P* 12½.
1412	2 c. Type **380** ..	..	..	5	5
1413	3 c. World map and oil tanker	..	..	5	5
1414	10 c. Cuban and Soviet technicians	..	..	10	5
1415	13 c. Cuban fruit-pickers and Soviet tractor technicians	..	..	15	8
1412/1415	*Set of 4* ..	..	..	30	20

381 A. Roldan and Music of "Fiesta Negra"   **382** Bacteriological Warfare

1966 (18 Nov). *Song Festival. T* **381** *and similar horiz designs. Litho. W* **324**. *P* 12½.
1416	1 c. brown, black and emerald	..	5	5
1417	2 c. brown, black and magenta	..	5	5
1418	3 c. brown, black and light blue	..	5	5
1419	7 c. brown, black and reddish violet ..		5	5
1420	9 c. brown, black and yellow-orange	..	8	5
1421	10 c. brown, black and red-orange	..	10	5
1422	13 c. brown, black and bright blue	..	15	8
1416/1422	*Set of 7* ..	..	..	45	30

Cuban composers and works:—2 c. E. S. de Fuentes and "Tu" (habanera, Cuban dance); 3 c. M. Simons and "El Manisero"; 7 c. J. Anckermann and "El arroyo que murmura"; 9 c. A. G. Caturla and "Pastoral Lullaby"; 10 c. E. Grenet and "Ay Mama Ines"; 13 c. E. Lecuona and "La Comparsa" (dance).

1966 (23 Nov). *"Genocide in Vietnam". T 382 and similar vert designs each black, red, yellow and blue. Litho.* W 324. P 12½.

1423	2 c. Type 382	..	..	5	5
1424	3 c. Gas warfare	..	..	5	5
1425	13 c. "Conventional" bombing	..	15	8

383 A. L. Fernandez ("Nico") and Beach Landing

1966 (30 Nov). *Tenth Anniv of 1956 Revolutionary Successes. T 383 and similar horiz designs. Portraits in black and light brown. Litho.* W 324. P 12½.

1426	1 c. light brown and bright green	..	5	5
1427	2 c. light brown and purple	..	5	5
1428	3 c. light brown and bright purple	..	5	5
1429	7 c. light brown and blue	..	8	5
1430	9 c. light brown and turquoise	..	10	5
1431	10 c. light brown and yellow-olive	..	12	5
1432	13 c. light brown and orange	..	15	8
1426/1432	*Set of 7*	.. .. ..	55	30

Heroes and scenes:—2 c. C. González and beach landing; 3 c. J. Tey and street fighting; 7 c. T. Aloma and street fighting; 9 c. O. Parellada and street fighting; 10 c. J. M. Marquez and beach landing; 13 c. F. Pais and trial scene.

384 Globe and Recreational Activities	385 Arrow and Telecommunications Symbols

1966 (2 Dec). *International Leisure Time and Recreation Seminar. T 384 and similar horiz designs. Multicoloured. Litho.* W 324. P 12½.

1433	3 c. Type 384	.. .. ..	..	5	5
1434	9 c. Clock, eye and world map	..	10	5
1435	13 c. Seminar poster	.. ..	15	8

1966 (12 Dec). *First National Telecommunications Forum. T 385 and similar vert designs. Multicoloured. Litho.* W 324. P 12½.

1436	3 c. Type 385	..		5	5
1437	10 c. Target and satellites	..	..	10	5
1438	13 c. Shell and satellites (larger, 28½ × 36 mm)	.. ..	12	8
MS1439	161 × 116 mm. Nos. 1436/8. Imperf (sold at 30 c.)	.. .. ..	45	45

386	387

1966 (20 Dec). *Christmas. Inscr "NAVIDAD 1966–67". Vert designs showing orchids. Litho.* P 12½. (a) As T 386.

1440	1 c. multicoloured (T 386)	..	..	5	5
1441	3 c. multicoloured	..	..	5	5
1442	13 c. multicoloured	..	..	12	8

(b) As T 387

1443	1 c. multicoloured	..	..	5	5
1444	3 c. multicoloured	..	..	5	5
1445	13 c. multicoloured	..	..	12	8

Nos. 1440 and 1443, 1441 and 1444, 1442 and 1445 were printed together in three sheets of 24, each comprising four stamps as T 386 plus *se-tenant* stamp-size labels showing pealing bells and four blocks of four different stamps as T 387. The four-stamp design incorporates different subjects, which together form a composite picture. (*Price for three sheets un £3.50.*)

388 Flag and Hands ("1959–Liberation")

1967 (2 Jan). *Eighth Anniv of Revolution. T 388 and similar multicoloured designs. Litho.* P 12½.

1446	3 c. Type 388	..	..	..	5	5
1447	3 c. Clenched fist ("1960—Agrarian Reform")	..	..	5	5
1448	3 c. Hands holding pencil ("1961—Education")	..	5	5
1449	3 c. Hand protecting plant ("1965—Agriculture")	..	5	5
1450	13 c. Head of Rodin's statue, "The Thinker", and arrows ("1962—Planification")	..	12	5
1451	13 c. Hands moving lever ("1963—Organisation")	..	12	5
1452	13 c. Hand holding plant within cogwheel ("1964—Economy")	..	12	5
1453	13 c. Hand holding rifle-butt, and part of Globe ("1966—Solidarity")	..	12	5
1446/1453	*Set of 8*	.. ..	60	30

Nos. 1450/3 are vertical.

Nos. 1446/9 and 1450/3 were issued respectively together se-tenant in rows of four (vert, 3 c., horiz, 13 c.) in the sheets.

389 "Spring" (after J. Arche)

1967 (27 Feb). *Paintings from the National Museum (1st series). T 389 and similar multicoloured designs. Litho.* P 12½.

1454	1 c. "Coffee-pot" (A. A. Leon) (vert)	..	5	5
1455	2 c. "Peasants" (E. Abela) (vert)	..	5	5
1456	3 c. Type 389	..	..	10	5
1457	13 c. "Still Life" (Amelia Paelez) (vert)	15	5
1458	30 c. "Landscape" (G. Escalante)	..	40	20
1454/1458	*Set of 5*	.. .. ..	70	35

See also Nos. 1648/54, 1785/91, 1871/7, 1900/6 and 2005/11.

390 Menelabo Mora, José A. Echeverria and Attack on Presidential Palace

391 *Homo habilis*

(Des R. Cordero. Litho)

1967 (13 Mar). *National Events of March* 13th 1957. *T* **390** *and similar horiz designs.* W **324**. P 12½.

1459	3 c. yellow-green and black	5	5
1460	13 c. brown and black	12	8
1461	30 c. blue and black	30	15

Designs: (36½ × 24½ *mm*)—13 c. Calixto Sanchez and *Corynthia* landing; 30 c. Dionisio San Roman and Cienfuegos revolt.

1967 (31 Mar). *"Prehistoric Man". T* **391** *and similar vert designs. Multicoloured. Litho.* P 12½.

1462	1 c. Type **391**	5	5
1463	2 c. *Australopithecus*	5	5
1464	3 c. *Pithecanthropus erectus*	5	5
1465	4 c. *Sinathropus pekinensis*	5	5
1466	5 c. Neanderthal man..	8	5
1467	13 c. Cro-Magnon man carving ivory tusk	15	8
1468	20 c. Cro-Magnon man painting on wall of cave ..	25	15
1462/1468	*Set of 7*	60	35

392 Victoria

1967 (24 Apr). *Stamp Day. T* **392** *and similar horiz designs showing carriages. Multicoloured. Litho.* P 12½.

1469	3 c. Type **392**	5	5
1470	9 c. Volanta	8	5
1471	13 c. Quitrin	12	8

393 Cuban Pavilion

394 *Eugenia malaccencis*

(Des G. Menendez. Litho)

1967 (28 Apr). *"EXPO 67" World Fair, Montreal. T* **393** *and similar horiz designs.* P 12½.

1472	1 c. multicoloured	5	5
1473	2 c. multicoloured	5	5
1474	3 c. multicoloured	5	5
1475	13 c. multicoloured	12	8
1476	20 c. multicoloured	20	12
1472/1476	*Set of 5*	40	25

Designs:—2 c. Bathysphere, satellite and met. balloon ("Man as Explorer"); 3 c. Ancient rock-drawing and tablet ("Man as Creator"); 13 c. Tractor, ear of wheat and electronic console ("Man as Producer"); 20 c. Olympic athletes ("Man in the Community").

(Des J. Delgado. Litho)

1967 (30 May). *150th Anniv of Cuban Botanical Gardens. T* **394** *and similar vert designs. Multicoloured.* P 12½.

1477	1 c. Type **394**	5	5
1478	2 c. *Jacaranda filicifolia*	5	5
1479	3 c. *Coroupita guianensis*	5	5
1480	4 c. *Spathodea campanulata*	5	5
1481	5 c. *Cassia fistula*	5	5
1482	13 c. *Plumieria alba*	12	8
1483	20 c. *Erythrina poeppigiana*	20	12
1477/1483	*Set of 7*	50	35

395 "Giselle"

397 L. A. Turcios Lima, Map and OLAS Emblem

396 Baseball

1967 (15 June). *International Ballet Festival, Havana. T* **395** *and similar vert designs. Multicoloured. Litho.* P 12½.

1484	1 c. Type **395**	5	5
1485	2 c. "Swan Lake"	5	5
1486	3 c. "Don Quixote"	5	5
1487	4 c. "Calaucan"	5	5
1488	13 c. "Swan Lake" (*different*)	12	8
1489	20 c. "Nutcracker"	20	12
1484/1489	*Set of 6*	45	30

(Des H. Echeverria. Litho)

1967 (22 July). *Pan-American Games, Winnipeg. T* **396** *and similar multicoloured designs.* P 12½.

1490	1 c. Type **396**	5	5
1491	2 c. Swimming	5	5
1492	3 c. Basketball (*vert*)	5	5
1493	4 c. Gymnastics (*vert*)	5	5
1494	5 c. Water-polo (*vert*)	5	5
1495	13 c. Weight-lifting	12	8
1496	20 c. Throwing the javelin	20	12
1490/1496	*Set of 7*	50	35

(Des G. Menendez. Litho)

1967 (28 July). *First Conference of Latin-American Solidarity Organisation (OLAS), Havana. T **397** and similar vert designs. W **324**. P 12½.*

1497	13 c. black, red and blue	..	..	15	8
1498	13 c. black, red and yellow-brown	..	15	8
1499	13 c. black, red and lilac	..	..	15	8
1500	13 c. black, red and light emerald	..	15	8
1497/1500	*Set of 4*	..	..	55	25

Designs:—No. 1497, T **397**; 1498, Fabricio Ojidia; 1499, L. de La Puente Uceda; 1500, Camilo Torres. Martyrs of Guatemala, Venezuela, Peru and Colombia respectively, Each with map and OLAS emblem

399 Octopus 400 "Sputnik 1"

(Des J. Delgado. Litho)

1967 (5 Sept). *World Underwater Fishing Championships. T **399** and similar horiz designs. Multicoloured. P 12½.*

1527	1 c. Green Moray eel ..	..	..	5	5
1528	2 c. Type **399** ..		..	5	5
1529	3 c. Great barracuda ..	..	..	5	5
1530	4 c. Bull shark ..		..	5	5
1531	5 c. Spotted Jewfish ..	..	..	8	5
1532	13 c. Ray ..	..	..	12	8
1533	20 c. Green turtle ..	..	..	20	10
1527/1533	*Set of 7* ..	..	..	55	35

398 "Portrait of Sonny Rollins" (Alan Davie)

1967 (29 July–Oct). *"Contemporary Art" Havana Exhibition from the Paris "Salon de Mayo". T **398** and various other designs showing modern paintings. Sizes given in millimetres. Multicoloured. Litho. P 12½.*

1501	1 c. Type **398** ..	..	..	5	5
1502	1 c. "Docena de Selenides" (Labisse) (39×41)	..	..	5	5
1503	1 c. "Noche de la Bebedora" (Hundertwasser) (53×41)	..	..	5	5
1504	1 c. "Figura" (Mariano) (48×41)	..		5	5
1505	1 c. "La Toussainte" (W. Lam) (45×41)	..	..	5	5
1506	2 c. "Gran Negro y Marron Agrietado" (Tapies) (37×54) ..	..		5	5
1507	2 c. "Banistas" (Singier) (37×54)	..		5	5
1508	2 c. "Torso de Musa" (Arp) (37×46) .	..		5	5
1509	2 c. "Figura" (M. W. Svanberg) (37×54)	..	..	5	5
1510	2 c. "El Informe Oppenheimer" (Erro) (37×41) ..	..	..	5	5
1511	3 c. "Donde Nacen los Cardenales" (Max Ernst) (37×52)	..	..	5	5
1512	3 c. "Paisaje de la Habana" (Portocarrero) (37×41)	..	..	5	5
1513	3 c. "EG 12" (Vasarely) (37×42)	..		5	5
1514	3 c. "Frisco" (Calder) (37×50)	..		5	5
1515	3 c. "El Hombre de la Pipa" (Picasso) (37×52)	..	..	5	5
1516	4 c. "Composicion Abstracta" (Poliakoff) (36×50)	..	..	8	5
1517	4 c. "Pintura" (Bram van Velde) (36×68)	..	..	8	5
1518	4 c. "Sembrador de Incendios" (detail, Matta) (36×47)	..	..	8	5
1519	4 c. "El Arte de Vivir" (Magritte) (36×50)	..	..	8	5
1520	4 c. "Poema" (Miro) (36×56) ..	..		8	5
1521	13 c. "Primpstempstigre" (Messagier) (50×33)	..	..	15	8
1522	13 c. "Pintura" (Vieira da Silva) (50×36)	..	..	15	8
1523	13 c. "Cobra Vivo" (Alechinsky) (50×35)	..	..	15	8
1524	13 c. "Stalingrad" (detail, Jorn) (50×46)	..	..	15	8
1525	30 c. "Los Hombres de Guerra" (Pignon) (55×32)	..	..	30	20
1501/1525	*Set of 25* ..	..	..	1·75	1·25
MS1526	128×90 mm 50 c. "Clausura" (mural representing "Salon de Mayo" pictures). Imperf (7.10) ..	..		60	45

The stamps in each denomination were issued together vert or horiz *se-tenant* in sheets of 20.

(Des C. Echenaguzia. Litho)

1967 (4 Oct). *Soviet Space Achievements. T **400** and similar vert designs. Multicoloured. W **324** (sideways). P 12½.*

1534	1 c. Type **400** ..	..	..	5	5
1535	2 c. "Lunik 3" ..	..	..	5	5
1536	3 c. "Venusik"	..	..	5	5
1537	4 c. "Cosmos"	..	..	5	5
1538	5 c. "Mars 1" ..	..	..	8	5
1539	9 c. "Electron 1, 2" ..	..	..	10	5
1540	10 c. "Luna 9" ..	..	..	12	5
1541	13 c. "Luna 10" ..	..	..	15	5
1534/1541	*Set of 8* ..	..	..	60	30
MS1542	164×132 mm. Nos. 1534/41. Imperf			50	60

401 "Storming the Winter Palace" (from painting by Sokolov, Skalia and Miasnikova)

1967 (7 Nov). *50th Anniv of October Revolution. T **401** and similar designs showing paintings. Sizes given in millimetres. Multicoloured. Litho. P 12½.*

1543	1 c. Type **401** ..	..	..	5	5
1544	2 c. "Lenin addressing Congress" (Serov) (48×36) ..	..		5	5
1545	3 c. "Lenin in the year 1919" (Nalbandian) (35×37)	..	..	5	5
1546	4 c. "Lenin explaining the Goerlo Map" (Schmatko) (48×36)	..		5	5
1547	5 c. "Dawn of the Five-Year Plan" (construction work, Romas) (50×36)	..		8	5
1548	13 c. "Kusnetzkroi Steel Furnace No. 1" (Kotov) (36×51) ..	..		15	8
1549	30 c. "Victory Jubilation" (rebels in the Palace, Krivonogov) (50×36)	..		35	20
1543/1549	*Set of 7* ..	..	..	70	40

HAVE YOU READ THE NOTES AT THE BEGINNING OF THIS CATALOGUE?

These often provide answers to the enquiries we receive.

402 Royal Force Castle, Havana

(Des F. Román. Litho)

1967 (22 Nov). *Historic Cuban Buildings. T **402** and similar multicoloured designs. Sizes given in millimetres. W **324** (sideways on 2 c.).*

1550	1 c. Type **402** ..	..	..	5	5
1551	2 c. Iznaga Tower, Trinidad (26½ × 47½)		5	5
1552	3 c. Castle of Our Lady of the Angels, Cienfuegos (41½ × 29) ..	..	5	5
1553	4 c. Church of St. Francis of Paula, Havana (41½ × 29) ..	..	..	5	5
1554	13 c. Convent of St. Francis, Havana		12	8
1555	30 c. Morro Castle, Santiago de Cuba (43 × 13) ..	..	..	25	15
1550/1555	*Set of 6* ..	..	..	..	50	35

403 Ostrich   **404** Golden Pheasant

(Des J. Delgado. Litho)

1967 (20 Dec). *Christmas. Inscr "NAVIDAD 1967–68". Vert designs showing birds of Havana Zoo. W **324** (sideways). P 12½. (a) As T **403**.*

1556	1 c. multicoloured (T **403**)	..	..	5	5
1557	3 c. multicoloured	..	..	5	5
1558	13 c. multicoloured	..	..	12	8

*(b) As T **404***

1559	1 c. multicoloured	..	..	5	5
1560	3 c. multicoloured	..	..	5	5
1561	13 c. multicoloured	..	..	12	8

Nos. 1556 and 1559, 1557 and 1560, 1558 and 1561 were printed together in three sheets of 24, each comprising four stamps as T **403** plus *se-tenant* stamp-size labels showing pealing bells and four blocks of four different stamps as T **404**. The four-stamp design incorporates different bird subjects, which together form a composite picture. (*Price for three sheets un.* £3.50.)

405 "Che" Guevara

1968 (3 Jan). *Ernesto "Che" Guevara Commemoration. Litho. W **324**. P 12½.*
1562	**405**	13 c. black and red ..	..	..	20	8

406 Man and Tree ("Problems of Artistic Creation, Scientific and Technical Work")

407 Canaries

1968 (4 Jan). *Cultural Congress, Havana. T **406** and similar multicoloured designs. Litho. W **324** (sideways on vert designs). P 12½.*

1563	3 c. Chainbreaker cradling flame ("Culture and Independence") ..	5	5
1564	3 c. Hand with spanner and rifle ("Integral Formation of Man") ..	5	5
1565	13 c. Demographic emblems ("Intellectual Responsibility") ..	12	5
1566	13 c. Hand with communications emblems ("Culture and Mass-Communications Media") ..	12	5
1567	30 c. Type **406** ..	25	15
1563/1567	*Set of 5* ..	55	30

The 3 and 13 c. values are all vertical designs.

(Des R. Cordero. Litho)

1968 (13 Apr). *Canary-breeding. T **407** and similar vert. designs. Multicoloured. W **324** (sideways). P 12½.*

1568	1 c. multicoloured	..	..	5	5
1569	2 c. multicoloured	..	..	5	5
1570	3 c. multicoloured	..	..	5	5
1571	4 c. multicoloured	..	..	5	5
1572	5 c. multicoloured	..	..	5	5
1573	13 c. multicoloured	..	..	12	5
1574	20 c. multicoloured	..	..	20	12
1568/1574	*Set of 7* ..	..	50	30

Designs:—Canaries and breeding cycle—mating, eggs, incubation and rearing young.

408 "The Village Postman" (after J. Harris)

409 Nurse tending Child ("Anti-Polio Campaign")

1968 (24 Apr). *Stamp Day. T **408** and similar vert design. Multicoloured. Litho. P 12½.*
1575	13 c. Type **408** ..	..	15	5
1576	30 c. "The Philatelist" (after G. Sciltian)	30	15

(Des H. Echeverria. Litho)

1968 (10 May). *20th Anniv of World Health Organisation. T **409** and similar horiz design. W **324**. P 12½.*
1577	13 c. black, red and light yellow-olive ..	10	5
1578	30 c. black, turquoise-blue & lt yell-ol ..	25	12

Design:—30 c. Two doctors ("Hospital Services").

ALBUM LISTS

Write for our latest lists of albums and accessories.

These will be sent free on request.

410 "Children"

411 "Four Winds" Aircraft and Route-map

(Des G. Menendez. Litho)

1968 (1 June). *International Children's Day.* W **324**. P 12½.
1579 **410** 3 c. multicoloured 5 5

(Des A. B. Sainz. Litho)

1968 (20 June). *35th Anniv of Seville–Camaguey Flight by Barberan and Collar. T* **411** *and similar horiz design. Multicoloured.* W **324**. P 12½.
1580 13 c. Type **411** 10 5
1581 30 c. Captain M. Barberan and Lieut. J.
Collar 25 12

412 "Canned Fish"

(Des R. Cordero. Litho)

1968 (29 June). *Cuban Food Products. T* **412** *and similar multicoloured designs.* W **324**. P 12½.
1582 1 c. Type **412** 5 5
1583 2 c. "Milk Products" 5 5
1584 3 c. "Poultry and Eggs" 5 5
1585 13 c. "Cuban Rum" 12 5
1586 20 c. "Canned Shell-fish" 20 12
1582/1586 *Set of* 5 .. .. 40 20

413 Siboney Farmhouse

414 Committee Members and Emblem

(Des G. Menendez. Litho)

1968 (26 July). *15th Anniv of Attack on Moncado Fortress. T* **413** *and similar horiz designs. Multicoloured.* W **324**. P 12½.
1587 3 c. Type **413** 5 5
1588 13 c. Map of Santiago de Cuba and
assault route 10 5
1589 30 c. Students and school building (on
site of Moncado fortress) .. 25 15

1968 (28 Sept). *Eighth Anniv of Committees for the Defence of the Revolution. Litho.* W **324** (*sideways*). P 12½.
1590 **414** 3 c. multicoloured 5 5

415 "Che" Guevara and Rifleman

1968 (8 Oct). *Guerillas Day. T* **415** *and similar horiz designs. Litho.* W **324**. P 12½.
1591 1 c. black, blue-green and gold .. 5 5
1592 3 c. black, orange-brown and gold .. 5 5
1593 9 c. black, red, orange and gold .. 10 5
1594 10 c. black, olive-green and gold .. 10 5
1595 13 c. black, pink and gold 12 5
1591/1595 *Set of* 5 .. .. .. 35 20
Designs: "Che" Guevara and—3 c. Machinegunners; 9 c. Riflemen; 10 c. Soldiers cheering; 13 c. Map of Caribbean and South America.

416 C. M. de Cespedes and Broken Wheel

(Des R. G. Parra. Litho)

1968 (10 Oct). *Centenary of Cuban War of Independence. T* **416** *and similar horiz designs. Multicoloured.* P 12½.
1596 1 c. Type **416** 5 5
1597 1 c. E. Betances and horsemen .. 5 5
1598 1 c. I. Agramonte and monument .. 5 5
1599 1 c. A. Maceo and "The Protest" .. 5 5
1600 1 c. J. Marti and patriots 5 5
1601 3 c. M. Gómez and "Invasion" .. 5 5
1602 3 c. J. A. Mella and declaration .. 5 5
1603 3 c. A. Guiteras and monument .. 5 5
1604 3 c. A. Santamaria and riflemen .. 5 5
1605 3 c. F. Pais and graffiti 5 5
1606 9 c. J. Echeverria and students .. 8 5
1607 13 c. C. Cienfuegos and rebels.. .. 12 5
1608 30 c. "Che" Guevara and Castro
addressing meeting 25 15
1596/1608 *Set of* 13 .. .. .. 65 50
Nos. 1596/1600 and 1601/5 were respectively issued together in *se-tenant* strips of five within the sheet.

417 "The Burning of Bayamo" (J. E. Hernandez Giro)

1968 (12 Oct). *National Philatelic Exhibition, Bayamo–Manzanillo. Sheet 137 × 84 mm. Litho. Imperf.*
MS1609 **417** 50 c. multicoloured 60 60

418 Parade of Athletes, Olympic Flag and Flame

(Des C. Echenaguzia. Litho)

1968 (21 Oct). *Olympic Games, Mexico. T* **418** *and similar multicoloured designs. P* 12½.
1610	1 c. Type **418** ..	..	5	5
1611	2 c. Basketball (*vert*) ..	..	5	5
1612	3 c. Throwing the hammer (*vert*)		5	5
1613	4 c. Boxing ..	..	5	5
1614	5 c. Water-polo	..	5	5
1615	13 c. Pistol-shooting ..		12	5
1616	30 c. Calendar-stone (*vert*)		25	15
1610/1616	Set of 7 ..	..	55	35

MS1617 125 × 84 mm 50 c. Runners and flags. Imperf 50 50
The 30 c. and 50 c. are larger, 32½ × 50 mm or 50 × 30 mm.

419 Aerial Crop-spraying

1968 (2 Dec). *Civil Activities of Cuban Armed Forces. T* **419** *and similar horiz designs. Litho. Multicoloured. W* **324**. *P* 12½.
1618	3 c. Type **419** ..	..	5	5
1619	9 c. "Che Guevara" Brigade ..		8	5
1620	10 c. Road-building Brigade ..		10	5
1621	13 c. Agricultural Brigade ..		12	5
1618/1621	Set of 4 ..	..	30	15

420 "Manrique de Lara's Family" (J.-B. Vermay)

421 Cuban Flag and Rifles

1968 (30 Dec). *150th Anniv of San Alejandro Painting School. T* **420** *and similar multicoloured designs. Sizes given in millimetres. Litho. P* 12½.
1622	1 c. Type **420** ..	..	5	5
1623	2 c. "Seascape" (L. Romanach) (48 × 37) ..		5	5
1624	3 c. "Wild Cane" (A. Rodriguez) (40 × 48) ..		5	5
1625	4 c. "Self-portrait" (M. Melero) (40 × 50) ..		5	5
1626	5 c. "The Lottery List" (J. J. Tejada) (48 × 37) ..		5	5
1627	13 c. "Portrait of Nina" (A. Menocal) (40 × 50) ..		12	5
1628	30 c. "Landscape" (E. S. Chartrand) (54 × 37) ..		30	15
1622/1628	Set of 7 ..	..	60	35

MS1629 63 × 97 mm. 50 c. "The Siesta" (G. Gollazo) (48 × 37) 60 60

(Des F. Román. Litho)

1969 (3 Jan). *Tenth Anniv of "The Triumph of the Rebellion". W* **324** (*sideways*). *P* 12½.
1630 **421** 13 c. multicoloured .. 12 5

422 Gutierrez and Sanchez

423 Mariana Grajales, Rose and Statue

(Des G. Menendez. Litho)

1969 (6 Feb). *Centenary of the Villaclarenos Patriots' Rebellion. W* **324**. *P* 12½.
1631 **422** 3 c. multicoloured .. 5 5

(Des F. Román. Litho)

1969 (8 Mar). *Cuban Women's Day. W* **324** (*sideways*). *P* 12½.
1632 **423** 3 c. multicoloured 5 5

424 Cuban Pioneers

(Des G. Menendez. Litho)

1969 (4 Apr). *Cuban Pioneers and Young Communist Unions. T* **424** *and similar horiz design. Multicoloured. W* **324**. *P* 12½.
1633	3 c. Type **424** ..	..	5	5
1634	13 c. Young Communists	..	12	5

425 Guaimaro Assembly

(Des R. G. Parra. Litho)

1969 (10 Apr). *Centenary of Guaimoro Assembly. Litho. W* **324**. *P* 12½.
1635 **425** 3 c. bistre-brown and sepia .. 5 5

426 "The Postman" (J. C. Cazin)

1969 (24 Apr). *Stamp Day.* T **426** *and similar painting. Multicoloured. Litho.* P 12½.
1636 13 c. Type **426** 15 5
1637 30 c. "Portrait of a Young Man" (G. Romney) (36×43 *mm*) 30 15

427 Agrarian Law, Headquarters, Eviction of Family and Tractor

(Des R. G. Parra. Litho)

1969 (17 May). 10th *Anniv of Agrarian Reform.* W **324**. P 12½.
1638 **427** 13 c. multicoloured 12 5

428 Hermit Crab   429 Factory and Peasants

1969 (20 May). *Crustaceans.* T **428** *and similar horiz designs. Multicoloured. Litho.* P 12½.
1639 1 c. Type **428** 5 5
1640 2 c. Spiny shrimp 5 5
1641 3 c. Spiny lobster 5 5
1642 4 c. Blue crab 5 5
1643 5 c. Land crab 5 5
1644 13 c. Freshwater prawn 12 5
1645 30 c. Pebble crab 25 15
1639/1645 Set of 7 .. .. .. 55 35

(Des G. Menendez. Litho)

1969 (6 June). *50th Anniv of International Labour Organization.* T **429** *and similar vert design. Multicoloured.* W **324** (*sideways*). P 12½.
1646 3 c. Type **429** 5 5
1647 13 c. Worker breaking chain .. 12 5

430 "Flowers" (R. Milian)

1969 (15 June). *Paintings from the National Museum (2nd series).* T **430** *and similar multicoloured designs. Litho.* P 12½.
1648 1 c. Type **430** 5 5
1649 2 c. "The Annunciation" (A. Eiriz) (*horiz*) 5 5
1650 3 c. "Factory" (M. Pogolotti) .. 5 5
1651 4 c. "Territorial Waters" (L. M. Pedro) 5 5
1652 5 c. "Miss Sarah Gale" (J. Hoppner) .. 5 5
1653 13 c. "Two Women in Mantillas" (I. Zuloaga) 12 5
1654 30 c. "Virgin and Child" (F. de Zurbaran) 25 15
1648/1654 Set of 7 .. .. .. 55 35
Sizes: As T **430**—1, 2, 3 c.; 40×44 *mm*—4 c.; 40×46 *mm*—5, 30 c.; 38×42 *mm*—13 c.

431 Television Cameras and Emblem

(Des R. Quintana. Litho)

1969 (5 July). *Cuban Radiodiffusion Institute.* T **431** *and similar horiz designs. Multicoloured.* W **324**. P 12½.
1655 3 c. Type **431** 5 5
1656 13 c. Broadcasting Tower and map .. 12 5
1657 1 p. Diagram of T.V. set 85 30

432 Spotted Cardinal   433 "Cuban Film Library"

(Des A. A. Fernandez. Litho)

1969 (20 July). *Cuban Pisciculture.* T **432** *and similar multicoloured designs, showing fish.* P 12½.
1658 1 c. Type **432** 5 5
1659 2 c. Spanish hogfish 5 5
1660 3 c. Yellowtail damsel fish .. 5 5
1661 4 c. Royal gramma 5 5
1662 5 c. Blue chromis 5 5
1663 13 c. Squirrel fish 12 5
1664 30 c. Portuguese man-o'-war fish (*vert*) 25 10
1658/1664 Set of 7 .. .. .. 50 30

Cuba 1969

1969 (5 Aug). *10th Anniv of Cuban Cinema Industry.* T 433 *and similar vert designs. Multicoloured. Litho.* W 324 *(sideways).* P 12½.

1665	1 c. Type 433 ..				5	5
1666	3 c. "Documentaries"..		..	..	5	5
1667	13 c. "Cartoons"	..	..	..	12	5
1668	30 c. "Full-length Features"		..	..	25	15
1665/1668	Set of 4 ..	..	..	..	40	20

434 "Napoleon in Milan" (A. Appiani (the Elder))

1969 (20 Aug). *Paintings from the Napoleonic Museum, Havana.* T 434 *and similar multicoloured designs. Litho.* P 12½.

1669	1 c. Type 434 ..	..	..	5	5
1670	2 c. "Hortense de Beauharnais" (F. Gerard) ..			5	5
1671	3 c. "Napoleon as First Consul" (J. B. Regnault) ..			5	5
1672	4 c. "Elisa Bonaparte" (R. Lefevre) ..			5	5
1673	5 c. "Napoleon planning the Coronation" (J. G. Vibert) (*horiz*) ..			5	5
1674	13 c. "Corporal of Cuirassiers" (J. Meissonier) ..			12	5
1675	30 c. "Napoleon Bonaparte" (R. Lefevre) ..	..	..	25	12
1669/1675	Set of 7 ..	..	..	55	30

Sizes: As T 434—1, 3 c.; 42½ × 55 mm—2 c.; 44 × 63 mm—4, 13 c.; 45½ × 60 mm—30 c.; 64 × 47 mm—5 c.

435 Baseball Players

(Des R. G. Parra. Litho)

1969 (11 Sept). *Cuba's Victory in World Amateur Baseball Championships, Dominican Republic.* P 12½.

1676	435	13 c. multicoloured	..	12	5

No. 1676 was issued in sheets vertically *se-tenant* with a stamp-sized label showing the Championships' result.

436 Von Humboldt, Book and Surinam Eel

(Des R. M. Parra. Litho)

1969 (14 Sept). *Birth Bicentenary of Alexander von Humboldt (naturalist).* T 436 *and similar horiz designs, each with portrait and book. Multicoloured.* P 12½.

1677	3 c. Type 436 ..			5	5
1678	13 c. Sleepy monkey ..			15	5
1679	30 c. Condors ..			30	12

1969. *As Nos. 686, 991 and 695, but colours changed. No wmk. Roul.*

1680	180	1 c. new blue	..	..	5	5
1681	–	2 c. yellow-green ..		..	5	5
1682	–	20 c. violet ..	..	..	20	5

437 Ancient Egyptians in Combat

(Des C. Echenaguzia. Litho)

1969 (2 Oct). *World Fencing Championships, Havana.* T 437 *and similar horiz designs. Multicoloured.* P 12½.

1683	1 c. Type 437 ..	..		5	5
1684	2 c. Roman gladiators	..		5	5
1685	3 c. Viking and Norman	..		5	5
1686	4 c. Medieval tournament	..		5	5
1687	5 c. French musketeers	..		5	5
1688	13 c. Japanese samurai	..		12	5
1689	30 c. Mounted Cubans, War of Independence	..		25	12
1683/1689	Set of 7 ..	..	..	55	30
MS1690	66 × 98 mm. 50 c. Modern fencing. Imperf ..	..	..	45	45

438 Militiaman   439 Major Cienfuegos, and Wreath on Sea

(Des R. Quintana. Litho)

1969 (26 Oct). *10th Anniv of National Revolutionary Militia.* W 324 *(sideways).* P 12½.

1691	438	3 c. multicoloured ..	..	..	5	5

(Des R. G. Parra. Litho)

1969 (28 Oct). *10th Death Anniv of Major Camilo Cienfuegos.* W 324 *(sideways).* P 12½.

1692	439	13 c. multicoloured	..	..	12	5

440 Strawberries and Grapes

(Des F. Román. Litho)

1969 (2 Nov). *Agricultural and Livestock Projects.* *T* **440** *and similar multicoloured designs.* *P* 12½.

1693	1 c. Type **440** ..	..	..	5	5
1694	1 c. Onion and asparagus	..	..	5	5
1695	1 c. Rice	..	..	5	5
1696	1 c. Bananas ..	..	..	5	5
1697	3 c. Pineapple (*vert*) ..	..	..	5	5
1698	3 c. Tobacco plant (*vert*)	..	..	5	5
1699	3 c. Citrus fruits (*vert*)..	..	..	5	5
1700	3 c. Coffee (*vert*)	..	..	5	5
1701	3 c. Rabbits (*vert*)	..	..	5	5
1702	10 c. Pigs (*vert*)..	..	..	8	5
1703	13 c. Sugar cane	..	..	12	5
1704	30 c. Cow	..	..	25	10
1693/1704	*Set of 12* ..	..	..	60	35

The 1 c. and 3 c. values were issued in *se-tenant* strips within their respective sheets.

441 Stadium and Map of Cuba (2nd National Games)

(Des R. G. Parra. Litho)

1969 (15 Nov). *Sporting Events of 1969.* *T* **441** *and similar multicoloured designs.* *P* 12½.

1705	1 c. Type **441** ..	..	..	5	5
1706	2 c. Throwing the discus (9th Anniversary Games)		..	5	5
1707	3 c. Running (Barrientos commemoration) (*vert*)		..	5	5
1708	10 c. Basketball (2nd Olympic Trial Games) (*vert*)		..	8	5
1709	13 c. Cycling (6th Cycle Race) (*vert*)		..	12	5
1710	30 c. Chessmen and globe (Capablanca commemoration) (*vert*)		..	25	10
1705/1710	*Set of 6* ..	..	..	50	30

442 *Plumbago capensis*

443 *Petrea volubilis*

(Des A. A. Fernandez. Litho)

1969 (1 Dec). *Christmas. Various vert flower designs as T* **442/3**, *inscr "NAVIDAD 1969/70".* *P* 12½. (*a*) *As Type* **442**.

1711	1 c. multicoloured (T **442**)	..	..	5	5
1712	3 c. multicoloured	..	..	5	5
1713	13 c. multicoloured	..	..	12	5

(*b*) *As Type* **443**

1714	1 c. multicoloured	..	..	5	5
1715	3 c. multicoloured	..	..	5	5
1716	13 c. multicoloured	..	..	12	5

Nos. 1711 and 1714, 1712 and 1715, 1713 and 1716, were printed together in three sheets of 24, each comprising four stamps as Type **442** plus *se-tenant* stamp-size labels showing bells, and four blocks of four different stamps as Type **443**. These blocks incorporate different flower designs, which together form a composite picture. (*Price for three sheets un* £3.50.)

444 River Snake

(Des F. Román. Litho)

1969 (15 Dec). *Fauna of Zapata Swamp.* *T* **444** *and similar multicoloured designs.* *P* 12½.

1717	1 c. Type **444** ..	..	..	5	5
1718	2 c. Banana frog	..	..	5	5
1719	3 c. Manjuari (fish)	..	..	5	5
1720	4 c. Cuban dwarf rat (*vert*)	..		5	5
1721	5 c. Alligator ..	..	..	5	5
1722	13 c. Parrot (*vert*)	..	..	12	5
1723	30 c. Swamp mayito (bird) (*vert*)	..		25	15
1717/1723	*Set of 7* ..	..	..	55	35

445 "Jibacoa Beach" (J. Hernandez)

446 Yamagua

1970 (25 Jan). *Tourist Centres.* *T* **445** *and similar vert designs, showing posters. Multicoloured. Litho.* *W* **324** (*sideways*). *P* 12½.

1724	1 c. Type **445** ..	..	..	5	5
1725	3 c. "Trinidad City" (J. Hernandez)		..	5	5
1726	13 c. "Santiago de Cuba" (A. Alonso) ..			12	5
1727	30 c. "Viñales Valley" (J. Hernandez) ..			25	15
1724/1727	*Set of 4* ..	..	..	40	25

(Des F. Román. Litho)

1970 (10 Feb). *Medicinal Plants.* *T* **446** *and similar vert designs. Multicoloured.* *P* 12½.

1728	1 c. Type **446** ..	..	..	5	5
1729	3 c. Albahaca Morada	..	..	5	5
1730	10 c. Curbana ..	..	..	8	5
1731	13 c. Romerillo ..	..	..	12	5
1732	30 c. Marilope ..	..	..	25	15
1733	50 c. Aguedita ..	..	..	45	20
1728/1733	*Set of 6* ..	..	..	90	45

447 Weightlifting

(Des F. Román. Litho)

1970 (28 Feb). 11th Central American and Caribbean Games, Panama. T **447** and similar horiz designs. Multicoloured. P 12½.

1734	1 c. Type **447**	..	..	5	5
1735	3 c. Boxing	..	..	5	5
1736	10 c. Gymnastics	..	..	8	5
1737	13 c. Athletics ..	..	..	12	5
1738	30 c. Fencing	..	..	25	15
1734/1738	Set of 5	..	..	50	25
MS1739	85×128 mm. 50 c. Baseball.				
Imperf	..	..	..	60	60

448 "Enjoyment of Life"

(Des G. Menendez. Litho)

1970 (15 Mar). "EXPO 70" World Fair, Osaka, Japan. T **448** and similar multicoloured designs. W **324** (sideways on vert designs). P 12½.

1740	1 c. Type **448**	..	..	5	5
1741	2 c. "Uses of Nature" (vert)	..	..	5	5
1742	3 c. "Better Living Standards"	..	5	5	
1743	13 c. "International Co-operation" (vert)	..	..	12	5
1744	30 c. Cuban pavilion	..	..	25	15
1740/1744	Set of 5	..	..	45	30

449 Oval Pictograph, Ambrosio Cave

450 J. D. Blino, Balloon and Spacecraft

(Des R. G. Parra. Litho)

1970 (28 Mar). 30th Anniv of Cuban Spelaeological Society. T **449** and similar designs, showing pictographs. P 12½.

1745	1 c. red, yellow-brown and brown	..	5	5
1746	2 c. black, yellow-brown and brown	..	5	5
1747	3 c. red, yellow-brown and brown	..	5	5
1748	4 c. black, yellow-brown and brown	..	5	5
1749	5 c. red, yellow-brown and brown	..	5	5
1750	13 c. blackish brown, yellow-brown and brown	..	12	5
1751	30 c. red, yellow-brown and brown	..	25	15
1745/1751	Set of 7	..	55	35

Designs: Horiz (42½×32 mm)—2 c. "Snake and Face", Cave 1, Punta del Este; 5 c. "Cross and Circles", Cave 1, Punta del Este; 30 c. "Fish", Cave 2, Punta del Este. Vert (as T **449**)—3 c. "Primitive God", Pichardo Cave; 4 c. "Conical Complex", Ambrosio Cave; 13 c. "Human Face", Garcia Robiou Cave.

(Des R. G. Parra. Litho)

1970 (10 Apr). Cuban Aviation Pioneers. T **450** and similar horiz portrait. Multicoloured. P 12½.

1752	3 c. Type **450** ..	..	5	5
1753	13 c. A. Théodore, balloon and satellite	15	5

451 "Lenin in Kazan" (O. Vishniakov)

1970 (22 Apr). Birth Centenary of Lenin. T **451** and similar horiz designs, showing paintings. Multicoloured. Litho. P 12½.

1754	1 c. Type **451** ..		5	5
1755	2 c. "Lenin's Youth" (V. Prager)		5	5
1756	3 c. "2nd Socialist Party Congress" (Y. Vinogradov)		5	5
1757	4 c. "The First Manifesto" (F. Golubkov)		5	5
1758	5 c. "First Day of Soviet Power" (N. Babasiuk) ..		5	5
1759	13 c. "Lenin in the Smolny Institute" (M. Sokolov)		12	5
1760	30 c. "Autumn at Gorky" (A. Varlamov)		25	15
1754/1760	Set of 7	..	55	35
MS1761	79×112 mm. 50 c. "Lenin at Gorky" (N. Barkakov). Imperf	..	60	60

Nos. 1755/6 and 1759/60 are smaller, 70×34 mm, and the stamp design of **MS**1761 is 45×43 mm.

452 "The Letter" (J. Arche)

1970 (24 Apr). Stamp Day. T **452** and similar vert painting. Multicoloured. Litho. P 12½.

1762	13 c. Type **452** ..	..	12	5
1763	30 c. "Portrait of a Cadet" (anon) (35×49 mm)	..	25	15

453 Da Vinci's Anatomical Drawing, Earth and Moon

(Des R. Quintana. Litho)

1970 (17 May). World Telecommunications Day. W **324**. P 12½.

1764	**453** 30 c. multicoloured	..	..	25	15

454 Vietnamese Fisherman

455 Tobacco Plantation and "Eden" Cigar-band

(Des R. M. Pazos. Litho)

1970 (19 May). *80th Birthday of Ho Chi-Minh (North Vietnamese leader). T 454 and similar vert designs. Multicoloured.* P 12½.

1765	1 c. Type **454** ..	..	..	5	5
1766	3 c. Cultivating rice-fields	..	..	5	5
1767	3 c. Two Vietnamese children		..	5	5
1768	3 c. Children entering air-raid shelter		5	5
1769	3 c. Camouflaged machine-shop	..		5	5
1770	3 c. Rice harvest	..	..	5	5
1771	13 c. Pres. Ho Chi-Minh	..	..	12	5
1765/1771	*Set of 7*	..	..	25	15

Sizes:—Nos. 1766/7, 33 × 44½ mm; Nos. 1768, 1770, 33½ × 46 mm; No. 1769, 35 × 42 mm; No. 1771, 34½ × 39½ mm.

(Des R. G. Parra. Litho)

1970 (5 July). *Cuban Cigar Industry. T 455 and similar vert designs. Multicoloured.* P 12½.

1772	3 c. Type **455** ..	..	..	5	5
1773	13 c. 19th-century cigar factory and "El Mambi" band		12	5
1774	30 c. Packing cigars (19th-century) and "Gran Pena" band		..	25	15

456 Cane-crushing Machinery

(Des G. Menendez. Litho)

1970 (26 July). *"Over 10 Million Tons" Sugar Production Target. T 456 and similar multicoloured designs.* P 12½.

1775	1 c. Type **456** ..	..	..	5	5
1776	2 c. Sowing and crop-spraying	..		5	5
1777	3 c. Cutting sugar-cane	..		5	5
1778	10 c. Ox-cart and diesel locomotive	..		8	5
1779	13 c. Modern cane-cutting machinery		12	5
1780	30 c. Cane-cutters and Globe (*vert*)	..		25	15
1781	1 p. Sugar warehouse	..	..	80	30
1775/1781	*Set of 7*	..	..	1·25	60

457 P. Figueredo and National Anthem (original version)

(Des F. Román. Litho)

1970 (17 Aug). *Death Centenary of Pedro Figueredo (composer of National Anthem). T 457 and similar horiz design, incorporating the same portrait. Multicoloured.* P 12½.

1782	3 c. Type **457** ..	..	..	5	5
1783	20 c. 1898 version of anthem	..	..	15	8

458 Cuban Girl, Flag and Federation Badge

(Des R. G. Parra. Litho)

1970 (23 Aug). *10th Anniv of Cuban Women's Federation.* P 12½.

1784	**458** 3 c. multicoloured ..	..	..	5	5

459 "Peasant Militia" (S. C. Moreno)

1970 (31 Aug). *National Museum Paintings (3rd series). T 459 and similar multicoloured designs. Litho.* P 12½.

1785	1 c. Type **459** ..	..	..	5	5
1786	2 c. "Washerwoman" (A. Fernandez)		5	5
1787	3 c. "Puerta del Sol, Madrid" (L. P. Alcazar)	..	..	5	5
1788	4 c. "Fishermen's Wives" (J. Sorolla) (*square*)	..	..	5	5
1789	5 c. "Portrait of a Lady" (T. de Keyser) (*vert*)	..	..	5	5
1790	13 c. "Mrs. Edward Foster" (Sir Thomas Lawrence) (*vert*)		12	5
1791	30 c. "Tropical Gipsy" (V. M. Garcia) (*vert*)	..	..	25	15
1785/1791	*Set of 7*	..	..	55	35

Sizes:—2 c., 3 c. 46 × 42 mm; 4 c. 41 × 41 mm; 5, 13, 30 c. 39 × 56 mm.

460 Crowd in José Marti Square, Havana

1970 (2 Sept). *10th Anniv of Havana Declaration. Litho.* P 12½.

1792	**460** 3 c. turquoise-blue, lt carmine & blk	5	5

461 C.D.R. Emblem

(Des G. Menendez. Litho)

1970 (28 Sept). *10th Anniv of Committees for the Defence of the Revolution.* P 12½.
1793 **461** 3 c. multicoloured 5 5

462 Laboratory, Emblem and Microscope

(Des G. Menendez. Litho)

1970 (11 Oct). *39th Sugar Technicians Association Conference (A.T.A.C.).* P 12½.
1794 **462** 30 c. multicoloured 25 15

463 Grey-breasted Guineafowl

(Des F. Román. Litho)

1970 (20 Oct). *Wildlife. T 463 and similar horiz designs. Multicoloured.* P 12½.
1795   1 c. Type **463** 5 5
1796   2 c. Whistling tree-duck 5 5
1797   3 c. Ring-necked pheasant 5 5
1798   4 c. Mourning dove 5 5
1799   5 c. Bobwhite quail 5 5
1800 13 c. Wild boar 12 5
1801 30 c. Virginia deer 25 15
1795/1801 *Set of 7* 55 35

464 "Black Magic Parade" (M. Puente)

1970 (5 Nov). *Afro-Cuban Folklore Paintings. T 464 and similar multicoloured designs.* Litho. P 12½.
1802   1 c. Type **464** 5 5
1803   3 c. "Zapateo Hat Dance" (V. P. Landaluze) (*vert*) 5 5
1804 10 c. "Los Hoyos Conga Dance" (D. Ravenet) 8 5
1805 13 c. "Climax of the Rumba" (E. Abela) (*vert*) 12 5
1802/1805 *Set of 4* 25 12
    Sizes:—3 c., 13 c. 37 × 49 mm; 10 c. 45 × 44 mm.

465 Zebra on Road Crossing

(Des F. Román. Litho)

1970 (15 Nov). *Road Safety Week. T 465 and similar horiz design. Multicoloured.* P 12½.
1806   3 c. Type **465** 5 5
1807   9 c. Prudence the Bear on point duty .. 8 5

466 Letter "a" and Abacus

(Des G. Menendez. Litho)

1970 (20 Nov). *International Education Year. T 466 and similar horiz design. Multicoloured.* P 12½.
1808 13 c. Type **466** 12 5
1809 30 c. Microscope and cow 25 15

467 Cuban Oriole   **468** Cuban Pigmy Owl

(Des F. Román. Litho)

1970 (1 Dec). *Christmas. Various vert bird designs as T 467/8 inscr "NAVIDAD 1970/71".* P 12½. (*a*) As Type **467**.
1810   1 c. multicoloured (T **467**) 5 5
1811   3 c. multicoloured 5 5
1812 13 c. multicoloured 12 5

(*b*) As Type **468**
1813   1 c. multicoloured 5 5
1814   3 c. multicoloured 5 5
1815 13 c. multicoloured 12 5
    Nos. 1810 and 1813, 1811 and 1814, 1812 and 1815 are printed together in three sheets of 24, each comprising four stamps as Type **467** plus se-tenant stamp-size labels showing bells, and four blocks of four different stamps as Type **468**. These blocks depict different birds, which together form a composite picture. (*Price for three sheets £3.25 un.*)

469 School Badge and Cadet Colour-party

1970 (2 Dec). *"Camilo Cienfuegos" Military School*. Litho.
P 12½.
1816 **469** 3 c. multicoloured 5 5

470 "Reporter" with Pen

472 Meteorological Class

471 Lockheed "Altair" Aircraft

(Des G. Menendez. Litho)

1971 (4 Jan). *7th International Organization of Journalists Conference, Havana*. P 12½.
1817 **470** 13 c. multicoloured 12 5

(Des R. Quintana. Litho)

1971 (12 Jan). *AIR. 35th Anniv of Camaguey–Seville Flight by Menendez Pelaez*. T **471** and similar horiz design. Multicoloured. P 12½.
1818 13 c. Type **471** 12 5
1819 30 c. Lieut. Menendez Pelaez and map . . 25 15

(Des G. Menendez. Litho)

1971 (16 Feb). *World Meteorological Day*. T **472** and similar multicoloured designs. P 12½.
1820 1 c. Type **472** 5 5
1821 3 c. Hurricane map (*horiz*) 5 5
1822 8 c. Meteorological equipment . . 8 5
1823 30 c. Weather radar systems (*horiz*) . . 25 15
1820/1823 *Set of 4* 35 25
Sizes:—1 c., 8 c., 30 c. As T **472**; 3 c. 40×36 mm.

473 Games Emblem

474 Paris Porcelain, 19th century

(Des R. Quintana. Litho)

1971 (20 Feb). *6th Pan-American Games, Cali, Colombia*. T **473** and similar multicoloured designs. P 12½.
1824 1 c. Type **473** 5 5
1825 2 c. Athletics 5 5
1826 3 c. Rifle-shooting (*horiz*) 5 5
1827 4 c. Gymnastics 5 5
1828 5 c. Boxing 5 5
1829 13 c. Water-polo (*horiz*) 12 5
1830 30 c. Baseball (*horiz*) 25 15
1824/1830 *Set of 7* 55 35

1971 (11 Mar). *Porcelain and Mosaics in Metropolitan Museum, Havana*. T **474** and similar multicoloured designs. Litho. P 12½.
1831 1 c. Type **474** 5 5
1832 3 c. 17th-century Mexican pottery bowl 5 5
1833 10 c. 19th-century Paris porcelain . . 8 5
1834 13 c. "Colosseum" (19th-century Italian mosaic) (*horiz*) . . 12 5
1835 20 c. 17th-century Mexican pottery dish 20 10
1836 30 c. "St. Peter's Square" (19th-cent Italian mosaic) (*horiz*) . . 25 15
1831/1836 *Set of 6* 65 40
Sizes:—1 c., 10 c. As T **474**; 3 c. 46×54 mm; 13 c., 30 c. 50×33 mm; 20 c. 43×49 mm.

475 Mother and Child

476 Cosmonaut in Training

(Des G. Menendez. Litho)

1971 (10 Apr). *10th Anniv of Cuban Infant Centres*. P 12½.
1837 **475** 3 c. multicoloured 5 5

(Des F. Román. Litho)

1971 (12 Apr). *10th Anniv of First Manned Space Flight*. T **476** and similar vert designs. Multicoloured. P 12½.
1838 1 c. Type **476** 5 5
1839 2 c. Speedometer test 5 5
1840 3 c. Medical examination 5 5
1841 4 c. Acceleration tower 5 5
1842 5 c. Pressurisation test 5 5
1843 13 c. Cosmonaut in gravity chamber . . 12 5
1844 30 c. Crew in flight simulator 25 15
1838/1844 *Set of 7* 55 35
MS1845 100×63 mm. 50 c. Yuri Gagarin.
Imperf 60 60

477 Cuban and Burning Ship

(Des G. Menendez. Litho)

1971 (17 Apr). *10th Anniv of Victory at Giron*. W **324**. P 12½.
1846 **477** 13 c. multicoloured 12 5

478 *Windsor Castle* attacked by *Jeune Richard* (1807)

(Des C. Echenaguzia. Litho)

1971 (24 Apr). *Stamp Day. T 478 and similar horiz design. Multicoloured. P 12½.*
1847	13 c. Type **478** ..	..	..	12	5
1848	30 c. Steam-packet *Orinoco*, 1851	..		25	15

479 Transmitter and Hemispheres

(Des R. Penate. Litho)

1971 (1 May). *10th Anniv of Cuban International Broadcasting Services. W 324. P 12½.*
1849	**479**	3 c. multicoloured	..	5	5
1850		50 c. multicoloured	..	50	25

480 *Cattleya skinnerii*

482 Larvae and Pupae

481 Loynaz del Castillo and "Invasion Hymn"

1971 (15 May). *Tropical Orchids (1st series). T 480 and similar vert designs. Multicoloured. Litho. P 12½.*
1851	1 c. Type **480** ..	..	..	5	5
1852	2 c. *Vanda hibrida* ..	..	..	5	5
1853	3 c. *Cypripedium callossum* ..	..	5	5
1854	4 c. *Cypripedium glaucophyllum*	..	5	5
1855	5 c. *Vanda tricolor* ..	..		5	5
1856	13 c. *Cypripedium mowgh* ..	..	12	5
1857	30 c. *Cypripedium solum* ..	..	25	15
1851/1857	*Set of 7* ..	..	..	55	35

See also Nos. 1908/14 and 2012/18.

(Des E. Rivadulla and R. Penate. Litho)

1971 (5 June). *Birth Centenary of Enrique Loynaz del Castillo (composer). W 324. P 12½.*
1858	**481**	3 c. multicoloured	..	5	5

(Des F. Román. Litho)

1971 (20 June). *Apiculture. T 482 and similar vert designs. Multicoloured. P 12½.*
1859	1 c. Type **482** ..			5	5
1860	3 c. Worker bee	..	..	5	5
1861	9 c. Drone ..	..	..	10	5
1862	13 c. Defending the hive	..	..	12	5
1863	30 c. Queen bee	..	..	25	15
1859/1863	*Set of 5* ..	..	..	50	30

483 "The Ship" (Lydia Rivera)

1971 (30 Aug). *Exhibition of Children's Drawings, Havana. T 483 and similar multicoloured designs. Litho. P 12½.*
1864	1 c. Type **483** ..	..	..	5	5
1865	3 c. "Little Train" (Yuri Ruiz) ..	..	5	5
1866	9 c. "Sugar-cane Cutter" (Horacio Carracedo)	..	..	10	5
1867	10 c. "Return of Cuban Fishermen" (Angela Munoz and Lazaro Hernandez)	..	..	10	5
1868	13 c. "The Zoo" (Victoria Castillo) ..		12	5
1869	20 c. "House and Garden" (Elsa Garcia)	15	8
1870	30 c. "Landscape" (Orestes Rodriguez) (vert)	..	..	25	15
1864/1870	*Set of 7* ..	..	..	75	40

Sizes:—1 c., 3 c. As T **483**; 9 c., 13 c. 45×35 mm; 10 c. 45×38 mm; 20 c. 47×42 mm; 30 c. 39×49 mm.

484 "The Cart" (F. Americo)

1971 (20 Sept). *National Museum Paintings (4th series). T 484 and similar multicoloured designs. Litho. P 12½.*
1871	1 c. "St. Catherine of Alexandria" (F. Zurbaran) (vert) ..	..	5	5
1872	2 c. Type **484** ..	..	..	5	5
1873	3 c. "St. Christopher and the Child" (J. Bassano) (vert) ..	..	5	5
1874	4 c. "Little Devil" (R. Portocarrero) (vert) ..	..	5	5
1875	5 c. "Portrait of a Lady" (N. Maes) (vert) ..	..	5	5
1876	13 c. "Phoenix" (R. Martinez) (vert) ..	15	5
1877	30 c. "Sir William Pitt" (T. Gainsborough) (vert) ..	..	30	15
1871/1877	*Set of 7* ..	..	..	60	35

Sizes:—1 c., 3 c. 30×56 mm; 4 c., 5 c. 37×49 mm; 13 c., 30 c. 39×49 mm.

485 Macabi

(Des F. Román. Litho)

1971 (30 Oct). *Sport Fishing.* T **485** *and similar horiz designs. Multicoloured. P* 12½.

1878	1 c.	Type **485** ..	..	5	5
1879	2 c.	Great amberjack ..	..	5	5
1880	3 c.	Large-mouthed black bass	..	5	5
1881	4 c.	Dorado ..	..	5	5
1882	5 c.	Tarpon ..	..	5	5
1883	13 c.	Waho ..	..	12	5
1884	30 c.	Swordfish ..	..	25	15
1878/1884		Set of 7 ..	..	55	35

486 Ball within "C"

(Des E. A. Borrego. Litho)

1971 (22 Nov). *World Amateur Baseball Championships.* T **486** *and similar diamond-shaped design. W* **324**. *P* 12½.

1885	3 c.	Type **486** ..	..	5	5
1886	1 p.	Hand holding Globe within "C"	..	90	50

487 "Dr. F. Valdes Dominguez" (artist unknown)   488 American Sparrowhawk

1971 (27 Nov). *Centenary of Medical Students' Execution.* T **487** *and similar multicoloured designs, showing paintings. Litho. P* 12½.

1887	3 c.	Type **487** ..	..	5	5
1888	13 c.	"Students' Execution" (M. Mesa) (horiz—62 × 47 mm)	..	12	5
1889	30 c.	"Captain Federico Capdevila" (artist unknown) ..	..	25	15

1971 (10 Dec). *Death Centenary of Ramon de la Sagra (naturalist).* T **488** *and similar multicoloured designs, showing birds. Litho. P* 12½.

1890	1 c.	Type **488** ..	..	..	5	5
1891	2 c.	Pygmy owl ..	..	..	5	5
1892	3 c.	Cuban trogon ..	..	..	5	5
1893	4 c.	Lizard cuckoo ..	..	..	5	5
1894	5 c.	Red-crowned woodpecker	..	..	5	5
1895	13 c.	Flycatcher (horiz) ..	..	..	12	5
1896	30 c.	Tyrant flycatcher (horiz)	..	..	25	15
1897	50 c.	Emerald and ruby-throated humming-birds (horiz—56 × 30 mm)	..	..	45	25
1890/1897		Set of 8 ..	..	..	95	55

489 Baseball Player, Stadium and Emblem

(Des R. Penate. Litho)

1971 (11 Dec). *Cuba's Victory in World Amateur Baseball Championships.* W **324**. *P* 12½.

1898	**489**	13 c. multicoloured	..	..	12	5

490 "Children of the World"   491 "Senora Malpica" (G. Collazo)

(Des R. Quintana. Litho)

1971 (11 Dec). *25th Anniv of U.N.I.C.E.F.* W **324** *(sideways). P* 12½.

1899	**490**	13 c. multicoloured	..	..	12	5

1972 (25 Jan). *National Museum Paintings (5th series).* T **491** *and similar multicoloured designs. Litho. P* 12½.

1900	1 c.	"Reception of Ambassadors" (V. Carpaccio) (horiz) ..	..	5	5
1901	2 c.	Type **491** ..	..	5	5
1902	3 c.	"La Chorrera Fortress" (E. Chartrand) (horiz)	..	5	5
1903	4 c.	"Creole Landscape" (C. Enriquez)	..	5	5
1904	5 c.	"Sir William Lemon" (G. Romney)	..	5	5
1905	13 c.	"La Tajona" (H. Cleenewek) (horiz)	..	12	5
1906	30 c.	"Valencia Beach" (J. Sorolla y Bastida) (horiz) ..	..	25	15
1900/1906		Set of 7 ..	..	55	35

Sizes:— 1 c., 3 c. 51 × 33 mm; 4 c., 5 c. 36 × 44 mm; 13, 30 c. 43 × 34 mm.

492 "Capitol" Stamp of 1929 (now Natural History Museum)

1972 (20 Feb). *10th Anniv of Academy of Sciences. Litho. W 324. P 12½.*
1907 **492** 13 c. maroon and greenish yellow   12   5

1972 (25 Feb). *Tropical Orchids (2nd series). Vert designs as T 480, but dated "1972". Multicoloured. Litho. P 12½.*
1908   1 c. *Brasso cattleya sindorossiana*   ..   5   5
1909   2 c. *Cypripedium doraeus*   5   5
1910   3 c. *Cypripedium exul*   5   5
1911   4 c. *Cypripedium Rosydawn*   5   5
1912   5 c. *Cypripedium Champolliom*   ..   5   5
1913   13 c. *Cypripedium Bucolique*   12   5
1914   30 c. *Cypripedium sullanum*   ..   25   15
1908/1914   *Set of 7*   55   35

493 "Eduardo Agramonte"   **494** Human Heart and
(F. Martinez)   Thorax

1972 (8 Mar). *Death Centenary of Dr. Eduardo Agramonte (surgeon and patriot). Litho. P 12½.*
1915 **493** 3 c. multicoloured   5   5

(Des J. S. Vargas. Litho)

1972 (7 Apr). *World Health Day. W 324 (sideways). P 12½.*
1916 **494** 13 c. multicoloured   12   5

495 "Sputnik 1"

(Des R. Quintana. Litho)

1972 (12 Apr). *Russian Space Exploration. T 495 and similar horiz designs. Multicoloured. P 12½.*
1917   1 c. Type **495**   5   5
1918   2 c. "Vostok 1"   5   5
1919   3 c. Valentina Tereshkova in capsule   5   5
1920   4 c. A. Leonov in Space   5   5
1921   5 c. "Lunokhod 1" moon vehicle   ..   5   5
1922   13 c. Linking of "Soyuz" capsules   ..   12   5
1923   30 c. Dobrovolsky, Volkov and Pataiev,
              victims of "Soyuz 11" disaster   ..   25   15
1917/1923   *Set of 7*   55   35

496 "Vicente Mora Pera"   **497** Cuban Workers
(Postmaster-General, War of
Independence) (R. Lov)

1972 (24 Apr). *Stamp Day. T 496 and similar multicoloured design. Litho. P 12½.*
1924   13 c. Type **496**   12   5
1925   30 c. Mambi Mail cover of 1897
              (*horiz—48 × 39 mm*)   25   15

(Des R. Quintana. Litho)

1972 (1 May). *Labour Day. W 324 (sideways). P 12½.*
1926 **497** 3 c. multicoloured   5   5

498 José Marti and Ho   **499** "Salvador del Muro" (J.
Chi-Minh   del Rio)

(Des R. Mederos. Litho)

1972 (19 May). *3rd Symposium on Indo-China War. T 498 and similar multicoloured designs. W 324 (sideways on 3 c., 30 c.). P 12½.*
1927   3 c. Type **498**   5   5
1928   13 c. Bombed house (*horiz—38 × 29 mm*)   12   5
1929   30 c. Symposium emblem   25   15

1972 (25 May). *Paintings from the Metropolitan Museum, Havana. T 499 and similar vert designs. Multicoloured. Litho. P 12½.*
1930   1 c. Type **499**   5   5
1931   2 c. "Luis de las Casas" (J. del Rio)   ..   5   5
1932   3 c. "Christopher Columbus"
              (unknown artist)   5   5
1933   4 c. "Tomas Gamba" (V. Escobar)   ..   5   5
1934   5 c. "Maria Galarraga" (V. Escobar)   ..   5   5
1935   13 c. "Isabella II of Spain" (F. Madrazo)   12   5
1936   30 c. "Carlos III of Spain" (M. Melero)   25   15
1930/1936   *Set of 7*   55   35
Nos. 1935/6 are larger, 34 × 52 mm.

500 Children in Boat

(Des J. S. Vargas. Litho)

1972 (5 June). *Children's Song Competition. W 324. P 12½.*
1937 **500** 3 c. multicoloured   5   5

501 Airliner, Map and Flags

(Des C. Echenaguzia. Litho)

1972 (26 June). *AIR. 1st Anniversary of Havana–Santiago de Chile Air Service. W 324. P 12½.*
1938 **501** 25 c. multicoloured   25   15

502 Tarpan

(Des F. Román. Litho)

1972 (30 June). *Thoroughbred Horses. T 502 and similar horiz designs. Multicoloured. P 12½.*

1939	1 c. Type 502	..	..	5	5
1940	2 c. Kertag	..	..	5	5
1941	3 c. Creole	..	..	5	5
1942	4 c. Andalusian	..	..	5	5
1943	5 c. Arab	..	..	5	5
1944	13 c. Quarter-horse	..	..	12	5
1945	30 c. Pursang	..	..	25	15
1939/1945	Set of 7	..	..	55	35

503 Frank Pais   504 Athlete and Emblem

1972 (25 July). *15th Death Anniversary of Frank Pais. Litho. W 324. P 12½.*

1946	503	13 c. multicoloured	..	12	5

(Des R. Quintana. Litho)

1972 (26 Aug). *Olympic Games, Munich. T 504 and similar designs. P 12½.*

1947	1 c. reddish brown and yellow-orange		5	5
1948	2 c. orange, reddish violet and cobalt		5	5
1949	3 c. black, olive-yell & sage-green	..	5	5
1950	4 c. orange-brown, ultramarine and yellow-bistre		5	5
1951	5 c. black, lemon and rosine	..	5	5
1952	13 c. olive-yellow, royal blue and lilac		12	5
1953	30 c. multicoloured		25	15
1947/1953	Set of 7	..	55	35
MS1954	58½×75 mm. 50 c. multicoloured. Imperf	..	60	60

Designs: *Horiz*—2 c. Boxing and "M"; 3 c. Weightlifting and "U"; 4 c. Fencing and "N"; 5 c. Rifle-shooting and "I"; 13 c. Running and "C"; 30 c. Basketball and "H"; 50 c. Gymnastics.

505 "Landscape with Tree-trunks" (D. Ramos)

(Des A. Franca. Litho)

1972 (20 Sept). *International Hydrological Decade. T 505 and similar multicoloured designs, showing paintings. P 12½.*

1955	1 c. Type 505	..	..	..	5	5
1956	3 c. "Cyclone" (T. Lorenzo)	..		5	5
1957	8 c. "Viñales" (D. Ramos)	..	..	10	5
1958	30 c. "Forest and Stream" (R. Morey) (vert)	..	..	25	15
1955/1958	Set of 4	..	..	..	40	25

506 *Papilio thoas oviedo*

(Des M. Durán and A. Franca. Litho)

1972 (25 Sept). *Butterflies from the Gundlach Collection. T 506 and similar horiz designs. Multicoloured. P 12½.*

1959	1 c. Type 506	..	..	5	5
1960	2 c. *Papilio devilliers*	..	..	5	5
1961	3 c. *Papilio polixenes polixenes*	..	5	5
1962	4 c. *Papilio androgeus epidaurus*	..	5	5
1963	5 c. *Papilio cayguanabus*	..	..	5	5
1964	13 c. *Papilio andraemon hernandezi*	..	12	5
1965	30 c. *Papilio celadon*	..	..	25	15
1959/1965	Set of 7	..	..	55	35

507 "In La Mancha" (A. Fernandez)   509 "Abwe" (shakers)

508 "Che" Guevara and Map of Bolivia

(Des M. A. Penate. Litho)

1972 (29 Sept). *425th Birth Anniv of Cervantes. T 507 and similar multicoloured designs, showing paintings. P 12½.*

1966	3 c. Type 507	..	..	5	5
1967	13 c. "Battle with the Wine-skins" (A. Fernandez) (horiz)		12	5
1968	30 c. "Don Quixote of La Mancha" (A. Fernandez)		25	15
MS1969	76×116 mm. 50 c. "Scene from Don Quixote" (J. M. Carbonero) ..	..	55	55

Sizes:—3 c., 30 c. As T 507; 13 c. 50×38 mm; 50 c. 47×29 mm.

The stamp within MS1969 is imperf along the bottom edge.

(Des M. Durán. Litho)

1972 (8 Oct). *5th Anniv of Guerillas' Day. T* **508** *and similar horiz designs, each with map of Bolivia. Multicoloured.* P 12½.

1970	3 c. Type **508** ..		5	5
1971	13 c. Tamara Bunke ("Tania") ..	..	12	5
1972	30 c. Guido Peredo ("Inti")	..	25	15

(Des M. Durán Litho)

1972 (25 Oct). *Traditional Musical Instruments. T* **509** *and similar vert designs. Multicoloured.* P 12½.

1973	3 c. Type **509** ..		5	5
1974	13 c. "Bonko-enchemiya" (drum)	..	12	5
1975	30 c. "Iya" (drum)	..	25	15

510 Cuban 2 c. Stamp of 1951

(Des M. A. Penate. Litho)

1972 (18 Nov). *3rd National Philatelic Exhibition, Matanzas. T* **510** *and similar horiz design. Multicoloured.* W **324** *(sideways).* P 12½.

1976	13 c. Type **510** ..	..	12	5
1977	30 c. Cuban 25 c. airmail stamp of 1951		25	15

Nos. 1976/7 were issued with *se-tenant* half stamp-size labels showing the Cuban Philatelic Federation emblem.

511 Viking Longship

(Des C. Echenaguzia. Litho)

1972 (30 Nov). *Maritime History. T* **511** *and similar multicoloured designs.* P 12½.

1978	1 c. Type **511** ..	..	..	5	5
1979	2 c. Caravel (*vert*)	..	..	5	5
1980	3 c. Galley	..	..	5	5
1981	4 c. Galleon (*vert*)	..	..	5	5
1982	5 c. Clipper	..	..	5	5
1983	13 c. Steam packet-boat	..	..	12	5
1984	30 c. Atomic icebreaker *Lenin* (53×29 mm)	..	..	25	15
1978/1984	*Set of 7* ..	..	..	55	35

512 Lion of St. Mark

513 Baseball Coach (poster)

1972 (8 Dec). *U.N.E.S.C.O. "Save Venice" Campaign. T* **512** *and similar multicoloured designs.* P 12½.

1985	3 c. Type **512** ..	..		5	5
1986	13 c. Bridge of Sighs (*vert*)	..	..	12	5
1987	30 c. St. Mark's Cathedral	..	..	25	15

(Des A. Franca. Litho)

1972 (15 Dec). *"Cuba, World Amateur Baseball Champions of 1972".* P 12½.

1988	513	3 c. reddish violet, flesh & orange ..	5	5

514 Various Sports (10th National Schoolchildren's Games)

515 Bronze Medal, Women's 100 Metres

(Des A. Franca. Litho)

1972 (22 Dec). *Sports Events of 1972. Posters. T* **513**/4 *and similar vert designs.* P 12½.

1989	1 c. multicoloured	..	..	5	5
1990	2 c. multicoloured	..	..	5	5
1991	3 c. black, orange & yellow-green		5	5
1992	4 c. red, black and blue	..	..	5	5
1993	5 c. yellow-orange, blue & lt blue		5	5
1994	13 c. multicoloured	..	..	12	5
1995	30 c. violet, black and new blue	..	25	15
1989/1995	*Set of 7* ..	..	..	55	35

Designs:—2 c. Pole-vaulting (Barrientos Memorial Athletics); 3 c. As T **513**, but inscr "XI serie nacional de beisbol aficionado" (11th National Amateur Baseball Competition); 4 c. Wrestling (Cerro Pelado International Tournament); 5 c. Foil (Central American and Caribbean Fencing tournament); 13 c. Boxing (Giraldo Cordova Tournament); 30 c. Fishes (Ernest Hemingway National Marlin Fishing Contest).

(Des M. Durán. Litho)

1973 (28 Jan). *Cuban Successes in Olympic Games, Munich. T* **515** *and similar horiz designs. Multicoloured.* P 12½.

1996	1 c. Type **515** ..	..	..	5	5
1997	2 c. Bronze medal, Women's 4×100 relay	..	..	5	5
1998	3 c. Gold medal, 54 kg Boxing	..	5	5
1999	4 c. Silver medal, 81 kg Boxing	..	5	5
2000	5 c. Bronze medal, 51 kg Boxing	..	5	5
2001	13 c. Gold medal, 67 kg Boxing	..	12	5
2002	30 c. Gold medal and silver cup award, 81 kg Boxing	..	..	25	15
1996/2002	*Set of 7* ..	..	..	55	35
MS2003	65×90 mm. 50 c. Bronze medal, Basketball. Imperf ..	..	..	55	55

516 "Gertrude G. de Avellaneda" (A. Esquivel)

517 "Bathers in the Lagoon" (C. Enriquez)

(Des M. Durán. Litho)

1973 (10 Feb). *Death Centenary of Gertrude Gomez de Avellanina (poetess).* P 12½.

2004	**516**	13 c. multicoloured	..	..	12	5

(Des M. A. Penate and J. Arriola. Litho)

1973 (26 Feb). *National Museum Paintings (6th series).*
T **517** *and similar multicoloured paintings. P* 12½.

2005	1 c. Type **517**	5	5
2006	2 c. "Still Life" (W. C. Heda)	5	5
2007	3 c. "Scene of Gallantry" (P. Landaluze)	5	5
2008	4 c. "Return at Evening" (C. Troyon) ..	5	5
2009	5 c. "Elizabeth Mascagni" (F. X. Fabre)	5	5
2010	13 c. "The Picador" (E. de Lucas Padilla) (horiz)	12	5
2011	30 c. "In the Garden" (J. A. Morell) ..	25	15
2005/2011	*Set of* 7	55	35

1973 (26 Mar). *Tropical Orchids (3rd series). Vert designs as
T* **480**, *but dated* "1973". *Multicoloured. Litho. P* 12½.

2012	1 c. Dendrobium (hybrid)	5	5
2013	2 c. Cypripedium exul O'Brien ..	5	5
2014	3 c. Vanda miss Joaquin	5	5
2015	4 c. Phalaenopsis schilleriana Reichb	5	5
2016	5 c. Vanda gilbert tribulet	5	5
2017	13 c. Dendrobium (hybrid) (different) ..	12	5
2018	30 c. Arachnis catherine	25	15
2012/2018	*Set of* 7	55	35

518 Medical Examination   **519** "Children and Vaccine"

(Des F. Román. Litho)

1973 (7 Apr). *25th Anniv of World Health Organization.
W* **324** *(sideways). P* 12½.

2019	**518** 10 c. multicoloured	10	5

(Des J. Medina. Litho)

1973 (9 Apr). *Freedom from Polio Campaign. P* 12½.

2020	**519** 3 c. multicoloured	5	5

520 "Soyuz" Rocket on   **521** Santiago de Cuba postmark,
Launch-pad   1839

(Des M. A. Penate. Litho)

1973 (12 Apr). *Cosmonauts Day. Russian Space Exploration. T* **520** *and similar multicoloured designs. P* 12½.

2021	1 c. Type **520**	5	5
2022	2 c. "Luna 1" in Moon orbit (horiz) ..	5	5
2023	3 c. "Luna 16" leaving Moon	5	5
2024	4 c. "Venus 7" probe (horiz)	5	5
2025	5 c. "Molnia 1" communications satellite	5	5
2026	13 c. "Mars 3" probe (horiz)	12	5
2027	30 c. Research ship Yuri Gagarin (horiz)	25	15
2021/2027	*Set of* 7	55	35

1973 (24 Apr). *Stamp Day. T* **521** *and similar horiz designs.
Multicoloured. Litho. P* 12½.

2028	13 c. Type **521**	12	5
2029	30 c. Havana postmark, 1760	25	15

522 "Ignacio Agramonte" (A. Espinosa)

(Des M. Durán. Litho)

1973 (11 May). *Death Centenary of Maj-Gen. Ignacio
Agramonte. P* 12½.

2030	**522** 13 c. multicoloured	12	5

CUNDINAMARCA. See under Colombian States.

CURAÇAO. See under Netherlands Antilles.

CYRENAICA. See under Libya.

Appendix

We record in this Appendix stamps from countries which either persist in issuing far more stamps than can be justified by postal need or have failed to maintain control over their distribution so that they have not been available to the public in reasonable quantities at face value.

A policy statement about this was published in the February 1968 issue of *Gibbons Stamp Monthly* and Stanley Gibbons Ltd. do not maintain stocks of the stamps recorded here. Hence no prices are quoted and the information is merely intended as a record. Miniature sheets and imperforate stamps are excluded.

The policy of the countries concerned is kept under continuous review and if circumstances improve or there is evidence of regular postal use of stamps in the Appendix consideration is given to including them in the body of the catalogue.

Afghanistan
1961

Agriculture Day. Fauna and Flora. 2, 2, 5, 10, 15, 25, 50, 100, 150, 175 p.

Child Welfare. Sports and Games. 2, 2, 5, 10, 15, 25, 50, 100, 150, 175 p.

U.N.I.C.E.F. Surch on 1961 Child Welfare issue. 2 + 25, 2 + 25, 5 + 25, 10 + 25, 15 p. + 25 p.

Women's Day. 50, 175 p.

Independence Day. Mohamed Nadir Shah. 50, 175 p.

International Exhibition, Kabul. 50, 175 p.

Pashtunistan Day. 50, 175 p.

National Assembly. 50, 175 p.

Anti-Malaria Campaign. 50, 175 p.

Shah's 47th Birthday. 50, 175 p.

Red Crescent Day. Fruits. 2, 2, 5, 10, 15, 25, 50, 100, 150, 175 p.

Afghan Red Crescent Fund. 1961 Red Crescent Day issue surch. 2 + 25, 2 + 25, 5 + 25, 10 + 25, 15 p. + 25 p.

United Nations Day. 1, 2, 3, 4, 50, 75, 175 p.

Teachers' Day. Flowers and Educational Scenes. 2, 2, 5, 10, 15, 25, 50, 100, 150, 175 p.

U.N.E.S.C.O. 1961 Teachers' Day issue surch. 2 + 25, 2 + 25, 5 + 25, 10 + 25, 15 p. + 25 p.

1962

15th Anniv of U.N.E.S.C.O. (1961). 2, 2, 5, 10, 15, 25, 50, 75, 100 p.

Ahmed Shah Baba. 50, 75, 100 p.

Agriculture Day. Animals and Products. 2, 2, 5, 10, 15, 25, 50, 75, 100, 125 p.

Independence Day. Marching Athletes. 25, 50, 150 p.

Women's Day. Postage 25, 50 p. ; *Air* 100, 175 p.

Pashtunistan Day. 25, 50, 150 p.

Malaria Eradication. 2, 2, 5, 10, 15, 25, 50, 75, 100, 150, 175 p.

National Assembly. 25, 50, 75, 100, 125 p.

4th Asian Games, Djakarta. Postage 1, 2, 3, 4, 5 p. ; *Air* 25, 50, 75, 100, 150, 175 p.

Children's Day. Sports and Produce. Postage 1, 2, 3, 4, 5 p. ; *Air* 75, 150, 200 p.

Shah's 48th Birthday. 25, 50, 75, 100 p.

Red Crescent Day. Fruits and Flowers. Postage 1, 2, 3, 4, 5 p. ; *Air* 25, 50, 100 p.

Boy Scouts' Day. Postage 1, 2, 3, 4 p. ; *Air* 25, 50, 75, 100 p.

1st Anniv of Hammarskjoeld's Death. Surch on 1961 U.N.E.S.C.O. issue. 2 + 20, 2 + 20, 5 + 20, 10 + 20, 15 + 20, 25 + 20, 50 + 20, 75 + 20, 100 p. + 20 p.

United Nations Day. Postage 1, 2, 3, 4, 5 p. ; *Air* 75, 100, 125 p.

Teachers' Day. Sport and Flowers. Postage 1, 2, 3, 4, 5 p. ; *Air* 100, 150 p.

World Meteorological Day. 50, 100 p.

1963

Famous Afghans Pantheon, Kabul. 50, 75, 100 p.

Agriculture Day. Sheep and Silkworms. Postage 1, 2, 3, 4, 5 p. ; *Air* 100, 150, 200 p.

Freedom from Hunger. Postage 2, 3, 300 p. ; *Air* 500 p.

Malaria Eradication Fund. 1962 Malaria Eradication issue surch. 2 + 15, 2 + 15, 5 + 15, 10 + 15, 15, 25 + 15, 50 + 15, 75 + 15, 100 + 15, 150 + 15, 175 p. + 15 p.

World Meteorological Day. Postage 1, 2, 3, 4, 5 p. ; *Air* 200, 300, 400, 500 p.

"GANEFO" Athletic Games, Djakarta. Postage 2, 3, 4, 5, 10 p. 9 a. ; *Air* 300, 500 p.

Red Cross Centenary. Postage 2, 3, 4, 5, 10 p. ; *Air* 100, 200 p., 4, 6 a.

Nubian Monuments Preservation. Postage 100, 200, 500 p. ; *Air* 5 a., 7 a. 50.

1964

Women's Day (1963). 2, 3, 4, 5, 10 p.

Afghan Boy Scouts and Girl Guides. Postage 2, 3, 4, 5, 10 p. ; *Air* 2, 2, 2 a. 50, 3, 4, 5, 12 a.

Child Welfare Day (1963). Sports and Games. Postage 2, 3, 4, 5, 10 p. ; *Air* 200, 300

Afghan Red Crescent Society. Postage 100, 200 p. ; *Air* 5 a., 7 a. 50.

Teachers' Day (1963). Flowers. Postage 2, 3, 4, 5, 10 p. ; *Air* 3 a., 3 a. 50.

United Nations Day (1963). Postage 2, 3, 4, 5, 10 p. ; *Air* 100 p., 2, 3 a.

15th Anniv of Human Rights Declaration. Surch on 1964 United Nations Day issue. Postage 2 + 50, 3 + 50, 4 + 50, 5 + 50, 10 p. + 50 p. ; *Air* 100 p. + 50 p., 2 a. + 50 p., 3 a. + 50 p.

U.N.I.C.E.F. (dated 1963). Postage 100, 200 p. ; *Air* 5 a., 7 a. 50.

Malaria Eradication (dated 1963). Postage 2, 3, 4, 5 p., 10 p. surch on 4 p. ; *Air* 2, 10 a.

Ajman
1967

Pres. J. Kennedy's 50th Birth Anniv. Air 10, 20, 40, 70 d., 1, 1 r. 50, 2, 3, 5 r.

Paintings. Postage. Arab Paintings 1, 2, 3, 4, 5, 30, 70 d. ; *Air. Asian Paintings* 1, 2, 3, 5 r. ; *Indian Painting* 10 r.

Tales from "The Arabian Nights". Postage 1, 2, 3, 10, 30, 50, 70 d. ; *Air* 90 d., 1, 2, 3 r.

World Scout Jamboree, Idaho. Postage 30, 70 d., 1 r.; Air 2, 3, 4 r.

Olympic Games. Mexico (1968). Postage 35, 65, 75 d., 1 r.; Air 1 r. 25, 2, 3, 4 r.

Winter Olympic Games, Grenoble (1968). Postage 5, 35, 60, 75 d.; Air 1, 1 r. 25, 2, 3 r.

Pres. J. Kennedy Memorial. Die-stamped on gold foil. Air 10 r.

Paintings by Renoir and Terbrugghen. Air 35, 65 d. 1, 2 r. × 3.

1968

Paintings by Velasquez. Air 1 r. × 2, 2 r. × 2

Winter Olympic Games, Grenoble. Die-stamped on gold foil. Air 7 r.

Paintings from Famous Galleries. Air 1 r. × 4, 2 r. × 6

Costumes. Air 30 d. × 2, 70 d. × 2, 1 r. × 2, 2 r. × 2

Olympic Games, Mexico. Postage 1 r. × 4; Air 2 r. × 4

Satellites and Spacecraft. Air 30 d. × 2, 70 d. × 2, 1 r. × 2, 2 r. × 2, 3 r. × 2

Paintings. Hunting Dogs. Air 2 r. × 6

Paintings. Adam and Eve. Air 2 r. × 4

Human Rights Year. Kennedy Brothers and Martin Luther King. Air 1 r. × 3, 2 r. × 3

Kennedy Brothers Memorial. Postage 2 r.; Air 5 r.

Sports Champions. Inter-Milano Football Club. Postage 5, 10, 15, 20, 25 d.; Air 10 r.

Sports Champions. Famous Footballers. Postage 15, 20, 50, 75 d., 1 r.; Air 10 r.

Cats. Postage 1, 2, 3 d.; Air 2, 3 r.

Olympic Games, Mexico. Die-stamped on gold foil. 5 r.

5th Death Anniv of Pres. J. Kennedy. On gold foil. Air 10 r.

Paintings of the Madonna. Air 30, 70 d., 1, 2, 3 r.

Space Exploration. Postage 5, 10, 15, 20, 25 d.; Air 15 r.

Olympic Games, Mexico. Gold Medals. Postage 2 r. × 4; Air 5 r. × 4

Christmas. Air 5 r.

1969

Sports Champions. Cyclists. Postage 1, 2, 5, 10, 15, 20 d.; Air 12 r.

Sports Champions. German Footballers. Postage 5, 10, 15, 20, 25 d.; Air 10 r.

Sports Champions. Motor-racing Drivers. Postage 1, 5, 10, 15, 25 d.; Air 10 r.

Motor-racing Cars. Postage 1, 5, 10, 15, 25 d.; Air 10 r.

Sports Champions. Boxers. Postage 5, 10, 15, 20 d.; Air 10 r.

Sports Champions. Baseball Players. Postage 1, 2, 5, 10, 15 d.; Air 10 r.

Birds. Air 1 r. × 11

Roses. 1 r. × 6

Wild Animals. Air 1 r. × 6

Paintings. Italian Old Masters. 5, 10, 15, 20 d., 10 r.

Paintings. Famous Composers. Air 5, 10, 25 d., 10 r.

Paintings. French Artists. 1 r. × 4

Paintings. Nudes. Air 2 r. × 4

Three Kings Mosaic. Postage 1 r. × 2; Air 3 r. × 2

Kennedy Brothers. Air 2, 3, 10 r.

Olympic Games, Mexico. Gold Medal Winners. Postage 1, 2 d., 10 r.; Air 10 d., 5, 10 r.

Paintings of the Madonna. Postage 10 d.; Air 10 r.

Space Flight of "Apollo 9". Optd on 1968 Space Exploration issue. Air 15 r.

Space Flight of "Apollo 10". Optd on 1968 Space Exploration issue. Air 15 r.

1st Death Anniv of Gagarin. Optd on 1968 Space Exploration issue. 5 d.

2nd Death Anniv of White. Optd on 1968 Space Exploration issue. 10 d.

1st Death Anniv of Robert Kennedy. Optd on 1969 Kennedy Brothers issue. Air 2 r.

European Football Championship. Optd on 1968 Famous Footballers issue. Air 10 r.

Olympic Games, Munich (1972). Optd on 1969 Mexico Gold Medal Winners issue. Air 10 d., 5, 10 r.

Moon Landing of "Apollo 11". Air 1, 2, 5 r.

Moon Landing of "Apollo 11". Circular designs on gold or silver foil. Air 3 r. × 3, 5 r. × 3, 10 r. × 14

Paintings. Christmas. Postage 1, 2, 3, 4, 5, 15 d.; Air 2, 3 r.

1970

"Apollo" Space Flights. Postage 1, 2, 4, 5, 10 d.; Air 3, 5 r.

Birth Bicent of Napoleon Bonaparte. Die-stamped on gold foil. Air 20 r.

Paintings. Easter. Postage 5, 10, 12, 30, 50, 70 d.; Air 1, 2 r.

Moon Landing. Die-stamped on gold foil. Air 20 r.

Paintings by Michelangelo. Postage 1, 2, 4, 5, 8, 10 d.; Air 3, 5 r.

World Football Cup, Mexico. Air 25, 50, 75 d., 1, 2, 3 r.

"Expo 70" World Fair, Osaka, Japan. Japanese Paintings. Postage 1, 2, 3, 4, 5, 10, 15 d.; Air 1, 5 r.

Birth Bicent of Napoleon Bonaparte. Postage 1, 2, 4, 5, 10 d.; Air 3, 5 r.

Paintings. Old Masters. Postage 1, 2, 5, 6, 10 d.; Air 1, 2, 3 r.

Space Flight of "Apollo 13". Air 50, 75, 80 d., 1, 2, 3 r.

World Football Cup, Mexico. Die-stamped on gold foil. Air 20 r.

Olympic Games, 1960–1972. Postage 15, 30, 50, 70 d.; Air 2, 5 r.

"Expo 70" World Fair, Osaka, Japan. Pavilions. 1, 2, 3, 4, 10, 15 d.; Air 1, 3 r.

Brazil, World Football Champions. Optd on 1970 World Football Cup issue. Air 25, 50, 75 d., 1, 2, 3 r.

"Gemini" and "Apollo" Space Flights. Postage 1, 2, 3, 4, 5, 6, 8, 10, 12, 15, 20, 25, 30, 35, 40, 50 d.; Air 1, 1 r. 50, 2, 3 r.

Vintage and Veteran Cars. Postage 1, 2, 4, 5, 8, 10 d.; Air 2, 3 r.

Pres. D. Eisenhower Commemoration. Postage 30, 50, 70 d.; Air 1, 2, 3 r.

Paintings by Ingres. Air 25, 30, 35, 50, 70, 85 d., 1, 2 r.

500th Birth Anniv of Dürer (1971). Air 25, 30, 35, 50, 70, 85 d., 1, 2 r.

Christmas Paintings. Air 25, 30, 35, 50, 70, 85 d., 1, 2 r.

Winter Olympic Games, Sapporo, Japan (1972). Die-stamped on gold foil. Air 20 r.

Meeting of Eisenhower and De Gaulle, 1942. Die-stamped on gold foil. Air 20 r.

General De Gaulle Commemoration. Air 25, 50, 75 d., 1, 2, 3 r.

Winter Olympic Games, Sapporo, Japan (1972). Sports. Postage 1, 2, 5, 10 d.; Air 3, 5 r.

J. Rindt, World Formula 1 Motor-racing Champion. Die-stamped on gold foil. Air 20 r.

1971

"Philatokyo" Stamp Exhib, Japan. Japanese Paintings. Air 25, 30, 35, 50, 70, 85 d., 1, 2 r.

Mars Space Project. Air 50, 75, 80 d., 1, 2, 3 r.

Napoleonic Military Uniforms. Postage 5, 10, 15, 20, 25, 30 d.; Air 2, 3 r.

Olympic Games, Munich (1972). Sports. Postage 10, 15, 25, 30, 40 d.; Air 1, 2, 3 r.

Paintings by Modern Artists. Air 25, 30, 35, 50, 70, 85 d.; 1, 2 r.

Paintings by Famous Artists. Air 25, 30, 35, 50, 70, 85 d., 1, 2 r.

25th Anniv of United Nations. Optd on *1971 Modern Artists* issue. Air 25, 30, 35, 50, 70, 85 d.; 1, 2 r.

Olympic Games, Munich (1972). *Sports.* Postage 1, 2, 3, 4, 5, 6, 8, 10, 12, 15, 20, 25, 30, 35, 40, 50 d.; Air 1, 1 r. 50, 2, 3 r.

Butterflies. Air 25, 30, 35, 50, 70, 85 d., 1, 2 r.

Space Flight of "Apollo 14". Postage 15, 25, 50, 60, 70 d.; Air 5 r.

Winter Olympic Games, 1908–1968. Postage 30, 40, 50, 75 d., 1 r.; Air 2 r.

Signs of the Zodiac. 1, 2, 5, 10, 12, 15, 25, 30, 35, 45, 50, 60 d.

Famous Men. Air 65, 70, 75, 80, 85, 90 d.; 1, 1 r. 25, 1 r. 50, 2, 2 r. 50, 3 r.

Death Bicent of Beethoven. 20, 30, 40, 60 d.; 1 r. 50, 2 r.

Albert Schweitzer Commem. 20, 30, 40, 60 d., 1 r. 50, 2 r.

Tropical Birds. Postage 1, 2, 3, 4, 5, 10 d.; Air 2, 3 r.

Paintings by French Artists. Postage 1, 2, 3, 4, 5, 10 d.; Air 2, 3 r.

Paintings by Modern Artists. Postage 1, 2, 3, 4, 5, 10 d.; Air 2, 3 r.

Paintings by Degas. Postage 1, 2, 3, 4, 5, 10 d.; Air 2, 3 r.

Paintings by Titian. Postage 1, 2, 3, 4, 5, 10 d.; Air 2, 3 r.

Paintings by Renoir. Postage 1, 2, 3, 4, 5, 10 d.; Air 2, 3 r.

Space Flight of "Apollo 15". Postage 25, 40, 50, 60 d., 1 r.; Air 6 r.

"Philatokyo" Stamp Exhib, Japan. Stamps. Postage 10, 15, 20, 30, 35, 50, 60, 80 d.; Air 1, 2 r.

Tropical Birds. Postage 1, 2, 3, 5, 7, 10, 12, 15, 20, 25, 30, 40 d.; Air 50, 80 d., 1, 3 r.

Paintings depicting Venus. Postage 1, 2, 3, 4, 5, 10 d.; Air 2, 3 r.

World Scout Jamboree, Japan. Scouts. Postage 1, 2, 3, 5, 7, 10, 12, 15, 20, 25, 30, 35, 40, 50, 65, 80 d.; Air 1, 1 r. 25, 1 r. 50, 2 r.

Lions International Clubs. Optd on *1971 Famous Paintings* issue. Air 25, 30, 35, 50, 70, 85 d.; 1, 2 r.

World Scout Jamboree, Japan. Japanese Paintings. Postage 20, 30, 40, 60, 75 d.; Air 3 r.

25th Anniv of U.N.I.C.E.F. Optd on *1971 Scout Jamboree (paintings)* issue. Postage 20, 30, 40, 60, 75 d.; Air 3 r.

Christmas 1971. Portraits of Popes. (*1st series*). Plain frames. Postage 1, 2, 3, 4, 5, 10 d.; Air 2, 3 r.

Modern Cars. Postage 10, 15, 25, 40, 50 d.; Air 3 r.

Olympic Games, Munich (1972). *Show-jumping.* Embossed on gold foil. Air 20 r.

Exploration of Outer Space. Postage 15, 25, 50, 60, 70 d.; Air 5 r.

Royal Visit of Queen Elizabeth II to Japan. Postage 1, 2, 3, 4, 5, 10 d.; Air 2, 3 r.

Meeting of Pres. Nixon and Emperor Hirohito of Japan, Alaska. Design as 3 r. value of 1970 *Eisenhower* issue, but value changed and optd with commemorative inscr. Air 5 r. (silver opt), 5 r. (gold opt)

"Apollo" Astronauts. Postage 5, 20, 35, 40, 50 d.; Air 1, 2, 3 r.

Discoverers of the Universe. Astronomers and Space-scientists. Postage 5, 10, 15, 20, 25, 30 d.; Air 2, 5 r.

"ANPHILEX 71" Stamp Exhibition, New York. Air 2 r. 50

Christmas 1971. Portraits of Popes (*2nd series*). Ornamental frames. Postage 1, 2, 3, 4, 5, 10 d.; Air 2, 3 r.

Silver Wedding of Queen Elizabeth II and Prince Philip (1972). Air 1, 2, 3 r.

Space Flight of "Apollo 16". Postage 20, 30, 40, 50, 60 d.; Air 3, 4 r.

Fairy Tales. "Baron Munchhausen" stories. Postage 1, 2, 4, 5, 10 d.; Air 3 r.

World Fair, Philadelphia (1976). *Paintings.* Postage 25, 50, 75 d.; Air 5 r.

Fairy Tales. Stories of the Brothers Grimm. Postage 1, 2, 4, 5, 10 d.; Air 3 r.

European Tour of Emperor Hirohito of Japan. Postage 1, 2, 4, 5, 10 d.; Air 6 r.

13th World Scout Jamboree, Asagiri, Japan. Postage 5, 10, 15, 20, 25 d.; Air 5 r.

Winter Olympic Games, Sapporo, Japan (1972). Postage 5, 10, 15, 20, 25 d.; Air 5 r.

Olympic Games, Munich (1972). Postage 5, 10, 15, 20, 25 d.; Air 5 r.

"Japanese Life". Postage 10 d. × 4, 20 d. × 4, 30 d. × 4, 40 d. × 4, 50 d. × 4; Air 3 r. × 4

Space Flight of "Apollo 15". Postage 5, 10, 15, 20, 25, 50 d.; Air 1, 2, 3, 5 r.

"Soyuz 11" Disaster. Air 50 d., 1 r., 1 r. 50

"The Future in Space". Postage 5, 10, 15, 20, 25, 50 d.

2500th Anniversary of Persian Empire. Postage 10, 20, 30, 40, 50 d.; Air 3 r.

Cats. Postage 10, 15, 20, 25 d.; Air 50 d., 1 r.

50th Anniversary of Tutankhamun Tomb Discovery, Postage 1, 2, 3, 4, 5, 6, 7, 8, 9, 10, 11, 12, 13, 14, 15, 16 d.; Air 1 r. × 4

400th Birth Anniv of Kepler. Postage 50 d.; Air 5 r.

Famous Men. Air 1 r. × 5

1972

150th Death Anniv of Napoleon (1971). Postage 10, 20, 30, 40 d.; Air 1, 2, 3, 4 r.

1st Death Anniv of General De Gaulle. Postage 10, 20, 30, 40 d.; Air 1, 2, 3, 4 r.

Wild Animals (*1st series*). Postage 5, 10, 15, 20, 25, 30, 35, 40 d.

Tropical Fish. Postage 5, 10, 15, 20, 25 d.; Air 50, 75 d., 1 r.

Famous Musicians. Postage 5 d. × 3, 10 d. × 3, 15 d. × 3, 20 d. × 3, 25 d. × 3, 30 d. × 3, 35 d. × 3, 40 d. × 3

Easter. Postage 5, 10, 15, 20, 25 d.; Air 5 r.

Wild Animals (*2nd series*). Postage 5, 10, 15, 20, 25 d.; Air 5 r.

"Tour de France" Cycle Race. Postage 5, 10, 15, 20, 25, 30, 35, 40, 45, 50, 55 d.; Air 60, 65, 70, 75, 80, 85, 90, 95 d., 1 r.

Many other issues were released between 1 September 1971 and 1 August 1972, but their authenticity has been denied by the Ajman Postmaster-General. Certain issues of 1967–69 exist overprinted to commemorate other events, but the Postmaster-General states that these are unofficial.

Ajman joined the United Arab Emirates on 1 August 1972 and the Federal Ministry of Communications assumed responsibility for the postal services. Further stamps inscribed "Ajman" issued after that date were released without authority and had no validity.

Manama
1966

New Currency Surcharges. Stamps of Ajman surch "Manama" in English and Arabic and new value.

(*a*) *Nos. 19/20 and 22/4* (*Kennedy*). 10 d. on 10 n.p., 15 d. on 15 n.p., 1 r. on 1 r., 2 r. on 2 r., 3 r on 3 r.

(*b*) *Nos. 27, 30 and 35/6* (*Olympics*). 5 d. on 5 n.p., 25 d. on 25 n.p., 3 r. on 3 r., 5 r. on 5 r.

(*c*) *Nos. 80/2 and 85* (*Churchill*). 50 d. on 50 n.p., 75 d. on 75 n.p., 1 r. on 1 r., 5 r. on 5 r.

(*d*) *Nos. 95/8* (*Space*). Air 50 d. on 50 n.p., 1 r. on 1 r., 3 r. on 3 r., 5 r. on 5 r.

1967

World Scout Jamboree, Idaho. Postage 30, 70 d., 1 r.; Air 2, 3, 4 r.

Olympic Games, Mexico (1968). Postage 35, 65, 75 d., 1 r., Air 1 r. 25, 2, 3, 4 r.

Winter Olympic Games, Grenoble (1968). Postage 5, 35, 60, 75 d.; Air 1, 1 r. 25, 2, 3 r.

Paintings by Renoir and Terbrugghen. Air 35, 65 d., 1, 2 r. × 3

1968

Paintings by Velasquez. Air 1 r. × 2, 2 r. × 2

Costumes. Air 30 d. × 2, 70 d. × 2, 1 r. × 2, 2 r. × 2

Olympic Games, Mexico. Postage 1 r. × 4; Air 2 r. × 4

Satellites and Spacecraft. Air 30 d. × 2, 70 d. × 2, 1 r. × 2, 2 r. × 2, 3 r. × 2

Human Rights Year. Kennedy Brothers and Martin Luther King. Air 1 r. × 3, 2 r. × 3

Sports Champions. Famous Footballers. Postage 15, 20, 50, 75 d., 1 r.; Air 10 r.

Heroes of Humanity. Circular designs on gold or silver foil. 60 d. × 12

Olympic Games, Mexico. Circular designs on gold or silver foil. Air 3 r. × 8

Mothers' Day. Paintings. Postage 1 r. × 6

Kennedy Brothers Commemoration. Postage 2 r.; Air 5 r.

Cats. Postage 1, 2, 3 d.; Air 2, 3 r.

5th Death Anniv of Pres. J. Kennedy. Air 10 r.

Space Exploration. Postage 5, 10, 15, 20, 25 d.; Air 15 r.

Olympic Games, Mexico. Gold Medals. Postage 2 r. × 4; Air 5 r. × 4

Christmas. Air 5 r.

1969

Sports Champions. Cyclists. Postage 1, 2, 5, 10, 15, 20 d.; Air 12 r.

Sports Champions. German Footballers. Postage 5, 10, 15, 20, 25 d.; Air 10 r.

Sports Champions. Motor-racing Drivers. Postage 1, 5, 10, 15, 25 d.; Air 10 r.

Motor-racing Cars. Postage 1, 5, 10, 15, 25 d.; Air 10 r.

Sports Champions. Boxers. Postage 5, 10, 15, 20 d.; Air 10 r.

Sports Champions. Baseball Players. Postage 1, 2, 5, 10, 15 d.; Air 10 r.

Birds. Air 1 r. × 11

Roses. Postage 1 r. × 6

Animals. Air 1 r. × 6

Paintings by Italian Artists. Postage 5, 10, 15, 20 d., 10 r.

Great Composers. Air 5, 10, 25 d., 10 r.

Paintings by French Artists. Postage 1 r. × 4

Nude Paintings. Air 2 r. × 4

Kennedy Brothers. Air 2, 3, 10 r.

Olympic Games, Mexico. Gold Medal Winners. Postage 1, 2 d., 10 r.; Air 10 d., 5, 10 r.

Paintings of the Madonna. Postage 10 d.; Air 10 r.

Space Flight of "Apollo 9". Optd on 1968 Space Exploration issue. Air 15 r.

Space Flight of "Apollo 10". Optd on 1968 Space Exploration issue. Air 15 r.

1st Death Anniv of Gagarin. Optd on 1968 Space Exploration issue. Postage 5 d.

2nd Death Anniv of White. Optd on 1968 Space Exploration issue. Postage 10 d.

1st Death Anniv of Robert Kennedy. Optd on 1969 Kennedy Brothers issue. Air 2 r.

Olympic Games, Munich (1972). Optd on 1969 Mexico Gold Medal Winners issue. Air 10 d., 5, 10 r.

Moon Mission of "Apollo 11". Air 1, 2, 3 r.

Christmas. Paintings by Brueghel. Postage 1, 2, 4, 5, 10 d.; Air 6 r.

1970

"Soyuz" and "Apollo" Space Programmes. Postage 1, 2, 4, 5, 10 d.; Air 3, 5 r.

Kennedy and Eisenhower Commem. Embossed on gold foil. Air 20 r.

Lord Baden-Powell Commem. Embossed on gold foil. Air 20 r.

World Cup Football Championships, Mexico. Postage 1, 20, 40, 60, 80 d.; Air 3 r.

Brazil, World Football Champions. Optd on 1970 World Cup issue. Postage 1, 20, 40, 60, 80 d.; Air 3 r.

Paintings by Michelangelo Postage. 1, 2, 4, 5, 10 d.; Air 6 r.

World Fair "EXPO 70", Osaka, Japan. Air 25, 50, 75 d., 1, 2, 3, 12 r.

Paintings by Renoir. Postage 1, 2, 5, 6, 10 d.; Air 5, 12 r.

Christmas. Flower Paintings by Brueghel. Postage 5, 20, 25, 30, 50 d.; Air 60 d., 1, 2 r

1971

Roses. Postage 5, 10, 25, 30, 50 d.; Air 60 d., 1, 2 r.

Birds. Postage 5, 20, 25, 30, 50 d.; Air 60 d., 1, 2 r.

Paintings by Modigliani. Air 25, 50, 60, 75 d., 1 r. 50, 3 r.

Paintings by Rubens. Postage 1, 2, 3, 4, 5, 10 d.; Air 3 r.

25th Anniversary of United Nations, Optd on 1970 Christmas issue. Postage 5, 20, 25, 30, 50 d.; Air 60 d., 1, 2 r.

British Military Uniforms. Postage 5, 20, 25, 30, 50 d.; Air 60 d., 1, 2 r.

Space Flight of "Apollo 14". Postage 15, 25, 50, 60, 70 d.; Air 5 r.

Space Flight of "Apollo 15". Postage 25, 40, 50, 60 d.; Air 1, 6 r.

13th World Scout Jamboree, Asagiri, Japan. Postage 1, 2, 3, 5, 7, 10, 12, 15, 20, 25, 30, 35, 40, 50, 65, 80 d.; Air 1, 1 r. 25, 1 r. 50, 2 r.

Lions International Clubs. Optd on 1971 Uniforms issue. Postage 5, 20, 25, 30, 50 d.; Air 60 d., 1, 2 r.

Royal Visit of Queen Elizabeth II to Japan. Postage 10, 20, 30, 40, 50 d.; Air 2, 3 r.

Fairy Tales. Stories by Hans Andersen. Postage 1, 2, 4, 5, 10 d.; Air 3 r.

World Fair, Philadelphia (1976). American Paintings. Postage 20, 25, 50, 60, 75 d.; Air 3 r.

Fairy Tales. Well-known stories. Postage 1, 2, 4, 5, 10 d.; Air 3 r.

Space Flight of "Apollo 16". Postage 20, 30, 40, 50, 60 d.; Air 3, 4 r.

European Tour of Emperor Hirohito of Japan. Postage 1, 2, 4, 5, 10 d.; Air 6 r.

Meeting of Pres. Nixon and Emperor Hirohito of Japan, Alaska. Optd on 1971 Emperor's Tour issue. Air 6 r.

2500th Anniversary of Persian Empire. Postage 10, 20, 30, 40, 50 d.; Air 3 r.

"Apollo 15" Mission and Future Developments in Space. Postage 10, 15, 20, 25, 50 d.; Air 1, 2 r.

1972

150th Death Anniv of Napoleon (1971). Postage 10, 20, 30, 40 d.; Air 1, 2, 3, 4 r.

1st Death Anniv of General De Gaulle. Postage 10, 20, 30, 40 d.; Air 1, 2, 3, 4 r.

Paintings from the "Alte Pinakothek", Munich. Postage 5, 10, 15, 20, 25 d.; Air 5 r.

"Tour de France" Cycle Race. Postage 5, 10, 15, 20, 25, 30, 35, 40, 45, 50, 55, 60 d.; Air 65, 70, 75, 80, 85, 90, 95 d., 1 r.

Many other issues inscribed "Manama" were made during this period, but we have yet to establish their authenticity.

The United Arab Emirates Ministry of Communications took over the Manama postal service on 1 August 1972. Further stamps inscribed "Manama" issued after that date were released without authority and had no validity.

Bhutan
1968

Bhutan Pheasants. 1, 2, 4, 8, 15 ch., 2, 4, 5, 7, 9 n.
Winter Olympic Games, Grenoble. Opts on 1966 Abominable Snowmen issue. 40 ch., 1 n. 25, 3, 6 n.
Mythological Creatures. Postage 2, 3, 4, 5, 15, 20, 30, 50 ch., 1 n. 50, 2 n. 50, 4, 5, 10 n.
Butterflies (plastic-surfaced). Postage 15, 50 ch., 1 n. 25, 2 n.; *Air* 3, 4, 5, 6 n.
Paintings (relief-printed). Postage 2, 4, 5, 10, 45, 80 ch., 1 n. 05, 1 n. 40, 2, 3, 4, 5 n.; *Air* 1 n. 50, 2 n. 50, 6, 8 n.
Olympic Games, Mexico. 5, 45, 60, 80 ch., 1 n. 05, 2, 3, 5 n.
Human Rights Year. Die-stamped surch on unissued "Coins". 15 ch. on 50 np., 33 ch. on 1 r., 9 n. on 3 r. 75
Flood Relief. Surch on 1968 Mexico Olympics issue. 5 ch. + 5 ch., 80 ch. + 25 ch., 2 n. + 50 ch.
Rare Birds. Postage 2, 3, 4, 5, 15, 20, 30, 50 ch., 1 n. 25, 2 n.; *Air* 1 n. 50, 2 n. 50, 4, 5, 10 n.

1969

Fish (plastic-surfaced). Postage 15, 20, 30 ch.; *Air* 5, 6, 7 n.
Insects (plastic-surfaced). Postage 10, 75 ch., 1 n. 25, 2 n.; *Air* 3, 4, 5, 6 n.
Admission of Bhutan to Universal Postal Union. 5, 10, 15, 45, 60 ch., 1 n. 05, 1 n. 40, 4 n.
5000 Years of Steel Industry. On steel foil. Postage 2, 5, 15, 45, 75 ch., 1 n. 50, 1 n. 75, 2 n.; *Air* 3, 4, 5, 6 n.
Birds (plastic-surfaced). Postage 15, 50 ch., 1 n. 25, 2 n.; *Air* 3, 4, 5, 6 n.
Buddhist Prayer Banners. On silk rayon. 15, 75 ch., 2, 5, 6 n.
Moon Landing by "Apollo 11" (plastic-surfaced). Postage 3, 5, 15, 20, 25, 45, 50 ch., 1 n. 75; *Air* 3, 4, 5, 6 n.

1970

Famous Paintings (plastic-surfaced). Postage 5, 10, 15 ch., 2 n. 75; *Air* 3, 4, 5, 6 n.
New U.P.U. Headquarters Building, Berne. 3, 10, 20 ch., 2 n. 50
Flower Paintings (relief-printed). Postage 2, 3, 5, 10, 15, 75 ch., 1 n., 1 n. 40; *Air* 80, 90 ch., 1 n. 10, 1 n. 40, 1 n. 60, 1 n. 70, 3 n., 3 n. 50
Animals (plastic-surfaced). Postage 5, 10, 20, 25, 30, 40, 65, 75, 85 ch.; *Air* 2, 3, 4, 5 n.
Conquest of Space (plastic-surfaced). Postage 2, 5, 15, 25, 30, 50, 75 ch., 1 n. 50; *Air* 2, 3, 6, 7 n.

1971

History of Sculpture (plastic-moulded). Postage 10, 75 ch., 1 n. 25, 2 n.; *Air* 3, 4, 5, 6 n.

Moon Vehicles (plastic-surfaced). Postage 10 ch., 1 n. 70; *Air* 2 n. 50, 4 n.
History of the Motor Car (plastic-surfaced). Postage 2, 5, 10, 15, 20, 30, 60, 75, 85 ch., 1 n., 1 n. 20, 1 n. 55, 1 n. 80, 2 n., 2 n. 50; *Air* 4, 6, 7, 9, 10 n.
Bhutan's Admission to United Nations. Postage 5, 10, 20 ch., 3 n.; *Air* 2 n. 50, 5, 6 n.
60th Anniv of Boy Scout Movement. 10, 20, 50, 75 ch., 2, 6 n.
World Refugee Year. Opt on 1971 United Nations issue. Postage 5, 10, 20 ch., 3 n.; *Air* 2 n. 50, 5, 6 n.

1972

Famous Paintings (relief-printed). Postage 15, 20, 90 ch., 2 n. 50; *Air* 1 n. 70, 4 n. 60, 5 n. 40, 6 n.
Famous Men (plastic-moulded). Postage 10, 15, 55 ch.; *Air* 2, 6, 8 n.
Olympic Games, Munich. Postage 10, 15, 20, 30, 45 ch.; *Air* 35 ch., 1 n. 35, 7 n.
Space Flight of "Apollo 16" (plastic-surfaced). Postage 15, 20, 90 ch., 2 n. 50; *Air* 1 n. 70, 4 n. 60, 5 n. 40, 6 n.
Bhutan Dogs. 5, 10, 15, 25, 55 ch., 8 n.

1973

Dogs of the World. 2, 3, 15, 20, 30, 99 ch., 2 n. 50, 4 n.
Roses (scent-impregnated paper). Postage 15, 25, 30 ch., 3 n.; *Air* 6, 7 n.
"Apollo 17" Moon Landing (plastic-surfaced). Postage 10, 15, 55 ch., 2 n.; *Air* 7, 9 n.
'Talking Stamps' (miniature records). Postage 10, 25 ch., 1 n. 25, 7, 8 n.; *Air* 3, 9 n.
Death of King Jigme Dorji Wangchuk. Embossed on gold foil. Postage 10, 25 ch., 3 n.; *Air* 6, 8 n.

Chad
1972

"Apollo 15" Moon Flight. Air 40, 80, 150, 250, 300, 500 f.
"Soyuz 11" Disaster. Air 30, 50, 100, 200, 300, 400 f.
President Tombalbaye. Postage 30, 40 f.; *Air* 70, 80 f.
Winter Olympic Games, Sapporo, Japan. Postage 25, 75, 150 f.; *Air* 130, 200 f.
Scout Jamboree. Postage 30, 70, 80 f.; *Air* 100, 120 f.
Medal-winners, Winter Olympic Games, Sapporo, Japan. Postage 25, 75, 100, 130 f.; *Air* 150, 200 f.
Olympic Games, Munich. Postage 20, 40, 60 f.; *Air* 100, 120, 150 f.
African Animals. Air 20, 30, 100, 130, 150 f.

1973

Medal-winners, Olympic Games, Munich (1st series). Postage 10, 20, 40, 60 f.; *Air* 150, 250 f.
Medal-winners, Olympic Games, Munich (2nd series. Gold frames). Postage 20, 30, 50 f.; *Air* 150, 250 f.

Index to all Foreign Overseas Countries and Places not in this Volume

Pending completion of the four-volume edition of the Foreign Overseas Countries, the following index includes all the stamp-issuing foreign countries not included in the three Europe volumes and not given in the present work.

Countries in the 1970–71 Sectional Catalogues are indicated by the Number of the Section, thus .. .. S 2

Countries still to be found in the 1970 Part III Catalogue (America, Asia and Africa) have the page numbers in roman figures, thus 332

Countries still to be found in the 1970 Part II Catalogue (Europe and Colonies) have their names and page numbers in italics, thus: *Belgian Congo* *91*

The 1970–71 Sectional Catalogues to which reference is made are as follows:

S 2 France
S 3 Germany
S 4 Israel and Middle East
S 5 Italy
S 6 Japan
S 7 Scandinavia
S 9 U.S.A.
S 11 Portugal
S 12 Spain

<table>
<tr><td>Abyssinia (see Ethiopia)</td><td>332</td></tr>
<tr><td>Abyssinia (Italian Occupation)</td><td>595</td></tr>
<tr><td>Acambaro (Mexico)</td><td>557</td></tr>
<tr><td>Acaponeta (Mexico)</td><td>557</td></tr>
<tr><td>Africa (Portuguese Colonies)</td><td>S 11</td></tr>
<tr><td>Aguascalientes (Mexico)</td><td>557</td></tr>
<tr><td>Alaouites (territory of the)</td><td>S 4</td></tr>
<tr><td>Alexandretta (see Hatay)</td><td>S 4</td></tr>
<tr><td>Alexandria (French P.O.)</td><td>S 2</td></tr>
<tr><td>Alexandria (United States)</td><td>S 9</td></tr>
<tr><td>Allende (Mexico)</td><td>557</td></tr>
<tr><td>Ancachs (Peru)</td><td>683</td></tr>
<tr><td>Annam (Indo-China) (French Colonies)</td><td>331</td></tr>
<tr><td>Annam and Tonquin (French Colonies)</td><td>331</td></tr>
<tr><td>Annapolis (United States)</td><td>S 9</td></tr>
<tr><td>Arabia (see Saudi Arabia)</td><td>731</td></tr>
<tr><td>Arequipa (Peru)</td><td>681</td></tr>
<tr><td>Athens (Confederate States)</td><td>S 9</td></tr>
<tr><td>Ayacucho (Peru)</td><td>683</td></tr>
<tr><td>Azerbaijan (see Persia)</td><td>680</td></tr>
<tr><td>Baja California (Mexico)</td><td>557, 578</td></tr>
<tr><td>Baltimore (United States)</td><td>S 9</td></tr>
<tr><td>Baton Rouge (Confederate States)</td><td>S 9</td></tr>
<tr><td>Beaumont (Confederate States)</td><td>S 9</td></tr>
<tr><td>Belgian Congo</td><td>91</td></tr>
<tr><td>Belgian Occupation of German East Africa</td><td>96</td></tr>
<tr><td>Benadir (Italian Colonies)</td><td>596</td></tr>
<tr><td>Benin (French Colonies)</td><td>265</td></tr>
<tr><td>Boscawen (United States)</td><td>S 9</td></tr>
<tr><td>Boston (United States)</td><td>S 9</td></tr>
<tr><td>Brattleboro (United States)</td><td>S 9</td></tr>
</table>

<table>
<tr><td>Bridgeville (Confederate States)</td><td>S 9</td></tr>
<tr><td>Cabo (Nicaragua)</td><td>620</td></tr>
<tr><td>Cambodia (Indo-China) (French Colonies)</td><td>331</td></tr>
<tr><td>Cambodia (Independent)</td><td>105</td></tr>
<tr><td>Campeche (Mexico)</td><td>577</td></tr>
<tr><td>Cape Juby (Spanish Colonies)</td><td>S 12</td></tr>
<tr><td>Carupano (Venezuela)</td><td>907</td></tr>
<tr><td>Chachapoyas (Peru)</td><td>683</td></tr>
<tr><td>Chala (Peru)</td><td>683</td></tr>
<tr><td>Charleston (Confederate States)</td><td>S 9</td></tr>
<tr><td>Charleston (United States)</td><td>S 9</td></tr>
<tr><td>Chiapas (Mexico)</td><td>577</td></tr>
<tr><td>Chiclayo (Peru)</td><td>683</td></tr>
<tr><td>Chihuahua (Mexico)</td><td>557</td></tr>
<tr><td>Ciudad Juarez (Mexico)</td><td>557</td></tr>
<tr><td>Coamo (Puerto Rico)</td><td>S 9</td></tr>
<tr><td>Cochin-China (French Colonies)</td><td>275</td></tr>
<tr><td>Colima (Mexico)</td><td>557</td></tr>
<tr><td>Comaygua (Honduras)</td><td>379</td></tr>
<tr><td>Confederate States (U.S.A.)</td><td>S 9</td></tr>
<tr><td>Congo (Belgian)</td><td>91</td></tr>
<tr><td>Congo (Independent)</td><td>219</td></tr>
<tr><td>Cuernavaca (Mexico)</td><td>578</td></tr>
<tr><td>Curacao (Netherlands Antilles)</td><td>685</td></tr>
<tr><td>Cuzco (Peru)</td><td>682</td></tr>
<tr><td>Cyrenaica (Italian Colonies)</td><td>592</td></tr>
<tr><td>Cyrenaica (Independent)</td><td>262</td></tr>
<tr><td>Dahomey (French Colonies)</td><td>282</td></tr>
<tr><td>Dahomey (Independent)</td><td>262</td></tr>
</table>

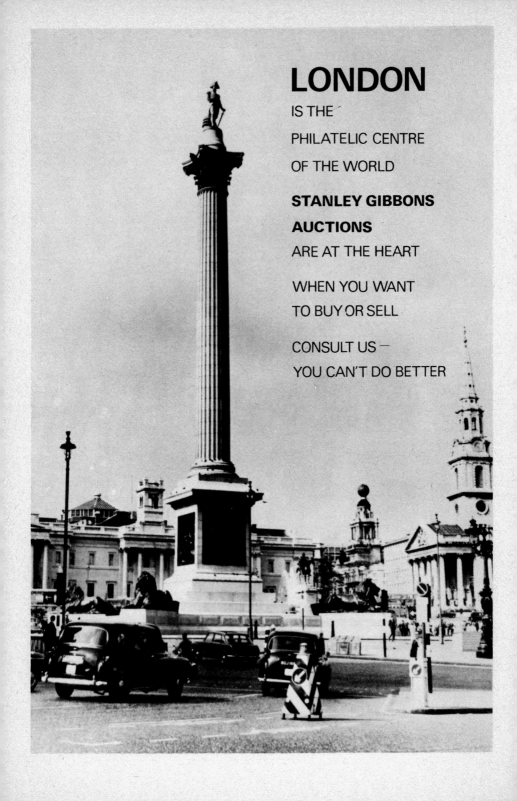

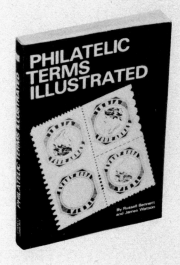

Gibbons' own monthly magazine, essential reading for **every** collector!

Detailed monthly Supplements update all Gibbons catalogues for you—and a special Stamp Market feature on price changes.

Informative articles cover all facets of philately, with regular notes on new discoveries, stamp designs, postmarks, market trends and news and views of the world of stamps.

Britain's LARGEST circulation of any stamp magazine—that fact speaks for itself!

Monthly from all dealers and news-agents or by post direct from Stanley Gibbons Magazines Ltd.—subscription rates on application.

PHILATELIC TERMS
ILLUSTRATED

This successful STAMP MONTHLY series has now been brought together in a snappy black and yellow binding and published as the latest addition to Stanley Gibbons range of essential handbooks for keen stamp collectors.
Within its 192 pages this handy limp-bound volume houses a veritable mine of useful information, on the words and phrases used in philately. It describes and illustrates printing processes and watermarks, papers and perforations, errors and varieties . . . and it does all this IN COLOUR. Indeed, there are 92 full page plates in colour, plus many black and white illustrations, making it

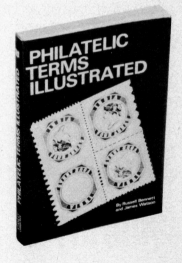

FANTASTIC VALUE AT ONLY A £1!

Index to the Contents of this Volume

StanGib Limited
StanGib House
595, Fifth Avenue
New York, NY 10017
USA

is
the
address
of
our
New York Office

All Stanley Gibbons Catalogues, Albums and Accessories are available here, and of course, a superb stock of all kinds of philatelic material is always available to our clients.

By Courtesy of the Post Office
we bring you

SG Approvals

Every pillar-box in the country is one of our branches! How else can we sell stamps to thousands of collectors all over the country, some of whom have never been to '391 Strand'?

Stanley Gibbons Approval Books make collecting easy. Furnish us with references and details of your requirements, and we send selections of stamps at intervals to suit you. You have the stamps on 14 days approval—time enough to browse at leisure in the comfort of your own home, with your albums close at hand. Compare the stamps with your own collection, check the watermarks and perforations— pick out the really fine copies which will make you proud of your collection! Stanley Gibbons Approvals bring the immense resources of the entire Gibbons stock into your own home. We've been running this service for nearly 100 years. How come you've never tried it before?

Stanley Gibbons Ltd, Approvals Dept, 391 Strand, London WC2R OLX.

Gibbons

NEW ISSUES. The first Supplement recording new stamps not in this Catalogue appeared in the June 1973 number of Gibbons *Stamp Monthly*

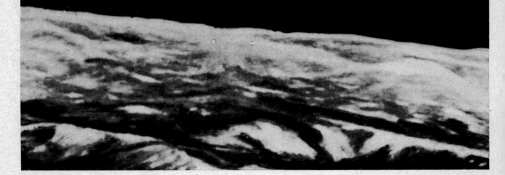